Title 37

Patents, Trademarks, and Copyrights

Revised as of July 1, 2013

Containing a codification of documents
of general applicability and future effect

As of July 1, 2013

Published by the Office of the Federal Register
National Archives and Records Administration
as a Special Edition of the Federal Register

Table of Contents

Cite this Code: CFR

To cite the regulations in this volume use title, part and section number. Thus, 37 CFR 1.1 *refers to title 37, part 1, section 1.*

Explanation

The Code of Federal Regulations is a codification of the general and permanent rules published in the Federal Register by the Executive departments and agencies of the Federal Government. The Code is divided into 50 titles which represent broad areas subject to Federal regulation. Each title is divided into chapters which usually bear the name of the issuing agency. Each chapter is further subdivided into parts covering specific regulatory areas.

Each volume of the Code is revised at least once each calendar year and issued on a quarterly basis approximately as follows:

Title 1 through Title 16..........as of January 1
Title 17 through Title 27..........as of April 1
Title 28 through Title 41..........as of July 1
Title 42 through Title 50..........as of October 1

The appropriate revision date is printed on the cover of each volume.

LEGAL STATUS

The contents of the Federal Register are required to be judicially noticed (44 U.S.C. 1507). The Code of Federal Regulations is prima facie evidence of the text of the original documents (44 U.S.C. 1510).

HOW TO USE THE CODE OF FEDERAL REGULATIONS

The Code of Federal Regulations is kept up to date by the individual issues of the Federal Register. These two publications must be used together to determine the latest version of any given rule.

To determine whether a Code volume has been amended since its revision date (in this case, July 1, 2013), consult the "List of CFR Sections Affected (LSA)," which is issued monthly, and the "Cumulative List of Parts Affected," which appears in the Reader Aids section of the daily Federal Register. These two lists will identify the Federal Register page number of the latest amendment of any given rule.

EFFECTIVE AND EXPIRATION DATES

Each volume of the Code contains amendments published in the Federal Register since the last revision of that volume of the Code. Source citations for the regulations are referred to by volume number and page number of the Federal Register and date of publication. Publication dates and effective dates are usually not the same and care must be exercised by the user in determining the actual effective date. In instances where the effective date is beyond the cut-off date for the Code a note has been inserted to reflect the future effective date. In those instances where a regulation published in the Federal Register states a date certain for expiration, an appropriate note will be inserted following the text.

OMB CONTROL NUMBERS

The Paperwork Reduction Act of 1980 (Pub. L. 96–511) requires Federal agencies to display an OMB control number with their information collection request.

Many agencies have begun publishing numerous OMB control numbers as amendments to existing regulations in the CFR. These OMB numbers are placed as close as possible to the applicable recordkeeping or reporting requirements.

PAST PROVISIONS OF THE CODE

Provisions of the Code that are no longer in force and effect as of the revision date stated on the cover of each volume are not carried. Code users may find the text of provisions in effect on any given date in the past by using the appropriate List of CFR Sections Affected (LSA). For the convenience of the reader, a "List of CFR Sections Affected" is published at the end of each CFR volume. For changes to the Code prior to the LSA listings at the end of the volume, consult previous annual editions of the LSA. For changes to the Code prior to 2001, consult the List of CFR Sections Affected compilations, published for 1949-1963, 1964-1972, 1973-1985, and 1986-2000.

"[RESERVED]" TERMINOLOGY

The term "[Reserved]" is used as a place holder within the Code of Federal Regulations. An agency may add regulatory information at a "[Reserved]" location at any time. Occasionally "[Reserved]" is used editorially to indicate that a portion of the CFR was left vacant and not accidentally dropped due to a printing or computer error.

INCORPORATION BY REFERENCE

What is incorporation by reference? Incorporation by reference was established by statute and allows Federal agencies to meet the requirement to publish regulations in the Federal Register by referring to materials already published elsewhere. For an incorporation to be valid, the Director of the Federal Register must approve it. The legal effect of incorporation by reference is that the material is treated as if it were published in full in the Federal Register (5 U.S.C. 552(a)). This material, like any other properly issued regulation, has the force of law.

What is a proper incorporation by reference? The Director of the Federal Register will approve an incorporation by reference only when the requirements of 1 CFR part 51 are met. Some of the elements on which approval is based are:

(a) The incorporation will substantially reduce the volume of material published in the Federal Register.

(b) The matter incorporated is in fact available to the extent necessary to afford fairness and uniformity in the administrative process.

(c) The incorporating document is drafted and submitted for publication in accordance with 1 CFR part 51.

What if the material incorporated by reference cannot be found? If you have any problem locating or obtaining a copy of material listed as an approved incorporation by reference, please contact the agency that issued the regulation containing that incorporation. If, after contacting the agency, you find the material is not available, please notify the Director of the Federal Register, National Archives and Records Administration, 8601 Adelphi Road, College Park, MD 20740-6001, or call 202-741-6010.

CFR INDEXES AND TABULAR GUIDES

A subject index to the Code of Federal Regulations is contained in a separate volume, revised annually as of January 1, entitled CFR INDEX AND FINDING AIDS. This volume contains the Parallel Table of Authorities and Rules. A list of CFR titles, chapters, subchapters, and parts and an alphabetical list of agencies publishing in the CFR are also included in this volume.

An index to the text of "Title 3—The President" is carried within that volume.

The Federal Register Index is issued monthly in cumulative form. This index is based on a consolidation of the "Contents" entries in the daily Federal Register.

A List of CFR Sections Affected (LSA) is published monthly, keyed to the revision dates of the 50 CFR titles.

REPUBLICATION OF MATERIAL

There are no restrictions on the republication of material appearing in the Code of Federal Regulations.

INQUIRIES

For a legal interpretation or explanation of any regulation in this volume, contact the issuing agency. The issuing agency's name appears at the top of odd-numbered pages.

For inquiries concerning CFR reference assistance, call 202–741–6000 or write to the Director, Office of the Federal Register, National Archives and Records Administration, 8601 Adelphi Road, College Park, MD 20740-6001 or e-mail *fedreg.info@nara.gov.*

SALES

The Government Printing Office (GPO) processes all sales and distribution of the CFR. For payment by credit card, call toll-free, 866-512-1800, or DC area, 202-512-1800, M-F 8 a.m. to 4 p.m. e.s.t. or fax your order to 202-512-2104, 24 hours a day. For payment by check, write to: US Government Printing Office – New Orders, P.O. Box 979050, St. Louis, MO 63197-9000.

ELECTRONIC SERVICES

The full text of the Code of Federal Regulations, the LSA (List of CFR Sections Affected), The United States Government Manual, the Federal Register, Public Laws, Public Papers of the Presidents of the United States, Compilation of Presidential Documents and the Privacy Act Compilation are available in electronic format via *www.ofr.gov*. For more information, contact the GPO Customer Contact Center, U.S. Government Printing Office. Phone 202-512-1800, or 866-512-1800 (toll-free). E-mail, *ContactCenter@gpo.gov.*

The Office of the Federal Register also offers a free service on the National Archives and Records Administration's (NARA) World Wide Web site for public law numbers, Federal Register finding aids, and related information. Connect to NARA's web site at *www.archives.gov/federal-register.*

The e-CFR is a regularly updated, unofficial editorial compilation of CFR material and Federal Register amendments, produced by the Office of the Federal Register and the Government Printing Office. It is available at *www.ecfr.gov.*

CHARLES A. BARTH,
Director,
Office of the Federal Register.
July 1, 2013.

THIS TITLE

Title 37—PATENTS, TRADEMARKS AND COPYRIGHTS is composed of one volume. The contents of this volume represent all current regulations codified under this title of the CFR as of July 1, 2013.

The parts in chapter I, subchapter A, are regrouped according to subject matter. All parts pertaining to patents—parts 1, 3, 4, and 5—appear sequentially. All parts pertaining to trademarks—parts 2, 6, and 7—follow, also in sequence. Part 3, which pertains to both patents and trademarks, follows the first part.

Indexes appear after parts 5, 7 and 41, within chapter I. An index to chapter II appears at the end of the chapter.

For this volume, Susannah C. Hurley was Chief Editor. The Code of Federal Regulations publication program is under the direction of Michael L. White, assisted by Ann Worley.

Title 37—Patents, Trademarks, and Copyrights

CHAPTER I—UNITED STATES PATENT AND TRADEMARK OFFICE, DEPARTMENT OF COMMERCE

EDITORIAL NOTE: Chapter I—United States Patent and Trademark Office, Department of Commerce, Subchapter A—General, contains patent and trademark regulations. Subchapter A has been restructured to allow parts pertaining to patent regulations and trademark regulations to be grouped separately. For further explanation see This Title, page ix.

SUBCHAPTER A—GENERAL

PATENTS

TRADEMARKS

PRACTICE BEFORE THE PATENT AND TRADEMARK OFFICE

SUBCHAPTER A—GENERAL

PATENTS

PART 1—RULES OF PRACTICE IN PATENT CASES

Subpart A—General Provisions

GENERAL INFORMATION AND CORRESPONDENCE

Sec.
1.1 Addresses for non-trademark correspondence with the United States Patent and Trademark Office.
1.2 Business to be transacted in writing.
1.3 Business to be conducted with decorum and courtesy.
1.4 Nature of correspondence and signature requirements.
1.5 Identification of patent, patent application, or patent-related proceeding.
1.6 Receipt of correspondence.
1.7 Times for taking action; Expiration on Saturday, Sunday or Federal holiday.
1.8 Certificate of mailing or transmission.
1.9 Definitions.
1.10 Filing of correspondence by "Express Mail."

RECORDS AND FILES OF THE PATENT AND TRADEMARK OFFICE

1.11 Files open to the public.
1.12 Assignment records open to public inspection.
1.13 Copies and certified copies.
1.14 Patent applications preserved in confidence.
1.15 Requests for identifiable records.

FEES AND PAYMENT OF MONEY

1.16 National application filing, search, and examination fees.
1.17 Patent application and reexamination processing fees.
1.18 Patent post allowance (including issue) fees.
1.19 Document supply fees.
1.20 Post issuance fees.
1.21 Miscellaneous fees and charges.
1.22 Fees payable in advance.
1.23 Methods of payment.
1.24 [Reserved]
1.25 Deposit accounts.
1.26 Refunds.
1.27 Definition of small entities and establishing status as a small entity to permit payment of small entity fees; when a determination of entitlement to small entity status and notification of loss of entitlement to small entity status are required; fraud on the Office.
1.28 Refunds when small entity status is later established; how errors in small entity status are excused.
1.29 Micro entity status.

Subpart B—National Processing Provisions

PROSECUTION OF APPLICATION AND APPOINTMENT OF ATTORNEY OR AGENT

1.31 Applicant may be represented by one or more patent practitioners or joint inventors.
1.32 Power of attorney.
1.33 Correspondence respecting patent applications, reexamination proceedings, and other proceedings.
1.34 Acting in a representative capacity.
1.36 Revocation of power of attorney; withdrawal of patent attorney or agent.

WHO MAY APPLY FOR A PATENT

1.41 Inventorship.
1.42 Applicant for patent.
1.43 Application for patent by a legal representative of a deceased or legally incapacitated inventor.
1.44 [Reserved]
1.45 Application for patent by joint inventors.
1.46 Application for patent by an assignee, obligated assignee, or a person who otherwise shows sufficient proprietary interest in the matter.
1.47 [Reserved]
1.48 Correction of inventorship pursuant to 35 U.S.C. 116 or correction of the name or order of names in a patent application, other than a reissue application.

THE APPLICATION

1.51 General requisites of an application.
1.52 Language, paper, writing, margins, compact disc specifications.
1.53 Application number, filing date, and completion of application.
1.54 Parts of application to be filed together; filing receipt.
1.55 Claim for foreign priority.
1.56 Duty to disclose information material to patentability.
1.57 Incorporation by reference.
1.58 Chemical and mathematical formulae and tables.
1.59 Expungement of information or copy of papers in application file.
1.60–162 [Reserved]

OATH OR DECLARATION

1.63 Inventor's oath or declaration.
1.64 Substitute statement in lieu of an oath or declaration.
1.66 Statements under oath.

AUTHORITY: 35 U.S.C. 2(b)(2), unless otherwise noted.

SOURCE: 24 FR 10332, Dec. 22, 1959, unless otherwise noted.

EDITORIAL NOTES: 1. In Patent and Trademark Office publications and usage the part number is omitted from the numbers of §§ 1.1 to 1.352 and the numbers to the right of the decimal point correspond with the respective rule numbers.

2. For nomenclature changes to part 1, see 68 FR 14335, Mar. 25, 2003.

Subpart A—General Provisions

GENERAL INFORMATION AND CORRESPONDENCE

§ 1.1 Addresses for non-trademark correspondence with the United States Patent and Trademark Office.

(a) *In general.* Except as provided in paragraphs (a)(3)(i), (a)(3)(ii), and (d)(1) of this section, all correspondence intended for the United States Patent and Trademark Office must be addressed to either "Director of the United States Patent and Trademark Office, P.O. Box 1450, Alexandria, Virginia 22313–1450" or to specific areas within the Office as set out in paragraphs (a)(1), and (a)(3)(iii) of this section. When appropriate, correspondence should also be marked for the attention of a particular office or individual.

(1) *Patent correspondence.*—(i) *In general.* All correspondence concerning patent matters processed by organizations reporting to the Commissioner for Patents should be addressed to: Commissioner for Patents, PO Box 1450, Alexandria, Virginia 22313–1450.

(ii) *Patent Trial and Appeal Board.* See § 41.10 or § 42.6 of this title. Notices of appeal, appeal briefs, reply briefs, requests for oral hearing, as well as all other correspondence in an application or a patent involved in an appeal to the Board for which an address is not otherwise specified, should be addressed as set out in paragraph (a)(1)(i) of this section.

(2) [Reserved]

(3) *Office of General Counsel correspondence*—(i) *Litigation and service.* Correspondence relating to pending litigation or otherwise within the scope of part 104 of this title shall be addressed as provided in § 104.2.

(ii) *Disciplinary proceedings.* Correspondence to counsel for the Director of the Office of Enrollment and Discipline relating to disciplinary proceedings pending before a Hearing Officer or the Director shall be mailed to: Mail Stop 8, Office of the Solicitor, United States Patent and Trademark Office, P.O. Box 1450, Alexandria, Virginia 22313–1450.

(iii) *Solicitor, in general.* Correspondence to the Office of the Solicitor not otherwise provided for shall be addressed to: Mail Stop 8, Office of the Solicitor, United States Patent and Trademark Office, P.O. Box 1450, Alexandria, Virginia 22313–1450.

(iv) *General Counsel.* Correspondence to the Office of the General Counsel not otherwise provided for, including correspondence to the General Counsel relating to disciplinary proceedings, shall be addressed to: General Counsel, United States Patent and Trademark Office, PO Box 1450, Alexandria, Virginia 22313–1450.

(v) *Improper correspondence.* Correspondence improperly addressed to a Post Office Box specified in paragraphs (a)(3)(i) and(a)(3)(ii) of this section will not be filed elsewhere in the United States Patent and Trademark Office, and may be returned.

(4) *Office of Public Records correspondence.* (i) Assignments. All patent-related documents submitted by mail to

be recorded by Assignment Services Division, except for documents filed together with a new application, should be addressed to: Mail Stop Assignment Recordation Services, Director of the United States Patent and Trademark Office, P.O. Box 1450, Alexandria, Virginia 22313–1450. *See* § 3.27.

(5) *Office of Enrollment and Discipline correspondence.* All correspondence directed to the Office of Enrollment and Discipline concerning enrollment, registration, and investigation matters should be addressed to Mail Stop OED, Director of the United States Patent and Trademark Office, P.O. Box 1450, Alexandria, Virginia 22313–1450.

(ii) *Documents.* All requests for certified or uncertified copies of patent documents should be addressed to: Mail Stop Document Services, Director of the United States Patent and Trademark Office, P.O. Box 1450, Alexandria, Virginia 22313–1450.

(b) *Patent Cooperation Treaty.* Letters and other communications relating to international applications during the international stage and prior to the assignment of a national serial number should be additionally marked "Mail Stop PCT."

(c) *For reexamination proceedings.* (1) Requests for *ex parte* reexamination (original request papers) and all subsequent *ex parte* reexamination correspondence filed in the Office, other than correspondence to the Office of the General Counsel pursuant to § 1.1(a)(3) and § 1.302(c), should be additionally marked "Mail Stop *Ex Parte* Reexam."

(2) Requests for *inter partes* reexamination (original request papers) and all subsequent *inter partes* reexamination correspondence filed in the Office, other than correspondence to the Office of the General Counsel pursuant to § 1.1(a)(3) and § 1.302(c), should be additionally marked "Mail Stop *Inter partes* Reexam."

(d) Payments of maintenance fees in patents not submitted electronically over the Internet, and correspondence related to maintenance fees may be addressed to: Director of the United States Patent and Trademark Office, Attn: Maintenance Fee, 2051 Jamieson Avenue, Suite 300, Alexandria, Virginia 22314.

(e) *Patent term extension.* All applications for extension of patent term under 35 U.S.C. 156 and any communications relating thereto intended for the United States Patent and Trademark Office should be additionally marked "Mail Stop Hatch-Waxman PTE." When appropriate, the communication should also be marked to the attention of a particular individual, as where a decision has been rendered.

(f) [Reserved]

[68 FR 14335, Mar. 25, 2003; 68 FR 19371, Apr. 21, 2003, as amended at 68 FR 48287, Aug. 13, 2003; 68 FR 71006, Dec. 22, 2003; 69 FR 29877, May 26, 2004; 69 FR 35451, June 24, 2004; 69 FR 49997, Aug. 12, 2004; 72 FR 18904, Apr. 16, 2007; 73 FR 47540, Aug. 14, 2008; 75 FR 36295, June 25, 2010; 77 FR 46624, Aug. 6, 2012; 77 FR 48811, Aug. 14, 2012]

§ 1.2 Business to be transacted in writing.

All business with the Patent and Trademark Office should be transacted in writing. The personal attendance of applicants or their attorneys or agents at the Patent and Trademark Office is unnecessary. The action of the Patent and Trademark Office will be based exclusively on the written record in the Office. No attention will be paid to any alleged oral promise, stipulation, or understanding in relation to which there is disagreement or doubt.

§ 1.3 Business to be conducted with decorum and courtesy.

Applicants and their attorneys or agents are required to conduct their business with the United States Patent and Trademark Office with decorum and courtesy. Papers presented in violation of this requirement will be submitted to the Director and will not be entered. A notice of the non-entry of the paper will be provided. Complaints against examiners and other employees must be made in correspondence separate from other papers.

[68 FR 38624, June 30, 2003]

§ 1.4 Nature of correspondence and signature requirements.

(a) Correspondence with the Patent and Trademark Office comprises:

(1) Correspondence relating to services and facilities of the Office, such as

general inquiries, requests for publications supplied by the Office, orders for printed copies of patents, orders for copies of records, transmission of assignments for recording, and the like, and

(2) *Correspondence in and relating to a particular application or other proceeding in the Office.* See particularly the rules relating to the filing, processing, or other proceedings of national applications in subpart B, §§1.31 to 1.378; of international applications in subpart C, §§1.401 to 1.499; of *ex parte* reexaminations of patents in subpart D, §§1.501 to 1.570; of extension of patent term in subpart F, §§1.710 to 1.785; of *inter partes* reexaminations of patents in subpart H, §§1.902 to 1.997; and of the Patent Trial and Appeal Board in parts 41 and 42 of this title.

(b) Since each file must be complete in itself, a separate copy of every paper to be filed in a patent application, patent file, or other proceeding must be furnished for each file to which the paper pertains, even though the contents of the papers filed in two or more files may be identical. The filing of duplicate copies of correspondence in the file of an application, patent, or other proceeding should be avoided, except in situations in which the Office requires the filing of duplicate copies. The Office may dispose of duplicate copies of correspondence in the file of an application, patent, or other proceeding.

(c) Since different matters may be considered by different branches or sections of the United States Patent and Trademark Office, each distinct subject, inquiry or order must be contained in a separate paper to avoid confusion and delay in answering papers dealing with different subjects.

(d)(1) *Handwritten signature.* Each piece of correspondence, except as provided in paragraphs (d)(2), (d)(3), (e) and (f) of this section, filed in an application, patent file, or other proceeding in the Office which requires a person's signature, must:

(i) Be an original, that is, have an original handwritten signature personally signed, in permanent dark ink or its equivalent, by that person; or

(ii) Be a direct or indirect copy, such as a photocopy or facsimile transmission (§1.6(d)), of an original. In the event that a copy of the original is filed, the original should be retained as evidence of authenticity. If a question of authenticity arises, the Office may require submission of the original.

(2) *S-signature.* An S-signature is a signature inserted between forward slash marks, but not a handwritten signature as defined by §1.4(d)(1). An S-signature includes any signature made by electronic or mechanical means, and any other mode of making or applying a signature not covered by a handwritten signature of §1.4(d)(1). Correspondence being filed in the Office in paper, by facsimile transmission as provided in §1.6(d), or via the Office electronic filing system as an attachment as provided in §1.6(a)(4), for a patent application, patent, or a reexamination proceeding may be S-signature signed instead of being personally signed (*i.e.*, with a handwritten signature) as provided for in paragraph (d)(1) of this section. The requirements for an S-signature under this paragraph (d)(2) of this section are as follows.

(i) The S-signature must consist only of letters, or Arabic numerals, or both, with appropriate spaces and commas, periods, apostrophes, or hyphens for punctuation, and the person signing the correspondence must insert his or her own S-signature with a first single forward slash mark before, and a second single forward slash mark after, the S-signature (e.g., /Dr. James T. Jones, Jr./); and

(ii) A patent practitioner (§1.32(a)(1)), signing pursuant to §§1.33(b)(1) or 1.33(b)(2), must supply his/her registration number either as part of the S-signature, or immediately below or adjacent to the S-signature. The number (#) character may be used only as part of the S-signature when appearing before a practitioner's registration number; otherwise the number character may not be used in an S-signature.

(iii) The signer's name must be:

(A) Presented in printed or typed form preferably immediately below or adjacent the S-signature, and

(B) Reasonably specific enough so that the identity of the signer can be readily recognized.

(3) *Forms.* The Office provides forms to the public to use in certain situations to assist in the filing of correspondence for a certain purpose and to meet certain requirements for patent applications and proceedings. Use of the forms for purposes for which they were not designed is prohibited. No changes to certification statements on the Office forms (e.g., oath or declaration forms, terminal disclaimer forms, petition forms, and nonpublication request form) may be made. The existing text of a form, other than a certification statement, may be modified, deleted, or added to, if all text identifying the form as an Office form is removed. The presentation to the Office (whether by signing, filing, submitting, or later advocating) of any Office form with text identifying the form as an Office form by a party, whether a practitioner or non-practitioner, constitutes a certification under § 11.18(b) of this chapter that the existing text and any certification statements on the form have not been altered other than permitted by EFS-Web customization.

(4) *Certifications*—(i) *Section 11.18 certifications.* The presentation to the Office (whether by signing, filing, submitting, or later advocating) of any paper by a party, whether a practitioner or non-practitioner, constitutes a certification under § 11.18(b) of this subchapter. Violations of § 11.18(b)(2) of this subchapter by a party, whether a practitioner or non-practitioner, may result in the imposition of sanctions under § 11.18(c) of this subchapter. Any practitioner violating § 11.18(b) of this subchapter may also be subject to disciplinary action. *See* § 11.18(d) of this subchapter.

(ii) *Certifications as to the signature:*—(A) *Of another:* A person submitting a document signed by another under paragraph (d)(2) of this section is obligated to have a reasonable basis to believe that the person whose signature is present on the document was actually inserted by that person, and should retain evidence of authenticity of the signature.

(B) *Self certification:* The person inserting a signature under paragraph (d)(2) of this section in a document submitted to the Office certifies that the inserted signature appearing in the document is his or her own signature.

(C) *Sanctions:* Violations of the certifications as to the signature of another or a person's own signature, set forth in paragraphs (d)(4)(ii)(A) and (B) of this section, may result in the imposition of sanctions under § 11.18(c) and (d) of this chapter.

(e) The following correspondence must be submitted with an original handwritten signature personally signed in permanent dark ink or its equivalent:

(1) Correspondence requiring a person's signature and relating to registration to practice before the Patent and Trademark Office in patent cases, enrollment and disciplinary investigations, or disciplinary proceedings; and

(2) Payments by credit cards where the payment is not being made via the Office's electronic filing systems.

(f) When a document that is required by statute to be certified must be filed, a copy, including a photocopy or facsimile transmission, of the certification is not acceptable.

(g) An applicant who has not made of record a registered attorney or agent may be required to state whether assistance was received in the preparation or prosecution of the patent application, for which any compensation or consideration was given or charged, and if so, to disclose the name or names of the person or persons providing such assistance. Assistance includes the preparation for the applicant of the specification and amendments or other papers to be filed in the Patent and Trademark Office, as well as other assistance in such matters, but does not include merely making drawings by draftsmen or stenographic services in typing papers.

(h) *Ratification/confirmation/evidence of authenticity:* The Office may require ratification, confirmation (which includes submission of a duplicate document but with a proper signature), or evidence of authenticity of a signature, such as when the Office has reasonable doubt as to the authenticity (veracity) of the signature, e.g., where there are variations of a signature, or where the signature and the typed or printed name, do not clearly identify the person signing.

(Pub. L. 94–131, 89 Stat. 685; 35 U.S.C. 6, Pub. L. 97–247)

EDITORIAL NOTE: For FEDERAL REGISTER citations affecting § 1.4, see the List of CFR Sections Affected, which appears in the Finding Aids section of the printed volume and at *www.fdsys.gov*.

§ 1.5 Identification of patent, patent application, or patent-related proceeding.

(a) No correspondence relating to an application should be filed prior to receipt of the application number from the Patent and Trademark Office. When a letter directed to the Patent and Trademark Office concerns a previously filed application for a patent, it must identify on the top page in a conspicuous location, the application number (consisting of the series code and the serial number; *e.g.*, 07/123,456), or the serial number and filing date assigned to that application by the Patent and Trademark Office, or the international application number of the international application. Any correspondence not containing such identification will be returned to the sender where a return address is available. The returned correspondence will be accompanied with a cover letter which will indicate to the sender that if the returned correspondence is resubmitted to the Patent and Trademark Office within two weeks of the mail date on the cover letter, the original date of receipt of the correspondence will be considered by the Patent and Trademark Office as the date of receipt of the correspondence. Applicants may use either the Certificate of Mailing or Transmission procedure under § 1.8 or the Express Mail procedure under § 1.10 for resubmissions of returned correspondence if they desire to have the benefit of the date of deposit in the United States Postal Service. If the returned correspondence is not resubmitted within the two-week period, the date of receipt of the resubmission will be considered to be the date of receipt of the correspondence. The two-week period to resubmit the returned correspondence will not be extended. In addition to the application number, all letters directed to the Patent and Trademark Office concerning applications for patent should also state the name of the first listed inventor, the title of the invention, the date of filing the same, and, if known, the group art unit or other unit within the Patent and Trademark Office responsible for considering the letter and the name of the examiner or other person to which it has been assigned.

(b) When the letter concerns a patent other than for purposes of paying a maintenance fee, it should state the number and date of issue of the patent, the name of the patentee, and the title of the invention. For letters concerning payment of a maintenance fee in a patent, see the provisions of § 1.366(c).

(c) Correspondence relating to a trial proceeding before the Patent Trial and Appeal Board (part 42 of this title) are governed by § 42.6 of this title.

(d) A letter relating to a reexamination proceeding should identify it as such by the number of the patent undergoing reexamination, the reexamination request control number assigned to such proceeding and, if known, the group art unit and name of the examiner to which it has been assigned.

(e) [Reserved]

(f) When a paper concerns a provisional application, it should identify the application as such and include the application number.

(Pub. L. 94–131, 89 Stat. 685; 35 U.S.C. 6, Pub. L. 97–247)

[24 FR 10332, Dec. 22, 1959, as amended at 46 FR 29181, May 29, 1981; 49 FR 552, Jan. 4, 1984; 49 FR 48451, Dec. 12, 1984; 53 FR 47807, Nov. 28, 1988; 58 FR 54501, Oct. 22, 1993; 61 FR 42802, Aug. 19, 1996; 61 FR 56446, Nov. 1, 1996; 64 FR 48917, Sept. 8, 1999; 68 FR 48288, Aug. 13, 2003; 69 FR 49997, Aug. 12, 2004; 77 FR 46624, Aug. 6, 2012; 77 FR 48812, Aug. 14, 2012]

§ 1.6 Receipt of correspondence.

(a) *Date of receipt and Express Mail date of deposit.* Correspondence received in the Patent and Trademark Office is stamped with the date of receipt except as follows:

(1) The Patent and Trademark Office is not open for the filing of correspondence on any day that is a Saturday, Sunday, or Federal holiday within the

District of Columbia. Except for correspondence transmitted by facsimile under paragraph (a)(3) of this section, or filed electronically under paragraph (a)(4) of this section, no correspondence is received in the Office on Saturdays, Sundays, or Federal holidays within the District of Columbia.

(2) Correspondence filed in accordance with § 1.10 will be stamped with the date of deposit as "Express Mail" with the United States Postal Service.

(3) Correspondence transmitted by facsimile to the Patent and Trademark Office will be stamped with the date on which the complete transmission is received in the Patent and Trademark Office unless that date is a Saturday, Sunday, or Federal holiday within the District of Columbia, in which case the date stamped will be the next succeeding day which is not a Saturday, Sunday, or Federal holiday within the District of Columbia.

(4) Correspondence may be submitted using the Office electronic filing system only in accordance with the Office electronic filing system requirements. Correspondence submitted to the Office by way of the Office electronic filing system will be accorded a receipt date, which is the date the correspondence is received at the correspondence address for the Office set forth in § 1.1 when it was officially submitted.

(b) [Reserved]

(c) *Correspondence delivered by hand.* In addition to being mailed, correspondence may be delivered by hand during hours the Office is open to receive correspondence.

(d) *Facsimile transmission.* Except in the cases enumerated below, correspondence, including authorizations to charge a deposit account, may be transmitted by facsimile. The receipt date accorded to the correspondence will be the date on which the complete transmission is received in the United States Patent and Trademark Office, unless that date is a Saturday, Sunday, or Federal holiday within the District of Columbia. See paragraph (a)(3) of this section. To facilitate proper processing, each transmission session should be limited to correspondence to be filed in a single application or other proceeding before the United States Patent and Trademark Office. The application number of a patent application, the control number of a reexamination proceeding, the interference number of an interference proceeding, the trial number of a trial proceeding before the Board, or the patent number of a patent should be entered as a part of the sender's identification on a facsimile cover sheet. Facsimile transmissions are not permitted and, if submitted, will not be accorded a date of receipt in the following situations:

(1) Correspondence as specified in § 1.4(e), requiring an original signature;

(2) Certified documents as specified in § 1.4(f);

(3) Correspondence which cannot receive the benefit of the certificate of mailing or transmission as specified in § 1.8(a)(2)(i)(A) through (D), (F), and (I), and § 1.8(a)(2)(iii)(A), except that a continued prosecution application under § 1.53(d) may be transmitted to the Office by facsimile;

(4) Color drawings submitted under §§ 1.81, 1.83 through 1.85, 1.152, 1.165, 1.173, or 1.437;

(5) A request for reexamination under § 1.510 or § 1.913;

(6) Correspondence to be filed in a patent application subject to a secrecy order under §§ 5.1 through 5.5 of this chapter and directly related to the secrecy order content of the application;

(7)–(8) [Reserved]

(9) In contested cases and trials before the Patent Trial and Appeal Board, except as the Board may expressly authorize.

(e) [Reserved]

(f) *Facsimile transmission of a patent application under § 1.53(d).* In the event that the Office has no evidence of receipt of an application under § 1.53(d) (a continued prosecution application) transmitted to the Office by facsimile transmission, the party who transmitted the application under § 1.53(d) may petition the Director to accord the application under § 1.53(d) a filing date as of the date the application under § 1.53(d) is shown to have been transmitted to and received in the Office,

(1) Provided that the party who transmitted such application under § 1.53(d):

(i) Informs the Office of the previous transmission of the application under

§ 1.53(d) promptly after becoming aware that the Office has no evidence of receipt of the application under § 1.53(d);

(ii) Supplies an additional copy of the previously transmitted application under § 1.53(d); and

(iii) Includes a statement which attests on a personal knowledge basis or to the satisfaction of the Director to the previous transmission of the application under § 1.53(d) and is accompanied by a copy of the sending unit's report confirming transmission of the application under § 1.53(d) or evidence that came into being after the complete transmission and within one business day of the complete transmission of the application under § 1.53(d).

(2) The Office may require additional evidence to determine if the application under § 1.53(d) was transmitted to and received in the Office on the date in question.

(g) *Submission of the national stage correspondence required by § 1.495 via the Office electronic filing system.* In the event that the Office has no evidence of receipt of the national stage correspondence required by § 1.495, which was submitted to the Office by the Office electronic filing system, the party who submitted the correspondence may petition the Director to accord the national stage correspondence a receipt date as of the date the correspondence is shown to have been officially submitted to the Office.

(1) The petition of this paragraph (g) requires that the party who submitted such national stage correspondence:

(i) Informs the Office of the previous submission of the correspondence promptly after becoming aware that the Office has no evidence of receipt of the correspondence under § 1.495;

(ii) Supplies an additional copy of the previously submitted correspondence;

(iii) Includes a statement that attests on a personal knowledge basis, or to the satisfaction of the Director, that the correspondence was previously officially submitted; and

(iv) Supplies a copy of an acknowledgment receipt generated by the Office electronic filing system, or equivalent evidence, confirming the submission to support the statement of paragraph (g)(1)(iii) of this section.

(2) The Office may require additional evidence to determine if the national stage correspondence was submitted to the Office on the date in question.

[58 FR 54501, Oct. 22, 1993; 58 FR 64154, Dec. 6, 1993; 61 FR 56447, Nov. 1, 1996; 62 FR 53180, Oct. 10, 1997; 64 FR 48917, Sept. 8, 1999; 65 FR 54657, Sept. 8, 2000; 65 FR 76772, Dec. 7, 2000; 68 FR 14336, Mar. 25, 2003; 68 FR 48288, Aug. 13, 2003; 69 FR 49997, Aug. 12, 2004; 69 FR 56536, Sept. 21, 2004; 72 FR 2775, Jan. 23, 2007; 77 FR 42173, July 17, 2012; 77 FR 46624, Aug. 6, 2012]

§ 1.7 Times for taking action; Expiration on Saturday, Sunday or Federal holiday.

(a) Whenever periods of time are specified in this part in days, calendar days are intended. When the day, or the last day fixed by statute or by or under this part for taking any action or paying any fee in the United States Patent and Trademark Office falls on Saturday, Sunday, or on a Federal holiday within the District of Columbia, the action may be taken, or the fee paid, on the next succeeding business day which is not a Saturday, Sunday, or a Federal holiday. See § 1.304 for time for appeal or for commencing civil action.

(b) If the day that is twelve months after the filing date of a provisional application under 35 U.S.C. 111(b) and § 1.53(c) falls on Saturday, Sunday, or on a Federal holiday within the District of Columbia, the period of pendency shall be extended to the next succeeding secular or business day which is not a Saturday, Sunday, or a Federal holiday.

[65 FR 14871, Mar. 20, 2000]

§ 1.8 Certificate of mailing or transmission.

(a) Except in the situations enumerated in paragraph (a)(2) of this section or as otherwise expressly excluded in this chapter, correspondence required to be filed in the U.S. Patent and Trademark Office within a set period of time will be considered as being timely filed if the procedure described in this section is followed. The actual date of receipt will be used for all other purposes.

(1) Correspondence will be considered as being timely filed if:

(i) The correspondence is mailed or transmitted prior to expiration of the set period of time by being:

(A) Addressed as set out in § 1.1(a) and deposited with the U.S. Postal Service with sufficient postage as first class mail;

(B) Transmitted by facsimile to the Patent and Trademark Office in accordance with § 1.6(d); or

(C) Transmitted via the Office electronic filing system in accordance with § 1.6(a)(4); and

(ii) The correspondence includes a certificate for each piece of correspondence stating the date of deposit or transmission. The person signing the certificate should have reasonable basis to expect that the correspondence would be mailed or transmitted on or before the date indicated.

(2) The procedure described in paragraph (a)(1) of this section does not apply to, and no benefit will be given to a Certificate of Mailing or Transmission on the following:

(i) *Relative to Patents and Patent Applications*—

(A) The filing of a national patent application specification and drawing or other correspondence for the purpose of obtaining an application filing date, including a request for a continued prosecution application under § 1.53(d);

(B) Papers filed in trials before the Patent Trial and Appeal Board, which are governed by § 42.6(b) of this title;

(C) Papers filed in contested cases before the Patent Trial and Appeal Board, which are governed by § 41.106 (f) of this title;

(D) The filing of an international application for patent;

(E) The filing of correspondence in an international application before the U.S. Receiving Office, the U.S. International Searching Authority, or the U.S. International Preliminary Examining Authority;

(F) The filing of a copy of the international application and the basic national fee necessary to enter the national stage, as specified in § 1.495(b).

(G) The filing of a written declaration of abandonment under § 1.138;

(H) The filing of a submission under § 1.217 for publication of a redacted copy of an application;

(I) The filing of a third-party submission under § 1.290; and

(J) The calculation of any period of adjustment, as specified in § 1.703(f).

(ii) [Reserved]

(iii) *Relative to Disciplinary Proceedings*—

(A) Correspondence filed in connection with a disciplinary proceeding under part 11 of this chapter.

(B) [Reserved]

(b) In the event that correspondence is considered timely filed by being mailed or transmitted in accordance with paragraph (a) of this section, but not received in the U.S. Patent and Trademark Office after a reasonable amount of time has elapsed from the time of mailing or transmitting of the correspondence, or after the application is held to be abandoned, or after the proceeding is dismissed or decided with prejudice, or the prosecution of a reexamination proceeding is terminated pursuant to § 1.550(d) or § 1.957(b) or limited pursuant to § 1.957(c), or a requester paper is refused consideration pursuant to § 1.957(a), the correspondence will be considered timely if the party who forwarded such correspondence:

(1) Informs the Office of the previous mailing or transmission of the correspondence promptly after becoming aware that the Office has no evidence of receipt of the correspondence;

(2) Supplies an additional copy of the previously mailed or transmitted correspondence and certificate; and

(3) Includes a statement that attests on a personal knowledge basis or to the satisfaction of the Director to the previous timely mailing, transmission or submission. If the correspondence was sent by facsimile transmission, a copy of the sending unit's report confirming transmission may be used to support this statement. If the correspondence was transmitted via the Office electronic filing system, a copy of an acknowledgment receipt generated by the Office electronic filing system confirming submission may be used to support this statement.

(c) The Office may require additional evidence to determine if the correspondence was timely filed.

[58 FR 54502, Oct. 22, 1993; 58 FR 64154, Dec. 6, 1993, as amended at 61 FR 56447, Nov. 1, 1996; 62 FR 53181, Oct. 10, 1997; 67 FR 523, Jan. 4, 2002; 68 FR 48288, Aug. 13, 2003; 69 FR 49997, Aug. 12, 2004; 69 FR 56536, Sept. 21, 2004; 72 FR 2775, Jan. 23, 2007; 72 FR 18904, Apr. 16, 2007; 73 FR 47684, Aug. 14, 2008; 77 FR 42173, July 17, 2012]

§ 1.9 Definitions.

(a)(1) A national application as used in this chapter means a U.S. application for patent which was either filed in the Office under 35 U.S.C. 111, or an international application filed under the Patent Cooperation Treaty in which the basic national fee under 35 U.S.C. 41(a)(1)(F) has been paid.

(2) A provisional application as used in this chapter means a U.S. national application for patent filed in the Office under 35 U.S.C. 111(b).

(3) A nonprovisional application as used in this chapter means a U.S. national application for patent which was either filed in the Office under 35 U.S.C. 111(a), or an international application filed under the Patent Cooperation Treaty in which the basic national fee under 35 U.S.C. 41(a)(1)(F) has been paid.

(b) An international application as used in this chapter means an international application for patent filed under the Patent Cooperation Treaty prior to entering national processing at the Designated Office stage.

(c) A published application as used in this chapter means an application for patent which has been published under 35 U.S.C. 122(b).

(d)(1) The term inventor or inventorship as used in this chapter means the individual or, if a joint invention, the individuals collectively who invented or discovered the subject matter of the invention.

(2) The term joint inventor or coinventor as used in this chapter means any one of the individuals who invented or discovered the subject matter of a joint invention.

(e) The term joint research agreement as used in this chapter means a written contract, grant, or cooperative agreement entered into by two or more persons or entities for the performance of experimental, developmental, or research work in the field of the claimed invention.

(f) The term claimed invention as used in this chapter means the subject matter defined by a claim in a patent or an application for a patent.

(g) For definitions in Patent Trial and Appeal Board proceedings, see parts 41 and 42 of this title.

(h) A *Federal holiday within the District of Columbia* as used in this chapter means any day, except Saturdays and Sundays, when the Patent and Trademark Office is officially closed for business for the entire day.

(i) National security classified as used in this chapter means specifically authorized under criteria established by an Act of Congress or Executive Order to be kept secret in the interest of national defense or foreign policy and, in fact, properly classified pursuant to such Act of Congress or Executive Order.

(j) Director as used in this chapter, except for part 11 of this chapter, means the Under Secretary of Commerce for Intellectual Property and Director of the United States Patent and Trademark Office.

(k) Paper as used in this chapter means a document that may exist in electronic form, or in physical form, and therefore does not necessarily imply physical sheets of paper.

(Pub. L. 94–131, 89 Stat. 685; 35 U.S.C. 6, Pub. L. 97–247; 15 U.S.C. 1113, 1123)

[43 FR 20461, May 11, 1978, as amended at 47 FR 40139, Sept. 10, 1982; 47 FR 43275, Sept. 30, 1982; 49 FR 48451, Dec. 12, 1984; 60 FR 20220, Apr. 25, 1995; 61 FR 56447, Nov. 1, 1996; 62 FR 53181, Oct. 10, 1997; 65 FR 54657, Sept. 8, 2000; 65 FR 57051, Sept. 20, 2000; 68 FR 14336, Mar. 25, 2003; 68 FR 38624, June 30, 2003; 69 FR 49997, Aug. 12, 2004; 73 FR 47685, Aug. 14, 2008; 77 FR 46624, Aug. 6, 2012; 77 FR 48812, Aug. 14, 2012; 78 FR 11052, Feb. 14, 2013]

§ 1.10 Filing of correspondence by "Express Mail."

(a)(1) Any correspondence received by the U.S. Patent and Trademark Office (USPTO) that was delivered by the "Express Mail Post Office to Addressee" service of the United States Postal Service (USPS) will be considered filed with the USPTO on the date of deposit with the USPS.

(2) The date of deposit with USPS is shown by the "date in" on the "Express Mail" label or other official USPS notation. If the USPS deposit date cannot be determined, the correspondence will be accorded the USPTO receipt date as the filing date. *See* § 1.6(a).

(b) Correspondence should be deposited directly with an employee of the USPS to ensure that the person depositing the correspondence receives a legible copy of the "Express Mail" mailing label with the "date-in" clearly marked. Persons dealing indirectly with the employees of the USPS (such as by deposit in an "Express Mail" drop box) do so at the risk of not receiving a copy of the "Express Mail" mailing label with the desired "date-in" clearly marked. The paper(s) or fee(s) that constitute the correspondence should also include the "Express Mail" mailing label number thereon. See paragraphs (c), (d) and (e) of this section.

(c) Any person filing correspondence under this section that was received by the Office and delivered by the "Express Mail Post Office to Addressee" service of the USPS, who can show that there is a discrepancy between the filing date accorded by the Office to the correspondence and the date of deposit as shown by the "date-in" on the "Express Mail" mailing label or other official USPS notation, may petition the Director to accord the correspondence a filing date as of the "date-in" on the "Express Mail" mailing label or other official USPS notation, provided that:

(1) The petition is filed promptly after the person becomes aware that the Office has accorded, or will accord, a filing date other than the USPS deposit date;

(2) The number of the "Express Mail" mailing label was placed on the paper(s) or fee(s) that constitute the correspondence prior to the original mailing by "Express Mail;" and

(3) The petition includes a true copy of the "Express Mail" mailing label showing the "date-in," and of any other official notation by the USPS relied upon to show the date of deposit.

(d) Any person filing correspondence under this section that was received by the Office and delivered by the "Express Mail Post Office to Addressee" service of the USPS, who can show that the "date-in" on the "Express Mail" mailing label or other official notation entered by the USPS was incorrectly entered or omitted by the USPS, may petition the Director to accord the correspondence a filing date as of the date the correspondence is shown to have been deposited with the USPS, provided that:

(1) The petition is filed promptly after the person becomes aware that the Office has accorded, or will accord, a filing date based upon an incorrect entry by the USPS;

(2) The number of the "Express Mail" mailing label was placed on the paper(s) or fee(s) that constitute the correspondence prior to the original mailing by "Express Mail"; and

(3) The petition includes a showing which establishes, to the satisfaction of the Director, that the requested filing date was the date the correspondence was deposited in the "Express Mail Post Office to Addressee" service prior to the last scheduled pickup for that day. Any showing pursuant to this paragraph must be corroborated by evidence from the USPS or that came into being after deposit and within one business day of the deposit of the correspondence in the "Express Mail Post Office to Addressee" service of the USPS.

(e) Any person mailing correspondence addressed as set out in § 1.1(a) to the Office with sufficient postage utilizing the "Express Mail Post Office to Addressee" service of the USPS but not received by the Office, may petition the Director to consider such correspondence filed in the Office on the USPS deposit date, provided that:

(1) The petition is filed promptly after the person becomes aware that the Office has no evidence of receipt of the correspondence;

(2) The number of the "Express Mail" mailing label was placed on the paper(s) or fee(s) that constitute the correspondence prior to the original mailing by "Express Mail";

(3) The petition includes a copy of the originally deposited paper(s) or

fee(s) that constitute the correspondence showing the number of the "Express Mail" mailing label thereon, a copy of any returned postcard receipt, a copy of the "Express Mail" mailing label showing the "date-in," a copy of any other official notation by the USPS relied upon to show the date of deposit, and, if the requested filing date is a date other than the "date-in" on the "Express Mail" mailing label or other official notation entered by the USPS, a showing pursuant to paragraph (d)(3) of this section that the requested filing date was the date the correspondence was deposited in the "Express Mail Post Office to Addressee" service prior to the last scheduled pickup for that day; and

(4) The petition includes a statement which establishes, to the satisfaction of the Director, the original deposit of the correspondence and that the copies of the correspondence, the copy of the "Express Mail" mailing label, the copy of any returned postcard receipt, and any official notation entered by the USPS are true copies of the originally mailed correspondence, original "Express Mail" mailing label, returned postcard receipt, and official notation entered by the USPS.

(f) The Office may require additional evidence to determine if the correspondence was deposited as "Express Mail" with the USPS on the date in question.

(g) Any person who mails correspondence addressed as set out in §1.1(a) to the Office with sufficient postage utilizing the "Express Mail Post Office to Addressee" service of the USPS, but has the correspondence returned by the USPS due to an interruption or emergency in "Express Mail" service, may petition the Director to consider such correspondence as filed on a particular date in the Office, provided that:

(1) The petition is filed promptly after the person becomes aware of the return of the correspondence;

(2) The number of the "Express Mail" mailing label was placed on the paper(s) or fee(s) that constitute the correspondence prior to the original mailing by "Express Mail";

(3) The petition includes the original correspondence or a copy of the original correspondence showing the number of the "Express Mail" mailing label thereon and a copy of the "Express Mail" mailing label showing the "date-in"; and

(4) The petition includes a statement which establishes, to the satisfaction of the Director, the original deposit of the correspondence and that the correspondence or copy of the correspondence is the original correspondence or a true copy of the correspondence originally deposited with the USPS on the requested filing date. The Office may require additional evidence to determine if the correspondence was returned by the USPS due to an interruption or emergency in "Express Mail" service.

(h) Any person who attempts to mail correspondence addressed as set out in §1.1(a) to the Office with sufficient postage utilizing the "Express Mail Post Office to Addressee" service of the USPS, but has the correspondence refused by an employee of the USPS due to an interruption or emergency in "Express Mail" service, may petition the Director to consider such correspondence as filed on a particular date in the Office, provided that:

(1) The petition is filed promptly after the person becomes aware of the refusal of the correspondence;

(2) The number of the "Express Mail" mailing label was placed on the paper(s) or fee(s) that constitute the correspondence prior to the attempted mailing by "Express Mail";

(3) The petition includes the original correspondence or a copy of the original correspondence showing the number of the "Express Mail" mailing label thereon; and

(4) The petition includes a statement by the person who originally attempted to deposit the correspondence with the USPS which establishes, to the satisfaction of the Director, the original attempt to deposit the correspondence and that the correspondence or copy of the correspondence is the original correspondence or a true copy of the correspondence originally attempted to be deposited with the USPS on the requested filing date. The Office may require additional evidence to determine if the correspondence was refused by an

employee of the USPS due to an interruption or emergency in "Express Mail" service.

(i) Any person attempting to file correspondence under this section that was unable to be deposited with the USPS due to an interruption or emergency in "Express Mail" service which has been so designated by the Director, may petition the Director to consider such correspondence as filed on a particular date in the Office, provided that:

(1) The petition is filed in a manner designated by the Director promptly after the person becomes aware of the designated interruption or emergency in "Express Mail" service;

(2) The petition includes the original correspondence or a copy of the original correspondence; and

(3) The petition includes a statement which establishes, to the satisfaction of the Director, that the correspondence would have been deposited with the USPS but for the designated interruption or emergency in "Express Mail" service, and that the correspondence or copy of the correspondence is the original correspondence or a true copy of the correspondence originally attempted to be deposited with the USPS on the requested filing date.

[61 FR 56447, Nov. 1, 1996 as amended at 62 FR 53181, Oct. 10, 1997; 67 FR 36101, May 23, 2002; 68 FR 48288, Aug. 13, 2003; 69 FR 56536, Sept. 21, 2004; 77 FR 46624, Aug. 6, 2012]

Records and Files of the Patent and Trademark Office

§ 1.11 Files open to the public.

(a) The specification, drawings, and all papers relating to the file of: A published application; a patent; or a statutory invention registration are open to inspection by the public, and copies may be obtained upon the payment of the fee set forth in § 1.19(b)(2). If an application was published in redacted form pursuant to § 1.217, the complete file wrapper and contents of the patent application will not be available if: The requirements of paragraphs (d)(1), (d)(2), and (d)(3) of § 1.217 have been met in the application; and the application is still pending. See § 2.27 of this title for trademark files.

(b) All reissue applications, all applications in which the Office has accepted a request to open the complete application to inspection by the public, and related papers in the application file, are open to inspection by the public, and copies may be furnished upon paying the fee therefor. The filing of reissue applications, other than continued prosecution applications under § 1.53(d) of reissue applications, will be announced in the *Official Gazette*. The announcement shall include at least the filing date, reissue application and original patent numbers, title, class and subclass, name of the inventor, name of the owner of record, name of the attorney or agent of record, and examining group to which the reissue application is assigned.

(c) All requests for reexamination for which all the requirements of § 1.510 or § 1.915 have been satisfied will be announced in the *Official Gazette*. Any reexaminations at the initiative of the Director pursuant to § 1.520 will also be announced in the *Official Gazette*. The announcement shall include at least the date of the request, if any, the reexamination request control number or the Director initiated order control number, patent number, title, class and subclass, name of the inventor, name of the patent owner of record, and the examining group to which the reexamination is assigned.

(d) All papers or copies thereof relating to a reexamination proceeding which have been entered of record in the patent or reexamination file are open to inspection by the general public, and copies may be furnished upon paying the fee therefor.

(e) Except as prohibited in § 41.6(b), § 42.14 or § 42.410(b), the file of any interference or trial before the Patent Trial and Appeal Board is open to public inspection and copies of the file may be obtained upon payment of the fee therefor.

(35 U.S.C. 6; 15 U.S.C. 1113, 1123)

[46 FR 29181, May 29, 1981, as amended at 47 FR 41272, Sept. 17, 1982; 50 FR 9378, Mar. 7, 1985; 60 FR 14518, Mar. 17, 1995; 62 FR 53181, Oct. 10, 1997; 65 FR 57051, Sept. 20, 2000; 69 FR 49997, Aug. 12, 2004; 70 FR 56126, Sept. 26, 2005; 71 FR 44223, Aug. 4, 2006; 77 FR 46624, Aug. 6, 2012]

§ 1.12 Assignment records open to public inspection.

(a)(1) Separate assignment records are maintained in the United States Patent and Trademark Office for patents and trademarks. The assignment records, relating to original or reissue patents, including digests and indexes (for assignments recorded on or after May 1, 1957), and published patent applications, are open to public inspection at the United States Patent and Trademark Office, and copies of patent assignment records may be obtained upon request and payment of the fee set forth in § 1.19 of this chapter. See § 2.200 of this chapter regarding trademark assignment records.

(2) All records of assignments of patents recorded before May 1, 1957, are maintained by the National Archives and Records Administration (NARA). The records are open to public inspection. Certified and uncertified copies of those assignment records are provided by NARA upon request and payment of the fees required by NARA.

(b) Assignment records, digests, and indexes relating to any pending or abandoned patent application, which is open to the public pursuant to § 1.11 or for which copies or access may be supplied pursuant to § 1.14, are available to the public. Copies of any assignment records, digests, and indexes that are not available to the public shall be obtainable only upon written authority of an inventor, the applicant, the assignee or an assignee of an undivided part interest, or a patent practitioner of record, or upon a showing that the person seeking such information is a bona fide prospective or actual purchaser, mortgagee, or licensee of such application, unless it shall be necessary to the proper conduct of business before the Office or as provided in this part.

(c) Any request by a member of the public seeking copies of any assignment records of any pending or abandoned patent application preserved in confidence under § 1.14, or any information with respect thereto, must:

(1) Be in the form of a petition including the fee set forth in § 1.17(g); or

(2) Include written authority granting access to the member of the public to the particular assignment records from an inventor, the applicant, the assignee or an assignee of an undivided part interest, or a patent practitioner of record.

(d) An order for a copy of an assignment or other document should identify the reel and frame number where the assignment or document is recorded. If a document is identified without specifying its correct reel and frame, an extra charge as set forth in § 1.21(j) will be made for the time consumed in making a search for such assignment.

(35 U.S.C. 6; 15 U.S.C. 1113, 1123)

[47 FR 41272, Sept. 17, 1982, as amended at 54 FR 6900, Feb. 15, 1989; 56 FR 65151, Dec. 13, 1991; 56 FR 66670, Dec. 24, 1991; 57 FR 29641, July 6, 1992; 60 FR 20221, Apr. 25, 1995; 61 FR 42802, Aug. 19, 1996; 65 FR 54657, Sept. 8, 2000; 65 FR 57051, Sept. 20, 2000; 68 FR 48288, Aug. 13, 2003; 69 FR 29877, May 26, 2004; 69 FR 56536, Sept. 21, 2004; 77 FR 48812, Aug. 14, 2012]

§ 1.13 Copies and certified copies.

(a) Non-certified copies of patents, and patent application publications and of any records, books, papers, or drawings within the jurisdiction of the United States Patent and Trademark Office and open to the public, will be furnished by the United States Patent and Trademark Office to any person, and copies of other records or papers will be furnished to persons entitled thereto, upon payment of the appropriate fee. See § 2.201 of this chapter regarding copies of trademark records.

(b) Certified copies of patents, patent application publications, and trademark registrations and of any records, books, papers, or drawings within the jurisdiction of the United States Patent and Trademark Office and open to the public or persons entitled thereto will be authenticated by the seal of the United States Patent and Trademark Office and certified by the Director, or in his or her name, upon payment of the fee for the certified copy.

[68 FR 48288, Aug. 13, 2003, as amended at 68 FR 71006, Dec. 22, 2003]

§ 1.14 Patent applications preserved in confidence.

(a) *Confidentiality of patent application information.* Patent applications that have not been published under 35 U.S.C.

122(b) are generally preserved in confidence pursuant to 35 U.S.C. 122(a). Information concerning the filing, pendency, or subject matter of an application for patent, including status information, and access to the application, will only be given to the public as set forth in § 1.11 or in this section.

(1) Records associated with patent applications (see paragraph (g) for international applications) may be available in the following situations:

(i) *Patented applications and statutory invention registrations.* The file of an application that has issued as a patent or published as a statutory invention registration is available to the public as set forth in § 1.11(a). A copy of the patent application-as-filed, the file contents of the application, or a specific document in the file of such an application may be provided upon request and payment of the appropriate fee set forth in § 1.19(b).

(ii) *Published abandoned applications.* The file of an abandoned application that has been published as a patent application publication is available to the public as set forth in § 1.11(a). A copy of the application-as-filed, the file contents of the published application, or a specific document in the file of the published application may be provided to any person upon request, and payment of the appropriate fee set forth in § 1.19(b).

(iii) *Published pending applications.* A copy of the application-as-filed, the file contents of the application, or a specific document in the file of a pending application that has been published as a patent application publication may be provided to any person upon request, and payment of the appropriate fee set forth in § 1.19(b). If a redacted copy of the application was used for the patent application publication, the copy of the specification, drawings, and papers may be limited to a redacted copy. The Office will not provide access to the paper file of a pending application that has been published, except as provided in paragraph (c) or (i) of this section.

(iv) *Unpublished abandoned applications (including provisional applications) that are identified or relied upon.* The file contents of an unpublished, abandoned application may be made available to the public if the application is identified in a U.S. patent, a statutory invention registration, a U.S. patent application publication, or an international patent application publication of an international application that was published in accordance with PCT Article 21(2). An application is considered to have been identified in a document, such as a patent, when the application number or serial number and filing date, first named inventor, title and filing date or other application specific information are provided in the text of the patent, but not when the same identification is made in a paper in the file contents of the patent and is not included in the printed patent. Also, the file contents may be made available to the public, upon a written request, if benefit of the abandoned application is claimed under 35 U.S.C. 119(e), 120, 121, or 365 in an application that has issued as a U.S. patent, or has published as a statutory invention registration, a U.S. patent application publication, or an international patent application that was published in accordance with PCT Article 21(2). A copy of the application-as-filed, the file contents of the application, or a specific document in the file of the application may be provided to any person upon written request, and payment of the appropriate fee (§ 1.19(b)).

(v) *Unpublished pending applications (including provisional applications) whose benefit is claimed.* A copy of the file contents of an unpublished pending application may be provided to any person, upon written request and payment of the appropriate fee (§ 1.19(b)), if the benefit of the application is claimed under 35 U.S.C. 119(e), 120, 121, or 365 in an application that has issued as a U.S. patent, an application that has published as a statutory invention registration, a U.S. patent application publication, or an international patent application publication that was published in accordance with PCT Article 21(2). A copy of the application-as-filed, or a specific document in the file of the pending application may also be provided to any person upon written request, and payment of the appropriate fee (§ 1.19(b)). The Office will not provide access to the paper file of a pending application, except as provided in paragraph (c) or (i) of this section.

(vi) *Unpublished pending applications (including provisional applications) that are incorporated by reference or otherwise identified.* A copy of the application as originally filed of an unpublished pending application may be provided to any person, upon written request and payment of the appropriate fee (§ 1.19(b)), if the application is incorporated by reference or otherwise identified in a U.S. patent, a statutory invention registration, a U.S. patent application publication, or an international patent application publication that was published in accordance with PCT Article 21(2). The Office will not provide access to the paper file of a pending application, except as provided in paragraph (c) or (i) of this section.

(vii) *When a petition for access or a power to inspect is required.* Applications that were not published or patented, that are not the subject of a benefit claim under 35 U.S.C. 119(e), 120, 121, or 365 in an application that has issued as a U.S. patent, an application that has published as a statutory invention registration, a U.S. patent application publication, or an international patent application publication that was published in accordance with PCT Article 21(2), or are not identified in a U.S. patent, a statutory invention registration, a U.S. patent application publication, or an international patent application that was published in accordance with PCT Article 21(2), are not available to the public. If an application is identified in the file contents of another application, but not the published patent application or patent itself, a granted petition for access (see paragraph (i)), or a power to inspect (see paragraph (c)) is necessary to obtain the application, or a copy of the application.

(2) Information concerning a patent application may be communicated to the public if the patent application is identified in a published patent document or in an application as set forth in paragraphs (a)(1)(i) through (a)(1)(vi) of this section. The information that may be communicated to the public (*i.e.*, status information) includes:

(i) Whether the application is pending, abandoned, or patented;

(ii) Whether the application has been published under 35 U.S.C. 122(b);

(iii) The application "numerical identifier" which may be:

(A) The eight-digit application number (the two-digit series code plus the six-digit serial number); or

(B) The six-digit serial number plus any one of the filing date of the national application, the international filing date, or date of entry into the national stage; and

(iv) Whether another application claims the benefit of the application (*i.e.*, whether there are any applications that claim the benefit of the filing date under 35 U.S.C. 119(e), 120, 121 or 365 of the application), and if there are any such applications, the numerical identifier of the application, the specified relationship between the applications (e.g., continuation), whether the application is pending, abandoned or patented, and whether the application has been published under 35 U.S.C. 122(b).

(b) *Electronic access to an application.* Where a copy of the application file or access to the application may be made available pursuant to this section, the Office may at its discretion provide access to only an electronic copy of the specification, drawings, and file contents of the application.

(c) *Power to inspect a pending or abandoned application.* Access to an application may be provided to any person if the application file is available, and the application contains written authority (*e.g.*, a power to inspect) granting access to such person. The written authority must be signed by:

(1) The applicant;

(2) A patent practitioner of record;

(3) The assignee or an assignee of an undivided part interest;

(4) The inventor or a joint inventor; or

(5) A registered attorney or agent named in the papers accompanying the application papers filed under § 1.53 or the national stage documents filed under § 1.495, if a power of attorney has not been appointed under § 1.32.

(d) *Applications reported to Department of Energy.* Applications for patents which appear to disclose, purport to disclose or do disclose inventions or discoveries relating to atomic energy are reported to the Department of Energy, which Department will be given access to the applications. Such reporting does not constitute a determination that the subject matter of each application so reported is in fact useful or is an invention or discovery, or that such application in fact discloses subject matter in categories specified by 42 U.S.C. 2181(c) and (d).

(e) *Decisions by the Director.* Any decision by the Director that would not otherwise be open to public inspection may be published or made available for public inspection if:

(1) The Director believes the decision involves an interpretation of patent laws or regulations that would be of precedential value; and

(2) The applicant is given notice and an opportunity to object in writing within two months on the ground that the decision discloses a trade secret or other confidential information. Any objection must identify the deletions in the text of the decision considered necessary to protect the information, or explain why the entire decision must be withheld from the public to protect such information. An applicant or party will be given time, not less than twenty days, to request reconsideration and seek court review before any portions of a decision are made public under this paragraph over his or her objection.

(f) *Notice to inventor of the filing of an application.* The Office may publish notice in the *Official Gazette* as to the filing of an application on behalf of an inventor by a person who otherwise shows sufficient proprietary interest in the matter.

(g) *International applications.* (1) Copies of international application files for international applications which designate the U.S. and which have been published in accordance with PCT Article 21(2), or copies of a document in such application files, will be furnished in accordance with PCT Articles 30 and 38 and PCT Rules 94.2 and 94.3, upon written request including a showing that the publication of the application has occurred and that the U.S. was designated, and upon payment of the appropriate fee (see § 1.19(b)), if:

(i) With respect to the Home Copy (the copy of the international application kept by the Office in its capacity as the Receiving Office, see PCT Article 12(1)), the international application was filed with the U.S. Receiving Office;

(ii) With respect to the Search Copy (the copy of an international application kept by the Office in its capacity as the International Searching Authority, see PCT Article 12(1)), the U.S. acted as the International Searching Authority, except for the written opinion of the International Searching Authority which shall not be available until the expiration of thirty months from the priority date; or

(iii) With respect to the Examination Copy (the copy of an international application kept by the Office in its capacity as the International Preliminary Examining Authority), the United States acted as the International Preliminary Examining Authority, an International Preliminary Examination Report has issued, and the United States was elected.

(2) A copy of an English language translation of a publication of an international application which has been filed in the United States Patent and Trademark Office pursuant to 35 U.S.C. 154(d)(4) will be furnished upon written request including a showing that the publication of the application in accordance with PCT Article 21(2) has occurred and that the U.S. was designated, and upon payment of the appropriate fee (§ 1.19(b)(4)).

(3) Access to international application files for international applications which designate the U.S. and which have been published in accordance with PCT Article 21(2), or copies of a document in such application files, will be permitted in accordance with PCT Articles 30 and 38 and PCT Rules 44*ter*.1, 94.2 and 94.3, upon written request including a showing that the publication of the application has occurred and that the U.S. was designated.

(4) In accordance with PCT Article 30, copies of an international application-as-filed under paragraph (a) of this section will not be provided prior to the international publication of the application pursuant to PCT Article 21(2).

(5) Access to international application files under paragraphs (a)(1)(i) through (a)(1)(vi) and (g)(3) of this section will not be permitted with respect to the Examination Copy in accordance with PCT Article 38.

(h) *Access by a Foreign Intellectual Property Office.* (1) Access to the application-as-filed may be provided to any foreign intellectual property office participating with the Office in a bilateral or multilateral priority document exchange agreement (participating foreign intellectual property office), if the application contains written authority granting such access. Written authority under this paragraph should be submitted prior to filing a subsequent foreign application with a participating intellectual property office in which priority is claimed to the patent application.

(2) Written authority provided under paragraph (h)(1) of this section must include the title of the invention (§ 1.71(a)), comply with the requirements of paragraph (c) of this section, and be submitted on a separate document (§ 1.4(c)).

(3) Written authority provided under paragraph (h)(1) of this section will be treated as authorizing the Office to provide to all participating foreign intellectual property offices indicated in the written authority in accordance with their respective agreements with the Office:

(i) A copy of the application-as-filed; and

(ii) A copy of the application-as-filed with respect to any application the filing date of which is claimed by the application in which written authority under paragraph (h)(1) of this section is filed.

(i) *Access or copies in other circumstances.* The Office, either *sua sponte* or on petition, may also provide access or copies of all or part of an application if necessary to carry out an Act of Congress or if warranted by other special circumstances. Any petition by a member of the public seeking access to, or copies of, all or part of any pending or abandoned application preserved in confidence pursuant to paragraph (a) of this section, or any related papers, must include:

(1) The fee set forth in § 1.17(g); and

(2) A showing that access to the application is necessary to carry out an Act of Congress or that special circumstances exist which warrant petitioner being granted access to all or part of the application.

[68 FR 38624, June 30, 2003, as amended at 68 FR 59886, Oct. 20, 2003; 68 FR 67805, Dec. 4, 2003; 68 FR 71006, Dec. 22, 2003; 69 FR 49997, Aug. 12, 2004; 69 FR 56536, Sept. 21, 2004; 72 FR 1667, Jan. 16, 2007; 77 FR 48812, Aug. 14, 2012; 78 FR 11052, Feb. 14, 2013]

§ 1.15 [Reserved]

FEES AND PAYMENT OF MONEY

AUTHORITY: Sections 1.16 through 1.22 also issued under 35 U.S.C. 41, 111, 119, 120, 132(b), 156, 157, 255, 302, and 311, Public Laws 103–465, 106–113, and 112–29.

§ 1.16 National application filing, search, and examination fees.

(a) Basic fee for filing each application under 35 U.S.C. 111 for an original patent, except design, plant, or provisional applications:

By a micro entity (§ 1.29)	$70.00
By a small entity (§ 1.27(a))	140.00
By a small entity (§ 1.27(a)) if the application is submitted in compliance with the Office electronic filing system (§ 1.27(b)(2))	70.00
By other than a small or micro entity	280.00

(b) Basic fee for filing each application for an original design patent:

By a micro entity (§ 1.29)	$45.00
By a small entity (§ 1.27(a))	90.00
By other than a small or micro entity	180.00

(c) Basic fee for filing each application for an original plant patent:

By a micro entity (§ 1.29)	$45.00
By a small entity (§ 1.27(a))	90.00
By other than a small or micro entity	180.00

(d) Basic fee for filing each provisional application:

By a micro entity (§ 1.29)	$65.00
By a small entity (§ 1.27(a))	130.00
By other than a small or micro entity	260.00

(e) Basic fee for filing each application for the reissue of a patent:

By a micro entity (§ 1.29) $70.00
By a small entity (§ 1.27(a)) 140.00
By other than a small or micro entity 280.00

(f) Surcharge for filing any of the basic filing fee, the search fee, the examination fee, or the oath or declaration on a date later than the filing date of the application, except provisional applications:

By a micro entity (§ 1.29) $35.00
By a small entity (§ 1.27(a)) 70.00
By other than a small or micro entity 140.00

(g) Surcharge for filing the basic filing fee or cover sheet (§ 1.51(c)(1)) on a date later than the filing date of the provisional application:

By a micro entity (§ 1.29) $15.00
By a small entity (§ 1.27(a)) 30.00
By other than a small or micro entity 60.00

(h) In addition to the basic filing fee in an application, other than a provisional application, for filing or later presentation at any other time of each claim in independent form in excess of 3:

By a micro entity (§ 1.29) $105.00
By a small entity (§ 1.27(a)) 210.00
By other than a small or micro entity 420.00

(i) In addition to the basic filing fee in an application, other than a provisional application, for filing or later presentation at any other time of each claim (whether dependent or independent) in excess of 20 (note that § 1.75(c) indicates how multiple dependent claims are considered for fee calculation purposes):

By a micro entity (§ 1.29) $20.00
By a small entity (§ 1.27(a)) 40.00
By other than a small or micro entity 80.00

(j) In addition to the basic filing fee in an application, other than a provisional application, that contains, or is amended to contain, a multiple dependent claim, per application:

By a micro entity (§ 1.29) $195.00
By a small entity (§ 1.27(a)) 390.00
By other than a small or micro entity 780.00

(k) Search fee for each application filed under 35 U.S.C. 111 for an original patent, except design, plant, or provisional applications:

By a micro entity (§ 1.29) $150.00
By a small entity (§ 1.27(a)) 300.00
By other than a small or micro entity 600.00

(l) Search fee for each application for an original design patent:

By a micro entity (§ 1.29) $30.00
By a small entity (§ 1.27(a)) 60.00
By other than a small or micro entity 120.00

(m) Search fee for each application for an original plant patent:

By a micro entity (§ 1.29) $95.00
By a small entity (§ 1.27(a)) 190.00
By other than a small or micro entity 380.00

(n) Search fee for each application for the reissue of a patent:

By a micro entity (§ 1.29) $150.00
By a small entity (§ 1.27(a)) 300.00
By other than a small or micro entity 600.00

(o) Examination fee for each application filed under 35 U.S.C. 111 for an original patent, except design, plant, or provisional applications:

By a micro entity (§ 1.29) $180.00
By a small entity (§ 1.27(a)) 360.00
By other than a small or micro entity 720.00

(p) Examination fee for each application for an original design patent:

By a micro entity (§ 1.29) $115.00
By a small entity (§ 1.27(a)) 230.00
By other than a small or micro entity 460.00

(q) Examination fee for each application for an original plant patent:

By a micro entity (§ 1.29) $145.00
By a small entity (§ 1.27(a)) 290.00
By other than a small or micro entity 580.00

(r) Examination fee for each application for the reissue of a patent:

By a micro entity (§ 1.29) $540.00
By a small entity (§ 1.27(a)) 1,080.00
By other than a small or micro entity 2,160.00

(s) Application size fee for any application filed under 35 U.S.C. 111 for the specification and drawings which exceed 100 sheets of paper, for each additional 50 sheets or fraction thereof:

By a micro entity (§ 1.29) $100.00
By a small entity (§ 1.27(a)) 200.00
By other than a small or micro entity 400.00

(t) Non-electronic filing fee for any application under 35 U.S.C. 111(a) that is filed on or after November 15, 2011, other than by the Office electronic filing system, except for a reissue, design, or plant application:

By a small entity (§ 1.27(a)) ... $200.00
By other than a small entity $400.00

NOTE TO § 1.16: See §§ 1.445, 1.482 and 1.492 for international application filing and processing fees.

[70 FR 3887, Jan. 27, 2005, as amended at 70 FR 30365, May 26, 2005; 72 FR 46901, Aug. 22, 2007; 73 FR 47540, Aug. 14, 2008; 76 FR 70653, Nov. 15, 2011; 77 FR 48812, Aug. 14, 2012; 77 FR 54365, Sept. 5, 2012; 78 FR 4284, Jan. 18, 2013]

§ 1.17 Patent application and reexamination processing fees.

(a) Extension fees pursuant to § 1.136(a):

(1) For reply within first month:
By a micro entity (§ 1.29) $50.00
By a small entity (§ 1.27(a)) $100.00
By other than a small or micro entity $200.00

(2) For reply within second month:
By a micro entity (§ 1.29) $150.00
By a small entity (§ 1.27(a)) $300.00
By other than a small or micro entity $600.00

(3) For reply within third month:
By a micro entity (§ 1.29) $350.00
By a small entity (§ 1.27(a)) $700.00
By other than a small or micro entity $1,400.00

(4) For reply within fourth month:.
By a micro entity (§ 1.29) $550.00
By a small entity (§ 1.27(a)) $1,100.00
By other than a small or micro entity $2,200.00

(5) For reply within fifth month:
By a micro entity (§ 1.29) $750.00
By a small entity (§ 1.27(a)) $1,500.00
By other than a small or micro entity $3,000.00

(b) For fees in proceedings before the Patent Trial and Appeal Board, *see* § 41.20 and § 42.15 of this title.

(c) For filing a request for prioritized examination under § 1.102(e):
By a micro entity (§ 1.29) $1,000.00
By a small entity (§ 1.27(a)) $2,000.00
By other than a small or micro entity $4,000.00

(d) For correction of inventorship in an application after the first action on the merits:
By a micro entity (§ 1.29) $150.00
By a small entity (§ 1.27(a)) $300.00
By other than a small or micro entity $600.00

(e) To request continued examination pursuant to § 1.114:

(1) For filing a first request for continued examination pursuant to § 1.114 in an application:
By a micro entity (§ 1.29) $300.00
By a small entity (§ 1.27(a)) $600.00
By other than a small or micro entity $1,200.00

(2) For filing a second or subsequent request for continued examination pursuant to § 1.114 in an application:
By a micro entity (§ 1.29) $425.00
By a small entity (§ 1.27(a)) $850.00

By other than a small or micro entity	$1,700.00
(f) For filing a petition under one of the following sections which refers to this paragraph:	
By a micro entity (§ 1.29)	$100.00
By a small entity (§ 1.27(a))	$200.00
By other than a small or micro entity	$400.00

§ 1.36(a)—for revocation of a power of attorney by fewer than all of the applicants.

§ 1.53(e)—to accord a filing date.

§ 1.57(a)—to accord a filing date.

§ 1.182—for decision on a question not specifically provided for.

§ 1.183—to suspend the rules.

§ 1.378(e)—for reconsideration of decision on petition refusing to accept delayed payment of maintenance fee in an expired patent.

§ 1.741(b)—to accord a filing date to an application under § 1.740 for extension of a patent term.

(g) For filing a petition under one of the following sections which refers to this paragraph:	
By a micro entity (§ 1.29)	$50.00
By a small entity (§ 1.27(a))	$100.00
By other than a small or micro entity	$200.00

§ 1.12—for access to an assignment record.

§ 1.14—for access to an application.

§ 1.46—for filing an application on behalf of an inventor by a person who otherwise shows sufficient proprietary interest in the matter.

§ 1.55(f)—for filing a belated certified copy of a foreign application.

§ 1.59—for expungement of information.

§ 1.103(a)—to suspend action in an application.

§ 1.136(b)—for review of a request for extension of time when the provisions of § 1.136(a) are not available.

§ 1.377—for review of decision refusing to accept and record payment of a maintenance fee filed prior to expiration of a patent.

§ 1.550(c)—for patent owner requests for extension of time in *ex parte* reexamination proceedings.

§ 1.956—for patent owner requests for extension of time in *inter partes* reexamination proceedings.

§ 5.12—for expedited handling of a foreign filing license.

§ 5.15—for changing the scope of a license.

§ 5.25—for retroactive license.

(h) For filing a petition under one of the following sections which refers to this paragraph:	
By a micro entity (§ 1.29)	$35.00
By a small entity (§ 1.27(a))	$70.00
By other than a small or micro entity	$140.00

§ 1.19(g)—to request documents in a form other than provided in this part.

§ 1.84—for accepting color drawings or photographs.

§ 1.91—for entry of a model or exhibit.

§ 1.102(d)—to make an application special.

§ 1.138(c)—to expressly abandon an application to avoid publication.

§ 1.313—to withdraw an application from issue.

§ 1.314—to defer issuance of a patent.

(i) Processing fees:	
(1) For taking action under one of the following sections which refers to this paragraph:	
By a micro entity (§ 1.29)	$35.00
By a small entity (§ 1.27(a))	$70.00
By other than a small or micro entity	$140.00

§ 1.28(c)(3)—for processing a non-itemized fee deficiency based on an error in small entity status.

§ 1.29(k)(3)—for processing a non-itemized fee deficiency based on an error in micro entity status.

§ 1.41(b)—for supplying the name or names of the inventor or joint inventors in an application without either an application data sheet or the inventor's oath or declaration, except in provisional applications.

§ 1.48—for correcting inventorship, except in provisional applications.

§ 1.52(d)—for processing a nonprovisional application filed with a specification in a language other than English.

§ 1.53(c)(3)—to convert a provisional application filed under § 1.53(c) into a nonprovisional application under § 1.53(b).

§ 1.55—for entry of a priority claim or certified copy of a foreign application after payment of the issue fee.

§ 1.71(g)(2)—for processing a belated amendment under § 1.71(g).

§ 1.102(e)—for requesting prioritized examination of an application.

§ 1.103(b)—for requesting limited suspension of action, continued prosecution application for a design patent (§ 1.53(d)).

§ 1.103(c)—for requesting limited suspension of action, request for continued examination (§ 1.114).

§ 1.103(d)—for requesting deferred examination of an application.

§ 1.291(c)(5)—for processing a second or subsequent protest by the same real party in interest.

§ 3.81—for a patent to issue to assignee, assignment submitted after payment of the issue fee.

(2) For taking action under one of the following sections which refers to this paragraph $130.00

§ 1.217—for processing a redacted copy of a paper submitted in the file of an application in which a redacted copy was submitted for the patent application publication.

§ 1.221—for requesting voluntary publication or republication of an application.

(j) [Reserved]

(k) For filing a request for expedited examination under § 1.155(a):

By a micro entity (§ 1.29) $225.00

By a small entity (§ 1.27(a)) $450.00

By other than a small or micro entity. $900.00

(l) For filing a petition for the revival of an unavoidably abandoned application under 35 U.S.C. 111, 133, 364, or 371, for the unavoidably delayed payment of the issue fee under 35 U.S.C. 151, or for the revival of an unavoidably terminated reexamination proceeding under 35 U.S.C. 133 (§ 1.137(a)):

By a micro entity (§ 1.29) $160.00

By a small entity (§ 1.27(a)) $320.00

By other than a small or micro entity $640.00

(m) For filing a petition for the revival of an unintentionally abandoned application, for the unintentionally delayed payment of the fee for issuing a patent, or for the revival of an unintentionally terminated reexamination proceeding under 35 U.S.C. 41(a)(7) (§ 1.137(b)):

By a micro entity (§ 1.29) $475.00

By a small entity (§ 1.27(a)) $950.00

By other than a small or micro entity $1,900.00

(n) [Reserved]

(o) [Reserved]

(p) For an information disclosure statement under § 1.97(c) or (d) or for the document fee for a submission under § 1.290:

By a micro entity (§ 1.29) $45.00

By a small entity (§ 1.27(a)) $90.00

By other than a small or micro entity $180.00

(q) Processing fee for taking action under one of the following sections which refers to this paragraph $50.00

§ 1.41—to supply the name or names of the inventor or inventors after the filing date without a cover sheet as prescribed by § 1.51(c)(1) in a provisional application.

§ 1.48—for correction of inventorship in a provisional application.

§ 1.53(c)(2)—to convert a nonprovisional application filed under § 1.53(b) to a provisional application under § 1.53(c).

(r) For entry of a submission after final rejection under § 1.129(a):

By a micro entity (§ 1.29)	$210.00
By a small entity (§ 1.27(a))	$420.00
By other than a small or micro entity	$840.00

(s) For each additional invention requested to be examined under § 1.129(b):

By a micro entity (§ 1.29)	$210.00
By a small entity (§ 1.27(a))	$420.00
By other than a small or micro entity	$840.00

(t) For the acceptance of an unintentionally delayed claim for priority under 35 U.S.C. 119, 120, 121, or 365(a) or (c) (§§ 1.55 and 1.78) or for filing a request for the restoration of the right of priority under § 1.452:

By a micro entity (§ 1.29)	$355.00
By a small entity (§ 1.27(a)).	$710.00
By other than a small or micro entity	$1,420.00

[78 FR 17105, Mar. 20, 2013]

§ 1.18 Patent post allowance (including issue) fees.

(a) Issue fee for issuing each original patent, except a design or plant patent, or for issuing each reissue patent:

(1) For an issue fee paid on or after January 1, 2014:

By a micro entity (§ 1.29)	$240.00
By a small entity (§ 1.27(a))	480.00
By other than a small or micro entity	960.00

(2) For an issue fee paid before January 1, 2014:

By a micro entity (§ 1.29)	$445.00
By a small entity (§ 1.27(a))	890.00
By other than a small or micro entity	1,780.00

(b) Issue fee for issuing an original design patent:

(1) For an issue fee paid on or after January 1, 2014:

By a micro entity (§ 1.29)	$140.00
By a small entity (§ 1.27(a))	280.00
By other than a small or micro entity	560.00

(2) For an issue fee paid before January 1, 2014:

By a micro entity (§ 1.29)	$255.00
By a small entity (§ 1.27(a))	510.00
By other than a small or micro entity	1,020.00

(c) Issue fee for issuing an original plant patent:

(1) For an issue fee paid on or after January 1, 2014:

By a micro entity (§ 1.29)	$190.00
By a small entity (§ 1.27(a))	380.00
By other than a small or micro entity	760.00

(2) For an issue fee paid before January 1, 2014:

By a micro entity (§ 1.29)	$350.00
By a small entity (§ 1.27(a))	700.00
By other than a small or micro entity	1,400.00

(d)

(1) Publication fee on or after January 1, 2014	$0.00
(2) Publication fee before January 1, 2014	300.00
(3) Republication fee (§ 1.221(a))	300.00

(e) For filing an application for patent term adjustment under § 1.705: $200.00.

(f) For filing a request for reinstatement of all or part of the term reduced pursuant to § 1.704(b) in an application for patent term adjustment under§ 1.705: $400.00.

[78 FR 4286, Jan. 18, 2013]

§ 1.19 Document supply fees.

The United States Patent and Trademark Office will supply copies of the following patent-related documents upon payment of the fees indicated. Paper copies will be in black and white unless the original document is in color, a color copy is requested and the fee for a color copy is paid.

(a) Uncertified copies of patent application publications and patents:

(1) Printed copy of the paper portion of a patent application publication or patent including a design patent, statutory invention registration, or defensive publication document. Service includes preparation of copies by the Office within two to three business days and delivery by United States Postal Service; and preparation of copies by the Office within one business day of receipt and delivery to an Office Box or by electronic means (e.g., facsimile, electronic mail): $3.00.

(2) Printed copy of a plant patent in color: $15.00.

(3) Color copy of a patent (other than a plant patent) or statutory invention registration containing a color drawing: $25.00.

(b) Copies of Office documents to be provided in paper, or in electronic form, as determined by the Director (for other patent-related materials *see* § 1.21(k)):

(1) Copy of a patent application as filed, or a patent-related file wrapper and contents, stored in paper in a paper file wrapper, in an image format in an image file wrapper, or if color documents, stored in paper in an Artifact Folder:

(i) If provided on paper:

(A) Application as filed: $20.00.

(B) File wrapper and contents of 400 or fewer pages: $200.00.

(C) Additional fee for each additional 100 pages or portion thereof of file wrapper and contents: $40.00.

(D) Individual application documents, other than application as filed, per document: $25.00.

(ii) If provided on compact disc or other physical electronic medium in single order:

(A) Application as filed: $20.00.

(B) File wrapper and contents, first physical electronic medium: $55.00.

(C) Additional fee for each continuing physical electronic medium in the single order of paragraph (b)(1)(ii)(B) of this section: $15.00.

(iii) If provided electronically (e.g., by electronic transmission) other than on a physical electronic medium as specified in paragraph (b)(1)(ii) of this section:

(A) Application as filed: $20.00.

(B) File wrapper and contents: $55.00.

(iv) If provided to a foreign intellectual property office pursuant to a priority document exchange agreement (*see* § 1.14 (h)(1)): $0.00.

(2) Copy of patent-related file wrapper contents that were submitted and are stored on compact disc or other electronic form (e.g., compact discs stored in an Artifact Folder), other than as available in paragraph (b)(1) of this section:

(i) If provided on compact disc or other physical electronic medium in a single order:

(A) First physical electronic medium in a single order: $55.00.

(B) Additional fee for each continuing physical electronic medium in the single order of this paragraph (b)(2)(i): $15.00.

(ii) If provided electronically other than on a physical electronic medium per order: $55.00.

(3) Copy of Office records, except copies available under paragraph (b)(1) or (2) of this section: $25.00.

(4) For assignment records, abstract of title and certification, per patent: $25.00.

(c) Library service (35 U.S.C. 13): For providing to libraries copies of all patents issued annually, per annum: $50.00.

(d) For list of all United States patents and statutory invention registrations in a subclass: $3.00.

(e) Uncertified statement as to status of the payment of maintenance fees due on a patent or expiration of a patent: $10.00.

(f) Uncertified copy of a non-United States patent document, per document: $25.00.

(g) Petitions for documents in a form other than that provided by this part, or in a form other than that generally provided by the Director, will be decided in accordance with the merits of each situation. Any petition seeking a decision under this section must be accompanied by the petition fee set forth in § 1.17(h) and, if the petition is granted, the documents will be provided at cost.

[78 FR 4287, Jan. 18, 2013]

§ 1.20 Post issuance fees.

(a) For providing a certificate of correction for applicant's mistake (§ 1.323) ... $100.00

(b) Processing fee for correcting inventorship in a patent (§ 1.324) ... $130.00

(c) In reexamination proceedings:

(1) For filing a request for *ex parte* reexamination (§ 1.510(a)):

By a micro entity (§ 1.29) ... $3,000.00

By a small entity (§ 1.27(a)) ... $6,000.00

By other than a small or micro entity ... $12,000.00

(2) [Reserved]

(3) For filing with a request for reexamination or later presentation at any other time of each claim in independent form in excess of 3 and also in excess of the number of claims in independent form in the patent under reexamination:

By a micro entity (§ 1.29) ... $105.00

By a small entity (§ 1.27(a)) ... $210.00

By other than a small or micro entity ... $420.00

(4) For filing with a request for reexamination or later presentation at any other time of each claim (whether dependent or independent) in excess of 20 and also in excess of the number of claims in the patent under reexamination (note that § 1.75(c) indicates how multiple dependent claims are considered for fee calculation purposes):

By a micro entity (§ 1.29) ... $20.00

By a small entity (§ 1.27(a)) ... $40.00

By other than a small or micro entity ... $80.00

(5) If the excess claims fees required by paragraphs (c)(3) and (4) of this section are not paid with the request for reexamination or on later presentation of the claims for which the excess claims fees are due, the fees required by paragraphs (c)(3) and (4) must be paid or the claims canceled by amendment prior to the expiration of the time period set for reply by the Office in any notice of fee deficiency in order to avoid abandonment.

(6) For filing a petition in a reexamination proceeding, except for those specifically enumerated in §§ 1.550(i) and 1.937(d):

By a micro entity (§ 1.29) ... $485.00

By a small entity (§ 1.27(a)) ... $970.00

By other than a small or micro entity ... $1,940.00

(7) For a refused request for *ex parte* reexamination under § 1.510 (included in the request for *ex parte* reexamination fee at § 1.20(c)(1)):

By a micro entity (§ 1.29) ... $900.00

By a small entity (§ 1.27(a)) ... $1,800.00

By other than a small or micro entity ... $3,600.00

(d) For filing each statutory disclaimer (§ 1.321) ... $160.00

(e) For maintaining an original or reissue patent, except a design or plant patent, based on an application filed on or after December 12, 1980, in force beyond four years, the fee being due by three years and six months after the original grant:

By a micro entity (§ 1.29) ... $400.00

By a small entity (§ 1.27(a)) ... $800.00

By other than a small or micro entity ... $1,600.00

(f) For maintaining an original or reissue patent, except a design or plant patent, based on an application filed on or after December 12, 1980, in force beyond eight years, the fee being due by seven years and six months after the original grant:	
By a micro entity (§ 1.29)	$900.00
By a small entity (§ 1.27(a))	$1,800.00
By other than a small or micro entity	$3,600.00
(g) For maintaining an original or reissue patent, except a design or plant patent, based on an application filed on or after December 12, 1980, in force beyond twelve years, the fee being due by eleven years and six months after the original grant:	
By a micro entity (§ 1.29)	$1,850.00
By a small entity (§ 1.27(a))	$3,700.00
By other than a small or micro entity	$7,400.00
(h) Surcharge for paying a maintenance fee during the six-month grace period following the expiration of three years and six months, seven years and six months, and eleven years and six months after the date of the original grant of a patent based on an application filed on or after December 12, 1980:	
By a micro entity (§ 1.29)	$40.00
By a small entity (§ 1.27(a))	$80.00
By other than a small or micro entity	$160.00
(i) Surcharge for accepting a maintenance fee after expiration of a patent for non-timely payment of a maintenance fee where the delay in payment is shown to the satisfaction of the Director to have been—	
(1) Unavoidable:	
By a micro entity (§ 1.29)	$175.00
By a small entity (§ 1.27(a))	$350.00
By other than a small or micro entity	$700.00
(2) Unintentional:	
By a micro entity (§ 1.29)	$410.00
By a small entity (§ 1.27(a))	$820.00
By other than a small or micro entity	$1,640.00
(j) For filing an application for extension of the term of a patent.	
Application for extension under § 1.740	$1,120.00
Initial application for interim extension under § 1.790	$420.00
Subsequent application for interim extension under § 1.790	$220.00
(k) In supplemental examination proceedings:	
(1) For processing and treating a request for supplemental examination:	
By a micro entity (§ 1.29)	$1,100.00
By a small entity (§ 1.27(a))	$2,200.00
By other than a small or micro entity	$4,400.00
(2) For *ex parte* reexamination ordered as a result of a supplemental examination proceeding:	
By a micro entity (§ 1.29)	$3,025.00
By a small entity (§ 1.27(a))	$6,050.00
By other than a small or micro entity	$12,100.00

(3) For processing and treating, in a supplemental examination proceeding, a non-patent document over 20 sheets in length, per document:	
(i) Between 21 and 50 sheets:	
By a micro entity (§ 1.29)	$45.00
By a small entity (§ 1.27(a))	$90.00
By other than a small or micro entity.	$180.00
(ii) For each additional 50 sheets or a fraction thereof:	
By a micro entity (§ 1.29)	$70.00
By a small entity (§ 1.27(a))	$140.00
By other than a small or micro entity	$280.00

[78 FR 17106, Mar. 20, 2013]

§ 1.21 Miscellaneous fees and charges.

The Patent and Trademark Office has established the following fees for the services indicated:

(a) Registration of attorneys and agents:

(1) For admission to examination for registration to practice:

(i) Application Fee (non-refundable): $40.00.

(ii) Registration examination fee.

(A) For test administration by commercial entity: $200.00.

(B) For test administration by the USPTO: $450.00.

(2) On registration to practice or grant of limited recognition under § 11.9(b) or (c): $100.00.

(3) [Reserved]

(4) For certificate of good standing as an attorney or agent: $10.00.

(i) Suitable for framing: $20.00.

(ii) [Reserved]

(5) For review of decision:

(i) By the Director of Enrollment and Discipline under § 11.2(c): $130.00.

(ii) Of the Director of Enrollment and Discipline under § 11.2(d): $130.00.

(6)–(8) [Reserved]

(9)(i) Delinquency fee: $50.00.

(ii) Administrative reinstatement fee: $100.00.

(10) On application by a person for recognition or registration after disbarment or suspension on ethical grounds, or resignation pending disciplinary proceedings in any other jurisdiction; on application by a person for recognition or registration who is asserting rehabilitation from prior conduct that resulted in an adverse decision in the Office regarding the person's moral character; and on application by a person for recognition or registration after being convicted of a felony or crime involving moral turpitude or breach of fiduciary duty; on petition for reinstatement by a person excluded or suspended on ethical grounds, or excluded on consent from practice before the Office: $1,600.00.

(b) Deposit accounts:

(1) For establishing a deposit account—$10.00

(2) Service charge for each month when the balance at the end of the month is below $1,000—$25.00

(3) Service charge for each month when the balance at the end of the month is below $300 for restricted subscription deposit accounts used exclusively for subscription order of patent copies as issued—$25.00

(c) [Reserved]

(d) [Reserved]

(e) International type search reports: For preparing an international type search report of an international type search made at the time of the first action on the merits in a national patent application: $40.00.

(f) [Reserved]

(g) Self-service copy charge, per page: $0.25.

(h) For recording each assignment, agreement, or other paper relating to the property in a patent or application, per property:

(1) If submitted electronically, on or after January 1, 2014: $0.00.

(2) If not submitted electronically: $40.00.

(i) Publication in Official Gazette: For publication in the Official Gazette of a notice of the availability of an application or a patent for licensing or sale: Each application or patent: $25.00.

(j) Labor charges for services, per hour or fraction thereof: $40.00.

(k) For items and services that the Director finds may be supplied, for which fees are not specified by statute or by this part, such charges as may be determined by the Director with respect to each such item or service: Actual cost.

(l) [Reserved]

(m) For processing each payment refused (including a check returned "unpaid") or charged back by a financial institution—$50.00.

(n) For handling an application in which proceedings are terminated pursuant to § 1.53(e): $130.00.

EDITORIAL NOTE: For FEDERAL REGISTER citations affecting § 1.21, see the List of CFR Sections Affected, which appears in the Finding Aids section of the printed volume and at *www.fdsys.gov*.

§ 1.22 Fees payable in advance.

(a) Patent fees and charges payable to the United States Patent and Trademark Office are required to be paid in advance; that is, at the time of requesting any action by the Office for which a fee or charge is payable, with the exception that under § 1.53 applications for patent may be assigned a filing date without payment of the basic filing fee.

(b) All fees paid to the United States Patent and Trademark Office must be itemized in each individual application, patent, or other proceeding in such a manner that it is clear for which purpose the fees are paid. The Office may return fees that are not itemized as required by this paragraph. The provisions of § 1.5(a) do not apply to the resubmission of fees returned pursuant to this paragraph.

[68 FR 48288, Aug. 13, 2003]

§ 1.23 Methods of payment.

(a) All payments of money required for United States Patent and Trademark Office fees, including fees for the processing of international applications (§ 1.445), shall be made in U.S. dollars and in the form of a cashier's or certified check, Treasury note, national bank notes, or United States Postal Service money order. If sent in any other form, the Office may delay or cancel the credit until collection is made. Checks and money orders must be made payable to the Director of the United States Patent and Trademark Office. (Checks made payable to the Commissioner of Patents and Trademarks will continue to be accepted.) Payments from foreign countries must be payable and immediately negotiable in the United States for the full amount of the fee required. Money sent to the Office by mail will be at the risk of the sender, and letters containing money should be registered with the United States Postal Service.

(b) Payments of money required for United States Patent and Trademark Office fees may also be made by credit card, except for replenishing a deposit account. Payment of a fee by credit card must specify the amount to be charged to the credit card and such other information as is necessary to process the charge, and is subject to collection of the fee. The Office will not accept a general authorization to charge fees to a credit card. If credit card information is provided on a form or document other than a form provided by the Office for the payment of fees by credit card, the Office will not be liable if the credit card number becomes public knowledge.

[65 FR 33455, May 24, 2000, as amended at 69 FR 43752, July 22, 2004]

§ 1.24 [Reserved]

§ 1.25 Deposit accounts.

(a) For the convenience of attorneys, and the general public in paying any fees due, in ordering services offered by the Office, copies of records, etc., deposit accounts may be established in the Patent and Trademark Office upon payment of the fee for establishing a deposit account (§ 1.21(b)(1)). A minimum deposit of $1,000 is required for paying any fees due or in ordering any services offered by the Office. However, a minimum deposit of $300 may be paid to establish a restricted subscription deposit account used exclusively for subscription order of patent copies as issued. At the end of each month, a deposit account statement will be rendered. A remittance must be made promptly upon receipt of the statement to cover the value of items or services charged to the account and thus restore the account to its established normal deposit. An amount sufficient to cover all fees, services, copies, etc., requested must always be on deposit. Charges to accounts with insufficient funds will not be accepted. A service charge (§ 1.21(b)(2)) will be assessed for each month that the balance at the end of the month is below $1,000. For restricted subscription deposit accounts, a service charge (§ 1.21(b)(3)) will be assessed for each month that the balance at the end of the month is below $300.

(b) Filing, issue, appeal, international-type search report, international application processing, petition, and post-issuance fees may be charged against these accounts if sufficient funds are on deposit to cover such fees. A general authorization to charge all fees, or only certain fees, set forth in §§ 1.16 to 1.18 to a deposit account containing sufficient funds may be filed in an individual application, either for the entire pendency of the application or with a particular paper filed. An authorization to charge fees under § 1.16 in an international application entering the national stage under 35 U.S.C. 371 will be treated as an authorization to charge fees under § 1.492. An authorization to charge fees set forth in § 1.18 to a deposit account is subject to the provisions of § 1.311(b). An authorization to charge to a deposit account the fee for a request for reexamination pursuant to § 1.510 or § 1.913 and any other fees required in a reexamination proceeding in a patent may also be filed with the request for reexamination. An authorization to charge a fee to a deposit account will not be considered payment of the fee on the date the authorization to charge the fee is effective as to the particular fee to be charged unless sufficient funds are present in the account to cover the fee.

(c) A deposit account holder may replenish the deposit account by submitting a payment to the United States Patent and Trademark Office. A payment to replenish a deposit account must be submitted by one of the methods set forth in paragraphs (c)(1), (c)(2), (c)(3), or (c)(4) of this section.

(1) A payment to replenish a deposit account may be submitted by electronic funds transfer through the Federal Reserve Fedwire System, which requires that the following information be provided to the deposit account holder's bank or financial institution:

(i) Name of the Bank, which is Treas NYC (Treasury New York City);

(ii) Bank Routing Code, which is 021030004;

(iii) United States Patent and Trademark Office account number with the Department of the Treasury, which is 13100001; and

(iv) The deposit account holder's company name and deposit account number.

(2) A payment to replenish a deposit account may be submitted by electronic funds transfer over the Office's Internet Web site (*www.uspto.gov*).

(3) A payment to replenish a deposit account may be addressed to: Director of the United States Patent and Trademark Office, Attn: Deposit Accounts, 2051 Jamieson Avenue, Suite 300, Alexandria, Virginia 22314.

(35 U.S.C. 6, Pub. L. 97–247)

[49 FR 553, Jan. 4, 1984, as amended at 50 FR 31826, Aug. 6, 1985; 65 FR 76772, Dec. 7, 2000; 67 FR 523, Jan. 4, 2002; 68 FR 14336, Mar. 25, 2003; 69 FR 43752, July 22, 2004; 70 FR 56127, Sept. 26, 2005; 73 FR 47541, Aug. 14, 2008]

§ 1.26 Refunds.

(a) The Director may refund any fee paid by mistake or in excess of that required. A change of purpose after the payment of a fee, such as when a party desires to withdraw a patent filing for which the fee was paid, including an application, an appeal, or a request for an oral hearing, will not entitle a party to a refund of such fee. The Office will not refund amounts of twenty-five dollars or less unless a refund is specifically requested, and will not notify the payor of such amounts. If a party paying a fee or requesting a refund does not provide the banking information necessary for making refunds by electronic funds transfer (31 U.S.C. 3332 and 31 CFR part 208), or instruct the Office that refunds are to be credited to a deposit account, the Director may require such information, or use the banking information on the payment instrument to make a refund. Any refund of a fee paid by credit card will be by a credit to the credit card account to which the fee was charged.

(b) Any request for refund must be filed within two years from the date the fee was paid, except as otherwise provided in this paragraph or in § 1.28(a). If the Office charges a deposit account by an amount other than an amount specifically indicated in an authorization (§ 1.25(b)), any request for refund based upon such charge must be filed within two years from the date of the deposit account statement indicating such charge, and include a copy of that deposit account statement. The time periods set forth in this paragraph are not extendable.

(c) If the Director decides not to institute a reexamination proceeding in response to a request for reexamination or supplemental examination, fees paid with the request for reexamination or supplemental examination will be refunded or returned in accordance with paragraphs (c)(1) through (c)(3) of this section. The reexamination requester or the patent owner who requested a supplemental examination proceeding, as appropriate, should indicate the form in which any refund should be made (*e.g.*, by check, electronic funds transfer, credit to a deposit account). Generally, refunds will be issued in the form that the original payment was provided.

(1) For an *ex parte* reexamination request, the *ex parte* reexamination filing fee paid by the reexamination requester, less the fee set forth in § 1.20(c)(7), will be refunded to the requester if the Director decides not to institute an *ex parte* reexamination proceeding.

(2) For an *inter partes* reexamination request, a refund of $7,970 will be made to the reexamination requester if the Director decides not to institute an *inter partes* reexamination proceeding.

(3) For a supplemental examination request, the fee for reexamination ordered as a result of supplemental examination, as set forth in § 1.20(k)(2), will be returned to the patent owner who requested the supplemental examination proceeding if the Director decides not to institute a reexamination proceeding.

(35 U.S.C. 6; 15 U.S.C. 1113, 1123)

[47 FR 41274, Sept. 17, 1982, as amended at 50 FR 31826, Aug. 6, 1985; 54 FR 6902, Feb. 15, 1989; 56 FR 65153, Dec. 13, 1991; 57 FR 38195, Aug. 21, 1992; 62 FR 53183, Oct. 10, 1997; 65 FR 54659, Sept. 8, 2000; 65 FR 76773, Dec. 7, 2000; 68 FR 48289, Aug. 13, 2003; 72 FR 46836, Aug. 21, 2007; 74 FR 52688, Oct. 14, 2009; 77 FR 48851, Aug. 14, 2012]

§ 1.27 Definition of small entities and establishing status as a small entity to permit payment of small entity fees; when a determination of entitlement to small entity status and notification of loss of entitlement to small entity status are required; fraud on the Office.

(a) *Definition of small entities.* A small entity as used in this chapter means any party (person, small business concern, or nonprofit organization) under paragraphs (a)(1) through (a)(3) of this section.

(1) *Person.* A person, as used in paragraph (c) of this section, means any inventor or other individual (e.g., an individual to whom an inventor has transferred some rights in the invention) who has not assigned, granted, conveyed, or licensed, and is under no obligation under contract or law to assign, grant, convey, or license, any rights in the invention. An inventor or other individual who has transferred some rights in the invention to one or more parties, or is under an obligation to transfer some rights in the invention to one or more parties, can also qualify for small entity status if all the parties who have had rights in the invention transferred to them also qualify for small entity status either as a person, small business concern, or nonprofit organization under this section.

(2) *Small business concern.* A small business concern, as used in paragraph (c) of this section, means any business concern that:

(i) Has not assigned, granted, conveyed, or licensed, and is under no obligation under contract or law to assign, grant, convey, or license, any rights in the invention to any person, concern, or organization which would not qualify for small entity status as a person, small business concern, or nonprofit organization; and

(ii) Meets the size standards set forth in 13 CFR 121.801 through 121.805 to be eligible for reduced patent fees. Questions related to standards for a small business concern may be directed to: Small Business Administration, Size Standards Staff, 409 Third Street, SW., Washington, DC 20416.

(3) *Nonprofit Organization.* A nonprofit organization, as used in paragraph (c) of this section, means any nonprofit organization that:

(i) Has not assigned, granted, conveyed, or licensed, and is under no obligation under contract or law to assign, grant, convey, or license, any rights in the invention to any person, concern, or organization which would not qualify as a person, small business concern, or a nonprofit organization; and

(ii) Is either:

(A) A university or other institution of higher education located in any country;

(B) An organization of the type described in section 501(c)(3) of the Internal Revenue Code of 1986 (26 U.S.C. 501(c)(3)) and exempt from taxation under section 501(a) of the Internal Revenue Code (26 U.S.C. 501(a));

(C) Any nonprofit scientific or educational organization qualified under a nonprofit organization statute of a state of this country (35 U.S.C. 201(i)); or

(D) Any nonprofit organization located in a foreign country which would qualify as a nonprofit organization under paragraphs (a)(3)(ii)(B) of this section or (a)(3)(ii)(C) of this section if it were located in this country.

(4) *License to a Federal agency.* (i) For persons under paragraph (a)(1) of this section, a license to the Government resulting from a rights determination under Executive Order 10096 does not constitute a license so as to prohibit claiming small entity status.

(ii) For small business concerns and nonprofit organizations under paragraphs (a)(2) and (a)(3) of this section, a license to a Federal agency resulting from a funding agreement with that agency pursuant to 35 U.S.C. 202(c)(4) does not constitute a license for the purposes of paragraphs (a)(2)(i) and (a)(3)(i) of this section.

(5) *Security Interest.* A security interest does not involve an obligation to transfer rights in the invention for the purposes of paragraphs (a)(1) through (a)(3) of this section unless the security interest is defaulted upon.

(b) *Establishment of small entity status permits payment of reduced fees.* (1) A small entity, as defined in paragraph (a) of this section, who has properly asserted entitlement to small entity status pursuant to paragraph (c) of this section will be accorded small entity status by the Office in the particular application or patent in which entitlement to small entity status was asserted. Establishment of small entity status allows the payment of certain reduced patent fees pursuant to 35 U.S.C. 41(h)(1).

(2) Submission of an original utility application in compliance with the Office electronic filing system by an applicant who has properly asserted entitlement to small entity status pursuant to paragraph (c) of this section in that application allows the payment of a reduced filing fee pursuant to 35 U.S.C. 41(h)(3).

(c) *Assertion of small entity status.* Any party (person, small business concern or nonprofit organization) should make a determination, pursuant to paragraph (f) of this section, of entitlement to be accorded small entity status based on the definitions set forth in paragraph (a) of this section, and must, in order to establish small entity status for the purpose of paying small entity fees, actually make an assertion of entitlement to small entity status, in the manner set forth in paragraphs (c)(1) or (c)(3) of this section, in the application or patent in which such small entity fees are to be paid.

(1) *Assertion by writing.* Small entity status may be established by a written assertion of entitlement to small entity status. A written assertion must:

(i) Be clearly identifiable;

(ii) Be signed (see paragraph (c)(2) of this section); and

(iii) Convey the concept of entitlement to small entity status, such as by stating that applicant is a small entity, or that small entity status is entitled to be asserted for the application or patent. While no specific words or wording are required to assert small entity status, the intent to assert small entity status must be clearly indicated in order to comply with the assertion requirement.

(2) *Parties who can sign the written assertion.* The written assertion can be signed by:

(i) The applicant (§ 1.42 or § 1.421);

(ii) A patent practitioner of record or a practitioner acting in a representative capacity under § 1.34;

(iii) The inventor or a joint inventor, if the inventor is the applicant; or

(iv) The assignee.

(3) Assertion by payment of the small entity basic filing, basic transmittal, basic national fee, or international search fee. The payment, by any party, of the exact amount of one of the small entity basic filing fees set forth in §§ 1.16(a), 1.16(b), 1.16(c), 1.16(d), 1.16(e), the small entity transmittal fee set forth in § 1.445(a)(1), the small entity international search fee set forth in § 1.445(a)(2) to a Receiving Office other than the United States Receiving Office in the exact amount established for that Receiving Office pursuant to PCT Rule 16, or the small entity basic national fee set forth in § 1.492(a), will be treated as a written assertion of entitlement to small entity status even if the type of basic filing, basic transmittal, or basic national fee is inadvertently selected in error.

(i) If the Office accords small entity status based on payment of a small entity basic filing or basic national fee under paragraph (c)(3) of this section that is not applicable to that application, any balance of the small entity fee that is applicable to that application will be due along with the appropriate surcharge set forth in § 1.16(f), or § 1.16(g).

(ii) The payment of any small entity fee other than those set forth in paragraph (c)(3) of this section (whether in the exact fee amount or not) will not be treated as a written assertion of entitlement to small entity status and will not be sufficient to establish small entity status in an application or a patent.

(4) *Assertion required in related, continuing, and reissue applications.* Status as a small entity must be specifically established by an assertion in each related, continuing and reissue application in which status is appropriate and desired. Status as a small entity in one application or patent does not affect the status of any other application or patent, regardless of the relationship of the applications or patents. The refiling of an application under § 1.53 as a continuation, divisional, or continuation-in-part application (including a continued prosecution application under § 1.53(d)), or the filing of a reissue application, requires a new assertion as to continued entitlement to small entity status for the continuing or reissue application.

(d) *When small entity fees can be paid.* Any fee, other than the small entity basic filing fees and the small entity national fees of paragraph (c)(3) of this section, can be paid in the small entity amount only if it is submitted with, or subsequent to, the submission of a written assertion of entitlement to small entity status, except when refunds are permitted by § 1.28(a).

(e) *Only one assertion required.* (1) An assertion of small entity status need only be filed once in an application or patent. Small entity status, once established, remains in effect until changed pursuant to paragraph (g)(1) of this section. Where an assignment of rights or an obligation to assign rights to other parties who are small entities occurs subsequent to an assertion of small entity status, a second assertion is not required.

(2) Once small entity status is withdrawn pursuant to paragraph (g)(2) of this section, a new written assertion is required to again obtain small entity status.

(f) *Assertion requires a determination of entitlement to pay small entity fees.* Prior to submitting an assertion of entitlement to small entity status in an application, including a related, continuing, or reissue application, a determination of such entitlement should be made pursuant to the requirements of paragraph (a) of this section. It should be determined that all parties holding rights in the invention qualify for small entity status. The Office will generally not question any assertion of small entity status that is made in accordance with the requirements of this section, but note paragraph (h) of this section.

(g)(1) *New determination of entitlement to small entity status is needed when issue and maintenance fees are due.* Once status as a small entity has been established in an application or patent, fees as a small entity may thereafter be paid in that application or patent without regard to a change in status until the issue fee is due or any maintenance fee is due.

(2) *Notification of loss of entitlement to small entity status is required when issue*

and maintenance fees are due. Notification of a loss of entitlement to small entity status must be filed in the application or patent prior to paying, or at the time of paying, the earliest of the issue fee or any maintenance fee due after the date on which status as a small entity as defined in paragraph (a) of this section is no longer appropriate. The notification that small entity status is no longer appropriate must be signed by a party identified in § 1.33(b). Payment of a fee in other than the small entity amount is not sufficient notification that small entity status is no longer appropriate.

(h) *Fraud attempted or practiced on the Office.* (1) Any attempt to fraudulently establish status as a small entity, or pay fees as a small entity, shall be considered as a fraud practiced or attempted on the Office.

(2) Improperly, and with intent to deceive, establishing status as a small entity, or paying fees as a small entity, shall be considered as a fraud practiced or attempted on the Office.

[65 FR 54659, Sept. 8, 2000, as amended at 69 FR 56538, Sept. 21, 2004; 70 FR 3889, Jan. 27, 2005; 77 FR 48813, Aug. 14, 2012; 78 FR 4289, Jan. 18, 2013]

§ 1.28 Refunds when small entity status is later established; how errors in small entity status are excused.

(a) *Refunds based on later establishment of small entity status.* A refund pursuant to § 1.26, based on establishment of small entity status, of a portion of fees timely paid in full prior to establishing status as a small entity may only be obtained if an assertion under § 1.27(c) and a request for a refund of the excess amount are filed within three months of the date of the timely payment of the full fee. The three-month time period is not extendable under § 1.136. Status as a small entity is waived for any fee by the failure to establish the status prior to paying, at the time of paying, or within three months of the date of payment of, the full fee.

(b) *Date of payment.* (1) The three-month period for requesting a refund, pursuant to paragraph (a) of this section, starts on the date that a full fee has been paid;

(2) The date when a deficiency payment is paid in full determines the amount of deficiency that is due, pursuant to paragraph (c) of this section.

(c) *How errors in small entity status are excused.* If status as a small entity is established in good faith, and fees as a small entity are paid in good faith, in any application or patent, and it is later discovered that such status as a small entity was established in error, or that through error the Office was not notified of a loss of entitlement to small entity status as required by § 1.27(g)(2), the error will be excused upon: compliance with the separate submission and itemization requirements of paragraphs (c)(1) and (c)(2) of this section, and the deficiency payment requirement of paragraph (c)(2) of this section:

(1) *Separate submission required for each application or patent.* Any paper submitted under this paragraph must be limited to the deficiency payment (all fees paid in error), required by paragraph (c)(2) of this section, for one application or one patent. Where more than one application or patent is involved, separate submissions of deficiency payments (e.g., checks) and itemizations are required for each application or patent. *See* § 1.4(b).

(2) *Payment of deficiency owed.* The deficiency owed, resulting from the previous erroneous payment of small entity fees, must be paid.

(i) *Calculation of the deficiency owed.* The deficiency owed for each previous fee erroneously paid as a small entity is the difference between the current fee amount (for other than a small entity) on the date the deficiency is paid in full and the amount of the previous erroneous (small entity) fee payment. The total deficiency payment owed is the sum of the individual deficiency owed amounts for each fee amount previously erroneously paid as a small entity. Where a fee paid in error as a small entity was subject to a fee decrease between the time the fee was paid in error and the time the deficiency is paid in full, the deficiency owed is equal to the amount (previously) paid in error;

(ii) *Itemization of the deficiency payment.* An itemization of the total deficiency payment is required. The itemization must include the following information:

(A) Each particular type of fee that was erroneously paid as a small entity, (e.g., basic statutory filing fee, two-month extension of time fee) along with the current fee amount for a non-small entity;

(B) The small entity fee actually paid, and when. This will permit the Office to differentiate, for example, between two one-month extension of time fees erroneously paid as a small entity but on different dates;

(C) The deficiency owed amount (for each fee erroneously paid); and

(D) The total deficiency payment owed, which is the sum or total of the individual deficiency owed amounts set forth in paragraph (c)(2)(ii)(C) of this section.

(3) *Failure to comply with requirements.* If the requirements of paragraphs (c)(1) and (c)(2) of this section are not complied with, such failure will either: be treated as an authorization for the Office to process the deficiency payment and charge the processing fee set forth in § 1.17(i), or result in a requirement for compliance within a one-month non-extendable time period under § 1.136(a) to avoid the return of the fee deficiency paper, at the option of the Office.

(d) *Payment of deficiency operates as notification of loss of status.* Any deficiency payment (based on a previous erroneous payment of a small entity fee) submitted under paragraph (c) of this section will be treated under § 1.27(g)(2) as a notification of a loss of entitlement to small entity status.

[65 FR 54661, Sept. 8, 2000]

§ 1.29 Micro entity status.

(a) To establish micro entity status under this paragraph, the applicant must certify that:

(1) The applicant qualifies as a small entity as defined in § 1.27;

(2) Neither the applicant nor the inventor nor a joint inventor has been named as the inventor or a joint inventor on more than four previously filed patent applications, other than applications filed in another country, provisional applications under 35 U.S.C. 111(b), or international applications for which the basic national fee under 35 U.S.C. 41(a) was not paid;

(3) Neither the applicant nor the inventor nor a joint inventor, in the calendar year preceding the calendar year in which the applicable fee is being paid, had a gross income, as defined in section 61(a) of the Internal Revenue Code of 1986 (26 U.S.C. 61(a)), exceeding three times the median household income for that preceding calendar year, as most recently reported by the Bureau of the Census; and

(4) Neither the applicant nor the inventor nor a joint inventor has assigned, granted, or conveyed, nor is under an obligation by contract or law to assign, grant, or convey, a license or other ownership interest in the application concerned to an entity that, in the calendar year preceding the calendar year in which the applicable fee is being paid, had a gross income, as defined in section 61(a) of the Internal Revenue Code of 1986, exceeding three times the median household income for that preceding calendar year, as most recently reported by the Bureau of the Census.

(b) An applicant, inventor, or joint inventor is not considered to be named on a previously filed application for purposes of paragraph (a)(2) of this section if the applicant, inventor, or joint inventor has assigned, or is under an obligation by contract or law to assign, all ownership rights in the application as the result of the applicant's, inventor's, or joint inventor's previous employment.

(c) If an applicant's, inventor's, joint inventor's, or entity's gross income in the preceding calendar year is not in United States dollars, the average currency exchange rate, as reported by the Internal Revenue Service, during that calendar year shall be used to determine whether the applicant's, inventor's, joint inventor's, or entity's gross income exceeds the threshold specified in paragraph (a)(3) or (4) of this section.

(d) To establish micro entity status under this paragraph, the applicant must certify that:

(1) The applicant qualifies as a small entity as defined in § 1.27; and

(2)(i) The applicant's employer, from which the applicant obtains the majority of the applicant's income, is an institution of higher education as defined in section 101(a) of the Higher Education Act of 1965 (20 U.S.C. 1001(a)); or

(ii) The applicant has assigned, granted, conveyed, or is under an obligation by contract or law, to assign, grant, or convey, a license or other ownership interest in the particular application to such an institution of higher education.

(e) Micro entity status is established in an application by filing a micro entity certification in writing complying with the requirements of either paragraph (a) or paragraph (d) of this section and signed in compliance with § 1.33(b). Status as a micro entity must be specifically established in each related, continuing and reissue application in which status is appropriate and desired. Status as a micro entity in one application or patent does not affect the status of any other application or patent, regardless of the relationship of the applications or patents. The refiling of an application under § 1.53 as a continuation, divisional, or continuation-in-part application (including a continued prosecution application under § 1.53(d)), or the filing of a reissue application, requires a new certification of entitlement to micro entity status for the continuing or reissue application.

(f) A fee may be paid in the micro entity amount only if it is submitted with, or subsequent to, the submission of a certification of entitlement to micro entity status.

(g) A certification of entitlement to micro entity status need only be filed once in an application or patent. Micro entity status, once established, remains in effect until changed pursuant to paragraph (i) of this section. However, a fee may be paid in the micro entity amount only if status as a micro entity as defined in paragraph (a) or (d) of this section is appropriate on the date the fee is being paid. Where an assignment of rights or an obligation to assign rights to other parties who are micro entities occurs subsequent to the filing of a certification of entitlement to micro entity status, a second certification of entitlement to micro entity status is not required.

(h) Prior to submitting a certification of entitlement to micro entity status in an application, including a related, continuing, or reissue application, a determination of such entitlement should be made pursuant to the requirements of this section. It should be determined that each applicant qualifies for micro entity status under paragraph (a) or (d) of this section, and that any other party holding rights in the invention qualifies for small entity status under § 1.27. The Office will generally not question certification of entitlement to micro entity status that is made in accordance with the requirements of this section.

(i) Notification of a loss of entitlement to micro entity status must be filed in the application or patent prior to paying, or at the time of paying, any fee after the date on which status as a micro entity as defined in paragraph (a) or (d) of this section is no longer appropriate. The notification that micro entity status is no longer appropriate must be signed by a party identified in § 1.33(b). Payment of a fee in other than the micro entity amount is not sufficient notification that micro entity status is no longer appropriate. A notification that micro entity status is no longer appropriate will not be treated as a notification that small entity status is also no longer appropriate unless it also contains a notification of loss of entitlement to small entity status under § 1.27(f)(2). Once a notification of a loss of entitlement to micro entity status is filed in the application or patent, a new certification of entitlement to micro entity status is required to again obtain micro entity status.

(j) Any attempt to fraudulently establish status as a micro entity, or pay fees as a micro entity, shall be considered as a fraud practiced or attempted on the Office. Improperly, and with intent to deceive, establishing status as a micro entity, or paying fees as a micro entity, shall be considered as a fraud practiced or attempted on the Office.

(k) If status as a micro entity is established in good faith in an application or patent, and fees as a micro entity are paid in good faith in the application or patent, and it is later discovered that such micro entity status either was established in error, or that the Office was not notified of a loss of entitlement to micro entity status as required by paragraph (i) of this section through error, the error will be excused upon compliance with the separate submission and itemization requirements of paragraph (k)(1) of this section and the deficiency payment requirement of paragraph (k)(2) of this section.

(1) Any paper submitted under this paragraph must be limited to the deficiency payment (all fees paid in error) required for a single application or patent. Where more than one application or patent is involved, separate submissions of deficiency payments are required for each application or patent (see §1.4(b)). The paper must contain an itemization of the total deficiency payment for the single application or patent and include the following information:

(i) Each particular type of fee that was erroneously paid as a micro entity, (*e.g.*, basic statutory filing fee, two-month extension of time fee) along with the current fee amount for a small or non-small entity, as applicable;

(ii) The micro entity fee actually paid, and the date on which it was paid;

(iii) The deficiency owed amount (for each fee erroneously paid); and

(iv) The total deficiency payment owed, which is the sum or total of the individual deficiency owed amounts as set forth in paragraph (k)(2) of this section.

(2) The deficiency owed, resulting from the previous erroneous payment of micro entity fees, must be paid. The deficiency owed for each previous fee erroneously paid as a micro entity is the difference between the current fee amount for a small entity or non-small entity, as applicable, on the date the deficiency is paid in full and the amount of the previous erroneous micro entity fee payment. The total deficiency payment owed is the sum of the individual deficiency owed amounts for each fee amount previously and erroneously paid as a micro entity.

(3) If the requirements of paragraphs (k)(1) and (2) of this section are not complied with, such failure will either be treated at the option of the Office as an authorization for the Office to process the deficiency payment and charge the processing fee set forth in §1.17(i), or result in a requirement for compliance within a one-month time period that is not extendable under §1.136(a) to avoid the return of the fee deficiency payment.

(4) Any deficiency payment (based on a previous erroneous payment of a micro entity fee) submitted under this paragraph will be treated as a notification of a loss of entitlement to micro entity status under paragraph (i) of this section, but payment of a deficiency based upon the difference between the current fee amount for a small entity and the amount of the previous erroneous micro entity fee payment will not be treated as an assertion of small entity status under §1.27(c). Once a deficiency payment is submitted under this paragraph, a written assertion of small entity status under §1.27(c)(1) is required to obtain small entity status.

[77 FR 75033, Dec. 19, 2012]

Subpart B—National Processing Provisions

Prosecution of Application and Appointment of Attorney or Agent

§1.31 Applicant may be represented by one or more patent practitioners or joint inventors.

An applicant for patent may file and prosecute the applicant's own case, or the applicant may give power of attorney so as to be represented by one or more patent practitioners or joint inventors, except that a juristic entity (*e.g.*, organizational assignee) must be represented by a patent practitioner even if the juristic entity is the applicant. The Office cannot aid in the selection of a patent practitioner.

[77 FR 48813, Aug. 14, 2012]

§ 1.32 Power of attorney.

(a) *Definitions.* (1) *Patent practitioner* means a registered patent attorney or registered patent agent under § 11.6.

(2) *Power of attorney* means a written document by which a principal authorizes one or more patent practitioners or joint inventors to act on the principal's behalf.

(3) *Principal* means the applicant (§ 1.42) for an application for patent and the patent owner for a patent, including a patent in a supplemental examination or reexamination proceeding. The principal executes a power of attorney designating one or more patent practitioners or joint inventors to act on the principal's behalf.

(4) *Revocation* means the cancellation by the principal of the authority previously given to a patent practitioner or joint inventor to act on the principal's behalf.

(5) *Customer Number* means a number that may be used to:

(i) Designate the correspondence address of a patent application or patent such that the correspondence address for the patent application, patent or other patent proceeding would be the address associated with the Customer Number;

(ii) Designate the fee address (§ 1.363) of a patent such that the fee address for the patent would be the address associated with the Customer Number; and

(iii) Submit a list of patent practitioners such that those patent practitioners associated with the Customer Number would have power of attorney.

(6) *Patent practitioner of record* means a patent practitioner who has been granted a power of attorney in an application, patent, or other proceeding in compliance with paragraph (b) of this section. The phrases practitioner of record and attorney or agent of record also mean a patent practitioner who has been granted a power of attorney in an application, patent, or other proceeding in compliance with paragraph (b) of this section.

(b) A power of attorney must:

(1) Be in writing;

(2) Name one or more representatives in compliance with paragraph (c) of this section;

(3) Give the representative power to act on behalf of the principal; and

(4) Be signed by the applicant for patent (§ 1.42) or the patent owner. A patent owner who was not the applicant under § 1.46 must appoint any power of attorney in compliance with §§ 3.71 and 3.73 of this chapter.

(c) A power of attorney may only name as representative:

(1) One or more joint inventors (§ 1.45);

(2) Those registered patent practitioners associated with a Customer Number;

(3) Ten or fewer patent practitioners, stating the name and registration number of each patent practitioner. Except as provided in paragraph (c)(1) or (c)(2) of this section, the Office will not recognize more than ten patent practitioners as being of record in an application or patent. If a power of attorney names more than ten patent practitioners, such power of attorney must be accompanied by a separate paper indicating which ten patent practitioners named in the power of attorney are to be recognized by the Office as being of record in the application or patent to which the power of attorney is directed.

(d) A power of attorney from a prior national application for which benefit is claimed under 35 U.S.C. 120, 121, or 365(c) in a continuing application may have effect in the continuing application if a copy of the power of attorney from the prior application is filed in the continuing application unless:

(1) The power of attorney was granted by the inventor; and

(2) The continuing application names an inventor who was not named as an inventor in the prior application.

(e) If the power of attorney was granted by the originally named inventive entity, and an added inventor pursuant to § 1.48 does not provide a power of attorney consistent with the power of attorney granted by the originally named inventive entity, the addition of the inventor results in the loss of that power of attorney upon grant of the § 1.48 request. This provision does not preclude a practitioner from acting pursuant to § 1.34, if applicable.

[69 FR 29877, May 26, 2004, as amended at 70 FR 56127, Sept. 26, 2005; 77 FR 48813, Aug. 14, 2012]

§ 1.33 Correspondence respecting patent applications, patent reexamination proceedings, and other proceedings.

(a) *Correspondence address and daytime telephone number.* When filing an application, a correspondence address must be set forth in either an application data sheet (§ 1.76), or elsewhere, in a clearly identifiable manner, in any paper submitted with an application filing. If no correspondence address is specified, the Office may treat the mailing address of the first named inventor (if provided, *see* §§ 1.76(b)(1) and 1.63(b)(2)) as the correspondence address. The Office will direct, or otherwise make available, all notices, official letters, and other communications relating to the application to the person associated with the correspondence address. For correspondence submitted via the Office's electronic filing system, however, an electronic acknowledgment receipt will be sent to the submitter. The Office will generally not engage in double correspondence with an applicant and a patent practitioner, or with more than one patent practitioner except as deemed necessary by the Director. If more than one correspondence address is specified, the Office will select one of the specified addresses for use as the correspondence address and, if given, may select the address associated with a Customer Number over a typed correspondence address. For the party to whom correspondence is to be addressed, a daytime telephone number should be supplied in a clearly identifiable manner and may be changed by any party who may change the correspondence address. The correspondence address may be changed by the parties set forth in paragraph (b)(1) or (b)(3) of this section. Prior to the appointment of any power of attorney under § 1.32(b), the correspondence address may also be changed by any patent practitioner named in the application transmittal papers who acts in a representative capacity under the provisions of § 1.34.

(b) *Amendments and other papers.* Amendments and other papers, except for written assertions pursuant to § 1.27(c)(2)(iii) or (c)(2)(iv), filed in the application must be signed by:

(1) A patent practitioner of record;

(2) A patent practitioner not of record who acts in a representative capacity under the provisions of § 1.34; or

(3) The applicant (§ 1.42). Unless otherwise specified, all papers submitted on behalf of a juristic entity must be signed by a patent practitioner.

(c) All notices, official letters, and other communications for the patent owner or owners in a reexamination proceeding will be directed to the correspondence address. Amendments and other papers filed in a reexamination proceeding on behalf of the patent owner must be signed by the patent owner, or if there is more than one owner by all the owners, or by an attorney or agent of record in the patent file, or by a registered attorney or agent not of record who acts in a representative capacity under the provisions of § 1.34. Double correspondence with the patent owner or owners and the patent owner's attorney or agent, or with more than one attorney or agent, will not be undertaken.

(d) A "correspondence address" or change thereto may be filed with the Patent and Trademark Office during the enforceable life of the patent. The "correspondence address" will be used in any correspondence relating to maintenance fees unless a separate "fee address" has been specified. See § 1.363 for "fee address" used solely for maintenance fee purposes.

(e) A change of address filed in a patent application or patent does not change the address for a patent practitioner in the roster of patent attorneys and agents. See § 11.11 of this title.

(f) Where application papers from a prior application are used in a continuing application and the correspondence address was changed during the prosecution of the prior application, an application data sheet or separate paper identifying the correspondence address to be used for the continuing application must be submitted. Otherwise, the Office may not recognize the change of correspondence address effected during the prosecution of the prior application.

(g) A patent practitioner acting in a representative capacity whose correspondence address is the correspondence address of record in an application may change the correspondence address after the patent has issued, provided that the change of correspondence address is accompanied by a statement that notice has been given to the patentee or owner.

[36 FR 12617, July 2, 1971, as amended at 46 FR 29181, May 29, 1981; 49 FR 34724, Aug. 31, 1984; 50 FR 5171, Feb. 6, 1985; 62 FR 53184, Oct. 10, 1997; 65 FR 54661, Sept. 8, 2000; 69 FR 29877, May 26, 2004; 69 FR 35452, June 24, 2004; 70 FR 3889, Jan. 27, 2005; 70 FR 56127, Sept. 26, 2005; 72 FR 2776, Jan. 23, 2007; 72 FR 18904, Apr. 16, 2007; 77 FR 48814, Aug. 14, 2012]

§ 1.34 Acting in a representative capacity.

When a patent practitioner acting in a representative capacity appears in person or signs a paper in practice before the United States Patent and Trademark Office in a patent case, his or her personal appearance or signature shall constitute a representation to the United States Patent and Trademark Office that under the provisions of this subchapter and the law, he or she is authorized to represent the particular party on whose behalf he or she acts. In filing such a paper, the patent practitioner must set forth his or her registration number, his or her name and signature. Further proof of authority to act in a representative capacity may be required.

[70 FR 56127, Sept. 26, 2005]

§ 1.36 Revocation of power of attorney; withdrawal of patent attorney or agent.

(a) A power of attorney, pursuant to § 1.32(b), may be revoked at any stage in the proceedings of a case by the applicant or patent owner. A power of attorney to the patent practitioners associated with a Customer Number will be treated as a request to revoke any powers of attorney previously given. Fewer than all of the applicants (or fewer than all patent owners in a supplemental examination or reexamination proceeding) may revoke the power of attorney only upon a showing of sufficient cause, and payment of the petition fee set forth in § 1.17(f). A patent practitioner will be notified of the revocation of the power of attorney. Where power of attorney is given to the patent practitioners associated with a Customer Number (§ 1.32(c)(2)), the practitioners so appointed will also be notified of the revocation of the power of attorney when the power of attorney to all of the practitioners associated with the Customer Number is revoked. The notice of revocation will be mailed to the correspondence address for the application (§ 1.33) in effect before the revocation. An assignment will not of itself operate as a revocation of a power previously given, but the assignee may become the applicant under § 1.46(c) and revoke any previous power of attorney and grant a power of attorney as provided in § 1.32(b).

(b) A registered patent attorney or patent agent who has been given a power of attorney pursuant to § 1.32(b) may withdraw as attorney or agent of record upon application to and approval by the Director. The applicant or patent owner will be notified of the withdrawal of the registered patent attorney or patent agent. Where power of attorney is given to the patent practitioners associated with a Customer Number, a request to delete all of the patent practitioners associated with the Customer Number may not be granted if an applicant has given power of attorney to the patent practitioners associated with the Customer Number in an application that has an Office action to which a reply is due, but insufficient time remains for the applicant to file a reply. See § 41.5 of this title for withdrawal during proceedings before the Patent Trial and Appeal Board.

[69 FR 49997, Aug. 12, 2004, as amended at 70 FR 56128, Sept. 26, 2005; 77 FR 46624, Aug. 6, 2012; 77 FR 48814, Aug. 14, 2012]

Who May Apply for a Patent

§ 1.41 Inventorship.

(a) An application must include, or be amended to include, the name of the inventor for any invention claimed in the application.

(b) The inventorship of a nonprovisional application under 35 U.S.C.

111(a) is the inventor or joint inventors set forth in the application data sheet in accordance with § 1.76 filed before or concurrently with the inventor's oath or declaration. If an application data sheet is not filed before or concurrently with the inventor's oath or declaration, the inventorship is the inventor or joint inventors set forth in the inventor's oath or declaration, except as provided for in §§ 1.53(d)(4) and 1.63(d). Once an application data sheet or the inventor's oath or declaration is filed in a nonprovisional application, any correction of inventorship must be pursuant to § 1.48. If neither an application data sheet nor the inventor's oath or declaration is filed during the pendency of a nonprovisional application, the inventorship is the inventor or joint inventors set forth in the application papers filed pursuant to § 1.53(b), unless the applicant files a paper, including the processing fee set forth in § 1.17(i), supplying the name or names of the inventor or joint inventors.

(c) The inventorship of a provisional application is the inventor or joint inventors set forth in the cover sheet as prescribed by § 1.51(c)(1). Once a cover sheet as prescribed by § 1.51(c)(1) is filed in a provisional application, any correction of inventorship must be pursuant to § 1.48. If a cover sheet as prescribed by § 1.51(c)(1) is not filed during the pendency of a provisional application, the inventorship is the inventor or joint inventors set forth in the application papers filed pursuant to § 1.53(c), unless applicant files a paper including the processing fee set forth in § 1.17(q), supplying the name or names of the inventor or joint inventors.

(d) In a nonprovisional application under 35 U.S.C. 111(a) filed without an application data sheet or the inventor's oath or declaration, or in a provisional application filed without a cover sheet as prescribed by § 1.51(c)(1), the name and residence of each person believed to be an actual inventor should be provided when the application papers pursuant to § 1.53(b) or § 1.53(c) are filed.

(e) The inventorship of an international application entering the national stage under 35 U.S.C. 371 is the inventor or joint inventors set forth in the application data sheet in accordance with § 1.76 filed with the initial submission under 35 U.S.C. 371. Unless the initial submission under 35 U.S.C. 371 is accompanied by an application data sheet in accordance with § 1.76 setting forth the inventor or joint inventors, the inventorship is the inventor or joint inventors set forth in the international application, which includes any change effected under PCT Rule 92 *bis*.

[77 FR 48814, Aug. 14, 2012]

§ 1.42 Applicant for patent.

(a) The word "applicant" when used in this title refers to the inventor or all of the joint inventors, or to the person applying for a patent as provided in §§ 1.43, 1.45, or 1.46.

(b) If a person is applying for a patent as provided in § 1.46, the word "applicant" refers to the assignee, the person to whom the inventor is under an obligation to assign the invention, or the person who otherwise shows sufficient proprietary interest in the matter, who is applying for a patent under § 1.46 and not the inventor.

(c) If fewer than all joint inventors are applying for a patent as provided in § 1.45, the phrase "the applicant" means the joint inventors who are applying for the patent without the omitted inventor(s).

(d) Any person having authority may deliver an application and fees to the Office on behalf of the applicant. However, an oath or declaration, or substitute statement in lieu of an oath or declaration, may be executed only in accordance with § 1.63 or 1.64, a correspondence address may be provided only in accordance with § 1.33(a), and amendments and other papers must be signed in accordance with § 1.33(b).

(e) The Office may require additional information where there is a question concerning ownership or interest in an application, and a showing may be required from the person filing the application that the filing was authorized where such authorization comes into question.

[77 FR 48815, Aug. 14, 2012]

§ 1.43 Application for patent by a legal representative of a deceased or legally incapacitated inventor.

If an inventor is deceased or under legal incapacity, the legal representative of the inventor may make an application for patent on behalf of the inventor. If an inventor dies during the time intervening between the filing of the application and the granting of a patent thereon, the letters patent may be issued to the legal representative upon proper intervention. *See* § 1.64 concerning the execution of a substitute statement by a legal representative in lieu of an oath or declaration.

[77 FR 48815, Aug. 14, 2012]

§ 1.44 [Reserved]

§ 1.45 Application for patent by joint inventors.

(a) Joint inventors must apply for a patent jointly, and each must make an inventor's oath or declaration as required by § 1.63, except as provided for in § 1.64. If a joint inventor refuses to join in an application for patent or cannot be found or reached after diligent effort, the other joint inventor or inventors may make the application for patent on behalf of themselves and the omitted inventor. *See* § 1.64 concerning the execution of a substitute statement by the other joint inventor or inventors in lieu of an oath or declaration.

(b) Inventors may apply for a patent jointly even though:

(1) They did not physically work together or at the same time;

(2) Each inventor did not make the same type or amount of contribution; or

(3) Each inventor did not make a contribution to the subject matter of every claim of the application.

(c) If multiple inventors are named in a nonprovisional application, each named inventor must have made a contribution, individually or jointly, to the subject matter of at least one claim of the application and the application will be considered to be a joint application under 35 U.S.C. 116. If multiple inventors are named in a provisional application, each named inventor must have made a contribution, individually or jointly, to the subject matter disclosed in the provisional application and the provisional application will be considered to be a joint application under 35 U.S.C. 116.

[77 FR 48815, Aug. 14, 2012]

§ 1.46 Application for patent by an assignee, obligated assignee, or a person who otherwise shows sufficient proprietary interest in the matter.

(a) A person to whom the inventor has assigned or is under an obligation to assign the invention may make an application for patent. A person who otherwise shows sufficient proprietary interest in the matter may make an application for patent on behalf of and as agent for the inventor on proof of the pertinent facts and a showing that such action is appropriate to preserve the rights of the parties.

(b) If an application under 35 U.S.C. 111 is made by a person other than the inventor under paragraph (a) of this section, the application must contain an application data sheet under § 1.76 specifying in the applicant information section (§ 1.76(b)(7)) the assignee, person to whom the inventor is under an obligation to assign the invention, or person who otherwise shows sufficient proprietary interest in the matter. If the application is the national stage of an international application, the person who is identified in the international stage as an applicant for the United States is the person specified as the original applicant for the national stage.

(1) If the applicant is the assignee or a person to whom the inventor is under an obligation to assign the invention, documentary evidence of ownership (*e.g.*, assignment for an assignee, employment agreement for a person to whom the inventor is under an obligation to assign the invention) should be recorded as provided for in part 3 of this chapter no later than the date the issue fee is paid in the application.

(2) If the applicant is a person who otherwise shows sufficient proprietary interest in the matter, such applicant must submit a petition including:

(i) The fee set forth in § 1.17(g);

(ii) A showing that such person has sufficient proprietary interest in the matter; and

(iii) A statement that making the application for patent by a person who otherwise shows sufficient proprietary interest in the matter on behalf of and as agent for the inventor is appropriate to preserve the rights of the parties.

(c) Any request to correct or update the name of the applicant after an applicant has been specified under paragraph (b) of this section must include an application data sheet under § 1.76 specifying the correct or updated name of the applicant in the applicant information section (§ 1.76(b)(7)). Any request to change the applicant after an original applicant has been specified under paragraph (b) of this section must include an application data sheet under § 1.76 specifying the applicant in the applicant information section (§ 1.76(b)(7)) and comply with §§ 3.71 and 3.73 of this title.

(d) Even if the whole or a part interest in the invention or in the patent to be issued is assigned or obligated to be assigned, an oath or declaration must be executed by the actual inventor or each actual joint inventor, except as provided for in § 1.64. *See* § 1.64 concerning the execution of a substitute statement by an assignee, person to whom the inventor is under an obligation to assign the invention, or a person who otherwise shows sufficient proprietary interest in the matter.

(e) If a patent is granted on an application filed under this section by a person other than the inventor, the patent shall be granted to the real party in interest. Otherwise, the patent may be issued to the assignee or jointly to the inventor and the assignee as provided in § 3.81. Where a real party in interest has filed an application under § 1.46, the applicant shall notify the Office of any change in the real party in interest no later than payment of the issue fee. The Office will treat the absence of such a notice as an indication that there has been no change in the real party in interest.

(f) The Office may publish notice of the filing of the application by a person who otherwise shows sufficient proprietary interest in the *Official Gazette*.

[77 FR 48815, Aug. 14, 2012]

§ 1.47 [Reserved]

§ 1.48 Correction of inventorship pursuant to 35 U.S.C. 116 or correction of the name or order of names in a patent application, other than a reissue application.

(a) *Nonprovisional application:* Any request to correct or change the inventorship once the inventorship has been established under § 1.41 must include:

(1) An application data sheet in accordance with § 1.76 that identifies each inventor by his or her legal name; and

(2) The processing fee set forth in § 1.17(i).

(b) *Inventor's oath or declaration for added inventor:* An oath or declaration as required by § 1.63, or a substitute statement in compliance with § 1.64, will be required for any actual inventor who has not yet executed such an oath or declaration.

(c) Any request to correct or change the inventorship under paragraph (a) of this section filed after the Office action on the merits has been given or mailed in the application must also be accompanied by the fee set forth in § 1.17(d), unless the request is accompanied by a statement that the request to correct or change the inventorship is due solely to the cancelation of claims in the application.

(d) *Provisional application.* Once a cover sheet as prescribed by § 1.51(c)(1) is filed in a provisional application, any request to correct or change the inventorship must include:

(1) A request, signed by a party set forth in § 1.33(b), to correct the inventorship that identifies each inventor by his or her legal name; and

(2) The processing fee set forth in § 1.17(q).

(e) *Additional information may be required.* The Office may require such other information as may be deemed appropriate under the particular circumstances surrounding the correction of inventorship.

(f) *Correcting or updating the name of an inventor:* Any request to correct or update the name of the inventor or a joint inventor, or the order of the names of joint inventors, in a nonprovisional application must include:

(1) An application data sheet in accordance with § 1.76 that identifies each

inventor by his or her legal name in the desired order; and

(2) The processing fee set forth in § 1.17(i).

(g) *Reissue applications not covered.* The provisions of this section do not apply to reissue applications. *See* §§ 1.171 and 1.175 for correction of inventorship in a patent via a reissue application.

(h) *Correction of inventorship in patent. See* § 1.324 for correction of inventorship in a patent.

(i) *Correction of inventorship in an interference or contested case before the Patent Trial and Appeal Board.* In an interference under part 41, subpart D, of this title, a request for correction of inventorship in an application must be in the form of a motion under § 41.121(a)(2) of this title. In a contested case under part 42, subpart D, of this title, a request for correction of inventorship in an application must be in the form of a motion under § 42.22 of this title. The motion under § 41.121(a)(2) or 42.22 of this title must comply with the requirements of paragraph (a) of this section.

[77 FR 48816, Aug. 14, 2012, as amended at 78 FR 4289, Jan. 18, 2013]

THE APPLICATION

§ 1.51 General requisites of an application.

(a) Applications for patents must be made to the Director of the United States Patent and Trademark Office.

(b) A complete application filed under § 1.53(b) or § 1.53(d) comprises:

(1) A specification as prescribed by 35 U.S.C. 112, including a claim or claims, see §§ 1.71 to 1.77;

(2) The inventor's oath or declaration, *see* §§ 1.63 and 1.64;

(3) Drawings, when necessary, see §§ 1.81 to 1.85; and

(4) The prescribed filing fee, search fee, examination fee, and application size fee, see § 1.16.

(c) A complete provisional application filed under § 1.53(c) comprises:

(1) A cover sheet identifying:

(i) The application as a provisional application,

(ii) The name or names of the inventor or inventors, (see § 1.41(a)(2)),

(iii) The residence of each named inventor,

(iv) The title of the invention,

(v) The name and registration number of the attorney or agent (if applicable),

(vi) The docket number used by the person filing the application to identify the application (if applicable),

(vii) The correspondence address, and

(viii) The name of the U.S. Government agency and Government contract number (if the invention was made by an agency of the U.S. Government or under a contract with an agency of the U.S. Government);

(2) A specification as prescribed by 35 U.S.C. 112(a), see § 1.71;

(3) Drawings, when necessary, see §§ 1.81 to 1.85; and

(4) The prescribed filing fee and application size fee, see § 1.16.

(d) Applicants are encouraged to file an information disclosure statement in nonprovisional applications. See § 1.97 and § 1.98. No information disclosure statement may be filed in a provisional application.

[62 FR 53185, Oct. 10, 1997, as amended at 65 FR 54664, Sept. 8, 2000; 68 FR 14336, Mar. 25, 2003; 70 FR 3889, Jan. 27, 2005; 77 FR 46624, Aug. 6, 2012; 77 FR 48816, Aug. 14, 2012]

§ 1.52 Language, paper, writing, margins, compact disc specifications.

(a) *Papers that are to become a part of the permanent United States Patent and Trademark Office records in the file of a patent application or a reexamination proceeding.* (1) All papers, other than drawings, that are submitted on paper or by facsimile transmission, and are to become a part of the permanent United States Patent and Trademark Office records in the file of a patent application or reexamination proceeding, must be on sheets of paper that are the same size, not permanently bound together, and:

(i) Flexible, strong, smooth, non-shiny, durable, and white;

(ii) Either 21.0 cm by 29.7 cm (DIN size A4) or 21.6 cm by 27.9 cm (8½ by 11 inches), with each sheet including a top margin of at least 2.0 cm (¾ inch), a left side margin of at least 2.5 cm (1 inch), a right side margin of at least 2.0 cm (¾ inch), and a bottom margin of at least 2.0 cm (¾ inch);

(iii) Written on only one side in portrait orientation;

(iv) Plainly and legibly written either by a typewriter or machine printer in permanent dark ink or its equivalent; and

(v) Presented in a form having sufficient clarity and contrast between the paper and the writing thereon to permit the direct reproduction of readily legible copies in any number by use of photographic, electrostatic, photo-offset, and microfilming processes and electronic capture by use of digital imaging and optical character recognition.

(2) All papers that are submitted on paper or by facsimile transmission and are to become a part of the permanent records of the United States Patent and Trademark Office should have no holes in the sheets as submitted.

(3) The provisions of this paragraph and paragraph (b) of this section do not apply to the pre-printed information on paper forms provided by the Office, or to the copy of the patent submitted on paper in double column format as the specification in a reissue application or request for reexamination.

(4) *See* § 1.58 for chemical and mathematical formulae and tables, and § 1.84 for drawings.

(5) Papers that are submitted electronically to the Office must be formatted and transmitted in compliance with the Office's electronic filing system requirements.

(b) *The application (specification, including the claims, drawings, and the inventor's oath or declaration) or supplemental examination or reexamination proceeding and any amendments or corrections to the application or reexamination proceeding.* (1) The application or proceeding and any amendments or corrections to the application (including any translation submitted pursuant to paragraph (d) of this section) or proceeding, except as provided for in § 1.69 and paragraph (d) of this section, must:

(i) Comply with the requirements of paragraph (a) of this section; and

(ii) Be in the English language or be accompanied by a translation of the application and a translation of any corrections or amendments into the English language together with a statement that the translation is accurate.

(2) The specification (including the abstract and claims) for other than reissue applications and reexamination proceedings, and any amendments for applications (including reissue applications) and reexamination proceedings to the specification, except as provided for in §§ 1.821 through 1.825, must have:

(i) Lines that are 1½ or double spaced;

(ii) Text written in a nonscript type font (e.g., Arial, Times Roman, or Courier, preferably a font size of 12) lettering style having capital letters which should be at least 0.3175 cm. (0.125 inch) high, but may be no smaller than 0.21 cm. (0.08 inch) high (e.g., a font size of 6); and

(iii) Only a single column of text.

(3) The claim or claims must commence on a separate physical sheet or electronic page (§ 1.75(h)).

(4) The abstract must commence on a separate physical sheet or electronic page or be submitted as the first page of the patent in a reissue application or reexamination proceeding (§ 1.72(b)).

(5) Other than in a reissue application or reexamination proceeding, the pages of the specification including claims and abstract must be numbered consecutively, starting with 1, the numbers being centrally located above or preferably, below, the text.

(6) Other than in a reissue application or reexamination proceeding, the paragraphs of the specification, other than in the claims or abstract, may be numbered at the time the application is filed, and should be individually and consecutively numbered using Arabic numerals, so as to unambiguously identify each paragraph. The number should consist of at least four numerals enclosed in square brackets, including leading zeros (e.g., [0001]). The numbers and enclosing brackets should appear to the right of the left margin as the first item in each paragraph, before the first word of the paragraph, and should be highlighted in bold. A gap, equivalent to approximately four spaces, should follow the number. Nontext elements (e.g., tables, mathematical or chemical formulae, chemical structures, and sequence data) are considered part of the numbered paragraph

around or above the elements, and should not be independently numbered. If a nontext element extends to the left margin, it should not be numbered as a separate and independent paragraph. A list is also treated as part of the paragraph around or above the list, and should not be independently numbered. Paragraph or section headers (titles), whether abutting the left margin or centered on the page, are not considered paragraphs and should not be numbered.

(c) Interlineation, erasure, cancellation, or other alteration of the application papers may be made before or after the signing of the inventor's oath or declaration referring to those application papers, provided that the statements in the inventor's oath or declaration pursuant to § 1.63 remain applicable to those application papers. A substitute specification (§ 1.125) may be required if the application papers do not comply with paragraphs (a) and (b) of this section.

(d) A nonprovisional or provisional application under 35 U.S.C. 111 may be in a language other than English.

(1) *Nonprovisional application.* If a nonprovisional application under 35 U.S.C. 111(a) is filed in a language other than English, an English language translation of the non-English language application, a statement that the translation is accurate, and the processing fee set forth in § 1.17(i) are required. If these items are not filed with the application, the applicant will be notified and given a period of time within which they must be filed in order to avoid abandonment.

(2) *Provisional application.* If a provisional application under 35 U.S.C. 111(b) is filed in a language other than English, an English language translation of the non-English language provisional application will not be required in the provisional application. *See* § 1.78(a) for the requirements for claiming the benefit of such provisional application in a nonprovisional application.

(e) *Electronic documents that are to become part of the permanent United States Patent and Trademark Office records in the file of a patent application or reexamination proceeding.* (1) The following documents may be submitted to the Office on a compact disc in compliance with this paragraph:

(i) A computer program listing (see § 1.96);

(ii) A "Sequence Listing" (submitted under § 1.821(c)); or

(iii) Any individual table (see § 1.58) if the table is more than 50 pages in length, or if the total number of pages of all the tables in an application exceeds 100 pages in length, where a table page is a page printed on paper in conformance with paragraph (b) of this section and § 1.58(c).

(2) A compact disc as used in this part means a Compact Disc-Read Only Memory (CD-ROM) or a Compact Disc-Recordable (CD-R) in compliance with this paragraph. A CD-ROM is a "read-only" medium on which the data is pressed into the disc so that it cannot be changed or erased. A CD-R is a "write once" medium on which once the data is recorded, it is permanent and cannot be changed or erased.

(3)(i) Each compact disc must conform to the International Standards Organization (ISO) 9660 standard, and the contents of each compact disc must be in compliance with the American Standard Code for Information Interchange (ASCII).

(ii) Each compact disc must be enclosed in a hard compact disc case within an unsealed padded and protective mailing envelope and accompanied by a transmittal letter on paper in accordance with paragraph (a) of this section. The transmittal letter must list for each compact disc the machine format (e.g., IBM-PC, Macintosh), the operating system compatibility (e.g., MS-DOS, MS-Windows, Macintosh, Unix), a list of files contained on the compact disc including their names, sizes in bytes, and dates of creation, plus any other special information that is necessary to identify, maintain, and interpret (e.g., tables in landscape orientation should be identified as landscape orientation or be identified when inquired about) the information on the compact disc. Compact discs submitted to the Office will not be returned to the applicant.

(4) Any compact disc must be submitted in duplicate unless it contains only the "Sequence Listing" in computer readable form required by

§ 1.821(e). The compact disc and duplicate copy must be labeled "Copy 1" and "Copy 2," respectively. The transmittal letter which accompanies the compact disc must include a statement that the two compact discs are identical. In the event that the two compact discs are not identical, the Office will use the compact disc labeled "Copy 1" for further processing. Any amendment to the information on a compact disc must be by way of a replacement compact disc in compliance with this paragraph containing the substitute information, and must be accompanied by a statement that the replacement compact disc contains no new matter. The compact disc and copy must be labeled "COPY 1 REPLACEMENT MM/DD/YYYY" (with the month, day and year of creation indicated), and "COPY 2 REPLACEMENT MM/DD/YYYY," respectively.

(5) The specification must contain an incorporation-by-reference of the material on the compact disc in a separate paragraph (§ 1.77(b)(5)), identifying each compact disc by the names of the files contained on each of the compact discs, their date of creation and their sizes in bytes. The Office may require applicant to amend the specification to include in the paper portion any part of the specification previously submitted on compact disc.

(6) A compact disc must also be labeled with the following information:

(i) The name of each inventor (if known);

(ii) Title of the invention;

(iii) The docket number, or application number if known, used by the person filing the application to identify the application; and

(iv) A creation date of the compact disc.

(v) If multiple compact discs are submitted, the label shall indicate their order (e.g., "1 of X").

(vi) An indication that the disk is "Copy 1" or "Copy 2" of the submission. See paragraph (b)(4) of this section.

(7) If a file is unreadable on both copies of the disc, the unreadable file will be treated as not having been submitted. A file is unreadable if, for example, it is of a format that does not comply with the requirements of paragraph (e)(3) of this section, it is corrupted by a computer virus, or it is written onto a defective compact disc.

(f)(1) Any sequence listing in an electronic medium in compliance with §§ 1.52(e) and 1.821(c) or (e), and any computer program listing filed in an electronic medium in compliance with §§ 1.52(e) and 1.96, will be excluded when determining the application size fee required by § 1.16(s) or § 1.492(j). For purposes of determining the application size fee required by § 1.16(s) or § 1.492(j), for an application the specification and drawings of which, excluding any sequence listing in compliance with § 1.821(c) or (e), and any computer program listing filed in an electronic medium in compliance with §§ 1.52(e) and 1.96, are submitted in whole or in part on an electronic medium other than the Office electronic filing system, each three kilobytes of content submitted on an electronic medium shall be counted as a sheet of paper.

(2) Except as otherwise provided in this paragraph, the paper size equivalent of the specification and drawings of an application submitted via the Office electronic filing system will be considered to be seventy-five percent of the number of sheets of paper present in the specification and drawings of the application when entered into the Office file wrapper after being rendered by the Office electronic filing system for purposes of determining the application size fee required by § 1.16(s). Any sequence listing in compliance with § 1.821(c) or (e), and any computer program listing in compliance with § 1.96, submitted via the Office electronic filing system will be excluded when determining the application size fee required by § 1.16(s) if the listing is submitted in ASCII text as part of an associated file.

(Pub. L. 94–131, 89 Stat. 685; 35 U.S.C. 6, Pub. L. 97–247; 15 U.S.C. 1113, 1123)

EDITORIAL NOTE: For FEDERAL REGISTER citations affecting § 1.52, see the List of CFR Sections Affected, which appears in the Finding Aids section of the printed volume and at *www.fdsys.gov*.

§ 1.53 Application number, filing date, and completion of application.

(a) *Application number*. Any papers received in the Patent and Trademark

Office which purport to be an application for a patent will be assigned an application number for identification purposes.

(b) *Application filing requirements—Nonprovisional application.* The filing date of an application for patent filed under this section, except for a provisional application under paragraph (c) of this section or a continued prosecution application under paragraph (d) of this section, is the date on which a specification as prescribed by 35 U.S.C. 112 containing a description pursuant to § 1.71 and at least one claim pursuant to § 1.75, and any drawing required by § 1.81(a) are filed in the Patent and Trademark Office. No new matter may be introduced into an application after its filing date. A continuing application, which may be a continuation, divisional, or continuation-in-part application, may be filed under the conditions specified in 35 U.S.C. 120, 121, or 365(c) and § 1.78(c) and (d).

(1) A continuation or divisional application that names as inventors the same or fewer than all of the inventors named in the prior application may be filed under this paragraph or paragraph (d) of this section.

(2) A continuation-in-part application (which may disclose and claim subject matter not disclosed in the prior application) or a continuation or divisional application naming an inventor not named in the prior application must be filed under this paragraph.

(c) *Application filing requirements—Provisional application.* The filing date of a provisional application is the date on which a specification as prescribed by 35 U.S.C. 112(a), and any drawing required by § 1.81(a) are filed in the Patent and Trademark Office. No amendment, other than to make the provisional application comply with the patent statute and all applicable regulations, may be made to the provisional application after the filing date of the provisional application.

(1) A provisional application must also include the cover sheet required by § 1.51(c)(1), which may be an application data sheet (§ 1.76), or a cover letter identifying the application as a provisional application. Otherwise, the application will be treated as an application filed under paragraph (b) of this section.

(2) An application for patent filed under paragraph (b) of this section may be converted to a provisional application and be accorded the original filing date of the application filed under paragraph (b) of this section. The grant of such a request for conversion will not entitle applicant to a refund of the fees that were properly paid in the application filed under paragraph (b) of this section. Such a request for conversion must be accompanied by the processing fee set forth in § 1.17(q) and be filed prior to the earliest of:

(i) Abandonment of the application filed under paragraph (b) of this section;

(ii) Payment of the issue fee on the application filed under paragraph (b) of this section; or

(iii) Expiration of twelve months after the filing date of the application filed under paragraph (b) of this section.

(3) A provisional application filed under paragraph (c) of this section may be converted to a nonprovisional application filed under paragraph (b) of this section and accorded the original filing date of the provisional application. The conversion of a provisional application to a nonprovisional application will not result in either the refund of any fee properly paid in the provisional application or the application of any such fee to the filing fee, or any other fee, for the nonprovisional application. Conversion of a provisional application to a nonprovisional application under this paragraph will result in the term of any patent to issue from the application being measured from at least the filing date of the provisional application for which conversion is requested. Thus, applicants should consider avoiding this adverse patent term impact by filing a nonprovisional application claiming the benefit of the provisional application under 35 U.S.C. 119(e) (rather than converting the provisional application into a nonprovisional application pursuant to this paragraph). A request to convert a provisional application to a nonprovisional application must be accompanied by the fee set forth in § 1.17(i) and an amendment including at least one claim as prescribed

by 35 U.S.C. 112(b), unless the provisional application under paragraph (c) of this section otherwise contains at least one claim as prescribed by 35 U.S.C. 112(b). The nonprovisional application resulting from conversion of a provisional application must also include the filing fee, search fee, and examination fee for a nonprovisional application, the inventor's oath or declaration, and the surcharge required by § 1.16(f) if either the basic filing fee for a nonprovisional application or the inventor's oath or declaration was not present on the filing date accorded the resulting nonprovisional application (*i.e.*, the filing date of the original provisional application). A request to convert a provisional application to a nonprovisional application must also be filed prior to the earliest of:

(i) Abandonment of the provisional application filed under paragraph (c) of this section; or

(ii) Expiration of twelve months after the filing date of the provisional application filed under paragraph (c) of this section.

(4) A provisional application is not entitled to the right of priority under 35 U.S.C. 119 or 365(a) or § 1.55, or to the benefit of an earlier filing date under 35 U.S.C. 120, 121, or 365(c) or § 1.78 of any other application. No claim for priority under 35 U.S.C. 119(e) or § 1.78(a) may be made in a design application based on a provisional application. The requirements of §§ 1.821 through 1.825 regarding application disclosures containing nucleotide and/or amino acid sequences are not mandatory for provisional applications.

(d) *Application filing requirements—Continued prosecution (nonprovisional) application.* (1) A continuation or divisional application (but not a continuation-in-part) of a prior nonprovisional application may be filed as a continued prosecution application under this paragraph, provided that:

(i) The application is for a design patent;

(ii) The prior nonprovisional application is a design application that is complete as defined by § 1.51(b); and

(iii) The application under this paragraph is filed before the earliest of:

(A) Payment of the issue fee on the prior application, unless a petition under § 1.313(c) is granted in the prior application;

(B) Abandonment of the prior application; or

(C) Termination of proceedings on the prior application.

(2) The filing date of a continued prosecution application is the date on which a request on a separate paper for an application under this paragraph is filed. An application filed under this paragraph:

(i) Must identify the prior application;

(ii) Discloses and claims only subject matter disclosed in the prior application;

(iii) Names as inventors the same inventors named in the prior application on the date the application under this paragraph was filed, except as provided in paragraph (d)(4) of this section;

(iv) Includes the request for an application under this paragraph, will utilize the file jacket and contents of the prior application, including the specification, drawings and the inventor's oath or declaration from the prior application, to constitute the new application, and will be assigned the application number of the prior application for identification purposes; and

(v) Is a request to expressly abandon the prior application as of the filing date of the request for an application under this paragraph.

(3) The filing fee, search fee, and examination fee for a continued prosecution application filed under this paragraph are the basic filing fee as set forth in § 1.16(b), the search fee as set forth in § 1.16(l), and the examination fee as set forth in § 1.16(p).

(4) An application filed under this paragraph may be filed by fewer than all the inventors named in the prior application, provided that the request for an application under this paragraph when filed is accompanied by a statement requesting deletion of the name or names of the person or persons who are not inventors of the invention being claimed in the new application. No person may be named as an inventor in an application filed under this paragraph who was not named as an inventor in the prior application on the

date the application under this paragraph was filed, except by way of correction of inventorship under § 1.48.

(5) Any new change must be made in the form of an amendment to the prior application as it existed prior to the filing of an application under this paragraph. No amendment in an application under this paragraph (a continued prosecution application) may introduce new matter or matter that would have been new matter in the prior application. Any new specification filed with the request for an application under this paragraph will not be considered part of the original application papers, but will be treated as a substitute specification in accordance with § 1.125.

(6) The filing of a continued prosecution application under this paragraph will be construed to include a waiver of confidentiality by the applicant under 35 U.S.C. 122 to the extent that any member of the public, who is entitled under the provisions of § 1.14 to access to, copies of, or information concerning either the prior application or any continuing application filed under the provisions of this paragraph, may be given similar access to, copies of, or similar information concerning the other application or applications in the file jacket.

(7) A request for an application under this paragraph is the specific reference required by 35 U.S.C. 120 to every application assigned the application number identified in such request. No amendment in an application under this paragraph may delete this specific reference to any prior application.

(8) In addition to identifying the application number of the prior application, applicant should furnish in the request for an application under this paragraph the following information relating to the prior application to the best of his or her ability:

(i) Title of invention;

(ii) Name of applicant(s); and

(iii) Correspondence address.

(9) See § 1.103(b) for requesting a limited suspension of action in an application filed under this paragraph.

(e) *Failure to meet filing date requirements.* (1) If an application deposited under paragraph (b), (c), or (d) of this section does not meet the requirements of such paragraph to be entitled to a filing date, applicant will be so notified, if a correspondence address has been provided, and given a period of time within which to correct the filing error. If, however, a request for an application under paragraph (d) of this section does not meet the requirements of that paragraph because the application in which the request was filed is not a design application, and if the application in which the request was filed was itself filed on or after June 8, 1995, the request for an application under paragraph (d) of this section will be treated as a request for continued examination under § 1.114.

(2) Any request for review of a notification pursuant to paragraph (e)(1) of this section, or a notification that the original application papers lack a portion of the specification or drawing(s), must be by way of a petition pursuant to this paragraph accompanied by the fee set forth in § 1.17(f). In the absence of a timely (§ 1.181(f)) petition pursuant to this paragraph, the filing date of an application in which the applicant was notified of a filing error pursuant to paragraph (e)(1) of this section will be the date the filing error is corrected.

(3) If an applicant is notified of a filing error pursuant to paragraph (e)(1) of this section, but fails to correct the filing error within the given time period or otherwise timely (§ 1.181(f)) take action pursuant to this paragraph, proceedings in the application will be considered terminated. Where proceedings in an application are terminated pursuant to this paragraph, the application may be disposed of, and any filing fees, less the handling fee set forth in § 1.21(n), will be refunded.

(f) *Completion of application subsequent to filing—Nonprovisional (including continued prosecution or reissue) application.*

(1) If an application which has been accorded a filing date pursuant to paragraph (b) or (d) of this section does not include the basic filing fee, the search fee, or the examination fee, or if an application which has been accorded a filing date pursuant to paragraph (b) of this section does not include the inventor's oath or declaration (§ 1.63, § 1.64, § 1.162 or § 1.175), and the applicant has provided a correspondence address (§ 1.33(a)), the applicant will be notified and given a period of time within

which to pay the basic filing fee, search fee, and examination fee, and pay the surcharge if required by §1.16(f) to avoid abandonment.

(2) If an application which has been accorded a filing date pursuant to paragraph (b) of this section does not include the basic filing fee, the search fee, the examination fee, or the inventor's oath or declaration, and the applicant has not provided a correspondence address (§1.33(a)), the applicant has two months from the filing date of the application within which to pay the basic filing fee, search fee, and examination fee, and pay the surcharge required by §1.16(f) to avoid abandonment.

(3) The inventor's oath or declaration in an application under §1.53(b) must also be filed within the period specified in paragraph (f)(1) or (f)(2) of this section, except that the filing of the inventor's oath or declaration may be postponed until the application is otherwise in condition for allowance under the conditions specified in paragraphs (f)(3)(i) and (f)(3)(ii) of this section.

(i) The application must be an original (non-reissue) application that contains an application data sheet in accordance with §1.76 identifying:

(A) Each inventor by his or her legal name;

(B) A mailing address where the inventor customarily receives mail, and residence, if an inventor lives at a location which is different from where the inventor customarily receives mail, for each inventor.

(ii) The applicant must file an oath or declaration in compliance with §1.63, or a substitute statement in compliance with §1.64, executed by or with respect to each actual inventor no later than the expiration of the time period set in the "Notice of Allowability" to avoid abandonment, when the applicant is notified in a "Notice of Allowability" that an application is otherwise in condition for allowance. The time period set in a "Notice of Allowability" is not extendable. *See* §1.136(c). The Office may dispense with the notice provided for in paragraph (f)(1) of this section if an oath or declaration under §1.63, or a substitute statement under §1.64, executed by or with respect to each actual inventor has been filed before the application is in condition for allowance.

(4) If the excess claims fees required by §1.16(h) and (i) and multiple dependent claim fee required by §1.16(j) are not paid on filing or on later presentation of the claims for which the excess claims or multiple dependent claim fees are due, the fees required by §1.16(h), (i) and (j) must be paid or the claims canceled by amendment prior to the expiration of the time period set for reply by the Office in any notice of fee deficiency. If the application size fee required by §1.16(s) (if any) is not paid on filing or on later presentation of the amendment necessitating a fee or additional fee under §1.16(s), the fee required by §1.16(s) must be paid prior to the expiration of the time period set for reply by the Office in any notice of fee deficiency in order to avoid abandonment.

(5) This paragraph applies to continuation or divisional applications under paragraphs (b) or (d) of this section and to continuation-in-part applications under paragraph (b) of this section. *See* §1.63(d) concerning the submission of a copy of the inventor's oath or declaration from the prior application for a continuing application under paragraph (b) of this section.

(6) If applicant does not pay the basic filing fee during the pendency of the application, the Office may dispose of the application.

(g) *Completion of application subsequent to filing—Provisional application.* (1) If a provisional application which has been accorded a filing date pursuant to paragraph (c) of this section does not include the cover sheet required by §1.51(c)(1) or the basic filing fee (§1.16(d)), and applicant has provided a correspondence address (§1.33(a)), applicant will be notified and given a period of time within which to pay the basic filing fee, file a cover sheet (§1.51(c)(1)), and pay the surcharge required by §1.16(g) to avoid abandonment.

(2) If a provisional application which has been accorded a filing date pursuant to paragraph (c) of this section does not include the cover sheet required by §1.51(c)(1) or the basic filing fee (§1.16(d)), and applicant has not provided a correspondence address

(§ 1.33(a)), applicant has two months from the filing date of the application within which to pay the basic filing fee, file a cover sheet (§ 1.51(c)(1)), and pay the surcharge required by § 1.16(g) to avoid abandonment.

(3) If the application size fee required by § 1.16(s) (if any) is not paid on filing, the fee required by § 1.16(s) must be paid prior to the expiration of the time period set for reply by the Office in any notice of fee deficiency in order to avoid abandonment.

(4) If applicant does not pay the basic filing fee during the pendency of the application, the Office may dispose of the application.

(h) *Subsequent treatment of application—Nonprovisional (including continued prosecution) application.* An application for a patent filed under paragraphs (b) or (d) of this section will not be placed on the files for examination until all its required parts, complying with the rules relating thereto, are received, except that the inventor's oath or declaration may be filed when the application is otherwise in condition for allowance pursuant to paragraph (f)(3) of this section and minor informalities may be waived subject to subsequent correction whenever required.

(i) *Subsequent treatment of application—Provisional application.* A provisional application for a patent filed under paragraph (c) of this section will not be placed on the files for examination and will become abandoned no later than twelve months after its filing date pursuant to 35 U.S.C. 111(b)(1).

[62 FR 53186, Oct. 10, 1997, as amended at 63 FR 5734, Feb. 4, 1998; 65 FR 14871, Mar. 20, 2000; 65 FR 50104, Aug. 16, 2000; 65 FR 54665, Sept. 8, 2000; 65 FR 78960, Dec. 18, 2000; 68 FR 14336, Mar. 25, 2003; 68 FR 32380, May 30, 2003; 69 FR 29878, May 26, 2004; 69 FR 56539, Sept. 21, 2004; 70 FR 3890, Jan. 27, 2005; 70 FR 30365, May 26, 2005; 72 FR 46836, Aug. 21, 2007; 74 FR 52688, Oct. 14, 2009; 77 FR 48817, Aug. 14, 2012; 78 FR 11053, Feb. 14, 2013]

§ 1.54 Parts of application to be filed together; filing receipt.

(a) It is desirable that all parts of the complete application be deposited in the Office together; otherwise, a letter must accompany each part, accurately and clearly connecting it with the other parts of the application. See § 1.53 (f) and (g) with regard to completion of an application.

(b) Applicant will be informed of the application number and filing date by a filing receipt, unless the application is an application filed under § 1.53(d).

[62 FR 53188, Oct. 10, 1997]

§ 1.55 Claim for foreign priority.

(a) *In general.* An applicant in a nonprovisional application may claim priority to one or more prior foreign applications under the conditions specified in 35 U.S.C. 119(a) through (d) and (f), 172, and 365(a) and (b) and this section.

(b) *Time for filing subsequent application.* The nonprovisional application must be filed not later than twelve months (six months in the case of a design application) after the date on which the foreign application was filed, or be entitled to claim the benefit under 35 U.S.C. 120, 121, or 365(c) of an application that was filed not later than twelve months (six months in the case of a design application) after the date on which the foreign application was filed. The twelve-month period is subject to 35 U.S.C. 21(b) (and § 1.7(a)) and PCT Rule 80.5, and the six-month period is subject to 35 U.S.C. 21(b) (and § 1.7(a)).

(c) *Time for filing priority claim and certified copy of foreign application in an application entering the national stage under 35 U.S.C. 371.* In an international application entering the national stage under 35 U.S.C. 371, the claim for priority must be made and a certified copy of the foreign application must be filed within the time limit set forth in the PCT and the Regulations under the PCT.

(d) *Time for filing priority claim in an application filed under 35 U.S.C. 111(a).* In an original application filed under 35 U.S.C. 111(a), the claim for priority must be filed within the later of four months from the actual filing date of the application or sixteen months from the filing date of the prior foreign application. The claim for priority must be presented in an application data sheet (§ 1.76(b)(6)), and must identify the foreign application for which priority is claimed, by specifying the application number, country (or intellectual property authority), day, month, and year of its filing. The time period in this paragraph does not apply in a design application.

(e) *Delayed priority claim in an application filed under 35 U.S.C. 111(a).* Unless such claim is accepted in accordance with the provisions of this paragraph, any claim for priority under 35 U.S.C. 119(a) through (d) or (f) or 365(a) in an original application filed under 35 U.S.C. 111(a) not presented in an application data sheet (§ 1.76(b)(6)) within the time period provided by paragraph (d) of this section is considered to have been waived. If a claim for priority is presented after the time period provided by paragraph (d) of this section, the claim may be accepted if the priority claim was unintentionally delayed. A petition to accept a delayed claim for priority under 35 U.S.C. 119(a) through (d) or (f) or 365(a) must be accompanied by:

(1) The priority claim under 35 U.S.C. 119(a) through (d) or (f) or 365(a) in an application data sheet (§ 1.76(b)(6)), identifying the foreign application for which priority is claimed, by specifying the application number, country (or intellectual property authority), day, month, and year of its filing, unless previously submitted;

(2) A certified copy of the foreign application if required by paragraph (f) of this section, unless previously submitted;

(3) The surcharge set forth in § 1.17(t); and

(4) A statement that the entire delay between the date the priority claim was due under paragraph (d) of this section and the date the priority claim was filed was unintentional. The Director may require additional information where there is a question whether the delay was unintentional.

(f) *Time for filing certified copy of foreign application in an application filed under 35 U.S.C. 111(a).* In an original application filed under 35 U.S.C. 111(a), a certified copy of the foreign application must be filed within the later of four months from the actual filing date of the application or sixteen months from the filing date of the prior foreign application, except as provided in paragraphs (h) and (i) of this section. If a certified copy of the foreign application is not filed within the later of four months from the actual filing date of the application or sixteen months from the filing date of the prior foreign application, and the exceptions in paragraphs (h) and (i) of this section are not applicable, the certified copy of the foreign application must be accompanied by a petition including a showing of good and sufficient cause for the delay and the petition fee set forth in § 1.17(g). The time period in this paragraph does not apply in a design application.

(g) *Requirement for filing priority claim, certified copy of foreign application, and translation in any application.* (1) The claim for priority and the certified copy of the foreign application specified in 35 U.S.C. 119(b) or PCT Rule 17 must, in any event, be filed within the pendency of the application and before the patent is granted. If the claim for priority or the certified copy of the foreign application is filed after the date the issue fee is paid, it must also be accompanied by the processing fee set forth in § 1.17(i), but the patent will not include the priority claim unless corrected by a certificate of correction under 35 U.S.C. 255 and § 1.323.

(2) The Office may require that the claim for priority and the certified copy of the foreign application be filed earlier than otherwise provided in this section:

(i) When the application is involved in an interference (see § 41.202 of this title) or derivation (see part 42 of this title) proceeding;

(ii) When necessary to overcome the date of a reference relied upon by the examiner; or

(iii) When deemed necessary by the examiner.

(3) An English language translation of a non-English language foreign application is not required except:

(i) When the application is involved in an interference (see § 41.202 of this title) or derivation (see part 42 of this title) proceeding;

(ii) When necessary to overcome the date of a reference relied upon by the examiner; or

(iii) When specifically required by the examiner.

(4) If an English language translation of a non-English language foreign application is required, it must be filed

together with a statement that the translation of the certified copy is accurate.

(h) *Foreign intellectual property office participating in a priority document exchange agreement.* The requirement in paragraphs (c), (f), and (g) of this section for a certified copy of the foreign application to be filed within the time limit set forth therein will be considered satisfied if:

(1) The foreign application was filed in a foreign intellectual property office participating with the Office in a bilateral or multilateral priority document exchange agreement (participating foreign intellectual property office), or a copy of the foreign application was filed in an application subsequently filed in a participating foreign intellectual property office that permits the Office to obtain such a copy;

(2) The claim for priority is presented in an application data sheet (§ 1.76(b)(6)), identifying the foreign application for which priority is claimed, by specifying the application number, country (or intellectual property authority), day, month, and year of its filing, and the applicant provides the information necessary for the participating foreign intellectual property office to provide the Office with access to the foreign application;

(3) The copy of the foreign application is received by the Office from the participating foreign intellectual property office, or a certified copy of the foreign application is filed, within the period specified in paragraph (g)(1) of this section; and

(4) The applicant files a request in a separate document that the Office obtain a copy of the foreign application from a participating intellectual property office that permits the Office to obtain such a copy if the foreign application was not filed in a participating foreign intellectual property office but a copy of the foreign application was filed in an application subsequently filed in a participating foreign intellectual property office that permits the Office to obtain such a copy. The request must identify the participating intellectual property office and the subsequent application by the application number, day, month, and year of its filing in which a copy of the foreign application was filed. The request must be filed within the later of sixteen months from the filing date of the prior foreign application or four months from the actual filing date of an application under 35 U.S.C. 111(a), within four months from the later of the date of commencement (§ 1.491(a)) or the date of the initial submission under 35 U.S.C. 371 in an application entering the national stage under 35 U.S.C. 371, or with a petition under paragraph (e) of this section.

(i) *Interim copy.* The requirement in paragraph (f) of this section for a certified copy of the foreign application to be filed within the time limit set forth therein will be considered satisfied if:

(1) A copy of the original foreign application clearly labeled as "Interim Copy," including the specification, and any drawings or claims upon which it is based, is filed in the Office together with a separate cover sheet identifying the foreign application by specifying the application number, country (or intellectual property authority), day, month, and year of its filing, and stating that the copy filed in the Office is a true copy of the original application as filed in the foreign country (or intellectual property authority);

(2) The copy of the foreign application and separate cover sheet is filed within the later of sixteen months from the filing date of the prior foreign application or four months from the actual filing date of an application under 35 U.S.C. 111(a), or with a petition under paragraph (e) of this section; and

(3) A certified copy of the foreign application is filed within the period specified in paragraph (g)(1) of this section.

(j) *Requirements for certain applications filed on or after March 16, 2013.* If a nonprovisional application filed on or after March 16, 2013, claims priority to a foreign application filed prior to March 16, 2013, and also contains, or contained at any time, a claim to a claimed invention that has an effective filing date on or after March 16, 2013, the applicant must provide a statement to that effect within the later of four months from the actual filing date of the nonprovisional application, four months from the date of entry into the national stage as set forth in § 1.491 in an international application, sixteen months from the filing date of the prior-filed foreign application, or the date that a first claim to a claimed invention that has an effective filing date on or after March 16, 2013, is presented in the nonprovisional application. An applicant is not required to provide such a statement if the applicant reasonably believes on the basis of information already known to the individuals designated in § 1.56(c) that the nonprovisional application does not, and did not at any time, contain a claim to a claimed invention that has an effective filing date on or after March 16, 2013.

(k) *Inventor's certificates.* An applicant in a nonprovisional application may under certain circumstances claim priority on the basis of one or more applications for an inventor's certificate in a country granting both inventor's certificates and patents. To claim the right of priority on the basis of an application for an inventor's certificate in such a country under 35 U.S.C. 119(d), the applicant when submitting a claim for such right as specified in this section, must include an affidavit or declaration. The affidavit or declaration must include a specific statement that, upon an investigation, he or she is satisfied that to the best of his or her knowledge, the applicant, when filing the application for the inventor's certificate, had the option to file an application for either a patent or an inventor's certificate as to the subject matter of the identified claim or claims forming the basis for the claim of priority.

(l) *Time periods not extendable.* The time periods set forth in this section are not extendable.

[78 FR 16182, Mar. 14, 2013]

§ 1.56 Duty to disclose information material to patentability.

(a) A patent by its very nature is affected with a public interest. The public interest is best served, and the most effective patent examination occurs when, at the time an application is being examined, the Office is aware of and evaluates the teachings of all information material to patentability. Each individual associated with the filing and prosecution of a patent application has a duty of candor and good faith in dealing with the Office, which includes a duty to disclose to the Office all information known to that individual to be material to patentability as defined in this section. The duty to disclose information exists with respect to each pending claim until the claim is cancelled or withdrawn from consideration, or the application becomes abandoned. Information material to the patentability of a claim that is cancelled or withdrawn from consideration need not be submitted if the information is not material to the patentability of any claim remaining under consideration in the application. There is no duty to submit information which is not material to the patentability of any existing claim. The duty to disclose all information known to be material to patentability is deemed to be satisfied if all information known to be material to patentability of any claim issued in a patent was cited by the Office or submitted to the Office in the manner prescribed by §§ 1.97(b)–(d) and 1.98. However, no patent will be granted on an application in connection with which fraud on the Office was practiced or attempted or the duty of disclosure was violated through bad faith or intentional misconduct. The Office encourages applicants to carefully examine:

(1) Prior art cited in search reports of a foreign patent office in a counterpart application, and

(2) The closest information over which individuals associated with the filing or prosecution of a patent application believe any pending claim patentably defines, to make sure that any material information contained therein is disclosed to the Office.

(b) Under this section, information is material to patentability when it is not cumulative to information already of record or being made of record in the application, and

(1) It establishes, by itself or in combination with other information, a prima facie case of unpatentability of a claim; or

(2) It refutes, or is inconsistent with, a position the applicant takes in:

(i) Opposing an argument of unpatentability relied on by the Office, or

(ii) Asserting an argument of patentability.

A prima facie case of unpatentability is established when the information compels a conclusion that a claim is unpatentable under the preponderance of evidence, burden-of-proof standard, giving each term in the claim its broadest reasonable construction consistent with the specification, and before any consideration is given to evidence which may be submitted in an attempt to establish a contrary conclusion of patentability.

(c) Individuals associated with the filing or prosecution of a patent application within the meaning of this section are:

(1) Each inventor named in the application;

(2) Each attorney or agent who prepares or prosecutes the application; and

(3) Every other person who is substantively involved in the preparation or prosecution of the application and who is associated with the inventor, the applicant, an assignee, or anyone to whom there is an obligation to assign the application.

(d) Individuals other than the attorney, agent or inventor may comply with this section by disclosing information to the attorney, agent, or inventor.

(e) In any continuation-in-part application, the duty under this section includes the duty to disclose to the Office all information known to the person to be material to patentability, as defined in paragraph (b) of this section, which became available between the filing date of the prior application and the national or PCT international filing date of the continuation-in-part application.

[57 FR 2034, Jan. 17, 1992, as amended at 65 FR 54666, Sept. 8, 2000; 77 FR 48818, Aug. 14, 2012]

§ 1.57 Incorporation by reference.

(a) Subject to the conditions and requirements of this paragraph, if all or a portion of the specification or drawing(s) is inadvertently omitted from an application, but the application contains a claim under § 1.55 for priority of a prior-filed foreign application, or a claim under § 1.78 for the benefit of a prior-filed provisional, nonprovisional, or international application, that was present on the filing date of the application, and the inadvertently omitted portion of the specification or drawing(s) is completely contained in the prior-filed application, the claim under § 1.55 or § 1.78 shall also be considered an incorporation by reference of the prior-filed application as to the inadvertently omitted portion of the specification or drawing(s).

(1) The application must be amended to include the inadvertently omitted portion of the specification or drawing(s) within any time period set by the Office, but in no case later than the close of prosecution as defined by § 1.114(b), or abandonment of the application, whichever occurs earlier. The applicant is also required to:

(i) Supply a copy of the prior-filed application, except where the prior-filed application is an application filed under 35 U.S.C. 111;

(ii) Supply an English language translation of any prior-filed application that is in a language other than English; and

(iii) Identify where the inadvertently omitted portion of the specification or drawings can be found in the prior-filed application.

(2) Any amendment to an international application pursuant to this paragraph shall be effective only as to the United States, and shall have no effect on the international filing date of the application. In addition, no request under this section to add the inadvertently omitted portion of the specification or drawings in an international application designating the United States will be acted upon by the Office prior to the entry and commencement of the national stage (§ 1.491) or the filing of an application under 35 U.S.C. 111(a) which claims benefit of the international application. Any omitted portion of the international application which applicant desires to be effective as to all designated States, subject to PCT Rule 20.8(b), must be submitted in accordance with PCT Rule 20.

(3) If an application is not otherwise entitled to a filing date under § 1.53(b),

the amendment must be by way of a petition pursuant to this paragraph accompanied by the fee set forth in § 1.17(f).

(b) Except as provided in paragraph (a) of this section, an incorporation by reference must be set forth in the specification and must:

(1) Express a clear intent to incorporate by reference by using the root words "incorporat(e)" and "reference" (e.g., "incorporate by reference"); and

(2) Clearly identify the referenced patent, application, or publication.

(c) "Essential material" may be incorporated by reference, but only by way of an incorporation by reference to a U.S. patent or U.S. patent application publication, which patent or patent application publication does not itself incorporate such essential material by reference. "Essential material" is material that is necessary to:

(1) Provide a written description of the claimed invention, and of the manner and process of making and using it, in such full, clear, concise, and exact terms as to enable any person skilled in the art to which it pertains, or with which it is most nearly connected, to make and use the same, and set forth the best mode contemplated by the inventor of carrying out the invention as required by 35 U.S.C. 112(a);

(2) Describe the claimed invention in terms that particularly point out and distinctly claim the invention as required by 35 U.S.C. 112(b); or

(3) Describe the structure, material, or acts that correspond to a claimed means or step for performing a specified function as required by 35 U.S.C. 112(f).

(d) Other material ("Nonessential material") may be incorporated by reference to U.S. patents, U.S. patent application publications, foreign patents, foreign published applications, prior and concurrently filed commonly owned U.S. applications, or non-patent publications. An incorporation by reference by hyperlink or other form of browser executable code is not permitted.

(e) The examiner may require the applicant to supply a copy of the material incorporated by reference. If the Office requires the applicant to supply a copy of material incorporated by reference, the material must be accompanied by a statement that the copy supplied consists of the same material incorporated by reference in the referencing application.

(f) Any insertion of material incorporated by reference into the specification or drawings of an application must be by way of an amendment to the specification or drawings. Such an amendment must be accompanied by a statement that the material being inserted is the material previously incorporated by reference and that the amendment contains no new matter.

(g) An incorporation of material by reference that does not comply with paragraphs (b), (c), or (d) of this section is not effective to incorporate such material unless corrected within any time period set by the Office, but in no case later than the close of prosecution as defined by § 1.114(b), or abandonment of the application, whichever occurs earlier. In addition:

(1) A correction to comply with paragraph (b)(1) of this section is permitted only if the application as filed clearly conveys an intent to incorporate the material by reference. A mere reference to material does not convey an intent to incorporate the material by reference.

(2) A correction to comply with paragraph (b)(2) of this section is only permitted for material that was sufficiently described to uniquely identify the document.

[69 FR 56539, Sept. 21, 2004, as amended at 72 FR 51563, Sept. 10, 2007; 77 FR 46624, Aug. 6, 2012]

§ 1.58 Chemical and mathematical formulae and tables.

(a) The specification, including the claims, may contain chemical and mathematical formulae, but shall not contain drawings or flow diagrams. The description portion of the specification may contain tables, but the same tables may only be included in both the drawings and description portion of the specification if the application was filed under 35 U.S.C. 371. Claims may contain tables either if necessary to conform to 35 U.S.C. 112 or if otherwise found to be desirable.

(b) Tables that are submitted in electronic form (§§ 1.96(c) and 1.821(c)) must maintain the spatial relationships (e.g., alignment of columns and rows) of the table elements when displayed so as to visually preserve the relational information they convey. Chemical and mathematical formulae must be encoded to maintain the proper positioning of their characters when displayed in order to preserve their intended meaning.

(c) Chemical and mathematical formulae and tables must be presented in compliance with § 1.52(a) and (b), except that chemical and mathematical formulae or tables may be placed in a landscape orientation if they cannot be presented satisfactorily in a portrait orientation. Typewritten characters used in such formulae and tables must be chosen from a block (nonscript) type font or lettering style having capital letters which should be at least 0.422 cm. (0.166 inch) high (e.g., preferably Arial, Times Roman, or Courier with a font size of 12), but may be no smaller than 0.21 cm. (0.08 inch) high (e.g., a font size of 6). A space at least 0.64 cm. (1/4 inch) high should be provided between complex formulae and tables and the text. Tables should have the lines and columns of data closely spaced to conserve space, consistent with a high degree of legibility.

[69 FR 56540, Sept. 21, 2004]

§ 1.59 Expungement of information or copy of papers in application file.

(a) (1) Information in an application will not be expunged, except as provided in paragraph (b) of this section or § 41.7(a) or § 42.7(a) of this title.

(2) Information forming part of the original disclosure (*i.e.*, written specification including the claims, drawings, and any preliminary amendment present on the filing date of the application) will not be expunged from the application file.

(b) An applicant may request that the Office expunge information, other than what is excluded by paragraph (a)(2) of this section, by filing a petition under this paragraph. Any petition to expunge information from an application must include the fee set forth in § 1.17(g) and establish to the satisfaction of the Director that the expungement of the information is appropriate in which case a notice granting the petition for expungement will be provided.

(c) Upon request by an applicant and payment of the fee specified in § 1.19(b), the Office will furnish copies of an application, unless the application has been disposed of (*see* §§ 1.53(e), (f) and (g)). The Office cannot provide or certify copies of an application that has been disposed of.

[68 FR 38628, June 30, 2003, as amended at 69 FR 49999, Aug. 12, 2004; 69 FR 56540, Sept. 21, 2004; 77 FR 46624, Aug. 6, 2012; 77 FR 48818, Aug. 14, 2012]

§§ 1.60–1.62 [Reserved]

Oath or Declaration

§ 1.63 Inventor's oath or declaration.

(a) The inventor, or each individual who is a joint inventor of a claimed invention, in an application for patent must execute an oath or declaration directed to the application, except as provided for in § 1.64. An oath or declaration under this section must:

(1) Identify the inventor or joint inventor executing the oath or declaration by his or her legal name;

(2) Identify the application to which it is directed;

(3) Include a statement that the person executing the oath or declaration believes the named inventor or joint inventor to be the original inventor or an original joint inventor of a claimed invention in the application for which the oath or declaration is being submitted; and

(4) State that the application was made or was authorized to be made by the person executing the oath or declaration.

(b) Unless the following information is supplied in an application data sheet in accordance with § 1.76, the oath or declaration must also identify:

(1) Each inventor by his or her legal name; and

(2) A mailing address where the inventor customarily receives mail, and residence, if an inventor lives at a location which is different from where the inventor customarily receives mail, for each inventor.

(c) A person may not execute an oath or declaration for an application unless that person has reviewed and understands the contents of the application, including the claims, and is aware of the duty to disclose to the Office all information known to the person to be material to patentability as defined in § 1.56. There is no minimum age for a person to be qualified to execute an oath or declaration, but the person must be competent to execute, *i.e.*, understand, the document that the person is executing.

(d)(1) A newly executed oath or declaration under § 1.63, or substitute statement under § 1.64, is not required under § 1.51(b)(2) and § 1.53(f) or § 1.497 for an inventor in a continuing application that claims the benefit under 35 U.S.C. 120, 121, or 365(c) in compliance with § 1.78 of an earlier-filed application, provided that an oath or declaration in compliance with this section, or substitute statement under § 1.64, was executed by or with respect to such inventor and was filed in the earlier-filed application, and a copy of such oath, declaration, or substitute statement showing the signature or an indication thereon that it was executed, is submitted in the continuing application.

(2) The inventorship of a continuing application filed under 35 U.S.C. 111(a) is the inventor or joint inventors specified in the application data sheet filed before or concurrently with the copy of the inventor's oath or declaration from the earlier-filed application. If an application data sheet is not filed before or concurrently with the copy of the inventor's oath or declaration from the earlier-filed application, the inventorship is the inventorship set forth in the copy of the inventor's oath or declaration from the earlier-filed application, unless it is accompanied by a statement signed pursuant to § 1.33(b) stating the name of each inventor in the continuing application.

(3) Any new joint inventor named in the continuing application must provide an oath or declaration in compliance with this section, except as provided for in § 1.64.

(e)(1) An assignment may also serve as an oath or declaration required by this section if the assignment as executed:

(i) Includes the information and statements required under paragraphs (a) and (b) of this section; and

(ii) A copy of the assignment is recorded as provided for in part 3 of this chapter.

(2) Any reference to an oath or declaration under this section includes an assignment as provided for in this paragraph.

(f) With respect to an application naming only one inventor, any reference to the inventor's oath or declaration in this chapter includes a substitute statement executed under § 1.64. With respect to an application naming more than one inventor, any reference to the inventor's oath or declaration in this chapter means the oaths, declarations, or substitute statements that have been collectively executed by or with respect to all of the joint inventors, unless otherwise clear from the context.

(g) An oath or declaration under this section, including the statement provided for in paragraph (e) of this section, must be executed (*i.e.*, signed) in accordance either with § 1.66 or with an acknowledgment that any willful false statement made in such declaration or statement is punishable under 18 U.S.C. 1001 by fine or imprisonment of not more than five (5) years, or both.

(h) An oath or declaration filed at any time pursuant to 35 U.S.C. 115(h)(1) will be placed in the file record of the application or patent, but may not necessarily be reviewed by the Office. Any request for correction of the named inventorship must comply with § 1.48 in an application and § 1.324 in a patent.

[77 FR 48818, Aug. 14, 2012]

§ 1.64 Substitute statement in lieu of an oath or declaration.

(a) An applicant under § 1.43, 1.45 or 1.46 may execute a substitute statement in lieu of an oath or declaration under § 1.63 if the inventor is deceased, is under a legal incapacity, has refused to execute the oath or declaration under § 1.63, or cannot be found or reached after diligent effort.

(b) A substitute statement under this section must:

(1) Comply with the requirements of § 1.63(a), identifying the inventor or joint inventor with respect to whom a substitute statement in lieu of an oath or declaration is executed, and stating upon information and belief the facts

which such inventor is required to state;

(2) Identify the person executing the substitute statement and the relationship of such person to the inventor or joint inventor with respect to whom the substitute statement is executed, and unless such information is supplied in an application data sheet in accordance with § 1.76, the residence and mailing address of the person signing the substitute statement;

(3) Identify the circumstances permitting the person to execute the substitute statement in lieu of an oath or declaration under § 1.63, namely whether the inventor is deceased, is under a legal incapacity, cannot be found or reached after a diligent effort was made, or has refused to execute the oath or declaration under § 1.63; and

(4) Unless the following information is supplied in an application data sheet in accordance with § 1.76, also identify:

(i) Each inventor by his or her legal name; and

(ii) The last known mailing address where the inventor customarily receives mail, and last known residence, if an inventor lives at a location which is different from where the inventor customarily receives mail, for each inventor who is not deceased or under a legal incapacity.

(c) A person may not execute a substitute statement provided for in this section for an application unless that person has reviewed and understands the contents of the application, including the claims, and is aware of the duty to disclose to the Office all information known to the person to be material to patentability as defined in § 1.56.

(d) Any reference to an inventor's oath or declaration includes a substitute statement provided for in this section.

(e) A substitute statement under this section must contain an acknowledgment that any willful false statement made in such statement is punishable under section 1001 of title 18 by fine or imprisonment of not more than 5 years, or both.

(f) A nonsigning inventor or legal representative may subsequently join in the application by submitting an oath or declaration under § 1.63. The submission of an oath or declaration by a nonsigning inventor or legal representative in an application filed under § 1.43, 1.45 or 1.46 will not permit the nonsigning inventor or legal representative to revoke or grant a power of attorney.

[77 FR 48819, Aug. 14, 2012]

§ 1.66 Statements under oath.

An oath or affirmation may be made before any person within the United States authorized by law to administer oaths. An oath made in a foreign country may be made before any diplomatic or consular officer of the United States authorized to administer oaths, or before any officer having an official seal and authorized to administer oaths in the foreign country in which the applicant may be, whose authority shall be proved by a certificate of a diplomatic or consular officer of the United States, or by an apostille of an official designated by a foreign country which, by treaty or convention, accords like effect to apostilles of designated officials in the United States. The oath shall be attested in all cases in this and other countries, by the proper official seal of the officer before whom the oath or affirmation is made. Such oath or affirmation shall be valid as to execution if it complies with the laws of the State or country where made. When the person before whom the oath or affirmation is made in this country is not provided with a seal, his official character shall be established by competent evidence, as by a certificate from a clerk of a court of record or other proper officer having a seal.

[77 FR 48819, Aug. 14, 2012]

§ 1.67 Supplemental oath or declaration.

(a) The applicant may submit an inventor's oath or declaration meeting the requirements of § 1.63, § 1.64, or § 1.162 to correct any deficiencies or inaccuracies present in an earlier-filed inventor's oath or declaration. Deficiencies or inaccuracies due to the failure to meet the requirements of § 1.63(b) in an oath or declaration may be corrected with an application data sheet in accordance with § 1.76, except that any correction of inventorship must be pursuant to § 1.48.

(b) A supplemental inventor's oath or declaration under this section must be executed by the person whose inventor's oath or declaration is being withdrawn, replaced, or otherwise corrected.

(c) The Office will not require a person who has executed an oath or declaration in compliance with 35 U.S.C. 115 and § 1.63 or 1.162 for an application to provide an additional inventor's oath or declaration for the application.

(d) No new matter may be introduced into a nonprovisional application after its filing date even if an inventor's oath or declaration is filed to correct deficiencies or inaccuracies present in the earlier-filed inventor's oath or declaration.

[77 FR 48819, Aug. 14, 2012]

§ 1.68 Declaration in lieu of oath.

Any document to be filed in the Patent and Trademark Office and which is required by any law, rule, or other regulation to be under oath may be subscribed to by a written declaration. Such declaration may be used in lieu of the oath otherwise required, if, and only if, the declarant is on the same document, warned that willful false statements and the like are punishable by fine or imprisonment, or both (18 U.S.C. 1001) and may jeopardize the validity of the application or any patent issuing thereon. The declarant must set forth in the body of the declaration that all statements made of the declarant's own knowledge are true and that all statements made on information and belief are believed to be true.

[49 FR 48452, Dec. 12, 1984]

§ 1.69 Foreign language oaths and declarations.

(a) Whenever an individual making an oath or declaration cannot understand English, the oath or declaration must be in a language that such individual can understand and shall state that such individual understands the content of any documents to which the oath or declaration relates.

(b) Unless the text of any oath or declaration in a language other than English is in a form provided by the Patent and Trademark Office or in accordance with PCT Rule 4.17(iv), it must be accompanied by an English translation together with a statement that the translation is accurate, except that in the case of an oath or declaration filed under § 1.63, the translation may be filed in the Office no later than two months from the date applicant is notified to file the translation.

(35 U.S.C. 6, Pub. L. 97–247)

[42 FR 5594, Jan. 28, 1977, as amended at 48 FR 2711, Jan. 20, 1983; 62 FR 53189, Oct. 10, 1997; 69 FR 56540, Sept. 21, 2004; 70 FR 3890, Jan. 27, 2005]

§ 1.70 [Reserved]

SPECIFICATION

AUTHORITY: Secs. 1.71 to 1.79 also issued under 35 U.S.C. 112.

§ 1.71 Detailed description and specification of the invention.

(a) The specification must include a written description of the invention or discovery and of the manner and process of making and using the same, and is required to be in such full, clear, concise, and exact terms as to enable any person skilled in the art or science to which the invention or discovery appertains, or with which it is most nearly connected, to make and use the same.

(b) The specification must set forth the precise invention for which a patent is solicited, in such manner as to distinguish it from other inventions and from what is old. It must describe completely a specific embodiment of the process, machine, manufacture, composition of matter or improvement invented, and must explain the mode of operation or principle whenever applicable. The best mode contemplated by the inventor of carrying out his invention must be set forth.

(c) In the case of an improvement, the specification must particularly point out the part or parts of the process, machine, manufacture, or composition of matter to which the improvement relates, and the description should be confined to the specific improvement and to such parts as necessarily cooperate with it or as may be necessary to a complete understanding or description of it.

(d) A copyright or mask work notice may be placed in a design or utility patent application adjacent to copyright and mask work material contained therein. The notice may appear at any appropriate portion of the patent application disclosure. For notices in drawings, see § 1.84(s). The content of the notice must be limited to only those elements provided for by law. For example, "© 1983 John Doe" (17 U.S.C. 401) and " *M* John Doe" (17 U.S.C. 909) would be properly limited and, under current statutes, legally sufficient notices of copyright and mask work, respectively. Inclusion of a copyright or mask work notice will be permitted only if the authorization language set forth in paragraph (e) of this section is included at the beginning (preferably as the first paragraph) of the specification.

(e) The authorization shall read as follows:

A portion of the disclosure of this patent document contains material which is subject to (copyright or mask work) protection. The (copyright or mask work) owner has no objection to the facsimile reproduction by anyone of the patent document or the patent disclosure, as it appears in the Patent and Trademark Office patent file or records, but otherwise reserves all (copyright or mask work) rights whatsoever.

(f) The specification must commence on a separate sheet. Each sheet including part of the specification may not include other parts of the application or other information. The claim(s), abstract and sequence listing (if any) should not be included on a sheet including any other part of the application.

(g)(1) The specification may disclose or be amended to disclose the names of the parties to a joint research agreement as defined in § 1.9(e).

(2) An amendment under paragraph (g)(1) of this section must be accompanied by the processing fee set forth in § 1.17(i) if not filed within one of the following time periods:

(i) Within three months of the filing date of a national application;

(ii) Within three months of the date of entry of the national stage as set forth in § 1.491 in an international application;

(iii) Before the mailing of a first Office action on the merits; or

(iv) Before the mailing of a first Office action after the filing of a request for continued examination under § 1.114.

(3) If an amendment under paragraph (g)(1) of this section is filed after the date the issue fee is paid, the patent as issued may not necessarily include the names of the parties to the joint research agreement. If the patent as issued does not include the names of the parties to the joint research agreement, the patent must be corrected to include the names of the parties to the joint research agreement by a certificate of correction under 35 U.S.C. 255 and § 1.323 for the amendment to be effective.

[24 FR 10332, Dec. 22, 1959, as amended at 53 FR 47808, Nov. 28, 1988; 58 FR 38723, July 20, 1993; 68 FR 38628, June 30, 2003; 70 FR 1823, Jan. 11, 2005; 70 FR 54266, Sept. 14, 2005; 78 FR 11055, Feb. 14, 2013]

§ 1.72 Title and abstract.

(a) The title of the invention may not exceed 500 characters in length and must be as short and specific as possible. Characters that cannot be captured and recorded in the Office's automated information systems may not be reflected in the Office's records in such systems or in documents created by the Office. Unless the title is supplied in an application data sheet (§ 1.76), the title of the invention should appear as a heading on the first page of the specification.

(b) A brief abstract of the technical disclosure in the specification must commence on a separate sheet, preferably following the claims, under the heading "Abstract" or "Abstract of the Disclosure." The sheet or sheets presenting the abstract may not include other parts of the application or other material. The abstract in an application filed under 35 U.S.C. 111 may not exceed 150 words in length. The purpose of the abstract is to enable the United States Patent and Trademark Office and the public generally to determine quickly from a cursory inspection the nature and gist of the technical disclosure.

[65 FR 54667, Sept. 8, 2000, as amended at 65 FR 57054, Sept. 20, 2000; 68 FR 38628, June 30, 2003]

§ 1.73 Summary of the invention.

A brief summary of the invention indicating its nature and substance, which may include a statement of the object of the invention, should precede the detailed description. Such summary should, when set forth, be commensurate with the invention as claimed and any object recited should be that of the invention as claimed.

§ 1.74 Reference to drawings.

When there are drawings, there shall be a brief description of the several views of the drawings and the detailed description of the invention shall refer to the different views by specifying the numbers of the figures and to the different parts by use of reference letters or numerals (preferably the latter).

§ 1.75 Claim(s).

(a) The specification must conclude with a claim particularly pointing out and distinctly claiming the subject matter which the applicant regards as his invention or discovery.

(b) More than one claim may be presented provided they differ substantially from each other and are not unduly multiplied.

(c) One or more claims may be presented in dependent form, referring back to and further limiting another claim or claims in the same application. Any dependent claim which refers to more than one other claim ("multiple dependent claim") shall refer to such other claims in the alternative only. A multiple dependent claim shall not serve as a basis for any other multiple dependent claim. For fee calculation purposes under § 1.16, a multiple dependent claim will be considered to be that number of claims to which direct reference is made therein. For fee calculation purposes also, any claim depending from a multiple dependent claim will be considered to be that number of claims to which direct reference is made in that multiple dependent claim. In addition to the other filing fees, any original application which is filed with, or is amended to include, multiple dependent claims must have paid therein the fee set forth in § 1.16(j). Claims in dependent form shall be construed to include all the limitations of the claim incorporated by reference into the dependent claim. A multiple dependent claim shall be construed to incorporate by reference all the limitations of each of the particular claims in relation to which it is being considered.

(d)(1) The claim or claims must conform to the invention as set forth in the remainder of the specification and the terms and phrases used in the claims must find clear support or antecedent basis in the description so that the meaning of the terms in the claims may be ascertainable by reference to the description. (See § 1.58(a).)

(2) See §§ 1.141 to 1.146 as to claiming different inventions in one application.

(e) Where the nature of the case admits, as in the case of an improvement, any independent claim should contain in the following order:

(1) A preamble comprising a general description of all the elements or steps of the claimed combination which are conventional or known,

(2) A phrase such as "wherein the improvement comprises," and

(3) Those elements, steps and/or relationships which constitute that portion of the claimed combination which the applicant considers as the new or improved portion.

(f) If there are several claims, they shall be numbered consecutively in Arabic numerals.

(g) The least restrictive claim should be presented as claim number 1, and all dependent claims should be grouped together with the claim or claims to which they refer to the extent practicable.

(h) The claim or claims must commence on a separate physical sheet or electronic page. Any sheet including a claim or portion of a claim may not contain any other parts of the application or other material.

(i) Where a claim sets forth a plurality of elements or steps, each element or step of the claim should be separated by a line indentation.

(35 U.S.C. 6; 15 U.S.C. 1113, 1126)

[31 FR 12922, Oct. 4, 1966, as amended at 36 FR 12690, July 3, 1971; 37 FR 21995, Oct. 18, 1972; 43 FR 4015, Jan. 31, 1978; 47 FR 41276, Sept. 17, 1982; 61 FR 42803, Aug. 19, 1996; 68 FR 38628, June 30, 2003; 70 FR 3891, Jan. 27, 2005; 72 FR 46836, Aug. 21, 2007; 74 FR 52688, Oct. 14, 2009]

§ 1.76 Application data sheet.

(a) *Application data sheet:* An application data sheet is a sheet or sheets, that may be submitted in a provisional application under 35 U.S.C. 111(b), a nonprovisional application under 35 U.S.C. 111(a), or a national stage application under 35 U.S.C. 371, and must be submitted when required by § 1.55 or 1.78 to claim priority to or the benefit of a prior-filed application under 35 U.S.C. 119, 120, 121, or 365. An application data sheet must be titled "Application Data Sheet." An application data sheet must contain all of the section headings listed in paragraph (b) of this section, except as provided in paragraph (c)(2) of this section, with any appropriate data for each section heading. If an application data sheet is provided, the application data sheet is part of the application for which it has been submitted.

(b) *Bibliographic data.* Bibliographic data as used in paragraph (a) of this section includes:

(1) *Inventor information.* This information includes the legal name, residence, and mailing address of the inventor or each joint inventor.

(2) *Correspondence information.* This information includes the correspondence address, which may be indicated by reference to a customer number, to which correspondence is to be directed (*see* § 1.33(a)).

(3) *Application information.* This information includes the title of the invention, the total number of drawing sheets, a suggested drawing figure for publication (in a nonprovisional application), any docket number assigned to the application, the type of application (*e.g.*, utility, plant, design, reissue, provisional), whether the application discloses any significant part of the subject matter of an application under a secrecy order pursuant to § 5.2 of this chapter (*see* § 5.2(c)), and, for plant applications, the Latin name of the genus and species of the plant claimed, as well as the variety denomination.

(4) *Representative information.* This information includes the registration number of each practitioner having a power of attorney in the application (preferably by reference to a customer number). Providing this information in the application data sheet does not constitute a power of attorney in the application (see § 1.32).

(5) *Domestic benefit information.* This information includes the application number, the filing date, the status (including patent number if available), and relationship of each application for which a benefit is claimed under 35 U.S.C. 119(e), 120, 121, or 365(c). Providing this information in the application data sheet constitutes the specific reference required by 35 U.S.C. 119(e) or 120, and § 1.78.

(6) *Foreign priority information.* This information includes the application number, country, and filing date of each foreign application for which priority is claimed. Providing this information in the application data sheet constitutes the claim for priority as required by 35 U.S.C. 119(b) and § 1.55.

(7) *Applicant information:* This information includes the name (either natural person or juristic entity) and address of the legal representative, assignee, person to whom the inventor is under an obligation to assign the invention, or person who otherwise shows sufficient proprietary interest in the matter who is the applicant under § 1.43 or § 1.46. Providing assignment information in the application data sheet does not substitute for compliance with any requirement of part 3 of this chapter to have an assignment recorded by the Office.

(c) *Correcting and updating an application data sheet.* (1) Information in a previously submitted application data sheet, inventor's oath or declaration under § 1.63, § 1.64 or § 1.67, or otherwise of record, may be corrected or updated until payment of the issue fee by a new application data sheet providing corrected or updated information, except that inventorship changes must comply with the requirements of § 1.48, foreign priority and domestic benefit information changes must comply with §§ 1.55 and 1.78, and correspondence address changes are governed by § 1.33(a).

(2) An application data sheet providing corrected or updated information may include all of the sections listed in paragraph (b) of this section or only those sections containing changed or updated information. The application data sheet must include the section headings listed in paragraph (b) of this section for each section included in the application data sheet, and must identify the information that is being changed, with underlining for insertions, and strike-through or brackets for text removed, except that identification of information being changed is not required for an application data sheet included with an initial submission under 35 U.S.C. 371.

(d) *Inconsistencies between application data sheet and other documents.* For inconsistencies between information that is supplied by both an application data sheet under this section and other documents:

(1) The most recent submission will govern with respect to inconsistencies as between the information provided in an application data sheet, a designation of a correspondence address, or by the inventor's oath or declaration, except that:

(i) The most recent application data sheet will govern with respect to foreign priority (§ 1.55) or domestic benefit (§ 1.78) claims; and

(ii) The naming of the inventorship is governed by § 1.41 and changes to inventorship or the names of the inventors is governed by § 1.48.

(2) The information in the application data sheet will govern when the inconsistent information is supplied at the same time by a designation of correspondence address or the inventor's oath or declaration.

(3) The Office will capture bibliographic information from the application data sheet. The Office will generally not review the inventor's oath or declaration to determine if the bibliographic information contained therein is consistent with the bibliographic information provided in an application data sheet. Incorrect bibliographic information contained in an application data sheet may be corrected as provided in paragraph (c)(1) of this section.

(e) *Signature requirement.* An application data sheet must be signed in compliance with § 1.33(b). An unsigned application data sheet will be treated only as a transmittal letter.

[65 FR 54668, Sept. 8, 2000, as amended at 65 FR 57054, Sept. 20, 2000; 69 FR 56540, Sept. 21, 2004; 70 FR 54266, Sept. 14, 2005;; 72 FR 46837, Aug. 21, 2007; 74 FR 52689, Oct. 14, 2009; 77 FR 48820, Aug. 14, 2012; 78 FR 11055, Feb. 14, 2013]

§ 1.77 Arrangement of application elements.

(a) The elements of the application, if applicable, should appear in the following order:

(1) Utility application transmittal form.

(2) Fee transmittal form.

(3) Application data sheet (see § 1.76).

(4) Specification.

(5) Drawings.

(6) The inventor's oath or declaration.

(b) The specification should include the following sections in order:

(1) Title of the invention, which may be accompanied by an introductory portion stating the name, citizenship, and residence of the applicant (unless included in the application data sheet).

(2) Cross-reference to related applications.

(3) Statement regarding federally sponsored research or development.

(4) The names of the parties to a joint research agreement.

(5) Reference to a "Sequence Listing," a table, or a computer program listing appendix submitted on a compact disc and an incorporation-by-reference of the material on the compact disc (see § 1.52(e)(5)). The total number of compact discs including duplicates and the files on each compact disc shall be specified.

(6) Statement regarding prior disclosures by the inventor or a joint inventor.

(7) Background of the invention.

(8) Brief summary of the invention.

(9) Brief description of the several views of the drawing.

(10) Detailed description of the invention.

(11) A claim or claims.

(12) Abstract of the disclosure.

(13) "Sequence Listing," if on paper (see §§ 1.821 through 1.825).

(c) The text of the specification sections defined in paragraphs (b)(1) through (b)(12) of this section, if applicable, should be preceded by a section heading in uppercase and without underlining or bold type.

[65 FR 54668, Sept. 8, 2000, as amended at 70 FR 1823, Jan. 11, 2005; 77 FR 48820, Aug. 14, 2012; 78 FR 11055, Feb. 14, 2013]

§ 1.78 Claiming benefit of earlier filing date and cross-references to other applications.

(a) *Claims under 35 U.S.C. 119(e) for the benefit of a prior-filed provisional application.* An applicant in a nonprovisional application, other than for a design patent, or an international application designating the United States of America may claim the benefit of one or more prior-filed provisional applications under the conditions set forth in 35 U.S.C. 119(e) and this section.

(1) The nonprovisional application or international application designating the United States of America must be filed not later than twelve months after the date on which the provisional application was filed, or be entitled to claim the benefit under 35 U.S.C. 120, 121, or 365(c) of an application that was filed not later than twelve months after the date on which the provisional application was filed. This twelve-month period is subject to 35 U.S.C. 21(b) (and § 1.7(a)).

(2) Each prior-filed provisional application must name the inventor or a joint inventor named in the later—filed application as the inventor or a joint inventor. In addition, each prior-filed provisional application must be entitled to a filing date as set forth in § 1.53(c), and the basic filing fee set forth in § 1.16(d) must have been paid for such provisional application within the time period set forth in § 1.53(g).

(3) Any nonprovisional application or international application designating the United States of America that claims the benefit of one or more prior-filed provisional applications must contain, or be amended to contain, a reference to each such prior-filed provisional application, identifying it by the provisional application number (consisting of series code and serial number). If the later-filed application is a nonprovisional application, the reference required by this paragraph must be included in an application data sheet (§ 1.76(b)(5)).

(4) The reference required by paragraph (a)(3) of this section must be submitted during the pendency of the later-filed application. If the later-filed application is an application filed under 35 U.S.C. 111(a), this reference must also be submitted within the later of four months from the actual filing date of the later-filed application or sixteen months from the filing date of the prior-filed provisional application. If the later-filed application is a nonprovisional application entering the national stage from an international application under 35 U.S.C. 371, this reference must also be submitted within the later of four months from the date on which the national stage commenced under 35 U.S.C. 371(b) or (f) in the later-filed international application or sixteen months from the filing date of the prior-filed provisional application. Except as provided in paragraph (b) of this section, failure to timely submit the reference is considered a waiver of any benefit under 35 U.S.C. 119(e) of the prior-filed provisional application.

(5) If the prior-filed provisional application was filed in a language other than English and both an English-language translation of the prior-filed provisional application and a statement that the translation is accurate were not previously filed in the prior-filed provisional application, the applicant will be notified and given a period of time within which to file, in the prior-filed provisional application, the translation and the statement. If the notice is mailed in a pending nonprovisional application, a timely reply to such a notice must include the filing in the nonprovisional application of either a confirmation that the translation and statement were filed in the provisional application, or an application data sheet eliminating the reference under paragraph (a)(3) of this section to the prior-filed provisional application, or

the nonprovisional application will be abandoned. The translation and statement may be filed in the provisional application, even if the provisional application has become abandoned.

(6) If a nonprovisional application filed on or after March 16, 2013, claims the benefit of the filing date of a provisional application filed prior to March 16, 2013, and also contains, or contained at any time, a claim to a claimed invention that has an effective filing date on or after March 16, 2013, the applicant must provide a statement to that effect within the later of four months from the actual filing date of the nonprovisional application, four months from the date of entry into the national stage as set forth in § 1.491 in an international application, sixteen months from the filing date of the prior-filed provisional application, or the date that a first claim to a claimed invention that has an effective filing date on or after March 16, 2013, is presented in the nonprovisional application. An applicant is not required to provide such a statement if the applicant reasonably believes on the basis of information already known to the individuals designated in § 1.56(c) that the nonprovisional application does not, and did not at any time, contain a claim to a claimed invention that has an effective filing date on or after March 16, 2013.

(b) *Delayed claims under 35 U.S.C. 119(e) for the benefit of a prior-filed provisional application.* If the reference required by 35 U.S.C. 119(e) and paragraph (a)(3) of this section is presented in a nonprovisional application after the time period provided by paragraph (a)(4) of this section, the claim under 35 U.S.C. 119(e) for the benefit of a prior-filed provisional application may be accepted if submitted during the pendency of the later-filed application and if the reference identifying the prior-filed application by provisional application number was unintentionally delayed. A petition to accept an unintentionally delayed claim under 35 U.S.C. 119(e) for the benefit of a prior-filed provisional application must be accompanied by:

(1) The reference required by 35 U.S.C. 119(e) and paragraph (a)(3) of this section to the prior-filed provisional application, unless previously submitted;

(2) The surcharge set forth in § 1.17(t); and

(3) A statement that the entire delay between the date the benefit claim was due under paragraph (a)(4) of this section and the date the benefit claim was filed was unintentional. The Director may require additional information where there is a question whether the delay was unintentional.

(c) *Claims under 35 U.S.C. 120, 121, or 365(c) for the benefit of a prior-filed nonprovisional or international application.* An applicant in a nonprovisional application (including an international application entering the national stage under 35 U.S.C. 371) or an international application designating the United States of America may claim the benefit of one or more prior-filed copending nonprovisional applications or international applications designating the United States of America under the conditions set forth in 35 U.S.C. 120, 121, or 365(c) and this section.

(1) Each prior-filed application must name the inventor or a joint inventor named in the later-filed application as the inventor or a joint inventor. In addition, each prior-filed application must either be:

(i) An international application entitled to a filing date in accordance with PCT Article 11 and designating the United States of America; or

(ii) A nonprovisional application under 35 U.S.C. 111(a) that is entitled to a filing date as set forth in § 1.53(b) or (d) for which the basic filing fee set forth in § 1.16 has been paid within the pendency of the application.

(2) Except for a continued prosecution application filed under § 1.53(d), any nonprovisional application, or international application designating the United States of America, that claims the benefit of one or more prior-filed nonprovisional applications or international applications designating the United States of America must contain or be amended to contain a reference to each such prior-filed application, identifying it by application number (consisting of the series code and serial number) or international application number and international filing date. If the later-filed application is a

nonprovisional application, the reference required by this paragraph must be included in an application data sheet (§1.76(b)(5)). The reference also must identify the relationship of the applications, namely, whether the later-filed application is a continuation, divisional, or continuation-in-part of the prior-filed nonprovisional application or international application.

(3) The reference required by 35 U.S.C. 120 and paragraph (c)(2) of this section must be submitted during the pendency of the later-filed application. If the later-filed application is an application filed under 35 U.S.C. 111(a), this reference must also be submitted within the later of four months from the actual filing date of the later-filed application or sixteen months from the filing date of the prior-filed application. If the later-filed application is a nonprovisional application entering the national stage from an international application under 35 U.S.C. 371, this reference must also be submitted within the later of four months from the date on which the national stage commenced under 35 U.S.C. 371(b) or (f) in the later-filed international application or sixteen months from the filing date of the prior-filed application. Except as provided in paragraph (d) of this section, failure to timely submit the reference required by 35 U.S.C. 120 and paragraph (c)(2) of this section is considered a waiver of any benefit under 35 U.S.C. 120, 121, or 365(c) to the prior-filed application. The time periods in this paragraph do not apply in a design application.

(4) The request for a continued prosecution application under §1.53(d) is the specific reference required by 35 U.S.C. 120 to the prior-filed application. The identification of an application by application number under this section is the identification of every application assigned that application number necessary for a specific reference required by 35 U.S.C. 120 to every such application assigned that application number.

(5) Cross-references to other related applications may be made when appropriate (see §1.14), but cross-references to applications for which a benefit is not claimed under title 35, United States Code, must not be included in an application data sheet (§1.76(b)(5)).

(6) If a nonprovisional application filed on or after March 16, 2013, claims the benefit of the filing date of a nonprovisional application or an international application designating the United States of America filed prior to March 16, 2013, and also contains, or contained at any time, a claim to a claimed invention that has an effective filing date on or after March 16, 2013, the applicant must provide a statement to that effect within the later of four months from the actual filing date of the later-filed application, four months from the date of entry into the national stage as set forth in §1.491 in an international application, sixteen months from the filing date of the prior-filed application, or the date that a first claim to a claimed invention that has an effective filing date on or after March 16, 2013, is presented in the later-filed application. An applicant is not required to provide such a statement if either:

(i) The application claims the benefit of a nonprovisional application in which a statement under §1.55(j), paragraph (a)(6) of this section, or this paragraph that the application contains, or contained at any time, a claim to a claimed invention that has an effective filing date on or after March 16, 2013 has been filed; or

(ii) The applicant reasonably believes on the basis of information already known to the individuals designated in §1.56(c) that the later filed application does not, and did not at any time, contain a claim to a claimed invention that has an effective filing date on or after March 16, 2013.

(d) *Delayed claims under 35 U.S.C. 120, 121, or 365(c) for the benefit of a prior-filed nonprovisional application or international application.* If the reference required by 35 U.S.C. 120 and paragraph (c)(2) of this section is presented after the time period provided by paragraph (c)(3) of this section, the claim under 35 U.S.C. 120, 121, or 365(c) for the benefit of a prior-filed copending nonprovisional application or international application designating the United States of America may be accepted if the reference identifying the prior-filed application by application number or international application number and international filing date was unintentionally delayed. A petition to accept an unintentionally delayed claim under 35 U.S.C. 120, 121, or 365(c) for the benefit of a prior-filed application must be accompanied by:

(1) The reference required by 35 U.S.C. 120 and paragraph (c)(2) of this section to the prior-filed application, unless previously submitted;

(2) The surcharge set forth in § 1.17(t); and

(3) A statement that the entire delay between the date the benefit claim was due under paragraph (c)(3) of this section and the date the benefit claim was filed was unintentional. The Director may require additional information where there is a question whether the delay was unintentional.

(e) *Applications containing patentably indistinct claims.* Where two or more applications filed by the same applicant contain patentably indistinct claims, elimination of such claims from all but one application may be required in the absence of good and sufficient reason for their retention during pendency in more than one application.

(f) *Applications or patents under reexamination naming different inventors and containing patentably indistinct claims.* If an application or a patent under reexamination and at least one other application naming different inventors are owned by the same person and contain patentably indistinct claims, and there is no statement of record indicating that the claimed inventions were commonly owned or subject to an obligation of assignment to the same person on the effective filing date (as defined in § 1.109), or on the date of the invention, as applicable, of the later claimed invention, the Office may require the applicant to state whether the claimed inventions were commonly owned or subject to an obligation of assignment to the same person on such date. Even if the claimed inventions were commonly owned, or subject to an obligation of assignment to the same person on the effective filing date (as defined in § 1.109), or on the date of the invention, as applicable, of the later claimed invention, the patentably indistinct claims may be rejected under the doctrine of double patenting in view of such commonly owned or assigned applications or patents under reexamination.

(g) *Time periods not extendable.* The time periods set forth in this section are not extendable.

[78 FR 11055, Feb. 14, 2013]

§ 1.79 Reservation clauses not permitted.

A reservation for a future application of subject matter disclosed but not claimed in a pending application will not be permitted in the pending application, but an application disclosing unclaimed subject matter may contain a reference to a later filed application of the same applicant or owned by a common assignee disclosing and claiming that subject matter.

The Drawings

AUTHORITY: Secs. 1.81 to 1.88 also issued under 35 U.S.C. 113.

§ 1.81 Drawings required in patent application.

(a) The applicant for a patent is required to furnish a drawing of the invention where necessary for the understanding of the subject matter sought to be patented; this drawing, or a high quality copy thereof, must be filed with the application. Since corrections are the responsibility of the applicant, the original drawing(s) should be retained by the applicant for any necessary future correction.

(b) Drawings may include illustrations which facilitate an understanding of the invention (for example, flow sheets in cases of processes, and diagrammatic views).

(c) Whenever the nature of the subject matter sought to be patented admits of illustration by a drawing without its being necessary for the understanding of the subject matter and the applicant has not furnished such a drawing, the examiner will require its submission within a time period of not less than two months from the date of the sending of a notice thereof.

(d) Drawings submitted after the filing date of the application may not be used to overcome any insufficiency of the specification due to lack of an enabling disclosure or otherwise inadequate disclosure therein, or to supplement the original disclosure thereof for the purpose of interpretation of the scope of any claim.

[43 FR 4015, Jan. 31, 1978, as amended at 53 FR 47808, Nov. 28, 1988; 77 FR 48821, Aug. 14, 2012]

§ 1.83 Content of drawing.

(a) The drawing in a nonprovisional application must show every feature of the invention specified in the claims. However, conventional features disclosed in the description and claims, where their detailed illustration is not essential for a proper understanding of the invention, should be illustrated in the drawing in the form of a graphical drawing symbol or a labeled representation (*e.g.*, a labeled rectangular box). In addition, tables and sequence listings that are included in the specification are, except for applications filed under 35 U.S.C. 371, not permitted to be included in the drawings.

(b) When the invention consists of an improvement on an old machine the drawing must when possible exhibit, in one or more views, the improved portion itself, disconnected from the old structure, and also in another view, so much only of the old structure as will suffice to show the connection of the invention therewith.

(c) Where the drawings in a nonprovisional application do not comply with the requirements of paragraphs (a) and (b) of this section, the examiner shall require such additional illustration within a time period of not less than two months from the date of the sending of a notice thereof. Such corrections are subject to the requirements of § 1.81(d).

[31 FR 12923, Oct. 4, 1966, as amended at 43 FR 4015, Jan. 31, 1978; 60 FR 20226, Apr. 25, 1995; 69 FR 56541, Sept. 21, 2004]

§ 1.84 Standards for drawings.

(a) *Drawings.* There are two acceptable categories for presenting drawings in utility and design patent applications.

(1) *Black ink.* Black and white drawings are normally required. India ink, or its equivalent that secures solid black lines, must be used for drawings; or

(2) *Color.* On rare occasions, color drawings may be necessary as the only practical medium by which to disclose the subject matter sought to be patented in a utility or design patent application. The color drawings must be of sufficient quality such that all details in the drawings are reproducible in black and white in the printed patent. Color drawings are not permitted in international applications (see PCT Rule 11.13), or in an application, or copy thereof, submitted under the Office electronic filing system. The Office will accept color drawings in utility or design patent applications only after granting a petition filed under this paragraph explaining why the color drawings are necessary. Any such petition must include the following:

(i) The fee set forth in § 1.17(h);

(ii) Three (3) sets of color drawings; and

(iii) An amendment to the specification to insert (unless the specification contains or has been previously amended to contain) the following language as the first paragraph of the brief description of the drawings:

The patent or application file contains at least one drawing executed in color. Copies of this patent or patent application publication with color drawing(s) will be provided by the Office upon request and payment of the necessary fee.

(b) *Photographs*—(1) *Black and white.* Photographs, including photocopies of photographs, are not ordinarily permitted in utility and design patent applications. The Office will accept photographs in utility and design patent applications, however, if photographs are the only practicable medium for illustrating the claimed invention. For example, photographs or photomicrographs of: electrophoresis gels, blots (*e.g.*, immunological, western, Southern, and northern), autoradiographs, cell cultures (stained and unstained), histological tissue cross sections (stained and unstained), animals, plants, in vivo imaging, thin layer chromatography plates, crystalline structures, and, in a design patent application, ornamental effects, are acceptable. If the subject matter of the application admits of illustration by a drawing, the examiner may require a drawing in place of the photograph. The photographs must be of sufficient quality so that all details in the photographs are reproducible in the printed patent.

(2) *Color photographs*. Color photographs will be accepted in utility and design patent applications if the conditions for accepting color drawings and black and white photographs have been satisfied. See paragraphs (a)(2) and (b)(1) of this section.

(c) *Identification of drawings*. Identifying indicia should be provided, and if provided, should include the title of the invention, inventor's name, and application number, or docket number (if any) if an application number has not been assigned to the application. If this information is provided, it must be placed on the front of each sheet within the top margin. Each drawing sheet submitted after the filing date of an application must be identified as either "Replacement Sheet" or "New Sheet" pursuant to § 1.121(d). If a marked-up copy of any amended drawing figure including annotations indicating the changes made is filed, such marked-up copy must be clearly labeled as "Annotated Sheet" pursuant to § 1.121(d)(1).

(d) *Graphic forms in drawings*. Chemical or mathematical formulae, tables, and waveforms may be submitted as drawings, and are subject to the same requirements as drawings. Each chemical or mathematical formula must be labeled as a separate figure, using brackets when necessary, to show that information is properly integrated. Each group of waveforms must be presented as a single figure, using a common vertical axis with time extending along the horizontal axis. Each individual waveform discussed in the specification must be identified with a separate letter designation adjacent to the vertical axis.

(e) *Type of paper*. Drawings submitted to the Office must be made on paper which is flexible, strong, white, smooth, non-shiny, and durable. All sheets must be reasonably free from cracks, creases, and folds. Only one side of the sheet may be used for the drawing. Each sheet must be reasonably free from erasures and must be free from alterations, overwritings, and interlineations. Photographs must be developed on paper meeting the sheet-size requirements of paragraph (f) of this section and the margin requirements of paragraph (g) of this section. See paragraph (b) of this section for other requirements for photographs.

(f) *Size of paper*. All drawing sheets in an application must be the same size. One of the shorter sides of the sheet is regarded as its top. The size of the sheets on which drawings are made must be:

(1) 21.0 cm. by 29.7 cm. (DIN size A4), or

(2) 21.6 cm. by 27.9 cm. (8½ by 11 inches).

(g) *Margins*. The sheets must not contain frames around the sight (*i.e.*, the usable surface), but should have scan target points (*i.e.*, cross-hairs) printed on two catercorner margin corners. Each sheet must include a top margin of at least 2.5 cm. (1 inch), a left side margin of at least 2.5 cm. (1 inch), a right side margin of at least 1.5 cm. (⅝ inch), and a bottom margin of at least 1.0 cm. (⅜ inch), thereby leaving a sight no greater than 17.0 cm. by 26.2 cm. on 21.0 cm. by 29.7 cm. (DIN size A4) drawing sheets, and a sight no greater than 17.6 cm. by 24.4 cm. (6 15/16 by 9⅝ inches) on 21.6 cm. by 27.9 cm. (8½ by 11 inch) drawing sheets.

(h) *Views*. The drawing must contain as many views as necessary to show the invention. The views may be plan, elevation, section, or perspective views. Detail views of portions of elements, on a larger scale if necessary, may also be used. All views of the drawing must be grouped together and arranged on the sheet(s) without wasting space, preferably in an upright position, clearly separated from one another, and must not be included in the sheets containing the specifications, claims, or abstract. Views must not be connected by projection lines and must not contain center lines. Waveforms of electrical signals may be connected by dashed lines to show the relative timing of the waveforms.

(1) *Exploded views*. Exploded views, with the separated parts embraced by a bracket, to show the relationship or order of assembly of various parts are permissible. When an exploded view is shown in a figure which is on the same

sheet as another figure, the exploded view should be placed in brackets.

(2) *Partial views.* When necessary, a view of a large machine or device in its entirety may be broken into partial views on a single sheet, or extended over several sheets if there is no loss in facility of understanding the view. Partial views drawn on separate sheets must always be capable of being linked edge to edge so that no partial view contains parts of another partial view. A smaller scale view should be included showing the whole formed by the partial views and indicating the positions of the parts shown. When a portion of a view is enlarged for magnification purposes, the view and the enlarged view must each be labeled as separate views.

(i) Where views on two or more sheets form, in effect, a single complete view, the views on the several sheets must be so arranged that the complete figure can be assembled without concealing any part of any of the views appearing on the various sheets.

(ii) A very long view may be divided into several parts placed one above the other on a single sheet. However, the relationship between the different parts must be clear and unambiguous.

(3) *Sectional views.* The plane upon which a sectional view is taken should be indicated on the view from which the section is cut by a broken line. The ends of the broken line should be designated by Arabic or Roman numerals corresponding to the view number of the sectional view, and should have arrows to indicate the direction of sight. Hatching must be used to indicate section portions of an object, and must be made by regularly spaced oblique parallel lines spaced sufficiently apart to enable the lines to be distinguished without difficulty. Hatching should not impede the clear reading of the reference characters and lead lines. If it is not possible to place reference characters outside the hatched area, the hatching may be broken off wherever reference characters are inserted. Hatching must be at a substantial angle to the surrounding axes or principal lines, preferably 45°. A cross section must be set out and drawn to show all of the materials as they are shown in the view from which the cross section was taken. The parts in cross section must show proper material(s) by hatching with regularly spaced parallel oblique strokes, the space between strokes being chosen on the basis of the total area to be hatched. The various parts of a cross section of the same item should be hatched in the same manner and should accurately and graphically indicate the nature of the material(s) that is illustrated in cross section. The hatching of juxtaposed different elements must be angled in a different way. In the case of large areas, hatching may be confined to an edging drawn around the entire inside of the outline of the area to be hatched. Different types of hatching should have different conventional meanings as regards the nature of a material seen in cross section.

(4) *Alternate position.* A moved position may be shown by a broken line superimposed upon a suitable view if this can be done without crowding; otherwise, a separate view must be used for this purpose.

(5) *Modified forms.* Modified forms of construction must be shown in separate views.

(i) *Arrangement of views.* One view must not be placed upon another or within the outline of another. All views on the same sheet should stand in the same direction and, if possible, stand so that they can be read with the sheet held in an upright position. If views wider than the width of the sheet are necessary for the clearest illustration of the invention, the sheet may be turned on its side so that the top of the sheet, with the appropriate top margin to be used as the heading space, is on the right-hand side. Words must appear in a horizontal, left-to-right fashion when the page is either upright or turned so that the top becomes the right side, except for graphs utilizing standard scientific convention to denote the axis of abscissas (of X) and the axis of ordinates (of Y).

(j) *Front page view.* The drawing must contain as many views as necessary to show the invention. One of the views should be suitable for inclusion on the front page of the patent application publication and patent as the illustration of the invention. Views must not be connected by projection lines and must not contain center lines. Applicant may suggest a single view (by figure number) for inclusion on the front page of the patent application publication and patent.

(k) *Scale.* The scale to which a drawing is made must be large enough to show the mechanism without crowding when the drawing is reduced in size to two-thirds in reproduction. Indications such as "actual size" or "scale ½" on the drawings are not permitted since these lose their meaning with reproduction in a different format.

(l) *Character of lines, numbers, and letters.* All drawings must be made by a process which will give them satisfactory reproduction characteristics. Every line, number, and letter must be durable, clean, black (except for color drawings), sufficiently dense and dark, and uniformly thick and well-defined. The weight of all lines and letters must be heavy enough to permit adequate reproduction. This requirement applies to all lines however fine, to shading, and to lines representing cut surfaces in sectional views. Lines and strokes of different thicknesses may be used in the same drawing where different thicknesses have a different meaning.

(m) *Shading.* The use of shading in views is encouraged if it aids in understanding the invention and if it does not reduce legibility. Shading is used to indicate the surface or shape of spherical, cylindrical, and conical elements of an object. Flat parts may also be lightly shaded. Such shading is preferred in the case of parts shown in perspective, but not for cross sections. See paragraph (h)(3) of this section. Spaced lines for shading are preferred. These lines must be thin, as few in number as practicable, and they must contrast with the rest of the drawings. As a substitute for shading, heavy lines on the shade side of objects can be used except where they superimpose on each other or obscure reference characters. Light should come from the upper left corner at an angle of 45°. Surface delineations should preferably be shown by proper shading. Solid black shading areas are not permitted, except when used to represent bar graphs or color.

(n) *Symbols.* Graphical drawing symbols may be used for conventional elements when appropriate. The elements for which such symbols and labeled representations are used must be adequately identified in the specification. Known devices should be illustrated by symbols which have a universally recognized conventional meaning and are generally accepted in the art. Other symbols which are not universally recognized may be used, subject to approval by the Office, if they are not likely to be confused with existing conventional symbols, and if they are readily identifiable.

(o) *Legends.* Suitable descriptive legends may be used subject to approval by the Office, or may be required by the examiner where necessary for understanding of the drawing. They should contain as few words as possible.

(p) *Numbers, letters, and reference characters.* (1) Reference characters (numerals are preferred), sheet numbers, and view numbers must be plain and legible, and must not be used in association with brackets or inverted commas, or enclosed within outlines, e.g., encircled. They must be oriented in the same direction as the view so as to avoid having to rotate the sheet. Reference characters should be arranged to follow the profile of the object depicted.

(2) The English alphabet must be used for letters, except where another alphabet is customarily used, such as the Greek alphabet to indicate angles, wavelengths, and mathematical formulas.

(3) Numbers, letters, and reference characters must measure at least .32 cm. (⅛ inch) in height. They should not be placed in the drawing so as to interfere with its comprehension. Therefore, they should not cross or mingle with the lines. They should not be placed upon hatched or shaded surfaces. When necessary, such as indicating a surface or cross section, a reference character may be underlined and a blank space may be left in the hatching or shading where the character occurs so that it appears distinct.

(4) The same part of an invention appearing in more than one view of the drawing must always be designated by the same reference character, and the same reference character must never be used to designate different parts.

(5) Reference characters not mentioned in the description shall not appear in the drawings. Reference characters mentioned in the description must appear in the drawings.

(q) *Lead lines.* Lead lines are those lines between the reference characters and the details referred to. Such lines may be straight or curved and should be as short as possible. They must originate in the immediate proximity of the reference character and extend to the feature indicated. Lead lines must not cross each other. Lead lines are required for each reference character except for those which indicate the surface or cross section on which they are placed. Such a reference character must be underlined to make it clear that a lead line has not been left out by mistake. Lead lines must be executed in the same way as lines in the drawing. See paragraph (l) of this section.

(r) *Arrows.* Arrows may be used at the ends of the lines, provided that their meaning is clear, as follows:

(1) On a lead line, a freestanding arrow to indicate the entire section towards which it points;

(2) On a lead line, an arrow touching a line to indicate the surface shown by the line looking along the direction of the arrow; or

(3) To show the direction of movement.

(s) *Copyright or Mask Work Notice.* A copyright or mask work notice may appear in the drawing, but must be placed within the sight of the drawing immediately below the figure representing the copyright or mask work material and be limited to letters having a print size of .32 cm. to .64 cm. (1/8 to 1/4 inches) high. The content of the notice must be limited to only those elements provided for by law. For example, "©1983 John Doe" (17 U.S.C. 401) and "*M* John Doe" (17 U.S.C. 909) would be properly limited and, under current statutes, legally sufficient notices of copyright and mask work, respectively. Inclusion of a copyright or mask work notice will be permitted only if the authorization language set forth in §1.71(e) is included at the beginning (preferably as the first paragraph) of the specification.

(t) *Numbering of sheets of drawings.* The sheets of drawings should be numbered in consecutive Arabic numerals, starting with 1, within the sight as defined in paragraph (g) of this section. These numbers, if present, must be placed in the middle of the top of the sheet, but not in the margin. The numbers can be placed on the right-hand side if the drawing extends too close to the middle of the top edge of the usable surface. The drawing sheet numbering must be clear and larger than the numbers used as reference characters to avoid confusion. The number of each sheet should be shown by two Arabic numerals placed on either side of an oblique line, with the first being the sheet number, and the second being the total number of sheets of drawings, with no other marking.

(u) *Numbering of views.* (1) The different views must be numbered in consecutive Arabic numerals, starting with 1, independent of the numbering of the sheets and, if possible, in the order in which they appear on the drawing sheet(s). Partial views intended to form one complete view, on one or several sheets, must be identified by the same number followed by a capital letter. View numbers must be preceded by the abbreviation "FIG." Where only a single view is used in an application to illustrate the claimed invention, it must not be numbered and the abbreviation "FIG." must not appear.

(2) Numbers and letters identifying the views must be simple and clear and must not be used in association with brackets, circles, or inverted commas. The view numbers must be larger than the numbers used for reference characters.

(v) *Security markings.* Authorized security markings may be placed on the drawings provided they are outside the sight, preferably centered in the top margin.

(w) *Corrections.* Any corrections on drawings submitted to the Office must be durable and permanent.

(x) *Holes.* No holes should be made by applicant in the drawing sheets.

(y) *Types of drawings.* See § 1.152 for design drawings, § 1.165 for plant drawings, and § 1.173(a)(2) for reissue drawings.

[58 FR 38723, July 20, 1993; 58 FR 45841, 45842, Aug. 31, 1993, as amended at 61 FR 42804, Aug. 19, 1996; 62 FR 53190, Oct. 10, 1997; 65 FR 54669, Sept. 8, 2000; 65 FR 57055, Sept. 20, 2000; 69 FR 56541, Sept. 21, 2004; 70 FR 3891, Jan. 27, 2005; 78 FR 11057, Feb. 14, 2013]

§ 1.85 Corrections to drawings.

(a) A utility or plant application will not be placed on the files for examination until objections to the drawings have been corrected. Except as provided in § 1.215(c), any patent application publication will not include drawings filed after the application has been placed on the files for examination. Unless applicant is otherwise notified in an Office action, objections to the drawings in a utility or plant application will not be held in abeyance, and a request to hold objections to the drawings in abeyance will not be considered a *bona fide* attempt to advance the application to final action (§ 1.135(c)). If a drawing in a design application meets the requirements of § 1.84(e), (f), and (g) and is suitable for reproduction, but is not otherwise in compliance with § 1.84, the drawing may be admitted for examination.

(b) The Office will not release drawings for purposes of correction. If corrections are necessary, new corrected drawings must be submitted within the time set by the Office.

(c) If a corrected drawing is required or if a drawing does not comply with § 1.84 at the time an application is allowed, the Office may notify the applicant and set a three-month period of time from the mail date of the notice of allowability within which the applicant must file a corrected drawing in compliance with § 1.84 to avoid abandonment. This time period is not extendable under § 1.136(a) or § 1.136(b).

[65 FR 54670, Sept. 8, 2000, as amended at 65 FR 57055, Sept. 20, 2000; 69 FR 56541, Sept. 21, 2004]

§ 1.88 [Reserved]

MODELS, EXHIBITS, SPECIMENS

AUTHORITY: Secs. 1.91 to 1.95 also issued under 35 U.S.C. 114.

§ 1.91 Models or exhibits not generally admitted as part of application or patent.

(a) A model or exhibit will not be admitted as part of the record of an application unless it:

(1) Substantially conforms to the requirements of § 1.52 or § 1.84;

(2) Is specifically required by the Office; or

(3) Is filed with a petition under this section including:

(i) The fee set forth in § 1.17(h); and

(ii) An explanation of why entry of the model or exhibit in the file record is necessary to demonstrate patentability.

(b) Notwithstanding the provisions of paragraph (a) of this section, a model, working model, or other physical exhibit may be required by the Office if deemed necessary for any purpose in examination of the application.

(c) Unless the model or exhibit substantially conforms to the requirements of § 1.52 or § 1.84 under paragraph (a)(1) of this section, it must be accompanied by photographs that show multiple views of the material features of the model or exhibit and that substantially conform to the requirements of § 1.84.

[62 FR 53190, Oct. 10, 1997, as amended at 65 FR 54670, Sept. 8, 2000; 69 FR 56541, Sept. 21, 2004]

§ 1.92 [Reserved]

§ 1.93 Specimens.

When the invention relates to a composition of matter, the applicant may be required to furnish specimens of the composition, or of its ingredients or intermediates, for the purpose of inspection or experiment.

§ 1.94 Return of models, exhibits or specimens.

(a) Models, exhibits, or specimens may be returned to the applicant if no longer necessary for the conduct of business before the Office. When applicant is notified that a model, exhibit, or specimen is no longer necessary for the conduct of business before the Office and will be returned, applicant must arrange for the return of the model, exhibit, or specimen at the applicant's expense. The Office will dispose of perishables without notice to applicant unless applicant notifies the Office upon submission of the model, exhibit or specimen that a return is desired and makes arrangements for its return promptly upon notification by the Office that the model, exhibit or specimen is no longer necessary for the conduct of business before the Office.

(b) Applicant is responsible for retaining the actual model, exhibit, or specimen for the enforceable life of any patent resulting from the application. The provisions of this paragraph do not apply to a model or exhibit that substantially conforms to the requirements of § 1.52 or § 1.84, where the model or exhibit has been described by photographs that substantially conform to § 1.84, or where the model, exhibit or specimen is perishable.

(c) Where applicant is notified, pursuant to paragraph (a) of this section, of the need to arrange for return of a model, exhibit or specimen, applicant must arrange for the return within the period set in such notice, to avoid disposal of the model, exhibit or specimen by the Office. Extensions of time are available under § 1.136, except in the case of perishables. Failure to establish that the return of the item has been arranged for within the period set or failure to have the item removed from Office storage within a reasonable amount of time notwithstanding any arrangement for return, will permit the Office to dispose of the model, exhibit or specimen.

[69 FR 56542, Sept. 21, 2004]

§ 1.95 Copies of exhibits.

Copies of models or other physical exhibits will not ordinarily be furnished by the Office, and any model or exhibit in an application or patent shall not be taken from the Office except in the custody of an employee of the Office specially authorized by the Director.

§ 1.96 Submission of computer program listings.

(a) *General.* Descriptions of the operation and general content of computer program listings should appear in the description portion of the specification. A computer program listing for the purpose of this section is defined as a printout that lists in appropriate sequence the instructions, routines, and other contents of a program for a computer. The program listing may be either in machine or machine-independent (object or source) language which will cause a computer to perform a desired procedure or task such as solve a problem, regulate the flow of work in a computer, or control or monitor events. Computer program listings may be submitted in patent applications as set forth in paragraphs (b) and (c) of this section.

(b) *Material which will be printed in the patent:* If the computer program listing is contained in 300 lines or fewer, with each line of 72 characters or fewer, it may be submitted either as drawings or as part of the specification.

(1) *Drawings.* If the listing is submitted as drawings, it must be submitted in the manner and complying with the requirements for drawings as provided in § 1.84. At least one figure numeral is required on each sheet of drawing.

(2) *Specification.* (i) If the listing is submitted as part of the specification, it must be submitted in accordance with the provisions of § 1.52.

(ii) Any listing having more than 60 lines of code that is submitted as part of the specification must be positioned at the end of the description but before the claims. Any amendment must be made by way of submission of a substitute sheet.

(c) *As an appendix which will not be printed:* Any computer program listing may, and any computer program listing having over 300 lines (up to 72 characters per line) must, be submitted on a compact disc in compliance with § 1.52(e). A compact disc containing such a computer program listing is to be referred to as a "computer program listing appendix." The "computer program listing appendix" will not be part of the printed patent. The specification must include a reference to the "computer program listing appendix" at the location indicated in § 1.77(b)(5).

(1) Multiple computer program listings for a single application may be placed on a single compact disc. Multiple compact discs may be submitted

for a single application if necessary. A separate compact disc is required for each application containing a computer program listing that must be submitted on a "computer program listing appendix."

(2) The "computer program listing appendix" must be submitted on a compact disc that complies with § 1.52(e) and the following specifications (no other format shall be allowed):

(i) Computer Compatibility: IBM PC/XT/AT, or compatibles, or Apple Macintosh;

(ii) Operating System Compatibility: MS-DOS, MS-Windows, Unix, or Macintosh;

(iii) Line Terminator: ASCII Carriage Return plus ASCII Line Feed;

(iv) Control Codes: the data must not be dependent on control characters or codes which are not defined in the ASCII character set; and

(v) Compression: uncompressed data.

[61 FR 42804, Aug. 19, 1996, as amended at 65 FR 54670, Sept. 8, 2000; 70 FR 54266, Sept. 14, 2005]

INFORMATION DISCLOSURE STATEMENT

§ 1.97 Filing of information disclosure statement.

(a) In order for an applicant for a patent or for a reissue of a patent to have an information disclosure statement in compliance with § 1.98 considered by the Office during the pendency of the application, the information disclosure statement must satisfy one of paragraphs (b), (c), or (d) of this section.

(b) An information disclosure statement shall be considered by the Office if filed by the applicant within any one of the following time periods:

(1) Within three months of the filing date of a national application other than a continued prosecution application under § 1.53(d);

(2) Within three months of the date of entry of the national stage as set forth in § 1.491 in an international application;

(3) Before the mailing of a first Office action on the merits; or

(4) Before the mailing of a first Office action after the filing of a request for continued examination under § 1.114.

(c) An information disclosure statement shall be considered by the Office if filed after the period specified in paragraph (b) of this section, provided that the information disclosure statement is filed before the mailing date of any of a final action under § 1.113, a notice of allowance under § 1.311, or an action that otherwise closes prosecution in the application, and it is accompanied by one of:

(1) The statement specified in paragraph (e) of this section; or

(2) The fee set forth in § 1.17(p).

(d) An information disclosure statement shall be considered by the Office if filed by the applicant after the period specified in paragraph (c) of this section, provided that the information disclosure statement is filed on or before payment of the issue fee and is accompanied by:

(1) The statement specified in paragraph (e) of this section; and

(2) The fee set forth in § 1.17(p).

(e) A statement under this section must state either:

(1) That each item of information contained in the information disclosure statement was first cited in any communication from a foreign patent office in a counterpart foreign application not more than three months prior to the filing of the information disclosure statement; or

(2) That no item of information contained in the information disclosure statement was cited in a communication from a foreign patent office in a counterpart foreign application, and, to the knowledge of the person signing the certification after making reasonable inquiry, no item of information contained in the information disclosure statement was known to any individual designated in § 1.56(c) more than three months prior to the filing of the information disclosure statement.

(f) No extensions of time for filing an information disclosure statement are permitted under § 1.136. If a bona fide attempt is made to comply with § 1.98, but part of the required content is inadvertently omitted, additional time may be given to enable full compliance.

(g) An information disclosure statement filed in accordance with this section shall not be construed as a representation that a search has been made.

(h) The filing of an information disclosure statement shall not be construed to be an admission that the information cited in the statement is, or is considered to be, material to patentability as defined in § 1.56(b).

(i) If an information disclosure statement does not comply with either this section or § 1.98, it will be placed in the file but will not be considered by the Office.

[57 FR 2034, Jan. 17, 1992, as amended at 59 FR 32658, June 24, 1994; 60 FR 20226, Apr. 25, 1995; 61 FR 42805, Aug. 19, 1996; 62 FR 53190, Oct. 10, 1997; 65 FR 14872, Mar. 20, 2000; 65 FR 54670, Sept. 8, 2000]

§ 1.98 Content of information disclosure statement.

(a) Any information disclosure statement filed under § 1.97 shall include the items listed in paragraphs (a)(1), (a)(2) and (a)(3) of this section.

(1) A list of all patents, publications, applications, or other information submitted for consideration by the Office. U.S. patents and U.S. patent application publications must be listed in a section separately from citations of other documents. Each page of the list must include:

(i) The application number of the application in which the information disclosure statement is being submitted;

(ii) A column that provides a space, next to each document to be considered, for the examiner's initials; and

(iii) A heading that clearly indicates that the list is an information disclosure statement.

(2) A legible copy of:

(i) Each foreign patent;

(ii) Each publication or that portion which caused it to be listed, other than U.S. patents and U.S. patent application publications unless required by the Office;

(iii) For each cited pending unpublished U.S. application, the application specification including the claims, and any drawing of the application, or that portion of the application which caused it to be listed including any claims directed to that portion; and

(iv) All other information or that portion which caused it to be listed.

(3)(i) A concise explanation of the relevance, as it is presently understood by the individual designated in § 1.56(c) most knowledgeable about the content of the information, of each patent, publication, or other information listed that is not in the English language. The concise explanation may be either separate from applicant's specification or incorporated therein.

(ii) A copy of the translation if a written English-language translation of a non-English-language document, or portion thereof, is within the possession, custody, or control of, or is readily available to any individual designated in § 1.56(c).

(b)(1) Each U.S. patent listed in an information disclosure statement must be identified by inventor, patent number, and issue date.

(2) Each U.S. patent application publication listed in an information disclosure statement shall be identified by applicant, patent application publication number, and publication date.

(3) Each U.S. application listed in an information disclosure statement must be identified by the inventor, application number, and filing date.

(4) Each foreign patent or published foreign patent application listed in an information disclosure statement must be identified by the country or patent office which issued the patent or published the application, an appropriate document number, and the publication date indicated on the patent or published application.

(5) Each publication listed in an information disclosure statement must be identified by publisher, author (if any), title, relevant pages of the publication, date, and place of publication.

(c) When the disclosures of two or more patents or publications listed in an information disclosure statement are substantively cumulative, a copy of one of the patents or publications as specified in paragraph (a) of this section may be submitted without copies of the other patents or publications, provided that it is stated that these other patents or publications are cumulative.

(d) A copy of any patent, publication, pending U.S. application or other information, as specified in paragraph (a) of this section, listed in an information disclosure statement is required to be provided, even if the patent, publication, pending U.S. application or other information was previously submitted to, or cited by, the Office in an earlier application, unless:

(1) The earlier application is properly identified in the information disclosure statement and is relied on for an earlier effective filing date under 35 U.S.C. 120; and

(2) The information disclosure statement submitted in the earlier application complies with paragraphs (a) through (c) of this section.

[65 FR 54671, Sept. 8, 2000, as amended at 65 FR 57055, Sept. 20, 2000; 68 FR 38628, June 30, 2003; 69 FR 56542, Sept. 21, 2004]

§ 1.99 [Reserved]

EXAMINATION OF APPLICATIONS

AUTHORITY: Secs. 1.101 to 1.108 also issued under 35 U.S.C. 131, 132.

§ 1.101 [Reserved]

§ 1.102 Advancement of examination.

(a) Applications will not be advanced out of turn for examination or for further action except as provided by this part, or upon order of the Director to expedite the business of the Office, or upon filing of a request under paragraph (b) or (e) of this section or upon filing a petition or request under paragraph (c) or (d) of this section with a showing which, in the opinion of the Director, will justify so advancing it.

(b) Applications wherein the inventions are deemed of peculiar importance to some branch of the public service and the head of some department of the Government requests immediate action for that reason, may be advanced for examination.

(c) A petition to make an application special may be filed without a fee if the basis for the petition is:

(1) The applicant's age or health; or

(2) That the invention will materially:

(i) Enhance the quality of the environment;

(ii) Contribute to the development or conservation of energy resources; or

(iii) Contribute to countering terrorism.

(d) A petition to make an application special on grounds other than those referred to in paragraph (c) of this section must be accompanied by the fee set forth in § 1.17(h).

(e) A request for prioritized examination under this paragraph must comply with the requirements of this paragraph and be accompanied by the prioritized examination fee set forth in § 1.17(c), the processing fee set forth in § 1.17(i), and if not already paid, the publication fee set forth in § 1.18(d). An application for which prioritized examination has been requested may not contain or be amended to contain more than four independent claims, more than thirty total claims, or any multiple dependent claim. Prioritized examination under this paragraph will not be accorded to international applications that have not entered the national stage under 35 U.S.C. 371, design applications, reissue applications, provisional applications, or reexamination proceedings. A request for prioritized examination must also comply with the requirements of paragraph (e)(1) or paragraph (e)(2) of this section.

(1) A request for prioritized examination may be filed with an original utility or plant nonprovisional application under 35 U.S.C. 111(a) that is complete as defined by § 1.51(b), with any fees due under § 1.16 paid on filing. If the application is a utility application, it must be filed via the Office's electronic filing system. The request for prioritized examination in compliance with this paragraph must be present upon filing of the application.

(2) A request for prioritized examination may be filed with or after a request for continued examination in compliance with § 1.114. If the application is a utility application, the request must be filed via the Office's electronic filing system. The request must be filed before the mailing of the first Office action after the filing of the request for continued examination under § 1.114. Only a single such request for prioritized examination under this paragraph may be granted in an application.

(36 U.S.C. 6; 15 U.S.C. 1113, 1123)

[24 FR 10332, Dec. 22, 1959, as amended at 47 FR 41276, Sept. 17, 1982; 54 FR 6903, Feb. 15, 1989; 60 FR 20226, Apr. 25, 1995; 62 FR 53191, Oct. 10, 1997; 65 FR 54671, Sept. 8, 2000; 69 FR 56542, Sept. 21, 2004; 76 FR 59054, Sept. 23, 2011; 76 FR 78569, Dec. 19, 2011]

§ 1.103 Suspension of action by the Office.

(a) *Suspension for cause.* On request of the applicant, the Office may grant a suspension of action by the Office under this paragraph for good and sufficient cause. The Office will not suspend action if a reply by applicant to an Office action is outstanding. Any petition for suspension of action under this paragraph must specify a period of suspension not exceeding six months. Any petition for suspension of action under this paragraph must also include:

(1) A showing of good and sufficient cause for suspension of action; and

(2) The fee set forth in § 1.17(g), unless such cause is the fault of the Office.

(b) *Limited suspension of action in a continued prosecution application (CPA) filed under § 1.53(d).* On request of the applicant, the Office may grant a suspension of action by the Office under this paragraph in a continued prosecution application filed under § 1.53(d) for a period not exceeding three months. Any request for suspension of action under this paragraph must be filed with the request for an application filed under § 1.53(d), specify the period of suspension, and include the processing fee set forth in § 1.17(i).

(c) *Limited suspension of action after a request for continued examination (RCE) under § 1.114.* On request of the applicant, the Office may grant a suspension of action by the Office under this paragraph after the filing of a request for continued examination in compliance with § 1.114 for a period not exceeding three months. Any request for suspension of action under this paragraph must be filed with the request for continued examination under § 1.114, specify the period of suspension, and include the processing fee set forth in § 1.17(i).

(d) *Deferral of examination.* On request of the applicant, the Office may grant a deferral of examination under the conditions specified in this paragraph for a period not extending beyond three years from the earliest filing date for which a benefit is claimed under title 35, United States Code. A request for deferral of examination under this paragraph must include the publication fee set forth in § 1.18(d) and the processing fee set forth in § 1.17(i). A request for deferral of examination under this paragraph will not be granted unless:

(1) The application is an original utility or plant application filed under § 1.53(b) or resulting from entry of an international application into the national stage after compliance with § 1.495;

(2) The applicant has not filed a nonpublication request under § 1.213(a), or has filed a request under § 1.213(b) to rescind a previously filed nonpublication request;

(3) The application is in condition for publication as provided in § 1.211(c); and

(4) The Office has not issued either an Office action under 35 U.S.C. 132 or a notice of allowance under 35 U.S.C. 151.

(e) *Notice of suspension on initiative of the Office.* The Office will notify applicant if the Office suspends action by the Office on an application on its own initiative.

(f) *Suspension of action for public safety or defense.* The Office may suspend action by the Office by order of the Director if the following conditions are met:

(1) The application is owned by the United States;

(2) Publication of the invention may be detrimental to the public safety or defense; and

(3) The appropriate department or agency requests such suspension.

[65 FR 50104, Aug. 16, 2000, as amended at 65 FR 57056, Sept. 20, 2000; 67 FR 523, Jan. 4, 2002; 69 FR 49999, Aug. 12, 2004; 69 FR 56542, Sept. 21, 2004; 78 FR 11057, Feb. 14, 2013]

§ 1.104 Nature of examination.

(a) *Examiner's action.* (1) On taking up an application for examination or a patent in a reexamination proceeding, the examiner shall make a thorough study thereof and shall make a thorough investigation of the available prior art relating to the subject matter of the claimed invention. The examination shall be complete with respect both to compliance of the application or patent under reexamination with the applicable statutes and rules and to the patentability of the invention as claimed, as well as with respect to matters of form, unless otherwise indicated.

(2) The applicant, or in the case of a reexamination proceeding, both the patent owner and the requester, will be notified of the examiner's action. The reasons for any adverse action or any objection or requirement will be stated in an Office action and such information or references will be given as may be useful in aiding the applicant, or in the case of a reexamination proceeding the patent owner, to judge the propriety of continuing the prosecution.

(3) An international-type search will be made in all national applications filed on and after June 1, 1978.

(4) Any national application may also have an international-type search report prepared thereon at the time of the national examination on the merits, upon specific written request therefor and payment of the international-type search report fee set forth in §1.21(e). The Patent and Trademark Office does not require that a formal report of an international-type search be prepared in order to obtain a search fee refund in a later filed international application.

(b) *Completeness of examiner's action.* The examiner's action will be complete as to all matters, except that in appropriate circumstances, such as misjoinder of invention, fundamental defects in the application, and the like, the action of the examiner may be limited to such matters before further action is made. However, matters of form need not be raised by the examiner until a claim is found allowable.

(c) *Rejection of claims.* (1) If the invention is not considered patentable, or not considered patentable as claimed, the claims, or those considered unpatentable will be rejected.

(2) In rejecting claims for want of novelty or for obviousness, the examiner must cite the best references at his or her command. When a reference is complex or shows or describes inventions other than that claimed by the applicant, the particular part relied on must be designated as nearly as practicable. The pertinence of each reference, if not apparent, must be clearly explained and each rejected claim specified.

(3) In rejecting claims the examiner may rely upon admissions by the applicant, or the patent owner in a reexamination proceeding, as to any matter affecting patentability and, insofar as rejections in applications are concerned, may also rely upon facts within his or her knowledge pursuant to paragraph (d)(2) of this section.

(4)(i) Subject matter which would otherwise qualify as prior art under 35 U.S.C. 102(a)(2) and a claimed invention will be treated as commonly owned for purposes of 35 U.S.C. 102(b)(2)(C) if the applicant or patent owner provides a statement to the effect that the subject matter and the claimed invention, not later than the effective filing date of the claimed invention, were owned by the same person or subject to an obligation of assignment to the same person.

(ii) Subject matter which would otherwise qualify as prior art under 35 U.S.C. 102(a)(2) and a claimed invention will be treated as commonly owned for purposes of 35 U.S.C. 102(b)(2)(C) on the basis of a joint research agreement under 35 U.S.C. 102(c) if:

(A) The applicant or patent owner provides a statement to the effect that the subject matter was developed and the claimed invention was made by or on behalf of one or more parties to a joint research agreement, within the meaning of 35 U.S.C. 100(h) and §1.9(e), that was in effect on or before the effective filing date of the claimed invention, and the claimed invention was made as a result of activities undertaken within the scope of the joint research agreement; and

(B) The application for patent for the claimed invention discloses or is amended to disclose the names of the parties to the joint research agreement.

(5)(i) Subject matter which qualifies as prior art under 35 U.S.C. 102(e), (f), or (g) in effect prior to March 16, 2013, and a claimed invention in an application filed on or after November 29, 1999, or any patent issuing thereon, in an application filed before November 29, 1999, but pending on December 10, 2004, or any patent issuing thereon, or in any patent granted on or after December 10, 2004, will be treated as commonly owned for purposes of 35 U.S.C. 103(c) in effect prior to March 16, 2013, if the applicant or patent owner provides a statement to the effect that the subject matter and the claimed invention, at the time the claimed invention was made, were owned by the same person or subject to an obligation of assignment to the same person.

(ii) Subject matter which qualifies as prior art under 35 U.S.C. 102(e), (f), or (g) in effect prior to March 16, 2013, and a claimed invention in an application pending on or after December 10, 2004, or in any patent granted on or after December 10, 2004, will be treated as commonly owned for purposes of 35 U.S.C. 103(c) in effect prior to March 16, 2013, on the basis of a joint research agreement under 35 U.S.C. 103(c)(2) in effect prior to March 16, 2013, if:

(A) The applicant or patent owner provides a statement to the effect that the subject matter and the claimed invention were made by or on behalf of the parties to a joint research agreement, within the meaning of 35 U.S.C. 100(h) and § 1.9(e), which was in effect on or before the date the claimed invention was made, and that the claimed invention was made as a result of activities undertaken within the scope of the joint research agreement; and

(B) The application for patent for the claimed invention discloses or is amended to disclose the names of the parties to the joint research agreement.

(6) Patents issued prior to December 10, 2004, from applications filed prior to November 29, 1999, are subject to 35 U.S.C. 103(c) in effect on November 28, 1999.

(d) *Citation of references.* (1) If domestic patents are cited by the examiner, their numbers and dates, and the names of the patentees will be stated. If domestic patent application publications are cited by the examiner, their publication number, publication date, and the names of the applicants will be stated. If foreign published applications or patents are cited, their nationality or country, numbers and dates, and the names of the patentees will be stated, and such other data will be furnished as may be necessary to enable the applicant, or in the case of a reexamination proceeding, the patent owner, to identify the published applications or patents cited. In citing foreign published applications or patents, in case only a part of the document is involved, the particular pages and sheets containing the parts relied upon will be identified. If printed publications are cited, the author (if any), title, date, pages or plates, and place of publication, or place where a copy can be found, will be given.

(2) When a rejection in an application is based on facts within the personal knowledge of an employee of the Office, the data shall be as specific as possible, and the reference must be supported, when called for by the applicant, by the affidavit of such employee, and such affidavit shall be subject to contradiction or explanation by the affidavits of the applicant and other persons.

(e) *Reasons for allowance.* If the examiner believes that the record of the prosecution as a whole does not make clear his or her reasons for allowing a claim or claims, the examiner may set forth such reasoning. The reasons shall be incorporated into an Office action rejecting other claims of the application or patent under reexamination or be the subject of a separate communication to the applicant or patent owner. The applicant or patent owner may file a statement commenting on the reasons for allowance within such time as may be specified by the examiner. Failure by the examiner to respond to any statement commenting on reasons for allowance does not give rise to any implication.

[62 FR 53191, Oct. 10, 1997, as amended at 65 FR 14872, Mar. 20, 2000; 65 FR 54671, Sept. 8, 2000; 65 FR 57056, Sept. 20, 2000; 70 FR 1823, Jan. 11, 2005; 70 FR 54266, Sept. 14, 2005; 72 FR 46841, Aug. 21, 2007; 74 FR 52690, Oct. 14, 2009; 78 FR 11057, Feb. 14, 2013]

§ 1.105 Requirements for information.

(a)(1) In the course of examining or treating a matter in a pending or abandoned application filed under 35 U.S.C. 111 or 371 (including a reissue application), in a patent, or in a reexamination proceeding, the examiner or other Office employee may require the submission, from individuals identified under § 1.56(c), or any assignee, of such information as may be reasonably necessary to properly examine or treat the matter, for example:

(i) *Commercial databases:* The existence of any particularly relevant commercial database known to any of the inventors that could be searched for a particular aspect of the invention.

(ii) *Search:* Whether a search of the prior art was made, and if so, what was searched.

(iii) *Related information:* A copy of any non-patent literature, published application, or patent (U.S. or foreign), by any of the inventors, that relates to the claimed invention.

(iv) *Information used to draft application:* A copy of any non-patent literature, published application, or patent (U.S. or foreign) that was used to draft the application.

(v) *Information used in invention process:* A copy of any non-patent literature, published application, or patent (U.S. or foreign) that was used in the invention process, such as by designing around or providing a solution to accomplish an invention result.

(vi) *Improvements:* Where the claimed invention is an improvement, identification of what is being improved.

(vii) *In use:* Identification of any use of the claimed invention known to any of the inventors at the time the application was filed notwithstanding the date of the use.

(viii) *Technical information known to applicant.* Technical information known to applicant concerning the related art, the disclosure, the claimed subject matter, other factual information pertinent to patentability, or concerning the accuracy of the examiner's stated interpretation of such items.

(2) Requirements for factual information known to applicant may be presented in any appropriate manner, for example:

(i) A requirement for factual information;

(ii) Interrogatories in the form of specific questions seeking applicant's factual knowledge; or

(iii) Stipulations as to facts with which the applicant may agree or disagree.

(3) Any reply to a requirement for information pursuant to this section that states either that the information required to be submitted is unknown to or is not readily available to the party or parties from which it was requested may be accepted as a complete reply.

(b) The requirement for information of paragraph (a)(1) of this section may be included in an Office action, or sent separately.

(c) A reply, or a failure to reply, to a requirement for information under this section will be governed by §§ 1.135 and 1.136.

[65 FR 54671, Sept. 8, 2000, as amended at 69 FR 56542, Sept. 21, 2004; 72 FR 46841, Aug. 21, 2007; 74 FR 52690, Oct. 14, 2009; 77 FR 48821, Aug. 14, 2012]

§§ 1.106–1.108 [Reserved]

§ 1.109 Effective filing date of a claimed invention under the Leahy-Smith America Invents Act.

(a) The effective filing date for a claimed invention in a patent or application for patent, other than in a reissue application or reissued patent, is the earliest of:

(1) The actual filing date of the patent or the application for the patent containing a claim to the invention; or

(2) The filing date of the earliest application for which the patent or application is entitled, as to such invention, to a right of priority or the benefit of an earlier filing date under 35 U.S.C. 119, 120, 121, or 365.

(b) The effective filing date for a claimed invention in a reissue application or a reissued patent is determined by deeming the claim to the invention to have been contained in the patent for which reissue was sought.

[78 FR 11057, Feb. 14, 2013]

§ 1.110 Inventorship and ownership of the subject matter of individual claims.

When one or more joint inventors are named in an application or patent, the Office may require an applicant or patentee to identify the inventorship and ownership or obligation to assign ownership, of each claimed invention on its effective filing date (as defined in § 1.109) or on its date of invention, as applicable, when necessary for purposes of an Office proceeding. The Office may also require an applicant or patentee to identify the invention dates of the subject matter of each claim when necessary for purposes of an Office proceeding.

[78 FR 11058, Feb. 14, 2013]

ACTION BY APPLICANT AND FURTHER CONSIDERATION

AUTHORITY: Secs. 1.111 to 1.113 also issued under 35 U.S.C. 132.

§ 1.111 Reply by applicant or patent owner to a non-final Office action.

(a)(1) If the Office action after the first examination (§ 1.104) is adverse in any respect, the applicant or patent owner, if he or she persists in his or her application for a patent or reexamination proceeding, must reply and request reconsideration or further examination, with or without amendment. See §§ 1.135 and 1.136 for time for reply to avoid abandonment.

(2) *Supplemental replies.* (i) A reply that is supplemental to a reply that is in compliance with § 1.111(b) will not be entered as a matter of right except as provided in paragraph (a)(2)(ii) of this section. The Office may enter a supplemental reply if the supplemental reply is clearly limited to:

(A) Cancellation of a claim(s);

(B) Adoption of the examiner suggestion(s);

(C) Placement of the application in condition for allowance;

(D) Reply to an Office requirement made after the first reply was filed;

(E) Correction of informalities (*e.g.*, typographical errors); or

(F) Simplification of issues for appeal.

(ii) A supplemental reply will be entered if the supplemental reply is filed within the period during which action by the Office is suspended under § 1.103(a) or (c).

(b) In order to be entitled to reconsideration or further examination, the applicant or patent owner must reply to the Office action. The reply by the applicant or patent owner must be reduced to a writing which distinctly and specifically points out the supposed errors in the examiner's action and must reply to every ground of objection and rejection in the prior Office action. The reply must present arguments pointing out the specific distinctions believed to render the claims, including any newly presented claims, patentable over any applied references. If the reply is with respect to an application, a request may be made that objections or requirements as to form not necessary to further consideration of the claims be held in abeyance until allowable subject matter is indicated. The applicant's or patent owner's reply must appear throughout to be a *bona fide* attempt to advance the application or the reexamination proceeding to final action. A general allegation that the claims define a patentable invention without specifically pointing out how the language of the claims patentably distinguishes them from the references does not comply with the requirements of this section.

(c) In amending in reply to a rejection of claims in an application or patent under reexamination, the applicant or patent owner must clearly point out the patentable novelty which he or she thinks the claims present in view of the state of the art disclosed by the references cited or the objections made. The applicant or patent owner must also show how the amendments avoid such references or objections.

[46 FR 29182, May 29, 1981, as amended at 62 FR 53192, Oct. 10, 1997; 65 FR 54672, Sept. 8, 2000; 69 FR 56542, Sept. 21, 2004; 70 FR 3891, Jan. 27, 2005]

§ 1.112 Reconsideration before final action.

After reply by applicant or patent owner (§ 1.111 or § 1.945) to a non-final action and any comments by an *inter partes* reexamination requester (§ 1.947), the application or the patent under reexamination will be reconsidered and again examined. The applicant, or in the case of a reexamination proceeding the patent owner and any third party requester, will be notified if claims are rejected, objections or requirements made, or decisions favorable to patentability are made, in the same manner as after the first examination (§ 1.104). Applicant or patent owner may reply to such Office action in the same manner provided in § 1.111 or § 1.945, with or without amendment, unless such Office action indicates that it is made final (§ 1.113) or an appeal (§ 41.31 of this title) has been taken (§ 1.116), or in an *inter partes* reexamination, that it is an action closing prosecution (§ 1.949) or a right of appeal notice (§ 1.953).

[69 FR 49999, Aug. 12, 2004]

§ 1.113 Final rejection or action.

(a) On the second or any subsequent examination or consideration by the examiner the rejection or other action may be made final, whereupon applicant's, or for *ex parte* reexaminations filed under § 1.510, patent owner's reply is limited to appeal in the case of rejection of any claim (§ 41.31 of this title), or to amendment as specified in § 1.114 or § 1.116. Petition may be taken to the Director in the case of objections or requirements not involved in the rejection of any claim (§ 1.181). Reply to a final rejection or action must comply with § 1.114 or paragraph (c) of this section. For final actions in an *inter partes* reexamination filed under § 1.913, see § 1.953.

(b) In making such final rejection, the examiner shall repeat or state all grounds of rejection then considered applicable to the claims in the application, clearly stating the reasons in support thereof.

(c) Reply to a final rejection or action must include cancellation of, or appeal from the rejection of, each rejected claim. If any claim stands allowed, the reply to a final rejection or action must comply with any requirements or objections as to form.

[65 FR 14872, Mar. 20, 2000, as amended at 65 FR 76773, Dec. 7, 2000; 69 FR 49999, Aug. 12, 2004]

§ 1.114 Request for continued examination.

(a) If prosecution in an application is closed, an applicant may request continued examination of the application by filing a submission and the fee set forth in § 1.17(e) prior to the earliest of:

(1) Payment of the issue fee, unless a petition under § 1.313 is granted;

(2) Abandonment of the application; or

(3) The filing of a notice of appeal to the U.S. Court of Appeals for the Federal Circuit under 35 U.S.C. 141, or the commencement of a civil action under 35 U.S.C. 145 or 146, unless the appeal or civil action is terminated.

(b) Prosecution in an application is closed as used in this section means that the application is under appeal, or that the last Office action is a final action (§ 1.113), a notice of allowance (§ 1.311), or an action that otherwise closes prosecution in the application.

(c) A submission as used in this section includes, but is not limited to, an information disclosure statement, an amendment to the written description, claims, or drawings, new arguments, or new evidence in support of patentability. If reply to an Office action under 35 U.S.C. 132 is outstanding, the submission must meet the reply requirements of § 1.111.

(d) If an applicant timely files a submission and fee set forth in § 1.17(e), the Office will withdraw the finality of any Office action and the submission will be entered and considered. If an applicant files a request for continued examination under this section after appeal, but prior to a decision on the appeal, it will be treated as a request to withdraw the appeal and to reopen prosecution of the application before the examiner. An appeal brief (§ 41.37 of this title) or a reply brief (§ 41.41 of this title), or related papers, will not be considered a submission under this section.

(e) The provisions of this section do not apply to:

(1) A provisional application;

(2) An application for a utility or plant patent filed under 35 U.S.C. 111(a) before June 8, 1995;

(3) An international application filed under 35 U.S.C. 363 before June 8, 1995;

(4) An application for a design patent; or

(5) A patent under reexamination.

[65 FR 50104, Aug. 16, 2000, as amended at 69 FR 49999, Aug. 12, 2004; 72 FR 46841, Aug. 21, 2007; 74 FR 52691, Oct. 14, 2009]

AMENDMENTS

AUTHORITY: Secs. 1.115 to 1.127 also issued under 35 U.S.C. 132.

§ 1.115 Preliminary amendments.

(a) A preliminary amendment is an amendment that is received in the Office (§ 1.6) on or before the mail date of the first Office action under § 1.104. The patent application publication may include preliminary amendments (§ 1.215(a)).

(1) A preliminary amendment that is present on the filing date of an application is part of the original disclosure of the application.

(2) A preliminary amendment filed after the filing date of the application is not part of the original disclosure of the application.

(b) A preliminary amendment in compliance with § 1.121 will be entered unless disapproved by the Director.

(1) A preliminary amendment seeking cancellation of all the claims without presenting any new or substitute claims will be disapproved.

(2) A preliminary amendment may be disapproved if the preliminary amendment unduly interferes with the preparation of a first Office action in an application. Factors that will be considered in disapproving a preliminary amendment include:

(i) The state of preparation of a first Office action as of the date of receipt (§ 1.6) of the preliminary amendment by the Office; and

(ii) The nature of any changes to the specification or claims that would result from entry of the preliminary amendment.

(3) A preliminary amendment will not be disapproved under (b)(2) of this section if it is filed no later than:

(i) Three months from the filing date of an application under § 1.53(b);

(ii) The filing date of a continued prosecution application under § 1.53(d); or

(iii) Three months from the date the national stage is entered as set forth in § 1.491 in an international application.

(4) The time periods specified in paragraph (b)(3) of this section are not extendable.

[69 FR 56543, Sept. 21, 2004]

§ 1.116 Amendments and affidavits or other evidence after final action and prior to appeal.

(a) An amendment after final action must comply with § 1.114 or this section.

(b) After a final rejection or other final action (§ 1.113) in an application or in an *ex parte* reexamination filed under § 1.510, or an action closing prosecution (§ 1.949) in an *inter partes* reexamination filed under § 1.913, but before or on the same date of filing an appeal (§ 41.31 or § 41.61 of this title):

(1) An amendment may be made canceling claims or complying with any requirement of form expressly set forth in a previous Office action;

(2) An amendment presenting rejected claims in better form for consideration on appeal may be admitted; or

(3) An amendment touching the merits of the application or patent under reexamination may be admitted upon a showing of good and sufficient reasons why the amendment is necessary and was not earlier presented.

(c) The admission of, or refusal to admit, any amendment after a final rejection, a final action, an action closing prosecution, or any related proceedings will not operate to relieve the application or reexamination proceeding from its condition as subject to appeal or to save the application from abandonment under § 1.135, or the reexamination prosecution from termination under § 1.550(d) or § 1.957(b) or limitation of further prosecution under § 1.957(c).

(d)(1) Notwithstanding the provisions of paragraph (b) of this section, no amendment other than canceling claims, where such cancellation does not affect the scope of any other pending claim in the proceeding, can be made in an *inter partes* reexamination proceeding after the right of appeal notice under § 1.953 except as provided in § 1.981 or as permitted by § 41.77(b)(1) of this title.

(2) Notwithstanding the provisions of paragraph (b) of this section, an amendment made after a final rejection or other final action (§ 1.113) in an *ex parte* reexamination filed under § 1.510, or an action closing prosecution (§ 1.949) in an *inter partes* reexamination filed under § 1.913 may not cancel claims where such cancellation affects the scope of any other pending claim in the reexamination proceeding except as provided in § 1.981 or as permitted by § 41.77(b)(1) of this title.

(e) An affidavit or other evidence submitted after a final rejection or other final action (§ 1.113) in an application or in an *ex parte* reexamination filed under § 1.510, or an action closing prosecution (§ 1.949) in an *inter partes* reexamination filed under § 1.913 but before or on the same date of filing an appeal (§ 41.31 or § 41.61 of this title), may be admitted upon a showing of good and sufficient reasons why the affidavit or other evidence is necessary and was not earlier presented.

(f) Notwithstanding the provisions of paragraph (e) of this section, no affidavit or other evidence can be made in an *inter partes* reexamination proceeding after the right of appeal notice under § 1.953 except as provided in § 1.981 or as permitted by § 41.77(b)(1) of this title.

(g) After decision on appeal, amendments, affidavits and other evidence can only be made as provided in §§ 1.198 and 1.981, or to carry into effect a recommendation under § 41.50(c) of this title.

[69 FR 49999, Aug. 12, 2004]

§§ 1.117–1.119 [Reserved]

§ 1.121 Manner of making amendments in applications.

(a) *Amendments in applications, other than reissue applications.* Amendments in applications, other than reissue applications, are made by filing a paper, in compliance with § 1.52, directing that specified amendments be made.

(b) *Specification.* Amendments to the specification, other than the claims, computer listings (§ 1.96) and sequence listings (§ 1.825), must be made by adding, deleting or replacing a paragraph, by replacing a section, or by a substitute specification, in the manner specified in this section.

(1) *Amendment to delete, replace, or add a paragraph.* Amendments to the specification, including amendment to a section heading or the title of the invention which are considered for amendment purposes to be an amendment of a paragraph, must be made by submitting:

(i) An instruction, which unambiguously identifies the location, to delete one or more paragraphs of the specification, replace a paragraph with one or more replacement paragraphs, or add one or more paragraphs;

(ii) The full text of any replacement paragraph with markings to show all the changes relative to the previous version of the paragraph. The text of any added subject matter must be shown by underlining the added text. The text of any deleted matter must be shown by strike-through except that double brackets placed before and after the deleted characters may be used to show deletion of five or fewer consecutive characters. The text of any deleted subject matter must be shown by being placed within double brackets if strike-through cannot be easily perceived;

(iii) The full text of any added paragraphs without any underlining; and

(iv) The text of a paragraph to be deleted must not be presented with strike-through or placed within double brackets. The instruction to delete may identify a paragraph by its paragraph number or include a few words from the beginning, and end, of the paragraph, if needed for paragraph identification purposes.

(2) *Amendment by replacement section.* If the sections of the specification contain section headings as provided in § 1.77(b), § 1.154(b), or § 1.163(c), amendments to the specification, other than the claims, may be made by submitting:

(i) A reference to the section heading along with an instruction, which unambiguously identifies the location, to delete that section of the specification and to replace such deleted section with a replacement section; and

(ii) A replacement section with markings to show all changes relative to the previous version of the section. The text of any added subject matter must be shown by underlining the added text. The text of any deleted matter must be shown by strike-through except that double brackets placed before and after the deleted characters may be used to show deletion of five or fewer consecutive characters. The text of any deleted subject matter must be shown by being placed within double brackets if strike-through cannot be easily perceived.

(3) *Amendment by substitute specification.* The specification, other than the claims, may also be amended by submitting:

(i) An instruction to replace the specification; and

(ii) A substitute specification in compliance with §§ 1.125(b) and (c).

(4) *Reinstatement of previously deleted paragraph or section.* A previously deleted paragraph or section may be reinstated only by a subsequent amendment adding the previously deleted paragraph or section.

(5) *Presentation in subsequent amendment document.* Once a paragraph or section is amended in a first amendment document, the paragraph or section shall not be re-presented in a subsequent amendment document unless it is amended again or a substitute specification is provided.

(c) *Claims.* Amendments to a claim must be made by rewriting the entire claim with all changes (*e.g.*, additions and deletions) as indicated in this subsection, except when the claim is being canceled. Each amendment document that includes a change to an existing claim, cancellation of an existing claim or addition of a new claim, must include a complete listing of all claims ever presented, including the text of all pending and withdrawn claims, in the application. The claim listing, including the text of the claims, in the amendment document will serve to replace all prior versions of the claims, in the application. In the claim listing, the status of every claim must be indicated after its claim number by using one of the following identifiers in a parenthetical expression: (Original), (Currently amended), (Canceled), (Withdrawn), (Previously presented), (New), and (Not entered).

(1) *Claim listing.* All of the claims presented in a claim listing shall be presented in ascending numerical order. Consecutive claims having the same status of "canceled" or "not entered" may be aggregated into one statement (*e.g.*, Claims 1–5 (canceled)). The claim listing shall commence on a separate sheet of the amendment document and the sheet(s) that contain the text of any part of the claims shall not contain any other part of the amendment.

(2) *When claim text with markings is required.* All claims being currently amended in an amendment paper shall be presented in the claim listing, indicate a status of "currently amended," and be submitted with markings to indicate the changes that have been made relative to the immediate prior version of the claims. The text of any added subject matter must be shown by underlining the added text. The text of any deleted matter must be shown by strike-through except that double brackets placed before and after the deleted characters may be used to show deletion of five or fewer consecutive characters. The text of any deleted subject matter must be shown by being placed within double brackets if strike-through cannot be easily perceived. Only claims having the status of "currently amended," or "withdrawn" if also being amended, shall include markings. If a withdrawn claim is currently amended, its status in the claim listing may be identified as "withdrawn—currently amended."

(3) *When claim text in clean version is required.* The text of all pending claims not being currently amended shall be presented in the claim listing in clean version, *i.e.*, without any markings in the presentation of text. The presentation of a clean version of any claim having the status of "original," "withdrawn" or "previously presented" will constitute an assertion that it has not been changed relative to the immediate prior version, except to omit markings that may have been present in the immediate prior version of the claims of the status of "withdrawn" or "previously presented." Any claim added by amendment must be indicated with the status of "new" and presented in clean version, *i.e.*, without any underlining.

(4) *When claim text shall not be presented; canceling a claim.* (i) No claim text shall be presented for any claim in the claim listing with the status of "canceled" or "not entered."

(ii) Cancellation of a claim shall be effected by an instruction to cancel a particular claim number. Identifying the status of a claim in the claim listing as "canceled" will constitute an instruction to cancel the claim.

(5) *Reinstatement of previously canceled claim.* A claim which was previously canceled may be reinstated only by adding the claim as a "new" claim with a new claim number.

(d) *Drawings:* One or more application drawings shall be amended in the following manner: Any changes to an application drawing must be in compliance with § 1.84 and must be submitted on a replacement sheet of drawings which shall be an attachment to the amendment document and, in the top margin, labeled "Replacement Sheet." Any replacement sheet of drawings shall include all of the figures appearing on the immediate prior version of the sheet, even if only one figure is amended. Any new sheet of drawings containing an additional figure must be labeled in the top margin as "New Sheet." All changes to the drawings shall be explained, in detail, in either the drawing amendment or remarks section of the amendment paper.

(1) A marked-up copy of any amended drawing figure, including annotations indicating the changes made, may be included. The marked-up copy must be clearly labeled as "Annotated Sheet" and must be presented in the amendment or remarks section that explains the change to the drawings.

(2) A marked-up copy of any amended drawing figure, including annotations indicating the changes made, must be provided when required by the examiner.

(e) *Disclosure consistency.* The disclosure must be amended, when required by the Office, to correct inaccuracies of description and definition, and to secure substantial correspondence between the claims, the remainder of the specification, and the drawings.

(f) *No new matter.* No amendment may introduce new matter into the disclosure of an application.

(g) *Exception for examiner's amendments.* Changes to the specification, including the claims, of an application made by the Office in an examiner's amendment may be made by specific instructions to insert or delete subject matter set forth in the examiner's amendment by identifying the precise point in the specification or the claim(s) where the insertion or deletion is to be made. Compliance with paragraphs (b)(1), (b)(2), or (c) of this section is not required.

(h) *Amendment sections.* Each section of an amendment document (*e.g.*, amendment to the claims, amendment to the specification, replacement drawings, and remarks) must begin on a separate sheet.

(i) *Amendments in reissue applications.* Any amendment to the description and claims in reissue applications must be made in accordance with § 1.173.

(j) *Amendments in reexamination proceedings.* Any proposed amendment to the description and claims in patents involved in reexamination proceedings must be made in accordance with § 1.530.

(k) *Amendments in provisional applications.* Amendments in provisional applications are not usually made. If an amendment is made to a provisional application, however, it must comply with the provisions of this section. Any amendments to a provisional application shall be placed in the provisional application file but may not be entered.

[68 FR 38628, June 30, 2003, as amended at 69 FR 56543, Sept. 21, 2004]

§§ 1.122–1.224 [Reserved]

§ 1.125 Substitute specification.

(a) If the number or nature of the amendments or the legibility of the application papers renders it difficult to consider the application, or to arrange the papers for printing or copying, the Office may require the entire specification, including the claims, or any part thereof, be rewritten.

(b) Subject to § 1.312, a substitute specification, excluding the claims, may be filed at any point up to payment of the issue fee if it is accompanied by a statement that the substitute specification includes no new matter.

(c) A substitute specification submitted under this section must be submitted with markings showing all the changes relative to the immediate prior version of the specification of record. The text of any added subject matter must be shown by underlining the added text. The text of any deleted matter must be shown by strike-through except that double brackets placed before and after the deleted characters may be used to show deletion of five or fewer consecutive characters. The text of any deleted subject matter must be shown by being placed within double brackets if strike-through cannot be easily perceived. An accompanying clean version (without markings) must also be supplied. Numbering the paragraphs of the specification of record is not considered a change that must be shown pursuant to this paragraph.

(d) A substitute specification under this section is not permitted in a reissue application or in a reexamination proceeding.

[62 FR 53193, Oct. 10, 1997, as amended at 65 FR 54673, Sept. 8, 2000; 68 FR 38630, June 30, 2003]

§ 1.126 Numbering of claims.

The original numbering of the claims must be preserved throughout the prosecution. When claims are canceled the remaining claims must not be renumbered. When claims are added, they must be numbered by the applicant consecutively beginning with the number next following the highest numbered claim previously presented (whether entered or not). When the application is ready for allowance, the examiner, if necessary, will renumber the claims consecutively in the order in which they appear or in such order as may have been requested by applicant.

[62 FR 53194, Oct. 10, 1997]

§ 1.127 Petition from refusal to admit amendment.

From the refusal of the primary examiner to admit an amendment, in whole or in part, a petition will lie to the Director under § 1.181.

TRANSITIONAL PROVISIONS

§ 1.129 Transitional procedures for limited examination after final rejection and restriction practice.

(a) An applicant in an application, other than for reissue or a design patent, that has been pending for at least two years as of June 8, 1995, taking into account any reference made in such application to any earlier filed application under 35 U.S.C. 120, 121 and 365(c), is entitled to have a first submission entered and considered on the merits after final rejection under the following circumstances: The Office will consider such a submission, if the first submission and the fee set forth in § 1.17(r) are filed prior to the filing of an appeal brief and prior to abandonment of the application. The finality of the final rejection is automatically withdrawn upon the timely filing of the submission and payment of the fee set forth in § 1.17(r). If a subsequent final rejection is made in the application, applicant is entitled to have a second submission entered and considered on the merits after the subsequent final rejection under the following circumstances: The Office will consider such a submission, if the second submission and a second fee set forth in § 1.17(r) are filed prior to the filing of an appeal brief and prior to abandonment of the application. The finality of the subsequent final rejection is automatically withdrawn upon the timely filing of the submission and payment of the second fee set forth in § 1.17(r). Any submission filed after a final rejection made in an application subsequent to the fee set forth in § 1.17(r) having been twice paid will be treated as set forth in § 1.116. A submission as used in this paragraph includes, but is not limited to, an information disclosure statement, an amendment to the written description, claims or drawings and a new substantive argument or new evidence in support of patentability.

(b)(1) In an application, other than for reissue or a design patent, that has been pending for at least three years as of June 8, 1995; taking into account any reference made in the application to any earlier filed application under 35 U.S.C. 120, 121, and 365(c), no requirement for restriction or for the filing of divisional applications shall be made or maintained in the application after June 8, 1995, except where:

(i) The requirement was first made in the application or any earlier filed application under 35 U.S.C. 120, 121 and 365(c) prior to April 8, 1995;

(ii) The examiner has not made a requirement for restriction in the present or parent application prior to April 8, 1995, due to actions by the applicant; or

(iii) The required fee for examination of each additional invention was not paid.

(2) If the application contains more than one independent and distinct invention and a requirement for restriction or for the filing of divisional applications cannot be made or maintained pursuant to this paragraph, applicant will be so notified and given a time period to:

(i) Elect the invention or inventions to be searched and examined, if no election has been made prior to the notice, and pay the fee set forth in § 1.17(s) for each independent and distinct invention claimed in the application in excess of one which applicant elects;

(ii) Confirm an election made prior to the notice and pay the fee set forth in § 1.17(s) for each independent and distinct invention claimed in the application in addition to the one invention which applicant previously elected; or

(iii) File a petition under this section traversing the requirement. If the required petition is filed in a timely manner, the original time period for electing and paying the fee set forth in § 1.17(s) will be deferred and any decision on the petition affirming or modifying the requirement will set a new time period to elect the invention or inventions to be searched and examined and to pay the fee set forth in § 1.17(s) for each independent and distinct invention claimed in the application in excess of one which applicant elects.

(3) The additional inventions for which the required fee has not been paid will be withdrawn from consideration under § 1.142(b). An applicant who desires examination of an invention so withdrawn from consideration can file a divisional application under 35 U.S.C. 121.

(c) The provisions of this section shall not be applicable to any application filed after June 8, 1995.

[60 FR 20226, Apr. 25, 1995]

AFFIDAVITS OVERCOMING REJECTIONS

§ 1.130 Affidavit or declaration of attribution or prior public disclosure under the Leahy-Smith America Invents Act.

(a) *Affidavit or declaration of attribution.* When any claim of an application or a patent under reexamination is rejected, the applicant or patent owner may submit an appropriate affidavit or declaration to disqualify a disclosure as prior art by establishing that the disclosure was made by the inventor or a joint inventor, or the subject matter disclosed was obtained directly or indirectly from the inventor or a joint inventor.

(b) *Affidavit or declaration of prior public disclosure.* When any claim of an application or a patent under reexamination is rejected, the applicant or patent owner may submit an appropriate affidavit or declaration to disqualify a disclosure as prior art by establishing that the subject matter disclosed had, before such disclosure was made or before such subject matter was effectively filed, been publicly disclosed by the inventor or a joint inventor or another who obtained the subject matter disclosed directly or indirectly from the inventor or a joint inventor. An affidavit or declaration under this paragraph must identify the subject matter publicly disclosed and provide the date such subject matter was publicly disclosed by the inventor or a joint inventor or another who obtained the subject matter disclosed directly or indirectly from the inventor or a joint inventor.

(1) If the subject matter publicly disclosed on that date was in a printed publication, the affidavit or declaration must be accompanied by a copy of the printed publication.

(2) If the subject matter publicly disclosed on that date was not in a printed publication, the affidavit or declaration must describe the subject matter with sufficient detail and particularity to determine what subject matter had been publicly disclosed on that date by the inventor or a joint inventor or another who obtained the subject matter disclosed directly or indirectly from the inventor or a joint inventor.

(c) *When this section is not available.* The provisions of this section are not available if the rejection is based upon a disclosure made more than one year before the effective filing date of the claimed invention. The provisions of this section may not be available if the rejection is based upon a U.S. patent or U.S. patent application publication of a patented or pending application naming another inventor, the patent or pending application claims an invention that is the same or substantially the same as the applicant's or patent owner's claimed invention, and the affidavit or declaration contends that an inventor named in the U.S. patent or U.S. patent application publication derived the claimed invention from the inventor or a joint inventor named in the application or patent, in which case an applicant or a patent owner may file a petition for a derivation proceeding pursuant to § 42.401 *et seq.* of this title.

(d) *Applications and patents to which this section is applicable.* The provisions of this section apply to any application for patent, and to any patent issuing thereon, that contains, or contained at any time:

(1) A claim to a claimed invention that has an effective filing date as defined in 35 U.S.C. 100(i) that is on or after March 16, 2013; or

(2) A specific reference under 35 U.S.C. 120, 121, or 365(c) to any patent or application that contains, or contained at any time, a claim to a claimed invention that has an effective filing date as defined in 35 U.S.C. 100(i) that is on or after March 16, 2013.

[78 FR 11058, Feb. 14, 2013]

§ 1.131 Affidavit or declaration of prior invention or to disqualify commonly owned patent or published application as prior art.

(a) When any claim of an application or a patent under reexamination is rejected, the inventor of the subject matter of the rejected claim, the owner of the patent under reexamination, or the party qualified under § 1.42 or § 1.46, may submit an appropriate oath or declaration to establish invention of the subject matter of the rejected claim prior to the effective date of the reference or activity on which the rejection is based. The effective date of a U.S. patent, U.S. patent application publication, or international application publication under PCT Article 21(2) is the earlier of its publication date or the date that it is effective as a reference under 35 U.S.C. 102(e) as in effect on March 15, 2013. Prior invention may not be established under this section in any country other than the United States, a NAFTA country, or a WTO member country. Prior invention may not be established under this section before December 8, 1993, in a NAFTA country other than the United States, or before January 1, 1996, in a WTO member country other than a NAFTA country. Prior invention may not be established under this section if either:

(1) The rejection is based upon a U.S. patent or U.S. patent application publication of a pending or patented application naming another inventor which claims interfering subject matter as defined in § 41.203(a) of this title, in which case an applicant may suggest an interference pursuant to § 41.202(a) of this title; or

(2) The rejection is based upon a statutory bar.

(b) The showing of facts for an oath or declaration under paragraph (a) of this section shall be such, in character and weight, as to establish reduction to practice prior to the effective date of the reference, or conception of the invention prior to the effective date of the reference coupled with due diligence from prior to said date to a subsequent reduction to practice or to the filing of the application. Original exhibits of drawings or records, or photocopies thereof, must accompany and form part of the affidavit or declaration or their absence must be satisfactorily explained.

(c) When any claim of an application or a patent under reexamination is rejected under 35 U.S.C. 103 as in effect on March 15, 2013, on a U.S. patent or U.S. patent application publication which is not prior art under 35 U.S.C. 102(b) as in effect on March 15, 2013, and the inventions defined by the claims in the application or patent under reexamination and by the claims in the patent or published application are not identical but are not patentably distinct, and the inventions are owned by the same party, the applicant or owner of the patent under reexamination may disqualify the patent or patent application publication as prior art. The patent or patent application publication can be disqualified as prior art by submission of:

(1) A terminal disclaimer in accordance with § 1.321(c); and

(2) An oath or declaration stating that the application or patent under reexamination and patent or published application are currently owned by the same party, and that the inventor named in the application or patent under reexamination is the prior inventor under 35 U.S.C. 104 as in effect on March 15, 2013.

(d) The provisions of this section apply to any application for patent, and to any patent issuing thereon, that contains, or contained at any time:

(1) A claim to an invention that has an effective filing date as defined in 35 U.S.C. 100(i) that is before March 16, 2013; or

(2) A specific reference under 35 U.S.C. 120, 121, or 365(c) to any patent or application that contains, or contained at any time, a claim to an invention that has an effective filing date as defined in 35 U.S.C. 100(i) that is before March 16, 2013.

(e) In an application for patent to which the provisions of § 1.130 apply, and to any patent issuing thereon, the provisions of this section are applicable only with respect to a rejection under 35 U.S.C. 102(g) as in effect on March 15, 2013.

[78 FR 11058, Feb. 14, 2013]

§ 1.132 Affidavits or declarations traversing rejections or objections.

When any claim of an application or a patent under reexamination is rejected or objected to, any evidence submitted to traverse the rejection or objection on a basis not otherwise provided for must be by way of an oath or declaration under this section.

[65 FR 57057, Sept. 20, 2000]

INTERVIEWS

§ 1.133 Interviews.

(a)(1) Interviews with examiners concerning applications and other matters pending before the Office must be conducted on Office premises and within Office hours, as the respective examiners may designate. Interviews will not be permitted at any other time or place without the authority of the Director.

(2) An interview for the discussion of the patentability of a pending application will not occur before the first Office action, unless the application is a continuing or substitute application or the examiner determines that such an interview would advance prosecution of the application.

(3) The examiner may require that an interview be scheduled in advance.

(b) In every instance where reconsideration is requested in view of an interview with an examiner, a complete written statement of the reasons presented at the interview as warranting favorable action must be filed by the applicant. An interview does not remove the necessity for reply to Office actions as specified in §§ 1.111 and 1.135.

(35 U.S.C. 132)

[24 FR 10332, Dec. 22, 1959, as amended at 62 FR 53194, Oct. 10, 1997; 65 FR 54674, Sept. 8, 2000; 70 FR 56128, Sept. 26, 2005]

TIME FOR REPLY BY APPLICANT; ABANDONMENT OF APPLICATION

AUTHORITY: Secs. 1.135 to 1.138 also issued under 35 U.S.C. 133.

§ 1.134 Time period for reply to an Office action.

An Office action will notify the applicant of any non-statutory or shortened statutory time period set for reply to an Office action. Unless the applicant is notified in writing that a reply is required in less than six months, a maximum period of six months is allowed.

[62 FR 53194, Oct. 10, 1997]

§ 1.135 Abandonment for failure to reply within time period.

(a) If an applicant of a patent application fails to reply within the time period provided under § 1.134 and § 1.136, the application will become abandoned unless an Office action indicates otherwise.

(b) Prosecution of an application to save it from abandonment pursuant to paragraph (a) of this section must include such complete and proper reply as the condition of the application may require. The admission of, or refusal to admit, any amendment after final rejection or any amendment not responsive to the last action, or any related proceedings, will not operate to save the application from abandonment.

(c) When reply by the applicant is a *bona fide* attempt to advance the application to final action, and is substantially a complete reply to the non-final Office action, but consideration of some matter or compliance with some requirement has been inadvertently omitted, applicant may be given a new time period for reply under § 1.134 to supply the omission.

[62 FR 53194, Oct. 10, 1997]

§ 1.136 Extensions of time.

(a)(1) If an applicant is required to reply within a nonstatutory or shortened statutory time period, applicant may extend the time period for reply up to the earlier of the expiration of any maximum period set by statute or five months after the time period set for reply, if a petition for an extension of time and the fee set in § 1.17(a) are filed, unless:

(i) Applicant is notified otherwise in an Office action;

(ii) The reply is a reply brief submitted pursuant to § 41.41 of this title;

(iii) The reply is a request for an oral hearing submitted pursuant to § 41.47(a) of this title;

(iv) The reply is to a decision by the Patent Trial and Appeal Board pursuant to § 1.304 or to § 41.50 or § 41.52 of this title; or

(v) The application is involved in a contested case (§ 41.101(a) of this title) or a derivation proceeding (§ 42.4(b) of this title).

(2) The date on which the petition and the fee have been filed is the date for purposes of determining the period of extension and the corresponding amount of the fee. The expiration of the time period is determined by the amount of the fee paid. A reply must be filed prior to the expiration of the period of extension to avoid abandonment of the application (§ 1.135), but in no situation may an applicant reply later than the maximum time period set by statute, or be granted an extension of time under paragraph (b) of this section when the provisions of this paragraph are available. See § 1.304 for extensions of time to appeal to the U.S. Court of Appeals for the Federal Circuit or to commence a civil action; § 1.550(c) for extensions of time in *ex parte* reexamination proceedings, § 1.956 for extensions of time in *inter partes* reexamination proceedings; §§ 41.4(a) and 41.121(a)(3) of this title for extensions of time in contested cases before the Patent Trial and Appeal Board; and § 42.5(c) of this title for extensions of time in trials before the Patent Trial and Appeal Board.

(3) A written request may be submitted in an application that is an authorization to treat any concurrent or future reply, requiring a petition for an extension of time under this paragraph for its timely submission, as incorporating a petition for extension of time for the appropriate length of time. An authorization to charge all required fees, fees under § 1.17, or all required extension of time fees will be treated as a constructive petition for an extension of time in any concurrent or future reply requiring a petition for an extension of time under this paragraph for its timely submission. Submission of the fee set forth in § 1.17(a) will also be treated as a constructive petition for an extension of time in any concurrent reply requiring a petition for an extension of time under this paragraph for its timely submission.

(b) When a reply cannot be filed within the time period set for such reply and the provisions of paragraph (a) of this section are not available, the period for reply will be extended only for sufficient cause and for a reasonable time specified. Any request for an extension of time under this paragraph must be filed on or before the day on which such reply is due, but the mere filing of such a request will not effect any extension under this paragraph. In no situation can any extension carry the date on which reply is due beyond the maximum time period set by statute. See § 1.304 for extensions of time to appeal to the U.S. Court of Appeals for the Federal Circuit or to commence a civil action; § 1.550(c) for extensions of time in *ex parte* reexamination proceedings; § 1.956 for extensions of time in *inter partes* reexamination proceedings; §§ 41.4(a) and 41.121(a)(3) of this title for extensions of time in contested cases before the Patent Trial and Appeal Board; and § 42.5(c) of this title for extensions of time in trials before the Patent Trial and Appeal Board. Any request under this section must be accompanied by the petition fee set forth in § 1.17(g).

(c) If an applicant is notified in a "Notice of Allowability" that an application is otherwise in condition for allowance, the following time periods are not extendable if set in the "Notice of Allowability" or in an Office action having a mail date on or after the mail date of the "Notice of Allowability":

(1) The period for submitting the inventor's oath or declaration;

(2) The period for submitting formal drawings set under § 1.85(c); and

(3) The period for making a deposit set under § 1.809(c).

[62 FR 53194, Oct. 10, 1997, as amended at 65 FR 54674, Sept. 8, 2000; 65 FR 76773, Dec. 7, 2000; 66 FR 21092, Apr. 27, 2001; 69 FR 50000, Aug. 12, 2004; 69 FR 56543, Sept. 21, 2004; 70 FR 3891, Jan. 27, 2005; 72 FR 46842, Aug. 21, 2007; 74 FR 52691, Oct. 14, 2009; 77 FR 46625, Aug. 6, 2012; 77 FR 48821, Aug. 14, 2012]

§ 1.137 Revival of abandoned application, terminated or limited reexamination prosecution, or lapsed patent.

(a) *Unavoidable.* If the delay in reply by applicant or patent owner was unavoidable, a petition may be filed pursuant to this paragraph to revive an abandoned application, a reexamination prosecution terminated under § 1.550(d) or § 1.957(b) or limited under § 1.957(c), or a lapsed patent. A grantable petition pursuant to this paragraph must be accompanied by:

(1) The reply required to the outstanding Office action or notice, unless previously filed;

(2) The petition fee as set forth in § 1.17(l);

(3) A showing to the satisfaction of the Director that the entire delay in filing the required reply from the due date for the reply until the filing of a grantable petition pursuant to this paragraph was unavoidable; and

(4) Any terminal disclaimer (and fee as set forth in § 1.20(d)) required pursuant to paragraph (d) of this section.

(b) *Unintentional.* If the delay in reply by applicant or patent owner was unintentional, a petition may be filed pursuant to this paragraph to revive an abandoned application, a reexamination prosecution terminated under § 1.550(d) or § 1.957(b) or limited under § 1.957(c), or a lapsed patent. A grantable petition pursuant to this paragraph must be accompanied by:

(1) The reply required to the outstanding Office action or notice, unless previously filed;

(2) The petition fee as set forth in § 1.17(m);

(3) A statement that the entire delay in filing the required reply from the due date for the reply until the filing of a grantable petition pursuant to this paragraph was unintentional. The Director may require additional information where there is a question whether the delay was unintentional; and

(4) Any terminal disclaimer (and fee as set forth in § 1.20(d)) required pursuant to paragraph (d) of this section.

(c) *Reply.* In a nonprovisional application abandoned for failure to prosecute, the required reply may be met by the filing of a continuing application. In a nonprovisional utility or plant application filed on or after June 8, 1995, and abandoned for failure to prosecute, the required reply may also be met by the filing of a request for continued examination in compliance with § 1.114. In an application or patent, abandoned or lapsed for failure to pay the issue fee or any portion thereof, the required reply must include payment of the issue fee or any outstanding balance. In an application, abandoned for failure to pay the publication fee, the required reply must include payment of the publication fee.

(d) *Terminal disclaimer.* (1) Any petition to revive pursuant to this section in a design application must be accompanied by a terminal disclaimer and fee as set forth in § 1.321 dedicating to the public a terminal part of the term of any patent granted thereon equivalent to the period of abandonment of the application. Any petition to revive pursuant to this section in either a utility or plant application filed before June 8, 1995, must be accompanied by a terminal disclaimer and fee as set forth in § 1.321 dedicating to the public a terminal part of the term of any patent granted thereon equivalent to the lesser of:

(i) The period of abandonment of the application; or

(ii) The period extending beyond twenty years from the date on which the application for the patent was filed in the United States or, if the application contains a specific reference to an earlier filed application(s) under 35 U.S.C. 120, 121, or 365(c), from the date on which the earliest such application was filed.

(2) Any terminal disclaimer pursuant to paragraph (d)(1) of this section must also apply to any patent granted on a continuing utility or plant application filed before June 8, 1995, or a continuing design application, that contains a specific reference under 35 U.S.C. 120, 121, or 365(c) to the application for which revival is sought.

(3) The provisions of paragraph (d)(1) of this section do not apply to applications for which revival is sought solely for purposes of copendency with a utility or plant application filed on or after June 8, 1995, to lapsed patents, to reissue applications, or to reexamination proceedings.

(e) *Request for reconsideration.* Any request for reconsideration or review of a decision refusing to revive an abandoned application, a terminated or limited reexamination prosecution, or lapsed patent upon petition filed pursuant to this section, to be considered timely, must be filed within two months of the decision refusing to revive or within such time as set in the decision. Unless a decision indicates otherwise, this time period may be extended under:

(1) The provisions of § 1.136 for an abandoned application or lapsed patent;

(2) The provisions of § 1.550(c) for a terminated *ex parte* reexamination prosecution, where the *ex parte* reexamination was filed under § 1.510; or

(3) The provisions of § 1.956 for a terminated *inter partes* reexamination prosecution or an *inter partes* reexamination limited as to further prosecution, where the *inter partes* reexamination was filed under § 1.913.

(f) *Abandonment for failure to notify the Office of a foreign filing:* A nonprovisional application abandoned pursuant to 35 U.S.C. 122(b)(2)(B)(iii) for failure to timely notify the Office of the filing of an application in a foreign country or under a multinational treaty that requires publication of applications eighteen months after filing, may be revived only pursuant to paragraph (b) of this section. The reply requirement of paragraph (c) of this section is met by the notification of such filing in a foreign country or under a multinational treaty, but the filing of a petition under this section will not operate to stay any period for reply that may be running against the application.

(g) *Provisional applications.* A provisional application, abandoned for failure to timely respond to an Office requirement, may be revived pursuant to this section. Subject to the provisions of 35 U.S.C. 119(e)(3) and § 1.7(b), a provisional application will not be regarded as pending after twelve months from its filing date under any circumstances.

[65 FR 57057, Sept. 20, 2000, as amended at 69 FR 56543, Sept. 21, 2004; 72 FR 18904, Apr. 16, 2007]

§ 1.138 Express abandonment.

(a) An application may be expressly abandoned by filing a written declaration of abandonment identifying the application in the United States Patent and Trademark Office. Express abandonment of the application may not be recognized by the Office before the date of issue or publication unless it is actually received by appropriate officials in time to act.

(b) A written declaration of abandonment must be signed by a party authorized under § 1.33(b)(1), (b)(3), or (b)(4) to sign a paper in the application, except as otherwise provided in this paragraph. A registered attorney or agent, not of record, who acts in a representative capacity under the provisions of § 1.34(a) when filing a continuing application, may expressly abandon the prior application as of the filing date granted to the continuing application.

(c) An applicant seeking to abandon an application to avoid publication of the application (see § 1.211(a)(1)) must submit a declaration of express abandonment by way of a petition under this paragraph including the fee set forth in § 1.17(h) in sufficient time to permit the appropriate officials to recognize the abandonment and remove the application from the publication process. Applicants should expect that the petition will not be granted and the application will be published in regular course unless such declaration of express abandonment and petition are received by the appropriate officials more than four weeks prior to the projected date of publication.

(d) An applicant seeking to abandon an application filed under 35 U.S.C. 111(a) and § 1.53(b) on or after December 8, 2004, to obtain a refund of the search fee and excess claims fee paid in the application, must submit a declaration of express abandonment by way of a petition under this paragraph before an examination has been made of the application. The date indicated on any certificate of mailing or transmission under § 1.8 will not be taken into account in determining whether a petition under § 1.138(d) was filed before an examination has been made of the application. If a request for refund of the search fee and excess claims fee paid in the application is not filed with the declaration of express abandonment under this paragraph or within two months from the date on which the declaration of express abandonment under this paragraph was filed, the Office may retain the entire search fee and excess claims fee paid in the application. This two-month period is not extendable. If a petition and declaration of express abandonment under this paragraph are not filed before an examination has been made of the application, the Office will not refund any part of the search fee and excess claims fee paid in the application except as provided in § 1.26.

[65 FR 54674, Sept. 8, 2000, as amended at 65 FR 57058, Sept. 20, 2000; 71 FR 12284, Mar. 10, 2006]

§ 1.139 [Reserved]

JOINDER OF INVENTIONS IN ONE APPLICATION; RESTRICTION

AUTHORITY: Secs. 1.141 to 1.147 also issued under 35 U.S.C. 121.

§ 1.141 Different inventions in one national application.

(a) Two or more independent and distinct inventions may not be claimed in one national application, except that more than one species of an invention, not to exceed a reasonable number, may be specifically claimed in different claims in one national application, provided the application also includes an allowable claim generic to all the claimed species and all the claims to species in excess of one are written in dependent form (§ 1.75) or otherwise include all the limitations of the generic claim.

(b) Where claims to all three categories, product, process of making, and process of use, are included in a national application, a three way requirement for restriction can only be made where the process of making is distinct from the product. If the process of making and the product are not distinct, the process of using may be joined with the claims directed to the product and the process of making the product even though a showing of distinctness between the product and process of using the product can be made.

[52 FR 20046, May 28, 1987]

§ 1.142 Requirement for restriction.

(a) If two or more independent and distinct inventions are claimed in a single application, the examiner in an Office action will require the applicant in the reply to that action to elect an invention to which the claims will be restricted, this official action being called a requirement for restriction (also known as a requirement for division). Such requirement will normally be made before any action on the merits; however, it may be made at any time before final action.

(b) Claims to the invention or inventions not elected, if not canceled, are nevertheless withdrawn from further consideration by the examiner by the election, subject however to reinstatement in the event the requirement for restriction is withdrawn or overruled.

[24 FR 10332, Dec. 22, 1959, as amended at 62 FR 53195, Oct. 10, 1997; 72 FR 46842, Aug. 21, 2007; 74 FR 52691, Oct. 14, 2009]

§ 1.143 Reconsideration of requirement.

If the applicant disagrees with the requirement for restriction, he may request reconsideration and withdrawal or modification of the requirement, giving the reasons therefor. (See § 1.111.) In requesting reconsideration the applicant must indicate a provisional election of one invention for prosecution, which invention shall be the one elected in the event the requirement becomes final The requirement for restriction will be reconsidered on such a request. If the requirement is repeated and made final the examiner will at the same time act on the claims to the invention elected.

§ 1.144 Petition from requirement for restriction.

After a final requirement for restriction, the applicant, in addition to making any reply due on the remainder of the action, may petition the Director to review the requirement. Petition may be deferred until after final action on or allowance of claims to the invention elected, but must be filed not later than appeal. A petition will not be considered if reconsideration of the requirement was not requested (see § 1.181).

[62 FR 53195, Oct. 10, 1997]

§ 1.145 Subsequent presentation of claims for different invention.

If, after an Office action on an application, the applicant presents claims directed to an invention distinct from and independent of the invention previously claimed, the applicant will be required to restrict the claims to the invention previously claimed if the amendment is entered, subject to reconsideration and review as provided in §§ 1.143 and 1.144.

[74 FR 52691, Oct. 14, 2009]

§ 1.146 Election of species.

In the first action on an application containing a generic claim to a generic invention (genus) and claims to more than one patentably distinct species embraced thereby, the examiner may require the applicant in the reply to that action to elect a species of his or her invention to which his or her claim will be restricted if no claim to the genus is found to be allowable. However, if such application contains claims directed to more than a reasonable number of species, the examiner may require restriction of the claims to not more than a reasonable number of species before taking further action in the application.

[62 FR 53195, Oct. 10, 1997]

DESIGN PATENTS

§ 1.151 Rules applicable.

The rules relating to applications for patents for other inventions or discoveries are also applicable to applications for patents for designs except as otherwise provided.

(35 U.S.C. 171)

§ 1.152 Design drawings.

The design must be represented by a drawing that complies with the requirements of § 1.84 and must contain a sufficient number of views to constitute a complete disclosure of the appearance of the design. Appropriate and adequate surface shading should be used to show the character or contour of the surfaces represented. Solid black surface shading is not permitted except when used to represent the color black as well as color contrast. Broken lines may be used to show visible environmental structure, but may not be used to show hidden planes and surfaces that cannot be seen through opaque materials. Alternate positions of a design component, illustrated by full and broken lines in the same view are not permitted in a design drawing. Photographs and ink drawings are not permitted to be combined as formal drawings in one application. Photographs submitted in lieu of ink drawings in design patent applications must not disclose environmental structure but must be limited to the design claimed for the article.

[65 FR 54674, Sept. 8, 2000]

§ 1.153 Title, description and claim, oath or declaration.

(a) The title of the design must designate the particular article. No description, other than a reference to the drawing, is ordinarily required. The claim shall be in formal terms to the ornamental design for the article (specifying name) as shown, or as shown and described. More than one claim is neither required nor permitted.

(b) The inventor's oath or declaration must comply with the requirements of § 1.63, or comply with the requirements of § 1.64 for a substitute statement.

(35 U.S.C. 6, Pub. L. 97–247)

[24 FR 10332, Dec. 22, 1959, as amended at 29 FR 18503, Dec. 29, 1964; 48 FR 2712, Jan. 20, 1983; 77 FR 48821, Aug. 14, 2012]

§ 1.154 Arrangement of application elements in a design application.

(a) The elements of the design application, if applicable, should appear in the following order:

(1) Design application transmittal form.

(2) Fee transmittal form.

(3) Application data sheet (see § 1.76).

(4) Specification.

(5) Drawings or photographs.

(6) The inventor's oath or declaration (*see* § 1.153(b)).

(b) The specification should include the following sections in order:

(1) Preamble, stating the name of the applicant, title of the design, and a brief description of the nature and intended use of the article in which the design is embodied.

(2) Cross-reference to related applications (unless included in the application data sheet).

(3) Statement regarding federally sponsored research or development.

(4) Description of the figure or figures of the drawing.

(5) Feature description.

(6) A single claim.

(c) The text of the specification sections defined in paragraph (b) of this section, if applicable, should be preceded by a section heading in uppercase letters without underlining or bold type.

[65 FR 54674, Sept. 8, 2000, as amended at 77 FR 48821, Aug. 14, 2012]

§ 1.155 Expedited examination of design applications.

(a) The applicant may request that the Office expedite the examination of a design application. To qualify for expedited examination:

(1) The application must include drawings in compliance with § 1.84;

(2) The applicant must have conducted a preexamination search; and

(3) The applicant must file a request for expedited examination including:

(i) The fee set forth in § 1.17(k); and

(ii) A statement that a preexamination search was conducted. The statement must also indicate the field of search and include an information disclosure statement in compliance with § 1.98.

(b) The Office will not examine an application that is not in condition for examination (*e.g.*, missing basic filing fee) even if the applicant files a request for expedited examination under this section.

[65 FR 54674, Sept. 8, 2000]

PLANT PATENTS

§ 1.161 Rules applicable.

The rules relating to applications for patent for other inventions or discoveries are also applicable to applications for patents for plants except as otherwise provided.

§ 1.162 Applicant, oath or declaration.

The inventor named for a plant patent application must be the person who has invented or discovered and asexually reproduced the new and distinct variety of plant for which a patent is sought. The inventor's oath or declaration, in addition to the averments required by § 1.63 or § 1.64, must state that the inventor has asexually reproduced the plant. Where the plant is a newly found plant, the inventor's oath or declaration must also state that it was found in a cultivated area.

[77 FR 48821, Aug. 14, 2012]

§ 1.163 Specification and arrangement of application elements in a plant application.

(a) The specification must contain as full and complete a disclosure as possible of the plant and the characteristics thereof that distinguish the same over related known varieties, and its antecedents, and must particularly point out where and in what manner the variety of plant has been asexually reproduced. For a newly found plant, the specification must particularly point out the location and character of the area where the plant was discovered.

(b) The elements of the plant application, if applicable, should appear in the following order:

(1) Plant application transmittal form.

(2) Fee transmittal form.

(3) Application data sheet (see § 1.76).

(4) Specification.

(5) Drawings (in duplicate).

(6) The inventor's oath or declaration (§ 1.162).

(c) The specification should include the following sections in order:

(1) Title of the invention, which may include an introductory portion stating the name, citizenship, and residence of the applicant.

(2) Cross-reference to related applications (unless included in the application data sheet).

(3) Statement regarding federally sponsored research or development.

(4) Latin name of the genus and species of the plant claimed.

(5) Variety denomination.

(6) Background of the invention.

(7) Brief summary of the invention.

(8) Brief description of the drawing.

(9) Detailed botanical description.

(10) A single claim.

(11) Abstract of the disclosure.

(d) The text of the specification or sections defined in paragraph (c) of this section, if applicable, should be preceded by a section heading in upper case, without underlining or bold type.

[65 FR 54675, Sept. 8, 2000, as amended at 77 FR 48821, Aug. 14, 2012]

§ 1.164 Claim.

The claim shall be in formal terms to the new and distinct variety of the specified plant as described and illustrated, and may also recite the principal distinguishing characteristics. More than one claim is not permitted.

(35 U.S.C. 162)

§ 1.165 Plant drawings.

(a) Plant patent drawings should be artistically and competently executed and must comply with the requirements of § 1.84. View numbers and reference characters need not be employed unless required by the examiner. The drawing must disclose all the distinctive characteristics of the plant capable of visual representation.

(b) The drawings may be in color. The drawing must be in color if color is a distinguishing characteristic of the new variety. Two copies of color drawings or photographs must be submitted.

[58 FR 38726, July 20, 1993, as amended at 65 FR 57058, Sept. 20, 2000; 69 FR 56543, Sept. 21, 2004]

§ 1.166 Specimens.

The applicant may be required to furnish specimens of the plant, or its flower or fruit, in a quantity and at a time in its stage of growth as may be designated, for study and inspection. Such specimens, properly packed, must be forwarded in conformity with instructions furnished to the applicant. When it is not possible to forward such specimens, plants must be made available for official inspection where grown.

(35 U.S.C. 114, 161)

§ 1.167 Examination.

Applications may be submitted by the Patent and Trademark Office to the Department of Agriculture for study and report.

[62 FR 53196, Oct. 10, 1997]

Reissues

AUTHORITY: Secs. 1.171 to 1.179 also issued under 35 U.S.C. 251.

§ 1.171 Application for reissue.

An application for reissue must contain the same parts required for an application for an original patent, complying with all the rules relating thereto except as otherwise provided, and in addition, must comply with the requirements of the rules relating to reissue applications.

[62 FR 53196, Oct. 10, 1997]

§ 1.172 Reissue applicant.

(a) The reissue applicant is the original patentee, or the current patent owner if there has been an assignment. A reissue application must be accompanied by the written consent of all assignees, if any, currently owning an undivided interest in the patent. All assignees consenting to the reissue must establish their ownership in the patent by filing in the reissue application a submission in accordance with the provisions of § 3.73(c) of this chapter.

(b) A reissue will be granted to the original patentee, his legal representatives or assigns as the interest may appear.

[77 FR 48821, Aug. 14, 2012]

§ 1.173 Reissue specification, drawings, and amendments.

(a) *Contents of a reissue application.* An application for reissue must contain the entire specification, including the claims, and the drawings of the patent. No new matter shall be introduced into the application. No reissue patent shall be granted enlarging the scope of the claims of the original patent unless applied for within two years from the grant of the original patent, pursuant to 35 U.S.C. 251.

(1) *Specification, including claims.* The entire specification, including the claims, of the patent for which reissue is requested must be furnished in the form of a copy of the printed patent, in double column format, each page on only one side of a single sheet of paper. If an amendment of the reissue application is to be included, it must be made pursuant to paragraph (b) of this section. The formal requirements for papers making up the reissue application other than those set forth in this section are set out in § 1.52. Additionally, a copy of any disclaimer (§ 1.321), certificate of correction (§§ 1.322 through 1.324), or reexamination certificate (§ 1.570) issued in the patent must be included. (See also § 1.178).

(2) *Drawings.* Applicant must submit a clean copy of each drawing sheet of the printed patent at the time the reissue application is filed. If such copy complies with § 1.84, no further drawings will be required. Where a drawing of the reissue application is to include any changes relative to the patent being reissued, the changes to the drawing must be made in accordance with paragraph (b)(3) of this section. The Office will not transfer the drawings from the patent file to the reissue application.

(b) *Making amendments in a reissue application.* An amendment in a reissue application is made either by physically incorporating the changes into the specification when the application is filed, or by a separate amendment paper. If amendment is made by incorporation, markings pursuant to paragraph (d) of this section must be used. If amendment is made by an amendment paper, the paper must direct that specified changes be made, as follows:

(1) *Specification other than the claims.* Changes to the specification, other than to the claims, must be made by submission of the entire text of an added or rewritten paragraph, including markings pursuant to paragraph (d) of this section, except that an entire paragraph may be deleted by a statement deleting the paragraph without presentation of the text of the paragraph. The precise point in the specification must be identified where any added or rewritten paragraph is located. This paragraph applies whether the amendment is submitted on paper or compact disc (*see* §§ 1.52(e)(1) and 1.821(c), but not for discs submitted under § 1.821(e)).

(2) *Claims.* An amendment paper must include the entire text of each claim being changed by such amendment paper and of each claim being added by such amendment paper. For any claim changed by the amendment paper, a parenthetical expression "amended," "twice amended," etc., should follow the claim number. Each changed patent claim and each added claim must include markings pursuant to paragraph (d) of this section, except that a patent claim or added claim should be canceled by a statement canceling the claim without presentation of the text of the claim.

(3) *Drawings.* One or more patent drawings shall be amended in the following manner: Any changes to a patent drawing must be submitted as a replacement sheet of drawings which shall be an attachment to the amendment document. Any replacement sheet of drawings must be in compliance with § 1.84 and shall include all of the figures appearing on the original version of the sheet, even if only one figure is amended. Amended figures must be identified as "Amended," and any added figure must be identified as "New." In the event that a figure is

canceled, the figure must be surrounded by brackets and identified as "Canceled." All changes to the drawing(s) shall be explained, in detail, beginning on a separate sheet accompanying the papers including the amendment to the drawings.

(i) A marked-up copy of any amended drawing figure, including annotations indicating the changes made, may be included. The marked-up copy must be clearly labeled as "Annotated Marked-up Drawings" and must be presented in the amendment or remarks section that explains the change to the drawings.

(ii) A marked-up copy of any amended drawing figure, including annotations indicating the changes made, must be provided when required by the examiner.

(c) *Status of claims and support for claim changes.* Whenever there is an amendment to the claims pursuant to paragraph (b) of this section, there must also be supplied, on pages separate from the pages containing the changes, the status (*i.e.*, pending or canceled), as of the date of the amendment, of all patent claims and of all added claims, and an explanation of the support in the disclosure of the patent for the changes made to the claims.

(d) *Changes shown by markings.* Any changes relative to the patent being reissued which are made to the specification, including the claims, upon filing, or by an amendment paper in the reissue application, must include the following markings:

(1) The matter to be omitted by reissue must be enclosed in brackets; and

(2) The matter to be added by reissue must be underlined, except for amendments submitted on compact discs (§§1.96 and 1.821(c)). Matter added by reissue on compact discs must be preceded with "<U>" and end with "</U>" to properly identify the material being added.

(e) *Numbering of patent claims preserved.* Patent claims may not be renumbered. The numbering of any claim added in the reissue application must follow the number of the highest numbered patent claim.

(f) *Amendment of disclosure may be required.* The disclosure must be amended, when required by the Office, to correct inaccuracies of description and definition, and to secure substantial correspondence between the claims, the remainder of the specification, and the drawings.

(g) *Amendments made relative to the patent.* All amendments must be made relative to the patent specification, including the claims, and drawings, which are in effect as of the date of filing of the reissue application.

[65 FR 54675, Sept. 8, 2000, as amended at 68 FR 38630, June 30, 2003; 69 FR 56543, Sept. 21, 2004]

§ 1.174 [Reserved]

§ 1.175 Inventor's oath or declaration for a reissue application.

(a) The inventor's oath or declaration for a reissue application, in addition to complying with the requirements of §1.63, §1.64, or §1.67, must also specifically identify at least one error pursuant to 35 U.S.C. 251 being relied upon as the basis for reissue and state that the applicant believes the original patent to be wholly or partly inoperative or invalid by reason of a defective specification or drawing, or by reason of the patentee claiming more or less than the patentee had the right to claim in the patent.

(b) If the reissue application seeks to enlarge the scope of the claims of the patent (a basis for the reissue is the patentee claiming less than the patentee had the right to claim in the patent), the inventor's oath or declaration for a reissue application must identify a claim that the application seeks to broaden. A claim is a broadened claim if the claim is broadened in any respect.

(c) The inventor, or each individual who is a joint inventor of a claimed invention, in a reissue application must execute an oath or declaration for the reissue application, except as provided for in §1.64, and except that the inventor's oath or declaration for a reissue application may be signed by the assignee of the entire interest if:

(1) The application does not seek to enlarge the scope of the claims of the original patent; or

(2) The application for the original patent was filed under §1.46 by the assignee of the entire interest.

(d) If errors previously identified in the inventor's oath or declaration for a reissue application pursuant to paragraph (a) of this section are no longer being relied upon as the basis for reissue, the applicant must identify an error being relied upon as the basis for reissue.

(e) The inventor's oath or declaration for a reissue application required by paragraph (a) of this section may be submitted under the provisions of § 1.53(f), except that the provisions of § 1.53(f)(3) do not apply to a reissue application.

(f)(1) The requirement for the inventor's oath or declaration for a continuing reissue application that claims the benefit under 35 U.S.C. 120, 121, or 365(c) in compliance with § 1.78 of an earlier-filed reissue application may be satisfied by a copy of the inventor's oath or declaration from the earlier-filed reissue application, provided that:

(i) The inventor, or each individual who is a joint inventor of a claimed invention, in the reissue application executed an inventor's oath or declaration for the earlier-filed reissue application, except as provided for in § 1.64;

(ii) The continuing reissue application does not seek to enlarge the scope of the claims of the original patent; or

(iii) The application for the original patent was filed under § 1.46 by the assignee of the entire interest.

(2) If all errors identified in the inventor's oath or declaration from the earlier-filed reissue application are no longer being relied upon as the basis for reissue, the applicant must identify an error being relied upon as the basis for reissue.

(g) An oath or declaration filed at any time pursuant to 35 U.S.C. 115(h)(1), will be placed in the file record of the reissue application, but may not necessarily be reviewed by the Office.

[77 FR 48821, Aug. 14, 2012]

§ 1.176 Examination of reissue.

(a) A reissue application will be examined in the same manner as a non-reissue, non-provisional application, and will be subject to all the requirements of the rules related to non-reissue applications. Applications for reissue will be acted on by the examiner in advance of other applications.

(b) Restriction between subject matter of the original patent claims and previously unclaimed subject matter may be required (restriction involving only subject matter of the original patent claims will not be required). If restriction is required, the subject matter of the original patent claims will be held to be constructively elected unless a disclaimer of all the patent claims is filed in the reissue application, which disclaimer cannot be withdrawn by applicant.

[65 FR 54676, Sept. 8, 2000]

§ 1.177 Issuance of multiple reissue patents.

(a) The Office may reissue a patent as multiple reissue patents. If applicant files more than one application for the reissue of a single patent, each such application must contain or be amended to contain in the first sentence of the specification a notice stating that more than one reissue application has been filed and identifying each of the reissue applications by relationship, application number and filing date. The Office may correct by certificate of correction under § 1.322 any reissue patent resulting from an application to which this paragraph applies that does not contain the required notice.

(b) If applicant files more than one application for the reissue of a single patent, each claim of the patent being reissued must be presented in each of the reissue applications as an amended, unamended, or canceled (shown in brackets) claim, with each such claim bearing the same number as in the patent being reissued. The same claim of the patent being reissued may not be presented in its original unamended form for examination in more than one of such multiple reissue applications. The numbering of any added claims in any of the multiple reissue applications must follow the number of the highest numbered original patent claim.

(c) If any one of the several reissue applications by itself fails to correct an error in the original patent as required by 35 U.S.C. 251 but is otherwise in condition for allowance, the Office may suspend action in the allowable application until all issues are resolved as to at least one of the remaining reissue applications. The Office may also merge two or more of the multiple reissue applications into a single reissue application. No reissue application containing only unamended patent claims and not correcting an error in the original patent will be passed to issue by itself.

[65 FR 54676, Sept. 8, 2000]

§ 1.178 Original patent; continuing duty of applicant.

(a) The application for reissue of a patent shall constitute an offer to surrender that patent, and the surrender shall take effect upon reissue of the patent. Until a reissue application is granted, the original patent shall remain in effect.

(b) In any reissue application before the Office, the applicant must call to the attention of the Office any prior or concurrent proceedings in which the patent (for which reissue is requested) is or was involved, such as interferences or trials before the Patent Trial and Appeal Board, reissues, reexaminations, or litigations and the results of such proceedings (see also § 1.173(a)(1)).

[65 FR 54676, Sept. 8, 2000, as amended at 69 FR 56544, Sept. 21, 2004; 77 FR 46625, Aug. 6, 2012]

§ 1.179 [Reserved]

PETITIONS AND ACTION BY THE DIRECTOR

AUTHORITY: 35 U.S.C. 6; 15 U.S.C. 1113, 1123.

§ 1.181 Petition to the Director.

(a) Petition may be taken to the Director:

(1) From any action or requirement of any examiner in the *ex parte* prosecution of an application, or in *ex parte* or *inter partes* prosecution of a reexamination proceeding which is not subject to appeal to the Patent Trial and Appeal Board or to the court;

(2) In cases in which a statute or the rules specify that the matter is to be determined directly by or reviewed by the Director; and

(3) To invoke the supervisory authority of the Director in appropriate circumstances. For petitions involving action of the Patent Trial and Appeal Board, see § 41.3 of this title.

(b) Any such petition must contain a statement of the facts involved and the point or points to be reviewed and the action requested. Briefs or memoranda, if any, in support thereof should accompany or be embodied in the petition; and where facts are to be proven, the proof in the form of affidavits or declarations (and exhibits, if any) must accompany the petition.

(c) When a petition is taken from an action or requirement of an examiner in the *ex parte* prosecution of an application, or in the *ex parte* or *inter partes* prosecution of a reexamination proceeding, it may be required that there have been a proper request for reconsideration (§ 1.111) and a repeated action by the examiner. The examiner may be directed by the Director to furnish a written statement, within a specified time, setting forth the reasons for his or her decision upon the matters averred in the petition, supplying a copy to the petitioner.

(d) Where a fee is required for a petition to the Director the appropriate section of this part will so indicate. If any required fee does not accompany the petition, the petition will be dismissed.

(e) Oral hearing will not be granted except when considered necessary by the Director.

(f) The mere filing of a petition will not stay any period for reply that may be running against the application, nor act as a stay of other proceedings. Any petition under this part not filed within two months of the mailing date of the action or notice from which relief is requested may be dismissed as untimely, except as otherwise provided. This two-month period is not extendable.

(g) The Director may delegate to appropriate Patent and Trademark Office officials the determination of petitions.

[24 FR 10332, Dec. 22, 1959, as amended at 34 FR 18857, Nov. 26, 1969; 47 FR 41278, Sept. 17, 1982; 49 FR 48452, Dec. 12, 1984; 65 FR 54676, Sept. 8, 2000; 65 FR 76774, Dec. 7, 2000; 69 FR 50000, Aug. 12, 2004; 77 FR 46625, Aug. 6, 2012]

§ 1.182 Questions not specifically provided for.

All situations not specifically provided for in the regulations of this part will be decided in accordance with the merits of each situation by or under the authority of the Director, subject to such other requirements as may be imposed, and such decision will be communicated to the interested parties in writing. Any petition seeking a decision under this section must be accompanied by the petition fee set forth in § 1.17(f).

[69 FR 56544, Sept. 21, 2004]

§ 1.183 Suspension of rules.

In an extraordinary situation, when justice requires, any requirement of the regulations in this part which is not a requirement of the statutes may be suspended or waived by the Director or the Director's designee, *sua sponte*, or on petition of the interested party, subject to such other requirements as may be imposed. Any petition under this section must be accompanied by the petition fee set forth in § 1.17(f).

[69 FR 56544, Sept. 21, 2004]

§ 1.184 [Reserved]

APPEAL TO THE PATENT TRIAL AND APPEAL BOARD

AUTHORITY: Secs. 1.191 to 1.198 also issued under 35 U.S.C. 134.

§ 1.191 Appeal to Patent Trial and Appeal Board.

Appeals to the Patent Trial and Appeal Board under 35 U.S.C. 134(a) and (b) are conducted according to part 41 of this title.

[77 FR 46625, Aug. 6, 2012]

§§ 1.192–1.196 [Reserved]

§ 1.197 Termination of proceedings.

(a) [Reserved]

(b) *Termination of proceedings.* (1) Proceedings on an application are considered terminated by the dismissal of an appeal or the failure to timely file an appeal to the court or a civil action (§ 1.304) except:

(i) Where claims stand allowed in an application; or

(ii) Where the nature of the decision requires further action by the examiner.

(2) The date of termination of proceedings on an application is the date on which the appeal is dismissed or the date on which the time for appeal to the U.S. Court of Appeals for the Federal Circuit or review by civil action (§ 1.304) expires in the absence of further appeal or review. If an appeal to the U.S. Court of Appeals for the Federal Circuit or a civil action has been filed, proceedings on an application are considered terminated when the appeal or civil action is terminated. A civil action is terminated when the time to appeal the judgment expires. An appeal to the U.S. Court of Appeals for the Federal Circuit, whether from a decision of the Board or a judgment in a civil action, is terminated when the mandate is issued by the Court.

[69 FR 50000, Aug. 12, 2004, as amended at 76 FR 72296, Nov. 22, 2011]

§ 1.198 Reopening after a final decision of the Patent Trial and Appeal Board.

When a decision by the Patent Trial and Appeal Board on appeal has become final for judicial review, prosecution of the proceeding before the primary examiner will not be reopened or reconsidered by the primary examiner except under the provisions of § 1.114 or § 41.50 of this title without the written authority of the Director, and then only for the consideration of matters not already adjudicated, sufficient cause being shown.

[77 FR 46625, Aug. 6, 2012]

PUBLICATION OF APPLICATIONS

SOURCE: 65 FR 57058, Sept. 20, 2000, unless otherwise noted.

§ 1.211 Publication of applications.

(a) Each U.S. national application for patent filed in the Office under 35 U.S.C. 111(a) and each international application in compliance with 35 U.S.C. 371 will be published promptly after the expiration of a period of eighteen months from the earliest filing date for which a benefit is sought under title 35, United States Code, unless:

(1) The application is recognized by the Office as no longer pending;

(2) The application is national security classified (see § 5.2(c)), subject to a secrecy order under 35 U.S.C. 181, or under national security review;

(3) The application has issued as a patent in sufficient time to be removed from the publication process; or

(4) The application was filed with a nonpublication request in compliance with § 1.213(a).

(b) Provisional applications under 35 U.S.C. 111(b) shall not be published, and design applications under 35 U.S.C. chapter 16 and reissue applications under 35 U.S.C. chapter 25 shall not be published under this section.

(c) An application filed under 35 U.S.C. 111(a) will not be published until it includes the basic filing fee (§ 1.16(a) or § 1.16(c)) and any English translation required by § 1.52(d). The Office may delay publishing any application until it includes any application size fee required by the Office under § 1.16(s) or § 1.492(j), a specification having papers in compliance with § 1.52 and an abstract (§ 1.72(b)), drawings in compliance with § 1.84, a sequence listing in compliance with §§ 1.821 through 1.825 (if applicable), and the inventor's oath or declaration or application data sheet containing the information specified in § 1.63(b).

(d) The Office may refuse to publish an application, or to include a portion of an application in the patent application publication (§ 1.215), if publication of the application or portion thereof would violate Federal or state law, or if the application or portion thereof contains offensive or disparaging material.

(e) The publication fee set forth in § 1.18(d) must be paid in each application published under this section before the patent will be granted. If an application is subject to publication under this section, the sum specified in the notice of allowance under § 1.311 will also include the publication fee which must be paid within three months from the date of mailing of the notice of allowance to avoid abandonment of the application. This three-month period is not extendable. If the application is not published under this section, the publication fee (if paid) will be refunded.

[65 FR 57058, Sept. 20, 2000, as amended at 70 FR 3891, Jan. 27, 2005; 77 FR 48822, Aug. 14, 2012]

§ 1.213 Nonpublication request.

(a) If the invention disclosed in an application has not been and will not be the subject of an application filed in another country, or under a multilateral international agreement, that requires publication of applications eighteen months after filing, the application will not be published under 35 U.S.C. 122(b) and § 1.211 provided:

(1) A request (nonpublication request) is submitted with the application upon filing;

(2) The request states in a conspicuous manner that the application is not to be published under 35 U.S.C. 122(b);

(3) The request contains a certification that the invention disclosed in the application has not been and will not be the subject of an application filed in another country, or under a multilateral international agreement, that requires publication at eighteen months after filing; and

(4) The request is signed in compliance with § 1.33(b).

(b) The applicant may rescind a nonpublication request at any time. A request to rescind a nonpublication request under paragraph (a) of this section must:

(1) Identify the application to which it is directed;

(2) State in a conspicuous manner that the request that the application is not to be published under 35 U.S.C. 122(b) is rescinded; and

(3) Be signed in compliance with § 1.33(b).

(c) If an applicant who has submitted a nonpublication request under paragraph (a) of this section subsequently files an application directed to the invention disclosed in the application in which the nonpublication request was submitted in another country, or under a multilateral international agreement, that requires publication of applications eighteen months after filing, the applicant must notify the Office of such filing within forty-five days after the date of the filing of such foreign or international application. The failure to timely notify the Office of the filing of such foreign or international application shall result in abandonment of the application in which the nonpublication request was submitted (35 U.S.C. 122(b)(2)(B)(iii)).

§ 1.215 Patent application publication.

(a) The publication of an application under 35 U.S.C. 122(b) shall include a patent application publication. The date of publication shall be indicated on the patent application publication. The patent application publication will be based upon the specification and drawings deposited on the filing date of the application, as well as the application data sheet and/or the inventor's oath or declaration. The patent application publication may also be based upon amendments to the specification (other than the abstract or the claims) that are reflected in a substitute specification under § 1.125(b), amendments to the abstract under § 1.121(b), amendments to the claims that are reflected in a complete claim listing under § 1.121(c), and amendments to the drawings under § 1.121(d), provided that such substitute specification or amendment is submitted in sufficient time to be entered into the Office file wrapper of the application before technical preparations for publication of the application have begun. Technical preparations for publication of an application generally begin four months prior to the projected date of publication. The patent application publication of an application that has entered the national stage under 35 U.S.C. 371 may also include amendments made during the international stage. *See* paragraph (c) of this section for publication of an application based upon a copy of the application submitted via the Office electronic filing system.

(b) The patent application publication will include the name of the assignee, person to whom the inventor is under an obligation to assign the invention, or person who otherwise shows sufficient proprietary interest in the matter if that information is provided in the application data sheet in an application filed under § 1.46. Assignee information may be included on the patent application publication in other applications if the assignee information is provided in an application data sheet submitted in sufficient time to be entered into the Office file wrapper of the application before technical preparations for publication of the application have begun. Providing assignee information in the application data sheet does not substitute for compliance with any requirement of part 3 of this chapter to have an assignment recorded by the Office.

(c) At applicant's option, the patent application publication will be based upon the copy of the application (specification, drawings, and the application data sheet and/or the inventor's oath or declaration) as amended, provided that applicant supplies such a copy in compliance with the Office electronic filing system requirements within one month of the mailing date of the first Office communication that includes a confirmation number for the application, or fourteen months of the earliest filing date for which a benefit is sought under title 35, United States Code, whichever is later.

(d) If the copy of the application submitted pursuant to paragraph (c) of this section does not comply with the Office electronic filing system requirements, the Office will publish the application as provided in paragraph (a) of this section. If, however, the Office has not started the publication process, the Office may use an untimely filed copy of the application supplied by the applicant under paragraph (c) of this section in creating the patent application publication.

[65 FR 57058, Sept. 20, 2000, as amended at 69 FR 56544, Sept. 21, 2004; 77 FR 48822, Aug. 14, 2012]

§ 1.217 Publication of a redacted copy of an application.

(a) If an applicant has filed applications in one or more foreign countries, directly or through a multilateral international agreement, and such foreign-filed applications or the description of the invention in such foreign-filed applications is less extensive than the application or description of the invention in the application filed in the Office, the applicant may submit a redacted copy of the application filed in the Office for publication, eliminating any part or description of the invention that is not also contained in any of the corresponding applications filed in a foreign country. The Office will publish the application as provided in § 1.215(a) unless the applicant files a redacted copy of the application in compliance with this section within sixteen months after the earliest filing date for which a benefit is sought under title 35, United States Code.

(b) The redacted copy of the application must be submitted in compliance with the Office electronic filing system requirements. The title of the invention in the redacted copy of the application must correspond to the title of the application at the time the redacted copy of the application is submitted to the Office. If the redacted copy of the application does not comply with the Office electronic filing system requirements, the Office will publish the application as provided in § 1.215(a).

(c) The applicant must also concurrently submit in paper (§ 1.52(a)) to be filed in the application:

(1) A certified copy of each foreign-filed application that corresponds to the application for which a redacted copy is submitted;

(2) A translation of each such foreign-filed application that is in a language other than English, and a statement that the translation is accurate;

(3) A marked-up copy of the application showing the redactions in brackets; and

(4) A certification that the redacted copy of the application eliminates only the part or description of the invention that is not contained in any application filed in a foreign country, directly or through a multilateral international agreement, that corresponds to the application filed in the Office.

(d) The Office will provide a copy of the complete file wrapper and contents of an application for which a redacted copy was submitted under this section to any person upon written request pursuant to § 1.14(c)(2), unless applicant complies with the requirements of paragraphs (d)(1), (d)(2), and (d)(3) of this section.

(1) Applicant must accompany the submission required by paragraph (c) of this section with the following:

(i) A copy of any Office correspondence previously received by applicant including any desired redactions, and a second copy of all Office correspondence previously received by applicant showing the redacted material in brackets; and

(ii) A copy of each submission previously filed by the applicant including any desired redactions, and a second copy of each submission previously filed by the applicant showing the redacted material in brackets.

(2) In addition to providing the submission required by paragraphs (c) and (d)(1) of this section, applicant must:

(i) Within one month of the date of mailing of any correspondence from the Office, file a copy of such Office correspondence including any desired redactions, and a second copy of such Office correspondence showing the redacted material in brackets; and

(ii) With each submission by the applicant, include a copy of such submission including any desired redactions, and a second copy of such submission showing the redacted material in brackets.

(3) Each submission under paragraph (d)(1) or (d)(2) of this paragraph must also be accompanied by the processing fee set forth in § 1.17(i) and a certification that the redactions are limited to the elimination of material that is relevant only to the part or description of the invention that was not contained in the redacted copy of the application submitted for publication.

(e) The provisions of § 1.8 do not apply to the time periods set forth in this section.

§ 1.219 Early publication.

Applications that will be published under § 1.211 may be published earlier than as set forth in § 1.211(a) at the request of the applicant. Any request for early publication must be accompanied by the publication fee set forth in § 1.18(d). If the applicant does not submit a copy of the application in compliance with the Office electronic filing system requirements pursuant to § 1.215(c), the Office will publish the application as provided in § 1.215(a). No consideration will be given to requests for publication on a certain date, and such requests will be treated as a request for publication as soon as possible.

§ 1.221 Voluntary publication or republication of patent application publication.

(a) Any request for publication of an application filed before, but pending on, November 29, 2000, and any request for republication of an application previously published under § 1.211, must include a copy of the application in compliance with the Office electronic filing system requirements and be accompanied by the publication fee set forth in § 1.18(d) and the processing fee set forth in § 1.17(i). If the request does not comply with the requirements of this paragraph or the copy of the application does not comply with the Office electronic filing system requirements, the Office will not publish the application and will refund the publication fee.

(b) The Office will grant a request for a corrected or revised patent application publication other than as provided in paragraph (a) of this section only when the Office makes a material mistake which is apparent from Office records. Any request for a corrected or revised patent application publication other than as provided in paragraph (a) of this section must be filed within two months from the date of the patent application publication. This period is not extendable.

MISCELLANEOUS PROVISIONS

§ 1.248 Service of papers; manner of service; proof of service in cases other than interferences and trials.

(a) Service of papers must be on the attorney or agent of the party if there be such or on the party if there is no attorney or agent, and may be made in any of the following ways:

(1) By delivering a copy of the paper to the person served;

(2) By leaving a copy at the usual place of business of the person served with someone in his employment;

(3) When the person served has no usual place of business, by leaving a copy at the person's residence, with some person of suitable age and discretion who resides there;

(4) Transmission by first class mail. When service is by mail the date of mailing will be regarded as the date of service;

(5) Whenever it shall be satisfactorily shown to the Director that none of the above modes of obtaining or serving the paper is practicable, service may be by notice published in the *Official Gazette*.

(b) Papers filed in the Patent and Trademark Office which are required to be served shall contain proof of service. Proof of service may appear on or be affixed to papers filed. Proof of service shall include the date and manner of service. In the case of personal service, proof of service shall also include the name of any person served, certified by the person who made service. Proof of service may be made by:

(1) An acknowledgement of service by or on behalf of the person served or

(2) A statement signed by the attorney or agent containing the information required by this section.

(c) See § 41.106(e) or § 42.6(e) of this title for service of papers in contested cases or trials before the Patent Trial and Appeal Board.

[46 FR 29184, May 29, 1981, as amended at 49 FR 48454, Dec. 12, 1984; 69 FR 50000, Aug. 12, 2004; 69 FR 58260, Sept. 30, 2004; 77 FR 46626, Aug. 6, 2012]

§ 1.251 Unlocatable file.

(a) In the event that the Office cannot locate the file of an application, patent, or other patent-related proceeding after a reasonable search, the Office will notify the applicant or patentee and set a time period within which the applicant or patentee must comply with the notice in accordance with one of paragraphs (a)(1), (a)(2), or (a)(3) of this section.

(1) Applicant or patentee may comply with a notice under this section by providing:

(i) A copy of the applicant's or patentee's record (if any) of all of the correspondence between the Office and the applicant or patentee for such application, patent, or other proceeding (except for U.S. patent documents);

(ii) A list of such correspondence; and

(iii) A statement that the copy is a complete and accurate copy of the applicant's or patentee's record of all of the correspondence between the Office and the applicant or patentee for such application, patent, or other proceeding (except for U.S. patent documents), and whether applicant or patentee is aware of any correspondence between the Office and the applicant or patentee for such application, patent, or other proceeding that is not among applicant's or patentee's records.

(2) Applicant or patentee may comply with a notice under this section by:

(i) Producing the applicant's or patentee's record (if any) of all of the correspondence between the Office and the applicant or patentee for such application, patent, or other proceeding for the Office to copy (except for U.S. patent documents); and

(ii) Providing a statement that the papers produced by applicant or patentee are applicant's or patentee's complete record of all of the correspondence between the Office and the applicant or patentee for such application, patent, or other proceeding (except for U.S. patent documents), and whether applicant or patentee is aware of any correspondence between the Office and the applicant or patentee for such application, patent, or other proceeding that is not among applicant's or patentee's records.

(3) If applicant or patentee does not possess any record of the correspondence between the Office and the applicant or patentee for such application, patent, or other proceeding, applicant or patentee must comply with a notice under this section by providing a statement that applicant or patentee does not possess any record of the correspondence between the Office and the applicant or patentee for such application, patent, or other proceeding.

(b) With regard to a pending application, failure to comply with one of paragraphs (a)(1), (a)(2), or (a)(3) of this section within the time period set in the notice will result in abandonment of the application.

[65 FR 69451, Nov. 17, 2000]

Preissuance Submissions and Protests by Third Parties

§ 1.290 Submissions by third parties in applications.

(a) A third party may submit, for consideration and entry in the record of a patent application, any patents, published patent applications, or other printed publications of potential relevance to the examination of the application if the submission is made in accordance with 35 U.S.C. 122(e) and this section. A third-party submission may not be entered or considered by the Office if any part of the submission is not in compliance with 35 U.S.C. 122(e) and this section.

(b) Any third-party submission under this section must be filed prior to the earlier of:

(1) The date a notice of allowance under § 1.311 is given or mailed in the application; or

(2) The later of:

(i) Six months after the date on which the application is first published by the Office under 35 U.S.C. 122(b) and § 1.211, or

(ii) The date the first rejection under § 1.104 of any claim by the examiner is given or mailed during the examination of the application.

(c) Any third-party submission under this section must be made in writing.

(d) Any third-party submission under this section must include:

(1) A document list identifying the documents, or portions of documents, being submitted in accordance with paragraph (e) of this section;

(2) A concise description of the asserted relevance of each item identified in the document list;

(3) A legible copy of each item identified in the document list, other than U.S. patents and U.S. patent application publications;

(4) An English language translation of any non-English language item identified in the document list; and

(5) A statement by the party making the submission that:

(i) The party is not an individual who has a duty to disclose information with respect to the application under § 1.56; and

(ii) The submission complies with the requirements of 35 U.S.C. 122(e) and this section.

(e) The document list required by paragraph (d)(1) of this section must include a heading that identifies the list as a third-party submission under § 1.290, identify on each page of the list the application number of the application in which the submission is being filed, list U.S. patents and U.S. patent application publications in a separate section from other items, and identify each:

(1) U.S. patent by patent number, first named inventor, and issue date;

(2) U.S. patent application publication by patent application publication number, first named inventor, and publication date;

(3) Foreign patent or published foreign patent application by the country or patent office that issued the patent or published the application; the applicant, patentee, or first named inventor; an appropriate document number; and the publication date indicated on the patent or published application; and

(4) Non-patent publication by author (if any), title, pages being submitted, publication date, and, where available, publisher and place of publication. If no publication date is known, the third party must provide evidence of publication.

(f) Any third-party submission under this section must be accompanied by the fee set forth in § 1.17(p) for every ten items or fraction thereof identified in the document list.

(g) The fee otherwise required by paragraph (f) of this section is not required for a submission listing three or fewer total items that is accompanied by a statement by the party making the submission that, to the knowledge of the person signing the statement after making reasonable inquiry, the submission is the first and only submission under 35 U.S.C. 122(e) filed in the application by the party or a party in privity with the party.

(h) In the absence of a request by the Office, an applicant need not reply to a submission under this section.

(i) The provisions of § 1.8 do not apply to the time periods set forth in this section.

[77 FR 42173, July 17, 2012]

§ 1.291 Protests by the public against pending applications.

(a) A protest may be filed by a member of the public against a pending application, and it will be matched with the application file if it adequately identifies the patent application. A protest submitted within the time frame of paragraph (b) of this section, which is not matched, or not matched in a timely manner to permit review by the examiner during prosecution, due to inadequate identification, may not be entered and may be returned to the protestor where practical, or, if return is not practical, discarded.

(b) The protest will be entered into the record of the application if, in addition to complying with paragraph (c) of this section, the protest has been served upon the applicant in accordance with § 1.248, or filed with the Office in duplicate in the event service is not possible; and, except for paragraph (b)(1) of this section, the protest was filed prior to the date the application was published under § 1.211, or the date a notice of allowance under § 1.311 was given or mailed, whichever occurs first:

(1) If a protest is accompanied by the written consent of the applicant, the protest will be considered if the protest is filed prior to the date a notice of allowance under § 1.311 is given or mailed in the application.

(2) A statement must accompany a protest that it is the first protest submitted in the application by the real party in interest who is submitting the protest; or the protest must comply with paragraph (c)(5) of this section. This section does not apply to the first protest filed in an application.

(c) In addition to compliance with paragraphs (a) and (b) of this section, a protest must include:

(1) An information list of the documents, portions of documents, or other information being submitted, where each:

(i) U.S. patent is identified by patent number, first named inventor, and issue date;

(ii) U.S. patent application publication is identified by patent application publication number, first named inventor, and publication date;

(iii) Foreign patent or published foreign patent application is identified by the country or patent office that issued the patent or published the application; an appropriate document number; the applicant, patentee, or first named inventor; and the publication date indicated on the patent or published application;

(iv) Non-patent publication is identified by author (if any), title, pages being submitted, publication date, and, where available, publisher and place of publication; and

(v) Item of other information is identified by date, if known.

(2) A concise explanation of the relevance of each item identified in the information list pursuant to paragraph (c)(1) of this section;

(3) A legible copy of each item identified in the information list, other than U.S. patents and U.S. patent application publications;

(4) An English language translation of any non-English language item identified in the information list; and

(5) If it is a second or subsequent protest by the same real party in interest, an explanation as to why the issue(s) raised in the second or subsequent protest are significantly different than those raised earlier and why the significantly different issue(s) were not presented earlier, and a processing fee under § 1.17(i) must be submitted.

(d) A member of the public filing a protest in an application under this section will not receive any communication from the Office relating to the protest, other than the return of a self-addressed postcard which the member of the public may include with the protest in order to receive an acknowledgment by the Office that the protest has been received. The limited involvement of the member of the public filing a protest pursuant to this section ends with the filing of the protest, and no further submission on behalf of the protestor will be considered, unless the submission is made pursuant to paragraph (c)(5) of this section.

(e) Where a protest raising inequitable conduct issues satisfies the provisions of this section for entry, it will be entered into the application file, generally without comment on the inequitable conduct issues raised in it.

(f) In the absence of a request by the Office, an applicant need not reply to a protest.

(g) Protests that fail to comply with paragraphs (b) or (c) of this section may not be entered, and if not entered, will be returned to the protestor, or discarded, at the option of the Office.

[69 FR 56544, Sept. 21, 2004, as amended at 77 FR 42173, July 17, 2012]

§§ 1.292–1.297 [Reserved]

REVIEW OF PATENT AND TRADEMARK OFFICE DECISIONS BY COURT

§§ 1.301–1.304 [Reserved]

ALLOWANCE AND ISSUE OF PATENT

§ 1.311 Notice of allowance.

(a) If, on examination, it appears that the applicant is entitled to a patent under the law, a notice of allowance will be sent to the applicant at the correspondence address indicated in § 1.33. The notice of allowance shall specify a sum constituting the issue fee which must be paid within three months from the date of mailing of the notice of allowance to avoid abandonment of the application. The sum specified in the notice of allowance may also include the publication fee, in which case the issue fee and publication fee (§ 1.211(e)) must both be paid within three months from the date of mailing of the notice of allowance to avoid abandonment of the application. This three-month period is not extendable.

(b) An authorization to charge the issue fee or other post-allowance fees set forth in § 1.18 to a deposit account may be filed in an individual application only after mailing of the notice of allowance. The submission of either of the following after the mailing of a notice of allowance will operate as a request to charge the correct issue fee or any publication fee due to any deposit account identified in a previously filed authorization to charge such fees:

(1) An incorrect issue fee or publication fee; or

(2) A fee transmittal form (or letter) for payment of issue fee or publication fee.

[65 FR 57060, Sept. 20, 2000, as amended at 66 FR 67096, Dec. 28, 2001; 69 FR 56545, Sept. 21, 2004]

§ 1.312 Amendments after allowance.

No amendment may be made as a matter of right in an application after the mailing of the notice of allowance. Any amendment filed pursuant to this section must be filed before or with the payment of the issue fee, and may be entered on the recommendation of the primary examiner, approved by the Director, without withdrawing the application from issue.

[65 FR 14873, Mar. 20, 2000]

§ 1.313 Withdrawal from issue.

(a) Applications may be withdrawn from issue for further action at the initiative of the Office or upon petition by the applicant. To request that the Office withdraw an application from issue, applicant must file a petition under this section including the fee set forth in § 1.17(h) and a showing of good and sufficient reasons why withdrawal of the application from issue is necessary. A petition under this section is not required if a request for continued examination under § 1.114 is filed prior to payment of the issue fee. If the Office withdraws the application from issue, the Office will issue a new notice of allowance if the Office again allows the application.

(b) Once the issue fee has been paid, the Office will not withdraw the application from issue at its own initiative for any reason except:

(1) A mistake on the part of the Office;

(2) A violation of § 1.56 or illegality in the application;

(3) Unpatentability of one or more claims; or

(4) For an interference or derivation proceeding.

(c) Once the issue fee has been paid, the application will not be withdrawn from issue upon petition by the applicant for any reason except:

(1) Unpatentability of one of more claims, which petition must be accompanied by an unequivocal statement that one or more claims are unpatentable, an amendment to such claim or claims, and an explanation as to how the amendment causes such claim or claims to be patentable;

(2) Consideration of a request for continued examination in compliance with § 1.114; or

(3) Express abandonment of the application. Such express abandonment may be in favor of a continuing application.

(d) A petition under this section will not be effective to withdraw the application from issue unless it is actually received and granted by the appropriate officials before the date of issue. Withdrawal of an application from issue after payment of the issue fee may not be effective to avoid publication of application information.

[65 FR 14873, Mar. 20, 2000, as amended at 65 FR 50105, Aug. 16, 2000; 77 FR 46626, Aug. 6, 2012]

§ 1.314 Issuance of patent.

If applicant timely pays the issue fee, the Office will issue the patent in regular course unless the application is withdrawn from issue (§ 1.313) or the Office defers issuance of the patent. To request that the Office defer issuance of a patent, applicant must file a petition under this section including the fee set forth in § 1.17(h) and a showing of good and sufficient reasons why it is necessary to defer issuance of the patent.

[65 FR 54677, Sept. 8, 2000]

§ 1.315 Delivery of patent.

The patent will be delivered or mailed upon issuance to the correspondence address of record. See § 1.33(a).

[61 FR 42807, Aug. 19, 1996]

§ 1.316 Application abandoned for failure to pay issue fee.

If the issue fee is not paid within three months from the date of the notice of allowance, the application will be regarded as abandoned. Such an abandoned application will not be considered as pending before the Patent and Trademark Office.

[62 FR 53198, Oct. 10, 1997]

§ 1.317 Lapsed patents; delayed payment of balance of issue fee.

If the issue fee paid is the amount specified in the notice of allowance, but a higher amount is required at the time the issue fee is paid, any remaining balance of the issue fee is to be paid within three months from the date of notice thereof and, if not paid, the patent will lapse at the termination of the three-month period.

[62 FR 53198, Oct. 10, 1997]

§ 1.318 [Reserved]

DISCLAIMER

§ 1.321 Statutory disclaimers, including terminal disclaimers.

(a) A patentee owning the whole or any sectional interest in a patent may disclaim any complete claim or claims in a patent. In like manner any patentee may disclaim or dedicate to the public the entire term, or any terminal part of the term, of the patent granted. Such disclaimer is binding upon the grantee and its successors or assigns. A notice of the disclaimer is published in the *Official Gazette* and attached to the printed copies of the specification. The disclaimer, to be recorded in the Patent and Trademark Office, must:

(1) Be signed by the patentee, or an attorney or agent of record;

(2) Identify the patent and complete claim or claims, or term being disclaimed. A disclaimer which is not a disclaimer of a complete claim or claims, or term will be refused recordation;

(3) State the present extent of patentee's ownership interest in the patent; and

(4) Be accompanied by the fee set forth in § 1.20(d).

(b) An applicant may disclaim or dedicate to the public the entire term, or any terminal part of the term, of a patent to be granted. Such terminal disclaimer is binding upon the grantee and its successors or assigns. The terminal disclaimer, to be recorded in the Patent and Trademark Office, must:

(1) Be signed by the applicant or an attorney or agent of record;

(2) Specify the portion of the term of the patent being disclaimed;

(3) State the present extent of applicant's ownership interest in the patent to be granted; and

(4) Be accompanied by the fee set forth in § 1.20(d).

(c) A terminal disclaimer, when filed to obviate judicially created double patenting in a patent application or in a reexamination proceeding except as provided for in paragraph (d) of this section, must:

(1) Comply with the provisions of paragraphs (b)(2) through (b)(4) of this section;

(2) Be signed in accordance with paragraph (b)(1) of this section if filed in a patent application or in accordance with paragraph (a)(1) of this section if filed in a reexamination proceeding; and

(3) Include a provision that any patent granted on that application or any patent subject to the reexamination proceeding shall be enforceable only for and during such period that said patent is commonly owned with the application or patent which formed the basis for the judicially created double patenting.

(d) A terminal disclaimer, when filed in a patent application or in a reexamination proceeding to obviate double patenting based upon a patent or application that is not commonly owned but was disqualified as prior art as set forth in either § 1.104(c)(4)(ii) or (c)(5)(ii) as the result of activities undertaken within the scope of a joint research agreement, must:

(1) Comply with the provisions of paragraphs (b)(2) through (b)(4) of this section;

(2) Be signed in accordance with paragraph (b)(1) of this section if filed in a patent application or be signed in accordance with paragraph (a)(1) of this section if filed in a reexamination proceeding; and

(3) Include a provision waiving the right to separately enforce any patent granted on that application or any patent subject to the reexamination proceeding and the patent or any patent granted on the application which formed the basis for the double patenting, and that any patent granted on that application or any patent subject to the reexamination proceeding shall be enforceable only for and during such

period that said patent and the patent, or any patent granted on the application, which formed the basis for the double patenting are not separately enforced.

[58 FR 54510, Oct. 22, 1993, as amended at 61 FR 42807, Aug. 19, 1996; 70 FR 1824, Jan. 11, 2005; 70 FR 54266, Sept. 14, 2005; 77 FR 48822, Aug. 14, 2012; 78 FR 11059, Feb. 14, 2013]

CORRECTION OF ERRORS IN PATENT

§ 1.322 Certificate of correction of Office mistake.

(a)(1) The Director may issue a certificate of correction pursuant to 35 U.S.C. 254 to correct a mistake in a patent, incurred through the fault of the Office, which mistake is clearly disclosed in the records of the Office:

(i) At the request of the patentee or the patentee's assignee;

(ii) Acting *sua sponte* for mistakes that the Office discovers; or

(iii) Acting on information about a mistake supplied by a third party.

(2)(i) There is no obligation on the Office to act on or respond to a submission of information or request to issue a certificate of correction by a third party under paragraph (a)(1)(iii) of this section.

(ii) Papers submitted by a third party under this section will not be made of record in the file that they relate to nor be retained by the Office.

(3) If the request relates to a patent involved in an interference or trial before the Patent Trial and Appeal Board, the request must comply with the requirements of this section and be accompanied by a motion under § 41.121(a)(2), § 41.121(a)(3), or § 42.20 of this title.

(4) The Office will not issue a certificate of correction under this section without first notifying the patentee (including any assignee of record) at the correspondence address of record as specified in § 1.33(a) and affording the patentee or an assignee an opportunity to be heard.

(b) If the nature of the mistake on the part of the Office is such that a certificate of correction is deemed inappropriate in form, the Director may issue a corrected patent in lieu thereof as a more appropriate form for certificate of correction, without expense to the patentee.

(35 U.S.C. 254)

[24 FR 10332, Dec. 22, 1959, as amended at 49 FR 48454, Dec. 12, 1984; 65 FR 54677, Sept. 8, 2000; 69 FR 50001, Aug. 12, 2004; 77 FR 46626, Aug. 6, 2012]

§ 1.323 Certificate of correction of applicant's mistake.

The Office may issue a certificate of correction under the conditions specified in 35 U.S.C. 255 at the request of the patentee or the patentee's assignee, upon payment of the fee set forth in § 1.20(a). If the request relates to a patent involved in an interference or trial before the Patent Trial and Appeal Board, the request must comply with the requirements of this section and be accompanied by a motion under § 41.121(a)(2), § 41.121(a)(3) or § 42.20 of this title.

[77 FR 46626, Aug. 6, 2012]

§ 1.324 Correction of inventorship in patent, pursuant to 35 U.S.C. 256.

(a) Whenever through error a person is named in an issued patent as the inventor, or an inventor is not named in an issued patent, the Director, pursuant to 35 U.S.C. 256, may, on application of all the parties and assignees, or on order of a court before which such matter is called in question, issue a certificate naming only the actual inventor or inventors.

(b) Any request to correct inventorship of a patent pursuant to paragraph (a) of this section must be accompanied by:

(1) A statement from each person who is being added as an inventor and each person who is currently named as an inventor either agreeing to the change of inventorship or stating that he or she has no disagreement in regard to the requested change;

(2) A statement from all assignees of the parties submitting a statement under paragraph (b)(1) of this section agreeing to the change of inventorship in the patent, which statement must comply with the requirements of § 3.73(c) of this chapter; and

(3) The fee set forth in § 1.20(b).

(c) For correction of inventorship in an application, *see* § 1.48.

(d) In an interference under part 41, subpart D, of this title, a request for correction of inventorship in a patent must be in the form of a motion under § 41.121(a)(2) of this title. In a contested case under part 42, subpart D, of this title, a request for correction of inventorship in a patent must be in the form of a motion under § 42.22 of this title. The motion under § 41.121(a)(2) or § 42.22 of this title must comply with the requirements of this section.

[77 FR 48822, Aug. 14, 2012]

§ 1.325 Other mistakes not corrected.

Mistakes other than those provided for in §§ 1.322, 1.323, 1.324, and not affording legal grounds for reissue or for reexamination, will not be corrected after the date of the patent.

(35 U.S.C. 6, Pub. L. 97–247)

[48 FR 2714, Jan. 20, 1983]

ARBITRATION AWARDS

§§ 1.331–1.334 [Reserved]

§ 1.335 Filing of notice of arbitration awards.

(a) Written notice of any award by an arbitrator pursuant to 35 U.S.C. 294 must be filed in the Patent and Trademark Office by the patentee, or the patentee's assignee or licensee. If the award involves more than one patent a separate notice must be filed for placement in the file of each patent. The notice must set forth the patent number, the names of the inventor and patent owner, and the names and addresses of the parties to the arbitration. The notice must also include a copy of the award.

(b) If an award by an arbitrator pursuant to 35 U.S.C. 294 is modified by a court, the party requesting the modification must file in the Patent and Trademark Office, a notice of the modification for placement in the file of each patent to which the modification applies. The notice must set forth the patent number, the names of the inventor and patent owner, and the names and addresses of the parties to the arbitration. The notice must also include a copy of the court's order modifying the award.

(c) Any award by an arbitrator pursuant to 35 U.S.C. 294 shall be unenforceable until any notices required by paragraph (a) or (b) of this section are filed in the Patent and Trademark Office. If any required notice is not filed by the party designated in paragraph (a) or (b) of this section, any party to the arbitration proceeding may file such a notice.

(35 U.S.C. 6, Pub. L. 97–247)

[48 FR 2714, Jan. 20, 1983]

AMENDMENT OF RULES

§ 1.351 Amendments to rules will be published.

All amendments to the regulations in this part will be published in the *Official Gazette* and in the FEDERAL REGISTER.

§ 1.352 [Reserved]

MAINTENANCE FEES

§ 1.362 Time for payment of maintenance fees.

(a) Maintenance fees as set forth in §§ 1.20 (e) through (g) are required to be paid in all patents based on applications filed on or after December 12, 1980, except as noted in paragraph (b) of this section, to maintain a patent in force beyond 4, 8 and 12 years after the date of grant.

(b) Maintenance fees are not required for any plant patents or for any design patents. Maintenance fees are not required for a reissue patent if the patent being reissued did not require maintenance fees.

(c) The application filing dates for purposes of payment of maintenance fees are as follows:

(1) For an application not claiming benefit of an earlier application, the actual United States filing date of the application.

(2) For an application claiming benefit of an earlier foreign application under 35 U.S.C. 119, the United States filing date of the application.

(3) For a continuing (continuation, division, continuation-in-part) application claiming the benefit of a prior patent application under 35 U.S.C. 120, the actual United States filing date of the continuing application.

(4) For a reissue application, including a continuing reissue application claiming the benefit of a reissue application under 35 U.S.C. 120, United States filing date of the original non-reissue application on which the patent reissued is based.

(5) For an international application which has entered the United States as a Designated Office under 35 U.S.C. 371, the international filing date granted under Article 11(1) of the Patent Cooperation Treaty which is considered to be the United States filing date under 35 U.S.C. 363.

(d) Maintenance fees may be paid in patents without surcharge during the periods extending respectively from:

(1) 3 years through 3 years and 6 months after grant for the first maintenance fee,

(2) 7 years through 7 years and 6 months after grant for the second maintenance fee, and

(3) 11 years through 11 years and 6 months after grant for the third maintenance fee.

(e) Maintenance fees may be paid with the surcharge set forth in § 1.20(h) during the respective grace periods after:

(1) 3 years and 6 months and through the day of the 4th anniversary of the grant for the first maintenance fee.

(2) 7 years and 6 months and through the day of the 8th anniversary of the grant for the second maintenance fee, and

(3) 11 years and 6 months and through the day of the 12th anniversary of the grant for the third maintenance fee.

(f) If the last day for paying a maintenance fee without surcharge set forth in paragraph (d) of this section, or the last day for paying a maintenance fee with surcharge set forth in paragraph (e) of this section, falls on a Saturday, Sunday, or a federal holiday within the District of Columbia, the maintenance fee and any necessary surcharge may be paid under paragraph (d) or paragraph (e) respectively on the next succeeding day which is not a Saturday, Sunday, or federal holiday.

(g) Unless the maintenance fee and any applicable surcharge is paid within the time periods set forth in paragraphs (d), (e) or (f) of this section, the patent will expire as of the end of the grace period set forth in paragraph (e) of this section. A patent which expires for the failure to pay the maintenance fee will expire at the end of the same date (anniversary date) the patent was granted in the 4th, 8th, or 12th year after grant.

(h) The periods specified in §§ 1.362 (d) and (e) with respect to a reissue application, including a continuing reissue application thereof, are counted from the date of grant of the original non-reissue application on which the reissued patent is based.

[49 FR 34724, Aug. 31, 1984, as amended at 56 FR 65154, Dec. 13, 1991; 58 FR 54511, Oct. 22, 1993]

§ 1.363 Fee address for maintenance fee purposes.

(a) All notices, receipts, refunds, and other communications relating to payment or refund of maintenance fees will be directed to the correspondence address used during prosecution of the application as indicated in § 1.33(a) unless:

(1) A fee address for purposes of payment of maintenance fees is set forth when submitting the issue fee, or

(2) A change in the correspondence address for all purposes is filed after payment of the issue fee, or

(3) A fee address or a change in the "fee address" is filed for purposes of receiving notices, receipts and other correspondence relating to the payment of maintenance fees after the payment of the issue fee, in which instance, the latest such address will be used.

(b) An assignment of a patent application or patent does not result in a change of the "correspondence address" or "fee address" for maintenance fee purposes.

(c) A fee address must be an address associated with a Customer Number.

[49 FR 34725, Aug. 31, 1984, as amended at 69 FR 29878, May 26, 2004]

§ 1.366 Submission of maintenance fees.

(a) The patentee may pay maintenance fees and any necessary surcharges, or any person or organization may pay maintenance fees and any necessary surcharges on behalf of a patentee. Authorization by the patentee need not be filed in the Patent and Trademark Office to pay maintenance fees and any necessary surcharges on behalf of the patentee.

(b) A maintenance fee and any necessary surcharge submitted for a patent must be submitted in the amount due on the date the maintenance fee and any necessary surcharge are paid. A maintenance fee or surcharge may be paid in the manner set forth in § 1.23 or by an authorization to charge a deposit account established pursuant to § 1.25. Payment of a maintenance fee and any necessary surcharge or the authorization to charge a deposit account must be submitted within the periods set forth in § 1.362 (d), (e), or (f). Any payment or authorization of maintenance fees and surcharges filed at any other time will not be accepted and will not serve as a payment of the maintenance fee except insofar as a delayed payment of the maintenance fee is accepted by the Director in an expired patent pursuant to a petition filed under § 1.378. Any authorization to charge a deposit account must authorize the immediate charging of the maintenance fee and any necessary surcharge to the deposit account. Payment of less than the required amount, payment in a manner other than that set forth § 1.23, or in the filing of an authorization to charge a deposit account having insufficient funds will not constitute payment of a maintenance fee or surcharge on a patent. The procedures set forth in § 1.8 or § 1.10 may be utilized in paying maintenance fees and any necessary surcharges.

(c) In submitting maintenance fees and any necessary surcharges, identification of the patents for which maintenance fees are being paid must include the patent number, and the application number of the United States application for the patent on which the maintenance fee is being paid. If the payment includes identification of only the patent number (*i.e.*, does not identify the application number of the United States application for the patent on which the maintenance fee is being paid), the Office may apply the payment to the patent identified by patent number in the payment or may return the payment.

(d) Payment of maintenance fees and any surcharges should identify the fee being paid for each patent as to whether it is the 3½-, 7½-, or 11½-year fee, whether small entity status is being changed or claimed, the amount of the maintenance fee and any surcharge being paid, and any assigned customer number. If the maintenance fee and any necessary surcharge is being paid on a reissue patent, the payment must identify the reissue patent by reissue patent number and reissue application number as required by paragraph (c) of this section and should also include the original patent number.

(e) Maintenance fee payments and surcharge payments relating thereto must be submitted separate from any other payments for fees or charges, whether submitted in the manner set forth in § 1.23 or by an authorization to charge a deposit account. If maintenance fee and surcharge payments for more than one patent are submitted together, they should be submitted on as few sheets as possible with the patent numbers listed in increasing patent number order. If the payment submitted is insufficient to cover the maintenance fees and surcharges for all the listed patents, the payment will be applied in the order the patents are listed, beginning at the top of the listing.

(f) Notification of any change in status resulting in loss of entitlement to small entity status must be filed in a patent prior to paying, or at the time of paying, the earliest maintenance fee due after the date on which status as a small entity is no longer appropriate. See § 1.27(g).

(g) Maintenance fees and surcharges relating thereto will not be refunded except in accordance with §§ 1.26 and 1.28(a).

[49 FR 34725, Aug. 31, 1984, as amended at 58 FR 54503, Oct. 22, 1993; 62 FR 53199, Oct. 10, 1997; 65 FR 54677, Sept. 8, 2000; 65 FR 78960, Dec. 18, 2000]

§ 1.377 Review of decision refusing to accept and record payment of a maintenance fee filed prior to expiration of patent.

(a) Any patentee who is dissatisfied with the refusal of the Patent and Trademark Office to accept and record a maintenance fee which was filed prior to the expiration of the patent may petition the Director to accept and record the maintenance fee.

(b) Any petition under this section must be filed within two months of the action complained of, or within such other time as may be set in the action complained of, and must be accompanied by the fee set forth in § 1.17(g). The petition may include a request that the petition fee be refunded if the refusal to accept and record the maintenance fee is determined to result from an error by the Patent and Trademark Office.

(c) Any petition filed under this section must comply with the requirements of § 1.181(b) and must be signed by an attorney or agent registered to practice before the Patent and Trademark Office, or by the patentee, the assignee, or other party in interest.

[49 FR 34725, Aug. 31, 1984, as amended at 62 FR 53199, Oct. 10, 1997; 69 FR 56545, Sept. 21, 2004]

§ 1.378 Acceptance of delayed payment of maintenance fee in expired patent to reinstate patent.

(a) The Director may accept the payment of any maintenance fee due on a patent after expiration of the patent if, upon petition, the delay in payment of the maintenance fee is shown to the satisfaction of the Director to have been unavoidable (paragraph (b) of this section) or unintentional (paragraph (c) of this section) and if the surcharge required by § 1.20(i) is paid as a condition of accepting payment of the maintenance fee. If the Director accepts payment of the maintenance fee upon petition, the patent shall be considered as not having expired, but will be subject to the conditions set forth in 35 U.S.C. 41(c)(2).

(b) Any petition to accept an unavoidably delayed payment of a maintenance fee filed under paragraph (a) of this section must include:

(1) The required maintenance fee set forth in § 1.20 (e) through (g);

(2) The surcharge set forth in § 1.20(i)(1); and

(3) A showing that the delay was unavoidable since reasonable care was taken to ensure that the maintenance fee would be paid timely and that the petition was filed promptly after the patentee was notified of, or otherwise became aware of, the expiration of the patent. The showing must enumerate the steps taken to ensure timely payment of the maintenance fee, the date and the manner in which patentee became aware of the expiration of the patent, and the steps taken to file the petition promptly.

(c) Any petition to accept an unintentionally delayed payment of a maintenance fee filed under paragraph (a) of this section must be filed within twenty-four months after the six-month grace period provided in § 1.362(e) and must include:

(1) The required maintenance fee set forth in § 1.20 (e) through (g);

(2) The surcharge set forth in § 1.20(i)(2); and

(3) A statement that the delay in payment of the maintenance fee was unintentional.

(d) Any petition under this section must be signed by an attorney or agent registered to practice before the Patent and Trademark Office, or by the patentee, the assignee, or other party in interest.

(e) Reconsideration of a decision refusing to accept a maintenance fee upon petition filed pursuant to paragraph (a) of this section may be obtained by filing a petition for reconsideration within two months of, or such other time as set in the decision refusing to accept the delayed payment of the maintenance fee. Any such petition for reconsideration must be accompanied by the petition fee set forth in § 1.17(f). After the decision on the petition for reconsideration, no further reconsideration or review of the matter will be undertaken by the Director. If the delayed payment of the maintenance fee is not accepted, the maintenance fee and the surcharge set forth in § 1.20(i) will be refunded following the decision on the petition for reconsideration, or after the expiration of the time for filing such a petition for reconsideration, if none is filed. Any petition fee under this section will not be refunded unless the refusal to accept and record the maintenance fee is determined to result from an error by the Patent and Trademark Office.

[49 FR 34726, Aug. 31, 1984, as amended at 50 FR 9383, Mar. 7, 1985; 58 FR 44282, Aug. 20, 1993; 62 FR 53199, Oct. 10, 1997; 69 FR 56545, Sept. 21, 2004]

Subpart C—International Processing Provisions

AUTHORITY: Secs. 1.401 to 1.499 also issued under 35 U.S.C. 41 and 351 through 376.

SOURCE: 43 FR 20466, May 11, 1978, unless otherwise noted.

GENERAL INFORMATION

§ 1.401 Definitions of terms under the Patent Cooperation Treaty.

(a) The abbreviation *PCT* and the term *Treaty* mean the Patent Cooperation Treaty.

(b) *International Bureau* means the World Intellectual Property Organization located in Geneva, Switzerland.

(c) *Administrative Instructions* means that body of instructions for operating under the Patent Cooperation Treaty referred to in PCT Rule 89.

(d) *Request*, when capitalized, means that element of the international application described in PCT Rules 3 and 4.

(e) *International application*, as used in this subchapter is defined in § 1.9(b).

(f) *Priority date* for the purpose of computing time limits under the Patent Cooperation Treaty is defined in PCT Art. 2 (xi). Note also § 1.465.

(g) *Demand*, when capitalized, means that document filed with the International Preliminary Examining Authority which requests an international preliminary examination.

(h) *Annexes* means amendments made to the claims, description or the drawings before the International Preliminary Examining Authority.

(i) Other terms and expressions in this subpart C not defined in this section are to be taken in the sense indicated in PCT Art. 2 and 35 U.S.C. 351.

[43 FR 20466, May 11, 1978, as amended at 52 FR 20047, May 28, 1987]

§ 1.412 The United States Receiving Office.

(a) The United States Patent and Trademark Office is a Receiving Office only for applicants who are residents or nationals of the United States of America.

(b) The Patent and Trademark Office, when acting as a Receiving Office, will be identified by the full title "United States Receiving Office" or by the abbreviation "RO/US."

(c) The major functions of the Receiving Office include:

(1) According of international filing dates to international applications meeting the requirements of PCT Art. 11(1), and PCT Rule 20;

(2) Assuring that international applications meet the standards for format and content of PCT Art. 14(1), PCT Rule 9, 26, 29.1, 37, 38, 91, and portions of PCT Rules 3 through 11;

(3) Collecting and, when required, transmitting fees due for processing international applications (PCT Rule 14, 15, 16);

(4) Transmitting the record and search copies to the International Bureau and International Searching Authority, respectively (PCT Rules 22 and 23); and

(5) Determining compliance with applicable requirements of part 5 of this chapter.

(6) Reviewing and, unless prescriptions concerning national security prevent the application from being so transmitted (PCT Rule 19.4), transmitting the international application to the International Bureau for processing in its capacity as a Receiving Office:

(i) Where the United States Receiving Office is not the competent Receiving Office under PCT Rule 19.1 or 19.2 and § 1.421(a); or

(ii) Where the international application is not in English but is in a language accepted under PCT Rule 12.1(a) by the International Bureau as a Receiving Office; or

(iii) Where there is agreement and authorization in accordance with PCT Rule 19.4(a)(iii).

[43 FR 20466, May 11, 1978, as amended at 60 FR 21439, May 2, 1995; 63 FR 29617, June 1, 1998]

§ 1.413 The United States International Searching Authority.

(a) Pursuant to appointment by the Assembly, the United States Patent and Trademark Office will act as an International Searching Authority for international applications filed in the United States Receiving Office and in other Receiving Offices as may be agreed upon by the Director, in accordance with the agreement between the Patent and Trademark Office and the International Bureau (PCT Art. 16(3)(b)).

(b) The Patent and Trademark Office, when acting as an International Searching Authority, will be identified by the full title "United States International Searching Authority" or by the abbreviation "ISA/US."

(c) The major functions of the International Searching Authority include:

(1) Approving or establishing the title and abstract;

(2) Considering the matter of unity of invention;

(3) Conducting international and international-type searches and preparing international and international-type search reports (PCT Art. 15, 17 and 18, and PCT Rules 25, 33 to 45 and 47), and issuing declarations that no international search report will be established (PCT Article 17(2)(a));

(4) Preparing written opinions of the International Searching Authority in accordance with PCT Rule 43*bis* (when necessary); and

(5) Transmitting the international search report and the written opinion of the International Searching Authority to the applicant and the International Bureau.

[43 FR 20466, May 11, 1978, as amended at 68 FR 59886, Oct. 20, 2003]

§ 1.414 The United States Patent and Trademark Office as a Designated Office or Elected Office.

(a) The United States Patent and Trademark Office will act as a Designated Office or Elected Office for international applications in which the United States of America has been designated or elected as a State in which patent protection is desired.

(b) The United States Patent and Trademark Office, when acting as a Designated Office or Elected Office during international processing will be identified by the full title "United States Designated Office" or by the abbreviation "DO/US" or by the full title "United States Elected Office" or by the abbreviation "EO/US".

(c) The major functions of the United States Designated Office or Elected Office in respect to international applications in which the United States of America has been designated or elected, include:

(1) Receiving various notifications throughout the international stage and

(2) National stage processing for international applications entering the national stage under 35 U.S.C. 371.

[52 FR 20047, May 28, 1987, as amended at 77 FR 48823, Aug. 14, 2012]

§ 1.415 The International Bureau.

(a) The International Bureau is the World Intellectual Property Organization located at Geneva, Switzerland. It is the international intergovernmental organization which acts as the coordinating body under the Treaty and the Regulations (PCT Art. 2 (xix) and 35 U.S.C. 351 (h)).

(b) The major functions of the International Bureau include:

(1) Publishing of international applications and the International Gazette;

(2) Transmitting copies of international applications to Designated Offices;

(3) Storing and maintaining record copies; and

(4) Transmitting information to authorities pertinent to the processing of specific international applications.

§ 1.416 The United States International Preliminary Examining Authority.

(a) Pursuant to appointment by the Assembly, the United States Patent and Trademark Office will act as an International Preliminary Examining Authority for international applications filed in the United States Receiving Office and in other Receiving Offices as may be agreed upon by the Director, in accordance with agreement between the Patent and Trademark Office and the International Bureau.

(b) The United States Patent and Trademark Office, when acting as an International Preliminary Examining Authority, will be identified by the full title "United States International Preliminary Examining Authority" or by the abbreviation "IPEA/US."

(c) The major functions of the International Preliminary Examining Authority include:

(1) Receiving and checking for defects in the Demand;

(2) Forwarding Demands in accordance with PCT Rule 59.3;

(3) Collecting the handling fee for the International Bureau and the preliminary examination fee for the United States International Preliminary Examining Authority;

(4) Informing applicant of receipt of the Demand;

(5) Considering the matter of unity of invention;

(6) Providing an international preliminary examination report which is a non-binding opinion on the questions of whether the claimed invention appears: to be novel, to involve an inventive step (to be nonobvious), and to be industrially applicable; and

(7) Transmitting the international preliminary examination report to applicant and the International Bureau.

[52 FR 20047, May 28, 1987, as amended at 63 FR 29617, June 1, 1998]

§ 1.417 Submission of translation of international publication.

The submission of an English language translation of the publication of an international application pursuant to 35 U.S.C. 154(d)(4) must clearly identify the international application to which it pertains (§ 1.5(a)) and be clearly identified as a submission pursuant to 35 U.S.C. 154(d)(4). Otherwise, the submission will be treated as a filing under 35 U.S.C. 111(a). Such submissions should be marked "Mail Stop PCT."

[68 FR 71007, Dec. 22, 2003]

§ 1.419 Display of currently valid control number under the Paperwork Reduction Act.

(a) Pursuant to the Paperwork Reduction Act of 1995 (44 U.S.C. 3501 *et seq.*), the collection of information in this subpart has been reviewed and approved by the Office of Management and Budget under control number 0651–0021.

(b) Notwithstanding any other provision of law, no person is required to respond to nor shall a person be subject to a penalty for failure to comply with a collection of information subject to the requirements of the Paperwork Reduction Act unless that collection of information displays a currently valid Office of Management and Budget control number. This section constitutes the display required by 44 U.S.C. 3512(a) and 5 CFR 1320.5(b)(2)(i) for the collection of information under Office of Management and Budget control number 0651–0021 (see 5 CFR 1320.5(b)(2)(ii)(D)).

[63 FR 29617, June 1, 1998]

WHO MAY FILE AN INTERNATIONAL APPLICATION

§ 1.421 Applicant for international application.

(a) Only residents or nationals of the United States of America may file international applications in the United States Receiving Office. If an international application does not include an applicant who is indicated as being a resident or national of the United States of America, and at least one applicant:

(1) Has indicated a residence or nationality in a PCT Contracting State, or

(2) Has no residence or nationality indicated, applicant will be so notified and, if the international application includes a fee amount equivalent to that required by § 1.445(a)(4), the international application will be forwarded for processing to the International Bureau acting as a Receiving Office (*see also* § 1.412(c)(6)).

(b) Although the United States Receiving Office will accept international applications filed by any applicant who is a resident or national of the United States of America for international processing, for the purposes of the designation of the United States, an international application will be accepted by the Patent and Trademark Office for the national stage only if the applicant is the inventor or other person as provided in § 1.422 or § 1.424. Joint inventors must jointly apply for an international application.

(c) A registered attorney or agent of the applicant may sign the international application Request and file the international application for the applicant. A separate power of attorney from each applicant may be required.

(d) Any indication of different applicants for the purpose of different Designated Offices must be shown on the Request portion of the international application.

(e) Requests for changes in the indications concerning the applicant, agent, or common representative of an international application shall be made in accordance with PCT Rule 92*bis* and may be required to be signed by all applicants.

(f) Requests for withdrawals of the international application, designations, priority claims, the Demand, or elections shall be made in accordance with PCT Rule 90*bis* and must be signed by all applicants. A separate power of attorney from the applicants will be required for the purposes of any request for a withdrawal in accordance with PCT Rule 90*bis* which is not signed by all applicants.

[77 FR 48823, Aug. 14, 2012]

§ 1.422 Legal representative as applicant in an international application.

If an inventor is deceased or under legal incapacity, the legal representative of the inventor may be an applicant in an international application which designates the United States of America.

[77 FR 48823, Aug. 14, 2012]

§ 1.423 [Reserved]

§ 1.424 Assignee, obligated assignee, or person having sufficient proprietary interest as applicant in an international application.

(a) A person to whom the inventor has assigned or is under an obligation to assign the invention may be an applicant in an international application which designates the United States of America. A person who otherwise shows sufficient proprietary interest in the matter may be an applicant in an international application which designates the United States of America on proof of the pertinent facts and a showing that such action is appropriate to preserve the rights of the parties.

(b) Neither any showing required under paragraph (a) of this section nor documentary evidence of ownership or proprietary interest will be required or considered by the Office in the international stage, but will be required in the national stage in accordance with the conditions and requirements of § 1.46.

[77 FR 48823, Aug. 14, 2012]

THE INTERNATIONAL APPLICATION

§ 1.431 International application requirements.

(a) An international application shall contain, as specified in the Treaty and the Regulations, a Request, a description, one or more claims, an abstract, and one or more drawings (where required). (PCT Art. 3(2) and section 207 of the Administrative Instructions.)

(b) An international filing date will be accorded by the United States Receiving Office, at the time to receipt of the international application, provided that:

(1) At least one applicant (§ 1.421) is a United States resident or national and the papers filed at the time of receipt of the international application so indicate (35 U.S.C. 361(a), PCT Art. 11(1)(i)).

(2) The international application is in the English language (35 U.S.C. 361(c), PCT Art. 11(1)(ii)).

(3) The international application contains at least the following elements (PCT Art. 11(1)(iii)):

(i) An indication that it is intended as an international application (PCT Rule 4.2);

(ii) The designation of at least one Contracting State of the International Patent Cooperation Union (§ 1.432);

(iii) The name of the applicant, as prescribed (note §§ 1.421, 1.422, and 1.424);

(iv) A part which on the face of it appears to be a description; and

(v) A part which on the face of it appears to be a claim.

(c) Payment of the international filing fee (PCT Rule 15.2) and the transmittal and search fees (§ 1.445) may be made in full at the time the international application papers required by paragraph (b) of this section are deposited or within one month thereafter. The international filing, transmittal, and search fee payable is the international filing, transmittal, and search fee in effect on the receipt date of the international application.

(1) If the international filing, transmittal and search fees are not paid within one month from the date of receipt of the international application and prior to the sending of a notice of deficiency which imposes a late payment fee, applicant will be notified and given one month within which to pay the deficient fees plus the late payment fee. Subject to paragraph (c)(2) of this section, the late payment fee will be equal to the greater of:

(i) Fifty percent of the amount of the deficient fees; or

(ii) An amount equal to the transmittal fee;

(2) The late payment fee shall not exceed an amount equal to fifty percent of the international filing fee not taking into account any fee for each sheet of the international application in excess of thirty sheets (PCT Rule 16*bis*).

(3) The one-month time limit set pursuant to paragraph (c) of this section to pay deficient fees may not be extended.

(d) If the payment needed to cover the transmittal fee, the international filing fee, the search fee, and the late payment fee pursuant to paragraph (c) of this section is not timely made in accordance with PCT Rule 16*bis*.1(e), the Receiving Office will declare the international application withdrawn under PCT Article 14(3)(a).

[43 FR 20466, May 11, 1978, as amended at 50 FR 9383, Mar. 7, 1985; 52 FR 20047, May 28, 1987; 58 FR 4344, Jan. 14, 1993; 63 FR 29618, June 1, 1998; 68 FR 59887, Oct. 20, 2003; 68 FR 67805, Dec. 4, 2003; 77 FR 48823, Aug. 14, 2012]

§ 1.432 Designation of States by filing an international application.

The filing of an international application request shall constitute:

(a) The designation of all Contracting States that are bound by the Treaty on the international filing date;

(b) An indication that the international application is, in respect of each designated State to which PCT Article 43 or 44 applies, for the grant of every kind of protection which is available by way of the designation of that State; and

(c) An indication that the international application is, in respect of each designated State to which PCT Article 45(1) applies, for the grant of a regional patent and also, unless PCT Article 45(2) applies, a national patent.

[68 FR 59887, Oct. 20, 2003]

§ 1.433 Physical requirements of international application.

(a) The international application and each of the documents that may be referred to in the check list of the Request (PCT Rule 3.3(a)(ii)) shall be filed in one copy only.

(b) All sheets of the international application must be on A4 size paper (21.0 × 29.7 cm.).

(c) Other physical requirements for international applications are set forth in PCT Rule 11 and sections 201–207 of the Administrative Instructions.

§ 1.434 The request.

(a) The request shall be made on a standardized form (PCT Rules 3 and 4). Copies of printed Request forms are available from the United States Patent and Trademark Office. Letters requesting printed forms should be marked "Mail Stop PCT."

(b) The Check List portion of the Request form should indicate each document accompanying the international application on filing.

(c) All information, for example, addresses, names of States and dates, shall be indicated in the Request as required by PCT Rule 4 and Administrative Instructions 110 and 201.

(d) For the purposes of the designation of the United States of America, an international application shall include:

(1) The name of the inventor; and

(2) A reference to any prior-filed national application or international application designating the United States of America, if the benefit of the filing date for the prior-filed application is to be claimed.

(e) An international application may also include in the Request a declaration of the inventors as provided for in PCT Rule 4.17(iv).

[43 FR 20466, May 11, 1978, as amended at 58 FR 4345, Jan. 14, 1993; 66 FR 16006, Mar. 22, 2001; 66 FR 67096, Dec. 28, 2001; 68 FR 14337, Mar. 25, 2003; 68 FR 59887, Oct. 20, 2003]

§ 1.435 The description.

(a) The application must meet the requirements as to the content and form of the description set forth in PCT Rules 5, 9, 10, and 11 and sections 204 and 208 of the Administrative Instructions.

(b) In international applications designating the United States the description must contain upon filing an indication of the best mode contemplated by the inventor for carrying out the claimed invention.

[43 FR 20466, May 11, 1978, as amended at 63 FR 29618, June 1, 1998]

§ 1.436 The claims.

The requirements as to the content and format of claims are set forth in PCT Art. 6 and PCT Rules 6, 9, 10 and 11 and shall be adhered to. The number of the claims shall be reasonable, considering the nature of the invention claimed.

§ 1.437 The drawings.

(a) Drawings are required when they are necessary for the understanding of the invention (PCT Art. 7).

(b) The physical requirements for drawings are set forth in PCT Rule 11 and shall be adhered to.

[72 FR 51563, Sept. 10, 2007]

§ 1.438 The abstract.

(a) Requirements as to the content and form of the abstract are set forth in PCT Rule 8, and shall be adhered to.

(b) Lack of an abstract upon filing of an international application will not affect the granting of a filing date. However, failure to furnish an abstract within one month from the date of the notification by the Receiving Office will result in the international appplication being declared withdrawn.

FEES

§ 1.445 International application filing, processing and search fees.

(a) The following fees and charges for international applications are established by law or by the Director under the authority of 35 U.S.C. 376:

(1) A transmittal fee (*see* 35 U.S.C. 361(d) and PCT Rule 14) consisting of:

(i) A basic portion:

(A) For an international application having a receipt date that is on or after January 1, 2014:	
By a micro entity (§ 1.29)	$60.00
By a small entity (§ 1.27(a))	$120.00
By other than a small or micro entity	$240.00
(B) For an international application having a receipt date that is before January 1, 2014	$240.00
(ii) A non-electronic filing fee portion for any international application designating the United States of America that is filed on or after November 15, 2011, other than by the Office electronic filing system, except for a plant application:	
By a small entity (§ 1.27(a))	$200.00
By other than a small entity	$400.00
(2) A search fee (*see* 35 U.S.C. 361(d) and PCT Rule 16):	
(i) For an international application having a receipt date that is on or after January 1, 2014:	
By a micro entity (§ 1.29)	$520.00
By a small entity (§ 1.27(a))	$1,040.00
By other than a small or micro entity	$2,080.00
(ii) For an international application having a receipt date that is before January 1, 2014	$2,080.00
(3) A supplemental search fee when required, per additional invention:	

(i) For an international application having a receipt date that is on or after January 1, 2014:

By a micro entity (§ 1.29)	$520.00
By a small entity (§ 1.27(a))	$1,040.00
By other than a small or micro entity	$2,080.00

(ii) For an international application having a receipt date that is before January 1, 2014	$2,080.00

(4) A fee equivalent to the transmittal fee in paragraph (a)(1) of this section that would apply if the USPTO was the Receiving Office for transmittal of an international application to the International Bureau for processing in its capacity as a Receiving Office (PCT Rule 19.4).

(b) The international filing fee shall be as prescribed in PCT Rule 15.

[78 FR 17107, Mar. 20, 2013]

§ 1.446 Refund of international application filing and processing fees.

(a) Money paid for international application fees, where paid by actual mistake or in excess, such as a payment not required by law or treaty and its regulations, may be refunded. A mere change of purpose after the payment of a fee will not entitle a party to a refund of such fee. The Office will not refund amounts of twenty-five dollars or less unless a refund is specifically requested and will not notify the payor of such amounts. If the payor or party requesting a refund does not provide the banking information necessary for making refunds by electronic funds transfer, the Office may use the banking information provided on the payment instrument to make any refund by electronic funds transfer.

(b) Any request for refund under paragraph (a) of this section must be filed within two years from the date the fee was paid. If the Office charges a deposit account by an amount other than an amount specifically indicated in an authorization under § 1.25(b), any request for refund based upon such charge must be filed within two years from the date of the deposit account statement indicating such charge and include a copy of that deposit account statement. The time periods set forth in this paragraph are not extendable.

(c) Refund of the supplemental search fees will be made if such refund is determined to be warranted by the Director or the Director's designee acting under PCT Rule 40.2(c).

(d) The international and search fees will be refunded if no international filing date is accorded or if the application is withdrawn before transmittal of the record copy to the International Bureau (PCT Rules 15.6 and 16.2). The search fee will be refunded if the application is withdrawn before transmittal of the search copy to the International Searching Authority. The transmittal fee will not be refunded.

(e) The handling fee (§ 1.482(b)) will be refunded (PCT Rule 57.6) only if:

(1) The Demand is withdrawn before the Demand has been sent by the International Preliminary Examining Authority to the International Bureau, or

(2) The Demand is considered not to have been submitted (PCT Rule 54.4(a)).

(35 U.S.C. 6; 15 U.S.C. 1113, 1123)

[43 FR 20466, May 11, 1978, as amended at 50 FR 9384, Mar. 7, 1985; 50 FR 31826, Aug. 6, 1985; 58 FR 4345, Jan. 14, 1993; 65 FR 54677, Sept. 8, 2000]

PRIORITY

§ 1.451 The priority claim and priority document in an international application.

(a) The claim for priority must, subject to paragraph (d) of this section, be made on the Request (PCT Rule 4.10) in a manner complying with sections 110 and 115 of the Administrative Instructions.

(b) Whenever the priority of an earlier United States national application or international application filed with the United States Receiving Office is claimed in an international application, the applicant may request in the Request or in a letter of transmittal accompanying the international application upon filing with the United States Receiving Office or in a separate letter filed in the United States Receiving Office not later than 16 months after the priority date, that the United States Patent and Trademark Office prepare a certified copy of the prior application for transmittal to the International Bureau (PCT Article 8 and PCT Rule 17). The fee for preparing a certified copy is set forth in § 1.19(b)(1).

(c) If a certified copy of the priority document is not submitted together with the international application on filing, or, if the priority application was filed in the United States and a request and appropriate payment for preparation of such a certified copy do not accompany the international application on filing or are not filed within 16 months of the priority date, the certified copy of the priority document must be furnished by the applicant to the International Bureau or to the United States Receiving Office within the time limit specified in PCT Rule 17.1(a).

(d) The applicant may correct or add a priority claim in accordance with PCT Rule 26bis.1.

(35 U.S.C. 6; 15 U.S.C. 1113, 1123)

[43 FR 20466, May 11, 1978, as amended at 50 FR 9384, Mar. 7, 1985; 50 FR 11366, Mar. 21, 1985; 54 FR 6903, Feb. 15, 1989; 58 FR 4345, Jan. 14, 1993; 63 FR 29619, June 1, 1998; 66 FR 16006, Mar. 22, 2001]

§ 1.452 Restoration of right of priority.

(a) If the international application has an international filing date which is later than the expiration of the priority period as defined by PCT Rule 2.4 but within two months from the expiration of the priority period, the right of priority in the international application may be restored upon request if the delay in filing the international application within the priority period was unintentional.

(b) A request to restore the right of priority in an international application under paragraph (a) of this section must be filed not later than two months from the expiration of the priority period and must include:

(1) A notice under PCT Rule 26*bis*.1(a) adding the priority claim, if the priority claim in respect of the earlier application is not contained in the international application;

(2) The fee set forth in § 1.17(t); and

(3) A statement that the delay in filing the international application within the priority period was unintentional. The Director may require additional information where there is a question whether the delay was unintentional.

(c) If the applicant makes a request for early publication under PCT Article 21(2)(b), any requirement under paragraph (b) of this section filed after the technical preparations for international publication have been completed by the International Bureau shall be considered as not having been submitted in time.

(d) Restoration of a right of priority to a prior application by the United States Receiving Office under this section, or by any other Receiving Office under the provisions of PCT Rule 26*bis*.3, will not entitle applicants to a right of priority in any application which has entered the national stage under 35 U.S.C. 371, or in any application filed under 35 U.S.C. 111(a) which claims benefit under 35 U.S.C. 120 and 365(c) to an international application in which the right to priority has been restored.

[72 FR 51563, Sept. 10, 2007]

REPRESENTATION

§ 1.455 Representation in international applications.

(a) Applicants of international applications may be represented by attorneys or agents registered to practice before the United States Patent and Trademark Office or by an applicant appointed as a common representative (PCT Art. 49, Rules 4.8 and 90 and § 11.9). If applicants have not appointed an attorney or agent or one of the applicants to represent them, and there is more than one applicant, the applicant first named in the request and who is entitled to file in the U.S. Receiving Office shall be considered to be the common representative of all the applicants. An attorney or agent having the right to practice before a national office with which an international application is filed and for which the United States is an International Searching Authority or International Preliminary Examining Authority may be appointed to represent the applicants in the international application before that authority. An attorney or agent may appoint an associate attorney or agent who shall also then be of record

(PCT Rule 90.1(d)). The appointment of an attorney or agent, or of a common representative, revokes any earlier appointment unless otherwise indicated (PCT Rule 90.6 (b) and (c)).

(b) Appointment of an agent, attorney or common representative (PCT Rule 4.8) must be effected either in the Request form, signed by applicant, in the Demand form, signed by applicant, or in a separate power of attorney submitted either to the United States Receiving Office or to the International Bureau.

(c) Powers of attorney and revocations thereof should be submitted to the United States Receiving Office until the issuance of the international search report.

(d) The addressee for correspondence will be as indicated in section 108 of the Administrative Instructions.

[43 FR 20466, May 11, 1978, as amended at 50 FR 5171, Feb. 6, 1985; 58 FR 4345, Jan. 14, 1993; 68 FR 59888, Oct. 20, 2003; 69 FR 35452, June 24, 2004]

TRANSMITTAL OF RECORD COPY

§ 1.461 Procedures for transmittal of record copy to the International Bureau.

(a) Transmittal of the record copy of the international application to the International Bureau shall be made by the United States Receiving Office or as provided by PCT Rule 19.4.

(b) [Reserved]

(c) No copy of an international application may be transmitted to the International Bureau, a foreign Designated Office, or other foreign authority by the United States Receiving Office or the applicant, unless the applicable requirements of part 5 of this chapter have been satisfied.

[43 FR 20466, May 11, 1978, as amended at 50 FR 9384, Mar. 7, 1985; 63 FR 29619, June 1, 1998]

TIMING

§ 1.465 Timing of application processing based on the priority date.

(a) For the purpose of computing time limits under the Treaty, the priority date shall be defined as in PCT Art. 2(xi).

(b) When a claimed priority date is corrected under PCT Rule 26*bis*.1(a), or a priority claim is added under PCT Rule 26*bis*.1(a), withdrawn under PCT Rule 90*bis*.3, or considered not to have been made under PCT Rule 26*bis*.2, the priority date for the purposes of computing any non-expired time limits will be the filing date of the earliest remaining priority claim under PCT Article 8 of the international application, or if none, the international filing date.

(c) When corrections under PCT Art. 11(2), Art. 14(2) or PCT Rule 20.2(a) (i) or (iii) are timely submitted, and the date of receipt of such corrections falls later than one year from the claimed priority date or dates, the Receiving Office shall proceed under PCT Rule 26bis.2.

[43 FR 20466, May 11, 1978, as amended at 63 FR 29619, June 1, 1998; 72 FR 51564, Sept. 10, 2007]

§ 1.468 Delays in meeting time limits.

Delays in meeting time limits during international processing of international applications may only be excused as provided in PCT Rule 82. For delays in meeting time limits in a national application, see § 1.137.

AMENDMENTS

§ 1.471 Corrections and amendments during international processing.

(a) Except as otherwise provided in this paragraph, all corrections submitted to the United States Receiving Office or United States International Searching Authority must be in English, in the form of replacement sheets in compliance with PCT Rules 10 and 11, and accompanied by a letter that draws attention to the differences between the replaced sheets and the replacement sheets. Replacement sheets are not required for the deletion of lines of text, the correction of simple typographical errors, and one addition or change of not more than five words per sheet. These changes may be stated in a letter and, if appropriate, the United States Receiving Office will make the deletion or transfer the correction to the international application, provided that such corrections do not adversely affect the clarity and direct reproducibility of the application (PCT Rule 26.4). Amendments that do not comply with PCT Rules 10 and 11.1 to 11.13 may not be entered.

(b) Amendments of claims submitted to the International Bureau shall be as prescribed by PCT Rule 46.

(c) Corrections or additions to the Request of any declarations under PCT Rule 4.17 should be submitted to the International Bureau as prescribed by PCT Rule 26*ter*.

[43 FR 20466, May 11, 1978, as amended at 63 FR 29619, June 1, 1998; 66 FR 16006, Mar. 22, 2001]

§ 1.472 Changes in person, name, or address of applicants and inventors.

All requests for a change in person, name or address of applicants and inventor be sent to the United States Receiving Office until the time of issuance of the international search report. Thereafter requests for such changes should be submitted to the International Bureau.

[43 FR 20466, May 11, 1978. Redesignated at 52 FR 20047, May 28, 1987]

UNITY OF INVENTION

§ 1.475 Unity of invention before the International Searching Authority, the International Preliminary Examining Authority and during the national stage.

(a) An international and a national stage application shall relate to one invention only or to a group of inventions so linked as to form a single general inventive concept ("requirement of unity of invention"). Where a group of inventions is claimed in an application, the requirement of unity of invention shall be fulfilled only when there is a technical relationship among those inventions involving one or more of the same or corresponding special technical features. The expression "special technical features" shall mean those technical features that define a contribution which each of the claimed inventions, considered as a whole, makes over the prior art.

(b) An international or a national stage application containing claims to different categories of invention will be considered to have unity of invention if the claims are drawn only to one of the following combinations of categories:

(1) A product and a process specially adapted for the manufacture of said product; or

(2) A product and a process of use of said product; or

(3) A product, a process specially adapted for the manufacture of the said product, and a use of the said product; or

(4) A process and an apparatus or means specifically designed for carrying out the said process; or

(5) A product, a process specially adapted for the manufacture of the said product, and an apparatus or means specifically designed for carrying out the said process.

(c) If an application contains claims to more or less than one of the combinations of categories of invention set forth in paragraph (b) of this section, unity of invention might not be present.

(d) If multiple products, processes of manufacture or uses are claimed, the first invention of the category first mentioned in the claims of the application and the first recited invention of each of the other categories related thereto will be considered as the main invention in the claims, see PCT Article 17(3)(a) and § 1.476(c).

(e) The determination whether a group of inventions is so linked as to form a single general inventive concept shall be made without regard to whether the inventions are claimed in separate claims or as alternatives within a single claim.

[58 FR 4345, Jan. 14, 1993]

§ 1.476 Determination of unity of invention before the International Searching Authority.

(a) Before establishing the international search report, the International Searching Authority will determine whether the international application complies with the requirement of unity of invention as set forth in § 1.475.

(b) If the International Searching Authority considers that the international application does not comply with the requirement of unity of invention, it shall inform the applicant accordingly and invite the payment of additional fees (note § 1.445 and PCT Art. 17(3)(a) and PCT Rule 40). The applicant will be given a time period in accordance with PCT Rule 40.3 to pay the additional fees due.

(c) In the case of non-compliance with unity of invention and where no additional fees are paid, the international search will be performed on the invention first mentioned ("main invention") in the claims.

(d) Lack of unity of invention may be directly evident before considering the claims in relation to any prior art, or after taking the prior art into consideration, as where a document discovered during the search shows the invention claimed in a generic or linking claim lacks novelty or is clearly obvious, leaving two or more claims joined thereby without a common inventive concept. In such a case the International Searching Authority may raise the objection of lack of unity of invention.

[43 FR 20466, May 11, 1978. Redesignated and amended at 52 FR 20048, May 28, 1987; 58 FR 4346, Jan. 14, 1993]

§ 1.477 Protest to lack of unity of invention before the International Searching Authority.

(a) If the applicant disagrees with the holding of lack of unity of invention by the International Searching Authority, additional fees may be paid under protest, accompanied by a request for refund and a statement setting forth reasons for disagreement or why the required additional fees are considered excessive, or both (PCT Rule 40.2(c)).

(b) Protest under paragraph (a) of this section will be examined by the Director or the Director's designee. In the event that the applicant's protest is determined to be justified, the additional fees or a portion thereof will be refunded.

(c) An applicant who desires that a copy of the protest and the decision thereon accompany the international search report when forwarded to the Designated Offices, may notify the International Searching Authority to that effect any time prior to the issuance of the international search report. Thereafter, such notification should be directed to the International Bureau (PCT Rule 40.2(c)).

[43 FR 20466, May 11, 1978. Redesignated and amended at 52 FR 20048, May 28, 1987]

INTERNATIONAL PRELIMINARY EXAMINATION

§ 1.480 Demand for international preliminary examination.

(a) On the filing of a proper Demand in an application for which the United States International Preliminary Examining Authority is competent and for which the fees have been paid, the international application shall be the subject of an international preliminary examination. The preliminary examination fee (§ 1.482(a)(1)) and the handling fee (§ 1.482(b)) shall be due within the applicable time limit set forth in PCT Rule 57.3.

(b) The Demand shall be made on a standardized form (PCT Rule 53). Copies of the printed Demand forms are available from the United States Patent and Trademark Office. Letters requesting printed Demand forms should be marked "Mail Stop PCT."

(c) Withdrawal of a proper Demand prior to the start of the international preliminary examination will entitle applicant to a refund of the preliminary examination fee minus the amount of the transmittal fee set forth in § 1.445(a)(1).

(d) The filing of a Demand shall constitute the election of all Contracting States which are designated and are bound by Chapter II of the Treaty on the international filing date (PCT Rule 53.7).

(e) Any Demand filed after the expiration of the applicable time limit set forth in PCT Rule 54*bis*.1(a) shall be considered as if it had not been submitted (PCT Rule 54*bis*.1(b)).

[52 FR 20048, May 28, 1987, as amended at 53 FR 47810, Nov. 28, 1988; 58 FR 4346, Jan. 14, 1993; 63 FR 29619, June 1, 1998; 67 FR 523, Jan. 4, 2002; 68 FR 14337, Mar. 25, 2003; 68 FR 59888, Oct. 20, 2003]

§ 1.481 Payment of international preliminary examination fees.

(a) The handling and preliminary examination fees shall be paid within the time period set in PCT Rule 57.3. The handling fee or preliminary examination fee payable is the handling fee or preliminary examination fee in effect on the date of payment.

(1) If the handling and preliminary examination fees are not paid within the time period set in PCT Rule 57.3, applicant will be notified and given one month within which to pay the deficient fees plus a late payment fee equal to the greater of:

(i) Fifty percent of the amount of the deficient fees, but not exceeding an amount equal to double the handling fee; or

(ii) An amount equal to the handling fee (PCT Rule 58*bis*.2).

(2) The one-month time limit set in this paragraph to pay deficient fees may not be extended.

(b) If the payment needed to cover the handling and preliminary examination fees, pursuant to paragraph (a) of this section, is not timely made in accordance with PCT Rule 58bis.1(d), the United States International Preliminary Examination Authority will declare the Demand to be considered as if it had not been submitted.

[63 FR 29619, June 1, 1998, as amended at 68 FR 59888, Oct. 20, 2003]

§ 1.482 International preliminary examination fees.

(a) The following fees and charges for international preliminary examination are established by the Director under the authority of 35 U.S.C. 376:

(1) The following preliminary examination fee is due on filing the Demand:

(i) If an international search fee as set forth in § 1.445(a)(2) has been paid on the international application to the United States Patent and Trademark Office as an International Searching Authority:

(A) For an international preliminary examination fee paid on or after January 1, 2014:	
By a micro entity (§ 1.29)	$150.00
By a small entity (§ 1.27(a))	$300.00
By other than a small or micro entity	$600.00
(B) For an international preliminary examination fee paid before January 1, 2014	$600.00
(ii) If the International Searching Authority for the international application was an authority other than the United States Patent and Trademark Office:	
(A) For an international preliminary examination fee paid on or after January 1, 2014:	
By a micro entity (§ 1.29)	$190.00
By a small entity (§ 1.27(a))	$380.00
By other than a small or micro entity	$760.00
(B) For an international preliminary examination fee paid before January 1, 2014 $750.00.	
(2) An additional preliminary examination fee when required, per additional invention:	
(i) If the international preliminary examination fee set forth in paragraph (a)(1) of this section was paid on or after January 1, 2014:	
By a micro entity (§ 1.29)	$150.00
By a small entity (§ 1.27(a))	$300.00
By other than a small or micro entity	$600.00
(ii) If the international preliminary examination fee set forth in paragraph (a)(1) of this section was paid before January 1, 2014	$600.00

(b) The handling fee is due on filing the Demand and shall be prescribed in PCT Rule 57.

[78 FR 17107, Mar. 20, 2013]

§ 1.484 Conduct of international preliminary examination.

(a) An international preliminary examination will be conducted to formulate a non-binding opinion as to whether the claimed invention has novelty, involves an inventive step (is non-obvious) and is industrially applicable.

(b) International preliminary examination will begin in accordance with PCT Rule 69.1.

(c) No international preliminary examination will be conducted on inventions not previously searched by an International Searching Authority.

(d) The International Preliminary Examining Authority will establish a written opinion if any defect exists or if the claimed invention lacks novelty, inventive step or industrial applicability and will set a non-extendable time limit in the written opinion for the applicant to reply.

(e) The written opinion established by the International Searching Authority under PCT Rule 43*bis*.1 shall be considered to be a written opinion of the United States International Preliminary Examining Authority for the purposes of paragraph (d) of this section.

(f) The International Preliminary Examining Authority may establish further written opinions under paragraph (d) of this section.

(g) If no written opinion under paragraph (d) of this section is necessary, or if no further written opinion under paragraph (f) of this section is to be established, or after any written opinion and the reply thereto or the expiration of the time limit for reply to such written opinion, an international preliminary examination report will be established by the International Preliminary Examining Authority. One copy will be submitted to the International Bureau and one copy will be submitted to the applicant.

(h) An applicant will be permitted a personal or telephone interview with the examiner, which may be requested after the filing of a Demand, and must be conducted during the period between the establishment of the written opinion and the establishment of the international preliminary examination report. Additional interviews may be conducted where the examiner determines that such additional interviews may be helpful to advancing the international preliminary examination procedure. A summary of any such personal or telephone interview must be filed by the applicant or, if not filed by applicant be made of record in the file by the examiner.

(i) If the application whose priority is claimed in the international application is in a language other than English, the United States International Preliminary Examining Authority may, where the validity of the priority claim is relevant for the formulation of the opinion referred to in Article 33(1), invite the applicant to furnish an English translation of the priority document within two months from the date of the invitation. If the translation is not furnished within that time limit, the international preliminary report may be established as if the priority had not been claimed.

[52 FR 20049, May 28, 1987, as amended at 58 FR 4346, Jan. 14, 1993; 62 FR 53199, Oct. 10, 1997; 63 FR 29619, June 1, 1998; 66 FR 16006, Mar. 22, 2001; 68 FR 59888, Oct. 20, 2003]

§ 1.485 Amendments by applicant during international preliminary examination.

The applicant may make amendments at the time of filing the Demand. The applicant may also make amendments within the time limit set by the International Preliminary Examining Authority for reply to any notification under § 1.484(b) or to any written opinion. Any such amendments must be made in accordance with PCT Rule 66.8.

[74 FR 31373, July 1, 2009]

§ 1.488 Determination of unity of invention before the International Preliminary Examining Authority.

(a) Before establishing any written opinion or the international preliminary examination report, the International Preliminary Examining Authority will determine whether the international application complies with the requirement of unity of invention as set forth in § 1.475.

(b) If the International Preliminary Examining Authority considers that the international application does not comply with the requirement of unity of invention, it may:

(1) Issue a written opinion and/or an international preliminary examination report, in respect of the entire international application and indicate that

unity of invention is lacking and specify the reasons therefor without extending an invitation to restrict or pay additional fees. No international preliminary examination will be conducted on inventions not previously searched by an International Searching Authority.

(2) Invite the applicant to restrict the claims or pay additional fees, pointing out the categories of invention found, within a set time limit which will not be extended. No international preliminary examination will be conducted on inventions not previously searched by an International Searching Authority, or

(3) If applicant fails to restrict the claims or pay additional fees within the time limit set for reply, the International Preliminary Examining Authority will issue a written opinion and/or establish an international preliminary examination report on the main invention and shall indicate the relevant facts in the said report. In case of any doubt as to which invention is the main invention, the invention first mentioned in the claims and previously searched by an International Searching Authority shall be considered the main invention.

(c) Lack of unity of invention may be directly evident before considering the claims in relation to any prior art, or after taking the prior art into consideration, as where a document discovered during the search shows the invention claimed in a generic or linking claim lacks novelty or is clearly obvious, leaving two or more claims joined thereby without a common inventive concept. In such a case the International Preliminary Examining Authority may raise the objection of lack of unity of invention.

[52 FR 20049, May 28, 1987, as amended at 58 FR 4346, Jan. 14, 1993; 62 FR 53200, Oct. 10, 1997]

§ 1.489 Protest to lack of unity of invention before the International Preliminary Examining Authority.

(a) If the applicant disagrees with the holding of lack of unity of invention by the International Preliminary Examining Authority, additional fees may be paid under protest, accompanied by a request for refund and a statement setting forth reasons for disagreement or why the required additional fees are considered excessive, or both.

(b) Protest under paragraph (a) of this section will be examined by the Director or the Director's designee. In the event that the applicant's protest is determined to be justified, the additional fees or a portion thereof will be refunded.

(c) An applicant who desires that a copy of the protest and the decision thereon accompany the international preliminary examination report when forwarded to the Elected Offices, may notify the International Preliminary Examining Authority to that effect any time prior to the issuance of the international preliminary examination report. Thereafter, such notification should be directed to the International Bureau.

[52 FR 20050, May 28, 1987]

National Stage

§ 1.491 National stage commencement, entry, and fulfillment.

(a) Subject to 35 U.S.C. 371(f), the national stage shall commence with the expiration of the applicable time limit under PCT Article 22 (1) or (2), or under PCT Article 39(1)(a).

(b) An international application enters the national stage when the applicant has filed the documents and fees required by 35 U.S.C. 371(c)(1) and (c)(2) within the period set in § 1.495.

(c) An international application fulfills the requirements of 35 U.S.C. 371 when the national stage has commenced under 35 U.S.C. 371(b) or (f) and all applicable requirements of 35 U.S.C. 371 have been satisfied.

[67 FR 523, Jan. 4, 2002, as amended at 77 FR 48823, Aug. 14, 2012]

§ 1.492 National stage fees.

The following fees and charges are established for international applications entering the national stage under 35 U.S.C. 371:

(a) The basic national fee for an international application entering the national stage under 35 U.S.C. 371:

By a micro entity (§ 1.29)	$70.00
By a small entity (§ 1.27(a))	140.00
By other than a small or micro entity	280.00

(b) Search fee for an international application entering the national stage under 35 U.S.C. 371:

(1) If an international preliminary examination report on the international application prepared by the United States International Preliminary Examining Authority or a written opinion on the international application prepared by the United States International Searching Authority states that the criteria of novelty, inventive step (non-obviousness), and industrial applicability, as defined in PCT Article 33(1) to (4) have been satisfied for all of the claims presented in the application entering the national stage:

By a micro entity (§ 1.29)	$0.00
By a small entity (§ 1.27(a))	0.00
By other than a small or micro entity	0.00

(2) If the search fee as set forth in § 1.445(a)(2) has been paid on the international application to the United States Patent and Trademark Office as an International Searching Authority:

By a micro entity (§ 1.29)	$30.00
By a small entity (§ 1.27(a))	60.00
By other than a small or micro entity	120.00

(3) If an international search report on the international application has been prepared by an International Searching Authority other than the United States International Searching Authority and is provided, or has been previously communicated by the International Bureau, to the Office:

By a micro entity (§ 1.29)	$120.00
By a small entity (§ 1.27(a))	240.00
By other than a small or micro entity	480.00

(4) In all situations not provided for in paragraphs (b)(1), (2), or (3) of this section:

By a micro entity (§ 1.29)	$150.00
By a small entity (§ 1.27(a))	300.00
By other than a small or micro entity	600.00

(c) The examination fee for an international application entering the national stage under 35 U.S.C. 371:

(1) If an international preliminary examination report on the international application prepared by the United States International Preliminary Examining Authority or a written opinion on the international application prepared by the United States International Searching Authority states that the criteria of novelty, inventive step (non-obviousness), and industrial applicability, as defined in PCT Article 33 (1) to (4) have been satisfied for all of the claims presented in the application entering the national stage:

By a micro entity (§ 1.29)	$0.00
By a small entity (§ 1.27(a))	0.00
By other than a small or micro entity	0.00

(2) In all situations not provided for in paragraph (c)(1) of this section:

By a micro entity (§ 1.29) $180.00.

By a small entity (§ 1.27(a))	$360.00
By other than a small or micro entity	720.00

(d) In addition to the basic national fee, for filing or on later presentation at any other time of each claim in independent form in excess of 3:

By a micro entity (§ 1.29)	$105.00
By a small entity (§ 1.27(a))	210.00
By other than a small or micro entity	420.00

(e) In addition to the basic national fee, for filing or on later presentation at any other time of each claim (whether dependent or independent) in excess of 20 (note that § 1.75(c) indicates how multiple dependent claims are considered for fee calculation purposes):

By a micro entity (§ 1.29)	$20.00
By a small entity (§ 1.27(a))	40.00
By other than a small or micro entity	80.00

(f) In addition to the basic national fee, if the application contains, or is amended to contain, a multiple dependent claim, per application:

By a micro entity (§ 1.29)	$195.00
By a small entity (§ 1.27(a))	390.00
By other than a small or micro entity	780.00

(g) If the excess claims fees required by paragraphs (d) and (e) of this section and multiple dependent claim fee required by paragraph (f) of this section are not paid with the basic national fee or on later presentation of the claims for which excess claims or multiple dependent claim fees are due, the fees required by paragraphs (d), (e), and (f) of this section must be paid or the claims canceled by amendment prior to the expiration of the time period set for reply by the Office in any notice of fee deficiency in order to avoid abandonment.

(h) Surcharge for filing any of the search fee, the examination fee, or the oath or declaration after the date of the commencement of the national stage (§ 1.491(a)) pursuant to § 1.495(c):

By a micro entity (§ 1.29)	$35.00
By a small entity (§ 1.27(a))	70.00
By other than a small or micro entity	140.00

(i) For filing an English translation of an international application or any annexes to an international preliminary examination report later than thirty months after the priority date (§ 1.495(c) and (e)):

By a micro entity (§ 1.29)	$35.00
By a small entity (§ 1.27(a))	70.00
By other than a small or micro entity	140.00

(j) Application size fee for any international application, the specification and drawings of which exceed 100 sheets of paper, for each additional 50 sheets or fraction thereof:

By a micro entity (§ 1.29)	$100.00
By a small entity (§ 1.27(a))	200.00
By other than a small or micro entity	400.00

[78 FR 4290, Jan. 18, 2013]

§ 1.495 Entering the national stage in the United States of America.

(a) The applicant in an international application must fulfill the requirements of 35 U.S.C. 371 within the time periods set forth in paragraphs (b) and (c) of this section in order to prevent the abandonment of the international application as to the United States of America. The thirty-month time period set forth in paragraphs (b), (c), (d), (e) and (h) of this section may not be extended.

(b) To avoid abandonment of the application, the applicant shall furnish to the United States Patent and Trademark Office not later than the expiration of thirty months from the priority date:

(1) A copy of the international application, unless it has been previously communicated by the International Bureau or unless it was originally filed in the United States Patent and Trademark Office; and

(2) The basic national fee (see § 1.492(a)).

(c)(1) If applicant complies with paragraph (b) of this section before expiration of thirty months from the priority date, the Office will notify the applicant if he or she has omitted any of:

(i) A translation of the international application, as filed, into the English language, if it was originally filed in another language and if any English language translation of the publication of the international application previously submitted under 35 U.S.C. 154(d) (§ 1.417) is not also a translation of the international application as filed (35 U.S.C. 371(c)(2));

(ii) The inventor's oath or declaration (35 U.S.C. 371(c)(4) and § 1.497), if a declaration of inventorship in compliance with § 1.63 has not been previously submitted in the international application under PCT Rule 4.17(iv) within the time limits provided for in PCT Rule 26*ter*.1;

(iii) The search fee set forth in § 1.492(b);

(iv) The examination fee set forth in § 1.492(c); and

(v) Any application size fee required by § 1.492(j).

(2) A notice under paragraph (c)(1) of this section will set a time period within which applicant must provide any omitted translation, search fee set forth in § 1.492(b), examination fee set forth in § 1.492(c), and any application size fee required by § 1.492(j) in order to avoid abandonment of the application.

(3) The inventor's oath or declaration must also be filed within the period specified in paragraph (c)(2) of this section, except that the filing of the inventor's oath or declaration may be postponed until the application is otherwise in condition for allowance under the conditions specified in paragraphs (c)(3)(i) through (c)(3)(iii) of this section.

(i) The application contains an application data sheet in accordance with

§ 1.76 filed prior to the expiration of the time period set in any notice under paragraph (c)(1) identifying:

(A) Each inventor by his or her legal name;

(B) A mailing address where the inventor customarily receives mail, and residence, if an inventor lives at a location which is different from where the inventor customarily receives mail, for each inventor.

(ii) The applicant must file an oath or declaration in compliance with § 1.63, or substitute statement in compliance with § 1.64, executed by or with respect to each actual inventor no later than the expiration of the time period set in the "Notice of Allowability" to avoid abandonment, when the applicant is notified in a "Notice of Allowability" that an application is otherwise in condition for allowance. The time period set in a "Notice of Allowability" is not extendable. *See* § 1.136(c). The Office may dispense with the notice provided for in paragraph (c)(1) of this section if an oath or declaration under § 1.63, or substitute statement under § 1.64, executed by or with respect to each actual inventor has been filed before the application is in condition for allowance.

(iii) An international application in which the basic national fee under 35 U.S.C. 41(a)(1)(F) has been paid and for which an application data sheet in accordance with § 1.76 has been filed may be treated as complying with 35 U.S.C. 371 for purposes of eighteen-month publication under 35 U.S.C. 122(b) and § 1.211 *et seq.*

(4) The payment of the processing fee set forth in § 1.492(i) is required for acceptance of an English translation later than the expiration of thirty months after the priority date. The payment of the surcharge set forth in § 1.492(h) is required for acceptance of any of the search fee, the examination fee, or the inventor's oath or declaration after the date of the commencement of the national stage (§ 1.491(a)).

(5) A "Sequence Listing" need not be translated if the "Sequence Listing" complies with PCT Rule 12.1(d) and the description complies with PCT Rule 5.2(b).

(d) A copy of any amendments to the claims made under PCT Article 19, and a translation of those amendments into English, if they were made in another language, must be furnished not later than the expiration of thirty months from the priority date. Amendments under PCT Article 19 which are not received by the expiration of thirty months from the priority date will be considered to be canceled.

(e) A translation into English of any annexes to an international preliminary examination report (if applicable), if the annexes were made in another language, must be furnished not later than the expiration of thirty months from the priority date. Translations of the annexes which are not received by the expiration of thirty months from the priority date may be submitted within any period set pursuant to paragraph (c) of this section accompanied by the processing fee set forth in § 1.492(f). Annexes for which translations are not timely received will be considered canceled.

(f) Verification of the translation of the international application or any other document pertaining to an international application may be required where it is considered necessary, if the international application or other document was filed in a language other than English.

(g) The documents and fees submitted under paragraphs (b) and (c) of this section must be identified as a submission to enter the national stage under 35 U.S.C. 371. If the documents and fees contain conflicting indications as between an application under 35 U.S.C. 111 and a submission to enter the national stage under 35 U.S.C. 371, the documents and fees will be treated as a submission to enter the national stage under 35 U.S.C. 371.

(h) An international application becomes abandoned as to the United States thirty months from the priority date if the requirements of paragraph (b) of this section have not been complied with within thirty months from the priority date.

[52 FR 20051, May 28, 1987, as amended at 58 FR 4347, Jan. 14, 1993; 63 FR 29620, June 1, 1998; 65 FR 57060, Sept. 20, 2000; 67 FR 523, Jan. 4, 2002; 68 FR 71007, Dec. 22, 2003; 70 FR 3892, Jan. 27, 2005; 70 FR 30365, May 26, 2005; 72 FR 46843, Aug. 21, 2007; 74 FR 52691, Oct. 14, 2009; 77 FR 48824, Aug. 14, 2012]

§ 1.496 Examination of international applications in the national stage.

National stage applications having paid therein the search fee as set forth in § 1.492(b)(1) and examination fee as set forth in § 1.492(c)(1) may be amended subsequent to the date of commencement of national stage processing only to the extent necessary to eliminate objections as to form or to cancel rejected claims. Such national stage applications will be advanced out of turn for examination.

[77 FR 48824, Aug. 14, 2012]

§ 1.497 Inventor's oath or declaration under 35 U.S.C. 371(c)(4).

(a) When an applicant of an international application desires to enter the national stage under 35 U.S.C. 371 pursuant to § 1.495, and a declaration in compliance with § 1.63 has not been previously submitted in the international application under PCT Rule 4.17(iv) within the time limits provided for in PCT Rule 26*ter*.1, the applicant must file the inventor's oath or declaration. The inventor, or each individual who is a joint inventor of a claimed invention, in an application for patent must execute an oath or declaration in accordance with the conditions and requirements of § 1.63, except as provided for in § 1.64.

(b) An oath or declaration under § 1.63 will be accepted as complying with 35 U.S.C. 371(c)(4) if it complies with the requirements of §§ 1.63(a), (c) and (g). A substitute statement under § 1.64 will be accepted as complying with 35 U.S.C. 371(c)(4) if it complies with the requirements of §§ 1.64(b)(1), (c) and (e) and identifies the person executing the substitute statement. If a newly executed inventor's oath or declaration under § 1.63 or substitute statement under § 1.64 is not required pursuant to § 1.63(d), submission of the copy of the previously executed oath, declaration, or substitute statement under § 1.63(d)(1) is required to comply with 35 U.S.C. 371(c)(4).

(c) If an oath or declaration under § 1.63, or substitute statement under § 1.64, meeting the requirements of § 1.497(b) does not also meet the requirements of § 1.63 or § 1.64, an oath, declaration, substitute statement, or application data sheet in accordance with § 1.76 to comply with § 1.63 or § 1.64 will be required.

[77 FR 48824, Aug. 14, 2012]

§ 1.499 Unity of invention during the national stage.

If the examiner finds that a national stage application lacks unity of invention under § 1.475, the examiner may in an Office action require the applicant in the response to that action to elect the invention to which the claims shall be restricted. Such requirement may be made before any action on the merits but may be made at any time before the final action at the discretion of the examiner. Review of any such requirement is provided under §§ 1.143 and 1.144.

[58 FR 4347, Jan. 14, 1993]

Subpart D—*Ex Parte* Reexamination of Patents

SOURCE: 46 FR 29185, May 29, 1981, unless otherwise noted.

CITATION OF PRIOR ART AND WRITTEN STATEMENTS

§ 1.501 Citation of prior art and written statements in patent files.

(a) *Information content of submission:* At any time during the period of enforceability of a patent, any person may file a written submission with the Office under this section, which is directed to the following information:

(1) Prior art consisting of patents or printed publications which the person making the submission believes to have a bearing on the patentability of any claim of the patent; or

(2) Statements of the patent owner filed by the patent owner in a proceeding before a Federal court or the Office in which the patent owner took a position on the scope of any claim of the patent. Any statement submitted under this paragraph must be accompanied by any other documents, pleadings, or evidence from the proceeding in which the statement was filed that address the written statement, and such statement and accompanying information under this paragraph must

be submitted in redacted form to exclude information subject to an applicable protective order.

(3) Submissions under paragraph (a)(2) of this section must identify:

(i) The forum and proceeding in which patent owner filed each statement;

(ii) The specific papers and portions of the papers submitted that contain the statements; and

(iii) How each statement submitted is a statement in which patent owner took a position on the scope of any claim in the patent.

(b) *Explanation:* A submission pursuant to paragraph (a) of this section:

(1) Must include an explanation in writing of the pertinence and manner of applying any prior art submitted under paragraph (a)(1) of this section and any written statement and accompanying information submitted under paragraph (a)(2) of this section to at least one claim of the patent, in order for the submission to become a part of the official file of the patent; and

(2) May, if the submission is made by the patent owner, include an explanation of how the claims differ from any prior art submitted under paragraph (a)(1) of this section or any written statements and accompanying information submitted under paragraph (a)(2) of this section.

(c) *Reexamination pending:* If a reexamination proceeding has been requested and is pending for the patent in which the submission is filed, entry of the submission into the official file of the patent is subject to the provisions of §§ 1.502 and 1.902.

(d) *Identity:* If the person making the submission wishes his or her identity to be excluded from the patent file and kept confidential, the submission papers must be submitted anonymously without any identification of the person making the submission.

(e) *Certificate of Service:* A submission under this section by a person other than the patent owner must include a certification that a copy of the submission was served in its entirety upon patent owner at the address as provided for in § 1.33 (c). A submission by a person other than the patent owner that fails to include proper proof of service as required by § 1.248(b) will not be entered into the patent file.

[77 FR 46626, Aug. 6, 2012]

§ 1.502 Processing of prior art citations during an *ex parte* reexamination proceeding.

Citations by the patent owner under § 1.555 and by an *ex parte* reexamination requester under either § 1.510 or § 1.535 will be entered in the reexamination file during a reexamination proceeding. The entry in the patent file of citations submitted after the date of an order to reexamine pursuant to § 1.525 by persons other than the patent owner, or an *ex parte* reexamination requester under either § 1.510 or § 1.535, will be delayed until the reexamination proceeding has been concluded by the issuance and publication of a reexamination certificate. See § 1.902 for processing of prior art citations in patent and reexamination files during an *inter partes* reexamination proceeding filed under § 1.913.

[72 FR 18905, Apr. 16, 2007]

REQUEST FOR *EX PARTE* REEXAMINATION

§ 1.510 Request for *ex parte* reexamination.

(a) Any person may, at any time during the period of enforceability of a patent, file a request for an *ex parte* reexamination by the Office of any claim of the patent on the basis of prior art patents or printed publications cited under § 1.501, unless prohibited by 35 U.S.C. 315(e)(1) or 35 U.S.C. 325(e)(1). The request must be accompanied by the fee for requesting reexamination set in § 1.20(c)(1).

(b) Any request for reexamination must include the following parts:

(1) A statement pointing out each substantial new question of patentability based on prior patents and printed publications.

(2) An identification of every claim for which reexamination is requested, and a detailed explanation of the pertinency and manner of applying the cited prior art to every claim for which reexamination is requested. For each statement of the patent owner and accompanying information submitted pursuant to § 1.501(a)(2) which is relied upon in the detailed explanation, the

request must explain how that statement is being used to determine the proper meaning of a patent claim in connection with the prior art applied to that claim and how each relevant claim is being interpreted. If appropriate, the party requesting reexamination may also point out how claims distinguish over cited prior art.

(3) A copy of every patent or printed publication relied upon or referred to in paragraph (b) (1) and (2) of this section accompanied by an English language translation of all the necessary and pertinent parts of any non-English language patent or printed publication.

(4) A copy of the entire patent including the front face, drawings, and specification/claims (in double column format) for which reexamination is requested, and a copy of any disclaimer, certificate of correction, or reexamination certificate issued in the patent. All copies must have each page plainly written on only one side of a sheet of paper.

(5) A certification that a copy of the request filed by a person other than the patent owner has been served in its entirety on the patent owner at the address as provided for in § 1.33(c). The name and address of the party served must be indicated. If service was not possible, a duplicate copy must be supplied to the Office.

(6) A certification by the third party requester that the statutory estoppel provisions of 35 U.S.C. 315(e)(1) or 35 U.S.C. 325(e)(1) do not prohibit the requester from filing the *ex parte* reexamination request.

(c) If the request does not include the fee for requesting *ex parte* reexamination required by paragraph (a) of this section and meet all the requirements by paragraph (b) of this section, then the person identified as requesting reexamination will be so notified and will generally be given an opportunity to complete the request within a specified time. Failure to comply with the notice will result in the *ex parte* reexamination request not being granted a filing date, and will result in placement of the request in the patent file as a citation if it complies with the requirements of § 1.501.

(d) The filing date of the request for *ex parte* reexamination is the date on which the request satisfies all the requirements of this section.

(e) A request filed by the patent owner may include a proposed amendment in accordance with § 1.530.

(f) If a request is filed by an attorney or agent identifying another party on whose behalf the request is being filed, the attorney or agent must have a power of attorney from that party or be acting in a representative capacity pursuant to § 1.34.

(35 U.S.C. 6; 15 U.S.C. 1113, 1123)

[46 FR 29185, May 29, 1981, as amended at 47 FR 41282, Sept. 17, 1982; 62 FR 53200, Oct. 10, 1997; 65 FR 54678, Sept. 8, 2000; 65 FR 76775, Dec 7, 2000; 71 FR 9262, Feb. 23, 2006; 71 FR 44223, Aug. 4, 2006; 72 FR 18905, Apr. 16, 2007; 77 FR 46626, Aug. 6, 2012]

§ 1.515 Determination of the request for *ex parte* reexamination.

(a) Within three months following the filing date of a request for an *ex parte* reexamination, an examiner will consider the request and determine whether or not a substantial new question of patentability affecting any claim of the patent is raised by the request and the prior art cited therein, with or without consideration of other patents or printed publications. A statement and any accompanying information submitted pursuant to § 1.501(a)(2) will not be considered by the examiner when making a determination on the request. The examiner's determination will be based on the claims in effect at the time of the determination, will become a part of the official file of the patent, and will be given or mailed to the patent owner at the address provided for in § 1.33(c) and to the person requesting reexamination.

(b) Where no substantial new question of patentability has been found, a refund of a portion of the fee for requesting *ex parte* reexamination will be made to the requester in accordance with § 1.26(c).

(c) The requester may seek review by a petition to the Director under § 1.181 within one month of the mailing date of the examiner's determination refusing *ex parte* reexamination. Any such petition must comply with § 1.181(b). If no petition is timely filed or if the decision on petition affirms that no substantial new question of patentability has been raised, the determination shall be final and nonappealable.

[65 FR 76775, Dec. 7, 2000, as amended at 77 FR 46626, Aug. 6, 2012]

§ 1.520 *Ex parte* reexamination at the initiative of the Director.

The Director, at any time during the period of enforceability of a patent, may determine whether or not a substantial new question of patentability is raised by patents or printed publications which have been discovered by the Director or which have been brought to the Director's attention, even though no request for reexamination has been filed in accordance with § 1.510 or § 1.913. The Director may initiate *ex parte* reexamination without a request for reexamination pursuant to § 1.510 or § 1.913. Normally requests from outside the Office that the Director undertake reexamination on his own initiative will not be considered. Any determination to initiate *ex parte* reexamination under this section will become a part of the official file of the patent and will be mailed to the patent owner at the address as provided for in § 1.33(c).

[65 FR 76775, Dec. 7, 2000]

Ex Parte REEXAMINATION

§ 1.525 Order for *ex parte* reexamination.

(a) If a substantial new question of patentability is found pursuant to § 1.515 or § 1.520, the determination will include an order for *ex parte* reexamination of the patent for resolution of the question. If the order for *ex parte* reexamination resulted from a petition pursuant to § 1.515(c), the *ex parte* reexamination will ordinarily be conducted by an examiner other than the examiner responsible for the initial determination under § 1.515(a).

(b) The notice published in the *Official Gazette* under § 1.11(c) will be considered to be constructive notice and *ex parte* reexamination will proceed.

[65 FR 76775, Dec. 7, 2000]

§ 1.530 Statement by patent owner in *ex parte* reexamination; amendment by patent owner in *ex parte* or *inter partes* reexamination; inventorship change in *ex parte* or *inter partes* reexamination.

(a) Except as provided in § 1.510(e), no statement or other response by the patent owner in an *ex parte* reexamination proceeding shall be filed prior to the determinations made in accordance with § 1.515 or § 1.520. If a premature statement or other response is filed by the patent owner, it will not be acknowledged or considered in making the determination, and it will be returned or discarded (at the Office's option).

(b) The order for *ex parte* reexamination will set a period of not less than two months from the date of the order within which the patent owner may file a statement on the new question of patentability, including any proposed amendments the patent owner wishes to make.

(c) Any statement filed by the patent owner shall clearly point out why the subject matter as claimed is not anticipated or rendered obvious by the prior art patents or printed publications, either alone or in any reasonable combinations. Where the reexamination request was filed by a third party requester, any statement filed by the patent owner must be served upon the *ex parte* reexamination requester in accordance with § 1.248.

(d) *Making amendments in a reexamination proceeding.* A proposed amendment in an *ex parte* or an *inter partes* reexamination proceeding is made by filing a paper directing that proposed specified changes be made to the patent specification, including the claims, or to the drawings. An amendment paper directing that proposed specified changes be made in a reexamination proceeding may be submitted as an accompaniment to a request filed by the patent owner in accordance with § 1.510(e), as part of a patent owner statement in accordance with paragraph (b) of this section, or, where permitted, during the prosecution of the reexamination proceeding pursuant to § 1.550(a) or § 1.937.

(1) *Specification other than the claims.* Changes to the specification, other

than to the claims, must be made by submission of the entire text of an added or rewritten paragraph including markings pursuant to paragraph (f) of this section, except that an entire paragraph may be deleted by a statement deleting the paragraph, without presentation of the text of the paragraph. The precise point in the specification must be identified where any added or rewritten paragraph is located. This paragraph applies whether the amendment is submitted on paper or compact disc (*see* §§ 1.96 and 1.825).

(2) *Claims.* An amendment paper must include the entire text of each patent claim which is being proposed to be changed by such amendment paper and of each new claim being proposed to be added by such amendment paper. For any claim changed by the amendment paper, a parenthetical expression "amended," "twice amended," etc., should follow the claim number. Each patent claim proposed to be changed and each proposed added claim must include markings pursuant to paragraph (f) of this section, except that a patent claim or proposed added claim should be canceled by a statement canceling the claim, without presentation of the text of the claim.

(3) *Drawings.* Any change to the patent drawings must be submitted as a sketch on a separate paper showing the proposed changes in red for approval by the examiner. Upon approval of the changes by the examiner, only new sheets of drawings including the changes and in compliance with § 1.84 must be filed. Amended figures must be identified as "Amended," and any added figure must be identified as "New." In the event a figure is canceled, the figure must be surrounded by brackets and identified as "Canceled."

(4) The formal requirements for papers making up the reexamination proceeding other than those set forth in this section are set out in § 1.52.

(e) *Status of claims and support for claim changes.* Whenever there is an amendment to the claims pursuant to paragraph (d) of this section, there must also be supplied, on pages separate from the pages containing the changes, the status (*i.e.*, pending or canceled), as of the date of the amendment, of all patent claims and of all added claims, and an explanation of the support in the disclosure of the patent for the changes to the claims made by the amendment paper.

(f) *Changes shown by markings.* Any changes relative to the patent being reexamined which are made to the specification, including the claims, must include the following markings:

(1) The matter to be omitted by the reexamination proceeding must be enclosed in brackets; and

(2) The matter to be added by the reexamination proceeding must be underlined.

(g) *Numbering of patent claims preserved.* Patent claims may not be renumbered. The numbering of any claims added in the reexamination proceeding must follow the number of the highest numbered patent claim.

(h) *Amendment of disclosure may be required.* The disclosure must be amended, when required by the Office, to correct inaccuracies of description and definition, and to secure substantial correspondence between the claims, the remainder of the specification, and the drawings.

(i) *Amendments made relative to patent.* All amendments must be made relative to the patent specification, including the claims, and drawings, which are in effect as of the date of filing the request for reexamination.

(j) *No enlargement of claim scope.* No amendment may enlarge the scope of the claims of the patent or introduce new matter. No amendment may be proposed for entry in an expired patent. Moreover, no amendment, other than the cancellation of claims, will be incorporated into the patent by a certificate issued after the expiration of the patent.

(k) *Amendments not effective until certificate.* Although the Office actions will treat proposed amendments as though they have been entered, the proposed amendments will not be effective until the reexamination certificate is issued and published.

(l) *Correction of inventorship in an ex parte or inter partes reexamination proceeding.* (1) When it appears in a patent being reexamined that the correct inventor or inventors were not named, the Director may, on petition of all the parties set forth in § 1.324(b)(1) and (b)(2), including the assignees, and satisfactory proof of the facts and payment of the fee set forth in § 1.20(b), or on order of a court before which such matter is called in question, include in the reexamination certificate to be issued under § 1.570 or § 1.997 an amendment naming only the actual inventor or inventors. The petition must be submitted as part of the reexamination proceeding and must satisfy the requirements of § 1.324.

(2) Notwithstanding paragraph (l)(1) of this section, if a petition to correct inventorship satisfying the requirements of § 1.324 is filed in a reexamination proceeding, and the reexamination proceeding is concluded other than by a reexamination certificate under § 1.570 or § 1.997, a certificate of correction indicating the change of inventorship stated in the petition will be issued upon request by the patentee.

[46 FR 29185, May 29, 1981, as amended at 62 FR 53200, Oct. 10, 1997; 65 FR 54678, Sept. 8, 2000; 65 FR 76775, Dec. 7, 2000; 72 FR 18905, Apr. 16, 2007; 77 FR 48825, Aug. 14, 2012]

§ 1.535 Reply by third party requester in *ex parte* reexamination.

A reply to the patent owner's statement under § 1.530 may be filed by the *ex parte* reexamination requester within two months from the date of service of the patent owner's statement. Any reply by the *ex parte* requester must be served upon the patent owner in accordance with § 1.248. If the patent owner does not file a statement under § 1.530, no reply or other submission from the *ex parte* reexamination requester will be considered.

[65 FR 76776, Dec. 7, 2000]

§ 1.540 Consideration of responses in *ex parte* reexamination.

The failure to timely file or serve the documents set forth in § 1.530 or in § 1.535 may result in their being refused consideration. No submissions other than the statement pursuant to § 1.530 and the reply by the *ex parte* reexamination requester pursuant to § 1.535 will be considered prior to examination.

[65 FR 76776, Dec. 7, 2000]

§ 1.550 Conduct of *ex parte* reexamination proceedings.

(a) All *ex parte* reexamination proceedings, including any appeals to the Board of Patent Appeals and Interferences, will be conducted with special dispatch within the Office. After issuance of the *ex parte* reexamination order and expiration of the time for submitting any responses, the examination will be conducted in accordance with §§ 1.104 through 1.116 and will result in the issuance of an *ex parte* reexamination certificate under § 1.570.

(b) The patent owner in an *ex parte* reexamination proceeding will be given at least thirty days to respond to any Office action. In response to any rejection, such response may include further statements and/or proposed amendments or new claims to place the patent in a condition where all claims, if amended as proposed, would be patentable.

(c) The time for taking any action by a patent owner in an *ex parte* reexamination proceeding will be extended only for sufficient cause and for a reasonable time specified. Any request for such extension must be filed on or before the day on which action by the patent owner is due, but in no case will the mere filing of a request effect any extension. Any request for such extension must be accompanied by the petition fee set forth in § 1.17(g). See § 1.304(a) for extensions of time for filing a notice of appeal to the U.S. Court of Appeals for the Federal Circuit or for commencing a civil action.

(d) If the patent owner fails to file a timely and appropriate response to any Office action or any written statement of an interview required under § 1.560(b), the prosecution in the *ex parte* reexamination proceeding will be a terminated prosecution, and the Director will proceed to issue and publish a certificate concluding the reexamination proceeding under § 1.570 in accordance with the last action of the Office.

(e) If a response by the patent owner is not timely filed in the Office,

(1) The delay in filing such response may be excused if it is shown to the satisfaction of the Director that the delay was unavoidable; a petition to

accept an unavoidably delayed response must be filed in compliance with § 1.137(a); or

(2) The response may nevertheless be accepted if the delay was unintentional; a petition to accept an unintentionally delayed response must be filed in compliance with § 1.137(b).

(f) The reexamination requester will be sent copies of Office actions issued during the *ex parte* reexamination proceeding. After filing of a request for *ex parte* reexamination by a third party requester, any document filed by either the patent owner or the third party requester must be served on the other party in the reexamination proceeding in the manner provided by § 1.248. The document must reflect service or the document may be refused consideration by the Office.

(g) The active participation of the *ex parte* reexamination requester ends with the reply pursuant to § 1.535, and no further submissions on behalf of the reexamination requester will be acknowledged or considered. Further, no submissions on behalf of any third parties will be acknowledged or considered unless such submissions are:

(1) in accordance with § 1.510 or § 1.535; or

(2) entered in the patent file prior to the date of the order for *ex parte* reexamination pursuant to § 1.525.

(h) Submissions by third parties, filed after the date of the order for *ex parte* reexamination pursuant to § 1.525, must meet the requirements of and will be treated in accordance with § 1.501(a).

(i) A petition in an *ex parte* reexamination proceeding must be accompanied by the fee set forth in § 1.20(c)(6), except for petitions under paragraph (c) of this section to extend the period for response by a patent owner, petitions under paragraph (e) of this section to accept a delayed response by a patent owner, petitions under § 1.78 to accept an unintentionally delayed benefit claim, and petitions under § 1.530(l) for correction of inventorship in a reexamination proceeding.

[65 FR 76776, Dec. 7, 2000, as amended at 69 FR 56545, Sept. 21, 2004; 72 FR 18905, Apr. 16, 2007; 77 FR 48851, Aug. 14, 2012]

§ 1.552 Scope of reexamination in *ex parte* reexamination proceedings.

(a) Claims in an *ex parte* reexamination proceeding will be examined on the basis of patents or printed publications and, with respect to subject matter added or deleted in the reexamination proceeding, on the basis of the requirements of 35 U.S.C. 112.

(b) Claims in an *ex parte* reexamination proceeding will not be permitted to enlarge the scope of the claims of the patent.

(c) Issues other than those indicated in paragraphs (a) and (b) of this section will not be resolved in a reexamination proceeding. If such issues are raised by the patent owner or third party requester during a reexamination proceeding, the existence of such issues will be noted by the examiner in the next Office action, in which case the patent owner may consider the advisability of filing a reissue application to have such issues considered and resolved.

(d) Any statement of the patent owner and any accompanying information submitted pursuant to § 1.501(a)(2) which is of record in the patent being reexamined (which includes any reexamination files for the patent) may be used after a reexamination proceeding has been ordered to determine the proper meaning of a patent claim when applying patents or printed publications.

[65 FR 76776, Dec. 7, 2000, as amended at 77 FR 46627, Aug. 6, 2012]

§ 1.555 Information material to patentability in *ex parte* reexamination and *inter partes* reexamination proceedings.

(a) A patent by its very nature is affected with a public interest. The public interest is best served, and the most effective reexamination occurs when, at the time a reexamination proceeding is being conducted, the Office is aware of and evaluates the teachings of all information material to patentability in a reexamination proceeding. Each individual associated with the patent owner in a reexamination proceeding has a duty of candor and good faith in dealing with the Office, which includes a duty to disclose to the Office all information known to that individual to be material to patentability in a reexamination proceeding. The individuals who have a duty to disclose to the Office all information known to them to be material to patentability in a reexamination proceeding are the patent owner, each attorney or agent who represents the patent owner, and every other individual who is substantively involved on behalf of the patent owner in a reexamination proceeding. The duty to disclose the information exists with respect to each claim pending in the reexamination proceeding until the claim is cancelled. Information material to the patentability of a cancelled claim need not be submitted if the information is not material to patentability of any claim remaining under consideration in the reexamination proceeding. The duty to disclose all information known to be material to patentability in a reexamination proceeding is deemed to be satisfied if all information known to be material to patentability of any claim in the patent after issuance of the reexamination certificate was cited by the Office or submitted to the Office in an information disclosure statement. However, the duties of candor, good faith, and disclosure have not been complied with if any fraud on the Office was practiced or attempted or the duty of disclosure was violated through bad faith or intentional misconduct by, or on behalf of, the patent owner in the reexamination proceeding. Any information disclosure statement must be filed with the items listed in §1.98(a) as applied to individuals associated with the patent owner in a reexamination proceeding, and should be filed within two months of the date of the order for reexamination, or as soon thereafter as possible.

(b) Under this section, information is material to patentability in a reexamination proceeding when it is not cumulative to information of record or being made of record in the reexamination proceeding, and

(1) It is a patent or printed publication that establishes, by itself or in combination with other patents or printed publications, a prima facie case of unpatentability of a claim; or

(2) It refutes, or is inconsistent with, a position the patent owner takes in:

(i) Opposing an argument of unpatentability relied on by the Office, or

(ii) Asserting an argument of patentability.

A prima facie case of unpatentability of a claim pending in a reexamination proceeding is established when the information compels a conclusion that a claim is unpatentable under the preponderance of evidence, burden-of-proof standard, giving each term in the claim its broadest reasonable construction consistent with the specification, and before any consideration is given to evidence which may be submitted in an attempt to establish a contrary conclusion of patentability.

(c) The responsibility for compliance with this section rests upon the individuals designated in paragraph (a) of this section and no evaluation will be made by the Office in the reexamination proceeding as to compliance with this section. If questions of compliance with this section are raised by the patent owner or the third party requester during a reexamination proceeding, they will be noted as unresolved questions in accordance with §1.552(c).

[57 FR 2036, Jan 17, 1992, as amended at 65 FR 76776, Dec. 7, 2000]

§1.560 Interviews in *ex parte* reexamination proceedings.

(a) Interviews in *ex parte* reexamination proceedings pending before the Office between examiners and the owners of such patents or their attorneys or agents of record must be conducted in the Office at such times, within Office hours, as the respective examiners may designate. Interviews will not be permitted at any other time or place without the authority of the Director. Interviews for the discussion of the patentability of claims in patents involved in *ex parte* reexamination proceedings will not be conducted prior to the first official action. Interviews should be arranged in advance. Requests that reexamination requesters participate in interviews with examiners will not be granted.

(b) In every instance of an interview with an examiner in an *ex parte* reexamination proceeding, a complete written statement of the reasons presented at the interview as warranting favorable action must be filed by the patent owner. An interview does not remove the necessity for response to Office actions as specified in § 1.111. Patent owner's response to an outstanding Office action after the interview does not remove the necessity for filing the written statement. The written statement must be filed as a separate part of a response to an Office action outstanding at the time of the interview, or as a separate paper within one month from the date of the interview, whichever is later.

[65 FR 76777, Dec. 7, 2000]

§ 1.565 Concurrent office proceedings which include an *ex parte* reexamination proceeding.

(a) In an *ex parte* reexamination proceeding before the Office, the patent owner must inform the Office of any prior or concurrent proceedings in which the patent is or was involved such as interferences, reissues, *ex parte* reexaminations, *inter partes* reexaminations, or litigation and the results of such proceedings. See § 1.985 for notification of prior or concurrent proceedings in an *inter partes* reexamination proceeding.

(b) If a patent in the process of *ex parte* reexamination is or becomes involved in litigation, the Director shall determine whether or not to suspend the reexamination. See § 1.987 for *inter partes* reexamination proceedings.

(c) If *ex parte* reexamination is ordered while a prior *ex parte* reexamination proceeding is pending and prosecution in the prior *ex parte* reexamination proceeding has not been terminated, the *ex parte* reexamination proceedings will usually be merged and result in the issuance and publication of a single certificate under § 1.570. For merger of *inter partes* reexamination proceedings, see § 1.989(a). For merger of *ex parte* reexamination and *inter partes* reexamination proceedings, see § 1.989(b).

(d) If a reissue application and an *ex parte* reexamination proceeding on which an order pursuant to § 1.525 has been mailed are pending concurrently on a patent, a decision will usually be made to merge the two proceedings or to suspend one of the two proceedings. Where merger of a reissue application and an *ex parte* reexamination proceeding is ordered, the merged examination will be conducted in accordance with §§ 1.171 through 1.179, and the patent owner will be required to place and maintain the same claims in the reissue application and the *ex parte* reexamination proceeding during the pendency of the merged proceeding. The examiner's actions and responses by the patent owner in a merged proceeding will apply to both the reissue application and the *ex parte* reexamination proceeding and will be physically entered into both files. Any *ex parte* reexamination proceeding merged with a reissue application shall be concluded by the grant of the reissued patent. For merger of a reissue application and an *inter partes* reexamination, see § 1.991.

(e) If a patent in the process of *ex parte* reexamination is or becomes involved in an interference, the Director may suspend the reexamination or the interference. The Director will not consider a request to suspend an interference unless a motion (§ 41.121(a)(3) of this title) to suspend the interference has been presented to, and denied by, an administrative patent judge, and the request is filed within ten (10) days of a decision by an administrative patent judge denying the motion for suspension or such other time as the administrative patent judge may set. For concurrent *inter partes* reexamination and interference of a patent, see § 1.993.

[65 FR 76776, Dec. 7, 2000, as amended at 69 FR 50001, Aug. 12, 2004; 72 FR 18905, Apr. 16, 2007]

Ex Parte REEXAMINATION CERTIFICATE

§ 1.570 Issuance and publication of *ex parte* reexamination certificate concludes *ex parte* reexamination proceeding.

(a) To conclude an *ex parte* reexamination proceeding, the Director will issue and publish an *ex parte* reexamination certificate in accordance with 35 U.S.C. 307 setting forth the results of the *ex parte* reexamination proceeding and the content of the patent following the *ex parte* reexamination proceeding.

(b) An *ex parte* reexamination certificate will be issued and published in each patent in which an *ex parte* reexamination proceeding has been ordered under § 1.525 and has not been merged with any *inter partes* reexamination proceeding pursuant to § 1.989(a). Any statutory disclaimer filed by the patent owner will be made part of the *ex parte* reexamination certificate.

(c) The *ex parte* reexamination certificate will be mailed on the day of its date to the patent owner at the address as provided for in § 1.33(c). A copy of the *ex parte* reexamination certificate will also be mailed to the requester of the *ex parte* reexamination proceeding.

(d) If an *ex parte* reexamination certificate has been issued and published which cancels all of the claims of the patent, no further Office proceedings will be conducted with that patent or any reissue applications or any reexamination requests relating thereto.

(e) If the *ex parte* reexamination proceeding is terminated by the grant of a reissued patent as provided in § 1.565(d), the reissued patent will constitute the *ex parte* reexamination certificate required by this section and 35 U.S.C. 307.

(f) A notice of the issuance of each *ex parte* reexamination certificate under this section will be published in the *Official Gazette* on its date of issuance.

[65 FR 76777, Dec. 7, 2000, as amended at 72 FR 18905, Apr. 16, 2007]

Subpart E—Supplemental Examination of Patents

SOURCE: 77 FR 48851, Aug. 14, 2012, unless otherwise noted.

§ 1.601 Filing of papers in supplemental examination.

(a) A request for supplemental examination of a patent must be filed by the owner(s) of the entire right, title, and interest in the patent.

(b) Any party other than the patent owner (*i.e.*, any third party) is prohibited from filing papers or otherwise participating in any manner in a supplemental examination proceeding.

(c) A request for supplemental examination of a patent may be filed at any time during the period of enforceability of the patent.

§ 1.605 Items of information.

(a) Each request for supplemental examination may include no more than twelve items of information believed to be relevant to the patent. More than one request for supplemental examination of the same patent may be filed at any time during the period of enforceability of the patent.

(b) An item of information includes a document submitted as part of the request that contains information, believed to be relevant to the patent, that the patent owner requests the Office to consider, reconsider, or correct. If the information to be considered, reconsidered, or corrected is not, at least in part, contained within or based on any document submitted as part of the request, the discussion within the body of the request relative to the information will be considered as an item of information.

(c) An item of information must be in writing in accordance with § 1.2. To be considered, any audio or video recording must be submitted in the form of a written transcript.

(d) If one item of information is combined in the request with one or more additional items of information, each item of information of the combination may be separately counted. Exceptions include the combination of a non-English language document and its translation, and the combination of a document that is over 50 pages in length and its summary pursuant to § 1.610(b)(8).

§ 1.610 Content of request for supplemental examination.

(a) A request for supplemental examination must be accompanied by the fee for filing a request for supplemental examination as set forth in § 1.20(k)(1), the fee for reexamination ordered as a result of a supplemental examination proceeding as set forth in § 1.20(k)(2), and any applicable document size fees as set forth in § 1.20(k)(3).

(b) A request for supplemental examination must include:

(1) An identification of the number of the patent for which supplemental examination is requested.

(2) A list of the items of information that are requested to be considered, reconsidered, or corrected. Where appropriate, the list must meet the requirements of § 1.98(b).

(3) A list identifying any other prior or concurrent post-patent Office proceedings involving the patent for which supplemental examination is being requested, including an identification of the type of proceeding, the identifying number of any such proceeding (*e.g.*, a control number or reissue application number), and the filing date of any such proceeding.

(4) An identification of each claim of the patent for which supplemental examination is requested.

(5) A separate, detailed explanation of the relevance and manner of applying each item of information to each claim of the patent for which supplemental examination is requested.

(6) A copy of the patent for which supplemental examination is requested and a copy of any disclaimer or certificate issued for the patent.

(7) A copy of each item of information listed in paragraph (b)(2) of this section, accompanied by a written English translation of all of the necessary and pertinent parts of any non-English language item of information. The patent owner is not required to submit copies of items of information that form part of the discussion within the body of the request as specified in § 1.605(b), or copies of U.S. patents and U.S. patent application publications.

(8) A summary of the relevant portions of any submitted document, other than the request, that is over 50 pages in length. The summary must include citations to the particular pages containing the relevant portions.

(9) An identification of the owner(s) of the entire right, title, and interest in the patent requested to be examined, and a submission by the patent owner in compliance with § 3.73(c) of this chapter establishing the entirety of the ownership in the patent requested to be examined.

(c) The request may also include:

(1) A cover sheet itemizing each component submitted as part of the request;

(2) A table of contents for the request;

(3) An explanation of how the claims patentably distinguish over the items of information; and

(4) An explanation of why each item of information submitted with the request does or does not raise a substantial new question of patentability.

(d) The filing date of a request for supplemental examination will not be granted if the request is not in compliance with §§ 1.605, 1.615, and this section, subject to the discretion of the Office. If the Office determines that the request, as originally submitted, is not entitled to a filing date, the patent owner will be so notified and will be given an opportunity to complete the request within a specified time. If the patent owner does not timely comply with the notice, the request for supplemental examination will not be granted a filing date and the fee for reexamination as set forth in § 1.20(k)(2) will be refunded. If the patent owner timely files a corrected request in response to the notice that properly addresses all of the defects set forth in the notice and that otherwise complies with all of the requirements of §§ 1.605, 1.615, and this section, the filing date of the supplemental examination request will be the receipt date of the corrected request.

§ 1.615 Format of papers filed in a supplemental examination proceeding.

(a) All papers submitted in a supplemental examination proceeding must be formatted in accordance with § 1.52.

(b) Court documents and non-patent literature may be redacted, but must otherwise be identical both in content and in format to the original documents, and, if a court document, to the document submitted in court, and must not otherwise be reduced in size or modified, particularly in terms of font type, font size, line spacing, and margins. Patents, patent application publications, and third-party-generated affidavits or declarations must not be reduced in size or otherwise modified in the manner described in this paragraph.

§ 1.620 Conduct of supplemental examination proceeding.

(a) Within three months after the filing date of a request for supplemental examination, the Office will determine whether a substantial new question of patentability affecting any claim of the patent is raised by any of the items of information presented in the request. The determination will generally be limited to a review of the item(s) of information identified in the request as applied to the identified claim(s) of the patent. The determination will be based on the claims in effect at the time of the determination and will become a part of the official record of the patent.

(b) The Office may hold in abeyance action on any petition or other paper filed in a supplemental examination proceeding until after the proceeding is concluded by the electronic issuance of the supplemental examination certificate as set forth in § 1.625.

(c) If an unauthorized or otherwise improper paper is filed in a supplemental examination proceeding, it will not be entered into the official file or considered, or if inadvertently entered, it will be expunged.

(d) The patent owner must, as soon as possible upon the discovery of any other prior or concurrent post-patent Office proceeding involving the patent for which the current supplemental examination is requested, file a paper limited to notifying the Office of the post- patent Office proceeding, if such notice has not been previously provided with the request. The notice shall be limited to an identification of the post-patent Office proceeding, including the type of proceeding, the identifying number of any such proceeding (*e.g.*, a control number or reissue application number), and the filing date of any such proceeding, without any discussion of the issues of the current supplemental examination proceeding or of the identified post-patent Office proceeding(s).

(e) Interviews are prohibited in a supplemental examination proceeding.

(f) No amendment may be filed in a supplemental examination proceeding.

(g) If the Office becomes aware, during the course of supplemental examination or of any reexamination ordered under 35 U.S.C. 257 as a result of the supplemental examination proceeding, that a material fraud on the Office may have been committed in connection with the patent requested to be examined, the supplemental examination proceeding or any reexamination proceeding ordered under 35 U.S.C. 257 will continue, and the matter will be referred to the U.S. Attorney General in accordance with 35 U.S.C. 257(e).

§ 1.625 Conclusion of supplemental examination; publication of supplemental examination certificate; procedure after conclusion.

(a) A supplemental examination proceeding will conclude with the electronic issuance of a supplemental examination certificate. The supplemental examination certificate will indicate the result of the determination whether any of the items of information presented in the request raised a substantial new question of patentability.

(b) If the supplemental examination certificate states that a substantial new question of patentability is raised by one or more items of information in the request, *ex parte* reexamination of the patent will be ordered under 35 U.S.C. 257. Upon the conclusion of the *ex parte* reexamination proceeding, an *ex parte* reexamination certificate, which will include a statement specifying that *ex parte* reexamination was ordered under 35 U.S.C. 257, will be published. The electronically issued supplemental examination certificate will remain as part of the public record of the patent.

(c) If the supplemental examination certificate indicates that no substantial new question of patentability is raised by any of the items of information in the request, and *ex parte* reexamination is not ordered under 35 U.S.C. 257, the electronically issued supplemental examination certificate will be published in due course. The fee for reexamination ordered as a result of supplemental examination, as set forth in § 1.20(k)(2), will be refunded in accordance with § 1.26(c).

(d) Any *ex parte* reexamination ordered under 35 U.S.C. 257 will be conducted in accordance with §§ 1.530 through 1.570, which govern *ex parte* reexamination, except that:

(1) The patent owner will not have the right to file a statement pursuant

to § 1.530, and the order will not set a time period within which to file such a statement;

(2) Reexamination of any claim of the patent may be conducted on the basis of any item of information as set forth in § 1.605, and is not limited to patents and printed publications or to subject matter that has been added or deleted during the reexamination proceeding, notwithstanding § 1.552(a);

(3) Issues in addition to those raised by patents and printed publications, and by subject matter added or deleted during a reexamination proceeding, may be considered and resolved, notwithstanding § 1.552(c); and

(4) Information material to patentability will be defined by § 1.56(b), notwithstanding § 1.555(b).

Subpart F—Adjustment and Extension of Patent Term

AUTHORITY: 35 U.S.C. 2(b)(2), 154, and 156.

SOURCE: 52 FR 9394, Mar. 24, 1987, unless otherwise noted.

ADJUSTMENT OF PATENT TERM DUE TO EXAMINATION DELAY

§ 1.701 Extension of patent term due to examination delay under the Uruguay Round Agreements Act (original applications, other than designs, filed on or after June 8, 1995, and before May 29, 2000).

(a) A patent, other than for designs, issued on an application filed on or after June 8, 1995, is entitled to extension of the patent term if the issuance of the patent was delayed due to:

(1) Interference or derivation proceedings under 35 U.S.C. 135(a); and/or

(2) The application being placed under a secrecy order under 35 U.S.C. 181; and/or

(3) Appellate review by the Patent Trial and Appeal Board or by a Federal court under 35 U.S.C. 141 or 145, if the patent was issued pursuant to a decision in the review reversing an adverse determination of patentability and if the patent is not subject to a terminal disclaimer due to the issuance of another patent claiming subject matter that is not patentably distinct from that under appellate review. If an application is remanded by a panel of the Patent Trial and Appeal Board and the remand is the last action by a panel of the Patent Trial and Appeal Board prior to the mailing of a notice of allowance under 35 U.S.C. 151 in the application, the remand shall be considered a decision in the review reversing an adverse determination of patentability as that phrase is used in 35 U.S.C. 154(b)(2) as amended by section 532(a) of the Uruguay Round Agreements Act, Public Law 103–465, 108 Stat. 4809, 4983–85 (1994), and a final decision in favor of the applicant under paragraph (c)(3) of this section. A remand by a panel of the Patent Trial and Appeal Board shall not be considered a decision in the review reversing an adverse determination of patentability as provided in this paragraph if there is filed a request for continued examination under 35 U.S.C. 132(b) that was not first preceded by the mailing, after such remand, of at least one of an action under 35 U.S.C. 132 or a notice of allowance under 35 U.S.C. 151.

(b) The term of a patent entitled to extension under paragraph (a) of this section shall be extended for the sum of the periods of delay calculated under paragraphs (c)(1), (c)(2), (c)(3) and (d) of this section, to the extent that these periods are not overlapping, up to a maximum of five years. The extension will run from the expiration date of the patent.

(c)(1) The period of delay under paragraph (a)(1) of this section for an application is the sum of the following periods, to the extent that the periods are not overlapping:

(i) With respect to each interference or derivation proceeding in which the application was involved, the number of days, if any, in the period beginning on the date the interference or derivation proceeding was instituted to involve the application in the interference or derivation proceeding and ending on the date that the interference or derivation proceeding was terminated with respect to the application; and

(ii) The number of days, if any, in the period beginning on the date prosecution in the application was suspended by the Patent and Trademark Office due to interference or derivation proceedings under 35 U.S.C. 135(a) not involving the application and ending on the date of the termination of the suspension.

(2) The period of delay under paragraph (a)(2) of this section for an application is the sum of the following periods, to the extent that the periods are not overlapping:

(i) The number of days, if any, the application was maintained in a sealed condition under 35 U.S.C. 181;

(ii) The number of days, if any, in the period beginning on the date of mailing of an examiner's answer under § 41.39 of this title in the application under secrecy order and ending on the date the secrecy order and any renewal thereof was removed;

(iii) The number of days, if any, in the period beginning on the date applicant was notified that an interference or derivation proceeding would be instituted but for the secrecy order and ending on the date the secrecy order and any renewal thereof was removed; and

(iv) The number of days, if any, in the period beginning on the date of notification under § 5.3(c) and ending on the date of mailing of the notice of allowance under § 1.311.

(3) The period of delay under paragraph (a)(3) of this section is the sum of the number of days, if any, in the period beginning on the date on which an appeal to the Patent Trial and Appeal Board was filed under 35 U.S.C. 134 and ending on the date of a final decision in favor of the applicant by the Patent Trial and Appeal Board or by a Federal court in an appeal under 35 U.S.C. 141 or a civil action under 35 U.S.C. 145.

(d) The period of delay set forth in paragraph (c)(3) shall be reduced by:

(1) Any time during the period of appellate review that occurred before three years from the filing date of the first national application for patent presented for examination; and

(2) Any time during the period of appellate review, as determined by the Director, during which the applicant for patent did not act with due diligence. In determining the due diligence of an applicant, the Director may examine the facts and circumstances of the applicant's actions during the period of appellate review to determine whether the applicant exhibited that degree of timeliness as may reasonably be expected from, and which is ordinarily exercised by, a person during a period of appellate review.

(e) The provisions of this section apply only to original patents, except for design patents, issued on applications filed on or after June 8, 1995, and before May 29, 2000.

[60 FR 20228, Apr. 25, 1995, as amended at 65 FR 56391, Sept. 18, 2000; 69 FR 21710, Apr. 22, 2004; 69 FR 50001, Aug. 12, 2004; 77 FR 46627, Aug. 6, 2012]

§ 1.702 Grounds for adjustment of patent term due to examination delay under the Patent Term Guarantee Act of 1999 (original applications, other than designs, filed on or after May 29, 2000).

(a) *Failure to take certain actions within specified time frames.* Subject to the provisions of 35 U.S.C. 154(b) and this subpart, the term of an original patent shall be adjusted if the issuance of the patent was delayed due to the failure of the Office to:

(1) Mail at least one of a notification under 35 U.S.C. 132 or a notice of allowance under 35 U.S.C. 151 not later than fourteen months after the date on which the application was filed under 35 U.S.C. 111(a) or the date the national stage commenced under 35 U.S.C. 371(b) or (f) in an international application;

(2) Respond to a reply under 35 U.S.C. 132 or to an appeal taken under 35 U.S.C. 134 not later than four months after the date on which the reply was filed or the appeal was taken;

(3) Act on an application not later than four months after the date of a decision by the Patent Trial and Appeal Board under 35 U.S.C. 134 or 135 or a decision by a Federal court under 35 U.S.C. 141, 145, or 146 where at least one allowable claim remains in the application; or

(4) Issue a patent not later than four months after the date on which the issue fee was paid under 35 U.S.C. 151 and all outstanding requirements were satisfied.

(b) *Three-year pendency.* Subject to the provisions of 35 U.S.C. 154(b) and this subpart, the term of an original patent shall be adjusted if the issuance of the patent was delayed due to the failure of the Office to issue a patent within three years after the date on which the application was filed under 35 U.S.C. 111(a) or the national stage commenced under 35 U.S.C. 371(b) or (f) in an international application, but not including:

(1) Any time consumed by continued examination of the application under 35 U.S.C. 132(b);

(2) Any time consumed by an interference or derivation proceeding under 35 U.S.C. 135(a);

(3) Any time consumed by the imposition of a secrecy order under 35 U.S.C. 181;

(4) Any time consumed by review by the Patent Trial and Appeal Board or a Federal court; or

(5) Any delay in the processing of the application by the Office that was requested by the applicant.

(c) *Delays caused by interference and derivation proceedings.* Subject to the provisions of 35 U.S.C. 154(b) and this subpart, the term of an original patent shall be adjusted if the issuance of the patent was delayed due to interference or derivation proceedings under 35 U.S.C. 135(a).

(d) *Delays caused by secrecy order.* Subject to the provisions of 35 U.S.C. 154(b) and this subpart, the term of an original patent shall be adjusted if the issuance of the patent was delayed due to the application being placed under a secrecy order under 35 U.S.C. 181.

(e) *Delays caused by successful appellate review.* Subject to the provisions of 35 U.S.C. 154(b) and this subpart, the term of an original patent shall be adjusted if the issuance of the patent was delayed due to review by the Patent Trial and Appeal Board under 35 U.S.C. 134 or by a Federal court under 35 U.S.C. 141 or 145, if the patent was issued under a decision in the review reversing an adverse determination of patentability. If an application is remanded by a panel of the Patent Trial and Appeal Board and the remand is the last action by a panel of the Patent Trial and Appeal Board prior to the mailing of a notice of allowance under 35 U.S.C. 151 in the application, the remand shall be considered a decision by the Patent Trial and Appeal Board as that phrase is used in 35 U.S.C. 154(b)(1)(A)(iii), a decision in the review reversing an adverse determination of patentability as that phrase is used in 35 U.S.C. 154(b)(1)(C)(iii), and a final decision in favor of the applicant under § 1.703(e). A remand by a panel of the Patent Trial and Appeal Board shall not be considered a decision in the review reversing an adverse determination of patentability as provided in this paragraph if there is filed a request for continued examination under 35 U.S.C. 132(b) that was not first preceded by the mailing, after such remand, of at least one of an action under 35 U.S.C. 132 or a notice of allowance under 35 U.S.C. 151.

(f) The provisions of this section and §§ 1.703 through 1.705 apply only to original applications, except applications for a design patent, filed on or after May 29, 2000, and patents issued on such applications.

[65 FR 56391, Sept. 18, 2000, as amended at 69 FR 21711, Apr. 22, 2004; 77 FR 46627, Aug. 6, 2012; 78 FR 19420, Apr. 1, 2013]

§ 1.703 Period of adjustment of patent term due to examination delay.

(a) The period of adjustment under § 1.702(a) is the sum of the following periods:

(1) The number of days, if any, in the period beginning on the day after the date that is fourteen months after the date on which the application was filed under 35 U.S.C. 111(a) or the date the national stage commenced under 35 U.S.C. 371(b) or (f) in an international application and ending on the date of mailing of either an action under 35 U.S.C. 132, or a notice of allowance under 35 U.S.C. 151, whichever occurs first;

(2) The number of days, if any, in the period beginning on the day after the date that is four months after the date a reply under § 1.111 was filed and ending on the date of mailing of either an action under 35 U.S.C. 132, or a notice of allowance under 35 U.S.C. 151, whichever occurs first;

(3) The number of days, if any, in the period beginning on the day after the date that is four months after the date a reply in compliance with § 1.113(c) was filed and ending on the date of mailing of either an action under 35 U.S.C. 132, or a notice of allowance

under 35 U.S.C. 151, whichever occurs first;

(4) The number of days, if any, in the period beginning on the day after the date that is four months after the date an appeal brief in compliance with § 41.37 of this title was filed and ending on the date of mailing of any of an examiner's answer under § 41.39 of this title, an action under 35 U.S.C. 132, or a notice of allowance under 35 U.S.C. 151, whichever occurs first;

(5) The number of days, if any, in the period beginning on the day after the date that is four months after the date of a final decision by the Patent Trial and Appeal Board or by a Federal court in an appeal under 35 U.S.C. 141 or a civil action under 35 U.S.C. 145 or 146 where at least one allowable claim remains in the application and ending on the date of mailing of either an action under 35 U.S.C. 132 or a notice of allowance under 35 U.S.C. 151, whichever occurs first; and

(6) The number of days, if any, in the period beginning on the day after the date that is four months after the date the issue fee was paid and all outstanding requirements were satisfied and ending on the date a patent was issued.

(b) The period of adjustment under § 1.702(b) is the number of days, if any, in the period beginning on the day after the date that is three years after the date on which the application was filed under 35 U.S.C. 111(a) or the national stage commenced under 35 U.S.C. 371(b) or (f) in an international application and ending on the date a patent was issued, but not including the sum of the following periods:

(1) The number of days, if any, in the period beginning on the date on which a request for continued examination of the application under 35 U.S.C. 132(b) was filed and ending on the date the patent was issued;

(2)(i) The number of days, if any, in the period beginning on the date an interference or derivation proceeding was instituted to involve the application in the interference or derivation proceeding under 35 U.S.C. 135(a) and ending on the date that the interference or derivation proceeding was terminated with respect to the application; and

(ii) The number of days, if any, in the period beginning on the date prosecution in the application was suspended by the Office due to interference or derivation proceedings under 35 U.S.C. 135(a) not involving the application and ending on the date of the termination of the suspension;

(3)(i) The number of days, if any, the application was maintained in a sealed condition under 35 U.S.C. 181;

(ii) The number of days, if any, in the period beginning on the date of mailing of an examiner's answer under § 41.39 of this title in the application under secrecy order and ending on the date the secrecy order was removed;

(iii) The number of days, if any, in the period beginning on the date applicant was notified that an interference or derivation proceeding under 35 U.S.C. 135(a) would be instituted but for the secrecy order and ending on the date the secrecy order was removed; and

(iv) The number of days, if any, in the period beginning on the date of notification under § 5.3(c) of this chapter and ending on the date of mailing of the notice of allowance under 35 U.S.C. 151; and,

(4) The number of days, if any, in the period beginning on the date on which jurisdiction over the application passes to the Patent Trial and Appeal Board under § 41.35(a) of this chapter and ending on the date that jurisdiction by the Patent Trial and Appeal Board ends under § 41.35(b) of this chapter or the date of the last decision by a Federal court in an appeal under 35 U.S.C. 141 or a civil action under 35 U.S.C. 145, whichever is later.

(c) The period of adjustment under § 1.702(c) is the sum of the following periods, to the extent that the periods are not overlapping:

(1) The number of days, if any, in the period beginning on the date an interference or derivation proceeding was instituted to involve the application in the interference or derivation proceeding under 35 U.S.C. 135(a) and ending on the date that the interference or derivation proceeding was terminated with respect to the application; and

(2) The number of days, if any, in the period beginning on the date prosecution in the application was suspended

by the Office due to interference or derivation proceedings under 35 U.S.C. 135(a) not involving the application and ending on the date of the termination of the suspension.

(d) The period of adjustment under § 1.702(d) is the sum of the following periods, to the extent that the periods are not overlapping:

(1) The number of days, if any, the application was maintained in a sealed condition under 35 U.S.C. 181;

(2) The number of days, if any, in the period beginning on the date of mailing of an examiner's answer under § 41.39 of this title in the application under secrecy order and ending on the date the secrecy order was removed;

(3) The number of days, if any, in the period beginning on the date applicant was notified that an interference or derivation proceeding under 35 U.S.C. 135(a) would be instituted but for the secrecy order and ending on the date the secrecy order was removed; and

(4) The number of days, if any, in the period beginning on the date of notification under § 5.3(c) of this chapter and ending on the date of mailing of the notice of allowance under 35 U.S.C. 151.

(e) The period of adjustment under § 1.702(e) is the sum of the number of days, if any, in the period beginning on the date on which jurisdiction over the application passes to the Patent Trial and Appeal Board under § 41.35(a) of this chapter and ending on the date of a final decision in favor of the applicant by the Patent Trial and Appeal Board or by a Federal court in an appeal under 35 U.S.C. 141 or a civil action under 35 U.S.C. 145.

(f) The adjustment will run from the expiration date of the patent as set forth in 35 U.S.C. 154(a)(2). To the extent that periods of delay attributable to the grounds specified in § 1.702 overlap, the period of adjustment granted under this section shall not exceed the actual number of days the issuance of the patent was delayed. The term of a patent entitled to adjustment under § 1.702 and this section shall be adjusted for the sum of the periods calculated under paragraphs (a) through (e) of this section, to the extent that such periods are not overlapping, less the sum of the periods calculated under § 1.704. The date indicated on any certificate of mailing or transmission under § 1.8 shall not be taken into account in this calculation.

(g) No patent, the term of which has been disclaimed beyond a specified date, shall be adjusted under § 1.702 and this section beyond the expiration date specified in the disclaimer.

[65 FR 56392, Sept. 18, 2000, as amended at 69 FR 21711, Apr. 22, 2004; 69 FR 50001, Aug. 12, 2004; 77 FR 46628, Aug. 6, 2012; 77 FR 49360, Aug. 16, 2012; 78 FR 19420, Apr. 1, 2013]

§ 1.704 Reduction of period of adjustment of patent term.

(a) The period of adjustment of the term of a patent under §§ 1.703(a) through (e) shall be reduced by a period equal to the period of time during which the applicant failed to engage in reasonable efforts to conclude prosecution (processing or examination) of the application.

(b) With respect to the grounds for adjustment set forth in §§ 1.702(a) through (e), and in particular the ground of adjustment set forth in § 1.702(b), an applicant shall be deemed to have failed to engage in reasonable efforts to conclude processing or examination of an application for the cumulative total of any periods of time in excess of three months that are taken to reply to any notice or action by the Office making any rejection, objection, argument, or other request, measuring such three-month period from the date the notice or action was mailed or given to the applicant, in which case the period of adjustment set forth in § 1.703 shall be reduced by the number of days, if any, beginning on the day after the date that is three months after the date of mailing or transmission of the Office communication notifying the applicant of the rejection, objection, argument, or other request and ending on the date the reply was filed. The period, or shortened statutory period, for reply that is set in the Office action or notice has no effect on the three-month period set forth in this paragraph.

(c) Circumstances that constitute a failure of the applicant to engage in reasonable efforts to conclude processing or examination of an application also include the following circumstances, which will result in the following reduction of the period of adjustment set forth in § 1.703 to the extent that the periods are not overlapping:

(1) Suspension of action under § 1.103 at the applicant's request, in which case the period of adjustment set forth in § 1.703 shall be reduced by the number of days, if any, beginning on the date a request for suspension of action under § 1.103 was filed and ending on the date of the termination of the suspension;

(2) Deferral of issuance of a patent under § 1.314, in which case the period of adjustment set forth in § 1.703 shall be reduced by the number of days, if any, beginning on the date a request for deferral of issuance of a patent under § 1.314 was filed and ending on the date the patent was issued;

(3) Abandonment of the application or late payment of the issue fee, in which case the period of adjustment set forth in § 1.703 shall be reduced by the number of days, if any, beginning on the date of abandonment or the date after the date the issue fee was due and ending on the earlier of:

(i) The date of mailing of the decision reviving the application or accepting late payment of the issue fee; or

(ii) The date that is four months after the date the grantable petition to revive the application or accept late payment of the issue fee was filed;

(4) Failure to file a petition to withdraw the holding of abandonment or to revive an application within two months from the mailing date of a notice of abandonment, in which case the period of adjustment set forth in § 1.703 shall be reduced by the number of days, if any, beginning on the day after the date two months from the mailing date of a notice of abandonment and ending on the date a petition to withdraw the holding of abandonment or to revive the application was filed;

(5) Conversion of a provisional application under 35 U.S.C. 111(b) to a nonprovisional application under 35 U.S.C. 111(a) pursuant to 35 U.S.C. 111(b)(5), in which case the period of adjustment set forth in § 1.703 shall be reduced by the number of days, if any, beginning on the date the application was filed under 35 U.S.C. 111(b) and ending on the date a request in compliance with § 1.53(c)(3) to convert the provisional application into a nonprovisional application was filed;

(6) Submission of a preliminary amendment or other preliminary paper less than one month before the mailing of an Office action under 35 U.S.C. 132 or notice of allowance under 35 U.S.C. 151 that requires the mailing of a supplemental Office action or notice of allowance, in which case the period of adjustment set forth in § 1.703 shall be reduced by the lesser of:

(i) The number of days, if any, beginning on the day after the mailing date of the original Office action or notice of allowance and ending on the date of mailing of the supplemental Office action or notice of allowance; or

(ii) Four months;

(7) Submission of a reply having an omission (§ 1.135(c)), in which case the period of adjustment set forth in § 1.703 shall be reduced by the number of days, if any, beginning on the day after the date the reply having an omission was filed and ending on the date that the reply or other paper correcting the omission was filed;

(8) Submission of a supplemental reply or other paper, other than a supplemental reply or other paper expressly requested by the examiner, after a reply has been filed, in which case the period of adjustment set forth in § 1.703 shall be reduced by the number of days, if any, beginning on the day after the date the initial reply was filed and ending on the date that the supplemental reply or other such paper was filed;

(9) Submission of an amendment or other paper after a decision by the Patent Trial and Appeal Board, other than a decision designated as containing a new ground of rejection under § 41.50 (b) of this title or statement under § 41.50(c) of this title, or a decision by a Federal court, less than one month before the mailing of an Office action under 35 U.S.C. 132 or notice of allowance under 35 U.S.C. 151 that requires the mailing of a supplemental Office action or supplemental notice of allowance, in which case the period of adjustment set forth in § 1.703 shall be reduced by the lesser of:

(i) The number of days, if any, beginning on the day after the mailing date of the original Office action or notice of allowance and ending on the mailing date of the supplemental Office action or notice of allowance; or

(ii) Four months;

(10) Submission of an amendment under § 1.312 or other paper after a notice of allowance has been given or mailed, in which case the period of adjustment set forth in § 1.703 shall be reduced by the lesser of:

(i) The number of days, if any, beginning on the date the amendment under § 1.312 or other paper was filed and ending on the mailing date of the Office action or notice in response to the amendment under § 1.312 or such other paper; or

(ii) Four months;

(11) Failure to file an appeal brief in compliance with § 41.37 of this chapter within three months from the date on which a notice of appeal to the Patent Trial and Appeal Board was filed under 35 U.S.C. 134 and § 41.31 of this chapter, in which case the period of adjustment set forth in § 1.703 shall be reduced by the number of days, if any, beginning on the day after the date three months from the date on which a notice of appeal to the Patent Trial and Appeal Board was filed under 35 U.S.C. 134 and § 41.31 of this chapter, and ending on the date an appeal brief in compliance with § 41.37 of this chapter or a request for continued examination in compliance with § 1.114 was filed; and

(12) Further prosecution via a continuing application, in which case the period of adjustment set forth in § 1.703 shall not include any period that is prior to the actual filing date of the application that resulted in the patent.

(d)(1) A paper containing only an information disclosure statement in compliance with §§ 1.97 and 1.98 will not be considered a failure to engage in reasonable efforts to conclude prosecution (processing or examination) of the application under paragraphs (c)(6), (c)(8), (c)(9), or (c)(10) of this section if it is accompanied by a statement that each item of information contained in the information disclosure statement:

(i) Was first cited in any communication from a patent office in a counterpart foreign or international application or from the Office, and this communication was not received by any individual designated in § 1.56(c) more than thirty days prior to the filing of the information disclosure statement; or

(ii) Is a communication that was issued by a patent office in a counterpart foreign or international application or by the Office, and this communication was not received by any individual designated in § 1.56(c) more than thirty days prior to the filing of the information disclosure statement.

(2) The thirty-day period set forth in paragraph (d)(1) of this section is not extendable.

(e) The submission of a request under § 1.705(c) for reinstatement of reduced patent term adjustment will not be considered a failure to engage in reasonable efforts to conclude prosecution (processing or examination) of the application under paragraph (c)(10) of this section.

[65 FR 56393, Sept. 18, 2000, as amended at 69 FR 21711, Apr. 22, 2004; 69 FR 50002, Aug. 12, 2004; 72 FR 46843, Aug. 21, 2007; 74 FR 52691, Oct. 14, 2009; 76 FR 74702, Dec. 1, 2011; 77 FR 46628, Aug. 6, 2012; 77 FR 49360, Aug. 16, 2012; 78 FR 19420, Apr. 1, 2013]

§ 1.705 Patent term adjustment determination.

(a) The patent will include notification of any patent term adjustment under 35 U.S.C. 154(b).

(b) Any request for reconsideration of the patent term adjustment indicated on the patent must be by way of an application for patent term adjustment filed no later than two months from the date the patent was granted. This two-month time period may be extended under the provisions of § 1.136(a). An application for patent term adjustment under this section must be accompanied by:

(1) The fee set forth in § 1.18(e); and

(2) A statement of the facts involved, specifying:

(i) The correct patent term adjustment and the basis or bases under § 1.702 for the adjustment;

(ii) The relevant dates as specified in §§ 1.703(a) through (e) for which an adjustment is sought and the adjustment as specified in § 1.703(f) to which the patent is entitled;

(iii) Whether the patent is subject to a terminal disclaimer and any expiration date specified in the terminal disclaimer; and

(iv)(A) Any circumstances during the prosecution of the application resulting in the patent that constitute a failure to engage in reasonable efforts to conclude processing or examination of such application as set forth in § 1.704; or

(B) That there were no circumstances constituting a failure to engage in reasonable efforts to conclude processing or examination of such application as set forth in § 1.704.

(c) Any request for reinstatement of all or part of the period of adjustment reduced pursuant to § 1.704(b) for failing to reply to a rejection, objection, argument, or other request within three months of the date of mailing of the Office communication notifying the applicant of the rejection, objection, argument, or other request must be filed prior to the issuance of the patent. This time period is not extendable. Any request for reinstatement of all or part of the period of adjustment reduced pursuant to § 1.704(b) under this paragraph must also be accompanied by:

(1) The fee set forth in § 1.18(f); and

(2) A showing to the satisfaction of the Director that, in spite of all due care, the applicant was unable to reply to the rejection, objection, argument, or other request within three months of the date of mailing of the Office communication notifying the applicant of the rejection, objection, argument, or other request. The Office shall not grant any request for reinstatement for more than three additional months for each reply beyond three months from the date of mailing of the Office communication notifying the applicant of the rejection, objection, argument, or other request.

(d) No submission or petition on behalf of a third party concerning patent term adjustment under 35 U.S.C. 154(b) will be considered by the Office. Any such submission or petition will be returned to the third party, or otherwise disposed of, at the convenience of the Office.

[65 FR 56394, Sept. 18, 2000, as amended at 69 FR 21711, Apr. 22, 2004; 78 FR 19420, Apr. 1, 2013]

Extension of Patent Term Due to Regulatory Review

§ 1.710 Patents subject to extension of the patent term.

(a) A patent is eligible for extension of the patent term if the patent claims a product as defined in paragraph (b) of this section, either alone or in combination with other ingredients that read on a composition that received permission for commercial marketing or use, or a method of using such a product, or a method of manufacturing such a product, and meets all other conditions and requirements of this subpart.

(b) The term *product* referred to in paragraph (a) of this section means—

(1) The active ingredient of a new human drug, antibiotic drug, or human biological product (as those terms are used in the Federal Food, Drug, and Cosmetic Act and the Public Health Service Act) including any salt or ester of the active ingredient, as a single entity or in combination with another active ingredient; or

(2) The active ingredient of a new animal drug or veterinary biological product (as those terms are used in the Federal Food, Drug, and Cosmetic Act and the Virus-Serum-Toxin Act) that is not primarily manufactured using recombinant DNA, recombinant RNA, hybridoma technology, or other processes including site specific genetic manipulation techniques, including any salt or ester of the active ingredient, as a single entity or in combination with another active ingredient; or

(3) Any medical device, food additive, or color additive subject to regulation under the Federal Food, Drug, and Cosmetic Act.

[54 FR 30379, July 20, 1989]

§ 1.720 Conditions for extension of patent term.

The term of a patent may be extended if:

(a) The patent claims a product or a method of using or manufacturing a product as defined in § 1.710;

(b) The term of the patent has never been previously extended, except for extensions issued pursuant to §§ 1.701, 1.760, or § 1.790;

(c) An application for extension is submitted in compliance with § 1.740;

(d) The product has been subject to a regulatory review period as defined in 35 U.S.C. 156(g) before its commercial marketing or use;

(e) The product has received permission for commercial marketing or use and—

(1) The permission for the commercial marketing or use of the product is the first received permission for commercial marketing or use under the provision of law under which the applicable regulatory review occurred, or

(2) In the case of a patent other than one directed to subject matter within § 1.710(b)(2) claiming a method of manufacturing the product that primarily uses recombinant DNA technology in the manufacture of the product, the permission for the commercial marketing or use is the first received permission for the commercial marketing or use of a product manufactured under the process claimed in the patent, or

(3) In the case of a patent claiming a new animal drug or a veterinary biological product that is not covered by the claims in any other patent that has been extended, and has received permission for the commercial marketing or use in non-food-producing animals and in food-producing animals, and was not extended on the basis of the regulatory review period for use in non-food-producing animals, the permission for the commercial marketing or use of the drug or product after the regulatory review period for use in food-producing animals is the first permitted commercial marketing or use of the drug or product for administration to a food-producing animal.

(f) The application is submitted within the sixty-day period beginning on the date the product first received permission for commercial marketing or use under the provisions of law under which the applicable regulatory review period occurred; or in the case of a patent claiming a method of manufacturing the product which primarily uses recombinant DNA technology in the manufacture of the product, the application for extension is submitted within the sixty-day period beginning on the date of the first permitted commercial marketing or use of a product manufactured under the process claimed in the patent; or in the case of a patent that claims a new animal drug or a veterinary biological product that is not covered by the claims in any other patent that has been extended, and said drug or product has received permission for the commercial marketing or use in non-food-producing animals, the application for extension is submitted within the sixty-day period beginning on the date of the first permitted commercial marketing or use of the drug or product for administration to a food-producing animal;

(g) The term of the patent, including any interim extension issued pursuant to § 1.790, has not expired before the submission of an application in compliance with § 1.741; and

(h) No other patent term has been extended for the same regulatory review period for the product.

[52 FR 9394, Mar. 24, 1987, as amended at 54 FR 30380, July 20, 1989; 65 FR 54679, Sept. 8, 2000]

§ 1.730 Applicant for extension of patent term; signature requirements.

(a) Any application for extension of a patent term must be submitted by the owner of record of the patent or its agent and must comply with the requirements of § 1.740.

(b) If the application is submitted by the patent owner, the application must be signed either by:

(1) The patent owner in compliance with § 3.73(c) of this chapter; or

(2) A registered practitioner on behalf of the patent owner.

(c) If the application is submitted on behalf of the patent owner by an agent of the patent owner (e.g., a licensee of the patent owner), the application must be signed by a registered practitioner on behalf of the agent. The Office may require proof that the agent is authorized to act on behalf of the patent owner.

(d) If the application is signed by a registered practitioner, the Office may require proof that the practitioner is authorized to act on behalf of the patent owner or agent of the patent owner.

[65 FR 54679, Sept. 8, 2000, as amended at 77 FR 48825, Aug. 14, 2012]

§ 1.740 Formal requirements for application for extension of patent term; correction of informalities.

(a) An application for extension of patent term must be made in writing to the Director. A formal application for the extension of patent term must include:

(1) A complete identification of the approved product as by appropriate chemical and generic name, physical structure or characteristics;

(2) A complete identification of the Federal statute including the applicable provision of law under which the regulatory review occurred;

(3) An identification of the date on which the product received permission for commercial marketing or use under the provision of law under which the applicable regulatory review period occurred;

(4) In the case of a drug product, an identification of each active ingredient in the product and as to each active ingredient, a statement that it has not been previously approved for commercial marketing or use under the Federal Food, Drug, and Cosmetic Act, the Public Health Service Act, or the Virus-Serum-Toxin Act, or a statement of when the active ingredient was approved for commercial marketing or use (either alone or in combination with other active ingredients), the use for which it was approved, and the provision of law under which it was approved.

(5) A statement that the application is being submitted within the sixty day period permitted for submission pursuant to § 1.720(f) and an identification of the date of the last day on which the application could be submitted;

(6) A complete identification of the patent for which an extension is being sought by the name of the inventor, the patent number, the date of issue, and the date of expiration;

(7) A copy of the patent for which an extension is being sought, including the entire specification (including claims) and drawings;

(8) A copy of any disclaimer, certificate of correction, receipt of maintenance fee payment, or reexamination certificate issued in the patent;

(9) A statement that the patent claims the approved product, or a method of using or manufacturing the approved product, and a showing which lists each applicable patent claim and demonstrates the manner in which at least one such patent claim reads on:

(i) The approved product, if the listed claims include any claim to the approved product;

(ii) The method of using the approved product, if the listed claims include any claim to the method of using the approved product; and

(iii) The method of manufacturing the approved product, if the listed claims include any claim to the method of manufacturing the approved product;

(10) A statement beginning on a new page of the relevant dates and information pursuant to 35 U.S.C. 156(g) in order to enable the Secretary of Health and Human Services or the Secretary of Agriculture, as appropriate, to determine the applicable regulatory review period as follows:

(i) For a patent claiming a human drug, antibiotic, or human biological product:

(A) The effective date of the investigational new drug (IND) application and the IND number;

(B) The date on which a new drug application (NDA) or a Product License Application (PLA) was initially submitted and the NDA or PLA number; and

(C) The date on which the NDA was approved or the Product License issued;

(ii) For a patent claiming a new animal drug:

(A) The date a major health or environmental effects test on the drug was initiated, and any available substantiation of that date, or the date of an exemption under subsection (j) of Section 512 of the Federal Food, Drug, and Cosmetic Act became effective for such animal drug;

(B) The date on which a new animal drug application (NADA) was initially submitted and the NADA number; and

(C) The date on which the NADA was approved;

(iii) For a patent claiming a veterinary biological product:

(A) The date the authority to prepare an experimental biological product under the Virus-Serum-Toxin Act became effective;

(B) The date an application for a license was submitted under the Virus-Serum-Toxin Act; and

(C) The date the license issued;

(iv) For a patent claiming a food or color additive:

(A) The date a major health or environmental effects test on the additive was initiated and any available substantiation of that date;

(B) The date on which a petition for product approval under the Federal Food, Drug and Cosmetic Act was initially submitted and the petition number; and

(C) The date on which the FDA published a FEDERAL REGISTER notice listing the additive for use;

(v) For a patent claiming a medical device:

(A) The effective date of the investigational device exemption (IDE) and the IDE number, if applicable, or the date on which the applicant began the first clinical investigation involving the device, if no IDE was submitted, and any available substantiation of that date;

(B) The date on which the application for product approval or notice of completion of a product development protocol under Section 515 of the Federal Food, Drug and Cosmetic Act was initially submitted and the number of the application; and

(C) The date on which the application was approved or the protocol declared to be completed;

(11) A brief description beginning on a new page of the significant activities undertaken by the marketing applicant during the applicable regulatory review period with respect to the approved product and the significant dates applicable to such activities;

(12) A statement beginning on a new page that in the opinion of the applicant the patent is eligible for the extension and a statement as to the length of extension claimed, including how the length of extension was determined;

(13) A statement that applicant acknowledges a duty to disclose to the Director of the United States Patent and Trademark Office and the Secretary of Health and Human Services or the Secretary of Agriculture any information which is material to the determination of entitlement to the extension sought (*see* § 1.765);

(14) The prescribed fee for receiving and acting upon the application for extension (see § 1.20(j)); and

(15) The name, address, and telephone number of the person to whom inquiries and correspondence relating to the application for patent term extension are to be directed.

(b) The application under this section must be accompanied by two additional copies of such application (for a total of three copies).

(c) If an application for extension of patent term is informal under this section, the Office will so notify the applicant. The applicant has two months from the mail date of the notice, or such time as is set in the notice, within which to correct the informality. Unless the notice indicates otherwise, this time period may be extended under the provisions of § 1.136.

[54 FR 9394, Mar. 24, 1987, as amended at 54 FR 30380, July 20, 1989; 56 FR 65155, Dec. 13, 1991; 65 FR 54679, Sept. 8, 2000; 68 FR 14337, Mar. 25, 2003]

§ 1.741 Complete application given a filing date; petition procedure.

(a) The filing date of an application for extension of a patent term is the date on which a complete application is received in the Office or filed pursuant to the procedures set forth in § 1.8 or § 1.10. A complete application must include:

(1) An identification of the approved product;

(2) An identification of each Federal statute under which regulatory review occurred;

(3) An identification of the patent for which an extension is being sought;

(4) An identification of each claim of the patent which claims the approved product or a method of using or manufacturing the approved product;

(5) Sufficient information to enable the Director to determine under subsections (a) and (b) of 35 U.S.C. 156 the eligibility of a patent for extension, and the rights that will be derived from the extension, and information to enable the Director and the Secretary of

Health and Human Services or the Secretary of Agriculture to determine the length of the regulatory review period; and

(6) A brief description of the activities undertaken by the marketing applicant during the applicable regulatory review period with respect to the approved product and the significant dates applicable to such activities.

(b) If an application for extension of patent term is incomplete under this section, the Office will so notify the applicant. If applicant requests review of a notice that an application is incomplete, or review of the filing date accorded an application under this section, applicant must file a petition pursuant to this paragraph accompanied by the fee set forth in § 1.17(f) within two months of the mail date of the notice that the application is incomplete, or the notice according the filing date complained of. Unless the notice indicates otherwise, this time period may be extended under the provisions of § 1.136.

[52 FR 9394, Mar. 24, 1987, as amended at 59 FR 54503, Oct. 22, 1993; 61 FR 64028, Dec. 3, 1996; 65 FR 54680, Sept. 8, 2000; 69 FR 56546, Sept. 21, 2004]

§ 1.750 Determination of eligibility for extension of patent term.

A determination as to whether a patent is eligible for extension may be made by the Director solely on the basis of the representations contained in the application for extension filed in compliance with § 1.740 or § 1.790. This determination may be delegated to appropriate Patent and Trademark Office officials and may be made at any time before the certificate of extension is issued. The Director or other appropriate officials may require from applicant further information or make such independent inquiries as desired before a final determination is made on whether a patent is eligible for extension. In an application for extension filed in compliance with § 1.740, a notice will be mailed to applicant containing the determination as to the eligibility of the patent for extension and the period of time of the extension, if any. This notice shall constitute the final determination as to the eligibility and any period of extension of the patent. A single request for reconsideration of a final determination may be made if filed by the applicant within such time as may be set in the notice of final determination or, if no time is set, within one month from the date of the final determination. The time periods set forth herein are subject to the provisions of § 1.136.

[60 FR 25618, May 12, 1995]

§ 1.760 Interim extension of patent term under 35 U.S.C. 156(e)(2).

An applicant who has filed a formal application for extension in compliance with § 1.740 may request one or more interim extensions for periods of up to one year each pending a final determination on the application pursuant to § 1.750. Any such request should be filed at least three months prior to the expiration date of the patent. The Director may issue interim extensions, without a request by the applicant, for periods of up to one year each until a final determination is made. The patent owner or agent will be notified when an interim extension is granted and notice of the extension will be published in the *Official Gazette of the United States Patent and Trademark Office*. The notice will be recorded in the official file of the patent and will be considered as part of the original patent. In no event will the interim extensions granted under this section be longer than the maximum period for extension to which the applicant would be eligible.

[65 FR 54680, Sept. 8, 2000]

§ 1.765 Duty of disclosure in patent term extension proceedings.

(a) A duty of candor and good faith toward the Patent and Trademark Office and the Secretary of Health and Human Services or the Secretary of Agriculture rests on the patent owner or its agent, on each attorney or agent who represents the patent owner and on every other individual who is substantively involved on behalf of the patent owner in a patent term extension proceeding. All such individuals who are aware, or become aware, of material information adverse to a determination of entitlement to the extension sought, which has not been previously made of record in the patent term extension proceeding must bring such information to the attention of the Office or the Secretary, as appropriate, in accordance with paragraph (b) of this section, as soon as it is practical to do so after the individual becomes aware of the information. Information is material where there is a substantial likelihood that the Office or the Secretary would consider it important in determinations to be made in the patent term extension proceeding.

(b) Disclosures pursuant to this section must be accompanied by a copy of each written document which is being disclosed. The disclosure must be made to the Office or the Secretary, as appropriate, unless the disclosure is material to determinations to be made by both the Office and the Secretary, in which case duplicate copies, certified as such, must be filed in the Office and with the Secretary. Disclosures pursuant to this section may be made to the Office or the Secretary, as appropriate, through an attorney or agent having responsibility on behalf of the patent owner or its agent for the patent term extension proceeding or through a patent owner acting on his or her own behalf. Disclosure to such an attorney, agent or patent owner shall satisfy the duty of any other individual. Such an attorney, agent or patent owner has no duty to transmit information which is not material to the determination of entitlement to the extension sought.

(c) No patent will be determined eligible for extension and no extension will be issued if it is determined that fraud on the Office or the Secretary was practiced or attempted or the duty of disclosure was violated through bad faith or gross negligence in connection with the patent term extension proceeding. If it is established by clear and convincing evidence that any fraud was practiced or attempted on the Office or the Secretary in connection with the patent term extension proceeding or that there was any violation of the duty of disclosure through bad faith or gross negligence in connection with the patent term extension proceeding, a final determination will be made pursuant to § 1.750 that the patent is not eligible for extension.

(d) The duty of disclosure pursuant to this section rests on the individuals identified in paragraph (a) of this section and no submission on behalf of third parties, in the form of protests or otherwise, will be considered by the Office. Any such submissions by third parties to the Office will be returned to the party making the submission, or otherwise disposed of, without consideration by the Office.

[24 FR 10332, Dec. 22, 1959, as amended at 54 FR 30381, July 20, 1989; 60 FR 25618, May 12, 1995]

§ 1.770 Express withdrawal of application for extension of patent term.

An application for extension of patent term may be expressly withdrawn before a determination is made pursuant to § 1.750 by filing in the Office, in duplicate, a written declaration of withdrawal signed by the owner of record of the patent or its agent. An application may not be expressly withdrawn after the date permitted for reply to the final determination on the application. An express withdrawal pursuant to this section is effective when acknowledged in writing by the Office. The filing of an express withdrawal pursuant to this section and its acceptance by the Office does not entitle applicant to a refund of the filing fee (§ 1.20(j)) or any portion thereof.

[62 FR 53201, Oct. 10, 1997]

§ 1.775 Calculation of patent term extension for a human drug, antibiotic drug or human biological product.

(a) If a determination is made pursuant to § 1.750 that a patent for a human drug, antibiotic drug or human biological product is eligible for extension, the term shall be extended by the time as calculated in days in the manner indicated by this section. The patent term extension will run from the original expiration date of the patent or any earlier date set by terminal disclaimer (§ 1.321).

(b) The term of the patent for a human drug, antibiotic drug or human biological product will be extended by the length of the regulatory review period for the product as determined by the Secretary of Health and Human Services, reduced as appropriate pursuant to paragraphs (d)(1) through (d)(6) of this section.

(c) The length of the regulatory review period for a human drug, antibiotic drug or human biological product will be determined by the Secretary of Health and Human Services. Under 35 U.S.C. 156(g)(1)(B), it is the sum of—

(1) The number of days in the period beginning on the date an exemption under subsection (i) of section 505 or subsection (d) of section 507 of the Federal Food, Drug, and Cosmetic Act became effective for the approved product and ending on the date the application was initially submitted for such product under those sections or under section 351 of the Public Health Service Act; and

(2) The number of days in the period beginning on the date the application was initially submitted for the approved product under section 351 of the Public Health Service Act, subsection (b) of section 505 or section 507 of the Federal Food, Drug, and Cosmetic Act and ending on the date such application was approved under such section.

(d) The term of the patent as extended for a human drug, antibiotic drug or human biological product will be determined by—

(1) Subtracting from the number of days determined by the Secretary of Health and Human Services to be in the regulatory review period:

(i) The number of days in the periods of paragraphs (c)(1) and (c)(2) of this section which were on and before the date on which the patent issued;

(ii) The number of days in the periods of paragraphs (c)(1) and (c)(2) of this section during which it is determined under 35 U.S.C. 156(d)(2)(B) by the Secretary of Health and Human Services that applicant did not act with due diligence;

(iii) One-half the number of days remaining in the period defined by paragraph (c)(1) of this section after that period is reduced in accordance with paragraphs (d)(1) (i) and (ii) of this section; half days will be ignored for purposes of subtraction;

(2) By adding the number of days determined in paragraph (d)(1) of this section to the original term of the patent as shortened by any terminal disclaimer;

(3) By adding 14 years to the date of approval of the application under section 351 of the Public Health Service Act, or subsection (b) of section 505 or section 507 of the Federal Food, Drug, and Cosmetic Act;

(4) By comparing the dates for the ends of the periods obtained pursuant to paragraphs (d)(2) and (d)(3) of this section with each other and selecting the earlier date;

(5) If the original patent was issued after September 24, 1984,

(i) By adding 5 years to the original expiration date of the patent or any earlier date set by terminal disclaimer; and

(ii) By comparing the dates obtained pursuant to paragraphs (d)(4) and (d)(5)(i) of this section with each other and selecting the earlier date;

(6) If the original patent was issued before September 24, 1984, and

(i) If no request was submitted for an exemption under subsection (i) of section 505 or subsection (d) of section 507 of the Federal Food, Drug, and Cosmetic Act before September 24, 1984, by—

(A) Adding 5 years to the original expiration date of the patent or earlier date set by terminal disclaimer; and

(B) By comparing the dates obtained pursuant to paragraphs (d)(4) and (d)(6)(i)(A) of this section with each other and selecting the earlier date; or

(ii) If a request was submitted for an exemption under subsection (i) of section 505 or subsection (d) of section 507 of the Federal Food, Drug, or Cosmetic Act before September 24, 1984 and the commercial marketing or use of the product was not approved before September 24, 1984, by—

(A) Adding 2 years to the original expiration date of the patent or earlier date set by terminal disclaimer, and

(B) By comparing the dates obtained pursuant to paragraphs (d)(4) and (d)(6)(ii)(A) of this section with each other and selecting the earlier date.

[52 FR 9394, Mar. 24, 1987, as amended at 54 FR 30381, July 20, 1989]

§ 1.776 Calculation of patent term extension for a food additive or color additive.

(a) If a determination is made pursuant to § 1.750 that a patent for a food additive or color additive is eligible for extension, the term shall be extended by the time as calculated in days in the manner indicated by this section. The patent term extension will run from the original expiration date of the patent or earlier date set by terminal disclaimer (§ 1.321).

(b) The term of the patent for a food additive or color additive will be extended by the length of the regulatory review period for the product as determined by the Secretary of Health and Human Services, reduced as appropriate pursuant to paragraphs (d)(1) through (d)(6) of this section.

(c) The length of the regulatory review period for a food additive or color additive will be determined by the Secretary of Health and Human Services. Under 35 U.S.C. 156(g)(2)(B), it is the sum of—

(1) The number of days in the period beginning on the date a major health or environmental effects test on the additive was initiated and ending on the date a petition was initially submitted with respect to the approved product under the Federal Food, Drug, and Cosmetic Act requesting the issuance of a regulation for use of the product; and

(2) The number of days in the period beginning on the date a petition was initially submitted with respect to the approved product under the Federal Food, Drug, and Cosmetic Act requesting the issuance of a regulation for use of the product, and ending on the date such regulation became effective or, if objections were filed to such regulation, ending on the date such objections were resolved and commercial marketing was permitted or, if commercial marketing was permitted and later revoked pending further proceedings as a result of such objections, ending on the date such proceedings were finally resolved and commercial marketing was permitted.

(d) The term of the patent as extended for a food additive or color additive will be determined by

(1) Subtracting from the number of days determined by the Secretary of Health and Human Services to be in the regulatory review period:

(i) The number of days in the periods of paragraphs (c)(1) and (c)(2) of this section which were on and before the date on which the patent issued;

(ii) The number of days in the periods of paragraphs (c)(1) and (c)(2) of this section during which it is determined under 35 U.S.C. 156(d)(2)(B) by the Secretary of Health and Human Services that applicant did not act with due diligence;

(iii) The number of days equal to one-half the number of days remaining in the period defined by paragraph (c)(1) of this section after that period is reduced in accordance with paragraphs (d)(1) (i) and (ii) of this section; half days will be ignored for purposes of subtraction;

(2) By adding the number of days determined in paragraph (d)(1) of this section to the original term of the patent as shortened by any terminal disclaimer;

(3) By adding 14 years to the date a regulation for use of the product became effective or, if objections were filed to such regulation, to the date such objections were resolved and commercial marketing was permitted or, if commercial marketing was permitted and later revoked pending further proceedings as a result of such objections, to the date such proceedings were finally resolved and commercial marketing was permitted;

(4) By comparing the dates for the ends of the periods obtained pursuant to paragraphs (d)(2) and (d)(3) of this section with each other and selecting the earlier date;

(5) If the original patent was issued after September 24, 1984,

(i) By adding 5 years to the original expiration date of the patent or earlier date set by terminal disclaimer; and

(ii) By comparing the dates obtained pursuant to paragraphs (d)(4) and (d)(5)(i) of this section with each other and selecting the earlier date;

(6) If the original patent was issued before September 24, 1984, and

(i) If no major health or environmental effects test was initiated and no petition for a regulation or application for registration was submitted before September 24, 1984, by—

(A) Adding 5 years to the original expiration date of the patent or earlier date set by terminal disclaimer, and

(B) By comparing the dates obtained pursuant to paragraphs (d)(4) and (d)(6)(i)(A) of this section with each other and selecting the earlier date; or

(ii) If a major health or environmental effects test was initiated or a petition for a regulation or application for registration was submitted by September 24, 1984, and the commercial marketing or use of the product was not approved before September 24, 1984, by—

(A) Adding 2 years to the original expiration date of the patent or earlier date set by terminal disclaimer, and

(B) By comparing the dates obtained pursuant to paragraphs (d)(4) and (d)(6)(ii)(A) of this section with each other and selecting the earlier date.

§ 1.777 Calculation of patent term extension for a medical device.

(a) If a determination is made pursuant to § 1.750 that a patent for a medical device is eligible for extension, the term shall be extended by the time as calculated in days in the manner indicated by this section. The patent term extension will run from the original expiration date of the patent or earlier date as set by terminal disclaimer (§ 1.321).

(b) The term of the patent for a medical device will be extended by the length of the regulatory review period for the product as determined by the Secretary of Health and Human Services, reduced as appropriate pursuant to paragraphs (d)(1) through (d)(6) of this section.

(c) The length of the regulatory review period for a medical device will be determined by the Secretary of Health and Human Services. Under 35 U.S.C. 156(g)(3)(B), it is the sum of

(1) The number of days in the period beginning on the date a clinical investigation on humans involving the device was begun and ending on the date an application was initially submitted with respect to the device under section 515 of the Federal Food, Drug, and Cosmetic Act; and

(2) The number of days in the period beginning on the date the application was initially submitted with respect to the device under section 515 of the Federal Food, Drug, and Cosmetic Act, and ending on the date such application was approved under such Act or the period beginning on the date a notice of completion of a product development protocol was initially submitted under section 515(f)(5) of the Act and ending on the date the protocol was declared completed under section 515(f)(6) of the Act.

(d) The term of the patent as extended for a medical device will be determined by—

(1) Substracting from the number of days determined by the Secretary of Health and Human Services to be in the regulatory review period pursuant to paragraph (c) of this section:

(i) The number of days in the periods of paragraphs (c)(1) and (c)(2) of this section which were on and before the date on which the patent issued;

(ii) The number of days in the periods of paragraphs (c)(1) and (c)(2) of this section during which it is determined under 35 U.S.C. 156(d)(2)(B) by the Secretary of Health and Human Services that applicant did not act with due diligence;

(iii) One-half the number of days remaining in the period defined by paragraph (c)(1) of this section after that period is reduced in accordance with paragraphs (d)(1) (i) and (ii) of this section; half days will be ignored for purposes of subtraction;

(2) By adding the number of days determined in paragraph (d)(1) of this section to the original term of the patent as shortened by any terminal disclaimer;

(3) By adding 14 years to the date of approval of the application under section 515 of the Federal Food, Drug, and Cosmetic Act or the date a product development protocol was declared completed under section 515(f)(6) of the Act;

(4) By comparing the dates for the ends of the periods obtained pursuant to paragraphs (d)(2) and (d)(3) of this section with each other and selecting the earlier date;

(5) If the original patent was issued after September 24, 1984,

(i) By adding 5 years to the original expiration date of the patent or earlier date set by terminal disclaimer; and

(ii) By comparing the dates obtained pursuant to paragraphs (d)(4) and (d)(5)(i) of this section with each other and selecting the earlier date;

(6) If the original patent was issued before September 24, 1984, and

(i) If no clinical investigation on humans involving the device was begun or no product development protocol was submitted under section 515(f)(5) of the Federal Food, Drug, and Cosmetic Act before September 24, 1984, by—

(A) Adding 5 years to the original expiration date of the patent or earlier date set by terminal disclaimer and

(B) By comparing the dates obtained pursuant to paragraphs (d)(4) and (d)(6)(i)(A) of this section with each other and selecting the earlier date; or

(ii) If a clinical investigation on humans involving the device was begun or a product development protocol was submitted under section 515(f)(5) of the Federal Food, Drug, and Cosmetic Act before September 24, 1984 and the commercial marketing or use of the product was not approved before September 24, 1984, by

(A) Adding 2 years to the original expiration date of the patent or earlier date set by terminal disclaimer, and

(B) By comparing the dates obtained pursuant to paragraphs (d)(4) and (d)(6)(ii)(A) of this section with each other and selecting the earlier date.

§ 1.778 Calculation of patent term extension for an animal drug product.

(a) If a determination is made pursuant to § 1.750 that a patent for an animal drug is eligible for extension, the term shall be extended by the time as calculated in days in the manner indicated by this section. The patent term extension will run from the original expiration date of the patent or any earlier date set by terminal disclaimer (§ 1.321).

(b) The term of the patent for an animal drug will be extended by the length of the regulatory review period for the drug as determined by the Secretary of Health and Human Services, reduced as appropriate pursuant to paragraphs (d)(1) through (d)(6) of this section.

(c) The length of the regulatory review period for an animal drug will be determined by the Secretary of Health and Human Services. Under 35 U.S.C. 156(g)(4)(B), it is the sum of—

(1) The number of days in the period beginning on the earlier of the date a major health or environmental effects test on the drug was initiated or the date an exemption under subsection (j) of section 512 of the Federal Food, Drug, and Cosmetic Act became effective for the approved animal drug and ending on the date an application was initially submitted for such animal drug under section 512 of the Federal Food, Drug, and Cosmetic Act; and

(2) The number of days in the period beginning on the date the application was initially submitted for the approved animal drug under subsection (b) of section 512 of the Federal Food, Drug, and Cosmetic Act and ending on the date such application was approved under such section.

(d) The term of the patent as extended for an animal drug will be determined by—

(1) Subtracting from the number of days determined by the Secretary of Health and Human Services to be in the regulatory review period:

(i) The number of days in the periods of paragraphs (c)(1) and (c)(2) of this section that were on and before the date on which the patent issued;

(ii) The number of days in the periods of paragraphs (c)(1) and (c)(2) of this section during which it is determined under 35 U.S.C. 156(d)(2)(B) by the Secretary of Health and Human Services that applicant did not act with due diligence;

(iii) One-half the number of days remaining in the period defined by paragraph (c)(1) of this section after that period is reduced in accordance with paragraphs (d)(1) (i) and (ii) of this section; half days will be ignored for purposes of subtraction;

(2) By adding the number of days determined in paragraph (d)(1) of this section to the original term of the patent as shortened by any terminal disclaimer;

(3) By adding 14 years to the date of approval of the application under section 512 of the Federal Food, Drug, and Cosmetic Act;

(4) By comparing the dates for the ends of the periods obtained pursuant to paragraphs (d)(2) and (d)(3) of this section with each other and selecting the earlier date;

(5) If the original patent was issued after November 16, 1988, by—

(i) Adding 5 years to the original expiration date of the patent or any earlier date set by terminal disclaimer; and

(ii) Comparing the dates obtained pursuant to paragraphs (d)(4) and (d)(5)(i) of this section with each other and selecting the earlier date;

(6) If the original patent was issued before November 16, 1988, and

(i) If no major health or environmental effects test on the drug was initiated and no request was submitted for an exemption under subsection (j) of section 512 of the Federal Food, Drug, and Cosmetic Act before November 16, 1988, by—

(A) Adding 5 years to the original expiration date of the patent or earlier date set by terminal disclaimer; and

(B) Comparing the dates obtained pursuant to paragraphs (d)(4) and (d)(6)(i)(A) of this section with each other and selecting the earlier date; or

(ii) If a major health or environmental effects test was initiated or a request for an exemption under subsection (j) of section 512 of the Federal Food, Drug, and Cosmetic Act was submitted before November 16, 1988, and the application for commercial marketing or use of the animal drug was not approved before November 16, 1988, by—

(A) Adding 3 years to the original expiration date of the patent or earlier date set by terminal disclaimer, and

(B) Comparing the dates obtained pursuant to paragraphs (d)(4) and (d)(6)(ii)(A) of this section with each other and selecting the earlier date.

[54 FR 30381, July 20, 1989]

§ 1.779 Calculation of patent term extension for a veterinary biological product.

(a) If a determination is made pursuant to § 1.750 that a patent for a veterinary biological product is eligible for extension, the term shall be extended by the time as calculated in days in the manner indicated by this section. The patent term extension will run from the original expiration date of the patent or any earlier date set by terminal disclaimer (§ 1.321).

(b) The term of the patent for a veterinary biological product will be extended by the length of the regulatory review period for the product as determined by the Secretary of Agriculture, reduced as appropriate pursuant to paragraphs (d)(1) through (d)(6) of this section.

(c) The length of the regulatory review period for a veterinary biological product will be determined by the Secretary of Agriculture. Under 35 U.S.C. 156(g)(5)(B), it is the sum of—

(1) The number of days in the period beginning on the date the authority to prepare an experimental biological product under the Virus-Serum-Toxin Act became effective and ending on the date an application for a license was submitted under the Virus-Serum-Toxin Act; and

(2) The number of days in the period beginning on the date an application for a license was initially submitted for approval under the Virus-Serum-Toxin Act and ending on the date such license was issued.

(d) The term of the patent as extended for a veterinary biological product will be determined by—

(1) Subtracting from the number of days determined by the Secretary of Agriculture to be in the regulatory review period:

(i) The number of days in the periods of paragraphs (c)(1) and (c)(2) of this section that were on and before the date on which the patent issued;

(ii) The number of days in the periods of paragraphs (c)(1) and (c)(2) of this section during which it is determined under 35 U.S.C. 156(d)(2)(B) by the Secretary of Agriculture that applicant did not act with due diligence;

(iii) One-half the number of days remaining in the period defined by paragraph (c)(1) of this section after that period is reduced in accordance with paragraphs (d)(1) (i) and (ii) of this section; half days will be ignored for purposes of subtraction;

(2) By adding the number of days determined in paragraph (d)(1) of this section to the original term of the patent

as shortened by any terminal disclaimer;

(3) By adding 14 years to the date of the issuance of a license under the Virus-Serum-Toxin Act;

(4) By comparing the dates for the ends of the periods obtained pursuant to paragraphs (d)(2) and (d)(3) of this section with each other and selecting the earlier date;

(5) If the original patent was issued after November 16, 1988, by—

(i) Adding 5 years to the original expiration date of the patent or any earlier date set by terminal disclaimer; and

(ii) Comparing the dates obtained pursuant to paragraphs (d)(4) and (d)(5)(i) of this section with each other and selecting the earlier date;

(6) If the original patent was issued before November 16, 1988, and

(i) If no request for the authority to prepare an experimental biological product under the Virus-Serum-Toxin Act was submitted before November 16, 1988, by—

(A) Adding 5 years to the original expiration date of the patent or earlier date set by terminal disclaimer; and

(B) Comparing the dates obtained pursuant to paragraphs (d)(4) and (d)(6)(i)(A) of this section with each other and selecting the earlier date; or

(ii) If a request for the authority to prepare an experimental biological product under the Virus-Serum-Toxin Act was submitted before November 16, 1988, and the commercial marketing or use of the product was not approved before November 16, 1988, by—

(A) Adding 3 years to the original expiration date of the patent or earlier date set by terminal disclaimer; and

(B) Comparing the dates obtained pursuant to paragraphs (d)(4) and (d)(6)(ii)(A) of this section with each other and selecting the earlier date.

[52 FR 9394, Mar. 24, 1987, as amended at 54 FR 30382, July 20, 1989]

§ 1.780 Certificate or order of extension of patent term.

If a determination is made pursuant to § 1.750 that a patent is eligible for extension and that the term of the patent is to be extended, a certificate of extension, under seal, or an order granting interim extension under 35 U.S.C. 156(d)(5), will be issued to the applicant for the extension of the patent term. Such certificate or order will be recorded in the official file of the patent and will be considered as part of the original patent. Notification of the issuance of the certificate or order of extension will be published in the *Official Gazette of the United States Patent and Trademark Office*. Notification of the issuance of the order granting an interim extension under 35 U.S.C. 156(d)(5), including the identity of the product currently under regulatory review, will be published in the *Official Gazette of the United States Patent and Trademark Office* and in the FEDERAL REGISTER. No certificate of, or order granting, an extension will be issued if the term of the patent cannot be extended, even though the patent is otherwise determined to be eligible for extension. In such situations, the final determination made pursuant to § 1.750 will indicate that no certificate or order will issue.

[65 FR 54680, Sept. 8, 2000]

§ 1.785 Multiple applications for extension of term of the same patent or of different patents for the same regulatory review period for a product.

(a) Only one patent may be extended for a regulatory review period for any product (§ 1.720(h)). If more than one application for extension of the same patent is filed, the certificate of extension of patent term, if appropriate, will be issued based upon the first filed application for extension.

(b) If more than one application for extension is filed by a single applicant which seeks the extension of the term of two or more patents based upon the same regulatory review period, and the patents are otherwise eligible for extension pursuant to the requirements of this subpart, in the absence of an election by the applicant, the certificate of extension of patent term, if appropriate, will be issued upon the application for extension of the patent term having the earliest date of issuance of those patents for which extension is sought.

(c) If an application for extension is filed which seeks the extension of the term of a patent based upon the same regulatory review period as that relied upon in one or more applications for extension pursuant to the requirements of this subpart, the certificate of extension of patent term will be issued on the application only if the patent owner or its agent is the holder of the regulatory approval granted with respect to the regulatory review period.

(d) An application for extension shall be considered complete and formal regardless of whether it contains the identification of the holder of the regulatory approval granted with respect to the regulatory review period. When an application contains such information, or is amended to contain such information, it will be considered in determining whether an application is eligible for an extension under this section. A request may be made of any applicant to supply such information within a non-extendable period of not less than one month whenever multiple applications for extension of more than one patent are received and rely upon the same regulatory review period. Failure to provide such information within the period for reply set shall be regarded as conclusively establishing that the applicant is not the holder of the regulatory approval.

(e) Determinations made under this section shall be included in the notice of final determination of eligibility for extension of the patent term pursuant to § 1.750 and shall be regarded as part of that determination.

[60 FR 25618, May 12, 1995, as amended at 62 FR 53201, Oct. 10, 1997]

§ 1.790 Interim extension of patent term under 35 U.S.C. 156(d)(5).

(a) An owner of record of a patent or its agent who reasonably expects that the applicable regulatory review period described in paragraph (1)(B)(ii), (2)(B)(ii), (3)(B)(ii), (4)(B)(ii), or (5)(B)(ii) of subsection (g) that began for a product that is the subject of such patent may extend beyond the expiration of the patent term in effect may submit one or more applications for interim extensions for periods of up to one year each. The initial application for interim extension must be filed during the period beginning 6 months and ending 15 days before the patent term is due to expire. Each subsequent application for interim extension must be filed during the period beginning 60 days before and ending 30 days before the expiration of the preceding interim extension. In no event will the interim extensions granted under this section be longer than the maximum period of extension to which the applicant would be entitled under 35 U.S.C. 156(c).

(b) A complete application for interim extension under this section shall include all of the information required for a formal application under § 1.740 and a complete application under § 1.741. Sections (a)(1), (a)(2), (a)(4), and (a)(6)–(a)(17) of § 1.740 and § 1.741 shall be read in the context of a product currently undergoing regulatory review. Sections (a)(3) and (a)(5) of § 1.740 are not applicable to an application for interim extension under this section.

(c) The content of each subsequent interim extension application may be limited to a request for a subsequent interim extension along with a statement that the regulatory review period has not been completed along with any materials or information required under §§ 1.740 and 1.741 that are not present in the preceding interim extension application.

[60 FR 25619, May 12, 1995]

§ 1.791 Termination of interim extension granted prior to regulatory approval of a product for commercial marketing or use.

Any interim extension granted under 35 U.S.C. 156(d)(5) terminates at the end of the 60-day period beginning on the date on which the product involved receives permission for commercial marketing or use. If within that 60-day period the patent owner or its agent files an application for extension under §§ 1.740 and 1.741 including any additional information required under 35 U.S.C. 156(d)(1) not contained in the application for interim extension, the patent shall be further extended in accordance with the provisions of 35 U.S.C. 156.

[60 FR 25619, May 12, 1995]

Subpart G—Biotechnology Invention Disclosures

DEPOSIT OF BIOLOGICAL MATERIAL

SOURCE: 54 FR 34880, Aug. 22, 1989, unless otherwise noted.

§ 1.801 Biological material.

For the purposes of these regulations pertaining to the deposit of biological material for purposes of patents for inventions under 35 U.S.C. 101, the term biological material shall include material that is capable of self-replication either directly or indirectly. Representative examples include bacteria, fungi including yeast, algae, protozoa, eukaryotic cells, cell lines, hybridomas, plasmids, viruses, plant tissue cells, lichens and seeds. Viruses, vectors, cell organelles and other non-living material existing in and reproducible from a living cell may be deposited by deposit of the host cell capable of reproducing the non-living material.

§ 1.802 Need or opportunity to make a deposit.

(a) Where an invention is, or relies on, a biological material, the disclosure may include reference to a deposit of such biological material.

(b) Biological material need not be deposited unless access to such material is necessary for the satisfaction of the statutory requirements for patentability under 35 U.S.C. 112. If a deposit is necessary, it shall be acceptable if made in accordance with these regulations. Biological material need not be deposited, inter alia, if it is known and readily avaliable to the public or can be made or isolated without undue experimentation. Once deposited in a depository complying with these regulations, a biological material will be considered to be readily available even though some requirement of law or regulation of the United States or of the country in which the depository institution is located permits access to the material only under conditions imposed for safety, public health or similar reasons.

(c) The reference to a biological material in a specification disclosure or the actual deposit of such material by an applicant or patent owner does not create any presumption that such material is necessary to satisfy 35 U.S.C. 112 or that deposit in accordance with these regulations is or was required.

§ 1.803 Acceptable depository.

(a) A deposit shall be recognized for the purposes of these regulations if made in

(1) Any International Depositary Authority (IDA) as established under the Budapest Treaty on the International Recognition of the Deposit of Microorganisms for the Purposes of Patent Procedure, or

(2) Any other depository recognized to be suitable by the Office. Suitability will be determined by the Director on the basis of the administrative and technical competence, and agreement of the depository to comply with the terms and conditions applicable to deposits for patent purposes. The Director may seek the advice of impartial consultants on the suitability of a depository. The depository must:

(i) Have a continuous existence;

(ii) Exist independent of the control of the depositor;

(iii) Possess the staff and facilities sufficient to examine the viability of a deposit and store the deposit in a manner which ensures that it is kept viable and uncontaminated;

(iv) Provide for sufficient safety measures to minimize the risk of losing biological material deposited with it;

(v) Be impartial and objective;

(vi) Furnish samples of the deposited material in an expeditious and proper manner; and

(vii) Promptly notify depositors of its inability to furnish samples, and the reasons why.

(b) A depository seeking status under paragraph (a)(2) of this section must direct a communication to the Director which shall:

(1) Indicate the name and address of the depository to which the communication relates;

(2) Contain detailed information as to the capacity of the depository to comply with the requirements of paragraph (a)(2) of this section, including information on its legal status, scientific standing, staff and facilities;

(3) Indicate that the depository intends to be available, for the purposes of deposit, to any depositor under these same conditions;

(4) Where the depository intends to accept for deposit only certain kinds of biological material, specify such kinds;

(5) Indicate the amount of any fees that the depository will, upon acquiring the status of suitable depository under paragraph (a)(2) of this section, charge for storage, viability statements and furnishings of samples of the deposit.

(c) A depository having status under paragraph (a)(2) of this section limited to certain kinds of biological material may extend such status to additional kinds of biological material by directing a communication to the Director in accordance with paragraph (b) of this section. If a previous communication under paragraph (b) of this section is of record, items in common with the previous communication may be incorporated by reference.

(d) Once a depository is recognized to be suitable by the Director or has defaulted or discontinued its performance under this section, notice thereof will be published in the Office Gazette of the Patent and Trademark Office.

§ 1.804 Time of making an original deposit.

(a) Whenever a biological material is specifically identified in an application for patent as filed, an original deposit thereof may be made at any time before filing the application for patent or, subject to § 1.809, during pendency of the application for patent.

(b) When the original deposit is made after the effective filing date of an application for patent, the applicant must promptly submit a statement from a person in a position to corroborate the fact, stating that the biological material which is deposited is a biological material specifically identified in the application as filed.

[54 FR 34880, Aug. 22, 1989, as amended at 62 FR 53202, Oct. 10, 1997]

§ 1.805 Replacement or supplement of deposit.

(a) A depositor, after receiving notice during the pendency of an application for patent, application for reissue patent or reexamination proceeding, that the depository possessing a deposit either cannot furnish samples thereof or can furnish samples thereof but the deposit has become contaminated or has lost its capability to function as described in the specification, shall notify the Office in writing, in each application for patent or patent affected. In such a case, or where the Office otherwise learns, during the pendency of an application for patent, application for reissue patent or reexamination proceeding, that the depository possessing a deposit either cannot furnish samples thereof or can furnish samples thereof but the deposit has become contaminated or has lost its capability to function as described in the specification, the need for making a replacement or supplemental deposit will be governed by the same considerations governing the need for making an original deposit under the provisions set forth in § 1.802(b). A replacement or supplemental deposit made during the pendency of an application for patent shall not be accepted unless it meets the requirements for making an original deposit under these regulations, including the requirement set forth under § 1.804(b). A replacement or supplemental deposit made in connection with a patent, whether or not made during the pendency of an application for reissue patent or a reexamination proceeding or both, shall not be accepted unless a certificate of correction under § 1.323 is requested by the patent owner which meets the terms of paragraphs (b) and (c) of this section.

(b) A request for certificate of correction under this section shall not be granted unless the certificate identifies:

(1) The accession number for the replacement or supplemental deposit;

(2) The date of the deposit; and

(3) The name and address of the depository.

(c) A request for a certificate of correction under this section shall not be granted unless the request is made promptly after the replacement or supplemental deposit has been made and the request:

(1) Includes a statement of the reason for making the replacement or supplemental deposit;

(2) Includes a statement from a person in a position to corroborate the fact, and stating that the replacement or supplemental deposit is of a biological material which is identical to that originally deposited;

(3) Includes a showing that the patent owner acted diligently—

(i) In the case of a replacement deposit, in making the deposit after receiving notice that samples could no longer be furnished from an earlier deposit; or

(ii) In the case of a supplemental deposit, in making the deposit after receiving notice that the earlier deposit had become contaminated or had lost its capability to function as described in the specification;

(4) Includes a statement that the term of the replacement or supplemental deposit expires no earlier than the term of the deposit being replaced or supplemented; and

(5) Otherwise establishes compliance with these regulations.

(d) A depositor's failure to replace a deposit, or in the case of a patent, to diligently replace a deposit and promptly thereafter request a certificate of correction which meets the terms of paragraphs (b) and (c) of this section, after being notified that the depository possessing the deposit cannot furnish samples thereof, shall cause the application or patent involved to be treated in any Office proceeding as if no deposit were made.

(e) In the event a deposit is replaced according to these regulations, the Office will apply a rebuttable presumption of identity between the original and the replacement deposit where a patent making reference to the deposit is relied upon during any Office proceeeding.

(f) A replacement or supplement deposit made during the pendency of an application for patent may be made for any reason.

(g) In no case is a replacement or supplemental deposit of a biological material necessary where the biological material, in accordance with § 1.802(b), need not be deposited.

(h) No replacement deposit of a biological material is necessary where a depository can furnish samples thereof but the depository for national security, health or environmental safety reasons is unable to provide samples to requesters outside of the jurisdiction where the depository is located.

(i) The Office will not recognize in any Office proceeding a replacement deposit of a biological material made by a patent owner where the depository could furnish samples of the deposit being replaced.

[54 FR 34880, Aug. 22, 1989, as amended at 62 FR 53202, Oct. 10, 1997]

§ 1.806 Term of deposit.

A deposit made before or during pendency of an application for patent shall be made for a term of at least thirty (30) years and at least five (5) years after the most recent request for the furnishing of a sample of the deposit was received by the depository. In any case, samples must be stored under agreements that would make them available beyond the enforceable life of the patent for which the deposit was made.

§ 1.807 Viability of deposit.

(a) A deposit of biological material that is capable of self-replication either directly or indirectly must be viable at the time of deposit and during the term of deposit. Viability may be tested by the depository. The test must conclude only that the deposited material is capable of reproduction. No evidence is necessarily required regarding the ability of the deposited material to perform any function described in the patent application.

(b) A viability statement for each deposit of a biological material defined in paragraph (a) of this section not made under the Budapest Treaty on the International Recognition of the Deposit of Microorganisms for the Purposes of Patent Procedure must be filed in the application and must contain:

(1) The name and address of the depository;

(2) The name and address of the depositor;

(3) The date of deposit;

(4) The identity of the deposit and the accession number given by the depository;

(5) The date of the viability test;

(6) The procedures used to obtain a sample if the test is not done by the depository; and

(7) A statement that the deposit is capable of reproduction.

(c) If a viability test indicates that the deposit is not viable upon receipt, or the examiner cannot, for scientific or other valid reasons, accept the statement of viability received from the applicant, the examiner shall proceed as if no deposit has been made. The examiner will accept the conclusion set forth in a viability statement issued by a depository recognized under § 1.803(a).

§ 1.808 Furnishing of samples.

(a) A deposit must be made under conditions that assure that:

(1) Access to the deposit will be available during pendency of the patent application making reference to the deposit to one determined by the Director to be entitled thereto under § 1.14 and 35 U.S.C. 122, and

(2) Subject to paragraph (b) of this section, all restrictions imposed by the depositor on the availability to the public of the deposited material will be irrevocably removed upon the granting of the patent.

(b) The depositor may contract with the depository to require that samples of a deposited biological material shall be furnished only if a request for a sample, during the term of the patent:

(1) Is in writing or other tangible form and dated;

(2) Contains the name and address of the requesting party and the accession number of the deposit; and

(3) Is communicated in writing by the depository to the depositor along with the date on which the sample was furnished and the name and address of the party to whom the sample was furnished.

(c) Upon request made to the Office, the Office will certify whether a deposit has been stated to have been made under conditions which make it available to the public as of the issue date of the patent grant provided the request contains:

(1) The name and address of the depository;

(2) The accession number given to the deposit;

(3) The patent number and issue date of the patent referring to the deposit; and

(4) The name and address of the requesting party.

§ 1.809 Examination procedures.

(a) The examiner shall determine pursuant to § 1.104 in each application for patent, application for reissue patent or reexamination proceeding if a deposit is needed, and if needed, if a deposit actually made is acceptable for patent purposes. If a deposit is needed and has not been made or replaced or supplemented in accordance with these regulations, the examiner, where appropriate, shall reject the affected claims under the appropriate provision of 35 U.S.C. 112, explaining why a deposit is needed and/or why a deposit actually made cannot be accepted.

(b) The applicant for patent or patent owner shall reply to a rejection under paragraph (a) of this section by—

(1) In the case of an applicant for patent, either making an acceptable original, replacement, or supplemental deposit, or assuring the Office in writing that an acceptable deposit will be made; or, in the case of a patent owner, requesting a certificate of correction of the patent which meets the terms of paragraphs (b) and (c) of § 1.805, or

(2) Arguing why a deposit is not needed under the circumstances of the application or patent considered and/or why a deposit actually made should be accepted. Other replies to the examiner's action shall be considered nonresponsive. The rejection will be repeated until either paragraph (b)(1) of this section is satisfied or the examiner is convinced that a deposit is not needed.

(c) If an application for patent is otherwise in condition for allowance except for a needed deposit and the Office has received a written assurance that an acceptable deposit will be made, applicant will be notified and given a period of time within which the deposit must be made in order to avoid abandonment. This time period is not extendable under § 1.136(a) or (b) if set forth in a "Notice of Allowability" or in an Office action having a mail date on or after the mail date of a "Notice of Allowability" (see § 1.136(c)).

(d) For each deposit made pursuant to these regulations, the specification shall contain:

(1) The accession number for the deposit;

(2) The date of the deposit;

(3) A description of the deposited biological material sufficient to specifically identify it and to permit examination; and

(4) The name and address of the depository.

(e) Any amendment required by paragraphs (d)(1), (d)(2) or (d)(4) of this section must be filed before or with the payment of the issue fee (see § 1.312).

[54 FR 34880, Aug. 22, 1989, as amended at 66 FR 21092, Apr. 27, 2001]

Application Disclosures Containing Nucleotide and/or Amino Acid Sequences

Source: Sections 1.821 through 1.825 appear at 55 FR 18245, May 1, 1990, unless otherwise noted.

§ 1.821 Nucleotide and/or amino acid sequence disclosures in patent applications.

(a) Nucleotide and/or amino acid sequences as used in §§ 1.821 through 1.825 are interpreted to mean an unbranched sequence of four or more amino acids or an unbranched sequence of ten or more nucleotides. Branched sequences are specifically excluded from this definition. Sequences with fewer than four specifically defined nucleotides or amino acids are specifically excluded from this section. "Specifically defined" means those amino acids other than "Xaa" and those nucleotide bases other than "n"defined in accordance with the World Intellectual Property Organization (WIPO) Handbook on Industrial Property Information and Documentation, Standard ST.25: Standard for the Presentation of Nucleotide and Amino Acid Sequence Listings in Patent Applications (1998), including Tables 1 through 6 in Appendix 2, herein incorporated by reference. (Hereinafter "WIPO Standard ST.25 (1998)"). This incorporation by reference was approved by the Director of the Federal Register in accordance with 5 U.S.C. 552(a) and 1 CFR part 51. Copies of WIPO Standard ST.25 (1998) may be obtained from the World Intellectual Property Organization; 34 chemin des Colombettes; 1211 Geneva 20 Switzerland. Copies may also be inspected at the National Archives and Records Administration (NARA). For information on the availability of this material at NARA, call 202–741–6030, or go to: *http://www.archives.gov/federal_register/code_of_federal_regulations/ibr_locations.html.* Nucleotides and amino acids are further defined as follows:

(1) *Nucleotides:* Nucleotides are intended to embrace only those nucleotides that can be represented using the symbols set forth in WIPO Standard ST.25 (1998), Appendix 2, Table 1. Modifications, e.g., methylated bases, may be described as set forth in WIPO Standard ST.25 (1998), Appendix 2, Table 2, but shall not be shown explicitly in the nucleotide sequence.

(2) *Amino acids:* Amino acids are those L-amino acids commonly found in naturally occurring proteins and are listed in WIPO Standard ST.25 (1998), Appendix 2, Table 3. Those amino acid sequences containing D-amino acids are not intended to be embraced by this definition. Any amino acid sequence that contains post-translationally modified amino acids may be described as the amino acid sequence that is initially translated using the symbols shown in WIPO Standard ST.25 (1998), Appendix 2, Table 3 with the modified positions; e.g., hydroxylations or glycosylations, being described as set forth in WIPO Standard ST.25 (1998), Appendix 2, Table 4, but these modifications shall not be shown explicitly in the amino acid sequence. Any peptide or protein that can be expressed as a sequence using the symbols in WIPO Standard ST.25 (1998), Appendix 2, Table 3 in conjunction with a description in the Feature section to describe, for example, modified linkages, cross links and end caps, non-peptidyl bonds, etc., is embraced by this definition.

(b) Patent applications which contain disclosures of nucleotide and/or amino acid sequences, in accordance with the definition in paragraph (a) of this section, shall, with regard to the manner in which the nucleotide and/or amino acid sequences are presented and described, conform exclusively to the requirements of §§ 1.821 through 1.825.

(c) Patent applications which contain disclosures of nucleotide and/or amino acid sequences must contain, as a separate part of the disclosure, a paper or compact disc copy (*see* § 1.52(e)) disclosing the nucleotide and/or amino acid sequences and associated information using the symbols and format in accordance with the requirements of §§ 1.822 and 1.823. This paper or compact disc copy is referred to elsewhere in this subpart as the "Sequence Listing." Each sequence disclosed must appear separately in the "Sequence Listing." Each sequence set forth in the "Sequence Listing" must be assigned a separate sequence identifier. The sequence identifiers must begin with 1 and increase sequentially by integers. If no sequence is present for a sequence identifier, the code "000" must be used in place of the sequence. The response for the numeric identifier <160> must include the total number of SEQ ID NOs, whether followed by a sequence or by the code "000."

(d) Where the description or claims of a patent application discuss a sequence that is set forth in the "Sequence Listing" in accordance with paragraph (c) of this section, reference must be made to the sequence by use of the sequence identifier, preceded by "SEQ ID NO:" in the text of the description or claims, even if the sequence is also embedded in the text of the description or claims of the patent application.

(e) A copy of the "Sequence Listing" referred to in paragraph (c) of this section must also be submitted in computer readable form (CRF) in accordance with the requirements of § 1.824. The computer readable form must be a copy of the "Sequence Listing" and may not be retained as a part of the patent application file. If the computer readable form of a new application is to be identical with the computer readable form of another application of the applicant on file in the Office, reference may be made to the other application and computer readable form in lieu of filing a duplicate computer readable form in the new application if the computer readable form in the other application was compliant with all of the requirements of this subpart. The new application must be accompanied by a letter making such reference to the other application and computer readable form, both of which shall be completely identified. In the new application, applicant must also request the use of the compliant computer readable "Sequence Listing" that is already on file for the other application and must state that the paper or compact disc copy of the "Sequence Listing" in the new application is identical to the computer readable copy filed for the other application.

(f) In addition to the paper or compact disc copy required by paragraph (c) of this section and the computer readable form required by paragraph (e) of this section, a statement that the "Sequence Listing" content of the paper or compact disc copy and the computer readable copy are the same must be submitted with the computer readable form, e.g., a statement that "the sequence listing information recorded in computer readable form is identical to the written (on paper or compact disc) sequence listing."

(g) If any of the requirements of paragraphs (b) through (f) of this section are not satisfied at the time of filing under 35 U.S.C. 111(a) or at the time of entering the national stage under 35 U.S.C. 371, applicant will be notified and given a period of time within which to comply with such requirements in order to prevent abandonment of the application. Any submission in reply to a requirement under this paragraph must be accompanied by a statement that the submission includes no new matter.

(h) If any of the requirements of paragraphs (b) through (f) of this section are not satisfied at the time of filing an international application under the Patent Cooperation Treaty (PCT), which application is to be searched by the United States International Searching Authority or examined by the United States International Preliminary Examining Authority, applicant will be sent a notice necessitating compliance with the requirements within a prescribed time period. Any submission in reply to a requirement under this paragraph must be accompanied by a statement that the submission does not include matter which goes beyond the disclosure in the international application as filed. If applicant fails to timely provide the required computer readable form, the United States International Searching Authority shall search only to the extent that a meaningful search can be performed without the computer readable form and the United States International Preliminary Examining Authority shall examine only to the extent that a meaningful examination can be performed without the computer readable form.

[63 FR 29634, June 1, 1998, as amended at 65 FR 54680, Sept. 8, 2000; 69 FR 18803, Apr. 9, 2004; 70 FR 10489, Mar. 4, 2005]

§ 1.822 Symbols and format to be used for nucleotide and/or amino acid sequence data.

(a) The symbols and format to be used for nucleotide and/or amino acid sequence data shall conform to the requirements of paragraphs (b) through (e) of this section.

(b) The code for representing the nucleotide and/or amino acid sequence characters shall conform to the code set forth in the tables in WIPO Standard ST.25 (1998), Appendix 2, Tables 1 and 3. This incorporation by reference was approved by the Director of the Federal Register in accordance with 5 U.S.C. 552(a) and 1 CFR part 51. Copies of ST.25 may be obtained from the World Intellectual Property Organization; 34 chemin des Colombettes; 1211 Geneva 20 Switzerland. Copies may also be inspected at the National Archives and Records Administration (NARA). For information on the availability of this material at NARA, call 202–741–6030, or go to: *http://www.archives.gov/federal_register/code_of_federal_regulations/ibr_locations.html*. No code other than that specified in these sections shall be used in nucleotide and amino acid sequences. A modified base or modified or unusual amino acid may be presented in a given sequence as the corresponding unmodified base or amino acid if the modified base or modified or unusual amino acid is one of those listed in WIPO Standard ST.25 (1998), Appendix 2, Tables 2 and 4, and the modification is also set forth in the Feature section. Otherwise, each occurrence of a base or amino acid not appearing in WIPO Standard ST.25 (1998), Appendix 2, Tables 1 and 3, shall be listed in a given sequence as "n" or "Xaa," respectively, with further information, as appropriate, given in the Feature section, preferably by including one or more feature keys listed in WIPO Standard ST.25 (1998), Appendix 2, Tables 5 and 6.

(c) *Format representation of nucleotides.* (1) A nucleotide sequence shall be listed using the lower-case letter for representing the one-letter code for the nucleotide bases set forth in WIPO Standard ST.25 (1998), Appendix 2, Table 1.

(2) The bases in a nucleotide sequence (including introns) shall be listed in groups of 10 bases except in the coding parts of the sequence. Leftover bases, fewer than 10 in number, at the end of noncoding parts of a sequence shall be grouped together and separated from adjacent groups of 10 or 3 bases by a space.

(3) The bases in the coding parts of a nucleotide sequence shall be listed as triplets (codons). The amino acids corresponding to the codons in the coding parts of a nucleotide sequence shall be typed immediately below the corresponding codons. Where a codon spans an intron, the amino acid symbol shall be typed below the portion of the codon containing two nucleotides.

(4) A nucleotide sequence shall be listed with a maximum of 16 codons or 60 bases per line, with a space provided between each codon or group of 10 bases.

(5) A nucleotide sequence shall be presented, only by a single strand, in the 5 to 3 direction, from left to right.

(6) The enumeration of nucleotide bases shall start at the first base of the sequence with number 1. The enumeration shall be continuous through the whole sequence in the direction 5 to 3. The enumeration shall be marked in the right margin, next to the line containing the one-letter codes for the bases, and giving the number of the last base of that line.

(7) For those nucleotide sequences that are circular in configuration, the

enumeration method set forth in paragraph (c)(6) of this section remains applicable with the exception that the designation of the first base of the nucleotide sequence may be made at the option of the applicant.

(d) *Representation of amino acids.* (1) The amino acids in a protein or peptide sequence shall be listed using the three-letter abbreviation with the first letter as an upper case character, as in WIPO Standard ST.25 (1998), Appendix 2, Table 3.

(2) A protein or peptide sequence shall be listed with a maximum of 16 amino acids per line, with a space provided between each amino acid.

(3) An amino acid sequence shall be presented in the amino to carboxy direction, from left to right, and the amino and carboxy groups shall not be presented in the sequence.

(4) The enumeration of amino acids may start at the first amino acid of the first mature protein, with the number 1. When presented, the amino acids preceding the mature protein, e.g., pre-sequences, pro-sequences, pre-pro-sequences and signal sequences, shall have negative numbers, counting backwards starting with the amino acid next to number 1. Otherwise, the enumeration of amino acids shall start at the first amino acid at the amino terminal as number 1. It shall be marked below the sequence every 5 amino acids. The enumeration method for amino acid sequences that is set forth in this section remains applicable for amino acid sequences that are circular in configuration, with the exception that the designation of the first amino acid of the sequence may be made at the option of the applicant.

(5) An amino acid sequence that contains internal terminator symbols (e.g., "Ter", "*", or ".", etc.) may not be represented as a single amino acid sequence, but shall be presented as separate amino acid sequences.

(e) A sequence with a gap or gaps shall be presented as a plurality of separate sequences, with separate sequence identifiers, with the number of separate sequences being equal in number to the number of continuous strings of sequence data. A sequence that is made up of one or more noncontiguous segments of a larger sequence or segments from different sequences shall be presented as a separate sequence.

[63 FR 29635, June 1, 1998, as amended at 69 FR 18803, Apr. 9, 2004; 70 FR 10489, Mar. 4, 2005]

§ 1.823 Requirements for nucleotide and/or amino acid sequences as part of the application.

(a)(1) If the "Sequence Listing" required by § 1.821(c) is submitted on paper: The "Sequence Listing," setting forth the nucleotide and/or amino acid sequence and associated information in accordance with paragraph (b) of this section, must begin on a new page and must be titled "Sequence Listing." The pages of the "Sequence Listing" preferably should be numbered independently of the numbering of the remainder of the application. Each page of the "Sequence Listing" shall contain no more than 66 lines and each line shall contain no more than 72 characters. The sheet or sheets presenting a sequence listing may not include material other than part of the sequence listing. A fixed-width font should be used exclusively throughout the "Sequence Listing."

(2) If the "Sequence Listing" required by § 1.821(c) is submitted on compact disc: The "Sequence Listing" must be submitted on a compact disc in compliance with § 1.52(e). The compact disc may also contain table information if the application contains table information that may be submitted on a compact disc (§ 1.52(e)(1)(iii)). The specification must contain an incorporation-by-reference of the Sequence Listing as required by § 1.52(e)(5). The presentation of the "Sequence Listing" and other materials on compact disc under § 1.821(c) does not substitute for the Computer Readable Form that must be submitted on disk, compact disc, or tape in accordance with § 1.824.

(b) The "Sequence Listing" shall, except as otherwise indicated, include the actual nucleotide and/or amino acid sequence, the numeric identifiers and their accompanying information as shown in the following table. The numeric identifier shall be used only in the "Sequence Listing." The order and presentation of the items of information in the "Sequence Listing" shall conform to the arrangement given below. Each item of information shall begin on a new line and shall begin with the numeric identifier enclosed in angle brackets as shown. The submission of those items of information designated with an "M" is mandatory. The submission of those items of information designated with an "O" is optional. Numeric identifiers <110> through <170> shall only be set forth at the beginning of the "Sequence Listing." The following table illustrates the numeric identifiers.

Numeric identifier	Definition	Comments and format	Mandatory (M) or optional (O).
<110>	Applicant	Preferably max. of 10 names; one name per line; preferable format: Surname, Other Names and/or Initials.	M.
<120>	Title of Invention		M.
<130>	File Reference	Personal file reference	M when filed prior to assignment of appl. number.
<140>	Current Application Number.	Specify as: US 07/999,999 or PCT/US96/99999.	M, if available.
<141>	Current Filing Date	Specify as: yyyy-mm-dd	M, if available.
<150>	Prior Application Number.	Specify as: US 07/999,999 or PCT/US96/99999.	M, if applicable include priority documents under 35 USC 119 and 120.
<151>	Prior Application Filing Date.	Specify as: yyyy-mm-dd	M, if applicable.
<160>	Number of SEQ ID NOs.	Count includes total number of SEQ ID NOs.	M.
<170>	Software	Name of software used to create the Sequence Listing.	O.
<210>	SEQ ID NO:#:	Response shall be an integer representing the SEQ ID NO shown.	M.
<211>	Length	Respond with an integer expressing the number of bases or amino acid residues.	M.
<212>	Type	Whether presented sequence molecule is DNA, RNA, or PRT (protein). If a nucleotide sequence contains both DNA and RNA fragments, the type shall be "DNA." In addition, the combined DNA/RNA molecule shall be further described in the <220> to <223> feature section.	M.
<213>	Organism	Scientific name, *i.e.*, Genus/ species, Unknown or Artificial Sequence. In addition, the "Unknown" or "Artificial Sequence" organisms shall be further described in the <220> to <223> feature section.	M
<220>	Feature	Leave blank after <220>. <221–223> provide for a description of points of biological significance in the sequence..	M, under the following conditions: if "n," "Xaa," or a modified or unusual L-amino acid or modified base was used in a sequence; if ORGANISM is "Artificial Sequence" or "Unknown"; if molecule is combined DNA/RNA"
<221>	Name/Key	Provide appropriate identifier for feature, preferably from WIPO Standard ST.25 (1998), Appendix 2, Tables 5 and 6.	M, under the following conditions: if "n," "Xaa," or a modified or unusual L-amino acid or modified base was used in a sequence.
<222>	Location	Specify location within sequence; where appropriate state number of first and last bases/amino acids in feature.	M, under the following conditions: if "n," "Xaa," or a modified or unusual L-amino acid or modified base was used in a sequence.
<223>	Other Information	Other relevant information; four lines maximum.	M, under the following conditions: if "n," "Xaa," or a modified or unusual L-amino acid or modified base was used in a sequence; if ORGANISM is "Artificial Sequence" or "Unknown"; if molecule is combined DNA/RNA.
<300>	Publication Information.	Leave blank after <300>	O.
<301>	Authors	Preferably max of ten named authors of publication; specify one name per line; preferable format: Surname, Other Names and/or Initials.	O.
<302>	Title		O.

Numeric identifier	Definition	Comments and format	Mandatory (M) or optional (O).
<303>	Journal		O.
<304>	Volume		O.
<305>	Issue		O.
<306>	Pages		O.
<307>	Date	Journal date on which data published; specify as yyyy-mm-dd, MMM-yyyy or Season-yyyy.	O.
<308>	Database Accession Number.	Accession number assigned by database including database name.	O.
<309>	Database Entry Date.	Date of entry in database; specify as yyyy-mm-dd or MMM-yyyy.	O.
<310>	Patent Document Number.	Document number; for patent-type citations only. Specify as, for example, US 07/999,999.	O.
<311>	Patent Filing Date	Document filing date, for patent-type citations only; specify as yyyy-mm-dd.	O.
<312>	Publication Date	Document publication date, for patent-type citations only; specify as yyyy-mm-dd.	O.
<313>	Relevant Residues	FROM (position) TO (position)	O.
<400>	Sequence	SEQ ID NO should follow the numeric identifier and should appear on the line preceding the actual sequence.	M.

[63 FR 29636, June 1, 1998, as amended at 65 FR 54681, Sept. 8, 2000; 68 FR 38630, June 30, 2003]

§ 1.824 Form and format for nucleotide and/or amino acid sequence submissions in computer readable form.

(a) The computer readable form required by § 1.821(e) shall meet the following requirements:

(1) The computer readable form shall contain a single "Sequence Listing" as either a diskette, series of diskettes, or other permissible media outlined in paragraph (c) of this section.

(2) The "Sequence Listing" in paragraph (a)(1) of this section shall be submitted in American Standard Code for Information Interchange (ASCII) text. No other formats shall be allowed.

(3) The computer readable form may be created by any means, such as word processors, nucleotide/amino acid sequence editors' or other custom computer programs; however, it shall conform to all requirements detailed in this section.

(4) File compression is acceptable when using diskette media, so long as the compressed file is in a self-extracting format that will decompress on one of the systems described in paragraph (b) of this section.

(5) Page numbering must not appear within the computer readable form version of the "Sequence Listing" file.

(6) All computer readable forms must have a label permanently affixed thereto on which has been hand-printed or typed: the name of the applicant, the title of the invention, the date on which the data were recorded on the computer readable form, the operating system used, a reference number, and an application number and filing date, if known. If multiple diskettes are submitted, the diskette labels must indicate their order (e.g., "1 of X").

(b) Computer readable form submissions must meet these format requirements:

(1) Computer Compatibility: IBM PC/XT/AT or Apple Macintosh;

(2) Operating System Compatibility: MS-DOS, MS-Windows, Unix or Macintosh;

(3) Line Terminator: ASCII Carriage Return plus ASCII Line Feed; and

(4) Pagination: Continuous file (no "hard page break" codes permitted).

(c) Computer readable form files submitted may be in any of the following media:

(1) Diskette: 3.50 inch, 1.44 Mb storage; 3.50 inch, 720 Kb storage; 5.25 inch, 1.2 Mb storage; 5.25 inch, 360 Kb storage.

(2) Magnetic tape: 0.5 inch, up to 24000 feet; Density: 1600 or 6250 bits per inch, 9 track; Format: Unix tar command; specify blocking factor (not "block size"); Line Terminator: ASCII Carriage Return plus ASCII Line Feed.

(3) 8mm Data Cartridge: Format: Unix tar command; specify blocking factor (not "block size"); Line Terminator: ASCII Carriage Return plus ASCII Line Feed.

(4) Compact disc: Format: ISO 9660 or High Sierra Format.

(5) Magneto Optical Disk: Size/Storage Specifications: 5.25 inch, 640 Mb.

(d) Computer readable forms that are submitted to the Office will not be returned to the applicant.

[65 FR 54681, Sept. 8, 2000]

§ 1.825 Amendments to or replacement of sequence listing and computer readable copy thereof.

(a) Any amendment to a paper copy of the "Sequence Listing" (§ 1.821(c)) must be made by the submission of substitute sheets and include a statement that the substitute sheets include no new matter. Any amendment to a compact disc copy of the "Sequence Listing" (§ 1.821(c)) must be made by the submission of a replacement compact disc (2 copies) in compliance with § 1.52(e). Amendments must also be accompanied by a statement that indicates support for the amendment in the application, as filed, and a statement that the replacement compact disc includes no new matter.

(b) Any amendment to the paper or compact disc copy of the "Sequence Listing," in accordance with paragraph (a) of this section, must be accompanied by a substitute copy of the computer readable form (§ 1.821(e)) including all previously submitted data with the amendment incorporated therein, accompanied by a statement that the copy in computer readable form is the same as the substitute copy of the "Sequence Listing."

(c) Any appropriate amendments to the "Sequence Listing" in a patent; e.g., by reason of reissue or certificate of correction, must comply with the requirements of paragraphs (a) and (b) of this section.

(d) If, upon receipt, the computer readable form is found to be damaged or unreadable, applicant must provide, within such time as set by the Director, a substitute copy of the data in computer readable form accompanied by a statement that the substitute data is identical to that originally filed.

[63 FR 29638, June 1, 1998, as amended at 65 FR 54681, Sept. 8, 2000]

APPENDIX A TO SUBPART G OF PART 1—SAMPLE SEQUENCE LISTING

```
<110> Smith, John

      Smith, Jane



<120> Example of a Sequence Listing



<130> 01-00001



<140> US 08/999,999

<141> 1998-02-28



<150> EP 91000000

<151> 1997-12-31
```

<160> 2

<170> PatentIn ver. 2.0

<210> 1

<211> 403

<212> DNA

<213> Paramecium aurelia

<220>

<221> CDS

<222> 341..394

<300>

<301> Doe, Richard

<302> Isolation and Characterization of a Gene Encoding a Protease from Paramecium sp.

<303> Journal of Fictional Genes

<304> 1

<305> 4

<306> 1 - 7

<307> 1988-06-20

<400> 1

```
ctactctact ctactctcat ctactatctt ctttggatct ctgagtctgc ctgagtggta   60

ctcttgagtc ctggagatct ctcctctcac atgtgatcgt cgagactgac cgatagatcg  120

ctgactgact ctgagatagt cgagcccgta cgagacccgt cgagggtgac agagagtggg  180

cgcgtgcgcg cagagcgccg cgccggtgcg cgcgcgagtg cgcggtgggc cgcgcgaggg  240

ctttcgcggc agcggcggcg ctttccggcg cgcgcccgtc cgcccctaga cctgagaggt  300

cttctcttcc ctcctcttca ctagagaggt ctatatatac atg gtt tca atg ttc    355
                                            Met Val Ser Met Phe
```

1 5

agc ttg tct ttc aaa tgg cct gga ttt tgt ttg ttt gtt tgtttgctc 403

Ser Leu Ser Phe Lys Trp Pro Gly Phe Cys Leu Phe Val

10 15

<210> 2

<211> 18

<212> PRT

<213> Paramecium aurelia

<400> 2

Met Val Ser Met Phe Ser Leu Ser Phe Lys Trp Pro Gly Phe Cys Leu

1 5 10 15

Phe Val

[63 FR 29639, June 1, 1998]

Subpart H—*Inter Partes* Reexamination of Patents That Issued From an Original Application Filed in the United States on or After November 29, 1999

SOURCE: 65 FR 76777, Dec. 7, 2000, unless otherwise noted.

PRIOR ART CITATIONS

§ 1.902 Processing of prior art citations during an *inter partes* reexamination proceeding.

Citations by the patent owner in accordance with § 1.933 and by an *inter partes* reexamination third party requester under § 1.915 or § 1.948 will be entered in the *inter partes* reexamination file. The entry in the patent file of other citations submitted after the date of an order for reexamination pursuant to § 1.931 by persons other than the patent owner, or the third party requester under either § 1.913 or § 1.948, will be delayed until the *inter partes* reexamination proceeding has been concluded by the issuance and publication of a reexamination certificate. See § 1.502 for processing of prior art citations in patent and reexamination files during an *ex parte* reexamination proceeding filed under § 1.510.

[72 FR 18906, Apr. 16, 2007]

REQUIREMENTS FOR *Inter Partes* REEXAMINATION PROCEEDINGS

§ 1.903 Service of papers on parties in *inter partes* reexamination.

The patent owner and the third party requester will be sent copies of Office actions issued during the *inter partes* reexamination proceeding. After filing of a request for *inter partes* reexamination by a third party requester, any document filed by either the patent owner or the third party requester must be served on every other party in the reexamination proceeding in the manner provided in § 1.248. Any document must reflect service or the document may be refused consideration by the Office. The failure of the patent owner or the third party requester to serve documents may result in their being refused consideration.

§ 1.904 Notice of *inter partes* reexamination in *Official Gazette.*

A notice of the filing of an *inter partes* reexamination request will be published in the *Official Gazette.* The notice published in the *Official Gazette* under § 1.11(c) will be considered to be constructive notice of the *inter partes* reexamination proceeding and *inter partes* reexamination will proceed.

§ 1.905 Submission of papers by the public in *inter partes* reexamination.

Unless specifically provided for, no submissions on behalf of any third parties other than third party requesters as defined in 35 U.S.C. 100(e) will be considered unless such submissions are in accordance with § 1.915 or entered in the patent file prior to the date of the order for reexamination pursuant to § 1.931. Submissions by third parties, other than third party requesters, filed after the date of the order for reexamination pursuant to § 1.931, must meet the requirements of § 1.501 and will be treated in accordance with § 1.902. Submissions which do not meet the requirements of § 1.501 will be returned.

§ 1.906 Scope of reexamination in *inter partes* reexamination proceeding.

(a) Claims in an *inter partes* reexamination proceeding will be examined on the basis of patents or printed publications and, with respect to subject matter added or deleted in the reexamination proceeding, on the basis of the requirements of 35 U.S.C. 112.

(b) Claims in an *inter partes* reexamination proceeding will not be permitted to enlarge the scope of the claims of the patent.

(c) Issues other than those indicated in paragraphs (a) and (b) of this section will not be resolved in an *inter partes* reexamination proceeding. If such issues are raised by the patent owner or the third party requester during a reexamination proceeding, the existence of such issues will be noted by the examiner in the next Office action, in which case the patent owner may desire to consider the advisability of filing a reissue application to have such issues considered and resolved.

§1.907 *Inter partes* reexamination prohibited.

(a) Once an order to reexamine has been issued under §1.931, neither the third party requester, nor its privies, may file a subsequent request for *inter partes* reexamination of the patent until an *inter partes* reexamination certificate is issued under §1.997, unless authorized by the Director.

(b) Once a final decision has been entered against a party in a civil action arising in whole or in part under 28 U.S.C. 1338 that the party has not sustained its burden of proving invalidity of any patent claim-in-suit, then neither that party nor its privies may thereafter request *inter partes* reexamination of any such patent claim on the basis of issues which that party, or its privies, raised or could have raised in such civil action, and an *inter partes* reexamination requested by that party, or its privies, on the basis of such issues may not thereafter be maintained by the Office.

(c) If a final decision in an *inter partes* reexamination proceeding instituted by a third party requester is favorable to patentability of any original, proposed amended, or new claims of the patent, then neither that party nor its privies may thereafter request *inter partes* reexamination of any such patent claims on the basis of issues which that party, or its privies, raised or could have raised in such *inter partes* reexamination proceeding.

§1.913 Persons eligible to file, and time for filing, a request for *inter partes* reexamination.

(a) Except as provided for in §1.907 and in paragraph (b) of this section, any person other than the patent owner or its privies may, at any time during the period of enforceability of a patent which issued from an original application filed in the United States on or after November 29, 1999, file a request for *inter partes* reexamination by the Office of any claim of the patent on the basis of prior art patents or printed publications cited under §1.501.

(b) Any request for an *inter partes* reexamination submitted on or after September 16, 2012, will not be accorded a filing date, and any such request will not be granted.

[76 FR 59057, Sept. 23, 2011]

§1.915 Content of request for *inter partes* reexamination.

(a) The request must be accompanied by the fee for requesting *inter partes* reexamination set forth in §1.20(c)(2).

(b) A request for *inter partes* reexamination must include the following parts:

(1) An identification of the patent by patent number and every claim for which reexamination is requested.

(2) A citation of the patents and printed publications which are presented to provide a showing that there is a reasonable likelihood that the requester will prevail with respect to at least one of the claims challenged in the request.

(3) A statement pointing out, based on the cited patents and printed publications, each showing of a reasonable likelihood that the requester will prevail with respect to at least one of the claims challenged in the request, and a detailed explanation of the pertinency and manner of applying the patents and printed publications to every claim for which reexamination is requested.

(4) A copy of every patent or printed publication relied upon or referred to in paragraphs (b)(1) through (3) of this section, accompanied by an English language translation of all the necessary and pertinent parts of any non-English language document.

(5) A copy of the entire patent including the front face, drawings, and specification/claims (in double column format) for which reexamination is requested, and a copy of any disclaimer, certificate of correction, or reexamination certificate issued in the patent. All copies must have each page plainly written on only one side of a sheet of paper.

(6) A certification by the third party requester that a copy of the request has been served in its entirety on the patent owner at the address provided for in §1.33(c). The name and address of the party served must be indicated. If service was not possible, a duplicate copy of the request must be supplied to the Office.

(7) A certification by the third party requester that the estoppel provisions of § 1.907 do not prohibit the *inter partes* reexamination.

(8) A statement identifying the real party in interest to the extent necessary for a subsequent person filing an *inter partes* reexamination request to determine whether that person is a privy.

(c) If an *inter partes* request is filed by an attorney or agent identifying another party on whose behalf the request is being filed, the attorney or agent must have a power of attorney from that party or be acting in a representative capacity pursuant to § 1.34.

(d) If the *inter partes* request does not include the fee for requesting *inter partes* reexamination required by paragraph (a) of this section and meet all the requirements of paragraph (b) of this section, then the person identified as requesting *inter partes* reexamination will be so notified and will generally be given an opportunity to complete the request within a specified time. Failure to comply with the notice will result in the *inter partes* reexamination request not being granted a filing date, and will result in placement of the request in the patent file as a citation if it complies with the requirements of § 1.501.

[65 FR 76777, Dec. 7, 2000, as amended at 71 FR 9262, Feb. 23, 2006; 71 FR 44223, Aug. 4, 2006; 72 FR 18906, Apr. 16, 2007; 76 FR 59058, Sept. 23, 2011]

§ 1.919 Filing date of request for *inter partes* reexamination.

(a) The filing date of a request for *inter partes* reexamination is the date on which the request satisfies all the requirements for the request set forth in § 1.915.

(b) If the request is not granted a filing date, the request will be placed in the patent file as a citation of prior art if it complies with the requirements of § 1.501.

[65 FR 76777, Dec. 7, 2000, as amended at 71 FR 9262, Feb. 23, 2006]

§ 1.923 Examiner's determination on the request for *inter partes* reexamination.

Within three months following the filing date of a request for *inter partes* reexamination under § 1.915, the examiner will consider the request and determine whether or not the request and the prior art establish a reasonable likelihood that the requester will prevail with respect to at least one of the claims challenged in the request. The examiner's determination will be based on the claims in effect at the time of the determination, will become a part of the official file of the patent, and will be mailed to the patent owner at the address as provided for in § 1.33(c) and to the third party requester. If the examiner determines that the request has not established a reasonable likelihood that the requester will prevail with respect to at least one of the challenged claims, the examiner shall refuse the request and shall not order *inter partes* reexamination.

[76 FR 59058, Sept. 23, 2011]

§ 1.925 Partial refund if request for *inter partes* reexamination is not ordered.

Where *inter partes* reexamination is not ordered, a refund of a portion of the fee for requesting *inter partes* reexamination will be made to the requester in accordance with § 1.26(c).

§ 1.927 Petition to review refusal to order *inter partes* reexamination.

The third party requester may seek review by a petition to the Director under § 1.181 within one month of the mailing date of the examiner's determination refusing to order *inter partes* reexamination. Any such petition must comply with § 1.181(b). If no petition is timely filed or if the decision on petition affirms that a reasonable likelihood that the requester will prevail with respect to at least one of the claims challenged in the request has not been established, the determination shall be final and nonappealable.

[76 FR 59058, Sept. 23, 2011]

Inter Partes REEXAMINATION OF PATENTS

§ 1.931 Order for *inter partes* reexamination.

(a) If it is found that there is a reasonable likelihood that the requester will prevail with respect to at least one of the claims challenged in the request, the determination will include an order for *inter partes* reexamination of the patent for resolution of the question of whether the requester will prevail.

(b) If the order for *inter partes* reexamination resulted from a petition pursuant to § 1.927, the *inter partes* reexamination will ordinarily be conducted by an examiner other than the examiner responsible for the initial determination under § 1.923.

[65 FR 76777, Dec. 7, 2000, as amended at 76 FR 59058, Sept. 23, 2011]

INFORMATION DISCLOSURE IN *Inter Partes* REEXAMINATION

§ 1.933 Patent owner duty of disclosure in *inter partes* reexamination proceedings.

(a) Each individual associated with the patent owner in an *inter partes* reexamination proceeding has a duty of candor and good faith in dealing with the Office, which includes a duty to disclose to the Office all information known to that individual to be material to patentability in a reexamination proceeding as set forth in § 1.555(a) and (b). The duty to disclose all information known to be material to patentability in an *inter partes* reexamination proceeding is deemed to be satisfied by filing a paper in compliance with the requirements set forth in § 1.555(a) and (b).

(b) The responsibility for compliance with this section rests upon the individuals designated in paragraph (a) of this section, and no evaluation will be made by the Office in the reexamination proceeding as to compliance with this section. If questions of compliance with this section are raised by the patent owner or the third party requester during a reexamination proceeding, they will be noted as unresolved questions in accordance with § 1.906(c).

OFFICE ACTIONS AND RESPONSES (BEFORE THE EXAMINER) IN *Inter Partes* REEXAMINATION

§ 1.935 Initial Office action usually accompanies order for *inter partes* reexamination.

The order for *inter partes* reexamination will usually be accompanied by the initial Office action on the merits of the reexamination.

§ 1.937 Conduct of *inter partes* reexamination.

(a) All *inter partes* reexamination proceedings, including any appeals to the Patent Trial and Appeal Board, will be conducted with special dispatch within the Office, unless the Director makes a determination that there is good cause for suspending the reexamination proceeding.

(b) The *inter partes* reexamination proceeding will be conducted in accordance with §§ 1.104 through 1.116, the sections governing the application examination process, and will result in the issuance of an *inter partes* reexamination certificate under § 1.997, except as otherwise provided.

(c) All communications between the Office and the parties to the *inter partes* reexamination which are directed to the merits of the proceeding must be in writing and filed with the Office for entry into the record of the proceeding.

(d) A petition in an *inter partes* reexamination proceeding must be accompanied by the fee set forth in § 1.20(c)(6), except for petitions under § 1.956 to extend the period for response by a patent owner, petitions under § 1.958 to accept a delayed response by a patent owner, petitions under § 1.78 to accept an unintentionally delayed benefit claim, and petitions under § 1.530(l) for correction of inventorship in a reexamination proceeding.

[65 FR 76777, as amended at 77 FR 46628, Aug. 6, 2012; 77 FR 48853, Aug. 14, 2012]

§ 1.939 Unauthorized papers in *inter partes* reexamination.

(a) If an unauthorized paper is filed by any party at any time during the *inter partes* reexamination proceeding it will not be considered and may be returned.

(b) Unless otherwise authorized, no paper shall be filed prior to the initial Office action on the merits of the *inter partes* reexamination.

§ 1.941 Amendments by patent owner in *inter partes* reexamination.

Amendments by patent owner in *inter partes* reexamination proceedings are made by filing a paper in compliance with §§ 1.530(d)–(k) and 1.943.

§ 1.943 Requirements of responses, written comments, and briefs in *inter partes* reexamination.

(a) The form of responses, written comments, briefs, appendices, and other papers must be in accordance with the requirements of § 1.52.

(b) Responses by the patent owner and written comments by the third party requester shall not exceed 50 pages in length, excluding amendments, appendices of claims, and reference materials such as prior art references.

(c) Appellant's briefs filed by the patent owner and the third party requester shall not exceed thirty pages or 14,000 words in length, excluding appendices of claims and reference materials such as prior art references. All other briefs filed by any party shall not exceed fifteen pages in length or 7,000 words. If the page limit for any brief is exceeded, a certificate is required stating the number of words contained in the brief.

§ 1.945 Response to Office action by patent owner in *inter partes* reexamination.

(a) The patent owner will be given at least thirty days to file a response to any Office action on the merits of the *inter partes* reexamination.

(b) Any supplemental response to the Office action will be entered only where the supplemental response is accompanied by a showing of sufficient cause why the supplemental response should be entered. The showing of sufficient cause must include:

(1) An explanation of how the requirements of § 1.111(a)(2)(i) are satisfied;

(2) An explanation of why the supplemental response was not presented together with the original response to the Office action; and

(3) A compelling reason to enter the supplemental response.

[72 FR 18906, Apr. 16, 2007]

§ 1.947 Comments by third party requester to patent owner's response in *inter partes* reexamination.

Each time the patent owner files a response to an Office action on the merits pursuant to § 1.945, a third party requester may once file written comments within a period of 30 days from the date of service of the patent owner's response. These comments shall be limited to issues raised by the Office action or the patent owner's response. The time for submitting comments by the third party requester may not be extended. For the purpose of filing the written comments by the third party requester, the comments will be considered as having been received in the Office as of the date of deposit specified in the certificate under § 1.8.

§ 1.948 Limitations on submission of prior art by third party requester following the order for *inter partes* reexamination.

(a) After the *inter partes* reexamination order, the third party requester may only cite additional prior art as defined under § 1.501 if it is filed as part of a comments submission under § 1.947 or § 1.951(b) and is limited to prior art:

(1) which is necessary to rebut a finding of fact by the examiner;

(2) which is necessary to rebut a response of the patent owner; or

(3) which for the first time became known or available to the third party requester after the filing of the request for *inter partes* reexamination proceeding. Prior art submitted under paragraph (a)(3) of this section must be accompanied by a statement as to when the prior art first became known or available to the third party requester and must include a discussion of the pertinency of each reference to the patentability of at least one claim.

(b) [Reserved]

§ 1.949 Examiner's Office action closing prosecution in *inter partes* reexamination.

Upon consideration of the issues a second or subsequent time, or upon a determination of patentability of all claims, the examiner shall issue an Office action treating all claims present in the *inter partes* reexamination, which may be an action closing prosecution. The Office action shall set forth all rejections and determinations not to make a proposed rejection, and the grounds therefor. An Office action will not usually close prosecution if it includes a new ground of rejection which was not previously addressed by the patent owner, unless the new ground was necessitated by an amendment.

§ 1.951 Options after Office action closing prosecution in *inter partes* reexamination.

(a) After an Office action closing prosecution in an *inter partes* reexamination, the patent owner may once file comments limited to the issues raised in the Office action closing prosecution. The comments can include a proposed amendment to the claims, which amendment will be subject to the criteria of § 1.116 as to whether or not it shall be admitted. The comments must be filed within the time set for response in the Office action closing prosecution.

(b) When the patent owner does file comments, a third party requester may once file comments responsive to the patent owner's comments within 30 days from the date of service of patent owner's comments on the third party requester.

§ 1.953 Examiner's Right of Appeal Notice in *inter partes* reexamination.

(a) Upon considering the comments of the patent owner and the third party requester subsequent to the Office action closing prosecution in an *inter partes* reexamination, or upon expiration of the time for submitting such comments, the examiner shall issue a Right of Appeal Notice, unless the examiner reopens prosecution and issues another Office action on the merits.

(b) Expedited Right of Appeal Notice: At any time after the patent owner's response to the initial Office action on the merits in an *inter partes* reexamination, the patent owner and all third party requesters may stipulate that the issues are appropriate for a final action, which would include a final rejection and/or a final determination favorable to patentability, and may request the issuance of a Right of Appeal Notice. The request must have the concurrence of the patent owner and all third party requesters present in the proceeding and must identify all of the appealable issues and the positions of the patent owner and all third party requesters on those issues. If the examiner determines that no other issues are present or should be raised, a Right of Appeal Notice limited to the identified issues shall be issued.

(c) The Right of Appeal Notice shall be a final action, which comprises a final rejection setting forth each ground of rejection and/or final decision favorable to patentability including each determination not to make a proposed rejection, an identification of the status of each claim, and the reasons for decisions favorable to patentability and/or the grounds of rejection for each claim. No amendment can be made in response to the Right of Appeal Notice. The Right of Appeal Notice shall set a one-month time period for either party to appeal. If no notice of appeal is filed, prosecution in the *inter partes* reexamination proceeding will be terminated, and the Director will proceed to issue and publish a certificate under § 1.997 in accordance with the Right of Appeal Notice.

[65 FR 76777, Dec. 7, 2000, as amended at 72 FR 18906, Apr. 16, 2007]

INTERVIEWS PROHIBITED IN *Inter Partes* REEXAMINATION

§ 1.955 Interviews prohibited in *inter partes* reexamination proceedings.

There will be no interviews in an *inter partes* reexamination proceeding which discuss the merits of the proceeding.

EXTENSIONS OF TIME, TERMINATING OF REEXAMINATION PROSECUTION, AND PETITIONS TO REVIVE IN *Inter Partes* REEXAMINATION

§ 1.956 Patent owner extensions of time in *inter partes* reexamination.

The time for taking any action by a patent owner in an *inter partes* reexamination proceeding will be extended only for sufficient cause and for a reasonable time specified. Any request for such extension must be filed on or before the day on which action by the patent owner is due, but in no case will the mere filing of a request effect any extension. Any request for such extension must be accompanied by the petition fee set forth in § 1.17(g). See § 1.304(a) for extensions of time for filing a notice of appeal to the U.S. Court of Appeals for the Federal Circuit.

[69 FR 56546, Sept. 21, 2004]

§ 1.957 Failure to file a timely, appropriate or complete response or comment in *inter partes* reexamination.

(a) If the third party requester files an untimely or inappropriate comment, notice of appeal or brief in an *inter partes* reexamination, the paper will be refused consideration.

(b) If no claims are found patentable, and the patent owner fails to file a timely and appropriate response in an *inter partes* reexamination proceeding, the prosecution in the reexamination proceeding will be a terminated prosecution and the Director will proceed to issue and publish a certificate concluding the reexamination proceeding under § 1.997 in accordance with the last action of the Office.

(c) If claims are found patentable and the patent owner fails to file a timely and appropriate response to any Office action in an *inter partes* reexamination proceeding, further prosecution will be limited to the claims found patentable at the time of the failure to respond, and to any claims added thereafter which do not expand the scope of the claims which were found patentable at that time.

(d) When action by the patent owner is a *bona fide* attempt to respond and to advance the prosecution and is substantially a complete response to the Office action, but consideration of some matter or compliance with some requirement has been inadvertently omitted, an opportunity to explain and supply the omission may be given.

[65 FR 76777, Dec. 7, 2000, as amended at 72 FR 18906, Apr. 16, 2007]

§ 1.958 Petition to revive *inter partes* reexamination prosecution terminated for lack of patent owner response.

(a) If a response by the patent owner is not timely filed in the Office, the delay in filing such response may be excused if it is shown to the satisfaction of the Director that the delay was unavoidable. A grantable petition to accept an unavoidably delayed response must be filed in compliance with § 1.137(a).

(b) Any response by the patent owner not timely filed in the Office may be accepted if the delay was unintentional. A grantable petition to accept an unintentionally delayed response must be filed in compliance with § 1.137(b).

APPEAL TO THE PATENT TRIAL AND APPEAL BOARD IN *Inter Partes* REEXAMINATION

§ 1.959 Appeal in *inter partes* reexamination.

Appeals to the Patent Trial and Appeal Board under 35 U.S.C. 134(c) are conducted according to part 41 of this title.

[77 FR 46628, Aug. 6, 2012]

§§ 1.961–1.977 [Reserved]

§ 1.979 Return of Jurisdiction from the Patent Trial and Appeal Board; termination of appeal proceedings.

(a) Jurisdiction over an *inter partes* reexamination proceeding passes to the examiner after a decision by the Patent Trial and Appeal Board upon transmittal of the file to the examiner, subject to each appellant's right of appeal or other review, for such further action as the condition of the *inter partes* reexamination proceeding may require, to carry into effect the decision of the Patent Trial and Appeal Board.

(b) Upon judgment in the appeal before the Patent Trial and Appeal Board, if no further appeal has been taken (§ 1.983), the prosecution in the *inter partes* reexamination proceeding will be terminated and the Director will issue and publish a certificate under § 1.997 concluding the proceeding. If an appeal to the U.S. Court of Appeals for the Federal Circuit has been filed, that appeal is considered terminated when the mandate is issued by the Court.

[77 FR 46628, Aug. 6, 2012]

§ 1.981 Reopening after a final decision of the Patent Trial and Appeal Board.

When a decision by the Patent Trial and Appeal Board on appeal has become final for judicial review, prosecution of the *inter partes* reexamination proceeding will not be reopened or reconsidered by the primary examiner except under the provisions of § 41.77 of this title without the written authority of the Director, and then only for the consideration of matters not already adjudicated, sufficient cause being shown.

[77 FR 46628, Aug. 6, 2012]

APPEAL TO THE UNITED STATES COURT OF APPEALS FOR THE FEDERAL CIRCUIT IN *Inter Partes* REEXAMINATION

§ 1.983 Appeal to the United States Court of Appeals for the Federal Circuit in *inter partes* reexamination.

(a) The patent owner or third party requester in an *inter partes* reexamination proceeding who is a party to an appeal to the Patent Trial and Appeal Board and who is dissatisfied with the decision of the Patent Trial and Appeal Board may, subject to § 41.81, appeal to the U.S. Court of Appeals for the Federal Circuit and may be a party to any appeal thereto taken from a reexamination decision of the Patent Trial and Appeal Board.

(b) The appellant must take the following steps in such an appeal:

(1) In the U.S. Patent and Trademark Office, timely file a written notice of appeal directed to the Director in accordance with §§ 1.302 and 1.304;

(2) In the U.S. Court of Appeals for the Federal Circuit, file a copy of the notice of appeal and pay the fee, as provided for in the rules of the U.S. Court of Appeals for the Federal Circuit; and

(3) Serve a copy of the notice of appeal on every other party in the reexamination proceeding in the manner provided in § 1.248.

(c) If the patent owner has filed a notice of appeal to the U.S. Court of Appeals for the Federal Circuit, the third party requester may cross appeal to the U.S. Court of Appeals for the Federal Circuit if also dissatisfied with the decision of the Patent Trial and Appeal Board.

(d) If the third party requester has filed a notice of appeal to the U.S. Court of Appeals for the Federal Circuit, the patent owner may cross appeal to the U.S. Court of Appeals for the Federal Circuit if also dissatisfied with the decision of the Patent Trial and Appeal Board.

(e) A party electing to participate in an appellant's appeal must, within fourteen days of service of the appellant's notice of appeal under paragraph (b) of this section, or notice of cross appeal under paragraphs (c) or (d) of this section, take the following steps:

(1) In the U.S. Patent and Trademark Office, timely file a written notice directed to the Director electing to participate in the appellant's appeal to the U.S. Court of Appeals for the Federal Circuit by mail to, or hand service on, the General Counsel as provided in § 104.2;

(2) In the U.S. Court of Appeals for the Federal Circuit, file a copy of the notice electing to participate in accordance with the rules of the U.S. Court of Appeals for the Federal Circuit; and

(3) Serve a copy of the notice electing to participate on every other party in the reexamination proceeding in the manner provided in § 1.248.

(f) Notwithstanding any provision of the rules, in any reexamination proceeding commenced prior to November 2, 2002, the third party requester is precluded from appealing and cross appealing any decision of the Patent Trial and Appeal Board to the U.S. Court of Appeals for the Federal Circuit, and the third party requester is precluded from participating in any appeal taken by the patent owner to the U.S. Court of Appeals for the Federal Circuit.

[68 FR 71008, Dec. 22, 2003, as amended at 72 FR 18907, Apr. 16, 2007; 77 FR 46628, Aug. 6, 2012]

CONCURRENT PROCEEDINGS INVOLVING SAME PATENT IN *Inter Partes* REEXAMINATION

§ 1.985 Notification of prior or concurrent proceedings in *inter partes* reexamination.

(a) In any *inter partes* reexamination proceeding, the patent owner shall call the attention of the Office to any prior or concurrent proceedings in which the patent is or was involved, including but not limited to interference or trial before the Patent Trial and Appeal Board, reissue, reexamination, or litigation and the results of such proceedings.

(b) Notwithstanding any provision of the rules, any person at any time may file a paper in an *inter partes* reexamination proceeding notifying the Office of a prior or concurrent proceeding in which the same patent is or was involved, including but not limited to interference or trial before the Patent Trial and Appeal Board, reissue, reexamination, or litigation and the results of such proceedings. Such paper must be limited to merely providing notice of the other proceeding without discussion of issues of the current *inter partes* reexamination proceeding.

[77 FR 46629, Aug. 6, 2012]

§ 1.987 Suspension of *inter partes* reexamination proceeding due to litigation.

If a patent in the process of *inter partes* reexamination is or becomes involved in litigation, the Director shall determine whether or not to suspend the *inter partes* reexamination proceeding.

§ 1.989 Merger of concurrent reexamination proceedings.

(a) If any reexamination is ordered while a prior *inter partes* reexamination proceeding is pending for the same patent and prosecution in the prior *inter partes* reexamination proceeding has not been terminated, a decision may be made to merge the two proceedings or to suspend one of the two proceedings. Where merger is ordered, the merged examination will normally result in the issuance and publication of a single reexamination certificate under § 1.997.

(b) An *inter partes* reexamination proceeding filed under § 1.913 which is merged with an *ex parte* reexamination proceeding filed under § 1.510 will result in the merged proceeding being governed by §§ 1.902 through 1.997, except that the rights of any third party requester of the *ex parte* reexamination shall be governed by §§ 1.510 through 1.560.

[65 FR 76777, Dec. 7, 2000, as amended at 72 FR 18907, Apr. 16, 2007]

§ 1.991 Merger of concurrent reissue application and *inter partes* reexamination proceeding.

If a reissue application and an *inter partes* reexamination proceeding on which an order pursuant to § 1.931 has been mailed are pending concurrently on a patent, a decision may be made to merge the two proceedings or to suspend one of the two proceedings. Where merger of a reissue application and an *inter partes* reexamination proceeding is ordered, the merged proceeding will be conducted in accordance with §§ 1.171 through 1.179, and the patent owner will be required to place and maintain the same claims in the reissue application and the *inter partes* reexamination proceeding during the pendency of the merged proceeding. In a merged proceeding the third party requester may participate to the extent provided under §§ 1.902 through 1.997 and 41.60 through 41.81, except that such participation shall be limited to issues within the scope of *inter partes* reexamination. The examiner's actions and any responses by the patent owner or third party requester in a merged proceeding will apply to both the reissue application and the *inter partes* reexamination proceeding and be physically entered into both files. Any *inter partes* reexamination proceeding merged with a reissue application shall be concluded by the grant of the reissued patent.

[72 FR 18907, Apr. 16, 2007]

§ 1.993 Suspension of concurrent interference and *inter partes* reexamination proceeding.

If a patent in the process of *inter partes* reexamination is or becomes involved in an interference or trial before the Patent Trial and Appeal Board, the Director may suspend the *inter partes* reexamination, interference, or trial. The Director will not consider a request to suspend an interference or trial unless a motion under § 41.121(a)(3) of this title to suspend the interference or trial has been presented to, and denied by, an administrative patent judge and the request is filed within ten (10) days of a decision by an administrative patent judge denying the motion for suspension or such other time as the administrative patent judge may set.

[77 FR 46629, Aug. 6, 2012]

§ 1.995 Third party requester's participation rights preserved in merged proceeding.

When a third party requester is involved in one or more proceedings, including an *inter partes* reexamination proceeding, the merger of such proceedings will be accomplished so as to preserve the third party requester's right to participate to the extent specifically provided for in these regulations. In merged proceedings involving different requesters, any paper filed by one party in the merged proceeding shall be served on all other parties of the merged proceeding.

REEXAMINATION CERTIFICATE IN *Inter Partes* REEXAMINATION

§ 1.997 Issuance and publication of *inter partes* reexamination certificate concludes *inter partes* reexamination proceeding.

(a) To conclude an *inter partes* reexamination proceeding, the Director will issue and publish an *inter partes* reexamination certificate in accordance with 35 U.S.C. 316 setting forth the results of the *inter partes* reexamination proceeding and the content of the patent following the *inter partes* reexamination proceeding.

(b) A certificate will be issued and published in each patent in which an *inter partes* reexamination proceeding has been ordered under § 1.931. Any statutory disclaimer filed by the patent owner will be made part of the certificate.

(c) The certificate will be sent to the patent owner at the address as provided for in § 1.33(c). A copy of the certificate will also be sent to the third party requester of the *inter partes* reexamination proceeding.

(d) If a certificate has been issued and published which cancels all of the claims of the patent, no further Office proceedings will be conducted with that patent or any reissue applications or any reexamination requests relating thereto.

(e) If the *inter partes* reexamination proceeding is terminated by the grant of a reissued patent as provided in § 1.991, the reissued patent will constitute the reexamination certificate required by this section and 35 U.S.C. 316.

(f) A notice of the issuance of each certificate under this section will be published in the *Official Gazette*.

[65 FR 76777, Dec. 7, 2000, as amended at 72 FR 18907, Apr. 16, 2007]

PART 2—RULES OF PRACTICE IN TRADEMARK CASES

EDITORIAL NOTE: Part 2 is placed in the separate grouping of parts pertaining to trademarks regulations.

PART 3—ASSIGNMENT, RECORDING AND RIGHTS OF ASSIGNEE

AUTHORITY: 15 U.S.C. 1123; 35 U.S.C. 2(b)(2).

SOURCE: 57 FR 29642, July 6, 1992, unless otherwise noted.

EDITORIAL NOTE: Nomenclature changes to part 3 appear at 68 FR 14337, Mar. 25, 2003.

§ 3.1 Definitions.

For purposes of this part, the following definitions shall apply:

Application means a national application for patent, an international patent application that designates the United States of America, or an application to register a trademark under section 1 or 44 of the Trademark Act, 15 U.S.C. 1051 or 15 U.S.C. 1126, unless otherwise indicated.

Assignment means a transfer by a party of all or part of its right, title and interest in a patent, patent application, registered mark or a mark for which an application to register has been filed.

Document means a document which a party requests to be recorded in the Office pursuant to § 3.11 and which affects some interest in an application, patent, or registration.

Office means the United States Patent and Trademark Office.

Recorded document means a document which has been recorded in the Office pursuant to § 3.11.

Registration means a trademark registration issued by the Office.

[69 FR 29878, May 26, 2004]

DOCUMENTS ELIGIBLE FOR RECORDING

§ 3.11 Documents which will be recorded.

(a) Assignments of applications, patents, and registrations, accompanied by completed cover sheets as specified in §§ 3.28 and 3.31, will be recorded in the Office. Other documents, accompanied by completed cover sheets as specified in §§ 3.28 and 3.31, affecting title to applications, patents, or registrations, will be recorded as provided in this part or at the discretion of the Director.

(b) Executive Order 9424 of February 18, 1944 (9 FR 1959, 3 CFR 1943–1948 Comp., p. 303) requires the several departments and other executive agencies of the Government, including Government-owned or Government-controlled corporations, to forward promptly to the Director for recording all licenses, assignments, or other interests of the Government in or under patents or patent applications. Assignments and other documents affecting title to patents or patent applications and documents not affecting title to patents or patent applications required by Executive Order 9424 to be filed will be recorded as provided in this part.

(c) A joint research agreement or an excerpt of a joint research agreement will also be recorded as provided in this part.

[62 FR 53202, Oct. 10, 1997, as amended at 70 FR 1824, Jan. 11, 2005; 70 FR 54267, Sept. 14, 2005]

§ 3.16 Assignability of trademarks prior to filing of an allegation of use.

Before an allegation of use under either 15 U.S.C. 1051(c) or 15 U.S.C. 1051(d) is filed, an applicant may only assign an application to register a mark under 15 U.S.C. 1051(b) to a successor to the applicant's business, or portion of the business to which the mark pertains, if that business is ongoing and existing.

[64 FR 48926, Sept. 8, 1999]

REQUIREMENTS FOR RECORDING

§ 3.21 Identification of patents and patent applications.

An assignment relating to a patent must identify the patent by the patent number. An assignment relating to a national patent application must identify the national patent application by the application number (consisting of the series code and the serial number, e.g., 07/123,456). An assignment relating to an international patent application which designates the United States of America must identify the international application by the international application number (e.g., PCT/US90/01234). If an assignment of a patent application filed under § 1.53(b) is executed concurrently with, or subsequent to, the execution of the patent application, but before the patent application is filed, it must identify the patent application by the name of each inventor and the title of the invention so that there can be no mistake as to the patent application intended. If an assignment of a provisional application under § 1.53(c) is executed before the provisional application is filed, it must identify the provisional application by the name of each inventor and the title of the invention so that there can be no mistake as to the provisional application intended.

[69 FR 29878, May 26, 2004]

§3.24 Requirements for documents and cover sheets relating to patents and patent applications.

(a) *For electronic submissions:* Either a copy of the original document or an extract of the original document may be submitted for recording. All documents must be submitted as digitized images in Tagged Image File Format (TIFF) or another form as prescribed by the Director. When printed to a paper size of either 21.6 by 27.9 cm (8½ by 11 inches) or 21.0 by 29.7 cm (DIN size A4), the document must be legible and a 2.5 cm (one-inch) margin must be present on all sides.

(b) *For paper or facsimile submissions:* Either a copy of the original document or an extract of the original document must be submitted for recording. Only one side of each page may be used. The paper size must be either 21.6 by 27.9 cm (8½ by 11 inches) or 21.0 by 29.7 cm (DIN size A4), and in either case, a 2.5 cm (one-inch) margin must be present on all sides. For paper submissions, the paper used should be flexible, strong white, non-shiny, and durable. The Office will not return recorded documents, so original documents must not be submitted for recording.

[69 FR 29879, May 26, 2004]

§3.25 Recording requirements for trademark applications and registrations.

(a) *Documents affecting title.* To record documents affecting title to a trademark application or registration, a legible cover sheet (*see* §3.31) and one of the following must be submitted:

(1) A copy of the original document;

(2) A copy of an extract from the document evidencing the effect on title; or

(3) A statement signed by both the party conveying the interest and the party receiving the interest explaining how the conveyance affects title.

(b) *Name changes.* Only a legible cover sheet is required (*See* §3.31).

(c) *All documents.* (1) *For electronic submissions:* All documents must be submitted as digitized images in Tagged Image File Format (TIFF) or another form as prescribed by the Director. When printed to a paper size of either 21.6 by 27.9 cm (8½ by 11 inches) or 21.0 by 29.7 cm (DIN size A4), a 2.5 cm (one-inch) margin must be present on all sides.

(2) *For paper or facsimile submissions:* All documents should be submitted on white and non-shiny paper that is either 8½ by 11 inches (21.6 by 27.9 cm) or DIN size A4 (21.0 by 29.7 cm) with a one-inch (2.5 cm) margin on all sides in either case. Only one side of each page may be used. The Office will not return recorded documents, so original documents should not be submitted for recording.

[69 FR 29879, May 26, 2004]

§3.26 English language requirement.

The Office will accept and record non-English language documents only if accompanied by an English translation signed by the individual making the translation.

[62 FR 53202, Oct. 10, 1997]

§3.27 Mailing address for submitting documents to be recorded.

Documents and cover sheets submitted by mail for recordation should be addressed to Mail Stop Assignment Recordation Services, Director of the United States Patent and Trademark Office, P.O. Box 1450, Alexandria, Virginia 22313–1450, unless they are filed together with new applications.

[69 FR 29879, May 26, 2004]

§3.28 Requests for recording.

Each document submitted to the Office for recording must include a single cover sheet (as specified in §3.31) referring either to those patent applications and patents, or to those trademark applications and registrations, against which the document is to be recorded. If a document to be recorded includes interests in, or transactions involving, both patents and trademarks, then separate patent and trademark cover sheets, each accompanied by a copy of the document to be recorded, must be submitted. If a document to be recorded is not accompanied by a completed cover sheet, the document and the incomplete cover sheet will be returned pursuant to §3.51 for proper completion, in which case the document and a completed cover sheet should be resubmitted.

[70 FR 56128, Sept. 26, 2005]

COVER SHEET REQUIREMENTS

§ 3.31 Cover sheet content.

(a) Each patent or trademark cover sheet required by § 3.28 must contain:

(1) The name of the party conveying the interest;

(2) The name and address of the party receiving the interest;

(3) A description of the interest conveyed or transaction to be recorded;

(4) Identification of the interests involved:

(i) *For trademark assignments and trademark name changes:* Each trademark registration number and each trademark application number, if known, against which the Office is to record the document. If the trademark application number is not known, a copy of the application or a reproduction of the trademark must be submitted, along with an estimate of the date that the Office received the application; or

(ii) *For any other document affecting title to a trademark or patent application, registration or patent:* Each trademark or patent application number or each trademark registration number or patent against which the document is to be recorded, or an indication that the document is filed together with a patent application;

(5) The name and address of the party to whom correspondence concerning the request to record the document should be mailed;

(6) The date the document was executed;

(7) The signature of the party submitting the document. For an assignment document or name change filed electronically, the person who signs the cover sheet must either:

(i) Place a symbol comprised of letters, numbers, and/or punctuation marks between forward slash marks (e.g., /Thomas O'Malley III/) in the signature block on the electronic submission; or

(ii) Sign the cover sheet using some other form of electronic signature specified by the Director.

(8) For trademark assignments, the entity and citizenship of the party receiving the interest. In addition, if the party receiving the interest is a domestic partnership or domestic joint venture, the cover sheet must set forth the names, legal entities, and national citizenship (or the state or country of organization) of all general partners or active members that compose the partnership or joint venture.

(b) A cover sheet should not refer to both patents and trademarks, since any information, including information about pending patent applications, submitted with a request for recordation of a document against a trademark application or trademark registration will become public record upon recordation.

(c) Each patent cover sheet required by § 3.28 seeking to record a governmental interest as provided by § 3.11(b) must:

(1) Indicate that the document relates to a Government interest; and

(2) Indicate, if applicable, that the document to be recorded is not a document affecting title (see § 3.41(b)).

(d) Each trademark cover sheet required by § 3.28 seeking to record a document against a trademark application or registration should include, in addition to the serial number or registration number of the trademark, identification of the trademark or a description of the trademark, against which the Office is to record the document.

(e) Each patent or trademark cover sheet required by § 3.28 should contain the number of applications, patents or registrations identified in the cover sheet and the total fee.

(f) Each trademark cover sheet should include the citizenship of the party conveying the interest.

(g) The cover sheet required by § 3.28 seeking to record a joint research agreement or an excerpt of a joint research agreement as provided by § 3.11(c) must:

(1) Identify the document as a "joint research agreement" (in the space provided for the description of the interest conveyed or transaction to be recorded if using an Office-provided form);

(2) Indicate the name of the owner of the application or patent (in the space provided for the name and address of

the party receiving the interest if using an Office-provided form);

(3) Indicate the name of each other party to the joint research agreement party (in the space provided for the name of the party conveying the interest if using an Office-provided form); and

(4) Indicate the date the joint research agreement was executed.

(h) The assignment cover sheet required by § 3.28 must contain a conspicuous indication of an intent to utilize the assignment as the required oath or declaration under § 1.63 of this chapter.

[57 FR 29642, July 6, 1992, as amended at 62 FR 53202, Oct. 10, 1997; 64 FR 48927, Sept. 8, 1999; 67 FR 79523, Dec. 30, 2002; 69 FR 29879, May 26, 2004; 70 FR 1824, Jan. 11, 2005; 70 FR 56128, Sept. 26, 2005; 73 FR 67775, Nov. 17, 2008; 77 FR 48825, Aug. 14, 2012]

§ 3.34 Correction of cover sheet errors.

(a) An error in a cover sheet recorded pursuant to § 3.11 will be corrected only if:

(1) The error is apparent when the cover sheet is compared with the recorded document to which it pertains, and

(2) A corrected cover sheet is filed for recordation.

(b) The corrected cover sheet must be accompanied by a copy of the document originally submitted for recording and by the recording fee as set forth in § 3.41.

[69 FR 29879, May 26, 2004]

FEES

§ 3.41 Recording fees.

(a) All requests to record documents must be accompanied by the appropriate fee. Except as provided in paragraph (b) of this section, a fee is required for each application, patent and registration against which the document is recorded as identified in the cover sheet. The recording fee is set in § 1.21(h) of this chapter for patents and in § 2.6(b)(6) of this chapter for trademarks.

(b) No fee is required for each patent application and patent against which a document required by Executive Order 9424 is to be filed if:

(1) The document does not affect title and is so identified in the cover sheet (see § 3.31(c)(2)); and

(2) The document and cover sheet are either: Faxed or electronically submitted as prescribed by the Director, or mailed to the Office in compliance with § 3.27.

[63 FR 52159, Sept. 30, 1998, as amended at 69 FR 29879, May 26, 2004]

DATE AND EFFECT OF RECORDING

§ 3.51 Recording date.

The date of recording of a document is the date the document meeting the requirements for recording set forth in this part is filed in the Office. A document which does not comply with the identification requirements of § 3.21 will not be recorded. Documents not meeting the other requirements for recording, for example, a document submitted without a completed cover sheet or without the required fee, will be returned for correction to the sender where a correspondence address is available. The returned papers, stamped with the original date of receipt by the Office, will be accompanied by a letter which will indicate that if the returned papers are corrected and resubmitted to the Office within the time specified in the letter, the Office will consider the original date of filing of the papers as the date of recording of the document. The procedure set forth in § 1.8 or § 1.10 of this chapter may be used for resubmissions of returned papers to have the benefit of the date of deposit in the United States Postal Service. If the returned papers are not corrected and resubmitted within the specified period, the date of filing of the corrected papers will be considered to be the date of recording of the document. The specified period to resubmit the returned papers will not be extended.

[62 FR 53203, Oct. 10, 1997]

§ 3.54 Effect of recording.

The recording of a document pursuant to § 3.11 is not a determination by the Office of the validity of the document or the effect that document has on the title to an application, a patent, or a registration. When necessary, the

Office will determine what effect a document has, including whether a party has the authority to take an action in a matter pending before the Office.

§ 3.56 Conditional assignments.

Assignments which are made conditional on the performance of certain acts or events, such as the payment of money or other condition subsequent, if recorded in the Office, are regarded as absolute assignments for Office purposes until cancelled with the written consent of all parties or by the decree of a court of competent jurisdiction. The Office does not determine whether such conditions have been fulfilled.

§ 3.58 Governmental registers.

(a) The Office will maintain a Departmental Register to record governmental interests required to be recorded by Executive Order 9424. This Departmental Register will not be open to public inspection but will be available for examination and inspection by duly authorized representatives of the Government. Governmental interests recorded on the Departmental Register will be available for public inspection as provided in § 1.12.

(b) The Office will maintain a Secret Register to record governmental interests required to be recorded by Executive Order 9424. Any instrument to be recorded will be placed on this Secret Register at the request of the department or agency submitting the same. No information will be given concerning any instrument in such record or register, and no examination or inspection thereof or of the index thereto will be permitted, except on the written authority of the head of the department or agency which submitted the instrument and requested secrecy, and the approval of such authority by the Director. No instrument or record other than the one specified may be examined, and the examination must take place in the presence of a designated official of the Patent and Trademark Office. When the department or agency which submitted an instrument no longer requires secrecy with respect to that instrument, it must be recorded anew in the Departmental Register.

[62 FR 53203, Oct. 10, 1997]

DOMESTIC REPRESENTATIVE

§ 3.61 Domestic representative.

If the assignee of a patent, patent application, trademark application or trademark registration is not domiciled in the United States, the assignee may designate a domestic representative in a document filed in the United States Patent and Trademark Office. The designation should state the name and address of a person residing within the United States on whom may be served process or notice of proceedings affecting the application, patent or registration or rights thereunder.

[67 FR 79522, Dec. 30, 2002]

ACTION TAKEN BY ASSIGNEE

§ 3.71 Prosecution by assignee.

(a) *Patents—conducting of prosecution.* One or more assignees as defined in paragraph (b) of this section may conduct prosecution of a national patent application as the applicant under § 1.46 of this title, or conduct prosecution of a supplemental examination or reexamination proceeding, to the exclusion of the inventor or previous applicant or patent owner. Conflicts between purported assignees are handled in accordance with § 3.73(c)(3).

(b) *Patents—assignee(s) who can prosecute.* The assignee(s) who may conduct either the prosecution of a national application for patent as the applicant under § 1.46 of this title or a supplemental examination or reexamination proceeding are:

(1) *A single assignee.* An assignee of the entire right, title and interest in the application or patent, or

(2) *Partial assignee(s) together or with inventor(s).* All partial assignees, or all partial assignees and inventors who have not assigned their right, title and interest in the application or patent, who together own the entire right, title and interest in the application or patent. A partial assignee is any assignee having less than the entire right, title and interest in the application or patent. The word "assignee" as used in this chapter means with respect to patent matters the single assignee of the entire right, title and interest in the application or patent if there is such a single assignee, or all of

the partial assignees, or all of the partial assignee and inventors who have not assigned their interest in the application or patent, who together own the entire right, title and interest in the application or patent.

(c) *Patents—Becoming of record.* An assignee becomes of record as the applicant in a national patent application under §1.46 of this title, and in a supplemental examination or reexamination proceeding, by filing a statement in compliance with §3.73(c) that is signed by a party who is authorized to act on behalf of the assignee.

(d) *Trademarks.* The assignee of a trademark application or registration may prosecute a trademark application, submit documents to maintain a trademark registration, or file papers against a third party in reliance on the assignee's trademark application or registration, to the exclusion of the original applicant or previous assignee. The assignee must establish ownership in compliance with §3.73(b).

[65 FR 54682, Sept. 8, 2000, as amended at 77 FR 48825, Aug. 14, 2012]

§3.73 Establishing right of assignee to take action.

(a) The original applicant is presumed to be the owner of an application for an original patent, and any patent that may issue therefrom, unless there is an assignment. The original applicant is presumed to be the owner of a trademark application or registration, unless there is an assignment.

(b) In order to request or take action in a trademark matter, the assignee must establish its ownership of the trademark property of paragraph (a) of this section to the satisfaction of the Director. The establishment of ownership by the assignee may be combined with the paper that requests or takes the action. Ownership is established by submitting to the Office a signed statement identifying the assignee, accompanied by either:

(1) Documentary evidence of a chain of title from the original owner to the assignee (*e.g.*, copy of an executed assignment). The documents submitted to establish ownership may be required to be recorded pursuant to §3.11 in the assignment records of the Office as a condition to permitting the assignee to take action in a matter pending before the Office; or

(2) A statement specifying where documentary evidence of a chain of title from the original owner to the assignee is recorded in the assignment records of the Office (*e.g.*, reel and frame number).

(c)(1) In order to request or take action in a patent matter, an assignee who is not the original applicant must establish its ownership of the patent property of paragraph (a) of this section to the satisfaction of the Director. The establishment of ownership by the assignee may be combined with the paper that requests or takes the action. Ownership is established by submitting to the Office a signed statement identifying the assignee, accompanied by either:

(i) Documentary evidence of a chain of title from the original owner to the assignee (*e.g.*, copy of an executed assignment). The submission of the documentary evidence must be accompanied by a statement affirming that the documentary evidence of the chain of title from the original owner to the assignee was or concurrently is being submitted for recordation pursuant to §3.11; or

(ii) A statement specifying where documentary evidence of a chain of title from the original owner to the assignee is recorded in the assignment records of the Office (*e.g.*, reel and frame number).

(2) If the submission is by an assignee of less than the entire right, title and interest (*e.g.*, more than one assignee exists) the Office may refuse to accept the submission as an establishment of ownership unless:

(i) Each assignee establishes the extent (by percentage) of its ownership interest, so as to account for the entire right, title and interest in the application or patent by all parties including inventors; or

(ii) Each assignee submits a statement identifying the parties including inventors who together own the entire right, title and interest and stating that all the identified parties own the entire right, title and interest.

(3) If two or more purported assignees file conflicting statements under paragraph (c)(1) of this section, the Director will determine which, if any, purported assignee will be permitted to control prosecution of the application.

(d) The submission establishing ownership under paragraph (b) or (c) of this section must show that the person signing the submission is a person authorized to act on behalf of the assignee by:

(1) Including a statement that the person signing the submission is authorized to act on behalf of the assignee;

(2) Being signed by a person having apparent authority to sign on behalf of the assignee; or

(3) For patent matters only, being signed by a practitioner of record.

[77 FR 48825, Aug. 14, 2012]

ISSUANCE TO ASSIGNEE

§ 3.81 Issue of patent to assignee.

(a) *With payment of the issue fee:* An application may issue in the name of the assignee consistent with the application's assignment where a request for such issuance is submitted with payment of the issue fee, provided the assignment has been previously recorded in the Office. If the assignment has not been previously recorded, the request must state that the document has been filed for recordation as set forth in § 3.11.

(b) *After payment of the issue fee:* Any request for issuance of an application in the name of the assignee submitted after the date of payment of the issue fee, and any request for a patent to be corrected to state the name of the assignee, must state that the assignment was submitted for recordation as set forth in § 3.11 before issuance of the patent, and must include a request for a certificate of correction under § 1.323 of this chapter (accompanied by the fee set forth in § 1.20(a)) and the processing fee set forth in § 1.17(i) of this chapter.

(c) *Partial assignees.* (1) If one or more assignee, together with one or more inventor, holds the entire right, title, and interest in the application, the patent may issue in the names of the assignee and the inventor.

(2) If multiple assignees hold the entire right, title, and interest to the exclusion of all the inventors, the patent may issue in the names of the multiple assignees.

[69 FR 29879, May 26, 2004]

§ 3.85 Issue of registration to assignee.

The certificate of registration may be issued to the assignee of the applicant, or in a new name of the applicant, provided that the party files a written request in the trademark application by the time the application is being prepared for issuance of the certificate of registration, and the appropriate document is recorded in the Office. If the assignment or name change document has not been recorded in the Office, then the written request must state that the document has been filed for recordation. The address of the assignee must be made of record in the application file.

PART 4—COMPLAINTS REGARDING INVENTION PROMOTERS

AUTHORITY: 35 U.S.C. 2(b)(2) and 297.

SOURCE: 65 FR 3129, Jan. 20, 2000, unless otherwise noted.

§ 4.1 Complaints regarding invention promoters.

These regulations govern the Patent and Trademark Office's (Office) responsibilities under the Inventors' Rights Act of 1999, which can be found in the U.S. Code at 35 U.S.C. 297. The Act requires the Office to provide a forum for the publication of complaints concerning invention promoters. The Office will not conduct any independent investigation of the invention promoter. Although the Act provides additional civil remedies for persons injured by invention promoters, those remedies must be pursued by the injured party without the involvement of the Office.

§4.2 Definitions.

(a) *Invention Promoter* means any person, firm, partnership, corporation, or other entity who offers to perform or performs invention promotion services for, or on behalf of, a customer, and who holds itself out through advertising in any mass media as providing such services, but does not include—

(1) Any department or agency of the Federal Government or of a State or local government;

(2) Any nonprofit, charitable, scientific, or educational organization qualified under applicable State law or described under section 170(b)(1)(A) of the Internal Revenue Code of 1986;

(3) Any person or entity involved in the evaluation to determine commercial potential of, or offering to license or sell, a utility patent or a previously filed nonprovisional utility patent application;

(4) Any party participating in a transaction involving the sale of the stock or assets of a business; or

(5) Any party who directly engages in the business of retail sales of products or the distribution of products.

(b) *Customer* means any individual who enters into a contract with an invention promoter for invention promotion services.

(c) *Contract for Invention Promotion Services* means a contract by which an invention promoter undertakes invention promotion services for a customer.

(d) *Invention Promotion Services* means the procurement or attempted procurement for a customer of a firm, corporation, or other entity to develop and market products or services that include the invention of the customer.

§4.3 Submitting complaints.

(a) A person may submit a complaint concerning an invention promoter with the Office. A person submitting a complaint should understand that the complaint may be forwarded to the invention promoter and may become publicly available. The Office will not accept any complaint that requests that it be kept confidential.

(b) A complaint must be clearly marked, or otherwise identified, as a complaint under these rules. The complaint must include:

(1) The name and address of the complainant;

(2) The name and address of the invention promoter;

(3) The name of the customer;

(4) The invention promotion services offered or performed by the invention promoter;

(5) The name of the mass media in which the invention promoter advertised providing such services;

(6) An explanation of the relationship between the customer and the invention promoter; and

(7) A signature of the complainant.

(c) The complaint should fairly summarize the action of the invention promoter about which the person complains. Additionally, the complaint should include names and addresses of persons believed to be associated with the invention promoter. Complaints, and any replies, must be addressed to: Mail Stop 24, Commissioner for Patents, P.O. Box 1450, Alexandria, Virginia 22313–1450.

(d) Complaints that do not provide the information requested in paragraphs (b) and (c) of this section will be returned. If complainant's address is not provided, the complaint will be destroyed.

(e) No originals of documents should be included with the complaint.

(f) A complaint can be withdrawn by the complainant or the named customer at any time prior to its publication.

[65 FR 3129, Jan. 20, 2000, as amended at 68 FR 14338, Mar. 25, 2003]

§4.4 Invention promoter reply.

(a) If a submission appears to meet the requirements of a complaint, the invention promoter named in the complaint will be notified of the complaint and given 30 days to respond. The invention promoter's response will be made available to the public along with the complaint. If the invention promoter fails to reply within the 30-day time period set by the Office, the complaint will be made available to the public. Replies sent after the complaint is made available to the public will also be published.

(b) A response must be clearly marked, or otherwise identified, as a response by an invention promoter. The response must contain:

(1) The name and address of the invention promoter;

(2) A reference to a complaint forwarded to the invention promoter or a complaint previously published;

(3) The name of the individual signing the response; and

(4) The title or authority of the individual signing the response.

§ 4.5 Notice by publication.

If the copy of the complaint that is mailed to the invention promoter is returned undelivered, then the USPTO will primarily publish a Notice of Complaint Received on the USPTO's Internet home page at *http://www.uspto.gov.* Only where the USPTO's Web site is unavailable for publication will the USPTO publish the Notice of Complaint in the *Official Gazette* and/or the FEDERAL REGISTER. The invention promoter will be given 30 days from such notice to submit a reply to the Notice of Complaint. If the USPTO does not receive a reply from the invention promoter within 30 days, the complaint alone will become publicly available.

[68 FR 9553, Feb. 28, 2003]

§ 4.6 Attorneys and Agents.

Complaints against registered patent attorneys and agents will not be treated under this section, unless a complaint fairly demonstrates that invention promotion services are involved. Persons having complaints about registered patent attorneys or agents should contact the Office of Enrollment and Discipline at Mail Stop OED, Director of the United States Patent and Trademark Office, PO Box 1450, Alexandria, Virginia 22313–1450, and the attorney discipline section of the attorney's state licensing bar if an attorney is involved.

[68 FR 14338, Mar. 25, 2003]

PART 5—SECRECY OF CERTAIN INVENTIONS AND LICENSES TO EXPORT AND FILE APPLICATIONS IN FOREIGN COUNTRIES

SECRECY ORDERS

Sec.

AUTHORITY: 35 U.S.C. 2(b)(2), 41, 181–188, as amended by the Patent Law Foreign Filing Amendments Act of 1988, Pub. L. 100–418, 102 Stat. 1567; the Arms Export Control Act, as amended, 22 U.S.C. 2571 *et seq.;* the Atomic Energy Act of 1954, as amended, 42 U.S.C. 2011 *et seq.;* the Nuclear Non Proliferation Act of 1978; 22 U.S.C. 3201 *et seq.;* and the delegations in the regulations under these Acts to the Director (15 CFR 734.3(b)(1)(v), 22 CFR 125.04, and 10 CFR 810.7), as well as the Export Administration Act of 1979, 50 U.S.C. app. 2401 *et seq.;* the International Emergency Economic Powers Act, 50 U.S.C. 1701 *et seq.;* E.O. 12938, 59 FR 59099, 3 CFR, 1994 Comp., p. 950; E.O. 13222, 66 FR 44025, 3 CFR, 2001 Comp., p. 783; Notice of August 2, 2005, 70 FR 45273 (August 5, 2005).

SOURCE: 24 FR 10381, Dec. 22, 1959, unless otherwise noted.

EDITORIAL NOTE: Nomenclature changes to part 5 appear at 68 FR 14338, Mar. 25, 2003.

SECRECY ORDERS

§ 5.1 Applications and correspondence involving national security.

(a) All correspondence in connection with this part, including petitions, should be addressed to: Mail Stop L&R, Commissioner for Patents, P.O. Box 1450, Alexandria, Virginia 22313–1450.

(b) Application as used in this part includes provisional applications filed under 35 U.S.C. 111(b) (§1.9(a)(2) of this chapter), nonprovisional applications filed under 35 U.S.C. 111(a) or entering the national stage from an international application after compliance with 35 U.S.C. 371 (§1.9(a)(3)), or international applications filed under the Patent Cooperation Treaty prior to entering the national stage of processing (§1.9(b)).

(c) Patent applications and documents relating thereto that are national security classified (see §1.9(i) of this chapter) and contain authorized national security markings (e.g., "Confidential," "Secret" or "Top Secret") are accepted by the Office. National security classified documents filed in the Office must be either hand-carried to Licensing and Review or mailed to the Office in compliance with paragraph (a) of this section.

(d) The applicant in a national security classified patent application must obtain a secrecy order pursuant to §5.2(a). If a national security classified patent application is filed without a notification pursuant to §5.2(a), the Office will set a time period within which either the application must be declassified, or the application must be placed under a secrecy order pursuant to §5.2(a), or the applicant must submit evidence of a good faith effort to obtain a secrecy order pursuant to §5.2(a) from the relevant department or agency in order to prevent abandonment of the application. If evidence of a good faith effort to obtain a secrecy order pursuant to §5.2(a) from the relevant department or agency is submitted by the applicant within the time period set by the Office, but the application has not been declassified or placed under a secrecy order pursuant to §5.2(a), the Office will again set a time period within which either the application must be declassified, or the application must be placed under a secrecy order pursuant to §5.2(a), or the applicant must submit evidence of a good faith effort to again obtain a secrecy order pursuant to §5.2(a) from the relevant department or agency in order to prevent abandonment of the application.

(e) An application will not be published under §1.211 of this chapter or allowed under §1.311 of this chapter if publication or disclosure of the application would be detrimental to national security. An application under national security review will not be published at least until six months from its filing date or three months from the date the application was referred to a defense agency, whichever is later. A national security classified patent application will not be published under §1.211 of this chapter or allowed under §1.311 of this chapter until the application is declassified and any secrecy order under §5.2(a) has been rescinded.

(f) Applications on inventions made outside the United States and on inventions in which a U.S. Government defense agency has a property interest will not be made available to defense agencies.

[65 FR 54682, Sept. 8, 2000, as amended at 65 FR 57060, Sept. 20, 2000; 68 FR 14338, Mar. 25, 2003; 69 FR 29880, May 26, 2004]

§5.2 Secrecy order.

(a) When notified by the chief officer of a defense agency that publication or disclosure of the invention by the granting of a patent would be detrimental to the national security, an order that the invention be kept secret will be issued by the Commissioner for Patents.

(b) Any request for compensation as provided in 35 U.S.C. 183 must not be made to the Patent and Trademark Office, but directly to the department or agency which caused the secrecy order to be issued.

(c) An application disclosing any significant part of the subject matter of an application under a secrecy order pursuant to paragraph (a) of this section also falls within the scope of such secrecy order. Any such application that is pending before the Office must be promptly brought to the attention of Licensing and Review, unless such application is itself under a secrecy order pursuant to paragraph (a) of this section. Any subsequently filed application containing any significant part of the subject matter of an application under a secrecy order pursuant to paragraph (a) of this section must either be hand-carried to Licensing and Review or mailed to the Office in compliance with § 5.1(a).

[24 FR 10381, Dec. 22, 1959, as amended at 62 FR 53203, Oct. 10, 1997; 65 FR 54683, Sept. 8, 2000]

§ 5.3 Prosecution of application under secrecy orders; withholding patent.

Unless specifically ordered otherwise, action on the application by the Office and prosecution by the applicant will proceed during the time an application is under secrecy order to the point indicated in this section:

(a) National applications under secrecy order which come to a final rejection must be appealed or otherwise prosecuted to avoid abandonment. Appeals in such cases must be completed by the applicant but unless otherwise specifically ordered by the Commissioner for Patents will not be set for hearing until the secrecy order is removed.

(b) An interference or derivation will not be instituted involving a national application under secrecy order. An applicant whose application is under secrecy order may suggest an interference (§ 41.202(a) of this title), but the Office will not act on the request while the application remains under a secrecy order.

(c) When the national application is found to be in condition for allowance except for the secrecy order the applicant and the agency which caused the secrecy order to be issued will be notified. This notice (which is not a notice of allowance under § 1.311 of this chapter) does not require reply by the applicant and places the national application in a condition of suspension until the secrecy order is removed. When the secrecy order is removed the Patent and Trademark Office will issue a notice of allowance under § 1.311 of this chapter, or take such other action as may then be warranted.

(d) International applications under secrecy order will not be mailed, delivered or otherwise transmitted to the international authorities or the applicant. International applications under secrecy order will be processed up to the point where, if it were not for the secrecy order, record and search copies would be transmitted to the international authorities or the applicant.

(Pub. L. 94–131, 89 Stat. 685)

[43 FR 20470, May 11, 1978, as amended at 53 FR 23736, June 23, 1988; 62 FR 53203, Oct. 10, 1997; 69 FR 50002, Aug. 12, 2004; 77 FR 46629, Aug. 6, 2012]

§ 5.4 Petition for rescission of secrecy order.

(a) A petition for rescission or removal of a secrecy order may be filed by, or on behalf of, any principal affected thereby. Such petition may be in letter form, and it must be in duplicate.

(b) The petition must recite any and all facts that purport to render the order ineffectual or futile if this is the basis of the petition. When prior publications or patents are alleged the petition must give complete data as to such publications or patents and should be accompanied by copies thereof.

(c) The petition must identify any contract between the Government and any of the principals, under which the subject matter of the application or any significant part thereof was developed, or to which the subject matter is otherwise related. If there is no such contract, the petition must so state.

(d) Appeal to the Secretary of Commerce, as provided by 35 U.S.C. 181, from a secrecy order cannot be taken until after a petition for rescission of the secrecy order has been made and denied. Appeal must be taken within sixty days from the date of the denial, and the party appealing, as well as the department or agency which caused the order to be issued, will be notified of the time and place of hearing.

[24 FR 10381, Dec. 22, 1959, as amended at 62 FR 53204, Oct. 10, 1997]

§ 5.5 Permit to disclose or modification of secrecy order.

(a) Consent to disclosure, or to the filing of an application abroad, as provided in 35 U.S.C. 182, shall be made by a "permit" or "modification" of the secrecy order.

(b) Petitions for a permit or modification must fully recite the reason or purpose for the proposed disclosure. Where any proposed disclosee is known to be cleared by a defense agency to receive classified information, adequate explanation of such clearance should be made in the petition including the name of the agency or department granting the clearance and the date and degree thereof. The petition must be filed in duplicate.

(c) In a petition for modification of a secrecy order to permit filing abroad, all countries in which it is proposed to file must be made known, as well as all attorneys, agents and others to whom the material will be consigned prior to being lodged in the foreign patent office. The petition should include a statement vouching for the loyalty and integrity of the proposed disclosees and where their clearance status in this or the foreign country is known all details should be given.

(d) Consent to the disclosure of subject matter from one application under secrecy order may be deemed to be consent to the disclosure of common subject matter in other applications under secrecy order so long as not taken out of context in a manner disclosing material beyond the modification granted in the first application.

(e) Organizations requiring consent for disclosure of applications under secrecy order to persons or organizations in connection with repeated routine operation may petition for such consent in the form of a general permit. To be successful such petitions must ordinarily recite the security clearance status of the disclosees as sufficient for the highest classification of material that may be involved.

[24 FR 10381, Dec. 22, 1959, as amended at 62 FR 53204 Oct. 10, 1997]

§§ 5.6–5.8 [Reserved]

Licenses for Foreign Exporting and Filing

§ 5.11 License for filing in a foreign country an application on an invention made in the United States or for transmitting an international application.

(a) A license from the Commissioner for Patents under 35 U.S.C. 184 is required before filing any application for patent including any modifications, amendments, or supplements thereto or divisions thereof or for the registration of a utility model, industrial design, or model, in a foreign patent office or any foreign patent agency or any international agency other than the United States Receiving Office, if the invention was made in the United States and:

(1) An application on the invention has been on file in the United States less than six months prior to the date on which the application is to be filed, or

(2) No application on the invention has been filed in the United States.

(b) The license from the Commissioner for Patents referred to in paragraph (a) would also authorize the export of technical data abroad for purposes relating to the preparation, filing or possible filing and prosecution of a foreign patent application without separately complying with the regulations contained in 22 CFR parts 121 through 130 (International Traffic in Arms Regulations of the Department of State), 15 CFR parts 730–774 (Regulations of the Bureau of Industry and Security, Department of Commerce) and 10 CFR part 810 (Foreign Atomic Energy Programs of the Department of Energy).

(c) Where technical data in the form of a patent application, or in any form, are being exported for purposes related to the preparation, filing or possible filing and prosecution of a foreign patent application, without the license from the Commissioner for Patents referred to in paragraphs (a) or (b) of this section, or on an invention not made in the United States, the export regulations contained in 22 CFR parts 120 through 130 (International Traffic in Arms Regulations of the Department of State), 15 CFR parts 730–774 (Bureau of Industry and Security Regulations, Department of Commerce) and 10 CFR part 810 (Assistance to Foreign Atomic Energy Activities Regulations of the Department of Energy) must be complied with unless a license is not required because a United States application was on file at the time of export for at least six months without a secrecy order under §5.2 being placed thereon. The term "exported" means export as it is defined in 22 CFR part 120, 15 CFR part 734 and activities covered by 10 CFR part 810.

(d) If a secrecy order has been issued under § 5.2, an application cannot be exported to, or filed in, a foreign country (including an international agency in a foreign country), except in accordance with § 5.5.

(e) No license pursuant to paragraph (a) of this section is required:

(1) If the invention was not made in the United States, or

(2) If the corresponding United States application is not subject to a secrecy order under § 5.2, and was filed at least six months prior to the date on which the application is filed in a foreign country, or

(3) For subsequent modifications, amendments and supplements containing additional subject matter to, or divisions of, a foreign patent application if:

(i) A license is not, or was not, required under paragraph (e)(2) of this section for the foreign patent application;

(ii) The corresponding United States application was not required to be made available for inspection under 35 U.S.C. 181; and

(iii) Such modifications, amendments, and supplements do not, or did not, change the general nature of the invention in a manner which would require any corresponding United States application to be or have been available for inspection under 35 U.S.C. 181.

(f) A license pursuant to paragraph (a) of this section can be revoked at any time upon written notification by the Patent and Trademark Office. An authorization to file a foreign patent application resulting from the passage of six months from the date of filing of a United States patent application may be revoked by the imposition of a secrecy order.

[49 FR 13461, Apr. 4, 1984, as amended at 56 FR 1928, Jan. 18, 1991; 62 FR 53204, Oct. 10, 1997; 70 FR 56129, Sept. 26, 2005]

§ 5.12 Petition for license.

(a) Filing of an application for patent for inventions made in the United States will be considered to include a petition for license under 35 U.S.C. 184 for the subject matter of the application. The filing receipt will indicate if a license is granted. If the initial automatic petition is not granted, a subsequent petition may be filed under paragraph (b) of this section.

(b) A petition for license must include the fee set forth in § 1.17(g) of this chapter, the petitioner's address, and full instructions for delivery of the requested license when it is to be delivered to other than the petitioner. The petition should be presented in letter form.

(35 U.S.C. 6, Pub. L. 97–247)

[48 FR 2714, Jan. 20, 1983, as amended at 49 FR 13462, Apr. 4, 1984; 62 FR 53204, Oct. 10, 1997; 65 FR 54683, Sept. 8, 2000; 69 FR 56546, Sept. 21, 2004]

§ 5.13 Petition for license; no corresponding application.

If no corresponding national or international application has been filed in the United States, the petition for license under § 5.12(b) must also be accompanied by a legible copy of the material upon which a license is desired. This copy will be retained as a measure of the license granted.

[62 FR 53204, Oct. 10, 1997]

§ 5.14 Petition for license; corresponding U.S. application.

(a) When there is a corresponding United States application on file, a petition for license under § 5.12(b) must also identify this application by application number, filing date, inventor, and title, but a copy of the material upon which the license is desired is not required. The subject matter licensed will be measured by the disclosure of the United States application.

(b) Two or more United States applications should not be referred to in the same petition for license unless they are to be combined in the foreign or international application, in which event the petition should so state and the identification of each United States application should be in separate paragraphs.

(c) When the application to be filed or exported abroad contains matter not disclosed in the United States application or applications, including the case where the combining of two or more United States applications introduces subject matter not disclosed in any of them, a copy of the application as it is to be filed in the foreign country or international application which is to be transmitted to a foreign international or national agency for filing in the Receiving Office, must be furnished with the petition. If however, all new matter in the foreign or international application to be filed is readily identifiable, the new matter may be submitted in detail and the remainder by reference to the pertinent United States application or applications.

(Pub. L. 94–131, 89 Stat. 685)

[43 FR 20471, May 11, 1978, as amended at 49 FR 13462, Apr. 4, 1984; 62 FR 53204, Oct. 10, 1997]

§5.15 Scope of license.

(a) Applications or other materials reviewed pursuant to §§5.12 through 5.14, which were not required to be made available for inspection by defense agencies under 35 U.S.C. 181, will be eligible for a license of the scope provided in this paragraph. This license permits subsequent modifications, amendments, and supplements containing additional subject matter to, or divisions of, a foreign patent application, if such changes to the application do not alter the general nature of the invention in a manner which would require the United States application to have been made available for inspection under 35 U.S.C. 181. Grant of this license authorizing the export and filing of an application in a foreign country or the transmitting of an international application to any foreign patent agency or international patent agency when the subject matter of the foreign or international application corresponds to that of the domestic application. This license includes authority:

(1) To export and file all duplicate and formal application papers in foreign countries or with international agencies;

(2) To make amendments, modifications, and supplements, including divisions, changes or supporting matter consisting of the illustration, exemplification, comparison, or explanation of subject matter disclosed in the application; and

(3) To take any action in the prosecution of the foreign or international application provided that the adding of subject matter or taking of any action under paragraphs (a)(1) or (2) of this section does not change the general nature of the invention disclosed in the application in a manner which would require such application to have been made available for inspection under 35 U.S.C. 181 by including technical data pertaining to:

(i) Defense services or articles designated in the United States Munitions List applicable at the time of foreign filing, the unlicensed exportation of which is prohibited pursuant to the Arms Export Control Act, as amended, and 22 CFR parts 121 through 130; or

(ii) Restricted Data, sensitive nuclear technology or technology useful in the production or utilization of special nuclear material or atomic energy, dissemination of which is subject to restrictions of the Atomic Energy Act of 1954, as amended, and the Nuclear Non-Proliferation Act of 1978, as implemented by the regulations for Unclassified Activities in Foreign Atomic Energy Programs, 10 CFR part 810, in effect at the time of foreign filing.

(b) Applications or other materials which were required to be made available for inspection under 35 U.S.C. 181 will be eligible for a license of the scope provided in this paragraph. Grant of this license authorizes the export and filing of an application in a foreign country or the transmitting of an international application to any foreign patent agency or international patent agency. Further, this license includes authority to export and file all duplicate and formal papers in foreign countries or with foreign and international patent agencies and to make amendments, modifications, and supplements to, file divisions of, and take any action in the prosecution of the foreign or international application, provided subject matter additional to that covered by the license is not involved.

(c) A license granted under §5.12(b) pursuant to §5.13 or §5.14 shall have the scope indicated in paragraph (a) of this section, if it is so specified in the license. A petition, accompanied by the required fee (§1.17(g) of this chapter), may also be filed to change a license having the scope indicated in paragraph (b) of this section to a license having the scope indicated in paragraph (a) of this section. No such petition will be granted if the copy of the material filed pursuant to § 5.13 or any corresponding United States application was required to be made available for inspection under 35 U.S.C. 181. The change in the scope of a license will be effective as of the date of the grant of the petition.

(d) In those cases in which no license is required to file the foreign application or transmit the international application, no license is required to file papers in connection with the prosecution of the foreign or international application not involving the disclosure of additional subject matter.

(e) Any paper filed abroad or transmitted to an international patent agency following the filing of a foreign or international application which changes the general nature of the subject matter disclosed at the time of filing in a manner which would require such application to have been made available for inspection under 35 U.S.C. 181 or which involves the disclosure of subject matter listed in paragraphs (a)(3)(i) or (ii) of this section must be separately licensed in the same manner as a foreign or international application. Further, if no license has been granted under § 5.12(a) on filing the corresponding United States application, any paper filed abroad or with an international patent agency which involves the disclosure of additional subject matter must be licensed in the same manner as a foreign or international application.

(f) Licenses separately granted in connection with two or more United States applications may be exercised by combining or dividing the disclosures, as desired, provided:

(1) Subject matter which changes the general nature of the subject matter disclosed at the time of filing or which involves subject matter listed in paragraph (a)(3) (i) or (ii) of this section is not introduced, and

(2) In the case where at least one of the licenses was obtained under § 5.12(b), additional subject matter is not introduced.

(g) A license does not apply to acts done before the license was granted. See § 5.25 for petitions for retroactive licenses.

[49 FR 13462, Apr. 4, 1984, as amended at 56 FR 1928, Jan. 18, 1991; 62 FR 53204, Oct. 10, 1997; 69 FR 56546, Sept. 21, 2004]

§§ 5.16–5.17 [Reserved]

§ 5.18 Arms, ammunition, and implements of war.

(a) The exportation of technical data relating to arms, ammunition, and implements of war generally is subject to the International Traffic in Arms Regulations of the Department of State (22 CFR parts 120 through 130); the articles designated as arms, ammunitions, and implements of war are enumerated in the U.S. Munitions List (22 CFR part 121). However, if a patent applicant complies with regulations issued by the Commissioner for Patents under 35 U.S.C. 184, no separate approval from the Department of State is required unless the applicant seeks to export technical data exceeding that used to support a patent application in a foreign country. This exemption from Department of State regulations is applicable regardless of whether a license from the Commissioner for Patents is required by the provisions of §§ 5.11 and 5.12 (22 CFR part 125).

(b) When a patent application containing subject matter on the Munitions List (22 CFR part 121) is subject to a secrecy order under § 5.2 and a petition is made under § 5.5 for a modification of the secrecy order to permit filing abroad, a separate request to the Department of State for authority to export classified information is not required (22 CFR part 125).

[62 FR 53205, Oct. 10, 1997]

§ 5.19 Export of technical data.

(a) Under regulations (15 CFR 734.3(b)(1)(v)) established by the Department of Commerce, a license is not required in any case to file a patent application or part thereof in a foreign country if the foreign filing is in accordance with the regulations (§§ 5.11 through 5.25) of the U.S. Patent and Trademark Office.

(b) An export license is not required for data contained in a patent application prepared wholly from foreign-origin technical data where such application is being sent to the foreign inventor to be executed and returned to the United States for subsequent filing in the U.S. Patent and Trademark Office (15 CFR 734.10(a)).

[70 FR 56129, Sept. 26, 2005]

§ 5.20 Export of technical data relating to sensitive nuclear technology.

Under regulations (10 CFR 810.7) established by the United States Department of Energy, an application filed in accordance with the regulations (§§ 5.11 through 5.25) of the Patent and Trademark Office and eligible for foreign filing under 35 U.S.C. 184, is considered to be information available to the public in published form and a generally authorized activity for the purposes of the Department of Energy regulations.

[62 FR 53205, Oct. 10, 1997]

§ 5.25 Petition for retroactive license.

(a) A petition for a retroactive license under 35 U.S.C. 184 shall be presented in accordance with § 5.13 or § 5.14(a), and shall include:

(1) A listing of each of the foreign countries in which the unlicensed patent application material was filed,

(2) The dates on which the material was filed in each country,

(3) A verified statement (oath or declaration) containing:

(i) An averment that the subject matter in question was not under a secrecy order at the time it was filed aboard, and that it is not currently under a secrecy order,

(ii) A showing that the license has been diligently sought after discovery of the proscribed foreign filing, and

(iii) An explanation of why the material was filed abroad through error without the required license under § 5.11 first having been obtained, and

(4) The required fee (§ 1.17(g) of this chapter).

(b) The explanation in paragraph (a) of this section must include a showing of facts rather than a mere allegation of action through error. The showing of facts as to the nature of the error should include statements by those persons having personal knowledge of the acts regarding filing in a foreign country and should be accompanied by copies of any necessary supporting documents such as letters of transmittal or instructions for filing. The acts which are alleged to constitute error should cover the period leading up to and including each of the proscribed foreign filings.

(c) If a petition for a retroactive license is denied, a time period of not less than thirty days shall be set, during which the petition may be renewed. Failure to renew the petition within the set time period will result in a final denial of the petition. A final denial of a petition stands unless a petition is filed under § 1.181 within two months of the date of the denial. If the petition for a retroactive license is denied with respect to the invention of a pending application and no petition under § 1.181 has been filed, a final rejection of the application under 35 U.S.C. 185 will be made.

[49 FR 13463, Apr. 4, 1984, as amended at 56 FR 1929, Jan. 18, 1991; 62 FR 53206, Oct. 10, 1997; 69 FR 56546, Sept. 21, 2004; 77 FR 48826, Aug. 14, 2012]

GENERAL

§§ 5.31–5.33 [Reserved]

PART 6—CLASSIFICATION OF GOODS AND SERVICES UNDER THE TRADEMARK ACT

EDITORIAL NOTE: Part 6 is placed in the separate grouping of parts pertaining to trademarks regulations.

PART 7—RULES OF PRACTICE IN FILINGS PURSUANT TO THE PROTOCOL RELATING TO THE MADRID AGREEMENT CONCERNING THE INTERNATIONAL REGISTRATION OF MARKS

EDITORIAL NOTE: Part 7 is placed in the separate grouping of parts pertaining to trademarks regulations.

INDEX I—RULES RELATING TO PATENTS

EDITORIAL NOTE: This listing is provided for informational purposes only. It is compiled and kept current by the Department of Commerce. This index is updated as of July 1, 2013.

Section

A

B

C

D

F

G

H

I

J

L

M

N

O

P

R

S

T

U

V

W

PART 1—RULES OF PRACTICE IN PATENT CASES

EDITORIAL NOTE: Part 1 is placed in the separate grouping of parts pertaining to patents regulations.

TRADEMARKS

PART 2—RULES OF PRACTICE IN TRADEMARK CASES

AUTHORITY: 15 U.S.C. 1123; 35 U.S.C. 2, unless otherwise noted.

SOURCE: 30 FR 13193, Oct. 16, 1965, unless otherwise noted.

EDITORIAL NOTE: Nomenclature changes to part 2 appear at 68 FR 14337, Mar. 25, 2003.

§ 2.1 [Reserved]

§ 2.2 Definitions.

(a) *The Act* as used in this part means the Trademark Act of 1946, 60 Stat. 427, as amended, codified in 15 U.S.C. 1051 *et seq*.

(b) *Entity* as used in this part includes both natural and juristic persons.

(c) *Director* as used in this chapter, except for part 11, means the Under Secretary of Commerce for Intellectual Property and Director of the United States Patent and Trademark Office.

(d) *Federal holiday within the District of Columbia* means any day, except Saturdays and Sundays, when the United States Patent and Trademark Office is officially closed for business for the entire day.

(e) The term *Office* means the United States Patent and Trademark Office.

(f) The acronym *TEAS* means the Trademark Electronic Application System, available online at *http://www.uspto.gov*.

(g) The acronym *ESTTA* means the Electronic System for Trademark Trials and Appeals, available at *www.uspto.gov*.

(h) The term *international application* means an application for international registration that is filed under the Protocol Relating to the Madrid Agreement Concerning the International Registration of Marks.

[54 FR 37588, Sept. 11, 1989, as amended at 68 FR 48289, Aug. 13, 2003; 68 FR 55762, Sept. 26, 2003; 73 FR 47685, Aug. 14, 2008; 78 FR 20197, Apr. 3, 2013]

§ 2.6 Trademark fees.

The Patent and Trademark Office requires the following fees and charges:

(a) Trademark process fees.

(1) Application filing fees.

(i) For filing an application on paper, per class $375.00

(ii) For filing an application through TEAS, per class $325.00

(iii) For filing a TEAS Plus application under § 2.22, per class $275.00

(iv) Additional processing fee under §§ 2.22(b) and 2.23(b), per class $50.00

(2) For filing an amendment to allege use under section 1(c) of the Act, per class $100.00

(3) For filing a statement of use under section 1(d)(1) of the Act, per class $100.00

(4) For filing a request under section 1(d)(2) of the Act for a six-month extension of time for filing a statement of use under section 1(d)(1) of the Act, per class $150.00

(5) For filing an application for renewal of a registration, per class

....$400.00

(6) Additional fee for filing a renewal application during the grace period, per class $100.00

(7) For filing to publish a mark under section 12(c), per class $100.00

(8) For issuing a new certificate of registration upon request of registrant—..$100.00

(9) For a certificate of correction of registrant's error $100.00

(10) For filing a disclaimer to a registration $100.00

(11) For filing an amendment to a registration $100.00

(12) For filing an affidavit under section 8 of the Act, per class $100.00

(13) For filing an affidavit under section 15 of the Act, per class $200.00

(14) Additional fee for filing a section 8 affidavit during the grace period, per class $100.00

(15) For petitions to the Director $100.00

(16) For filing a petition to cancel, per class $300.00

(17) For filing a notice of opposition, per class $300.00

(18) For *ex parte* appeal to the Trademark Trial and Appeal Board, per class $100.00

(19) Dividing an application, per new application created $100.00

(20) For correcting a deficiency in a section 8 affidavit $100.00

(21) For correcting a deficiency in a renewal application $100.00

(b) Trademark service fees.

(1) For printed copy of registered mark, copy only. Service includes preparation of copies by the Office within two to three business days and delivery by United States Postal Service; and preparation of copies by the Office within one business day of receipt and delivery to an Office Box or by electronic means (e.g., facsimile, electronic mail)— $3.00

(2) Certified or uncertified copy of trademark application as filed processed within seven calendar days— $15.00

(3) Certified or uncertified copy of a trademark-related official record— $50.00

(4) Certified copy of a registered mark, showing title and/or status:

(i) Regular service $15.00

(ii) Expedited local service $30.00

(5) Certified or uncertified copy of trademark records, per document except as otherwise provided in this section $25.00

(6) For recording each trademark assignment, agreement or other document relating to the property in a registration or application

(i) First property in a document $40.00

(ii) For each additional property in the same document $25.00

(7) For assignment records, abstract of title and certification, per registration $25.00

(8) Marginal cost, paid in advance, for each hour of terminal session time, including print time, using X-Search capabilities, prorated for the actual time used. The Director may waive the payment by an individual for access to X-Search upon a showing of need or hardship, and if such waiver is in the public interest $40.00

(9) Self-service copy charge, per page $0.25

(10) Labor charges for services, per hour or fraction thereof $40.00

(11) For items and services that the Director finds may be supplied, for which fees are not specified by statute or by this part, such charges as may be determined by the Director with respect to each such item or service ....Actual Cost

(12) For processing each payment refused (including a check returned "unpaid") or charged back by a financial institution $50.00

(13) Deposit accounts:

(i) For establishing a deposit account $10.00

(ii) Service charge for each month when the balance at the end of the month is below $1,000 ....$25.00

[56 FR 65155, Dec. 13, 1991; 56 FR 66670, Dec. 24, 1991, as amended at 57 FR 38196, Aug. 21, 1992; 59 FR 257, Jan. 4, 1994; 60 FR 41023, Aug. 11, 1995; 62 FR 40453, July 29, 1997; 64 FR 48918, Sept. 8, 1999; 64 FR 67486, Dec. 2, 1999; 64 FR 67777, Dec. 3, 1999; 67 FR 79522, Dec. 30, 2002; 67 FR 70850, Nov. 27, 2002; 68 FR 48289, Aug. 13, 2003; 70 FR 2953, Jan. 19, 2005; 70 FR 38773, July 6, 2005; 73 FR 67767, Nov. 17, 2008]

§ 2.7 Fastener recordal fees.

(a) Application fee for recordal of insignia $20.00

(b) Renewal of insignia recordal............$20.00

(c) Surcharge for late renewal of insignia recordal $20.00

[61 FR 55223, Oct. 25, 1996]

REPRESENTATION BY ATTORNEYS OR OTHER AUTHORIZED PERSONS

AUTHORITY: Secs. 2.11 to 2.19 also issued under 35 U.S.C. 31, 32.

§2.11 Applicants may be represented by an attorney.

Representation before the Office is governed by §11.14 of this chapter. The Office cannot aid in the selection of an attorney.

[73 FR 47685, Aug. 14, 2008]

§§2.12–2.16 [Reserved]

§2.17 Recognition for representation.

(a) *Authority to practice in trademark cases.* Only an individual qualified to practice under §11.14 of this chapter may represent an applicant, registrant, or party to a proceeding before the Office in a trademark case.

(b)(1) *Recognition of practitioner as representative.* To be recognized as a representative in a trademark case, a practitioner qualified under §11.14 of this chapter may:

(i) File a power of attorney that meets the requirements of paragraph (c) of this section;

(ii) Sign a document on behalf of an applicant, registrant, or party to a proceeding who is not already represented by a practitioner qualified under §11.14 of this chapter from a different firm; or

(iii) Appear in person on behalf of an applicant, registrant, or party to a proceeding who is not already represented by a practitioner qualified under §11.14 of this chapter from a different firm.

(2) *Signature as certificate of authorization to represent.* When a practitioner qualified under §11.14 of this chapter appears in person or signs a document pursuant to paragraph (b) of this section, his or her personal appearance or signature shall constitute a representation to the Office that he or she is authorized to represent the person or entity on whose behalf he or she acts. The Office may require further proof of authority to act in a representative capacity.

(c) *Requirements for power of attorney.* A power of attorney must:

(1) Designate by name at least one practitioner meeting the requirements of §11.14 of this chapter; and

(2) Be signed by the individual applicant, registrant, or party to a proceeding pending before the Office, or by someone with legal authority to bind the applicant, registrant, or party (e.g., a corporate officer or general partner of a partnership). In the case of joint applicants or joint registrants, all must sign. Once the applicant, registrant, or party has designated a practitioner(s) qualified to practice under §11.14 of this chapter, that practitioner may sign an associate power of attorney appointing another qualified practitioner(s) as an additional person(s) authorized to represent the applicant, registrant, or party. If the applicant, registrant, or party revokes the original power of attorney (§2.19(a)), the revocation discharges any associate power signed by the practitioner whose power has been revoked. If the practitioner who signed an associate power withdraws (§2.19(b)), the withdrawal discharges any associate power signed by the withdrawing practitioner upon acceptance of the request for withdrawal by the Office.

(d) *Power of attorney relating to multiple applications or registrations.* (1) The owner of an application or registration may appoint a practitioner(s) qualified to practice under §11.14 of this chapter for up to twenty applications or registrations that have the identical owner name and attorney through TEAS.

(2) The owner of an application or registration may file a power of attorney that relates to more than one trademark application or registration, or to all existing and future applications and registrations of that owner, on paper. A person relying on such a power of attorney must:

(i) Include a copy of the previously filed power of attorney; or

(ii) Refer to the power of attorney, specifying the filing date of the previously filed power of attorney; the application serial number (if known), registration number, or *inter partes* proceeding number for which the original power of attorney was filed; and the name of the person who signed the power of attorney; or, if the application serial number is not known, submit a copy of the application or a copy of the mark, and specify the filing date.

(e) *Canadian attorneys and agents.* (1) A Canadian patent agent who is registered and in good standing as a patent agent under §11.6(c) may represent parties located in Canada before the Office in trademark matters.

(2) A Canadian attorney or agent who is registered or in good standing with the Canadian Intellectual Property Office, but not registered as a patent agent under § 11.6(c), may represent parties located in Canada if he or she has been authorized to do so by the Director of the Office of Enrollment and Discipline, pursuant to § 11.14(f) of this chapter.

(f) *Non-lawyers.* A non-lawyer may not act as a representative except in the limited circumstances set forth in § 11.14(b) of this chapter. Before any non-lawyer who meets the requirements of § 11.14(b) of this chapter may take action of any kind with respect to an application, registration or proceeding, a written authorization must be filed, signed by the applicant, registrant, or party to the proceeding, or by someone with legal authority to bind the applicant, registrant, or party (e.g., a corporate officer or general partner of a partnership).

(g) *Duration of power of attorney.* (1) For purposes of recognition as a representative, the Office considers a power of attorney filed while an application is pending to end when the mark registers, when ownership changes, or when the application is abandoned.

(2) The Office considers a power of attorney filed after registration to end when the mark is cancelled or expired, or when ownership changes. If the power was filed in connection with an affidavit under section 8, 12(c), 15 or 71 of the Trademark Act, renewal application under section 9 of the Act, or request for amendment or correction under section 7 of the Act, the power is deemed to end upon acceptance or final rejection of the filing.

[74 FR 54906, Oct. 26, 2009]

§ 2.18 Correspondence, with whom held.

(a) *Establishing the correspondence address.* (1) If a written power of attorney that meets the requirements of § 2.17 is filed, the Office will send correspondence to the practitioner designated in the power.

(2) If a practitioner qualified under § 11.14 of this chapter transmits a document(s) on behalf of an applicant, registrant, or party to a proceeding who is not already represented by another qualified practitioner from a different firm, the Office will send correspondence to the practitioner transmitting the documents.

(3) If an application, registration or proceeding is not being prosecuted by a practitioner qualified under § 11.14 of this chapter and the applicant, registrant, or party to the proceeding designates a correspondence address in writing, the Office will send correspondence to the designated address if appropriate.

(4) If an application, registration or proceeding is not being prosecuted by a practitioner qualified under § 11.14 of this chapter and the applicant, registrant, or party to the proceeding has not designated a correspondence address in writing, but a domestic representative has been appointed, the Office will send correspondence to the domestic representative if appropriate.

(5) If the application, registration or proceeding is not being prosecuted by a practitioner qualified under § 11.14 of this chapter, the applicant, registrant, or party to the proceeding has not designated a correspondence address, and no domestic representative has been appointed, the Office will send correspondence directly to the applicant, registrant, or party to the proceeding.

(6) The Office will send correspondence to only one address in an *ex parte* matter.

(7) Once the Office has recognized a practitioner qualified under § 11.14 of this chapter as the representative of an applicant or registrant, the Office will communicate and conduct business only with that practitioner, or with another qualified practitioner from the same firm. The Office will not conduct business directly with the applicant or registrant, or with another practitioner from a different firm, unless the applicant or registrant files a revocation of the power of attorney under § 2.19(a), and/or a new power of attorney that meets the requirements of § 2.17(c). A written request to change the correspondence address does not revoke a power of attorney.

(b) *Changing the correspondence address.* (1) If a physical or e-mail correspondence address changes, the applicant, registrant, or party to a proceeding must file a written request to change the correspondence address. The request should be promptly filed.

(2) A request to change the correspondence address must be made in writing, signed by the applicant, registrant, or party to a proceeding, someone with legal authority to bind the applicant, registrant, or party (e.g., a corporate officer or general partner of a partnership), or a practitioner qualified to practice under §11.14 of this chapter, in accordance with §2.193(e)(9).

(3) If an applicant or registrant files a new power of attorney that meets the requirements of §2.17(c), the Office will change the correspondence address to that of the practitioner named in the power.

(4) If a practitioner qualified under §11.14 of this chapter transmits a document(s) on behalf of an applicant, registrant, or party to a proceeding who is not already represented by another qualified practitioner, the Office will construe this as including a request to change the correspondence address to that of the practitioner, and will send correspondence to the practitioner.

(c) *Post registration filings under sections 7, 8, 9, 12(c), 15, and 71.* (1) Even if there is no new power of attorney or written request to change the correspondence address, the Office will change the correspondence address upon the examination of an affidavit under section 8, 12(c), 15 or 71 of the Trademark Act, renewal application under section 9 of the Act, or request for amendment or correction under section 7 of the Act. If a practitioner qualified under §11.14 of this chapter transmits the affidavit, renewal application, or section 7 request, the Office will send correspondence to the practitioner. If the owner of the registration is not represented by a qualified practitioner, the Office will send correspondence directly to the owner, or to the domestic representative if appropriate, in accordance with paragraph (a).

(2) Once the Office establishes a correspondence address upon examination of an affidavit, renewal application, or section 7 request, a written request to change the address in accordance with the requirements of paragraph (b)(2) of this section is required to change the address during the pendency of that filing.

[74 FR 54906, Oct. 26, 2009]

§2.19 Revocation or withdrawal of attorney.

(a) *Revocation.* (1) Authority to represent an applicant, registrant or party to a proceeding before the Office may be revoked at any stage in the proceedings of a trademark case, upon written notification signed by the applicant, registrant, or party to the proceeding, or by someone with legal authority to bind the applicant, registrant, or party (e.g., a corporate officer or general partner of a partnership). In the case of joint applicants or joint registrants, all must sign.

(2) When a power of attorney is revoked, the Office will communicate directly with the applicant, registrant, or party to the proceeding, or with the new attorney or domestic representative if appropriate.

(3) A request to change the correspondence address does not revoke a power of attorney.

(4) A new power of attorney that meets the requirements of §2.17(c) will be treated as a revocation of the previous power.

(b) *Withdrawal of attorney.* If the requirements of §10.40 of this chapter are met, a practitioner authorized to represent an applicant, registrant, or party to a proceeding in a trademark case may withdraw upon application to and approval by the Director or, when applicable, upon motion granted by the Trademark Trial and Appeal Board. The practitioner should file the request to withdraw soon after the practitioner notifies the client of his/her intent to withdraw. The request must include the following:

(1) The application serial number, registration number, or proceeding number;

(2) A statement of the reason(s) for the request to withdraw; and

(3) Either

(i) A statement that the practitioner has given notice to the client that the practitioner is withdrawing from employment and will be filing the necessary documents with the Office; that the client was given notice of the withdrawal at least two months before the expiration of the response period, if applicable; that the practitioner has delivered to the client all documents and property in the practitioner's file concerning the application, registration or proceeding to which the client is entitled; and that the practitioner has notified the client of any responses that may be due, and of the deadline for response; or

(ii) If more than one qualified practitioner is of record, a statement that representation by co-counsel is ongoing.

[74 FR 54907, Oct. 26, 2009]

DECLARATIONS

§ 2.20 Declarations in lieu of oaths.

Instead of an oath, affidavit, verification, or sworn statement, the language of 28 U.S.C. 1746, or the following language, may be used:

The undersigned being warned that willful false statements and the like are punishable by fine or imprisonment, or both, under 18 U.S.C. 1001, and that such willful false statements and the like may jeopardize the validity of the application or document or any registration resulting therefrom, declares that all statements made of his/her own knowledge are true; and all statements made on information and belief are believed to be true.

[64 FR 48918, Sept. 8, 1999]

APPLICATION FOR REGISTRATION

AUTHORITY: Secs. 2.21 to 2.47 also issued under sec. 1, 60 Stat. 427; 15 U.S.C. 1051.

§ 2.21 Requirements for receiving a filing date.

(a) The Office will grant a filing date to an application under section 1 or section 44 of the Act that is in the English language and contains all of the following:

(1) The name of the applicant;

(2) A name and address for correspondence;

(3) A clear drawing of the mark;

(4) A listing of the goods or services; and

(5) The filing fee for at least one class of goods or services, required by § 2.6.

(b) If the applicant does not submit all the elements required in paragraph (a) of this section, the Office will deny a filing date and issue a notice explaining why the filing date was denied.

[64 FR 48918, Sept. 8, 1999, as amended at 68 FR 55762, Sept. 26, 2003; 73 FR 67767, Nov. 17, 2008]

§ 2.22 Filing requirements for a TEAS Plus application.

(a) A trademark/service mark application for registration on the Principal Register under section 1 and/or section 44 of the Act will be entitled to a reduced filing fee under § 2.6(a)(1)(iii) if it is filed through TEAS and includes:

(1) The applicant's name and address;

(2) The applicant's legal entity;

(3) The citizenship of an individual applicant, or the state or country of incorporation or organization of a juristic applicant;

(4) If the applicant is a partnership, the names and citizenship of the applicant's general partners;

(5) A name and address for correspondence;

(6) An e-mail address for correspondence, and an authorization for the Office to send correspondence concerning the application to the applicant or applicant's attorney by e-mail;

(7) One or more bases for filing that satisfy all the requirements of § 2.34. If more than one basis is set forth, the applicant must comply with the requirements of § 2.34 for each asserted basis;

(8) Correctly classified goods and/or services, with an identification of goods and/or services from the Office's Acceptable Identification of Goods and Services Manual, available through the TEAS Plus form and at *http://www.uspto.gov*. In an application based on section 44 of the Act, the scope of the goods and/or services covered by the section 44 basis may not exceed the scope of the goods and/or services in the foreign application or registration;

(9) If the application contains goods and/or services in more than one class, compliance with § 2.86;

(10) A filing fee for each class of goods and/or services, as required by § 2.6(a)(1)(iii);

(11) A verified statement that meets the requirements of § 2.33, dated and signed by a person properly authorized to sign on behalf of the owner pursuant to § 2.193(e)(1);

(12) A clear drawing of the mark. If the applicant does not claim standard characters, the applicant must attach a digitized image of the mark in .jpg format. If the mark includes color, the drawing must show the mark in color;

(13) If the mark is in standard characters, a mark comprised of only characters in the Office's standard character set, currently available at *http://www.uspto.gov*, typed in the appropriate field of the TEAS Plus form;

(14) If the mark includes color, a statement naming the color(s) and describing where the color(s) appears on the mark, and a claim that the color(s) is a feature of the mark;

(15) If the mark is not in standard characters, a description of the mark;

(16) If the mark includes non-English wording, an English translation of that wording;

(17) If the mark includes non-Latin characters, a transliteration of those characters;

(18) If the mark includes an individual's name or portrait, either (i) a statement that identifies the living individual whose name or likeness the mark comprises and written consent of the individual, or (ii) a statement that the name or portrait does not identify a living individual (*see* section 2(c) of the Act);

(19) If the applicant owns one or more registrations for the same mark, a claim of ownership of the registration(s) identified by the registration number(s), pursuant to § 2.36; and

(20) If the application is a concurrent use application, compliance with § 2.42.

(b) If an application does not meet the requirements of paragraph (a) of this section at the time of filing, the applicant must pay the fee required by § 2.6(a)(1)(iv). The application will retain its original filing date, provided that when filed, the application met the filing date requirements of § 2.21.

(c) The following types of applications cannot be filed as TEAS Plus applications under paragraph (a) of this section:

(1) Applications for certification marks (*see* § 2.45);

(2) Applications for collective marks (*see* § 2.44);

(3) Applications for collective membership marks (*see* § 2.44); and

(4) Applications for registration on the Supplemental Register (*see* § 2.47).

[70 FR 38773, July 6, 2005, as amended at 74 FR 54907, Oct. 26, 2009]

§ 2.23 Additional requirements for TEAS Plus application.

(a) In addition to the filing requirements under § 2.22(a), the applicant must:

(1) File the following communications through TEAS:

(i) Responses to Office actions (except notices of appeal under section 20 of the Trademark Act);

(ii) Requests to change the correspondence address and owner's address;

(iii) Appointment and/or revocation of power of attorney;

(iv) Appointment and/or revocation of domestic representative;

(v) Preliminary amendments;

(vi) Amendments to allege use under section 1(c) of the Act or statements of use under section 1(d) of the Act;

(vii) Request(s) for extensions of time to file a statement of use under section 1(d) of the Act; and

(viii) Request(s) to delete a section 1(b) basis.

(2) Maintain a valid e-mail correspondence address, and continue to receive communications from the Office by electronic mail.

(b) If an application does not meet the requirements of paragraph (a) of this section, the applicant must pay the fee required by § 2.6(a)(1)(iv).

[70 FR 38773, July 6, 2005, as amended at 73 FR 67768, Nov. 17, 2008]

§ 2.24 Designation and revocation of domestic representative by foreign applicant.

(a)(1) If an applicant is not domiciled in the United States, the applicant may designate a domestic representative (*i.e.*, a person residing in the United States on whom notices or process in proceedings affecting the mark may be served) by either:

(i) Setting forth the name and address of the domestic representative in the initial application; or

(ii) Filing a separate designation setting forth the name and address of the domestic representative, signed by the applicant, someone with legal authority to bind the applicant (e.g., a corporate officer or general partner of a partnership), or a practitioner qualified to practice under § 11.14 of this chapter.

(2) If the applicant does not file a document designating the name and address of a person residing in the United States on whom notices or process in proceedings affecting the mark may be served, or if the last person designated cannot be found at the address given in the designation, then notices or process in proceedings affecting the mark may be served on the Director.

(3) The mere designation of a domestic representative does not authorize the person designated to represent the applicant unless qualified under § 11.14 of this chapter.

(b) A request to change or revoke a designation of domestic representative must be signed by the applicant, someone with legal authority to bind the applicant (e.g., a corporate officer or general partner of a partnership), or a practitioner qualified to practice under § 11.14 of this chapter.

[74 FR 54907, Oct. 26, 2009]

§ 2.25 Documents not returnable.

Except as provided in § 2.27(e), documents filed in the Office by the applicant or registrant become part of the official record and will not be returned or removed.

[73 FR 67768, Nov. 17, 2008]

§ 2.27 Pending trademark application index; access to applications.

(a) An index of pending applications including the name and address of the applicant, a reproduction or description of the mark, the goods or services with which the mark is used, the class number, the dates of use, and the serial number and filing date of the application will be available for public inspection as soon as practicable after filing.

(b) Except as provided in paragraph (e) of this section, access to the file of a particular pending application will be permitted prior to publication under § 2.80 upon written request.

(c) Decisions of the Director and the Trademark Trial and Appeal Board in applications and proceedings relating thereto are published or available for inspection or publication.

(d) Except as provided in paragraph (e) of this section, the official records of applications and all proceedings relating thereto are available for public inspection and copies of the documents may be furnished upon payment of the fee required by § 2.6.

(e) Anything ordered to be filed under seal pursuant to a protective order issued or made by any court or by the Trademark Trial and Appeal Board in any proceeding involving an application or a registration shall be kept confidential and shall not be made available for public inspection or copying unless otherwise ordered by the court or the Board, or unless the party protected by the order voluntarily discloses the matter subject thereto. When possible, only confidential portions of filings with the Board shall be filed under seal.

[36 FR 25406, Dec. 31, 1971, as amended at 48 FR 23134, May 23, 1983; 48 FR 27225, June 14, 1983; 73 FR 67768, Nov. 17, 2008]

The Written Application

§ 2.31 [Reserved]

§ 2.32 Requirements for a complete application.

(a) The application must be in English and include the following:

(1) A request for registration;

(2) The name of the applicant(s);

(3)(i) The citizenship of the applicant(s); or

(ii) If the applicant is a corporation, association, partnership or other juristic person, the jurisdiction (usually state or nation) under the laws of which the applicant is organized; and

(iii) If the applicant is a domestic partnership, the names and citizenship of the general partners;

(iv) If the applicant is a domestic joint venture, the names and citizenship of the active members of the joint venture;

(4) The address of the applicant;

(5) One or more bases, as required by § 2.34(a);

(6) A list of the particular goods or services on or in connection with which the applicant uses or intends to use the mark. In a United States application filed under section 44 of the Act, the scope of the goods and/or services covered by the section 44 basis may not exceed the scope of the goods and/or services in the foreign application or registration;

(7) The international class of goods or services, if known. See § 6.1 of this chapter for a list of the international classes of goods and services.

(8) If the mark is not in standard characters, a description of the mark;

(9) If the mark includes non-English wording, an English translation of that wording; and

(10) If the mark includes non-Latin characters, a transliteration of those characters, and either a translation of the transliterated term in English, or a statement that the transliterated term has no meaning in English.

(b) The application must include a verified statement that meets the requirements of § 2.33.

(c) The application must include a drawing that meets the requirements of §§ 2.51 and 2.52.

(d) The application must include fee required by § 2.6 for each class of goods or services.

(e) For the requirements for a multiple class application, see § 2.86.

[64 FR 48918, Sept. 8, 1999, as amended at 73 FR 13784, Mar. 14, 2008; 73 FR 67768, Nov. 17, 2008]

§ 2.33 Verified statement.

(a) The application must include a statement that is signed in accordance with the requirements of § 2.193 and verified (sworn to) or supported by a declaration under § 2.20 by a person properly authorized to sign on behalf of the applicant under § 2.193(e)(1).

(b)(1) In an application under section 1(a) of the Act, the verified statement must allege:

That the applicant believes it is the owner of the mark; that the mark is in use in commerce; that to the best of the declarant's knowledge and belief, no other person has the right to use the mark in commerce, either in the identical form or in such near resemblance as to be likely, when applied to the goods or services of the other person, to cause confusion or mistake, or to deceive; that the specimen shows the mark as used on or in connection with the goods or services; and that the facts set forth in the application are true.

(2) In an application under section 1(b) or section 44 of the Act, the verified statement must allege:

That the applicant has a bona fide intention to use the mark shown in the accompanying drawing in commerce on or in connection with the specified goods or services; that the applicant believes it is entitled to use the mark in commerce; that to the best of the declarant's knowledge and belief, no other person has the right to use the mark in commerce, either in the identical form or in such near resemblance as to be likely, when applied to the goods or services of the other person, to cause confusion or mistake, or to deceive; and that the facts set forth in the application are true.

(c) If the verified statement is not filed within a reasonable time after it is signed, the Office may require the applicant to submit a substitute verification or declaration under § 2.20 of the applicant's continued use or bona fide intention to use the mark in commerce.

(d) [Reserved]

(e) In an application under section 66(a) of the Act, the verified statement is part of the international registration on file at the International Bureau. The verified statement must allege that:

(1) The applicant/holder has a bona fide intention to use the mark in commerce that the United States Congress can regulate on or in connection with the goods/services identified in the international application/subsequent designation;

(2) The signatory is properly authorized to execute this declaration on behalf of the applicant/holder;

(3) The signatory believes the applicant/holder to be entitled to use the mark in commerce that the United States Congress can regulate on or in connection with the goods/services identified in the international application/registration; and

(4) To the best of his/her knowledge and belief, no other person, firm, corporation, association, or other legal entity has the right to use the mark in

commerce that the United States Congress can regulate, either in the identical form thereof or in such near resemblance thereto as to be likely, when used on or in connection with the goods/services of such other person, firm, corporation, association, or other legal entity, to cause confusion, or to cause mistake, or to deceive.

[64 FR 48918, Sept. 8, 1999, as amended at 67 FR 79522, Dec. 30, 2002; 68 FR 55762, Sept. 26, 2003; 73 FR 47685, Aug. 14, 2008; 73 FR 67768, Nov. 17, 2008; 74 FR 54908, Oct. 26, 2009]

§ 2.34 Bases for filing.

(a) The application must include one or more of the following five filing bases:

(1) *Use in commerce under section 1(a) of the Act.* The requirements for an application based on section 1(a) of the Act are:

(i) The trademark owner's verified statement that the mark is in use in commerce on or in connection with the goods or services listed in the application. If the verification is not filed with the initial application, the verified statement must also allege that the mark was in use in commerce on or in connection with the goods or services listed in the application as of the application filing date;

(ii) The date of the applicant's first use of the mark anywhere on or in connection with the goods or services;

(iii) The date of the applicant's first use of the mark in commerce as a trademark or service mark; and

(iv) One specimen per class showing how the applicant actually uses the mark in commerce. When requested by the Office, additional specimens must be provided.

(v) If more than one item of goods or services is specified in the application, the dates of use required in paragraphs (ii) and (iii) of this section need be for only one of the items specified in each class, provided that the particular item to which the dates apply is designated.

(2) *Intent-to-use under section 1(b) of the Act.* In an application under section 1(b) of the Act, the applicant must verify that it has a bona fide intention to use the mark in commerce on or in connection with the goods or services listed in the application. If the verification is not filed with the initial application, the verified statement must also allege that the applicant had a bona fide intention to use the mark in commerce on or in connection with the goods or services listed in the application as of the filing date of the application.

(3) *Registration of a mark in a foreign applicant's country of origin under section 44(e) of the Act.* The requirements for an application under section 44(e) of the Act are:

(i) The applicant's verified statement that it has a bona fide intention to use the mark in commerce on or in connection with the goods or services listed in the application. If the verification is not filed with the initial application, the verified statement must also allege that the applicant had a bona fide intention to use the mark in commerce on or in connection with the goods or services listed in the application as of the filing date of the application.

(ii) A true copy, a photocopy, a certification, or a certified copy of a registration in the applicant's country of origin showing that the mark has been registered in that country, and that the registration is in full force and effect. The certification or copy of the foreign registration must show the name of the owner, the mark, and the goods or services for which the mark is registered. If the foreign registration is not in the English language, the applicant must submit a translation.

(iii) If the record indicates that the foreign registration will expire before the United States registration will issue, the applicant must submit a true copy, a photocopy, a certification, or a certified copy from the country of origin to establish that the foreign registration has been renewed and will be in force at the time the United States registration will issue. If the foreign registration is not in the English language, the applicant must submit a translation.

(4) *Claim of priority, based upon an earlier-filed foreign application, under section 44(d) of the Act.* The requirements for an application under section 44(d) of the Act are:

(i) A claim of priority, filed within six months of the filing date of the foreign application. Before publication or registration on the Supplemental Register, the applicant must either:

(A) Specify the filing date, serial number and country of the first regularly filed foreign application; or

(B) State that the application is based upon a subsequent regularly filed application in the same foreign country, and that any prior-filed application has been withdrawn, abandoned or otherwise disposed of, without having been laid open to public inspection and without having any rights outstanding, and has not served as a basis for claiming a right of priority.

(ii) Include the applicant's verified statement that it has a bona fide intention to use the mark in commerce on or in connection with the goods or services listed in the application. If the verification is not filed with the initial application, the verified statement must also allege that the applicant had a bona fide intention to use the mark in commerce on or in connection with the goods or services listed in the application as of the filing date of the application.

(iii) Before the application can be approved for publication, or for registration on the Supplemental Register, the applicant must establish a basis under section 1(a), section 1(b) or section 44(e) of the Act.

(5) *Extension of protection of an international registration under section 66(a) of the Act.* In an application under section 66(a) of the Act, the international application or subsequent designation requesting an extension of protection to the United States must contain a signed declaration that meets the requirements of § 2.33.

(b)(1) In an application under section 1 or section 44 of the Act, an applicant may claim more than one basis, provided the applicant satisfies all requirements for the bases claimed. However, the applicant may not claim both sections 1(a) and 1(b) for the identical goods or services in the same application.

(2) In an application under section 1 or section 44 of the Act, if an applicant claims more than one basis, the applicant must list each basis, followed by the goods or services to which that basis applies. If some or all of the goods or services are covered by more than one basis, this must be stated.

(3) A basis under section 66(a) of the Act cannot be combined with any other basis.

(c) The word "commerce" means commerce that Congress may lawfully regulate, as specified in section 45 of the Act.

[64 FR 48919, Sept. 8, 1999, as amended at 67 FR 79522, Dec. 30, 2002; 68 FR 55763, Sept. 26, 2003; 73 FR 67768, Nov. 17, 2008; 77 FR 30207, May 22, 2012]

§ 2.35 Adding, deleting, or substituting bases.

(a) In an application under section 66(a) of the Act, an applicant may not add, substitute or delete a basis, unless the applicant meets the requirements for transformation under section 70(c) of the Act and § 7.31 of this chapter.

(b) In an application under section 1 or section 44 of the Act:

(1) Before publication for opposition, an applicant may add or substitute a basis, if the applicant meets all requirements for the new basis, as stated in § 2.34. The applicant may delete a basis at any time.

(2) After publication, an applicant may add or substitute a basis in an application that is not the subject of an *inter partes* proceeding before the Trademark Trial and Appeal Board, but only with the express permission of the Director, after consideration on petition. Republication will be required. The amendment of an application that is the subject of an *inter partes* proceeding before the Board is governed by § 2.133(a).

(3) When an applicant substitutes one basis for another, the Office will presume that there was a continuing valid basis, unless there is contradictory evidence in the record, and the application will retain the original filing date, including a priority filing date under section 44(d), if appropriate.

(4) If an applicant properly claims a section 44(d) basis in addition to another basis, the applicant will retain the priority filing date under section 44(d) no matter which basis the applicant perfects.

(5) The applicant may add or substitute a section 44(d) basis only within the six-month priority period following

the filing date of the foreign application.

(6) When the applicant adds or substitutes a basis, the applicant must list each basis, followed by the goods or services to which that basis applies.

(7) When the applicant deletes a basis, the applicant must also delete any goods or services covered solely by the deleted basis.

(8) Once an applicant claims a section 1(b) basis as to any or all of the goods or services, the applicant may not amend the application to seek registration under section 1(a) of the Act for those goods or services unless the applicant files an allegation of use under section 1(c) or section 1(d) of the Act.

[68 FR 55763, Sept. 26, 2003]

§ 2.36 Identification of prior registrations.

Prior registrations of the same or similar marks owned by the applicant should be identified in the application.

§ 2.37 Description of mark.

A description of the mark must be included if the mark is not in standard characters. In an application where the mark is in standard characters, a description may be included and must be included if required by the trademark examining attorney.

[73 FR 13784, Mar. 14, 2008]

§ 2.38 Use by predecessor or by related companies.

(a) If the first use of the mark was by a predecessor in title or by a related company (sections 5 and 45 of the Act), and the use inures to the benefit of the applicant, the dates of first use (§§ 2.34(a)(1) (ii) and (iii)) may be asserted with a statement that first use was by the predecessor in title or by the related company, as appropriate.

(b) If the mark is not in fact being used by the applicant but is being used by one or more related companies whose use inures to the benefit of the applicant under section 5 of the Act, such facts must be indicated in the application.

(c) The Office may require such details concerning the nature of the relationship and such proofs as may be necessary and appropriate for the purpose of showing that the use by related companies inures to the benefit of the applicant and does not affect the validity of the mark.

(Sec. 5, 60 Stat. 429; 15 U.S.C. 1055)

[30 FR 13193, Oct. 16, 1965, as amended at 54 FR 37589, Sept. 11, 1989; 64 FR 48920, Sept. 8, 1999]

§ 2.39 [Reserved]

§ 2.41 Proof of distinctiveness under section 2(f).

(a) When registration is sought of a mark which would be unregistrable by reason of section 2(e) of the Act but which is said by applicant to have become distinctive in commerce of the goods or services set forth in the application, applicant may, in support of registrability, submit with the application, or in response to a request for evidence or to a refusal to register, affidavits, or declarations in accordance with § 2.20, depositions, or other appropriate evidence showing duration, extent and nature of use in commerce and advertising expenditures in connection therewith (identifying types of media and attaching typical advertisements), and affidavits, or declarations in accordance with § 2.20, letters or statements from the trade or public, or both, or other appropriate evidence tending to show that the mark distinguishes such goods or services.

(b) In appropriate cases, ownership of one or more prior registrations on the Principal Register or under the Act of 1905 of the same mark may be accepted as prima facie evidence of distinctiveness. Also, if the mark is said to have become distinctive of applicant's goods by reason of substantially exclusive and continuous use in commerce thereof by applicant for the five years before the date on which the claim of distinctiveness is made, a showing by way of statements which are verified or which include declarations in accordance with § 2.20, in the application may, in appropriate cases, be accepted as prima facie evidence of distinctiveness. In each of these situations, however, further evidence may be required.

[54 FR 37590, Sept. 11, 1989, as amended at 73 FR 67768, Nov. 17, 2008]

§ 2.42 Concurrent use.

An application for registration as a lawful concurrent user shall specify and contain all the elements required by the preceding sections. The applicant in addition shall state in the application the area, the goods, and the mode of use for which applicant seeks registration; and also shall state, to the extent of the applicant's knowledge, the concurrent lawful use of the mark by others, setting forth their names and addresses; registrations issued to or applications filed by such others, if any; the areas of such use; the goods on or in connection with which such use is made; the mode of such use; and the periods of such use.

[54 FR 34897, Aug. 22, 1989]

§ 2.43 Service mark.

In an application to register a service mark, the application shall specify and contain all the elements required by the preceding sections for trademarks, but shall be modified to relate to services instead of to goods wherever necessary.

(Sec. 3, 60 Stat. 429; 15 U.S.C. 1052)

§ 2.44 Collective mark.

(a) In an application to register a collective mark under section 1(a) of the Act, the application shall specify and contain all applicable elements required by the preceding sections for trademarks, but shall, in addition, specify the class of persons entitled to use the mark, indicating their relationship to the applicant, and the nature of the applicant's control over the use of the mark.

(b) In an application to register a collective mark under section 1(b), section 44 or section 66(a) of the Act, the application shall specify and contain all applicable elements required by the preceding sections for trademarks, but shall also specify the class of persons intended to be entitled to use the mark, indicating what their relationship to the applicant will be, and the nature of the control applicant intends to exercise over the use of the mark.

[54 FR 37590, Sept. 11, 1989, as amended at 73 FR 67769, Nov. 17, 2008]

§ 2.45 Certification mark.

(a) In an application to register a certification mark under section 1(a) of the Act, the application shall include all applicable elements required by the preceding sections for trademarks. In addition, the application must: Specify the conditions under which the certification mark is used; allege that the applicant exercises legitimate control over the use of the mark; allege that the applicant is not engaged in the production or marketing of the goods or services to which the mark is applied; and include a copy of the standards that determine whether others may use the certification mark on their goods and/or in connection with their services.

(b) In an application to register a certification mark under section 1(b), section 44 or section 66(a) of the Act, the application shall include all applicable elements required by the preceding sections for trademarks. In addition, the application must: specify the conditions under which the certification mark is intended to be used; allege that the applicant intends to exercise legitimate control over the use of the mark; and allege that the applicant will not engage in the production or marketing of the goods or services to which the mark is applied. When the applicant files an allegation of use under § 2.76 or § 2.88, the applicant must submit a copy of the standards that determine whether others may use the certification mark on their goods and/or in connection with their services.

[64 FR 48920, Sept. 8, 1999, as amended at 73 FR 67769, Nov. 17, 2008]

§ 2.46 Principal Register.

All applications will be treated as seeking registration on the Principal Register unless otherwise stated in the application. Service marks, collective marks, and certification marks, registrable in accordance with the applicable provisions of section 2 of the Act, are registered on the Principal Register.

§ 2.47 Supplemental Register.

(a) In an application to register on the Supplemental Register under section 23 of the Act, the application shall so indicate and shall specify that the mark has been in use in commerce.

(b) In an application to register on the Supplemental Register under section 44 of the Act, the application shall so indicate. The statement of lawful use in commerce may be omitted.

(c) An application under section 66(a) of the Act is not eligible for registration on the Supplemental Register.

(d) A mark in an application to register on the Principal Register under section 1(b) of the Act is eligible for registration on the Supplemental Register only after an acceptable amendment to allege use under § 2.76 or statement of use under § 2.88 has been timely filed.

(e) An application for registration on the Supplemental Register must conform to the requirements for registration on the Principal Register under section 1(a) of the Act, so far as applicable.

[54 FR 37590, Sept. 11, 1989, as amended at 68 FR 55763, Sept. 26, 2003; 73 FR 67769, Nov. 17, 2008]

§ 2.48 Office does not issue duplicate registrations.

If two applications on the same register would result in registrations that are exact duplicates, the Office will permit only one application to mature into registration, and will refuse registration in the other application.

[73 FR 67769, Nov. 17, 2008]

DRAWING

AUTHORITY: Secs. 2.51 to 2.55 also issued under sec. 1, 60 Stat. 427; 15 U.S.C. 1051.

§ 2.51 Drawing required.

(a) In an application under section 1(a) of the Act, the drawing of the mark must be a substantially exact representation of the mark as used on or in connection with the goods and/or services.

(b) In an application under section 1(b) of the Act, the drawing of the mark must be a substantially exact representation of the mark as intended to be used on or in connection with the goods and/or services specified in the application, and once an amendment to allege use under § 2.76 or a statement of use under § 2.88 has been filed, the drawing of the mark must be a substantially exact representation of the mark as used on or in connection with the goods and/or services.

(c) In an application under section 44 of the Act, the drawing of the mark must be a substantially exact representation of the mark as it appears in the drawing in the registration certificate of a mark duly registered in the applicant's country of origin.

(d) In an application under section 66(a) of the Act, the drawing of the mark must be a substantially exact representation of the mark as it appears in the international registration.

[68 FR 55763, Sept. 26, 2003]

§ 2.52 Types of drawings and format for drawings.

A drawing depicts the mark sought to be registered. The drawing must show only one mark. The applicant must include a clear drawing of the mark when the application is filed. There are two types of drawings:

(a) *Standard character (typed) drawing.* Applicants who seek to register words, letters, numbers, or any combination thereof without claim to any particular font style, size, or color must submit a standard character drawing that shows the mark in black on a white background. An applicant may submit a standard character drawing if:

(1) The application includes a statement that the mark is in standard characters and no claim is made to any particular font style, size, or color;

(2) The mark does not include a design element;

(3) All letters and words in the mark are depicted in Latin characters;

(4) All numerals in the mark are depicted in Roman or Arabic numerals; and

(5) The mark includes only common punctuation or diacritical marks.

(b) *Special form drawing.* Applicants who seek to register a mark that includes a two or three-dimensional design; color; and/or words, letters, or numbers or the combination thereof in a particular font style or size must submit a special form drawing. The drawing should show the mark in black on a white background, unless the mark includes color.

(1) *Marks that include color.* If the mark includes color, the drawing must show the mark in color, and the applicant must name the color(s), describe where the color(s) appear on the mark, and submit a claim that the color(s) is a feature of the mark.

(2) *Three dimensional marks.* If the mark has three-dimensional features, the drawing must depict a single rendition of the mark, and the applicant must indicate that the mark is three-dimensional.

(3) *Motion marks.* If the mark has motion, the drawing may depict a single point in the movement, or the drawing may depict up to five freeze frames showing various points in the movement, whichever best depicts the commercial impression of the mark. The applicant must also describe the mark.

(4) *Broken lines to show placement.* If necessary to adequately depict the commercial impression of the mark, the applicant may be required to submit a drawing that shows the placement of the mark by surrounding the mark with a proportionately accurate broken-line representation of the particular goods, packaging, or advertising on which the mark appears. The applicant must also use broken lines to show any other matter not claimed as part of the mark. For any drawing using broken lines to indicate placement of the mark, or matter not claimed as part of the mark, the applicant must describe the mark and explain the purpose of the broken lines.

(5) *Description of mark.* A description of the mark must be included.

(c) *TEAS drawings.* A drawing filed through TEAS must meet the requirements of § 2.53.

(d) *Paper drawings.* A paper drawing must meet the requirements of § 2.54.

(e) *Sound, scent, and non-visual marks.* An applicant is not required to submit a drawing if the mark consists only of a sound, a scent, or other completely non-visual matter. For these types of marks, the applicant must submit a detailed description of the mark.

[68 FR 55763, Sept. 26, 2003, as amended at 73 FR 13784, Mar. 14, 2008; 73 FR 67769, Nov. 17, 2008]

§ 2.53 Requirements for drawings filed through the TEAS.

The drawing must meet the requirements of § 2.52. In addition, in a TEAS submission, the drawing must meet the following requirements:

(a) *Standard character drawings.* If an applicant seeks registration of a standard character mark, the applicant must enter the mark in the appropriate field on the TEAS form, and check the box to claim that the mark consists of standard characters.

(b) *Special form drawings:* If an applicant is filing a special form drawing, the applicant must attach a digitized image of the mark to the TEAS submission that meets the requirements of paragraph (c) of this section.

(c) *Requirements for digitized image:* The image must be in .jpg format and scanned at no less than 300 dots per inch and no more than 350 dots per inch with a length and width of no less than 250 pixels and no more than 944 pixels. All lines must be clean, sharp and solid, not fine or crowded, and produce a high quality image when copied.

[68 FR 55764, Sept. 26, 2003, as amended at 70 FR 38774, July 6, 2005; 73 FR 67769, Nov. 17, 2008]

§ 2.54 Requirements for drawings submitted on paper.

The drawing must meet the requirements of § 2.52. In addition, in a paper submission, the drawing should:

(a) Be on non-shiny white paper that is separate from the application;

(b) Be on paper that is 8 to 8.5 inches (20.3 to 21.6 cm.) wide and 11 to 11.69 inches (27.9 to 29.7 cm.) long. One of the shorter sides of the sheet should be regarded as its top edge. The image must be no larger than 3.15 inches (8 cm) high by 3.15 inches (8 cm) wide;

(c) Include the caption "DRAWING PAGE" at the top of the drawing beginning one inch (2.5 cm.) from the top edge; and

(d) Depict the mark in black ink, or in color if color is claimed as a feature of the mark.

(e) Drawings must be typed or made with a pen or by a process that will provide high definition when copied. A photolithographic, printer's proof copy, or other high quality reproduction of the mark may be used. All lines must be clean, sharp and solid, and must not be fine or crowded.

[68 FR 55764, Sept. 26, 2003]

§ 2.56 Specimens.

(a) An application under section 1(a) of the Act, an amendment to allege use under § 2.76, and a statement of use under § 2.88 must each include one specimen per class showing the mark as used on or in connection with the goods or services. When requested by the Office as reasonably necessary to proper examination, additional specimens must be provided.

(b)(1) A trademark specimen is a label, tag, or container for the goods, or a display associated with the goods. The Office may accept another document related to the goods or the sale of the goods when it is impracticable to place the mark on the goods, packaging for the goods, or displays associated with the goods.

(2) A service mark specimen must show the mark as actually used in the sale or advertising of the services.

(3) A collective trademark or collective service mark specimen must show how a member uses the mark on the member's goods or in the sale or advertising of the member's services.

(4) A collective membership mark specimen must show use by members to indicate membership in the collective organization.

(5) A certification mark specimen must show how a person other than the owner uses the mark to certify regional or other origin, material, mode of manufacture, quality, accuracy, or other characteristics of that person's goods or services; or that members of a union or other organization performed the work or labor on the goods or services.

(c) A photocopy or other reproduction of a specimen of the mark as actually used on or in connection with the goods, or in the sale or advertising of the services, is acceptable. However, a photocopy of the drawing required by § 2.51 is not a proper specimen.

(d)(1) The specimen should be flat, and not larger than 8½ inches (21.6 cm.) wide by 11.69 inches (29.7 cm.) long. If a specimen of this size is not available, the applicant may substitute a suitable photograph or other facsimile.

(2) If the applicant files a specimen exceeding these size requirements (a "bulky specimen"), the Office will create a digital facsimile of the specimen that meets the requirements of the rule (*i.e.*, is flat and no larger than 8½ inches (21.6 cm.) wide by 11.69 inches (29.7 cm.) long) and put it in the record. The Office may destroy the original bulky specimen.

(3) In the absence of non-bulky alternatives, the Office may accept an audio or video cassette tape recording, CD-ROM, or other appropriate medium.

(4) For a TEAS submission, the specimen must be a digitized image in .jpg or .pdf format.

[64 FR 48921, Sept. 8, 1999, as amended at 68 FR 55764, Sept. 26, 2003; 73 FR 67769, Nov. 17, 2008; 77 FR 30207, May 22, 2012]

§§ 2.57–2.58 [Reserved]

§ 2.59 Filing substitute specimen(s).

(a) In an application under section 1(a) of the Act, the applicant may submit substitute specimens of the mark as used on or in connection with the goods, or in the sale or advertising of the services. The applicant must verify by an affidavit or declaration under § 2.20 that the substitute specimens were in use in commerce at least as early as the filing date of the application. Verification is not required if the specimen is a duplicate or facsimile of a specimen already of record in the application.

(b) In an application under section 1(b) of the Act, after filing either an amendment to allege use under § 2.76 or a statement of use under § 2.88, the applicant may submit substitute specimens of the mark as used on or in connection with the goods, or in the sale or advertising of the services. If the applicant submits substitute specimen(s), the applicant must:

(1) For an amendment to allege use under § 2.76, verify by affidavit or declaration under § 2.20 that the applicant used the substitute specimen(s) in commerce prior to filing the amendment to allege use.

(2) For a statement of use under § 2.88, verify by affidavit or declaration under § 2.20 that the applicant used the substitute specimen(s) in commerce either prior to filing the statement of

use or prior to the expiration of the deadline for filing the statement of use.

[64 FR 48921, Sept. 8, 1999]

EXAMINATION OF APPLICATION AND ACTION BY APPLICANTS

AUTHORITY: Secs. 2.61 to 2.69 also issued under sec. 12, 60 Stat. 432; 15 U.S.C. 1062.

§2.61 Action by examiner.

(a) Applications for registration, including amendments to allege use under section 1(c) of the Act, and statements of use under section 1(d) of the Act, will be examined and, if the applicant is found not entitled to registration for any reason, applicant will be notified and advised of the reasons therefor and of any formal requirements or objections.

(b) The Office may require the applicant to furnish such information, exhibits, affidavits or declarations, and such additional specimens as may be reasonably necessary to the proper examination of the application.

(c) Whenever it shall be found that two or more parties whose interests are in conflict are represented by the same attorney, each party and also the attorney shall be notified of this fact.

[30 FR 13193, Oct. 16, 1965, as amended at 37 FR 2880, Feb. 9, 1972; 54 FR 37592, Sept. 11, 1989; 77 FR 30207, May 22, 2012]

§2.62 Procedure for filing response.

(a) *Deadline.* The applicant's response to an Office action must be received within six months from the date of issuance.

(b) *Signature.* The response must be signed by the applicant, someone with legal authority to bind the applicant (e.g., a corporate officer or general partner of a partnership), or a practitioner qualified to practice under §11.14 of this chapter, in accordance with the requirements of §2.193(e)(2).

[73 FR 67769, Nov. 17, 2008, as amended at 74 FR 54908, Oct. 26, 2009]

§2.63 Reexamination.

(a) After response by the applicant, the application will be reexamined or reconsidered. If registration is again refused or any formal requirement[s] is repeated, but the examiner's action is not stated to be final, the applicant may respond again.

(b) After reexamination the applicant may respond by filing a timely petition to the Director for relief from a formal requirement if: (1) The requirement is repeated, but the examiner's action is not made final, and the subject matter of the requirement is appropriate for petition to the Director (see §2.146(b)); or (2) the examiner's action is made final and such action is limited to subject matter appropriate for petition to the Director. If the petition is denied, the applicant shall have until six months from the date of the Office action which repeated the requirement or made it final or thirty days from the date of the decision on the petition, whichever date is later, to comply with the requirement. A formal requirement which is the subject of a petition decided by the Director may not subsequently be the subject of an appeal to the Trademark Trial and Appeal Board.

[48 FR 23134, May 23, 1983]

§2.64 Final action.

(a) On the first or any subsequent reexamination or reconsideration the refusal of the registration or the insistence upon a requirement may be stated to be final, whereupon applicant's response is limited to an appeal, or to a compliance with any requirement, or to a petition to the Director if permitted by §2.63(b).

(b) During the period between a final action and expiration of the time for filing an appeal, the applicant may request the examiner to reconsider the final action. The request must be signed by the applicant, someone with legal authority to bind the applicant (e.g., a corporate officer or general partner of a partnership), or a practitioner qualified to practice under §11.14, in accordance with the requirements of §2.193(e)(2). The filing of a request for reconsideration will not extend the time for filing an appeal or petitioning the Director, but normally the examiner will reply to a request for reconsideration before the end of the six-month period if the request is filed within three months after the date of the final action. The Office will enter amendments accompanying requests for reconsideration after final action if the amendments comply with the rules of practice in trademark cases and the Act.

(c)(1) If an applicant in an application under section 1(b) of the Act files an amendment to allege use under § 2.76 during the six-month response period after issuance of a final action, the examiner shall examine the amendment. The filing of an amendment to allege use does not extend the deadline for filing a response to an outstanding Office action, appeal to the Trademark Trial and Appeal Board, or petition to the Director.

(2) If the amendment to allege use under § 2.76 is acceptable in all respects, the applicant will be notified of its acceptance.

(3) If, as a result of the examination of the amendment to allege use under § 2.76, the applicant is found not entitled to registration for any reason not previously stated, applicant will be notified and advised of the reasons and of any formal requirements or refusals. The Trademark Examining Attorney shall withdraw the final action previously issued and shall incorporate all unresolved refusals or requirements previously stated in the new non-final action.

[48 FR 23134, May 23, 1983, as amended at 54 FR 37592, Sept. 11, 1989; 73 FR 67769, Nov. 17, 2008; 74 FR 54908, Oct. 26, 2009]

§ 2.65 Abandonment.

(a) If an applicant fails to respond, or to respond completely, within six months after the date an action is issued, the application shall be deemed abandoned unless the refusal or requirement is expressly limited to only certain goods and/or services. If the refusal or requirement is expressly limited to only certain goods and/or services, the application will be abandoned only as to those particular goods and/or services. A timely petition to the Director pursuant to §§ 2.63(b) and 2.146 or notice of appeal to the Trademark Trial and Appeal Board pursuant to § 2.142, if appropriate, is a response that avoids abandonment of an application.

(b) When action by the applicant filed within the six-month response period is a bona fide attempt to advance the examination of the application and is substantially a complete response to the examiner's action, but consideration of some matter or compliance with some requirement has been inadvertently omitted, opportunity to explain and supply the omission may be given before the question of abandonment is considered.

(c) If an applicant in an application under section 1(b) of the Act fails to timely file a statement of use under § 2.88, the application shall be deemed to be abandoned.

[48 FR 23134, May 23, 1983, as amended at 54 FR 37592, Sept. 11, 1989; 68 FR 55764, Sept. 26, 2003; 73 FR 67769, Nov. 17, 2008]

§ 2.66 Revival of abandoned applications.

(a) The applicant may file a petition to revive an application abandoned because the applicant did not timely respond to an Office action or notice of allowance, if the delay was unintentional. The applicant must file the petition:

(1) Within two months of the date of issuance of the notice of abandonment; or

(2) Within two months of actual knowledge of the abandonment, if the applicant did not receive the notice of abandonment, and the applicant was diligent in checking the status of the application every six months in accordance with § 2.146(i).

(b) The requirements for filing a petition to revive an application abandoned because the applicant did not timely respond to an Office action are:

(1) The petition fee required by § 2.6;

(2) A statement, signed by someone with firsthand knowledge of the facts, that the delay in filing the response on or before the due date was unintentional; and

(3) Unless the applicant alleges that it did not receive the Office action, the proposed response.

(c) The requirements for filing a petition to revive an application abandoned because the applicant did not timely respond to a notice of allowance are:

(1) The petition fee required by § 2.6;

(2) A statement, signed by someone with firsthand knowledge of the facts, that the delay in filing the statement of use (or request for extension of time

to file a statement of use) on or before the due date was unintentional;

(3) Unless the applicant alleges that it did not receive the notice of allowance and requests cancellation of the notice of allowance, the required fees for the number of requests for extensions of time to file a statement of use that the applicant should have filed under § 2.89 if the application had never been abandoned;

(4) Unless the applicant alleges that it did not receive the notice of allowance and requests cancellation of the notice of allowance, either a statement of use under § 2.88 or a request for an extension of time to file a statement of use under § 2.89; and

(5) Unless a statement of use is filed with or before the petition, or the applicant alleges that it did not receive the notice of allowance and requests cancellation of the notice of allowance, the applicant must file any further requests for extensions of time to file a statement of use under § 2.89 that become due while the petition is pending, or file a statement of use under § 2.88.

(d) In an application under section 1(b) of the Act, the Director will not grant the petition if this would permit the filing of a statement of use more than 36 months after the date of issuance of the notice of allowance under section 13(b)(2) of the Act.

(e) The Director will grant the petition to revive if the applicant complies with the requirements listed above and establishes that the delay in responding was unintentional.

(f) If the Director denies a petition, the applicant may request reconsideration, if the applicant:

(1) Files the request within two months of the date of issuance of the decision denying the petition; and

(2) Pays a second petition fee under § 2.6.

[64 FR 48921, Sept. 8, 1999, as amended at 68 FR 55764, Sept. 26, 2003; 73 FR 67769, Nov. 17, 2008]

§ 2.67 Suspension of action by the Patent and Trademark Office.

Action by the Patent and Trademark Office may be suspended for a reasonable time for good and sufficient cause. The fact that a proceeding is pending before the Patent and Trademark Office or a court which is relevant to the issue of registrability of the applicant's mark, or the fact that the basis for registration is, under the provisions of section 44(e) of the Act, registration of the mark in a foreign country and the foreign application is still pending, will be considered prima facie good and sufficient cause. An applicant's request for a suspension of action under this section filed within the 6-month response period (see § 2.62) may be considered responsive to the previous Office action. The first suspension is within the discretion of the Examiner of Trademarks and any subsequent suspension must be approved by the Director.

[37 FR 3898, Feb. 24, 1972]

§ 2.68 Express abandonment (withdrawal) of application.

(a) *Written document required.* An applicant may expressly abandon an application by filing a written request for abandonment or withdrawal of the application, signed by the applicant, someone with legal authority to bind the applicant (e.g., a corporate officer or general partner of a partnership), or a practitioner qualified to practice under § 11.14 of this chapter, in accordance with the requirements of § 2.193(e)(2).

(b) *Rights in the mark not affected.* Except as provided in § 2.135, the fact that an application has been expressly abandoned shall not, in any proceeding in the Office, affect any rights that the applicant may have in the mark in the abandoned application.

[74 FR 54908, Oct. 26, 2009]

§ 2.69 Compliance with other laws.

When the sale or transportation of any product for which registration of a trademark is sought is regulated under an Act of Congress, the Patent and Trademark Office may make appropriate inquiry as to compliance with such Act for the sole purpose of determining lawfulness of the commerce recited in the application.

[54 FR 37592, Sept. 11, 1989]

AMENDMENT OF APPLICATION

§ 2.71 Amendments to correct informalities.

The applicant may amend the application during the course of examination, when required by the Office or for other reasons.

(a) The applicant may amend the application to clarify or limit, but not to broaden, the identification of goods and/or services.

(b)(1) If the declaration or verification of an application under § 2.33 is unsigned or signed by the wrong party, the applicant may submit a substitute verification or declaration under § 2.20.

(2) If the declaration or verification of a statement of use under § 2.88, or a request for extension of time to file a statement of use under § 2.89, is unsigned or signed by the wrong party, the applicant must submit a substitute verification before the expiration of the statutory deadline for filing the statement of use.

(c) The applicant may amend the dates of use, provided that the applicant supports the amendment with an affidavit or declaration under § 2.20, except that the following amendments are not permitted:

(1) In an application under section 1(a) of the Act, the applicant may not amend the application to specify a date of use that is subsequent to the filing date of the application;

(2) In an application under section 1(b) of the Act, after filing a statement of use under § 2.88, the applicant may not amend the statement of use to specify a date of use that is subsequent to the expiration of the deadline for filing the statement of use.

(d) The applicant may amend the application to correct the name of the applicant, if there is a mistake in the manner in which the name of the applicant is set out in the application. The amendment must be supported by an affidavit or declaration under § 2.20, signed by the applicant. However, the application cannot be amended to set forth a different entity as the applicant. An application filed in the name of an entity that did not own the mark as of the filing date of the application is void.

[64 FR 48922, Sept. 8, 1999]

§ 2.72 Amendments to description or drawing of the mark.

(a) In an application based on use in commerce under section 1(a) of the Act, the applicant may amend the description or drawing of the mark only if:

(1) The specimens originally filed, or substitute specimens filed under § 2.59(a), support the proposed amendment; and

(2) The proposed amendment does not materially alter the mark. The Office will determine whether a proposed amendment materially alters a mark by comparing the proposed amendment with the description or drawing of the mark filed with the original application.

(b) In an application based on a bona fide intention to use a mark in commerce under section 1(b) of the Act, the applicant may amend the description or drawing of the mark only if:

(1) The specimens filed with an amendment to allege use or statement of use, or substitute specimens filed under § 2.59(b), support the proposed amendment; and

(2) The proposed amendment does not materially alter the mark. The Office will determine whether a proposed amendment materially alters a mark by comparing the proposed amendment with the description or drawing of the mark filed with the original application.

(c) In an application based on a claim of priority under section 44(d) of the Act, or on a mark duly registered in the country of origin of the foreign applicant under section 44(e) of the Act, the applicant may amend the description or drawing of the mark only if:

(1) The description or drawing of the mark in the foreign registration certificate supports the amendment; and

(2) The proposed amendment does not materially alter the mark. The Office will determine whether a proposed amendment materially alters a mark by comparing the proposed amendment with the description or drawing of the

mark filed with the original application.

[64 FR 48922, Sept. 8, 1999]

§2.73 Amendment to recite concurrent use.

An application that includes section 1(a) of the Trademark Act as a filing basis, or for which an acceptable allegation of use under §2.76 or §2.88 has been filed, may be amended to an application for concurrent use registration, provided that the application as amended meets the requirements of §2.42. The trademark examining attorney will determine whether the application, as amended, is acceptable.

[73 FR 67770, Nov. 17, 2008]

§2.74 Form and signature of amendment.

(a) *Form of Amendment.* Amendments should be set forth clearly and completely. Applicant should either set forth the entire wording, including the proposed changes, or, if it would be more efficient, indicate which words should be added and which words should be deleted. The examining attorney may require the applicant to rewrite the entire amendment, if necessary for clarification of the record.

(b) *Signature.* A request for amendment of an application must be signed by the applicant, someone with legal authority to bind the applicant (e.g., a corporate officer or general partner of a partnership), or a practitioner qualified to practice under §11.14 of this chapter, in accordance with the requirements of §2.193(e)(2). If the amendment requires verification, the verification must be sworn to or supported by a declaration under §2.20 by a person properly authorized to sign on behalf of the applicant under §2.193(e)(1).

[73 FR 67770, Nov. 17, 2008, as amended at 74 FR 54908, Oct. 26, 2009]

§2.75 Amendment to change application to different register.

(a) An application for registration on the Principal Register under section 1(a) or 44 of the Act may be changed to an application for registration on the Supplemental Register and vice versa by amending the application to comply with the rules relating to the appropriate register, as the case may be.

(b) An application under section 1(b) of the Act may be amended to change the application to a different register only after submission of an acceptable amendment to allege use under §2.76 or statement of use under §2.88. When such an application is changed from the Principal Register to the Supplemental Register, the effective filing date of the application is the date of the filing of the allegation of use under section 1(c) or 1(d) of the Act.

(c) In an application under section 66(a) of the Act, the applicant may not amend the application to the Supplemental Register.

[54 FR 37593, Sept. 11, 1989, as amended at 68 FR 55765, Sept. 26, 2003]

§2.76 Amendment to allege use.

(a) An application under section 1(b) of the Act may be amended to allege use of the mark in commerce under section 1(c) of the Act at any time between the filing of the application and the date the examiner approves the mark for publication. Thereafter, an allegation of use may be submitted only as a statement of use under §2.88 after the issuance of a notice of allowance under section 13(b)(2) of the Act. If an amendment to allege use is filed outside the time period specified in this paragraph, it will be returned to the applicant.

(b) A complete amendment to allege use must include:

(1) A statement that is signed and verified (sworn to) or supported by a declaration under §2.20 by a person properly authorized to sign on behalf of the applicant (*see* §2.193(e)(1)) that:

(i) The applicant believes it is the owner of the mark; and

(ii) The mark is in use in commerce, specifying the date of the applicant's first use of the mark and first use of the mark in commerce, and those goods or services specified in the application on or in connection with which the applicant uses the mark in commerce.

(2) One specimen per class showing the mark as actually used in commerce. When requested by the Office, additional specimens must be provided.

See § 2.56 for the requirements for specimens; and

(3) The fee per class required by § 2.6.

(c) An amendment to allege use may be filed only when the applicant has made use of the mark in commerce on or in connection with all of the goods or services, as specified in the application, for which applicant will seek registration in that application unless the amendment to allege use is accompanied by a request in accordance with § 2.87 to divide out from the application the goods or services to which the amendment pertains. If more than one item of goods or services is specified in the amendment to allege use, the dates of use required in paragraph (b)(1) of this section need be for only one of the items specified in each class, provided the particular item to which the dates apply is designated.

(d) The title "Allegation of Use" should appear at the top of the document.

(e) The Office will review a timely filed amendment to allege use to determine whether it meets the following minimum requirements:

(1) The fee prescribed in § 2.6;

(2) One specimen or facsimile of the mark as used in commerce; and

(3) A statement that is signed and verified (sworn to) or supported by a declaration under § 2.20 by a person properly authorized to sign on behalf of the applicant that the mark is in use in commerce.

(f) A timely filed amendment to allege use which meets the minimum requirements specified in paragraph (e) of this section will be examined in accordance with §§ 2.61 through 2.69. If, as a result of the examination of the amendment to allege use, applicant is found not entitled to registration for any reason not previously stated, applicant will be so notified and advised of the reasons and of any formal requirements or refusals. The notification shall restate or incorporate by reference all unresolved refusals or requirements previously stated. The amendment to allege use may be amended in accordance with §§ 2.59 and 2.71 through 2.75. If the amendment to allege use is acceptable in all respects, the applicant will be notified of its acceptance. The filing of such an amendment shall not constitute a response to any outstanding action by the Trademark Examining Attorney.

(g) If the amendment to allege use is filed within the permitted time period but does not meet the minimum requirements specified in paragraph (e) of this section, applicant will be notified of the deficiency. The deficiency may be corrected provided the mark has not been approved for publication. If an acceptable amendment to correct the deficiency is not filed prior to approval of the mark for publication, the amendment will not be examined.

(h) An amendment to allege use may be withdrawn for any reason prior to approval of a mark for publication.

(i) If the applicant does not file the amendment to allege use within a reasonable time after it is signed, the Office may require a substitute verification or declaration under § 2.20 stating that the mark is still in use in commerce.

(j) For the requirements for a multiple class application, see § 2.86.

[54 FR 37593, Sept. 11, 1989, as amended at 63 FR 48097, Sept. 9, 1998; 64 FR 48922, Sept. 8, 1999; 64 FR 51245, Sept. 22, 1999; 73 FR 67770, Nov. 17, 2008; 74 FR 54908, Oct. 26, 2009; 77 FR 30207, May 22, 2012]

§ 2.77 Amendments between notice of allowance and statement of use.

(a) The only amendments that can be entered in an application between the issuance of the notice of allowance and the submission of a statement of use are:

(1) The deletion of specified goods or services from the identification of goods/services;

(2) The deletion of a basis in a multiple-basis application; and

(3) A change of attorney or change of address.

(b) Other amendments filed during this period will be placed in the application file and considered when the statement of use is examined.

[73 FR 67770, Nov. 17, 2008]

Publication and Post Publication

§ 2.80 Publication for opposition.

If, on examination or reexamination of an application for registration on the Principal Register, it appears that the applicant is entitled to have his mark registered, the mark will be published in the *Official Gazette* for opposition. The mark will also be published in the case of an application to be placed in interference or concurrent use proceedings, if otherwise registrable.

[41 FR 758, Jan. 5, 1976]

§2.81 Post publication.

(a) Except in an application under section 1(b) of the Act for which no amendment to allege use under §2.76 has been submitted and accepted, if no opposition is filed within the time permitted or all oppositions filed are dismissed, and if no interference is declared and no concurrent use proceeding is instituted, the application will be prepared for issuance of the certificate of registration as provided in §2.151.

(b) In an application under section 1(b) of the Act for which no amendment to allege use under §2.76 has been submitted and accepted, if no opposition is filed within the time permitted or all oppositions filed are dismissed, and if no interference is declared, a notice of allowance will issue. The notice of allowance will state the serial number of the application, the name of the applicant, the correspondence address, the mark, the identification of goods and/or services, and the issue date of the notice of allowance. Thereafter, the applicant must submit a statement of use as provided in §2.88.

[54 FR 37594, Sept. 11, 1989, as amended at 73 FR 67770, Nov. 17, 2008]

§2.82 Marks on Supplemental Register published only upon registration.

In the case of an application for registration on the Supplemental Register the mark will not be published for opposition but if it appears, after examination or reexamination, that the applicant is entitled to have the mark registered, a certificate of registration will issue as provided in §2.151. The mark will be published in the *Official Gazette* when registered.

[54 FR 37594, Sept. 11, 1989]

§2.83 Conflicting marks.

(a) Whenever an application is made for registration of a mark which so resembles another mark or marks pending registration as to be likely to cause confusion or mistake or to deceive, the mark with the earliest effective filing date will be published in the *Official Gazette* for opposition if eligible for the Principal Register, or issued a certificate of registration if eligible for the Supplemental Register.

(b) In situations in which conflicting applications have the same effective filing date, the application with the earliest date of execution will be published in the *Official Gazette* for opposition or issued on the Supplemental Register.

(c) Action on the conflicting application which is not published in the *Official Gazette* for opposition or not issued on the Supplemental Register will be suspended by the Examiner of Trademarks until the published or issued application is registered or abandoned.

[37 FR 2880, Feb. 9, 1972, as amended at 54 FR 37594, Sept. 11, 1989]

§2.84 Jurisdiction over published applications.

(a) The trademark examining attorney may exercise jurisdiction over an application up to the date the mark is published in the *Official Gazette*. After publication of an application under section 1(a), 44 or 66(a) of the Act, the trademark examining attorney may, with the permission of the Director, exercise jurisdiction over the application. After publication of an application under section 1(b) of the Act, the trademark examining attorney may exercise jurisdiction over the application after the issuance of the notice of allowance under section 13(b)(2) of the Act. After publication, and prior to issuance of a notice of allowance in an application under section 1(b), the trademark examining attorney may, with the permission of the Director, exercise jurisdiction over the application.

(b) After publication, but before the certificate of registration is issued in an application under section 1(a), 44, or 66(a) of the Act, or before the notice of allowance is issued in an application under section 1(b) of the Act, an application that is not the subject of an *inter partes* proceeding before the Trademark Trial and Appeal Board may be amended if the amendment does not necessitate republication of the mark or issuance of an Office action. Otherwise, an amendment to such an application may be submitted only upon petition to the Director to restore jurisdiction over the application to the trademark examining attorney for consideration of the amendment and further examination. The amendment of an application that is the subject of an *inter partes* proceeding before the Trademark Trial and Appeal Board is governed by § 2.133.

[68 FR 55765, Sept. 26, 2003, as amended at 73 FR 67770, Nov. 17, 2008]

CLASSIFICATION

§ 2.85 Classification schedules.

(a) *International classification system.* Section 6.1 of this chapter sets forth the international system of classification for goods and services, which applies for all statutory purposes to:

(1) Applications filed in the Office on or after September 1, 1973, and resulting registrations; and

(2) Registrations resulting from applications filed on or before August 31, 1973, that have been amended to adopt international classification pursuant to § 2.85(e)(3).

(b) *Prior United States classification system.* Section 6.2 of this chapter sets forth the prior United States system of classification for goods and services, which applies for all statutory purposes to registrations resulting from applications filed on or before August 31, 1973, unless:

(1) The registration has been amended to adopt international classification pursuant to § 2.85(e)(3); or

(2) The registration was issued under a classification system prior to that set forth in § 6.2.

(c) *Certification marks and collective membership marks.* Sections 6.3 and 6.4 specify the system of classification which applies to certification marks and collective membership marks in applications based on sections 1 and 44 of the Act, and to registrations resulting from applications based on sections 1 and 44. These sections do not apply to applications under section 66(a) or to registered extensions of protection.

(d) *Section 66(a) applications and registered extensions of protection.* In an application under section 66(a) of the Act or registered extension of protection, the classification cannot be changed from the classification assigned by the International Bureau of the World Intellectual Property Organization, unless the International Bureau corrects the classification. Classes cannot be added, and goods or services cannot be transferred from one class to another in a multiple-class application.

(e) *Changes to Nice Agreement.* The international classification system changes periodically, pursuant to the Nice Agreement Concerning the International Classification of Goods and Services for the Purposes of the Registration of Marks. These changes are listed in the *International Classification of Goods and Services for the Purposes of the Registration of Marks*, which is published by the World Intellectual Property Organization.

(1) If international classification changes pursuant to the Nice Agreement, the new classification applies only to applications filed on or after the effective date of the change.

(2) In a section 1 or section 44 application filed before the effective date of a change to the Nice Agreement, the applicant may amend the application to comply with the requirements of the current edition. The applicant must comply with the current edition for all goods or services identified in the application. The applicant must pay the fees for any added class(es).

(3) In a registration resulting from a section 1 or section 44 application that was filed before the effective date of a change to the Nice Agreement, the owner may amend the registration to comply with the requirements of the current edition. The owner must reclassify all goods or services identified in the registration to the current edition. The owner must pay the fee required by § 2.6 for amendments under section 7 of the Act. The owner may reclassify registrations from multiple United States classes (§ 2.85(b)) into a single international classification, where appropriate.

(f) Classification schedules shall not limit or extend the applicant's rights, except that in a section 66(a) application, the scope of the identification of goods or services for purposes of permissible amendments (*see* § 2.71(a)) is limited by the class, pursuant to § 2.85(d).

[73 FR 67770, Nov. 17, 2008]

§ 2.86 Application may include multiple classes.

(a) In a single application, an applicant may apply to register the same mark for goods and/or services in multiple classes. The applicant must:

(1) Specifically identify the goods or services in each class;

(2) Submit an application filing fee for each class, as set forth in § 2.6(a)(1); and

(3) Include either dates of use (see §§ 2.34(a)(1)(ii) and (iii)) and one specimen for each class, or a statement of a bona fide intention to use the mark in commerce on or in connection with all the goods or services specified in each class. When requested by the Office, additional specimens must be provided. The applicant may not claim both use in commerce and a bona fide intention to use the mark in commerce for the identical goods or services in one application.

(b) An amendment to allege use under § 2.76 or a statement of use under § 2.88 must include, for each class, the required fee, dates of use, and one specimen. When requested by the Office, additional specimens must be provided. The applicant may not file the amendment to allege use or statement of use until the applicant has used the mark on all the goods or services, unless the applicant files a request to divide. See § 2.87 for information regarding requests to divide.

(c) The Office will issue a single certificate of registration for the mark, unless the applicant files a request to divide. See § 2.87 for information regarding requests to divide.

[64 FR 48923, Sept. 8, 1999, as amended at 70 FR 2953, Jan. 19, 2005; 73 FR 67771, Nov. 17, 2008; 77 FR 30207, May 22, 2012]

§ 2.87 Dividing an application.

(a) *Application may be divided.* An application may be divided into two or more separate applications upon the payment of a fee for each new application created and submission by the applicant of a request in accordance with paragraph (d) of this section.

(b) *Fee.* In the case of a request to divide out one or more entire classes from an application, only the fee for dividing an application as set forth in § 2.6(a)(19) will be required. However, in the case of a request to divide out some, but not all, of the goods or services in a class, the applicant must submit the application filing fee as set forth in § 2.6(a)(1) for each new separate application to be created by the division, in addition to the fee for dividing an application.

(c) *Time for filing.* (1) A request to divide an application may be filed at any time between the application filing date and the date on which the trademark examining attorney approves the mark for publication; or during an opposition, concurrent use, or interference proceeding, upon motion granted by the Trademark Trial and Appeal Board.

(2) In an application under section 1(b) of the Act, a request to divide may also be filed with a statement of use under § 2.88 or at any time between the filing of a statement of use and the date on which the trademark examining attorney approves the mark for registration.

(3) In a multiple-basis application, a request to divide out goods or services having a particular basis may also be filed during the period between the issuance of the notice of allowance under section 13(b)(2) of the Act and the filing of a statement of use under § 2.88.

(d) *Form.* A request to divide an application should be made in a separate document from any other amendment or response in the application. The title "Request to Divide Application" should appear at the top of the first page of the document.

(e) *Outstanding time periods apply to newly created applications.* Any time period for action by the applicant which is outstanding in the original application at the time of the division will apply to each separate new application created by the division, except as follows:

(1) If an Office action pertaining to less than all the classes in a multiple-class application is outstanding, and the applicant files a request to divide out the goods, services, and/or class(es) to which the Office action does not pertain before the response deadline, a response to the Office action is not due in the new (child) application(s) created by the division of the application;

(2) If an Office action pertaining to less than all the bases in a multiple-basis application is outstanding, and the applicant files a request to divide out the goods/services having the basis or bases to which the Office action does not pertain before the response deadline, a response to the Office action is not due in the new (child) application(s) created by the division of the application; or

(3) In a multiple-basis application in which a notice of allowance has issued, if the applicant files a request to divide out the goods/services having the basis or bases to which the notice of allowance does not pertain before the deadline for filing the statement of use, the new (child) applications created by the division are not affected by the notice of allowance.

(f) *Signature*. The request to divide must be signed by the applicant, someone with legal authority to bind the applicant (e.g., a corporate officer or general partner of a partnership), or a practitioner who meets the requirements of § 11.14, in accordance with the requirements of § 2.193(e)(2).

(g) *Section 66(a) applications—change of ownership with respect to some but not all of the goods or services*. (1) When the International Bureau of the World Intellectual Property Organization notifies the Office that an international registration has been divided as the result of a change of ownership with respect to some but not all of the goods or services, the Office will construe the International Bureau's notice as a request to divide. The Office will record the partial change of ownership in the Assignment Services Branch, and divide out the assigned goods/services from the original (parent) application. The Office will create a new (child) application serial number, and enter the information about the new application in its automated records.

(2) To obtain a certificate of registration in the name of the new owner for the goods/services that have been divided out, the new owner must pay the fee(s) for the request to divide, as required by § 2.6 and paragraph (b) of this section. The examining attorney will issue an Office action in the child application requiring the new owner to pay the required fee(s). If the owner of the child application fails to respond, the child application will be abandoned. It is not necessary for the new owner to file a separate request to divide.

(3) The Office will not divide a section 66(a) application based upon a change of ownership unless the International Bureau notifies the Office that the international registration has been divided.

[73 FR 67771, Nov. 17, 2008, as amended at 74 FR 54908, Oct. 26, 2009]

POST NOTICE OF ALLOWANCE

§ 2.88 Filing statement of use after notice of allowance.

(a) In an application under section 1(b) of the Act, a statement of use, required under section 1(d) of the Act, must be filed within six months after issuance of a notice of allowance under section 13(b)(2) of the Act, or within an extension of time granted under § 2.89. A statement of use that is filed prior to issuance of a notice of allowance is premature, will not be considered, and will be returned to the applicant.

(b) A complete statement of use must include:

(1) A statement that is signed and verified (sworn to) or supported by a declaration under § 2.20 by a person properly authorized to sign on behalf of the applicant (*see* § 2.193(e)(1)) that:

(i) The applicant believes it is the owner of the mark; and

(ii) The mark is in use in commerce, specifying the date of the applicant's first use of the mark and first use of the mark in commerce on or in connection with the goods or services identified in the notice of allowance, and setting forth or incorporating by reference those goods/services identified in the notice of allowance on or in connection with which the mark is in use in commerce. Where an applicant claims section 1(a) of the Act for some goods/services in a class and section 1(b) of the Act for other goods/services in the same class, the statement of use must include dates for the section 1(b) of the Act goods/services;

(2) One specimen of the mark as actually used in commerce. When requested by the Office, additional specimens must be provided. See §2.56 for the requirements for specimens; and

(3) The fee per class required by §2.6. The applicant must pay a filing fee sufficient to cover at least one class within the statutory time for filing the statement of use, or the application will be abandoned. If the applicant submits a fee insufficient to cover all the classes in a multiple-class application, the applicant must specify the classes to be abandoned. If the applicant submits a fee sufficient to pay for at least one class, but insufficient to cover all the classes, and the applicant has not specified the class(es) to be abandoned, the Office will issue a notice granting the applicant additional time to submit the fee(s) for the remaining class(es), or specify the class(es) to be abandoned. If the applicant does not submit the required fee(s) or specify the class(es) to be abandoned within the set time period, the Office will apply the fees paid, beginning with the lowest numbered class(es), in ascending order. The Office will delete the goods/services in the remaining class(es) not covered by the fees submitted.

(c) The statement of use may be filed only when the applicant has made use of the mark in commerce on or in connection with all of the goods or services, as specified in the notice of allowance, for which applicant will seek registration in that application, unless the statement of use is accompanied by a request in accordance with §2.87 to divide out from the application the goods or services to which the statement of use pertains. If more than one item of goods or services is specified in the statement of use, the dates of use required in paragraph (b)(1) of this section need be for only one of the items specified in each class, provided the particular item to which the dates apply is designated.

(d) The title "Allegation of Use" should appear at the top of the first page of the document.

(e) The Office will review a timely filed statement of use to determine whether it meets the following minimum requirements:

(1) The fee for at least a single class, required by §2.6;

(2) One specimen of the mark as used in commerce;

(3) A statement that is signed and verified (sworn to) or supported by a declaration under §2.20 by a person properly authorized to sign on behalf of the applicant that the mark is in use in commerce. If the verification or declaration is unsigned or signed by the wrong party, the applicant must submit a substitute verification on or before the statutory deadline for filing the statement of use.

(f) A timely filed statement of use which meets the minimum requirements specified in paragraph (e) of this section will be examined in accordance with §§2.61 through 2.69. If, as a result of the examination of the statement of use, applicant is found not entitled to registration, applicant will be notified and advised of the reasons and of any formal requirements or refusals. The statement of use may be amended in accordance with §§2.59 and 2.71 through 2.75. If the statement of use is acceptable in all respects, the applicant will be notified of its acceptance.

(g) If the statement of use does not meet the minimum requirements specified in paragraph (e) of this section, applicant will be notified of the deficiency. If the time permitted for applicant to file a statement of use has not expired, applicant may correct the deficiency. After the filing of a statement of use during a permitted time period for such filing, the applicant may not withdraw the statement to return to the previous status of awaiting submission of a statement of use, regardless of whether it is in compliance with paragraph (e) of this section.

(h) The failure to timely file a statement of use which meets the minimum requirements specified in paragraph (e) of this section shall result in the abandonment of the application.

(i)(1) The goods or services specified in a statement of use must conform to those goods or services identified in the notice of allowance. An applicant may specify the goods or services by stating "those goods or services identified in the notice of allowance" or, if appropriate, "those goods or services identified in the notice of allowance except * * *" followed by an identification of the goods or services to be deleted.

(2) If any goods or services specified in the notice of allowance are omitted from the identification of goods or services in the statement of use, the Office will delete the omitted goods/services from the application. The applicant may not thereafter reinsert these goods/services.

(3) The statement of use may be accompanied by a separate request to amend the identification of goods or services in the application, as stated in the notice of allowance, in accordance with § 2.71(a).

(j) The statement of use may be accompanied by a separate request to amend the drawing in the application, in accordance with §§ 2.51 and 2.72.

(k) If the statement of use is not filed within a reasonable time after the date it is signed, the Office may require a substitute verification or declaration under § 2.20 stating that the mark is still in use in commerce.

(l) For the requirements for a multiple class application, see § 2.86.

[54 FR 37595, Sept. 11, 1989, as amended at 64 FR 48923, Sept. 8, 1999; 64 FR 51245, Sept. 22, 1999; 68 FR 55765, Sept. 26, 2003; 73 FR 67771, Nov. 17, 2008; 74 FR 54908, Oct. 26, 2009; 77 FR 30207, May 22, 2012]

§ 2.89 Extensions of time for filing a statement of use.

(a) The applicant may request a six-month extension of time to file the statement of use required by § 2.88. The extension request must be filed within six months of the date of issuance of the notice of allowance under section 13(b)(2) of the Act and must include the following:

(1) A written request for an extension of time to file the statement of use;

(2) The fee per class required by § 2.6. The applicant must pay a filing fee sufficient to cover at least one class within the statutory time for filing the extension request, or the request will be denied. If the applicant timely submits a fee sufficient to pay for at least one class, but insufficient to cover all the classes, and the applicant has not specified the class(es) to which the fee applies, the Office will issue a notice granting the applicant additional time to submit the fee(s) for the remaining classes, or specify the class(es) to be abandoned. If the applicant does not submit the required fee(s) or specify the class(es) to be abandoned within the set time period, the Office will apply the fees paid, beginning with the lowest numbered class(es), in ascending order. The Office will delete the goods/services in the remaining classes not covered by the fees submitted; and

(3) A statement that the applicant still has a bona fide intention to use the mark in commerce, specifying the relevant goods or services, signed and verified (sworn to) or supported by a declaration under § 2.20 by a person properly authorized to sign on behalf of the applicant (*see* § 2.193(e)(1)). If the verification is unsigned or signed by the wrong party, the applicant must submit a substitute verification within six months of the date of issuance of the notice of allowance.

(b) Before the expiration of the previously granted extension of time, the applicant may request further six month extensions of time to file the statement of use by submitting the following:

(1) A written request for an extension of time to file the statement of use;

(2) The fee per class required by § 2.6. The applicant must pay a filing fee sufficient to cover at least one class within the statutory time for filing the extension request, or the request will be denied. If the applicant submits a fee insufficient to cover all the classes in a multiple-class application, the applicant must specify the classes to be abandoned. If the applicant submits a fee sufficient to pay for at least one class, but insufficient to cover all the classes, and the applicant has not specified the class(es) to which the fee applies, the Office will issue a notice granting the applicant additional time to submit the fee(s) for the remaining classes, or specify the class(es) to be

abandoned. If the applicant does not submit the required fee(s) or specify the class(es) to be abandoned within the set time period, the Office will apply the fees, beginning with the lowest numbered class(es), in ascending order. The Office will delete the remaining goods/services not covered by the fees submitted;

(3) A statement that the applicant still has a bona fide intention to use the mark in commerce, specifying the relevant goods or services, signed and verified (sworn to) or supported by a declaration under §2.20 by a person properly authorized to sign on behalf of the applicant (*see* §2.193(e)(1)). If the verification is unsigned or signed by the wrong party, the applicant must submit a substitute verification before the expiration of the previously granted extension; and

(4) A showing of good cause, as specified in paragraph (d) of this section.

(c) Extensions of time under paragraph (b) of this section will be granted only in six-month increments and may not aggregate more than 24 months.

(d) The showing of good cause must include a statement of the applicant's ongoing efforts to make use of the mark in commerce on or in connection with each of the relevant goods or services. Those efforts may include product or service research or development, market research, manufacturing activities, promotional activities, steps to acquire distributors, steps to obtain governmental approval, or other similar activities. In the alternative, the applicant must submit a satisfactory explanation for the failure to make efforts to use the mark in commerce.

(e)(1) At the time of the filing of a statement of use, or during any time remaining in the existing six-month period in which a statement of use is filed, applicant may file one request, in accordance with paragraph (a) or (b) of this section, for a six-month extension of time for filing a statement of use, provided that the time requested would not extend beyond 36 months from the issuance of the notice of allowance. Thereafter, applicant may not request any further extensions of time.

(2) A request for an extension of time that is filed at the time of the filing of a statement of use, or during any time remaining in the existing six-month period in which a statement of use is filed, must comply with all the requirements of paragraph (a) of this section, if it is applicant's first extension request, or paragraph (b) of this section, if it is a second or subsequent extension request. However, in a request under paragraph (b) of this section, applicant may satisfy the requirement for a showing of good cause by asserting that applicant believes that it has made valid use of the mark in commerce, as evidenced by the submitted statement of use, but that if the statement of use is found by the Patent and Trademark Office to be fatally defective, applicant will need additional time in which to file a new statement of use.

(f) The goods or services specified in a request for an extension of time for filing a statement of use must conform to those goods or services identified in the notice of allowance. Any goods or services specified in the notice of allowance which are omitted from the identification of goods or services in the request for extension of time will be presumed to be deleted and the applicant may not thereafter request that the deleted goods or services be reinserted in the application. If appropriate, an applicant may specify the goods or services by stating "those goods or services identified in the notice of allowance" or "those goods or services identified in the notice of allowance except * * *" followed by an identification of the goods or services to be deleted.

(g) The applicant will be notified of the grant or denial of a request for an extension of time, and of the reasons for a denial. Failure to notify the applicant of the grant or denial of the request prior to the expiration of the existing period or requested extension does not relieve the applicant of the responsibility of timely filing a statement of use under §2.88. If, after denial of an extension request, there is time remaining in the existing six-month period for filing a statement of use, applicant may submit a substitute request for extension of time. Otherwise, the only recourse available after denial of a request for an extension of time is a petition to the Director in accordance with § 2.66 or § 2.146. A petition from the denial of an extension request must be filed within two months of the date of issuance of the denial of the request. If the petition is granted, the term of the requested six-month extension that was the subject of the petition will run from the date of expiration of the previously existing six-month period for filing a statement of use.

(h) If the extension request is not filed within a reasonable time after it is signed, the Office may require a substitute verification or declaration under § 2.20 stating that the applicant still has a bona fide intention to use the mark in commerce.

[54 FR 37595, Sept. 11, 1989, as amended at 64 FR 48923, Sept. 8, 1999; 64 FR 51245, Sept. 22, 1999; 73 FR 67772, Nov. 17, 2008; 74 FR 54908, Oct. 26, 2009]

INTERFERENCES AND CONCURRENT USE PROCEEDINGS

AUTHORITY: Secs. 2.91 to 2.99 also issued under secs. 16, 17, 60 Stat. 434; 15 U.S.C. 1066, 1067.

§ 2.91 Declaration of interference.

(a) An interference will not be declared between two applications or between an application and a registration except upon petition to the Director. Interferences will be declared by the Director only upon a showing of extraordinary circumstances which would result in a party being unduly prejudiced without an interference. In ordinary circumstances, the availability of an opposition or cancellation proceeding to the party will be deemed to remove any undue prejudice.

(b) Registrations and applications to register on the Supplemental Register, registrations under the Act of 1920, and registrations of marks the right to use of which has become incontestable are not subject to interference.

[37 FR 2881, Feb. 9, 1972, as amended at 54 FR 34897, Aug. 22, 1989]

§ 2.92 Preliminary to interference.

An interference which has been declared by the Director will not be instituted by the Trademark Trial and Appeal Board until the Examiner of Trademarks has determined that the marks which are to form the subject matter of the controversy are registrable, and all of the marks have been published in the *Official Gazette* for opposition.

[54 FR 34897, Aug. 22, 1989]

§ 2.93 Institution of interference.

An interference is instituted by the issuance of a notice of interference to the parties. The notice shall be sent to each applicant, in care of the applicant's attorney or other representative of record, if any, and if one of the parties is a registrant, the notice shall be sent to the registrant or the registrant's assignee of record. The notice shall give the name and address of every adverse party and of the adverse party's attorney or other authorized representative, if any, together with the serial number and date of filing and publication of each of the applications, or the registration number and date of issuance of each of the registrations, involved.

[73 FR 67772, Nov. 17, 2008]

§§ 2.94–2.95 [Reserved]

§ 2.96 Issue; burden of proof.

The issue in an interference between applications is normally priority of use, but the rights of the parties to registration may also be determined. The party whose application involved in the interference has the latest filing date is the junior party and has the burden of proof. When there are more than two parties to an interference, a party shall be a junior party to and shall have the burden of proof as against every other party whose application involved in the interference has an earlier filing date. If the involved applications of any parties have the same filing date, the application with the latest date of execution will be deemed to have the latest filing date and that applicant will be the junior party. The issue in an interference between an application and a registration shall be the same, but in the event the final decision is adverse to the registrant, a registration to the applicant will not be authorized so long as the interfering registration remains on the register.

[48 FR 23135, May 23, 1983; 48 FR 27225, June 14, 1983]

§ 2.97 [Reserved]

§ 2.98 Adding party to interference.

A party may be added to an interference only upon petition to the Director by that party. If an application which is or might be the subject of a petition for addition to an interference is not added, the examiner may suspend action on the application pending termination of the interference proceeding.

[48 FR 23135, May 23, 1983]

§ 2.99 Application to register as concurrent user.

(a) An application for registration as a lawful concurrent user will be examined in the same manner as other applications for registration.

(b) If it appears that the applicant is entitled to have the mark registered, subject to a concurrent use proceeding, the mark will be published in the Official Gazette as provided by § 2.80.

(c) If no opposition is filed, or if all oppositions that are filed are dismissed or withdrawn, the Trademark Trial and Appeal Board will send a notification to the applicant for concurrent use registration (plaintiff) and to each applicant, registrant or user specified as a concurrent user in the application (defendants). The notification for each defendant shall state the name and address of the plaintiff and of the plaintiff's attorney or other authorized representative, if any, together with the serial number and filing date of the application. If a party has provided the Office with an e-mail address, the notification may be transmitted via e-mail.

(d)(1) Within ten days from the date of the Board's notification, the applicant for concurrent use registration must serve copies of its application, specimens and drawing on each applicant, registrant or user specified as a concurrent user in the application for registration, as directed by the Board. If any service copy is returned to the concurrent use applicant as undeliverable, the concurrent use applicant must notify the Board within ten days of receipt of the returned copy.

(2) An answer to the notice is not required in the case of an applicant or registrant whose application or registration is specified as a concurrent user in the application, but a statement, if desired, may be filed within forty days after the issuance of the notice; in the case of any other party specified as a concurrent user in the application, an answer must be filed within forty days after the issuance of the notice.

(3) If an answer, when required, is not filed, judgment will be entered precluding the specified user from claiming any right more extensive than that acknowledged in the application(s) for concurrent use registration, but the applicant(s) will remain with the burden of proving entitlement to registration(s).

(e) The applicant for a concurrent use registration has the burden of proving entitlement thereto. If there are two or more applications for concurrent use registration involved in a proceeding, the party whose application has the latest filing date is the junior party. A party whose application has a filing date between the filing dates of the earliest involved application and the latest involved application is a junior party to every party whose involved application has an earlier filing date. If any applications have the same filing date, the application with the latest date of execution will be deemed to have the latest filing date and that applicant will be the junior party. A person specified as an excepted user in a concurrent use application but who has not filed an application shall be considered a party senior to every party that has an application involved in the proceeding.

(f) When a concurrent use registration is sought on the basis that a court of competent jurisdiction has finally determined that the parties are entitled to use the same or similar marks in commerce, a concurrent use registration proceeding will not be instituted if all of the following conditions are fulfilled:

(1) The applicant is entitled to registration subject only to the concurrent lawful use of a party to the court proceeding; and

(2) The court decree specifies the rights of the parties; and

(3) A true copy of the court decree is submitted to the examiner; and

(4) The concurrent use application complies fully and exactly with the court decree; and

(5) The excepted use specified in the concurrent use application does not involve a registration, or any involved registration has been restricted by the Director in accordance with the court decree.

If any of the conditions specified in this paragraph is not satisfied, a concurrent use registration proceeding shall be prepared and instituted as provided in paragraphs (a) through (e) of this section.

(g) Registrations and applications to register on the Supplemental Register and registrations under the Act of 1920 are not subject to concurrent use registration proceedings. Applications under section 1(b) of the Act of 1946 are subject to concurrent use registration proceedings only after the applicant files an acceptable allegation of use under § 2.76 or § 2.88. Applications based solely on section 44 or section 66(a) of the Act are not subject to concurrent use registration proceedings.

(h) The Trademark Trial and Appeal Board will consider and determine concurrent use rights only in the context of a concurrent use registration proceeding.

[48 FR 23135, May 23, 1983; 48 FR 27225, 27226, June 14, 1983, as amended at 54 FR 37596, Sept. 11, 1989; 72 FR 42258, Aug. 1, 2007; 73 FR 67772, Nov. 17, 2008]

OPPOSITION

AUTHORITY: Secs. 2.101 to 2.106 also issued under secs. 13, 17, 60 Stat. 433, 434; 15 U.S.C. 1063, 1067.

§ 2.101 Filing an opposition.

(a) An opposition proceeding is commenced by filing in the Office a timely notice of opposition with the required fee. The notice must include proof of service on the applicant, or its attorney or domestic representative of record, at the correspondence address of record in the Office, as detailed in §§ 2.101(b) and 2.119.

(b) Any person who believes that he, she or it would be damaged by the registration of a mark on the Principal Register may file an opposition addressed to the Trademark Trial and Appeal Board and must serve a copy of the opposition, including any exhibits, on the attorney of record for the applicant or, if there is no attorney, on the applicant or on the applicant's domestic representative, if one has been appointed, at the correspondence address of record in the Office. The opposer must include with the opposition proof of service pursuant to § 2.119 at the correspondence address of record in the Office. If any service copy of the opposition is returned to the opposer as undeliverable, the opposer must notify the Board within ten days of receipt of the returned copy. The opposition need not be verified, but must be signed by the opposer or the opposer's attorney, as specified in § 11.1 of this chapter, or other authorized representative, as specified in § 11.14(b) of this chapter. Electronic signatures pursuant to § 2.193(c) are required for oppositions filed through ESTTA under paragraphs (b)(1) or (2) of this section.

(1) An opposition to an application based on section 1 or 44 of the Act must be filed either on paper or through ESTTA.

(2) An opposition to an application based on section 66(a) of the Act must be filed through ESTTA.

(c) The opposition must be filed within thirty days after publication (§ 2.80) of the application being opposed or within an extension of time (§ 2.102) for filing an opposition.

(d)(1) The opposition must be accompanied by the required fee for each party joined as opposer for each class in the application for which registration is opposed (*see* § 2.6).

(2) An otherwise timely opposition will not be accepted via ESTTA unless the opposition is accompanied by a fee that is sufficient to pay in full for each named party opposer to oppose the registration of a mark in each class specified in the opposition.

(3) If an otherwise timely opposition is submitted on paper, the following is

applicable if less than all required fees are submitted:

(i) If the opposition is accompanied by no fee or a fee insufficient to pay for one person to oppose the registration of a mark in at least one class, the opposition will be refused.

(ii) If the opposition is accompanied by fees sufficient to pay for one person to oppose registration in at least one class, but fees are insufficient to oppose registration in all the classes in the application, and the particular class or classes against which the opposition is filed is not specified, the opposition will be presumed to be against the class or classes in ascending numerical order, including only the number of classes in the application for which sufficient fees have been submitted.

(iii) If persons are joined as party opposers, each must submit a fee for each class for which opposition is sought. If the fees submitted are sufficient to pay for one person to oppose registration in at least one class, but are insufficient for each named party opposer, the first-named party will be presumed to be the party opposer. Additional parties will be deemed to be party opposers only to the extent that the fees submitted are sufficient to pay the fee due for each party opposer. If persons are joined as party opposers against a multiple class application, the fees submitted are insufficient, and no specification of opposers and classes is made at the time the party is joined, the fees submitted will be applied first on behalf of the first-named opposer against as many of the classes in the application as the submitted fees are sufficient to pay. Any excess will be applied on behalf of the second-named party to the opposition against the classes in the application in ascending numerical order.

(4) The filing date of an opposition is the date of receipt in the Office of the notice of opposition, with proof of service on the applicant, or its attorney or domestic representative of record, if one has been appointed, at the correspondence address of record in the Office, and the required fee, unless the notice is filed in accordance with § 2.198.

[68 FR 55765, Sept. 26, 2003, as amended at 72 FR 42258, Aug. 1, 2007; 73 FR 47685, Aug. 14, 2008; 74 FR 54909, Oct. 26, 2009]

§ 2.102 Extension of time for filing an opposition.

(a) Any person who believes that he, she or it would be damaged by the registration of a mark on the Principal Register may file in the Office a written request, addressed to the Trademark Trial and Appeal Board, to extend the time for filing an opposition. The written request need not be verified, but must be signed by the potential opposer or by the potential opposer's attorney, as specified in § 11.1 of this chapter, or authorized representative, as specified in § 11.14(b) of this chapter. Electronic signatures pursuant to § 2.193(c) are required for electronically filed extension requests.

(1) A written request to extend the time for filing an opposition to an application filed under section 1 or 44 of the Act must be filed either on paper or through ESTTA.

(2) A written request to extend the time for filing an opposition to an application filed under section 66(a) of the Act must be filed through ESTTA.

(b) A written request to extend the time for filing an opposition must identify the potential opposer with reasonable certainty. Any opposition filed during an extension of time should be in the name of the person to whom the extension was granted. An opposition may be accepted if the person in whose name the extension was requested was misidentified through mistake or if the opposition is filed in the name of a person in privity with the person who requested and was granted the extension of time.

(c) The time for filing an opposition shall not be extended beyond 180 days from the date of publication. Any request to extend the time for filing an opposition must be filed before thirty days have expired from the date of publication or before the expiration of a previously granted extension of time, as appropriate. Requests to extend the time for filing an opposition must be filed as follows:

(1) A person may file a first request for either a thirty-day extension of time, which will be granted upon request, or a ninety-day extension of time, which will be granted only for good cause shown.

(2) If a person was granted a thirty-day extension of time, that person may file a request for an additional sixty-day extension of time, which will be granted only for good cause shown.

(3) After receiving one or two extensions of time totaling ninety days, a person may file one final request for an extension of time for an additional sixty days. The Board will grant this request only upon written consent or stipulation signed by the applicant or its authorized representative, or a written request by the potential opposer or its authorized representative stating that the applicant or its authorized representative has consented to the request, or a showing of extraordinary circumstances. No further extensions of time to file an opposition will be granted under any circumstances.

[68 FR 55765, Sept. 26, 2003, as amended at 73 FR 47685, Aug. 14, 2008; 74 FR 54909, Oct. 26, 2009]

§ 2.104 Contents of opposition.

(a) The opposition must set forth a short and plain statement showing why the opposer believes he, she or it would be damaged by the registration of the opposed mark and state the grounds for opposition.

(b) Oppositions to different applications owned by the same party may be joined in a consolidated opposition when appropriate, but the required fee must be included for each party joined as opposer for each class in which registration is opposed in each application against which the opposition is filed.

[54 FR 34897, Aug. 22, 1989, as amended at 68 FR 55766, Sept. 26, 2003]

§ 2.105 Notification to parties of opposition proceeding(s).

(a) When an opposition in proper form (see §§ 2.101 and 2.104), with proof of service in accordance with § 2.101(b), has been filed and the correct fee has been submitted, the Trademark Trial and Appeal Board shall prepare a notification, which shall identify the title and number of the proceeding and the application involved and shall designate a time, not less than thirty days from the mailing date of the notification, within which an answer must be filed. If a party has provided the Office with an e-mail address, the notification may be transmitted via e-mail.

(b) The Board shall forward a copy of the notification to opposer, as follows:

(1) If the opposition is transmitted by an attorney, or a written power of attorney is filed, the Board will send the notification to the attorney transmitting the opposition or to the attorney designated in the power of attorney, provided that the person is an "attorney" as defined in § 11.1 of this chapter.

(2) If opposer is not represented by an attorney in the opposition, but opposer has appointed a domestic representative, the Board will send the notification to the domestic representative, unless opposer designates in writing another correspondence address.

(3) If opposer is not represented by an attorney in the opposition, and no domestic representative has been appointed, the Board will send the notification directly to opposer, unless opposer designates in writing another correspondence address.

(c) The Board shall forward a copy of the notification to applicant, as follows:

(1) If the opposed application contains a clear indication that the application is being prosecuted by an attorney, as defined in § 11.1 of this chapter, the Board shall send the documents described in this section to applicant's attorney.

(2) If the opposed application is not being prosecuted by an attorney but a domestic representative has been appointed, the Board will send the documents described in this section to the domestic representative, unless applicant designates in writing another correspondence address.

(3) If the opposed application is not being prosecuted by an attorney, and no domestic representative has been appointed, the Board will send the documents described in this section directly to applicant, unless applicant

designates in writing another correspondence address.

[68 FR 55766, Sept. 26, 2003, as amended at 72 FR 42258, Aug. 1, 2007; 73 FR 47685, Aug. 14, 2008]

§2.106 Answer.

(a) If no answer is filed within the time set, the opposition may be decided as in case of default.

(b)(1) An answer shall state in short and plain terms the applicant's defenses to each claim asserted and shall admit or deny the averments upon which the opposer relies. If the applicant is without knowledge or information sufficient to form a belief as to the truth of an averment, applicant shall so state and this will have the effect of a denial. Denials may take any of the forms specified in Rule 8(b) of the Federal Rules of Civil Procedure. An answer may contain any defense, including the affirmative defenses of unclean hands, laches, estoppel, acquiescence, fraud, mistake, prior judgment, or any other matter constituting an avoidance or affirmative defense. When pleading special matters, the Federal Rules of Civil Procedure shall be followed. A reply to an affirmative defense need not be filed. When a defense attacks the validity of a registration pleaded in the opposition, paragraph (b)(2) of this section shall govern. A pleaded registration is a registration identified by number and date of issuance in an original notice of opposition or in any amendment thereto made under Rule 15, Federal Rules of Civil Procedure.

(2)(i) A defense attacking the validity of any one or more of the registrations pleaded in the opposition shall be a compulsory counterclaim if grounds for such counterclaim exist at the time when the answer is filed. If grounds for a counterclaim are known to the applicant when the answer to the opposition is filed, the counterclaim shall be pleaded with or as part of the answer. If grounds for a counterclaim are learned during the course of the opposition proceeding, the counterclaim shall be pleaded promptly after the grounds therefor are learned. A counterclaim need not be filed if it is the subject of another proceeding between the same parties or anyone in privity therewith.

(ii) An attack on the validity of a registration pleaded by an opposer will not be heard unless a counterclaim or separate petition is filed to seek the cancellation of such registration.

(iii) The provisions of §§2.111 through 2.115, inclusive, shall be applicable to counterclaims. A time, not less than thirty days, will be designated within which an answer to the counterclaim must be filed.

(iv) The times for pleading, discovery, testimony, briefs or oral argument will be reset or extended when necessary, upon motion by a party, to enable a party fully to present or meet a counterclaim or separate petition for cancellation of a registration.

(c) The opposition may be withdrawn without prejudice before the answer is filed. After the answer is filed, the opposition may not be withdrawn without prejudice except with the written consent of the applicant or the applicant's attorney or other authorized representative.

[30 FR 13193, Oct. 16, 1965, as amended at 46 FR 6940, Jan. 22, 1981; 48 FR 23136, May 23, 1983; 54 FR 34897, Aug. 22, 1989]

§2.107 Amendment of pleadings in an opposition proceeding.

(a) Pleadings in an opposition proceeding against an application filed under section 1 or 44 of the Act may be amended in the same manner and to the same extent as in a civil action in a United States district court, except that, after the close of the time period for filing an opposition including any extension of time for filing an opposition, an opposition may not be amended to add to the goods or services opposed.

(b) Pleadings in an opposition proceeding against an application filed under section 66(a) of the Act may be amended in the same manner and to the same extent as in a civil action in a United States district court, except that, once filed, the opposition may not be amended to add to the grounds for opposition or to add to the goods or services subject to opposition.

[68 FR 55766, Sept. 26, 2003]

CANCELLATION

AUTHORITY: Secs. 2.111 to 2.114 also issued under secs. 14, 17, 24, 60 Stat. 433, 434, 436; 15 U.S.C. 1064, 1067, 1092.

§ 2.111 Filing petition for cancellation.

(a) A cancellation proceeding is commenced by filing in the Office a timely petition for cancellation with the required fee. The petition must include proof of service on the owner of record for the registration, or the owner's domestic representative of record, at the correspondence address of record in the Office, as detailed in §§ 2.111(b) and 2.119.

(b) Any person who believes that he, she or it is or will be damaged by a registration may file a petition, addressed to the Trademark Trial and Appeal Board, for cancellation of the registration in whole or in part. Petitioner must serve a copy of the petition, including any exhibits, on the owner of record for the registration, or on the owner's domestic representative of record, if one has been appointed, at the correspondence address of record in the Office. The petitioner must include with the petition for cancellation proof of service, pursuant to § 2.119, on the owner of record, or on the owner's domestic representative of record, if one has been appointed, at the correspondence address of record in the Office. If any service copy of the petition for cancellation is returned to the petitioner as undeliverable, the petitioner must notify the Board within ten days of receipt of the returned copy. The petition for cancellation need not be verified, but must be signed by the petitioner or the petitioner's attorney, as specified in § 11.1 of this chapter, or other authorized representative, as specified in § 11.14(b) of this chapter. Electronic signatures pursuant to § 2.193(c) are required for petitions submitted electronically via ESTTA. The petition for cancellation may be filed at any time in the case of registrations on the Supplemental Register or under the Act of 1920, or registrations under the Act of 1881 or the Act of 1905 which have not been published under section 12(c) of the Act, or on any ground specified in section 14(3) or (5) of the Act. In all other cases, the petition for cancellation and the required fee must be filed within five years from the date of registration of the mark under the Act or from the date of publication under section 12(c) of the Act.

(c)(1) The petition for cancellation must be accompanied by the required fee for each party joined as petitioner for each class in the registration for which cancellation is sought (*see* § 2.6).

(2) An otherwise timely petition for cancellation will not be accepted via ESTTA unless the petition for cancellation is accompanied by a fee that is sufficient to pay in full for each named party petitioner to petition for cancellation of the registration of a mark in each class specified in the petition for cancellation.

(3) If an otherwise timely petition for cancellation is submitted on paper, the following is applicable if less than all required fees are submitted:

(i) If the petition for cancellation is accompanied by no fee or a fee insufficient to pay for one person to petition for cancellation against at least one class in the registration, the petition for cancellation will be refused.

(ii) If the petition for cancellation is accompanied by fees sufficient to pay for one person to petition for cancellation against at least one class in the registration, but fees are insufficient for a petition for cancellation against all the classes in the registration, and the particular class or classes against which the petition for cancellation is filed is not specified, the petition for cancellation will be presumed to be against the class or classes in ascending numerical order, including only the number of classes in the registration for which sufficient fees have been submitted.

(iii) If persons are joined as party petitioners, each must submit a fee for each class for which cancellation is sought. If the fees submitted are sufficient to pay for one person to petition for cancellation of the registration in at least one class but are insufficient for each named party petitioner, the first-named party will be presumed to be the party petitioner. Additional parties will be deemed to be party petitioners only to the extent that the fees submitted are sufficient to pay the fee due for each party petitioner. If persons are joined as party petitioners against a multiple class registration, the fees submitted are insufficient, and no specification of parties and classes is made at the time the party is joined, the fees submitted will be applied first on behalf of the first-named petitioner against as many of the classes in the registration as the submitted fees are sufficient to pay. Any excess will be applied on behalf of the second-named party to the cancellation against the classes in the registration in ascending numerical order.

(4) The filing date of a petition for cancellation is the date of receipt in the Office of the petition for cancellation, with proof of service on the owner of record, or on the owner's domestic representative, if one has been appointed, at the correspondence address of record in the Office, and with the required fee, unless the petition is filed in accordance with § 2.198.

[68 FR 55766, Sept. 26, 2003, as amended at 72 FR 42258, Aug. 1, 2007; 73 FR 47686, Aug. 14, 2008; 74 FR 54909, Oct. 26, 2009]

§ 2.112 Contents of petition for cancellation.

(a) The petition for cancellation must set forth a short and plain statement showing why the petitioner believes he, she or it is or will be damaged by the registration, state the ground for cancellation, and indicate, to the best of petitioner's knowledge, the name and address of the current owner of the registration.

(b) When appropriate, petitions for cancellation of different registrations owned by the same party may be joined in a consolidated petition for cancellation. The required fee must be included for each party joined as a petitioner for each class sought to be cancelled in each registration against which the petition for cancellation is filed.

[68 FR 55767, Sept. 26, 2003]

§ 2.113 Notification to parties of cancellation proceeding.

(a) When a petition for cancellation in proper form (see §§ 2.111 and 2.112), with proof of service in accordance with § 2.111(b), has been filed and the correct fee has been submitted, the Trademark Trial and Appeal Board shall prepare a notification which shall identify the title and number of the proceeding and the registration(s) involved and shall designate a time, not less than thirty days from the mailing date of the notification, within which an answer must be filed. If a party has provided the Office with an e-mail address, the notification may be transmitted via e-mail.

(b) The Board shall forward a copy of the notification to petitioner, as follows:

(1) If the petition for cancellation is transmitted by an attorney, or a written power of attorney is filed, the Board will send the notification to the attorney transmitting the petition for cancellation or to the attorney designated in the power of attorney, provided that person is an "attorney" as defined in § 11.1 of this chapter.

(2) If petitioner is not represented by an attorney in the cancellation proceeding, but petitioner has appointed a domestic representative, the Board will send the notification to the domestic representative, unless petitioner designates in writing another correspondence address.

(3) If petitioner is not represented by an attorney in the cancellation proceeding, and no domestic representative has been appointed, the Board will send the notification directly to petitioner, unless petitioner designates in writing another correspondence address.

(c) The Board shall forward a copy of the notification to the respondent (see § 2.118). The respondent shall be the party shown by the records of the Office to be the current owner of the registration(s) sought to be cancelled, except that the Board, in its discretion, may join or substitute as respondent a party who makes a showing of a current ownership interest in such registration(s).

(d) When the party alleged by the petitioner, pursuant to § 2.112(a), as the current owner of the registration(s) is not the record owner, a courtesy copy of the petition for cancellation shall be forwarded with a copy of the notification to the alleged current owner. The alleged current owner may file a motion to be joined or substituted as respondent.

[68 FR 55767, Sept. 26, 2003, as amended at 72 FR 42259, Aug. 1, 2007; 73 FR 47686, Aug. 14, 2008]

§ 2.114 Answer.

(a) If no answer is filed within the time set, the petition may be decided as in case of default.

(b)(1) An answer shall state in short and plain terms the respondent's defenses to each claim asserted and shall admit or deny the averments upon which the petitioner relies. If the respondent is without knowledge or information sufficient to form a belief as to the truth of an averment, respondent shall so state and this will have the effect of a denial. Denials may take any of the forms specified in Rule 8(b) of the Federal Rules of Civil Procedure. An answer may contain any defense, including the affirmative defenses of unclean hands, laches, estoppel, acquiescence, fraud, mistake, prior judgment, or any other matter constituting an avoidance or affirmative defense. When pleading special matters, the Federal Rules of Civil Procedure shall be followed. A reply to an affirmative defense need not be filed. When a defense attacks the validity of a registration pleaded in the petition, paragraph (b)(2) of this section shall govern. A pleaded registration is a registration identified by number and date of issuance in an original petition for cancellation or in any amendment thereto made under Rule 15, Federal Rules of Civil Procedure.

(2)(i) A defense attacking the validity of any one or more of the registrations pleaded in the petition shall be a compulsory counterclaim if grounds for such counterclaim exist at the time when the answer if filed. If grounds for a counterclaim are known to respondent when the answer to the petition is filed, the counterclaim shall be pleaded with or as part of the answer. If grounds for a counterclaim are learned during the course of the cancellation proceeding, the counterclaim shall be pleaded promptly after the grounds therefor are learned. A counterclaim need not be filed if it is the subject of another proceeding between the same parties or anyone in privity therewith.

(ii) An attack on the validity of a registration pleaded by a petitioner for cancellation will not be heard unless a counterclaim or separate petition is filed to seek the cancellation of such registration.

(iii) The provisions of §§ 2.111 through 2.115, inclusive, shall be applicable to counterclaims. A time, not less than thirty days, will be designated within which an answer to the counterclaim must be filed.

(iv) The times for pleading, discovery, testimony, briefs, or oral argument will be reset or extended when necessary, upon motion by a party, to enable a party fully to present or meet a counterclaim or separate petition for cancellation of a registration.

(c) The petition for cancellation may be withdrawn without prejudice before the answer is filed. After the answer is filed, the petition may not be withdrawn without prejudice except with the written consent of the registrant or the registrant's attorney or other authorized representative.

[30 FR 13193, Oct. 16, 1965, as amended at 46 FR 6940, Jan. 22, 1981; 46 FR 11548, Feb. 9, 1981; 51 FR 28710, Aug. 11, 1986; 54 FR 34898, Aug. 22, 1989]

§ 2.115 Amendment of pleadings in a cancellation proceeding.

Pleadings in a cancellation proceeding may be amended in the same manner and to the same extent as in a civil action in a United States district court.

[48 FR 23136, May 23, 1983]

Procedure in *Inter Partes* Proceedings

Authority: Secs. 2.116 to 2.136 also issued under sec. 17, 60 Stat. 434; 15 U.S.C. 1067.

§ 2.116 Federal Rules of Civil Procedure.

(a) Except as otherwise provided, and wherever applicable and appropriate, procedure and practice in *inter partes* proceedings shall be governed by the Federal Rules of Civil Procedure.

(b) The opposer in an opposition proceeding or the petitioner in a cancellation proceeding shall be in the position of plaintiff, and the applicant in an opposition proceeding or the respondent in a cancellation proceeding shall be in the position of defendant. A party that is a junior party in an interference proceeding or in a concurrent use registration proceeding shall be in the position of plaintiff against every party that is senior, and the party that is a senior party in an interference proceeding or in a concurrent use registration proceeding shall be a defendant against every party that is junior.

(c) The opposition or the petition for cancellation and the answer correspond to the complaint and answer in a court proceeding.

(d) The assignment of testimony periods corresponds to setting a case for trial in court proceedings.

(e) The taking of depositions during the assigned testimony periods corresponds to the trial in court proceedings.

(f) Oral hearing corresponds to oral summation in court proceedings.

(g) The Trademark Trial and Appeal Board's standard protective order is applicable during disclosure, discovery and at trial in all opposition, cancellation, interference and concurrent use registration proceedings, unless the parties, by stipulation approved by the Board, agree to an alternative order, or a motion by a party to use an alternative order is granted by the Board. The standard protective order is available at the Office's Web site, or upon request, a copy will be provided. No material disclosed or produced by a party, presented at trial, or filed with the Board, including motions or briefs which discuss such material, shall be treated as confidential or shielded from public view unless designated as protected under the Board's standard protective order, or under an alternative order stipulated to by the parties and approved by the Board, or under an order submitted by motion of a party granted by the Board.

[30 FR 13193, Oct. 16, 1965. Redesignated and amended at 37 FR 7606, Apr. 18, 1972; 48 FR 23136, May 23, 1983; 72 FR 42259, Aug. 1, 2007]

§2.117 Suspension of proceedings.

(a) Whenever it shall come to the attention of the Trademark Trial and Appeal Board that a party or parties to a pending case are engaged in a civil action or another Board proceeding which may have a bearing on the case, proceedings before the Board may be suspended until termination of the civil action or the other Board proceeding.

(b) Whenever there is pending before the Board both a motion to suspend and a motion which is potentially dispositive of the case, the potentially dispositive motion may be decided before the question of suspension is considered regardless of the order in which the motions were filed.

(c) Proceedings may also be suspended, for good cause, upon motion or a stipulation of the parties approved by the Board.

[48 FR 23136, May 23, 1983, as amended at 63 FR 48097, Sept. 9, 1998]

§2.118 Undelivered Office notices.

When a notice sent by the Office to any registrant or applicant is returned to the Office undelivered, additional notice may be given by publication in the Official Gazette for the period of time prescribed by the Director.

[72 FR 42259, Aug. 1, 2007]

§2.119 Service and signing of papers.

(a) Every paper filed in the United States Patent and Trademark Office in *inter partes* cases, including notices of appeal, must be served upon the other parties. Proof of such service must be made before the paper will be considered by the Office. A statement signed by the attorney or other authorized representative, attached to or appearing on the original paper when filed, clearly stating the date and manner in which service was made will be accepted as prima facie proof of service.

(b) Service of papers must be on the attorney or other authorized representative of the party if there be such or on the party if there is no attorney or other authorized representative, and may be made in any of the following ways:

(1) By delivering a copy of the paper to the person served;

(2) By leaving a copy at the usual place of business of the person served, with someone in the person's employment;

(3) When the person served has no usual place of business, by leaving a copy at the person's residence, with a member of the person's family over 14 years of age and of discretion;

(4) Transmission by the "Express Mail Post Office to Addressee" service of the United States Postal Service or by first-class mail, which may also be certified or registered;

(5) Transmission by overnight courier.

Whenever it shall be satisfactorily shown to the Director that none of the above modes of obtaining service or serving the paper is practicable, service may be by notice published in the *Official Gazette*.

(6) Electronic transmission when mutually agreed upon by the parties.

(c) When service is made by first-class mail, "Express Mail," or overnight courier, the date of mailing or of delivery to the overnight courier will be considered the date of service. Whenever a party is required to take some action within a prescribed period after the service of a paper upon the party by another party and the paper is served by first-class mail, "Express Mail," or overnight courier, 5 days shall be added to the prescribed period.

(d) If a party to an *inter partes* proceeding is not domiciled in the United States and is not represented by an attorney or other authorized representative located in the United States, the party may designate by document filed in the United States Patent and Trademark Office the name and address of a person residing in the United States on whom may be served notices or process in the proceeding. If the party has appointed a domestic representative, official communications of the United States Patent and Trademark Office will be addressed to the domestic representative unless the proceeding is being prosecuted by an attorney at law or other qualified person duly authorized under §11.14(c) of this subchapter. If the party has not appointed a domestic representative and the proceeding is not being prosecuted by an attorney at law or other qualified person, the Office will send correspondence directly to the party, unless the party designates in writing another address to which correspondence is to be sent. The mere designation of a domestic representative does not authorize the person designated to prosecute the proceeding unless qualified under §11.14(a), or qualified under §11.14(b) and authorized under §2.17(f).

(e) Every paper filed in an *inter partes* proceeding, and every request for an extension of time to file an opposition, must be signed by the party filing it, or by the party's attorney or other authorized representative, but an unsigned paper will not be refused consideration if a signed copy is submitted to the Patent and Trademark Office within the time limit set in the notification of this defect by the Office.

[37 FR 7606, Apr. 18, 1972, as amended at 41 FR 760, Jan. 5, 1976; 54 FR 34898, Aug. 22, 1989; 54 FR 38041, Sept. 14, 1989; 63 FR 48097, Sept. 9, 1998; 67 FR 79523, Dec. 30, 2002; 72 FR 42259, Aug. 1, 2007; 73 FR 47686, Aug. 14, 2008; 74 FR 54909, Oct. 26, 2009]

§2.120 Discovery.

(a) *In general.* (1) Wherever appropriate, the provisions of the Federal Rules of Civil Procedure relating to disclosure and discovery shall apply in opposition, cancellation, interference and concurrent use registration proceedings except as otherwise provided in this section. The provisions of Federal Rule of Civil Procedure 26 relating to required disclosures, the conference of the parties to discuss settlement and to develop a disclosure and discovery plan, the scope, timing and sequence of discovery, protective orders, signing of disclosures and discovery responses, and supplementation of disclosures and discovery responses, are applicable to Board proceedings in modified form, as noted in these rules and as may be detailed in any order instituting an *inter partes* proceeding or subsequent scheduling order. The Board will specify the deadline for a discovery conference, the opening and closing dates for the taking of discovery, and the deadlines within the discovery period for making initial disclosures and expert disclosure. The trial order setting these deadlines and dates will be included with the notice of institution of the proceeding.

(2) The discovery conference shall occur no later than the opening of the discovery period, and the parties must

discuss the subjects set forth in Federal Rule of Civil Procedure 26(f) and any subjects set forth in the Board's institution order. A Board Interlocutory Attorney or Administrative Trademark Judge will participate in the conference upon request of any party made after answer but no later than ten days prior to the deadline for the conference. The participating attorney or judge may expand or reduce the number or nature of subjects to be discussed in the conference as may be deemed appropriate. The discovery period will be set for a period of 180 days. Initial disclosures must be made no later than thirty days after the opening of the discovery period. Disclosure of expert testimony must occur in the manner and sequence provided in Federal Rule of Civil Procedure 26(a)(2), unless alternate directions have been provided by the Board in an institution order or any subsequent order resetting disclosure, discovery or trial dates. If the expert is retained after the deadline for disclosure of expert testimony, the party must promptly file a motion for leave to use expert testimony. Upon disclosure by any party of plans to use expert testimony, whether before or after the deadline for disclosing expert testimony, the Board may issue an order regarding expert discovery and/or set a deadline for any other party to disclose plans to use a rebuttal expert. The parties may stipulate to a shortening of the discovery period. The discovery period may be extended upon stipulation of the parties approved by the Board, or upon motion granted by the Board, or by order of the Board. If a motion for an extension is denied, the discovery period may remain as originally set or as reset. Disclosure deadlines and obligations may be modified upon written stipulation of the parties approved by the Board, or upon motion granted by the Board, or by order of the Board. If a stipulation or motion for modification is denied, disclosure deadlines may remain as originally set or reset and obligations may remain unaltered. The parties are not required to prepare or transmit to the Board a written report outlining their discovery conference discussions, unless the parties have agreed to alter disclosure or discovery obligations set forth by these rules or applicable Federal Rules of Civil Procedure, or unless directed to file such a report by a participating Board Interlocutory Attorney or Administrative Trademark Judge.

(3) A party must make its initial disclosures prior to seeking discovery, absent modification of this requirement by a stipulation of the parties approved by the Board, or a motion granted by the Board, or by order of the Board. Discovery depositions must be taken, and interrogatories, requests for production of documents and things, and requests for admission must be served, on or before the closing date of the discovery period as originally set or as reset. Responses to interrogatories, requests for production of documents and things, and requests for admission must be served within thirty days from the date of service of such discovery requests. The time to respond may be extended upon stipulation of the parties, or upon motion granted by the Board, or by order of the Board. The resetting of a party's time to respond to an outstanding request for discovery will not result in the automatic rescheduling of the discovery and/or testimony periods; such dates will be rescheduled only upon stipulation of the parties approved by the Board, or upon motion granted by the Board, or by order of the Board.

(b) *Discovery deposition within the United States.* The deposition of a natural person shall be taken in the Federal judicial district where the person resides or is regularly employed or at any place on which the parties agree by stipulation. The responsibility rests wholly with the party taking discovery to secure the attendance of a proposed deponent other than a party or anyone who, at the time set for the taking of the deposition, is an officer, director, or managing agent of a party, or a person designated under Rule 30(b)(6) or Rule 31(a) of the Federal Rules of Civil Procedure. See 35 U.S.C. 24.

(c) *Discovery deposition in foreign countries.* (1) The discovery deposition of a natural person residing in a foreign country who is a party or who, at the time set for the taking of the deposition, is an officer, director, or managing agent of a party, or a person designated under Rule 30(b)(6) or Rule

31(a) of the Federal Rules of Civil Procedure, shall, if taken in a foreign country, be taken in the manner prescribed by § 2.124 unless the Trademark Trial and Appeal Board, upon motion for good cause, orders or the parties stipulate, that the deposition be taken by oral examination.

(2) Whenever a foreign party is or will be, during a time set for discovery, present within the United States or any territory which is under the control and jurisdiction of the United States, such party may be deposed by oral examination upon notice by the party seeking discovery. Whenever a foreign party has or will have, during a time set for discovery, an officer, director, managing agent, or other person who consents to testify on its behalf, present within the United States or any territory which is under the control and jurisdiction of the United States, such officer, director, managing agent, or other person who consents to testify in its behalf may be deposed by oral examination upon notice by the party seeking discovery. The party seeking discovery may have one or more officers, directors, managing agents, or other persons who consent to testify on behalf of the adverse party, designated under Rule 30(b)(6) of the Federal Rules of Civil Procedure. The deposition of a person under this paragraph shall be taken in the Federal judicial district where the witness resides or is regularly employed, or, if the witness neither resides nor is regularly employed in a Federal judicial district, where the witness is at the time of the deposition. This paragraph does not preclude the taking of a discovery deposition of a foreign party by any other procedure provided by paragraph (c)(1) of this section.

(d) *Interrogatories; request for production.* (1) The total number of written interrogatories which a party may serve upon another party pursuant to Rule 33 of the Federal Rules of Civil Procedure, in a proceeding, shall not exceed seventy-five, counting subparts, except that the Trademark Trial and Appeal Board, in its discretion, may allow additional interrogatories upon motion therefor showing good cause, or upon stipulation of the parties, approved by the Board. A motion for leave to serve additional interrogatories must be filed and granted prior to the service of the proposed additional interrogatories and must be accompanied by a copy of the interrogatories, if any, which have already been served by the moving party, and by a copy of the interrogatories proposed to be served. If a party upon which interrogatories have been served believes that the number of interrogatories exceeds the limitation specified in this paragraph, and is not willing to waive this basis for objection, the party shall, within the time for (and instead of) serving answers and specific objections to the interrogatories, serve a general objection on the ground of their excessive number. If the inquiring party, in turn, files a motion to compel discovery, the motion must be accompanied by a copy of the set(s) of the interrogatories which together are said to exceed the limitation, and must otherwise comply with the requirements of paragraph (e) of this section.

(2) The production of documents and things under the provisions of Rule 34 of the Federal Rules of Civil Procedure will be made at the place where the documents and things are usually kept, or where the parties agree, or where and in the manner which the Trademark Trial and Appeal Board, upon motion, orders.

(e) *Motion for an order to compel disclosure or discovery.* (1) If a party fails to make required initial disclosures or expert testimony disclosure, or fails to designate a person pursuant to Rule 30(b)(6) or Rule 31(a) of the Federal Rules of Civil Procedure, or if a party, or such designated person, or an officer, director or managing agent of a party fails to attend a deposition or fails to answer any question propounded in a discovery deposition, or any interrogatory, or fails to produce and permit the inspection and copying of any document or thing, the party entitled to disclosure or seeking discovery may file a motion to compel disclosure, a designation, or attendance at a deposition, or an answer, or production and an opportunity to inspect and copy. A motion to compel initial disclosures or expert testimony disclosure must be filed prior to the close of the discovery period. A motion to compel discovery must be filed prior to the commencement of the first testimony period as originally set or as reset. A motion to compel discovery shall include a copy of the request for designation or of the relevant portion of the discovery deposition; or a copy of the interrogatory with any answer or objection that was made; or a copy of the request for production, any proffer of production or objection to production in response to the request, and a list and brief description of the documents or things that were not produced for inspection and copying. A motion to compel initial disclosures, expert testimony disclosure, or discovery must be supported by a written statement from the moving party that such party or the attorney therefor has made a good faith effort, by conference or correspondence, to resolve with the other party or the attorney therefor the issues presented in the motion but the parties were unable to resolve their differences. If issues raised in the motion are subsequently resolved by agreement of the parties, the moving party should inform the Board in writing of the issues in the motion which no longer require adjudication.

(2) When a party files a motion for an order to compel initial disclosures, expert testimony disclosure, or discovery, the case will be suspended by the Board with respect to all matters not germane to the motion. After the motion is filed and served, no party should file any paper that is not germane to the motion, except as otherwise specified in the Board's suspension order. Nor may any party serve any additional discovery until the period of suspension is lifted or expires by or under order of the Board. The filing of a motion to compel any disclosure or discovery shall not toll the time for a party to comply with any disclosure requirement or to respond to any outstanding discovery requests or to appear for any noticed discovery deposition.

(f) *Motion for a protective order.* Upon motion by a party obligated to make initial disclosures or expert testimony disclosure or from whom discovery is sought, and for good cause, the Trademark Trial and Appeal Board may make any order which justice requires to protect a party from annoyance, embarrassment, oppression, or undue burden or expense, including one or more of the types of orders provided by clauses (1) through (8), inclusive, of Rule 26(c) of the Federal Rules of Civil Procedure. If the motion for a protective order is denied in whole or in part, the Board may, on such conditions (other than an award of expenses to the party prevailing on the motion) as are just, order that any party comply with disclosure obligations or provide or permit discovery.

(g) *Sanctions.* (1) If a party fails to participate in the required discovery conference, or if a party fails to comply with an order of the Trademark Trial and Appeal Board relating to disclosure or discovery, including a protective order, the Board may make any appropriate order, including those provided in Rule 37(b)(2) of the Federal Rules of Civil Procedure, except that the Board will not hold any person in contempt or award expenses to any party. The Board may impose against a party any of the sanctions provided in Rule 37(b)(2) in the event that said party or any attorney, agent, or designated witness of that party fails to comply with a protective order made pursuant to Rule 26(c) of the Federal Rules of Civil Procedure. A motion for sanctions against a party for its failure to participate in the required discovery conference must be filed prior to the deadline for any party to make initial disclosures.

(2) If a party fails to make required initial disclosures or expert testimony disclosure, and such party or the party's attorney or other authorized representative informs the party or parties entitled to receive disclosures that required disclosures will not be made, the Board may make any appropriate order, as specified in paragraph (g)(1) of this section. If a party, or an officer, director, or managing agent of a party, or a person designated under Rule 30(b)(6) or 31(a) of the Federal Rules of Civil Procedure to testify on behalf of a party, fails to attend the party's or person's discovery deposition, after being served with proper notice, or fails to provide any response to a set of interrogatories or to a set of requests for production of documents and

things, and such party or the party's attorney or other authorized representative informs the party seeking discovery that no response will be made thereto, the Board may make any appropriate order, as specified in paragraph (g)(1) of this section.

(h)(1) Any motion by a party to determine the sufficiency of an answer or objection to a request made by that party for an admission must be filed prior to the commencement of the first testimony period, as originally set or as reset. The motion shall include a copy of the request for admission and any exhibits thereto and of the answer or objection. The motion must be supported by a written statement from the moving party that such party or the attorney therefor has made a good faith effort, by conference or correspondence, to resolve with the other party or the attorney therefor the issues presented in the motion and has been unable to reach agreement. If issues raised in the motion are subsequently resolved by agreement of the parties, the moving party should inform the Board in writing of the issues in the motion which no longer require adjudication.

(2) When a party files a motion to determine the sufficiency of an answer or objection to a request for an admission, the case will be suspended by the Board with respect to all matters not germane to the motion. After filing and service of the motion, no party should file any paper that is not germane to the motion, except as otherwise specified in the Board's suspension order. Nor may any party thereafter serve any additional discovery until the period of suspension is lifted or expires by or under order of the Board. The filing of a motion to determine the sufficiency of an answer or objection to a request for admission shall not toll the time for a party to comply with any disclosure requirement or to respond to any outstanding discovery requests or to appear for any noticed discovery deposition.

(i) *Telephone and pretrial conferences.* (1) Whenever it appears to the Trademark Trial and Appeal Board that a stipulation or motion filed in an *inter partes* proceeding is of such nature that its approval or resolution by correspondence is not practical, the Board may, upon its own initiative or upon request made by one or both of the parties, address the stipulation or resolve the motion by telephone conference.

(2) Whenever it appears to the Trademark Trial and Appeal Board that questions or issues arising during the interlocutory phase of an *inter partes* proceeding have become so complex that their resolution by correspondence or telephone conference is not practical and that resolution would likely be facilitated by a conference in person of the parties or their attorneys with an Administrative Trademark Judge or an Interlocutory Attorney of the Board, the Board may, upon its own initiative or upon motion made by one or both of the parties, request that the parties or their attorneys, under circumstances which will not result in undue hardship for any party, meet with the Board at its offices for a disclosure, discovery or pretrial conference.

(j) *Use of discovery deposition, answer to interrogatory, admission or written disclosure.* (1) The discovery deposition of a party or of anyone who at the time of taking the deposition was on officer, director or managing agent of a party, or a person designated by a party pursuant to Rule 30(b)(6) or Rule 31(a) of the Federal Rules of Civil Procedure, may be offered in evidence by an adverse party.

(2) Except as provided in paragraph (j)(1) of this section, the discovery deposition of a witness, whether or not a party, shall not be offered in evidence unless the person whose deposition was taken is, during the testimony period of the party offering the deposition, dead; or out of the United States (unless it appears that the absence of the witness was procured by the party offering the deposition); or unable to testify because of age, illness, infirmity, or imprisonment; or cannot be served with a subpoena to compel attendance at a testimonial deposition; or there is a stipulation by the parties; or upon a showing that such exceptional circumstances exist as to make it desirable, in the interest of justice, to allow the deposition to be used. The use of a discovery deposition by any party under this paragraph will be allowed

only by stipulation of the parties approved by the Trademark Trial and Appeal Board, or by order of the Board on motion, which shall be filed at the time of the purported offer of the deposition in evidence, unless the motion is based upon a claim that such exceptional circumstances exist as to make it desirable, in the interest of justice, to allow the deposition to be used, in which case the motion shall be filed promptly after the circumstances claimed to justify use of the deposition became known.

(3)(i) A discovery deposition, an answer to an interrogatory, an admission to a request for admission, or a written disclosure (but not a disclosed document), which may be offered in evidence under the provisions of paragraph (j) of this section, may be made of record in the case by filing the deposition or any part thereof with any exhibit to the part that is filed, or a copy of the interrogatory and answer thereto with any exhibit made part of the answer, or a copy of the request for admission and any exhibit thereto and the admission (or a statement that the party from which an admission was requested failed to respond thereto), or a copy of the written disclosure, together with a notice of reliance. The notice of reliance and the material submitted thereunder should be filed during the testimony period of the party that files the notice of reliance. An objection made at a discovery deposition by a party answering a question subject to the objection will be considered at final hearing.

(ii) A party that has obtained documents from another party through disclosure or under Rule 34 of the Federal Rules of Civil Procedure may not make the documents of record by notice of reliance alone, except to the extent that they are admissible by notice of reliance under the provisions of § 2.122(e).

(4) If only part of a discovery deposition is submitted and made part of the record by a party, an adverse party may introduce under a notice of reliance any other part of the deposition which should in fairness be considered so as to make not misleading what was offered by the submitting party. A notice of reliance filed by an adverse party must be supported by a written statement explaining why the adverse party needs to rely upon each additional part listed in the adverse party's notice, failing which the Board, in its discretion, may refuse to consider the additional parts.

(5) Written disclosures, an answer to an interrogatory, or an admission to a request for admission, may be submitted and made part of the record only by the receiving or inquiring party except that, if fewer than all of the written disclosures, answers to interrogatories, or fewer than all of the admissions, are offered in evidence by the receiving or inquiring party, the disclosing or responding party may introduce under a notice of reliance any other written disclosures, answers to interrogatories, or any other admissions, which should in fairness be considered so as to make not misleading what was offered by the receiving or inquiring party. The notice of reliance filed by the disclosing or responding party must be supported by a written statement explaining why the disclosing or responding party needs to rely upon each of the additional written disclosures or discovery responses listed in the disclosing or responding party's notice, and absent such statement the Board, in its discretion, may refuse to consider the additional written disclosures or responses.

(6) Paragraph (j) of this section will not be interpreted to preclude reading or use of written disclosures or documents, a discovery deposition, or answer to an interrogatory, or admission as part of the examination or cross-examination of any witness during the testimony period of any party.

(7) When a written disclosure, a discovery deposition, or a part thereof, or an answer to an interrogatory, or an admission, has been made of record by one party in accordance with the provisions of paragraph (j)(3) of this section, it may be referred to by any party for any purpose permitted by the Federal Rules of Evidence.

(8) Written disclosures or disclosed documents, requests for discovery, responses thereto, and materials or depositions obtained through the disclosure or discovery process should not be filed with the Board, except when submitted

with a motion relating to disclosure or discovery, or in support of or in response to a motion for summary judgment, or under a notice of reliance, when permitted, during a party's testimony period.

[48 FR 23136, May 23, 1983, as amended at 54 FR 34898, Aug. 22, 1989; 54 FR 38041, Sept. 14, 1989; 56 FR 46379, Sept. 12, 1991; 56 FR 54917, Oct. 23, 1991; 63 FR 48098, Sept. 9, 1998; 63 FR 52159, Sept. 30, 1998; 72 FR 42259, Aug. 1, 2007]

§2.121 Assignment of times for taking testimony.

(a) The Trademark Trial and Appeal Board will issue a trial order setting a deadline for each party's required pretrial disclosures and assigning to each party its time for taking testimony. No testimony shall be taken except during the times assigned, unless by stipulation of the parties approved by the Board, or upon motion granted by the Board, or by order of the Board. The deadlines for pretrial disclosures and the testimony periods may be rescheduled by stipulation of the parties approved by the Board, or upon motion granted by the Board, or by order of the Board. If a motion to reschedule any pretrial disclosure deadline and/or testimony period is denied, the pretrial disclosure deadline or testimony period and any subsequent remaining periods may remain as set. The resetting of the closing date for discovery will result in the rescheduling of pretrial disclosure deadlines and testimony periods without action by any party.

(b)(1) The Trademark Trial and Appeal Board will schedule a testimony period for the plaintiff to present its case in chief, a testimony period for the defendant to present its case and to meet the case of the plaintiff, and a testimony period for the plaintiff to present evidence in rebuttal.

(2) When there is a counterclaim, or when proceedings have been consolidated and one party is in the position of plaintiff in one of the involved proceedings and in the position of defendant in another of the involved proceedings, or when there is an interference or a concurrent use registration proceeding involving more than two parties, the Board will schedule testimony periods so that each party in the position of plaintiff will have a period for presenting its case in chief against each party in the position of defendant, each party in the position of defendant will have a period for presenting its case and meeting the case of each plaintiff, and each party in the position of plaintiff will have a period for presenting evidence in rebuttal.

(c) A testimony period which is solely for rebuttal will be set for fifteen days. All other testimony periods will be set for thirty days. The periods may be extended by stipulation of the parties approved by the Trademark Trial and Appeal Board, or upon motion granted by the Board, or by order of the Board. If a motion for an extension is denied, the testimony periods may remain as set.

(d) When parties stipulate to the rescheduling of a deadline for pretrial disclosures and subsequent testimony periods or to the rescheduling of the closing date for discovery and the rescheduling of subsequent deadlines for pretrial disclosures and testimony periods, a stipulation presented in the form used in a trial order, signed by the parties, or a motion in said form signed by one party and including a statement that every other party has agreed thereto, shall be submitted to the Board.

(e) A party need not disclose, prior to its testimony period, any notices of reliance it intends to file during its testimony period. However, no later than fifteen days prior to the opening of each testimony period, or on such alternate schedule as may be provided by order of the Board, the party scheduled to present evidence must disclose the name and, if not previously provided, the telephone number and address of each witness from whom it intends to take testimony, or may take testimony if the need arises, general identifying information about the witness, such as relationship to any party, including job title if employed by a party, or, if neither a party nor related to a party, occupation and job title, a general summary or list of subjects on which the witness is expected to testify, and a general summary or list of the types of documents and things which may be introduced as exhibits during the testimony of the witness. Pretrial disclosure of a witness under this subsection does not substitute for issuance of a proper notice of examination under § 2.123(c) or § 2.124(b). If a party does not plan to take testimony from any witnesses, it must so state in its pretrial disclosure. When a party fails to make required pretrial disclosures, any adverse party or parties may have remedy by way of a motion to the Board to delay or reset any subsequent pretrial disclosure deadlines and/or testimony periods.

[48 FR 23138, May 23, 1983; 48 FR 27226, June 14, 1983, as amended at 54 FR 34899, Aug. 22, 1989; 63 FR 48099, Sept. 9, 1998; 68 FR 55767, Sept. 26, 2003; 72 FR 42262, Aug. 1, 2007]

§ 2.122 Matters in evidence.

(a) *Rules of evidence.* The rules of evidence for proceedings before the Trademark Trial and Appeal Board are the Federal Rules of Evidence, the relevant provisions of the Federal Rules of Civil Procedure, the relevant provisions of Title 28 of the United States Code, and the provisions of this part of title 37 of the Code of Federal Regulations.

(b) *Application files.* (1) The file of each application or registration specified in a notice of interference, of each application or registration specified in the notice of a concurrent use registration proceeding, of the application against which a notice of opposition is filed, or of each registration against which a petition or counterclaim for cancellation is filed forms part of the record of the proceeding without any action by the parties and reference may be made to the file for any relevant and competent purpose.

(2) The allegation in an application for registration, or in a registration, of a date of use is not evidence on behalf of the applicant or registrant; a date of use of a mark must be established by competent evidence. Specimens in the file of an application for registration, or in the file of a registration, are not evidence on behalf of the applicant or registrant unless identified and introduced in evidence as exhibits during the period for the taking of testimony.

(c) *Exhibits to pleadings.* Except as provided in paragraph (d)(1) of this section, an exhibit attached to a pleading is not evidence on behalf of the party to whose pleading the exhibit is attached unless identified and introduced in evidence as an exhibit during the period for the taking of testimony.

(d) *Registrations.* (1) A registration of the opposer or petitioner pleaded in an opposition or petition to cancel will be received in evidence and made part of the record if the opposition or petition is accompanied by an original or photocopy of the registration prepared and issued by the United States Patent and Trademark Office showing both the current status of and current title to the registration, or by a current printout of information from the electronic database records of the USPTO showing the current status and title of the registration. For the cost of a copy of a registration showing status and title, see § 2.6(b)(4).

(2) A registration owned by any party to a proceeding may be made of record in the proceeding by that party by appropriate identification and introduction during the taking of testimony or by filing a notice of reliance, which shall be accompanied by a copy (original or photocopy) of the registration prepared and issued by the Patent and Trademark Office showing both the current status of and current title to the registration. The notice of reliance shall be filed during the testimony period of the party that files the notice.

(e) *Printed publications and official records.* Printed publications, such as books and periodicals, available to the general public in libraries or of general circulation among members of the public or that segment of the public which is relevant under an issue in a proceeding, and official records, if the publication of official record is competent evidence and relevant to an issue, may be introduced in evidence by filing a notice of reliance on the material being offered. The notice shall specify the printed publication (including information sufficient to identify the source and the date of the publication) or the official record and the pages to be read; indicate generally the relevance of the material being offered; and be accompanied by the official record or a copy thereof whose authenticity is established under the Federal Rules of Evidence, or by the printed publication or a copy of the relevant portion thereof. A copy of an official record of the Patent and Trademark

Office need not be certified to be offered in evidence. The notice of reliance shall be filed during the testimony period of the party that files the notice.

(f) *Testimony from other proceedings.* By order of the Trademark Trial and Appeal Board, on motion, testimony taken in another proceeding, or testimony taken in a suit or action in a court, between the same parties or those in privity may be used in a proceeding, so far as relevant and material, subject, however, to the right of any adverse party to recall or demand the recall for examination or cross-examination of any witness whose prior testimony has been offered and to rebut the testimony.

[48 FR 23138, May 23, 1983, as amended at 54 FR 34899, Aug. 22, 1989; 54 FR 38041, Sept. 14, 1989; 63 FR 48099, Sept. 9, 1998; 72 FR 42262, Aug. 1, 2007]

§ 2.123 Trial testimony in *inter partes* cases.

(a)(1) The testimony of witnesses in *inter partes* cases may be taken by depositions upon oral examination as provided by this section or by depositions upon written questions as provided by § 2.124. If a party serves notice of the taking of a testimonial deposition upon written questions of a witness who is, or will be at the time of the deposition, present within the United States or any territory which is under the control and jurisdiction of the United States, any adverse party may, within fifteen days from the date of service of the notice, file a motion with the Trademark Trial and Appeal Board, for good cause, for an order that the deposition be taken by oral examination.

(2) A testimonial deposition taken in a foreign country shall be taken by deposition upon written questions as provided by § 2.124, unless the Board, upon motion for good cause, orders that the deposition be taken by oral examination, or the parties so stipulate.

(b) *Stipulations.* If the parties so stipulate in writing, depositions may be taken before any person authorized to administer oaths, at any place, upon any notice, and in any manner, and when so taken may be used like other depositions. By written agreement of the parties, the testimony of any witness or witnesses of any party, may be submitted in the form of an affidavit by such witness or witnesses. The parties may stipulate in writing what a particular witness would testify to if called, or the facts in the case of any party may be stipulated in writing.

(c) *Notice of examination of witnesses.* Before the depositions of witnesses shall be taken by a party, due notice in writing shall be given to the opposing party or parties, as provided in § 2.119(b), of the time when and place where the depositions will be taken, of the cause or matter in which they are to be used, and the name and address of each witness to be examined; if the name of a witness is not known, a general description sufficient to identify the witness or the particular class or group to which the witness belongs, together with a satisfactory explanation, may be given instead. Depositions may be noticed for any reasonable time and place in the United States. A deposition may not be noticed for a place in a foreign country except as provided in paragraph (a)(2) of this section. No party shall take depositions in more than one place at the same time, nor so nearly at the same time that reasonable opportunity for travel from one place of examination to the other is not available.

(d) *Persons before whom depositions may be taken.* Depositions may be taken before persons designated by Rule 28 of the Federal Rules of Civil Procedure.

(e) *Examination of witnesses.* (1) Each witness before testifying shall be duly sworn according to law by the officer before whom his deposition is to be taken.

(2) The deposition shall be taken in answer to questions, with the questions and answers recorded in their regular order by the officer, or by some other person (who shall be subject to the provisions of Rule 28 of the Federal Rules of Civil Procedure) in the presence of the officer except when the officer's presence is waived on the record by agreement of the parties. The testimony shall be taken stenographically and transcribed, unless the parties present agree otherwise. In the absence

of all opposing parties and their attorneys or other authorized representatives, depositions may be taken in longhand, typewriting, or stenographically. Exhibits which are marked and identified at the deposition will be deemed to have been offered into evidence, without any formal offer thereof, unless the intention of the party marking the exhibits is clearly expressed to the contrary.

(3) Every adverse party shall have full opportunity to cross-examine each witness. If pretrial disclosures or the notice of examination of witnesses served pursuant to paragraph (c) of this section are improper or inadequate with respect to any witness, an adverse party may cross-examine that witness under protest while reserving the right to object to the receipt of the testimony in evidence. Promptly after the testimony is completed, the adverse party, to preserve the objection, shall move to strike the testimony from the record, which motion will be decided on the basis of all the relevant circumstances. A motion to strike the testimony of a witness for lack of proper or adequate pretrial disclosure may seek exclusion of the entire testimony, when there was no pretrial disclosure, or may seek exclusion of that portion of the testimony that was not adequately disclosed in accordance with § 2.121(e). A motion to strike the testimony of a witness for lack of proper or adequate notice of examination must request the exclusion of the entire testimony of that witness and not only a part of that testimony.

(4) All objections made at the time of the examination to the qualifications of the officer taking the deposition, or to the manner of taking it, or to the evidence presented, or to the conduct of any party, and any other objection to the proceedings, shall be noted by the officer upon the deposition. Evidence objected to shall be taken subject to the objections.

(5) When the deposition has been transcribed, the deposition shall be carefully read over by the witness or by the officer to him, and shall then be signed by the witness in the presence of any officer authorized to administer oaths unless the reading and the signature be waived on the record by agreement of all parties.

(f) *Certification and filing of deposition.* (1) The officer shall annex to the deposition his certificate showing:

(i) Due administration of the oath by the officer to the witness before the commencement of his deposition;

(ii) The name of the person by whom the deposition was taken down, and whether, if not taken down by the officer, it was taken down in his presence;

(iii) The presence or absence of the adverse party;

(iv) The place, day, and hour of commencing and taking the deposition;

(v) The fact that the officer was not disqualified as specified in Rule 28 of the Federal Rules of Civil Procedure.

(2) If any of the foregoing requirements in paragraph (f)(1) of this section are waived, the certificate shall so state. The officer shall sign the certificate and affix thereto his seal of office, if he has such a seal. Unless waived on the record by an agreement, he shall then securely seal in an envelope all the evidence, notices, and paper exhibits, inscribe upon the envelope a certificate giving the number and title of the case, the name of each witness, and the date of sealing. The officer or the party taking the deposition, or its attorney or other authorized representative, shall then promptly forward the package to the address set out in § 2.190. If the weight or bulk of an exhibit shall exclude it from the envelope, it shall, unless waived on the record by agreement of all parties, be authenticated by the officer and transmitted by the officer or the party taking the deposition, or its attorney or other authorized representative, in a separate package marked and addressed as provided in this section.

(g) *Form of deposition.* (1) The pages of each deposition must be numbered consecutively, and the name of the witness plainly and conspicuously written at the top of each page. A deposition must be in written form. The questions propounded to each witness must be consecutively numbered unless the pages have numbered lines. Each question must be followed by its answer.

(2) Exhibits must be numbered or lettered consecutively and each must be marked with the number and title of

the case and the name of the party offering the exhibit. Entry and consideration may be refused to improperly marked exhibits.

(3) Each deposition must contain an index of the names of the witnesses, giving the pages where their examination and cross-examination begin, and an index of the exhibits, briefly describing their nature and giving the pages at which they are introduced and offered in evidence.

(h) *Depositions must be filed.* All depositions which are taken must be duly filed in the Patent and Trademark Office. On refusal to file, the Office at its discretion will not further hear or consider the contestant with whom the refusal lies; and the Office may, at its discretion, receive and consider a copy of the withheld deposition, attested by such evidence as is procurable.

(i) *Inspection of depositions.* After the depositions are filed in the Office, they may be inspected by any party to the case, but they cannot be withdrawn for the purpose of printing. They may be printed by someone specially designated by the Office for that purpose, under proper restrictions.

(j) *Effect of errors and irregularities in depositions.* Rule 32(d) (1), (2), and (3) (A) and (B) of the Federal Rules of Civil Procedure shall apply to errors and irregularities in depositions. Notice will not be taken of merely formal or technical objections which shall not appear to have wrought a substantial injury to the party raising them; and in case of such injury it must be made to appear that the objection was raised at the time specified in said rule.

(k) *Objections to admissibility:* Subject to the provisions of paragraph (j) of this section, objection may be made to receiving in evidence any deposition, or part thereof, or any other evidence, for any reason which would require the exclusion of the evidence from consideration. Objections to the competency of a witness or to the competency, relevancy, or materiality of testimony must be raised at the time specified in Rule 32(d)(3)(A) of the Federal Rules of Civil Procedure. Such objections will not be considered until final hearing.

(l) *Evidence not considered.* Evidence not obtained and filed in compliance with these sections will not be considered.

[37 FR 7607, Apr. 18, 1972, as amended at 41 FR 760, Jan. 5, 1976; 48 FR 23139, May 23, 1983; 54 FR 34899, Aug. 22, 1989; 54 FR 38041, Sept. 14, 1989; 63 FR 48099, Sept. 9, 1998; 68 FR 14337, Mar. 25, 2003; 68 FR 48289, Aug. 13, 2003; 68 FR 55767, Sept. 26, 2003; 72 FR 42262, Aug. 1, 2007]

§ 2.124 Depositions upon written questions.

(a) A deposition upon written questions may be taken before any person before whom depositions may be taken as provided by Rule 28 of the Federal Rules of Civil Procedure.

(b)(1) A party desiring to take a testimonial deposition upon written questions shall serve notice thereof upon each adverse party within ten days from the opening date of the testimony period of the party who serves the notice. The notice shall state the name and address of the witness. A copy of the notice, but not copies of the questions, shall be filed with the Trademark Trial and Appeal Board.

(2) A party desiring to take a discovery deposition upon written questions shall serve notice thereof upon each adverse party and shall file a copy of the notice, but not copies of the questions, with the Board. The notice shall state the name and address, if known, of the person whose deposition is to be taken. If the name of the person is not known, a general description sufficient to identify him or the particular class or group to which he belongs shall be stated in the notice, and the party from whom the discovery deposition is to be taken shall designate one or more persons to be deposed in the same manner as is provided by Rule 30(b)(6) of the Federal Rules of Civil Procedure.

(c) Every notice given under the provisions of paragraph (b) of this section shall be accompanied by the name or descriptive title of the officer before whom the deposition is to be taken.

(d)(1) Every notice served on any adverse party under the provisions of paragraph (b) of this section shall be accompanied by the written questions to be propounded on behalf of the party who proposes to take the deposition. Within twenty days from the date of service of the notice, any adverse party may serve cross questions upon the party who proposes to take the deposition; any party who serves cross questions shall also serve every other adverse party. Within ten days from the date of service of the cross questions, the party who proposes to take the deposition may serve redirect questions on every adverse party. Within ten days from the date of service of the redirect questions, any party who served cross questions may serve recross questions upon the party who proposes to take the deposition; any party who serves recross questions shall also serve every other adverse party. Written objections to questions may be served on a party propounding questions; any party who objects shall serve a copy of the objections on every other adverse party. In response to objections, substitute questions may be served on the objecting party within ten days of the date of service of the objections; substitute questions shall be served on every other adverse party.

(2) Upon motion for good cause by any party, or upon its own initiative, the Trademark Trial and Appeal Board may extend any of the time periods provided by paragraph (d)(1) of this section. Upon receipt of written notice that one or more testimonial depositions are to be taken upon written questions, the Trademark Trial and Appeal Board shall suspend or reschedule other proceedings in the matter to allow for the orderly completion of the depositions upon written questions.

(e) Within ten days after the last date when questions, objections, or substitute questions may be served, the party who proposes to take the deposition shall mail a copy of the notice and copies of all the questions to the officer designated in the notice; a copy of the notice and of all the questions mailed to the officer shall be served on every adverse party. The officer designated in the notice shall take the testimony of the witness in response to the questions and shall record each answer immediately after the corresponding question. The officer shall then certify the transcript and mail the transcript and exhibits to the party who took the deposition.

(f) The party who took the deposition shall promptly serve a copy of the transcript, copies of documentary exhibits, and duplicates or photographs of physical exhibits on every adverse party. It is the responsibility of the party who takes the deposition to assure that the transcript is correct (see §2.125(b)). If the deposition is a discovery deposition, it may be made of record as provided by §2.120(j). If the deposition is a testimonial deposition, the original, together with copies of documentary exhibits and duplicates or photographs of physical exhibits, shall be filed promptly with the Trademark Trial and Appeal Board.

(g) Objections to questions and answers in depositions upon written questions may be considered at final hearing.

[48 FR 23139, May 23, 1983]

§2.125 Filing and service of testimony.

(a) One copy of the transcript of testimony taken in accordance with §2.123, together with copies of documentary exhibits and duplicates or photographs of physical exhibits, shall be served on each adverse party within thirty days after completion of the taking of that testimony. If the transcript with exhibits is not served on each adverse party within thirty days or within an extension of time for the purpose, any adverse party which was not served may have remedy by way of a motion to the Trademark Trial and Appeal Board to reset such adverse party's testimony and/or briefing periods, as may be appropriate. If the deposing party fails to serve a copy of the transcript with exhibits on an adverse party after having been ordered to do so by the Board, the Board, in its discretion, may strike the deposition, or enter judgment as by default against the deposing party, or take any such other action as may be deemed appropriate.

(b) The party who takes testimony is responsible for having all typographical errors in the transcript and all errors of arrangement, indexing and form of the transcript corrected, on notice to each adverse party, prior to the filing of one certified transcript with the Trademark Trial and Appeal Board. The party who takes testimony is responsible for serving on each adverse party one copy of the corrected transcript or, if reasonably feasible, corrected pages to be inserted into the transcript previously served.

(c) One certified transcript and exhibits shall be filed with the Trademark Trial and Appeal Board. Notice of such filing shall be served on each adverse party and a copy of each notice shall be filed with the Board.

(d) Each transcript shall comply with § 2.123(g) with respect to arrangement, indexing and form.

(e) Upon motion by any party, for good cause, the Trademark Trial and Appeal Board may order that any part of a deposition transcript or any exhibits that directly disclose any trade secret or other confidential research, development, or commercial information may be filed under seal and kept confidential under the provisions of § 2.27(e). If any party or any attorney or agent of a party fails to comply with an order made under this paragraph, the Board may impose any of the sanctions authorized by § 2.120(g).

[48 FR 23140, May 23, 1983, as amended at 54 FR 34900, Aug. 22, 1989; 63 FR 48099, Sept. 9, 1998]

§ 2.126 Form of submissions to the Trademark Trial and Appeal Board.

(a) Submissions may be made to the Trademark Trial and Appeal Board on paper where Board practice or the rules in this part permit. A paper submission, including exhibits and depositions, must meet the following requirements:

(1) A paper submission must be printed in at least 11-point type and double-spaced, with text on one side only of each sheet;

(2) A paper submission must be 8 to 8.5 inches (20.3 to 21.6 cm.) wide and 11 to 11.69 inches (27.9 to 29.7 cm.) long, and contain no tabs or other such devices extending beyond the edges of the paper;

(3) If a paper submission contains dividers, the dividers must not have any extruding tabs or other devices, and must be on the same size and weight paper as the submission;

(4) A paper submission must not be stapled or bound;

(5) All pages of a paper submission must be numbered and exhibits shall be identified in the manner prescribed in § 2.123(g)(2);

(6) Exhibits pertaining to a paper submission must be filed on paper and comply with the requirements for a paper submission.

(b) Submissions may be made to the Trademark Trial and Appeal Board electronically via the Internet where the rules in this part or Board practice permit, according to the parameters established by the Board and published on the Web site of the Office. Text in an electronic submission must be in at least 11-point type and double-spaced. Exhibits pertaining to an electronic submission must be made electronically as an attachment to the submission.

(c) To be handled as confidential, submissions to the Trademark Trial and Appeal Board that are confidential in whole or part pursuant to § 2.125(e) must be submitted under a separate cover. Both the submission and its cover must be marked confidential and must identify the case number and the parties. A copy of the submission with the confidential portions redacted must be submitted.

[68 FR 55767, Sept. 26, 2003, as amended at 72 FR 42262, Aug. 1, 2007]

§ 2.127 Motions.

(a) Every motion must be submitted in written form and must meet the requirements prescribed in § 2.126. It shall contain a full statement of the grounds, and shall embody or be accompanied by a brief. Except as provided in paragraph (e)(1) of this section, a brief in response to a motion shall be filed within fifteen days from the date of service of the motion unless another time is specified by the Trademark Trial and Appeal Board, or the time is extended by stipulation of the parties approved by the Board, or upon motion granted by the Board, or upon order of the Board. If a motion for an extension is denied, the time for responding to the motion remains as specified under this section, unless otherwise ordered. Except as provided in paragraph (e)(1) of this section, a reply brief, if filed, shall be filed within fifteen days from the date of service of the brief in response to the motion. The time for filing a reply brief will not be extended. The Board will consider no further papers in support of or in opposition to a motion. Neither the brief in support of a motion nor the brief in response to a motion shall exceed twenty-five pages in length in its entirety, including table of contents, index of cases, description of the record, statement of the issues, recitation of the facts, argument, and summary. A reply brief shall not exceed ten pages in length in its entirety. Exhibits submitted in support of or in opposition to a motion are not considered part of the brief for purposes of determining the length of the brief. When a party fails to file a brief in response to a motion, the Board may treat the motion as conceded. An oral hearing will not be held on a motion except on order by the Board.

(b) Any request for reconsideration or modification of an order or decision issued on a motion must be filed within one month from the date thereof. A brief in response must be filed within 15 days from the date of service of the request.

(c) Interlocutory motions, requests, and other matters not actually or potentially dispositive of a proceeding may be acted upon by a single Administrative Trademark Judge of the Trademark Trial and Appeal Board or by an Interlocutory Attorney of the Board to whom authority so to act has been delegated.

(d) When any party files a motion to dismiss, or a motion for judgment on the pleadings, or a motion for summary judgment, or any other motion which is potentially dispositive of a proceeding, the case will be suspended by the Trademark Trial and Appeal Board with respect to all matters not germane to the motion and no party should file any paper which is not germane to the motion except as otherwise specified in the Board's suspension order. If the case is not disposed of as a result of the motion, proceedings will be resumed pursuant to an order of the Board when the motion is decided.

(e)(1) A party may not file a motion for summary judgment until the party has made its initial disclosures, except for a motion asserting claim or issue preclusion or lack of jurisdiction by the Trademark Trial and Appeal Board. A motion for summary judgment, if filed, should be filed prior to the commencement of the first testimony period, as originally set or as reset, and the Board, in its discretion, may deny as untimely any motion for summary judgment filed thereafter. A motion under Rule 56(f) of the Federal Rules of Civil Procedure, if filed in response to a motion for summary judgment, shall be filed within thirty days from the date of service of the summary judgment motion. The time for filing a motion under Rule 56(f) will not be extended. If no motion under Rule 56(f) is filed, a brief in response to the motion for summary judgment shall be filed within thirty days from the date of service of the motion unless the time is extended by stipulation of the parties approved by the Board, or upon motion granted by the Board, or upon order of the Board. If a motion for an extension is denied, the time for responding to the motion for summary judgment may remain as specified under this section. A reply brief, if filed, shall be filed within fifteen days from the date of service of the brief in response to the motion. The time for filing a reply brief will not be extended. The Board will consider no further papers in support of or in opposition to a motion for summary judgment.

(2) For purposes of summary judgment only, the Board will consider any of the following, if a copy is provided with the party's brief on the summary judgment motion: written disclosures or disclosed documents, a discovery deposition or any part thereof with any exhibit to the part that is filed, an interrogatory and answer thereto with any exhibit made part of the answer, a request for production and the documents or things produced in response thereto, or a request for admission and any exhibit thereto and the admission (or a statement that the party from which an admission was requested failed to respond thereto).

(f) The Board will not hold any person in contempt, or award attorneys' fees or other expenses to any party.

[48 FR 23140, May 23, 1983, as amended at 54 FR 34900, Aug. 22, 1989; 63 FR 48099, Sept. 9, 1998; 63 FR 52159, Sept. 30, 1998; 68 FR 55768, Sept. 26, 2003; 72 FR 42262, Aug. 1, 2007]

§ 2.128 Briefs at final hearing.

(a)(1) The brief of the party in the position of plaintiff shall be due not later than sixty days after the date set for the close of rebuttal testimony. The brief of the party in the position of defendant, if filed, shall be due not later than thirty days after the due date of the first brief. A reply brief by the party in the position of plaintiff, if filed, shall be due not later than fifteen days after the due date of the defendant's brief.

(2) When there is a counterclaim, or when proceedings have been consolidated and one party is in the position of plaintiff in one of the involved proceedings and in the position of defendant in another of the involved proceedings, or when there is an interference or a concurrent use registration proceeding involving more than two parties, the Trademark Trial and Appeal Board will set the due dates for the filing of the main brief, and the answering brief, and the rebuttal brief by the parties.

(3) When a party in the position of plaintiff fails to file a main brief, an order may be issued allowing plaintiff until a set time, not less than fifteen days, in which to show cause why the Board should not treat such failure as a concession of the case. If plaintiff fails to file a response to the order, or files a response indicating that he has lost interest in the case, judgment may be entered against plaintiff.

(b) Briefs must be submitted in written form and must meet the requirements prescribed in § 2.126. Each brief shall contain an alphabetical index of cited cases. Without prior leave of the Trademark Trial and Appeal Board, a main brief on the case shall not exceed fifty-five pages in length in its entirety, including the table of contents, index of cases, description of the record, statement of the issues, recitation of the facts, argument, and summary; and a reply brief shall not exceed twenty-five pages in its entirety.

[48 FR 23140, May 23, 1983; 48 FR 27226, June 14, 1983, as amended at 54 FR 34900, Aug. 22, 1989; 68 FR 55768, Sept. 26, 2003]

§ 2.129 Oral argument; reconsideration.

(a) If a party desires to have an oral argument at final hearing, the party shall request such argument by a separate notice filed not later than ten days after the due date for the filing of the last reply brief in the proceeding. Oral arguments will be heard by at least three Administrative Trademark Judges of the Trademark Trial and Appeal Board at the time specified in the notice of hearing. If any party appears at the specified time, that party will be heard. If the Board is prevented from hearing the case at the specified time, a new hearing date will be set. Unless otherwise permitted, oral arguments in an *inter partes* case will be limited to thirty minutes for each party. A party in the position of plaintiff may reserve part of the time allowed for oral argument to present a rebuttal argument.

(b) The date or time of a hearing may be reset, so far as is convenient and proper, to meet the wishes of the parties and their attorneys or other authorized representatives.

(c) Any request for rehearing or reconsideration or modification of a decision issued after final hearing must be filed within one month from the date of the decision. A brief in response must be filed within fifteen days from the date of service of the request. The times specified may be extended by order of the Trademark Trial and Appeal Board on motion for good cause.

(d) When a party to an *inter partes* proceeding before the Trademark Trial and Appeal Board cannot prevail without establishing constructive use pursuant to section 7(c) of the Act in an application under section 1(b) of the Act, the Trademark Trial and Appeal Board will enter a judgment in favor of that party, subject to the party's establishment of constructive use. The time for filing an appeal or for commencing a civil action under section 21 of the Act shall run from the date of the entry of the judgment.

[48 FR 23141, May 23, 1983, as amended at 54 FR 29554, July 13, 1989; 54 FR 34900, Aug. 22, 1989; 54 FR 37597, Sept. 11, 1989; 72 FR 42263, Aug. 1, 2007]

§2.130 New matter suggested by the trademark examining attorney.

If, while an *inter partes* proceeding involving an application under section 1 or 44 of the Act is pending, facts appear which, in the opinion of the trademark examining attorney, render the mark in the application unregistrable, the facts should be called to the attention of the Trademark Trial and Appeal Board. The Board may suspend the proceeding and refer the application to the trademark examining attorney for an *ex parte* determination of the question of registrability. A copy of the trademark examining attorney's final action will be furnished to the parties to the *inter partes* proceeding following the final determination of registrability by the trademark examining attorney or the Board on appeal. The Board will consider the application for such further *inter partes* action as may be appropriate.

[68 FR 55768, Sept. 26, 2003]

§2.131 Remand after decision in *inter partes* proceeding.

If, during an *inter partes* proceeding involving an application under section 1 or 44 of the Act, facts are disclosed which appear to render the mark unregistrable, but such matter has not been tried under the pleadings as filed by the parties or as they might be deemed to be amended under Rule 15(b) of the Federal Rules of Civil Procedure to conform to the evidence, the Trademark Trial and Appeal Board, in lieu of determining the matter in the decision on the proceeding, may remand the application to the trademark examining attorney for reexamination in the event the applicant ultimately prevails in the *inter partes* proceeding. Upon remand, the trademark examining attorney shall reexamine the application in light of the reference by the Board. If, upon reexamination, the trademark examining attorney finally refuses registration to the applicant, an appeal may be taken as provided by §§2.141 and 2.142.

[68 FR 55768, Sept. 26, 2003]

§2.132 Involuntary dismissal for failure to take testimony.

(a) If the time for taking testimony by any party in the position of plaintiff has expired and that party has not taken testimony or offered any other evidence, any party in the position of defendant may, without waiving the right to offer evidence in the event the motion is denied, move for dismissal on the ground of the failure of the plaintiff to prosecute. The party in the position of plaintiff shall have fifteen days from the date of service of the motion to show cause why judgment should not be rendered against him. In the absence of a showing of good and sufficient cause, judgment may be rendered against the party in the position of plaintiff. If the motion is denied, testimony periods will be reset for the party in the position of defendant and for rebuttal.

(b) If no evidence other than a copy or copies of Patent and Trademark Office records is offered by any party in the position of plaintiff, any party in the position of defendant may, without waiving the right to offer evidence in the event the motion is denied, move for dismissal on the ground that upon the law and the facts the party in the position of plaintiff has shown no right to relief. The party in the position of plaintiff shall have fifteen days from the date of service of the motion to file a brief in response to the motion. The Trademark Trial and Appeal Board may render judgment against the party in the position of plaintiff, or the Board may decline to render judgment until all of the evidence is in the record. If judgment is not rendered, testimony periods will be reset for the party in the position of defendant and for rebuttal.

(c) A motion filed under paragraph (a) or (b) of this section must be filed before the opening of the testimony period of the moving party, except that the Trademark Trial and Appeal Board may in its discretion grant a motion under paragraph (a) even if the motion was filed after the opening of the testimony period of the moving party.

[48 FR 23141, May 23, 1983, as amended at 51 FR 28710, Aug. 11, 1986]

§ 2.133 Amendment of application or registration during proceedings.

(a) An application subject to an opposition may not be amended in substance nor may a registration subject to a cancellation be amended or disclaimed in part, except with the consent of the other party or parties and the approval of the Trademark Trial and Appeal Board, or upon motion granted by the Board.

(b) If, in an *inter partes* proceeding, the Trademark Trial and Appeal Board finds that a party whose application or registration is the subject of the proceeding is not entitled to registration in the absence of a specified restriction to the application or registration, the Board will allow the party time in which to file a motion that the application or registration be amended to conform to the findings of the Board, failing which judgment will be entered against the party.

(c) Geographic limitations will be considered and determined by the Trademark Trial and Appeal Board only in the context of a concurrent use registration proceeding.

(d) A plaintiff's pleaded registration will not be restricted in the absence of a counterclaim to cancel the registration in whole or in part, except that a counterclaim need not be filed if the registration is the subject of another proceeding between the same parties or anyone in privity therewith.

[54 FR 37597, Sept. 11, 1989, as amended at 72 FR 42263, Aug. 1, 2007]

§ 2.134 Surrender or voluntary cancellation of registration.

(a) After the commencement of a cancellation proceeding, if the respondent applies for cancellation of the involved registration under section 7(e) of the Act of 1946 without the written consent of every adverse party to the proceeding, judgment shall be entered against the respondent. The written consent of an adverse party may be signed by the adverse party or by the adverse party's attorney or other authorized representative.

(b) After the commencement of a cancellation proceeding, if it comes to the attention of the Trademark Trial and Appeal Board that the respondent has permitted his involved registration to be cancelled under section 8 of the Act of 1946 or has failed to renew his involved registration under section 9 of the Act of 1946, an order may be issued allowing respondent until a set time, not less than fifteen days, in which to show cause why such cancellation or failure to renew should not be deemed to be the equivalent of a cancellation by request of respondent without the consent of the adverse party and should not result in entry of judgment against respondent as provided by paragraph (a) of this section. In the absence of a showing of good and sufficient cause, judgment may be entered against respondent as provided by paragraph (a) of this section.

[48 FR 23141, May 23, 1983, as amended at 54 FR 34900, Aug. 22, 1989; 63 FR 48100, Sept. 9, 1998]

§ 2.135 Abandonment of application or mark.

After the commencement of an opposition, concurrent use, or interference proceeding, if the applicant files a written abandonment of the application or of the mark without the written consent of every adverse party to the proceeding, judgment shall be entered against the applicant. The written consent of an adverse party may be signed by the adverse party or by the adverse party's attorney or other authorized representative.

[54 FR 34900, Aug. 22, 1989]

§ 2.136 Status of application on termination of proceeding.

On termination of a proceeding involving an application, the application, if the judgment is not adverse, returns to the status it had before the institution of the proceedings. If the judgment is adverse to the applicant, the application stands refused without further action and all proceedings thereon are considered terminated.

Appeals

§ 2.141 Ex parte appeals from action of trademark examining attorney.

(a) An applicant may, upon final refusal by the trademark examining attorney, appeal to the Trademark Trial and Appeal Board upon payment of the prescribed fee for each class in the application for which an appeal is taken, within six months of the date of issuance of the final action. A second refusal on the same grounds may be considered as final by the applicant for purpose of appeal.

(b) The applicant must pay an appeal fee for each class from which the appeal is taken. If the applicant does not pay an appeal fee for at least one class of goods or services before expiration of the six-month statutory filing period, the application will be abandoned. In a multiple-class application, if an appeal fee is submitted for fewer than all classes, the applicant must specify the class(es) in which the appeal is taken. If the applicant timely submits a fee sufficient to pay for an appeal in at least one class, but insufficient to cover all the classes, and the applicant has not specified the class(es) to which the fee applies, the Board will issue a written notice setting a time limit in which the applicant may either pay the additional fees or specify the class(es) being appealed. If the applicant does not submit the required fee or specify the class(es) being appealed within the set time period, the Board will apply the fee(s) to the class(es) in ascending order, beginning with the lowest numbered class.

[73 FR 67772, Nov. 17, 2008]

§2.142 Time and manner of *ex parte* appeals.

(a) Any appeal filed under the provisions of §2.141 must be filed within six months from the date of the final refusal or the date of the action from which the appeal is taken. An appeal is taken by filing a notice of appeal in written form, as prescribed in §2.126, and paying the appeal fee.

(b)(1) The brief of appellant shall be filed within sixty days from the date of appeal. If the brief is not filed within the time allowed, the appeal may be dismissed. The examiner shall, within sixty days after the brief of appellant is sent to the examiner, file with the Trademark Trial and Appeal Board a written brief answering the brief of appellant and shall mail a copy of the brief to the appellant. The appellant may file a reply brief within twenty days from the date of mailing of the brief of the examiner.

(2) Briefs must be submitted in written form and must meet the requirements prescribed in §2.126. Each brief shall contain an alphabetical index of cited cases. Without prior leave of the Trademark Trial and Appeal Board, a brief shall not exceed twenty-five pages in length in its entirety, including the table of contents, index of cases, description of the record, statement of the issues, recitation of the facts, argument, and summary.

(c) All requirements made by the examiner and not the subject of appeal shall be complied with prior to the filing of an appeal.

(d) The record in the application should be complete prior to the filing of an appeal. The Trademark Trial and Appeal Board will ordinarily not consider additional evidence filed with the Board by the appellant or by the examiner after the appeal is filed. After an appeal is filed, if the appellant or the examiner desires to introduce additional evidence, the appellant or the examiner may request the Board to suspend the appeal and to remand the application for further examination.

(e)(1) If the appellant desires an oral hearing, a request should be made by a separate notice filed not later than ten days after the due date for a reply brief. Oral argument will be heard by at least three Administrative Trademark Judges of the Trademark Trial and Appeal Board at the time specified in the notice of hearing, which may be reset if the Board is prevented from hearing the argument at the specified time or, so far as is convenient and proper, to meet the wish of the appellant or the appellant's attorney or other authorized representative.

(2) If the appellant requests an oral argument, the examiner who issued the refusal of registration or the requirement from which the appeal is taken, or in lieu thereof another examiner from the same examining division as designated by the supervisory attorney thereof, shall present an oral argument. If no request for an oral hearing is made by the appellant, the appeal will be decided on the record and briefs.

(3) Oral argument will be limited to twenty minutes by the appellant and

ten minutes by the examiner. The appellant may reserve part of the time allowed for oral argument to present a rebuttal argument.

(f)(1) If, during an appeal from a refusal of registration, it appears to the Trademark Trial and Appeal Board that an issue not previously raised may render the mark of the appellant unregistrable, the Board may suspend the appeal and remand the application to the examiner for further examination to be completed within thirty days.

(2) If the further examination does not result in an additional ground for refusal of registration, the examiner shall promptly return the application to the Board, for resumption of the appeal, with a written statement that further examination did not result in an additional ground for refusal of registration.

(3) If the further examination does result in an additional ground for refusal of registration, the examiner and appellant shall proceed as provided by §§ 2.61, 2.62, 2.63 and 2.64. If the ground for refusal is made final, the examiner shall return the application to the Board, which shall thereupon issue an order allowing the appellant sixty days from the date of the order to file a supplemental brief limited to the additional ground for the refusal of registration. If the supplemental brief is not filed by the appellant within the time allowed, the appeal may be dismissed.

(4) If the supplemental brief of the appellant is filed, the examiner shall, within sixty days after the supplemental brief of the appellant is sent to the examiner, file with the Board a written brief answering the supplemental brief of appellant and shall mail a copy of the brief to the appellant. The appellant may file a reply brief within twenty days from the date of mailing of the brief of the examiner.

(5) If an oral hearing on the appeal had been requested prior to the remand of the application but not yet held, an oral hearing will be set and heard as provided in paragraph (e) of this section. If an oral hearing had been held prior to the remand or had not been previously requested by the appellant, an oral hearing may be requested by the appellant by a separate notice filed not later than ten days after the due date for a reply brief on the additional ground for refusal of registration. If the appellant files a request for an oral hearing, one will be set and heard as provided in paragraph (e) of this section.

(6) If, during an appeal from a refusal of registration, it appears to the examiner that an issue not involved in the appeal may render the mark of the appellant unregistrable, the examiner may, by written request, ask the Board to suspend the appeal and to remand the application to the examiner for further examination. If the request is granted, the examiner and appellant shall proceed as provided by §§ 2.61, 2.62, 2.63 and 2.64. After the additional ground for refusal of registration has been withdrawn or made final, the examiner shall return the application to the Board, which shall resume proceedings in the appeal and take further appropriate action with respect thereto.

(g) An application which has been considered and decided on appeal will not be reopened except for the entry of a disclaimer under section 6 of the Act of 1946 or upon order of the Director, but a petition to the Director to reopen an application will be considered only upon a showing of sufficient cause for consideration of any matter not already adjudicated.

[48 FR 23141, May 23, 1983, as amended at 54 FR 34901, Aug. 22, 1989; 68 FR 55768, Sept. 26, 2003; 72 FR 42263, Aug. 1, 2007]

§ 2.144 Reconsideration of decision on *ex parte* appeal.

Any request for rehearing or reconsideration, or modification of the decision, must be filed within one month from the date of the decision. Such time may be extended by the Trademark Trial and Appeal Board upon a showing of sufficient cause.

[54 FR 29554, July 13, 1989]

§ 2.145 Appeal to court and civil action.

(a) *Appeal to U.S. Court of Appeals for the Federal Circuit.* An applicant for registration, or any party to an interference, opposition, or cancellation proceeding or any party to an application to register as a concurrent user, hereinafter referred to as *inter partes* proceedings, who is dissatisfied with the decision of the Trademark Trial and Appeal Board and any registrant who has filed an affidavit or declaration under section 8 of the Act or who has filed an application for renewal and is dissatisfied with the decision of the Director (§§2.165, 2.184), may appeal to the U.S. Court of Appeals for the Federal Circuit. The appellant must take the following steps in such an appeal:

(1) In the Patent and Trademark Office give written notice of appeal to the Director (see paragraphs (b) and (d) of this section);

(2) In the court, file a copy of the notice of appeal and pay the fee for appeal, as provided by the rules of the Court.

(b) *Notice of appeal.* (1) When an appeal is taken to the U.S. Court of Appeals for the Federal Circuit, the appellant shall give notice thereof in writing to the Director, which notice shall be filed in the Patent and Trademark Office, within the time specified in paragraph (d) of this section. The notice shall specify the party or parties taking the appeal and shall designate the decision or part thereof appealed from.

(2) In *inter partes* proceedings, the notice must be served as provided in §2.119.

(3) Notices of appeal directed to the Director shall be mailed to or served by hand on the General Counsel, according to part 104 of this chapter, with a duplicate copy mailed or served by hand on the Trademark Trial and Appeal Board.

(c) *Civil action.* (1) Any person who may appeal to the U.S. Court of Appeals for the Federal Circuit (paragraph (a) of this section), may have remedy by civil action under section 21(b) of the Act. Such civil action must be commenced within the time specified in paragraph (d) of this section.

(2) Any applicant or registrant in an *ex parte* case who takes an appeal to the U.S. Court of Appeals for the Federal Circuit waives any right to proceed under section 21(b) of the Act.

(3) Any adverse party to an appeal taken to the U.S. Court of Appeals for the Federal Circuit by a defeated party in an *inter partes* proceeding may file a notice with the Office, addressed to the Office of the General Counsel, according to part 104 of this chapter, within twenty days after the filing of the defeated party's notice of appeal to the court (paragraph (b) of this section), electing to have all further proceedings conducted as provided in section 21(b) of the Act. The notice of election must be served as provided in §2.119.

(4) In order to avoid premature termination of a proceeding, a party who commences a civil action, pursuant to section 21(b) of the Act, must file written notice thereof at the Trademark Trial and Appeal Board.

(d) *Time for appeal or civil action.* (1) The time for filing the notice of appeal to the U.S. Court of Appeals for the Federal Circuit (paragraph (b) of this section), or for commencing a civil action (paragraph (c) of this section), is two months from the date of the decision of the Trademark Trial and Appeal Board or the Director, as the case may be. If a request for rehearing or reconsideration or modification of the decision is filed within the time specified in §2.127(b), 2.129(c) or 2.144, or within any extension of time granted thereunder, the time for filing an appeal or commencing a civil action shall expire two months after action on the request. In *inter partes* cases, the time for filing a cross-action or a notice of a cross-appeal expires

(i) 14 days after service of the notice of appeal or the summons and complaint; or

(ii) Two months from the date of the decision of the Trademark Trial and Appeal Board or the Director, whichever is later.

(2) The times specified in this section in days are calendar days. The times specified herein in months are calendar months except that one day shall be added to any two-month period which includes February 28. If the last day of time specified for an appeal, or commencing a civil action falls on a Saturday, Sunday or Federal holiday in the District of Columbia, the time is extended to the next day which is neither a Saturday, Sunday nor a Federal holiday.

(3) If a party to an *inter partes* proceeding has taken an appeal to the U.S.

Court of Appeals for the Federal Circuit and an adverse party has filed notice under section 21(a)(1) of the Act electing to have all further proceedings conducted under section 21(b) of the Act, the time for filing a civil action thereafter is specified in section 21(a)(1) of the Act. The time for filing a cross-action expires 14 days after service of the summons and complaint.

(e) *Extensions of time to commence judicial review.* The Director may extend the time for filing an appeal or commencing a civil action (1) for good cause shown if requested in writing before the expiration of the period for filing an appeal or commencing a civil action, or (2) upon written request after the expiration of the period for filing an appeal or commencing a civil action upon a showing that the failure to act was the result of excusable neglect.

[47 FR 47382, Oct. 26, 1982, as amended at 53 FR 16414, May 9, 1988; 54 FR 29554, July 13, 1989; 54 FR 34901, Aug. 22, 1989; 58 FR 54503, Oct. 22, 1993; 68 FR 14337, Mar. 25, 2003; 68 FR 55769, Sept. 26, 2003]

PETITIONS AND ACTION BY THE DIRECTOR

§ 2.146 Petitions to the Director.

(a) Petition may be taken to the Director:

(1) From any repeated or final formal requirement of the examiner in the *ex parte* prosecution of an application if permitted by § 2.63(b);

(2) In any case for which the Act of 1946, or title 35 of the United States Code, or this part of title 37 of the Code of Federal Regulations specifies that the matter is to be determined directly or reviewed by the Director;

(3) To invoke the supervisory authority of the Director in appropriate circumstances;

(4) In any case not specifically defined and provided for by this part of title 37 of the Code of Federal Regulations;

(5) In an extraordinary situation, when justice requires and no other party is injured thereby, to request a suspension or waiver of any requirement of the rules not being a requirement of the Act of 1946.

(b) Questions of substance arising during the *ex parte* prosecution of applications, including, but not limited to, questions arising under sections 2, 3, 4, 5, 6 and 23 of the Act of 1946, are not considered to be appropriate subject matter for petitions to the Director.

(c) Every petition to the Director shall include a statement of the facts relevant to the petition, the points to be reviewed, the action or relief requested, and the fee required by § 2.6. Any brief in support of the petition shall be embodied in or accompany the petition. The petition must be signed by the petitioner, someone with legal authority to bind the petitioner (e.g., a corporate officer or general partner of a partnership), or a practitioner qualified to practice under § 11.14 of this chapter, in accordance with the requirements of § 2.193(e)(5). When facts are to be proved on petition, the petitioner must submit proof in the form of affidavits or declarations in accordance with § 2.20, signed by someone with firsthand knowledge of the facts to be proved, and any exhibits.

(d) A petition must be filed within two months of the date of issuance of the action from which relief is requested, unless a different deadline is specified elsewhere in this chapter.

(e)(1) A petition from the grant or denial of a request for an extension of time to file a notice of opposition must be filed within fifteen days from the date of issuance of the grant or denial of the request. A petition from the grant of a request must be served on the attorney or other authorized representative of the potential opposer, if any, or on the potential opposer. A petition from the denial of a request must be served on the attorney or other authorized representative of the applicant, if any, or on the applicant. Proof of service of the petition must be made as provided by § 2.119. The potential opposer or the applicant, as the case may be, may file a response within fifteen days from the date of service of the petition and must serve a copy of the response on the petitioner, with proof of service as provided by § 2.119. No further document relating to the petition may be filed.

(2) A petition from an interlocutory order of the Trademark Trial and Appeal Board must be filed within thirty

days after the date of issuance of the order from which relief is requested. Any brief in response to the petition must be filed, with any supporting exhibits, within fifteen days from the date of service of the petition. Petitions and responses to petitions, and any documents accompanying a petition or response under this subsection must be served on every adverse party pursuant to § 2.119.

(f) An oral hearing will not be held on a petition except when considered necessary by the Director.

(g) The mere filing of a petition to the Director will not act as a stay in any appeal or *inter partes* proceeding that is pending before the Trademark Trial and Appeal Board nor stay the period for replying to an Office action in an application except when a stay is specifically requested and is granted or when §§ 2.63(b) and 2.65 are applicable to an *ex parte* application.

(h) Authority to act on petitions, or on any petition, may be delegated by the Director.

(i) Where a petitioner seeks to reactivate an application or registration that was abandoned, cancelled or expired because documents were lost or mishandled, the Director may deny the petition if the petitioner was not diligent in checking the status of the application or registration. To be considered diligent, a petitioner must:

(1) During the pendency of an application, check the status of the application every six months between the filing date of the application and issuance of a registration;

(2) After registration, check the status of the registration every six months from the filing of an affidavit of use or excusable nonuse under section 8 or 71 of the Act, or a renewal application under section 9 of the Act, until the petitioner receives notice that the affidavit or renewal application has been accepted; and

(3) If the status check reveals that the Office has not received a document filed by the petitioner, or that the Office has issued an action or notice that the petitioner has not received, the petitioner must promptly request corrective action.

(j) If the Director denies a petition, the petitioner may request reconsideration, if the petitioner:

(1) Files the request within two months of the date of issuance of the decision denying the petition; and

(2) Pays a second petition fee under § 2.6.

[48 FR 23142, May 23, 1983; 48 FR 27226, June 14, 1983, as amended at 63 FR 48100, Sept. 9, 1998; 64 FR 48924, Sept. 8, 1999; 68 FR 55769, Sept. 26, 2003; 73 FR 67773, Nov. 17, 2008; 74 FR 54909, Oct. 26, 2009]

§ 2.147 [Reserved]

§ 2.148 Director may suspend certain rules.

In an extraordinary situation, when justice requires and no other party is injured thereby, any requirement of the rules in this part not being a requirement of the statute may be suspended or waived by the Director.

CERTIFICATE

§ 2.151 Certificate.

When the Office determines that a mark is registrable, the Office will issue a certificate stating that the applicant is entitled to registration on the Principal Register or on the Supplemental Register. The certificate will state the application filing date, the act under which the mark is registered, the date of issue, and the number of the registration. A reproduction of the mark and pertinent data from the application will be sent with the certificate. A notice of the requirements of sections 8 and 71 of the Act will accompany the certificate.

[68 FR 55769, Sept. 26, 2003]

PUBLICATION OF MARKS REGISTERED UNDER 1905 ACT

AUTHORITY: Secs. 2.153 to 2.156 also issued under sec. 12, 60 Stat. 432; 15 U.S.C. 1062.

§ 2.153 Publication requirements.

The owner of a mark registered under the provisions of the Trademark Act of 1881 or 1905 may at any time prior to the expiration of the period for which the registration was issued or renewed, upon the payment of the prescribed fee, file an affidavit or declaration in accordance with § 2.20 setting forth those goods or services in the registration on or in connection with which said mark is in use in commerce, and stating that the owner claims the benefits of the Act of 1946. The affidavit or declaration must be signed by a person properly authorized to sign on behalf of the owner under § 2.193(e)(1).

[74 FR 54909, Oct. 26, 2009]

§ 2.154 Publication in *Official Gazette.*

A notice of the claim of benefits under the Act of 1946 and a reproduction of the mark will then be published in the *Official Gazette* as soon as practicable. The published mark will retain its original registration number.

§ 2.155 Notice of publication.

The Office will send the registrant a notice of publication of the mark and of the requirement for filing the affidavit or declaration required by section 8 of the Act.

[64 FR 48924, Sept. 8, 1999]

§ 2.156 Not subject to opposition; subject to cancellation.

The published mark is not subject to opposition, but is subject to petitions to cancel as specified in § 2.111 and to cancellation for failure to file the affidavit or declaration required by section 8 of the Act.

[64 FR 48924, Sept. 8, 1999]

Reregistration of Marks Registered Under Prior Acts

§ 2.158 Reregistration of marks registered under Acts of 1881, 1905, and 1920.

Trademarks registered under the Act of 1881, the Act of 1905 or the Act of 1920 may be reregistered under the Act of 1946, either on the Principal Register, if eligible, or on the Supplemental Register, but a new complete application for registration must be filed complying with the rules relating thereto, and such application will be subject to examination and other proceedings in the same manner as other applications filed under the Act of 1946. See § 2.26 for use of old drawing.

Cancellation for Failure To File Affidavit or Declaration

Authority: Secs. 2.161 to 2.165 also issued under sec. 8, 60 Stat. 431; 15 U.S.C. 1058.

§ 2.160 Affidavit or declaration of continued use or excusable nonuse required to avoid cancellation of registration.

(a) During the following time periods, the owner of the registration must file an affidavit or declaration of continued use or excusable nonuse, or the registration will be cancelled:

(1)(i) For registrations issued under the Trademark Act of 1946, on or after the fifth anniversary and no later than the sixth anniversary after the date of registration; or

(ii) For registrations issued under prior Acts, on or after the fifth anniversary and no later than the sixth anniversary after the date of publication under section 12(c) of the Act; and

(2) For all registrations, within the year before the end of every ten-year period after the date of registration.

(3) The affidavit or declaration may be filed within a grace period of six months after the end of the deadline set forth in paragraphs (a)(1) and (a)(2) of this section, with payment of the grace period surcharge per class required by section 8(a)(3) of the Act and § 2.6.

(b) For the requirements for the affidavit or declaration, see § 2.161.

[64 FR 48924, Sept. 8, 1999, as amended at 75 FR 35976, June 24, 2010]

§ 2.161 Requirements for a complete affidavit or declaration of continued use or excusable nonuse.

A complete affidavit or declaration under section 8 of the Act must:

(a) Be filed by the owner within the period set forth in § 2.160(a);

(b) Include a statement that is signed and verified (sworn to) or supported by a declaration under § 2.20 by a person properly authorized to sign on behalf of the owner under § 2.193(e)(1), attesting to the use or excusable nonuse of the mark within the period set forth in section 8 of the Act. The verified statement must be executed on or after the beginning of the filing period specified in § 2.160(a).

(c) Include the registration number;

(d)(1) Include the fee required by § 2.6 for each class of goods or services that the affidavit or declaration covers;

(2) If the affidavit or declaration is filed during the grace period under section 8(a)(3) of the Act, include the grace period surcharge per class required by § 2.6;

(3) If at least one fee is submitted for a multi-class registration, but the class(es) to which the fee(s) should be applied are not specified, the Office will issue a notice requiring either the submission of additional fee(s) or an indication of the class(es) to which the original fee(s) should be applied. Additional fee(s) may be submitted if the requirements of § 2.164 are met. If the required fee(s) are not submitted and the class(es) to which the original fee(s) should be applied are not specified, the Office will presume that the fee(s) cover the classes in ascending order, beginning with the lowest numbered class;

(e)(1) Specify the goods or services for which the mark is in use in commerce, and/or the goods or services for which excusable nonuse is claimed under § 2.161(f)(2);

(2) If the affidavit or declaration covers less than all the goods or services, or less than all the classes in the registration, specify the goods or services being deleted from the registration;

(f)(1) State that the registered mark is in use in commerce on or in connection with the goods or services in the registration; or

(2) If the registered mark is not in use in commerce on or in connection with all the goods or services in the registration, set forth the date when use of the mark in commerce stopped and the approximate date when use is expected to resume; and recite facts to show that nonuse as to those goods or services is due to special circumstances that excuse the nonuse and is not due to an intention to abandon the mark;

(g) Include one specimen showing current use of the mark for each class of goods or services, unless excusable nonuse is claimed under § 2.161(f)(2). When requested by the Office, additional specimens must be provided. The specimen must:

(1) Show the mark as actually used on or in connection with the goods or in the sale or advertising of the services. A photocopy or other reproduction of the specimen showing the mark as actually used is acceptable. However, a photocopy that merely reproduces the registration certificate is not a proper specimen;

(2) Be flat and no larger than 8.5 inches (21.6 cm.) wide by 11.69 inches (29.7 cm.) long. If a specimen exceeds these size requirements (a "bulky specimen"), the Office will create a facsimile of the specimen that meets the requirements of the rule (*i.e.*, is flat and no larger than 8.5 inches (21.6 cm.) wide by 11.69 inches (29.7 cm.) long) and put it in the record. In the absence of non-bulky alternatives, the Office may accept an audio or video cassette tape recording, CD-ROM, or a specimen in another appropriate medium.

(3) Be a digitized image in .jpg or .pdf format, if transmitted through TEAS.

(h) The Office may require the owner to furnish such information, exhibits, affidavits or declarations, and such additional specimens:

(1) As may be reasonably necessary to the proper examination of the affidavit or declaration under section 8 of the Act; or

(2) For the Office to assess the accuracy and integrity of the register.

(3) The provisions of paragraph (h)(2) of this section will no longer be applied after June 21, 2014.

[64 FR 48924, Sept. 8, 1999, as amended at 67 FR 79522, Dec. 30, 2002; 68 FR 55769, Sept. 26, 2003; 73 FR 47686, Aug. 14, 2008; 73 FR 67773, Nov. 17, 2008; 74 FR 54910, Oct. 26, 2009; 75 FR 35976, June 24, 2010; 77 FR 30207, May 22, 2012]

§ 2.162 Notice to registrant.

When a certificate of registration is originally issued, the Office includes a notice of the requirement for filing the affidavit or declaration of use or excusable nonuse under section 8 of the Act. However the affidavit or declaration must be filed within the time period required by section 8 of the Act even if this notice is not received.

[64 FR 48925, Sept. 8, 1999]

§ 2.163 Acknowledgment of receipt of affidavit or declaration.

The Office will issue a notice as to whether an affidavit or declaration is acceptable, or the reasons for refusal.

(a) If the affidavit or declaration is filed within the time periods set forth in section 8 of the Act, deficiencies may be corrected after notification from the Office if the requirements of § 2.164 are met.

(b) A response to the refusal must be filed within six months of the date of issuance of the Office action, or before the end of the filing period set forth in section 8(a) of the Act, whichever is later. The response must be signed by the owner, someone with legal authority to bind the owner (e.g., a corporate officer or general partner of a partnership), or a practitioner qualified to practice under § 11.14 of this chapter, in accordance with the requirements of § 2.193(e)(2).

(c) If no response is filed within this time period, the registration will be cancelled, unless time remains in the grace period under section 8(a)(3) of the Act. If time remains in the grace period, the owner may file a complete, new affidavit.

[75 FR 35976, June 24, 2010, as amended at 76 FR 69133, Nov. 8, 2011]

§ 2.164 Correcting deficiencies in affidavit or declaration.

(a) If the affidavit or declaration is filed within the time periods set forth in section 8 of the Act, deficiencies may be corrected after notification from the Office, as follows:

(1) *Correcting deficiencies in affidavits or declarations timely filed within the periods set forth in sections 8(a)(1) and 8(a)(2) of the Act.* If the affidavit or declaration is timely filed within the relevant filing period set forth in section 8(a)(1) or section 8(a)(2) of the Act, deficiencies may be corrected before the end of this filing period without paying a deficiency surcharge. Deficiencies may be corrected after the end of this filing period with payment of the deficiency surcharge required by section 8(c) of the Act and § 2.6.

(2) *Correcting deficiencies in affidavits or declarations filed during the grace period.* If the affidavit or declaration is filed during the six-month grace period provided by section 8(a)(3) of the Act, deficiencies may be corrected before the expiration of the grace period without paying a deficiency surcharge. Deficiencies may be corrected after the expiration of the grace period with payment of the deficiency surcharge required by section 8(c) of the Act and § 2.6.

(b) If the affidavit or declaration is not filed within the time periods set forth in section 8 of the Act, the registration will be cancelled.

[75 FR 35976, June 24, 2010, as amended at 76 FR 69133, Nov. 8, 2011]

§ 2.165 Petition to Director to review refusal.

(a) A response to the examiner's initial refusal to accept an affidavit or declaration is required before filing a petition to the Director, unless the examiner directs otherwise. See § 2.163(b) for the deadline for responding to an examiner's Office action.

(b) If the examiner maintains the refusal of the affidavit or declaration, the owner may file a petition to the Director to review the action. The petition must be filed within six months of the date of issuance of the action maintaining the refusal, or the Office will cancel the registration and issue a notice of the cancellation.

(c) A decision by the Director is necessary before filing an appeal or commencing a civil action in any court.

[64 FR 48925, Sept. 8, 1999, as amended at 73 FR 67773, Nov. 17, 2008]

§ 2.166 Affidavit of continued use or excusable nonuse combined with renewal application.

An affidavit or declaration under section 8 of the Act and a renewal application under section 9 of the Act may be combined into a single document, provided that the document meets the requirements of both sections 8 and 9 of the Act.

[64 FR 48925, Sept. 8, 1999]

AFFIDAVIT OR DECLARATION UNDER SECTION 15

§ 2.167 Affidavit or declaration under section 15.

The affidavit or declaration in accordance with § 2.20 provided by section 15 of the Act for acquiring incontestability for a mark registered on the Principal Register or a mark registered under the Act of 1881 or 1905 and published under section 12(c) of the Act (§ 2.153) must:

(a) Be verified (sworn to) or supported by a declaration under § 2.20, signed by the owner of the registration or a person properly authorized to sign on behalf of the owner under § 2.193(e)(1);

(b) Identify the certificate of registration by the certificate number and date of registration;

(c) Recite the goods or services stated in the registration on or in connection with which the mark has been in continuous use in commerce for a period of five years after the date of registration or date of publication under section 12(c) of the Act, and is still in use in commerce;

(d) Specify that there has been no final decision adverse to the owner's claim of ownership of such mark for such goods or services, or to the owner's right to register the same or to keep the same on the register;

(e) Specify that there is no proceeding involving said rights pending in the Patent and Trademark Office or in a court and not finally disposed of;

(f) Be filed within one year after the expiration of any five-year period of continuous use following registration or publication under section 12(c). The Office will issue a notice acknowledging receipt of the affidavit or declaration.

The registrant will be notified of the receipt of the affidavit or declaration.

(g) Include the required fee for each class to which the affidavit or declaration pertains in the registration. If no fee, or a fee insufficient to cover at least one class, is filed at an appropriate time, the affidavit or declaration will not be refused if the required fee(s) (see § 2.6) are filed in the Patent and Trademark Office within the time limit set forth in the notification of this defect by the Office. If insufficient fees are included to cover all classes in the registration, the particular class or classes to which the affidavit or declaration pertains should be specified.

(Sec. 15, 60 Stat. 433; 15 U.S.C. 1065; 35 U.S.C. 6; 15 U.S.C. 1113, 1123)

[30 FR 13193, Oct. 16, 1965, as amended at 47 FR 41282, Sept. 17, 1982; 64 FR 48925, Sept. 8, 1999; 73 FR 67773, Nov. 17, 2008; 74 FR 54910, Oct. 26, 2009]

§ 2.168 Affidavit or declaration under section 15 combined with affidavit or declaration under sections 8 or 71, or with renewal application.

(a) The affidavit or declaration filed under section 15 of the Act may also be used as the affidavit or declaration required by section 8, if the affidavit or declaration meets the requirements of both sections 8 and 15. The affidavit or declaration filed under section 15 of the Act may also be used as the affidavit or declaration required by section 71, if the affidavit or declaration meets the requirements of both sections 71 and 15.

(b) The affidavit or declaration filed under section 15 of the Act may be combined with an application for renewal of a registration under section 9 of the Act, if the requirements of both sections 9 and 15 are met.

[64 FR 48925, Sept. 8, 1999, as amended at 75 FR 35976, June 24, 2010]

CORRECTION, DISCLAIMER, SURRENDER, ETC.

§ 2.171 New certificate on change of ownership.

(a) *Full change of ownership.* If the ownership of a registered mark changes, the new owner may request that a new certificate of registration be issued in the name of the new owner. The assignment or other document changing title must be recorded in the Office. The request for the new certificate must include the fee required by § 2.6(a)(8) and be signed by the owner of the registration, someone with legal authority to bind the owner (e.g., a corporate officer or general partner of a partnership), or a practitioner qualified to practice under § 11.14 of this chapter. In a registered extension of protection, the assignment must be recorded with the International Bureau of the World Intellectual Property Organization before it can be recorded in the Office (see § 7.22).

(b) *Partial change of ownership.* (1) In a registration resulting from an application based on section 1 or section 44 of the Act, if ownership of a registration has changed with respect to some but not all of the goods and/or services, the owner(s) may file a request that the registration be divided into two or more separate registrations. The assignment or other document changing title must be recorded in the Office. The request to divide must include the fee required by § 2.6(a)(8) for each new registration created by the division, and be signed by the owner of the registration, someone with legal authority to bind the owner (e.g., a corporate officer or general partner of a partnership), or a practitioner qualified to practice under § 11.14 of this chapter, in accordance with § 2.193(e)(2) of this chapter.

(2)(i) When the International Bureau of the World Intellectual Property Organization notifies the Office that an international registration has been divided as the result of a change of ownership with respect to some but not all of the goods or services, the Office will construe the International Bureau's notice as a request to divide. The Office will record the partial change of ownership in the Assignment Services Branch, and divide out the assigned goods/services from the registered extension of protection (parent registration), issue an updated certificate for the parent registration, and publish notice of the parent registration in the *Official Gazette.*

(ii) The Office will create a new registration number for the child registration, and enter the information about the new registration in its automated records. The Office will notify the new owner that the new owner must pay the fee required by § 2.6 to obtain a new registration certificate for the child registration. It is not necessary for the new owner to file a separate request to divide.

(iii) The Office will not divide a registered extension of protection unless the International Bureau notifies the Office that the international registration has been divided.

[73 FR 67774, Nov. 17, 2008, as amended at 74 FR 54910, Oct. 26, 2009]

§ 2.172 Surrender for cancellation.

Upon application by the owner, the Director may permit any registration to be surrendered for cancellation. The application for surrender must be signed by the owner of the registration, someone with legal authority to bind the owner (e.g., a corporate officer or general partner of a partnership), or a practitioner qualified to practice under § 11.14 of this chapter. When a registration has more than one class, one or more entire class(es) but fewer than the total number of classes may be surrendered. Deletion of fewer than all the goods or services in a single class constitutes amendment of the registration as to that class (*see* § 2.173), not surrender.

[74 FR 54910, Oct. 26, 2009]

§ 2.173 Amendment of registration.

(a) *Form of amendment.* The owner of a registration may apply to amend a registration or to disclaim part of the mark in the registration. The owner must submit a written request specifying the amendment or disclaimer. If the registration is involved in an *inter partes* proceeding before the Trademark Trial and Appeal Board, the request must be filed by appropriate motion to the Board.

(b) *Requirements for request.* A request for amendment or disclaimer must:

(1) Include the fee required by § 2.6;

(2) Be signed by the owner of the registration, someone with legal authority to bind the owner (e.g., a corporate officer or general partner of a partnership), or a practitioner who meets the requirements of § 11.14, and verified or supported by a declaration under § 2.20; and

(3) If the amendment involves a change in the mark: one new specimen per class showing the mark as used on or in connection with the goods or services; an affidavit or declaration under § 2.20 stating that the specimen was in use in commerce at least as

early as the filing date of the amendment; and a new drawing of the amended mark. When requested by the Office, additional specimens must be provided.

(4) The Office may require the owner to furnish such specimens, information, exhibits, and affidavits or declarations as may be reasonably necessary to the proper examination of the amendment.

(c) *Registration must still contain registrable matter.* The registration as amended must still contain registrable matter, and the mark as amended must be registrable as a whole.

(d) *Amendment may not materially alter the mark.* An amendment or disclaimer must not materially alter the character of the mark.

(e) *Amendment of identification of goods.* No amendment in the identification of goods or services in a registration will be permitted except to restrict the identification or to change it in ways that would not require republication of the mark.

(f) *Conforming amendments may be required.* If the registration includes a disclaimer, description of the mark, or other miscellaneous statement, any request to amend the registration must include a request to make any necessary conforming amendments to the disclaimer, description, or other statement.

(g) *Elimination of disclaimer.* No amendment seeking the elimination of a disclaimer will be permitted, unless deletion of the disclaimed portion of the mark is also sought.

[73 FR 67774, Nov. 17, 2008, as amended at 77 FR 30207, May 22, 2012]

§ 2.174 Correction of Office mistake.

Whenever Office records clearly disclose a material mistake in a registration, incurred through the fault of the Office, the Office will issue a certificate of correction stating the fact and nature of the mistake, signed by the Director or by an employee designated by the Director, without charge. Thereafter, the corrected certificate shall have the same effect as if it had been originally issued in the corrected form. In the discretion of the Director, the Office may issue a new certificate of registration without charge.

[73 FR 67774, Nov. 17, 2008]

§ 2.175 Correction of mistake by owner.

(a) Whenever a mistake has been made in a registration and a showing has been made that the mistake occurred in good faith through the fault of the owner, the Director may issue a certificate of correction. In the discretion of the Director, the Office may issue a new certificate upon payment of the required fee, provided that the correction does not involve such changes in the registration as to require republication of the mark.

(b) An application for such action must:

(1) Include the following:

(i) Specification of the mistake for which correction is sought;

(ii) Description of the manner in which it arose; and

(iii) A showing that it occurred in good faith;

(2) Be signed by the owner of the registration, someone with legal authority to bind the owner (e.g., a corporate officer or general partner of a partnership), or a practitioner who meets the requirements of § 11.14 of this chapter, and verified or include a declaration in accordance with § 2.20; and

(3) Be accompanied by the required fee.

(Sec. 7, 60 Stat. 430, as amended; 15 U.S.C. 1057)

[30 FR 13193, Oct. 16, 1965, as amended at 31 FR 5262, Apr. 1, 1966; 69 FR 51364, Aug. 19, 2004; 73 FR 67774, Nov. 17, 2008]

§ 2.176 Consideration of above matters.

The matters in §§ 2.171 to 2.175 will be considered in the first instance by the Post Registration examiners, except for requests to amend registrations involved in *inter partes* proceedings before the Trademark Trial and Appeal Board, as specified in § 2.173(a), which shall be considered by the Board. If an action of the examiner is adverse, the owner of the registration may petition the Director to review the action under § 2.146. If the owner does not respond to an adverse action of the examiner within six months of the date of issuance, the matter will be considered abandoned.

[73 FR 67774, Nov. 17, 2008]

TERM AND RENEWAL

AUTHORITY: Secs. 2.181 to 2.184 also issued under sec. 9, 60 Stat. 431; 15 U.S.C. 1059.

§ 2.181 Term of original registrations and renewals.

(a)(1) Subject to the provisions of section 8 of the Act requiring an affidavit or declaration of continued use or excusable nonuse, registrations issued or renewed prior to November 16, 1989, whether on the Principal Register or on the Supplemental Register, remain in force for twenty years from their date of issue or the date of renewal, and may be further renewed for periods of ten years, unless previously cancelled or surrendered.

(2) Subject to the provisions of section 8 of the Act requiring an affidavit or declaration of continued use or excusable nonuse, registrations issued or renewed on or after November 16, 1989, whether on the Principal Register or on the Supplemental Register, remain in force for ten years from their date of issue or the date of renewal, and may be further renewed for periods of ten years, unless previously cancelled or surrendered.

(b) Registrations issued under the Acts of 1905 and 1881 remain in force for their unexpired terms and may be renewed in the same manner as registrations under the Act of 1946.

(c) Registrations issued under the Act of 1920 cannot be renewed unless renewal is required to support foreign registrations and in such case may be renewed on the Supplemental Register in the same manner as registrations under the Act of 1946.

[30 FR 13193, Oct. 16, 1965, as amended at 54 FR 37597, Sept. 11, 1989; 64 FR 48926, Sept. 8, 1999]

§ 2.182 Time for filing renewal application.

An application for renewal must be filed within one year before the expiration date of the registration, or within the six-month grace period after the expiration date of the registration. If no renewal application is filed within this period, the registration will expire.

[64 FR 48926, Sept. 8, 1999]

§ 2.183 Requirements for a complete renewal application.

A complete renewal application must include:

(a) A request for renewal of the registration, signed by the registrant or the registrant's representative;

(b) The fee required by § 2.6 for each class;

(c) The additional fee required by § 2.6 for each class if the renewal application is filed during the six-month grace period set forth in section 9(a) of the Act;

(d) If the renewal application covers less than all the goods or services in the registration, a list of the particular goods or services to be renewed.

(e) If at least one fee is submitted for a multi-class registration, but the class(es) to which the fee(s) should be applied are not specified, the Office will issue a notice requiring either the submission of additional fee(s) or an indication of the class(es) to which the original fee(s) should be applied. Additional fee(s) may be submitted if the requirements of § 2.185 are met. If the required fee(s) are not submitted and the class(es) to which the original fee(s) should be applied are not specified, the Office will presume that the fee(s) cover the classes in ascending order, beginning with the lowest numbered class.

(f) Renewals of registrations issued under a prior classification system will be processed on the basis of that system, unless the registration has been amended to adopt international classification pursuant to § 2.85(e)(3).

[64 FR 48926, Sept. 8, 1999, as amended at 67 FR 79523, Dec. 30, 2002; 73 FR 67775, Nov. 17, 2008]

§ 2.184 Refusal of renewal.

(a) If the renewal application is not acceptable, the Office will issue a notice stating the reason(s) for refusal.

(b)(1) The registrant must file a response to the refusal of renewal within six months of the date of issuance of the Office action, or before the expiration date of the registration, whichever is later. If no response is filed within this time period, the registration will expire, unless time remains in the grace period under section 9(a) of the Act. If time remains in the grace period, the registrant may file a complete new renewal application.

(2) The response must be signed by the registrant, someone with legal authority to bind the registrant (e.g., a corporate officer or general partner of a partnership), or a practitioner who meets the requirements of §11.14 of this chapter, in accordance with the requirements of §2.193(e)(2).

(c) If the renewal application is not filed within the time periods set forth in section 9(a) of the Act, the registration will expire.

[64 FR 48926, Sept. 8, 1999, as amended at 73 FR 67775, Nov. 17, 2008; 74 FR 54910, Oct. 26, 2009]

§2.185 Correcting deficiencies in renewal application.

(a) If the renewal application is filed within the time periods set forth in section 9(a) of the Act, deficiencies may be corrected, as follows:

(1) *Correcting deficiencies in renewal applications filed within one year before the expiration date of the registration.* If the renewal application is filed within one year before the expiration date of the registration, deficiencies may be corrected before the expiration date of the registration without paying a deficiency surcharge. Deficiencies may be corrected after the expiration date of the registration with payment of the deficiency surcharge required by section 9(a) of the Act and §2.6.

(2) *Correcting deficiencies in renewal applications filed during the grace period.* If the renewal application is filed during the six-month grace period, deficiencies may be corrected before the expiration of the grace period without paying a deficiency surcharge. Deficiencies may be corrected after the expiration of the grace period with payment of the deficiency surcharge required by section 9(a) of the Act and §2.6.

(b) If the renewal application is not filed within the time periods set forth in section 9(a) of the Act, the registration will expire. This deficiency cannot be cured.

[64 FR 48926, Sept. 8, 1999]

§2.186 Petition to Director to review refusal of renewal.

(a) A response to the examiner's initial refusal of the renewal application is required before filing a petition to the Director, unless the examiner directs otherwise. See §2.184(b) for the deadline for responding to an examiner's Office action.

(b) If the examiner maintains the refusal of the renewal application, a petition to the Director to review the refusal may be filed. The petition must be filed within six months of the date of issuance of the Office action maintaining the refusal, or the renewal application will be abandoned and the registration will expire.

(c) A decision by the Director is necessary before filing an appeal or commencing a civil action in any court.

[64 FR 48926, Sept. 8, 1999, as amended at 73 FR 67775, Nov. 17, 2008]

General Information and Correspondence in Trademark Cases

Source: 68 FR 48289, Aug. 13, 2003, unless otherwise noted.

§§2.188–2.189 [Reserved]

§2.190 Addresses for trademark correspondence with the United States Patent and Trademark Office.

(a) *Trademark correspondence. In general.* All trademark-related documents filed on paper, except documents sent to the Assignment Services Division for recordation; requests for copies of trademark documents; and certain documents filed under the Madrid Protocol as specified in paragraph (e) of this section, should be addressed to: Commissioner for Trademarks, P.O. Box 1451, Alexandria, VA 22313–1451. All trademark-related documents may be delivered by hand, during the hours the Office is open to receive correspondence, to the Trademark Assistance Center, James Madison Building—East Wing, Concourse Level, 600 Dulany Street, Alexandria, Virginia 22314.

(b) *Electronic trademark documents.* An applicant may transmit a trademark document through TEAS, at *http://www.uspto.gov.*

(c) *Trademark assignments.* Requests to record documents in the Assignment Services Division may be filed through the Office's web site, at *http://www.uspto.gov.* Paper documents and cover sheets to be recorded in the Assignment Services Division should be addressed to: Mail Stop Assignment Recordation Services, Director of the United States Patent and Trademark Office, P.O. Box 1450, Alexandria, Virginia 22313–1450. See § 3.27 of this chapter.

(d) *Requests for copies of trademark documents.* Copies of trademark documents can be ordered through the Office's web site at *www.uspto.gov.* Paper requests for certified or uncertified copies of trademark documents should be addressed to: Mail Stop Document Services, Director of the United States Patent and Trademark Office, P.O. Box 1450, Alexandria, Virginia 22313–1450.

(e) *Certain Documents Relating to International Applications and Registrations.* International applications under § 7.11, subsequent designations under § 7.21, responses to notices of irregularity under § 7.14, requests to record changes in the International Register under § 7.23 and § 7.24, requests to note replacements under § 7.28, requests for transformation under § 7.31, and petitions to the Director to review an action of the Office's Madrid Processing Unit, when filed by mail, must be mailed to: Madrid Processing Unit, 600 Dulany Street, MDE–7B87, Alexandria, VA 22314–5793.

[68 FR 48289, Aug. 13, 2003, as amended at 69 FR 57184, Sept. 24, 2004; 69 FR 63321, Nov. 1, 2004; 72 FR 18908, Apr. 16, 2007]

§ 2.191 Business to be transacted in writing.

All business with the Office should be transacted in writing. The personal appearance of applicants or their representatives at the Office is unnecessary. The action of the Office will be based exclusively on the written record. No attention will be paid to any alleged oral promise, stipulation, or understanding in relation to which there is disagreement or doubt. The Office encourages parties to file documents through TEAS wherever possible.

§ 2.192 Business to be conducted with decorum and courtesy.

Trademark applicants, registrants, and parties to proceedings before the Trademark Trial and Appeal Board and their attorneys or agents are required to conduct their business with decorum and courtesy. Documents presented in violation of this requirement will be submitted to the Director and will be returned by the Director's direct order. Complaints against trademark examining attorneys and other employees must be made in correspondence separate from other documents.

§ 2.193 Trademark correspondence and signature requirements.

(a) *Signature required.* Each piece of correspondence that requires a signature must bear:

(1) A handwritten signature personally signed in permanent ink by the person named as the signatory, or a true copy thereof; or

(2) An electronic signature that meets the requirements of paragraph (c) of this section, personally entered by the person named as the signatory. The Office will accept an electronic signature that meets the requirements of paragraph (c) of this section on correspondence filed on paper, by facsimile transmission (§ 2.195(c)), or through TEAS or ESTTA.

(b) *Copy of original signature.* If a copy, such as a photocopy or facsimile copy of an original signature is filed, the filer should retain the original as evidence of authenticity. If a question of authenticity arises, the Office may require submission of the original.

(c) *Requirements for electronic signature.* A person signing a document electronically must:

(1) Personally enter any combination of letters, numbers, spaces and/or punctuation marks that he or she has adopted as a signature, placed between two forward slash ("/") symbols in the signature block on the electronic submission; or

(2) Sign the verified statement using some other form of electronic signature specified by the Director.

(d) *Signatory must be identified.* The name of the person who signs a document in connection with a trademark application, registration, or proceeding before the Trademark Trial and Appeal Board must be set forth in printed or typed form immediately below or adjacent to the signature, or identified elsewhere in the filing (e.g., in a cover letter or other document that accompanies the filing).

(e) *Proper person to sign.* Documents filed in connection with a trademark application or registration must be signed by a proper person. Unless otherwise specified by law, the following requirements apply:

(1) *Verification of facts.* A verification in support of an application for registration, amendment to an application for registration, allegation of use under §2.76 or §2.88, request for extension of time to file a statement of use under §2.89, or an affidavit under section 8, 12(c), 15, or 71 of the Trademark Act must be sworn to or supported by a declaration under §2.20, signed by the owner or a person properly authorized to sign on behalf of the owner. A person who is properly authorized to verify facts on behalf of an owner is:

(i) A person with legal authority to bind the owner (e.g., a corporate officer or general partner of a partnership);

(ii) A person with firsthand knowledge of the facts and actual or implied authority to act on behalf of the owner; or

(iii) An attorney as defined in §11.1 of this chapter who has an actual written or verbal power of attorney or an implied power of attorney from the owner.

(2) *Responses, amendments to applications, requests for express abandonment, requests for reconsideration of final actions, and requests to divide.* Responses to Office actions, amendments to applications, requests for express abandonment, requests for reconsideration of final actions, and requests to divide must be signed by the owner of the application or registration, someone with legal authority to bind the owner (e.g., a corporate officer or general partner of a partnership), or a practitioner qualified to practice under §11.14 of this chapter, in accordance with the following guidelines:

(i) If the owner is represented by a practitioner qualified to practice before the Office under §11.14 of this chapter, the practitioner must sign, except where the owner is required to sign the correspondence; or

(ii) If the owner is not represented by a practitioner qualified to practice under §11.14 of this chapter, the individual owner or someone with legal authority to bind the owner (e.g., a corporate officer or general partner of a partnership) must sign. In the case of joint owners who are not represented by a qualified practitioner, all must sign.

(3) *Powers of attorney and revocations of powers of attorney.* Powers of attorney and revocations of powers of attorney must be signed by the individual applicant, registrant or party to a proceeding pending before the Office, or by someone with legal authority to bind the applicant, registrant, or party (e.g., a corporate officer or general partner of a partnership). In the case of joint applicants, registrants, or parties, all must sign. Once the applicant, registrant or party has designated a qualified practitioner(s), the named practitioner may sign an associate power of attorney appointing another qualified practitioner(s) as an additional person(s) authorized to prosecute the application or registration. If the applicant, registrant, or party revokes the original power of attorney, the revocation discharges any associate power signed by the practitioner whose power has been revoked. If the practitioner who signed an associate power withdraws, the withdrawal discharges any associate power signed by the withdrawing practitioner upon acceptance of the request for withdrawal by the Office.

(4) *Petitions to revive under §2.66.* A petition to revive under §2.66 must be signed by someone with firsthand knowledge of the facts regarding unintentional delay.

(5) *Petitions to Director under §2.146.* A petition to the Director under §2.146 must be signed by the petitioner, someone with legal authority to bind the petitioner (e.g., a corporate officer or general partner of a partnership), or a practitioner qualified to practice under

§ 11.14 of this chapter, in accordance with the following guidelines:

(i) If the petitioner is represented by a practitioner qualified to practice before the Office under § 11.14 of this chapter, the practitioner must sign; or

(ii) If the petitioner is not represented by a practitioner authorized to practice before the Office under § 11.14 of this chapter, the individual petitioner or someone with legal authority to bind the petitioner (e.g., a corporate officer or general partner of a partnership) must sign. In the case of joint petitioners, all must sign.

(6) *Requests for correction, amendment or surrender of registrations.* A request for correction, amendment or surrender of a registration must be signed by the owner of the registration, someone with legal authority to bind the owner (e.g., a corporate officer or general partner of a partnership), or a practitioner qualified to practice before the Office under § 11.14 of this chapter. In the case of joint owners who are not represented by a qualified practitioner, all must sign.

(7) *Renewal applications.* A renewal application must be signed by the registrant or the registrant's representative.

(8) *Designations and revocations of domestic representative.* A designation or revocation of a domestic representative must be signed by the applicant or registrant, someone with legal authority to bind the applicant or registrant (e.g., a corporate officer or general partner of a partnership), or a practitioner qualified to practice under § 11.14 of this chapter. In the case of joint applicants or registrants, all must sign.

(9) *Requests to change correspondence address in an application or registration.* A notice of change of correspondence address in an application or registration must be signed by the applicant or registrant, someone with legal authority to bind the applicant or registrant (e.g., a corporate officer or general partner of a partnership), or a practitioner qualified to practice under § 11.14 of this chapter, in accordance with the following guidelines:

(i) If the applicant or registrant is represented by a practitioner qualified to practice before the Office under § 11.14 of this chapter, the practitioner must sign; or

(ii) If the applicant or registrant is not represented by a practitioner qualified to practice before the Office under § 11.14, the individual applicant or registrant or someone with legal authority to bind the applicant or registrant (e.g., a corporate officer or general partner of a partnership) must sign. In the case of joint applicants or joint registrants, all must sign.

(10) *Cover letters.* A person transmitting paper documents to the Office may sign a cover letter or transmittal letter. The Office neither requires cover letters nor questions the authority of a person who signs a communication that merely transmits paper documents.

(f) *Signature as certification.* The presentation to the Office (whether by signing, filing, submitting, or later advocating) of any document by any person, whether a practitioner or non-practitioner, constitutes a certification under § 11.18(b) of this chapter. Violations of § 11.18(b) of this chapter may jeopardize the validity of the application or registration, and may result in the imposition of sanctions under § 11.18(c) of this chapter. Any practitioner violating § 11.18(b) of this chapter may also be subject to disciplinary action. *See* §§ 10.23(c)(15) and 11.18(d) of this chapter.

(g) *Separate copies for separate files.* (1) Since each file must be complete in itself, a separate copy of every document to be filed in connection with a trademark application, registration, or *inter partes* proceeding must be furnished for each file to which the document pertains, even though the contents of the documents filed in multiple files may be identical.

(2) Parties should not file duplicate copies of correspondence in a single application, registration, or proceeding file, unless the Office requires the filing of duplicate copies. The Office may dispose of duplicate copies of correspondence.

(h) *Separate documents for separate branches of the Office.* Since different branches or sections of the Office may consider different matters, each distinct subject, inquiry or order must be contained in a separate document to avoid confusion and delay in answering correspondence.

(i) *Certified documents required by statute.* When a statute requires that a document be certified, a copy or facsimile transmission of the certification is not acceptable.

[74 FR 54910, Oct. 26, 2009]

§2.194 Identification of trademark application or registration.

(a) No correspondence relating to a trademark application should be filed prior to receipt of the application serial number.

(b) (1) A letter about a trademark application should identify the serial number, the name of the applicant, and the mark.

(2) A letter about a registered trademark should identify the registration number, the name of the registrant, and the mark.

§2.195 Receipt of trademark correspondence.

(a) *Date of receipt and Express Mail date of deposit.* Trademark correspondence received in the Office is given a filing date as of the date of receipt except as follows:

(1) The Office is not open for the filing of correspondence on any day that is a Saturday, Sunday, or Federal holiday within the District of Columbia. Except for correspondence transmitted electronically under paragraph (a)(2) of this section or transmitted by facsimile under paragraph (a)(3) of this section, no correspondence is received in the Office on Saturdays, Sundays, or Federal holidays within the District of Columbia.

(2) Trademark-related correspondence transmitted electronically will be given a filing date as of the date on which the Office receives the transmission.

(3) Correspondence transmitted by facsimile will be given a filing date as of the date on which the complete transmission is received in the Office unless that date is a Saturday, Sunday, or Federal holiday within the District of Columbia, in which case the filing date will be the next succeeding day that is not a Saturday, Sunday, or Federal holiday within the District of Columbia.

(4) Correspondence filed in accordance with §2.198 will be given a filing date as of the date of deposit as "Express Mail" with the United States Postal Service.

(b) *Correspondence delivered by hand.* Correspondence may be delivered by hand during hours the Office is open to receive correspondence.

(c) *Facsimile transmission.* Except in the cases enumerated in paragraph (d) of this section, correspondence, including authorizations to charge a deposit account, may be transmitted by facsimile. The receipt date accorded to the correspondence will be the date on which the complete transmission is received in the Office, unless that date is a Saturday, Sunday, or Federal holiday within the District of Columbia. See §2.196. To facilitate proper processing, each transmission session should be limited to correspondence to be filed in a single application, registration or proceeding before the Office. The application serial number, registration number, or proceeding number should be entered as a part of the sender's identification on a facsimile cover sheet.

(d) Facsimile transmissions are not permitted and if submitted, will not be accorded a date of receipt, in the following situations:

(1) Applications for registration of marks;

(2) Drawings submitted under §2.51, §2.52, §2.72, or §2.173;

(3) Correspondence to be filed with the Trademark Trial and Appeal Board, except notices of *ex parte* appeal;

(4) Requests for cancellation or amendment of a registration under section 7(e) of the Trademark Act; and certificates of registration surrendered for cancellation or amendment under section 7(e) of the Trademark Act; and

(5) Madrid-related correspondence submitted under §7.11, §7.21, §7.14, §7.23, §7.24, or §7.31 of this title.

(e) *Interruptions in U.S. Postal Service.* (1) If the Director designates a postal service interruption or emergency within the meaning of 35 U.S.C. 21(a), any person attempting to file correspondence by "Express Mail Post Office to Addressee" service who was unable to deposit the correspondence with the United States Postal Service due to the interruption or emergency may petition the Director to consider such correspondence as filed on a particular date in the Office.

(2) The petition must:

(i) Be filed promptly after the ending of the designated interruption or emergency;

(ii) Include the original correspondence or a copy of the original correspondence; and

(iii) Include a statement that the correspondence would have been deposited with the United States Postal Service on the requested filing date but for the designated interruption or emergency in "Express Mail" service; and that the correspondence attached to the petition is the original correspondence or a true copy of the correspondence originally attempted to be deposited as Express Mail on the requested filing date.

(3) Paragraphs (e)(1) and (e)(2) of this section do not apply to correspondence that is excluded from the Express Mail procedure pursuant to § 2.198(a)(1).

[68 FR 48289, Aug. 13, 2003, as amended at 69 FR 57185, Sept. 24, 2004; 73 FR 67775, Nov. 17, 2008]

§ 2.196 Times for taking action: Expiration on Saturday, Sunday or Federal holiday.

Whenever periods of time are specified in this part in days, calendar days are intended. When the day, or the last day fixed by statute or by regulation under this part for taking any action or paying any fee in the Office falls on a Saturday, Sunday, or Federal holiday within the District of Columbia, the action may be taken, or the fee paid, on the next succeeding day that is not a Saturday, Sunday, or a Federal holiday.

§ 2.197 Certificate of mailing or transmission.

(a) Except in the cases enumerated in paragraph (a)(2) of this section, correspondence required to be filed in the Office within a set period of time will be considered as being timely filed if the procedure described in this section is followed. The actual date of receipt will be used for all other purposes.

(1) Correspondence will be considered as being timely filed if:

(i) The correspondence is mailed or transmitted prior to expiration of the set period of time by being:

(A) Addressed as set out in § 2.190 and deposited with the U.S. Postal Service with sufficient postage as first class mail; or

(B) Transmitted by facsimile to the Office in accordance with § 2.195(c); and

(ii) The correspondence includes a certificate for each piece of correspondence stating the date of deposit or transmission. The person signing the certificate should have a reasonable basis to expect that the correspondence would be mailed or transmitted on or before the date indicated.

(2) The procedure described in paragraph (a)(1) of this section does not apply to:

(i) Applications for the registration of marks under 15 U.S.C. 1051 or 1126; and

(ii) Madrid-related correspondence filed under § 7.11, § 7.21, § 7.14, § 7.23, § 7.24 or § 7.31 of this title.

(b) In the event that correspondence is considered timely filed by being mailed or transmitted in accordance with paragraph (a) of this section, but not received in the Office, and an application is abandoned, a registration is cancelled or expired, or a proceeding is dismissed, terminated, or decided with prejudice, the correspondence will be considered timely if the party who forwarded such correspondence:

(1) Informs the Office of the previous mailing or transmission of the correspondence within two months after becoming aware that the Office has no evidence of receipt of the correspondence;

(2) Supplies an additional copy of the previously mailed or transmitted correspondence and certificate; and

(3) Includes a statement that attests on a personal knowledge basis or to the satisfaction of the Director to the previous timely mailing or transmission. If the correspondence was sent by facsimile transmission, a copy of the sending unit's report confirming transmission may be used to support this statement.

(c) The Office may require additional evidence to determine whether the correspondence was timely filed.

[68 FR 48289, Aug. 13, 2003, as amended at 69 FR 57185, Sept. 24, 2004]

§ 2.198 Filing of correspondence by "Express Mail."

(a)(1) Except for documents listed in paragraphs (a)(1)(i) through (vii) of this section, any correspondence received by the Office that was delivered by the "Express Mail Post Office to Addressee" service of the United States Postal Service (USPS) will be considered filed with the Office on the date of deposit with the USPS. The Express Mail procedure does not apply to:

(i) Applications for registration of marks;

(ii) Amendments to allege use under section 1(c) of the Act;

(iii) Statements of use under section 1(d) of the Act;

(iv) Requests for extension of time to file a statement of use under section 1(d) of the Act;

(v) Affidavits of continued use under section 8 of the Act;

(vi) Renewal requests under section 9 of the Act; and

(vii) Requests to change or correct addresses.

(2) The date of deposit with USPS is shown by the "date in" on the "Express Mail" label or other official USPS notation. If the USPS deposit date cannot be determined, the correspondence will be accorded the date of receipt in the Office as the filing date.

(b) Correspondence should be deposited directly with an employee of the USPS to ensure that the person depositing the correspondence receives a legible copy of the "Express Mail" mailing label with the "date-in" clearly marked. Persons dealing indirectly with the employees of the USPS (such as by deposit in an "Express Mail" drop box) do so at the risk of not receiving a copy of the "Express Mail" mailing label with the desired "date-in" clearly marked. The paper(s) or fee(s) that constitute the correspondence should also include the "Express Mail" mailing label number thereon. See paragraphs (c), (d) and (e) of this section.

(c) Any person filing correspondence under this section that was received by the Office and delivered by the "Express Mail Post Office to Addressee" service of the USPS, who can show that there is a discrepancy between the filing date accorded by the Office to the correspondence and the date of deposit as shown by the "date-in" on the "Express Mail" mailing label or other official USPS notation, may petition the Director to accord the correspondence a filing date as of the "date-in" on the "Express Mail" mailing label or other official USPS notation, provided that:

(1) The petition is filed within two months after the person becomes aware that the Office has accorded, or will accord, a filing date other than the USPS deposit date;

(2) The number of the "Express Mail" mailing label was placed on the paper(s) or fee(s) that constitute the correspondence prior to the original mailing; and

(3) The petition includes a true copy of the "Express Mail" mailing label showing the "date-in," and of any other official notation by the USPS relied upon to show the date of deposit.

(d) Any person filing correspondence under this section that was received by the Office and delivered by the "Express Mail Post Office to Addressee" service of the USPS, who can show that the "date-in" on the "Express Mail" mailing label or other official notation entered by the USPS was incorrectly entered or omitted by the USPS, may petition the Director to accord the correspondence a filing date as of the date the correspondence is shown to have been deposited with the USPS, provided that:

(1) The petition is filed within two months after the person becomes aware that the Office has accorded, or will accord, a filing date based upon an incorrect entry by the USPS;

(2) The number of the "Express Mail" mailing label was placed on the paper(s) or fee(s) prior to the original mailing; and

(3) The petition includes a showing that establishes, to the satisfaction of the Director, that the correspondence was deposited in the "Express Mail Post Office to Addressee" service prior

to the last scheduled pickup on the requested filing date. Any showing pursuant to this paragraph must be corroborated by evidence from the USPS or evidence that came into being within one business day after the deposit of the correspondence in the "Express Mail Post Office to Addressee" service of the USPS.

(e) If correspondence is properly addressed to the Office pursuant to § 2.190 and deposited with sufficient postage in the "Express Mail Post Office to Addressee" service of the USPS, but not received by the Office, the party who mailed the correspondence may petition the Director to consider such correspondence filed in the Office on the USPS deposit date, provided that:

(1) The petition is filed within two months after the person becomes aware that the Office has no evidence of receipt of the correspondence;

(2) The number of the "Express Mail" mailing label was placed on the paper(s) or fee(s) prior to the original mailing;

(3) The petition includes a copy of the originally deposited paper(s) or fee(s) showing the number of the "Express Mail" mailing label thereon, a copy of any returned postcard receipt, a copy of the "Express Mail" mailing label showing the "date-in," a copy of any other official notation by the USPS relied upon to show the date of deposit, and, if the requested filing date is a date other than the "date-in" on the "Express Mail" mailing label or other official notation entered by the USPS, a showing pursuant to paragraph (d)(3) of this section that the correspondence was deposited in the "Express Mail Post Office to Addressee" service prior to the last scheduled pickup on the requested filing date; and

(4) The petition includes a statement that establishes, to the satisfaction of the Director, the original deposit of the correspondence and that the copies of the correspondence, the copy of the "Express Mail" mailing label, the copy of any returned postcard receipt, and any official notation entered by the USPS are true copies of the originally mailed correspondence, original "Express Mail" mailing label, returned postcard receipt, and official notation entered by the USPS.

(f) The Office may require additional evidence to determine whether the correspondence was deposited as "Express Mail" with the USPS on the date in question.

[68 FR 48289, Aug. 13, 2003; 68 FR 56557, Oct. 1, 2003]

TRADEMARK RECORDS AND FILES OF THE PATENT AND TRADEMARK OFFICE

SOURCE: 68 FR 48292, Aug. 13, 2003, unless otherwise noted.

§ 2.200 Assignment records open to public inspection.

(a)(1) Separate assignment records are maintained in the Office for patents and trademarks. The assignment records relating to trademark applications and registrations (for assignments recorded on or after January 1, 1955) are open to public inspection at the Office, and copies of those assignment records may be obtained upon request and payment of the fee set forth in § 2.6 of this chapter.

(2) All records of trademark assignments recorded before January 1, 1955, are maintained by the National Archives and Records Administration (NARA). The records are open to public inspection. Certified and uncertified copies of those assignment records are provided by NARA upon request and payment of the fees required by NARA.

(b) An order for a copy of an assignment or other document should identify the reel and frame number where the assignment or document is recorded. If a document is identified without specifying its correct reel and frame, an extra charge as set forth in § 2.6(b)(10) will be made for the time consumed in making a search for such assignment.

§ 2.201 Copies and certified copies.

(a) Non-certified copies of trademark registrations and of any trademark records or trademark documents within the jurisdiction of the Office and open to the public, will be furnished by the Office to any person entitled thereto, upon payment of the appropriate fee required by § 2.6.

(b) Certified copies of trademark registrations and of any trademark records or trademark documents within the jurisdiction of the Office and open to the public will be authenticated by the seal of the Office and certified by the Director, or in his or her name attested by an officer of the Office authorized by the Director, upon payment of the fee required by § 2.6.

FEES AND PAYMENT OF MONEY IN TRADEMARK CASES

SOURCE: 68 FR 48292, Aug. 13, 2003, unless otherwise noted.

§ 2.206 Trademark fees payable in advance.

(a) Trademark fees and charges payable to the Office are required to be paid in advance; that is, at the time of requesting any action by the Office for which a fee or charge is payable.

(b) All fees paid to the Office must be itemized in each individual trademark application or registration file, or trademark proceeding, so that the purpose for which the fees are paid is clear. The Office may return fees that are not itemized as required by this paragraph.

§ 2.207 Methods of payment.

(a) All payments of money required in trademark cases, including fees for the processing of international trademark applications and registrations that are paid through the Office, shall be made in U.S. dollars and in the form of a cashier's or certified check, Treasury note, national bank note, or United States Postal Service money order. If sent in any other form, the Office may delay or cancel the credit until collection is made. Checks and money orders must be made payable to the Director of the United States Patent and Trademark Office. (Checks made payable to the Commissioner of Patents and Trademarks will continue to be accepted.) Payments from foreign countries must be payable and immediately negotiable in the United States for the full amount of the fee required. Money sent to the Office by mail will be at the risk of the sender, and letters containing money should be registered with the United States Postal Service.

(b) Payments of money required for trademark fees may also be made by credit card, except for replenishing a deposit account. Payment of a fee by credit card must specify the amount to be charged to the credit card and such other information as is necessary to process the charge, and is subject to collection of the fee. The Office will not accept a general authorization to charge fees to a credit card. If credit card information is provided on a form or document other than a form provided by the Office for the payment of fees by credit card, the Office will not be liable if the credit card number becomes public knowledge.

[68 FR 48292, Aug. 13, 2003, as amended at 69 FR 43752, July 22, 2004]

§ 2.208 Deposit accounts.

(a) For the convenience of attorneys, and the general public in paying any fees due, in ordering copies of records, or services offered by the Office, deposit accounts may be established in the Office upon payment of the fee for establishing a deposit account (§ 2.6(b)(13)). A minimum deposit of $1,000 is required for paying any fees due or in ordering any services offered by the Office. The Office will issue a deposit account statement at the end of each month. A remittance must be made promptly upon receipt of the statement to cover the value of items or services charged to the account and thus restore the account to its established normal deposit. An amount sufficient to cover all fees, copies, or services requested must always be on deposit. Charges to accounts with insufficient funds will not be accepted. A service charge (§ 2.6(b)(13)) will be assessed for each month that the balance at the end of the month is below $1,000.

(b) A general authorization to charge all fees, or only certain fees to a deposit account containing sufficient funds may be filed in an individual application, either for the entire pendency of the application or with respect to a particular document filed. An authorization to charge a fee to a deposit account will not be considered payment of the fee on the date the authorization to charge the fee is effective as to the particular fee to be charged unless sufficient funds are present in the account to cover the fee.

(c) A deposit account holder may replenish the deposit account by submitting a payment to the Office. A payment to replenish a deposit account must be submitted by one of the methods set forth in paragraphs (c)(1), (c)(2), (c)(3), or (c)(4) of this section.

(1) A payment to replenish a deposit account may be submitted by electronic funds transfer through the Federal Reserve Fedwire System, which requires that the following information be provided to the deposit account holder's bank or financial institution:

(i) Name of the Bank, which is Treas NYC (Treasury New York City);

(ii) Bank Routing Code, which is 021030004;

(iii) United States Patent and Trademark Office account number with the Department of the Treasury, which is 13100001; and

(iv) The deposit account holder's company name and deposit account number.

(2) A payment to replenish a deposit account may be submitted by electronic funds transfer over the Office's Internet Web site (*www.uspto.gov*).

(3) A payment to replenish a deposit account may be addressed to: Director of the United States Patent and Trademark Office, Attn: Deposit Accounts, 2051 Jamieson Avenue, Suite 300, Alexandria, Virginia 22314.

[68 FR 48292, Aug. 13, 2003, as amended at 69 FR 43752, July 22, 2004; 70 FR 56128, Sept. 26, 2005; 73 FR 67775, Nov. 17, 2008]

§ 2.209 Refunds.

(a) The Director may refund any fee paid by mistake or in excess of that required. A change of purpose after the payment of a fee, such as when a party desires to withdraw a trademark application, appeal or other trademark filing for which a fee was paid, will not entitle a party to a refund of such fee. The Office will not refund amounts of twenty-five dollars or less unless a refund is specifically requested, and will not notify the payor of such amounts. If a party paying a fee or requesting a refund does not provide the banking information necessary for making refunds by electronic funds transfer (31 U.S.C. 3332 and 31 CFR part 208), or instruct the Office that refunds are to be credited to a deposit account, the Director may require such information, or use the banking information on the payment instrument to make a refund. Any refund of a fee paid by credit card will be by a credit to the credit card account to which the fee was charged.

(b) Any request for refund must be filed within two years from the date the fee was paid, except as otherwise provided in this paragraph. If the Office charges a deposit account by an amount other than an amount specifically indicated in an authorization (§ 2.208(b)), any request for refund based upon such charge must be filed within two years from the date of the deposit account statement indicating such charge, and include a copy of that deposit account statement. The time periods set forth in this paragraph are not extendable.

PART 3—ASSIGNMENT, RECORDING AND RIGHTS OF ASSIGNEE

EDITORIAL NOTE: Part 3 pertaining to both patents and trademarks is placed in the grouping pertaining to patents regulations.

PART 4—COMPLAINTS REGARDING INVENTION PROMOTERS

EDITORIAL NOTE: Part 4 is placed in the separate grouping of parts pertaining to patents regulations.

PART 5—SECRECY OF CERTAIN INVENTIONS AND LICENSES TO EXPORT AND FILE APPLICATIONS IN FOREIGN COUNTRIES

EDITORIAL NOTE: Part 5 is placed in the separate grouping of parts pertaining to patents regulations.

PART 6—CLASSIFICATION OF GOODS AND SERVICES UNDER THE TRADEMARK ACT

Sec.

6.3 Schedule for certification marks.
6.4 Schedule for collective membership marks.

AUTHORITY: Secs. 30, 41, 60 Stat. 436, 440; 15 U.S.C. 1112, 1123.

§6.1 International schedule of classes of goods and services.

GOODS

1. Chemicals used in industry, science and photography, as well as in agriculture, horticulture and forestry; unprocessed artificial resins, unprocessed plastics; manures; fire extinguishing compositions; tempering and soldering preparations; chemical substances for preserving foodstuffs; tanning substances; adhesives used in industry.

2. Paints, varnishes, lacquers; preservatives against rust and against deterioration of wood; colorants; mordants; raw natural resins; metals in foil and powder form for painters, decorators, printers and artists.

3. Bleaching preparations and other substances for laundry use; cleaning, polishing, scouring and abrasive preparations; soaps; perfumery, essential oils, cosmetics, hair lotions; dentifrices.

4. Industrial oils and greases; lubricants; dust absorbing, wetting and binding compositions; fuels (including motor spirit) and illuminants; candles and wicks for lighting.

5. Pharmaceutical and veterinary preparations; sanitary preparations for medical purposes; dietetic food and substances adapted for medical use, food for babies; dietary supplements for humans and animals; plasters, materials for dressings; material for stopping teeth, dental wax; disinfectants; preparations for destroying vermin; fungicides, herbicides.

6. Common metals and their alloys; metal building materials; transportable buildings of metal; materials of metal for railway tracks; non-electric cables and wires of common metal; ironmongery, small items of metal hardware; pipes and tubes of metal; safes; goods of common metal not included in other classes; ores.

7. Machines and machine tools; motors and engines (except for land vehicles); machine coupling and transmission components (except for land vehicles); agricultural implements other than hand-operated; incubators for eggs; automatic vending machines.

8. Hand tools and implements (hand-operated); cutlery; side arms; razors.

9. Scientific, nautical, surveying, photographic, cinematographic, optical, weighing, measuring, signalling, checking (supervision), life-saving and teaching apparatus and instruments; apparatus and instruments for conducting, switching, transforming, accumulating, regulating or controlling electricity; apparatus for recording, transmission or reproduction of sound or images; magnetic data carriers, recording discs; compact discs, DVDs and other digital recording media; mechanisms for coin-operated apparatus; cash registers, calculating machines, data processing equipment, computers; computer software; fire-extinguishing apparatus.

10. Surgical, medical, dental and veterinary apparatus and instruments, artificial limbs, eyes and teeth; orthopedic articles; suture materials.

11. Apparatus for lighting, heating, steam generating, cooking, refrigerating, drying, ventilating, water supply and sanitary purposes.

12. Vehicles; apparatus for locomotion by land, air or water.

13. Firearms; ammunition and projectiles; explosives; fireworks.

14. Precious metals and their alloys and goods in precious metals or coated therewith, not included in other classes; jewellery, precious stones; horological and chronometric instruments.

15. Musical instruments.

16. Paper, cardboard and goods made from these materials, not included in other classes; printed matter; bookbinding material; photographs; stationery; adhesives for stationery or household purposes; artists' materials; paint brushes; typewriters and office requisites (except furniture); instructional and teaching material (except apparatus); plastic materials for packaging (not included in other classes); printers' type; printing blocks.

17. Rubber, gutta-percha, gum, asbestos, mica and goods made from these materials and not included in other classes; plastics in extruded form for use in manufacture; packing, stopping

and insulating materials; flexible pipes, not of metal.

18. Leather and imitations of leather, and goods made of these materials and not included in other classes; animal skins, hides; trunks and travelling bags; umbrellas and parasols; walking sticks; whips, harness and saddlery.

19. Building materials (non-metallic); non-metallic rigid pipes for building; asphalt, pitch and bitumen; non-metallic transportable buildings; monuments, not of metal.

20. Furniture, mirrors, picture frames; goods (not included in other classes) of wood, cork, reed, cane, wicker, horn, bone, ivory, whalebone, shell, amber, mother-of-pearl, meerschaum and substitutes for all these materials, or of plastics.

21. Household or kitchen utensils and containers; combs and sponges; brushes (except paint brushes); brush-making materials; articles for cleaning purposes; steelwool; unworked or semi-worked glass (except glass used in building); glassware, porcelain and earthenware not included in other classes.

22. Ropes, string, nets, tents, awnings, tarpaulins, sails, sacks and bags (not included in other classes); padding and stuffing materials (except of rubber or plastics); raw fibrous textile materials.

23. Yarns and threads, for textile use.

24. Textiles and textile goods, not included in other classes; bed covers; table covers.

25. Clothing, footwear, headgear.

26. Lace and embroidery, ribbons and braid; buttons, hooks and eyes, pins and needles; artificial flowers.

27. Carpets, rugs, mats and matting, linoleum and other materials for covering existing floors; wall hangings (non-textile).

28. Games and playthings; gymnastic and sporting articles not included in other classes; decorations for Christmas trees.

29. Meat, fish, poultry and game; meat extracts; preserved, frozen, dried and cooked fruits and vegetables; jellies, jams, compotes; eggs; milk and milk products; edible oils and fats.

30. Coffee, tea, cocoa and artificial coffee; rice; tapioca and sago; flour and preparations made from cereals; bread, pastry and confectionery; ices; sugar, honey, treacle; yeast, baking-powder; salt; mustard; vinegar, sauces (condiments); spices; ice.

31. Grains and agricultural, horticultural and forestry products not included in other classes; live animals; fresh fruits and vegetables; seeds, natural plants and flowers; foodstuffs for animals, malt.

32. Beers; mineral and aerated waters and other non-alcoholic beverages; fruit beverages and fruit juices; syrups and other preparations for making beverages.

33. Alcoholic beverages (except beers).

34. Tobacco; smokers' articles; matches.

SERVICES

35. Advertising; business management; business administration; office functions.

36. Insurance; financial affairs; monetary affairs; real estate affairs.

37. Building construction; repair; installation services.

38. Telecommunications.

39. Transport; packaging and storage of goods; travel arrangement.

40. Treatment of materials.

41. Education; providing of training; entertainment; sporting and cultural activities.

42. Scientific and technological services and research and design relating thereto; industrial analysis and research services; design and development of computer hardware and software.

43. Services for providing food and drink; temporary accommodation.

44. Medical services; veterinary services; hygienic and beauty care for human beings or animals; agriculture, horticulture and forestry services.

45. Legal services; security services for the protection of property and individuals; personal and social services rendered by others to meet the needs of individuals.

[77 FR 47529, Aug. 9, 2012]

§ 6.2 Prior U.S. schedule of classes of goods and services.

Class	Title
	GOODS
1	Raw or partly prepared materials.
2	Receptacles.
3	Baggage, animal equipments, portfolios, and pocket books.
4	Abrasives and polishing materials.
5	Adhesives.
6	Chemicals and chemical compositions.
7	Cordage.
8	Smokers' articles, not including tobacco products.
9	Explosives, firearms, equipments, and projectiles.
10	Fertilizers.
11	Inks and inking materials.
12	Construction materials.
13	Hardware and plumbing and steamfitting supplies.
14	Metals and metal castings and forgings.
15	Oils and greases.
16	Protective and decorative coatings.
17	Tobacco products.
18	Medicines and pharmaceutical preparations.
19	Vehicles.
20	Linoleum and oiled cloth.
21	Electrical apparatus, machines, and supplies.
22	Games, toys, and sporting goods.
23	Cutlery, machinery, and tools, and parts thereof.
24	Laundry appliances and machines.
25	Locks and safes.
26	Measuring and scientific appliances.
27	Horological instruments.
28	Jewelry and precious-metal ware.
29	Brooms, brushes, and dusters.
30	Crockery, earthenware, and porcelain.
31	Filters and refrigerators.
32	Furniture and upholstery.
33	Glassware.
34	Heating, lighting, and ventilating apparatus.
35	Belting, hose, machinery packing, and nonmetallic tires.
36	Musical instruments and supplies.
37	Paper and stationery.
38	Prints and publications.
39	Clothing.
40	Fancy goods, furnishings, and notions.
41	Canes, parasols, and umbrellas.
42	Knitted, netted, and textile fabrics, and substitutes therefor.
43	Thread and yarn.
44	Dental, medical, and surgical appliances.
45	Soft drinks and carbonated waters.
46	Foods and ingredients of foods.
47	Wines.
48	Malt beverages and liquors.
49	Distilled alcoholic liquors.
50	Merchandise not otherwise classified.
51	Cosmetics and toilet preparations.
52	Detergents and soaps.
	SERVICES
100	Miscellaneous.
101	Advertising and business.
102	Insurance and financial.
103	Construction and repair.
104	Communication.
105	Transportation and storage.
106	Material treatment.
107	Education and entertainment.

[24 FR 10383, Dec. 22, 1959. Redesignated at 38 FR 14681, June 4, 1973]

§ 6.3 Schedule for certification marks.

In applications for registration of certification marks based on sections 1 and 44 of the Trademark Act and registrations resulting from such applications, goods and services are classified in two classes as follows:

A. Goods.

B. Services.

[73 FR 67775, Nov. 15, 2008]

§ 6.4 Schedule for collective membership marks.

All collective membership marks in applications based on sections 1 and 44 of the Trademark Act and registrations resulting from such applications are classified as follows:

Class	Title
200	Collective Membership.

[73 FR 67775, Nov. 17, 2008]

PART 7—RULES OF PRACTICE IN FILINGS PURSUANT TO THE PROTOCOL RELATING TO THE MADRID AGREEMENT CONCERNING THE INTERNATIONAL REGISTRATION OF MARKS

Subpart A—General Information

Subpart B—International Application Originating From the United States

Subpart C—Subsequent Designation Submitted Through the Office

AUTHORITY: 15 U.S.C. 1123, 35 U.S.C. 2, unless othe rwise noted.

SOURCE: 68 FR 55769, Sept. 26, 2003, unless otherwise noted.

Subpart A—General Information

§ 7.1 Definitions of terms as used in this part.

(a) *the Act* means the Trademark Act of 1946, 60 Stat. 427, as amended, codified in 15 U.S.C. 1051 *et seq.*

(b) *Subsequent designation* means a request for extension of protection of an international registration to a Contracting Party made after the International Bureau registers the mark.

(c) The acronym *TEAS* means the Trademark Electronic Application System available on-line through the Office's Web site at: *www.uspto.gov.*

(d) The term *Office* means the United States Patent and Trademark Office.

(e) All references to sections in this part refer to 37 Code of Federal Regulations, except as otherwise stated.

§ 7.2 [Reserved]

§ 7.3 Correspondence must be in English.

International applications and registrations, requests for extension of protection and all other related correspondence with the Office must be in English. The Office will not process correspondence that is in a language other than English.

§ 7.4 Receipt of correspondence.

(a) *Correspondence Filed Through TEAS.* Correspondence relating to international applications and registrations and requests for extension of protection submitted through TEAS will be accorded the date and time on which the complete transmission is received in the Office based on Eastern Time. Eastern Time means eastern standard time or eastern daylight time, as appropriate.

(b) *Correspondence Filed By Mail.* International applications under § 7.11, subsequent designations under § 7.21, responses to notices of irregularity under § 7.14, requests to record changes in the International Register under § 7.23 and § 7.24, requests to note replacement under § 7.28, requests for transformation under § 7.31, and petitions to the Director to review an action of the Office's Madrid Processing Unit, when filed by mail, must be addressed to: Madrid Processing Unit, 600

Dulany Street, MDE–7B87, Alexandria, VA 22314–5793.

(1) International applications under §7.11, subsequent designations under §7.21, requests to record changes in the International Register under §7.23 and §7.24, and petitions to the Director to review an action of the Office's Madrid Processing Unit, when filed by mail, will be accorded the date of receipt in the Office, unless they are sent by Express Mail pursuant to §2.198 of this title, in which case they will be accorded the date of deposit with the United States Postal Service.

(2) Responses to notices of irregularity under §7.14, requests to note replacement under §7.28, and requests for transformation under §7.31, when filed by mail, will be accorded the date of receipt in the Office.

(c) *Hand-Delivered Correspondence.* International applications under §7.11, subsequent designations under §7.21, responses to notices of irregularity under §7.14, requests to record changes in the International Register under §§7.23 and 7.24, requests to note replacement under §7.28, requests for transformation under §7.31, and petitions to the Director to review an action of the Office's Madrid Processing Unit, may be delivered by hand during the hours the Office is open to receive correspondence. Madrid-related hand-delivered correspondence must be delivered to the Trademark Assistance Center, James Madison Building—East Wing, Concourse Level, 600 Dulany Street, Alexandria, VA 22314, Attention: MPU.

(d) *Facsimile Transmission Not Permitted.* The following documents may not be sent by facsimile transmission, and will not be accorded a date of receipt if sent by facsimile transmission:

(1) International applications under §7.11;

(2) Subsequent designations under §7.21;

(3) Responses to notices of irregularity under §7.14;

(4) Requests to record changes of ownership under §7.23;

(5) Requests to record restrictions of the holder's right of disposal, or the release of such restrictions, under §7.24; and

(6) Requests for transformation under §7.31.

(e) *Certificate of Mailing or Transmission Procedure Does Not Apply.* The certificate of mailing or transmission procedure provided in §2.197 does not apply to the documents specified in paragraph (d) of this section.

[69 FR 57185, Sept. 24, 2004, as amended at 69 FR 63321, Nov. 1, 2004; 72 FR 18908, Apr. 16, 2007]

§7.5 [Reserved]

§7.6 Schedule of U.S. process fees.

(a) The Office requires the following process fees:

(1) For certifying an international application based on a single basic application or registration, per class—$100.00

(2) For certifying an international application based on more than one basic application or registration, per class—$150.00

(3) For transmitting a subsequent designation under §7.21—$100.00

(4) For transmitting a request to record an assignment or restriction, or release of a restriction, under §7.23 or §7.24—$100.00

(5) For filing a notice of replacement under §7.28, per class—$100.00

(6) For filing an affidavit under §71 of the Act, per class—$100.00

(7) Surcharge for filing an affidavit under §71 of the Act during the grace period, per class—$100.00

(8) For correcting a deficiency in a section 71 affidavit—$100.00

(b) The fees required in paragraph (a) of this section must be paid in U.S. dollars at the time of submission of the requested action. *See* §2.207 of this chapter for acceptable forms of payment and §2.208 of this chapter for payments using a deposit account established in the Office.

[68 FR 55769, Sept. 26, 2003, as amended at 75 FR 35977, June 24, 2010]

§7.7 Payments of fees to International Bureau.

(a) For documents filed through TEAS, the following fees may be paid either directly to the International Bureau or through the Office:

(1) International application fees;

(2) Subsequent designation fees; and

(3) Recording fee for an assignment of an international registration under § 7.23.

(b) The fees in paragraph (a) of this section may be paid as follows:

(1)(i) Directly to the International Bureau by debit to a current account with the International Bureau. In this case, an applicant or holder's submission to the Office must include the International Bureau account number; or

(ii) Directly to the International Bureau using any other acceptable method of payment. In this case, an applicant or holder's submission to the Office must include the International Bureau receipt number for payment of the fees; or

(2) Through the Office. Fees paid through the Office must be paid in U.S. dollars at the time of submission. See § 2.207 of this chapter for acceptable forms of payment and § 2.208 of this chapter for payments using a deposit account established in the Office.

(c) All fees for paper filings must be paid directly to the International Bureau.

(d) The International Bureau fee calculator may be viewed on the Web site of the World Intellectual Property Organization, currently available at: *http://www.wipo.int/madrid/en/*.

[68 FR 55769, Sept. 26, 2003, as amended at 69 FR 57185, Sept. 24, 2004]

Subpart B—International Application Originating From the United States

§ 7.11 Requirements for international application originating from the United States.

(a) The Office will grant a date of receipt to an international application That is either filed through TEAS, or typed on the official paper form issued by the International Bureau. The international application must include all of the following:

(1) The filing date and serial number of the basic application and/or the registration date and registration number of the basic registration;

(2) The name and entity of the international applicant that is identical to the name and entity of the applicant or registrant in the basic application or basic registration, and the applicant's current address;

(3) A reproduction of the mark that is the same as the mark in the basic application and/or registration and that meets the requirements of § 2.52 of this title.

(i) If the mark in the basic application and/or registration is depicted in black and white and the basic application or registration does not include a color claim, the reproduction of the mark in the international application must be black and white.

(ii) If the mark in the basic application or registration is depicted in black and white and includes a color claim, the international application must include both a black and white reproduction of the mark and a color reproduction of the mark.

(iii) If the mark in the basic application and/or registration is depicted in color, the reproduction of the mark in the international application must be in color.

(iv) If the international application is filed on paper, the mark must be no more than 3.15 inches (8 cm) high by 3.15 inches (8 cm) wide, and must appear in the box designated by the International Bureau on the International Bureau's official form;

(4) A color claim as set out in § 7.12, if appropriate;

(5) A description of the mark that is the same as the description of the mark in the basic application or registration, as appropriate;

(6) An indication of the type of mark if the mark in the basic application and/or registration is a three-dimensional mark, a sound mark, a collective mark or a certification mark;

(7) A list of the goods and/or services that is identical to or narrower than the list of goods and/or services in each claimed basic application or registration and classified according to the *Nice Agreement Concerning the International Classification of Goods and Services for the Purposes of the Registration of Marks*;

(8) A list of the designated Contracting Parties. If the goods and/or services in the international application are not the same for each designated Contracting Party, the application must list the goods and/or services

in the international application that pertain to each designated Contracting Party;

(9) The certification fee required by §7.6;

(10) If the application is filed through TEAS, the international application fees for all classes, and the fees for all designated Contracting Parties identified in the international application (see §7.7);

(11) A statement that the applicant is entitled to file an international application in the Office, specifying that applicant: is a national of the United States; has a domicile in the United States; or has a real and effective industrial or commercial establishment in the United States. Where an applicant's address is not in the United States, the applicant must provide the address of its U.S. domicile or establishment; and

(12) If the international application is filed through TEAS, an e-mail address for receipt of correspondence from the Office.

(b) For requirements for certification, *see* §7.13.

[68 FR 55769, Sept. 26, 2003, as amended at 69 FR 57185, Sept. 24, 2004; 73 FR 67775, Nov. 17, 2008]

§7.12 Claim of color.

(a) If color is claimed as a feature of the mark in the basic application and/or registration, the international application must include a statement that color is claimed as a feature of the mark and set forth the same name(s) of the color(s) claimed in the basic application and/or registration.

(b) If color is not claimed as a feature of the mark in the basic application and/or registration, color may not be claimed as a feature of the mark in the international application.

§7.13 Certification of international application.

(a) When an international application contains all the elements set forth in §7.11(a), the Office will certify to the International Bureau that the information contained in the international application corresponds to the information contained in the basic application(s) and/or basic registration(s) at the time of certification, and will then forward the international application to the International Bureau.

(b) When an international application does not meet the requirements of §7.11(a), the Office will not certify or forward the international application. If the international applicant paid the international application fees (see §7.7) through the Office, the Office will refund the international fees. The Office will not refund the certification fee.

§7.14 Correcting irregularities in international application.

(a) *Response period.* Upon receipt of a notice of irregularities in an international application from the International Bureau, the applicant must respond to the International Bureau within the period set forth in the notice.

(b) *Classification and Identification of Goods and Services.* Responses to International Bureau notices of irregularities in the classification or identification of goods or services in an international application must be submitted through the Office for forwarding to the International Bureau. The Office will review an applicant's response to a notice of irregularities in the identification of goods or services to ensure that the response does not identify goods or services that are broader than the scope of the goods or services in the basic application or registration.

(c) *Fees.* If the International Bureau notice of irregularities requires the payment of fees, the fees for correcting irregularities in the international application must be paid directly to the International Bureau.

(d) *Other Irregularities Requiring Response from Applicant.* Except for responses to irregularities mentioned in paragraph (b) of this section and payment of fees for correcting irregularities mentioned in paragraph (c) of this section, all other responses may be submitted through the Office in accordance with §7.14(e), or filed directly at the International Bureau. The Office will forward timely responses to the International Bureau, but will not review the responses or respond to any irregularities on behalf of the international applicant.

(e) *Procedure for response.* To be considered timely, a response must be received by the International Bureau before the end of the response period set forth in the International Bureau's notice. Receipt in the Office does not fulfill this requirement. Any response submitted through the Office for forwarding to the International Bureau should be submitted as soon as possible, but at least one month before the end of the response period in the International Bureau's notice. The Office will not process any response received in the Office after the International Bureau's response deadline.

[68 FR 55769, Sept. 26, 2003, as amended at 69 FR 57186, Sept. 24, 2004; 73 FR 67776, Nov. 17, 2008]

Subpart C—Subsequent Designation Submitted Through the Office

§ 7.21 Subsequent designation.

(a) A subsequent designation may be filed directly with the International Bureau, or, if it meets the requirements of paragraph (b) of this section, submitted through the Office.

(b) The Office will grant a date of receipt to a subsequent designation that is either filed through TEAS, or typed on the official paper form issued by the International Bureau. The subsequent designation must contain all of the following:

(1) The international registration number;

(2) The serial number of the U.S. application or registration number of the U.S. registration that formed the basis of the international registration;

(3) The name and address of the holder of the international registration;

(4) A statement that the holder is entitled to file a subsequent designation in the Office, specifying that holder: Is a national of the United States; has a domicile in the United States; or has a real and effective industrial or commercial establishment in the United States. Where a holder's address is not in the United States, the holder must provide the address of its U.S. domicile or establishment;

(5) A list of goods and/or services that is identical to or narrower than the list of goods and/or services in the international registration;

(6) A list of the designated Contracting Parties. If the goods and/or services in the subsequent designation are not the same for each designated Contracting Party, the holder must list the goods and/or services covered by the subsequent designation that pertain to each designated Contracting Party;

(7) The U.S. transmittal fee required by § 7.6;

(8) If the subsequent designation is filed through TEAS, the subsequent designation fees (*see* § 7.7); and

(9) If the subsequent designation is filed through TEAS, an e-mail address for receipt of correspondence from the Office.

(c) If the subsequent designation is accorded a date of receipt, the Office will then forward the subsequent designation to the International Bureau.

(d) If the subsequent designation fails to contain all the elements set forth in paragraph (b) of this section, the Office will not forward the subsequent designation to the International Bureau. The Office will notify the holder of the reason(s). If the holder paid the subsequent designation fees (see § 7.7) through the Office, the Office will refund the subsequent designation fees. The Office will not refund the transmittal fee.

(e) Correspondence to correct any irregularities in a subsequent designation must be made directly with the International Bureau.

[68 FR 55769, Sept. 26, 2003, as amended at 69 FR 57186, Sept. 24, 2004]

Subpart D—Recording Changes to International Registration

§ 7.22 Recording changes to international registration.

Except as provided in §§ 7.23 and 7.24, requests to record changes to an international registration must be filed with the International Bureau. If a request to record an assignment or restriction of a holder's right of disposal of an international registration or the release of such a restriction meets the requirements of § 7.23 or 7.24, the Office will forward the request to the International Bureau. Section 10 of the Act and part 3 of this chapter are not applicable to assignments or restrictions of international registrations.

§7.23 Requests for recording assignments at the International Bureau.

A request to record an assignment of an international registration may be submitted through the Office for forwarding to the International Bureau only if the assignee cannot obtain the assignor's signature for the request to record the assignment.

(a) A request to record an assignment submitted through the Office must include all of the following:

(1) The international registration number;

(2) The name and address of the holder of the international registration;

(3) The name and address of the assignee of the international registration;

(4) A statement that the assignee: Is a national of the United States; has a domicile in the United States; or has a real and effective industrial or commercial establishment in the United States. Where an assignee's address is not in the United States, the assignee must provide the address of its U.S. domicile or establishment;

(5) A statement that the assignee could not obtain the assignor's signature for the request to record the assignment;

(6) An indication that the assignment applies to the designation to the United States;

(7) A statement that the assignment applies to all the goods and/or services in the international registration, or if less, a list of the goods and/or services in the international registration that have been assigned that pertain to the designation to the United States; and

(8) The U.S. transmittal fee required by §7.6.

(b) If a request to record an assignment contains all the elements set forth in paragraph (a) of this section, the Office will forward the request to the International Bureau. Forwarding the request to the International Bureau is not a determination by the Office of the validity of the assignment or the effect that the assignment has on the title of the international registration.

(c) If the request fails to contain all the elements set forth in paragraph (a) of this section, the Office will not forward the request to the International Bureau. The Office will notify the assignee(s) of the reason(s). If the assignee paid the fees to record the assignment (*see* §7.7) through the Office, the Office will refund the recording fee. The Office will not refund the transmittal fee.

(d) Correspondence to correct any irregularities in a request to record an assignment must be made directly with the International Bureau.

[68 FR 55769, Sept. 26, 2003, as amended at 69 FR 57186, Sept. 24, 2004]

§7.24 Requests to record security interest or other restriction of holder's rights of disposal or release of such restriction submitted through the Office.

(a) A party who obtained a security interest or other restriction of a holder's right to dispose of an international registration, or the release of such a restriction, may submit a request to record the restriction or release through the Office for forwarding to the International Bureau only if:

(1) The restriction or release:

(i) Is the result of a court order; or

(ii) Is the result of an agreement between the holder of the international registration and the party restricting the holder's right of disposal, and the signature of the holder cannot be obtained for the request to record the restriction or release;

(2) The party who obtained the restriction is a national of, is domiciled in, or has a real and effective industrial or commercial establishment in the United States; and

(3) The restriction or release applies to the holder's right to dispose of the international registration in the United States.

(b) A request to record a restriction or the release of a restriction must be submitted by the party who obtained the restriction of the holder's right of disposal and include all the following:

(1) The international registration number;

(2) The name and address of the holder of the international registration;

(3) The name and address of the party who obtained the restriction;

(4) A statement that the party who submitted the request: Is a national of the United States; has a domicile in the United States; or has a real and effective industrial or commercial establishment in the United States. Where a party's address is not in the United States, the party must provide the address of its U.S. domicile or establishment;

(5) (i) A statement that the restriction is the result of a court order, or

(ii) Where the restriction is the result of an agreement between the holder of the international registration and the party restricting the holder's right of disposal, a statement that the signature of the holder of the international registration could not be obtained for the request to record the restriction or release of the restriction;

(6) A summary of the main facts concerning the restriction;

(7) An indication that the restriction, or the release of the restriction, of the holder's right of disposal of the international registration applies to the designation to the United States; and

(8) The U.S. transmittal fee required by § 7.6.

(c) If a request to record a restriction, or the release of a restriction, contains all the elements set forth in paragraph (b) of this section, the Office will forward the request to the International Bureau. Forwarding the request to the International Bureau is not a determination by the Office of the validity of the restriction, or its release, or the effect that the restriction has on the holder's right to dispose of the international registration.

(d) If the request fails to contain all the elements set forth in paragraph (b) of this section, the Office will not forward the request. The Office will notify the party who submitted the request of the reason(s). The Office will not refund the transmittal fee.

(e) Correspondence to correct any irregularities in a request to record a restriction of a holder's right to dispose of an international registration or the release of such a restriction must be made directly with the International Bureau.

Subpart E—Extension of Protection to the United States

§ 7.25 Sections of part 2 applicable to extension of protection.

(a) Except for §§ 2.22–2.23, 2.130–2.131, 2.160–2.166, 2.168, 2.173, 2.175, 2.181–2.186 and 2.197, all sections in part 2 and all sections in part 11 of this chapter shall apply to an extension of protection of an international registration to the United States, including sections related to proceedings before the Trademark Trial and Appeal Board, unless otherwise stated.

(b) The Office will refer to a request for an extension of protection to the United States as an application under section 66(a) of the Act, and references to applications and registrations in part 2 of this chapter include extensions of protection to the United States.

(c) Upon registration in the United States under section 69 of the Act, an extension of protection to the United States is referred to as a registration, a registered extension of protection, or a section 66(a) registration.

[68 FR 55769, Sept. 26, 2003, as amended at 69 FR 57186, Sept. 24, 2004; 70 FR 38774, July 6, 2005; 73 FR 47686, Aug. 14, 2008; 73 FR 67776, Nov. 17, 2008; 75 FR 35977, June 24, 2010; 78 FR 20197, Apr. 3, 2013]

§ 7.26 Filing date of extension of protection for purposes of examination in the Office.

(a) If a request for extension of protection of an international registration to the United States is made in an international application and the request includes a declaration of a bona fide intention to use the mark in commerce as set out in § 2.33(e) of this chapter, the filing date of the extension of protection to the United States is the international registration date.

(b) If a request for extension of protection of an international registration to the United States is made in a subsequent designation and the request includes a declaration of a bona fide intention to use the mark in commerce as set out in § 2.33(e), the filing date of the extension of protection to the United States is the date that the International Bureau records the subsequent designation.

§ 7.27 Priority claim of extension of protection for purposes of examination in the Office.

An extension of protection of an international registration to the United States is entitled to a claim of priority under section 67 of the Act if:

(a) The request for extension of protection contains a claim of priority;

(b) The request for extension of protection specifies the filing date, serial number and the country of the application that forms the basis for the claim of priority; and

(c) The date of the international registration or the date of recording of the subsequent designation at the International Bureau of the request for extension of protection to the United States is not later than six months after the filing date of the application that forms the basis for the claim of priority.

§ 7.28 Replacement of U.S. registration by registered extension of protection.

(a) A registered extension of protection affords the same rights as those afforded to a previously issued U.S. registration if:

(1) Both registrations are owned by the same person and identify the same mark; and

(2) All the goods and/or services listed in the U.S. registration are also listed in the registered extension of protection.

(b) The holder of an international registration with a registered extension of protection to the United States that meets the requirements of paragraph (a) of this section may file a request to note replacement of the U.S. registration with the extension of protection. If the request contains all of the following, the Office will take note of the replacement in its automated records:

(1) The serial number or registration number of the extension of protection;

(2) The registration number of the replaced U.S. registration; and

(3) The fee required by § 7.6.

(c) If the request to note replacement is denied, the Office will notify the holder of the reason(s) for refusal.

§ 7.29 Effect of replacement on U.S. registration.

A U.S. registration that has been replaced by a registered extension of protection under section 74 of the Act and § 7.28 will remain in force, unless cancelled, expired or surrendered, as long as:

(a) The owner of the replaced U.S. registration continues to file affidavits or declarations of use in commerce or excusable nonuse under section 8 of the Act; and

(b) The replaced U.S. registration is renewed under section 9 of the Act.

§ 7.30 Effect of cancellation or expiration of international registration.

When the International Bureau notifies the Office of the cancellation or expiration of an international registration, in whole or in part, the Office shall cancel, in whole or in part, the corresponding pending or registered extension of protection to the United States. The date of cancellation of an extension of protection or relevant part shall be the date of cancellation or expiration of the corresponding international registration or relevant part.

§ 7.31 Requirements for transformation of an extension of protection to the United States into a U.S. application.

If the International Bureau cancels an international registration in whole or in part, under Article 6(4) of the Madrid Protocol, the holder of that international registration may file a request to transform the corresponding pending or registered extension of protection to the United States into an application under section 1 or 44 of the Act.

(a) The holder of the international registration must file a request for transformation within three months of the date of cancellation of the international registration and include:

(1) The serial number or registration number of the extension of protection to the United States;

(2) The name and address of the holder of the international registration;

(3) The application filing fee for at least one class of goods or services required by § 2.6(a)(1) of this chapter; and

(4) An e-mail address for receipt of correspondence from the Office.

(b) If the request for transformation contains all the elements set forth in paragraph (a) of this section, the extension of protection shall be transformed into an application under section 1 and/or 44 of the Act and accorded the same filing date and the same priority that was accorded to the extension of protection.

(c) The application under section 1 and/or 44 of the Act that results from a transformed extension of protection will be examined under part 2 of this chapter.

(d) A request for transformation that fails to contain all the elements set forth in paragraph (a) of this section will not be accepted.

[68 FR 55769, Sept. 26, 2003, as amended at 69 FR 57186, Sept. 24, 2004]

Subpart F—Affidavit Under Section 71 of the Act for Extension of Protection to the United States

§ 7.36 Affidavit or declaration of use in commerce or excusable nonuse required to avoid cancellation of an extension of protection to the United States.

(a) Subject to the provisions of section 71 of the Act, a registered extension of protection shall remain in force for the term of the international registration upon which it is based unless the international registration expires or is cancelled under section 70 of the Act due to cancellation of the international registration by the International Bureau.

(b) During the following time periods, the holder of an international registration must file an affidavit or declaration of use or excusable nonuse, or the registered extension of protection will be cancelled under section 71 of the Act:

(1) On or after the fifth anniversary and no later than the sixth anniversary after the date of registration in the United States; and

(2) Within the year before the end of every ten-year period after the date of registration in the United States.

(3) The affidavit or declaration may be filed within a grace period of six months after the end of the deadline set forth in paragraphs (b)(1) and (b)(2) of this section, with payment of the grace period surcharge per class required by section 71(a)(3) of the Act and § 7.6.

(c) For the requirements for the affidavit or declaration, see § 7.37.

[68 FR 55769, Sept. 26, 2003, as amended at 75 FR 35977, June 24, 2010]

§ 7.37 Requirements for a complete affidavit or declaration of use in commerce or excusable nonuse.

A complete affidavit or declaration under section 71 of the Act must:

(a) Be filed by the holder of the international registration within the period set forth in § 7.36(b);

(b) Include a statement that is signed and verified (sworn to) or supported by a declaration under § 2.20 of this chapter by a person properly authorized to sign on behalf of the holder, attesting to the use in commerce or excusable nonuse of the mark within the period set forth in section 71 of the Act. The verified statement must be executed on or after the beginning of the filing period specified in § 7.36(b). A person who is properly authorized to sign on behalf of the holder is:

(1) A person with legal authority to bind the holder; or

(2) A person with firsthand knowledge of the facts and actual or implied authority to act on behalf of the holder; or

(3) An attorney as defined in § 11.1 of this chapter who has an actual written or verbal power of attorney or an implied power of attorney from the holder.

(c) Include the U.S. registration number;

(d)(1) Include the fee required by § 7.6 for each class of goods or services that the affidavit or declaration covers;

(2) If the affidavit or declaration is filed during the grace period under section 71(a)(3) of the Act, include the grace period surcharge per class required by § 7.6;

(3) If at least one fee is submitted for a multi-class registration, but the class(es) to which the fee(s) should be applied are not specified, the Office will issue a notice requiring either the

submission of additional fee(s) or an indication of the class(es) to which the original fee(s) should be applied. If the required fee(s) are not submitted within the time period set out in the Office action and the class(es) to which the original fee(s) should be applied are not specified, the Office will presume that the fee(s) cover the classes in ascending order, beginning with the lowest numbered class;

(e)(1) Specify the goods or services for which the mark is in use in commerce, and/or the goods or services for which excusable nonuse is claimed under § 7.37(f)(2);

(2) Specify the goods or services being deleted from the registration, if the affidavit or declaration covers less than all the goods or services or less than all the classes in the registration;

(f)(1) State that the registered mark is in use in commerce on or in connection with the goods or services in the registration; or

(2) If the registered mark is not in use in commerce on or in connection with all the goods or services in the registration, set forth the date when use of the mark in commerce stopped and the approximate date when use is expected to resume and recite facts to show that nonuse as to those goods or services is due to special circumstances that excuse the nonuse and is not due to an intention to abandon the mark; and

(g) Include a specimen showing current use of the mark for each class of goods or services, unless excusable nonuse is claimed under § 7.37(f)(2). When requested by the Office, additional specimens must be provided. The specimen must meet the requirements of § 2.56 of this chapter.

(h) The Office may require the holder to furnish such information, exhibits, affidavits or declarations, and such additional specimens:

(1) As may be reasonably necessary to the proper examination of the affidavit or declaration under section 71 of the Act; or

(2) For the Office to assess the accuracy and integrity of the register.

(3) The provisions of paragraph (h)(2) of this section will no longer be applied after June 21, 2014.

[68 FR 55769, Sept. 26, 2003, as amended at 73 FR 47686, Aug. 14, 2008; 75 FR 35977, June 24, 2010; 77 FR 30208, May 22, 2012]

§ 7.38 Notice to holder of extension of protection.

The registration certificate for an extension of protection to the United States includes a notice of the requirement for filing the affidavit or declaration of use or excusable nonuse under section 71 of the Act. However, the affidavit or declaration must be filed within the time period required by section 71 of the Act regardless of whether this notice is received.

§ 7.39 Acknowledgment of receipt of and correcting deficiencies in affidavit or declaration of use in commerce or excusable nonuse.

The Office will issue a notice as to whether an affidavit or declaration is acceptable, or the reasons for refusal.

(a) A response to the refusal must be filed within six months of the date of issuance of the Office action, or before the end of the filing period set forth in section 71(a) of the Act, whichever is later. The response must be signed by the holder, someone with legal authority to bind the holder (e.g., a corporate officer or general partner of a partnership), or a practitioner qualified to practice under § 11.14 of this chapter, in accordance with the requirements of § 2.193(e)(2).

(b) If no response is filed within this time period, the extension of protection will be cancelled, unless time remains in the grace period under section 71(a)(3) of the Act. If time remains in the grace period, the holder may file a complete, new affidavit.

(c) If the affidavit or declaration is filed within the time periods set forth in section 71 of the Act, deficiencies may be corrected after notification from the Office, as follows:

(1) *Correcting deficiencies in affidavits or declarations timely filed within the periods set forth in sections 71(a)(1) and 71(a)(2) of the Act.* If the affidavit or declaration is timely filed within the relevant filing period set forth in section 71(a)(1) or section 71(a)(2) of the

Act, deficiencies may be corrected before the end of this filing period without paying a deficiency surcharge. Deficiencies may be corrected after the end of this filing period with payment of the deficiency surcharge required by section 71(c) of the Act and § 7.6.

(2) *Correcting deficiencies in affidavits or declarations filed during the grace period.* If the affidavit or declaration is filed during the six-month grace period provided by section 71(a)(3) of the Act, deficiencies may be corrected before the expiration of the grace period without paying a deficiency surcharge. Deficiencies may be corrected after the expiration of the grace period with payment of the deficiency surcharge required by section 71(c) of the Act and § 7.6.

(d) If the affidavit or declaration is not filed within the time periods set forth in section 71 of the Act, the registration will be cancelled.

[75 FR 35977, June 24, 2010, as amended at 76 FR 69133, Nov. 8, 2011]

§ 7.40 Petition to Director to review refusal.

(a) A response to the examiner's initial refusal to accept an affidavit or declaration is required before filing a petition to the Director, unless the examiner directs otherwise. *See* § 7.39(b) for the deadline for responding to an examiner's Office action.

(b) If the examiner maintains the refusal of the affidavit or declaration, the holder may file a petition to the Director to review the examiner's action. The petition must be filed within six months of the date of issuance of the action maintaining the refusal, or the Office will cancel the registration.

(c) A decision by the Director is necessary before filing an appeal or commencing a civil action in any court.

[68 FR 55769, Sept. 26, 2003, as amended at 73 FR 67776, Nov. 17, 2008]

Subpart G—Renewal of International Registration and Extension of Protection

§ 7.41 Renewal of international registration and extension of protection.

(a) Any request to renew an international registration and its extension of protection to the United States must be made at the International Bureau in accordance with Article 7 of the Madrid Protocol.

(b) A request to renew an international registration or extension of protection to the United States submitted through the Office will not be processed.

INDEX II—RULES RELATING TO TRADEMARKS

EDITORIAL NOTE: This listing is provided for information purposes only. It is compiled and kept up-to-date by the Department of Commerce. This index is updated as of July 1, 2013.

Section

A

B

C

D

E

F

J

L

M

N

O

P

R

S

T

PRACTICE BEFORE THE PATENT AND TRADEMARK OFFICE

PART 10 [RESERVED]

PART 11—REPRESENTATION OF OTHERS BEFORE THE UNITED STATES PATENT AND TRADEMARK OFFICE

Subpart A—General Provisions

GENERAL INFORMATION

Subpart B—Recognition To Practice Before the USPTO

PATENTS, TRADEMARKS, AND OTHER NON-PATENT LAW

Subpart C—Investigations and Disciplinary Proceedings; Jurisdiction, Sanctions, Investigations, and Proceedings

Subpart D—USPTO Rules of Professional Conduct

CLIENT-PRACTITIONER RELATIONSHIP

AUTHORITY: 5 U.S.C. 500, 15 U.S.C. 1123, 35 U.S.C. 2(b)(2), 32, 41.

SOURCE: 69 FR 35452, June 24, 2004, unless otherwise noted.

Subpart A—General Provisions

GENERAL INFORMATION

§ 11.1 Definitions.

This part governs solely the practice of patent, trademark, and other law before the United States Patent and Trademark Office. Nothing in this part shall be construed to preempt the authority of each State to regulate the practice of law, except to the extent necessary for the United States Patent and Trademark Office to accomplish its Federal objectives. Unless otherwise clear from the context, the following definitions apply to this part:

Attorney or lawyer means an individual who is a member in good standing of the highest court of any State, including an individual who is in good standing of the highest court of one State and not under an order of any court or Federal agency suspending, enjoining, restraining, disbarring or otherwise restricting the attorney from practice before the bar of another State or Federal agency. A *non-lawyer* means a person who is not an attorney or lawyer.

Belief or *believes* means that the person involved actually supposed the fact in question to be true. A person's belief may be inferred from circumstances.

Confirmed in writing, when used in reference to the informed consent of a person, means informed consent that is given in writing by the person or a writing that a practitioner promptly transmits to the person confirming an oral informed consent. If it is not feasible to obtain or transmit the writing at the time the person gives informed consent, then the practitioner must obtain or transmit it within a reasonable time thereafter.

Conviction or *convicted* means any confession to a crime; a verdict or judgment finding a person guilty of a crime; any entered plea, including *nolo contendre* or Alford plea, to a crime; or receipt of deferred adjudication (whether judgment or sentence has been entered or not) for an accused or pled crime.

Crime means any offense declared to be a felony or misdemeanor by Federal or State law in the jurisdiction where the act occurs.

Data sheet means a form used to collect the name, address, and telephone information from individuals recognized to practice before the Office in patent matters.

Disqualified means any action that prohibits a practitioner from participating in or appearing before the program or agency, regardless of how long the prohibition lasts or the specific terminology used.

Federal agency means any authority of the executive branch of the Government of the United States.

Federal program means any program established by an Act of Congress or administered by a Federal agency.

Firm or *law firm* means a practitioner or practitioners in a law partnership, professional corporation, sole proprietorship or other association authorized to practice law; or practitioners employed in a legal services organization or the legal department of a corporation or other organization.

Fiscal year means the time period from October 1st through the ensuing September 30th.

Fraud or *fraudulent* means conduct that involves a misrepresentation of material fact made with intent to deceive or a state of mind so reckless respecting consequences as to be the equivalent of intent, where there is justifiable reliance on the misrepresentation by the party deceived, inducing the party to act thereon, and where there is injury to the party deceived resulting from reliance on the misrepresentation. Fraud also may be established by a purposeful omission or failure to state a material fact, which omission or failure to state makes other statements misleading, and where the other elements of justifiable reliance and injury are established.

Good moral character and reputation means the possession of honesty and truthfulness, trustworthiness and reliability, and a professional commitment to the legal process and the administration of justice, as well as the condition of being regarded as possessing such qualities.

Grievance means a written submission from any source received by the OED Director that presents possible grounds for discipline of a specified practitioner.

Informed consent means the agreement by a person to a proposed course of conduct after the practitioner has communicated adequate information and explanation about the material risks of and reasonably available alternatives to the proposed course of conduct.

Knowingly, known, or *knows* means actual knowledge of the fact in question. A person's knowledge may be inferred from circumstances.

Law-related services means services that might reasonably be performed in conjunction with and in substance are related to the provision of legal services, and that are not prohibited as unauthorized practice of law when provided by a non-lawyer.

OED means the Office of Enrollment and Discipline.

OED Director means the Director of the Office of Enrollment and Discipline.

OED Director's representatives means attorneys within the USPTO Office of General Counsel who act as representatives of the OED Director.

Office means the United States Patent and Trademark Office.

Partner means a member of a partnership, a shareholder in a law firm organized as a professional corporation, or a member of an association authorized to practice law.

Person means an individual, a corporation, an association, a trust, a partnership, and any other organization or legal entity.

Practitioner means:

(1) An attorney or agent registered to practice before the Office in patent matters,

(2) An individual authorized under 5 U.S.C. 500(b), or otherwise as provided by § 11.14(a), (b), and (c), to practice before the Office in trademark matters or other non-patent matters, or

(3) An individual authorized to practice before the Office in a patent case or matters under § 11.9(a) or (b).

Proceeding before the Office means an application for patent, an application for reissue, a reexamination, a protest, a public use matter, an *inter partes* patent matter, correction of a patent, correction of inventorship, an application to register a trademark, an *inter partes* trademark matter, an appeal, a petition, and any other matter that is pending before the Office.

Reasonable or *reasonably* when used in relation to conduct by a practitioner means the conduct of a reasonably prudent and competent practitioner.

Reasonable belief or *reasonably believes* when used in reference to a practitioner means that the practitioner believes the matter in question and that the circumstances are such that the belief is reasonable.

Reasonably should know when used in reference to a practitioner means that a practitioner of reasonable prudence and competence would ascertain the matter in question.

Registration means registration to practice before the Office in patent proceedings.

Roster means a list of individuals who have been registered as either a patent attorney or patent agent.

Screened means the isolation of a practitioner from any participation in a matter through the timely imposition of procedures within a firm that are reasonably adequate under the circumstances to protect information that the isolated practitioner is obligated to protect under these USPTO Rules of Professional Conduct or other law.

Serious crime means:

(1) Any criminal offense classified as a felony under the laws of the United States, any state or any foreign country where the crime occurred; or

(2) Any crime a necessary element of which, as determined by the statutory or common law definition of such crime in the jurisdiction where the crime occurred, includes interference with the administration of justice, false swearing, misrepresentation, fraud, willful failure to file income tax returns, deceit, bribery, extortion, misappropriation, theft, or an attempt or a conspiracy or solicitation of another to commit a "serious crime."

Significant evidence of rehabilitation means satisfactory evidence that is significantly more probable than not that there will be no recurrence in the foreseeable future of the practitioner's prior disability or addiction.

State means any of the 50 states of the United States of America, the District of Columbia, and any Commonwealth or territory of the United States of America.

Substantial when used in reference to degree or extent means a material matter of clear and weighty importance.

Suspend or *suspension* means a temporary debarring from practice before the Office or other jurisdiction.

Tribunal means the Office, a court, an arbitrator in a binding arbitration proceeding or a legislative body, administrative agency or other body acting in an adjudicative capacity. A legislative body, administrative agency or other body acts in an adjudicative capacity when a neutral official, after the presentation of evidence or legal argument by a party or parties, will render a binding legal judgment directly affecting a party's interests in a particular matter.

United States means the United States of America, and the territories and possessions the United States of America.

USPTO Director means the Director of the United States Patent and Trademark Office, or an employee of the Office delegated authority to act for the Director of the United States Patent and Trademark Office in matters arising under this part.

Writing or *written* means a tangible or electronic record of a communication or representation, including handwriting, typewriting, printing, photostating, photography, audio or video recording and electronic communications. A "signed" writing includes an electronic sound, symbol or process attached to or logically associated with a writing and executed or adopted by a person with the intent to sign the writing.

[69 FR 35452, June 24, 2004, as amended at 73 FR 47687, Aug. 14, 2008; 77 FR 45251, July 31, 2012; 78 FR 20197, Apr. 3, 2013]

§11.2 Director of the Office of Enrollment and Discipline.

(a) *Appointment.* The USPTO Director shall appoint a Director of the Office of Enrollment and Discipline (OED Director). In the event of a vacancy in the office of the OED Director, the USPTO Director may designate an employee of the Office to serve as acting OED Director. The OED Director shall be an active member in good standing of the bar of the highest court of a State.

(b) *Duties.* The OED Director shall:

(1) Supervise staff as may be necessary for the performance of the OED Director's duties.

(2) Receive and act upon applications for registration, prepare and grade the examination provided for in §11.7(b), maintain the register provided for in §11.5, and perform such other duties in connection with enrollment and recognition of attorneys and agents as may be necessary.

(3) Conduct investigations into the moral character and reputation of any individual seeking to be registered as an attorney or agent, or of any individual seeking limited recognition, deny registration or recognition of individuals failing to demonstrate possession of good moral character and reputation, and perform such other duties in connection with enrollment matters and investigations as may be necessary.

(4) Conduct investigations of matters involving possible grounds for discipline of practitioners coming to the attention of the OED Director. Except in matters meriting summary dismissal, no disposition under §11.22(h) shall be recommended or undertaken by the OED Director until the accused practitioner shall have been afforded an opportunity to respond to a reasonable inquiry by the OED Director.

(5) With the consent of a panel of three members of the Committee on Discipline, initiate disciplinary proceedings under §11.32 and perform such other duties in connection with investigations and disciplinary proceedings as may be necessary.

(6) Oversee the preliminary screening of information and close investigations as provided for in §11.22.

(7) [Reserved]

(c) *Petition to OED Director regarding enrollment or recognition.* Any petition from any action or requirement of the staff of OED reporting to the OED Director shall be taken to the OED Director accompanied by payment of the fee set forth in §1.21(a)(5)(i) of this chapter. Any such petition not filed within sixty days from the mailing date of the action or notice from which relief is requested will be dismissed as untimely. The filing of a petition will neither stay the period for taking other action which may be running, nor stay other proceedings. The petitioner may file a single request for reconsideration of a decision within thirty days of the date of the decision. Filing a request for reconsideration stays the period for seeking review of the OED Director's decision until a final decision on the request for reconsideration is issued.

(d) *Review of OED Director's decision regarding enrollment or recognition.* A party dissatisfied with a final decision of the OED Director regarding enrollment or recognition shall seek review of the decision upon petition to the USPTO Director accompanied by payment of the fee set forth in §1.21(a)(5)(ii) of this chapter. By filing such petition to the USPTO Director, the party waives any right to seek reconsideration from the OED Director. Any petition not filed within thirty days after the final decision of the OED Director may be dismissed as untimely. Briefs or memoranda, if any, in support of the petition shall accompany the petition. The petition will be decided on the basis of the record made before the OED Director. The USPTO Director in deciding the petition will consider no new evidence. Copies of documents already of record before the OED Director shall not be submitted with the petition. An oral hearing will not be granted except when considered necessary by the USPTO Director. Any request for reconsideration of the decision of the USPTO Director may be dismissed as untimely if not filed within thirty days after the date of said decision. Only a decision of the USPTO Director regarding denial of a petition constitutes a final decision for the purpose of judicial review.

(e) *Petition to USPTO Director in disciplinary matters.* A party dissatisfied with any action or notice of any employee of the Office of Enrollment and Discipline during or at the conclusion of a disciplinary investigation shall seek review of the action or notice upon petition to the OED Director. A petition from any action or notice of the staff reporting to the OED Director shall be taken to the OED Director. A party dissatisfied with the OED Director's final decision shall seek review of the final decision upon petition to the USPTO Director to invoke the supervisory authority of the USPTO Director in appropriate circumstances in disciplinary matters. Any petition under this paragraph must contain a statement of the facts involved and the point or points to be reviewed and the action requested. Briefs or memoranda, if any, in support of the petition must accompany the petition. Where facts are to be proven, the proof in the form of affidavits or declarations (and exhibits, if any) must accompany the petition. The OED Director may be directed by the USPTO Director to file a reply to the petition to the USPTO Director, supplying a copy to the petitioner. An oral hearing on petition taken to the USPTO Director will not be granted except when considered necessary by the USPTO Director. The filing of a petition under this paragraph will not stay an investigation, disciplinary proceeding, or other proceedings. Any petition under this part not filed within thirty days of the mailing date of the action or notice from which relief is requested may be dismissed as untimely. Any request for reconsideration of the decision of the OED Director or the USPTO Director may be dismissed as untimely if not filed within thirty days after the date of said decision. Only a decision of the USPTO Director regarding denial of a petition constitutes a final decision for the purpose of judicial review.

[69 FR 35452, June 24, 2004, as amended at 73 FR 47687, Aug. 14, 2008; 78 FR 20198, Apr. 3, 2013]

§ 11.3 Suspension of rules.

(a) In an extraordinary situation, when justice requires, any requirement of the regulations of this Part which is not a requirement of statute may be suspended or waived by the USPTO Director or the designee of the USPTO Director, *sua sponte*, or on petition by any party, including the OED Director or the OED Director's representative, subject to such other requirements as may be imposed.

(b) No petition under this section shall stay a disciplinary proceeding unless ordered by the USPTO Director or a hearing officer.

[73 FR 47688, Aug. 14, 2008]

Subpart B—Recognition To Practice Before the USPTO

PATENTS, TRADEMARKS, AND OTHER NON-PATENT LAW

§ 11.4 [Reserved]

§ 11.5 Register of attorneys and agents in patent matters; practice before the Office.

(a) A register of attorneys and agents is kept in the Office on which are entered the names of all individuals recognized as entitled to represent applicants having prospective or immediate business before the Office in the preparation and prosecution of patent applications. Registration in the Office under the provisions of this part shall entitle the individuals so registered to practice before the Office only in patent matters.

(b) *Practice before the Office.* Practice before the Office includes, but is not limited to, law-related service that comprehends any matter connected with the presentation to the Office or any of its officers or employees relating to a client's rights, privileges, duties, or responsibilities under the laws or regulations administered by the Office for the grant of a patent or registration of a trademark, or for enrollment or disciplinary matters. Such presentations include preparing necessary documents in contemplation of filing the documents with the Office, corresponding and communicating with the Office, and representing a client through documents or at interviews, hearings, and meetings, as well as communicating with and advising a client concerning matters pending or contemplated to be presented before the Office. Nothing in this section proscribes a practitioner from employing or retaining non-practitioner assistants under the supervision of the practitioner to assist the practitioner in matters pending or contemplated to be presented before the Office.

(1) *Practice before the Office in patent matters.* Practice before the Office in patent matters includes, but is not limited to, preparing and prosecuting any patent application, consulting with or giving advice to a client in contemplation of filing a patent application or other document with the Office, drafting the specification or claims of a patent application; drafting an amendment or reply to a communication from the Office that may require written argument to establish the patentability of a claimed invention; drafting a reply to a communication from the Office regarding a patent application; and drafting a communication for a public use, interference, reexamination proceeding, petition, appeal to or any other proceeding before the Patent Trial and Appeal Board, or other proceeding. Registration to practice before the Office in patent cases sanctions the performance of those services which are reasonably necessary and incident to the preparation and prosecution of patent applications or other proceeding before the Office involving a patent application or patent in which the practitioner is authorized to participate. The services include:

(i) Considering the advisability of relying upon alternative forms of protection which may be available under state law, and

(ii) Drafting an assignment or causing an assignment to be executed for the patent owner in contemplation of filing or prosecution of a patent application for the patent owner, where the practitioner represents the patent owner after a patent issues in a proceeding before the Office, and when drafting the assignment the practitioner does no more than replicate the terms of a previously existing oral or written obligation of assignment from one person or party to another person or party.

(2) *Practice before the Office in trademark matters.* Practice before the Office in trademark matters includes, but is not limited to, consulting with or giving advice to a client in contemplation of filing a trademark application or other document with the Office; preparing and prosecuting an application for trademark registration; preparing an amendment which may require written argument to establish the registrability of the mark; and conducting an opposition, cancellation, or concurrent use proceeding; or conducting an appeal to the Trademark Trial and Appeal Board.

[73 FR 47688, Aug. 14, 2008, as amended at 77 FR 46629, Aug. 6, 2012]

§ 11.6 Registration of attorneys and agents.

(a) *Attorneys.* Any citizen of the United States who is an attorney and who fulfills the requirements of this part may be registered as a patent attorney to practice before the Office. When appropriate, any alien who is an attorney, who lawfully resides in the United States, and who fulfills the requirements of this part may be registered as a patent attorney to practice before the Office, provided that such registration is not inconsistent with the terms upon which the alien was admitted to, and resides in, the United States and further provided that the alien may remain registered only:

(1) If the alien continues to lawfully reside in the United States and registration does not become inconsistent with the terms upon which the alien continues to lawfully reside in the United States, or

(2) If the alien ceases to reside in the United States, the alien is qualified to be registered under paragraph (c) of this section. *See also* § 11.9(b).

(b) *Agents.* Any citizen of the United States who is not an attorney, and who fulfills the requirements of this part may be registered as a patent agent to practice before the Office. When appropriate, any alien who is not an attorney, who lawfully resides in the United States, and who fulfills the requirements of this part may be registered as a patent agent to practice before the Office, provided that such registration is not inconsistent with the terms upon which the alien was admitted to, and resides in, the United States, and further provided that the alien may remain registered only:

(1) If the alien continues to lawfully reside in the United States and registration does not become inconsistent with the terms upon which the alien continues to lawfully reside in the United States or

(2) If the alien ceases to reside in the United States, the alien is qualified to be registered under paragraph (c) of this section. *See also* § 11.9(b).

(c) *Foreigners.* Any foreigner not a resident of the United States who shall file proof to the satisfaction of the OED Director that he or she is registered and in good standing before the patent office of the country in which he or she resides and practices, and who is possessed of the qualifications stated in § 11.7, may be registered as a patent agent to practice before the Office for the limited purpose of presenting and prosecuting patent applications of applicants located in such country, provided that the patent office of such country allows substantially reciprocal privileges to those admitted to practice before the Office. Registration as a patent agent under this paragraph shall continue only during the period that the conditions specified in this paragraph obtain. Upon notice by the patent office of such country that a patent agent registered under this section is no longer registered or no longer in good standing before the patent office of such country, and absent a showing of cause why his or her name should not be removed from the register, the OED Director shall promptly remove the name of the patent agent from the register and publish the fact of removal. Upon ceasing to reside in such country, the patent agent registered under this section is no longer qualified to be registered under this section, and the OED Director shall promptly remove the name of the patent agent from the register and publish the fact of removal.

(d) *Patent Trial and Appeal Board matters.* For action by a person who is not registered in a proceeding before the Patent Trial and Appeal Board, see § 41.5(a) or § 42.10(c) of this title.

[69 FR 35452, June 24, 2004, as amended at 69 FR 50003, Aug. 12, 2004; 77 FR 46629, Aug. 6, 2012]

§ 11.7 Requirements for registration.

(a) No individual will be registered to practice before the Office unless he or she has:

(1) Applied to the USPTO Director in writing by completing an application for registration form supplied by the OED Director and furnishing all requested information and material; and

(2) Established to the satisfaction of the OED Director that he or she:

(i) Possesses good moral character and reputation;

(ii) Possesses the legal, scientific, and technical qualifications necessary for him or her to render applicants valuable service; and

(iii) Is competent to advise and assist patent applicants in the presentation and prosecution of their applications before the Office.

(b)(1) To enable the OED Director to determine whether an individual has the qualifications specified in paragraph (a)(2) of this section, the individual shall:

(i) File a complete application for registration each time admission to the registration examination is requested. A complete application for registration includes:

(A) An application for registration form supplied by the OED Director wherein all requested information and supporting documents are furnished,

(B) Payment of the fees required by § 1.21(a)(1) of this subchapter,

(C) Satisfactory proof of scientific and technical qualifications, and

(D) For aliens, provide proof that recognition is not inconsistent with the terms of their visa or entry into the United States;

(ii) Pass the registration examination, unless the taking and passing of the examination is waived as provided in paragraph (d) of this section. Unless examination is waived pursuant to paragraph (d) of this section, each individual seeking registration must take and pass the registration examination to enable the OED Director to determine whether the individual possesses the legal and competence qualifications specified in paragraphs (a)(2)(ii) and (a)(2)(iii) of this section. An individual failing the examination may, upon receipt of notice of failure from OED, reapply for admission to the examination. An individual failing the examination must wait thirty days after the date the individual last took the examination before retaking the examination. An individual reapplying shall:

(A) File a completed application for registration form wherein all requested information and supporting documents are furnished,

(B) Pay the fees required by § 1.21(a)(1) of this subchapter, and

(C) For aliens, provide proof that recognition is not inconsistent with the terms of their visa or entry into the United States; and

(iii) Provide satisfactory proof of possession of good moral character and reputation.

(2) An individual failing to file a complete application for registration will not be admitted to the examination and will be notified of the incompleteness. Applications for registration that are incomplete as originally submitted will be considered only when they have been completed and received by OED, provided that this occurs within sixty days of the mailing date of the notice of incompleteness. Thereafter, a new and complete application for registration must be filed. Only an individual approved as satisfying the requirements of paragraphs (b)(1)(i)(A), (b)(1)(i)(B), (b)(1)(i)(C) and (b)(1)(i)(D) of this section may be admitted to the examination.

(3) If an individual does not reapply until more than one year after the mailing date of a notice of failure, that individual must again comply with paragraph (b)(1)(i) of this section.

(c) Each individual seeking registration is responsible for updating all information and answers submitted in or with the application for registration based upon anything occurring between the date the application for registration is signed by the individual, and the date he or she is registered or recognized to practice before the Office in patent matters. The update shall be filed within thirty days after the date of the occasion that necessitates the update.

(d) *Waiver of the Registration Examination for Former Office Employees*—(1) *Former patent examiners who by July 26, 2004, had not actively served four years in the patent examining corps, and were serving in the corps at the time of their separation.* The OED Director may waive the taking of a registration examination in the case of any individual meeting the requirements of paragraph (b)(1)(i)(C) of this section who is a former patent examiner but by July 26, 2004, had not served four years in the patent examining corps, if the individual demonstrates that he or she:

(i) Actively served in the patent examining corps of the Office and was serving in the corps at the time of separation from the Office;

(ii) Received a certificate of legal competency and negotiation authority;

(iii) After receiving the certificate of legal competency and negotiation authority, was rated at least fully successful in each quality performance element of his or her performance plan for the last two complete fiscal years as a patent examiner; and

(iv) Was not under an oral or written warning regarding the quality performance elements at the time of separation from the patent examining corps.

(2) *Former patent examiners who on July 26, 2004, had actively served four years in the patent examining corps, and were serving in the corps at the time of their separation.* The OED Director may waive the taking of a registration examination in the case of any individual meeting the requirements of paragraph (b)(1)(i)(C) of this section who is a former patent examiner and by July 26, 2004, had served four years in the patent examining corps, if the individual demonstrates that he or she:

(i) Actively served for at least four years in the patent examining corps of the Office by July 26, 2004, and was serving in the corps at the time of separation from the Office;

(ii) Was rated at least fully successful in each quality performance element of his or her performance plan for the last two complete fiscal years as a patent examiner in the Office; and

(iii) Was not under an oral or written warning regarding the quality performance elements at the time of separation from the patent examining corps.

(3) *Certain former Office employees who were not serving in the patent examining corps upon their separation from the Office.* The OED Director may waive the taking of a registration examination in the case of a former Office employee meeting the requirements of paragraph (b)(1)(i)(C) of this section who by petition demonstrates possession of the necessary legal qualifications to render to patent applicants and others valuable service and assistance in the preparation and prosecution of their applications or other business before the Office by showing that he or she has:

(i) Exhibited comprehensive knowledge of patent law equivalent to that shown by passing the registration examination as a result of having been in a position of responsibility in the Office in which he or she:

(A) Provided substantial guidance on patent examination policy, including the development of rule or procedure changes, patent examination guidelines, changes to the Manual of Patent Examining Procedure, development of training or testing materials for the patent examining corps, or development of materials for the registration examination or continuing legal education; or

(B) Represented the Office in patent cases before Federal courts; and

(ii) Was rated at least fully successful in each quality performance element of his or her performance plan for said position for the last two complete rating periods in the Office, and was not under an oral or written warning regarding such performance elements at the time of separation from the Office.

(4) To be eligible for consideration for waiver, an individual formerly employed by the Office within the scope of one of paragraphs (d)(1), (d)(2) or (d)(3) of this section must file a complete application for registration and pay the fee required by § 1.21(a)(1)(i) of this subchapter within two years of the individual's date of separation from the Office. All other individuals formerly employed by the Office, including former examiners, filing an application for registration or fee more than two years after separation from the Office, are required to take and pass the registration examination. The individual or former examiner must pay the examination fee required by § 1.21(a)(1)(ii) of this subchapter within thirty days after notice of non-waiver.

(e) *Examination results.* Notification of the examination results is final. Within sixty days of the mailing date of a notice of failure, the individual is entitled to inspect, but not copy, the questions and answers he or she incorrectly answered. Review will be under supervision. No notes may be taken during such review. Substantive review of the answers or questions may not be pursued by petition for regrade. An individual who failed the examination has the right to retake the examination an unlimited number of times upon payment of the fees required by § 1.21(a)(1)(i) and (ii) of this subchapter, and a fee charged by a commercial entity administering the examination.

(f) *Application for reciprocal recognition.* An individual seeking reciprocal recognition under § 11.6(c), in addition to satisfying the provisions of paragraphs (a) and (b) of this section, and the provisions of § 11.8(c), shall pay the application fee required by § 1.21(a)(1)(i) of this subchapter upon filing an application for registration.

(g) *Investigation of good moral character and reputation.* (1) Every individual seeking recognition shall answer all questions in the application for registration and request(s) for comments issued by OED; disclose all relevant facts, dates and information; and provide verified copies of documents relevant to his or her good moral character and reputation. An individual who is an attorney shall submit a certified copy of each of his or her State bar applications and moral character determinations, if available.

(2)(i) If the OED Director receives information from any source that reflects adversely on the good moral character or reputation of an individual seeking registration or recognition, the OED Director shall conduct an investigation into the good moral character and reputation of that individual. The investigation will be conducted after the individual has passed the registration examination, or after the registration examination has been waived for the individual, as applicable. An individual failing to timely answer questions or respond to an inquiry by OED shall be deemed to have withdrawn his or her application, and shall be required to reapply, pass the examination, and otherwise satisfy all the requirements of this section. No individual shall be certified for registration or recognition by the OED Director until, to the satisfaction of the OED Director, the individual demonstrates his or her possession of good moral character and reputation.

(ii) The OED Director, in considering an application for registration by an attorney, may accept a State bar's character determination as meeting the requirements set forth in paragraph (g) of this section if, after review, the Office finds no substantial discrepancy between the information provided with his or her application for registration and the State bar application and moral character determination, provided that acceptance is not inconsistent with other rules and the requirements of 35 U.S.C. 2(b)(2)(D).

(h) *Good moral character and reputation.* Evidence showing lack of good moral character and reputation may include, but is not limited to, conviction of a felony or a misdemeanor identified in paragraph (h)(1) of this section, drug or alcohol abuse; lack of candor; suspension or disbarment on ethical grounds from a State bar; and resignation from a State bar while under investigation.

(1) *Conviction of felony or misdemeanor.* An individual who has been convicted of a felony or a misdemeanor involving moral turpitude, breach of trust, interference with the administration of justice, false swearing, misrepresentation, fraud, deceit, bribery, extortion, misappropriation, theft, or conspiracy to commit any felony or misdemeanor, is presumed not to be of good moral character and reputation in the absence of a pardon or a satisfactory showing of reform and rehabilitation, and shall file with his or her application for registration the fees required by § 1.21(a)(1)(ii) and (a)(10) of this subchapter. The OED Director shall determine whether individuals convicted of said felony or misdemeanor provided satisfactory proof of reform and rehabilitation.

(i) An individual who has been convicted of a felony or a misdemeanor identified in paragraph (h)(1) of this section shall not be eligible to apply for registration during the time of any sentence (including confinement or commitment to imprisonment), deferred adjudication, and period of probation or parole as a result of the conviction, and for a period of two years after the date of completion of the sentence, deferred adjudication, and period of probation or parole, whichever is later.

(ii) The following presumptions apply to the determination of good moral character and reputation of an individual convicted of said felony or misdemeanor:

(A) The court record or docket entry of conviction is conclusive evidence of guilt in the absence of a pardon or a satisfactory showing of reform or rehabilitation; and

(B) An individual convicted of a felony or any misdemeanor identified in paragraph (h)(1) of this section is conclusively deemed not to have good moral character and reputation, and shall not be eligible to apply for registration for a period of two years after completion of the sentence, deferred adjudication, and period of probation or parole, whichever is later.

(iii) The individual, upon applying for registration, shall provide satisfactory evidence that he or she is of good moral character and reputation.

(iv) Upon proof that a conviction has been set aside or reversed, the individual shall be eligible to file a complete application for registration and the fee required by § 1.21(a)(1)(ii) of this subchapter and, upon passing the registration examination, have the OED Director determine, in accordance with paragraph (h)(1) of this section, whether, absent the conviction, the individual possesses good moral character and reputation.

(2) *Good moral character and reputation involving drug or alcohol abuse.* An individual's record is reviewed as a whole to see if there is a drug or alcohol abuse issue. An individual appearing to abuse drugs or alcohol may be asked to undergo an evaluation, at the individual's expense, by a qualified professional approved by the OED Director. In instances where, before an investigation commences, there is evidence of a present abuse or an individual has not established a record of recovery, the OED Director may request the individual to withdraw his or her application, and require the individual to satisfactorily demonstrate that he or she is complying with treatment and undergoing recovery.

(3) *Moral character and reputation involving lack of candor.* An individual's lack of candor in disclosing facts bearing on or relevant to issues concerning good moral character and reputation when completing the application or any time thereafter may be found to be cause to deny registration on moral character and reputation grounds.

(4) *Moral character and reputation involving suspension, disbarment, or resignation from a profession.* (i) An individual who has been disbarred or suspended from practice of law or other profession, or has resigned in lieu of a disciplinary proceeding (excluded or disbarred on consent) shall be ineligible to apply for registration as follows:

(A) An individual who has been disbarred from practice of law or other profession, or has resigned in lieu of a disciplinary proceeding (excluded or disbarred on consent) shall be ineligible to apply for registration for a period of five years from the date of disbarment or resignation.

(B) An individual who has been suspended on ethical grounds from the practice of law or other profession shall be ineligible to apply for registration until expiration of the period of suspension.

(C) An individual who was not only disbarred, suspended or resigned in lieu of a disciplinary proceeding, but also convicted in a court of a felony, or of a crime involving moral turpitude or breach of trust, shall be ineligible to apply for registration until the conditions in paragraphs (h)(1) and (h)(4) of this section are fully satisfied.

(ii) An individual who has been disbarred or suspended, or who resigned in lieu of a disciplinary proceeding shall file an application for registration and the fees required by § 1.21(a)(1)(ii) and (a)(10) of this subchapter; provide a full and complete copy of the proceedings that led to the disbarment, suspension, or resignation; and provide satisfactory proof that he or she possesses good moral character and reputation. The following presumptions shall govern the determination of good moral character and reputation of an individual who has been licensed to practice law or other profession in any jurisdiction and has been disbarred, suspended on ethical grounds, or allowed to resign in lieu of discipline, in that jurisdiction:

(A) A copy of the record resulting in disbarment, suspension or resignation is *prima facie* evidence of the matters contained in the record, and the imposition of disbarment or suspension, or the acceptance of the resignation of the individual shall be deemed conclusive that the individual has committed professional misconduct.

(B) The individual is ineligible for registration and is deemed not to have good moral character and reputation during the period of the imposed discipline.

(iii) The only defenses available with regard to an underlying disciplinary matter resulting in disbarment, suspension on ethical grounds, or resignation in lieu of a disciplinary proceeding are set out below, and must be shown to the satisfaction of the OED Director:

(A) The procedure in the disciplinary court was so lacking in notice or opportunity to be heard as to constitute a deprivation of due process;

(B) There was such infirmity of proof establishing the misconduct as to give rise to the clear conviction that the Office could not, consistently with its duty, accept as final the conclusion on that subject; or

(C) The finding of lack of good moral character and reputation by the Office would result in grave injustice.

(i) *Factors that may be taken into consideration when evaluating rehabilitation of an individual seeking a moral character and reputation determination.* The factors enumerated below are guidelines to assist the OED Director in determining whether an individual has demonstrated rehabilitation from an act of misconduct or moral turpitude. The factors include:

(1) The nature of the act of misconduct, including whether it involved moral turpitude, whether there were aggravating or mitigating circumstances, and whether the activity was an isolated event or part of a pattern;

(2) The age and education of the individual at the time of the misconduct and the age and education of the individual at the present time;

(3) The length of time that has passed between the misconduct and the present, absent any involvement in any further acts of moral turpitude, the amount of time and the extent of rehabilitation being dependent upon the nature and seriousness of the act of misconduct under consideration;

(4) Restitution by the individual to any person who suffered monetary losses through acts or omissions of the individual;

(5) Expungement of a conviction;

(6) Successful completion or early discharge from probation or parole;

(7) Abstinence from the use of controlled substances or alcohol for not less than two years if the specific misconduct was attributable in part to the use of a controlled substance or alcohol, where abstinence may be demonstrated by, but is not necessarily limited to, enrolling in and complying with a self-help or professional treatment program;

(8) If the specific misconduct was attributable in part to a medically recognized mental disease, disorder or illness, proof that the individual sought professional assistance, and complied with the treatment program prescribed by the professional, and submitted letters from the treating psychiatrist/psychologist verifying that the medically recognized mental disease, disorder or illness will not impede the individual's ability to competently practice before the Office;

(9) Payment of the fine imposed in connection with any criminal conviction;

(10) Correction of behavior responsible in some degree for the misconduct;

(11) Significant and conscientious involvement in programs designed to provide social benefits or to ameliorate social problems; and

(12) Change in attitude from that which existed at the time of the act of misconduct in question as evidenced by any or all of the following:

(i) Statements of the individual;

(ii) Statements from persons familiar with the individual's previous misconduct and with subsequent attitudes and behavioral patterns;

(iii) Statements from probation or parole officers or law enforcement officials as to the individual's social adjustments; and

(iv) Statements from persons competent to testify with regard to neuropsychiatry or emotional disturbances.

(j) *Notice to Show Cause.* The OED Director shall inquire into the good moral character and reputation of an individual seeking registration, providing the individual with the opportunity to create a record on which a decision is made. If, following inquiry and consideration of the record, the OED Director is of the opinion that the individual seeking registration has not satisfactorily established that he or she possesses good moral character and reputation, the OED Director shall issue to the individual a notice to show cause why the individual's application for registration should not be denied.

(1) The individual shall be given no less than ten days from the date of the notice to reply. The notice shall be given by certified mail at the address appearing on the application if the address is in the United States, and by any other reasonable means if the address is outside the United States.

(2) Following receipt of the individual's response, or in the absence of a response, the OED Director shall consider the individual's response, if any, and the record, and determine whether,

in the OED Director's opinion, the individual has sustained his or her burden of satisfactorily demonstrating that he or she possesses good moral character and reputation.

(k) *Reapplication for registration.* An individual who has been refused registration for lack of good moral character or reputation may reapply for registration two years after the date of the decision, unless a shorter period is otherwise ordered by the USPTO Director. An individual, who has been notified that he or she is under investigation for good moral character and reputation may elect to withdraw his or her application for registration, and may reapply for registration two years after the date of withdrawal. Upon reapplication for registration, the individual shall pay the fees required by § 1.21(a)(1)(ii) and (a)(10) of this subchapter, and has the burden of showing to the satisfaction of the OED Director his or her possession of good moral character and reputation as prescribed in paragraph (b) of this section. Upon reapplication for registration, the individual also shall complete successfully the examination prescribed in paragraph (b) of this section, even though the individual has previously passed a registration examination.

§ 11.8 Oath and registration fee.

(a) After an individual passes the examination, or the examination is waived, the OED Director shall promptly publish a solicitation for information concerning the individual's good moral character and reputation. The solicitation shall include the individual's name, and business or communication postal address.

(b) An individual shall not be registered as an attorney under § 11.6(a), registered as an agent under § 11.6(b) or (c), or granted limited recognition under § 11.9(b) unless within two years of the mailing date of a notice of passing registration examination or of waiver of the examination the individual files with the OED Director a completed Data Sheet, an oath or declaration prescribed by the USPTO Director, and the registration fee set forth in § 1.21(a)(2) of this subchapter. An individual seeking registration as an attorney under § 11.6(a) must provide a certificate of good standing of the bar of the highest court of a State that is no more than six months old.

(c) An individual who does not comply with the requirements of paragraph (b) of this section within the two-year period will be required to retake the registration examination.

(d) [Reserved]

[69 FR 35452, June 24, 2004, as amended at 73 FR 67757, Nov. 17, 2008; 78 FR 20198, Apr. 3, 2013]

§ 11.9 Limited recognition in patent matters.

(a) Any individual not registered under § 11.6 may, upon a showing of circumstances which render it necessary or justifiable, and that the individual is of good moral character and reputation, be given limited recognition by the OED Director to prosecute as attorney or agent a specified patent application or specified patent applications. Limited recognition under this paragraph shall not extend further than the application or applications specified. Limited recognition shall not be granted while individuals who have passed the examination or for whom the examination has been waived are awaiting registration to practice before the Office in patent matters.

(b) A nonimmigrant alien residing in the United States and fulfilling the provisions of § 11.7(a) and (b) may be granted limited recognition if the nonimmigrant alien is authorized by the United States Government to be employed or trained in the United States in the capacity of representing a patent applicant by presenting or prosecuting a patent application. Limited recognition shall be granted for a period consistent with the terms of authorized employment or training. Limited recognition shall not be granted or extended to a non-United States citizen residing abroad. If granted, limited recognition shall automatically expire upon the nonimmigrant alien's departure from the United States.

(c) An individual not registered under § 11.6 may, if appointed by an applicant, prosecute an international patent application only before the United States International Searching Authority and the United States International Preliminary Examining Authority, provided that the individual has the right to practice before the national office with which the international application is filed as provided in PCT Art. 49, Rule 90 and §1.455 of this subchapter, or before the International Bureau when the USPTO is acting as Receiving Office pursuant to PCT Rules 83.1 bis and 90.1.

[69 FR 35452, June 24, 2004, as amended at 78 FR 20198, Apr. 3, 2013]

§11.10 Restrictions on practice in patent matters.

(a) Only practitioners who are registered under §11.6 or individuals given limited recognition under §11.9(a) or (b) are permitted to prosecute patent applications of others before the Office; or represent others in any proceedings before the Office.

(b) *Post employment agreement of former Office employee.* No individual who has served in the patent examining corps or elsewhere in the Office may practice before the Office after termination of his or her service, unless he or she signs a written undertaking agreeing:

(1) To not knowingly act as agent or attorney for, or otherwise represent, or assist in any manner the representation of, any other person:

(i) Before the Office,

(ii) In connection with any particular patent or patent application,

(iii) In which said employee participated personally and substantially as an employee of the Office; and

(2) To not knowingly act within two years after terminating employment by the Office as agent or attorney for, or otherwise represent, or assist in any manner the representation of any other person:

(i) Before the Office,

(ii) In connection with any particular patent or patent application,

(iii) If such patent or patent application was pending under the employee's official responsibility as an officer or employee within a period of one year prior to the termination of such responsibility.

(3) The words and phrases in paragraphs (b)(1) and (b)(2) of this section are construed as follows:

(i) *Represent* and *representation* mean acting as patent attorney or patent agent or other representative in any appearance before the Office, or communicating with an employee of the Office with intent to influence.

(ii) *Assist in any manner* means aid or help another person on a particular patent or patent application involving representation.

(iii) Particular patent or patent application means any patent or patent application, including, but not limited to, a provisional, substitute, international, continuation, divisional, continuation-in-part, or reissue patent application, as well as any protest, reexamination, petition, appeal, interference, or trial proceeding based on the patent or patent application.

(iv) *Participate personally and substantially.* (A) Basic requirements. The restrictions of §11.10(a)(1) apply only to those patents and patent applications in which a former Office employee had "personal and substantial participation," exercised "through decision, approval, disapproval, recommendation, the rendering of advice, investigation or otherwise." To *participate personally* means directly, and includes the participation of a subordinate when actually directed by the former Office employee in the patent or patent application. *Substantially* means that the employee's involvement must be of significance to the matter, or form a basis for a reasonable appearance of such significance. It requires more than official responsibility, knowledge, perfunctory involvement, or involvement on an administrative or peripheral issue. A finding of substantiality should be based not only on the effort devoted to a patent or patent application, but also on the importance of the effort. While a series of peripheral involvements may be insubstantial, the single act of approving or participation in a critical step may be substantial. It is essential that the participation be related to a "particular patent or patent application." (*See* paragraph (b)(3)(iii) of this section.)

(B) Participation on ancillary matters. An Office employee's participation on subjects not directly involving the substantive merits of a patent or patent application may not be "substantial," even if it is time-consuming. An employee whose official responsibility is the review of a patent or patent application solely for compliance with administrative control or budgetary considerations and who reviews a particular patent or patent application for such a purpose should not be regarded as having participated substantially in the patent or patent application, except when such considerations also are the subject of the employee's proposed representation.

(C) Role of official responsibility in determining substantial participation. *Official responsibility* is defined in paragraph (b)(3)(v) of this section. "Personal and substantial participation" is different from "official responsibility." One's responsibility may, however, play a role in determining the "substantiality" of an Office employee's participation.

(v) *Official responsibility* means the direct administrative or operating authority, whether intermediate or final, and either exercisable alone or with others, and either personally or through subordinates, to approve, disapprove, or otherwise direct Government actions.

(A) Determining official responsibility. Ordinarily, those areas assigned by statute, regulation, Executive Order, job description, or delegation of authority determine the scope of an employee's "official responsibility". All particular matters under consideration in the Office are under the "official responsibility" of the Director of the Office, and each is under that of any intermediate supervisor having responsibility for an employee who actually participates in the patent or patent application within the scope of his or her duties. A patent examiner would have "official responsibility" for the patent applications assigned to him or her.

(B) Ancillary matters and official responsibility. *Administrative* authority as used in paragraph (v) of this section means authority for planning, organizing and controlling a patent or patent application rather than authority to review or make decisions on ancillary aspects of a patent or patent application such as the regularity of budgeting procedures, public or community relations aspects, or equal employment opportunity considerations. Responsibility for such an ancillary consideration does not constitute official responsibility for the particular patent or patent application, except when such a consideration is also the subject of the employee's proposed representation.

(C) Duty to inquire. In order for a former employee, e.g., former patent examiner, to be barred from representing or assisting in representing another as to a particular patent or patent application, he or she need not have known, while employed by the Office, that the patent or patent application was pending under his or her official responsibility. The former employee has a reasonable duty of inquiry to learn whether the patent or patent application had been under his or her official responsibility. Ordinarily, a former employee who is asked to represent another on a patent or patent application will become aware of facts sufficient to suggest the relationship of the prior matter to his or her former office, e.g., technology center, group or art unit. If so, he or she is under a duty to make further inquiry. It would be prudent for an employee to maintain a record of only patent application numbers of the applications actually acted upon by decision or recommendation, as well as those applications under the employee's official responsibility which he or she has not acted upon.

(D) Self-disqualification. A former employee, e.g., former patent examiner, cannot avoid the restrictions of this section through self-disqualification with respect to a patent or patent application for which he or she otherwise had official responsibility. However, an employee who through self-disqualification does not participate personally and substantially in a particular patent or patent application is not subject to the lifetime restriction of paragraph (b)(1) of this section.

(vi) *Pending* means that the matter was in fact referred to or under consideration by persons within the employee's area of official responsibility.

(4) Measurement of the two-year restriction period. The two-year period under paragraph (b)(2) of this section is

measured from the date when the employee's official responsibility in a particular area ends, not from the termination of service in the Office, unless the two occur simultaneously. The prohibition applies to all particular patents or patent applications subject to such official responsibility in the one-year period before termination of such responsibility.

(c) *Former employees of the Office.* This section imposes restrictions generally parallel to those imposed in 18 U.S.C. 207(a) and (b)(1). This section, however, does not interpret these statutory provisions or any other post-employment restrictions that may apply to former Office employees, and such former employees should not assume that conduct not prohibited by this section is otherwise permissible. Former employees of the Office, whether or not they are practitioners, are encouraged to contact the Department of Commerce for information concerning applicable post-employment restrictions.

(d) An employee of the Office may not prosecute or aid in any manner in the prosecution of any patent application before the Office.

(e) Practice before the Office by Government employees is subject to any applicable conflict of interest laws, regulations or codes of professional responsibility.

[69 FR 35452, June 24, 2004, as amended at 77 FR 46630, Aug. 6, 2012]

§ 11.11 Administrative suspension, inactivation, resignation, and readmission.

(a) *Contact information.* (1) A registered practitioner must notify the OED Director of his or her postal address for his or her office, up to three email addresses where he or she receives email, and a business telephone number, as well as every change to any of said addresses or telephone number within thirty days of the date of the change. A registered practitioner shall, in addition to any notice of change of address and telephone number filed in individual patent applications, separately file written notice of the change of address or telephone number to the OED Director. A registered practitioner who is an attorney in good standing with the bar of the highest court of one or more States shall provide the OED Director with the State bar identification number associated with each membership. The OED Director shall publish from the roster a list containing the name, postal business addresses, business telephone number, registration number, and registration status as an attorney or agent of each registered practitioner recognized to practice before the Office in patent cases.

(2) A letter may be addressed to any registered practitioner, at the address of which separate notice was last received by the OED Director, for the purpose of ascertaining whether such practitioner desires to remain on the register. Any registered practitioner failing to reply and give any information requested by the OED Director within a time limit specified will be subject to administrative suspension under paragraph (b) of this section.

(b) *Administrative suspension.* (1) Whenever it appears that a registered practitioner or a person granted limited recognition under § 11.9(b) has failed to comply with § 11.8(d) or paragraph (a)(2) of this section, the OED Director shall publish and send a notice to the registered practitioner or person granted limited recognition advising of the noncompliance, the consequence of being administratively suspended under paragraph (b)(5) of this section if noncompliance is not timely remedied, and the requirements for reinstatement under paragraph (f) of this section. The notice shall be published and sent to the registered practitioner or person granted limited recognition by mail to the last postal address furnished under paragraph (a) of this section or by email addressed to the last email addresses furnished under paragraph (a) of this section. The notice shall demand compliance and payment of a delinquency fee set forth in § 1.21(a)(9)(i) of this subchapter within sixty days after the date of such notice.

(2) In the event a registered practitioner or person granted limited recognition fails to comply with the notice of paragraph (b)(1) of this section within the time allowed, the OED Director shall publish and send in the manner provided for in paragraph (b)(1)

of this section to the registered practitioner or person granted limited recognition a Rule to Show Cause why his or her registration or recognition should not be administratively suspended, and he or she no longer be permitted to practice before the Office in patent matters or in any way hold himself or herself out as being registered or authorized to practice before the Office in patent matters. The OED Director shall file a copy of the Rule to Show Cause with the USPTO Director.

(3) Within 30 days of the OED Director's sending the Rule to Show Cause identified in paragraph (b)(2) of this section, the registered practitioner or person granted limited recognition may file a response to the Rule to Show Cause with the USPTO Director. The response must set forth the factual and legal bases why the person should not be administratively suspended. The registered practitioner or person granted limited recognition shall serve the OED Director with a copy of the response at the time it is filed with the USPTO Director. Within ten days of receiving a copy of the response, the OED Director may file a reply with the USPTO Director that includes documents demonstrating that the notice identified in paragraph (b)(1) of this section was published and sent to the practitioner in accordance with paragraph (b)(1) of this section. A copy of the reply by the OED Director shall be served on the registered practitioner or person granted limited recognition. When acting on the Rule to Show Cause, if the USPTO Director determines that there are no genuine issues of material fact regarding the Office's compliance with the notice requirements under this section or the failure of the person to pay the requisite fees, the USPTO Director shall enter an order administratively suspending the registered practitioner or person granted limited recognition. Otherwise, the USPTO Director shall enter an appropriate order dismissing the Rule to Show Cause. Nothing herein shall permit an administratively suspended registered practitioner or person granted limited recognition to seek a stay of the administrative suspension during the pendency of any review of the USPTO Director's final decision.

(4) [Reserved]

(5) An administratively suspended registered practitioner or person granted limited recognition is subject to investigation and discipline for his or her conduct prior to, during, or after the period he or she was administratively suspended.

(6) An administratively suspended registered practitioner or person granted limited recognition is prohibited from practicing before the Office in patent cases while administratively suspended. A registered practitioner or person granted limited recognition who knows he or she has been administratively suspended under this section will be subject to discipline for failing to comply with the provisions of this paragraph (b).

(c) *Administrative inactivation.* (1) Any registered practitioner who shall become employed by the Office shall comply with § 11.116 for withdrawal from the applications, patents, and trademark matters wherein he or she represents an applicant or other person, and notify the OED Director in writing of said employment on the first day of said employment. The name of any registered practitioner employed by the Office shall be endorsed on the roster as administratively inactive. Upon separation from the Office, the administratively inactive practitioner may request reactivation by completing and filing an application, Data Sheet, signing a written undertaking required by § 11.10, and paying the fee set forth in § 1.21(a)(1)(i) of this subchapter. An administratively inactive practitioner remains subject to the provisions of the USPTO Rules of Professional Conduct and to proceedings and sanctions under §§ 11.19 through 11.58 for conduct that violates a provision of the USPTO Rules of Professional Conduct prior to or during employment at the Office. If, within 30 days after separation from the Office, the registered practitioner does not request active status or another status, the registered practitioner will be endorsed on the roster as voluntarily inactive and be subject to the provisions of paragraph (d) of this section.

(2) Any registered practitioner who is a judge of a court of record, full-time court commissioner, U.S. bankruptcy

judge, U.S. magistrate judge, or a retired judge who is eligible for temporary judicial assignment and is not engaged in the practice of law may request, in writing, that his or her name be endorsed on the roster as administratively inactive. Upon acceptance of the request, the OED Director shall endorse the name of the practitioner as administratively inactive. Following separation from the bench, the practitioner may request restoration to active status by completing and filing an application, Data Sheet, and signing a written undertaking required by §11.10.

(d) *Voluntary inactivation.* (1) Except as provided in paragraph (d)(4) of this section, any registered practitioner may voluntarily enter inactive status by filing a request, in writing, that his or her name be endorsed on the roster as voluntarily inactive. Upon acceptance of the request, the OED Director shall endorse the name as voluntarily inactive.

(2) [Reserved]

(3) A registered practitioner who seeks or enters into voluntary inactive status is subject to investigation and discipline for his or her conduct prior to, during, or after the period of his or her inactivation.

(4) [Reserved]

(5) A registered practitioner in voluntary inactive status is prohibited from practicing before the Office in patent cases while in voluntary inactive status. A registered practitioner in voluntary inactive status will be subject to discipline for failing to comply with the provisions of this paragraph. Upon acceptance of the request for voluntary inactive status, the practitioner must comply with the provisions of §11.116.

(6) Any registered practitioner whose name has been endorsed as voluntarily inactive pursuant to paragraph (d)(1) of this section and is not under investigation and not subject to a disciplinary proceeding may be restored to active status on the register as may be appropriate provided that the practitioner files a written request for restoration, a completed application for registration on a form supplied by the OED Director furnishing all requested information and material, including information and material pertaining to the practitioner's moral character and reputation under §11.7(a)(2)(i) during the period of inactivation, a declaration or affidavit attesting to the fact that the practitioner has read the most recent revisions of the patent laws and the rules of practice before the Office, and pays the fees set forth in §1.21(a)(7)(iii) and (iv) of this subchapter.

(e) *Resignation.* A registered practitioner or a practitioner recognized under §11.14(c), who is not under investigation under §11.22 for a possible violation of the USPTO Rules of Professional Conduct, subject to discipline under §§11.24 or 11.25, or a practitioner against whom probable cause has been found by a panel of the Committee on Discipline under §11.23(b), may resign by notifying the OED Director in writing that he or she desires to resign. Upon acceptance in writing by the OED Director of such notice, that registered practitioner or practitioner under §11.14 shall no longer be eligible to practice before the Office in patent matters but shall continue to file a change of address for five years thereafter in order that he or she may be located in the event information regarding the practitioner's conduct comes to the attention of the OED Director or any grievance is made about his or her conduct while he or she engaged in practice before the Office. The name of any registered practitioner whose resignation is accepted shall be removed from the register, endorsed as resigned, and notice thereof published in the Official Gazette. Upon acceptance of the resignation by the OED Director, the registered practitioner must comply with the provisions of §11.116.

(f) *Administrative reinstatement.* (1) Any registered practitioner who has been administratively suspended pursuant to paragraph (b) of this section, or who has resigned pursuant to paragraph (e) of this section, may be reinstated on the register provided the practitioner has applied for reinstatement on an application form supplied by the OED Director, demonstrated compliance with the provisions of §11.7(a)(2)(i) and (iii), and paid the fees set forth in §1.21(a)(9)(i) and (a)(9)(ii) of this subchapter. Any person granted limited recognition who has been administratively suspended pursuant to paragraph (b) of this section may have their recognition reactivated provided the practitioner has applied for reinstatement on an application form supplied by the OED Director, demonstrated compliance with the provisions of § 11.7(a)(2)(i) and (iii), and paid the fees set forth in § 1.21(a)(9)(i) and (a)(9)(ii) of this subchapter. A practitioner who has resigned or was administratively suspended for two or more years before the date the Office receives a completed application from the person who resigned or was administratively suspended must also pass the registration examination under § 11.7(b)(1)(ii). Any reinstated practitioner is subject to investigation and discipline for his or her conduct that occurred prior to, during, or after the period of his or her administrative suspension or resignation.

(2) Any registered practitioner whose registration has been administratively inactivated pursuant to paragraph (c) of this section may be reinstated to the register as may be appropriate provided within two years after his or her employment with the Office ceases or within two years after his or her employment in a judicial capacity ceases the following is filed with the OED Director: a request for reinstatement, a completed application for registration on a form supplied by the OED Director furnishing all requested information and material, and the fee set forth in § 1.21(a)(9)(ii) of this subchapter. Any registered practitioner inactivated or reinstated is subject to investigation and discipline for his or her conduct before, during, or after the period of his or her inactivation.

[73 FR 67757, Nov. 17, 2008, as amended at 78 FR 20198, Apr. 3, 2013]

§§ 11.12–11.13 [Reserved]

§ 11.14 Individuals who may practice before the Office in trademark and other non-patent matters.

(a) *Attorneys.* Any individual who is an attorney as defined in § 11.1 may represent others before the Office in trademark and other non-patent matters. An attorney is not required to apply for registration or recognition to practice before the Office in trademark and other non-patent matters. Registration as a patent practitioner does not itself entitle an individual to practice before the Office in trademark matters.

(b) *Non-lawyers.* Individuals who are not attorneys are not recognized to practice before the Office in trademark and other non-patent matters, except that individuals not attorneys who were recognized to practice before the Office in trademark matters under this chapter prior to January 1, 1957, will be recognized as agents to continue practice before the Office in trademark matters. Except as provided in the preceding sentence, registration as a patent agent does not itself entitle an individual to practice before the Office in trademark matters.

(c) *Foreigners.* Any foreign attorney or agent not a resident of the United States who shall file a written application for reciprocal recognition under paragraph (f) of this section and prove to the satisfaction of the OED Director that he or she is registered or in good standing before the patent or trademark office of the country in which he or she resides and practices and is possessed of good moral character and reputation, may be recognized for the limited purpose of representing parties located in such country before the Office in the presentation and prosecution of trademark matters, provided: the patent or trademark office of such country allows substantially reciprocal privileges to those permitted to practice in trademark matters before the Office. Recognition under this paragraph shall continue only during the period that the conditions specified in this paragraph obtain.

(d) Recognition of any individual under this section shall not be construed as sanctioning or authorizing the performance of any act regarded in the jurisdiction where performed as the unauthorized practice of law.

(e) No individual other than those specified in paragraphs (a), (b), and (c) of this section will be permitted to practice before the Office in trademark matters on behalf of a client. Any individual may appear in a trademark or other non-patent matter in his or her own behalf. Any individual may appear in a trademark matter for:

(1) A firm of which he or she is a member,

(2) A partnership of which he or she is a partner, or

(3) A corporation or association of which he or she is an officer and which he or she is authorized to represent, if such firm, partnership, corporation, or association is a party to a trademark proceeding pending before the Office.

(f) *Application for reciprocal recognition.* An individual seeking reciprocal recognition under paragraph (c) of this section, in addition to providing evidence satisfying the provisions of paragraph (c) of this section, shall apply in writing to the OED Director for reciprocal recognition, and shall pay the application fee required by §1.21(a)(1)(i) of this subchapter.

[73 FR 47688, Aug. 14, 2008]

§11.15 Refusal to recognize a practitioner.

Any practitioner authorized to appear before the Office may be suspended, excluded, or reprimanded in accordance with the provisions of this Part. Any practitioner who is suspended or excluded under this Part shall not be entitled to practice before the Office in patent, trademark, or other non-patent matters while suspended or excluded.

[73 FR 47688, Aug. 14, 2008]

§§11.16–11.17 [Reserved]

§11.18 Signature and certificate for correspondence filed in the Office.

(a) For all documents filed in the Office in patent, trademark, and other non-patent matters, and all documents filed with a hearing officer in a disciplinary proceeding, except for correspondence that is required to be signed by the applicant or party, each piece of correspondence filed by a practitioner in the Office must bear a signature, personally signed or inserted by such practitioner, in compliance with §1.4(d)(1), §1.4(d)(2), or §2.193(a) of this chapter.

(b) By presenting to the Office or hearing officer in a disciplinary proceeding (whether by signing, filing, submitting, or later advocating) any paper, the party presenting such paper, whether a practitioner or non-practitioner, is certifying that—

(1) All statements made therein of the party's own knowledge are true, all statements made therein on information and belief are believed to be true, and all statements made therein are made with the knowledge that whoever, in any matter within the jurisdiction of the Office, knowingly and willfully falsifies, conceals, or covers up by any trick, scheme, or device a material fact, or knowingly and willfully makes any false, fictitious, or fraudulent statements or representations, or knowingly and willfully makes or uses any false writing or document knowing the same to contain any false, fictitious, or fraudulent statement or entry, shall be subject to the penalties set forth under 18 U.S.C. 1001 and any other applicable criminal statute, and violations of the provisions of this section may jeopardize the probative value of the paper; and

(2) To the best of the party's knowledge, information and belief, formed after an inquiry reasonable under the circumstances,

(i) The paper is not being presented for any improper purpose, such as to harass someone or to cause unnecessary delay or needless increase in the cost of any proceeding before the Office;

(ii) The other legal contentions therein are warranted by existing law or by a nonfrivolous argument for the extension, modification, or reversal of existing law or the establishment of new law;

(iii) The allegations and other factual contentions have evidentiary support or, if specifically so identified, are likely to have evidentiary support after a reasonable opportunity for further investigation or discovery; and

(iv) The denials of factual contentions are warranted on the evidence, or if specifically so identified, are reasonably based on a lack of information or belief.

(c) Violations of any of paragraphs (b)(2)(i) through (iv) of this section are, after notice and reasonable opportunity to respond, subject to such sanctions or actions as deemed appropriate by the USPTO Director, which may include, but are not limited to, any combination of—

(1) Striking the offending paper;

(2) Referring a practitioner's conduct to the Director of Enrollment and Discipline for appropriate action;

(3) Precluding a party or practitioner from submitting a paper, or presenting or contesting an issue;

(4) Affecting the weight given to the offending paper; or

(5) Terminating the proceedings in the Office.

(d) Any practitioner violating the provisions of this section may also be subject to disciplinary action.

[73 FR 47689, Aug. 14, 2008, as amended at 74 FR 54912, Oct. 26, 2009]

Subpart C—Investigations and Disciplinary Proceedings; Jurisdiction, Sanctions, Investigations, and Proceedings

SOURCE: 73 FR 47689, Aug. 14, 2008, unless otherwise noted.

§ 11.19 Disciplinary jurisdiction; Jurisdiction to transfer to disability inactive status.

(a) All practitioners engaged in practice before the Office; all practitioners administratively suspended; all practitioners registered to practice before the Office in patent cases; all practitioners inactivated; all practitioners authorized under § 11.6(d) to take testimony; and all practitioners transferred to disability inactive status, reprimanded, suspended, or excluded from the practice of law by a duly constituted authority, including by the USPTO Director, are subject to the disciplinary jurisdiction of the Office. Practitioners who have resigned shall also be subject to such jurisdiction with respect to conduct undertaken prior to the resignation and conduct in regard to any practice before the Office following the resignation. A person not registered or recognized to practice before the Office is also subject to the disciplinary authority of the Office if the person provides or offers to provide any legal services before the Office.

(b) *Grounds for discipline; Grounds for transfer to disability inactive status.* The following, whether done individually by a practitioner or in concert with any other person or persons and whether or not done in the course of providing legal services to a client, or in a matter pending before the Office, constitute grounds for discipline or grounds for transfer to disability inactive status.

(1) Grounds for discipline include:

(i) Conviction of a serious crime;

(ii) Discipline on ethical grounds imposed in another jurisdiction or disciplinary disqualification from participating in or appearing before any Federal program or agency;

(iii) Failure to comply with any order of a Court disciplining a practitioner, or any final decision of the USPTO Director in a disciplinary matter;

(iv) Violation of any USPTO Rule of Professional Conduct; or

(v) Violation of the oath or declaration taken by the practitioner. See § 11.8.

(2) Grounds for transfer to disability inactive status include:

(i) Being transferred to disability inactive status in another jurisdiction;

(ii) Being judicially declared incompetent, being judicially ordered to be involuntarily committed after a hearing on the grounds of insanity, incompetency or disability, or being placed by court order under guardianship or conservatorship; or

(iii) Filing a motion requesting a disciplinary proceeding be held in abeyance because the practitioner is suffering from a disability or addiction that makes it impossible for the practitioner to adequately defend the charges in the disciplinary proceeding.

(c) Petitions to disqualify a practitioner in *ex parte* or *inter partes* matters in the Office are not governed by §§ 11.19 through 11.60 and will be handled on a case-by-case basis under such conditions as the USPTO Director deems appropriate.

(d) The OED Director may refer the existence of circumstances suggesting unauthorized practice of law to the authorities in the appropriate jurisdiction(s).

[73 FR 47689, Aug. 14, 2008, as amended at 78 FR 20200, Apr. 3, 2013]

§ 11.20 Disciplinary sanctions; Transfer to disability inactive status.

(a) *Types of discipline.* The USPTO Director, after notice and opportunity for a hearing, and where grounds for discipline exist, may impose on a practitioner the following types of discipline:

(1) Exclusion from practice before the Office;

(2) Suspension from practice before the Office for an appropriate period of time;

(3) Reprimand or censure; or

(4) *Probation.* Probation may be imposed *in lieu* of or in addition to any other disciplinary sanction. Any conditions of probation shall be stated in writing in the order imposing probation. The order shall also state whether, and to what extent, the practitioner shall be required to notify clients of the probation. Violation of any condition of probation shall be cause for imposition of the disciplinary sanction. Imposition of the disciplinary sanction predicated upon violation of probation shall occur only after an order to show cause why the disciplinary sanction should not be imposed is resolved adversely to the practitioner.

(b) *Conditions imposed with discipline.* When imposing discipline, the USPTO Director may condition reinstatement upon the practitioner making restitution, successfully completing a professional responsibility course or examination, or any other condition deemed appropriate under the circumstances.

(c) *Transfer to disability inactive status.* The USPTO Director, after notice and opportunity for a hearing may, and where grounds exist to believe a practitioner has been transferred to disability inactive status in another jurisdiction, or has been judicially declared incompetent; judicially ordered to be involuntarily committed after a hearing on the grounds of incompetency or disability, or placed by court order under guardianship or conservatorship, transfer the practitioner to disability inactive status.

[73 FR 47689, Aug. 14, 2008, as amended at 78 FR 20200, Apr. 3, 2013]

§ 11.21 Warnings.

A warning is neither public nor a disciplinary sanction. The OED Director may conclude an investigation with the issuance of a warning. The warning shall contain a brief statement of facts and USPTO Rules of Professional Conduct relevant to the facts.

[78 FR 20200, Apr. 3, 2013]

§ 11.22 Disciplinary investigations.

(a) The OED Director is authorized to investigate possible grounds for discipline. An investigation may be initiated when the OED Director receives a grievance, information or evidence from any source suggesting possible grounds for discipline. Neither unwillingness nor neglect by a grievant to prosecute a charge, nor settlement, compromise, or restitution with the grievant, shall in itself justify abatement of an investigation.

(b) Any person possessing information or evidence concerning possible grounds for discipline of a practitioner may report the information or evidence to the OED Director. The OED Director may request that the report be presented in the form of an affidavit or declaration.

(c) [Reserved]

(d) *Preliminary screening of information or evidence.* The OED Director shall examine all information or evidence concerning possible grounds for discipline of a practitioner.

(e) *Notification of investigation.* The OED Director shall notify the practitioner in writing of the initiation of an investigation into whether a practitioner has engaged in conduct constituting possible grounds for discipline.

(f) *Request for information and evidence by OED Director.*

(1) In the course of the investigation, the OED Director may request information and evidence regarding possible grounds for discipline of a practitioner from:

(i) The grievant,

(ii) The practitioner, or

(iii) Any person who may reasonably be expected to provide information and evidence needed in connection with the grievance or investigation.

(2) The OED Director may request information and evidence regarding possible grounds for discipline of a practitioner from a non-grieving client either after obtaining the consent of the practitioner or upon a finding by a

Contact Member of the Committee on Discipline, appointed in accordance with § 11.23(d), that good cause exists to believe that the possible ground for discipline alleged has occurred with respect to non-grieving clients. Neither a request for, nor disclosure of, such information shall constitute a violation of any USPTO Rules of Professional Conduct.

(g) Where the OED Director makes a request under paragraph (f)(2) of this section to a Contact Member of the Committee on Discipline, such Contact Member shall not, with respect to the practitioner connected to the OED Director's request, participate in the Committee on Discipline panel that renders a probable cause determination under paragraph (b)(1) of this section concerning such practitioner, and that forwards the probable cause finding and recommendation to the OED Director under paragraph (b)(2) of this section.

(h) *Disposition of investigation.* Upon the conclusion of an investigation, the OED Director may:

(1) Close the investigation without issuing a warning, or taking disciplinary action;

(2) Issue a warning to the practitioner;

(3) Institute formal charges upon the approval of the Committee on Discipline; or

(4) Enter into a settlement agreement with the practitioner and submit the same for approval of the USPTO Director.

(i) *Closing investigation.* The OED Director shall terminate an investigation and decline to refer a matter to the Committee on Discipline if the OED Director determines that:

(1) The information or evidence is unfounded;

(2) The information or evidence relates to matters not within the jurisdiction of the Office;

(3) As a matter of law, the conduct about which information or evidence has been obtained does not constitute grounds for discipline, even if the conduct may involve a legal dispute; or

(4) The available evidence is insufficient to conclude that there is probable cause to believe that grounds exist for discipline.

[73 FR 47689, Aug. 14, 2008, as amended at 77 FR 45251, July 31, 2012; 78 FR 20200, Apr. 3, 2013]

§ 11.23 Committee on Discipline.

(a) The USPTO Director shall appoint a Committee on Discipline. The Committee on Discipline shall consist of at least three employees of the Office. None of the Committee members shall report directly or indirectly to the OED Director or any employee designated by the USPTO Director to decide disciplinary matters. Each Committee member shall be a member in good standing of the bar of the highest court of a State. The Committee members shall select a Chairperson from among themselves. Three Committee members will constitute a panel of the Committee.

(b) *Powers and duties of the Committee on Discipline.* The Committee shall have the power and duty to:

(1) Meet in panels at the request of the OED Director and, after reviewing evidence presented by the OED Director, by majority vote of the panel, determine whether there is probable cause to bring charges under § 11.32 against a practitioner; and

(2) Prepare and forward its own probable cause findings and recommendations to the OED Director.

(c) No discovery shall be authorized of, and no member of the Committee on Discipline shall be required to testify about deliberations of, the Committee on Discipline or of any panel.

(d) The Chairperson shall appoint the members of the panels and a Contact Member of the Committee on Discipline.

§ 11.24 Reciprocal discipline.

(a) *Notification of OED Director.* Within thirty days of being publicly censured, publicly reprimanded, subjected to probation, disbarred or suspended by another jurisdiction, or being disciplinarily disqualified from participating in or appearing before any Federal program or agency, a practitioner subject to the disciplinary jurisdiction of the Office shall notify the OED Director in writing of the same. A practitioner is deemed to be disbarred if he or she is disbarred, excluded on consent, or has resigned in lieu of a disciplinary proceeding. Upon receiving notification from any source or otherwise learning that a practitioner subject to the disciplinary jurisdiction of the Office has been so publicly censured, publicly reprimanded, subjected to probation, disbarred, suspended or disciplinarily disqualified, the OED Director shall obtain a certified copy of the record or order regarding the public censure, public reprimand, probation, disbarment, suspension or disciplinary disqualification and file the same with the USPTO Director. The OED Director shall, in addition, without Committee on Discipline authorization, file with the USPTO Director a complaint complying with § 11.34 against the practitioner predicated upon the public censure, public reprimand, probation, disbarment, suspension or disciplinary disqualification. The OED Director shall request the USPTO Director to issue a notice and order as set forth in paragraph (b) of this section.

(b) *Notification served on practitioner.* Upon receipt of a certified copy of the record or order regarding the practitioner being so publicly censured, publicly reprimanded, subjected to probation, disbarred, suspended or disciplinarily disqualified together with the complaint, the USPTO Director shall issue a notice directed to the practitioner in accordance with § 11.35 and to the OED Director containing:

(1) A copy of the record or order regarding the public censure, public reprimand, probation, disbarment, suspension or disciplinary disqualification;

(2) A copy of the complaint; and

(3) An order directing the practitioner to file a response with the USPTO Director and the OED Director, within forty days of the date of the notice establishing a genuine issue of material fact predicated upon the grounds set forth in paragraphs (d)(1)(i) through (d)(1)(iv) of this section that the imposition of the identical public censure, public reprimand, probation, disbarment, suspension or disciplinary disqualification would be unwarranted and the reasons for that claim.

(c) *Effect of stay in another jurisdiction.* In the event the public censure, public reprimand, probation, disbarment, suspension imposed by another jurisdiction or disciplinary disqualification imposed in the Federal program or agency has been stayed, any reciprocal discipline imposed by the USPTO may be deferred until the stay expires.

(d) *Hearing and discipline to be imposed.* (1) The USPTO Director shall hear the matter on the documentary record unless the USPTO Director determines that an oral hearing is necessary. After expiration of the forty days from the date of the notice pursuant to provisions of paragraph (b) of this section, the USPTO Director shall consider any timely filed response and shall impose the identical public censure, public reprimand, probation, disbarment, suspension or disciplinary disqualification unless the practitioner clearly and convincingly demonstrates, and the USPTO Director finds there is a genuine issue of material fact that:

(i) The procedure elsewhere was so lacking in notice or opportunity to be heard as to constitute a deprivation of due process;

(ii) There was such infirmity of proof establishing the conduct as to give rise to the clear conviction that the Office could not, consistently with its duty, accept as final the conclusion on that subject;

(iii) The imposition of the same public censure, public reprimand, probation, disbarment, suspension or disciplinary disqualification by the Office would result in grave injustice; or

(iv) Any argument that the practitioner was not publicly censured, publicly reprimanded, placed on probation, disbarred, suspended or disciplinarily disqualified.

(2) If the USPTO Director determines that there is no genuine issue of material fact, the USPTO Director shall enter an appropriate final order. If the USPTO Director is unable to make such determination because there is a genuine issue of material fact, the USPTO Director shall enter an appropriate order:

(i) Referring the complaint to a hearing officer for a formal hearing and entry of an initial decision in accordance with the other rules in this part, and

(ii) Directing the practitioner to file an answer to the complaint in accordance with § 11.36.

(e) *Adjudication in another jurisdiction or Federal agency or program.* In all other respects, a final adjudication in another jurisdiction or Federal agency or program that a practitioner, whether or not admitted in that jurisdiction, has been guilty of misconduct shall establish a prima facie case by clear and convincing evidence that the practitioner has engaged in misconduct under § 11.804.

(f) *Reciprocal discipline—action where practice has ceased.* Upon request by the practitioner, reciprocal discipline may be imposed *nunc pro tunc* only if the practitioner promptly notified the OED Director of his or her censure, public reprimand, probation, disbarment, suspension or disciplinary disqualification in another jurisdiction, and establishes by clear and convincing evidence that the practitioner voluntarily ceased all activities related to practice before the Office and complied with all provisions of § 11.58. The effective date of any public censure, public reprimand, probation, suspension, disbarment or disciplinary disqualification imposed *nunc pro tunc* shall be the date the practitioner voluntarily ceased all activities related to practice before the Office and complied with all provisions of § 11.58.

(g) *Reinstatement following reciprocal discipline proceeding.* A practitioner may petition for reinstatement under conditions set forth in § 11.60 no sooner than completion of the period of reciprocal discipline imposed, and compliance with all provisions of § 11.58.

[73 FR 47689, Aug. 14, 2008, as amended at 78 FR 20200, Apr. 3, 2013]

§ 11.25 Interim suspension and discipline based upon conviction of committing a serious crime.

(a) *Notification of OED Director.* Upon being convicted of a crime in a court of the United States, any State, or a foreign country, a practitioner subject to the disciplinary jurisdiction of the Office shall notify the OED Director in writing of the same within thirty days from the date of such conviction. Upon being advised or learning that a practitioner subject to the disciplinary jurisdiction of the Office has been convicted of a crime, the OED Director shall make a preliminary determination whether the crime constitutes a serious crime warranting interim suspension. If the crime is a serious crime, the OED Director shall file with the USPTO Director proof of the conviction and request the USPTO Director to issue a notice and order set forth in paragraph (b)(2) of this section. The OED Director shall in addition, without Committee on Discipline authorization, file with the USPTO Director a complaint against the practitioner complying with § 11.34 predicated upon the conviction of a serious crime. If the crime is not a serious crime, the OED Director shall process the matter in the same manner as any other information or evidence of a possible violation of any USPTO Rule of Professional Conduct coming to the attention of the OED Director.

(b) *Interim suspension and referral for disciplinary proceeding.* All proceedings under this section shall be handled as expeditiously as possible.

(1) The USPTO Director has authority to place a practitioner on interim suspension after hearing the request for interim suspension on the documentary record.

(2) *Notification served on practitioner.* Upon receipt of a certified copy of the court record, docket entry or judgment demonstrating that the practitioner has been so convicted together with the complaint, the USPTO Director shall forthwith issue a notice directed to the practitioner in accordance with §§ 11.35(a), (b) or (c), and to the OED Director, containing:

(i) A copy of the court record, docket entry, or judgment of conviction;

(ii) A copy of the complaint; and

(iii) An order directing the practitioner to file a response with the USPTO Director and the OED Director, within forty days of the date of the notice, establishing that there is a genuine issue of material fact that the crime did not constitute a serious crime, the practitioner is not the individual found guilty of the crime, or that the conviction was so lacking in notice or opportunity to be heard as to constitute a deprivation of due process.

(3) *Hearing and final order on request for interim suspension.* The request for interim suspension shall be heard by the USPTO Director on the documentary record unless the USPTO Director determines that the practitioner's response establishes a genuine issue of material fact that: The crime did not constitute a serious crime, the practitioner is not the person who committed the crime, or that the conviction was so lacking in notice or opportunity to be heard as to constitute a deprivation of due process. If the USPTO Director determines that there is no genuine issue of material fact regarding the defenses set forth in the preceding sentence, the USPTO Director shall enter an appropriate final order regarding the OED Director's request for interim suspension regardless of the pendency of any criminal appeal. If the USPTO Director is unable to make such determination because there is a genuine issue of material fact, the USPTO Director shall enter a final order dismissing the request and enter a further order referring the complaint to a hearing officer for a hearing and entry of an initial decision in accordance with the other rules in this part and directing the practitioner to file an answer to the complaint in accordance with § 11.36.

(4) *Termination.* The USPTO Director has authority to terminate an interim suspension. In the interest of justice, the USPTO Director may terminate an interim suspension at any time upon a showing of extraordinary circumstances, after affording the OED Director an opportunity to respond to the request to terminate interim suspension.

(5) *Referral for disciplinary proceeding.* Upon entering a final order imposing interim suspension, the USPTO Director shall refer the complaint to a hearing officer to conduct a formal disciplinary proceeding. The formal disciplinary proceeding, however, shall be stayed by the hearing officer until all direct appeals from the conviction are concluded. Review of the initial decision of the hearing officer shall be pursuant to § 11.55.

(c) *Proof of conviction and guilt*—(1) *Conviction in the United States.* For purposes of a hearing for interim suspension and a hearing on the formal charges in a complaint filed as a consequence of the conviction, a certified copy of the court record, docket entry, or judgment of conviction in a court of the United States or any State shall establish a prima facie case by clear and convincing evidence that the practitioner was convicted of a serious crime and that the conviction was not lacking in notice or opportunity to be heard as to constitute a deprivation of due process.

(2) *Conviction in a foreign country.* For purposes of a hearing for interim suspension and on the formal charges filed as a result of a finding of guilt, a certified copy of the court record, docket entry, or judgment of conviction in a court of a foreign country shall establish a *prima facie* case by clear and convincing evidence that the practitioner was convicted of a serious crime and that the conviction was not lacking in notice or opportunity to be heard as to constitute a deprivation of due process. However, nothing in this paragraph shall preclude the practitioner from demonstrating by clear and convincing evidence in any hearing on a request for interim suspension there is a genuine issue of material fact to be considered when determining if the elements of a serious crime were committed in violating the criminal law of the foreign country and whether a disciplinary sanction should be entered.

(d) *Crime determined not to be serious crime.* If the USPTO Director determines that the crime is not a serious crime, the complaint shall be referred to the OED Director for investigation under § 11.22 and processing as is appropriate.

(e) *Reinstatement*—(1) *Upon reversal or setting aside a finding of guilt or a conviction.* If a practitioner suspended solely under the provisions of paragraph (b) of this section demonstrates that the underlying finding of guilt or conviction of serious crimes has been reversed or vacated, the order for interim suspension shall be vacated and the practitioner shall be placed on active status unless the finding of guilt was reversed or the conviction was set aside with respect to less than all serious crimes for which the practitioner was found guilty or convicted. The vacating of the interim suspension will not terminate any other disciplinary proceeding then pending against the practitioner, the disposition of which shall be determined by the hearing officer before whom the matter is pending, on the basis of all available evidence other than the finding of guilt or conviction.

(2) *Following conviction of a serious crime.* Any practitioner convicted of a serious crime and disciplined in whole or in part in regard to that conviction, may petition for reinstatement under conditions set forth in § 11.60 no sooner than five years after being discharged following completion of service of his or her sentence, or after completion of service under probation or parole, whichever is later.

(f) *Notice to clients and others of interim suspension.* An interim suspension under this section shall constitute a suspension of the practitioner for the purpose of § 11.58.

[73 FR 47689, Aug. 14, 2008, as amended at 78 FR 20200, Apr. 3, 2013]

§ 11.26 Settlement.

Before or after a complaint under § 11.34 is filed, a settlement conference may occur between the OED Director and the practitioner. Any offers of compromise and any statements made during the course of settlement discussions shall not be admissible in subsequent proceedings. The OED Director may recommend to the USPTO Director any settlement terms deemed appropriate, including steps taken to correct or mitigate the matter forming the basis of the action, or to prevent recurrence of the same or similar conduct. A settlement agreement shall be effective only upon entry of a final decision by the USPTO Director.

§ 11.27 Exclusion on consent.

(a) *Required affidavit.* The OED Director may confer with a practitioner concerning possible violations by the practitioner of the Rules of Professional Conduct whether or not a disciplinary proceeding has been instituted. A practitioner who is the subject of an investigation or a pending disciplinary proceeding based on allegations of grounds for discipline, and who desires to resign, may only do so by consenting to exclusion and delivering to the OED Director an affidavit declaring the consent of the practitioner to exclusion and stating:

(1) That the practitioner's consent is freely and voluntarily rendered, that the practitioner is not being subjected to coercion or duress, and that the practitioner is fully aware of the implications of consenting to exclusion;

(2) That the practitioner is aware that there is currently pending an investigation into, or a proceeding involving allegations of misconduct, the nature of which shall be specifically set forth in the affidavit to the satisfaction of the OED Director;

(3) That the practitioner acknowledges that, if and when he or she applies for reinstatement under § 11.60, the OED Director will conclusively presume, for the limited purpose of determining the application for reinstatement, that:

(i) The facts upon which the investigation or complaint is based are true, and

(ii) The practitioner could not have successfully defended himself or herself against the allegations in the investigation or charges in the complaint.

(b) *Action by the USPTO Director.* Upon receipt of the required affidavit, the OED Director shall file the affidavit and any related papers with the USPTO Director for review and approval. Upon such approval, the USPTO Director will enter an order excluding the practitioner on consent and providing other appropriate actions. Upon entry of the order, the excluded practitioner shall comply with the requirements set forth in § 11.58.

(c) When an affidavit under paragraph (a) of this section is received after a complaint under § 11.34 has been filed, the OED Director shall notify the hearing officer. The hearing officer shall enter an order transferring the disciplinary proceeding to the USPTO Director, who may enter an order excluding the practitioner on consent.

(d) *Reinstatement.* Any practitioner excluded on consent under this section may not petition for reinstatement for five years. A practitioner excluded on consent who intends to reapply for admission to practice before the Office must comply with the provisions of

§11.58, and apply for reinstatement in accordance with §11.60. Failure to comply with the provisions of §11.58 constitutes grounds for denying an application for reinstatement.

§11.28 Incapacitated practitioners in a disciplinary proceeding.

(a) *Holding in abeyance a disciplinary proceeding because of incapacitation due to a current disability or addiction*—(1) *Practitioner's motion.* In the course of a disciplinary proceeding under §11.32, but before the date set by the hearing officer for a hearing, the practitioner may file a motion requesting the hearing officer to enter an order holding such proceeding in abeyance based on the contention that the practitioner is suffering from a disability or addiction that makes it impossible for the practitioner to adequately defend the charges in the disciplinary proceeding.

(i) *Content of practitioner's motion.* The practitioner's motion shall, in addition to any other requirement of §11.43, include or have attached thereto:

(A) A brief statement of all material facts;

(B) Affidavits, medical reports, official records, or other documents and the opinion of at least one medical expert setting forth and establishing any of the material facts on which the practitioner is relying;

(C) A statement that the practitioner acknowledges the alleged incapacity by reason of disability or addiction;

(D) Written consent that the practitioner be transferred to disability inactive status if the motion is granted; and

(E) A written agreement by the practitioner to not practice before the Office in patent, trademark or other non-patent cases while on disability inactive status.

(ii) *Response.* The OED Director's response to any motion hereunder shall be served and filed within thirty days after service of the practitioner's motion unless such time is shortened or enlarged by the hearing officer for good cause shown, and shall set forth the following:

(A) All objections, if any, to the actions requested in the motion;

(B) An admission, denial or allegation of lack of knowledge with respect to each of the material facts in the practitioner's motion and accompanying documents; and

(C) Affidavits, medical reports, official records, or other documents setting forth facts on which the OED Director intends to rely for purposes of disputing or denying any material fact set forth in the practitioner's papers.

(2) *Disposition of practitioner's motion.* The hearing officer shall decide the motion and any response thereto. The motion shall be granted upon a showing of good cause to believe the practitioner to be incapacitated as alleged. If the required showing is made, the hearing officer shall enter an order holding the disciplinary proceeding in abeyance. In the case of addiction to drugs or intoxicants, the order may provide that the practitioner will not be returned to active status absent satisfaction of specified conditions. Upon receipt of the order, the OED Director shall transfer the practitioner to disability inactive status, give notice to the practitioner, cause notice to be published, and give notice to appropriate authorities in the Office that the practitioner has been placed on disability inactive status. The practitioner shall comply with the provisions of §11.58, and shall not engage in practice before the Office in patent, trademark and other non-patent law until a determination is made of the practitioner's capability to resume practice before the Office in a proceeding under paragraph (c) or paragraph (d) of this section. A practitioner on disability inactive status must seek permission from the OED Director to engage in an activity authorized under §11.58(e). Permission will be granted only if the practitioner has complied with all the conditions of §§11.58(a) through 11.58(d) applicable to disability inactive status. In the event that permission is granted, the practitioner shall fully comply with the provisions of §11.58(e).

(b) *Motion for reactivation.* Any practitioner transferred to disability inactive status in a disciplinary proceeding may file with the hearing officer a motion for reactivation once a year beginning at any time not less than one year after the initial effective date of inactivation, or once during any shorter interval provided by the order issued pursuant to paragraph (a)(2) of this section or any modification thereof. If the motion is granted, the disciplinary proceeding shall resume under such schedule as may be established by the hearing officer.

(c) *Contents of motion for reactivation.* A motion by the practitioner for reactivation alleging that a practitioner has recovered from a prior disability or addiction shall be accompanied by all available medical reports or similar documents relating thereto. The hearing officer may require the practitioner to present such other information as is necessary.

(d) *OED Director's motion to resume disciplinary proceeding held in abeyance.* (1) The OED Director, having good cause to believe a practitioner is no longer incapacitated, may file a motion requesting the hearing officer to terminate a prior order holding in abeyance any pending proceeding because of the practitioner's disability or addiction. The hearing officer shall decide the matter presented by the OED Director's motion hereunder based on the affidavits and other admissible evidence attached to the OED Director's motion and the practitioner's response. The OED Director bears the burden of showing by clear and convincing evidence that the practitioner is able to defend himself or herself. If there is any genuine issue as to one or more material facts, the hearing officer will hold an evidentiary hearing.

(2) The hearing officer, upon receipt of the OED Director's motion under paragraph (d)(1) of this section, may direct the practitioner to file a response. If the hearing officer requires the practitioner to file a response, the practitioner must present clear and convincing evidence that the prior self-alleged disability or addiction continues to make it impossible for the practitioner to defend himself or herself in the underlying proceeding being held in abeyance.

(e) *Action by the hearing officer.* If, in deciding a motion under paragraph (b) or (d) of this section, the hearing officer determines that there is good cause to believe the practitioner is not incapacitated from defending himself or herself, or is not incapacitated from practicing before the Office, the hearing officer shall take such action as is deemed appropriate, including the entry of an order directing the reactivation of the practitioner and resumption of the disciplinary proceeding.

§ 11.29 Reciprocal transfer or initial transfer to disability inactive status.

(a) *Notification of OED Director.* (1) Transfer to disability inactive status in another jurisdiction as grounds for reciprocal transfer by the Office. Within thirty days of being transferred to disability inactive status in another jurisdiction, a practitioner subject to the disciplinary jurisdiction of the Office shall notify the OED Director in writing of the transfer. Upon notification from any source that a practitioner subject to the disciplinary jurisdiction of the Office has been transferred to disability inactive status in another jurisdiction, the OED Director shall obtain a certified copy of the order. The OED Director shall file with the USPTO Director:

(i) The order;

(ii) A request that the practitioner be transferred to disability inactive status, including the specific grounds therefor; and

(iii) A request that the USPTO Director issue a notice and order as set forth in paragraph (b) of this section.

(2) *Involuntary commitment, adjudication of incompetency or court ordered placement under guardianship or conservatorship as grounds for initial transfer to disability inactive status.* Within thirty days of being judicially declared incompetent, being judicially ordered to be involuntarily committed after a hearing on the grounds of incompetency or disability, or being placed by court order under guardianship or conservatorship in another jurisdiction, a practitioner subject to the disciplinary jurisdiction of the Office shall notify the OED Director in writing of such judicial action. Upon notification from any source that a practitioner subject to the disciplinary jurisdiction of the Office has been subject to such judicial action, the OED Director

shall obtain a certified copy of the order. The OED Director shall file with the USPTO Director:

(i) The order;

(ii) A request that the practitioner be transferred to disability inactive status, including the specific grounds therefor; and

(iii) A request that the USPTO Director issue a notice and order as set forth in paragraph (b) of this section.

(b) *Notice served on practitioner.* Upon receipt of a certified copy of an order or declaration issued by another jurisdiction demonstrating that a practitioner subject to the disciplinary jurisdiction of the Office has been transferred to disability inactive status, judicially declared incompetent, judicially ordered to be involuntarily committed after a judicial hearing on the grounds of incompetency or disability, or placed by court order under guardianship or conservatorship, together with the OED Director's request, the USPTO Director shall issue a notice, comporting with § 11.35, directed to the practitioner containing:

(1) A copy of the order or declaration from the other jurisdiction,

(2) A copy of the OED Director's request; and

(3) An order directing the practitioner to file a response with the USPTO Director and the OED Director, within 30 days from the date of the notice, establishing a genuine issue of material fact supported by an affidavit and predicated upon the grounds set forth in § 11.29(d) (1) through (4) that a transfer to disability inactive status would be unwarranted and the reasons therefor.

(c) *Effect of stay of transfer, judicially declared incompetence, judicially ordered involuntarily commitment on the grounds of incompetency or disability, or court-ordered placement under guardianship or conservatorship.* In the event the transfer, judicially declared incompetence, judicially ordered involuntary commitment on the grounds of incompetency or disability, or court-ordered placement under guardianship or conservatorship in the other jurisdiction has been stayed there, any reciprocal transfer or transfer by the Office may be deferred until the stay expires.

(d) *Hearing and transfer to disability inactive status.* The request for transfer to disability inactive status shall be heard by the USPTO Director on the documentary record unless the USPTO Director determines that there is a genuine issue of material fact, in which case the USPTO Director may deny the request. Upon the expiration of 30 days from the date of the notice pursuant to the provisions of paragraph (b) of this section, the USPTO Director shall consider any timely filed response and impose the identical transfer to disability inactive status based on the practitioner's transfer to disability status in another jurisdiction, or shall transfer the practitioner to disability inactive status based on judicially declared incompetence, judicially ordered involuntary commitment on the grounds of incompetency or disability, or court-ordered placement under guardianship or conservatorship, unless the practitioner demonstrates by clear and convincing evidence, or the USPTO Director finds there is a genuine issue of material fact by clear and convincing evidence that:

(1) The procedure was so lacking in notice or opportunity to be heard as to constitute a deprivation of due process;

(2) There was such infirmity of proof establishing the transfer to disability status, judicial declaration of incompetence, judicial order for involuntary commitment on the grounds of incompetency or disability, or placement by court order under guardianship or conservatorship that the USPTO Director could not, consistent with Office's duty, accept as final the conclusion on that subject;

(3) The imposition of the same disability status or transfer to disability status by the USPTO Director would result in grave injustice; or

(4) The practitioner is not the individual transferred to disability status, judicially declared incompetent, judicially ordered for involuntary commitment on the grounds of incompetency or disability, or placed by court order under guardianship or conservatorship.

(5) If the USPTO Director determines that there is no genuine issue of material fact with regard to any of the elements of paragraphs (d)(1) through (4) of this section, the USPTO Director

shall enter an appropriate final order. If the USPTO Director is unable to make that determination because there is a genuine issue of material fact, the USPTO Director shall enter an appropriate order dismissing the OED Director's request for such reason.

(e) *Adjudication in other jurisdiction.* In all other aspects, a final adjudication in another jurisdiction that a practitioner be transferred to disability inactive status, is judicially declared incompetent, is judicially ordered to be involuntarily committed on the grounds of incompetency or disability, or is placed by court order under guardianship or conservatorship shall establish the disability for purposes of a reciprocal transfer to or transfer to disability status before the Office.

(f) A practitioner who is transferred to disability inactive status under this section shall be deemed to have been refused recognition to practice before the Office for purposes of 35 U.S.C. 32.

(g) *Order imposing reciprocal transfer to disability inactive status or order imposing initial transfer to disability inactive status.* An order by the USPTO Director imposing reciprocal transfer to disability inactive status, or transferring a practitioner to disability inactive status shall be effective immediately, and shall be for an indefinite period until further order of the USPTO Director. A copy of the order transferring a practitioner to disability inactive status shall be served upon the practitioner, the practitioner's guardian, and/or the director of the institution to which the practitioner has been committed in the manner the USPTO Director may direct. A practitioner reciprocally transferred or transferred to disability inactive status shall comply with the provisions of § 11.58, and shall not engage in practice before the Office in patent, trademark and other non-patent law unless and until reinstated to active status.

(h) *Confidentiality of proceeding; Orders to be public*—(1) *Confidentiality of proceeding.* All proceedings under this section involving allegations of disability of a practitioner shall be kept confidential until and unless the USPTO Director enters an order reciprocally transferring or transferring the practitioner to disability inactive status.

(2) *Orders to be public.* The OED Director shall publicize any reciprocal transfer to disability inactive status or transfer to disability inactive status in the same manner as for the imposition of public discipline.

(i) *Employment of practitioners on disability inactive status.* A practitioner on disability inactive status must seek permission from the OED Director to engage in an activity authorized under § 11.58(e). Permission will be granted only if the practitioner has complied with all the conditions of §§ 11.58(a) through 11.58(d) applicable to disability inactive status. In the event that permission is granted, the practitioner shall fully comply with the provisions of § 11.58(e).

(j) *Reinstatement from disability inactive status.* (1) *Generally.* No practitioner reciprocally transferred or transferred to disability inactive status under this section may resume active status except by order of the OED Director.

(2) *Petition.* A practitioner reciprocally transferred or transferred to disability inactive status shall be entitled to petition the OED Director for transfer to active status once a year, or at whatever shorter intervals the USPTO Director may direct in the order transferring or reciprocally transferring the practitioner to disability inactive status or any modification thereof.

(3) *Examination.* Upon the filing of a petition for transfer to active status, the OED Director may take or direct whatever action is deemed necessary or proper to determine whether the incapacity has been removed, including a direction for an examination of the practitioner by qualified medical or psychological experts designated by the OED Director. The expense of the examination shall be paid and borne by the practitioner.

(4) *Required disclosure, waiver of privilege.* With the filing of a petition for reinstatement to active status, the practitioner shall be required to disclose the name of each psychiatrist, psychologist, physician and hospital or other institution by whom or in which the practitioner has been examined or

treated for the disability since the transfer to disability inactive status. The practitioner shall furnish to the OED Director written consent to the release of information and records relating to the incapacity if requested by the OED Director.

(5) *Learning in the law, examination.* The OED Director may direct that the practitioner establish proof of competence and learning in law, which proof may include passing the registration examination.

(6) *Granting of petition for transfer to active status.* The OED Director shall grant the petition for transfer to active status upon a showing by clear and convincing evidence that the incapacity has been removed.

(7) *Reinstatement in other jurisdiction.* If a practitioner is reciprocally transferred to disability inactive status on the basis of a transfer to disability inactive status in another jurisdiction, the OED Director may dispense with further evidence that the disability has been removed and may immediately direct reinstatement to active status upon such terms as are deemed proper and advisable.

(8) *Judicial declaration of competency.* If a practitioner is transferred to disability inactive status on the basis of a judicially declared incompetence, judicially ordered involuntary commitment on the grounds of incompetency or disability, or court-ordered placement under guardianship or conservatorship has been declared to be competent, the OED Director may dispense with further evidence that the incapacity to practice law has been removed and may immediately direct reinstatement to active status.

§§ 11.30–11.31 [Reserved]

§ 11.32 Instituting a disciplinary proceeding.

If after conducting an investigation under § 11.22(a), the OED Director is of the opinion that grounds exist for discipline under § 11.19(b), the OED Director, after complying where necessary with the provisions of 5 U.S.C. 558(c), may convene a meeting of a panel of the Committee on Discipline. If convened, the panel of the Committee on Discipline shall then determine as specified in § 11.23(b) whether there is probable cause to bring disciplinary charges. If the panel of the Committee on Discipline determines that probable cause exists to bring charges, the OED Director may institute a disciplinary proceeding by filing a complaint under § 11.34.

[78 FR 20201, Apr. 3, 2013]

§ 11.33 [Reserved]

§ 11.34 Complaint.

(a) A complaint instituting a disciplinary proceeding shall:

(1) Name the person who is the subject of the complaint who may then be referred to as the "respondent";

(2) Give a plain and concise description of the respondent's alleged grounds for discipline;

(3) State the place and time, not less than thirty days from the date the complaint is filed, for filing an answer by the respondent;

(4) State that a decision by default may be entered if an answer is not timely filed by the respondent; and

(5) Be signed by the OED Director.

(b) A complaint will be deemed sufficient if it fairly informs the respondent of any grounds for discipline, and where applicable, the USPTO Rules of Professional Conduct that form the basis for the disciplinary proceeding so that the respondent is able to adequately prepare a defense.

(c) The complaint shall be filed in the manner prescribed by the USPTO Director.

(d) *Time for filing a complaint.* A complaint shall be filed within one year after the date on which the OED Director receives a grievance forming the basis of the complaint. No complaint shall be filed more than ten years after the date on which the misconduct forming the basis for the proceeding occurred.

(e) *Tolling agreements.* The one-year period for filing a complaint under paragraph (d) of this section shall be tolled if the involved practitioner and the OED Director agree in writing to such tolling.

[73 FR 47689, Aug. 14, 2008, as amended at 77 FR 45251, July 31, 2012; 78 FR 20201, Apr. 3, 2013]

§ 11.35 Service of complaint.

(a) A complaint may be served on a respondent in any of the following methods:

(1) By delivering a copy of the complaint personally to the respondent, in which case the individual who gives the complaint to the respondent shall file an affidavit with the OED Director indicating the time and place the complaint was delivered to the respondent.

(2) By mailing a copy of the complaint by "Express Mail," first-class mail, or any delivery service that provides ability to confirm delivery or attempted delivery to:

(i) A respondent who is a registered practitioner at the address provided to OED pursuant to § 11.11, or

(ii) A respondent who is not registered at the last address for the respondent known to the OED Director.

(3) By any method mutually agreeable to the OED Director and the respondent.

(4) In the case of a respondent who resides outside the United States, by sending a copy of the complaint by any delivery service that provides ability to confirm delivery or attempted delivery, to:

(i) A respondent who is a registered practitioner at the address provided to OED pursuant to § 11.11; or

(ii) A respondent who is not registered at the last address for the respondent known to the OED Director.

(b) If a copy of the complaint cannot be delivered to the respondent through any one of the procedures in paragraph (a) of this section, the OED Director shall serve the respondent by causing an appropriate notice to be published in the Official Gazette for two consecutive weeks, in which case, the time for filing an answer shall be thirty days from the second publication of the notice. Failure to timely file an answer will constitute an admission of the allegations in the complaint in accordance with paragraph (d) of § 11.36, and the hearing officer may enter an initial decision on default.

(c) If the respondent is known to the OED Director to be represented by an attorney under § 11.40(a), a copy of the complaint shall be served on the attorney in lieu of service on the respondent in the manner provided for in paragraph (a) or (b) of this section.

[73 FR 47689, Aug. 14, 2008, as amended at 78 FR 20201, Apr. 3, 2013]

§ 11.36 Answer to complaint.

(a) *Time for answer.* An answer to a complaint shall be filed within the time set in the complaint but in no event shall that time be less than thirty days from the date the complaint is filed.

(b) *With whom filed.* The answer shall be filed in writing with the hearing officer at the address specified in the complaint. The hearing officer may extend the time for filing an answer once for a period of no more than thirty days upon a showing of good cause, provided a motion requesting an extension of time is filed within thirty days after the date the complaint is served on respondent. A copy of the answer, and any exhibits or attachments thereto, shall be served on the OED Director.

(c) *Content.* The respondent shall include in the answer a statement of the facts that constitute the grounds of defense and shall specifically admit or deny each allegation set forth in the complaint. The respondent shall not deny a material allegation in the complaint that the respondent knows to be true or state that respondent is without sufficient information to form a belief as to the truth of an allegation, when in fact the respondent possesses that information. The respondent shall also state affirmatively in the answer special matters of defense and any intent to raise a disability as a mitigating factor. If respondent intends to raise a special matter of defense or disability, the answer shall specify the defense or disability, its nexus to the misconduct, and the reason it provides a defense or mitigation. A respondent who fails to do so cannot rely on a special matter of defense or disability. The hearing officer may, for good cause, allow the respondent to file the statement late, grant additional hearing preparation time, or make other appropriate orders.

(d) *Failure to deny allegations in complaint.* Every allegation in the complaint that is not denied by a respondent in the answer shall be deemed to be admitted and may be considered proven. The hearing officer at any hearing need receive no further evidence with respect to that allegation.

(e) *Default judgment.* Failure to timely file an answer will constitute an admission of the allegations in the complaint and may result in entry of default judgment.

§11.37 [Reserved]

§11.38 Contested case.

Upon the filing of an answer by the respondent, a disciplinary proceeding shall be regarded as a contested case within the meaning of 35 U.S.C. 24. Evidence obtained by a subpoena issued under 35 U.S.C. 24 shall not be admitted into the record or considered unless leave to proceed under 35 U.S.C. 24 was previously authorized by the hearing officer.

§11.39 Hearing officer; appointment; responsibilities; review of interlocutory orders; stays.

(a) *Appointment.* A hearing officer, appointed by the USPTO Director under 5 U.S.C. 3105 or 35 U.S.C. 32, shall conduct disciplinary proceedings as provided by this Part.

(b) *Independence of the Hearing Officer.* (1) A hearing officer appointed in accordance with paragraph (a) of this section shall not be subject to first level or second level supervision by either the USPTO Director or OED Director, or his or her designee.

(2) A hearing officer appointed in accordance with paragraph (a) of this section shall not be subject to supervision of the person(s) investigating or prosecuting the case.

(3) A hearing officer appointed in accordance with paragraph (a) of this section shall be impartial, shall not be an individual who has participated in any manner in the decision to initiate the proceedings, and shall not have been employed under the immediate supervision of the practitioner.

(4) A hearing officer appointed in accordance with paragraph (a) of this section shall be admitted to practice law and have suitable experience and training conducting hearings, reaching a determination, and rendering an initial decision in an equitable manner.

(c) *Responsibilities.* The hearing officer shall have authority, consistent with specific provisions of these regulations, to:

(1) Administer oaths and affirmations;

(2) Make rulings upon motions and other requests;

(3) Rule upon offers of proof, receive relevant evidence, and examine witnesses;

(4) Authorize the taking of a deposition of a witness in lieu of personal appearance of the witness before the hearing officer;

(5) Determine the time and place of any hearing and regulate its course and conduct;

(6) Hold or provide for the holding of conferences to settle or simplify the issues;

(7) Receive and consider oral or written arguments on facts or law;

(8) Adopt procedures and modify procedures for the orderly disposition of proceedings;

(9) Make initial decisions under §§11.25 and 11.54; and

(10) Perform acts and take measures as necessary to promote the efficient, timely, and impartial conduct of any disciplinary proceeding.

(d) *Time for making initial decision.* The hearing officer shall set times and exercise control over a disciplinary proceeding such that an initial decision under §11.54 is normally issued within nine months of the date a complaint is filed. The hearing officer may, however, issue an initial decision more than nine months after a complaint is filed if there exist circumstances, in his or her opinion, that preclude issuance of an initial decision within nine months of the filing of the complaint.

(e) *Review of interlocutory orders.* The USPTO Director will not review an interlocutory order of a hearing officer except:

(1) When the hearing officer shall be of the opinion:

(i) That the interlocutory order involves a controlling question of procedure or law as to which there is a substantial ground for a difference of opinion, and

(ii) That an immediate decision by the USPTO Director may materially advance the ultimate termination of the disciplinary proceeding, or

(2) In an extraordinary situation where the USPTO Director deems that justice requires review.

(f) *Stays pending review of interlocutory order.* If the OED Director or a respondent seeks review of an interlocutory order of a hearing officer under paragraph (b)(2) of this section, any time period set by the hearing officer for taking action shall not be stayed unless ordered by the USPTO Director or the hearing officer.

(g) The hearing officer shall engage in no *ex parte* discussions with any party on the merits of the complaint, beginning with appointment and ending when the final agency decision is issued.

§ 11.40 Representative for OED Director or respondent.

(a) A respondent may represent himself or herself, or be represented by an attorney before the Office in connection with an investigation or disciplinary proceeding. The attorney shall file a written declaration that he or she is an attorney within the meaning of § 11.1 and shall state:

(1) The address to which the attorney wants correspondence related to the investigation or disciplinary proceeding sent, and

(2) A telephone number where the attorney may be reached during normal business hours.

(b) The Deputy General Counsel for Intellectual Property and Solicitor, and attorneys in the Office of the Solicitor shall represent the OED Director. The attorneys representing the OED Director in disciplinary proceedings shall not consult with the USPTO Director, the General Counsel, the Deputy General Counsel for General Law, or an individual designated by the USPTO Director to decide disciplinary matters regarding the proceeding. The General Counsel and the Deputy General Counsel for General Law shall remain screened from the investigation and prosecution of all disciplinary proceedings in order that they shall be available as counsel to the USPTO Director in deciding disciplinary proceedings unless access is appropriate to perform their duties. After a final decision is entered in a disciplinary proceeding, the OED Director and attorneys representing the OED Director shall be available to counsel the USPTO Director, the General Counsel, and the Deputy General Counsel for General Law in any further proceedings.

§ 11.41 Filing of papers.

(a) The provisions of §§ 1.8 and 2.197 of this subchapter do not apply to disciplinary proceedings. All papers filed after the complaint and prior to entry of an initial decision by the hearing officer shall be filed with the hearing officer at an address or place designated by the hearing officer.

(b) All papers filed after entry of an initial decision by the hearing officer shall be filed with the USPTO Director. A copy of the paper shall be served on the OED Director. The hearing officer or the OED Director may provide for filing papers and other matters by hand, by "Express Mail," or by other means.

§ 11.42 Service of papers.

(a) All papers other than a complaint shall be served on a respondent who is represented by an attorney by:

(1) Delivering a copy of the paper to the office of the attorney; or

(2) Mailing a copy of the paper by first-class mail, "Express Mail," or other delivery service to the attorney at the address provided by the attorney under § 11.40(a)(1); or

(3) Any other method mutually agreeable to the attorney and a representative for the OED Director.

(b) All papers other than a complaint shall be served on a respondent who is not represented by an attorney by:

(1) Delivering a copy of the paper to the respondent; or

(2) Mailing a copy of the paper by first-class mail, "Express Mail," or other delivery service to the respondent at the address to which a complaint may be served or such other address as may be designated in writing by the respondent; or

(3) Any other method mutually agreeable to the respondent and a representative of the OED Director.

(c) A respondent shall serve on the representative for the OED Director one copy of each paper filed with the hearing officer or the OED Director. A paper may be served on the representative for the OED Director by:

(1) Delivering a copy of the paper to the representative; or

(2) Mailing a copy of the paper by first-class mail, "Express Mail," or other delivery service to an address designated in writing by the representative; or

(3) Any other method mutually agreeable to the respondent and the representative.

(d) Each paper filed in a disciplinary proceeding shall contain therein a certificate of service indicating:

(1) The date on which service was made; and

(2) The method by which service was made.

(e) The hearing officer or the USPTO Director may require that a paper be served by hand or by "Express Mail."

(f) Service by mail is completed when the paper mailed in the United States is placed into the custody of the U.S. Postal Service.

§ 11.43 Motions.

Motions, including all prehearing motions commonly filed under the Federal Rules of Civil Procedure, shall be filed with the hearing officer. The hearing officer will determine whether replies to responses will be authorized and the time period for filing such a response. No motion shall be filed with the hearing officer unless such motion is supported by a written statement by the moving party that the moving party or attorney for the moving party has conferred with the opposing party or attorney for the opposing party in an effort in good faith to resolve by agreement the issues raised by the motion and has been unable to reach agreement. If, prior to a decision on the motion, the parties resolve issues raised by a motion presented to the hearing officer, the parties shall promptly notify the hearing officer.

§ 11.44 Hearings.

(a) The hearing officer shall preside over hearings in disciplinary proceedings. The hearing officer shall set the time and place for the hearing. In cases involving an incarcerated respondent, any necessary oral hearing may be held at the location of incarceration. Oral hearings will be stenographically recorded and transcribed, and the testimony of witnesses will be received under oath or affirmation. The hearing officer shall conduct the hearing as if the proceeding were subject to 5 U.S.C. 556. A copy of the transcript of the hearing shall become part of the record. A copy of the transcript shall be provided to the OED Director and the respondent at the expense of the Office.

(b) If the respondent to a disciplinary proceeding fails to appear at the hearing after a notice of hearing has been given by the hearing officer, the hearing officer may deem the respondent to have waived the right to a hearing and may proceed with the hearing in the absence of the respondent.

(c) A hearing under this section will not be open to the public except that the hearing officer may grant a request by a respondent to open his or her hearing to the public and make the record of the disciplinary proceeding available for public inspection, *provided*, a protective order is entered to exclude from public disclosure information which is privileged or confidential under applicable laws or regulations.

§ 11.45 Amendment of pleadings.

The OED Director may, without Committee on Discipline authorization, but with the authorization of the hearing officer, amend the complaint to include additional charges based upon conduct committed before or after the complaint was filed. If amendment of the complaint is authorized, the hearing officer shall authorize amendment of the answer. Any party who would otherwise be prejudiced by the amendment will be given reasonable opportunity to meet the allegations in the complaint or answer as amended, and the hearing officer shall make findings on any issue presented by the complaint or answer as amended.

§§ 11.46–11.48 [Reserved]

§ 11.49 Burden of proof.

In a disciplinary proceeding, the OED Director shall have the burden of proving the violation by clear and convincing evidence and a respondent shall have the burden of proving any affirmative defense by clear and convincing evidence.

§ 11.50 Evidence.

(a) *Rules of evidence.* The rules of evidence prevailing in courts of law and equity are not controlling in hearings in disciplinary proceedings. However, the hearing officer shall exclude evidence that is irrelevant, immaterial, or unduly repetitious.

(b) *Depositions.* Depositions of witnesses taken pursuant to § 11.51 may be admitted as evidence.

(c) *Government documents.* Official documents, records, and papers of the Office, including, but not limited to, all papers in the file of a disciplinary investigation, are admissible without extrinsic evidence of authenticity. These documents, records, and papers may be evidenced by a copy certified as correct by an employee of the Office.

(d) *Exhibits.* If any document, record, or other paper is introduced in evidence as an exhibit, the hearing officer may authorize the withdrawal of the exhibit subject to any conditions the hearing officer deems appropriate.

(e) *Objections.* Objections to evidence will be in short form, stating the grounds of objection. Objections and rulings on objections will be a part of the record. No exception to the ruling is necessary to preserve the rights of the parties.

§ 11.51 Depositions.

(a) Depositions for use at the hearing in lieu of personal appearance of a witness before the hearing officer may be taken by respondent or the OED Director upon a showing of good cause and with the approval of, and under such conditions as may be deemed appropriate by, the hearing officer. Depositions may be taken upon oral or written questions, upon not less than ten days' written notice to the other party, before any officer authorized to administer an oath or affirmation in the place where the deposition is to be taken. The parties may waive the requirement of ten days' notice and depositions may then be taken of a witness at a time and place mutually agreed to by the parties. When a deposition is taken upon written questions, copies of the written questions will be served upon the other party with the notice, and copies of any written cross-questions will be served by hand or "Express Mail" not less than five days before the date of the taking of the deposition unless the parties mutually agree otherwise. A party on whose behalf a deposition is taken shall file a copy of a transcript of the deposition signed by a court reporter with the hearing officer and shall serve one copy upon the opposing party. Expenses for a court reporter and preparing, serving, and filing depositions shall be borne by the party at whose instance the deposition is taken. Depositions may not be taken to obtain discovery, except as provided for in paragraph (b) of this section.

(b) When the OED Director and the respondent agree in writing, a deposition of any witness who will appear voluntarily may be taken under such terms and conditions as may be mutually agreeable to the OED Director and the respondent. The deposition shall not be filed with the hearing officer and may not be admitted in evidence before the hearing officer unless he or she orders the deposition admitted in evidence. The admissibility of the deposition shall lie within the discretion of the hearing officer who may reject the deposition on any reasonable basis including the fact that demeanor is involved and that the witness should have been called to appear personally before the hearing officer.

§ 11.52 Discovery.

Discovery shall not be authorized except as follows:

(a) After an answer is filed under § 11.36 and when a party establishes that discovery is reasonable and relevant, the hearing officer, under such conditions as he or she deems appropriate, may order an opposing party to:

(1) Answer a reasonable number of written requests for admission or interrogatories;

(2) Produce for inspection and copying a reasonable number of documents; and

(3) Produce for inspection a reasonable number of things other than documents.

(b) Discovery shall not be authorized under paragraph (a) of this section of any matter which:

(1) Will be used by another party solely for impeachment;

(2) Is not available to the party under 35 U.S.C. 122;

(3) Relates to any other disciplinary proceeding;

(4) Relates to experts except as the hearing officer may require under paragraph (e) of this section;

(5) Is privileged; or

(6) Relates to mental impressions, conclusions, opinions, or legal theories of any attorney or other representative of a party.

(c) The hearing officer may deny discovery requested under paragraph (a) of this section if the discovery sought:

(1) Will unduly delay the disciplinary proceeding;

(2) Will place an undue burden on the party required to produce the discovery sought; or

(3) Consists of information that is available:

(i) Generally to the public;

(ii) Equally to the parties; or

(iii) To the party seeking the discovery through another source.

(d) Prior to authorizing discovery under paragraph (a) of this section, the hearing officer shall require the party seeking discovery to file a motion (§ 11.43) and explain in detail, for each request made, how the discovery sought is reasonable and relevant to an issue actually raised in the complaint or the answer.

(e) The hearing officer may require parties to file and serve, prior to any hearing, a pre-hearing statement that contains:

(1) A list (together with a copy) of all proposed exhibits to be used in connection with a party's case-in-chief;

(2) A list of proposed witnesses;

(3) As to each proposed expert witness:

(i) An identification of the field in which the individual will be qualified as an expert;

(ii) A statement as to the subject matter on which the expert is expected to testify; and

(iii) A statement of the substance of the facts and opinions to which the expert is expected to testify;

(4) Copies of memoranda reflecting respondent's own statements to administrative representatives.

§ 11.53 Proposed findings and conclusions; post-hearing memorandum.

Except in cases in which the respondent has failed to answer the complaint or amended complaint, the hearing officer, prior to making an initial decision, shall afford the parties a reasonable opportunity to submit proposed findings and conclusions and a post-hearing memorandum in support of the proposed findings and conclusions.

§ 11.54 Initial decision of hearing officer.

(a) The hearing officer shall make an initial decision in the case. The decision will include:

(1) A statement of findings of fact and conclusions of law, as well as the reasons or bases for those findings and conclusions with appropriate references to the record, upon all the material issues of fact, law, or discretion presented on the record, and

(2) An order of default judgment, of suspension or exclusion from practice, of reprimand, of probation or an order dismissing the complaint. The order also may impose any conditions deemed appropriate under the circumstances. The hearing officer shall transmit a copy of the decision to the OED Director and to the respondent. After issuing the decision, the hearing officer shall transmit the entire record to the OED Director. In the absence of an appeal to the USPTO Director, the decision of the hearing officer, including a default judgment, will, without further proceedings, become the decision of the USPTO Director thirty days from the date of the decision of the hearing officer.

(b) The initial decision of the hearing officer shall explain the reason for any default judgment, reprimand, suspension, exclusion, or probation, and shall explain any conditions imposed with discipline. In determining any sanction, the following four factors must be considered if they are applicable:

(1) Whether the practitioner has violated a duty owed to a client, to the public, to the legal system, or to the profession;

(2) Whether the practitioner acted intentionally, knowingly, or negligently;

(3) The amount of the actual or potential injury caused by the practitioner's misconduct; and

(4) The existence of any aggravating or mitigating factors.

[73 FR 47689, Aug. 14, 2008, as amended at 78 FR 20201, Apr. 3, 2013]

§ 11.55 Appeal to the USPTO Director.

(a) Within thirty days after the date of the initial decision of the hearing officer under §§ 11.25 or 11.54, either party may appeal to the USPTO Director. The appeal shall include the appellant's brief. If more than one appeal is filed, the party who files the appeal first is the appellant for purpose of this rule. If appeals are filed on the same day, the respondent is the appellant. If an appeal is filed, then the OED Director shall transmit the entire record to the USPTO Director. Any cross-appeal shall be filed within fourteen days after the date of service of the appeal pursuant to § 11.42, or thirty days after the date of the initial decision of the hearing officer, whichever is later. The cross-appeal shall include the cross-appellant's brief. Any appellee or cross-appellee brief must be filed within thirty days after the date of service pursuant to § 11.42 of an appeal or cross-appeal. Any reply brief must be filed within fourteen days after the date of service of any appellee or cross-appellee brief.

(b) An appeal or cross-appeal must include exceptions to the decisions of the hearing officer and supporting reasons for those exceptions. Any exception not raised will be deemed to have been waived and will be disregarded by the USPTO Director in reviewing the initial decision.

(c) All briefs shall:

(1) Be filed with the USPTO Director at the address set forth in § 1.1(a)(3)(ii) of this subchapter and served on the opposing party;

(2) Include separate sections containing a concise statement of the disputed facts and disputed points of law; and

(3) Be typed on 8½ by 11-inch paper, and comply with Rule 32(a)(4)–(6) of the Federal Rules of Appellate Procedure.

(d) An appellant's, cross-appellant's, appellee's, and cross-appellee's brief shall be no more than thirty pages in length, and comply with Rule 28(a)(2), (3), and (5) through (10) of the Federal Rules of Appellate Procedure. Any reply brief shall be no more than fifteen pages in length, and shall comply with Rule 28(a)(2), (3), (8), and (9) of the Federal Rules of Appellate Procedure.

(e) The USPTO Director may refuse entry of a nonconforming brief.

(f) The USPTO Director will decide the appeal on the record made before the hearing officer.

(g) Unless the USPTO Director permits, no further briefs or motions shall be filed.

(h) The USPTO Director may order reopening of a disciplinary proceeding in accordance with the principles that govern the granting of new trials. Any request to reopen a disciplinary proceeding on the basis of newly discovered evidence must demonstrate that the newly discovered evidence could not have been discovered by due diligence.

(i) In the absence of an appeal by the OED Director, failure by the respondent to appeal under the provisions of this section shall result in the initial decision being final and effective thirty days from the date of the initial decision of the hearing officer.

§ 11.56 Decision of the USPTO Director.

(a) The USPTO Director shall decide an appeal from an initial decision of the hearing officer. On appeal from the initial decision, the USPTO Director has authority to conduct a de novo review of the factual record. The USPTO Director may affirm, reverse, or modify the initial decision or remand the matter to the hearing officer for such further proceedings as the USPTO Director may deem appropriate. In making a final decision, the USPTO Director shall review the record or the portions of the record designated by the parties. The USPTO Director shall transmit a copy of the final decision to the OED Director and to the respondent.

(b) A final decision of the USPTO Director may dismiss a disciplinary proceeding, reverse or modify the initial decision, reprimand a practitioner, or may suspend or exclude the practitioner from practice before the Office. A final decision suspending or excluding a practitioner shall require compliance with the provisions of § 11.58. The final decision may also condition the reinstatement of the practitioner upon a showing that the practitioner has taken steps to correct or mitigate the matter forming the basis of the action, or to prevent recurrence of the same or similar conduct.

(c) The respondent or the OED Director may make a single request for reconsideration or modification of the decision by the USPTO Director if filed within twenty days from the date of entry of the decision. No request for reconsideration or modification shall be granted unless the request is based on newly discovered evidence or error of law or fact, and the requestor must demonstrate that any newly discovered evidence could not have been discovered any earlier by due diligence. Such a request shall have the effect of staying the effective date of the order of discipline in the final decision. The decision by the USPTO Director is effective on its date of entry.

§ 11.57 Review of final decision of the USPTO Director.

(a) Review of the final decision by the USPTO Director in a disciplinary case may be had, subject to § 11.55(d), by a petition filed in accordance with 35 U.S.C. 32. The Respondent must serve the USPTO Director with the petition. Respondent must serve the petition in accordance with Rule 4 of the Federal Rules of Civil Procedure and § 104.2 of this Title.

(b) Except as provided for in § 11.56(c), an order for discipline in a final decision will not be stayed except on proof of exceptional circumstances.

§ 11.58 Duties of disciplined or resigned practitioner, or practitioner on disability inactive status.

(a) An excluded, suspended or resigned practitioner, or practitioner transferred to disability inactive status shall not engage in any practice of patent, trademark and other non-patent law before the Office. An excluded, suspended or resigned practitioner will not be automatically reinstated at the end of his or her period of exclusion or suspension. An excluded, suspended or resigned practitioner, or practitioner transferred to disability inactive status must comply with the provisions of this section and § 11.60 to be reinstated. Failure to comply with the provisions of this section may constitute both grounds for denying reinstatement or readmission; and cause for further action, including seeking further exclusion, suspension, and for revocation of any pending probation.

(b) Unless otherwise ordered by the USPTO Director, any excluded, suspended or resigned practitioner, or practitioner transferred to disability inactive status shall:

(1) Within thirty days after the date of entry of the order of exclusion, suspension, acceptance of resignation, or transfer to disability inactive status:

(i) File a notice of withdrawal as of the effective date of the exclusion, suspension, acceptance of resignation, or transfer to disability inactive status in each pending patent and trademark application, each pending reexamination and interference or trial proceeding, and every other matter pending in the Office, together with a copy of the notices sent pursuant to paragraphs (b) and (c) of this section;

(ii) Provide notice to all State and Federal jurisdictions and administrative agencies to which the practitioner is admitted to practice and all clients the practitioner represents having immediate or prospective business before the Office in patent, trademark and other non-patent matters of the order of exclusion, suspension, acceptance of resignation, or transferred to disability inactive status and of the practitioner's consequent inability to act as a practitioner after the effective date of the order; and that, if not represented by another practitioner, the client should act promptly to substitute another practitioner, or to seek legal advice elsewhere, calling attention to any urgency arising from the circumstances of the case;

(iii) Provide notice to the practitioner(s) for all opposing parties (or, to the parties in the absence of a practitioner representing the parties) in matters pending before the Office of the practitioner's exclusion, suspension, resignation, or transfer to disability inactive status and, that as a consequence, the practitioner is disqualified from acting as a practitioner regarding matters before the Office after the effective date of the suspension, exclusion, resignation or transfer to disability inactive status, and state in the notice the mailing address of each client of the excluded, suspended or resigned practitioner, or practitioner transferred to disability inactive status who is a party in the pending matter;

(iv) Deliver to all clients having immediate or prospective business before the Office in patent, trademark or other non-patent matters any papers or other property to which the clients are entitled, or shall notify the clients and any co-practitioner of a suitable time and place where the papers and other property may be obtained, calling attention to any urgency for obtaining the papers or other property;

(v) Relinquish to the client, or other practitioner designated by the client, all funds for practice before the Office, including any legal fees paid in advance that have not been earned and any advanced costs not expended;

(vi) Take any necessary and appropriate steps to remove from any telephone, legal, or other directory any advertisement, statement, or representation which would reasonably suggest that the practitioner is authorized to practice patent, trademark, or other non-patent law before the Office; and

(vii) Serve all notices required by paragraphs (b)(1)(ii) and (b)(1)(iii) of this section by certified mail, return receipt requested, unless mailed abroad. If mailed abroad, all notices shall be served with a receipt to be signed and returned to the practitioner.

(2) Within forty-five days after entry of the order of suspension, exclusion, or of acceptance of resignation, the practitioner shall file with the OED Director an affidavit of compliance certifying that the practitioner has fully complied with the provisions of the order, this section, and with § 11.116 for withdrawal from representation. Appended to the affidavit of compliance shall be:

(i) A copy of each form of notice, the names and addresses of the clients, practitioners, courts, and agencies to which notices were sent, and all return receipts or returned mail received up to the date of the affidavit. Supplemental affidavits shall be filed covering subsequent return receipts and returned mail. Such names and addresses of clients shall remain confidential unless otherwise ordered by the USPTO Director;

(ii) A schedule showing the location, title and account number of every bank account designated as a client or trust account, deposit account in the Office, or other fiduciary account, and of every account in which the practitioner holds or held as of the entry date of the order any client, trust, or fiduciary funds for practice before the Office;

(iii) A schedule describing the practitioner's disposition of all client and fiduciary funds for practice before the Office in the practitioner's possession, custody or control as of the date of the order or thereafter;

(iv) Such proof of the proper distribution of said funds and the closing of such accounts as has been requested by the OED Director, including copies of checks and other instruments;

(v) A list of all other State, Federal, and administrative jurisdictions to which the practitioner is admitted to practice; and

(vi) An affidavit describing the precise nature of the steps taken to remove from any telephone, legal, or other directory any advertisement, statement, or representation which would reasonably suggest that the practitioner is authorized to practice patent, trademark, or other non-patent law before the Office. The affidavit shall also state the residence or other address of the practitioner to which communications may thereafter be directed, and list all State and Federal jurisdictions, and administrative agencies to which the practitioner is admitted to practice. The OED Director may require such additional proof as is deemed necessary. In addition, for the period of discipline, an excluded or suspended practitioner, or a practitioner transferred to disability inactive status shall continue to file a statement in accordance with §11.11, regarding any change of residence or other address to which communications may thereafter be directed, so that the excluded or suspended practitioner, or practitioner transferred to disability inactive status may be located if a grievance is received regarding any conduct occurring before or after the exclusion or suspension. The practitioner shall retain copies of all notices sent and shall maintain complete records of the steps taken to comply with the notice requirements.

(3) Not hold himself or herself out as authorized to practice law before the Office.

(4) Not advertise the practitioner's availability or ability to perform or render legal services for any person having immediate or prospective business before the Office as to that business.

(5) Not render legal advice or services to any person having immediate or prospective business before the Office as to that business.

(6) Promptly take steps to change any sign identifying the practitioner's or the practitioner's firm's office and the practitioner's or the practitioner's firm's stationery to delete therefrom any advertisement, statement, or representation which would reasonably suggest that the practitioner is authorized to practice law before the Office.

(c) An excluded, suspended or resigned practitioner, or practitioner transferred to disability inactive status after entry of the order of exclusion or suspension, acceptance of resignation, or transfer to disability inactive status shall not accept any new retainer regarding immediate or prospective business before the Office, or engage as a practitioner for another in any new case or legal matter regarding practice before the Office. The excluded, suspended or resigned practitioner, or practitioner transferred to disability inactive status shall be granted limited recognition for a period of thirty days. During the thirty-day period of limited recognition, the excluded, suspended or resigned practitioner, or practitioner transferred to disability inactive status shall conclude work on behalf of a client on any matters that were pending before the Office on the date of entry of the order of exclusion or suspension, or acceptance of resignation. If such work cannot be concluded, the excluded, suspended or resigned practitioner, or practitioner transferred to disability inactive status shall so advise the client so that the client may make other arrangements.

(d) *Required records.* An excluded, suspended or resigned practitioner, or practitioner transferred to disability inactive status shall keep and maintain records of the various steps taken under this section, so that in any subsequent proceeding proof of compliance with this section and with the exclusion or suspension order will be available. The OED Director will require the practitioner to submit such proof as a condition precedent to the granting of any petition for reinstatement.

(e) An excluded, suspended or resigned practitioner, or practitioner on disability inactive status who aids another practitioner in any way in the other practitioner's practice of law before the Office, may, under the direct supervision of the other practitioner, act as a paralegal for the other practitioner or perform other services for the other practitioner which are normally performed by laypersons, provided:

(1) The excluded, suspended or resigned practitioner, or practitioner transferred to disability inactive status is a salaried employee of:

(i) The other practitioner;

(ii) The other practitioner's law firm; or

(iii) A client-employer who employs the other practitioner as a salaried employee;

(2) The other practitioner assumes full professional responsibility to any client and the Office for any work performed by the excluded, suspended or

resigned practitioner for the other practitioner;

(3) The excluded, suspended or resigned practitioner, or practitioner transferred to disability inactive status does not:

(i) Communicate directly in writing, orally, or otherwise with a client of the other practitioner in regard to any immediate or prospective business before the Office;

(ii) Render any legal advice or any legal services to a client of the other practitioner in regard to any immediate or prospective business before the Office; or

(iii) Meet in person or in the presence of the other practitioner in regard to any immediate or prospective business before the Office, with:

(A) Any Office employee in connection with the prosecution of any patent, trademark, or other case;

(B) Any client of the other practitioner, the other practitioner's law firm, or the client-employer of the other practitioner; or

(C) Any witness or potential witness whom the other practitioner, the other practitioner's law firm, or the other practitioner's client-employer may or intends to call as a witness in any proceeding before the Office. The term "witness" includes individuals who will testify orally in a proceeding before, or sign an affidavit or any other document to be filed in, the Office.

(f) When an excluded, suspended or resigned practitioner, or practitioner transferred to disability inactive status acts as a paralegal or performs services under paragraph (e) of this section, the practitioner shall not thereafter be reinstated to practice before the Office unless:

(1) The practitioner shall have filed with the OED Director an affidavit which:

(i) Explains in detail the precise nature of all paralegal or other services performed by the excluded, suspended or resigned practitioner, or practitioner transferred to disability inactive status, and

(ii) Shows by clear and convincing evidence that the excluded, suspended or resigned practitioner, or practitioner transferred to disability inactive status has complied with the provisions of this section and all USPTO Rules of Professional Conduct; and

(2) The other practitioner shall have filed with the OED Director a written statement which:

(i) Shows that the other practitioner has read the affidavit required by paragraph (d)(1) of this section and that the other practitioner believes every statement in the affidavit to be true, and

(ii) States why the other practitioner believes that the excluded, suspended or resigned practitioner, or practitioner transferred to disability inactive status has complied with paragraph (c) of this section.

[73 FR 47689, Aug. 14, 2008, as amended at 77 FR 46630, Aug. 6, 2012; 78 FR 20201, Apr. 3, 2013]

§ 11.59 Dissemination of disciplinary and other information.

(a) The OED Director shall inform the public of the disposition of each matter in which public discipline has been imposed, and of any other changes in a practitioner's registration status. Public discipline includes exclusion, as well as exclusion on consent; suspension; and public reprimand. Unless otherwise ordered by the USPTO Director, the OED Director shall give notice of public discipline and the reasons for the discipline to disciplinary enforcement agencies in the State where the practitioner is admitted to practice, to courts where the practitioner is known to be admitted, and the public. If public discipline is imposed, the OED Director shall cause a final decision of the USPTO Director to be published. Final decisions of the USPTO Director include default judgments. See § 11.54(a)(2). If a private reprimand is imposed, the OED Director shall cause a redacted version of the final decision to be published.

(b) *Records available to the public.* Unless the USPTO Director orders that the proceeding or a portion of the record be kept confidential, the OED Director's records of every disciplinary proceeding where a practitioner is reprimanded, suspended, or excluded, including when said sanction is imposed by default judgment, shall be made available to the public upon written request, except that information may be withheld as necessary to protect the privacy of third parties or as directed in a protective order issued pursuant to § 11.44(c). The record of a proceeding that results in a practitioner's transfer to disability inactive status shall not be available to the public.

(c) *Access to records of exclusion by consent.* Unless the USPTO Director orders that the proceeding or a portion of the record be kept confidential, an order excluding a practitioner on consent under § 11.27 and the affidavit required under paragraph (a) of § 11.27 shall be available to the public, except that information in the order or affidavit may be withheld as necessary to protect the privacy of third parties or as directed in a protective order under § 11.44(c). The affidavit required under paragraph (a) of § 11.27 shall not be used in any other proceeding except by order of the USPTO Director or upon written consent of the practitioner.

§ 11.60 Petition for reinstatement.

(a) *Restrictions on reinstatement.* An excluded, suspended or resigned practitioner shall not resume practice of patent, trademark, or other non-patent law before the Office until reinstated by order of the OED Director or the USPTO Director.

(b) *Petition for reinstatement.* An excluded or suspended practitioner shall be eligible to apply for reinstatement only upon expiration of the period of suspension or exclusion and the practitioner's full compliance with § 11.58. An excluded practitioner shall be eligible to apply for reinstatement no earlier than at least five years from the effective date of the exclusion. A resigned practitioner shall be eligible to petition for reinstatement and must show compliance with § 11.58 no earlier than at least five years from the date the practitioner's resignation is accepted and an order is entered excluding the practitioner on consent.

(c) *Review of reinstatement petition.* An excluded, suspended or resigned practitioner shall file a petition for reinstatement accompanied by the fee required by § 1.21(a)(10) of this subchapter. The petition for reinstatement shall be filed with the OED Director. An excluded or suspended practitioner who has violated any provision of § 11.58 shall not be eligible for reinstatement until a continuous period of the time in compliance with § 11.58 that is equal to the period of suspension or exclusion has elapsed. A resigned practitioner shall not be eligible for reinstatement until compliance with § 11.58 is shown. If the excluded, suspended or resigned practitioner is not eligible for reinstatement, or if the OED Director determines that the petition is insufficient or defective on its face, the OED Director may dismiss the petition. Otherwise the OED Director shall consider the petition for reinstatement. The excluded, suspended or resigned practitioner seeking reinstatement shall have the burden of proof by clear and convincing evidence. Such proof shall be included in or accompany the petition, and shall establish:

(1) That the excluded, suspended or resigned practitioner has the good moral character and reputation, competency, and learning in law required under § 11.7 for admission;

(2) That the resumption of practice before the Office will not be detrimental to the administration of justice or subversive to the public interest; and

(3) That the suspended practitioner has complied with the provisions of § 11.58 for the full period of suspension, that the excluded practitioner has complied with the provisions of § 11.58 for at least five continuous years, or that the resigned practitioner has complied with § 11.58 upon acceptance of the resignation.

(d) *Petitions for reinstatement—Action by the OED Director granting reinstatement.* (1) If the excluded, suspended or resigned practitioner is found to have complied with paragraphs (c)(1) through (c)(3) of this section, the OED Director shall enter an order of reinstatement, which shall be conditioned on payment of the costs of the disciplinary proceeding to the extent set forth in paragraphs (d)(2) and (3) of this section.

(2) *Payment of costs of disciplinary proceedings.* Prior to reinstatement to practice, the excluded or suspended practitioner shall pay the costs of the disciplinary proceeding. The costs imposed pursuant to this section include all of the following:

(i) The actual expense incurred by the OED Director or the Office for the original and copies of any reporter's transcripts of the disciplinary proceeding, and any fee paid for the services of the reporter;

(ii) All expenses paid by the OED Director or the Office which would qualify as taxable costs recoverable in civil proceedings; and

(iii) The charges determined by the OED Director to be "reasonable costs" of investigation, hearing, and review. These amounts shall serve to defray the costs, other than fees for services of attorneys and experts, of the Office of Enrollment and Discipline in the preparation or hearing of the disciplinary proceeding, and costs incurred in the administrative processing of the disciplinary proceeding.

(3) An excluded or suspended practitioner may be granted relief, in whole or in part, only from an order assessing costs under this section or may be granted an extension of time to pay these costs, in the discretion of the OED Director, upon grounds of hardship, special circumstances, or other good cause.

(e) *Petitions for reinstatement—Action by the OED Director denying reinstatement.* If the excluded, suspended or resigned practitioner is found unfit to resume the practice of patent law before the Office, the OED Director shall first provide the excluded, suspended or resigned practitioner with an opportunity to show cause in writing why the petition should not be denied. Failure to comply with § 11.12(c) shall constitute unfitness. If unpersuaded by the showing, the OED Director shall deny the petition. The OED Director may require the excluded, suspended or resigned practitioner, in meeting the requirements of § 11.7, to take and pass an examination under § 11.7(b), ethics courses, and/or the Multistate Professional Responsibility Examination. The OED Director shall provide findings, together with the record. The findings shall include on the first page, immediately beneath the caption of the case, a separate section entitled "Prior Proceedings" which shall state the docket number of the original disciplinary proceeding in which the exclusion or suspension was ordered.

(f) *Resubmission of petitions for reinstatement.* If a petition for reinstatement is denied, no further petition for reinstatement may be filed until the expiration of at least one year following the denial unless the order of denial provides otherwise.

(g) *Reinstatement proceedings open to public.* Proceedings on any petition for reinstatement shall be open to the public. Before reinstating any excluded or suspended practitioner, the OED Director shall publish a notice of the excluded or suspended practitioner's petition for reinstatement and shall permit the public a reasonable opportunity to comment or submit evidence with respect to the petition for reinstatement.

§§ 11.61–11.99 [Reserved]

Subpart D—USPTO Rules of Professional Conduct

SOURCE: 78 FR 20201, Apr. 3, 2013, unless otherwise noted.

§ 11.100 [Reserved]

CLIENT-PRACTITIONER RELATIONSHIP

§ 11.101 Competence.

A practitioner shall provide competent representation to a client. Competent representation requires the legal, scientific, and technical knowledge, skill, thoroughness and preparation reasonably necessary for the representation.

§ 11.102 Scope of representation and allocation of authority between client and practitioner.

(a) Subject to paragraphs (c) and (d) of this section, a practitioner shall abide by a client's decisions concerning the objectives of representation and, as required by § 11.104, shall consult with the client as to the means by which they are to be pursued. A practitioner may take such action on behalf of the client as is impliedly authorized to carry out the representation. A practitioner shall abide by a client's decision whether to settle a matter.

(b) [Reserved]

(c) A practitioner may limit the scope of the representation if the limitation is reasonable under the circumstances and the client gives informed consent.

(d) A practitioner shall not counsel a client to engage, or assist a client, in conduct that the practitioner knows is criminal or fraudulent, but a practitioner may discuss the legal consequences of any proposed course of conduct with a client and may counsel or assist a client to make a good-faith effort to determine the validity, scope, meaning or application of the law.

§ 11.103 Diligence.

A practitioner shall act with reasonable diligence and promptness in representing a client.

§ 11.104 Communication.

(a) A practitioner shall:

(1) Promptly inform the client of any decision or circumstance with respect to which the client's informed consent is required by the USPTO Rules of Professional Conduct;

(2) Reasonably consult with the client about the means by which the client's objectives are to be accomplished;

(3) Keep the client reasonably informed about the status of the matter;

(4) Promptly comply with reasonable requests for information from the client; and

(5) Consult with the client about any relevant limitation on the practitioner's conduct when the practitioner knows that the client expects assistance not permitted by the USPTO Rules of Professional Conduct or other law.

(b) A practitioner shall explain a matter to the extent reasonably necessary to permit the client to make informed decisions regarding the representation.

§ 11.105 Fees.

(a) A practitioner shall not make an agreement for, charge, or collect an unreasonable fee or an unreasonable amount for expenses. The factors to be considered in determining the reasonableness of a fee include the following:

(1) The time and labor required, the novelty and difficulty of the questions involved, and the skill requisite to perform the legal service properly;

(2) The likelihood, if apparent to the client, that the acceptance of the particular employment will preclude other employment by the practitioner;

(3) The fee customarily charged in the locality for similar legal services;

(4) The amount involved and the results obtained;

(5) The time limitations imposed by the client or by the circumstances;

(6) The nature and length of the professional relationship with the client;

(7) The experience, reputation, and ability of the practitioner or practitioners performing the services; and

(8) Whether the fee is fixed or contingent.

(b) The scope of the representation and the basis or rate of the fee and expenses for which the client will be responsible shall be communicated to the client, preferably in writing, before or within a reasonable time after commencing the representation, except when the practitioner will charge a regularly represented client on the same basis or rate. Any changes in the basis or rate of the fee or expenses shall also be communicated to the client.

(c) A fee may be contingent on the outcome of the matter for which the service is rendered, except in a matter in which a contingent fee is prohibited by law. A contingent fee agreement shall be in a writing signed by the client and shall state the method by which the fee is to be determined, including the percentage or percentages that shall accrue to the practitioner in the event of settlement, trial or appeal; litigation and other expenses to be deducted from the recovery; and whether such expenses are to be deducted before or after the contingent fee is calculated. The agreement must clearly notify the client of any expenses for which the client will be liable whether or not the client is the prevailing party. Upon conclusion of a contingent fee matter, the practitioner shall provide the client with a written statement stating the outcome of the matter and, if there is a recovery, showing the remittance to the client and the method of its determination.

(d) [Reserved]

(e) A division of a fee between practitioners who are not in the same firm may be made only if:

(1) The division is in proportion to the services performed by each practitioner or each practitioner assumes joint responsibility for the representation;

(2) The client agrees to the arrangement, including the share each practitioner will receive, and the agreement is confirmed in writing; and

(3) The total fee is reasonable.

§ 11.106 Confidentiality of information.

(a) A practitioner shall not reveal information relating to the representation of a client unless the client gives informed consent, the disclosure is impliedly authorized in order to carry out the representation, the disclosure is permitted by paragraph (b) of this section, or the disclosure is required by paragraph (c) of this section.

(b) A practitioner may reveal information relating to the representation of a client to the extent the practitioner reasonably believes necessary:

(1) To prevent reasonably certain death or substantial bodily harm;

(2) To prevent the client from engaging in inequitable conduct before the Office or from committing a crime or fraud that is reasonably certain to result in substantial injury to the financial interests or property of another and in furtherance of which the client has used or is using the practitioner's services;

(3) To prevent, mitigate or rectify substantial injury to the financial interests or property of another that is reasonably certain to result or has resulted from the client's commission of a crime, fraud, or inequitable conduct before the Office in furtherance of which the client has used the practitioner's services;

(4) To secure legal advice about the practitioner's compliance with the USPTO Rules of Professional Conduct;

(5) To establish a claim or defense on behalf of the practitioner in a controversy between the practitioner and the client, to establish a defense to a criminal charge or civil claim against the practitioner based upon conduct in which the client was involved, or to respond to allegations in any proceeding concerning the practitioner's representation of the client; or

(6) To comply with other law or a court order.

(c) A practitioner shall disclose to the Office information necessary to comply with applicable duty of disclosure provisions.

§ 11.107 Conflict of interest; Current clients.

(a) Except as provided in paragraph (b) of this section, a practitioner shall not represent a client if the representation involves a concurrent conflict of interest. A concurrent conflict of interest exists if:

(1) The representation of one client will be directly adverse to another client; or

(2) There is a significant risk that the representation of one or more clients will be materially limited by the practitioner's responsibilities to another client, a former client or a third person or by a personal interest of the practitioner.

(b) Notwithstanding the existence of a concurrent conflict of interest under paragraph (a) of this section, a practitioner may represent a client if:

(1) The practitioner reasonably believes that the practitioner will be able to provide competent and diligent representation to each affected client;

(2) The representation is not prohibited by law;

(3) The representation does not involve the assertion of a claim by one client against another client represented by the practitioner in the same litigation or other proceeding before a tribunal; and

(4) Each affected client gives informed consent, confirmed in writing.

§ 11.108 Conflict of interest; Current clients; Specific rules.

(a) A practitioner shall not enter into a business transaction with a client or knowingly acquire an ownership, possessory, security or other pecuniary interest adverse to a client unless:

(1) The transaction and terms on which the practitioner acquires the interest are fair and reasonable to the client and are fully disclosed and transmitted in writing in a manner that can be reasonably understood by the client;

(2) The client is advised in writing of the desirability of seeking and is given a reasonable opportunity to seek the advice of independent legal counsel in the transaction; and

(3) The client gives informed consent, in a writing signed by the client, to the essential terms of the transaction and the practitioner's role in the transaction, including whether the practitioner is representing the client in the transaction.

(b) A practitioner shall not use information relating to representation of a client to the disadvantage of the client unless the client gives informed consent, except as permitted or required by the USPTO Rules of Professional Conduct.

(c) A practitioner shall not solicit any substantial gift from a client, including a testamentary gift, or prepare on behalf of a client an instrument giving the practitioner or a person related to the practitioner any substantial gift unless the practitioner or other recipient of the gift is related to the client. For purposes of this paragraph, related persons include a spouse, child, grandchild, parent, grandparent or other relative or individual with whom the practitioner or the client maintains a close, familial relationship.

(d) Prior to the conclusion of representation of a client, a practitioner shall not make or negotiate an agreement giving the practitioner literary or media rights to a portrayal or account based in substantial part on information relating to the representation.

(e) A practitioner shall not provide financial assistance to a client in connection with pending or contemplated litigation or a proceeding before the Office, except that:

(1) A practitioner may advance court costs and expenses of litigation, the repayment of which may be contingent on the outcome of the matter;

(2) A practitioner representing an indigent client may pay court costs and expenses of litigation or a proceeding before the Office on behalf of the client;

(3) A practitioner may advance costs and expenses in connection with a proceeding before the Office provided the client remains ultimately liable for such costs and expenses; and

(4) A practitioner may also advance any fee required to prevent or remedy an abandonment of a client's application by reason of an act or omission attributable to the practitioner and not to the client, whether or not the client is ultimately liable for such fee.

(f) A practitioner shall not accept compensation for representing a client from one other than the client unless:

(1) The client gives informed consent;

(2) There is no interference with the practitioner's independence of professional judgment or with the client-practitioner relationship; and

(3) Information relating to representation of a client is protected as required by § 11.106.

(g) A practitioner who represents two or more clients shall not participate in making an aggregate settlement of the claims of or against the clients, unless each client gives informed consent, in a writing signed by the client. The practitioner's disclosure shall include the existence and nature of all the claims involved and of the participation of each person in the settlement.

(h) A practitioner shall not:

(1) Make an agreement prospectively limiting the practitioner's liability to a client for malpractice unless the client is independently represented in making the agreement; or

(2) Settle a claim or potential claim for such liability with an unrepresented client or former client unless that person is advised in writing of the desirability of seeking and is given a reasonable opportunity to seek the advice of independent legal counsel in connection therewith.

(i) A practitioner shall not acquire a proprietary interest in the cause of action, subject matter of litigation, or a proceeding before the Office which the practitioner is conducting for a client, except that the practitioner may, subject to the other provisions in this section:

(1) Acquire a lien authorized by law to secure the practitioner's fee or expenses;

(2) Contract with a client for a reasonable contingent fee in a civil case; and

(3) In a patent case or a proceeding before the Office, take an interest in the patent or patent application as part or all of his or her fee.

(j) [Reserved]

(k) While practitioners are associated in a firm, a prohibition in paragraphs (a) through (i) of this section that applies to any one of them shall apply to all of them.

§ 11.109 Duties to former clients.

(a) A practitioner who has formerly represented a client in a matter shall not thereafter represent another person in the same or a substantially related matter in which that person's interests are materially adverse to the interests of the former client unless the former client gives informed consent, confirmed in writing.

(b) A practitioner shall not knowingly represent a person in the same or a substantially related matter in which a firm with which the practitioner formerly was associated had previously represented a client:

(1) Whose interests are materially adverse to that person; and

(2) About whom the practitioner had acquired information protected by §§ 11.106 and 11.109(c) that is material to the matter; unless the former client gives informed consent, confirmed in writing.

(c) A practitioner who has formerly represented a client in a matter or whose present or former firm has formerly represented a client in a matter shall not thereafter:

(1) Use information relating to the representation to the disadvantage of the former client except as the USPTO Rules of Professional Conduct would permit or require with respect to a client, or when the information has become generally known; or

(2) Reveal information relating to the representation except as the USPTO Rules of Professional Conduct would permit or require with respect to a client.

§ 11.110 Imputation of conflicts of interest; General rule.

(a) While practitioners are associated in a firm, none of them shall knowingly represent a client when any one of them practicing alone would be prohibited from doing so by §§ 11.107 or 11.109, unless:

(1) The prohibition is based on a personal interest of the disqualified practitioner and does not present a significant risk of materially limiting the representation of the client by the remaining practitioners in the firm; or

(2) The prohibition is based upon § 11.109(a) or (b), and arises out of the disqualified practitioner's association with a prior firm, and

(i) The disqualified practitioner is timely screened from any participation in the matter and is apportioned no part of the fee therefrom; and

(ii) Written notice is promptly given to any affected former client to enable the former client to ascertain compliance with the provisions of this section, which shall include a description of the screening procedures employed; a statement of the firm's and of the screened practitioner's compliance with the USPTO Rules of Professional Conduct; a statement that review may be available before a tribunal; and an agreement by the firm to respond promptly to any written inquiries or objections by the former client about the screening procedures.

(b) When a practitioner has terminated an association with a firm, the firm is not prohibited from thereafter representing a person with interests materially adverse to those of a client represented by the formerly associated practitioner and not currently represented by the firm, unless:

(1) The matter is the same or substantially related to that in which the formerly associated practitioner represented the client; and

(2) Any practitioner remaining in the firm has information protected by §§ 11.106 and 11.109(c) that is material to the matter.

(c) A disqualification prescribed by this section may be waived by the affected client under the conditions stated in § 11.107.

(d) The disqualification of practitioners associated in a firm with former or current Federal Government lawyers is governed by § 11.111.

§11.111 Former or current Federal Government employees.

A practitioner who is a former or current Federal Government employee shall not engage in any conduct which is contrary to applicable Federal ethics law, including conflict of interest statutes and regulations of the department, agency or commission formerly or currently employing said practitioner.

§11.112 Former judge, arbitrator, mediator or other third-party neutral.

(a) Except as stated in paragraph (d) of this section, a practitioner shall not represent anyone in connection with a matter in which the practitioner participated personally and substantially as a judge or other adjudicative officer or law clerk to such a person or as an arbitrator, mediator or other third-party neutral, unless all parties to the proceeding give informed consent, confirmed in writing.

(b) A practitioner shall not negotiate for employment with any person who is involved as a party or as practitioner for a party in a matter in which the practitioner is participating personally and substantially as a judge or other adjudicative officer or as an arbitrator, mediator or other third-party neutral. A practitioner serving as a law clerk to a judge or other adjudicative officer may negotiate for employment with a party or practitioner involved in a matter in which the clerk is participating personally and substantially, but only after the practitioner has notified the judge, or other adjudicative officer.

(c) If a practitioner is disqualified by paragraph (a) of this section, no practitioner in a firm with which that practitioner is associated may knowingly undertake or continue representation in the matter unless:

(1) The disqualified practitioner is timely screened from any participation in the matter and is apportioned no part of the fee therefrom; and

(2) Written notice is promptly given to the parties and any appropriate tribunal to enable them to ascertain compliance with the provisions of this section.

(d) An arbitrator selected as a partisan of a party in a multimember arbitration panel is not prohibited from subsequently representing that party.

§11.113 Organization as client.

(a) A practitioner employed or retained by an organization represents the organization acting through its duly authorized constituents.

(b) If a practitioner for an organization knows that an officer, employee or other person associated with the organization is engaged in action, intends to act or refuses to act in a matter related to the representation that is a violation of a legal obligation to the organization, or a violation of law that reasonably might be imputed to the organization, and that is likely to result in substantial injury to the organization, then the practitioner shall proceed as is reasonably necessary in the best interest of the organization. Unless the practitioner reasonably believes that it is not necessary in the best interest of the organization to do so, the practitioner shall refer the matter to higher authority in the organization, including, if warranted by the circumstances, to the highest authority that can act on behalf of the organization as determined by applicable law.

(c) Except as provided in paragraph (d) of this section, if

(1) Despite the practitioner's efforts in accordance with paragraph (b) of this section the highest authority that can act on behalf of the organization insists upon or fails to address in a timely and appropriate manner an action, or a refusal to act, that is clearly a violation of law, and

(2) The practitioner reasonably believes that the violation is reasonably certain to result in substantial injury to the organization, then the practitioner may reveal information relating to the representation whether or not §11.106 permits such disclosure, but only if and to the extent the practitioner reasonably believes necessary to prevent substantial injury to the organization.

(d) Paragraph (c) of this section shall not apply with respect to information relating to a practitioner's representation of an organization to investigate an alleged violation of law, or to defend the organization or an officer, employee or other constituent associated with the organization against a claim arising out of an alleged violation of law.

(e) A practitioner who reasonably believes that he or she has been discharged because of the practitioner's actions taken pursuant to paragraphs (b) or (c) of this section, or who withdraws under circumstances that require or permit the practitioner to take action under either of those paragraphs, shall proceed as the practitioner reasonably believes necessary to assure that the organization's highest authority is informed of the practitioner's discharge or withdrawal.

(f) In dealing with an organization's directors, officers, employees, members, shareholders, or other constituents, a practitioner shall explain the identity of the client when the practitioner knows or reasonably should know that the organization's interests are adverse to those of the constituents with whom the practitioner is dealing.

(g) A practitioner representing an organization may also represent any of its directors, officers, employees, members, shareholders or other constituents, subject to the provisions of § 11.107. If the organization's consent to the dual representation is required by § 11.107, the consent shall be given by an appropriate official of the organization other than the individual who is to be represented, or by the shareholders.

§ 11.114 Client with diminished capacity.

(a) When a client's capacity to make adequately considered decisions in connection with a representation is diminished, whether because of minority, mental impairment or for some other reason, the practitioner shall, as far as reasonably possible, maintain a normal client-practitioner relationship with the client.

(b) When the practitioner reasonably believes that the client has diminished capacity, is at risk of substantial physical, financial or other harm unless action is taken and cannot adequately act in the client's own interest, the practitioner may take reasonably necessary protective action, including consulting with individuals or entities that have the ability to take action to protect the client and, in appropriate cases, seeking the appointment of a guardian ad litem, conservator or guardian.

(c) Information relating to the representation of a client with diminished capacity is protected under § 11.106. When taking protective action pursuant to paragraph (b) of this section, the practitioner is impliedly authorized under § 11.106(a) to reveal information about the client, but only to the extent reasonably necessary to protect the client's interests.

§ 11.115 Safekeeping property.

(a) A practitioner shall hold property of clients or third persons that is in a practitioner's possession in connection with a representation separate from the practitioner's own property. Funds shall be kept in a separate account maintained in the state where the practitioner's office is situated, or elsewhere with the consent of the client or third person. Where the practitioner's office is situated in a foreign country, funds shall be kept in a separate account maintained in that foreign country or elsewhere with the consent of the client or third person. Other property shall be identified as such and appropriately safeguarded. Complete records of such account funds and other property shall be kept by the practitioner and shall be preserved for a period of five years after termination of the representation.

(b) A practitioner may deposit the practitioner's own funds in a client trust account for the sole purpose of paying bank service charges on that account, but only in an amount necessary for that purpose.

(c) A practitioner shall deposit into a client trust account legal fees and expenses that have been paid in advance, to be withdrawn by the practitioner only as fees are earned or expenses incurred.

(d) Upon receiving funds or other property in which a client or third person has an interest, a practitioner shall promptly notify the client or third person. Except as stated in this section or otherwise permitted by law or by agreement with the client, a practitioner shall promptly deliver to the client or third person any funds or other property that the client or third person is entitled to receive and, upon request by the client or third person, shall promptly render a full accounting regarding such property.

(e) When in the course of representation a practitioner is in possession of property in which two or more persons (one of whom may be the practitioner) claim interests, the property shall be kept separate by the practitioner until the dispute is resolved. The practitioner shall promptly distribute all portions of the property as to which the interests are not in dispute.

(f) All separate accounts for clients or third persons kept by a practitioner must also comply with the following provisions:

(1) *Required records.* The records to be kept include:

(i) Receipt and disbursement journals containing a record of deposits to and withdrawals from client trust accounts, specifically identifying the date, source, and description of each item deposited, as well as the date, payee and purpose of each disbursement;

(ii) Ledger records for all client trust accounts showing, for each separate trust client or beneficiary, the source of all funds deposited, the names of all persons for whom the funds are or were held, the amount of such funds, the descriptions and amounts of charges or withdrawals, and the names of all persons or entities to whom such funds were disbursed;

(iii) Copies of retainer and compensation agreements with clients;

(iv) Copies of accountings to clients or third persons showing the disbursement of funds to them or on their behalf;

(v) Copies of bills for legal fees and expenses rendered to clients;

(vi) Copies of records showing disbursements on behalf of clients;

(vii) The physical or electronic equivalents of all checkbook registers, bank statements, records of deposit, pre-numbered canceled checks, and substitute checks provided by a financial institution;

(viii) Records of all electronic transfers from client trust accounts, including the name of the person authorizing transfer, the date of transfer, the name of the recipient and confirmation from the financial institution of the trust account number from which money was withdrawn and the date and the time the transfer was completed;

(ix) Copies of monthly trial balances and quarterly reconciliations of the client trust accounts maintained by the practitioner; and

(x) Copies of those portions of client files that are reasonably related to client trust account transactions.

(2) *Client trust account safeguards.* With respect to client trust accounts required by paragraphs (a) through (e) of this section:

(i) Only a practitioner or a person under the direct supervision of the practitioner shall be an authorized signatory or authorize transfers from a client trust account;

(ii) Receipts shall be deposited intact and records of deposit should be sufficiently detailed to identify each item; and

(iii) Withdrawals shall be made only by check payable to a named payee and not to cash, or by authorized electronic transfer.

(3) *Availability of records.* Records required by paragraph (f)(1) of this section may be maintained by electronic, photographic, or other media provided that they otherwise comply with paragraphs (f)(1) and (f)(2) of this section and that printed copies can be produced. These records shall be readily accessible to the practitioner.

(4) *Lawyers.* The records kept by a lawyer are deemed to be in compliance with this section if the types of records that are maintained meet the recordkeeping requirements of a state in which the lawyer is licensed and in good standing, the recordkeeping requirements of the state where the lawyer's principal place of business is located, or the recordkeeping requirements of this section.

(5) *Patent agents and persons granted limited recognition who are employed in the United States by a law firm.* The records kept by a law firm employing one or more registered patent agents or persons granted limited recognition under § 11.9 are deemed to be in compliance with this section if the types of records that are maintained meet the recordkeeping requirements of the

state where at least one practitioner of the law firm is licensed and in good standing, the recordkeeping requirements of the state where the law firm's principal place of business is located, or the recordkeeping requirements of this section.

§ 11.116 Declining or terminating representation.

(a) Except as stated in paragraph (c) of this section, a practitioner shall not represent a client, or where representation has commenced, shall withdraw from the representation of a client if:

(1) The representation will result in violation of the USPTO Rules of Professional Conduct or other law;

(2) The practitioner's physical or mental condition materially impairs the practitioner's ability to represent the client; or

(3) The practitioner is discharged.

(b) Except as stated in paragraph (c) of this section, a practitioner may withdraw from representing a client if:

(1) Withdrawal can be accomplished without material adverse effect on the interests of the client;

(2) The client persists in a course of action involving the practitioner's services that the practitioner reasonably believes is criminal or fraudulent;

(3) The client has used the practitioner's services to perpetrate a crime or fraud;

(4) A client insists upon taking action that the practitioner considers repugnant or with which the practitioner has a fundamental disagreement;

(5) The client fails substantially to fulfill an obligation to the practitioner regarding the practitioner's services and has been given reasonable warning that the practitioner will withdraw unless the obligation is fulfilled;

(6) The representation will result in an unreasonable financial burden on the practitioner or has been rendered unreasonably difficult by the client; or

(7) Other good cause for withdrawal exists.

(c) A practitioner must comply with applicable law requiring notice to or permission of a tribunal when terminating a representation. When ordered to do so by a tribunal, a practitioner shall continue representation notwithstanding good cause for terminating the representation.

(d) Upon termination of representation, a practitioner shall take steps to the extent reasonably practicable to protect a client's interests, such as giving reasonable notice to the client, allowing time for employment of other counsel, surrendering papers and property to which the client is entitled and refunding any advance payment of fee or expense that has not been earned or incurred. The practitioner may retain papers relating to the client to the extent permitted by other law.

§ 11.117 Sale of law practice.

A practitioner or a law firm may sell or purchase a law practice, or an area of law practice, including good will, if the following conditions are satisfied:

(a) The seller ceases to engage in the private practice of law, or in the area of practice that has been sold, in a geographic area in which the practice has been conducted;

(b)(1) Except as provided in paragraph (b)(2) of this section, the entire practice, or the entire area of practice, is sold to one or more lawyers or law firms;

(2) To the extent the practice or the area of practice involves patent proceedings before the Office, that practice or area of practice may be sold only to one or more registered practitioners or law firms that include at least one registered practitioner;

(c)(1) The seller gives written notice to each of the seller's clients regarding:

(i) The proposed sale;

(ii) The client's right to retain other counsel or to take possession of the file; and

(iii) The fact that the client's consent to the transfer of the client's files will be presumed if the client does not take any action or does not otherwise object within ninety (90) days after receipt of the notice.

(2) If a client cannot be given notice, the representation of that client may be transferred to the purchaser only upon entry of an order so authorizing by a court having jurisdiction. The

seller may disclose to the court in camera information relating to the representation only to the extent necessary to obtain an order authorizing the transfer of a file; and

(d) The fees charged clients shall not be increased by reason of the sale.

§ 11.118 Duties to prospective client.

(a) A person who discusses with a practitioner the possibility of forming a client-practitioner relationship with respect to a matter is a prospective client.

(b) Even when no client-practitioner relationship ensues, a practitioner who has had discussions with the prospective client shall not use or reveal information learned in the consultation, except as § 11.109 would permit with respect to information of a former client.

(c) A practitioner subject to paragraph (b) of this section shall not represent a client with interests materially adverse to those of a prospective client in the same or a substantially related matter if the practitioner received information from the prospective client that could be significantly harmful to that person in the matter, except as provided in paragraph (d) of this section. If a practitioner is disqualified from representation under this paragraph, no practitioner in a firm with which that practitioner is associated may knowingly undertake or continue representation in such a matter, except as provided in paragraph (d) of this section.

(d) When the practitioner has received disqualifying information as defined in paragraph (c) of this section, representation is permissible if:

(1) Both the affected client and the prospective client have given informed consent, confirmed in writing; or

(2) The practitioner who received the information took reasonable measures to avoid exposure to more disqualifying information than was reasonably necessary to determine whether to represent the prospective client; and

(i) The disqualified practitioner is timely screened from any participation in the matter and is apportioned no part of the fee therefrom; and

(ii) Written notice is promptly given to the prospective client.

§§ 11.119–11.200 [Reserved]

COUNSELOR

§ 11.201 Advisor.

In representing a client, a practitioner shall exercise independent professional judgment and render candid advice. In rendering advice, a practitioner may refer not only to law but to other considerations such as moral, economic, social and political factors that may be relevant to the client's situation.

§ 11.202 [Reserved]

§ 11.203 Evaluation for use by third persons.

(a) A practitioner may provide an evaluation of a matter affecting a client for the use of someone other than the client if the practitioner reasonably believes that making the evaluation is compatible with other aspects of the practitioner's relationship with the client.

(b) When the practitioner knows or reasonably should know that the evaluation is likely to affect the client's interests materially and adversely, the practitioner shall not provide the evaluation unless the client gives informed consent.

(c) Except as disclosure is authorized in connection with a report of an evaluation, information relating to the evaluation is otherwise protected by § 11.106.

§ 11.204 Practitioner serving as third-party neutral.

(a) A practitioner serves as a third-party neutral when the practitioner assists two or more persons who are not clients of the practitioner to reach a resolution of a dispute or other matter that has arisen between them. Service as a third-party neutral may include service as an arbitrator, a mediator or in such other capacity as will enable the practitioner to assist the parties to resolve the matter.

(b) A practitioner serving as a third-party neutral shall inform unrepresented parties that the practitioner is not representing them. When the practitioner knows or reasonably should know that a party does not understand the practitioner's role in the matter, the practitioner shall explain the difference between the practitioner's role as a third-party neutral and a practitioner's role as one who represents a client.

§§ 11.205–11.300 [Reserved]

ADVOCATE

§ 11.301 Meritorious claims and contentions.

A practitioner shall not bring or defend a proceeding, or assert or controvert an issue therein, unless there is a basis in law and fact for doing so that is not frivolous, which includes a good-faith argument for an extension, modification or reversal of existing law.

§ 11.302 Expediting proceedings.

A practitioner shall make reasonable efforts to expedite proceedings before a tribunal consistent with the interests of the client.

§ 11.303 Candor toward the tribunal.

(a) A practitioner shall not knowingly:

(1) Make a false statement of fact or law to a tribunal or fail to correct a false statement of material fact or law previously made to the tribunal by the practitioner;

(2) Fail to disclose to the tribunal legal authority in the controlling jurisdiction known to the practitioner to be directly adverse to the position of the client and not disclosed by opposing counsel in an *inter partes* proceeding, or fail to disclose such authority in an *ex parte* proceeding before the Office if such authority is not otherwise disclosed; or

(3) Offer evidence that the practitioner knows to be false. If a practitioner, the practitioner's client, or a witness called by the practitioner, has offered material evidence and the practitioner comes to know of its falsity, the practitioner shall take reasonable remedial measures, including, if necessary, disclosure to the tribunal. A practitioner may refuse to offer evidence that the practitioner reasonably believes is false.

(b) A practitioner who represents a client in a proceeding before a tribunal and who knows that a person intends to engage, is engaging or has engaged in criminal or fraudulent conduct related to the proceeding shall take reasonable remedial measures, including, if necessary, disclosure to the tribunal.

(c) The duties stated in paragraphs (a) and (b) of this section continue to the conclusion of the proceeding, and apply even if compliance requires disclosure of information otherwise protected by § 11.106.

(d) In an *ex parte* proceeding, a practitioner shall inform the tribunal of all material facts known to the practitioner that will enable the tribunal to make an informed decision, whether or not the facts are adverse.

(e) In a proceeding before the Office, a practitioner shall disclose to the Office information necessary to comply with applicable duty of disclosure provisions.

§ 11.304 Fairness to opposing party and counsel.

A practitioner shall not:

(a) Unlawfully obstruct another party's access to evidence or unlawfully alter, destroy or conceal a document or other material having potential evidentiary value. A practitioner shall not counsel or assist another person to do any such act;

(b) Falsify evidence, counsel or assist a witness to testify falsely, or offer an inducement to a witness that is prohibited by law;

(c) Knowingly disobey an obligation under the rules of a tribunal except for an open refusal based on an assertion that no valid obligation exists;

(d) Make a frivolous discovery request or fail to make a reasonably diligent effort to comply with a legally proper discovery request by an opposing party;

(e) In a proceeding before a tribunal, allude to any matter that the practitioner does not reasonably believe is relevant or that will not be supported by admissible evidence, assert personal knowledge of facts in issue except when testifying as a witness, or state a personal opinion as to the justness of a cause, the credibility of a witness, the culpability of a civil litigant or the guilt or innocence of an accused; or

(f) Request a person other than a client to refrain from voluntarily giving relevant information to another party unless:

(1) The person is a relative or an employee or other agent of a client; and

(2) The practitioner reasonably believes that the person's interests will not be adversely affected by refraining from giving such information.

§ 11.305 Impartiality and decorum of the tribunal.

A practitioner shall not:

(a) Seek to influence a judge, hearing officer, administrative law judge, administrative patent judge, administrative trademark judge, juror, prospective juror, employee or officer of the Office, or other official by means prohibited by law;

(b) Communicate *ex parte* with such a person during the proceeding unless authorized to do so by law, rule or court order; or

(c) [Reserved]

(d) Engage in conduct intended to disrupt any proceeding before a tribunal.

§ 11.306 Trial publicity.

(a) A practitioner who is participating or has participated in the investigation or litigation of a matter shall not make an extrajudicial statement that the practitioner knows or reasonably should know will be disseminated by means of public communication and will have a substantial likelihood of materially prejudicing an adjudicative proceeding in the matter.

(b) Notwithstanding paragraph (a) of this section, a practitioner may state:

(1) The claim, offense or defense involved and, except when prohibited by law, the identity of the persons involved;

(2) Information contained in a public record;

(3) That an investigation of a matter is in progress;

(4) The scheduling or result of any step in litigation;

(5) A request for assistance in obtaining evidence and information necessary thereto; and

(6) A warning of danger concerning the behavior of a person involved, when there is reason to believe that there exists the likelihood of substantial harm to an individual or to the public interest.

(c) Notwithstanding paragraph (a) of this section, a practitioner may make a statement that a reasonable practitioner would believe is required to protect a client from the substantial undue prejudicial effect of recent publicity not initiated by the practitioner or the practitioner's client. A statement made pursuant to this paragraph shall be limited to such information as is necessary to mitigate the recent adverse publicity.

(d) No practitioner associated in a firm or government agency with a practitioner subject to paragraph (a) of this section shall make a statement prohibited by paragraph (a).

§ 11.307 Practitioner as witness.

(a) A practitioner shall not act as advocate at a proceeding before a tribunal in which the practitioner is likely to be a necessary witness unless:

(1) The testimony relates to an uncontested issue;

(2) The testimony relates to the nature and value of legal services rendered in the case; or

(3) Disqualification of the practitioner would work substantial hardship on the client.

(b) A practitioner may act as advocate in a proceeding before a tribunal in which another practitioner in the practitioner's firm is likely to be called as a witness unless precluded from doing so by §§ 11.107 or 11.109.

§ 11.308 [Reserved]

§ 11.309 Advocate in nonadjudicative proceedings.

A practitioner representing a client before a legislative body or administrative agency in a nonadjudicative proceeding shall disclose that the appearance is in a representative capacity and shall conform to the provisions of §§ 11.303(a) through (c), 11.304(a) through (c), and 11.305.

§§ 11.310—11.400 [Reserved]

TRANSACTIONS WITH PERSONS OTHER THAN CLIENTS

§ 11.401 Truthfulness in statements to others.

In the course of representing a client, a practitioner shall not knowingly:

(a) Make a false statement of material fact or law to a third person; or

(b) Fail to disclose a material fact to a third person when disclosure is necessary to avoid assisting a criminal or fraudulent act by a client, unless disclosure is prohibited by § 11.106.

§ 11.402 Communication with person represented by a practitioner.

(a) In representing a client, a practitioner shall not communicate about the subject of the representation with a person the practitioner knows to be represented by another practitioner in the matter, unless the practitioner has the consent of the other practitioner or is authorized to do so by law, rule, or a court order.

(b) This section does not prohibit communication by a practitioner with government officials who are otherwise represented by counsel and who have the authority to redress the grievances of the practitioner's client, provided that, if the communication relates to a matter for which the government official is represented, then prior to the communication the practitioner must disclose to such government official both the practitioner's identity and the fact that the practitioner represents a party with a claim against the government.

§ 11.403 Dealing with unrepresented person.

In dealing on behalf of a client with a person who is not represented by a practitioner, a practitioner shall not state or imply that the practitioner is disinterested. When the practitioner knows or reasonably should know that the unrepresented person misunderstands the practitioner's role in the matter, the practitioner shall make reasonable efforts to correct the misunderstanding. The practitioner shall not give legal advice to an unrepresented person, other than the advice to secure counsel, if the practitioner knows or reasonably should know that the interests of such a person are or have a reasonable possibility of being in conflict with the interests of the client.

§ 11.404 Respect for rights of third persons.

(a) In representing a client, a practitioner shall not use means that have no substantial purpose other than to embarrass, delay, or burden a third person, or use methods of obtaining evidence that violate the legal rights of such a person.

(b) A practitioner who receives a document or electronically stored information relating to the representation of the practitioner's client and knows or reasonably should know that the document or electronically stored information was inadvertently sent shall promptly notify the sender.

§§ 11.405—11.500 [Reserved]

LAW FIRMS AND ASSOCIATIONS

§ 11.501 Responsibilities of partners, managers, and supervisory practitioners.

(a) A practitioner who is a partner in a law firm, and a practitioner who individually or together with other practitioners possesses comparable managerial authority in a law firm, shall make reasonable efforts to ensure that the firm has in effect measures giving reasonable assurance that all practitioners in the firm conform to the USPTO Rules of Professional Conduct.

(b) A practitioner having direct supervisory authority over another practitioner shall make reasonable efforts to ensure that the other practitioner conforms to the USPTO Rules of Professional Conduct.

(c) A practitioner shall be responsible for another practitioner's violation of the USPTO Rules of Professional Conduct if:

(1) The practitioner orders or, with knowledge of the specific conduct, ratifies the conduct involved; or

(2) The practitioner is a partner or has comparable managerial authority in the law firm in which the other practitioner practices, or has direct supervisory authority over the other

practitioner, and knows of the conduct at a time when its consequences can be avoided or mitigated but fails to take reasonable remedial action.

§ 11.502 Responsibilities of a subordinate practitioner.

(a) A practitioner is bound by the USPTO Rules of Professional Conduct notwithstanding that the practitioner acted at the direction of another person.

(b) A subordinate practitioner does not violate the USPTO Rules of Professional Conduct if that practitioner acts in accordance with a supervisory practitioner's reasonable resolution of an arguable question of professional duty.

§ 11.503 Responsibilities regarding non-practitioner assistance.

With respect to a non-practitioner assistant employed or retained by or associated with a practitioner:

(a) A practitioner who is a partner, and a practitioner who individually or together with other practitioners possesses comparable managerial authority in a law firm shall make reasonable efforts to ensure that the firm has in effect measures giving reasonable assurance that the person's conduct is compatible with the professional obligations of the practitioner;

(b) A practitioner having direct supervisory authority over the non-practitioner assistant shall make reasonable efforts to ensure that the person's conduct is compatible with the professional obligations of the practitioner; and

(c) A practitioner shall be responsible for conduct of such a person that would be a violation of the USPTO Rules of Professional Conduct if engaged in by a practitioner if:

(1) The practitioner orders or, with the knowledge of the specific conduct, ratifies the conduct involved; or

(2) The practitioner is a partner or has comparable managerial authority in the law firm in which the person is employed, or has direct supervisory authority over the person, and knows of the conduct at a time when its consequences can be avoided or mitigated but fails to take reasonable remedial action.

§ 11.504 Professional independence of a practitioner.

(a) A practitioner or law firm shall not share legal fees with a non-practitioner, except that:

(1) An agreement by a practitioner with the practitioner's firm, partner, or associate may provide for the payment of money, over a reasonable period of time after the practitioner's death, to the practitioner's estate or to one or more specified persons;

(2) A practitioner who purchases the practice of a deceased, disabled, or disappeared practitioner may, pursuant to the provisions of § 11.117, pay to the estate or other representative of that practitioner the agreed-upon purchase price;

(3) A practitioner or law firm may include non-practitioner employees in a compensation or retirement plan, even though the plan is based in whole or in part on a profit-sharing arrangement; and

(4) A practitioner may share legal fees, whether awarded by a tribunal or received in settlement of a matter, with a nonprofit organization that employed, retained or recommended employment of the practitioner in the matter and that qualifies under Section 501(c)(3) of the Internal Revenue Code.

(b) A practitioner shall not form a partnership with a non-practitioner if any of the activities of the partnership consist of the practice of law.

(c) A practitioner shall not permit a person who recommends, employs, or pays the practitioner to render legal services for another to direct or regulate the practitioner's professional judgment in rendering such legal services.

(d) A practitioner shall not practice with or in the form of a professional corporation or association authorized to practice law for a profit, if:

(1) A non-practitioner owns any interest therein, except that a fiduciary representative of the estate of a practitioner may hold the stock or interest of the practitioner for a reasonable time during administration;

(2) A non-practitioner is a corporate director or officer thereof or occupies the position of similar responsibility in

any form of association other than a corporation; or

(3) A non-practitioner has the right to direct or control the professional judgment of a practitioner.

§ 11.505 Unauthorized practice of law.

A practitioner shall not practice law in a jurisdiction in violation of the regulation of the legal profession in that jurisdiction, or assist another in doing so.

§ 11.506 Restrictions on right to practice.

A practitioner shall not participate in offering or making:

(a) A partnership, shareholders, operating, employment, or other similar type of agreement that restricts the right of a practitioner to practice after termination of the relationship, except an agreement concerning benefits upon retirement; or

(b) An agreement in which a restriction on the practitioner's right to practice is part of the settlement of a client controversy.

§ 11.507 Responsibilities regarding law-related services.

A practitioner shall be subject to the USPTO Rules of Professional Conduct with respect to the provision of law-related services if the law-related services are provided:

(a) By the practitioner in circumstances that are not distinct from the practitioner's provision of legal services to clients; or

(b) In other circumstances by an entity controlled by the practitioner individually or with others if the practitioner fails to take reasonable measures to assure that a person obtaining the law-related services knows that the services are not legal services and that the protections of the client-practitioner relationship do not exist.

§§ 11.508—11.700 [Reserved]

INFORMATION ABOUT LEGAL SERVICES

§ 11.701 Communications concerning a practitioner's services.

A practitioner shall not make a false or misleading communication about the practitioner or the practitioner's services. A communication is false or misleading if it contains a material misrepresentation of fact or law, or omits a fact necessary to make the statement considered as a whole not materially misleading.

§ 11.702 Advertising.

(a) Subject to the requirements of §§ 11.701 and 11.703, a practitioner may advertise services through written, recorded or electronic communication, including public media.

(b) A practitioner shall not give anything of value to a person for recommending the practitioner's services except that a practitioner may:

(1) Pay the reasonable costs of advertisements or communications permitted by this section;

(2) [Reserved]

(3) Pay for a law practice in accordance with § 11.117; and

(4) Refer clients to another practitioner or a non-practitioner professional pursuant to an agreement not otherwise prohibited under the USPTO Rules of Professional Conduct that provides for the other person to refer clients or customers to the practitioner, if:

(i) The reciprocal referral agreement is not exclusive, and

(ii) The client is informed of the existence and nature of the agreement.

(c) Any communication made pursuant to this section shall include the name and office address of at least one practitioner or law firm responsible for its content.

§ 11.703 Direct contact with prospective clients.

(a) A practitioner shall not by in-person, live telephone or real-time electronic contact solicit professional employment from a prospective client when a significant motive for the practitioner's doing so is the practitioner's pecuniary gain, unless the person contacted:

(1) Is a practitioner; or

(2) Has a family, close personal, or prior professional relationship with the practitioner.

(b) A practitioner shall not solicit professional employment from a prospective client by written, recorded or electronic communication or by in-person, telephone or real-time electronic contact even when not otherwise prohibited by paragraph (a) of this section, if:

(1) The prospective client has made known to the practitioner a desire not to be solicited by the practitioner; or

(2) The solicitation involves coercion, duress or harassment.

(c) Every written, recorded or electronic communication from a practitioner soliciting professional employment from a prospective client known to be in need of legal services in a particular matter shall include the words "Advertising Material" on the outside envelope, if any, and at the beginning and ending of any recorded or electronic communication, unless the recipient of the communication is a person specified in paragraphs (a)(1) or (a)(2) of this section.

(d) Notwithstanding the prohibitions in paragraph (a) of this section, a practitioner may participate with a prepaid or group legal service plan operated by an organization not owned or directed by the practitioner that uses in-person or telephone contact to solicit memberships or subscriptions for the plan from persons who are not known to need legal services in a particular matter covered by the plan.

§ 11.704 Communication of fields of practice and specialization.

(a) A practitioner may communicate the fact that the practitioner does or does not practice in particular fields of law.

(b) A registered practitioner who is an attorney may use the designation "Patents," "Patent Attorney," "Patent Lawyer," "Registered Patent Attorney," or a substantially similar designation. A registered practitioner who is not an attorney may use the designation "Patents," "Patent Agent," "Registered Patent Agent," or a substantially similar designation. Unless authorized by § 11.14(b), a registered patent agent shall not hold himself or herself out as being qualified or authorized to practice before the Office in trademark matters or before a court.

(c) [Reserved]

(d) A practitioner shall not state or imply that a practitioner is certified as a specialist in a particular field of law, unless:

(1) The practitioner has been certified as a specialist by an organization that has been approved by an appropriate state authority or that has been accredited by the American Bar Association; and

(2) The name of the certifying organization is clearly identified in the communication.

(e) An individual granted limited recognition under § 11.9 may use the designation "Limited Recognition."

§ 11.705 Firm names and letterheads.

(a) A practitioner shall not use a firm name, letterhead or other professional designation that violates § 11.701. A trade name may be used by a practitioner in private practice if it does not imply a connection with a government agency or with a public or charitable legal services organization and is not otherwise in violation of § 11.701.

(b) [Reserved]

(c) The name of a practitioner holding a public office shall not be used in the name of a law firm, or in communications on its behalf, during any substantial period in which the practitioner is not actively and regularly practicing with the firm.

§§ 11.706–11.800 [Reserved]

MAINTAINING THE INTEGRITY OF THE PROFESSION

§ 11.801 Registration, recognition and disciplinary matters.

An applicant for registration or recognition to practice before the Office, or a practitioner in connection with an application for registration or recognition, or a practitioner in connection with a disciplinary or reinstatement matter, shall not:

(a) Knowingly make a false statement of material fact; or

(b) Fail to disclose a fact necessary to correct a misapprehension known by the person to have arisen in the matter, fail to cooperate with the Office of Enrollment and Discipline in an investigation of any matter before it, or knowingly fail to respond to a lawful demand or request for information from an admissions or disciplinary authority, except that the provisions of this section do not require disclosure of information otherwise protected by § 11.106.

§ 11.802 Judicial and legal officials.

(a) A practitioner shall not make a statement that the practitioner knows to be false or with reckless disregard as to its truth or falsity concerning the qualifications or integrity of a judge, adjudicatory officer or public legal officer, or of a candidate for election or appointment to judicial or legal office.

(b) A practitioner who is a candidate for judicial office shall comply with the applicable provisions of the Code of Judicial Conduct.

§ 11.803 Reporting professional misconduct.

(a) A practitioner who knows that another practitioner has committed a violation of the USPTO Rules of Professional Conduct that raises a substantial question as to that practitioner's honesty, trustworthiness or fitness as a practitioner in other respects, shall inform the OED Director and any other appropriate professional authority.

(b) A practitioner who knows that a judge, hearing officer, administrative law judge, administrative patent judge, or administrative trademark judge has committed a violation of applicable rules of judicial conduct that raises a substantial question as to the individual's fitness for office shall inform the appropriate authority.

(c) The provisions of this section do not require disclosure of information otherwise protected by § 11.106 or information gained while participating in an approved lawyers assistance program.

§ 11.804 Misconduct.

It is professional misconduct for a practitioner to:

(a) Violate or attempt to violate the USPTO Rules of Professional Conduct, knowingly assist or induce another to do so, or do so through the acts of another;

(b) Commit a criminal act that reflects adversely on the practitioner's honesty, trustworthiness or fitness as a practitioner in other respects;

(c) Engage in conduct involving dishonesty, fraud, deceit or misrepresentation;

(d) Engage in conduct that is prejudicial to the administration of justice;

(e) State or imply an ability to influence improperly a government agency or official or to achieve results by means that violate the USPTO Rules of Professional Conduct or other law;

(f) Knowingly assist a judge, hearing officer, administrative law judge, administrative patent judge, administrative trademark judge, or judicial officer in conduct that is a violation of applicable rules of judicial conduct or other law;

(g) Knowingly assist an officer or employee of the Office in conduct that is a violation of applicable rules of conduct or other law;

(h) Be publicly disciplined on ethical or professional misconduct grounds by any duly constituted authority of:

(1) A State,

(2) The United States, or

(3) The country in which the practitioner resides; or

(i) Engage in other conduct that adversely reflects on the practitioner's fitness to practice before the Office.

§§ 11.805–11.900 [Reserved]

§ 11.901 Savings clause.

(a) A disciplinary proceeding based on conduct engaged in prior to the effective date of these regulations may be instituted subsequent to such effective date, if such conduct would continue to justify disciplinary sanctions under the provisions of this part.

(b) No practitioner shall be subject to a disciplinary proceeding under this part based on conduct engaged in before the effective date hereof if such conduct would not have been subject to disciplinary action before such effective date.

PARTS 15–15a [RESERVED]

PART 41—PRACTICE BEFORE THE PATENT TRIAL AND APPEAL BOARD

Subpart A—General Provisions

Subpart B—*Ex Parte* Appeals

Subpart C—*Inter Partes* Appeals

Subpart D—Contested Cases

Subpart E—Patent Interferences

AUTHORITY: 35 U.S.C. 2(b)(2), 3(a)(2)(A), 21, 23, 32, 41, 134, 135, and Public Law 112–29.

SOURCE: 69 FR 50003, Aug. 12, 2004, unless otherwise noted.

Subpart A—General Provisions

§41.1 Policy.

(a) *Scope.* Part 41 governs appeals and interferences before the Patent Trial and Appeal Board. Sections 1.1 to 1.36 and 1.181 to 1.183 of this title also apply to practice before the Board, as do other sections of part 1 of this title that are incorporated by reference into part 41.

(b) *Construction.* The provisions of Part 41 shall be construed to secure the just, speedy, and inexpensive resolution of every proceeding before the Board.

(c) *Decorum.* Each party must act with courtesy and decorum in all proceedings before the Board, including interactions with other parties.

[69 FR 50003, Aug. 12, 2004, as amended at 77 FR 46630, Aug. 6, 2012]

§41.2 Definitions.

Unless otherwise clear from the context, the following definitions apply to proceedings under this part:

Affidavit means affidavit, declaration under §1.68 of this title, or statutory declaration under 28 U.S.C. 1746. A transcript of an *ex parte* deposition may be used as an affidavit in a contested case.

Board means the Patent Trial and Appeal Board and includes:

(1) For a final Board action:

(i) In an appeal or contested case, a panel of the Board.

(ii) In a proceeding under §41.3, the Chief Administrative Patent Judge or another official acting under an express delegation from the Chief Administrative Patent Judge.

(2) For non-final actions, a Board member or employee acting with the authority of the Board.

Board member means the Under Secretary of Commerce for Intellectual Property and Director of the United States Patent and Trademark Office, the Deputy Under Secretary of Commerce for Intellectual Property and Deputy Director of the United States Patent and Trademark Office, the Commissioner for Patents, the Commissioner for Trademarks, and the administrative patent judges.

Contested case means a Board proceeding other than an appeal under 35 U.S.C. 134 or a petition under §41.3. An appeal in an *inter partes* reexamination is not a contested case.

Final means, with regard to a Board action, final for the purposes of judicial review. A decision is final only if:

(1) *In a panel proceeding.* The decision is rendered by a panel, disposes of all issues with regard to the party seeking judicial review, and does not indicate that further action is required; and

(2) *In other proceedings.* The decision disposes of all issues or the decision states it is final.

Hearing means consideration of the issues of record. *Rehearing* means reconsideration.

Office means United States Patent and Trademark Office.

Panel means at least three Board members acting in a panel proceeding.

Panel proceeding means a proceeding in which final action is reserved by statute to at least three Board members, but includes a non-final portion of such a proceeding whether administered by a panel or not.

Party, in this part, means any entity participating in a Board proceeding, other than officers and employees of the Office, including:

(1) An appellant;

(2) A participant in a contested case;

(3) A petitioner; and

(4) Counsel for any of the above, where context permits.

[69 FR 50003, Aug. 12, 2004, as amended at 77 FR 46630, Aug. 6, 2012]

§41.3 Petitions.

(a) *Deciding official.* Petitions must be addressed to the Chief Administrative Patent Judge. A panel or an administrative patent judge may certify a question of policy to the Chief Administrative Patent Judge for decision. The Chief Administrative Patent Judge may delegate authority to decide petitions.

(b) *Scope.* This section covers petitions on matters pending before the Board (§§41.35, 41.64, 41.103, and 41.205); otherwise, see §§1.181 to 1.183 of this title. The following matters are not subject to petition:

(1) Issues committed by statute to a panel, and

(2) In pending contested cases, procedural issues. See §41.121(a)(3) and §41.125(c).

(c) *Petition fee.* The fee set in §41.20(a) must accompany any petition under this section except no fee is required for a petition under this section seeking supervisory review.

(d) *Effect on proceeding.* The filing of a petition does not stay the time for any other action in a Board proceeding.

(e) *Time for action.* (1) Except as otherwise provided in this part or as the Board may authorize in writing, a party may:

(i) File the petition within 14 days from the date of the action from which the party is requesting relief, and

(ii) File any request for reconsideration of a petition decision within 14 days of the decision on petition or such other time as the Board may set.

(2) A party may not file an opposition or a reply to a petition without Board authorization.

[69 FR 50003, Aug. 12, 2004, as amended at 69 FR 58260, Sept. 30, 2004]

§41.4 Timeliness.

(a) *Extensions of time.* Extensions of time will be granted only on a showing of good cause except as otherwise provided by rule.

(b) *Late filings.* (1) A late filing that results in either an application becoming abandoned or a reexamination prosecution becoming terminated under §1.550(d) or §1.957(b) of this title or limited under §1.957(c) of this title may be revived as set forth in §1.137 of this title.

(2) A late filing that does not result in either an application becoming abandoned or a reexamination prosecution becoming terminated under §1.550(d) or §1.957(b) of this title or limited under §1.957(c) of this title will be excused upon a showing of excusable neglect or a Board determination that consideration on the merits would be in the interest of justice.

(c) *Scope.* This section governs all proceedings before the Board, but does not apply to filings related to Board proceedings before or after the Board has jurisdiction, such as:

(1) Extensions during prosecution (see §1.136 of this title),

(2) Filing of a brief or request for oral hearing (see §§41.37, 41.41, 41.47, 41.67, 41.68, 41.71 and 41.73), or

(3) Seeking judicial review (see §§1.301 to 1.304 of this title).

[69 FR 50003, Aug. 12, 2004, as amended at 72 FR 18907, Apr. 16, 2007]

§41.5 Counsel.

While the Board has jurisdiction:

(a) *Appearance pro hac vice.* The Board may authorize a person other than a registered practitioner to appear as counsel in a specific proceeding.

(b) *Disqualification.* (1) The Board may disqualify counsel in a specific proceeding after notice and an opportunity to be heard.

(2) A decision to disqualify is not final for the purposes of judicial review until certified by the Chief Administrative Patent Judge.

(c) *Withdrawal.* Counsel may not withdraw from a proceeding before the Board unless the Board authorizes such withdrawal. *See* §11.116 of this subchapter regarding conditions for withdrawal.

(d) *Procedure.* The Board may institute a proceeding under this section on its own or a party in a contested case may request relief under this section.

(e) *Referral to the Director of Enrollment and Discipline.* Possible violations of the disciplinary rules in part 11 of this subchapter may be referred to the Office of Enrollment and Discipline for investigation. See §11.22 of this subchapter.

[69 FR 50003, Aug. 12, 2004, as amended at 73 FR 47704, Aug. 14, 2008; 78 FR 20211, Apr. 3, 2013]

§41.6 Public availability of Board records.

(a) *Publication*—(1) *Generally.* Any Board action is available for public inspection without a party's permission if rendered in a file open to the public pursuant to §1.11 of this title or in an application that has been published in accordance with §§1.211 to 1.221 of this title. The Office may independently publish any Board action that is available for public inspection.

(2) *Determination of special circumstances.* Any Board action not publishable under paragraph (a)(1) of this section may be published or made available for public inspection if the Director believes that special circumstances warrant publication and a party does not, within two months after being notified of the intention to make the action public, object in writing on the ground that the action discloses the objecting party's trade secret or other confidential information and states with specificity that such information is not otherwise publicly available. If the action discloses such information, the party shall identify the deletions in the text of the action considered necessary to protect the information. If the affected party considers that the entire action must be withheld from the public to protect such information, the party must explain why. The party will be given time, not less than twenty days, to request reconsideration and seek court review before any contested portion of the action is made public over its objection.

(b) *Record of proceeding.* (1) The record of a Board proceeding is available to the public unless a patent application not otherwise available to the public is involved.

(2) Notwithstanding paragraph (b)(1) of this section, after a final Board action in or judgment in a Board proceeding, the record of the Board proceeding will be made available to the public if any involved file is or becomes open to the public under § 1.11 of this title or an involved application is or becomes published under §§ 1.211 to 1.221 of this title.

§ 41.7 Management of the record.

(a) The Board may expunge any paper directed to a Board proceeding, or filed while an application or patent is under the jurisdiction of the Board, that is not authorized under this part or in a Board order, or that is filed contrary to a Board order.

(b) A party may not file a paper previously filed in the same Board proceeding, not even as an exhibit or appendix, without Board authorization or as required by rule.

§ 41.8 Mandatory notices.

(a) In an appeal brief (§§ 41.37, 41.67, or 41.68) or at the initiation of a contested case (§ 41.101), and within 20 days of any change during the proceeding, a party must identify:

(1) Its real party-in-interest, and

(2) Each judicial or administrative proceeding that could affect, or be affected by, the Board proceeding.

(b) For contested cases, a party seeking judicial review of a Board proceeding must file a notice with the Board of the judicial review within 20 days of the filing of the complaint or the notice of appeal. The notice to the Board must include a copy of the complaint or notice of appeal. See also §§ 1.301 to 1.304 of this title.

§ 41.9 Action by owner.

(a) *Entire interest.* An owner of the entire interest in an application or patent involved in a Board proceeding may act in the proceeding to the exclusion of the inventor (*see* §§ 3.71 and 3.73 of this title).

(b) *Part interest.* An owner of a part interest in an application or patent involved in a Board proceeding may petition to act in the proceeding to the exclusion of an inventor or a co-owner. The petition must show the inability or refusal of an inventor or co-owner to prosecute the proceeding or other cause why it is in the interest of justice to permit the owner of a part interest to act in the proceeding. An order granting the petition may set conditions on the actions of the parties during the proceeding.

[69 FR 50003, Aug. 12, 2004, as amended at 77 FR 48826, Aug. 14, 2012]

§ 41.10 Correspondence addresses.

Except as the Board may otherwise direct,

(a) *Appeals.* Correspondence in an application or a patent involved in an appeal (subparts B and C of this part) during the period beginning when an appeal docketing notice is issued and ending when a decision has been rendered by the Board, as well as any request for rehearing of a decision by the Board, shall be mailed to: Patent Trial and Appeal Board, United States Patent and Trademark Office, PO Box 1450, Alexandria, Virginia 22313–1450. Notices of appeal, appeal briefs, reply briefs, requests for oral hearing, as well as all other correspondence in an application or a patent involved in an appeal to the Board for which an address is not otherwise specified, should be addressed as set out in § 1.1(a)(1)(i) of this title.

(b) *Interferences.* Mailed correspondence in interference (subpart D of this part) shall be sent to Mail Stop INTERFERENCE, Patent Trial and Appeal Board, United States Patent and Trademark Office, PO Box 1450, Alexandria, Virginia 22313–1450.

(c) *Trial Proceedings.* Correspondence in trial proceedings (part 42 of this title) are governed by § 42.6(b) of this title.

[77 FR 46630, Aug. 6, 2012]

§ 41.11 *Ex Parte* communications in *inter partes* proceedings.

An *ex parte* communication about an *inter partes* reexamination (subpart C of this part) or about a contested case (subparts D and E of this part) with a

Board member, or with a Board employee assigned to the proceeding, is not permitted.

§41.12 Citation of authority.

(a) For any United States Supreme Court decision, citation to the United States Reports is preferred.

(b) For any decision other than a United States Supreme Court decision, citation to the West Reporter System is preferred.

(c) Citations to authority must include pinpoint citations whenever a specific holding or portion of an authority is invoked.

(d) Non-binding authority should be used sparingly. If the authority is not an authority of the Office and is not reproduced in the United States Reports or the West Reporter System, a copy of the authority should be provided.

[76 FR 72296, Nov. 22, 2011]

§41.20 Fees.

(a) *Petition fee.* The fee for filing a petition under this part is: $400.00.

(b) *Appeal fees.* (1) For filing a notice of appeal from the examiner to the Patent Trial and Appeal Board:

By a micro entity (§1.29)	$200.00
By a small entity (§1.27(a))	400.00
By other than a small or micro entity	800.00

(2)(i) For filing a brief in support of an appeal in an application or *ex parte* reexamination proceeding: $0.00.

(ii) In addition to the fee for filing a notice of appeal, for filing a brief in support of an appeal in an *inter partes* reexamination proceeding:

By a micro entity (§1.29)	$500.00
By a small entity (§1.27(a))	1,000.00
By other than a small or micro entity	2,000.00

(3) For filing a request for an oral hearing before the Board in an appeal under 35 U.S.C. 134:

By a micro entity (§1.29)	$325.00
By a small entity (§1.27(a))	650.00
By other than a small or micro entity	1,300.00

(4) In addition to the fee for filing a notice of appeal, for forwarding an appeal in an application or *ex parte* reexamination proceeding to the Board:

By a micro entity (§1.29)	$500.00
By a small entity (§1.27(a))	1,000.00
By other than a small or micro entity	2,000.00

[78 FR 4290, Jan. 18, 2013]

Subpart B—*Ex Parte* Appeals

§41.30 Definitions.

In addition to the definitions in §41.2, the following definitions apply to proceedings under this subpart unless otherwise clear from the context:

Applicant means either the applicant in a national application for a patent or the applicant in an application for reissue of a patent.

Evidence means something (including testimony, documents and tangible objects) that tends to prove or disprove the existence of an alleged fact, except that for the purpose of this subpart *Evidence* does not include dictionaries, which may be cited before the Board.

Owner means the owner of the patent undergoing *ex parte* reexamination under §1.510 of this title.

Proceeding means either a national application for a patent, an application for reissue of a patent, an *ex parte* reexamination proceeding, or a trial before the Patent Trial and Appeal Board. Appeal to the Board in an *inter partes* reexamination proceeding is controlled by subpart C of this part.

Record means the items listed in the content listing of the Image File Wrapper of the official file of the application or reexamination proceeding on appeal or the official file of the Office if other than the Image File Wrapper, excluding amendments, Evidence, and other documents that were not entered. In the case of an issued patent being reissued or reexamined, the *Record* further includes the *Record* of the patent being reissued or reexamined.

[69 FR 50003, Aug. 12, 2004, as amended at 76 FR 72296, Nov. 22, 2011; 77 FR 46630, Aug. 6, 2012]

§41.31 Appeal to Board.

(a) *Who may appeal and how to file an appeal.* An appeal is taken to the Board by filing a notice of appeal.

(1) Every applicant, any of whose claims has been twice rejected, may

appeal from the decision of the examiner to the Board by filing a notice of appeal accompanied by the fee set forth in § 41.20(b)(1) within the time period provided under § 1.134 of this title for reply.

(2) Every owner of a patent under *ex parte* reexamination filed under § 1.510 of this title before November 29, 1999, any of whose claims has been twice rejected, may appeal from the decision of the examiner to the Board by filing a notice of appeal accompanied by the fee set forth in § 41.20(b)(1) within the time period provided under § 1.134 of this title for reply.

(3) Every owner of a patent under *ex parte* reexamination filed under § 1.510 of this title on or after November 29, 1999, any of whose claims has been finally (§ 1.113 of this title) rejected, may appeal from the decision of the examiner to the Board by filing a notice of appeal accompanied by the fee set forth in § 41.20(b)(1) within the time period provided under § 1.134 of this title for reply.

(b) The signature requirements of §§ 1.33 and 11.18(a) of this title do not apply to a notice of appeal filed under this section.

(c) An appeal, when taken, is presumed to be taken from the rejection of all claims under rejection unless cancelled by an amendment filed by the applicant and entered by the Office. Questions relating to matters not affecting the merits of the invention may be required to be settled before an appeal can be considered.

(d) The time periods set forth in paragraphs (a)(1) through (a)(3) of this section are extendable under the provisions of § 1.136 of this title for patent applications and § 1.550(c) of this title for *ex parte* reexamination proceedings.

[69 FR 50003, Aug. 12, 2004, as amended at 76 FR 72296, Nov. 22, 2011]

§ 41.33 Amendments and affidavits or other Evidence after appeal.

(a) Amendments filed after the date of filing an appeal pursuant to § 41.31(a)(1) through (a)(3) and prior to the date a brief is filed pursuant to § 41.37 may be admitted as provided in § 1.116 of this title.

(b) Amendments filed on or after the date of filing a brief pursuant to § 41.37 may be admitted:

(1) To cancel claims, where such cancellation does not affect the scope of any other pending claim in the proceeding, or

(2) To rewrite dependent claims into independent form.

(c) All other amendments filed after the date of filing an appeal pursuant to § 41.31(a)(1) through (a)(3) will not be admitted except as permitted by §§ 41.39(b)(1), 41.50(a)(2)(i), and 41.50(b)(1).

(d)(1) An affidavit or other Evidence filed after the date of filing an appeal pursuant to § 41.31(a)(1) through (a)(3) and prior to the date of filing a brief pursuant to § 41.37 may be admitted if the examiner determines that the affidavit or other Evidence overcomes all rejections under appeal and that a showing of good and sufficient reasons why the affidavit or other Evidence is necessary and was not earlier presented has been made.

(2) All other affidavits or other Evidence filed after the date of filing an appeal pursuant to § 41.31(a)(1) through (a)(3) will not be admitted except as permitted by §§ 41.39(b)(1), 41.50(a)(2)(i), and 41.50(b)(1).

[69 FR 50003, Aug. 12, 2004, as amended at 76 FR 72296, Nov. 22, 2011]

§ 41.35 Jurisdiction over appeal.

(a) *Beginning of jurisdiction.* Jurisdiction over the proceeding passes to the Board upon the filing of a reply brief under § 41.41 or the expiration of the time in which to file such a reply brief, whichever is earlier.

(b) *End of jurisdiction.* The jurisdiction of the Board ends when:

(1) The Director or the Board enters a remand order (*see* §§ 41.35(c), 41.35(e), and 41.50(a)(1)),

(2) The Board enters a final decision (*see* § 41.2) and judicial review is sought or the time for seeking judicial review has expired,

(3) An express abandonment which complies with § 1.138 of this title is recognized,

(4) A request for continued examination is filed which complies with § 1.114 of this title,

(5) Appellant fails to take any required action under §§41.39(b), 41.50(a)(2), 41.50(b), or 41.50(d), and the Board enters an order of dismissal, or

(6) Appellant reopens prosecution pursuant to §41.40(b) or in response to a new ground of rejection entered in a decision of the Board (*see* §41.50(b)(1)).

(c) *Remand ordered by the Director.* Prior to the entry of a decision on the appeal by the Board (*see* §41.50), the Director may sua sponte order the proceeding remanded to the examiner.

(d) *Documents filed during Board's jurisdiction.* Except for petitions authorized by this part, consideration of any information disclosure statement or petition filed while the Board possesses jurisdiction over the proceeding will be held in abeyance until the Board's jurisdiction ends.

(e) *Administrative remands ordered by the Board.* If, after receipt and review of the proceeding, the Board determines that the file is not complete or is not in compliance with the requirements of this subpart, the Board may relinquish jurisdiction to the examiner or take other appropriate action to permit completion of the file.

[76 FR 72297, Nov. 22, 2011]

§41.37 Appeal brief.

(a) *Timing.* Appellant must file a brief under this section within two months from the date of filing the notice of appeal under §41.31. The appeal brief fee in an application or *ex parte* reexamination proceeding is $0.00, but if the appeal results in an examiner's answer, the appeal forwarding fee set forth in §41.20(b)(4) must be paid within the time period specified in §41.45 to avoid dismissal of an appeal.

(b) *Failure to file a brief.* On failure to file the brief within the period specified in paragraph (a) of this section, the appeal will stand dismissed.

(c) *Content of appeal brief.* (1) Except as otherwise provided in this paragraph, the brief shall contain the following items under appropriate headings and in the order indicated in paragraphs (c)(1)(i) through (v) of this section, except that a brief filed by an appellant who is not represented by a registered practitioner need only substantially comply with paragraphs (c)(1)(i), (c)(1)(ii), (c)(1)(iv), and (c)(1)(v) of this section:

(i) *Real party in interest.* A statement identifying by name the real party in interest at the time the appeal brief is filed, except that such statement is not required if the named inventor or inventors are themselves the real party in interest. If an appeal brief does not contain a statement of the real party in interest, the Office may assume that the named inventor or inventors are the real party in interest.

(ii) *Related appeals, interferences, and trials.* A statement identifying by application, patent, appeal, interference, or trial number all other prior and pending appeals, interferences, trials before the Board, or judicial proceedings (collectively, "related cases") which satisfy all of the following conditions: involve an application or patent owned by the appellant or assignee, are known to appellant, the appellant's legal representative, or assignee, and may be related to, directly affect or be directly affected by or have a bearing on the Board's decision in the pending appeal, except that such statement is not required if there are no such related cases. If an appeal brief does not contain a statement of related cases, the Office may assume that there are no such related cases.

(iii) *Summary of claimed subject matter.* A concise explanation of the subject matter defined in each of the rejected independent claims, which shall refer to the specification in the Record by page and line number or by paragraph number, and to the drawing, if any, by reference characters. For each rejected independent claim, and for each dependent claim argued separately under the provisions of paragraph (c)(1)(iv) of this section, if the claim contains a means plus function or step plus function recitation as permitted by 35 U.S.C. 112(f), then the concise explanation must identify the structure, material, or acts described in the specification in the Record as corresponding to each claimed function with reference to the specification in the Record by page and line number or by paragraph number, and to the drawing, if any, by reference characters. Reference to the patent application publication does not satisfy the requirements of this paragraph.

(iv) *Argument.* The arguments of appellant with respect to each ground of rejection, and the basis therefor, with citations of the statutes, regulations, authorities, and parts of the Record relied on. The arguments shall explain why the examiner erred as to each ground of rejection contested by appellant. Except as provided for in §§ 41.41, 41.47 and 41.52, any arguments or authorities not included in the appeal brief will be refused consideration by the Board for purposes of the present appeal. Each ground of rejection contested by appellant must be argued under a separate heading, and each heading shall reasonably identify the ground of rejection being contested (*e.g.*, by claim number, statutory basis, and applied reference, if any). For each ground of rejection applying to two or more claims, the claims may be argued separately (claims are considered by appellant as separately patentable), as a group (all claims subject to the ground of rejection stand or fall together), or as a subgroup (a subset of the claims subject to the ground of rejection stand or fall together). When multiple claims subject to the same ground of rejection are argued as a group or subgroup by appellant, the Board may select a single claim from the group or subgroup and may decide the appeal as to the ground of rejection with respect to the group or subgroup on the basis of the selected claim alone. Notwithstanding any other provision of this paragraph, the failure of appellant to separately argue claims which appellant has grouped together shall constitute a waiver of any argument that the Board must consider the patentability of any grouped claim separately. Under each heading identifying the ground of rejection being contested, any claim(s) argued separately or as a subgroup shall be argued under a separate subheading that identifies the claim(s) by number. A statement which merely points out what a claim recites will not be considered an argument for separate patentability of the claim.

(v) *Claims appendix.* An appendix containing a copy of the claims involved in the appeal.

(2) A brief shall not include any new or non-admitted amendment, or any new or non-admitted affidavit or other Evidence. *See* § 1.116 of this title for treatment of amendments, affidavits or other evidence filed after final action but before or on the same date of filing an appeal and § 41.33 for treatment of amendments, affidavits or other Evidence filed after the date of filing the appeal. Review of an examiner's refusal to admit an amendment or Evidence is by petition to the Director. *See* § 1.181 of this title.

(d) *Notice of non-compliance.* If a brief is filed which does not comply with all the requirements of paragraph (c) of this section, appellant will be notified of the reasons for non-compliance and given a time period within which to file an amended brief. If appellant does not, within the set time period, file an amended brief that overcomes all the reasons for non-compliance stated in the notification, the appeal will stand dismissed. Review of a determination of non-compliance is by petition to the Chief Administrative Patent Judge. *See* § 41.3.

(e) *Extensions of time.* The time periods set forth in this section are extendable under the provisions of § 1.136 of this title for patent applications and § 1.550(c) of this title for *ex parte* reexamination proceedings.

[69 FR 50003, Aug. 12, 2004, as amended at 76 FR 72297, Nov. 22, 2011; 77 FR 46630, Aug. 6, 2012; 78 FR 4291, Jan. 18, 2013; 78 FR 17107, Mar. 20, 2013]

§ 41.39 Examiner's answer.

(a) *Content of examiner's answer.* The primary examiner may, within such time as may be directed by the Director, furnish a written answer to the appeal brief.

(1) An examiner's answer is deemed to incorporate all of the grounds of rejection set forth in the Office action from which the appeal is taken (as modified by any advisory action and pre-appeal brief conference decision), unless the examiner's answer expressly indicates that a ground of rejection has been withdrawn.

(2) An examiner's answer may include a new ground of rejection. For purposes of the examiner's answer, any rejection that relies upon any Evidence not relied upon in the Office action from which the appeal is taken (as modified by any advisory action) shall be designated by the primary examiner as a new ground of rejection. The examiner must obtain the approval of the Director to furnish an answer that includes a new ground of rejection.

(b) *Appellant's response to new ground of rejection.* If an examiner's answer contains a rejection designated as a new ground of rejection, appellant must within two months from the date of the examiner's answer exercise one of the following two options to avoid sua sponte dismissal of the appeal as to the claims subject to the new ground of rejection:

(1) *Reopen prosecution.* Request that prosecution be reopened before the primary examiner by filing a reply under §1.111 of this title with or without amendment or submission of affidavits (§§1.130, 1.131 or 1.132 of this of this title) or other Evidence. Any amendment or submission of affidavits or other Evidence must be relevant to the new ground of rejection. A request that complies with this paragraph will be entered and the application or the patent under *ex parte* reexamination will be reconsidered by the examiner under the provisions of §1.112 of this title. Any request that prosecution be reopened under this paragraph will be treated as a request to withdraw the appeal.

(2) *Maintain appeal.* Request that the appeal be maintained by filing a reply brief as set forth in §41.41. Such a reply brief must address as set forth in §41.37(c)(1)(iv) each new ground of rejection and should follow the other requirements of a brief as set forth in §41.37(c). A reply brief may not be accompanied by any amendment, affidavit (§§1.130, 1.131 or 1.132 of this of this title) or other Evidence. If a reply brief filed pursuant to this section is accompanied by any amendment, affidavit or other Evidence, it shall be treated as a request that prosecution be reopened before the primary examiner under paragraph (b)(1) of this section.

(c) *Extensions of time.* Extensions of time under §1.136(a) of this title for patent applications are not applicable to the time period set forth in this section. See §1.136(b) of this title for extensions of time to reply for patent applications and §1.550(c) of this title for extensions of time to reply for *ex parte* reexamination proceedings.

[69 FR 50003, Aug. 12, 2004, as amended at 76 FR 72298, Nov. 22, 2011]

§41.40 Tolling of time period to file a reply brief.

(a) *Timing.* Any request to seek review of the primary examiner's failure to designate a rejection as a new ground of rejection in an examiner's answer must be by way of a petition to the Director under §1.181 of this title filed within two months from the entry of the examiner's answer and before the filing of any reply brief. Failure of appellant to timely file such a petition will constitute a waiver of any arguments that a rejection must be designated as a new ground of rejection.

(b) *Petition granted and prosecution reopened.* A decision granting a petition under §1.181 to designate a new ground of rejection in an examiner's answer will provide a two-month time period in which appellant must file a reply under §1.111 of this title to reopen the prosecution before the primary examiner. On failure to timely file a reply under §1.111, the appeal will stand dismissed.

(c) *Petition not granted and appeal maintained.* A decision refusing to grant a petition under §1.181 of this title to designate a new ground of rejection in an examiner's answer will provide a two-month time period in which appellant may file only a single reply brief under §41.41.

(d) *Withdrawal of petition and appeal maintained.* If a reply brief under §41.41 is filed within two months from the date of the examiner's answer and on or after the filing of a petition under §1.181 to designate a new ground of rejection in an examiner's answer, but before a decision on the petition, the reply brief will be treated as a request to withdraw the petition and to maintain the appeal.

(e) *Extensions of time.* Extensions of time under §1.136(a) of this title for patent applications are not applicable to the time period set forth in this section. See § 1.136(b) of this title for extensions of time to reply for patent applications and § 1.550(c) of this title for extensions of time to reply for *ex parte* reexamination proceedings.

[76 FR 72298, Nov. 22, 2011]

§ 41.41 Reply brief.

(a) *Timing.* Appellant may file only a single reply brief to an examiner's answer within the later of two months from the date of either the examiner's answer, or a decision refusing to grant a petition under § 1.181 of this title to designate a new ground of rejection in an examiner's answer.

(b) *Content.* (1) A reply brief shall not include any new or non-admitted amendment, or any new or non-admitted affidavit or other Evidence. See § 1.116 of this title for amendments, affidavits or other evidence filed after final action but before or on the same date of filing an appeal and § 41.33 for amendments, affidavits or other Evidence filed after the date of filing the appeal.

(2) Any argument raised in the reply brief which was not raised in the appeal brief, or is not responsive to an argument raised in the examiner's answer, including any designated new ground of rejection, will not be considered by the Board for purposes of the present appeal, unless good cause is shown.

(c) *Extensions of time.* Extensions of time under § 1.136(a) of this title for patent applications are not applicable to the time period set forth in this section. See § 1.136(b) of this title for extensions of time to reply for patent applications and § 1.550(c) of this title for extensions of time to reply for *ex parte* reexamination proceedings.

[69 FR 50003, Aug. 12, 2004, as amended at 76 FR 72298, Nov. 22, 2011]

§ 41.45 Appeal forwarding fee.

(a) *Timing.* Appellant in an application or *ex parte* reexamination proceeding must pay the fee set forth in § 41.20(b)(4) within the later of two months from the date of either the examiner's answer, or a decision refusing to grant a petition under § 1.181 of this chapter to designate a new ground of rejection in an examiner's answer.

(b) *Failure to pay appeal forwarding fee.* On failure to pay the fee set forth in § 41.20(b)(4) within the period specified in paragraph (a) of this section, the appeal will stand dismissed.

(c) *Extensions of time.* Extensions of time under § 1.136(a) of this title for patent applications are not applicable to the time period set forth in this section. *See* § 1.136(b) of this title for extensions of time to reply for patent applications and § 1.550(c) of this title for extensions of time to reply for *ex parte* reexamination proceedings.

[78 FR 17107, Mar. 20, 2013]

§ 41.47 Oral hearing.

(a) An oral hearing should be requested only in those circumstances in which appellant considers such a hearing necessary or desirable for a proper presentation of the appeal. An appeal decided on the briefs without an oral hearing will receive the same consideration by the Board as appeals decided after an oral hearing.

(b) If appellant desires an oral hearing, appellant must file, as a separate paper captioned "REQUEST FOR ORAL HEARING," a written request for such hearing accompanied by the fee set forth in § 41.20(b)(3) within two months from the date of the examiner's answer or on the date of filing of a reply brief, whichever is earlier.

(c) If no request and fee for oral hearing have been timely filed by appellant as required by paragraph (b) of this section, the appeal will be assigned for consideration and decision on the briefs without an oral hearing.

(d) If appellant has complied with all the requirements of paragraph (b) of this section, a date for the oral hearing will be set, and due notice thereof given to appellant. If an oral hearing is held, an oral argument may be presented by, or on behalf of, the primary examiner if considered desirable by either the primary examiner or the Board. A hearing will be held as stated in the notice, and oral argument will ordinarily be limited to twenty minutes for appellant and fifteen minutes for the primary examiner unless otherwise ordered.

(e)(1) Appellant will argue first and may reserve time for rebuttal. At the oral hearing, appellant may only rely on Evidence that has been previously entered and considered by the primary examiner and present argument that has been relied upon in the brief or reply brief except as permitted by paragraph (e)(2) of this section. The primary examiner may only rely on argument and Evidence relied upon in an answer except as permitted by paragraph (e)(2) of this section.

(2) Upon a showing of good cause, appellant and/or the primary examiner may rely on a new argument based upon a recent relevant decision of either the Board or a Federal Court.

(f) Notwithstanding the submission of a request for oral hearing complying with this rule, if the Board decides that a hearing is not necessary, the Board will so notify appellant.

(g) Extensions of time under §1.136(a) of this title for patent applications are not applicable to the time periods set forth in this section. See §1.136(b) of this title for extensions of time to reply for patent applications and §1.550(c) of this title for extensions of time to reply for *ex parte* reexamination proceedings.

[69 FR 50003, Aug. 12, 2004, as amended at 76 FR 72298, Nov. 22, 2011]

§41.50 Decisions and other actions by the Board.

(a)(1) *Affirmance and reversal.* The Board, in its decision, may affirm or reverse the decision of the examiner in whole or in part on the grounds and on the claims specified by the examiner. The affirmance of the rejection of a claim on any of the grounds specified constitutes a general affirmance of the decision of the examiner on that claim, except as to any ground specifically reversed. The Board may also remand an application to the examiner.

(2) If a substitute examiner's answer is written in response to a remand by the Board for further consideration of a rejection pursuant to paragraph (a)(1) of this section, the appellant must within two months from the date of the substitute examiner's answer exercise one of the following two options to avoid sua sponte dismissal of the appeal as to the claims subject to the rejection for which the Board has remanded the proceeding:

(i) *Reopen prosecution.* Request that prosecution be reopened before the examiner by filing a reply under §1.111 of this title with or without amendment or submission of affidavits (§§1.130, 1.131 or 1.132 of this title) or other Evidence. Any amendment or submission of affidavits or other Evidence must be relevant to the issues set forth in the remand or raised in the substitute examiner's answer. A request that complies with this paragraph (a) will be entered and the application or the patent under *ex parte* reexamination will be reconsidered by the examiner under the provisions of §1.112 of this title. Any request that prosecution be reopened under this paragraph will be treated as a request to withdraw the appeal.

(ii) *Maintain appeal.* Request that the appeal be maintained by filing a reply brief as provided in §41.41. If such a reply brief is accompanied by any amendment, affidavit or other Evidence, it shall be treated as a request that prosecution be reopened before the examiner under paragraph (a)(2)(i) of this section.

(b) *New ground of rejection.* Should the Board have knowledge of any grounds not involved in the appeal for rejecting any pending claim, it may include in its opinion a statement to that effect with its reasons for so holding, and designate such a statement as a new ground of rejection of the claim. A new ground of rejection pursuant to this paragraph shall not be considered final for judicial review. When the Board enters such a non-final decision, the appellant, within two months from the date of the decision, must exercise one of the following two options with respect to the new ground of rejection to avoid termination of the appeal as to the rejected claims:

(1) *Reopen prosecution.* Submit an appropriate amendment of the claims so rejected or new Evidence relating to the claims so rejected, or both, and have the matter reconsidered by the examiner, in which event the prosecution will be remanded to the examiner. The new ground of rejection is binding upon the examiner unless an amendment or new Evidence not previously of Record is made which, in the opinion of

the examiner, overcomes the new ground of rejection designated in the decision. Should the examiner reject the claims, appellant may again appeal to the Board pursuant to this subpart.

(2) *Request rehearing.* Request that the proceeding be reheard under § 41.52 by the Board upon the same Record. The request for rehearing must address any new ground of rejection and state with particularity the points believed to have been misapprehended or overlooked in entering the new ground of rejection and also state all other grounds upon which rehearing is sought.

(c) *Review of undesignated new ground of rejection.* Any request to seek review of a panel's failure to designate a new ground of rejection in its decision must be raised by filing a request for rehearing as set forth in § 41.52. Failure of appellant to timely file such a request for rehearing will constitute a waiver of any arguments that a decision contains an undesignated new ground of rejection.

(d) *Request for briefing and information.* The Board may order appellant to additionally brief any matter that the Board considers to be of assistance in reaching a reasoned decision on the pending appeal. Appellant will be given a time period within which to respond to such an order. Failure to timely comply with the order may result in the sua sponte dismissal of the appeal.

(e) *Remand not final action.* Whenever a decision of the Board includes a remand, that decision shall not be considered final for judicial review. When appropriate, upon conclusion of proceedings on remand before the examiner, the Board may enter an order otherwise making its decision final for judicial review.

(f) *Extensions of time.* Extensions of time under § 1.136(a) of this title for patent applications are not applicable to the time periods set forth in this section. See § 1.136(b) of this title for extensions of time to reply for patent applications and § 1.550(c) of this title for extensions of time to reply for *ex parte* reexamination proceedings.

[76 FR 72299, Nov. 22, 2011]

§ 41.52 Rehearing.

(a)(1) Appellant may file a single request for rehearing within two months of the date of the original decision of the Board. No request for rehearing from a decision on rehearing will be permitted, unless the rehearing decision so modified the original decision as to become, in effect, a new decision, and the Board states that a second request for rehearing would be permitted. The request for rehearing must state with particularity the points believed to have been misapprehended or overlooked by the Board. Arguments not raised, and Evidence not previously relied upon, pursuant to §§ 41.37, 41.41, or 41.47 are not permitted in the request for rehearing except as permitted by paragraphs (a)(2) through (a)(4) of this section. When a request for rehearing is made, the Board shall render a decision on the request for rehearing. The decision on the request for rehearing is deemed to incorporate the earlier opinion reflecting its decision for appeal, except for those portions specifically withdrawn on rehearing, and is final for the purpose of judicial review, except when noted otherwise in the decision on rehearing.

(2) Appellant may present a new argument based upon a recent relevant decision of either the Board or a Federal Court.

(3) New arguments responding to a new ground of rejection designated pursuant to § 41.50(b) are permitted.

(4) New arguments that the Board's decision contains an undesignated new ground of rejection are permitted.

(b) Extensions of time under § 1.136(a) of this title for patent applications are not applicable to the time period set forth in this section. See § 1.136(b) of this title for extensions of time to reply for patent applications and § 1.550(c) of this title for extensions of time to reply for *ex parte* reexamination proceedings.

[69 FR 50003, Aug. 12, 2004, as amended at 76 FR 72299, Nov. 22, 2011]

§ 41.54 Action following decision.

After decision by the Board, jurisdiction over an application or patent under *ex parte* reexamination proceeding passes to the examiner, subject to appellant's right of appeal or other review, for such further action by appellant or by the examiner, as the condition of the application or patent under *ex parte* reexamination proceeding may require, to carry into effect the decision.

[76 FR 72299, Nov. 22, 2011]

Subpart C—*Inter Partes* Appeals

§41.60 Definitions.

In addition to the definitions in §41.2, the following definitions apply to proceedings under this subpart unless otherwise clear from the context:

Appellant means any party, whether the owner or a requester, filing a notice of appeal or cross appeal under §41.61. If more than one party appeals or cross appeals, each appealing or cross appealing party is an appellant with respect to the claims to which his or her appeal or cross appeal is directed.

Filing means filing with a certificate indicating service of the document under §1.903 of this title.

Owner means the owner of the patent undergoing *inter partes* reexamination under §1.915 of this title.

Proceeding means an *inter partes* reexamination proceeding. Appeal to the Board in an *ex parte* reexamination proceeding is controlled by subpart B of this part. An *inter partes* reexamination proceeding is not a contested case subject to subpart D.

Requester means each party, other than the owner, who requested that the patent undergo *inter partes* reexamination under §1.915 of this title.

Respondent means any requester responding under §41.68 to the appellant's brief of the owner, or the owner responding under §41.68 to the appellant's brief of any requester. No requester may be a respondent to the appellant brief of any other requester.

§41.61 Notice of appeal and cross appeal to Board.

(a)(1) Upon the issuance of a Right of Appeal Notice under §1.953 of this title, the owner may appeal to the Board with respect to the final rejection of any claim of the patent by filing a notice of appeal within the time provided in the Right of Appeal Notice and paying the fee set forth in §41.20(b)(1).

(2) Upon the issuance of a Right of Appeal Notice under §1.953 of this title, the requester may appeal to the Board with respect to any final decision favorable to the patentability, including any final determination not to make a proposed rejection, of any original, proposed amended, or new claim of the patent by filing a notice of appeal within the time provided in the Right of Appeal Notice and paying the fee set forth in §41.20(b)(1).

(b)(1) Within fourteen days of service of a requester's notice of appeal under paragraph (a)(2) of this section and upon payment of the fee set forth in §41.20(b)(1), an owner who has not filed a notice of appeal may file a notice of cross appeal with respect to the final rejection of any claim of the patent.

(2) Within fourteen days of service of an owner's notice of appeal under paragraph (a)(1) of this section and upon payment of the fee set forth in §41.20(b)(1), a requester who has not filed a notice of appeal may file a notice of cross appeal with respect to any final decision favorable to the patentability, including any final determination not to make a proposed rejection, of any original, proposed amended, or new claim of the patent.

(c) The notice of appeal or cross appeal in the proceeding must identify the appealed claim(s) and must be signed by the owner, the requester, or a duly authorized attorney or agent.

(d) An appeal or cross appeal, when taken, must be taken from all the rejections of the claims in a Right of Appeal Notice which the patent owner proposes to contest or from all the determinations favorable to patentability, including any final determination not to make a proposed rejection, in a Right of Appeal Notice which a requester proposes to contest. Questions relating to matters not affecting the merits of the invention may be required to be settled before an appeal is decided.

(e) The time periods for filing a notice of appeal or cross appeal may not be extended.

(f) If a notice of appeal or cross appeal is timely filed but does not comply with any requirement of this section, appellant will be notified of the reasons for non-compliance and given a non-extendable time period within which to file an amended notice of appeal or cross appeal. If the appellant does not then file an amended notice of appeal or cross appeal within the set time period, or files a notice which does not overcome all the reasons for non-compliance stated in the notification of the reasons for non-compliance, that appellant's appeal or cross appeal will stand dismissed.

§ 41.63 Amendments and affidavits or other evidence after appeal.

(a) Amendments filed after the date of filing an appeal pursuant to § 41.61 canceling claims may be admitted where such cancellation does not affect the scope of any other pending claim in the proceeding.

(b) All other amendments filed after the date of filing an appeal pursuant to § 41.61 will not be admitted except as permitted by § 41.77(b)(1).

(c) Affidavits or other evidence filed after the date of filing an appeal pursuant to § 41.61 will not be admitted except as permitted by reopening prosecution under § 41.77(b)(1).

§ 41.64 Jurisdiction over appeal in *inter partes* reexamination.

(a) Jurisdiction over the proceeding passes to the Board upon transmittal of the file, including all briefs and examiner's answers, to the Board.

(b) If, after receipt and review of the proceeding, the Board determines that the file is not complete or is not in compliance with the requirements of this subpart, the Board may relinquish jurisdiction to the examiner or take other appropriate action to permit completion of the file.

(c) Prior to the entry of a decision on the appeal by the Board, the Director may sua sponte order the proceeding remanded to the examiner.

§ 41.66 Time for filing briefs.

(a) An appellant's brief must be filed no later than two months from the latest filing date of the last-filed notice of appeal or cross appeal or, if any party to the proceeding is entitled to file an appeal or cross appeal but fails to timely do so, no later than two months from the expiration of the time for filing (by the last party entitled to do so) such notice of appeal or cross appeal. The time for filing an appellant's brief or an amended appellant's brief may not be extended.

(b) Once an appellant's brief has been properly filed, any brief must be filed by respondent within one month from the date of service of the appellant's brief. The time for filing a respondent's brief or an amended respondent's brief may not be extended.

(c) The examiner will consider both the appellant's and respondent's briefs and may prepare an examiner's answer under § 41.69.

(d) Any appellant may file a rebuttal brief under § 41.71 within one month of the date of the examiner's answer. The time for filing a rebuttal brief or an amended rebuttal brief may not be extended.

(e) No further submission will be considered and any such submission will be treated in accordance with § 1.939 of this title.

§ 41.67 Appellant's brief.

(a)(1) Appellant(s) may once, within time limits for filing set forth in § 41.66, file a brief and serve the brief on all other parties to the proceeding in accordance with § 1.903 of this title.

(2) The brief must be signed by the appellant, or the appellant's duly authorized attorney or agent and must be accompanied by the requisite fee set forth in § 41.20(b)(2).

(b) An appellant's appeal shall stand dismissed upon failure of that appellant to file an appellant's brief, accompanied by the requisite fee, within the time allowed under § 41.66(a).

(c)(1) The appellant's brief shall contain the following items under appropriate headings and in the order indicated in paragraphs (c)(1)(i) through (c)(1)(xi) of this section.

(i) *Real party in interest.* A statement identifying by name the real party in interest.

(ii) *Related appeals, interferences, and trials.* A statement identifying by application, patent, appeal, interference, or trial number all other prior and pending appeals, interferences, trials before the Board, or judicial proceedings known to appellant, the appellant's legal representative, or assignee which may be related to, directly affect or be directly affected by or have a bearing on the Board's decision in the pending appeal. Copies of any decisions rendered by a court or the Board in any proceeding identified under this paragraph must be included in an appendix as required by paragraph (c)(1)(xi) of this section.

(iii) *Status of claims.* A statement of the status of all the claims in the proceeding (e.g., rejected, allowed or confirmed, withdrawn, objected to, canceled). If the appellant is the owner, the appellant must also identify the rejected claims whose rejection is being appealed. If the appellant is a requester, the appellant must identify the claims that the examiner has made a determination favorable to patentability, which determination is being appealed.

(iv) *Status of amendments.* A statement of the status of any amendment filed subsequent to the close of prosecution.

(v) *Summary of claimed subject matter.* A concise explanation of the subject matter defined in each of the independent claims involved in the appeal, which shall refer to the specification by column and line number, and to the drawing(s), if any, by reference characters. For each independent claim involved in the appeal and for each dependent claim argued separately under the provisions of paragraph (c)(1)(vii) of this section, every means plus function and step plus function as permitted by 35 U.S.C. 112(f), must be identified and the structure, material, or acts described in the specification as corresponding to each claimed function must be set forth with reference to the specification by page and line number, and to the drawing, if any, by reference characters.

(vi) *Issues to be reviewed on appeal.* A concise statement of each issue presented for review. No new ground of rejection can be proposed by a third party requester appellant, unless such ground was withdrawn by the examiner during the prosecution of the proceeding, and the third party requester has not yet had an opportunity to propose it as a third party requester proposed ground of rejection.

(vii) *Argument.* The contentions of appellant with respect to each issue presented for review in paragraph (c)(1)(vi) of this section, and the basis therefor, with citations of the statutes, regulations, authorities, and parts of the record relied on. Any arguments or authorities not included in the brief permitted under this section or §§41.68 and 41.71 will be refused consideration by the Board, unless good cause is shown. Each issue must be treated under a separate heading. If the appellant is the patent owner, for each ground of rejection in the Right of Appeal Notice which appellant contests and which applies to two or more claims, the claims may be argued separately or as a group. When multiple claims subject to the same ground of rejection are argued as a group by appellant, the Board may select a single claim from the group of claims that are argued together to decide the appeal with respect to the group of claims as to the ground of rejection on the basis of the selected claim alone. Notwithstanding any other provision of this paragraph, the failure of appellant to separately argue claims which appellant has grouped together shall constitute a waiver of any argument that the Board must consider the patentability of any grouped claim separately. Any claim argued separately should be placed under a subheading identifying the claim by number. Claims argued as a group should be placed under a subheading identifying the claims by number. A statement which merely points out what a claim recites will not be considered an argument for separate patentability of the claim.

(viii) *Claims appendix.* An appendix containing a copy of the claims to be reviewed on appeal.

(ix) *Evidence appendix.* An appendix containing copies of any evidence submitted pursuant to §§1.130, 1.131, or 1.132 of this title or of any other evidence entered by the examiner and relied upon by appellant in the appeal, along with a statement setting forth where in the record that evidence was entered in the record by the examiner.

Reference to unentered evidence is not permitted in the brief. See § 41.63 for treatment of evidence submitted after appeal. This appendix may also include copies of the evidence relied upon by the examiner in any ground of rejection to be reviewed on appeal.

(x) *Related proceedings appendix.* An appendix containing copies of decisions rendered by a court or the Board in any proceeding identified pursuant to paragraph (c)(1)(ii) of this section.

(xi) *Certificate of service.* A certification that a copy of the brief has been served in its entirety on all other parties to the reexamination proceeding. The names and addresses of the parties served must be indicated.

(2) A brief shall not include any new or non-admitted amendment, or any new or non-admitted affidavit or other evidence. See § 1.116 of this title for amendments, affidavits or other evidence filed after final action but before or on the same date of filing an appeal and § 41.63 for amendments, affidavits or other evidence after the date of filing the appeal.

(d) If a brief is filed which does not comply with all the requirements of paragraph (a) and paragraph (c) of this section, appellant will be notified of the reasons for non-compliance and given a non-extendable time period within which to file an amended brief. If appellant does not file an amended brief within the set time period, or files an amended brief which does not overcome all the reasons for non-compliance stated in the notification, that appellant's appeal will stand dismissed.

[69 FR 50003, Aug. 12, 2004, as amended at 77 FR 46630, Aug. 6, 2012]

§ 41.68 Respondent's brief.

(a)(1) Respondent(s) in an appeal may once, within the time limit for filing set forth in § 41.66, file a respondent brief and serve the brief on all parties in accordance with § 1.903 of this title.

(2) The brief must be signed by the party, or the party's duly authorized attorney or agent, and must be accompanied by the requisite fee set forth in § 41.20(b)(2).

(3) The respondent brief shall be limited to issues raised in the appellant brief to which the respondent brief is directed.

(4) A requester's respondent brief may not address any brief of any other requester.

(b)(1) The respondent brief shall contain the following items under appropriate headings and in the order here indicated, and may include an appendix containing only those portions of the record on which reliance has been made.

(i) *Real Party in Interest.* A statement identifying by name the real party in interest.

(ii) *Related Appeals, Interferences, and trials.* A statement identifying by application, patent, appeal, interference, or trial number all other prior and pending appeals, interferences or judicial proceedings known to respondent, the respondent's legal representative, or assignee which may be related to, directly affect or be directly affected by or have a bearing on the Board's decision in the pending appeal. Copies of any decisions rendered by a court or the Board in any proceeding identified under this paragraph must be included in an appendix as required by paragraph (b)(1)(ix) of this section.

(iii) *Status of claims.* A statement accepting or disputing appellant's statement of the status of claims. If appellant's statement of the status of claims is disputed, the errors in appellant's statement must be specified with particularity.

(iv) *Status of amendments.* A statement accepting or disputing appellant's statement of the status of amendments. If appellant's statement of the status of amendments is disputed, the errors in appellant's statement must be specified with particularity.

(v) *Summary of claimed subject matter.* A statement accepting or disputing appellant's summary of the subject matter defined in each of the independent claims involved in the appeal. If appellant's summary of the subject matter is disputed, the errors in appellant's summary must be specified.

(vi) *Issues to be reviewed on appeal.* A statement accepting or disputing appellant's statement of the issues presented for review. If appellant's statement of the issues presented for review is disputed, the errors in appellant's statement must be specified. A counter statement of the issues for review may be made. No new ground of rejection can be proposed by a requester respondent.

(vii) *Argument.* A statement accepting or disputing the contentions of appellant with each of the issues presented by the appellant for review. If a contention of the appellant is disputed, the errors in appellant's argument must be specified, stating the basis therefor, with citations of the statutes, regulations, authorities, and parts of the record relied on. Each issue must be treated under a separate heading. An argument may be made with each of the issues stated in the counter statement of the issues, with each counter-stated issue being treated under a separate heading.

(viii) *Evidence appendix.* An appendix containing copies of any evidence submitted pursuant to §§1.130, 1.131, or 1.132 of this title or of any other evidence entered by the examiner and relied upon by respondent in the appeal, along with a statement setting forth where in the record that evidence was entered in the record by the examiner. Reference to unentered evidence is not permitted in the respondent's brief. See §41.63 for treatment of evidence submitted after appeal.

(ix) *Related proceedings appendix.* An appendix containing copies of decisions rendered by a court or the Board in any proceeding identified pursuant to paragraph (b)(1)(ii) of this section.

(x) *Certificate of service.* A certification that a copy of the respondent brief has been served in its entirety on all other parties to the reexamination proceeding. The names and addresses of the parties served must be indicated.

(2) A respondent brief shall not include any new or non-admitted amendment, or any new or non-admitted affidavit or other evidence. See §1.116 of this title for amendments, affidavits or other evidence filed after final action but before or on the same date of filing an appeal and §41.63 for amendments, affidavits or other evidence filed after the date of filing the appeal.

(c) If a respondent brief is filed which does not comply with all the requirements of paragraph (a) and paragraph (b) of this section, respondent will be notified of the reasons for non-compliance and given a non-extendable time period within which to file an amended brief. If respondent does not file an amended respondent brief within the set time period, or files an amended respondent brief which does not overcome all the reasons for non-compliance stated in the notification, the respondent brief and any amended respondent brief by that respondent will not be considered.

[69 FR 50003, Aug. 12, 2004, as amended at 77 FR 46631, Aug. 6, 2012]

§41.69 Examiner's answer.

(a) The primary examiner may, within such time as directed by the Director, furnish a written answer to the owner's and/or requester's appellant brief or respondent brief including, as may be necessary, such explanation of the invention claimed and of the references relied upon, the grounds of rejection, and the reasons for patentability, including grounds for not adopting any proposed rejection. A copy of the answer shall be supplied to the owner and all requesters. If the primary examiner determines that the appeal does not comply with the provisions of §§41.61, 41.66, 41.67 and 41.68 or does not relate to an appealable action, the primary examiner shall make such determination of record.

(b) An examiner's answer may not include a new ground of rejection.

(c) An examiner's answer may not include a new determination not to make a proposed rejection of a claim.

(d) Any new ground of rejection, or any new determination not to make a proposed rejection, must be made in an Office action reopening prosecution.

§41.71 Rebuttal brief.

(a) Within one month of the examiner's answer, any appellant may once file a rebuttal brief.

(b)(1) The rebuttal brief of the owner may be directed to the examiner's answer and/or any respondent brief.

(2) The rebuttal brief of the owner shall not include any new or non-admitted amendment, or an affidavit or other evidence. See §1.116 of this title for amendments, affidavits or other

evidence filed after final action but before or on the same date of filing an appeal and § 41.63 for amendments, affidavits or other evidence filed after the date of filing the appeal.

(c)(1) The rebuttal brief of any requester may be directed to the examiner's answer and/or the respondent brief of the owner.

(2) The rebuttal brief of a requester may not be directed to the respondent brief of any other requester.

(3) No new ground of rejection can be proposed by a requester.

(4) The rebuttal brief of a requester shall not include any new or non-admitted affidavit or other evidence. See § 1.116(d) of this title for affidavits or other evidence filed after final action but before or on the same date of filing an appeal and § 41.63(c) for affidavits or other evidence filed after the date of filing the appeal.

(d) The rebuttal brief must include a certification that a copy of the rebuttal brief has been served in its entirety on all other parties to the proceeding. The names and addresses of the parties served must be indicated.

(e) If a rebuttal brief is timely filed under paragraph (a) of this section but does not comply with all the requirements of paragraphs (a) through (d) of this section, appellant will be notified of the reasons for non-compliance and provided with a non-extendable period of one month within which to file an amended rebuttal brief. If the appellant does not file an amended rebuttal brief during the one-month period, or files an amended rebuttal brief which does not overcome all the reasons for non-compliance stated in the notification, that appellant's rebuttal brief and any amended rebuttal brief by that appellant will not be considered.

§ 41.73 Oral hearing.

(a) An oral hearing should be requested only in those circumstances in which an appellant or a respondent considers such a hearing necessary or desirable for a proper presentation of the appeal. An appeal decided on the briefs without an oral hearing will receive the same consideration by the Board as an appeal decided after an oral hearing.

(b) If an appellant or a respondent desires an oral hearing, he or she must file, as a separate paper captioned "REQUEST FOR ORAL HEARING," a written request for such hearing accompanied by the fee set forth in § 41.20(b)(3) within two months after the date of the examiner's answer. The time for requesting an oral hearing may not be extended. The request must include a certification that a copy of the request has been served in its entirety on all other parties to the proceeding. The names and addresses of the parties served must be indicated.

(c) If no request and fee for oral hearing have been timely filed by appellant or respondent as required by paragraph (b) of this section, the appeal will be assigned for consideration and decision on the briefs without an oral hearing.

(d) If appellant or respondent has complied with all the requirements of paragraph (b) of this section, a hearing date will be set, and notice given to the owner and all requesters. If an oral hearing is held, an oral argument may be presented by, or on behalf of, the primary examiner if considered desirable by either the primary examiner or the Board. The notice shall set a non-extendable period within which all requests for oral hearing shall be submitted by any other party to the appeal desiring to participate in the oral hearing. A hearing will be held as stated in the notice, and oral argument will be limited to thirty minutes for each appellant or respondent who has requested an oral hearing, and twenty minutes for the primary examiner unless otherwise ordered. No appellant or respondent will be permitted to participate in an oral hearing unless he or she has requested an oral hearing and submitted the fee set forth in § 41.20(b)(3).

(e)(1) At the oral hearing, each appellant and respondent may only rely on evidence that has been previously entered and considered by the primary examiner and present argument that has been relied upon in the briefs except as permitted by paragraph (e)(2) of this section. The primary examiner may only rely on argument and evidence relied upon in an answer except as permitted by paragraph (e)(2) of this section. The Board will determine the order of the arguments presented at the oral hearing.

(2) Upon a showing of good cause, appellant, respondent and/or the primary examiner may rely on a new argument based upon a recent relevant decision of either the Board or a Federal Court.

(f) Notwithstanding the submission of a request for oral hearing complying with this rule, if the Board decides that a hearing is not necessary, the Board will so notify the owner and all requesters.

§41.77 Decisions and other actions by the Board.

(a) The Patent Trial and Appeal Board, in its decision, may affirm or reverse each decision of the examiner on all issues raised on each appealed claim, or remand the reexamination proceeding to the examiner for further consideration. The reversal of the examiner's determination not to make a rejection proposed by the third party requester constitutes a decision adverse to the patentability of the claims which are subject to that proposed rejection which will be set forth in the decision of the Patent Trial and Appeal Board as a new ground of rejection under paragraph (b) of this section. The affirmance of the rejection of a claim on any of the grounds specified constitutes a general affirmance of the decision of the examiner on that claim, except as to any ground specifically reversed.

(b) Should the Board reverse the examiner's determination not to make a rejection proposed by a requester, the Board shall set forth in the opinion in support of its decision a new ground of rejection; or should the Board have knowledge of any grounds not raised in the appeal for rejecting any pending claim, it may include in its opinion a statement to that effect with its reasons for so holding, which statement shall constitute a new ground of rejection of the claim. Any decision which includes a new ground of rejection pursuant to this paragraph shall not be considered final for judicial review. When the Board makes a new ground of rejection, the owner, within one month from the date of the decision, must exercise one of the following two options with respect to the new ground of rejection to avoid termination of the appeal proceeding as to the rejected claim:

(1) *Reopen prosecution.* The owner may file a response requesting reopening of prosecution before the examiner. Such a response must be either an amendment of the claims so rejected or new evidence relating to the claims so rejected, or both.

(2) *Request rehearing.* The owner may request that the proceeding be reheard under §41.79 by the Board upon the same record. The request for rehearing must address any new ground of rejection and state with particularity the points believed to have been misapprehended or overlooked in entering the new ground of rejection and also state all other grounds upon which rehearing is sought.

(c) Where the owner has filed a response requesting reopening of prosecution under paragraph (b)(1) of this section, any requester, within one month of the date of service of the owner's response, may once file comments on the response. Such written comments must be limited to the issues raised by the Board's opinion reflecting its decision and the owner's response. Any requester that had not previously filed an appeal or cross appeal and is seeking under this subsection to file comments or a reply to the comments is subject to the appeal and brief fees under §41.20(b)(1) and (2), respectively, which must accompany the comments or reply.

(d) Following any response by the owner under paragraph (b)(1) of this section and any written comments from a requester under paragraph (c) of this section, the proceeding will be remanded to the examiner. The statement of the Board shall be binding upon the examiner unless an amendment or new evidence not previously of record is made which, in the opinion of the examiner, overcomes the new ground of rejection stated in the decision. The examiner will consider any owner response under paragraph (b)(1) of this section and any written comments by a requester under paragraph (c) of this section and issue a determination that the rejection is maintained or has been overcome.

(e) Within one month of the examiner's determination pursuant to paragraph (d) of this section, the owner or any requester may once submit comments in response to the examiner's determination. Within one month of the date of service of comments in response to the examiner's determination, the owner and any requesters may file a reply to the comments. No requester reply may address the comments of any other requester reply. Any requester that had not previously filed an appeal or cross appeal and is seeking under this subsection to file comments or a reply to the comments is subject to the appeal and brief fees under § 41.20(b)(1) and (2), respectively, which must accompany the comments or reply.

(f) After submission of any comments and any reply pursuant to paragraph (e) of this section, or after time has expired, the proceeding will be returned to the Board which shall reconsider the matter and issue a new decision. The new decision is deemed to incorporate the earlier decision, except for those portions specifically withdrawn.

(g) The time period set forth in paragraph (b) of this section is subject to the extension of time provisions of § 1.956 of this title when the owner is responding under paragraph (b)(1) of this section. The time period set forth in paragraph (b) of this section may not be extended when the owner is responding under paragraph (b)(2) of this section. The time periods set forth in paragraphs (c) and (e) of this section may not be extended.

[69 FR 50003, Aug. 12, 2004, as amended at 77 FR 46631, Aug. 6, 2012]

§ 41.79 Rehearing.

(a) Parties to the appeal may file a request for rehearing of the decision within one month of the date of:

(1) The original decision of the Board under § 41.77(a),

(2) The original § 41.77(b) decision under the provisions of § 41.77(b)(2),

(3) The expiration of the time for the owner to take action under § 41.77(b)(2), or

(4) The new decision of the Board under § 41.77(f).

(b)(1) The request for rehearing must state with particularity the points believed to have been misapprehended or overlooked in rendering the Board's opinion reflecting its decision. Arguments not raised in the briefs before the Board and evidence not previously relied upon in the briefs are not permitted in the request for rehearing except as permitted by paragraphs (b)(2) and (b)(3) of this section.

(2) Upon a showing of good cause, appellant and/or respondent may present a new argument based upon a recent relevant decision of either the Board or a Federal Court.

(3) New arguments responding to a new ground of rejection made pursuant to § 41.77(b) are permitted.

(c) Within one month of the date of service of any request for rehearing under paragraph (a) of this section, or any further request for rehearing under paragraph (d) of this section, the owner and all requesters may once file comments in opposition to the request for rehearing or the further request for rehearing. The comments in opposition must be limited to the issues raised in the request for rehearing or the further request for rehearing.

(d) If a party to an appeal files a request for rehearing under paragraph (a) of this section, or a further request for rehearing under this section, the Board shall render a decision on the request for rehearing. The decision on the request for rehearing is deemed to incorporate the earlier opinion reflecting its decision for appeal, except for those portions specifically withdrawn on rehearing and is final for the purpose of judicial review, except when noted otherwise in the decision on rehearing. If the Board opinion reflecting its decision on rehearing becomes, in effect, a new decision, and the Board so indicates, then any party to the appeal may, within one month of the new decision, file a further request for rehearing of the new decision under this subsection. Such further request for rehearing must comply with paragraph (b) of this section.

(e) The times for requesting rehearing under paragraph (a) of this section, for requesting further rehearing under paragraph (c) of this section, and for submitting comments under paragraph (b) of this section may not be extended.

§41.81 Action following decision.

The parties to an appeal to the Board may not appeal to the U.S. Court of Appeals for the Federal Circuit under §1.983 of this title until all parties' rights to request rehearing have been exhausted, at which time the decision of the Board is final and appealable by any party to the appeal to the Board.

Subpart D—Contested Cases

§41.100 Definitions.

In addition to the definitions in §41.2, the following definitions apply to proceedings under this subpart:

Business day means a day other than a Saturday, Sunday, or Federal holiday within the District of Columbia.

Involved means the Board has declared the patent application, patent, or claim so described to be a subject of the contested case.

§41.101 Notice of proceeding.

(a) Notice of a contested case will be sent to every party to the proceeding. The entry of the notice initiates the proceeding.

(b) When the Board is unable to provide actual notice of a contested case on a party through the correspondence address of record for the party, the Board may authorize other modes of notice, including:

(1) Sending notice to another address associated with the party, or

(2) Publishing the notice in the *Official Gazette of the United States Patent and Trademark Office.*

§41.102 Completion of examination.

Before a contested case is initiated, except as the Board may otherwise authorize, for each involved application and patent:

(a) Examination or reexamination must be completed, and

(b) There must be at least one claim that:

(1) Is patentable but for a judgment in the contested case, and

(2) Would be involved in the contested case.

§41.103 Jurisdiction over involved files.

The Board acquires jurisdiction over any involved file when the Board initiates a contested case. Other proceedings for the involved file within the Office are suspended except as the Board may order.

§41.104 Conduct of contested case.

(a) The Board may determine a proper course of conduct in a proceeding for any situation not specifically covered by this part and may enter non-final orders to administer the proceeding.

(b) An administrative patent judge may waive or suspend in a proceeding the application of any rule in this subpart, subject to such conditions as the administrative patent judge may impose.

(c) Times set in this subpart are defaults. In the event of a conflict between a time set by rule and a time set by order, the time set by order is controlling. Action due on a day other than a business day may be completed on the next business day unless the Board expressly states otherwise.

§41.106 Filing and service.

(a) *General format requirements.* (1) The paper used for filings must be durable and white. A party must choose to file on either A4-sized paper or 8½ inch × 11 inch paper except in the case of exhibits that require a larger size in order to preserve details of the original. A party may not switch between paper sizes in a single proceeding. Only one side of the paper may be used.

(2) In papers, including affidavits, created for the proceeding:

(i) Markings must be in black ink or must otherwise provide an equivalently permanent, dark, high-contrast image on the paper. The quality of printing must be equivalent to the quality produced by a laser printer. Either a proportional or monospaced font may be used, but the proportional font must be 12-point or larger and a monospaced font must not contain more than 4 characters per centimeter (10 characters per inch). Case names must be underlined or italicized.

(ii) Double spacing must be used except in headings, tables of contents, tables of authorities, indices, signature blocks, and certificates of service. Block quotations may be single-spaced and must be indented. Margins must be at least 2.5 centimeters (1 inch) on all sides.

(b) *Papers other than exhibits*—(1) *Cover sheet.* (i) The cover sheet must include the caption the Board specifies for the proceeding, a header indicating the party and contact information for the party, and a title indicating the sequence and subject of the paper. For example, "JONES MOTION 2, For benefit of an earlier application".

(ii) If the Board specifies a color other than white for the cover sheet, the cover sheet must be that color.

(2) Papers must have two 0.5 cm (¼ inch) holes with centers 1 cm (½ inch) from the top of the page and 7 cm (2 ¾ inch) apart, centered horizontally on the page.

(3) *Incorporation by reference; combined papers.* Arguments must not be incorporated by reference from one paper into another paper. Combined motions, oppositions, replies, or other combined papers are not permitted.

(4) *Exhibits.* Additional requirements for exhibits appear in § 41.154(c).

(c) *Working copy.* Every paper filed must be accompanied by a working copy marked "APJ Copy".

(d) *Specific filing forms*—(1) *Filing by mail.* A paper filed using the EXPRESS MAIL® service of the United States Postal Service will be deemed to be filed as of "date-in" on the EXPRESS MAIL® mailing label; otherwise, mail will be deemed to be filed as of the stamped date of receipt at the Board.

(2) *Other modes of filing.* The Board may authorize other modes of filing, including electronic filing and hand filing, and may set conditions for the use of such other modes.

(e) *Service.* (1) Papers filed with the Board, if not previously served, must be served simultaneously on every opposing party except as the Board expressly directs.

(2) If a party is represented by counsel, service must be on counsel.

(3) Service must be by EXPRESS MAIL® or by means at least as fast and reliable as EXPRESS MAIL®. Electronic service is not permitted without Board authorization.

(4) The date of service does not count in computing the time for responding.

(f) *Certificate of service.* (1) Papers other than exhibits must include a certificate of service as a separate page at the end of each paper that must be served on an opposing party.

(2) Exhibits must be accompanied by a certificate of service, but a single certificate may accompany any group of exhibits submitted together.

(3) A certificate of service must state:

(i) The date and manner of service,

(ii) The name and address of every person served, and

(iii) For exhibits filed as a group, the name and number of each exhibit served.

(4) A certificate made by a person other than a registered patent practitioner must be in the form of an affidavit.

§ 41.108 Lead counsel.

(a) A party may be represented by counsel. The Board may require a party to appoint a lead counsel. If counsel is not of record in a party's involved application or patent, then a power of attorney for that counsel for the party's involved application or patent must be filed with the notice required in paragraph (b) of this section.

(b) Within 14 days of the initiation of each contested case, each party must file a separate notice identifying its counsel, if any, and providing contact information for each counsel identified or, if the party has no counsel, then for the party. Contact information must, at a minimum, include:

(1) A mailing address;

(2) An address for courier delivery when the mailing address is not available for such delivery (for example, when the mailing address is a Post Office box);

(3) A telephone number;

(4) A facsimile number; and

(5) An electronic mail address.

(c) A party must promptly notify the Board of any change in the contact information required in paragraph (b) of this section.

§41.109 Access to and copies of Office records.

(a) *Request for access or copies.* Any request from a party for access to or copies of Office records directly related to a contested case must be filed with the Board. The request must precisely identify the records and in the case of copies include the appropriate fee set under §1.19(b) of this title.

(b) *Authorization of access and copies.* Access and copies will ordinarily only be authorized for the following records:

(1) The application file for an involved patent;

(2) An involved application; and

(3) An application for which a party has been accorded benefit under subpart E of this part.

(c) *Missing or incomplete copies.* If a party does not receive a complete copy of a record within 21 days of the authorization, the party must promptly notify the Board.

§41.110 Filing claim information.

(a) *Clean copy of claims.* Within 14 days of the initiation of the proceeding, each party must file a clean copy of its involved claims and, if a biotechnology material sequence is a limitation, a clean copy of the sequence.

(b) *Annotated copy of claims.* Within 28 days of the initiation of the proceeding, each party must:

(1) For each involved claim having a limitation that is illustrated in a drawing or biotechnology material sequence, file an annotated copy of the claim indicating in bold face between braces ({}) where each limitation is shown in the drawing or sequence.

(2) For each involved claim that contains a means-plus-function or step-plus-function limitation in the form permitted under 35 U.S.C. 112(f), file an annotated copy of the claim indicating in bold face between braces ({ }) the specific portions of the specification that describe the structure, material, or acts corresponding to each claimed function.

(c) Any motion to add or amend a claim must include:

(1) A clean copy of the claim,

(2) A claim chart showing where the disclosure of the patent or application provides written description of the subject matter of the claim, and

(3) Where applicable, a copy of the claims annotated according to paragraph (b) of this section.

[69 FR 50003, Aug. 12, 2004, as amended at 77 FR 46631, Aug. 6, 2012]

§41.120 Notice of basis for relief.

(a) The Board may require a party to provide a notice stating the relief it requests and the basis for its entitlement to relief. The Board may provide for the notice to be maintained in confidence for a limited time.

(b) *Effect.* If a notice under paragraph (a) of this section is required, a party will be limited to filing substantive motions consistent with the notice. Ambiguities in the notice will be construed against the party. A notice is not evidence except as an admission by a party-opponent.

(c) *Correction.* A party may move to correct its notice. The motion should be filed promptly after the party becomes aware of the basis for the correction. A correction filed after the time set for filing notices will only be entered if entry would serve the interests of justice.

§41.121 Motions.

(a) *Types of motions*—(1) *Substantive motions.* Consistent with the notice of requested relief, if any, and to the extent the Board authorizes, a party may file a motion:

(i) To redefine the scope of the contested case,

(ii) To change benefit accorded for the contested subject matter, or

(iii) For judgment in the contested case.

(2) *Responsive motions.* The Board may authorize a party to file a motion to amend or add a claim, to change inventorship, or otherwise to cure a defect raised in a notice of requested relief or in a substantive motion.

(3) *Miscellaneous motions.* Any request for relief other than a substantive or responsive motion must be filed as a miscellaneous motion.

(b) *Burden of proof.* The party filing the motion has the burden of proof to establish that it is entitled to the requested relief.

(c) *Content of motions; oppositions and replies.* (1) Each motion must be filed as a separate paper and must include:

(i) A statement of the precise relief requested,

(ii) A statement of material facts (see paragraph (d) of this section), and

(iii) A full statement of the reasons for the relief requested, including a detailed explanation of the significance of the evidence and the governing law, rules, and precedent.

(2) *Compliance with rules.* Where a rule in part 1 of this title ordinarily governs the relief sought, the motion must make any showings required under that rule in addition to any showings required in this part.

(3) The Board may order additional showings or explanations as a condition for filing a motion.

(d) *Statement of material facts.* (1) Each material fact shall be set forth as a separate numbered sentence with specific citations to the portions of the record that support the fact.

(2) The Board may require that the statement of material facts be submitted as a separate paper.

(e) *Claim charts.* Claim charts must be used in support of any paper requiring the comparison of a claim to something else, such as another claim, prior art, or a specification. Claim charts must accompany the paper as an appendix. Claim charts are not a substitute for appropriate argument and explanation in the paper.

(f) The Board may order briefing on any issue that could be raised by motion.

§ 41.122 Oppositions and replies.

(a) Oppositions and replies must comply with the content requirements for motions and must include a statement identifying material facts in dispute. Any material fact not specifically denied shall be considered admitted.

(b) All arguments for the relief requested in a motion must be made in the motion. A reply may only respond to arguments raised in the corresponding opposition.

§ 41.123 Default filing times.

(a) A *motion*, other than a miscellaneous motion, may only be filed according to a schedule the Board sets. The default times for acting are:

(1) An *opposition* is due 30 days after service of the motion.

(2) A *reply* is due 30 days after service of the opposition.

(3) A *responsive motion* is due 30 days after the service of the motion.

(b) *Miscellaneous motions.* (1) If no time for filing a specific miscellaneous motion is provided in this part or in a Board order:

(i) The opposing party must be consulted prior to filing the miscellaneous motion, and

(ii) If an opposing party plans to oppose the miscellaneous motion, the movant may not file the motion without Board authorization. Such authorization should ordinarily be obtained through a telephone conference including the Board and every other party to the proceeding. Delay in seeking relief may justify a denial of the motion.

(2) An opposition may not be filed without authorization. The default times for acting are:

(i) An *opposition* to a miscellaneous motion is due five business days after service of the motion.

(ii) A *reply* to a miscellaneous motion opposition is due three business days after service of the opposition.

(c) *Exhibits.* Each exhibit must be filed and served with the first paper in which it is cited except as the Board may otherwise order.

§ 41.124 Oral argument.

(a) *Request for oral argument.* A party may request an oral argument on an issue raised in a paper within five business days of the filing of the paper. The request must be filed as a separate paper and must specify the issues to be considered.

(b) *Copies for panel.* If an oral argument is set for a panel, the movant on any issue to be argued must provide three working copies of the motion, the opposition, and the reply. Each party is responsible for providing three working copies of its exhibits relating to the motion.

(c) *Length of argument.* If a request for oral argument is granted, each party will have a total of 20 minutes to present its arguments, including any time for rebuttal.

(d) *Demonstrative exhibits* must be served at least five business days before the oral argument and filed no later than the time of the oral argument.

(e) *Transcription.* The Board encourages the use of a transcription service at oral arguments but, if such a service is to be used, the Board must be notified in advance to ensure adequate facilities are available and a transcript must be filed with the Board promptly after the oral argument.

§41.125 Decision on motions.

(a) *Order of consideration.* The Board may take up motions for decisions in any order, may grant, deny, or dismiss any motion, and may take such other action appropriate to secure the just, speedy, and inexpensive determination of the proceeding. A decision on a motion may include deferral of action on an issue until a later point in the proceeding.

(b) *Interlocutory decisions.* A decision on motions without a judgment is not final for the purposes of judicial review. A panel decision on an issue will govern further proceedings in the contested case.

(c) *Rehearing*—(1) *Time for request.* A request for rehearing of a decision on a motion must be filed within fourteen days of the decision.

(2) *No tolling.* The filing of a request for rehearing does not toll times for taking action.

(3) *Burden on rehearing.* The burden of showing a decision should be modified lies with the party attacking the decision. The request must specifically identify:

(i) All matters the party believes to have been misapprehended or overlooked, and

(ii) The place where the matter was previously addressed in a motion, opposition, or reply.

(4) *Opposition; reply.* Neither an opposition nor a reply to a request for rehearing may be filed without Board authorization.

(5) *Panel rehearing.* If a decision is not a panel decision, the party requesting rehearing may request that a panel rehear the decision. A panel rehearing a procedural decision will review the decision for an abuse of discretion.

§41.126 Arbitration.

(a) Parties to a contested case may resort to binding arbitration to determine any issue in a contested case. The Office is not a party to the arbitration. The Board is not bound and may independently determine questions of patentability, jurisdiction, and Office practice.

(b) The Board will not authorize arbitration unless:

(1) It is to be conducted according to Title 9 of the United States Code.

(2) The parties notify the Board in writing of their intention to arbitrate.

(3) The agreement to arbitrate:

(i) Is in writing,

(ii) Specifies the issues to be arbitrated,

(iii) Names the arbitrator, or provides a date not more than 30 days after the execution of the agreement for the selection of the arbitrator, and

(iv) Provides that the arbitrator's award shall be binding on the parties and that judgment thereon can be entered by the Board.

(4) A copy of the agreement is filed within 20 days after its execution.

(5) The arbitration is completed within the time the Board sets.

(c) The parties are solely responsible for the selection of the arbitrator and the conduct of proceedings before the arbitrator.

(d) Issues not disposed of by the arbitration will be resolved in accordance with the procedures established in this subpart.

(e) The Board will not consider the arbitration award unless it:

(1) Is binding on the parties,

(2) Is in writing,

(3) States in a clear and definite manner each issue arbitrated and the disposition of each issue, and

(4) Is filed within 20 days of the date of the award.

(f) Once the award is filed, the parties to the award may not take actions inconsistent with the award. If the award is dispositive of the contested subject matter for a party, the Board may enter judgment as to that party.

§41.127 Judgment.

(a) *Effect within Office*—(1) *Estoppel.* A judgment disposes of all issues that were, or by motion could have properly been, raised and decided. A losing party who could have properly moved for relief on an issue, but did not so move, may not take action in the Office after the judgment that is inconsistent with that party's failure to move, except that a losing party shall not be estopped with respect to any contested subject matter for which that party was awarded a favorable judgment.

(2) *Final disposal of claim.* Adverse judgment against a claim is a final action of the Office requiring no further action by the Office to dispose of the claim permanently.

(b) *Request for adverse judgment.* A party may at any time in the proceeding request judgment against itself. Actions construed to be a request for adverse judgment include:

(1) Abandonment of an involved application such that the party no longer has an application or patent involved in the proceeding,

(2) Cancellation or disclaiming of a claim such that the party no longer has a claim involved in the proceeding,

(3) Concession of priority or unpatentability of the contested subject matter, and

(4) Abandonment of the contest.

(c) *Recommendation.* The judgment may include a recommendation for further action by the examiner or by the Director. If the Board recommends rejection of a claim of an involved application, the examiner must enter and maintain the recommended rejection unless an amendment or showing of facts not previously of record is filed which, in the opinion of the examiner, overcomes the recommended rejection.

(d) *Rehearing.* A party dissatisfied with the judgment may file a request for rehearing within 30 days of the entry of the judgment. The request must specifically identify all matters the party believes to have been misapprehended or overlooked, and the place where the matter was previously addressed in a motion, opposition, or reply.

[69 FR 50003, Aug. 12, 2004, as amended at 69 FR 58260, Sept. 30, 2004]

§41.128 Sanctions.

(a) The Board may impose a sanction against a party for misconduct, including:

(1) Failure to comply with an applicable rule or order in the proceeding;

(2) Advancing a misleading or frivolous request for relief or argument; or

(3) Engaging in dilatory tactics.

(b) Sanctions include entry of:

(1) An order holding certain facts to have been established in the proceeding;

(2) An order expunging, or precluding a party from filing, a paper;

(3) An order precluding a party from presenting or contesting a particular issue;

(4) An order precluding a party from requesting, obtaining, or opposing discovery;

(5) An order excluding evidence;

(6) An order awarding compensatory expenses, including attorney fees;

(7) An order requiring terminal disclaimer of patent term; or

(8) Judgment in the contested case.

§41.150 Discovery.

(a) *Limited discovery.* A party is not entitled to discovery except as authorized in this subpart. The parties may agree to discovery among themselves at any time.

(b) *Automatic discovery.* (1) Within 21 days of a request by an opposing party, a party must:

(i) Serve a legible copy of every requested patent, patent application, literature reference, and test standard mentioned in the specification of the party's involved patent or application, or application upon which the party will rely for benefit, and, if the requested material is in a language other than English, a translation, if available, and

(ii) File with the Board a notice (without copies of the requested materials) of service of the requested materials.

(2) Unless previously served, or the Board orders otherwise, any exhibit cited in a motion or in testimony must be served with the citing motion or testimony.

(c) *Additional discovery.* (1) A party may request additional discovery. The requesting party must show that such additional discovery is in the interests of justice. The Board may specify conditions for such additional discovery.

(2) When appropriate, a party may obtain production of documents and things during cross examination of an opponent's witness or during testimony authorized under §41.156.

§41.151 Admissibility.

Evidence that is not taken, sought, or filed in accordance with this subpart shall not be admissible.

§41.152 Applicability of the Federal Rules of Evidence.

(a) *Generally.* Except as otherwise provided in this subpart, the Federal Rules of Evidence shall apply to contested cases.

(b) *Exclusions.* Those portions of the Federal Rules of Evidence relating to criminal proceedings, juries, and other matters not relevant to proceedings under this subpart shall not apply.

(c) *Modifications in terminology.* Unless otherwise clear from context, the following terms of the Federal Rules of Evidence shall be construed as indicated:

Appellate court means United States Court of Appeals for the Federal Circuit or a United States district court when judicial review is under 35 U.S.C. 146.

Civil action, civil proceeding, action, and *trial* mean contested case.

Courts of the United States, U.S. Magistrate, court, trial court, and *trier of fact* mean Board.

Hearing means:

(i) In Federal Rule of Evidence 703, the time when the expert testifies.

(ii) In Federal Rule of Evidence 804(a)(5), the time for taking testimony.

Judge means the Board.

Judicial notice means official notice.

Trial or hearing means, in Federal Rule of Evidence 807, the time for taking testimony.

(d) The Board, in determining foreign law, may consider any relevant material or source, including testimony, whether or not submitted by a party or admissible under the Federal Rules of Evidence.

§41.153 Records of the Office.

Certification is not necessary as a condition to admissibility when the evidence to be submitted is a record of the Office to which all parties have access.

§41.154 Form of evidence.

(a) Evidence consists of affidavits, transcripts of depositions, documents, and things. All evidence must be submitted in the form of an exhibit.

(b) *Translation required.* When a party relies on a document or is required to produce a document in a language other than English, a translation of the document into English and an affidavit attesting to the accuracy of the translation must be filed with the document.

(c) An exhibit must conform with the requirements for papers in §41.106 of this subpart and the requirements of this paragraph.

(1) Each exhibit must have an exhibit label with a unique number in a range assigned by the Board, the names of the parties, and the proceeding number in the following format:

JONES EXHIBIT 2001

Jones v. Smith

Contested Case 104,999

(2) When the exhibit is a paper:

(i) Each page must be uniquely numbered in sequence, and

(ii) The exhibit label must be affixed to the lower right corner of the first page of the exhibit without obscuring information on the first page or, if obscuring is unavoidable, affixed to a duplicate first page.

(d) *Exhibit list.* Each party must maintain an exhibit list with the exhibit number and a brief description of each exhibit. If the exhibit is not filed, the exhibit list should note that fact. The Board may require the filing of a current exhibit list prior to acting on a motion.

[69 FR 50003, Aug. 12, 2004, as amended at 69 FR 58260, Sept. 30, 2004]

§41.155 Objection; motion to exclude; motion in limine.

(a) *Deposition.* Objections to deposition evidence must be made during the deposition. Evidence to cure the objection must be provided during the deposition unless the parties to the deposition stipulate otherwise on the deposition record.

(b) *Other than deposition.* For evidence other than deposition evidence:

(1) *Objection.* Any objection must be served within five business days of service of evidence, other than deposition evidence, to which the objection is directed.

(2) *Supplemental evidence.* The party relying on evidence for which an objection is timely served may respond to the objection by serving supplemental evidence within ten business days of service of the objection.

(c) *Motion to exclude.* A miscellaneous motion to exclude evidence must be filed to preserve any objection. The motion must identify the objections in the record in order and must explain the objections.

(d) *Motion in limine.* A party may file a miscellaneous motion in limine for a ruling on the admissibility of evidence.

[69 FR 50003, Aug. 12, 2004, as amended at 69 FR 58260, Sept. 30, 2004]

§ 41.156 Compelling testimony and production.

(a) *Authorization required.* A party seeking to compel testimony or production of documents or things must file a miscellaneous motion for authorization. The miscellaneous motion must describe the general relevance of the testimony, document, or thing and must:

(1) In the case of testimony, identify the witness by name or title, and

(2) In the case of a document or thing, the general nature of the document or thing.

(b) *Outside the United States.* For testimony or production sought outside the United States, the motion must also:

(1) *In the case of testimony.* (i) Identify the foreign country and explain why the party believes the witness can be compelled to testify in the foreign country, including a description of the procedures that will be used to compel the testimony in the foreign country and an estimate of the time it is expected to take to obtain the testimony; and

(ii) Demonstrate that the party has made reasonable efforts to secure the agreement of the witness to testify in the United States but has been unsuccessful in obtaining the agreement, even though the party has offered to pay the expenses of the witness to travel to and testify in the United States.

(2) *In the case of production of a document or thing.* (i) Identify the foreign country and explain why the party believes production of the document or thing can be compelled in the foreign country, including a description of the procedures that will be used to compel production of the document or thing in the foreign country and an estimate of the time it is expected to take to obtain production of the document or thing; and

(ii) Demonstrate that the party has made reasonable efforts to obtain the agreement of the individual or entity having possession, custody, or control of the document to produce the document or thing in the United States but has been unsuccessful in obtaining that agreement, even though the party has offered to pay the expenses of producing the document or thing in the United States.

§ 41.157 Taking testimony.

(a) *Form.* Direct testimony must be submitted in the form of an affidavit except when the testimony is compelled under 35 U.S.C. 24, in which case it may be in the form of a deposition transcript.

(b) *Time and location.* (1) *Uncompelled direct testimony* may be taken at any time; otherwise, testimony may only be taken during such time period as the Board may authorize.

(2) *Other testimony.* (i) Except as the Board otherwise orders, authorized testimony may be taken at any reasonable time and location within the United States before any disinterested official authorized to administer oaths at that location.

(ii) Testimony outside the United States may only be taken as the Board specifically directs.

(c) *Notice of deposition.* (1) Prior to the taking of testimony, all parties to the proceeding must agree on the time and place for taking testimony. If the parties cannot agree, the party seeking the testimony must initiate a conference with the Board to set a time and place.

(2) Cross-examination should ordinarily take place after any supplemental evidence relating to the direct testimony has been filed and more than a week before the filing date for any paper in which the cross-examination testimony is expected to be used. A party requesting cross-examination testimony of more than one witness may choose the order in which the witnesses are to be cross-examined.

(3) In the case of direct testimony, at least three business days prior to the conference in paragraph (c)(1) of this section, the party seeking the direct testimony must serve:

(i) A list and copy of each document under the party's control and on which the party intends to rely, and

(ii) A list of, and proffer of reasonable access to, any thing other than a document under the party's control and on which the party intends to rely.

(4) Notice of the deposition must be filed at least two business days before a deposition. The notice limits the scope of the testimony and must list:

(i) The time and place of the deposition,

(ii) The name and address of the witness,

(iii) A list of the exhibits to be relied upon during the deposition, and

(iv) A general description of the scope and nature of the testimony to be elicited.

(5) *Motion to quash.* Objection to a defect in the notice is waived unless a miscellaneous motion to quash is promptly filed.

(d) *Deposition in a foreign language.* If an interpreter will be used during the deposition, the party calling the witness must initiate a conference with the Board at least five business days before the deposition.

(e) *Manner of taking testimony.* (1) Each witness before giving a deposition shall be duly sworn according to law by the officer before whom the deposition is to be taken. The officer must be authorized to take testimony under 35 U.S.C. 23.

(2) The testimony shall be taken in answer to interrogatories with any questions and answers recorded in their regular order by the officer, or by some other disinterested person in the presence of the officer, unless the presence of the officer is waived on the record by agreement of all parties.

(3) Any exhibits relied upon must be numbered according to the numbering scheme assigned for the contested case and must, if not previously served, be served at the deposition.

(4) All objections made at the time of the deposition to the qualifications of the officer taking the deposition, the manner of taking it, the evidence presented, the conduct of any party, and any other objection to the proceeding shall be noted on the record by the officer. Evidence objected to shall be taken subject to a ruling on the objection.

(5) When the testimony has been transcribed, the witness shall read and sign (in the form of an affidavit) a transcript of the deposition unless:

(i) The parties otherwise agree in writing, (ii) The parties waive reading and signature by the witness on the record at the deposition, or

(iii) The witness refuses to read or sign the transcript of the deposition.

(6) The officer shall prepare a certified transcript by attaching to the transcript of the deposition a certificate in the form of an affidavit signed and sealed by the officer. Unless the parties waive any of the following requirements, in which case the certificate shall so state, the certificate must state:

(i) The witness was duly sworn by the officer before commencement of testimony by the witness;

(ii) The transcript is a true record of the testimony given by the witness;

(iii) The name of the person who recorded the testimony and, if the officer did not record it, whether the testimony was recorded in the presence of the officer;

(iv) The presence or absence of any opponent;

(v) The place where the deposition was taken and the day and hour when the deposition began and ended;

(vi) The officer has no disqualifying interest, personal or financial, in a party; and

(vii) If a witness refuses to read or sign the transcript, the circumstances under which the witness refused.

(7) The officer must promptly provide a copy of the transcript to all parties.

The proponent of the testimony must file the original as an exhibit.

(8) Any objection to the content, form, or manner of taking the deposition, including the qualifications of the officer, is waived unless made on the record during the deposition and preserved in a timely filed miscellaneous motion to exclude.

(f) *Costs.* Except as the Board may order or the parties may agree in writing, the proponent of the testimony shall bear all costs associated with the testimony, including the reasonable costs associated with making the witness available for the cross-examination.

§ 41.158 Expert testimony; tests and data.

(a) Expert testimony that does not disclose the underlying facts or data on which the opinion is based is entitled to little or no weight. Testimony on United States patent law will not be admitted.

(b) If a party relies on a technical test or data from such a test, the party must provide an affidavit explaining:

(1) Why the test or data is being used,

(2) How the test was performed and the data was generated,

(3) How the data is used to determine a value,

(4) How the test is regarded in the relevant art, and

(5) Any other information necessary for the Board to evaluate the test and data.

Subpart E—Patent Interferences

§ 41.200 Procedure; pendency.

(a) A patent interference is a contested case subject to the procedures set forth in subpart D of this part.

(b) [Reserved]

(c) Patent interferences shall be administered such that pendency before the Board is normally no more than two years.

[69 FR 50003, Aug. 12, 2004, as amended at 75 FR 19559, Apr. 15, 2010]

§ 41.201 Definitions.

In addition to the definitions in §§ 41.2 and 41.100, the following definitions apply to proceedings under this subpart:

Accord benefit means Board recognition that a patent application provides a proper constructive reduction to practice under 35 U.S.C. 102(g)(1).

Constructive reduction to practice means a described and enabled anticipation under 35 U.S.C. 102(g)(1) in a patent application of the subject matter of a count. *Earliest constructive reduction to practice* means the first constructive reduction to practice that has been continuously disclosed through a chain of patent applications including in the involved application or patent. For the chain to be continuous, each subsequent application must have been co-pending under 35 U.S.C. 120 or 121 or timely filed under 35 U.S.C. 119 or 365(a).

Count means the Board's description of the interfering subject matter that sets the scope of admissible proofs on priority. Where there is more than one count, each count must describe a patentably distinct invention.

Involved claim means, for the purposes of 35 U.S.C. 135(a), a claim that has been designated as corresponding to the count.

Senior party means the party entitled to the presumption under § 41.207(a)(1) that it is the prior inventor. Any other party is a *junior party*.

Threshold issue means an issue that, if resolved in favor of the movant, would deprive the opponent of standing in the interference. Threshold issues may include:

(1) No interference-in-fact, and

(2) In the case of an involved application claim first made after the publication of the movant's application or issuance of the movant's patent:

(i) Repose under 35 U.S.C. 135(b) in view of the movant's patent or published application, or

(ii) Unpatentability for lack of written description under 35 U.S.C. 112(a) of an involved application claim where the applicant suggested, or could have suggested, an interference under § 41.202(a).

[69 FR 50003, Aug. 12, 2004, as amended at 77 FR 46631, Aug. 6, 2012]

§41.202 Suggesting an interference.

(a) *Applicant.* An applicant, including a reissue applicant, may suggest an interference with another application or a patent. The suggestion must:

(1) Provide sufficient information to identify the application or patent with which the applicant seeks an interference,

(2) Identify all claims the applicant believes interfere, propose one or more counts, and show how the claims correspond to one or more counts,

(3) For each count, provide a claim chart comparing at least one claim of each party corresponding to the count and show why the claims interfere within the meaning of §41.203(a),

(4) Explain in detail why the applicant will prevail on priority,

(5) If a claim has been added or amended to provoke an interference, provide a claim chart showing the written description for each claim in the applicant's specification, and

(6) For each constructive reduction to practice for which the applicant wishes to be accorded benefit, provide a chart showing where the disclosure provides a constructive reduction to practice within the scope of the interfering subject matter.

(b) *Patentee.* A patentee cannot suggest an interference under this section but may, to the extent permitted under §1.291 of this title, alert the examiner of an application claiming interfering subject matter to the possibility of an interference.

(c) *Examiner.* An examiner may require an applicant to add a claim to provoke an interference. Failure to satisfy the requirement within a period (not less than one month) the examiner sets will operate as a concession of priority for the subject matter of the claim. If the interference would be with a patent, the applicant must also comply with paragraphs (a)(2) through (a)(6) of this section. The claim the examiner proposes to have added must, apart from the question of priority under 35 U.S.C. 102(g):

(1) Be patentable to the applicant, and

(2) Be drawn to patentable subject matter claimed by another applicant or patentee.

(d) *Requirement to show priority under 35 U.S.C. 102(g).* (1) When an applicant has an earliest constructive reduction to practice that is later than the apparent earliest constructive reduction to practice for a patent or published application claiming interfering subject matter, the applicant must show why it would prevail on priority.

(2) If an applicant fails to show priority under paragraph (d)(1) of this section, an administrative patent judge may nevertheless declare an interference to place the applicant under an order to show cause why judgment should not be entered against the applicant on priority. New evidence in support of priority will not be admitted except on a showing of good cause. The Board may authorize the filing of motions to redefine the interfering subject matter or to change the benefit accorded to the parties.

(e) *Sufficiency of showing.* (1) A showing of priority under this section is not sufficient unless it would, if unrebutted, support a determination of priority in favor of the party making the showing.

(2) When testimony or production necessary to show priority is not available without authorization under §41.150(c) or §41.156(a), the showing shall include:

(i) Any necessary interrogatory, request for admission, request for production, or deposition request, and

(ii) A detailed proffer of what the response to the interrogatory or request would be expected to be and an explanation of the relevance of the response to the question of priority.

[69 FR 50003, Aug. 12, 2004, as amended at 77 FR 42174, July 17, 2012]

§41.203 Declaration.

(a) *Interfering subject matter.* An interference exists if the subject matter of a claim of one party would, if prior art, have anticipated or rendered obvious the subject matter of a claim of the opposing party and vice versa.

(b) *Notice of declaration.* An administrative patent judge declares the patent interference on behalf of the Director. A notice declaring an interference identifies:

(1) The interfering subject matter;

(2) The involved applications, patents, and claims;

(3) The accorded benefit for each count; and

(4) The claims corresponding to each count.

(c) *Redeclaration.* An administrative patent judge may redeclare a patent interference on behalf of the Director to change the declaration made under paragraph (b) of this section.

(d) A party may suggest the addition of a patent or application to the interference or the declaration of an additional interference. The suggestion should make the showings required under § 41.202(a) of this part.

§ 41.204 Notice of basis for relief.

(a) *Priority statement.* (1) A party may not submit evidence of its priority in addition to its accorded benefit unless it files a statement setting forth all bases on which the party intends to establish its entitlement to judgment on priority.

(2) The priority statement must:

(i) State the date and location of the party's earliest corroborated conception,

(ii) State the date and location of the party's earliest corroborated actual reduction to practice,

(iii) State the earliest corroborated date on which the party's diligence began, and

(iv) Provide a copy of the earliest document upon which the party will rely to show conception.

(3) If a junior party fails to file a priority statement overcoming a senior party's accorded benefit, judgment shall be entered against the junior party absent a showing of good cause.

(b) *Other substantive motions.* The Board may require a party to list the motions it intends to file, including sufficient detail to place the Board and the opponent on notice of the precise relief sought.

(c) *Filing and service.* The Board will set the times for filing and serving statements required under this section.

§ 41.205 Settlement agreements.

(a) *Constructive notice; time for filing.* Pursuant to 35 U.S.C. 135(c), an agreement or understanding, including collateral agreements referred to therein, made in connection with or in contemplation of the termination of an interference must be filed prior to the termination of the interference between the parties to the agreement. After a final decision is entered by the Board, an interference is considered terminated when no appeal (35 U.S.C. 141) or other review (35 U.S.C. 146) has been or can be taken or had. If an appeal to the U.S. Court of Appeals for the Federal Circuit (under 35 U.S.C. 141) or a civil action (under 35 U.S.C. 146) has been filed the interference is considered terminated when the appeal or civil action is terminated. A civil action is terminated when the time to appeal the judgment expires. An appeal to the U.S. Court of Appeals for the Federal Circuit, whether from a decision of the Board or a judgment in a civil action, is terminated when the mandate is issued by the Court.

(b) *Untimely filing.* The Chief Administrative Patent Judge may permit the filing of an agreement under paragraph (a) of this section up to six months after termination upon petition and a showing of good cause for the failure to file prior to termination.

(c) *Request to keep separate.* Any party to an agreement under paragraph (a) of this section may request that the agreement be kept separate from the interference file. The request must be filed with or promptly after the agreement is filed.

(d) *Access to agreement.* Any person, other than a representative of a Government agency, may have access to an agreement kept separate under paragraph (c) of this section only upon petition and on a showing of good cause. The agreement will be available to Government agencies on written request.

§ 41.206 Common interests in the invention.

An administrative patent judge may decline to declare, or if already declared the Board may issue judgment in, an interference between an application and another application or patent that are commonly owned.

§ 41.207 Presumptions.

(a) *Priority*—(1) *Order of invention.* Parties are presumed to have invented interfering subject matter in the order of the dates of their accorded benefit for each count. If two parties are accorded the benefit of the same earliest date of constructive reduction to practice, then neither party is entitled to a presumption of priority with respect to the other such party.

(2) *Evidentiary standard.* Priority may be proved by a preponderance of the evidence except a party must prove priority by clear and convincing evidence if the date of its earliest constructive reduction to practice is after the issue date of an involved patent or the publication date under 35 U.S.C. 122(b) of an involved application or patent.

(b) *Claim correspondence.* (1) For the purposes of determining priority and derivation, all claims of a party corresponding to the count are presumed to stand or fall together. To challenge this presumption, a party must file a timely substantive motion to have a corresponding claim designated as not corresponding to the count. No presumption based on claim correspondence regarding the grouping of claims exists for other grounds of unpatentability.

(2) A claim corresponds to a count if the subject matter of the count, treated as prior art to the claim, would have anticipated or rendered obvious the subject matter of the claim.

(c) *Cross-applicability of prior art.* When a motion for judgment of unpatentability against an opponent's claim on the basis of prior art is granted, each of the movant's claims corresponding to the same count as the opponent's claim will be presumed to be unpatentable in view of the same prior art unless the movant in its motion rebuts this presumption.

§ 41.208 Content of substantive and responsive motions.

The general requirements for motions in contested cases are stated at § 41.121(c).

(a) In an interference, substantive motions must:

(1) Raise a threshold issue,

(2) Seek to change the scope of the definition of the interfering subject matter or the correspondence of claims to the count,

(3) Seek to change the benefit accorded for the count, or

(4) Seek judgment on derivation or on priority.

(b) To be sufficient, a motion must provide a showing, supported with appropriate evidence, such that, if unrebutted, it would justify the relief sought. The burden of proof is on the movant.

(c) *Showing patentability.* (1) A party moving to add or amend a claim must show the claim is patentable.

(2) A party moving to add or amend a count must show the count is patentable over prior art.

PART 42—TRIAL PRACTICE BEFORE THE PATENT TRIAL AND APPEAL BOARD

Subpart A—Trial Practice and Procedure

GENERAL

FEES

PETITION AND MOTION PRACTICE

TESTIMONY AND PRODUCTION

AUTHORITY: 35 U.S.C. 2(b)(2), 6, 21, 23, 41,135, 311, 312, 316, 321–326 and Public Law 112–29.

SOURCE: 77 FR 48669, Aug. 14, 2012, unless otherwise noted.

Subpart A—Trial Practice and Procedure

GENERAL

§ 42.1 Policy.

(a) *Scope.* Part 42 governs proceedings before the Patent Trial and Appeal Board. Sections 1.4, 1.7, 1.14, 1.16, 1.22, 1.23, 1.25, 1.26, 1.32, 1.34, and 1.36 of this chapter also apply to proceedings before the Board, as do other sections of part 1 of this chapter that are incorporated by reference into this part.

(b) *Construction.* This part shall be construed to secure the just, speedy, and inexpensive resolution of every proceeding.

(c) *Decorum.* Every party must act with courtesy and decorum in all proceedings before the Board, including in interactions with other parties.

(d) *Evidentiary standard.* The default evidentiary standard is a preponderance of the evidence.

§ 42.2 Definitions.

The following definitions apply to this part:

Affidavit means affidavit or declaration under § 1.68 of this chapter. A transcript of an *ex parte* deposition or a declaration under 28 U.S.C. 1746 may be used as an affidavit.

Board means the Patent Trial and Appeal Board. Board means a panel of the Board, or a member or employee acting with the authority of the Board, including:

(1) For petition decisions and interlocutory decisions, a Board member or employee acting with the authority of the Board.

(2) For final written decisions under 35 U.S.C. 135(d), 318(a), and 328(a), a panel of the Board.

Business day means a day other than a Saturday, Sunday, or Federal holiday within the District of Columbia.

Confidential information means trade secret or other confidential research, development, or commercial information.

Final means final for the purpose of judicial review to the extent available. A decision is final only if it disposes of all necessary issues with regard to the party seeking judicial review, and does not indicate that further action is required.

Hearing means consideration of the trial.

Involved means an application, patent, or claim that is the subject of the proceeding.

Judgment means a final written decision by the Board, or a termination of a proceeding.

Motion means a request for relief other than by petition.

Office means the United States Patent and Trademark Office.

Panel means at least three members of the Board.

Party means at least the petitioner and the patent owner and, in a derivation proceeding, any applicant or assignee of the involved application.

Petition is a request that a trial be instituted.

Petitioner means the party filing a petition requesting that a trial be instituted.

Preliminary Proceeding begins with the filing of a petition for instituting a trial and ends with a written decision as to whether a trial will be instituted.

Proceeding means a trial or preliminary proceeding.

Rehearing means reconsideration.

Trial means a contested case instituted by the Board based upon a petition. A trial begins with a written decision notifying the petitioner and patent owner of the institution of the trial. The term trial specifically includes a derivation proceeding under 35 U.S.C. 135; an *inter partes* review under Chapter 31 of title 35, United States Code; a post-grant review under Chapter 32 of title 35, United States Code; and a transitional business-method review under section 18 of the Leahy-Smith America Invents Act. Patent interferences are administered under part 41 and not under part 42 of this title, and therefore are not trials.

§ 42.3 Jurisdiction.

(a) The Board may exercise exclusive jurisdiction within the Office over every involved application and patent during the proceeding, as the Board may order.

(b) A petition to institute a trial must be filed with the Board consistent with any time period required by statute.

§ 42.4 Notice of trial.

(a) *Institution of trial.* The Board institutes the trial on behalf of the Director.

(b) Notice of a trial will be sent to every party to the proceeding. The entry of the notice institutes the trial.

(c) The Board may authorize additional modes of notice, including:

(1) Sending notice to another address associated with the party, or

(2) Publishing the notice in the Official Gazette of the United States Patent and Trademark Office or the FEDERAL REGISTER.

§ 42.5 Conduct of the proceeding.

(a) The Board may determine a proper course of conduct in a proceeding for any situation not specifically covered by this part and may enter non-final orders to administer the proceeding.

(b) The Board may waive or suspend a requirement of parts 1, 41, and 42 and may place conditions on the waiver or suspension.

(c) *Times.* (1) *Setting times.* The Board may set times by order. Times set by rule are default and may be modified by order. Any modification of times will take any applicable statutory pendency goal into account.

(2) *Extension of time.* A request for an extension of time must be supported by a showing of good cause.

(3) *Late action.* A late action will be excused on a showing of good cause or upon a Board decision that consideration on the merits would be in the interests of justice.

(d) *Ex parte communications.* Communication regarding a specific proceeding with a Board member defined in 35 U.S.C. 6(a) is not permitted unless both parties have an opportunity to be involved in the communication.

§ 42.6 Filing of documents, including exhibits; service.

(a) *General format requirements.* (1) Page size must be 8½ inch × 11 inch except in the case of exhibits that require a larger size in order to preserve details of the original.

(2) In documents, including affidavits, created for the proceeding:

(i) Markings must be in black or must otherwise provide an equivalent dark, high-contrast image;

(ii) Either a proportional or monospaced font may be used:

(A) The proportional font must be 14-point or larger, and

(B) The monospaced font must not contain more than four characters per centimeter (ten characters per inch);

(iii) Double spacing must be used except in claim charts, headings, tables of contents, tables of authorities, indices, signature blocks, and certificates of service. Block quotations may be 1.5 spaced, but must be indented from both the left and the right margins; and

(iv) Margins must be at least 2.5 centimeters (1 inch) on all sides.

(3) *Incorporation by reference; combined documents.* Arguments must not be incorporated by reference from one document into another document. Combined motions, oppositions, replies, or other combined documents are not permitted.

(4) *Signature; identification.* Documents must be signed in accordance with §§ 1.33 and 11.18(a) of this title, and should be identified by the trial number (where known).

(b) *Modes of filing.* (1) *Electronic filing.* Unless otherwise authorized, submissions are to be made to the Board electronically via the Internet according to the parameters established by the Board and published on the Web site of the Office.

(2)(i) *Filing by means other than electronic filing.* A document filed by means other than electronic filing must:

(A) Be accompanied by a motion requesting acceptance of the submission; and

(B) Identify a date of transmission where a party seeks a filing date other than the date of receipt at the Board.

(ii) Mailed correspondence shall be sent to: Mail Stop PATENT BOARD, Patent Trial and Appeal Board, United States Patent and Trademark Office, PO Box 1450, Alexandria, Virginia 22313–1450.

(c) *Exhibits.* Each exhibit must be filed with the first document in which it is cited except as the Board may otherwise order.

(d) *Previously filed paper.* A document already in the record of the proceeding must not be filed again, not even as an exhibit or an appendix, without express Board authorization.

(e) *Service.* (1) *Electronic or other mode.* Service may be made electronically upon agreement of the parties. Otherwise, service may be by EXPRESS MAIL® or by means at least as fast and reliable as EXPRESS MAIL®.

(2) *Simultaneous with filing.* Each document filed with the Board, if not previously served, must be served simultaneously on each opposing party.

(3) *Counsel of record.* If a party is represented by counsel of record in the proceeding, service must be on counsel.

(4) *Certificate of service.* (i) Each document, other than an exhibit, must include a certificate of service at the end of that document. Any exhibit filed with the document may be included in the certification for the document.

(ii) For an exhibit filed separately, a transmittal letter incorporating the certificate of service must be filed. If more than one exhibit is filed at one time, a single letter should be used for all of the exhibits filed together. The letter must state the name and exhibit number for every exhibit filed with the letter.

(iii) The certificate of service must state:

(A) The date and manner of service; and

(B) The name and address of every person served.

§42.7 Management of the record.

(a) The Board may expunge any paper directed to a proceeding or filed while an application or patent is under the jurisdiction of the Board that is not authorized under this part or in a Board order or that is filed contrary to a Board order.

(b) The Board may vacate or hold in abeyance any non-Board action directed to a proceeding while an application or patent is under the jurisdiction of the Board unless the action was authorized by the Board.

§42.8 Mandatory notices.

(a) Each notice listed in paragraph (b) of this section must be filed with the Board:

(1) By the petitioner, as part of the petition;

(2) By the patent owner, or applicant in the case of derivation, within 21 days of service of the petition; or

(3) By either party, within 21 days of a change of the information listed in paragraph (b) of this section stated in an earlier paper.

(b) Each of the following notices must be filed:

(1) *Real party-in-interest.* Identify each real party-in-interest for the party.

(2) *Related matters.* Identify any other judicial or administrative matter that would affect, or be affected by, a decision in the proceeding.

(3) *Lead and back-up counsel.* If the party is represented by counsel, then counsel must be identified.

(4) *Service information.* Identify (if applicable):

(i) An electronic mail address;

(ii) A postal mailing address;

(iii) A hand-delivery address, if different than the postal mailing address;

(iv) A telephone number; and

(v) A facsimile number.

§42.9 Action by patent owner.

(a) *Entire interest.* An owner of the entire interest in an involved application or patent may act to the exclusion of the inventor (*see* §3.71 of this title).

(b) *Part interest.* An owner of a part interest in the subject patent may move to act to the exclusion of an inventor or a co-owner. The motion must show the inability or refusal of an inventor or co-owner to prosecute the proceeding or other cause why it is in the interests of justice to permit the owner of a part interest to act in the trial. In granting the motion, the Board may set conditions on the actions of the parties.

§42.10 Counsel.

(a) If a party is represented by counsel, the party must designate a lead counsel and a back-up counsel who can conduct business on behalf of the lead counsel.

(b) A power of attorney must be filed with the designation of counsel, except the patent owner should not file an additional power of attorney if the designated counsel is already counsel of record in the subject patent or application.

(c) The Board may recognize counsel *pro hac vice* during a proceeding upon a showing of good cause, subject to the condition that lead counsel be a registered practitioner and to any other conditions as the Board may impose. For example, where the lead counsel is a registered practitioner, a motion to appear *pro hac vice* by counsel who is not a registered practitioner may be granted upon showing that counsel is an experienced litigating attorney and has an established familiarity with the subject matter at issue in the proceeding.

(d) A panel of the Board may disqualify counsel for cause after notice and opportunity for hearing. A decision to disqualify is not final for the purposes of judicial review until certified by the Chief Administrative Patent Judge.

(e) Counsel may not withdraw from a proceeding before the Board unless the Board authorizes such withdrawal.

§42.11 Duty of candor.

Parties and individuals involved in the proceeding have a duty of candor and good faith to the Office during the course of a proceeding.

§42.12 Sanctions.

(a) The Board may impose a sanction against a party for misconduct, including:

(1) Failure to comply with an applicable rule or order in the proceeding;

(2) Advancing a misleading or frivolous argument or request for relief;

(3) Misrepresentation of a fact;

(4) Engaging in dilatory tactics;

(5) Abuse of discovery;

(6) Abuse of process; or

(7) Any other improper use of the proceeding, including actions that harass or cause unnecessary delay or an unnecessary increase in the cost of the proceeding.

(b) Sanctions include entry of one or more of the following:

(1) An order holding facts to have been established in the proceeding;

(2) An order expunging or precluding a party from filing a paper;

(3) An order precluding a party from presenting or contesting a particular issue;

(4) An order precluding a party from requesting, obtaining, or opposing discovery;

(5) An order excluding evidence;

(6) An order providing for compensatory expenses, including attorney fees;

(7) An order requiring terminal disclaimer of patent term; or

(8) Judgment in the trial or dismissal of the petition.

§42.13 Citation of authority.

(a) For any United States Supreme Court decision, citation to the United States Reports is preferred.

(b) For any decision other than a United States Supreme Court decision, citation to the West Reporter System is preferred.

(c) Citations to authority must include pinpoint citations whenever a specific holding or portion of an authority is invoked.

(d) Non-binding authority should be used sparingly. If the authority is not an authority of the Office and is not reproduced in the United States Reports or the West Reporter System, a copy of the authority should be provided.

§42.14 Public availability.

The record of a proceeding, including documents and things, shall be made available to the public, except as otherwise ordered. A party intending a document or thing to be sealed shall file a motion to seal concurrent with the filing of the document or thing to be sealed. The document or thing shall be provisionally sealed on receipt of the motion and remain so pending the outcome of the decision on the motion.

FEES

§42.15 Fees.

(a) On filing a petition for *inter partes* review of a patent, payment of the following fees are due:

(1) *Inter Partes* Review request fee: $9,000.00.

(2) *Inter Partes* Review Post-Institution fee: $14,000.00.

(3) In addition to the *Inter Partes* Review request fee, for requesting review of each claim in excess of 20: $200.00.

(4) In addition to the *Inter Partes* Post-Institution request fee, for requesting review of each claim in excess of 15: $400.00.

(b) On filing a petition for post-grant review or covered business method patent review of a patent, payment of the following fees are due:

(1) Post-Grant or Covered Business Method Patent Review request fee: $12,000.00.

(2) Post-Grant or Covered Business Method Patent Review Post-Institution fee: $18,000.00.

(3) In addition to the Post-Grant or Covered Business Method Patent Review request fee, for requesting review of each claim in excess of 20: $250.00.

(4) In addition to the Post-Grant or Covered Business Method Patent Review request fee Post-Institution request fee, for requesting review of each claim in excess of 15: $550.00.

(c) On the filing of a petition for a derivation proceeding, payment of the following fees is due:

(1) Derivation petition fee: $400.00.

(d) Any request requiring payment of a fee under this part, including a written request to make a settlement agreement available: $400.00.

[78 FR 4291, Jan. 18, 2013]

PETITION AND MOTION PRACTICE

§42.20 Generally.

(a) *Relief.* Relief, other than a petition requesting the institution of a trial, must be requested in the form of a motion.

(b) *Prior authorization.* A motion will not be entered without Board authorization. Authorization may be provided in an order of general applicability or during the proceeding.

(c) *Burden of proof.* The moving party has the burden of proof to establish that it is entitled to the requested relief.

(d) *Briefing.* The Board may order briefing on any issue involved in the trial.

§42.21 Notice of basis for relief.

(a) *Notice of request for relief.* The Board may require a party to file a notice stating the relief it requests and the basis for its entitlement to relief. A notice must include sufficient detail to place the Board and each opponent on notice of the precise relief requested. A notice is not evidence except as an admission by a party-opponent.

(b) *Filing and service.* The Board may set the times and conditions for filing and serving notices required under this section. The Board may provide for the notice filed with the Board to be maintained in confidence for a limited time.

(c) *Effect.* If a notice under paragraph (a) of this section is required:

(1) A failure to state a sufficient basis for relief may result in a denial of the relief requested;

(2) A party will be limited to filing motions consistent with the notice; and

(3) Ambiguities in the notice will be construed against the party.

(d) *Correction.* A party may move to correct its notice. The motion should be filed promptly after the party becomes aware of the basis for the correction. A correction filed after the time set for filing notices will only be entered if entry would serve the interests of justice.

§42.22 Content of petitions and motions.

(a) Each petition or motion must be filed as a separate paper and must include:

(1) A statement of the precise relief requested; and

(2) A full statement of the reasons for the relief requested, including a detailed explanation of the significance of the evidence including material facts, and the governing law, rules, and precedent.

(b) *Relief requested.* Where a rule in part 1 of this title ordinarily governs the relief sought, the petition or motion must make any showings required under that rule in addition to any showings required in this part.

(c) *Statement of material facts.* Each petition or motion may include a statement of material fact. Each material fact preferably shall be set forth as a separately numbered sentence with specific citations to the portions of the record that support the fact.

(d) The Board may order additional showings or explanations as a condition for authorizing a motion (*see* §42.20(b)).

§42.23 Oppositions and replies.

(a) Oppositions and replies must comply with the content requirements for motions and must include a statement identifying material facts in dispute. Any material fact not specifically denied may be considered admitted.

(b) All arguments for the relief requested in a motion must be made in the motion. A reply may only respond to arguments raised in the corresponding opposition or patent owner response.

§42.24 Page limits for petitions, motions, oppositions, and replies.

(a) *Petitions and motions.* (1) The following page limits for petitions and motions apply and include any statement of material facts to be admitted or denied in support of the petition or motion. The page limit does not include a table of contents, a table of authorities, a certificate of service, or appendix of exhibits.

(i) Petition requesting *inter partes* review: 60 pages.

(ii) Petition requesting post-grant review: 80 pages.

(iii) Petition requesting covered business method patent review: 80 pages.

(iv) Petition requesting derivation proceeding: 60 pages.

(v) Motions: 15 pages.

(2) Petitions to institute a trial must comply with the stated page limits but may be accompanied by a motion to waive the page limits. The petitioner must show in the motion how a waiver of the page limits is in the interests of justice and must append a copy of proposed petition exceeding the page limit to the motion. If the motion is not granted, the proposed petition exceeding the page limit may be expunged or returned. Any other motion to waive page limits must be granted in advance of filing a motion, opposition, or reply for which the waiver is necessary.

(b) *Patent owner responses and oppositions*. The page limits set forth in this paragraph do not include a listing of facts which are admitted, denied, or cannot be admitted or denied.

(1) The page limits for a patent owner preliminary response to petition are the same as the page limits for the petition.

(2) The page limits for a patent owner response to petition are the same as the page limits for the petition.

(3) The page limits for oppositions are the same as those for corresponding motions.

(c) *Replies*. The following page limits for replies apply and include the required statement of facts in support of the reply. The page limits do not include a table of contents, a table of authorities, a listing of facts which are admitted, denied, or cannot be admitted or denied, a certificate of service, or appendix of exhibits.

(1) Replies to patent owner responses to petitions: 15 pages.

(2) Replies to oppositions: 5 pages.

§ 42.25 Default filing times.

(a) A motion may only be filed according to a schedule set by the Board. The default times for acting are:

(1) An opposition is due one month after service of the motion; and

(2) A reply is due one month after service of the opposition.

(b) A party should seek relief promptly after the need for relief is identified. Delay in seeking relief may justify a denial of relief sought.

TESTIMONY AND PRODUCTION

§ 42.51 Discovery.

(a) *Mandatory initial disclosures.*

(1) *With agreement.* Parties may agree to mandatory discovery requiring the initial disclosures set forth in the Office Patent Trial Practice Guide.

(i) The parties must submit any agreement reached on initial disclosures by no later than the filing of the patent owner preliminary response or the expiration of the time period for filing such a response. The initial disclosures of the parties shall be filed as exhibits.

(ii) Upon the institution of a trial, parties may automatically take discovery of the information identified in the initial disclosures.

(2) *Without agreement.* Where the parties fail to agree to the mandatory discovery set forth in paragraph (a)(1), a party may seek such discovery by motion.

(b) *Limited discovery.* A party is not entitled to discovery except as provided in paragraph (a) of this section, or as otherwise authorized in this subpart.

(1) *Routine discovery.* Except as the Board may otherwise order:

(i) Unless previously served or otherwise by agreement of the parties, any exhibit cited in a paper or in testimony must be served with the citing paper or testimony.

(ii) Cross examination of affidavit testimony is authorized within such time period as the Board may set.

(iii) Unless previously served, a party must serve relevant information that is inconsistent with a position advanced by the party during the proceeding concurrent with the filing of the documents or things that contains the inconsistency. This requirement does not make discoverable anything otherwise protected by legally recognized privileges such as attorney-client or attorney work product. This requirement extends to inventors, corporate officers, and persons involved in the preparation or filing of the documents or things.

(2) *Additional discovery.* (i) The parties may agree to additional discovery between themselves. Where the parties fail to agree, a party may move for additional discovery. The moving party must show that such additional discovery is in the interests of justice, except in post-grant reviews where additional discovery is limited to evidence directly related to factual assertions advanced by either party in the proceeding (*see* §42.224). The Board may specify conditions for such additional discovery.

(ii) When appropriate, a party may obtain production of documents and things during cross examination of an opponent's witness or during authorized compelled testimony under §42.52.

(c) *Production of documents.* Except as otherwise ordered by the Board, a party producing documents and things shall either provide copies to the opposing party or make the documents and things available for inspection and copying at a reasonable time and location in the United States.

§42.52 Compelling testimony and production.

(a) *Authorization required.* A party seeking to compel testimony or production of documents or things must file a motion for authorization. The motion must describe the general relevance of the testimony, document, or thing, and must:

(1) In the case of testimony, identify the witness by name or title; and

(2) In the case of a document or thing, the general nature of the document or thing.

(b) *Outside the United States.* For testimony or production sought outside the United States, the motion must also:

(1) *In the case of testimony.* (i) Identify the foreign country and explain why the party believes the witness can be compelled to testify in the foreign country, including a description of the procedures that will be used to compel the testimony in the foreign country and an estimate of the time it is expected to take to obtain the testimony; and

(ii) Demonstrate that the party has made reasonable efforts to secure the agreement of the witness to testify in the United States but has been unsuccessful in obtaining the agreement, even though the party has offered to pay the travel expenses of the witness to testify in the United States.

(2) *In the case of production of a document or thing.* (i) Identify the foreign country and explain why the party believes production of the document or thing can be compelled in the foreign country, including a description of the procedures that will be used to compel production of the document or thing in the foreign country and an estimate of the time it is expected to take to obtain production of the document or thing; and

(ii) Demonstrate that the party has made reasonable efforts to obtain the agreement of the individual or entity having possession, custody, or control of the document or thing to produce the document or thing in the United States but has been unsuccessful in obtaining that agreement, even though the party has offered to pay the expenses of producing the document or thing in the United States.

§42.53 Taking testimony.

(a) *Form.* Uncompelled direct testimony must be submitted in the form of an affidavit. All other testimony, including testimony compelled under 35 U.S.C. 24, must be in the form of a deposition transcript. Parties may agree to video-recorded testimony, but may not submit such testimony without prior authorization of the Board. In addition, the Board may authorize or require live or video-recorded testimony.

(b) *Time and location.* (1) Uncompelled direct testimony may be taken at any time to support a petition, motion, opposition, or reply; otherwise, testimony may only be taken during a testimony period set by the Board.

(2) Except as the Board otherwise orders, during the testimony period, deposition testimony may be taken at any reasonable time and location within the United States before any disinterested official authorized to administer oaths at that location.

(3) Uncompelled deposition testimony outside the United States may only be taken upon agreement of the parties or as the Board specifically directs.

(c) *Duration.* (1) Unless stipulated by the parties or ordered by the Board, direct examination, cross-examination, and redirect examination for compelled deposition testimony shall be subject to the following time limits: Seven hours for direct examination, four hours for cross-examination, and two hours for redirect examination.

(2) Unless stipulated by the parties or ordered by the Board, cross-examination, redirect examination, and re-cross examination for uncompelled direct deposition testimony shall be subject to the following time limits: Seven hours for cross-examination, four hours for redirect examination, and two hours for re-cross examination.

(d) *Notice of deposition.* (1) Prior to the taking of deposition testimony, all parties to the proceeding must agree on the time and place for taking testimony. If the parties cannot agree, the party seeking the testimony must initiate a conference with the Board to set a time and place.

(2) Cross-examination should ordinarily take place after any supplemental evidence relating to the direct testimony has been filed and more than a week before the filing date for any paper in which the cross-examination testimony is expected to be used. A party requesting cross-examination testimony of more than one witness may choose the order in which the witnesses are to be cross-examined.

(3) In the case of direct deposition testimony, at least three business days prior to the conference in paragraph (d)(1) of this section, or if there is no conference, at least ten days prior to the deposition, the party seeking the direct testimony must serve:

(i) A list and copy of each document under the party's control and on which the party intends to rely; and

(ii) A list of, and proffer of reasonable access to, anything other than a document under the party's control and on which the party intends to rely.

(4) The party seeking the deposition must file a notice of the deposition at least ten business days before a deposition.

(5) *Scope and content*—(i) For direct deposition testimony, the notice limits the scope of the testimony and must list:

(A) The time and place of the deposition;

(B) The name and address of the witness;

(C) A list of the exhibits to be relied upon during the deposition; and

(D) A general description of the scope and nature of the testimony to be elicited.

(ii) For cross-examination testimony, the scope of the examination is limited to the scope of the direct testimony.

(iii) The notice must list the time and place of the deposition.

(iv) Where an additional party seeks to take direct testimony of a third party witness at the time and place noticed in paragraph (d)(5) of this section, the additional party must provide a counter notice that lists the exhibits to be relied upon in the deposition and a general description of the scope and nature of the testimony to be elicited.

(6) *Motion to quash*—Objection to a defect in the notice is waived unless the objecting party promptly seeks authorization to file a motion to quash.

(e) *Deposition in a foreign language.* If an interpreter will be used during the deposition, the party calling the witness must initiate a conference with the Board at least five business days before the deposition.

(f) *Manner of taking deposition testimony.* (1) Before giving deposition testimony, each witness shall be duly sworn according to law by the officer before whom the deposition is to be taken. The officer must be authorized to take testimony under 35 U.S.C. 23.

(2) The testimony shall be taken with any questions and answers recorded in their regular order by the officer, or by some other disinterested person in the presence of the officer, unless the presence of the officer is waived on the record by agreement of all parties.

(3) Any exhibits used during the deposition must be numbered as required by § 42.63(c), and must, if not previously served, be served at the deposition. Exhibits objected to shall be accepted pending a decision on the objection.

(4) All objections made at the time of the deposition to the qualifications of the officer taking the deposition, the manner of taking it, the evidence presented, the conduct of any party, and any other objection to the deposition shall be noted on the record by the officer.

(5) When the testimony has been transcribed, the witness shall read and sign (in the form of an affidavit) a transcript of the deposition unless:

(i) The parties otherwise agree in writing;

(ii) The parties waive reading and signature by the witness on the record at the deposition; or

(iii) The witness refuses to read or sign the transcript of the deposition.

(6) The officer shall prepare a certified transcript by attaching a certificate in the form of an affidavit signed and sealed by the officer to the transcript of the deposition. Unless the parties waive any of the following requirements, in which case the certificate shall so state, the certificate must state:

(i) The witness was duly sworn by the officer before commencement of testimony by the witness;

(ii) The transcript is a true record of the testimony given by the witness;

(iii) The name of the person who recorded the testimony, and if the officer did not record it, whether the testimony was recorded in the presence of the officer;

(iv) The presence or absence of any opponent;

(v) The place where the deposition was taken and the day and hour when the deposition began and ended;

(vi) The officer has no disqualifying interest, personal or financial, in a party; and

(vii) If a witness refuses to read or sign the transcript, the circumstances under which the witness refused.

(7) Except where the parties agree otherwise, the proponent of the testimony must arrange for providing a copy of the transcript to all other parties. The testimony must be filed by proponent as an exhibit.

(8) Any objection to the content, form, or manner of taking the deposition, including the qualifications of the officer, is waived unless made on the record during the deposition and preserved in a timely filed motion to exclude.

(g) *Costs.* Except as the Board may order or the parties may agree in writing, the proponent of the direct testimony shall bear all costs associated with the testimony, including the reasonable costs associated with making the witness available for the cross-examination.

§ 42.54 Protective order.

(a) A party may file a motion to seal where the motion to seal contains a proposed protective order, such as the default protective order set forth in the Office Patent Trial Practice Guide. The motion must include a certification that the moving party has in good faith conferred or attempted to confer with other affected parties in an effort to resolve the dispute. The Board may, for good cause, issue an order to protect a party or person from disclosing confidential information, including, but not limited to, one or more of the following:

(1) Forbidding the disclosure or discovery;

(2) Specifying terms, including time and place, for the disclosure or discovery;

(3) Prescribing a discovery method other than the one selected by the party seeking discovery;

(4) Forbidding inquiry into certain matters, or limiting the scope of disclosure or discovery to certain matters;

(5) Designating the persons who may be present while the discovery is conducted;

(6) Requiring that a deposition be sealed and opened only by order of the Board;

(7) Requiring that a trade secret or other confidential research, development, or commercial information not be revealed or be revealed only in a specified way; and

(8) Requiring that the parties simultaneously file specified documents or information in sealed envelopes, to be opened as the Board directs.

(b) [Reserved]

§ 42.55 Confidential information in a petition.

A petitioner filing confidential information with a petition may, concurrent with the filing of the petition, file a motion to seal with a proposed protective order as to the confidential information. The institution of the requested trial will constitute a grant of the motion to seal unless otherwise ordered by the Board.

(a) *Default protective order.* Where a motion to seal requests entry of the default protective order set forth in the Office Patent Trial Practice Guide, the petitioner must file, but need not serve, the confidential information under seal. The patent owner may only access the filed sealed information prior to the institution of the trial by agreeing to the terms of the default protective order or obtaining relief from the Board.

(b) *Protective orders other than default protective order.* Where a motion to seal requests entry of a protective order other than the default protective order, the petitioner must file, but need not serve, the confidential information under seal. The patent owner may only access the sealed confidential information prior to the institution of the trial by:

(1) agreeing to the terms of the protective order requested by the petitioner;

(2) agreeing to the terms of a protective order that the parties file jointly; or

(3) obtaining entry of a protective order (*e.g.*, the default protective order).

§ 42.56 Expungement of confidential information.

After denial of a petition to institute a trial or after final judgment in a trial, a party may file a motion to expunge confidential information from the record.

§ 42.61 Admissibility.

(a) Evidence that is not taken, sought, or filed in accordance with this subpart is not admissible.

(b) *Records of the Office.* Certification is not necessary as a condition to admissibility when the evidence to be submitted is a record of the Office to which all parties have access.

(c) *Specification and drawings.* A specification or drawing of a United States patent application or patent is admissible as evidence only to prove what the specification or drawing describes. If there is data in the specification or a drawing upon which a party intends to rely to prove the truth of the data, an affidavit by an individual having first-hand knowledge of how the data was generated must be filed.

§ 42.62 Applicability of the Federal rules of evidence.

(a) *Generally.* Except as otherwise provided in this subpart, the Federal Rules of Evidence shall apply to a proceeding.

(b) *Exclusions.* Those portions of the Federal Rules of Evidence relating to criminal proceedings, juries, and other matters not relevant to proceedings under this subpart shall not apply.

(c) *Modifications in terminology.* Unless otherwise clear from context, the following terms of the Federal Rules of Evidence shall be construed as indicated:

Appellate court means United States Court of Appeals for the Federal Circuit.

Civil action, civil proceeding, and *action* mean a proceeding before the Board under part 42.

Courts of the United States, U.S. Magistrate, court, trial court, trier of fact, and *judge* mean Board.

Hearing means, as defined in Federal Rule of Evidence 804(a)(5), the time for taking testimony.

Judicial notice means official notice.

Trial or *hearing* in Federal Rule of Evidence 807 means the time for taking testimony.

(d) In determining foreign law, the Board may consider any relevant material or source, including testimony, whether or not submitted by a party or admissible under the Federal Rules of Evidence.

§ 42.63 Form of evidence.

(a) *Exhibits required.* Evidence consists of affidavits, transcripts of depositions, documents, and things. All evidence must be filed in the form of an exhibit.

(b) *Translation required.* When a party relies on a document or is required to produce a document in a language other than English, a translation of the document into English and an affidavit attesting to the accuracy of the translation must be filed with the document.

(c) *Exhibit numbering.* Each party's exhibits must be uniquely numbered sequentially in a range the Board specifies. For the petitioner, the range is 1001–1999, and for the patent owner, the range is 2001–2999.

(d) *Exhibit format.* An exhibit must conform with the requirements for papers in §42.6 and the requirements of this paragraph.

(1) Each exhibit must have an exhibit label.

(i) An exhibit filed with the petition must include the petitioner's name followed by a unique exhibit number.

(ii) For exhibits not filed with the petition, the exhibit label must include the party's name followed by a unique exhibit number, the names of the parties, and the trial number.

(2) When the exhibit is a paper:

(i) Each page must be uniquely numbered in sequence; and

(ii) The exhibit label must be affixed to the lower right corner of the first page of the exhibit without obscuring information on the first page or, if obscuring is unavoidable, affixed to a duplicate first page.

(e) *Exhibit list.* Each party must maintain an exhibit list with the exhibit number and a brief description of each exhibit. If the exhibit is not filed, the exhibit list should note that fact. A current exhibit list must be served whenever evidence is served and the current exhibit list must be filed when filing exhibits.

§42.64 Objection; motion to exclude; motion in limine.

(a) *Deposition evidence.* An objection to the admissibility of deposition evidence must be made during the deposition. Evidence to cure the objection must be provided during the deposition, unless the parties to the deposition stipulate otherwise on the deposition record.

(b) *Other evidence.* For evidence other than deposition evidence:

(1) *Objection.* Any objection to evidence submitted during a preliminary proceeding must be served within ten business days of the institution of the trial. Once a trial has been instituted, any objection must be served within five business days of service of evidence to which the objection is directed. The objection must identify the grounds for the objection with sufficient particularity to allow correction in the form of supplemental evidence.

(2) *Supplemental evidence.* The party relying on evidence to which an objection is timely served may respond to the objection by serving supplemental evidence within ten business days of service of the objection.

(c) *Motion to exclude.* A motion to exclude evidence must be filed to preserve any objection. The motion must identify the objections in the record in order and must explain the objections. The motion may be filed without prior authorization from the Board.

§42.65 Expert testimony; tests and data.

(a) Expert testimony that does not disclose the underlying facts or data on which the opinion is based is entitled to little or no weight. Testimony on United States patent law or patent examination practice will not be admitted.

(b) If a party relies on a technical test or data from such a test, the party must provide an affidavit explaining:

(1) Why the test or data is being used;

(2) How the test was performed and the data was generated;

(3) How the data is used to determine a value;

(4) How the test is regarded in the relevant art; and

(5) Any other information necessary for the Board to evaluate the test and data.

Oral Argument, Decision, and Settlement

§42.70 Oral argument.

(a) *Request for oral argument.* A party may request oral argument on an issue raised in a paper at a time set by the Board. The request must be filed as a separate paper and must specify the issues to be argued.

(b) Demonstrative exhibits must be served at least five business days before the oral argument and filed no later than the time of the oral argument.

§ 42.71 Decision on petitions or motions.

(a) *Order of consideration.* The Board may take up petitions or motions for decisions in any order, may grant, deny, or dismiss any petition or motion, and may enter any appropriate order.

(b) *Interlocutory decisions.* A decision on a motion without a judgment is not final for the purposes of judicial review. If a decision is not a panel decision, the party may request that a panel rehear the decision. When rehearing a non-panel decision, a panel will review the decision for an abuse of discretion. A panel decision on an issue will govern the trial.

(c) *Petition decisions.* A decision by the Board on whether to institute a trial is final and nonappealable. A party may request rehearing on a decision by the Board on whether to institute a trial pursuant to paragraph (d) of this section. When rehearing a decision on petition, a panel will review the decision for an abuse of discretion.

(d) *Rehearing.* A party dissatisfied with a decision may file a request for rehearing, without prior authorization from the Board. The burden of showing a decision should be modified lies with the party challenging the decision. The request must specifically identify all matters the party believes the Board misapprehended or overlooked, and the place where each matter was previously addressed in a motion, an opposition, or a reply. A request for rehearing does not toll times for taking action. Any request must be filed:

(1) Within 14 days of the entry of a non-final decision or a decision to institute a trial as to at least one ground of unpatentability asserted in the petition; or

(2) Within 30 days of the entry of a final decision or a decision not to institute a trial.

§ 42.72 Termination of trial.

The Board may terminate a trial without rendering a final written decision, where appropriate, including where the trial is consolidated with another proceeding or pursuant to a joint request under 35 U.S.C. 317(a) or 327(a).

§ 42.73 Judgment.

(a) A judgment, except in the case of a termination, disposes of all issues that were, or by motion reasonably could have been, raised and decided.

(b) *Request for adverse judgment.* A party may request judgment against itself at any time during a proceeding. Actions construed to be a request for adverse judgment include:

(1) Disclaimer of the involved application or patent;

(2) Cancellation or disclaimer of a claim such that the party has no remaining claim in the trial;

(3) Concession of unpatentability or derivation of the contested subject matter; and

(4) Abandonment of the contest.

(c) *Recommendation.* The judgment may include a recommendation for further action by an examiner or by the Director.

(d) *Estoppel.* (1) *Petitioner other than in derivation proceeding.* A petitioner, or the real party in interest or privy of the petitioner, is estopped in the Office from requesting or maintaining a proceeding with respect to a claim for which it has obtained a final written decision on patentability in an *inter partes* review, post-grant review, or a covered business method patent review, on any ground that the petitioner raised or reasonably could have raised during the trial, except that estoppel shall not apply to a petitioner, or to the real party in interest or privy of the petitioner who has settled under 35 U.S.C. 317 or 327.

(2) *In a derivation,* the losing party who could have properly moved for relief on an issue, but did not so move, may not take action in the Office after the judgment that is inconsistent with that party's failure to move, except that a losing party shall not be estopped with respect to any contested subject matter for which that party was awarded a favorable judgment.

(3) *Patent applicant or owner.* A patent applicant or owner is precluded from

taking action inconsistent with the adverse judgment, including obtaining in any patent:

(i) A claim that is not patentably distinct from a finally refused or canceled claim; or

(ii) An amendment of a specification or of a drawing that was denied during the trial proceeding, but this provision does not apply to an application or patent that has a different written description.

§42.74 Settlement.

(a) *Board role.* The parties may agree to settle any issue in a proceeding, but the Board is not a party to the settlement and may independently determine any question of jurisdiction, patentability, or Office practice.

(b) *Agreements in writing.* Any agreement or understanding between the parties made in connection with, or in contemplation of, the termination of a proceeding shall be in writing and a true copy shall be filed with the Board before the termination of the trial.

(c) *Request to keep separate.* A party to a settlement may request that the settlement be treated as business confidential information and be kept separate from the files of an involved patent or application. The request must be filed with the settlement. If a timely request is filed, the settlement shall only be available:

(1) To a Government agency on written request to the Board; or

(2) To any other person upon written request to the Board to make the settlement agreement available, along with the fee specified in §42.15(d) and on a showing of good cause.

CERTIFICATE

§42.80 Certificate.

After the Board issues a final written decision in an *inter partes* review, post-grant review, or covered business method patent review and the time for appeal has expired or any appeal has terminated, the Office will issue and publish a certificate canceling any claim of the patent finally determined to be unpatentable, confirming any claim of the patent determined to be patentable, and incorporating in the patent any new or amended claim determined to be patentable by operation of the certificate.

Subpart B—*Inter Partes* Review

GENERAL

SOURCE: 77 FR 48727, Aug. 14, 2012, unless otherwise noted.

§42.100 Procedure; pendency.

(a) An *inter partes* review is a trial subject to the procedures set forth in subpart A of this part.

(b) A claim in an unexpired patent shall be given its broadest reasonable construction in light of the specification of the patent in which it appears.

(c) An *inter partes* review proceeding shall be administered such that pendency before the Board after institution is normally no more than one year. The time can be extended by up to six months for good cause by the Chief Administrative Patent Judge, or adjusted by the Board in the case of joinder.

§42.101 Who may petition for *inter partes* review.

A person who is not the owner of a patent may file with the Office a petition to institute an *inter partes* review of the patent unless:

(a) Before the date on which the petition for review is filed, the petitioner or real party-in-interest filed a civil action challenging the validity of a claim of the patent;

(b) The petition requesting the proceeding is filed more than one year after the date on which the petitioner, the petitioner's real party-in-interest, or a privy of the petitioner is served with a complaint alleging infringement of the patent; or

(c) The petitioner, the petitioner's real party-in-interest, or a privy of the petitioner is estopped from challenging the claims on the grounds identified in the petition.

§42.102 Time for filing.

(a) A petition for *inter partes* review of a patent must be filed after the later of the following dates, where applicable:

(1) If the patent is a patent described in section 3(n)(1) of the Leahy-Smith America Invents Act, the date that is

nine months after the date of the grant of the patent;

(2) If the patent is a patent that is not described in section 3(n)(1) of the Leahy-Smith American Invents Act, the date of the grant of the patent; or

(3) If a post-grant review is instituted as set forth in subpart C of this part, the date of the termination of such post-grant review.

(b) The Director may impose a limit on the number of *inter partes* reviews that may be instituted during each of the first four one-year periods in which the amendment made to chapter 31 of title 35, United States Code, is in effect by providing notice in the Office's Official Gazette or FEDERAL REGISTER. Petitions filed after an established limit has been reached will be deemed untimely.

[77 FR 48727, Aug. 14, 2012, as amended at 78 FR 17874, Mar. 25, 2013]

§ 42.103 *Inter partes* review fee.

(a) An *inter partes* review fee set forth in § 42.15(a) must accompany the petition. (b) No filing date will be accorded to the petition until full payment is received.

§ 42.104 Content of petition.

In addition to the requirements of §§ 42.6, 42.8, 42.22, and 42.24, the petition must set forth:

(a) *Grounds for standing.* The petitioner must certify that the patent for which review is sought is available for *inter partes* review and that the petitioner is not barred or estopped from requesting an *inter partes* review challenging the patent claims on the grounds identified in the petition.

(b) *Identification of challenge.* Provide a statement of the precise relief requested for each claim challenged. The statement must identify the following:

(1) The claim;

(2) The specific statutory grounds under 35 U.S.C. 102 or 103 on which the challenge to the claim is based and the patents or printed publications relied upon for each ground;

(3) How the challenged claim is to be construed. Where the claim to be construed contains a means-plus-function or step-plus-function limitation as permitted under 35 U.S.C. 112(f), the construction of the claim must identify the specific portions of the specification that describe the structure, material, or acts corresponding to each claimed function;

(4) How the construed claim is unpatentable under the statutory grounds identified in paragraph (b)(2) of this section. The petition must specify where each element of the claim is found in the prior art patents or printed publications relied upon; and

(5) The exhibit number of the supporting evidence relied upon to support the challenge and the relevance of the evidence to the challenge raised, including identifying specific portions of the evidence that support the challenge. The Board may exclude or give no weight to the evidence where a party has failed to state its relevance or to identify specific portions of the evidence that support the challenge.

(c) A motion may be filed that seeks to correct a clerical or typographical mistake in the petition. The grant of such a motion does not change the filing date of the petition.

§ 42.105 Service of petition.

In addition to the requirements of § 42.6, the petitioner must serve the petition and exhibits relied upon in the petition as follows:

(a) The petition and supporting evidence must be served on the patent owner at the correspondence address of record for the subject patent. The petitioner may additionally serve the petition and supporting evidence on the patent owner at any other address known to the petitioner as likely to effect service.

(b) Upon agreement of the parties, service may be made electronically. Service may be by EXPRESS MAIL® or by means at least as fast and reliable as EXPRESS MAIL®. Personal service is not required.

§ 42.106 Filing date.

(a) *Complete petition.* A petition to institute *inter partes* review will not be accorded a filing date until the petition satisfies all of the following requirements:

(1) Complies with § 42.104;

(2) Effects service of the petition on the correspondence address of record as provided in § 42.105(a); and

(3) Is accompanied by the fee to institute required in §42.15(a).

(b) *Incomplete petition.* Where a party files an incomplete petition, no filing date will be accorded, and the Office will dismiss the petition if the deficiency in the petition is not corrected within one month from the notice of an incomplete petition.

§42.107 Preliminary response to petition.

(a) The patent owner may file a preliminary response to the petition. The response is limited to setting forth the reasons why no *inter partes* review should be instituted under 35 U.S.C. 314. The response can include evidence except as provided in paragraph (c) of this section. The preliminary response is subject to the page limits under §42.24.

(b) *Due date.* The preliminary response must be filed no later than three months after the date of a notice indicating that the request to institute an *inter partes* review has been granted a filing date. A patent owner may expedite the proceeding by filing an election to waive the patent owner preliminary response.

(c) *No new testimonial evidence.* The preliminary response shall not present new testimony evidence beyond that already of record, except as authorized by the Board.

(d) *No amendment.* The preliminary response shall not include any amendment.

(e) *Disclaim Patent Claims.* The patent owner may file a statutory disclaimer under 35 U.S.C. 253(a) in compliance with §1.321(a) of this chapter, disclaiming one or more claims in the patent. No *inter partes* review will be instituted based on disclaimed claims.

INSTITUTING *Inter Partes* REVIEW

§42.108 Institution of *inter partes* review.

(a) When instituting *inter partes* review, the Board may authorize the review to proceed on all or some of the challenged claims and on all or some of the grounds of unpatentability asserted for each claim.

(b) At any time prior to institution of *inter partes* review, the Board may deny some or all grounds for unpatentability for some or all of the challenged claims. Denial of a ground is a Board decision not to institute *inter partes* review on that ground.

(c) Sufficient grounds. *Inter partes* review shall not be instituted for a ground of unpatentability unless the Board decides that the petition supporting the ground would demonstrate that there is a reasonable likelihood that at least one of the claims challenged in the petition is unpatentable. The Board's decision will take into account a patent owner preliminary response where such a response is filed.

AFTER INSTITUTION OF *Inter Partes* REVIEW

§42.120 Patent owner response.

(a) *Scope.* A patent owner may file a response to the petition addressing any ground for unpatentability not already denied. A patent owner response is filed as an opposition and is subject to the page limits provided in §42.24.

(b) *Due date for response.* If no time for filing a patent owner response to a petition is provided in a Board order, the default date for filing a patent owner response is three months from the date the *inter partes* review was instituted.

§42.121 Amendment of the patent.

(a) *Motion to amend.* A patent owner may file one motion to amend a patent, but only after conferring with the Board.

(1) *Due date.* Unless a due date is provided in a Board order, a motion to amend must be filed no later than the filing of a patent owner response.

(2) *Scope.* A motion to amend may be denied where:

(i) The amendment does not respond to a ground of unpatentability involved in the trial; or

(ii) The amendment seeks to enlarge the scope of the claims of the patent or introduce new subject matter.

(3) *A reasonable number of substitute claims.* A motion to amend may cancel a challenged claim or propose a reasonable number of substitute claims. The presumption is that only one substitute claim would be needed to replace each challenged claim, and it

may be rebutted by a demonstration of need.

(b) *Content.* A motion to amend claims must include a claim listing, show the changes clearly, and set forth:

(1) The support in the original disclosure of the patent for each claim that is added or amended; and

(2) The support in an earlier-filed disclosure for each claim for which benefit of the filing date of the earlier filed disclosure is sought.

(c) *Additional motion to amend.* In addition to the requirements set forth in paragraphs (a) and (b) of this section, any additional motion to amend may not be filed without Board authorization. An additional motion to amend may be authorized when there is a good cause showing or a joint request of the petitioner and the patent owner to materially advance a settlement. In determining whether to authorize such an additional motion to amend, the Board will consider whether a petitioner has submitted supplemental information after the time period set for filing a motion to amend in paragraph (a)(1) of this section.

§ 42.122 Multiple proceedings and Joinder.

(a) *Multiple proceedings.* Where another matter involving the patent is before the Office, the Board may during the pendency of the *inter partes* review enter any appropriate order regarding the additional matter including providing for the stay, transfer, consolidation, or termination of any such matter.

(b) *Request for joinder.* Joinder may be requested by a patent owner or petitioner. Any request for joinder must be filed, as a motion under § 42.22, no later than one month after the institution date of any *inter partes* review for which joinder is requested. The time period set forth in § 42.101(b) shall not apply when the petition is accompanied by a request for joinder.

§ 42.123 Filing of supplemental information.

(a) *Motion to submit supplemental information.* Once a trial has been instituted, a party may file a motion to submit supplemental information in accordance with the following requirements:

(1) A request for the authorization to file a motion to submit supplemental information is made within one month of the date the trial is instituted.

(2) The supplemental information must be relevant to a claim for which the trial has been instituted.

(b) *Late submission of supplemental information.* A party seeking to submit supplemental information more than one month after the date the trial is instituted, must request authorization to file a motion to submit the information. The motion to submit supplemental information must show why the supplemental information reasonably could not have been obtained earlier, and that consideration of the supplemental information would be in the interests-of-justice.

(c) *Other supplemental information.* A party seeking to submit supplemental information not relevant to a claim for which the trial has been instituted must request authorization to file a motion to submit the information. The motion must show why the supplemental information reasonably could not have been obtained earlier, and that consideration of the supplemental information would be in the interests-of-justice.

Subpart C—Post-Grant Review

SOURCE: 77 FR 48729, Aug. 14, 2012, unless otherwise noted.

GENERAL

§ 42.200 Procedure; pendency.

(a) A post-grant review is a trial subject to the procedures set forth in subpart A of this part.

(b) A claim in an unexpired patent shall be given its broadest reasonable construction in light of the specification of the patent in which it appears.

(c) A post-grant review proceeding shall be administered such that pendency before the Board after institution is normally no more than one year. The time can be extended by up to six months for good cause by the Chief Administrative Patent Judge, or adjusted by the Board in the case of joinder.

(d) Interferences commenced before September 16, 2012, shall proceed under part 41 of this chapter except as the Chief Administrative Patent Judge, acting on behalf of the Director, may otherwise order in the interests-of-justice.

§42.201 Who may petition for a post-grant review.

A person who is not the owner of a patent may file with the Office a petition to institute a post-grant review of the patent unless:

(a) Before the date on which the petition for review is filed, the petitioner or real party-in-interest filed a civil action challenging the validity of a claim of the patent; or

(b) The petitioner, the petitioner's real party-in-interest, or a privy of the petitioner is estopped from challenging the claims on the grounds identified in the petition.

§42.202 Time for filing.

(a) A petition for a post-grant review of a patent must be filed no later than the date that is nine months after the date of the grant of a patent or of the issuance of a reissue patent. A petition, however, may not request a post-grant review for a claim in a reissue patent that is identical to or narrower than a claim in the original patent from which the reissue patent was issued unless the petition is filed not later than the date that is nine months after the date of the grant of the original patent.

(b) The Director may impose a limit on the number of post-grant reviews that may be instituted during each of the first four one-year periods in which 35 U.S.C. 321 is in effect by providing notice in the Office's Official Gazette or FEDERAL REGISTER. Petitions filed after an established limit has been reached will be deemed untimely.

§42.203 Post-grant review fee.

(a) A post-grant review fee set forth in §42.15(b) must accompany the petition.

(b) No filing date will be accorded to the petition until full payment is received.

§42.204 Content of petition.

In addition to the requirements of §§42.6, 42.8, 42.22, and 42.24, the petition must set forth:

(a) *Grounds for standing.* The petitioner must certify that the patent for which review is sought is available for post-grant review and that the petitioner is not barred or estopped from requesting a post-grant review challenging the patent claims on the grounds identified in the petition.

(b) *Identification of challenge.* Provide a statement of the precise relief requested for each claim challenged. The statement must identify the following:

(1) The claim;

(2) The specific statutory grounds permitted under 35 U.S.C. 282(b)(2) or (3) on which the challenge to the claim is based;

(3) How the challenged claim is to be construed. Where the claim to be construed contains a means-plus-function or step-plus-function limitation as permitted under 35 U.S.C. 112(f), the construction of the claim must identify the specific portions of the specification that describe the structure, material, or acts corresponding to each claimed function;

(4) How the construed claim is unpatentable under the statutory grounds identified in paragraph (b)(2) of this section. Where the grounds for unpatentability are based on prior art, the petition must specify where each element of the claim is found in the prior art. For all other grounds of unpatentability, the petition must identify the specific part of the claim that fails to comply with the statutory grounds raised and state how the identified subject matter fails to comply with the statute; and

(5) The exhibit number of the supporting evidence relied upon to support the challenge and the relevance of the evidence to the challenge raised, including identifying specific portions of the evidence that support the challenge. The Board may exclude or give no weight to the evidence where a party has failed to state its relevance or to identify specific portions of the evidence that support the challenge.

(c) A motion may be filed that seeks to correct a clerical or typographical mistake in the petition. The grant of such a motion does not change the filing date of the petition.

§ 42.205 Service of petition.

In addition to the requirements of § 42.6, the petitioner must serve the petition and exhibits relied upon in the petition as follows:

(a) The petition and supporting evidence must be served on the patent owner at the correspondence address of record for the subject patent. The petitioner may additionally serve the petition and supporting evidence on the patent owner at any other address known to the petitioner as likely to effect service.

(b) Upon agreement of the parties, service may be made electronically. Service may be by EXPRESS MAIL® or by means at least as fast and reliable as EXPRESS MAIL®. Personal service is not required.

§ 42.206 Filing date.

(a) *Complete petition.* A petition to institute a post-grant review will not be accorded a filing date until the petition satisfies all of the following requirements:

(1) Complies with § 42.204 or § 42.304, as the case may be,

(2) Effects service of the petition on the correspondence address of record as provided in § 42.205(a); and

(3) Is accompanied by the filing fee in § 42.15(b).

(b) *Incomplete petition.* Where a party files an incomplete petition, no filing date will be accorded and the Office will dismiss the request if the deficiency in the petition is not corrected within the earlier of either one month from the notice of an incomplete petition, or the expiration of the statutory deadline in which to file a petition for post-grant review.

§ 42.207 Preliminary response to petition.

(a) The patent owner may file a preliminary response to the petition. The response is limited to setting forth the reasons why no post-grant review should be instituted under 35 U.S.C. 324. The response can include evidence except as provided in paragraph (c) of this section. The preliminary response is subject to the page limits under § 42.24.

(b) *Due date.* The preliminary response must be filed no later than three months after the date of a notice indicating that the request to institute a post-grant review has been granted a filing date. A patent owner may expedite the proceeding by filing an election to waive the patent owner preliminary response.

(c) *No new testimonial evidence.* The preliminary response shall not present new testimony evidence beyond that already of record, except as authorized by the Board.

(d) *No amendment.* The preliminary response shall not include any amendment.

(e) *Disclaim Patent Claims.* The patent owner may file a statutory disclaimer under 35 U.S.C. 253(a) in compliance with § 1.321(a), disclaiming one or more claims in the patent. No post-grant review will be instituted based on disclaimed claims.

INSTITUTING POST-GRANT REVIEW

§ 42.208 Institution of post-grant review.

(a) When instituting post-grant review, the Board may authorize the review to proceed on all or some of the challenged claims and on all or some of the grounds of unpatentability asserted for each claim.

(b) At any time prior to institution of post-grant review, the Board may deny some or all grounds for unpatentability for some or all of the challenged claims. Denial of a ground is a Board decision not to institute post-grant review on that ground.

(c) *Sufficient grounds.* Post-grant review shall not be instituted for a ground of unpatentability, unless the Board decides that the petition supporting the ground would, if unrebutted, demonstrate that it is more likely than not that at least one of the claims challenged in the petition is unpatentable. The Board's decision will take into account a patent owner preliminary response where such a response is filed.

(d) *Additional grounds.* Sufficient grounds under § 42.208(c) may be a showing that the petition raises a novel or unsettled legal question that is important to other patents or patent applications.

AFTER INSTITUTION OF POST-GRANT REVIEW

§ 42.220 Patent owner response.

(a) *Scope.* A patent owner may file a response to the petition addressing any ground for unpatentability not already denied. A patent owner response is filed as an opposition and is subject to the page limits provided in § 42.24.

(b) *Due date for response.* If no date for filing a patent owner response to a petition is provided in a Board order, the default date for filing a patent owner response is three months from the date the post-grant review is instituted.

§ 42.221 Amendment of the patent.

(a) *Motion to amend.* A patent owner may file one motion to amend a patent, but only after conferring with the Board.

(1) *Due date.* Unless a due date is provided in a Board order, a motion to amend must be filed no later than the filing of a patent owner response.

(2) *Scope.* A motion to amend may be denied where:

(i) The amendment does not respond to a ground of unpatentability involved in the trial; or

(ii) The amendment seeks to enlarge the scope of the claims of the patent or introduce new subject matter.

(3) *A reasonable number of substitute claims.* A motion to amend may cancel a challenged claim or propose a reasonable number of substitute claims. The presumption is that only one substitute claim would be needed to replace each challenged claim, and it may be rebutted by a demonstration of need.

(b) *Content.* A motion to amend claims must include a claim listing, show the changes clearly, and set forth:

(1) The support in the original disclosure of the patent for each claim that is added or amended; and

(2) The support in an earlier-filed disclosure for each claim for which benefit of the filing date of the earlier filed disclosure is sought.

(c) *Additional motion to amend.* In addition to the requirements set forth in paragraphs (a) and (b) of this section, any additional motion to amend may not be filed without Board authorization. An additional motion to amend may be authorized when there is a good cause showing or a joint request of the petitioner and the patent owner to materially advance a settlement. In determining whether to authorize such an additional motion to amend, the Board will consider whether a petitioner has submitted supplemental information after the time period set for filing a motion to amend in paragraph (a)(1) of this section.

§ 42.222 Multiple proceedings and Joinder.

(a) *Multiple proceedings.* Where another matter involving the patent is before the Office, the Board may during the pendency of the post-grant review enter any appropriate order regarding the additional matter including providing for the stay, transfer, consolidation, or termination of any such matter.

(b) *Request for joinder.* Joinder may be requested by a patent owner or petitioner. Any request for joinder must be filed, as a motion under § 42.22, no later than one month after the institution date of any post-grant review for which joinder is requested.

§ 42.223 Filing of supplemental information.

(a) *Motion to submit supplemental information.* Once a trial has been instituted, a party may file a motion to submit supplemental information in accordance with the following requirements:

(1) A request for the authorization to file a motion to submit supplemental information is made within one month of the date the trial is instituted.

(2) The supplemental information must be relevant to a claim for which the trial has been instituted.

(b) *Late submission of supplemental information.* A party seeking to submit supplemental information more than one month after the date the trial is instituted, must request authorization to file a motion to submit the information. The motion to submit supplemental information must show why the supplemental information reasonably could not have been obtained earlier, and that consideration of the supplemental information would be in the interests-of-justice.

(c) *Other supplemental information.* A party seeking to submit supplemental information not relevant to a claim for which the trial has been instituted must request authorization to file a motion to submit the information. The motion must show why the supplemental information reasonably could not have been obtained earlier, and that consideration of the supplemental information would be in the interests-of-justice.

§ 42.224 Discovery.

Notwithstanding the discovery provisions of subpart A:

(a) Requests for additional discovery may be granted upon a showing of good cause as to why the discovery is needed; and

(b) Discovery is limited to evidence directly related to factual assertions advanced by either party in the proceeding.

Subpart D—Transitional Program for Covered Business Method Patents

§ 42.300 Procedure; pendency.

(a) A covered business method patent review is a trial subject to the procedures set forth in subpart A of this part and is also subject to the post-grant review procedures set forth in subpart C except for §§ 42.200, 42.201, 42.202, and 42.204.

(b) A claim in an unexpired patent shall be given its broadest reasonable construction in light of the specification of the patent in which it appears.

(c) A covered business method patent review proceeding shall be administered such that pendency before the Board after institution is normally no more than one year. The time can be extended by up to six months for good cause by the Chief Administrative Patent Judge.

(d) The rules in this subpart are applicable until September 15, 2020, except that the rules shall continue to apply to any petition for a covered business method patent review filed before the date of repeal.

§ 42.301 Definitions.

In addition to the definitions in § 42.2, the following definitions apply to proceedings under this subpart D:

(a) *Covered business method patent* means a patent that claims a method or corresponding apparatus for performing data processing or other operations used in the practice, administration, or management of a financial product or service, except that the term does not include patents for technological inventions.

(b) *Technological invention.* In determining whether a patent is for a technological invention solely for purposes of the Transitional Program for Covered Business Methods (section 42.301(a)), the following will be considered on a case-by-case basis: whether the claimed subject matter as a whole recites a technological feature that is novel and unobvious over the prior art; and solves a technical problem using a technical solution.

[77 FR 48753, Aug. 14, 2012]

§ 42.302 Who may petition for a covered business method patent review.

(a) A petitioner may not file with the Office a petition to institute a covered business method patent review of the patent unless the petitioner, the petitioner's real party-in-interest, or a privy of the petitioner has been sued for infringement of the patent or has been charged with infringement under that patent. Charged with infringement means a real and substantial controversy regarding infringement of a covered business method patent exists such that the petitioner would have standing to bring a declaratory judgment action in Federal court.

(b) A petitioner may not file a petition to institute a covered business method patent review of the patent where the petitioner, the petitioner's real party-in-interest, or a privy of the petitioner is estopped from challenging the claims on the grounds identified in the petition.

§42.303 Time for filing.

A petition requesting a covered business method patent review may be filed any time except during the period in which a petition for a post-grant review of the patent would satisfy the requirements of 35 U.S.C. 321(c).

§42.304 Content of petition.

In addition to any other notices required by subparts A and C of this part, a petition must request judgment against one or more claims of a patent identified by patent number. In addition to the requirements of §§42.6, 42.8, 42.22, and 42.24 the petition must set forth:

(a) *Grounds for standing.* The petitioner must demonstrate that the patent for which review is sought is a covered business method patent, and that the petitioner meets the eligibility requirements of §42.302.

(b) *Identification of challenge.* Provide a statement of the precise relief requested for each claim challenged. The statement must identify the following:

(1) The claim;

(2) The specific statutory grounds permitted under paragraph (2) or (3) of 35 U.S.C. 282(b), except as modified by section 18(a)(1)(C) of the Leahy-Smith America Invents Act (Pub. L. 112–29, 125 Stat. 284 (2011)), on which the challenge to the claim is based;

(3) How the challenged claim is to be construed. Where the claim to be construed contains a means-plus-function or step-plus-function limitation as permitted under 35 U.S.C. 112(f), the construction of the claim must identify the specific portions of the specification that describe the structure, material, or acts corresponding to each claimed function;

(4) How the construed claim is unpatentable under the statutory grounds identified in paragraph (b)(2) of this section. Where the grounds for unpatentability are based on prior art, the petition must specify where each element of the claim is found in the prior art. For all other grounds of unpatentability, the petition must identify the specific part of the claim that fails to comply with the statutory grounds raised and state how the identified subject matter fails to comply with the statute; and

(5) The exhibit number of supporting evidence relied upon to support the challenge and the relevance of the evidence to the challenge raised, including identifying specific portions of the evidence that support the challenge. The Board may exclude or give no weight to the evidence where a party has failed to state its relevance or to identify specific portions of the evidence that support the challenge.

(c) A motion may be filed that seeks to correct a clerical or typographical mistake in the petition. The grant of such a motion does not change the filing date of the petition.

Subpart E—Derivation

SOURCE: 77 FR 56090, Sep. 11, 2012, unless otherwise noted.

§42.400 Procedure; pendency

(a) A derivation proceeding is a trial subject to the procedures set forth in subpart A of this part.

(b) The Board may for good cause authorize or direct the parties to address patentability issues that arise in the course of the derivation proceeding.

§42.401 Definitions.

In addition to the definitions in §42.2, the following definitions apply to proceedings under this subpart:

Agreement or *understanding under 35 U.S.C. 135(e)* means settlement for the purposes of §42.74.

Applicant includes a reissue applicant.

Application includes both an application for an original patent and an application for a reissued patent.

First publication means either a patent or an application publication under 35 U.S.C. 122(b), including a publication of an international application designating the United States as provided by 35 U.S.C. 374.

Petitioner means a patent applicant who petitions for a determination that another party named in an earlier-filed patent application allegedly derived a claimed invention from an inventor named in the petitioner's application and filed the earlier application without authorization.

Respondent means a party other than the petitioner.

Same or substantially the same means patentably indistinct.

§ 42.402 Who may file a petition for a derivation proceeding.

An applicant for patent may file a petition to institute a derivation proceeding in the Office.

§ 42.403 Time for filing.

A petition for a derivation proceeding must be filed within the one-year period beginning on the date of the first publication of a claim to an invention that is the same or substantially the same as the earlier application's claim to the allegedly derived invention.

§ 42.404 Derivation fee.

(a) A derivation fee set forth in § 42.15(c) must accompany the petition.

(b) No filing date will be accorded to the petition until payment is complete.

§ 42.405 Content of petition.

(a) *Grounds for standing.* The petition must:

(1) Demonstrate compliance with §§ 42.402 and 42.403; and

(2) Show that the petitioner has at least one claim that is:

(i) The same or substantially the same as the respondent's claimed invention; and

(ii) The same or substantially the same as the invention disclosed to the respondent.

(b) In addition to the requirements of §§ 42.8 and 42.22, the petition must:

(1) Provide sufficient information to identify the application or patent for which the petitioner seeks a derivation proceeding;

(2) Demonstrate that a claimed invention was derived from an inventor named in the petitioner's application, and that the inventor from whom the invention was derived did not authorize the filing of the earliest application claiming such invention; and

(3) For each of the respondent's claims to the derived invention,

(i) Show why the claimed invention is the same or substantially the same as the invention disclosed to the respondent, and

(ii) Identify how the claim is to be construed. Where the claim to be construed contains a means-plus-function or step-plus-function limitation as permitted under 35 U.S.C. 112(f), the construction of the claim must identify the specific portions of the specification that describe the structure, material, or acts corresponding to each claimed function.

(c) *Sufficiency of showing.* A derivation showing is not sufficient unless it is supported by substantial evidence, including at least one affidavit addressing communication of the derived invention and lack of authorization that, if unrebutted, would support a determination of derivation. The showing of communication must be corroborated.

§ 42.406 Service of petition.

In addition to the requirements of § 42.6, the petitioner must serve the petition and exhibits relied upon in the petition as follows:

(a) The petition and supporting evidence must be served on the respondent at the correspondence address of record for the earlier application or subject patent. The petitioner may additionally serve the petition and supporting evidence on the respondent at any other address known to the petitioner as likely to effect service.

(b) Upon agreement of the parties, service may be made electronically. Service may be by EXPRESS MAIL® or by means at least as fast and reliable as EXPRESS MAIL®. Personal service is not required.

§ 42.407 Filing date.

(a) *Complete petition.* A petition to institute a derivation proceeding will not be accorded a filing date until the petition satisfies all of the following requirements:

(1) Complies with §§ 42.404 and 42.405, and

(2) Service of the petition on the correspondence address of record as provided in § 42.406.

(b) *Incomplete petition.* Where the petitioner files an incomplete petition, no filing date will be accorded, and the Office will dismiss the petition if the deficiency in the petition is not corrected within the earlier of either one month from notice of the incomplete petition, or the expiration of the statutory deadline in which to file a petition for derivation.

INSTITUTING DERIVATION PROCEEDING

§42.408 Institution of derivation proceeding.

(a) An administrative patent judge institutes, and may as necessary reinstitute, the derivation proceeding on behalf of the Director.

(b) *Additional derivation proceeding.* The petitioner may suggest the addition of a patent or application to the derivation proceeding. The suggestion should make the showings required under §42.405 and explain why the suggestion could not have been made in the original petition.

AFTER INSTITUTION OF DERIVATION PROCEEDING

§42.409 Settlement agreements.

An agreement or understanding under 35 U.S.C. 135(e) is a settlement for the purposes of §42.74.

§42.410 Arbitration.

(a) Parties may resort to binding arbitration to determine any issue. The Office is not a party to the arbitration. The Board is not bound by, and may independently determine, any question of patentability.

(b) The Board will not set a time for, or otherwise modify the proceeding for, an arbitration unless:

(1) It is to be conducted according to Title 9 of the United States Code;

(2) The parties notify the Board in writing of their intention to arbitrate;

(3) The agreement to arbitrate:

(i) Is in writing;

(ii) Specifies the issues to be arbitrated;

(iii) Names the arbitrator, or provides a date not more than 30 days after the execution of the agreement for the selection of the arbitrator;

(iv) Provides that the arbitrator's award shall be binding on the parties and that judgment thereon can be entered by the Board;

(v) Provides that a copy of the agreement is filed within 20 days after its execution; and

(vi) Provides that the arbitration is completed within the time the Board sets.

(c) The parties are solely responsible for the selection of the arbitrator and the conduct of the arbitration.

(d) The Board may determine issues the arbitration does not resolve.

(e) The Board will not consider the arbitration award unless it:

(1) Is binding on the parties;

(2) Is in writing;

(3) States in a clear and definite manner each issue arbitrated and the disposition of each issue; and

(4) Is filed within 20 days of the date of the award.

(f) Once the award is filed, the parties to the award may not take actions inconsistent with the award. If the award is dispositive of the contested subject matter for a party, the Board may enter judgment as to that party.

§42.411 Common interests in the invention.

The Board may decline to institute, or if already instituted the Board may issue judgment in, a derivation proceeding between an application and a patent or another application that are commonly owned.

§42.412 Public availability of Board records.

(a) *Publication.* (1) *Generally.* Any Board decision is available for public inspection without a party's permission if rendered in a file open to the public pursuant to §1.11 of this chapter or in an application that has been published in accordance with §§1.211 to 1.221 of this chapter. The Office may independently publish any Board decision that is available for public inspection.

(2) *Determination of special circumstances.* Any Board decision not publishable under paragraph (a)(1) of this section may be published or made available for public inspection if the Director believes that special circumstances warrant publication and a party does not petition within two months after being notified of the intention to make the decision public, objecting in writing on the ground that the decision discloses the objecting

party's trade secret or other confidential information and stating with specificity that such information is not otherwise publicly available.

(b) *Record of proceeding.* (1) The record of a Board proceeding is available to the public, unless a patent application not otherwise available to the public is involved.

(2) Notwithstanding paragraph (b)(1) of this section, after a final Board decision in or judgment in a Board proceeding, the record of the Board proceeding will be made available to the public if any involved file is or becomes open to the public under § 1.11 of this chapter or an involved application is or becomes published under §§ 1.211 to 1.221 of this chapter.

PART 90—JUDICIAL REVIEW OF PATENT TRIAL AND APPEAL BOARD DECISIONS

AUTHORITY: 35 U.S.C. 2(b)(2).

SOURCE: 77 FR 48677, Aug. 14, 2012, unless otherwise noted.

§ 90.1 Scope.

The provisions herein govern judicial review for Patent Trial and Appeal Board decisions under chapter 13 of title 35, United States Code. Judicial review of decisions arising out of *inter partes* reexamination proceedings that are requested under 35 U.S.C. 311, and where available, judicial review of decisions arising out of interferences declared pursuant to 35 U.S.C. 135 continue to be governed by the pertinent regulations in effect on July 1, 2012.

§ 90.2 Notice; service.

(a) *For an appeal under 35 U.S.C. 141.* (1) In all appeals, the notice of appeal required by 35 U.S.C. 142 must be filed with the Director of the United States Patent and Trademark Office as provided in § 104.2 of this title. A copy of the notice of appeal must also be filed with the Patent Trial and Appeal Board in the appropriate manner provided in § 41.10(a), 41.10(b), or 42.6(b).

(2) In all appeals, the party initiating the appeal must comply with the requirements of the Federal Rules of Appellate Procedure and Rules for the United States Court of Appeals for the Federal Circuit, including:

(i) Serving the requisite number of copies on the Court; and

(ii) Paying the requisite fee for the appeal.

(3) *Additional requirements.* (i) In appeals arising out of an *ex parte* reexamination proceeding ordered pursuant to § 1.525, notice of the appeal must be served as provided in § 1.550(f) of this title.

(ii) In appeals arising out of an *inter partes* review, a post-grant review, a covered business method patent review, or a derivation proceeding, notice of the appeal must provide sufficient information to allow the Director to determine whether to exercise the right to intervene in the appeal pursuant to 35 U.S.C. 143, and it must be served as provided in § 42.6(e) of this title.

(b) *For a notice of election under 35 U.S.C. 141(d) to proceed under 35 U.S.C. 146.* (1) Pursuant to 35 U.S.C. 141(d), if an adverse party elects to have all further review proceedings conducted under 35 U.S.C. 146 instead of under 35 U.S.C. 141, that party must file a notice of election with the United States Patent and Trademark Office as provided in § 104.2.

(2) A copy of the notice of election must also be filed with the Patent Trial and Appeal Board in the manner provided in § 42.6(b).

(3) A copy of the notice of election must also be served where necessary pursuant to § 42.6(e).

(c) *For a civil action under 35 U.S.C. 146.* The party initiating an action under 35 U.S.C. 146 must file a copy of the complaint no later than five business days after filing the complaint in district court with the Patent Trial and Appeal Board in the manner provided in § 42.6(b), and the Office of the Solicitor pursuant to § 104.2. Failure to comply with this requirement can result in further action within the United States Patent and Trademark Office consistent with the final Board decision.

§90.3 Time for appeal or civil action.

(a) *Filing deadline.* (1) *For an appeal under 35 U.S.C. 141.* The notice of appeal filed pursuant to 35 U.S.C. 142 must be filed with the Director of the United States Patent and Trademark Office no later than sixty-three (63) days after the date of the final Board decision. Any notice of cross-appeal is controlled by Rule 4(a)(3) of the Federal Rules of Appellate Procedure, and any other requirement imposed by the Rules of the United States Court of Appeals for the Federal Circuit.

(2) *For a notice of election under 35 U.S.C. 141(d).* The time for filing a notice of election under 35 U.S.C. 141(d) is governed by 35 U.S.C. 141(d).

(3) *For a civil action under 35 U.S.C. 145 or 146.* (i) A civil action must be commenced no later than sixty-three (63) days after the date of the final Board decision.

(ii) The time for commencing a civil action pursuant to a notice of election under 35 U.S.C. 141(d) is governed by 35 U.S.C. 141(d).

(b) *Time computation.* (1) *Rehearing.* A timely request for rehearing will reset the time for appeal or civil action to no later than sixty-three (63) days after action on the request. Any subsequent request for rehearing from the same party in the same proceeding will not reset the time for seeking judicial review, unless the additional request is permitted by order of the Board.

(2) *Holidays.* If the last day for filing an appeal or civil action falls on a Federal holiday in the District of Columbia, the time is extended pursuant to 35 U.S.C. 21(b).

(c) *Extension of time.* (1) The Director, or his designee, may extend the time for filing an appeal, or commencing a civil action, upon written request if:

(i) Requested before the expiration of the period for filing an appeal or commencing a civil action, and upon a showing of good cause; or

(ii) Requested after the expiration of the period for filing an appeal of commencing a civil action, and upon a showing that the failure to act was the result of excusable neglect.

(2) The request must be filed as provided in §104.2 of this title.

INDEX III—RULES RELATING TO PRACTICE BEFORE THE PATENT AND TRADEMARK OFFICE

EDITORIAL NOTE: This listing is provided for informational purposes only. It is compiled and kept current by the Department of Commerce. This index is updated as of July 1, 2013.

S

T

U

V

W

Z

SUBCHAPTER B—ADMINISTRATION

PARTS 100–101 [RESERVED]

PART 102—DISCLOSURE OF GOVERNMENT INFORMATION

Subpart A—Freedom of Information Act

Subpart B—Privacy Act

AUTHORITY: 5 U.S.C. 552; 5 U.S.C. 552a; 5 U.S.C. 553; 31 U.S.C. 3717; 35 U.S.C. 2(b)(2), 21, 41, 42, 122; 44 U.S.C. 3101.

SOURCE: 65 FR 52917, Aug. 31, 2000, unless otherwise noted.

Subpart A—Freedom of Information Act

§ 102.1 General.

(a) The information in this part is furnished for the guidance of the public and in compliance with the requirements of the Freedom of Information Act (FOIA), as amended (5 U.S.C. 552). This part sets forth the procedures the United States Patent and Trademark Office (USPTO) follows to make publicly available the materials and indices specified in 5 U.S.C. 552(a)(2) and records requested under 5 U.S.C. 552(a)(3). Information routinely provided to the public as part of a regular USPTO activity (for example, press releases issued by the Office of Public Affairs) may be provided to the public without following this part. USPTO's policy is to make discretionary disclosures of records or information exempt from disclosure under FOIA whenever disclosure would not foreseeably harm an interest protected by a FOIA exemption, but this policy does not create any right enforceable in court.

(b) As used in this subpart, *FOIA Officer* means the USPTO employee designated to administer FOIA for USPTO. To ensure prompt processing of a request, correspondence should be addressed to the FOIA Officer, United States Patent and Trademark Office, P.O. Box 1450, Alexandria, Virginia 22313–1450, or delivered by hand to 10B20, Madison Building East, 600 Dulany Street, Alexandria, Virginia.

[65 FR 52917, Aug. 31, 2000, as amended at 68 FR 14338, Mar. 25, 2003; 70 FR 10489, Mar. 4, 2005]

§ 102.2 Public reference facilities.

(a) USPTO maintains a public reference facility that contains the records FOIA requires to be made regularly available for public inspection and copying; furnishes information and otherwise assists the public concerning USPTO operations under FOIA; and receives and processes requests for records under FOIA. The FOIA Officer is responsible for determining which of USPTO's records are required to be made available for public inspection and copying, and for making those records available in USPTO's reference and records inspection facility. The FOIA Officer shall maintain and make available for public inspection and copying a current subject-matter index of USPTO's public inspection facility records. Each index shall be updated regularly, at least quarterly, with respect to newly included records. In accordance with 5 U.S.C. 552(a)(2), USPTO has determined that it is unnecessary and impracticable to publish quarterly, or more frequently, and distribute copies of the index and supplements thereto. The public reference facility is located in the Public Search Room, Madison Building East, First Floor, 600 Dulany Street, Alexandria, Virginia.

(b) The FOIA Officer shall also make public inspection facility records created by USPTO on or after November 1, 1996, available electronically through USPTO's World Wide Web site (*http://www.uspto.gov*). Information available at the site shall include:

(1) The FOIA Officer's index of the public inspection facility records, which indicates which records are available electronically; and

(2) The general index referred to in paragraph (c)(3) of this section.

(c) USPTO maintains and makes available for public inspection and copying:

(1) A current index providing identifying information for the public as to any matter that is issued, adopted, or promulgated after July 4, 1967, and that is retained as a record and is required to be made available or published. Copies of the index are available upon request after payment of the direct cost of duplication;

(2) Copies of records that have been released and that the FOIA Officer determines, because of their subject matter, have become or are likely to become the subject of subsequent requests for substantially the same records;

(3) A general index of the records described in paragraph (c)(2) of this section;

(4) Final opinions and orders, including concurring and dissenting opinions made in the adjudication of cases;

(5) Those statements of policy and interpretations that have been adopted by USPTO and are not published in the FEDERAL REGISTER; and

(6) Administrative staff manuals and instructions to staff that affect a member of the public.

[65 FR 52917, Aug. 31, 2000, as amended at 75 FR 36295, June 25, 2010]

§ 102.3 Records under FOIA.

(a) Records under FOIA include all Government records, regardless of format, medium or physical characteristics, and include electronic records and information, audiotapes, videotapes, and photographs.

(b) There is no obligation to create, compile, or obtain from outside USPTO a record to satisfy a FOIA request. With regard to electronic data, the issue of whether records are created or merely extracted from an existing database is not always apparent. When responding to FOIA requests for electronic data where creation of a record or programming becomes an issue, USPTO shall undertake reasonable efforts to search for the information in electronic format.

(c) USPTO officials may, upon request, create and provide new information pursuant to user fee statutes, such as the first paragraph of 15 U.S.C. 1525, or in accordance with authority otherwise provided by law. This is outside the scope of FOIA.

(d) The FOIA Officer shall preserve all correspondence pertaining to the requests received under this subpart, as well as copies of all requested records, until disposition or destruction is authorized by Title 44 of the United States Code or a National Archives and Records Administration's General Records Schedule. The FOIA Officer shall not dispose of records while they are the subject of a pending request, appeal, or lawsuit under FOIA.

§ 102.4 Requirements for making requests.

(a) A request for USPTO records that are not customarily made available to the public as part of USPTO's regular informational services must be in writing, and shall be processed under FOIA, regardless of whether FOIA is mentioned in the request. Requests should be sent to the USPTO FOIA Officer, United States Patent and Trademark Office, P.O. Box 1450, Alexandria, Virginia 22313–1450 (records FOIA requires to be made regularly available for public inspection and copying are addressed in § 102.2(c)). For the quickest handling, the request letter and envelope should be marked "Freedom of Information Act Request." For requests for records about oneself, § 102.24 contains additional requirements. For requests for records about another individual, either a written authorization signed by that individual permitting disclosure of those records to the requester or proof that individual is deceased (for example, a copy of a death certificate or an obituary) facilitates processing the request.

(b) The records requested must be described in enough detail to enable USPTO personnel to locate them with a reasonable amount of effort. Whenever possible, a request should include specific information about each record sought, such as the date, title or name, author, recipient, and subject matter of the record, and the name and location of the office where the record is located. Also, if records about a court case are sought, the title of the case, the court in which the case was filed, and the nature of the case should be included. If known, any file designations or descriptions for the requested records should be included. In general, the more specifically the request describes the records sought, the greater the likelihood that USPTO will locate those records. If the FOIA Officer determines that a request does not reasonably describe records, the FOIA Officer will inform the requester what additional information is needed or why the request is otherwise insufficient. The FOIA Officer also may give the requester an opportunity to discuss the request so that it may be modified to meet the requirements of this section.

[65 FR 52917, Aug. 31, 2000, as amended at 68 FR 14338, Mar. 25, 2003]

§ 102.5 Responsibility for responding to requests.

(a) *In general.* Except as stated in paragraph (b) of this section, the USPTO will process FOIA requests directed to USPTO. In determining records responsive to a request, the FOIA Officer shall include only those records within USPTO's possession and control as of the date the FOIA Officer receives the request.

(b) *Consultations and referrals.* If the FOIA Officer receives a request for a record in USPTO's possession in which another Federal agency subject to FOIA has the primary interest, the FOIA Officer shall refer the record to that agency for direct response to the requester. The FOIA Officer shall consult with another Federal agency before responding to a requester if the FOIA Officer receives a request for a record in which another Federal agency subject to FOIA has a significant interest, but not the primary interest; or another Federal agency not subject to FOIA has the primary interest or a significant interest. Ordinarily, the agency that originated a record will be presumed to have the primary interest in it.

(c) *Notice of referral.* Whenever a FOIA Officer refers a document to another Federal agency for direct response to the requester, the FOIA Officer will ordinarily notify the requester in writing of the referral and inform the requester of the name of the agency to which the document was referred.

(d) *Timing of responses to consultations and referrals.* All consultations and referrals shall be handled according to the date the FOIA request was received by the first Federal agency.

(e) *Agreements regarding consultations and referrals.* The FOIA Officer may make agreements with other Federal agencies to eliminate the need for consultations or referrals for particular types of records.

§ 102.6 Time limits and expedited processing.

(a) *In general.* The FOIA Officer ordinarily shall respond to requests according to their order of receipt.

(b) *Initial response and appeal.* Subject to paragraph (c)(1) of this section, an initial response shall be made within 20 working days (*i.e.*, excluding Saturdays, Sundays, and legal public holidays) of the receipt of a request for a record under this part by the proper FOIA Officer identified in accordance with § 102.5(a), and an appeal shall be decided within 20 working days of its receipt by the Office of the General Counsel.

(c) *Unusual circumstances.* (1) In unusual circumstances as specified in paragraph (c)(2) of this section, the FOIA Officer may extend the time limits in paragraph (b) of this section by notifying the requester in writing as soon as practicable of the unusual circumstances and of the date by which processing of the request is expected to be completed. Extensions of time for the initial determination and extensions on appeal may not exceed a total of ten working days, unless the requester agrees to a longer extension, or the FOIA Officer provides the requester with an opportunity either to limit the scope of the request so that it may be processed within the applicable time limit, or to arrange an alternative time frame for processing the request or a modified request.

(2) As used in this section, *unusual circumstances* means, but only to the extent reasonably necessary to properly process the particular request:

(i) The need to search for and collect the requested records from field facilities or other establishments separate from the office processing the request;

(ii) The need to search for, collect, and appropriately examine a voluminous amount of separate and distinct records that are the subject of a single request; or

(iii) The need for consultation, which shall be conducted with all practicable speed, with another Federal agency having a substantial interest in the determination of the request.

(3) Unusual circumstances do not include a delay that results from a predictable workload of requests, unless USPTO demonstrates reasonable progress in reducing its backlog of pending requests. Refusal to reasonably modify the scope of a request or arrange an alternate time frame may affect a requester's ability to obtain judicial review.

(4) If the FOIA Officer reasonably believes that multiple requests submitted by a requester, or by a group of requesters acting in concert, constitute a single request that would otherwise involve unusual circumstances, and the requests involve clearly related matters, the FOIA Officer may aggregate them. Multiple requests involving unrelated matters will not be aggregated.

(d) *Multitrack processing.* (1) The FOIA Officer may use two or more processing tracks by distinguishing between simple and more complex requests based on the number of pages involved, or some other measure of the amount of work and/or time needed to process the request, and whether the request qualifies for expedited processing as described in paragraph (e) of this section.

(2) The FOIA Officer may provide requesters in a slower track with an opportunity to limit the scope of their requests in order to qualify for faster processing. The FOIA Officer may contact the requester by telephone or by letter, whichever is most efficient in each case.

(e) *Expedited processing.* (1) Requests and appeals shall be taken out of order and given expedited treatment whenever it is determined they involve:

(i) Circumstances in which the lack of expedited treatment could reasonably be expected to pose an imminent threat to the life or physical safety of an individual;

(ii) The loss of substantial due process rights;

(iii) A matter of widespread and exceptional media interest in which there exist questions about the Government's integrity that affect public confidence; or

(iv) An urgency to inform the public about an actual or alleged Federal Government activity, if made by a person primarily engaged in disseminating information.

(2) A request for expedited processing may be made at the time of the initial request for records or at any later time. For a prompt determination, a request for expedited processing should be sent to the FOIA Officer.

(3) A requester who seeks expedited processing must submit a statement, certified to be true and correct to the best of that person's knowledge and belief, explaining in detail the basis for requesting expedited processing. For example, a requester within the category described in paragraph (e)(1)(iv) of this section, if not a full-time member of the news media, must establish that he or she is a person whose main professional activity or occupation is information dissemination, though it need not be his or her sole occupation.

A requester within the category described in paragraph (e)(1)(iv) of this section must also establish a particular urgency to inform the public about the Government activity involved in the request, beyond the public's right to know about Government activity generally. The formality of certification may be waived as a matter of administrative discretion.

(4) Within ten calendar days of receipt of a request for expedited processing, the FOIA Officer will decide whether to grant it and shall notify the requester of the decision. If a request for expedited treatment is granted, the request shall be given priority and processed as soon as practicable. If a request for expedited processing is denied, any appeal of that decision shall be acted on expeditiously.

§ 102.7 Responses to requests.

(a) *Grants of requests.* If the FOIA Officer makes a determination to grant a request in whole or in part, the FOIA Officer will notify the requester in writing. The FOIA Officer will inform the requester in the notice of any fee charged under § 102.11 and disclose records to the requester promptly upon payment of any applicable fee. Records disclosed in part shall be marked or annotated to show each applicable FOIA exemption and the amount of information deleted, unless doing so would harm an interest protected by an applicable exemption. The location of the information deleted shall also be indicated on the record, if feasible.

(b) *Adverse determinations of requests.* If the FOIA Officer makes an adverse determination regarding a request, the FOIA Officer will notify the requester of that determination in writing. An adverse determination is a denial of a request in any respect, namely: A determination to withhold any requested record in whole or in part; a determination that a requested record does not exist or cannot be located; a determination that a record is not readily reproducible in the form or format sought by the requester; a determination that what has been requested is not a record subject to FOIA (except that a determination under § 102.11(j) that records are to be made available under a fee statute other than FOIA is not an adverse determination); a determination against the requester on any disputed fee matter, including a denial of a request for a fee waiver; or a denial of a request for expedited treatment. Each denial letter shall be signed by the FOIA Officer and shall include:

(1) The name and title or position of the denying official;

(2) A brief statement of the reason(s) for the denial, including applicable FOIA exemption(s);

(3) An estimate of the volume of records or information withheld, in number of pages or some other reasonable form of estimation. This estimate need not be provided if the volume is otherwise indicated through deletions on records disclosed in part, or if providing an estimate would harm an interest protected by an applicable FOIA exemption; and

(4) A statement that the denial may be appealed, and a list of the requirements for filing an appeal under § 102.10(b).

§ 102.9 Business Information.

(a) *In general.* Business information obtained by USPTO from a submitter will be disclosed under FOIA only under this section.

(b) *Definitions.* For the purposes of this section:

(1) *Business information* means commercial or financial information, obtained by USPTO from a submitter, which may be protected from disclosure under FOIA exemption 4 (5 U.S.C. 552(b)(4)).

(2) *Submitter* means any person or entity outside the Federal Government from whom USPTO obtains business information, directly or indirectly. The term includes corporations; state, local and tribal governments; and foreign governments.

(c) *Designation of business information.* A submitter of business information should designate by appropriate markings, either at the time of submission or at a reasonable time thereafter, any portions of its submission that it considers to be protected from disclosure under FOIA exemption 4. These designations will expire ten years after the date of the submission unless the submitter requests, and provides justification for, a longer designation period.

(d) *Notice to submitters.* The FOIA Officer shall provide a submitter with prompt written notice of a FOIA request or administrative appeal that seeks its business information whenever required under paragraph (e) of this section, except as provided in paragraph (h) of this section, in order to give the submitter an opportunity under paragraph (f) of this section to object to disclosure of any specified portion of that information. Such written notice shall be sent via certified mail, return receipt requested, or similar means. The notice shall either describe the business information requested or include copies of the requested records containing the information. When notification of a large number of submitters is required, notification may be made by posting or publishing the notice in a place reasonably likely to accomplish notification.

(e) *When notice is required.* Notice shall be given to the submitter whenever:

(1) The information has been designated in good faith by the submitter as protected from disclosure under FOIA exemption 4; or

(2) The FOIA Officer has reason to believe that the information may be protected from disclosure under FOIA exemption 4.

(f) *Opportunity to object to disclosure.* The FOIA Officer shall allow a submitter seven working days (*i.e.*, excluding Saturdays, Sundays, and legal public holidays) from the date of receipt of the written notice described in paragraph (d) of this section to provide the FOIA Officer with a detailed statement of any objection to disclosure. The statement must specify all grounds for withholding any portion of the information under any exemption of FOIA and, in the case of exemption 4, it must show why the information is a trade secret or commercial or financial information that is privileged or confidential. If a submitter fails to respond to the notice within the time specified, the submitter will be considered to have no objection to disclosure of the information. Information a submitter provides under this paragraph may itself be subject to disclosure under FOIA.

(g) *Notice of intent to disclose.* The FOIA Officer shall consider a submitter's objections and specific grounds under FOIA for nondisclosure in deciding whether to disclose business information. If the FOIA Officer decides to disclose business information over the objection of a submitter, the FOIA Officer shall give the submitter written notice via certified mail, return receipt requested, or similar means, which shall include:

(1) A statement of reason(s) why the submitter's objections to disclosure were not sustained;

(2) A description of the business information to be disclosed; and

(3) A statement that the FOIA Officer intends to disclose the information seven working days from the date the submitter receives the notice.

(h) *Exceptions to notice requirements.* The notice requirements of paragraphs (d) and (g) of this section shall not apply if:

(1) The FOIA Officer determines that the information should not be disclosed;

(2) The information has been lawfully published or has been officially made available to the public;

(3) Disclosure of the information is required by statute (other than FOIA) or by a regulation issued in accordance with Executive Order 12600; or

(4) The designation made by the submitter under paragraph (c) of this section appears obviously frivolous, in which case the FOIA Officer shall provide the submitter written notice of any final decision to disclose the information seven working days from the date the submitter receives the notice.

(i) *Notice of FOIA lawsuit.* Whenever a requester files a lawsuit seeking to compel the disclosure of business information, the FOIA Officer shall promptly notify the submitter.

(j) *Corresponding notice to requesters.* Whenever a FOIA Officer provides a submitter with notice and an opportunity to object to disclosure under paragraph (d) of this section, the FOIA Officer shall also notify the requester(s). Whenever a submitter files a lawsuit seeking to prevent the disclosure of business information, the FOIA Officer shall notify the requester(s).

§ 102.10 Appeals from initial determinations or untimely delays.

(a) If a request for records is initially denied in whole or in part, or has not been timely determined, or if a requester receives an adverse initial determination regarding any other matter under this subpart (as described in § 102.7(b)), the requester may file a written appeal, which must be received by the Office of General Counsel within thirty calendar days of the date of the written denial or, if there has been no determination, may be submitted anytime after the due date, including the last extension under § 102.6(c), of the determination.

(b) Appeals shall be decided by a Deputy General Counsel. Appeals should be addressed to the General Counsel, United States Patent and Trademark Office, PO Box 1450, Alexandria, Virginia 22313–1450. Both the letter and the appeal envelope should be clearly marked "Freedom of Information Appeal". The appeal must include a copy of the original request and the initial denial, if any, and may include a statement of the reasons why the records requested should be made available and why the initial denial, if any, was in error. No opportunity for personal appearance, oral argument or hearing on appeal is provided.

(c) If an appeal is granted, the person making the appeal shall be immediately notified and copies of the releasable documents shall be made available promptly thereafter upon receipt of appropriate fees determined in accordance with § 102.11.

(d) If no determination of an appeal has been sent to the requester within the twenty-working-day period specified in § 102.6(b) or the last extension thereof, the requester is deemed to have exhausted his administrative remedies with respect to the request, giving rise to a right of judicial review under 5 U.S.C. 552(a)(6)(C). If the person making a request initiates a civil action against USPTO based on the provision in this paragraph, the administrative appeal process may continue.

(e) A determination on appeal shall be in writing and, when it denies records in whole or in part, the letter to the requester shall include:

(1) A brief explanation of the basis for the denial, including a list of applicable FOIA exemptions and a description of how the exemptions apply;

(2) A statement that the decision is final;

(3) Notification that judicial review of the denial is available in the United States district court for the district in which the requester resides or has its principal place of business, the United States District Court for the Eastern District of Virginia, or the District of Columbia; and

(4) The name and title or position of the official responsible for denying the appeal.

[65 FR 52917, Aug. 31, 2000, as amended at 68 FR 14338, Mar. 25, 2003]

§ 102.11 Fees.

(a) *In general.* USPTO shall charge for processing requests under FOIA in accordance with paragraph (c) of this section, except when fees are limited under paragraph (d) of this section or when a waiver or reduction of fees is granted under paragraph (k) of this section. USPTO shall collect all applicable fees before sending copies of requested records to a requester. Requesters must pay fees by check or money order made payable to the Treasury of the United States.

(b) *Definitions.* For purposes of this section:

(1) *Commercial use request* means a request from or on behalf of a person who seeks information for a use or purpose that furthers his or her commercial, trade, or profit interests, which can include furthering those interests through litigation. The FOIA Officer shall determine, whenever reasonably possible, the use to which a requester will put the requested records. When it appears that the requester will put the records to a commercial use, either because of the nature of the request itself or because the FOIA Officer has reasonable cause to doubt a requester's stated use, the FOIA Officer shall provide the requester a reasonable opportunity to submit further clarification.

(2) *Direct costs* means those expenses USPTO incurs in searching for and duplicating (and, in the case of commercial use requests, reviewing) records to respond to a FOIA request. Direct costs include, for example, the labor costs of the employee performing the work (the basic rate of pay for the employee, plus 16 percent of that rate to cover benefits). Not included in direct costs are overhead expenses such as the costs of space and heating or lighting of the facility in which the records are kept.

(3) *Duplication* means the making of a copy of a record, or of the information contained in it, necessary to respond to a FOIA request. Copies may take the form of paper, microform, audiovisual materials, or electronic records (for example, magnetic tape or disk), among others. The FOIA Officer shall honor a requester's specified preference of form or format of disclosure if the record is readily reproducible with reasonable efforts in the requested form or format.

(4) *Educational institution* means a preschool, a public or private elementary or secondary school, an institution of undergraduate higher education, an institution of graduate higher education, an institution of professional education, or an institution of vocational education, that operates a program of scholarly research. To be in this category, a requester must show that the request is authorized by and is made under the auspices of a qualifying institution, and that the records are sought to further scholarly research rather than for a commercial use.

(5) *Noncommercial scientific institution* means an institution that is not operated on a "commercial" basis, as that term is defined in paragraph (b)(1) of this section, and that is operated solely for the purpose of conducting scientific research, the results of which are not intended to promote any particular product or industry. To be in this category, a requester must show that the request is authorized by and is made under the auspices of a qualifying institution and that the records are sought to further scientific research rather than for a commercial use.

(6) *Representative of the news media, or news media requester* means any person actively gathering news for an entity that is organized and operated to publish or broadcast news to the public. The term "news" means information that is about current events or that would be of current interest to the public. Examples of news media entities include television or radio stations broadcasting to the public at large and publishers of periodicals (but only if they can qualify as disseminators of "news") that make their products available for purchase or subscription by the general public. For "freelance" journalists to be regarded as working for a news organization, they must demonstrate a solid basis for expecting publication through that organization. A publication contract would be the clearest proof, but the FOIA Officer shall also look to the past publication record of a requester in making this determination. To be in this category, a requester must not be seeking the requested records for a commercial use. However, a request for records supporting the news-dissemination function of the requester shall not be considered to be for a commercial use.

(7) *Review* means the examination of a record located in response to a request in order to determine whether any portion of it is exempt from disclosure. It also includes processing any record for disclosure—for example, doing all that is necessary to redact it and prepare it for disclosure. Review costs are recoverable even if a record ultimately is not disclosed. Review time does not include time spent resolving general legal or policy issues regarding the application of exemptions.

(8) *Search* means the process of looking for and retrieving records or information responsive to a request. It includes page-by-page or line-by-line identification of information within records and also includes reasonable efforts to locate and retrieve information from records maintained in electronic form or format. The FOIA Officer shall ensure that searches are done in the most efficient and least expensive manner reasonably possible.

(c) *Fees.* In responding to FOIA requests, the FOIA Officer shall charge the fees summarized in chart form in paragraphs (c)(1) and (c)(2) of this section and explained in paragraphs (c)(3) through (c)(5) of this section, unless a waiver or reduction of fees has been granted under paragraph (k) of this section.

(1) The four categories and chargeable fees are:

Category	Chargeable fees
(i) Commercial Use Requesters	Search, Review, and Duplication.
(ii) Educational and Non-commercial Scientific Institution Requesters.	Duplication (excluding the cost of the first 100 pages).
(iii) Representatives of the News Media	Duplication (excluding the cost of the first 100 pages).
(iv) All Other Requesters	Search and Duplication (excluding the cost of the first 2 hours of search and 100 pages).

(2) *Uniform fee schedule.*

Service	Rate
(i) Manual search	Actual salary rate of employee involved, plus 16 percent of salary rate.
(ii) Computerized search	Actual direct cost, including operator time.
(iii) Duplication of records:	
(A) Paper copy reproduction	$.15 per page
(B) Other reproduction (e.g., computer disk or printout, microfilm, microfiche, or microform).	Actual direct cost, including operator time.
(iv) Review of records (includes preparation for release, *i.e.* excising).	Actual salary rate of employee conducting review, plus 16 percent of salary rate.

(3) *Search.* (i) Search fees shall be charged for all requests—other than requests made by educational institutions, noncommercial scientific institutions, or representatives of the news media—subject to the limitations of paragraph (d) of this section. The FOIA Officer will charge for time spent searching even if no responsive records are located or if located records are entirely exempt from disclosure. Search fees shall be the direct costs of conducting the search by the involved employees.

(ii) For computer searches of records, requesters will be charged the direct costs of conducting the search, although certain requesters (as provided in paragraph (d)(1) of this section) will be charged no search fee and certain other requesters (as provided in paragraph (d)(3) of this section) are entitled to the cost equivalent of two hours of manual search time without charge. These direct costs include the costs, attributable to the search, of operating a central processing unit and operator/programmer salary.

(4) *Duplication.* Duplication fees will be charged to all requesters, subject to the limitations of paragraph (d) of this section. For a paper photocopy of a record (no more than one copy of which need be supplied), the fee shall be $.15 cents per page. For copies produced by computer, such as tapes or printouts, the FOIA Officer shall charge the direct costs, including operator time, of producing the copy. For other forms of duplication, the FOIA Officer will charge the direct costs of that duplication.

(5) *Review.* Review fees shall be charged to requesters who make a commercial use request. Review fees shall be charged only for the initial record review—the review done when the FOIA Officer determines whether an exemption applies to a particular record at the initial request level. No charge will be made for review at the administrative appeal level for an exemption already applied. However, records withheld under an exemption that is subsequently determined not to apply may be reviewed again to determine whether any other exemption not previously considered applies, and the costs of that review are chargeable. Review fees shall be the direct costs of conducting the review by the involved employees.

(d) *Limitations on charging fees.* (1) No search fee will be charged for requests by educational institutions, noncommercial scientific institutions, or representatives of the news media.

(2) No search fee or review fee will be charged for a quarter-hour period unless more than half of that period is required for search or review.

(3) Except for requesters seeking records for a commercial use, the FOIA Officer will provide without charge:

(i) The first 100 pages of duplication (or the cost equivalent); and

(ii) The first two hours of search (or the cost equivalent).

(4) Whenever a total fee calculated under paragraph (c) of this section is $20.00 or less for any request, no fee will be charged.

(5) The provisions of paragraphs (d) (3) and (4) of this section work together. This means that for requesters other than those seeking records for a commercial use, no fee will be charged unless the cost of the search in excess of two hours plus the cost of duplication in excess of 100 pages totals more than $20.00.

(e) *Notice of anticipated fees over $20.00.* When the FOIA Officer determines or estimates that the fees to be charged under this section will be more than $20.00, the FOIA Officer shall notify the requester of the actual or estimated fees, unless the requester has indicated a willingness to pay fees as high as those anticipated. If only a portion of the fee can be estimated readily, the FOIA Officer shall advise the requester that the estimated fee may be only a portion of the total fee. If the FOIA Officer has notified a requester that actual or estimated fees are more than $20.00, the FOIA Officer shall not consider the request received or process it further until the requester agrees to pay the anticipated total fee. Any such agreement should be in writing. A notice under this paragraph shall offer the requester an opportunity to discuss the matter with USPTO personnel in order to reformulate the request to meet the requester's needs at a lower cost.

(f) *Charges for other services.* Apart from the other provisions of this section, the FOIA Officer shall ordinarily charge the direct cost of special services. Such special services could include certifying that records are true copies or sending records by other than ordinary mail.

(g) *Charging interest.* The FOIA Officer shall charge interest on any unpaid bill starting on the 31st calendar day following the date of billing the requester. Interest charges shall be assessed at the rate provided in 31 U.S.C. 3717 and accrue from the date of the billing until payment is received by the FOIA Officer. The FOIA Officer shall follow the provisions of the Debt Collection Improvement Act of 1996 (Pub. L. 104–134), as amended, and its administrative procedures, including the use of consumer reporting agencies, collection agencies, and offset.

(h) *Aggregating requests.* If a FOIA Officer reasonably believes that a requester or a group of requesters acting together is attempting to divide a request into a series of requests for the purpose of avoiding fees, the FOIA Officer may aggregate those requests and charge accordingly. The FOIA Officer may presume that multiple requests of this type made within a 30-calendar-day period have been made in order to avoid fees. If requests are separated by a longer period, the FOIA Officer shall aggregate them only if a solid basis exists for determining that aggregation is warranted under all the circumstances involved. Multiple requests involving unrelated matters shall not be aggregated.

(i) *Advance payments.* (1) For requests other than those described in paragraphs (i)(2) and (3) of this section, the FOIA Officer shall not require the requester to make an advance payment: a payment made before work is begun or continued on a request. Payment owed for work already completed (*i.e.*, a payment before copies are sent to a requester) is not an advance payment.

(2) If the FOIA Officer determines or estimates that a total fee to be charged under this section will be more than $250.00, the requester must pay the entire anticipated fee before beginning to process the request, unless the FOIA Officer receives a satisfactory assurance of full payment from a requester who has a history of prompt payment.

(3) If a requester has previously failed to pay a properly charged FOIA fee to USPTO or another responsible Federal agency within 30 calendar days of the date of billing, the FOIA Officer shall require the requester to pay the full

amount due, plus any applicable interest, and to make an advance payment of the full amount of any anticipated fee, before the FOIA Officer begins to process a new request or continues to process a pending request from that requester.

(4) In cases in which the FOIA Officer requires payment under paragraphs (i)(2) or (3) of this section, the request shall not be considered received and further work will not be done on it until the required payment is received.

(5) Upon the completion of processing of a request, when a specific fee is determined to be payable and appropriate notice has been given to the requester, the FOIA Officer shall make records available to the requester only upon receipt of full payment of the fee.

(j) *Other statutes specifically providing for fees.* The fee schedule of this section does not apply to fees charged under any statute (except for FOIA) that specifically requires USPTO or another responsible Federal agency to set and collect fees for particular types of records. If records responsive to requests are maintained for distribution by agencies operating such statutorily based fee schedule programs, the FOIA Officer shall inform requesters of how to obtain records from those sources.

(k) *Requirements for waiver or reduction of fees.* (1) Records responsive to a request will be furnished without charge or at a charge reduced below that established under paragraph (c) of this section if the FOIA Officer determines, based on all available information, that the requester has demonstrated that:

(i) Disclosure of the requested information is in the public interest because it is likely to contribute significantly to public understanding of the operations or activities of the Government; and

(ii) Disclosure of the information is not primarily in the commercial interest of the requester.

(2) To determine whether the first fee waiver requirement is met, the FOIA Officer shall consider the following factors:

(i) *The subject of the request:* whether the subject of the requested records concerns the operations or activities of the Government. The subject of the requested records must concern identifiable operations or activities of the Federal Government, with a connection that is direct and clear, not remote or attenuated.

(ii) *The informative value of the information to be disclosed:* whether the disclosure is "likely to contribute" to an understanding of Government operations or activities. The disclosable portions of the requested records must be meaningfully informative about Government operations or activities in order to be "likely to contribute" to an increased public understanding of those operations or activities. The disclosure of information that already is in the public domain, in either a duplicative or a substantially identical form, would not be likely to contribute to such understanding.

(iii) *The contribution to an understanding of the subject by the public likely to result from disclosure:* whether disclosure of the requested information will contribute to the understanding of a reasonably broad audience of persons interested in the subject, as opposed to the individual understanding of the requester. A requester's expertise in the subject area and ability and intention to effectively convey information to the public shall be considered. It shall be presumed that a representative of the news media satisfies this consideration. It shall be presumed that a requester who merely provides information to media sources does not satisfy this consideration.

(iv) *The significance of the contribution to public understanding:* whether the disclosure is likely to contribute "significantly" to public understanding of Government operations or activities. The public's understanding of the subject in question prior to the disclosure must be significantly enhanced by the disclosure.

(3) To determine whether the second fee waiver requirement is met, the FOIA Officer shall consider the following factors:

(i) *The existence and magnitude of a commercial interest:* whether the requester has a commercial interest that would be furthered by the requested disclosure. The FOIA Officer shall consider any commercial interest of the requester (with reference to the definition of "commercial use request" in paragraph (b)(1) of this section), or of any person on whose behalf the requester may be acting, that would be furthered by the requested disclosure. Requesters shall be given an opportunity to provide explanatory information regarding this consideration.

(ii) *The primary interest in disclosure:* whether any identified commercial interest of the requester is sufficiently large, in comparison with the public interest in disclosure, that disclosure is "primarily in the commercial interest of the requester." A fee waiver or reduction is justified if the public interest standard (paragraph (k)(1)(i) of this section) is satisfied and the public interest is greater than any identified commercial interest in disclosure. The FOIA Officer ordinarily shall presume that if a news media requester has satisfied the public interest standard, the public interest is the primary interest served by disclosure to that requester. Disclosure to data brokers or others who merely compile and market Government information for direct economic return shall not be presumed to primarily serve the public interest.

(4) If only some of the records to be released satisfy the requirements for a fee waiver, a waiver shall be granted for those records.

(5) Requests for the waiver or reduction of fees should address the factors listed in paragraphs (k)(2) and (3) of this section, insofar as they apply to each request.

Subpart B—Privacy Act

§ 102.21 Purpose and scope.

(a) The purpose of this subpart is to establish policies and procedures for implementing the Privacy Act of 1974, as amended (5 U.S.C. 552a) (the Act). The main objectives are to facilitate full exercise of rights conferred on individuals under the Act and to ensure the protection of privacy as to individuals on whom USPTO maintains records in systems of records under the Act. USPTO accepts the responsibility to act promptly and in accordance with the Act upon receipt of any inquiry, request or appeal from a citizen of the United States or an alien lawfully admitted for permanent residence into the United States, regardless of the age of the individual. Further, USPTO accepts the obligations to maintain only such information on individuals as is relevant and necessary to the performance of its lawful functions, to maintain that information with such accuracy, relevancy, timeliness, and completeness as is reasonably necessary to assure fairness in determinations made by USPTO about the individual, to obtain information from the individual to the extent practicable, and to take every reasonable step to protect that information from unwarranted disclosure. USPTO will maintain no record describing how an individual exercises rights guaranteed by the First Amendment unless expressly authorized by statute or by the individual about whom the record is maintained or unless pertinent to and within the scope of an authorized law enforcement activity. An individual's name and address will not be sold or rented by USPTO unless such action is specifically authorized by law; however, this provision shall not be construed to require the withholding of names and addresses otherwise permitted to be made public.

(b) This subpart is administered by the Privacy Officer of USPTO.

(c) Matters outside the scope of this subpart include the following:

(1) Requests for records which do not pertain to the individual making the request, or to the individual about whom the request is made if the requester is the parent or guardian of the individual;

(2) Requests involving information pertaining to an individual which is in a record or file but not within the scope of a system of records notice published in the FEDERAL REGISTER;

(3) Requests to correct a record where a grievance procedure is available to the individual either by regulation or by provision in a collective bargaining agreement with USPTO, and the individual has initiated, or has expressed in writing the intention of initiating, such grievance procedure. An individual selecting the grievance procedure waives the use of the procedures in this subpart to correct or amend a record; and,

(4) Requests for employee-employer services and counseling which were routinely granted prior to enactment of the Act, including, but not limited to, test calculations of retirement benefits, explanations of health and life insurance programs, and explanations of tax withholding options.

(d) Any request for records which pertains to the individual making the request, or to the individual about whom the request is made if the requester is the parent or guardian of the individual, shall be processed under the Act and this subpart and under the Freedom of Information Act and USPTO's implementing regulations at Subpart A of this part, regardless whether the Act or the Freedom of Information Act is mentioned in the request.

§ 102.22 Definitions.

(a) All terms used in this subpart which are defined in 5 U.S.C. 552a shall have the same meaning herein.

(b) As used in this subpart:

(1) *Act* means the "Privacy Act of 1974, as amended (5 U.S.C. 552a)".

(2) *Appeal* means a request by an individual to review and reverse an initial denial of a request by that individual for correction or amendment.

(3) *USPTO* means the United States Patent and Trademark Office.

(4) *Inquiry* means either a request for general information regarding the Act and this subpart or a request by an individual (or that individual's parent or guardian) that USPTO determine whether it has any record in a system of records which pertains to that individual.

(5) *Person* means any human being and also shall include but not be limited to, corporations, associations, partnerships, trustees, receivers, personal representatives, and public or private organizations.

(6) *Privacy Officer* means a USPTO employee designated to administer this subpart.

(7) *Request for access* means a request by an individual or an individual's parent or guardian to see a record which is in a particular system of records and which pertains to that individual.

(8) *Request for correction or amendment* means the request by an individual or an individual's parent or guardian that USPTO change (either by correction, amendment, addition or deletion) a particular record in a system of records which pertains to that individual.

§ 102.23 Procedures for making inquiries.

(a) Any individual, regardless of age, who is a citizen of the United States or an alien lawfully admitted for permanent residence into the United States may submit an inquiry to USPTO. The inquiry should be made either in person at 10B20, Madison Building East, 600 Dulany Street, Alexandria, Virginia, or by mail addressed to the Privacy Officer, United States Patent and Trademark Office, P.O. Box 1450, Alexandria, Virginia 22313–1450, or to the official identified in the notification procedures paragraph of the systems of records notice published in the FEDERAL REGISTER. If an individual believes USPTO maintains a record pertaining to that individual but does not know which system of records might contain such a record, the USPTO Privacy Officer will provide assistance in person or by mail.

(b) Inquiries submitted by mail should include the words "PRIVACY ACT INQUIRY" in capital letters at the top of the letter and on the face of the envelope. If the inquiry is for general information regarding the Act and this subpart, no particular information is required. USPTO reserves the right to require compliance with the identification procedures appearing at § 102.24(d) where circumstances warrant. If the inquiry is a request that USPTO determine whether it has, in a given system of records, a record which pertains to the individual, the following information should be submitted:

(1) Name of individual whose record is sought;

(2) Individual whose record is sought is either a U.S. citizen or an alien lawfully admitted for permanent residence;

(3) Identifying data that will help locate the record (for example, maiden name, occupational license number, period or place of employment, etc.);

(4) Record sought, by description and by record system name, if known;

(5) Action requested (that is, sending information on how to exercise rights under the Act; determining whether requested record exists; gaining access to requested record; or obtaining copy of requested record);

(6) Copy of court guardianship order or minor's birth certificate, as provided in §102.24(f)(3), but only if requester is guardian or parent of individual whose record is sought;

(7) Requester's name (printed), signature, address, and telephone number (optional);

(8) Date; and,

(9) Certification of request by notary or other official, but only if

(i) Request is for notification that requested record exists, for access to requested record or for copy of requested record;

(ii) Record is not available to any person under 5 U.S.C. 552; and

(iii) Requester does not appear before an employee of USPTO for verification of identity.

(c) Any inquiry which is not addressed as specified in paragraph (a) of this section or which is not marked as specified in paragraph (b) of this section will be so addressed and marked by USPTO personnel and forwarded immediately to the Privacy Officer. An inquiry which is not properly addressed by the individual will not be deemed to have been "received" for purposes of measuring the time period for response until actual receipt by the Privacy Officer. In each instance when an inquiry so forwarded is received, the Privacy Officer shall notify the individual that his or her inquiry was improperly addressed and the date the inquiry was received at the proper address.

(d)(1) Each inquiry received shall be acted upon promptly by the Privacy Officer. Every effort will be made to respond within ten working days (*i.e.*, excluding Saturdays, Sundays and legal public holidays) of the date of receipt. If a response cannot be made within ten working days, the Privacy Officer shall send an acknowledgment during that period providing information on the status of the inquiry and asking for such further information as may be necessary to process the inquiry. The first correspondence sent by the Privacy Officer to the requester shall contain USPTO's control number assigned to the request, as well as a note that the requester should use that number in all future contacts in order to facilitate processing. USPTO shall use that control number in all subsequent correspondence.

(2) If the Privacy Officer fails to send an acknowledgment within ten working days, as provided above, the requester may ask the General Counsel to take corrective action. No failure of the Privacy Officer to send an acknowledgment shall confer administrative finality for purposes of judicial review.

(e) An individual shall not be required to state a reason or otherwise justify his or her inquiry.

(f) Special note should be taken of the fact that certain agencies are responsible for publishing notices of systems of records having Government-wide application to other agencies, including USPTO. The agencies known to be publishing these general notices and the types of records covered therein appear in an appendix to this part. The provisions of this section, and particularly paragraph (a) of this section, should be followed in making inquiries with respect to such records. Such records in USPTO are subject to the provisions of this part to the extent indicated in the appendix to this part. The exemptions, if any, determined by an agency publishing a general notice shall be invoked and applied by USPTO after consultation, as necessary, with that other agency.

[65 FR 52917, Aug. 31, 2000, as amended at 68 FR 14338, Mar. 25, 2003; 70 FR 10489, Mar. 4, 2005]

§ 102.24 Procedures for making requests for records.

(a) Any individual, regardless of age, who is a citizen of the United States or an alien lawfully admitted for permanent residence into the United States may submit a request to the USPTO for access to records. The request should be made either in person at 10B20, Madison Building East, 600 Dulany Street, Alexandria, Virginia, or by mail addressed to the Privacy Officer, United States Patent and Trademark Office, P.O. Box 1450, Alexandria, Virginia 22313–1450.

(b) Requests submitted by mail should include the words "PRIVACY ACT REQUEST" in capital letters at the top of the letter and on the face of the envelope. Any request which is not addressed as specified in paragraph (a) of this section or which is not marked as specified in this paragraph will be so addressed and marked by USPTO personnel and forwarded immediately to the Privacy Officer. A request which is not properly addressed by the individual will not be deemed to have been "received" for purposes of measuring time periods for response until actual receipt by the Privacy Officer. In each instance when a request so forwarded is received, the Privacy Officer shall notify the individual that his or her request was improperly addressed and the date when the request was received at the proper address.

(c) If the request follows an inquiry under § 102.23 in connection with which the individual's identity was established by USPTO, the individual need only indicate the record to which access is sought, provide the USPTO control number assigned to the request, and sign and date the request. If the request is not preceded by an inquiry under § 102.23, the procedures of this section should be followed.

(d) The requirements for identification of individuals seeking access to records are as follows:

(1) *In person.* Each individual making a request in person shall be required to present satisfactory proof of identity. The means of proof, in the order of preference and priority, are:

(i) A document bearing the individual's photograph (for example, driver's license, passport or military or civilian identification card);

(ii) A document, preferably issued for participation in a federally sponsored program, bearing the individual's signature (for example, unemployment insurance book, employer's identification card, national credit card, and professional, craft or union membership card); and

(iii) A document bearing neither the photograph nor the signature of the individual, preferably issued for participation in a federally sponsored program (for example, Medicaid card). In the event the individual can provide no suitable documentation of identity, USPTO will require a signed statement asserting the individual's identity and stipulating that the individual understands the penalty provision of 5 U.S.C. 552a(i)(3) recited in § 102.32(a). In order to avoid any unwarranted disclosure of an individual's records, USPTO reserves the right to determine the adequacy of proof of identity offered by any individual, particularly when the request involves a sensitive record.

(2) *Not in person.* If the individual making a request does not appear in person before the Privacy Officer or other employee authorized to determine identity, a certification of a notary public or equivalent officer empowered to administer oaths must accompany the request under the circumstances prescribed in § 102.23(b)(9). The certification in or attached to the letter must be substantially in accordance with the following text:

City of ______
County of ______ :ss
(Name of individual), who affixed (his) (her) signature below in my presence, came before me, a (title), in and for the aforesaid County and State, this _____ day of _____, 20__, and established (his) (her) identity to my satisfaction.
My commission expires ______.
(Signature)

(3) *Parents of minors and legal guardians.* An individual acting as the parent of a minor or the legal guardian of the individual to whom a record pertains shall establish his or her personal identity in the same manner prescribed in either paragraph (d)(1) or (d)(2) of this section. In addition, such other individual shall establish his or her identity in the representative capacity of parent or legal guardian. In the case of the parent of a minor, the proof of identity shall be a certified or authenticated copy of the minor's birth certificate. In the case of a legal guardian of an individual who has been declared incompetent due to physical or mental incapacity or age by a court of competent jurisdiction, the proof of identity shall be a certified or authenticated copy of the court's order. For purposes of the Act, a parent or legal guardian may represent only a living individual, not a decedent. A parent or legal guardian may be accompanied

during personal access to a record by another individual, provided the provisions of § 102.25(f) are satisfied.

(e) When the provisions of this subpart are alleged to impede an individual in exercising his or her right to access, USPTO will consider, from an individual making a request, alternative suggestions regarding proof of identity and access to records.

(f) An individual shall not be required to state a reason or otherwise justify his or her request for access to a record.

[65 FR 52917, Aug. 31, 2000, as amended at 68 FR 14338, Mar. 25, 2003; 70 FR 10490, Mar. 4, 2005]

§ 102.25 Disclosure of requested records to individuals.

(a)(1) The Privacy Officer shall act promptly upon each request. Every effort will be made to respond within ten working days (*i.e.*, excluding Saturdays, Sundays, and legal public holidays) of the date of receipt. If a response cannot be made within ten working days due to unusual circumstances, the Privacy Officer shall send an acknowledgment during that period providing information on the status of the request and asking for any further information that may be necessary to process the request. "Unusual circumstances" shall include circumstances in which

(i) A search for and collection of requested records from inactive storage, field facilities or other establishments is required;

(ii) A voluminous amount of data is involved;

(iii) Information on other individuals must be separated or expunged from the particular record; or

(iv) Consultations with other agencies having a substantial interest in the determination of the request are necessary.

(2) If the Privacy Officer fails to send an acknowledgment within ten working days, as provided above in paragraph (a) of this section, the requester may ask the General Counsel to take corrective action. No failure of the Privacy Officer to send an acknowledgment shall confer administrative finality for purposes of judicial review.

(b) *Grant of access*—(1) *Notification.* An individual shall be granted access to a record pertaining to him or her, except where the provisions of paragraph (g)(1) of this section apply. The Privacy Officer will notify the individual of a determination to grant access, and provide the following information:

(i) The methods of access, as set forth in paragraph (b)(2) of this section;

(ii) The place at which the record may be inspected;

(iii) The earliest date on which the record may be inspected and the period of time that the records will remain available for inspection. In no event shall the earliest date be later than thirty calendar days from the date of notification;

(iv) The estimated date by which a copy of the record could be mailed and the estimate of fees pursuant to § 102.31. In no event shall the estimated date be later than thirty calendar days from the date of notification;

(v) The fact that the individual, if he or she wishes, may be accompanied by another individual during personal access, subject to the procedures set forth in paragraph (f) of this section; and,

(vi) Any additional requirements needed to grant access to a specific record.

(2) *Methods of access.* The following methods of access to records by an individual may be available depending on the circumstances of a given situation:

(i) Inspection in person may be had in a location specified by the Privacy Officer during business hours;

(ii) Transfer of records to a Federal facility more convenient to the individual may be arranged, but only if the Privacy Officer determines that a suitable facility is available, that the individual's access can be properly supervised at that facility, and that transmittal of the records to that facility will not unduly interfere with operations of USPTO or involve unreasonable costs, in terms of both money and manpower; and

(iii) Copies may be mailed at the request of the individual, subject to payment of the fees prescribed in § 102.31. USPTO, on its own initiative, may elect to provide a copy by mail, in which case no fee will be charged the individual.

(c) Access to medical records is governed by the provisions of § 102.26.

(d) USPTO will supply such other information and assistance at the time of access as to make the record intelligible to the individual.

(e) USPTO reserves the right to limit access to copies and abstracts of original records, rather than the original records. This election would be appropriate, for example, when the record is in an automated data media such as tape or diskette, when the record contains information on other individuals, and when deletion of information is permissible under exemptions (for example, 5 U.S.C. 552a(k)(2)). In no event shall original records of USPTO be made available to the individual except under the immediate supervision of the Privacy Officer or the Privacy Officer's designee.

(f) Any individual who requests access to a record pertaining to that individual may be accompanied by another individual of his or her choice. "Accompanied" includes discussion of the record in the presence of the other individual. The individual to whom the record pertains shall authorize the presence of the other individual in writing. The authorization shall include the name of the other individual, a specific description of the record to which access is sought, the USPTO control number assigned to the request, the date, and the signature of the individual to whom the record pertains. The other individual shall sign the authorization in the presence of the Privacy Officer. An individual shall not be required to state a reason or otherwise justify his or her decision to be accompanied by another individual during personal access to a record.

(g) *Initial denial of access*—(1) *Grounds.* Access by an individual to a record which pertains to that individual will be denied only upon a determination by the Privacy Officer that:

(i) The record is exempt under § 102.33 or § 102.34, or exempt by determination of another agency publishing notice of the system of records, as described in § 102.23(f);

(ii) The record is information compiled in reasonable anticipation of a civil action or proceeding;

(iii) The provisions of § 102.26 pertaining to medical records temporarily have been invoked; or

(iv) The individual has unreasonably failed to comply with the procedural requirements of this part.

(2) *Notification.* The Privacy Officer shall give notice of denial of access to records to the individual in writing and shall include the following information:

(i) The Privacy Officer's name and title or position;

(ii) The date of the denial;

(iii) The reasons for the denial, including citation to the appropriate section of the Act and this part;

(iv) The individual's opportunities, if any, for further administrative consideration, including the identity and address of the responsible official. If no further administrative consideration within USPTO is available, the notice shall state that the denial is administratively final; and

(v) If stated to be administratively final within USPTO, the individual's right to judicial review provided under 5 U.S.C. 552a(g)(1), as limited by 5 U.S.C. 552a(g)(5).

(3) *Administrative review.* When an initial denial of a request is issued by the Privacy Officer, the individual's opportunities for further consideration shall be as follows:

(i) As to denial under paragraph (g)(1)(i) of this section, two opportunities for further consideration are available in the alternative:

(A) If the individual contests the application of the exemption to the records, review procedures in § 102.25(g)(3)(ii) shall apply; or

(B) If the individual challenges the exemption itself, the procedure is a petition for the issuance, amendment, or repeal of a rule under 5 U.S.C. 553(e). If the exemption was determined by USPTO, such petition shall be filed with the General Counsel. If the exemption was determined by another agency (as described in § 102.23(f)), USPTO will provide the individual with the name and address of the other agency and any relief sought by the individual shall be that provided by the regulations of the other agency. Within USPTO, no such denial is administratively final until such a petition has been filed by the individual and disposed of on the merits by the General Counsel.

(ii) As to denial under paragraphs (g)(1)(ii) of this section, (g)(1)(iv) of this section or (to the limited extent provided in paragraph (g)(3)(i)(A) of this section) paragraph (g)(1)(i) of this section, the individual may file for review with the General Counsel, as indicated in the Privacy Officer's initial denial notification. The procedures appearing in § 102.28 shall be followed by both the individual and USPTO to the maximum extent practicable.

(iii) As to denial under paragraph (g)(1)(iii) of this section, no further administrative consideration within USPTO is available because the denial is not administratively final until expiration of the time period indicated in § 102.26(a).

(h) If a request is partially granted and partially denied, the Privacy Officer shall follow the appropriate procedures of this section as to the records within the grant and the records within the denial.

§ 102.26 Special procedures: Medical records.

(a) No response to any request for access to medical records by an individual will be issued by the Privacy Officer for a period of seven working days (*i.e.*, excluding Saturdays, Sundays, and legal public holidays) from the date of receipt.

(b) USPTO has published as a routine use, for all systems of records containing medical records, consultations with an individual's physician or psychologist if, in the sole judgment of USPTO, disclosure could have an adverse effect upon the individual. The mandatory waiting period set forth in paragraph (a) of this section will permit exercise of this routine use in appropriate cases. USPTO will pay no cost of any such consultation.

(c) In every case of a request by an individual for access to medical records, the Privacy Officer shall:

(1) Inform the individual of the waiting period prescribed in paragraph (a) of this section;

(2) Obtain the name and address of the individual's physician and/or psychologist, if the individual consents to give them;

(3) Obtain specific, written consent for USPTO to consult the individual's physician and/or psychologist in the event that USPTO believes such consultation is advisable, if the individual consents to give such authorization;

(4) Obtain specific, written consent for USPTO to provide the medical records to the individual's physician or psychologist in the event that USPTO believes access to the record by the individual is best effected under the guidance of the individual's physician or psychologist, if the individual consents to give such authorization; and

(5) Forward the individual's medical record to USPTO's medical expert for review and a determination on whether consultation with or transmittal of the medical records to the individual's physician or psychologist is warranted. If the consultation with or transmittal of such records to the individual's physician or psychologist is determined to be warranted, USPTO's medical expert shall so consult or transmit. Whether or not such a consultation or transmittal occurs, USPTO's medical officer shall provide instruction to the Privacy Officer regarding the conditions of access by the individual to his or her medical records.

(d) If an individual refuses in writing to give the names and consents set forth in paragraphs (c)(2) through (c)(4) of this section and USPTO has determined that disclosure could have an adverse effect upon the individual, USPTO shall give the individual access to said records by means of a copy, provided without cost to the requester, sent registered mail return receipt requested.

§ 102.27 Procedures for making requests for correction or amendment.

(a) Any individual, regardless of age, who is a citizen of the United States or an alien lawfully admitted for permanent residence into the United States may submit a request for correction or amendment to USPTO. The request should be made either in person or by mail addressed to the Privacy Officer who processed the individual's request for access to the record, and to whom is delegated authority to make initial determinations on requests for correction or amendment. The office of the Privacy Officer is open to the public between the hours of 9 a.m. and 4 p.m., Monday through Friday (excluding legal public holidays).

(b) Requests submitted by mail should include the words "PRIVACY ACT REQUEST" in capital letters at the top of the letter and on the face of the envelope. Any request which is not addressed as specified in paragraph (a) of this section or which is not marked as specified in this paragraph will be so addressed and marked by USPTO personnel and forwarded immediately to the Privacy Officer. A request which is not properly addressed by the individual will not be deemed to have been "received" for purposes of measuring the time period for response until actual receipt by the Privacy Officer. In each instance when a request so forwarded is received, the Privacy Officer shall notify the individual that his or her request was improperly addressed and the date the request was received at the proper address.

(c) Since the request, in all cases, will follow a request for access under § 102.25, the individual's identity will be established by his or her signature on the request and use of the USPTO control number assigned to the request.

(d) A request for correction or amendment should include the following:

(1) Specific identification of the record sought to be corrected or amended (for example, description, title, date, paragraph, sentence, line and words);

(2) The specific wording to be deleted, if any;

(3) The specific wording to be inserted or added, if any, and the exact place at which to be inserted or added; and

(4) A statement of the basis for the requested correction or amendment, with all available supporting documents and materials which substantiate the statement. The statement should identify the criterion of the Act being invoked, that is, whether the information in the record is unnecessary, inaccurate, irrelevant, untimely or incomplete.

§ 102.28 Review of requests for correction or amendment.

(a)(1)(i) Not later than ten working days (*i.e.*, excluding Saturdays, Sundays and legal public holidays) after receipt of a request to correct or amend a record, the Privacy Officer shall send an acknowledgment providing an estimate of time within which action will be taken on the request and asking for such further information as may be necessary to process the request. The estimate of time may take into account unusual circumstances as described in § 102.25(a). No acknowledgment will be sent if the request can be reviewed, processed, and the individual notified of the results of review (either compliance or denial) within the ten working days. Requests filed in person will be acknowledged in writing at the time submitted.

(ii) If the Privacy Officer fails to send the acknowledgment within ten working days, as provided in paragraph (a)(1)(i) of this section, the requester may ask the General Counsel to take corrective action. No failure of the Privacy Officer to send an acknowledgment shall confer administrative finality for purposes of judicial review.

(2) Promptly after acknowledging receipt of a request, or after receiving such further information as might have been requested, or after arriving at a decision within the ten working days, the Privacy Officer shall either:

(i) Make the requested correction or amendment and advise the individual in writing of such action, providing either a copy of the corrected or amended record or a statement as to the means whereby the correction or amendment was effected in cases where a copy cannot be provided (for example, erasure of information from a record maintained only in magnetically recorded computer files); or

(ii) Inform the individual in writing that his or her request is denied and provide the following information:

(A) The Privacy Officer's name and title or position;

(B) The date of the denial;

(C) The reasons for the denial, including citation to the appropriate sections of the Act and this subpart; and

(D) The procedures for appeal of the denial as set forth in § 102.29, including the address of the General Counsel.

(3) The term *promptly* in this section means within thirty working days (*i.e.*, excluding Saturdays, Sundays, and legal public holidays). If the Privacy Officer cannot make the determination within thirty working days, the individual will be advised in writing of the reason therefor and of the estimated date by which the determination will be made.

(b) Whenever an individual's record is corrected or amended pursuant to a request by that individual, the Privacy Officer shall be responsible for notifying all persons and agencies to which the corrected or amended portion of the record had been disclosed prior to its correction or amendment, if an accounting of such disclosure required by the Act was made. The notification shall require a recipient agency maintaining the record to acknowledge receipt of the notification, to correct or amend the record, and to apprise any agency or person to which it had disclosed the record of the substance of the correction or amendment.

(c) The following criteria will be considered by the Privacy Officer in reviewing a request for correction or amendment:

(1) The sufficiency of the evidence submitted by the individual;

(2) The factual accuracy of the information;

(3) The relevance and necessity of the information in terms of purpose for which it was collected;

(4) The timeliness and currency of the information in light of the purpose for which it was collected;

(5) The completeness of the information in terms of the purpose for which it was collected;

(6) The degree of risk that denial of the request could unfairly result in determinations adverse to the individual;

(7) The character of the record sought to be corrected or amended; and

(8) The propriety and feasibility of complying with the specific means of correction or amendment requested by the individual.

(d) USPTO will not undertake to gather evidence for the individual, but does reserve the right to verify the evidence which the individual submits.

(e) Correction or amendment of a record requested by an individual will be denied only upon a determination by the Privacy Officer that:

(1) The individual has failed to establish, by a preponderance of the evidence, the propriety of the correction or amendment in light of the criteria set forth in paragraph (c) of this section;

(2) The record sought to be corrected or amended is part of the official record in a terminated judicial, quasi-judicial, or quasi-legislative proceeding to which the individual was a party or participant;

(3) The information in the record sought to be corrected or amended, or the record sought to be corrected or amended, is the subject of a pending judicial, quasi-judicial, or quasi-legislative proceeding to which the individual is a party or participant;

(4) The correction or amendment would violate a duly enacted statute or promulgated regulation; or

(5) The individual has unreasonably failed to comply with the procedural requirements of this part.

(f) If a request is partially granted and partially denied, the Privacy Officer shall follow the appropriate procedures of this section as to the records within the grant and the records within the denial.

§ 102.29 Appeal of initial adverse determination on correction or amendment.

(a) When a request for correction or amendment has been denied initially under § 102.28, the individual may submit a written appeal within thirty working days (*i.e.*, excluding Saturdays, Sundays and legal public holidays) after the date of the initial denial. When an appeal is submitted by mail, the postmark is conclusive as to timeliness.

(b) An appeal should be addressed to the General Counsel, United States Patent and Trademark Office, PO Box 1450, Alexandria, Virginia 22313–1450. An appeal should include the words

"PRIVACY APPEAL" in capital letters at the top of the letter and on the face of the envelope. An appeal not addressed and marked as provided herein will be so marked by USPTO personnel when it is so identified and will be forwarded immediately to the General Counsel. An appeal which is not properly addressed by the individual will not be deemed to have been "received" for purposes of measuring the time periods in this section until actual receipt by the General Counsel. In each instance when an appeal so forwarded is received, the General Counsel shall notify the individual that his or her appeal was improperly addressed and the date when the appeal was received at the proper address.

(c) The individual's appeal shall include a statement of the reasons why the initial denial is believed to be in error and USPTO's control number assigned to the request. The appeal shall be signed by the individual. The record which the individual requests be corrected or amended and all correspondence between the Privacy Officer and the requester will be furnished by the Privacy Officer who issued the initial denial. Although the foregoing normally will comprise the entire record on appeal, the General Counsel may seek additional information necessary to assure that the final determination is fair and equitable and, in such instances, disclose the additional information to the individual to the greatest extent possible, and provide an opportunity for comment thereon.

(d) No personal appearance or hearing on appeal will be allowed.

(e) The General Counsel shall act upon the appeal and issue a final determination in writing not later than thirty working days (*i.e.*, excluding Saturdays, Sundays and legal public holidays) from the date on which the appeal is received, except that the General Counsel may extend the thirty days upon deciding that a fair and equitable review cannot be made within that period, but only if the individual is advised in writing of the reason for the extension and the estimated date by which a final determination will issue. The estimated date should not be later than the sixtieth working day after receipt of the appeal unless unusual circumstances, as described in §102.25(a), are met.

(f) If the appeal is determined in favor of the individual, the final determination shall include the specific corrections or amendments to be made and a copy thereof shall be transmitted promptly both to the individual and to the Privacy Officer who issued the initial denial. Upon receipt of such final determination, the Privacy Officer promptly shall take the actions set forth in §102.28(a)(2)(i) and (b).

(g) If the appeal is denied, the final determination shall be transmitted promptly to the individual and state the reasons for the denial. The notice of final determination also shall inform the individual of the following:

(1) The right of the individual under the Act to file a concise statement of reasons for disagreeing with the final determination. The statement ordinarily should not exceed one page and USPTO reserves the right to reject a statement of excessive length. Such a statement shall be filed with the General Counsel. It should provide the USPTO control number assigned to the request, indicate the date of the final determination and be signed by the individual. The General Counsel shall acknowledge receipt of such statement and inform the individual of the date on which it was received.

(2) The facts that any such disagreement statement filed by the individual will be noted in the disputed record, that the purposes and uses to which the statement will be put are those applicable to the record in which it is noted, and that a copy of the statement will be provided to persons and agencies to which the record is disclosed subsequent to the date of receipt of such statement;

(3) The fact that USPTO will append to any such disagreement statement filed by the individual, a copy of the final determination or summary thereof which also will be provided to persons and agencies to which the disagreement statement is disclosed; and,

(4) The right of the individual to judicial review of the final determination under 5 U.S.C. 552a(g)(1)(A), as limited by 5 U.S.C. 552a(g)(5).

(h) In making the final determination, the General Counsel shall employ the criteria set forth in § 102.28(c) and shall deny an appeal only on the grounds set forth in § 102.28(e).

(i) If an appeal is partially granted and partially denied, the General Counsel shall follow the appropriate procedures of this section as to the records within the grant and the records within the denial.

(j) Although a copy of the final determination or a summary thereof will be treated as part of the individual's record for purposes of disclosure in instances where the individual has filed a disagreement statement, it will not be subject to correction or amendment by the individual.

(k) The provisions of paragraphs (g)(1) through (g)(3) of this section satisfy the requirements of 5 U.S.C. 552a(e)(3).

[65 FR 52917, Aug. 31, 2000, as amended at 68 FR 14339, Mar. 25, 2003]

§ 102.30 Disclosure of record to person other than the individual to whom it pertains.

(a) USPTO may disclose a record pertaining to an individual to a person other than the individual to whom it pertains only in the following instances:

(1) Upon written request by the individual, including authorization under § 102.25(f);

(2) With the prior written consent of the individual;

(3) To a parent or legal guardian under 5 U.S.C. 552a(h);

(4) When required by the Act and not covered explicitly by the provisions of 5 U.S.C. 552a(b); and

(5) When permitted under 5 U.S.C. 552a(b)(1) through (12), which read as follows: [1]

(i) To those officers and employees of the agency which maintains the record who have a need for the record in the performance of their duties;

(ii) Required under 5 U.S.C. 552 ;

(iii) For a routine use as defined in 5 U.S.C. 552a(a)(7) and described under 5 U.S.C. 552a(e)(4)(D);

(iv) To the Bureau of the Census for purposes of planning or carrying out a census or survey or related activity pursuant to the provisions of Title 13;

(v) To a recipient who has provided the agency with advance adequate written assurance that the record will be used solely as a statistical research or reporting record, and the record is to be transferred in a form that is not individually identifiable;

(vi) To the National Archives and Records Administration as a record which has sufficient historical or other value to warrant its continued preservation by the United States Government, or for evaluation by the Archivist of the United States or the designee of the Archivist to determine whether the record has such value;

(vii) To another agency or to an instrumentality of any governmental jurisdiction within or under the control of the United States for a civil or criminal law enforcement activity if the activity is authorized by law, and if the head of the agency or instrumentality has made a written request to the agency which maintains the record specifying the particular portion desired and the law enforcement activity for which the record is sought;

(viii) To a person pursuant to a showing of compelling circumstances affecting the health or safety of an individual if upon such disclosure notification is transmitted to the last known address of such individual;

(ix) To either House of Congress, or, to the extent of matter within its jurisdiction, any committee or subcommittee thereof, any joint committee of Congress or subcommittee of any such joint committee;

(x) To the Comptroller General, or any of his authorized representatives, in the course of the performance of the duties of the General Accounting Office;

(xi) Pursuant to the order of a court of competent jurisdiction; or

(xii) To a consumer reporting agency in accordance with section 3711(e) of Title 31.

(b) The situations referred to in paragraph (a)(4) of this section include the following:

(1) 5 U.S.C. 552a(c)(4) requires dissemination of a corrected or amended record or notation of a disagreement

[1] 5 U.S.C. 552a(b)(4) has no application within USPTO.

statement by USPTO in certain circumstances;

(2) 5 U.S.C. 552a(d) requires disclosure of records to the individual to whom they pertain, upon request; and

(3) 5 U.S.C. 552a(g) authorizes civil action by an individual and requires disclosure by USPTO to the court.

(c) The Privacy Officer shall make an accounting of each disclosure by him of any record contained in a system of records in accordance with 5 U.S.C. 552a(c) (1) and (2). Except for a disclosure made under 5 U.S.C. 552a(b)(7), the Privacy Officer shall make such accounting available to any individual, insofar as it pertains to that individual, on request submitted in accordance with § 102.24. The Privacy Officer shall make reasonable efforts to notify any individual when any record in a system of records is disclosed to any person under compulsory legal process, promptly upon being informed that such process has become a matter of public record.

§ 102.31 Fees.

The only fees to be charged to or collected from an individual under the provisions of this part are for duplication of records at the request of the individual. The Privacy Officer shall charge fees for duplication of records under the Act in the same way in which they charge duplication fees under § 102.11, except as provided in this section.

(a) No fees shall be charged or collected for the following: Search for and retrieval of the records; review of the records; copying at the initiative of USPTO without a request from the individual; transportation of records and personnel; and first-class postage.

(b) It is the policy of USPTO to provide an individual with one copy of each record corrected or amended pursuant to his or her request without charge as evidence of the correction or amendment.

(c) As required by the United States Office of Personnel Management in its published regulations implementing the Act, USPTO will charge no fee for a single copy of a personnel record covered by that agency's Government-wide published notice of systems of records.

§ 102.32 Penalties.

(a) The Act provides, in pertinent part:

> Any person who knowingly and willfully requests or obtains any record concerning an individual from an agency under false pretenses shall be guilty of a misdemeanor and fined not more than $5,000. (5 U.S.C. 552a(i)(3)).

(b) A person who falsely or fraudulently attempts to obtain records under the Act also may be subject to prosecution under such other criminal statutes as 18 U.S.C. 494, 495 and 1001.

§ 102.33 General exemptions.

(a) Individuals may not have access to records maintained by USPTO but which were provided by another agency which has determined by regulation that such information is subject to general exemption under 5 U.S.C. 552a(j). If such exempt records are within a request for access, USPTO will advise the individual of their existence and of the name and address of the source agency. For any further information concerning the record and the exemption, the individual must contact that source agency.

(b) The general exemption determined to be necessary and proper with respect to systems of records maintained by USPTO, including the parts of each system to be exempted, the provisions of the Act from which they are exempted, and the justification for the exemption, is as follows: *Investigative Records—Contract and Grant Frauds and Employee Criminal Misconduct—COMMERCE/DEPT.—12.* Pursuant to 5 U.S.C. 552a(j)(2), these records are hereby determined to be exempt from all provisions of the Act, except 5 U.S.C. 552a (b), (c) (1) and (2), (e)(4) (A) through (F), (e) (6), (7), (9), (10), and (11), and (i). These exemptions are necessary to ensure the proper functions of the law enforcement activity, to protect confidential sources of information, to fulfill promises of confidentiality, to prevent interference with law enforcement proceedings, to avoid the disclosure of investigative techniques, to avoid the endangering of law enforcement personnel, to avoid premature disclosure of the knowledge of criminal activity and the evidentiary bases of possible enforcement actions, and to maintain the integrity of the law enforcement process.

§ 102.34 Specific exemptions.

(a)(1) Some systems of records under the Act which are maintained by USPTO contain, from time-to-time, material subject to the exemption appearing at 5 U.S.C. 552a(k)(1), relating to national defense and foreign policy materials. The systems of records published in the FEDERAL REGISTER by USPTO which are within this exemption are: COMMERCE/PAT-TM-6, COMMERCE/PAT-TM-7, COMMERCE/PAT-TM-8, COMMERCE/PAT-TM-9.

(2) USPTO hereby asserts a claim to exemption of such materials wherever they might appear in such systems of records, or any systems of records, at present or in the future. The materials would be exempt from 5 U.S.C. 552a (c)(3), (d), (e)(1), (e)(4) (G), (H), and (I), and (f) to protect materials required by Executive order to be kept secret in the interest of the national defense and foreign policy.

(b) The specific exemptions determined to be necessary and proper with respect to systems of records maintained by USPTO, including the parts of each system to be exempted, the provisions of the Act from which they are exempted, and the justification for the exemption, are as follows:

(1)(i) Exempt under 5 U.S.C. 552a(k)(2). The systems of records exempt (some only conditionally), the sections of the Act from which exempted, and the reasons therefor are as follows:

(A) Investigative Records—Contract and Grant Frauds and Employee Criminal Misconduct—COMMERCE/DEPT-12, but only on condition that the general exemption claimed in § 102.33(b)(3) is held to be invalid;

(B) Investigative Records—Persons Within the Investigative Jurisdiction of USPTO—COMMERCE/DEPT-13;

(C) Litigation, Claims and Administrative Proceeding Records—COMMERCE/DEPT-14;

(D) Attorneys and Agents Registered to Practice Before the Office—COMMERCE/PAT-TM-1;

(E) Complaints, Investigations and Disciplinary Proceedings Relating to Registered Patent Attorneys and Agents—COMMERCE/PAT-TM-2; and

(F) Non-Registered Persons Rendering Assistance to Patent Applicants—COMMERCE/PAT-TM-5.

(ii) The foregoing are exempted from 5 U.S.C. 552a (c)(3), (d), (e)(1), (e)(4)(G), (H), and (I), and (f). The reasons for asserting the exemption are to prevent subjects of investigation from frustrating the investigatory process, to insure the proper functioning and integrity of law enforcement activities, to prevent disclosure of investigative techniques, to maintain the ability to obtain necessary information, to fulfill commitments made to sources to protect their identities and the confidentiality of information and to avoid endangering these sources and law enforcement personnel. Special note is taken of the fact that the proviso clause in this exemption imports due process and procedural protections for the individual. The existence and general character of the information exempted will be made known to the individual to whom it pertains.

(2)(i) Exempt under 5 U.S.C. 552a(k)(5). The systems of records exempt (some only conditionally), the sections of the act from which exempted, and the reasons therefor are as follows:

(A) Investigative Records—Contract and Grant Frauds and Employee Criminal Misconduct—COMMERCE/DEPT–12, but only on condition that the general exemption claimed in § 102.33(b)(3) is held to be invalid;

(B) Investigative Records—Persons Within the Investigative Jurisdiction of USPTO—COMMERCE/DEPT–13; and

(C) Litigation, Claims, and Administrative Proceeding Records—COMMERCE/DEPT–14.

(ii) The foregoing are exempted from 5 U.S.C. 552a (c)(3), (d), (e)(1), (e)(4) (G), (H), and (I), and (f). The reasons for asserting the exemption are to maintain the ability to obtain candid and necessary information, to fulfill commitments made to sources to protect the confidentiality of information, to avoid endangering these sources and, ultimately, to facilitate proper selection or continuance of the best applicants or persons for a given position or contract. Special note is made of the limitation on the extent to which this exemption may be asserted. The existence and general character of the information exempted will be made known to the individual to whom it pertains.

(c) At the present time, USPTO claims no exemption under 5 U.S.C. 552a(k) (3), (4), (6) and (7).

APPENDIX TO PART 102—SYSTEMS OF RECORDS NOTICED BY OTHER FEDERAL AGENCIES[1] AND APPLICABLE TO USPTO RECORDS AND APPLICABILITY OF THIS PART THERETO

Category of records	Other federal agency
Federal Personnel Records	Office of Personnel Management.[2]
Federal Employee Compensation Act Program	Department of Labor.[3]
Equal Employment Opportunity Appeal Complaints	Equal Employment Opportunity Commission.[4]
Formal Complaints/Appeals of Adverse Personnel Actions	Merit Systems Protection Board.[5]

[1] Other than systems of records noticed by the Department of Commerce. Where the system of records applies only to USPTO, these regulations apply. Where the system of records applies generally to components of the Department of Commerce, the regulations of that department attach at the point of any denial for access or for correction or amendment.

[2] The provisions of this part do not apply to these records covered by notices of systems of records published by the Office of Personnel Management for all agencies. The regulations of OPM alone apply.

[3] The provisions of this part apply only initially to these records covered by notices of systems of records published by the U.S. Department of Labor for all agencies. The regulations of that department attach at the point of any denial for access or for correction or amendment.

[4] The provisions of this part do not apply to these records covered by notices of systems of records published by the Equal Employment Opportunity Commission for all agencies. The regulations of the Commission alone apply.

[5] The provisions of this part do not apply to these records covered by notices of systems of records published by the Merit Systems Protection Board for all agencies. The regulations of the Board alone apply.

PART 104—LEGAL PROCESSES

AUTHORITY: 35 U.S.C. 2(b)(2), 10, 23, 25; 44 U.S.C. 3101, except as otherwise indicated.

SOURCE: 66 FR 47389, Sept. 12, 2001, unless otherwise noted.

Subpart A—General Provisions

§ 104.1 Definitions.

Demand means a request, order, or subpoena for testimony or documents for use in a legal proceeding.

Director means the Under Secretary of Commerce for Intellectual Property and Director of the United States Patent and Trademark Office (*see* § 1.9(j)).

Document means any record, paper, and other property held by the Office, including without limitation, official letters, telegrams, memoranda, reports, studies, calendar and diary entries, maps, graphs, pamphlets, notes, charts, tabulations, analyses, statistical or informational accumulations, any kind of summaries of meetings and conversations, film impressions, magnetic tapes, and sound or mechanical reproductions.

Employee means any current or former officer or employee of the Office.

Legal proceeding means any pretrial, trial, and posttrial stages of existing or reasonably anticipated judicial or administrative actions, hearings, investigations, or similar proceedings before courts, commissions, boards or other tribunals, foreign or domestic. This phrase includes all phases of discovery as well as responses to formal or informal requests by attorneys or others involved in legal proceedings.

Office means the United States Patent and Trademark Office, including any operating unit in the United States Patent and Trademark Office, and its predecessors, the Patent Office and the Patent and Trademark Office.

Official business means the authorized business of the Office.

General Counsel means the General Counsel of the Office.

Testimony means a statement in any form, including personal appearances before a court or other legal tribunal, interviews, depositions, telephonic, televised, or videotaped statements or any responses given during discovery or similar proceedings, which response would involve more than the production of documents, including a declaration under 35 U.S.C. 25 or 28 U.S.C. 1746.

United States means the Federal Government, its departments and agencies, individuals acting on behalf of the Federal Government, and parties to the extent they are represented by the United States.

[66 FR 47389, Sept. 12, 2001, as amended at 68 FR 14339, Mar. 25, 2003]

§ 104.2 Address for mail and service; telephone number.

(a) Mail under this part should be addressed to the Office of the General Counsel, United States Patent and Trademark Office, P.O. Box 1450, Alexandria, Virginia 22313–1450.

(b) Service by hand should be made during business hours to the Office of the General Counsel, 10B20, Madison Building East, 600 Dulany Street, Alexandria, Virginia.

(c) The Office of the General Counsel may be reached by telephone at 571–272–7000 during business hours.

[66 FR 47389, Sept. 12, 2001, as amended at 70 FR 10490, Mar. 4, 2005; 75 FR 36295, June 25, 2010]

§ 104.3 Waiver of rules.

In extraordinary situations, when the interest of justice requires, the General Counsel may waive or suspend the rules of this part, *sua sponte* or on petition of an interested party to the Director, subject to such requirements as the General Counsel may impose. Any such petition must be accompanied by a petition fee of $130.00.

[69 FR 56546, Sept. 21, 2004]

§ 104.4 Relationship of this Part to the Federal Rules of Civil or Criminal Procedure.

Nothing in this part waives or limits any requirement under the Federal Rules of Civil or Criminal Procedure.

Subpart B—Service of Process

§ 104.11 Scope and purpose.

(a) This subpart sets forth the procedures to be followed when a summons and complaint is served on the Office or on the Director or an employee in his or her official capacity.

(b) This subpart is intended, and should be construed, to ensure the efficient administration of the Office and not to impede any legal proceeding.

(c) This subpart does not apply to subpoenas, the procedures for which are set out in subpart C.

(d) This subpart does not apply to service of process made on an employee personally on matters not related to official business of the Office or to the official responsibilities of the employee.

§ 104.12 Acceptance of service of process.

(a) Any summons and complaint to be served in person or by registered or certified mail or as otherwise authorized by law on the Office, on the Director, or on an employee in his or her official capacity, shall be served as indicated in § 104.2.

(b) Any employee of the Office served with a summons and complaint shall immediately notify, and shall deliver the summons and complaint to, the Office of the General Counsel.

(c) Any employee receiving a summons and complaint shall note on the summons and complaint the date, hour, and place of service and whether service was by hand or by mail.

(d) When a legal proceeding is brought to hold an employee personally liable in connection with an action taken in the conduct of official business, rather than liable in an official capacity, the employee by law is to be served personally with process. *See Fed. R. Civ. P.* 4(e). An employee sued personally for an action taken in the conduct of official business shall immediately notify and deliver a copy of the summons and complaint to the General Counsel.

(e) An employee sued personally in connection with official business may be represented by the Department of Justice at its discretion (28 CFR 50.15 and 50.16).

(f) The Office will only accept service of process for an employee in the employee's official capacity.

Subpart C—Employee Testimony and Production of Documents in Legal Proceedings

§ 104.21 Scope and purpose.

(a) This subpart sets forth the policies and procedures of the Office regarding the testimony of employees as witnesses in legal proceedings and the production or disclosure of information contained in Office documents for use in legal proceedings pursuant to a demand.

(b) *Exceptions.* This subpart does not apply to any legal proceeding in which:

(1) An employee is to testify regarding facts or events that are unrelated to official business; or

(2) A former employee is to testify as an expert in connection with a particular matter in which the former employee did not participate personally while at the Office.

§ 104.22 Demand for testimony or production of documents.

(a) Whenever a demand for testimony or for the production of documents is made upon an employee, the employee shall immediately notify the Office of the General Counsel at the telephone number or addresses in § 104.2 and make arrangements to send the subpoena to the General Counsel promptly.

(b) An employee may not give testimony, produce documents, or answer inquiries from a person not employed by the Office regarding testimony or documents subject to a demand or a potential demand under the provisions of this subpart without the approval of the General Counsel. The General Counsel may authorize the provision of certified copies not otherwise available under Part 1 of this title subject to payment of applicable fees under § 1.19.

(c)(1) *Demand for testimony or documents.* A demand for the testimony of an employee under this subpart shall be addressed to the General Counsel as indicated in § 104.2.

(2) *Subpoenas.* A subpoena for employee testimony or for a document shall be served in accordance with the Federal Rules of Civil or Criminal Procedure or applicable state procedure, and a copy of the subpoena shall be sent to the General Counsel as indicated in § 104.2.

(3) *Affidavits.* Except when the United States is a party, every demand shall be accompanied by an affidavit or declaration under 28 U.S.C. 1746 or 35 U.S.C. 25(b) setting forth the title of the legal proceeding, the forum, the requesting party's interest in the legal proceeding, the reason for the demand, a showing that the desired testimony or document is not reasonably available from any other source, and, if testimony is requested, the intended use of the testimony, a general summary of the desired testimony, and a showing that no document could be provided and used in lieu of testimony.

(d) Failure of the attorney to cooperate in good faith to enable the General Counsel to make an informed determination under this subpart may serve as a basis for a determination not to comply with the demand.

(e) A determination under this subpart to comply or not to comply with a demand is not a waiver or an assertion of any other ground for noncompliance, including privilege, lack of relevance, or technical deficiency.

(f) *Noncompliance.* If the General Counsel makes a determination not to comply, he or she will seek Department of Justice representation for the employee and will attempt to have the subpoena modified or quashed. If Department of Justice representation cannot be arranged, the employee should appear at the time and place set forth in the subpoena. In such a case, the employee should produce a copy of these rules and state that the General Counsel has advised the employee not to provide the requested testimony nor to produce the requested document. If a legal tribunal rules that the demand in the subpoena must be complied with, the employee shall respectfully decline to comply with the demand, citing *United States ex rel. Touhy* v. *Ragen*, 340 U.S. 462 (1951).

§ 104.23 Expert or opinion testimony.

(a)(1) If the General Counsel authorizes an employee to give testimony in a legal proceeding not involving the United States, the testimony, if otherwise proper, shall be limited to facts within the personal knowledge of the employee. Employees, with or without compensation, shall not provide expert testimony in any legal proceedings regarding Office information, subjects, or activities except on behalf of the United States or a party represented by the United States Department of Justice.

(2) The General Counsel may authorize an employee to appear and give the expert or opinion testimony upon the requester showing, pursuant to § 104.3 of this part, that exceptional circumstances warrant such testimony and that the anticipated testimony will not be adverse to the interest of the Office or the United States.

(b)(1) If, while testifying in any legal proceeding, an employee is asked for expert or opinion testimony regarding Office information, subjects, or activities, which testimony has not been approved in advance in writing in accordance with the regulations in this subpart, the witness shall:

(i) Respectfully decline to answer on the grounds that such expert or opinion testimony is forbidden by this subpart;

(ii) Request an opportunity to consult with the General Counsel before giving such testimony; and

(iii) Explain that upon such consultation, approval for such testimony may be provided.

(2) If the tribunal conducting the proceeding then orders the employee to provide expert or opinion testimony regarding Office information, subjects, or activities without the opportunity to consult with the General Counsel, the employee shall respectfully refuse to provide such testimony, citing *United States ex rel. Touhy v. Ragen*, 340 U.S. 462 (1951).

(c) If an employee is unaware of the regulations in this subpart and provides expert or opinion testimony regarding Office information, subjects, or activities in a legal proceeding without the aforementioned consultation, the employee shall, as soon after testifying as possible, inform the General Counsel that such testimony was given and provide a written summary of the expert or opinion testimony provided.

(d) *Proceeding where the United States is a party.* In a proceeding in which the United States is a party or is representing a party, an employee may not testify as an expert or opinion witness for any party other than the United States.

§ 104.24 Demands or requests in legal proceedings for records protected by confidentiality statutes.

Demands in legal proceedings for the production of records, or for the testimony of employees regarding information protected by the confidentiality provisions of the Patent Act (35 U.S.C. 122), the Privacy Act (5 U.S.C. 552a), the Trade Secrets Act (18 U.S.C. 1905), or any other confidentiality statute, must satisfy the requirements for disclosure set forth in those statutes and associated rules before the records may be provided or testimony given.

Subpart D—Employee Indemnification

§ 104.31 Scope.

The procedure in this subpart shall be followed if a civil action or proceeding is brought, in any court, against an employee (including the employee's estate) for personal injury, loss of property, or death, resulting from the employee's activities while acting within the scope of the employee's office or employment. When the employee is incapacitated or deceased, actions required of an employee should be performed by the employee's executor, administrator, or comparable legal representative.

§ 104.32 Procedure for requesting indemnification.

(a) After being served with process or pleadings in such an action or proceeding, the employee shall within five (5) calendar days of receipt, deliver to the General Counsel all such process and pleadings or an attested true copy thereof, together with a fully detailed report of the circumstances of the incident giving rise to the court action or proceeding.

(b)(1) An employee may request indemnification to satisfy a verdict, judgment, or award entered against that employee only if the employee has timely satisfied the requirements of paragraph (a) of this section.

(2) No request for indemnification will be considered unless the employee has submitted a written request through the employee's supervisory chain to the General Counsel with:

(i) Appropriate documentation, including copies of the verdict, judgment, appeal bond, award, or settlement proposal;

(ii) The employee's explanation of how the employee was acting within the scope of the employee's employment; and

(iii) The employee's statement of whether the employee has insurance or any other source of indemnification.

Subpart E—Tort Claims

AUTHORITY: 28 U.S.C. 2672; 35 U.S.C. 2(b)(2); 44 U.S.C. 3101; 28 CFR Part 14.

§ 104.41 Procedure for filing claims.

Administrative claims against the Office filed pursuant to the administrative claims provision of the Federal Tort Claims Act (28 U.S.C. 2672) and the corresponding Department of Justice regulations (28 CFR Part 14) shall be filed with the General Counsel as indicated in § 104.2.

§ 104.42 Finality of settlement or denial of claims.

Only a decision of the Director or the General Counsel regarding settlement or denial of any claim under this subpart may be considered final for the purpose of judicial review.

SUBCHAPTER C—PROTECTION OF FOREIGN MASK WORKS

PART 150—REQUESTS FOR PRESIDENTIAL PROCLAMATIONS PURSUANT TO 17 U.S.C. 902(a)(2)

AUTHORITY: 35 U.S.C. 2(b)(2); E.O. 12504, 50 FR 4849; 3 CFR, 1985 Comp., p. 335.

SOURCE: 53 FR 24447, June 29, 1988, unless otherwise noted.

EDITORIAL NOTE: Nomenclature changes to part 150 appear at 68 FR 14339, Mar. 25, 2003.

§ 150.1 Definitions.

(a) *Director* means the Under Secretary of Commerce for Intellectual Property and Director of the United States Patent and Trademark Office (*see* § 1.9(j)).

(b) *Foreign government* means the duly-constituted executive of a foreign nation, or an international or regional intergovernmental organization which has been empowered by its member states to request issuance of Presidential proclamations on their behalf under this part.

(c) *Interim order* means an order issued by the Secretary of Commerce under 17 U.S.C. 914.

(d) *Mask work* means a series of related images, however fixed or encoded—

(1) Having or representing the predetermined, three-dimensional pattern of metallic, insulating, or semiconductor material present or removed from the layers of a semiconductor chip product; and

(2) In which series the relation of the images to one another is that each image has the pattern of the surface of one form of the semiconductor chip product.

(e) *Presidential proclamation* means an action by the President extending to foreign nationals, domiciliaries and sovereign authorities the privilege of applying for registrations for mask works pursuant to 17 U.S.C. 902.

(f) *Request* means a request by a foreign government for the issuance of a Presidential proclamation.

(g) *Proceeding* means a proceeding to issue an interim order extending protection to foreign nationals, domiciliaries and sovereign authorities under 17 U.S.C. Chapter 9.

(h) *Secretary* means the Secretary of Commerce.

[53 FR 24447, June 29, 1988, as amended at 68 Fr 14339, Mar. 25, 2003]

§ 150.2 Initiation of evaluation.

(a) The Director independently or as directed by the Secretary, may initiate an evaluation of the propriety of recommending the issuance, revision, suspension or revocation of a section 902 proclamation.

(b) The Director shall initiate an evaluation of the propriety of recommending the issuance of a section 902 proclamation upon receipt of a request from a foreign government.

§ 150.3 Submission of requests.

(a) Requests for the issuance of a section 902 proclamation shall be submitted by foreign governments for review by the Director.

(b) Requests for issuance of a proclamation shall include:

(1) A copy of the foreign law or legal rulings that provide protection for U.S. mask works which provide a basis for the request.

(2) A copy of any regulations or administrative orders implementing the protection.

(3) A copy of any laws, regulations or administrative orders establishing or regulating the registration (if any) of mask works.

(4) Any other relevant laws, regulations or administrative orders.

(5) All copies of laws, legal rulings, regulations or administrative orders submitted must be in unedited, full-text form, and if possible, must be reproduced from the original document.

(6) All material submitted must be in the original language, and if not in English, must be accompanied by a certified English translation.

§ 150.4 Evaluation.

(a) Upon submission of a request by a foreign government for the issuance of a section 902 proclamation, if an interim order under section 914 has not been issued, the Director may initiate a section 914 proceeding if additional information is required.

(b) If an interim order under section 914 has been issued, the information obtained during the section 914 proceeding will be used in evaluating the request for a section 902 proclamation.

(c) After the Director receives the request of a foreign government for a section 902 proclamation, or after a determination is made by the Director to initiate independently an evaluation pursuant to § 150.2(a) of this part, a notice will be published in the FEDERAL REGISTER to request relevant and material comments on the adequacy and effectiveness of the protection afforded U.S. mask works under the system of law described in the notice. Comments should include detailed explanations of any alleged deficiencies in the foreign law or any alleged deficiencies in its implementation. If the alleged deficiencies include problems in administration such as registration, the respondent should include as specifically as possible full detailed explanations, including dates for and the nature of any alleged problems. Comments shall be submitted to the Director within sixty (60) days of publication of the FEDERAL REGISTER notice.

(d) The Director shall notify the Register of Copyrights and the Committees on the Judiciary of the Senate and the House of Representatives of the initiation of an evaluation under these regulations.

(e) If the written comments submitted by any party present relevant and material reasons why a proclamation should not issue, the Director will:

(1) Contact the party raising the issue for verification and any needed additional information;

(2) Contact the requesting foreign government to determine if the issues raised by the party can be resolved; and,

(i) If the issues are resolved, continue with the evaluation; or,

(ii) If the issues cannot be resolved on this basis, hold a public hearing to gather additional information.

(f) The comments, the section 902 request, information obtained from a section 914 proceeding, if any, and information obtained in a hearing held pursuant to paragraph (e)(ii) of this section, if any, will be evaluated by the Director.

(g) The Director will forward the information to the Secretary, together with an evaluation and a draft recommendation.

(h) The Secretary will forward a recommendation regarding the issuance of a section 902 proclamation to the President.

§ 150.5 Duration of proclamation.

(a) The recommendation for the issuance of a proclamation may include terms and conditions regarding the duration of the proclamation.

(b) Requests for the revision, suspension or revocation of a proclamation may be submitted by any interested party. Requests for revision, suspension or revocation of a proclamation will be considered in substantially the same manner as requests for the issuance of a section 902 proclamation.

§ 150.6 Mailing address.

Requests and all correspondence pursuant to these guidelines shall be addressed to: Mail Stop Congressional Relations, Director of the United States Patent and Trademark Office, P.O. Box 1450, Alexandria, Virginia 22313–1450.

[70 FR 10490, Mar. 4, 2005]

CHAPTER II—COPYRIGHT OFFICE, LIBRARY OF CONGRESS

SUBCHAPTER A—COPYRIGHT OFFICE AND PROCEDURES

SUBCHAPTER B—COPYRIGHT ARBITRATION ROYALTY PANEL RULES AND PROCEDURES

SUBCHAPTER A—COPYRIGHT OFFICE AND PROCEDURES

PART 201—GENERAL PROVISIONS

AUTHORITY: 17 U.S.C. 702.

Section 201.10 also issued under 17 U.S.C. 304.

§ 201.1 Communication with the Copyright Office.

(a) *General purpose addresses.* Members of the public must use the correct address in order to facilitate timely receipt by the copyright division or section to which an inquiry should be directed. The following addresses may be used for general inquiries made to a particular division or section of the Copyright Office. Addresses for special, limited purposes are provided below in paragraph (b) of this section. Anyone who is not certain where a particular inquiry should be directed, should inquire about the proper address through the "Contact us" section on the Office's Web site (*http://*

www.copyright.gov) or call the Public Information Office at (202) 707–3000.

(1) *In general.* Mail and other communications which do not come under the areas listed in paragraph (a) or (b) of this section shall be addressed to the Library of Congress, Copyright Office, 101 Independence Avenue, SE., Washington, DC 20559–6000.

(2) *Inquiries to Licensing Division.* Inquiries about filings related to the compulsory licenses (17 U.S.C. 111, 112, 114, 115, 118, 119, 122 and chapter 10) should be addressed to the Library of Congress, Copyright Office, Licensing Division, 101 Independence Avenue, SE., Washington, DC 20557–6400.

(3) *Copies of records or deposits.* Requests for copies of records or deposits for use in litigation or other authorized purposes should be addressed to the Records Research and Certification Section, LM–455, Library of Congress, Copyright Office, 101 Independence Avenue, SE., Washington, DC 20559–6302.

(4) *Search of records.* Requests for searches of registrations and recordations in the completed catalogs, indexes, and other records of the Copyright Office should be addressed to the Records Research and Certification Section, LM–455, Library of Congress, Copyright Office, 101 Independence Avenue, SE., Washington, DC 20559–6306. Records dating from January 1, 1978, forward are available for searching on the Copyright Office's Web site at *http://www.copyright.gov:* COHM, which includes information on all registrations except serials; COHD, which includes information on recordations; and COHS, which includes information on serials.

(b) *Limited purpose addresses.* The following addresses may be used only in the special, limited circumstances given for a particular Copyright Office service:

(1) *Time sensitive requests.* Freedom of Information (FOIA) requests; notices of filing of copyright infringement lawsuits;[3] comments for rulemaking proceedings; requests for Copyright Office speakers; requests for approvals of computer generated application forms; requests for expedited service from either the Records Research and Certification Section to meet the needs of pending or prospective litigation, customs matters or contract or publishing deadlines should be addressed to: Copyright GC/I&R, P.O. Box 70400, Washington, DC 20024–0400.

(2) *Notices of termination.* Notices of termination submitted for recordation should be mailed to Copyright Office, Notices of Termination, P.O. Box 71537, Washington, DC 20024–1537.

[69 FR 39331, June 30, 2004, as amended at 73 FR 37838, July 2, 2008; 74 FR 12556, Mar. 25, 2009]

§ 201.2 Information given by the Copyright Office.

(a) *In general.* (1) Information relative to the operations of the Copyright Office is supplied without charge. A search of the records, indexes, and deposits will be made for such information as they may contain relative to copyright claims upon application and payment of the statutory fee. The Copyright Office, however, does not undertake the making of comparisons of copyright deposits to determine similarity between works.

(2) The Copyright Office does not furnish the names of copyright attorneys, publishers, agents, or other similar information.

(3) In the administration of the Copyright Act in general, the Copyright Office interprets the Act. The Copyright Office, however, does not give specific legal advice on the rights of persons, whether in connection with particular uses of copyrighted works, cases of alleged foreign or domestic copyright infringement, contracts between authors and publishers, or other matters of a similar nature.

(b) *Inspection and copying of records.* (1) Inspection and copying of completed records and indexes relating to a registration or a recorded document, and inspection of copies or identifying material deposited in connection with a completed copyright registration may be undertaken in the Records Research and Certification Section. Since some of these materials are not stored on the immediate premises of the Copyright Office, it is advisable to consult the

[3] All litigation material is time sensitive and must be addressed to the appropriate section of the Copyright Office; the Office is also publishing new regulations governing legal process.

Certifications and Documents Section to determine the length of time necessary to produce the requested materials.

(2) It is the general policy of the Copyright Office to deny direct public access to in-process files and to any work (or other) areas where they are kept. However, direct public use of computers intended to access the automated equivalent of limited portions of these files is permitted on a specified terminal in the Records Management Section, LM B–14, Monday through Friday, upon payment of applicable fees.

(3) Information contained in Copyright Office in-process files may be obtained by anyone upon payment of applicable fees and request to the Information and Records Division, in accordance with the following procedures:

(i) In general, all requests by the public for information in the in-process and open unfinished business files should be made to the Records Research and Certification Section, which upon receipt of applicable fees will give a report that provides the following for each request:

(A) The date(s) of receipt of:

(*1*) The application(s) for registration that may have been submitted and is (are) in process;

(*2*) The document(s) that may have been submitted for recordation and is (are) in process;

(*3*) The copy or copies (or phonorecords) that may have been submitted;

(B) The title of the work(s); and

(C) The name of the remitter.

(ii) Such searches of the in-process files will be given priority to the extent permitted by the demands of normal work flow of the affected sections of the Copyright Office.

(4) Access will be afforded as follows to pending applications for registration, the deposit material accompanying them, and pending documents for recordation that were submitted within the twelve month period immediately preceding the request for access:

(i) In the case of applications for registration and deposits accompanying them, upon the request of the copyright claimant or his/her authorized representative, and

(ii) In the case of documents, upon the request of at least one of the persons who executed the document or by an authorized representative of that person.

These requests should be made to the Copyright Information Section, and the review of the materials will be permitted there. No charge will be made for reviewing these materials; the appropriate search fee identified in § 201.3(c) or § 201.3(d) will be assessed, and the appropriate copying fee identified in § 201.3(c) or § 201.3(d) will be assessed if the claimant wants and is entitled to a copy of the material.

(5) In exceptional circumstances, the Register of Copyrights may allow inspection of pending applications and open correspondence files by someone other than the copyright claimant, upon submission of a written request which is deemed by the Register to show good cause for such access and establishes that the person making the request is one properly and directly concerned. The written request should be addressed to Copyright GC/I&R, P.O. Box 70400, Washington, DC 20024.

(6) Direct public access will not be permitted to any financial or accounting records, including records maintained on Deposit Accounts.

(7) The Copyright Office maintains administrative staff manuals referred to as its "Compendium of Office Practices I" and "Compendium of Office Practices II" for the general guidance of its staff in making registrations and recording documents. The manuals, as amended and supplemented from time to time, are available for purchase from the National Technical Information Service (Compendium I) and the Government Printing Office (Compendium II). They are also available for public inspection and copying in the Records Research and Certifications Section. As the Office updates and revises certain chapters of Compendium II, it will make the information available on the Copyright Office's Web site. This information is also available for public inspection and copying in the Records Research and Certifications Section.

(c) *Correspondence.* (1) Official correspondence, including preliminary applications, between copyright claimants or their agents and the Copyright Office, and directly relating to a completed registration, a recorded document, a rejected application for registration, or a document for which recordation was refused is available for public inspection. Included in the correspondence available for public inspection is that portion of the file directly relating to a completed registration, recorded document, a rejected application for registration, or a document for which recordation was refused which was once open to public inspection as a closed case, even if the case is subsequently reopened. Public inspection is available only for the correspondence contained in the file during the time it was closed because of one of the aforementioned actions. Correspondence relating to the reopening of the file and reconsideration of the case is considered part of an in-process file until final action is taken, and public inspection of that correspondence is governed by § 201.2(b). Requests for reproductions of the correspondence shall be made pursuant to paragraph (d) of this section.

(2) Correspondence, application forms, and any accompanying material forming a part of a pending application are considered in-process files and access to them is governed by paragraph (b) of this section.

(3) Correspondence, memoranda, reports, opinions, and similar material relating to internal matters of personnel and procedures, office administration, security matters, and internal consideration of policy and decisional matters including the work product of an attorney, are not open to public inspection.

(4) The Copyright Office will not respond to any abusive or scurrilous correspondence or correspondence where the intent is unknown.

(d) *Requests for copies.* (1) Requests for copies of records should include the following:

(i) A clear identification of the type of records desired (for example, additional certificates of registration, copies of correspondence, copies of deposits).

(ii) A specification of whether the copies are to be certified or uncertified.

(iii) A clear identification of the specific records to be copied. Requests should include the following specific information, if possible:

(A) The type of work involved (for example, novel, lyrics, photograph);

(B) The registration number;

(C) The year date or approximate year date of registration;

(D) The complete title of the work;

(E) The author(s) including any pseudonym by which the author may be known; and

(F) The claimant(s); and

(G) If the requested copy is of an assignment, license, contract, or other recorded document, the volume and page number of the recorded document.

(iv) If the copy requested is an additional certificate of registration, include the fee. The Records Research and Certifications Section will review requests for copies of other records and quote fees for each.

(v) The telephone number and address of the requestor.

(2) Requests for certified or uncertified reproductions of the copies, phonorecords, or identifying material deposited in connection with a copyright registration of published or unpublished works in the custody of the Copyright Office will be granted only when one of the following three conditions has been met:

(i) The Copyright Office receives written authorization from the copyright claimant of record or his or her designated agent, or from the owner of any of the exclusive rights in the copyright as long as this ownership can be demonstrated by written documentation of the transfer of ownership.

(ii) The Copyright Office receives a written request from an attorney on behalf of either the plaintiff or defendant in connection with litigation, actual or prospective, involving the copyrighted work. The following information must be included in such a request:

(A) The names of all the parties involved and the nature of the controversy;

(B) The name of the court in which the actual case is pending or, in the case of a prospective proceeding, a full statement of the facts of the controversy in which the copyrighted work is involved; and

(C) Satisfactory assurance that the requested reproduction will be used only in connection with the specified litigation.

(iii) The Copyright Office receives a court order for reproduction of the deposited copies, phonorecords, or identifying material of a registered work which is the subject of litigation. The order must be issued by a court having jurisdiction of the case in which the reproduction is to be submitted as evidence.

(3) When a request is made for a reproduction of a phonorecord, such as an audiotape or cassette, in which either a sound recording or the underlying musical, dramatic, or literary work is embodied, the Copyright Office will provide proximate reproduction. The Copyright Office reserves the right to substitute a monaural reproduction for a stereo, quadraphonic, or any other type of fixation of the work accepted for deposit.

[50 FR 30170, July 24, 1985, as amended at 51 FR 30062, Aug. 22, 1986; 62 FR 35421, July 1, 1997; 64 FR 29520, June 1, 1999; 69 FR 39332, June 30, 2004; 69 FR 70377, Dec. 6, 2004; 73 FR 37838, July 2, 2008]

§ 201.3 Fees for registration, recordation, and related services, special services, and services performed by the Licensing Division.

(a) *General.* This section prescribes the fees for registration, recordation, and related services, special services, and services performed by the Licensing Division.

(b) *Definitions.* For purposes of this section, the following definitions apply:

(1) *Registration, recordation, and related service fee.* This is the fee for a registration or recordation service that the Office is required to perform under 17 U.S.C., or a directly related service. It includes those services described in section 708(a)(1)–(9) and authorized by Pub. L. 105–80.

(2) *Special service fee.* This is a fee for a special service not specified in title 17, which the Register of Copyrights may fix at any time on the basis of the cost of providing the service, as provided by 17 U.S.C. 708(a).

(3) *Licensing Division service fee.* This is a fee for a service performed by the Licensing Division.

(c) *Registration, recordation and related service fees.* The Copyright Office has established the following fees for these services:

Registration, Recordation and Related Services	Fees
(1) Registration of a basic claim in an original work of authorship:	
Electronic Filing	$35
Forms PA, SR, TX, VA, SE	65
(2) Registration of a claim in a group of contributions to periodicals (Form GR/CP), published photographs, or database updates:	
Electronic filing of automated databases that predominantly consist of photographs and updates thereto or group registration of published photographs	35
Forms GR/CP, PA, SR, VA and SE (paper filing)	65
(3) Registration of a renewal claim (Form RE):	
Claim without Addendum	115
Addendum	220
(4) Registration of a claim in a group of serials (Form SE/Group)(per issue, minimum 2 issues)	25
(5) Registration of a claim in a group of daily newspapers and qualified newsletters (Form G/DN)	80
(6) Registration of a claim in a restored copyright (Form GATT)	65
(7) Preregistration of certain unpublished works	115
(8) Registration of a correction or amplification to a claim (Form CA and Form DC)	100
(9) Registration of a claim in a mask work (Form MW)	105
(10) Registration of a claim in a vessel hull (Form D/VH)	220
(11) Providing an additional certificate of registration	35
(12) Certification of other Copyright Office records (per hour)	165
(13) Search report prepared from official records (per hour) (minimum: 2 hours)	165
Estimate of search fee	115
(14) Location and retrieval of Copyright Office materials or records (per hour)	165
Fee for location and retrieval of electronic records (per quarter hour) (minimum: ½ hour)	41.25
(15) Recordation of document, including a Notice of Intention to Enforce (NIE) (single title)	105
Additional titles (per group of 10 titles)	30
(16) Recordation of an Interim Designation of Agent to Receive Notification of Claimed Infringement under § 512(c)(2) (single name)	105
Additional domain names (per group of 10)	30
(17) Recordation of a Notice of Intention to Make and Distribute Phonorecords (17 U.S.C. 115) (single title)	60
Additional titles (per group of 10)	20

Registration, Recordation and Related Services	Fees
(18) Issuance of a receipt for § 407 deposit	30

(d) *Special Service Fees.* The Copyright Office has established the following fees for special services:

Special Services	Fees
(1) Service charge for deposit account overdraft	$165
(2) Service charge for dishonored deposit account replenishment check	85
(3) Service charge for an uncollectible or non-negotiable check	25
(4) Appeals:	
(i) First appeal	250
Additional claim in related group	25
(ii) Second appeal	500
Additional claim in related group	25
(5) Secure test processing charge (per hour)	165
(6) Copying of Copyright Office records by staff:	
Photocopy (b&w, 8½ × 11) (per page, minimum $12)	0.50
Photocopy (b&w, 11 × 17) (per page, minimum $12)	1
Photocopy (color, 8½ × 11) (per page, minimum $12)	2
Photocopy (color, 11 × 17) (per page, minimum $12)	4
Photograph (Polaroid)	15
Photograph (digital)	45
Slide	3
Audiocassette (first 30 minutes)	75
Additional 15 minute increments	20
Videocassette (first 30 minutes)	75
Additional 15 minute increments	25
CD or DVD	100
Zip or floppy disk	100
(7) Special handling fee for a claim	760
Additional fee for each claim using the same deposit	50
(8) Special handling fee for recordation of a document	480
(9) Handling fee of extra deposit copy for certification	45
(10) Full-term retention of a published deposit	470
(11) Expedited search report service (per hour) (minimum 2 hours)	445
(12) Expedited location and retrieval, certification, and copying services (surcharge, per hour)	265
(13) Notice to Libraries and Archives	50
Each additional title	20
(14) Service charge for Federal Express mailing	40
(15) Service charge for delivery of documents via facsimile (per page, 7 page maximum)	1

(e) *Licensing Division service fees.* The Copyright Office has established the following fees for certain services performed by the Licensing Division:

Licensing Division Services	Fees
(1) Recordation of a Notice of Intention to Make and Distribute Phonorecords (17 U.S.C. 115) (single title)	$60
Additional titles (per group of 10)	20
(2) Recordation of a licensing agreement for use of certain works in connection with noncommercial broadcasting (17 U.S.C. 118)	140
(3) Recordation of certain contracts by cable TV systems located outside the 48 contiguous states	50
(4) Amendment to Statement of Account filed pursuant to 17 U.S.C. 111, 119 or 1003)	100
(5) Notice of Digital Transmission of Sound Recording (17 U.S.C. 112 and 114)	25
Amended Notice of Digital Transmission of Sound Recording	25
(6) Photocopy of record by staff (b&w) (per page) (minimum $12)	0.50
(7) Search and report services (per hour)	165
(8) Certification of search report (per hour)	165

(f) *Fees for travel in connection with educational activities.* For travel expenses in connection with Copyright Office educational activities when participation by Copyright Office personnel has been requested by another organization or person and that organization or person has agreed to pay such expenses, collection of the fee shall be subject to, and the amount of the fee shall be no greater than, the amount authorized under the Federal Travel Regulations found in Chapters 300 through 304 of Title 41.

[64 FR 29520, June 1, 1999, as amended at 64 FR 36574, July 7, 1999; 65 FR 39819, June 28, 2000; 67 FR 38005, May 31, 2002; 71 FR 31090, June 1, 2006; 71 FR 46402, Aug. 14, 2006; 72 FR 33691, June 19, 2007; 74 FR 12556, Mar. 25, 2009, 74 FR 32807, July 9, 2009; 77 FR 18705, Mar. 28, 2012; 77 FR 18707, Mar. 28, 2012]

§201.4 Recordation of transfers and certain other documents.

(a) *General.* (1) This section prescribes conditions for the recordation of transfers of copyright ownership and other documents pertaining to a copyright under section 205 of title 17 of the United States Code, as amended by Pub. L. 94–553. The filing or recordation of the following documents is not within the provisions of this section:

(i) Certain contracts entered into by cable systems located outside of the 48 contiguous States (17 U.S.C. 111(e); see 37 CFR 201.12);

(ii) Notices of identity and signal carriage complement, and statements of account of cable systems and satellite carriers and for digital audio recording devices and media (17 U.S.C. 111(d), 119(b) and 1003(c); see 37 CFR 201.11; 201.17; 201.28);

(iii) Notices of intention to obtain compulsory license to make and distribute phonorecords of nondramatic musical works (17 U.S.C. 115(b); see 37 CFR 201.18);

(iv) License agreements, and terms and rates of royalty payments, voluntarily negotiated between one or more public broadcasting entities and certain owners of copyright (17 U.S.C. 118; see 37 CFR 201.9);

(v) Notices of termination (17 U.S.C. 203, 304(c) and (d); see 37 CFR 201.10); and

(vi) Statements regarding the identity of authors of anonymous and pseudonymous works, and statements relating to the death of authors (17 U.S.C. 302).

(2) A *transfer of copyright ownership* has the meaning set forth in section 101 of title 17 of the United States Code, as amended by Pub. L. 94–553. A document shall be considered to "pertain to a copyright" if it has a direct or indirect relationship to the existence, scope, duration, or identification of a copyright, or to the ownership, division, allocation, licensing, transfer, or exercise of rights under a copyright. That relationship may be past, present, future, or potential.

(3) For purposes of this section:

(i) A *sworn certification* is an affidavit under the official seal of any officer authorized to administer oaths within the United States, or if the original is located outside of the United States, under the official seal of any diplomatic or consular officer of the United States or of a person authorized to administer oaths whose authority is proved by the certificate of such an officer, or a statement in accordance with section 1746 of title 28 of the United States Code; and

(ii) An *official certification* is a certification, by the appropriate Government official, that the original of the document is on file in a public office and that the reproduction is a true copy or the original.

(b) *Forms.* The Copyright Office does not provide forms for the use of persons recording documents.

(c) *Recordable documents.* Any transfer of copyright ownership (including any instrument of conveyance, or note or memorandum of the transfer), or any other document pertaining to a copyright, may be recorded in the Copyright Office if it is accompanied by the fee set forth in paragraph (d) of this section, and if the requirements of this paragraph with respect to signatures, completeness, and legibility are met.

(1) To be recordable, the document must bear the actual signature or signatures of the person or persons who executed it. Alternatively, the document may be recorded if it is a legible photocopy or other legible facsimile reproduction of the signed document, accompanied by a sworn certification or

an official certification that the reproduction is a true copy of the signed document. Any sworn certification accompanying a reproduction shall be signed by at least one of the parties to the signed document, or by an authorized representative of that person.

(2) To be recordable, the document must be complete by its own terms.

(i) A document that contains a reference to any schedule, appendix, exhibit, addendum, or other material as being attached to the document or made a part of it shall be recordable only if the attachment is also submitted for recordation with the document or if the reference is deleted by the parties to the document. If a document has been submitted for recordation and has been returned by the Copyright Office at the request of the sender for deletion of the reference to an attachment, the document will be recorded only if the deletion is signed or initialed by the persons who executed the document or by their authorized representatives. In exceptional cases a document containing a reference to an attachment will be recorded without the attached material and without deletion of the reference if the person seeking recordation submits a written request specifically asserting that:

(A) The attachment is completely unavailable for recordation; and

(B) The attachment is not essential to the identification of the subject matter of the document; and

(C) It would be impossible or wholly impracticable to have the parties to the document sign or initial a deletion of the reference.

In such exceptional cases, the Copyright Office records of the document will be annotated to show that recordation was made in response to a specific request under this paragraph.

(ii) If a document otherwise recordable under this title indicates on its face that it is a self-contained part of a larger instrument (for example: if it is designated "Attachment A" or "Exhibit B"), the Copyright Office will raise the question of completeness, but will record the document if the person requesting recordation asserts that the document is sufficiently complete as it stands.

(iii) When the document submitted for recordation merely identifies or incorporates by reference another document, or certain terms of another document, the Copyright Office will raise no question of completeness, and will not require recordation of the other document.

(3) To be recordable, the document must be legible and capable of being imaged or otherwise reproduced in legible copies by the technology employed by the Office at the time of submission.

(d) *Fees.* The fees for recordation of a document are prescribed in § 201.3(c).

(e) *Recordation.* The date of recordation is the date when a proper document under paragraph (c) of this section and a proper fee under paragraph (d) of this section are all received in the Copyright Office. After recordation the document is returned to the sender with a certificate of record.

(17 U.S.C. 205, 702, 708)

[43 FR 35044, Aug. 8, 1978, as amended at 53 FR 123, Jan. 5, 1988; 56 FR 59885, Nov. 26, 1991; 64 FR 29521, June 1, 1999; 65 FR 39819, June 28, 2000; 67 FR 69136, Nov. 15, 2002; 70 FR 38022, July 1, 2005; 74 FR 12556, Mar. 25, 2009; 77 FR 71103, Nov. 29, 2012]

§ 201.5 Corrections and amplifications of copyright registrations; applications for supplementary registration.

(a) *General.* (1) This section prescribes conditions relating to the filing of an application for supplementary registration, to correct an error in a copyright registration or to amplify the information given in a registration, under section 408(d) of title 17 of the United States Code, as amended by Pub. L. 94–553. For the purposes of this section:

(i) A *basic registration* means any of the following:

(A) A copyright registration made under sections 408, 409, and 410 of title 17 of the United States Code, as amended by Pub. L. 94–553;

(B) A renewal registration made under section 304 of title 17 of the United States Code, as so amended;

(C) A registration of claim to copyright made under title 17 of the United States Code as it existed before January 1, 1978; or

(D) A renewal registration made under title 17 of the United States Code as it existed before January 1, 1978; and

(ii) A *supplementary registration* means a registration made upon application under section 408(d) of title 17 of the United States Code, as amended by Pub. L. 94–553, and the provisions of this section.

(2) No correction or amplification of the information in a basic registration will be made except pursuant to the provisions of this §201.5. As an exception, where it is discovered that the record of a basic registration contains an error that the Copyright Office itself should have recognized at the time registration was made, the Office will take appropriate measures to rectify its error.

(b) *Persons entitled to file an application for supplementary registration; grounds of application.* (1) Supplementary registration can be made only if a basic copyright registration for the same work has already been completed. After a basic registration has been completed, any author or other copyright claimant of the work, or the owner of any exclusive right in the work, or the duly authorized agent of any such author, other claimant, or owner, who wishes to correct or amplify the information given in the basic registration for the work may file an application for supplementary registration.[1]

(2) Supplementary registration may be made either to correct or to amplify the information in a basic registration. For the purposes of this section:

(i) A *correction* is appropriate if information in the basic registration was incorrect at the time that basic registration was made, and the error is not one that the Copyright Office itself should have recognized;

(ii) An *amplification* is appropriate:

(A) To supplement or clarify the information that was required by the application for the basic registration and should have been provided, such as the identity of a co-author or co-claimant, but was omitted at the time the basic registration was made, or

(B) To reflect changes in facts, other than those relating to transfer, license, or ownership of rights in the work, that have occurred since the basic registration was made.

(iii) Supplementary registration is not appropriate:

(A) As an amplification, to reflect a change in ownership that occurred on or after the effective date of the basic registration or to reflect the division, allocation, licensing or transfer of rights in a work; or

(B) To correct errors in statements or notices on the copies of phonorecords of a work, or to reflect changes in the content of a work; and

(iv) Where a basic renewal registration has been made for a work during the last year of the relevant first-term copyright, supplementary registration to correct the renewal claimant or basis of claim or to add a renewal claimant is ordinarily possible only if the application for supplementary registration and fee are received in the Copyright Office within the last year of the relevant first-term copyright. If the error or omission in a basic renewal registration is extremely minor, and does not involve the identity of the renewal claimant or the legal basis of the claim, supplementary registration may be made at any time. In an exceptional case, however, supplementary registration may be made to correct the name of the renewal claimant and the legal basis of the claim at any time if clear, convincing, objective documentation is submitted to the Copyright Office which proves that an inadvertent error was made in failing to designate the correct living statutory renewal claimant in the basic renewal registration.

(c) *Form and content of application for supplementary registration.* (1) An application for supplementary registration shall be made on a form prescribed by the Copyright Office, shall be accompanied by the appropriate fee identified in §201.3(c) and shall contain the following information:

[1] If the person who, or on whose behalf, an application for supplementary registration is submitted is the same as the person identified as the copyright claimant in the basic registration, the Copyright Office will place a note referring to the supplementary registration on its records of the basic registration.

(i) The title of the work as it appears in the basic registration, including previous or alternative titles if they appear;

(ii) The registration number of the basic registration;

(iii) The year when the basic registration was completed;

(iv) The name or names of the author or authors of the work, and the copyright claimant or claimants in the work, as they appear in the basic registration;

(v) In the case of a correction:

(A) The line number and heading or description of the part of the basic registration where the error occurred;

(B) A transcription of the erroneous information as it appears in the basic registration;

(C) A statement of the correct information as it should have appeared; and

(D) If desired, an explanation of the error or its correction;

(vi) In the case of an amplification:

(A) The line number and heading or description of the part of the basic registration where the information to be amplified appears;

(B) A clear and succinct statement of the information to be added; and

(C) If desired, an explanation of the amplification;

(vii) The name and address:

(A) To which correspondence concerning the application should be sent; and

(B) To which the certificate of supplementary registration should be mailed; and

(viii) The certification shall consist of:

(A) The handwritten signature of the author, other copyright claimant, or owner of exclusive right(s) in the work, or of the duly authorized agent of such author, other claimant or owner (who shall also be identified);

(B) The typed or printed name of the person whose signature appears, and the date of signature; and

(C) A statement that the person signing the application is the author, other copyright claimant, or owner of exclusive right(s) in the work, or the authorized agent of such author, other claimant, or owner, and that the statements made in the application are correct to the best of that person's knowledge.

(2) The form prescribed by the Copyright Office for the foregoing purposes is designated "Application for Supplementary Copyright Registration (Form CA)". Copies of the form are available free upon request to the Copyright Information Section, Library of Congress, Copyright Office, 101 Independence Avenue, SE, Washington, DC 20559-6000.

(3) Copies, phonorecords or supporting documents cannot be made part of the record of a supplementary registration and should not be submitted with the application.

(d) *Effect of supplementary registration.* (1) When a supplementary registration is completed, the Copyright Office will assign it a new registration number in the appropriate class, and issue a certificate of supplementary registration under that number.

(2) As provided in section 408(d) of title 17, the information contained in a supplementary registration augments but does not supersede that contained in the basic registration. The basic registration will not be expunged or cancelled.

(Pub. L. 94–553; 17 U.S.C. 205, 408(d), 601(b), 702, 708)

[43 FR 773, Jan. 4, 1978, as amended at 56 FR 59885, Nov. 26, 1991; 57 FR 60482, Dec. 21, 1992; 60 FR 34168, June 30, 1995; 62 FR 35421, July 1, 1997; 63 FR 59236, Nov. 3, 1998; 63 FR 66042, Dec. 1, 1998; 64 FR 29521, June 1, 1999; 65 FR 39819, June 28, 2000; 65 FR 48914, Aug. 10, 2000; 66 FR 34372, June 28, 2001; 73 FR 37838, July 2, 2008]

§ 201.6 Payment and refund of Copyright Office fees.

(a) *In general.* All fees sent to the Copyright Office should be in the form of a money order, check or bank draft payable to the Register of Copyrights. Coin or currency sent to the Office in letters or packages will be at the remitter's risk. Remittances from foreign countries should be in the form of an International Money Order or Bank Draft payable and immediately negotiable in the United States for the full amount of the fee required. Uncertified checks are accepted subject to collection. Where the statutory fee is submitted in the form of a check, the registration of the copyright claim or other record made by the Office is provisional until payment in money is received. In the event the fee is not paid, the registration or other record shall be expunged.

(b) *Deposit accounts.* (1) Persons or firms having 12 or more transactions a year with the Copyright Office may prepay copyright expenses by establishing a Deposit Account. The Office and the Deposit Account holder will cooperatively determine an appropriate minimum balance for the Deposit Account which, in no case, can be less than $450, and the Office will automatically notify the Deposit Account holder when the account goes below that balance.

(2) The Copyright Office will close a Deposit Account the second time the Deposit Account holder overdraws his or her account within any 12-month period. An account closed for this reason can be re-opened only if the holder elects to fund it through automatic replenishment.

(3) In order to ensure that a Deposit Account's funds are sufficiently maintained, a Deposit Account holder may authorize the Copyright Office to automatically replenish the account from the holder's bank account or credit card. The amount by which a Deposit Account will be replenished will be determined by the deposit account holder. Automatic replenishment will be triggered when the Deposit Account goes below the minimum level of funding established pursuant to paragraph (b)(1) of this section, and Deposit Account holders will be automatically notified that their accounts will be replenished. Funding through automatic replenishment is required if a Deposit Account holder, who has had an account closed because it has been overdrawn twice within any 12 month period, wishes to re-open the account.

(c) *Refunds.* (1) Money remitted to the Copyright Office for basic, supplementary or renewal registration, including mask works and vessel hulls, will not be refunded if the claim is rejected because the material deposited does not constitute copyrightable subject matter or because the claim is invalid for any other reason. Payments made by mistake or in excess of the fee will be refunded, but amounts of $50 or less will not be refunded unless specifically requested, and refunds of less than $2 may be made in postage stamps. Except for services specified in paragraphs (c)(2) and (3) of this section, before making any refund for fees remitted in relation to non-registration copyright services, the Copyright Office shall deduct an administrative processing fee in an amount equivalent to one hour of the requested service, or the minimum charge for the service.

(2) In instances where money has been remitted to pay for recordation of a document, and it is determined that the document cannot be recorded, the basic recordation fee covering one title will be retained as a filing fee. Any additional money over the basic fee for one title will be refunded, but amounts of $50 or less will not be refunded unless specifically requested, and refunds of less than $2 may be made in postage stamps.

(3) For services where fees are calculated on an hourly basis, such as preparation of a search report, certification of certain Copyright Office records, or location and retrieval of records, in instances where the request is withdrawn before work is begun by the staff member responsible for providing the service, the Copyright Office will retain half of the hourly charge for administrative expenses, and refund the remaining portion of the fee subject to paragraph (c)(1) of this section. In addition, the fee for an estimate of a search fee is non-refundable. This policy applies to requests to the Records, Research and Certification Section, and requests to the Licensing Division.

(d) *Return of deposit copies.* Copies of works deposited in the Copyright Office pursuant to law are either retained in the Copyright Office, transferred for the permanent collections or other uses of the Library of Congress, or disposed of according to law. When an application is rejected, the Copyright Office reserves the right to retain the deposited copies.

(17 U.S.C. 702, 708(c))

[24 FR 4955, June 18, 1959, as amended at 46 FR 25442, May 7, 1981; 56 FR 7813, Feb. 26, 1991; 59 FR 38371, July 28, 1994; 74 FR 32809, July 9, 2009; 76 FR 9231, Feb. 17, 2011]

§ 201.7 Cancellation of completed registrations.

(a) *Definition.* Cancellation is an action taken by the Copyright Office whereby either the registration is eliminated on the ground that the registration is invalid under the applicable law and regulations, or the registration number is eliminated and a new registration is made under a different class and number.

(b) *General policy.* The Copyright Office will cancel a completed registration only in those cases where:

(1) It is clear that no registration should have been made because the work does not constitute copyrightable subject matter or fails to satisfy the other legal and formal requirements for obtaining copyright;

(2) Registration may be authorized but the application, deposit material, or fee does not meet the requirements of the law and Copyright Office regulations, and the Office is unable to get the defect corrected; or

(3) An existing registration in the wrong class is to be replaced by a new registration in the correct class.

(c) *Circumstances under which a registration will be cancelled.* (1) Where the Copyright Office becomes aware after registration that a work is not copyrightable, either because the authorship is *de minimis* or the work does not contain authorship subject to copyright, the registration will be cancelled. The copyright claimant will be notified by correspondence of the proposed cancellation and the reasons therefor, and be given 30 days, from the date the Copyright Office letter is mailed, to show cause in writing why the cancellation should not be made. If the claimant fails to respond within the 30 day period, or if the Office after considering the response, determines that the registration was made in error and not in accordance with title 17 U.S.C., Chapters 1 through 8, the registration will be cancelled.

(2) When a check received in payment of a registration fee is returned to the Copyright Office marked "insufficient funds" or is otherwise uncollectible the Copyright Office will immediately cancel any registration(s) for which the dishonored check was submitted and will notify the remitter the registration has been cancelled because the check was returned as uncollectible.

(3) Where registration is made in the wrong class, the Copyright Office will cancel the first registration, replace it with a new registration in the correct class, and issue a corrected certificate.

(4) Where registration has been made for a work which appears to be copyrightable but after registration the Copyright Office becomes aware that, on the administrative record before the Office, the statutory requirements have apparently not been satisfied, or that information essential to registration has been omitted entirely from the application or is questionable, or correct deposit material has not been deposited, the Office will correspond with the copyright claimant in an attempt to secure the required information or deposit material or to clarify the information previously given on the application. If the Copyright Office receives no reply to its correspondence within 30 days of the date the letter is mailed, or the response does not resolve the substantive defect, the registration will be cancelled. The correspondence will include the reason for the cancellation. The following are instances where a completed registration will be cancelled unless the substantive defect in the registration can be cured:

(i) Eligibility for registration has not been established;

(ii) A work published before March 1, 1989, was registered more than 5 years after the date of first publication and the deposit copy or phonorecord does not contain a statutory copyright notice;

(iii) The deposit copies or phonorecords of a work published before January 1, 1978 do not contain a copyright notice or the notice is defective;

(iv) A renewal claim was registered after the statutory time limits for registration had apparently expired;

(v) The application and copy(s) or phonorecord(s) do not match each other and the Office cannot locate a copy or phonorecord as described in the application elsewhere in the Copyright Office or the Library of Congress;

(vi) The application for registration does not identify a copyright claimant or it appears from the transfer statement on the application or elsewhere that the "claimant" named in the application does not have the right to claim copyright;

(vii) A claim to copyright is based on material added to a preexisting work and a reading of the application in its totality indicates that there is no copyrightable new material on which to base a claim;

(viii) A work subject to the manufacturing provisions of the Act of 1909 was apparently published in violation of those provisions;

(ix) For a work published after January 1, 1978, the only claimant given on the application was deceased on the date the application was certified;

(x) A work is not anonymous or pseudonymous and statements on the application and/or copy vary so much that the author cannot be identified; and

(xi) Statements on the application conflict or are so unclear that the claimant cannot be adequately identified.

(d) *Minor substantive errors.* Where a registration includes minor substantive errors or omissions which would generally have been rectified before registration, the Copyright Office will attempt to rectify the error through correspondence with the remitter. Except in those cases enumerated in paragraph (c) of this section, if the Office is unable for any reason to obtain the correct information or deposit copy, the registration record will be annotated to state the nature of the informality and show that the Copyright Office attempted to correct the registration.

[50 FR 40835, Oct. 7, 1985, as amended at 60 FR 34168, June 30, 1995; 65 FR 39819, June 28, 2000; 66 FR 34372, June 28, 2001]

§201.8 Disruption of postal or other transportation or communication services.

(a) For purposes of 17 U.S.C. 709, when the Register has determined that there is or has been a general disruption or suspension of postal or other transportation or communications services that has delayed the receipt by the Copyright Office of deposits, applications, fees, or any other materials, the Register shall publish an announcement of that determination, stating the date on which the disruption or suspension commenced. The announcement may, if appropriate, limit the means of delivery that are subject to relief pursuant to section 709. Following the cessation of the disruption or suspension of services, the Register shall publish an announcement stating the date on which the disruption or suspension has terminated.

(b) At the request of any person who provides satisfactory evidence that he or she has attempted to deliver a deposit, application, fee or other material to the Copyright Office but that receipt by the Copyright Office was delayed due to a general disruption or suspension of postal or other transportation or communications services, the Register shall assign, as the date of receipt of the deposit, application, fee or other material, the date on which the Register determines the material would have been received but for the disruption or suspension of services, if the deposit, application, fee or other material was actually received in the Copyright Office within one month after the disruption or suspension of services has terminated.

(c) *Timing.* The request shall be made:

(1) With respect to an application for copyright registration, no earlier than the date on which the claimant receives the certificate of registration and no later than one year after the date on which the claimant receives the certificate of registration; provided, however, that a request may be made prior to receipt of a certificate of registration—

(i) If the Copyright Office has communicated with the claimant relating to the application and the claimant makes the request as part of a response to the communication from the Office; or

(ii) If the Register determines that good cause exists to entertain a request prior to the issuance of a certificate of registration;

(2) With respect to a transfer of copyright ownership or other document submitted for recordation pursuant to 17 U.S.C. 205, no later than one year after the date on which the person submitting the transfer or document receives the certificate of recordation;

(3) With respect to any other material, no later than one year after the date on which the material was actually received in the Copyright Office.

(d) In cases in which a certificate or registration or a certificate of recordation has already been issued, the original certificate must be returned to the Copyright Office along with the request.

(e) For purposes of paragraph (b) of this section, satisfactory evidence shall consist of:

(1) A receipt from the United States Postal Service indicating the date on which the United States Postal Service received material for delivery to the Copyright Office by means of first class mail, Priority Mail or Express Mail;

(2) A receipt from a delivery service such as, or comparable to, United Parcel Service, Federal Express, or Airborne Express, indicating the date on which the delivery service received material for delivery to the Copyright Office and

(i) The date on which delivery was to be made to the Copyright Office, or

(ii) The period of time (e.g., overnight, or 2 days) from receipt by the delivery service to the date on which delivery was to be made to the Copyright Office;

(3) Other documentary evidence which the Register deems equivalent to the evidence set forth in paragraphs (e)(1) and (2) of this section; or

(4) A sworn statement from a person with actual knowledge of the facts relating to the attempt to deliver the material to the Copyright Office, setting forth with particularity facts which satisfy the Register that in the absence of the general disruption or suspension of postal or other transportation or communications services, the material would have been received by the Copyright Office by a particular date.

(f) For purposes of paragraph (b) of this section, the Register shall presume that but for the general disruption or suspension of postal or other transportation or communications services,

(1) Materials deposited with the United States Postal Service for delivery by means of first class mail would have been received in the Copyright Office seven days after deposit with the United States Postal Service;

(2) Materials deposited with the United States Postal Service for delivery by means of Priority mail would have been received in the Copyright Office three days after deposit with the United States Postal Service;

(3) Materials deposited with the United States Postal Service for delivery by means of Express mail would have been received in the Copyright Office one day after deposit with the United States Postal Service;

(4) Materials deposited with a delivery service such as, or comparable to, United Parcel Service, Federal Express, or Airborne Express, would have been received in the Copyright Office on the date indicated on the receipt from the delivery service.

(g) Requests pursuant to paragraph (b) of this section shall be addressed to: Chief, Copyright Office Receipt, Analysis and Control Division, Copyright Office, and if delivered by hand they should be brought to the Copyright Information Section, Library of Congress, James Madison Memorial Building, Room 401, First and Independence Avenue, SE., Washington, DC. If mailed, the request should be addressed to Chief, Receipt, Analysis and Control Division, P.O. Box 71380, Washington, DC 20024–1380.

[66 FR 62944, Dec. 4, 2001; 66 FR 63920, Dec. 11, 2001; 73 FR 37838, July 2, 2008]

§ 201.9 Recordation of agreements between copyright owners and public broadcasting entities.

(a) License agreements voluntarily negotiated between one or more owners of copyright in published nondramatic musical works and published pictorial, graphic, and sculptural works, and one or more public broadcasting entities, and terms and rates of royalty payments agreed to among owners of copyright in nondramatic literary works and public broadcasting entities will be filed in the Copyright Office, Licensing Division by recordation upon payment of the fee prescribed by § 201.3. The document submitted for recordation shall meet the following requirements:

(1) It shall be an original instrument of agreement; or it shall be a legible photocopy or other full-size facsimile

reproduction of an original, accompanied by a certification signed by at least one of the parties to the agreement, or an authorized representative of that party, that the reproduction is a true copy;

(2) It shall bear the signatures of all persons identified as parties to the agreement, or of their authorized agents or representatives;

(3) It shall be complete on its face, and shall include any schedules, appendixes, or other attachments referred to in the instrument as being part of it; and

(4) It shall be clearly identified, in its body or a covering transmittal letter, as being submitted for recordation under 17 U.S.C. 118.

(b) The fee for recordation of a voluntary license agreement under this section is the basic recordation fee as prescribed in § 201.3(c).

(c) The date of recordation is the date when all of the elements required for recordation, including the prescribed fee, have been received in the Copyright Office. A document is filed in the Copyright Office, and a filing in the Copyright Office takes place on the date of recordation. After recordation the document is returned to the sender with a certificate of record.

(17 U.S.C. 207 and 17 U.S.C. 118, 702, 708(11), as amended by Pub. L. 94–553)

[42 FR 16777, Mar. 30, 1977, as amended at 46 FR 33249, June 29, 1981; 56 FR 59885, Nov. 26, 1991; 64 FR 29521, June 1, 1999]

§ 201.10 Notices of termination of transfers and licenses.

This section covers notices of termination of transfers and licenses under sections 203, 304(c) and 304(d) of title 17, of the United States Code. A termination under section 304(d) is possible only if no termination was made under section 304(c), and federal copyright was originally secured on or between January 1, 1923, and October 26, 1939.

(a) *Form.* The Copyright Office does not provide printed forms for the use of persons serving notices of termination.

(b) *Contents.* (1) A notice of termination covering the extended renewal term under sections 304(c) and 304(d) of title 17, U.S.C., must include a clear identification of each of the following:

(i) Whether the termination is made under section 304(c) or under section 304(d);

(ii) The name of each grantee whose rights are being terminated, or the grantee's successor in title, and each address at which service of the notice is being made;

(iii) The title and the name of at least one author of, and the date copyright was originally secured in, each work to which the notice of termination applies; and, if possible and practicable, the original copyright registration number;

(iv) A brief statement reasonably identifying the grant to which the notice of termination applies;

(v) The effective date of termination;

(vi) If termination is made under section 304(d), a statement that termination of renewal term rights under section 304(c) has not been previously exercised; and

(vii) In the case of a termination of a grant executed by a person or persons other than the author, a listing of the surviving person or persons who executed the grant. In the case of a termination of a grant executed by one or more of the authors of the work where the termination is exercised by the successors of a deceased author, a listing of the names and relationships to that deceased author of all of the following, together with specific indication of the person or persons executing the notice who constitute more than one-half of that author's termination interest: That author's surviving widow or widower; and all of that author's surviving children; and, where any of that author's children are dead, all of the surviving children of any such deceased child of that author; however, instead of the information required by this paragraph (vii), the notice may contain both of the following:

(A) A statement of as much of such information as is currently available to the person or persons signing the notice, with a brief explanation of the reasons why full information is or may be lacking; together with

(B) A statement that, to the best knowledge and belief of the person or persons signing the notice, the notice has been signed by all persons whose signature is necessary to terminate the grant under section 304 of title 17, U.S.C., or by their duly authorized agents.

(2) A notice of termination of an exclusive or nonexclusive grant of a transfer or license of copyright or of any right under a copyright, executed by the author on or after January 1, 1978, under section 203 of title 17, U.S.C., must include a clear identification of each of the following:

(i) A statement that the termination is made under section 203;

(ii) The name of each grantee whose rights are being terminated, or the grantee's successor in title, and each address at which service of the notice is being made;

(iii) The date of execution of the grant being terminated and, if the grant covered the right of publication of a work, the date of publication of the work under the grant;

(iv) For each work to which the notice of termination applies, the title of the work and the name of the author or, in the case of a joint work, the authors who executed the grant being terminated; and, if possible and practicable, the original copyright registration number;

(v) A brief statement reasonably identifying the grant to which the notice of termination applies;

(vi) The effective date of termination; and

(vii) In the case of a termination of a grant executed by one or more of the authors of the work where the termination is exercised by the successors of a deceased author, a listing of the names and relationships to that deceased author of all of the following, together with specific indication of the person or persons executing the notice who constitute more than one-half of that author's termination interest: That author's surviving widow or widower; and all of that author's surviving children; and, where any of that author's children are dead, all of the surviving children of any such deceased child of that author; however, instead of the information required by this paragraph (b)(2)(vii), the notice may contain both of the following:

(A) A statement of as much of such information as is currently available to the person or persons signing the notice, with a brief explanation of the reasons why full information is or may be lacking; together with

(B) A statement that, to the best knowledge and belief of the person or persons signing the notice, the notice has been signed by all persons whose signature is necessary to terminate the grant under section 203 of title 17, U.S.C., or by their duly authorized agents.

(3) Clear identification of the information specified by paragraphs (b)(1) and (b)(2) of this section requires a complete and unambiguous statement of facts in the notice itself, without incorporation by reference of information in other documents or records.

(c) *Signature.* (1) In the case of a termination of a grant under section 304(c) or section 304(d) executed by a person or persons other than the author, the notice shall be signed by all of the surviving person or persons who executed the grant, or by their duly authorized agents.

(2) In the case of a termination of a grant under section 304(c) or section 304(d) executed by one or more of the authors of the work, the notice as to any one author's share shall be signed by that author or by his or her duly authorized agent. If that author is dead, the notice shall be signed by the number and proportion of the owners of that author's termination interest required under section 304(c) or section 304(d), whichever applies, of title 17, U.S.C., or by their duly authorized agents, and shall contain a brief statement of their relationship or relationships to that author.

(3) In the case of a termination of a grant under section 203 executed by one or more of the authors of the work, the notice shall be signed by each author who is terminating the grant or by his or her duly authorized agent. If that author is dead, the notice shall be signed by the number and proportion of the owners of that author's termination interest required under section 203 of title 17, U.S.C., or by their duly authorized agents, and shall contain a brief statement of their relationship or relationships to that author.

(4) Where a signature is by a duly authorized agent, it shall clearly identify

the person or persons on whose behalf the agent is acting.

(5) The handwritten signature of each person effecting the termination shall either be accompanied by a statement of the full name and address of that person, typewritten or printed legibly by hand, or shall clearly correspond to such a statement elswhere in the notice.

(d) *Service.* (1) The notice of termination shall be served upon each grantee whose rights are being terminated, or the grantee's successor in title, by personal service, or by first-class mail sent to an address which, after a reasonable investigation, is found to be the last known address of the grantee or successor in title.

(2) The service provision of section 203, section 304(c) or section 304(d) of title 17, U.S.C., whichever applies, will be satisfied if, before the notice of termination is served, a reasonable investigation is made by the person or persons executing the notice as to the current ownership of the rights being terminated, and based on such investigation:

(i) If there is no reason to believe that such rights have been transferred by the grantee to a successor in title, the notice is served on the grantee; or

(ii) If there is reason to believe that such rights have been transferred by the grantee to a particular successor in title, the notice is served on such successor in title.

(3) For purposes of paragraph (d)(2) of this section, a *reasonable investigation* includes, but is not limited to, a search of the records in the Copyright Office; in the case of a musical composition with respect to which performing rights are licensed by a performing rights society, a "reasonable investigation" also includes a report from that performing rights society identifying the person or persons claiming current ownership of the rights being terminated.

(4) Compliance with the provisions of paragraphs (d)(2) and (d)(3) of this section will satisfy the service requirements of section 203, section 304(c), or section 304(d) of title 17, U.S.C., whichever applies. However, as long as the statutory requirements have been met, the failure to comply with the regulatory provisions of paragraph (d)(2) or (d)(3) of this section will not affect the validity of the service.

(e) *Harmless errors.* (1) Harmless errors in a notice that do not materially affect the adequacy of the information required to serve the purposes of section 203, section 304(c), or section 304(d) of title 17, U.S.C., whichever applies, shall not render the notice invalid.

(2) Without prejudice to the general rule provided by paragraph (e)(1) of this section, errors made in giving the date or registration number referred to in paragraph (b)(1)(iii), (b)(2)(iii), or (b)(2)(iv) of this section, or in complying with the provisions of paragraph (b)(1)(vii) or (b)(2)(vii) of this section, or in describing the precise relationships under paragraph (c)(2) or (c)(3) of this section, shall not affect the validity of the notice if the errors were made in good faith and without any intention to deceive, mislead, or conceal relevant information.

(f) *Recordation.* (1) A copy of the notice of termination will be recorded in the Copyright Office upon payment of the fee prescribed by paragraph (2) of this paragraph (f) and upon compliance with the following provisions:

(i) The copy submitted for recordation shall be a complete and exact duplicate of the notice of termination as served and shall include the actual signature or signatures, or a reproduction of the actual signature or signatures, appearing on the notice; where separate copies of the same notice were served on more than one grantee or successor in title, only one copy need be submitted for recordation; and

(ii) The copy submitted for recordation shall be accompanied by a statement setting forth the date on which the notice was served and the manner of service, unless such information is contained in the notice. In instances where service is made by first-class mail, the date of service shall be the day the notice of termination was deposited with the United States Postal Service.

(iii) The copy submitted for recordation must be legible per the requirements of § 201.4(c)(3).

(2) The fee for recordation of a document is prescribed in § 201.3(c).

(3) The date of recordation is the date when all of the elements required for recordation, including the prescribed fee and, if required, the statement referred to in paragraph (f)(1)(ii) of this section, have been received in the Copyright Office. After recordation, the document, including any accompanying statement, is returned to the sender with a certificate of record.

(4) Notwithstanding anything to the contrary in this section, the Copyright Office reserves the right to refuse recordation of a notice of termination as such if, in the judgment of the Copyright Office, such notice of termination is untimely. Conditions under which a notice of termination will be considered untimely include: the effective date of termination does not fall within the five-year period described in section 203(a)(3) or section 304(c)(3), as applicable, of title 17, United States Code; or the documents submitted indicate that the notice of termination was served less than two or more than ten years before the effective date of termination. If a notice of termination is untimely or if a document is submitted for recordation as a notice of termination on or after the effective date of termination, the Office will offer to record the document as a "document pertaining to copyright" pursuant to § 201.4(c)(3), but the Office will not index the document as a notice of termination.

(5) In any case where an author agreed, prior to January 1, 1978, to a grant of a transfer or license of rights in a work that was not created until on or after January 1, 1978, a notice of termination of a grant under section 203 of title 17 may be recorded if it recites, as the date of execution, the date on which the work was created.

(6) A copy of the notice of termination shall be recorded in the Copyright Office before the effective date of termination, as a condition to its taking effect. However, the fact that the Office has recorded the notice does not mean that it is otherwise sufficient under the law. Recordation of a notice of termination by the Copyright Office is without prejudice to any party claiming that the legal and formal requirements for issuing a valid notice have not been met, including before a court of competent jurisdiction.

(7) Notices of termination should be submitted to the address specified in § 201.1(b)(2).

(Pub. L. 94–553; 17 U.S.C. 304(c), 702, 708(11))

[42 FR 45920, Sept. 13, 1977, as amended at 56 FR 59885, Nov. 26, 1991; 60 FR 34168, June 30, 1995; 64 FR 29521, June 1, 1999; 64 FR 36574, July 7, 1999; 66 FR 34372, June 28, 2001; 67 FR 69136, Nov. 15, 2002; 67 FR 78176, Dec. 23, 2002; 68 FR 16959, Apr. 8, 2003; 71 FR 36486, June 27, 2006; 74 FR 12556, Mar. 25, 2009; 76 FR 32320, June 6, 2011]

§ 201.11 Satellite carrier statements of account covering statutory licenses for secondary transmissions.

(a) *General.* This section prescribes rules pertaining to the deposit of Statements of Account and royalty fees in the Copyright Office as required by the satellite carrier license of section 119(b)(1) and Section 122(a) of title 17 of the United States Code, as amended by Pub. L. No. 111–175, in order that certain secondary transmissions by satellite carriers for private home viewing be subject to statutory licensing.

(b) *Definitions.* (1) The terms *distributor, network station, private home viewing, satellite carrier, subscribe, subscriber, non-network station, unserved household, primary stream, and multicast stream,* have the meanings set forth in Section 119(d) of title 17 of the United States Code, as amended by Pub. L. No. 111–175.

(2) The terms *primary transmission* and *secondary transmission* have the meanings set forth in section 111(f) of title 17 of the United States Code.

(c) *Accounting periods and deposit.* (1) Statements of Account shall cover semiannual accounting periods of January 1 through June 30, and July 1 through December 31, and shall be deposited in the Copyright Office, together with the total statutory royalty fee or the confirmed arbitration royalty fee for such accounting periods as prescribed by section 119(b)(1)(B) and (c)(3) of title 17, by not later than July 30, if the Statement of Account covers the January 1 through June 30 accounting period, and by not later than the immediately following January 30, if the Statement of Account covers the

July 1 through December 31 accounting period.

(2) Upon receiving a Statement of Account and royalty fee, the Copyright Office will make an official record of the actual date when such statement and fee were physically received in the Copyright Office. Thereafter, the Licensing Division of the Copyright Office will examine the statement and fee for obvious errors or omissions appearing on the face of the documents, and will require that any such obvious errors or omissions be corrected before final processing of the documents is completed. If, as the result of communications between the Copyright Office and the satellite carrier, an additional fee is deposited or changes or additions are made in the Statement of Account, the date that additional deposit or information was actually received in the Office will be added to the official record of the case. However, completion by the Copyright Office of the final processing of a Statement of Account and royalty fee deposit shall establish only the fact of such completion and the date or dates of receipt shown in the official record. It shall in no case be considered a determination that the Statement of Account was, in fact, properly prepared and accurate, that the correct amount of the royalty fee had been deposited, that the statutory time limits for filing had been met, or that any other requirements to qualify for a statutory license have been satisfied.

(3) Statements of Account and royalty fees received before the end of the particular accounting period they purport to cover will not be processed by the Copyright Office. Statements of Account and royalty fees received after the filing deadlines of July 30 or January 30, respectively, will be accepted for whatever legal effect they may have, if any.

(4) In the Register's discretion, four years after the close of any calendar year, the Register may close out the royalty payments account for that calendar year, and may treat any funds remaining in such account and any subsequent deposits that would otherwise be attributable to that calendar year as attributable to the succeeding calendar year.

(d) *Forms.* (1) Each Statement of Account shall be furnished on an appropriate form prescribed by the Copyright Office, and shall contain the information required by that form and its accompanying instructions. Computation of the copyright royalty fee shall be in accordance with the procedures set forth in the forms. Copies of Statement of Account forms are available free upon request to the Library of Congress, Copyright Office, Licensing Division, 101 Independence Avenue, SE, Washington, DC 20557–6400.

(2) The form prescribed by the Copyright Office is designated "Statement of Account for Secondary Transmissions by Satellite Carriers to Home Viewers."

(e) *Contents.* Each Statement of Account shall contain the following information:

(1) A clear designation of the accounting period covered by the Statement.

(2) The designation "Owner" followed by:

(i) The full legal name of the satellite carrier. If the owner is a partnership, the name of the partnership is to be followed by the name of at least one individual partner;

(ii) Any other name or names under which the owner conducts the business of the satellite carrier; and

(iii) The full mailing address of the owner. Ownership, other names under which the owner conducts the business of the satellite carrier, and the owner's mailing address shall reflect facts existing on the last day of the accounting period covered by the Statement of Account.

(3) The designation "Primary Transmitters," followed by the call signs, broadcast channel numbers, station locations (city and state of license), and a notation whether that primary transmitter is a "non-network station" or "network station" transmitted to any or all of the subscribers of the satellite carrier during any portion of the period covered by the Statement of Account.

(4) The designation "non-network station," followed by:

(i) The call sign of each non-network station signal carried for each month of the period covered by the Statement, and

(ii) The total number of subscribers to each non-network station for each month of the period covered by the Statement. This number is the number of subscribers to each non-network station receiving the retransmission on the last day of each month.

(5) The designation "Network Stations," followed by:

(i) The call sign of each network station carried for each month of the period covered by the Statement, and

(ii) The total number of subscribers to each network station for each month of the period covered by the Statement. This number is the number of subscribers to each network station receiving the retransmission on the last day of each month.

(6) The total number of subscribers to each non-network station for the six-month period covered by the Statement multiplied by the statutory royalty rate prescribed in § 258.3 of this chapter.

(7) The total number of subscribers to each network station for the six-month period covered by the Statement multiplied by the statutory royalty rate prescribed in § 258.3 of this chapter.

(8) The name, address, business title, and telephone number of the individual or individuals to be contacted for information or questions concerning the content of the Statement of Account.

(9) The handwritten signature of:

(i) The owner of the satellite carrier or a duly authorized agent of the owner, if the owner is not a partnership or a corporation; or

(ii) A partner, if the owner is a partnership; or

(iii) An officer of the corporation, if the owner is a corporation. The signature shall be accompanied by:

(A) The printed or typewritten name of the person signing the Statement of Account;

(B) The date of signature;

(C) If the owner of the satellite carrier is a partnership or a corporation, by the title or official position held in the partnership or corporation by the person signing the Statement of Account;

(D) A certification of the capacity of the person signing; and

(E) The following statement:

I, the undersigned Owner or Agent of the Satellite Carrier, or Officer or Partner, if the Satellite Carrier is a Corporation or Partnership, have examined this Statement of Account and hereby declare under penalty of law that all statements of fact contained herein are true, complete, and correct to the best of my knowledge, information, and belief, and are made in good faith.

(18 U.S.C., section 1001 (1986))

(f) *Royalty fee payment.* (1) All royalty fees shall be paid by a single electronic funds transfer and payment must be received in the designated bank by the filing deadline for the relevant accounting period. The following information shall be provided as part of the EFT and/or as part of the remittance advice as provided for in circulars issued by the Copyright Office:

(i) Remitter's name and address;

(ii) Name of a contact person, telephone number and extension, and email address;

(iii) The actual or anticipated date that the EFT will be transmitted;

(iv) Type of royalty payment (*i.e.*, satellite);

(v) Total amount submitted via the EFT;

(vi) Total amount to be paid by year and period;

(vii) Number of Statements of Account that the EFT covers;

(viii) ID numbers assigned by the Licensing Division;

(ix) Legal name of the owner for each Statement of Account.

(2) The remittance advice shall be attached to the Statement(s) of Account. In addition, a copy of the remittance advice shall be emailed or sent by facsimile to the Licensing Division.

(3) The Office may waive the requirement for payment by electronic funds transfer as set forth in paragraph (f)(1) of this section. To obtain a waiver, the remitter shall submit to the Licensing Division at least 60 days prior to the royalty fee due date a certified statement setting forth the reasons explaining why payment by an electronic funds transfer would be virtually impossible or, alternatively, why it would impose a financial or other hardship on the remitter. The certified statement must be signed by a duly authorized representative of the entity making the payment. A waiver shall cover only

a single payment period. Failure to obtain a waiver may result in the remittance being returned to the remitter.

(g) *Copies of statements of account.* A licensee shall file an original and one copy of the statement of account with the Licensing Division of the Copyright Office.

(h) *Corrections, supplemental payments, and refunds.* (1) Upon compliance with the procedures and within the time limits set forth in paragraph (h)(3) of this section, corrections to Statements of Account will be placed on record, supplemental royalty fee payments will be received for deposit, or refunds will be issued, in the following cases:

(i) Where, with respect to the accounting period covered by a Statement of Account, any of the information given in the Statement filed in the Copyright Office is incorrect or incomplete; or

(ii) Where calculation of the royalty fee payable for a particular accounting period was incorrect, and the amount deposited in the Copyright Office for that period was either too high or too low.

(2) Corrections to Statements of Account will not be placed on record, supplemental royalty fee payments will not be received for deposit, and refunds will not be issued, where the information in the Statements of Account, the royalty fee calculations, or the payments were correct as of the date on which the accounting period ended, but changes (for example, addition or deletion of a signal) took place later.

(3) Requests that corrections to a Statement of Account be placed on record, that fee payments be accepted, or requests for the issuance of refunds, shall be made only in the cases mentioned in paragraph (h)(1) of this section. Such requests shall be addressed to the Licensing Division of the Copyright Office, and shall meet the following conditions:

(i) The request must be in writing, must clearly identify its purpose, and, in the case of a request for a refund, must be received in the Copyright Office before the expiration of 30 days from the last day of the applicable Statement of Account filing period, or before the expiration of 30 days from the date of receipt at the Copyright Office of the royalty payment that is the subject of the request, whichever time period is longer. A telegraphic or similar unsigned communication will be considered to meet this requirement if it clearly identifies the basis of the request, if it is received in the Copyright Office within the required 30-day period, and if a written request meeting all the conditions of this paragraph (h)(3) is also received in the Copyright Office within 14 days after the end of such 30-day period:

(ii) The Statement of Account to which the request pertains must be sufficiently identified in the request (by inclusion of the name of the owner of the satellite carrier and the accounting period in question) so that it can be readily located in the records of the Copyright Office;

(iii) The request must contain a clear statement of the facts on which it is based and provide a clear basis on which a refund may be granted, in accordance with the following procedures:

(A) In the case of a request filed under paragraph (h)(1)(i) of this section, where the information given in the Statement of Account is incorrect or incomplete, the request must clearly identify the erroneous or incomplete information and provide the correct or additional information:

(B) In the case of a request filed under paragraph (h)(1)(ii) of this section, where the royalty fee was miscalculated and the amount deposited in the Copyright Office was either too high or too low, the request must be accompanied by an affidavit under the official seal of any officer authorized to administer oaths within the United States, or a statement in accordance with section 1746 of title 28 of the United States Code, made and signed in accordance with paragraph (e)(9) of this section. The affidavit or statement shall describe the reasons why the royalty fee was improperly calculated and include a detailed analysis of the proper royalty calculation.

(iv)(A) All requests filed under this paragraph (h) must be accompanied by a filing fee in the amount prescribed in § 201.3(e) of this part for each Statement of Account involved. Payment of this fee may be in the form of a personal or company check, or of a certified check, cashier's check or money order, payable to: Register of Copyrights. No request will be processed until the appropriate filing fees are received.

(B) All requests that a supplemental royalty fee payment be received for deposit under this paragraph (h) must be accompanied by a remittance in the full amount of such fee. Payment of the supplemental royalty fee must be in the form of certified check, cashier's check, or money order, payable to: Register of Copyrights; or electronic payment. No such request will be processed until an acceptable remittance in the full amount of the supplemental royalty fee has been received.

(v) All requests submitted under this paragraph (h) must be signed by the satellite carrier owner named in the Statement of Account, or the duly authorized agent of the owner, in accordance with paragraph (e)(9) of this section.

(vi) A request for a refund is not necessary where the Licensing Division, during its examination of a Statement of Account or related document, discovers an error that has resulted in a royalty overpayment. In this case, the Licensing Division will forward the royalty refund to the satellite carrier owner named in the Statement of Account without regard to the time limitations provided for in paragraph (h)(3)(i) of this section.

(4) Following final processing, all requests submitted under this paragraph (h) will be filed with the original Statement of Account in the records of the Copyright Office. Nothing contained in this paragraph shall be considered to relieve satellite carriers from their full obligations under title 17 of the United States Code, and the filing of a correction or supplemental payment shall have only such effect as may be attributed to it by a court of competent jurisdiction.

(i) *Interest.* (1) Royalty fee payments submitted as a result of late or amended filings will include interest. Interest will begin to accrue beginning on the first day after the close of the period for filing statements of account for all underpayments or late payments of royalties for the satellite carrier statutory license for secondary transmissions for private home viewing and viewing in commercial establishments occurring within that accounting period. The accrual period shall end on the date the electronic payment submitted by a satellite carrier is received by the Copyright Office. In cases where a waiver of the electronic funds transfer requirement is approved by the Copyright Office, and royalties payments are either late or underpaid, the accrual period shall end on the date the payment is postmarked. If the payment is not received by the Copyright Office within five business days of its date, then the accrual period shall end on the date of the actual receipt by the Copyright Office.

(2)(i) The interest rate applicable to a specific accounting period beginning with the 1992/2 period shall be the Current Value of Funds Rate, as established by section 8025.40 of the Treasury Financial Manual and published in the FEDERAL REGISTER, in effect on the first business day after the close of the filing deadline for that accounting period. Satellite carriers wishing to obtain the interest rate for a specific accounting period may do so by consulting the FEDERAL REGISTER for the applicable Current Value of Funds Rate, or by contacting the Licensing Division of the Copyright Office.

(ii) The interest rate applicable to a specific accounting period earlier than the 1992/2 period shall be the rate fixed by the Licensing Division of the Copyright Office pursuant to 37 CFR 201.11(h) in effect on June 30, 1992.

(3) Interest is not required to be paid on any royalty underpayment or late payment from a particular accounting period if the interest charge is less than or equal to five dollars ($5.00).

[54 FR 27877, July 3, 1989, as amended at 55 FR 49998, Dec. 4, 1990; 56 FR 29589, June 28, 1991; 57 FR 61834, Dec. 29, 1992; 59 FR 67635, Dec. 30, 1994; 60 FR 34168, June 30, 1995; 60 FR 57937, Nov. 24, 1995; 63 FR 30635, June 5, 1998; 64 FR 36574, July 7, 1999; 70 FR 30366, May 26, 2005; 70 FR 38022, July 1, 2005; 71 FR 45739, Aug. 10, 2006; 72 FR 33691, June 19, 2007; 73 FR 29072, May 20, 2008; 75 FR 56872, Sept. 17, 2010]

§ 201.12 Recordation of certain contracts by cable systems located outside of the forty-eight contiguous States.

(a) Written, nonprofit contracts providing for the equitable sharing of costs of videotapes and their transfer, as identified in section 111(e)(2) of title 17 of the United States Code as amended by Pub. L. 94–553, will be filed in the Copyright Office Licensing Division by recordation upon payment of the prescribed fee. The document submitted for recordation shall meet the following requirements:

(1) It shall be an original instrument of contract; or it shall be a legible photocopy or other full-size facsimile reproduction of an original, accompanied by a certification signed by at least one of the parties to the contract, or an authorized representative of that party, that the reproduction is a true copy;

(2) It shall bear the signatures of all persons identified as parties to the contract, or of their authorized agents or representatives;

(3) It shall be complete on its face, and shall include any schedules, appendixes, or other attachments referred to in the instrument as being part of it; and

(4) It shall be clearly identified, in its body or a covering transmittal letter, as being submitted for recordation under 17 U.S.C. 111(e).

(b) The fee for recordation of a document is prescribed in § 201.3.

(c) The date of recordation is the date when all of the elements required for recordation, including the prescribed fee, have been received in the Copyright Office. A document is filed in the Copyright Office and a filing in the Copyright Office takes place on the date of recordation. After recordation the document is returned to the sender with a certificate of record.

(Pub. L. 94–553; 17 U.S.C. 111, 702, 708(11))

[42 FR 53961, Oct. 4, 1977, as amended at 56 FR 59885, Nov. 26, 1991; 64 FR 29521, June 1, 1999]

§ 201.13 Notices of objection to certain noncommercial performances of nondramatic literary or musical works.

(a) *Definitions.* (1) A *Notice of Objection* is a notice, as required by section 110(4) of title 17 of the United States Code as amended by Pub. L. 94–553, to be served as a condition of preventing the noncommercial performance of a nondramatic literary or musical work under certain circumstances.

(2) For purposes of this section, the *copyright owner* of a nondramatic literary or musical work is the author of the work (including, in the case of a work made for hire, the employer or other person for whom the work was prepared), or a person or organization that has obtained ownership of the exclusive right, initially owned by the author of performance of the type referred to in 17 U.S.C. 110(4). If the other requirements of this section are met, a Notice of Objection may cover the works of more than one copyright owner.

(b) *Form.* The Copyright Office does not provide printed forms for the use of persons serving Notices of Objection.

(c) *Contents.* (1) A Notice of Objection must clearly state that the copyright owner objects to the performance, and must include all of the following:

(i) Reference to the statutory authority on which the Notice of Objection is based, either by citation of 17 U.S.C. 110(4) or by a more general characterization or description of that statutory provision;

(ii) The date and place of the performance to which an objection is being made; however, if the exact date or place of a particular performance, or both, are not known to the copyright owner, it is sufficient if the Notice describes whatever information the copyright owner has about the date and place of a particular performance, and the source of that information unless the source was considered private or confidential;

(iii) Clear identification, by title and at least one author, of the particular nondramatic literary or musical work or works, to the performance of which the copyright owner thereof is lodging objection; a Notice may cover any number of separately identified copyrighted works owned by the copyright owner or owners serving the objection. Alternatively, a blanket notice, with or without separate identification of certain copyrighted works, and purporting to cover one or more groups of copyrighted works not separately identified by title and author, shall have effect if the conditions specified in paragraph (c)(2) of this section are met; and

(iv) A concise statement of the reasons for the objection.

(2) A blanket notice purporting to cover one or more groups of copyrighted works not separately identified by title and author shall be valid only if all of the following conditions are met:

(i) The Notice shall identify each group of works covered by the blanket notice by a description of any common characteristics distinguishing them from other copyrighted works, such as common author, common copyright owner, common publisher, or common licensing agent;

(ii) The Notice shall identify a particular individual whom the person responsible for the performance can contact for more detailed information about the works covered by the blanket notice and to determine whether a particular work planned for performance is in fact covered by the Notice. Such identification shall include the full name and business and residence addresses of the individual, telephone numbers at which the individual can be reached throughout the period between service of the notice and the performance, and name, addresses, and telephone numbers of another individual to contact during that period in case the first cannot be reached.

(iii) If the copyright owner or owners of all works covered by the blanket notice is not identified in the Notice, the Notice shall include an offer to identify, by name and last known address, the owner or owners of any and all such works, upon request made to the individual referred to in paragraph (c)(2)(ii) of this section.

(3) A Notice of Objection must also include clear and prominent statements explaining that:

(i) A failure to exclude the works identified in the Notice from the performance in question may subject the person responsible for the performance to liability for copyright infringement; and

(ii) The objection is without legal effect if there is no direct or indirect admission charge for the performance, and if the other conditions of 17 U.S.C. 110(4) are met.

(d) *Signature and identification.* (1) A Notice of Objection shall be in writing and signed by each copyright owner, or such owner's duly authorized agent, as required by 17 U.S.C. 110(4)(B)(i).

(2) The signature of each owner or agent shall be an actual handwritten signature of an individual, accompanied by the date of signature and the full name, address, and telephone number of that person, typewritten or printed legibly by hand.

(3) If a Notice of Objection is initially served in the form of a telegram or similar communication, as provided by paragraph (e) of this section, the requirement for an individual's handwritten signature shall be considered waived if the further conditions of said paragraph (e) are met.

(e) *Service.* (1) A Notice of Objection shall be served on the person responsible for the performance at least seven days before the date of the performance, as provided by 17 U.S.C. 110 (4)(B)(ii).

(2) Service of the Notice may be effected by any of the following methods:

(i) Personal service;

(ii) First-class mail;

(iii) Telegram, cablegram, or similar form of communication, if:

(A) The Notice meets all of the other conditions provided by this section; and

(B) Before the performance takes place, the person responsible for the performance receives written confirmation of the Notice, bearing the actual handwritten signature of each copyright owner or duly authorized agent.

(3) The date of service is the date the Notice of Objection is received by the person responsible for the performance or any agent or employee of that person.

(Pub. L. 94–553; 17 U.S.C. 110(4), 702)

[42 FR 64684, Dec. 28, 1977]

§ 201.14 Warnings of copyright for use by certain libraries and archives.

(a) *Definitions.* (1) A *Display Warning of Copyright* is a notice under paragraphs (d)(2) and (e)(2) of section 108 of title 17 of the United States Code as amended by Pub. L. 94–553. As required by those sections the "Display Warning of Copyright" is to be displayed at the place where orders for copies or phonorecords are accepted by certain libraries and archives.

(2) An *Order Warning of Copyright* is a notice under paragraphs (d)(2) and (e)(2) of section 108 of title 17 of the United States Code as amended by Pub. L. 94–553. As required by those sections the "Order Warning of Copyright" is to be included on printed forms supplied by certain libraries and archives and used by their patrons for ordering copies or phonorecords.

(b) *Contents.* A Display Warning of Copyright and an Order Warning of Copyright shall consist of a verbatim reproduction of the following notice, printed in such size and form and displayed in such manner as to comply with paragraph (c) of this section:

NOTICE WARNING CONCERNING COPYRIGHT RESTRICTIONS

The copyright law of the United States (title 17, United States Code) governs the making of photocopies or other reproductions of copyrighted material.

Under certain conditions specified in the law, libraries and archives are authorized to furnish a photocopy or other reproduction. One of these specific conditions is that the photocopy or reproduction is not to be "used for any purpose other than private study, scholarship, or research." If a user makes a request for, or later uses, a photocopy or reproduction for purposes in excess of "fair use," that user may be liable for copyright infringement.

This institution reserves the right to refuse to accept a copying order if, in its judgment, fulfillment of the order would involve violation of copyright law.

(c) *Form and manner of use.* (1) A Display Warning of Copyright shall be printed on heavy paper or other durable material in type at least 18 points in size, and shall be displayed prominently, in such manner and location as to be clearly visible, legible, and comprehensible to a casual observer within the immediate vicinity of the place where orders are accepted.

(2) An Order Warning of Copyright shall be printed within a box located prominently on the order form itself, either on the front side of the form or immediately adjacent to the space calling for the name or signature of the person using the form. The notice shall be printed in type size no smaller than that used predominantly throughout the form, and in no case shall the type size be smaller than 8 points. The notice shall be printed in such manner as to be clearly legible, comprehensible, and readily apparent to a casual reader of the form.

(Pub. L. 94–553; 17 U.S.C. 108, 702)

[42 FR 59265, Nov. 16, 1977]

§ 201.16 [Reserved]

§ 201.17 Statements of Account covering compulsory licenses for secondary transmissions by cable systems.

(a) *General.* This section prescribes rules pertaining to the deposit of Statements of Account and royalty fees in the Coypright Office as required by section 111(d)(2) of title 17 of the United States Code in order for secondary transmissions of cable systems to be subject to compulsory licensing.

(b) *Definitions.* (1) Gross receipts for the "basic service of providing secondary transmissions of primary broadcast transmitters" include the full amount of monthly (or other periodic) service fees for any and all services or tiers of services which include one or more secondary transmissions of television or radio broadcast signals, for additional set fees, and for converter fees. In no case shall gross receipts be less than the cost of obtaining the signals of primary broadcast transmitters for subsequent retransmission. All such gross receipts shall be aggregated and the distant signal equivalent (DSE) calculations shall be made against the aggregated amount. Gross receipts for secondary transmission services do not include installation (including connection, relocation, disconnection, or reconnection) fees, separate charges for security, alarm or facsimile services, charges for late payments, or charges for pay cable or other program origination services: *Provided* That, the origination services are not offered in combination with secondary transmission service for a single fee.

(2) A *cable system* is a facility, located in any State, Territory, Trust Territory, or Possession, that in whole or in part receives signals transmitted or

programs broadcast by one or more television broadcast stations licensed by the Federal Communications Commission, and makes secondary transmissions of such signals or programs by wires, cables, microwave, or other communications channels to subscribing members of the public who pay for such service. A system that meets this definition is considered a "cable system" for copyright purposes, even if the FCC excludes it from being considered a "cable system" because of the number or nature of its subscribers or the nature of its secondary transmissions. The Statements of Account and royalty fees to be deposited under § 201.17 of this section, shall be recorded and deposited by each individual cable system desiring its secondary transmissions to be subject to compulsory licensing. The owner of each individual cable system on the last day of the accounting period covered by a Statement of Account is responsible for depositing the Statement of Account and remitting the copyright royalty fees. For these purposes, and the purpose of § 201.17 of this section, an "individual" cable system is each cable system recognized as a distinct entity under the rules, regulations, and practices of the Federal Communications Commission in effect on the last day of the accounting period covered by a Statement of Account, in the case of the preparation and deposit of a Statement of Account and copyright royalty fee. For these purposes, two or more cable facilities are considered as one individual cable system if the facilities are either:

(i) In contiguous communities under common ownership or control or

(ii) Operating from one headend.

(3) *FCC* means the Federal Communications Commission.

(4) In the case of cable systems which make secondary transmissions of all available FM radio signals, which signals are not electronically processed by the system as separate and discrete signals, an FM radio signal is "generally receivable" if:

(i) It is usually carried by the system whenever it is received at the system's headend, and

(ii) As a result of monitoring at reasonable times and intervals, it can be expected to be received at the system's headend, with the system's FM antenna, at least three consecutive hours each day at the same time each day, five or more days a week, for four or more weeks during any calendar quarter, with a strength of not less than fifty microvolts per meter measured at the foot of the tower or pole to which the antenna is attached.

(5) The terms *primary transmission, secondary transmission, local service area of a primary transmitter, distant signal equivalent, network station, independent station, noncommercial educational station, primary stream, multicast stream, simulcast, primary transmitter, subscriber,* and *subscribe* have the meanings set forth in Section 111(f) of title 17 of the United States Code, as amended by Pub. L. No. 94–553, Pub. L. No. 103–369, and Pub. L. No. 111–175.

(6) A primary transmitter is a "distant" station, for purposes of this section, if the programming of such transmitter is carried by the cable system in whole or in part beyond the local service area of such primary transmitter.

(7) A translator station is, with respect to programs both originally transmitted and retransmitted by it, a primary transmitter for the purposes of this section. A translator station which retransmits the programs of a network station will be considered a network station; a translator station which retransmits the programs of an independent station shall be considered an independent station; and a translator station which retransmits the programs of a noncommercial educational station shall be considered a noncommercial educational station. The determination of whether a translator station should be identified as a "distant" station depends on the local service area of the translator station.

(8) For purposes of this section, the "rules and regulations of the FCC in effect on October 19, 1976," which permitted a cable system, at its election, to omit the retransmission of a particular program and substitute another program in its place, refers to that portion of former 47 CFR 76.61(b)(2), revised June 25, 1981, and § 76.63 (referring to § 76.61(b)(2)), deleted June 25, 1981, concerning the substitution of a program that is primarily of local interest

to the distant community (e.g., a local news or public affairs program).

(9) For purposes of this section, the "rules and regulations of the FCC", which require a cable system to omit the retransmission of a particular program and substitute another program in its place, refers to 47 CFR 76.67.

(10) For purposes of this section, a cable system "lacks the activated channel capacity to retransmit on a full-time basis all signals which it is authorized to carry" only if:

(i) All of its activated television channels are used exclusively for the secondary transmission of television signals; and

(ii) The number of primary television transmitters secondarily transmitted by the cable system exceeds the number of its activated television channels.

(c) *Accounting periods and deposit.* (1) Statements of Account shall cover semiannual accounting periods of (i) January 1 through June 30, and (ii) July 1 through December 31, and shall be deposited in the Copyright Office, together with the total royalty fee for such accounting periods as prescribed by section 111(d)(1) (B), (C), or (D) of title 17, by not later than the immediately following August 29, if the Statement of Account covers the January 1 through June 30 accounting period, and by not later than the immediately following March 1, if the Statement of Account covers the July 1 through December 31 accounting period.

(2) Upon receiving a Statement of Account and royalty fee, the Copyright Office will make an official record of the actual date when such Statement and fee were physically received in the Copyright Office. Thereafter, the Office will examine the Statement and fee for obvious errors or omissions appearing on the face of the documents, and will require that any such obvious errors or omissions be corrected before final processing of the documents is completed. If, as the result of communications between the Copyright Office and the cable system, an additional fee is deposited or changes or additions are made in the Statement of Account, the date that additional deposit or information was actually received in the Office will be added to the official record of the case. However, completion by the Copyright Office of the final processing of a Statement of Account and royalty fee deposit shall establish only the fact of such completion and the date or dates of receipt shown in the official record. It shall in no case be considered a determination that the Statement of Account was, in fact, properly prepared and accurate, that the correct amount of the royalty fee had been deposited, that the statutory time limits for filing had been met, or that any other requirements to qualify for a compulsory license have been satisfied.

(3) Statements of Account and royalty fees received before the end of the particular accounting period they purport to cover will not be processed by the Copyright Office. Statements of Account and royalty fees received after the filing deadlines of August 29 or March 1, respectively, will be accepted for whatever legal effect they may have, if any.

(4) In the Register's discretion, four years after the close of any calendar year, the Register may, close out the royalty payments account for that calendar year, and may treat any funds remaining in such account and any subsequent deposits that would otherwise be attributable to that calendar year as attributable to the succeeding calendar year.

(d) *Forms.* (1) Each Statement of Account shall be furnished on an appropriate form prescribed by the Copyright Office, and shall contain the information required by that form and its accompanying instructions. Computation of distant signal equivalents and the copyright royalty fee shall be in accordance with the procedures set forth in the forms. Copies of Statement of Account forms are available free upon request to the Library of Congress, Copyright Office, Licensing Division, 101 Independence Avenue, SE, Washington, DC 20557–6400.

(2) The forms prescribed by the Copyright Office are designated "Statement of Account for Secondary Transmissions By Cable Systems":

(i) Form SA1–2—"Short Form" for use by cable systems whose semiannual gross receipts for secondary transmission total less than $527,600; and

(ii) Form SA3—"Long Form" for use by cable systems whose semiannual gross receipts for secondary transmission total $527,600 or more.

(e) *Contents*. Each Statement of Account shall contain the following information:

(1) A clear designation of the accounting period covered by the Statement.

(2) The designation "Owner," followed by:

(i) The full legal name of the owner of the cable system. The owner of the cable system is the individual or entity that provides the retransmission service and collects payment from the end user either directly or indirectly through a third party. If the owner is a partnership, the name of the partnership is to be followed by the name of at least one individual partner;

(ii) Any other name or names under which the owner conducts the business of the cable system; and

(iii) The full mailing address of the owner.

Ownership, other names under which the owner conducts the business of the cable system, and the owner's mailing address shall reflect facts existing on the last day of the accounting period covered by the Statement of Account.

(3) The designation "System," followed by:

(i) Any business or trade names used to identify the business and operation of the system, unless these names have already been given under the designation "Owner"; and

(ii) The full mailing address of the system, unless such address is the same as the address given under the designation "Owner".

Business or trade names used to identify the business and operation of the system, and the system's mailing address, shall reflect the facts existing on the last day of the accounting period covered by the Statement of Account.

(4) The designation "Area Served", followed by the name of the community or communities served by the system. For this purpose a "community" is the same as a "community unit" as defined in FCC rules and regulations.

(5) The designation "Channels," followed by:

(i) The number of channels, including multicast streams on which the cable system made secondary transmissions to its subscribers, and

(ii) The cable system's total activated channel capacity, in each case during the period covered by the Statement.

(iii) A multicast stream is considered a channel for purposes of this section

(6) The designation "Secondary Transmission Service: Subscribers and Rates", followed by:

(i) A brief description of each subscriber category for which a charge is made by the cable system for the basic service of providing secondary transmissions of primary broadcast transmitters;

(ii) The number of subscribers to the cable system in each such subscriber category; and

(iii) The charge or charges made per subscriber to each such subscriber category for the basic service of providing such secondary transmissions. Standard rate variations within a particular category should be summarized; discounts allowed for advance payment should not be included. For these purposes:

(A) The description, the number of subscribers, and the charge or charges made shall reflect the facts existing on the last day of the period covered by the Statement; and

(B) Each entity (for example, the owner of a private home, the resident of an apartment, the owner of a motel, or the owner of an apartment house) which is charged by the cable system for the basic service of providing secondary transmissions shall be considered one subscriber.

(7) The designation "Gross Receipts", followed by the gross amount paid to the cable system by subscribers for the basic service of providing secondary transmissions of primary broadcast transmissions during the period covered by the Statement of Account. If the cable system maintains its revenue accounts on an accrual basis, gross receipts for any accounting period includes all such amounts accrued for secondary transmission service furnished during that period, regardless of when accrued:

(i) Less the amount of any bad debts actually written-off during that accounting period, excluding bad debts for secondary transmission service furnished before January 1, 1978;

(ii) Plus the amount of any previously written-off bad debts for secondary transmission service which were actually recovered during that accounting period, excluding bad debt recoveries for secondary transmission service furnished before January 1, 1978.

If the cable system maintains its revenue accounts on a cash basis, gross receipts for any accounting period includes all such amounts actually received by the cable system during that accounting period, excluding amounts paid for secondary transmission service furnished before January 1, 1978; however, amounts received before January 1, 1978, for secondary transmission service furnished after that date, are to be considered as if they had been received during the accounting period in which the service covered by such payments was furnished.

(8) The designation "Services Other Than Secondary Transmissions: Rates," followed by a description of each package of service which consists solely of services other than secondary transmission services, for which a separate charge was made or established, and which the cable system furnished or made available to subscribers during the period covered by the Statement of Account, together with the amount of such charge. However, no information need be given concerning services furnished at cost. Specific amounts charged for pay cable programming need not be given if the rates are on a variable, per-program basis. (The fact of such variable charge shall be indicated.)

(9) The designation "Primary Transmitters: Television", followed by an identification of all primary television transmitters whose signals were carried by the cable system during the period covered by the Statement of Account, other than primary transmitters of programs carried by the cable system exclusively pursuant to rules, regulations, or authorizations of the FCC in effect on October 19, 1976, permitting the substitution of signals under certain circumstances, and required to be specially identified by paragraph (e)(11) of this section, together with the information listed below:

(i) The station call sign of the primary transmitter.

(ii) The name of the community to which that primary transmitter is licensed by the FCC (in the case of domestic signals) or with which that primary transmitter is identified (in the case of foreign signals).

(iii) The number of the channel upon which that primary transmitter broadcasts in the community to which that primary transmitter is licensed by the FCC (in the case of domestic signals) or with which that primary transmitter is identified (in the case of foreign signals).

(iv) A designation as to whether that primary transmitter is a "network station", an "independent station", or a "noncommercial educational station".

(v) A designation as to whether that primary transmitter is a "distant" station.

(vi) If that primary transmitter is a "distant" station, a specification of whether the signals of that primary transmitter are carried:

(A) On a part-time basis where full-time carriage is not possible because the cable system lacks the activated channel capacity to retransmit on a full-time basis all signals which it is authorized to carry; or

(B) On any other basis.

If the signals of that primary transmitter are carried on a part-time basis because of lack of activated channel capacity, the Statement shall also include a log showing the dates on which such carriage occurred, and the hours during which such carriage occurred on those dates. Hours of carriage shall be accurate to the nearest quarter-hour, except that, in any case where such part-time carriage extends to the end of the broadcast day of the primary transmitter, an approximate ending hour may be given if it is indicated as an estimate.

(vii) A designation as to whether the channel carried is a multicast stream, and if so, the sub-channel number assigned to that stream by the television broadcast licensee.

(viii) Simulcasts must be reported and labeled on the Statement of Accounts form in an easily identifiable manner (e.g., WETA-simulcast).

(ix) The information indicated by paragraph (e)(9), paragraphs (v) through (viii) of this section, is not required to be given by any cable system that appropriately completed Form SA1–2 for the period covered by the Statement.

(x) Notwithstanding the requirements of this section, where a cable system carried a distant primary transmitter under FCC rules and regulations in effect on October 19, 1976 which permitted carriage of specific network programs on a part-time basis in certain circumstances (former 47 CFR 76.59 (d) (2) and (4), 76.61(e) (2) and (4), and 76.63, referring to § 76.61(e) (2) and (4), all of which were deleted June 25, 1981), carriage of that primary transmitter on that basis need not be reported, and that carriage is to be excluded in computing the distant signal equivalent of that primary transmitter.

(10) The designation "Primary Transmitters: Radio", followed by an identification of primary radio transmitters whose signals were carried by the cable system during the period covered by the Statement of Account, together with the information listed below:

(i) A designation as to whether each primary transmitter was electronically processed by the system as a separate and discrete signal.

(ii) The station call sign of each:

(A) AM primary transmitter;

(B) FM primary transmitter, the signals of which were electronically processed by the system as separate and discrete signals; and

(C) FM primary transmitter carried on an all-band retransmission basis, the signals of which were generally receivable by the system.

(iii) A designation as to whether the primary transmitter is AM or FM.

(iv) The name of the community to which that primary transmitter is licensed by the FCC (in the case of domestic signals) or with which that primary transmitter is identified (in the case of foreign signals).

(11) A special statement and program log, which shall consist of the information indicated below for all nonnetwork television programming that, during the period covered by the Statement, was carried in whole or in part beyond the local service area of the primary transmitter of such programming under (i) rules or regulations of the FCC requiring a cable system to omit the further transmission of a particular program and permitting the substitution of another program in place of the omitted transmission; or (ii) rules, regulations, or authorizations of the FCC in effect on October 19, 1976, permitting a cable system, at its election, to omit the further transmission of a particular program and permitting the substitution of another program in place of the omitted transmission:

(A) The name or title of the substitute program.

(B) Whether the substitute program was transmitted live by its primary transmitter.

(C) The station call sign of the primary transmitter of the substitute program.

(D) The name of the community to which the primary transmitter of the substitute program is licensed by the FCC (in the case of domestic signals) or with which that primary transmitter is identified (in the case of foreign signals).

(E) The date when the secondary transmission of the substitute program occurred, and the hours during which such secondary transmission occurred on that date accurate to the nearest 5 minutes.

(F) A designation as to whether deletion of the omitted program was permitted by the rules, regulations, or authorizations of the FCC in effect on October 19, 1976, or was required by the rules, regulations, or authorizations of the FCC.

(12) A statement of the total royalty fee payable for the period covered by the Statement of Account, together with a royalty fee analysis which gives a clear, complete, and detailed presentation of the determination of such fee. This analysis shall present in appropriate sequence all facts, figures, and mathematical processes used in determining such fee, and shall do so in such manner as required in the appropriate

form so as to permit the Copyright Office to verify readily, from the face of the Statement of Account, the accuracy of such determination and fee. The royalty fee analysis is not required to be given by any cable system whose gross receipts from subscribers for the period covered by the Statement of Account, for the basic service of providing secondary transmissions of primary broadcast transmissions, total $137,100 or less.

(13) The name, address, and telephone number of an individual who may be contacted by the Copyright Office for further information about the Statement of Account.

(14) The handwritten signature of:

(i) The owner of the cable system or a duly authorized agent of the owner, if the owner is not a partnership or a corporation; or

(ii) A partner, if the owner is a partnership; or

(iii) An officer of the corporation, if the owner is a corporation. The signature shall be accompanied by:

(A) The printed or typewritten name of the person signing the Statement of Account;

(B) The date of signature;

(C) If the owner of the cable system is a partnership or a corporation, by the title or official position held in the partnership or corporation by the person signing the Statement of Account;

(D) A certification of the capacity of the person signing; and

(E) A declaration of the veracity of the statements of fact contained in the Statement of Account and the good faith of the person signing in making such statement of fact.

(f) *Computation of distant signal equivalents.* (1) A cable system that elects to delete a particular television program and substitute for that program another television program ("substitute program") under rules, regulations, or authorizations of the FCC in effect on October 19, 1976, which permit a cable system, at its election, to omit the retransmission of a particular program and substitute another program in its place shall compute the distant signal equivalent ("DSE") of each primary transmitter that broadcasts one or more substitute programs by dividing:

(i) The number of the primary transmitter's live, nonnetwork, substitute programs that were carried by the cable system, during the period covered by the Statement of Account, in substitution for programs deleted at the option of the system; by

(ii) The number of days in the year in which the substitution occurred.

(2)(i) Where a cable system carries a primary transmitter on a full-time basis during any portion of an accounting period, the system shall compute a DSE for that primary transmitter as if it was carried full-time during the entire accounting period.

(ii) Where a cable system carries a primary transmitter solely on a substitute or part-time basis, in accordance with paragraph (f)(3) of this section, the system shall compute a DSE for that primary transmitter based on its cumulative carriage on a substitute or part-time basis. If that primary transmitter is carried on a full-time basis as well as on a substitute or part-time basis, the full DSE for that primary transmitter shall be the full DSE type value for that primary transmitter, for the entire accounting period.

(3)(i) In computing the DSE of a primary transmitter in a particular case of carriage before July 1, 1981, the cable system may make no prorated adjustments other than those specified as permissible "exceptions and limitations" in the definition of "distant signal equivalent" in the fifth paragraph of section 111(f) of title 17 of the United States Code, as amended by Pub. L. 94-553. Four prorated adjustments, as prescribed in the fourth and fifth sentences of said definition, are permitted under certain conditions where:

(A) A station is carried pursuant to the late-night programming rules of the Federal Communications Commission in effect on the date of carriage;

(B) A station is carried pursuant to the specialty programming rules of the Federal Communications Commission in effect on the date of carriage;

(C) A station is carried on a part-time basis where full-time carriage is not possible because the cable system lacks the activated channel capacity to retransmit on a full-time basis all signals which it is authorized to carry; and

(D) A station is carried on a "substitute" basis under rules, regulations, or authorizations of the Federal Communications Commission in effect on October 19, 1976.

(ii) In computing the DSE of a primary transmitter in a particular case of carriage on or after July 1, 1981, the cable system may make no prorated adjustments other than those specified as permissible "exceptions and limitations" in the definition of "distant signal equivalent" in the fifth paragraph of section 111(f) of title 17 of the United States Code, as amended by Pub. L. 94–553, and which remain in force under that provision. Two prorated adjustments, as prescribed in the fourth and fifth sentences of said definition, are permitted under certain conditions where:

(A) A station is carried on a part-time basis where full-time carriage is not possible because the cable system lacks the activated channel capacity to retransmit on a full-time basis all signals which it is authorized to carry; and

(B) A station is carried on a "substitute" basis under rules, regulations, or authorizations of the Federal Communications Commission in effect on October 19, 1976, which permitted a cable system, at its election, to omit the retransmission of a particular program and substitute another program in its place.

(4) In computing a DSE, a cable system may round off to the third decimal point. If a DSE is rounded off in any case in a Statement of Account, it must be rounded off throughout the Statement. Where a cable system has chosen to round off, and the fourth decimal point for a particular DSE value would, without rounding off, have been 1, 2, 3, or 4, the third decimal point remains unchanged; if, in such a case, the fourth decimal point would, without rounding off, be 5, 6, 7, 8, or 9, the third decimal point must be rounded off to the next higher number.

(5) For the purposes of computing DSE values, specialty primary television transmitters in the United States and all Canadian and Mexican primary television transmitters shall be assigned a value of one.

(g) *Computation of copyright royalty fee: subscriber groups.* (1) If a cable system provides a secondary transmission of a primary transmitter to some, but not all, communities served by that cable system—

(i) The gross receipts and the distant signal equivalent values for such secondary transmission shall be derived solely on the basis of the subscribers in those communities where the cable system provides such secondary transmission; and

(ii) The total royalty fee for the period paid by such system shall not be less than the minimum fee multiplied by the gross receipts from all subscribers to the system.

(2) A cable system that, on a statement submitted before the date of the enactment of the Satellite Television Extension and Localism Act of 2010, computed its royalty fee consistent with the methodology under paragraph (i)(1) of this section or that amends a statement filed before such date of enactment to compute the royalty fee due using such methodology, shall not be subject to an action for infringement, or eligible for any royalty refund or offset, arising out of the use of such methodology on such statement.

(3) Any royalty fee payments received by the Copyright Office from cable systems for the secondary transmission of primary transmissions that are in addition to the payments calculated and deposited in accordance with this subsection shall be deemed to have been deposited for the particular accounting period for which they are received and shall be distributed as specified under subsection 111(d) of title 17, United States Code. Such payments shall be considered as part of the base rate royalty fund.

(4) The royalty fee rates established by the Satellite Television Extension and Localism Act shall take effect commencing with the first accounting period occurring in 2010.

(h) *Computation of the copyright royalty fee: Partially distant stations.* A cable system located partly within and partly without the local service area of a primary television transmitter ("partially distant station") computes the royalty fee specified in section 111(d)(1)(B) (ii), (iii), and (iv) of the Copyright Act ("DSE fee") by excluding gross receipts from subscribers located within that station's local service area from total gross receipts. A cable system which carries two or more partially distant stations with local service areas that do not exactly coincide shall compute a separate DSE fee for each group of subscribers who are located outside of the local service areas of exactly the same complement of distant stations. Computation of the DSE fee for each subscriber group is to be based on:

(1) The total distant signal equivalents of that group's complement of distant stations, and

(2) The total gross receipts from that group of subscribers. The copyright royalty fee for that cable system is:

(i) The total of the subscriber group royalty fees thus computed, or

(ii) 1.013 of 1 percent of the system's gross receipts from all subscribers, whichever is larger.

(i) *Computation of the copyright royalty fee pursuant to the 1982 cable rate adjustment.* (1) For the purposes of this paragraph, in addition to the definitions of paragraph (b) of this section, the following definitions shall also apply:

(i) *Current base rate* means the applicable royalty rates in effect on December 31, 1982, as reflected in 37 CFR 256.2(a).

(ii) If the 3.75% rate does not apply to certain DSE's in the case of a cable system located wholly or in part within a top 100 television market, the current base rate together with the surcharge shall apply. However, the surcharge shall not apply for carriage of a particular signal first carried prior to March 31, 1972. With respect to statements of account covering the filing period beginning January 1, 1990, and subsequent filing periods, the current base rate together with the surcharge shall apply only to those DSE's that represent commercial VHF signals which place a predicted Grade B contour, in whole or in part, over a cable system. The surcharge will not apply if the signal is exempt from the syndicated exclusivity rules in effect on June 24, 1981.

(iii) The *3.75% rate* means the rate established by 37 CFR 256.2(c), in effect on March 15, 1983.

(iv) *Top 100 television market* means a television market defined or interpreted as being within either the "top 50 television markets" or "second 50 television markets" in accordance with 47 CFR 76.51, in effect on June 24, 1981.

(v) The *1982 cable rate adjustment* means the rate adjustment adopted by the Copyright Royalty Tribunal on October 20, 1982 (CRT Docket No. 81–2, 47 FR 52146, November 19, 1982).

(vi) The terms *DSE* or *DSE's* mean "distant signal equivalent(s)" as defined in 17 U.S.C. 111(f) and any fraction thereof.

(2) A cable system filing Form SA3 shall compute its royalty fee in the following manner:

(i) The cable system shall first determine those DSE's to which the 3.75% rate established by 37 CFR 256.2(c) applies.

(ii) If the 3.75% rate does not apply to certain DSE's in the case of a cable system located wholly or in part within a top 100 television market, the current base rate together with the surcharge shall apply. However, the surcharge shall not apply for carriage of a particular signal first carried prior to March 31, 1972. With respect to statements of account covering the filing period beginning January 1, 1990, and subsequent filing periods, the current base rate together with the surcharge shall apply only to those DSE's that represent commercial VHF signals which place a predicted Grade B contour, in whole or in part, over a cable system. The surcharge will not apply if the signal is exempt from the syndicated exclusivity rules in effect on June 24, 1981.

(iii) If the 3.75% rate does not apply to certain DSE's, in the case of a cable system located wholly outside a top 100 television market, the current base rate shall apply.

(iv) Commencing with the semiannual accounting period of January 1, 1998, through June 30, 1998, the 3.75% rate applies to certain DSE's with respect to the communities within the cable system where carriage would not have been permitted under the rules and regulations of the Federal Communications Commission in effect on June 24, 1981, but in all other communities within the cable system, the current base rate and the syndicated exclusivity surcharge, where applicable, shall apply. Such computation shall be made as provided for on Form SA3. The calculations shall be based upon the gross receipts from all subscribers, within the relevant communities, for the basic service of providing secondary transmissions of primary broadcast transmitters, without regard to whether those subscribers actually received the station in question. For partially-distant stations, gross receipts shall be the total gross receipts from subscribers outside the local service area.

(3) A cable system whose semiannual gross receipts for secondary transmissions totalled $214,000 or more during the period January 1, 1983, through June 30, 1983, shall compute its royalty fee for carriage during that period in the following manner:

(i) Copyright royalty fees must be paid on the basis of carriage for the entire accounting period except where proration of the DSE is permitted as described in paragraph (f)(3) of this section.

(ii) Where a distant signal was carried at any time only between January 1, 1983, and March 14, 1983;

(A) In the case of a cable system located wholly or in part within a top 100 television market, the current base rate, together with the surcharge shall apply. However, the surcharge shall not apply for carriage of a particular signal first carried prior to March 31, 1972.

(B) In case of a cable system located wholly outside a top 100 television market, the current base rate shall apply.

(iii) Where a distant signal was carried at any time after March 14, 1983;

(A) The cable system shall first determine those DSE's to which the 3.75% rate established by 37 CFR 256.2(c) applies.

(B) If the 3.75% rate is applicable to a particular DSE, it shall be applied against the per centum .5967 (representing the number of days from March 15, 1983, through June 30, 1983, inclusive, in relation to the entire accounting period); and either

(*1*) In the case of a cable system located wholly or in part within a top 100 television market, the current base rate, together with the surcharge, applied against the per centum .4033 (representing the number of days from January 1, 1983, through March 14, 1983, inclusive, in relation to the entire accounting period); however, the surcharge shall not apply for carriage of a particular signal first carried prior to March 31, 1972; or

(*2*) In the case of a cable system located wholly outside a top 100 television market, the current base rate applied against the per centum .4033.

(C) If the 3.75% rate does not apply to certain DSE's, in the case of a cable system located wholly or in part within a top 100 television market, the current base rate together with the surcharge shall apply. However, the surcharge shall not apply for carriage of a particular signal first carried prior to March 31, 1972.

(D) If the 3.75% rate does not apply to certain DSE's, in the case of a cable system located wholly outside a top 100 television market, the current base rate shall apply.

(4)(i) Separate Supplemental DSE Schedules as prescribed by the Copyright Office shall be completed and filed by a cable system affected by the 1982 cable rate adjustment for the accounting periods January 1, 1983, through June 30, 1983 (83–1), and July 1, 1983, through December 31, 1983 (83–2). Each Supplemental DSE schedule shall contain the information required by that form and its accompanying instructions.

(ii) The Supplemental DSE Schedule will be mailed to all cable systems whose gross receipts for secondary transmissions total $214,000 or more either for accounting period 83–1 or for 83–2, and shall be completed and returned to the Copyright Office with the supplemental royalty fee due, if any, within sixty-five (65) days from the date of mailing by the Copyright Office.

(iii) Cable systems located wholly outside all major and smaller television markets as defined by the FCC are not affected by the 1982 cable rate adjustment. Such systems shall complete a certifying statement provided in the Supplemental DSE Schedule and return it within sixty-five (65) days from the date of mailing by the Copyright Office.

(5)(i) It shall be presumed that the 3.75% rate of 37 CFR 308.2(c) applies to DSE's accruing from newly added distant signals, carried for the first time by a cable system after June 24, 1981.

(ii) The presumption of paragraph (h)(5)(i) of this section can be rebutted in whole or in part:

(A) By actual carriage of a particular distant signal prior to June 25, 1981, as reported in Statements of Account duly filed with the Copyright Office ("actual carriage"), unless the prior carriage was not permitted by the FCC; or

(B) By carriage of no more than the number of distant signals which was or would have been allotted to the cable system under the FCC's quota for importation of network and nonspecialty independent stations (47 CFR 76.59(b), 76.61 (b) and (c) and 76.63, referring to 76.61 (b) and (c), in effect on June 24, 1981).

(6) To qualify as an FCC-permitted signal on the ground of individual waiver of the FCC rules (47 CFR 76.7 in effect on June 24, 1981), the waiver must have actually been granted by the FCC, and the signal must have been first carried by the cable system after April 15, 1976.

(7) Expanded geographic carriage after June 24, 1981, of a signal previously carried within only certain parts of a cable system is governed by the current base rate and the surcharge, if applicable.

(8) In cases of expanded temporal carriage of the same signal, previously carried pursuant to the FCC's former part-time or substitute carriage rules (47 CFR 76.61(b)(2), 76.61 (e)(1) and (e)(3), and 76.63, referring to 76.61 (e)(1) and (e)(3), in effect on June 24, 1981), the 3.75% rate shall be applied to any additional fraction of a DSE accruing from the expanded temporal carriage of that signal. To identify such additional DSE's, a comparison shall be made of DSE's reported for that signal in any single accounting period prior to the July 1, 1981, to December 31, 1981, period (81–2), as designated by the cable system, with the DSE's for that same signal reported in the current relevant accounting period.

(9) Substitution of like signals pursuant to 37 CFR 256.2(c) is possible at the relevant non-3.75% rate (the surcharge together with the current base rate, or the current base rate alone) only if the substitution does not exceed the number of distant signals which was or would have been allotted to the cable system under the FCC's television market quota for importation of network and nonspecialty independent stations (47 CFR 76.59(b), 76.61 (b) and (c), and 76.63, referring to 76.61 (b) and (c), in effect on June 24, 1981.

(10) The 3.75% rate does not apply to distant multicast streams retransmitted by cable systems.

(j) *Multicasting.* (1) A royalty payment shall be made for the retransmission of non-network television programming carried on each multicast stream of a distant digital television signal under the following circumstances:

(i) If the distant multicast stream was first retransmitted by a cable system on or after February 27, 2010, or

(ii) If the distant multicast stream is retransmitted by a cable operator on or after July 1, 2010.

(2) In any case in which a distant multicast stream is the subject of a written agreement entered into on or before June 30, 2009, between a cable system or an association representing the cable system and a primary transmitter or an association representing the primary transmitter, a distant signal equivalent value shall not be assigned to a distant multicast stream that is made on or before the date on which such written agreement expires.

(3) No royalties are due for carrying a distant multicast stream that "simulcasts" (i.e., duplicates) a primary stream or another multicast stream of the same station that the cable system is carrying. However, simulcast streams must be reported on the Statement of Accounts.

(4) Multicast streams of digital broadcast programming shall not be subject to the 3.75% fee or the syndicated exclusivity surcharge.

(k) *Royalty fee payment.* (1) All royalty fees must be paid by a single electronic funds transfer, and must be received in the designated bank by the filing deadline for the relevant accounting period. The following information must be provided as part of the EFT and/or as part of the remittance advice as provided for in circulars issued by the Copyright Office:

(i) Remitter's name and address;

(ii) Name of a contact person, telephone number and extension, and e-mail address;

(iii) The actual or anticipated date that the EFT will be transmitted;

(iv) Type of royalty payment (*i.e.*, cable);

(v) Total amount submitted via the EFT;

(vi) Total amount to be paid by year and period;

(vii) Number of Statements of Account that the EFT covers;

(viii) ID numbers assigned by the Licensing Division;

(ix) Legal name of the owner for each Statement of Account;

(x) Identification of the first community served (city and state).

(2) The remittance advice shall be attached to the Statement(s) of Account. In addition, a copy of the remittance advice shall be emailed or sent by facsimile to the Licensing Division.

(3) The Office may waive the requirement for payment by electronic funds transfer as set forth in paragraph (i)(1) of this section. To obtain a waiver, the remitter shall submit to the Licensing Division at least 60 days prior to the royalty fee due date a certified statement setting forth the reasons explaining why payment by an electronic funds transfer would be virtually impossible or, alternatively, why it would impose a financial or other hardship on the remitter. The certified statement must be signed by a duly authorized representative of the entity making the payment. A waiver shall cover only a single payment period. Failure to obtain a waiver may result in the remittance being returned to the remitter.

(4) Royalty fee payments submitted as a result of late or amended filings shall include interest. Interest shall begin to accrue beginning on the first day after the close of the period for filing statements of account for all late payments and underpayments of royalties for the cable statutory license occurring within that accounting period. The accrual period shall end on the date the electronic payment submitted by a cable operator is received. The accrual period shall end on the date the electronic payment submitted by a satellite carrier is received by the Copyright Office. In cases where a waiver of the electronic funds transfer requirement is approved by the Copyright Office, and royalties payments are either late or underpaid, the accrual period shall end on the date the payment is postmarked. If the payment is not received by the Copyright Office within five business days of its date, then the accrual period shall end on the date of the actual receipt by the Copyright Office. Interest is not required to be paid on any royalty underpayment or late payment from a particular accounting period if the interest charge is less than or equal to five dollars.

(l) *Copies of statements of account.* A licensee shall file an original and one copy of the statement of account with the Licensing Division of the Copyright Office.

(m) *Corrections, supplemental payments, and refunds.* (1) Royalty fee obligations under 17 U.S.C. 111 prior to the effective date of the Satellite Television Extension and Localism Act of 2010, Public Law 111–175, are determined based on carriage of each distant signal on a system-wide basis. Refunds for an overpayment of royalty fees for an accounting period prior to January 1, 2010, shall be made only when all outstanding royalty fee obligations have been met, including those for carriage of each distant signal on a system-wide basis.

(2) Upon compliance with the procedures and within the time limits set forth in paragraph (m)(3) of this section, corrections to Statements of Account will be placed on record, supplemental royalty fee payments will be received for deposit, or refunds will be issued, in the following cases:

(i) Where, with respect to the accounting period covered by a Statement of Account, any of the information given in the Statement filed in the

Copyright Office is incorrect or incomplete;

(ii) Where, for any reason except that mentioned in paragraph (m)(1)(iii) of this section, calculation of the royalty fee payable for a particular accounting period was incorrect, and the amount deposited in the Copyright Office for that period was either too high or too low; or

(iii) Where, for the semiannual accounting period of January 1, 1978, through June 30, 1978, the total royalty fee deposited was incorrect because the cable operator failed to compute royalties attributable to carriage of late-night, specialty, or part-time programming between January 1, 1978, and February 9, 1978.

(3) Corrections to Statements of Account will not be placed on record, supplemental royalty fee payments will not be received for deposit, and refunds will not be issued, where the information in the Statements of Account, the royalty fee calculations, or the payments were correct as of the date on which the accounting period ended, but changes (for example, addition or deletion of a distant signal) took place later.

(4) Requests that corrections to a Statement of Account be placed on record, that fee payments be accepted, or requests for the issuance of refunds, shall be made only in the cases mentioned in paragraph (m)(1) of this section. Such requests shall be addressed to the Licensing Division of the Copyright Office, and shall meet the following conditions:

(i) The request must be in writing, must clearly identify its purpose, and, in the case of a request for a refund, must be received in the Copyright Office before the expiration of 60 days from the last day of the applicable Statement of Account filing period, or before the expiration of 60 days from the date of receipt at the Copyright Office of the royalty payment that is the subject of the request, whichever time period is longer. A request made by telephone or by telegraphic or similar unsigned communication, will be considered to meet this requirement if it clearly identifies the basis of the request, if it is received in the Copyright Office within the required 60-day period, and if a written request meeting all the conditions of this paragraph (m)(3) is also received in the Copyright Office within 14 days after the end of such 60-day period;

(ii) The Statement of Account to which the request pertains must be sufficiently identified in the request (by inclusion of the name of the owner of the cable system, the community or communities served, and the accounting period in question) so that it can be readily located in the records of the Copyright Office;

(iii) The request must contain a clear statement of the facts on which it is based and provide a clear basis on which a refund may be granted, in accordance with the following procedures:

(A) In the case of a request filed under paragraph (m)(1)(i) of this section, where the information given in the Statement of Account is incorrect or incomplete, the request must clearly identify the erroneous or incomplete information and provide the correct or additional information;

(B) In the case of a request filed under paragraph (m)(1)(ii) of this section, where the royalty fee was miscalculated and the amount deposited in the Copyright Office was either too high or too low, the request must be accompanied by an affidavit under the official seal of any officer authorized to administer oaths within the United States, or a statement in accordance with section 1746 of title 28 of the United States Code, made and signed in accordance with paragraph (e)(14) of this section. The affidavit or statement shall describe the reasons why the royalty fee was improperly calculated and include a detailed analysis of the proper royalty calculations;

(C) In the case of a request filed under paragraph (m)(1)(iii) of this section, the request shall be identified as "Transitional and Supplemental Royalty Fee Payment" and include a detailed analysis of the proper royalty calculations;

(iv)(A) All requests filed under this paragraph (m) (except those filed under paragraph (m)(1)(iii) of this section) must be accompanied by a filing fee in the amount prescribed in §201.3(e) of this part for each Statement of Account involved. Payment of this fee may be in the form of a personal or company check, or of a certified check, cashier's check or money order, payable to: Register of Copyrights. No request will be processed until the appropriate filing fees are received.

(B) All requests that a supplemental royalty fee payment be received for deposit under this paragraph (m), must be accompanied by a remittance in the full amount of such fee. Payment of the supplemental royalty fee must be in the form of a certified check, cashier's check, or money order, payable to: Register of Copyrights; or an electronic payment. No such request will be processed until an acceptable remittance in the full amount of the supplemental royalty fee has been received.

(v) All requests submitted under this paragraph (m) must be signed by the cable system owner named in the Statement of Account, or the duly authorized agent of the owner, in accordance with paragraph (e)(14) of this section.

(vi) A request for a refund is not necessary where the Licensing Division, during its examination of a Statement of Account or related document, discovers an error that has resulted in a royalty overpayment. In this case, the Licensing Division will forward the royalty refund to the cable system owner named in the Statement of Account without regard to the time limitations provided for in paragraph (m)(3)(i) of this section.

(5) Following final processing, all requests submitted under this paragraph (m) will be filed with the original Statement of Account in the records of the Copyright Office. Nothing contained in this paragraph shall be considered to relieve cable systems from their full obligations under title 17 of the United States Code, and the filing of a correction or supplemental payment shall have only such effect as may be attributed to it by a court of competent jurisdiction.

(n) *Satellite carriers not eligible.* Satellite carriers and satellite resale carriers are not eligible for the cable compulsory license based upon an interpretation of the whole of section 111 of title 17 of the United States Code.

(17 U.S.C. 111, 702, 708)

[43 FR 27832, June 27, 1978]

EDITORIAL NOTE: For FEDERAL REGISTER citations affecting § 201.17, see the List of CFR Sections Affected, which appears in the Finding Aids section of the printed volume and at *www.fdsys.gov*.

§ 201.18 Notice of intention to obtain a compulsory license for making and distributing phonorecords of nondramatic musical works.

(a) *General.* (1) A "Notice of Intention" is a Notice identified in section 115(b) of title 17 of the United States Code, and required by that section to be served on a copyright owner or, in certain cases, to be filed in the Copyright Office, before or within thirty days after making, and before distributing any phonorecords of the work, in order to obtain a compulsory license to make and distribute phonorecords of nondramatic musical works.

(2) A person is entitled to serve or file a Notice of Intention and thereby obtain a compulsory license pursuant to 17 U.S.C. 115 only if his primary purpose in making phonorecords is to distribute them to the public for private use, including by means of a digital phonorecord delivery.

(3) For the purposes of this section, a "digital phonorecord delivery" is each individual delivery of a phonorecord by digital transmission of a sound recording which results in a specifically identifiable reproduction by or for any transmission recipient of a phonorecord of that sound recording, regardless of whether the digital transmission is also a public performance of the sound recording or any nondramatic musical work embodied therein. The reproduction of the phonorecord must be sufficiently permanent or stable to permit it to be perceived, reproduced, or otherwise communicated for a period of more than transitory duration. Such a phonorecord may be permanent or it may be made available to the transmission recipient for a limited period of time or for a specified number of performances. A digital phonorecord delivery includes all phonorecords that are made for the

purpose of making the digital phonorecord delivery.

(4) A Notice of Intention shall be served or filed for nondramatic musical works embodied, or intended to be embodied, in phonorecords made under the compulsory license. For purposes of this section and subject to subparagraphs (ii) and (iii), a Notice filed with the Copyright Office which lists multiple works shall be considered a single Notice and fees shall be paid in accordance with the fee schedule set forth in §201.3(e)(1) if filed in the Copyright Office under paragraph (f)(3) of this section. Payment of the applicable fees for a Notice submitted electronically under this paragraph shall be made through a deposit account established under §201.6(b).

(i) Except as provided for in paragraph (a)(7), a Notice of Intention served on a copyright owner or agent of a copyright owner may designate any number of nondramatic musical works provided that that the information required under paragraphs (d)(1)(i) through (iv) of this section does not vary and that the copyright owner of each designated work is the same, or in the case of any work having more than one copyright owner, that any one of the copyright owners is the same and is the copyright owner served.

(ii) A Notice of Intention filed in the Copyright Office in paper form may designate any number of nondramatic musical works provided that that the information required under paragraphs (d)(1)(i) through (iv) of this section does not vary, and that the copyright owner of each designated work (or, in the case of works having more than one copyright owner, any one of the copyright owners) is the same and the registration records or other public records of the Copyright Office do not identify the copyright owner(s) of such work(s) and include an address for any such owner(s) at which notice can be served. For purposes of this subparagraph, in the case of works having more than one copyright owner, a single Notice must identify an actual person or entity as the common copyright owner; the common copyright owner may not be identified as "unknown." However, a single Notice may include multiple works for which no copyright owners can be identified for any of the listed works.

(iii) A Notice of Intention filed in the Copyright Office through its electronic filing system may designate multiple nondramatic musical works, regardless of whether the copyright owner of each designated work (or, in the case of any work having more than one copyright owner, any one of the copyright owners) is the same, provided that the information required under paragraphs (d)(1)(i) through (iv) of this section does not vary, and that for any designated work, the records of the Copyright Office do not include an address at which notice can be served.

(5) For the purposes of this section, the term *copyright owner*, in the case of any work having more than one copyright owner, means any one of the co-owners.

(6) For the purposes of this section, service of a Notice of Intention on a copyright owner may be accomplished by means of service of the Notice on either the copyright owner or an agent of the copyright owner with authority to receive the Notice. In the case where the work has more than one copyright owner, the service of the Notice on any one of the co-owners of the nondramatic musical work or upon an authorized agent of one of the co-owners identified in the Notice of Intention shall be sufficient with respect to all co-owners. Notwithstanding paragraph (a)(2) of this section, a single Notice may designate works not owned by the same copyright owner in the case where the Notice is served on a common agent of multiple copyright owners, and where each of the works designated in the Notice is owned by any of the copyright owners who have authorized that agent to receive Notices.

(7) For purposes of this section, a copyright owner or an agent of a copyright owner with authority to receive Notices of Intention may make public a written policy that it will accept Notices of Intention to make and distribute phonorecords pursuant to 17 U.S.C. 115 which include less than all of the information required by this section, in a form different than required by this section, or delivered by means (including electronic transmission)

other than those required by this section. Any Notice provided in accordance with such policy shall not be rendered invalid for failing to comply with the specific requirements of this section.

(8) For the purposes of this section, a digital phonorecord delivery shall be treated as a type of phonorecord configuration, and a digital phonorecord delivery shall be treated as a phonorecord manufactured, made, and distributed on the date the phonorecord is digitally transmitted.

(b) *Agent.* An agent who has been authorized to accept Notices of Intention in accordance with paragraph (a)(4) of this section and who has received a Notice of Intention on behalf of a copyright owner shall provide within two weeks of the receipt of that Notice of Intention the name and address of the copyright owner or its agent upon whom the person or entity intending to obtain the compulsory license shall serve Statements of Account and the monthly royalty in accordance with § 201.19(a)(4).

(c) *Form.* The Copyright Office does not provide printed forms for the use of persons serving or filing Notices of Intention.

(d) *Content.* (1) A Notice of Intention shall be clearly and prominently designated, at the head of the notice, as a "Notice of Intention to Obtain a Compulsory License for Making and Distributing Phonorecords," and shall include a clear statement of the following information:

(i) The full legal name of the person or entity intending to obtain the compulsory license, together with all fictitious or assumed names used by such person or entity for the purpose of conducting the business of making and distributing phonorecords;

(ii) The telephone number, the full address, including a specific number and street name or rural route of the place of business, and an e-mail address, if available, of the person or entity intending to obtain the compulsory license, and if a business organization intends to obtain the compulsory license, the name and title of the chief executive officer, managing partner, sole proprietor or other person similarly responsible for the management of such entity. A post office box or similar designation will not be sufficient for this purpose except where it is the only address that can be used in that geographic location.

(iii) The information specified in paragraphs (d)(1)(i) and (ii) of this section for the primary entity expected to be engaged in the business of making and distributing phonorecords under the license or of authorizing such making and distribution (for example: a record company or digital music service), if an entity intending to obtain the compulsory license is a holding company, trust or other entity that is not expected to be actively engaged in the business of making and distributing phonorecords under the license or of authorizing such making and distribution;

(iv) The fiscal year of the person or entity intending to obtain the compulsory license. If that fiscal year is a calendar year, the Notice shall state that this is the case;

(v) For each nondramatic musical work embodied or intended to be embodied in phonorecords made under the compulsory license:

(A) The title of the nondramatic musical work;

(B) The name of the author or authors, if known;

(C) A copyright owner of the work, if known;

(D) The types of all phonorecord configurations already made (if any) and expected to be made under the compulsory license (for example: single disk, long-playing disk, cassette, cartridge, reel-to-reel, a digital phonorecord delivery, or a combination of them);

(E) The expected date of initial distribution of phonorecords already made (if any) or expected to be made under the compulsory license;

(F) The name of the principal recording artist or group actually engaged or expected to be engaged in rendering the performances fixed on phonorecords already made (if any) or expected to be made under the compulsory license;

(G) The catalog number or numbers, and label name or names, used or expected to be used on phonorecords already made (if any) or expected to be made under the compulsory license; and

(H) In the case of phonorecords already made (if any) under the compulsory license, the date or dates of such manufacture.

(vi) In the case where the Notice will be filed with the Copyright Office pursuant to paragraph (f)(3) of this section, the Notice shall include an affirmative statement that with respect to the nondramatic musical work named in the Notice of Intention, the registration records or other public records of the Copyright Office have been searched and found not to identify the name and address of the copyright owner of such work.

(2) A "clear statement" of the information listed in paragraph (d)(1) of this section requires a clearly intelligible, legible, and unambiguous statement in the Notice itself and without incorporation by reference of facts or information contained in other documents or records.

(3) Where information is required to be given by paragraph (d)(1) of this section "if known" or as "expected," such information shall be given in good faith and on the basis of the best knowledge, information, and belief of the person signing the Notice. If so given, later developments affecting the accuracy of such information shall not affect the validity of the Notice.

(e) *Signature.* The Notice shall be signed by the person or entity intending to obtain the compulsory license or by a duly authorized agent of such person or entity.

(1) If the person or entity intending to obtain the compulsory license is a corporation, the signature shall be that of a duly authorized officer or agent of the corporation.

(2) If the person or entity intending to obtain the compulsory license is a partnership, the signature shall be that of a partner or of a duly authorized agent of the partnership.

(3) If the Notice is signed by a duly authorized agent for the person or entity intending to obtain the compulsory license, the Notice shall include an affirmative statement that the agent is authorized to execute the Notice of Intention on behalf of the person or entity intending to obtain the compulsory license.

(4) If the Notice is served electronically, the person or entity intending to obtain the compulsory license and the copyright owner shall establish a procedure to verify that the Notice is being submitted upon the authority of the person or entity intending to obtain the compulsory license.

(5) If the Notice is filed in the Office electronically, the person or entity intending to obtain the compulsory license or a duly authorized agent of such person or entity shall, rather than signing the Notice, attest that he or she has the appropriate authority of the licensee, including any related entities listed, if applicable, to submit the electronically filed Notice on behalf of the licensee.

(f) *Filing and service.* (1) If the registration records or other public records of the Copyright Office identify the copyright owner of the nondramatic musical works named in the Notice of Intention and include an address for such owner, the Notice may be served on such owner by mail sent to, or by reputable courier service at, the last address for such owner shown by the records of the Office. It shall not be necessary to file a copy of the Notice in the Copyright Office in this case.

(2) If the Notice is sent by mail or delivered by reputable courier service to the last address for the copyright owner shown by the records of the Copyright Office and the Notice is returned to the sender because the copyright owner is no longer located at the address or has refused to accept delivery, the original Notice as sent shall be filed in the Copyright Office. Notices of Intention submitted for filing under this paragraph (f)(2) shall be submitted to the Licensing Division of the Copyright Office, shall be accompanied by a brief statement that the Notice was sent to the last address for the copyright owner shown by the records of the Copyright Office but was returned, and may be accompanied by appropriate evidence that it was mailed to, or that delivery by reputable courier service was attempted at, that address. In these cases, the Copyright Office will specially mark its records to consider the date the original Notice was mailed, or the date delivery by courier service was attempted, if shown by the

evidence mentioned above, as the date of filing. An acknowledgment of receipt and filing will be provided to the sender.

(3) If, with respect to the nondramatic musical works named in the Notice of Intention, the registration records or other public records of the Copyright Office do not identify the copyright owner of such work and include an address for such owner, the Notice may be filed in the Copyright Office. Notices of Intention submitted for filing shall be accompanied by the fee specified in § 201.3(e). A separate fee shall be assessed for each title listed in the Notice. Notices of Intention will be filed by being placed in the appropriate public records of the Licensing Division of the Copyright Office. The date of filing will be the date when the Notice and fee are both received in the Copyright Office. An acknowledgment of receipt and filing will be provided to the sender.

(4) Alternatively, if the person or entity intending to obtain the compulsory license knows the name and address of the copyright owner of the nondramatic musical work, or the agent of the copyright owner as described in paragraph (a)(4) of this section, the Notice of Intention may be served on the copyright owner or the agent of the copyright owner by sending the Notice by mail or delivering it by reputable courier service to the address of the copyright owner or agent of the copyright owner. For purposes of section 115(b)(1) of title 17 of the United States Code, the Notice will not be considered properly served if the Notice is not sent to the copyright owner or the agent of the copyright owner as described in paragraph (a)(4) of this section, or if the Notice is sent to an incorrect address.

(5) If a Notice of Intention is sent by certified mail or registered mail, a mailing receipt shall be sufficient to prove that service was timely. If a Notice of Intention is delivered by a reputable courier, documentation from the courier showing the first date of attempted delivery shall also be sufficient to prove that service was timely. In the absence of a receipt from the United States Postal Service showing the date of delivery or documentation showing the first date of attempted delivery by a reputable courier, the compulsory licensee shall bear the burden of proving that the Notice of Intention was served in a timely manner.

(6) If a Notice served upon a copyright owner or an authorized agent of a copyright owner identifies more than 50 works that are embodied or intended to be embodied in phonorecords made under the compulsory license, the copyright owner or the authorized agent may send the person who served the Notice a demand that a list of each of the works so identified be resubmitted in an electronic format, along with a copy of the original Notice. The person who served the Notice must submit such a list, which shall include all of the information required in paragraph (d)(1)(v) of this section, within 30 days after receipt of the demand from the copyright owner or authorized agent. The list shall be submitted on magnetic disk or another medium widely used at the time for electronic storage of data, in the form of a flat file, word processing document or spreadsheet readable with computer software in wide use at such time, with the required information identified and/or delimited so as to be readily discernible. The list may be submitted by means of electronic transmission (such as e-mail) if the demand from the copyright owner or authorized agent states that such submission will be accepted.

(g) *Filing date and legal sufficiency of Notices.* The Copyright Office will notify a prospective licensee when a Notice was not accompanied by payment of the required fee. Notices shall be deemed filed as of the date the Office receives both the Notice and the fee, if applicable. If the prospective licensee fails to remit the required fee, the Notice will be deemed not to have been filed with the Office. However, the Copyright Office does not review Notices for legal sufficiency or interpret the content of any Notice filed with the Copyright Office under this section. Furthermore, the Copyright Office does not screen Notices for errors or discrepancies and it does not generally correspond with a prospective licensee about the sufficiency of a Notice. If any issue (other than an issue related to fees) arises as to whether a Notice filed in the Copyright Office is sufficient as a matter of law under this section, that issue shall be determined not by the Copyright Office, but shall be subject to a determination of legal sufficiency by a court of competent jurisdiction. Prospective licensees are therefore cautioned to review and scrutinize Notices to assure their legal sufficiency before filing them in the Copyright Office.

(h) *Harmless errors.* Harmless errors in a Notice that do not materially affect the adequacy of the information required to serve the purposes of section 115(b)(1) of title 17 of the United States Code, shall not render the Notice invalid.

(i) *Privacy Act Advisory Statement.* The authority for receiving the personally identifying information included within a Notice of Intention to obtain a compulsory license is found in 17 U.S.C. 115 and §201.18. Personally identifying information is any personal information that can be used to identify or trace an individual, such as name, address or telephone numbers. Furnishing the information set forth in §201.18 is voluntary. However, if the information is not furnished, it may affect the sufficiency of Notice of Intention to obtain a compulsory license and may not entitle the prospective licensee to the benefits available under 17 U.S.C. 115. The principal uses of the requested information are the establishment and maintenance of a public record of the Notices of Intention to obtain a compulsory license received in the Licensing Division of the Copyright Office. Other routine uses include public inspection and copying, preparation of public indexes, preparation of public catalogs of copyright records including online catalogs, and preparation of search reports upon request.

[69 FR 34582, June 22, 2004, as amended at 73 FR 66181, Nov. 7, 2008; 77 FR 71103, Nov. 29, 2012]

§201.19 Royalties and statements of account under compulsory license for making and distributing phonorecords of nondramatic musical works.

(a) *Definitions.* (1) A *Monthly Statement of Account* is a statement accompanying monthly royalty payments identified in section 115(c)(5) of title 17 of the United States Code, as amended by Pub. L. 94–553, and required by that section to be made under the compulsory license to make and distribute phonorecords of nondramatic musical works, including by means of a digital phonorecord delivery.

(2) An *Annual Statement of Account* is a statement identified in section 115(c)(5) of title 17 of the United States Code, as amended by Pub. L. 94–553, and required by that section to be filed for every compulsory license to make and distribute phonorecords of nondramatic musical works.

(3) For the purposes of this section, a "digital phonorecord delivery" is each individual delivery of a phonorecord by digital transmission of a sound recording which results in a specifically identifiable reproduction by or for any transmission recipient of a phonorecord of that sound recording, regardless of whether the digital transmission is also a public performance of the sound recording or any nondramatic musical work embodied therein. The reproduction of the phonorecord must be sufficiently permanent or stable to permit it to be perceived, reproduced, or otherwise communicated for a period of more than transitory duration. Such a phonorecord may be permanent or it may be made available to the transmission recipient for a limited period of time or for a specified number of performances. A digital phonorecord delivery includes all phonorecords that are made for the purpose of making the digital phonorecord delivery.

(4) For the purposes of this section, the term *copyright owner*, in the case of any work having more than one copyright owner, means any one of the co-owners.

(5) For the purposes of this section, the service of a Statement of Account on a copyright owner under paragraph (e)(7) or (f)(7) of this section may be accomplished by means of service on either the copyright owner or an agent of the copyright owner with authority to receive Statements of Account on behalf of the copyright owner. In the case where the work has more than one copyright owner, the service of the Statement of Account on one co-owner

or upon an agent of one of the co-owners shall be sufficient with respect to all co-owners.

(6) For the purposes of this section, a *compulsory licensee* is a person or entity exercising the compulsory license to make and distribute phonorecords of nondramatic musical works as provided under section 115 of title 17 of the United States Code.

(7) For the purposes of this section, a digital phonorecord delivery shall be treated as a type of phonorecord configuration, and a digital phonorecord delivery shall be treated as a phonorecord, with the following clarifications:

(i) A digital phonorecord delivery shall be treated as a phonorecord made and distributed on the date the phonorecord is digitally transmitted; and

(ii) A digital phonorecord delivery shall be treated as having been *voluntarily distributed* and *relinquished from possession*, and a compulsory licensee shall be treated as having *permanently parted with possession* of a digital phonorecord delivery, on the date that the phonorecord is digitally transmitted.

(8) Except as provided in paragraph (a)(6) of this section, a phonorecord is considered *voluntarily distributed* if the compulsory licensee has voluntarily and permanently parted with possession of the phonorecord. For this purpose, and subject to the provisions of paragraph (d) of this section, a compulsory licensee shall be considered to have "permanently parted with possession" of a phonorecord made under the license:

(i) In the case of phonorecords relinquished from possession for purposes other than sale, at the time at which the compulsory licensee actually first parts with possession;

(ii) In the case of phonorecords relinquished from possession for purposes of sale without a privilege of returning unsold phonorecords for credit or exchange, at the time at which the compulsory licensee actually first parts with possession;

(iii) In the case of phonorecords relinquished from possession for purposes of sale accompanied by a privilege of returning unsold phonorecords for credit or exchange:

(A) At the time when revenue from a sale of the phonorecord is "recognized" by the compulsory licensee; or

(B) Nine months from the month in which the compulsory licensee actually first parted with possession, whichever occurs first.

For these purposes, a compulsory licensee shall be considered to "recognize" revenue from the sale of a phonorecord when sales revenue would be recognized in accordance with generally accepted accounting principles as expressed by the American Institute of Certified Public Accountants or the Financial Accounting Standards Board, whichever would cause sales revenue to be recognized first.

(9) To the extent that the terms *reserve*, *credit* and *return* appear in this section, such provisions shall not apply to digital phonorecord deliveries.

(10) A *phonorecord reserve* comprises the number of phonorecords, if any, that have been relinquished from possession for purposes of sale in a given month accompanied by a privilege of return, as described in paragraph (a)(5)(iii) of this section, and that have not been considered voluntarily distributed during the month in which the compulsory licensee actually first parted with their possession. The initial number of phonorecords comprising a phonorecord reserve shall be determined in accordance with generally accepted accounting principles as expressed by the American Institute of Certified Public Accountants or the Financial Accounting Standards Board.

(11) A *negative reserve balance* comprises the aggregate number of phonorecords, if any, that have been relinquished from possession for purposes of sale accompanied by a privilege of return, as described in paragraph (a)(5)(iii) of this section, and that have been returned to the compulsory licensee, but because all available phonorecord reserves have been eliminated, have not been used to reduce a phonorecord reserve.

(12) An *incomplete transmission* is any digital transmission of a sound recording which, as determined by means within the sole control of the distributor, does not result in a specifically identifiable reproduction of the

entire sound recording by or for any transmission recipient.

(13) A *retransmission* is a subsequent digital transmission of the same sound recording initially transmitted to an identified recipient for the purpose of completing the delivery of a complete and usable reproduction of that sound recording to that recipient.

(b) *Accounting requirements where sales revenue is "recognized".* Where under paragraph (a)(5)(iii)(A) of this section, revenue from the sale of phonorecords is "recognized" during any month after the month in which the compulsory licensee actually first parted with their possession, said compulsory licensee shall reduce particular phonorecord reserves by the number of phonorecords for which revenue is being "recognized," as follows:

(1) If the number of phonorecords for which revenue is being "recognized" is smaller than the number of phonorecords comprising the earliest eligible phonorecord reserve, this phonorecord reserve shall be reduced by the number of phonorecords for which revenue is being "recognized." Subject to the time limitations of paragraph (a)(7)(iii)(B) of this section, the number of phonorecords remaining in this reserve shall be available for use in subsequent months.

(2) If the number of phonorecords for which revenue is being "recognized" is greater than the number of phonorecords comprising the earliest eligible phonorecord reserve but less than the total number of phonorecords comprising all eligible phonorecord reserves, the compulsory licensee shall first eliminate those phonorecord reserves, beginning with the earliest eligible phonorecord reserve and continuing to the next succeeding phonorecord reserves, that are completely offset by phonorecords for which revenue is being "recognized." Said licensee shall then reduce the next succeeding phonorecord reserve by the number of phonorecords for which revenue is being "recognized" that have not been used to eliminate a phonorecord reserve. Subject to the time limitations of paragraph (a)(7)(iii)(B) of this section, the number of phonorecords remaining in this reserve shall be available for use in subsequent months.

(3) If the number of phonorecords for which revenue is being "recognized" equals the number of phonorecords comprising all eligible phonorecord reserves, the person or entity exercising the compulsory license shall eliminate all of the phonorecord reserves.

(c) *Accounting requirements for offsetting phonorecord reserves with returned phonorecords.* (1) In the case of a phonorecord that has been relinquished from possession for purposes of sale accompanied by a privilege of return, as described in paragraph (a)(5)(iii) of this section, where the phonorecord is returned to the compulsory licensee for credit or exchange before said compulsory licensee is considered to have "permanently parted with possession" of the phonorecord under paragraph (a)(5) of this section, the compulsory licensee may use such phonorecord to reduce a "phonorecord reserve," as defined in paragraph (a)(6) of this section.

(2) In such cases, the compulsory licensee shall reduce particular phonorecord reserves by the number of phonorecords that are returned during the month covered by the Monthly Statement of Account in the following manner:

(i) If the number of phonorecords that are returned during the month covered by the Monthly Statement is smaller than the number comprising the earliest eligible phonorecord reserve, the compulsory licensee shall reduce this phonorecord reserve by the total number of returned phonorecords. Subject to the time limitations of paragraph (B) of §201.19(a)(5)(iii), the number of phonorecords remaining in this reserve shall be available for use in subsequent months.

(ii) If the number of phonorecords that are returned during the month covered by the Monthly Statement is greater than the number of phonorecords comprising the earliest eligible phonorecord reserve but less than the total number of phonorecords comprising all eligible phonorecord reserves, the compulsory licensee shall first eliminate those phonorecord reserves, beginning with the earliest eligible phonorecord reserve, and continuing to the next succeeding phonorecord reserves, that are completely offset by returned phonorecords. Said licensee shall then reduce the next succeeding phonorecord reserve by the number of returned phonorecords that have not been used to eliminate a phonorecord reserve. Subject to the time limitations of paragraph (B) of § 201.19(a)(5)(iii), the number of phonorecords remaining in this reserve shall be available for use in subsequent months.

(iii) If the number of phonorecords that are returned during the month covered by the Monthly Statement is equal to or is greater than the total number of phonorecords comprising all eligible phonorecord reserves, the compulsory licensee shall eliminate all eligible phonorecord reserves. Where said number is greater than the total number of phonorecords comprising all eligible phonorecord reserves, said compulsory licensee shall establish a "negative reserve balance," as defined in paragraph (a)(10) of this section.

(3) Except where a negative reserve balance exists, a separate and distinct phonorecord reserve shall be established for each month during which the compulsory licensee relinquishes phonorecords from possession for purposes of sale accompanied by a privilege of return, as described in paragraph (a)(5)(iii) of this section. In accordance with paragraph (B) of § 201.19(a)(5)(iii), any phonorecord remaining in a particular phonorecord reserve nine months from the month in which the particular reserve was established shall be considered "voluntarily distributed"; at that point, the particular monthly phonorecord reserve shall lapse and royalties for the phonorecords remaining in it shall be paid as provided in paragraph (e)(4)(ii) of this section.

(4) Where a negative reserve balance exists, the aggregate total of phonorecords comprising it shall be accumulated into a single balance rather than being separated into distinct monthly balances. Following the establishment of a negative reserve balance, any phonorecords relinquished from possession by the compulsory licensee for purposes of sale or otherwise, shall be credited against such negative balance, and the negative reserve balance shall be reduced accordingly. The nine-month limit provided by paragraph (B) of § 201.19(a)(5)(iii) shall have no effect upon a negative reserve balance; where a negative reserve balance exists, relinquishment from possession of a phonorecord by the compulsory licensee at any time shall be used to reduce such balance, and shall not be considered a "voluntary distribution" within the meaning of paragraph (a)(5) of this section.

(5) In no case shall a phonorecord reserve be established while a negative reserve balance is in existence; conversely, in no case shall a negative reserve balance be established before all available phonorecord reserves have been eliminated.

(d) *Situations in which a compulsory licensee is barred from maintaining reserves.* Notwithstanding any other provisions of this section, in any case where, within three years before the phonorecord was relinquished from possession, the compulsory licensee has had final judgment entered against it for failure to pay royalties for the reproduction of copyrighted music on phonorecords, or within such period has been definitively found in any proceeding involving bankruptcy, insolvency, receivership, assignment for the benefit of creditors, or similar action, to have failed to pay such royalties, that compulsory licensee shall be considered to have "Permanently parted with possession" of a phonorecord made under the license at the time at which that licensee actually first parts with possession. For these purposes the "compulsory licensee," as defined in paragraph (a)(5) of this section, shall include:

(1) In the case of any corporation, the corporation or any director, officer, or beneficial owner of twenty-five percent (25%) or more of the outstanding securities of the corporation;

(2) In all other cases, any entity or individual owning a beneficial interest of twenty-five percent (25%) or more in the entity exercising the compulsory license.

(e) *Monthly statements of account*—(1) *Forms*. The Copyright Office does not provide printed forms for the use of persons serving Monthly Statements of Account.

(2) *General content*. A Monthly Statement of Account shall be clearly and prominently identified as a "Monthly Statement of Account Under Compulsory License for Making and Distributing Phonorecords," and shall include a clear statement of the following information:

(i) The period (month and year) covered by the Monthly Statement;

(ii) The full legal name of the compulsory licensee, together with all fictitious or assumed names used by such person or entity for the purpose of conducting the business of making and distributing phonorecords;

(iii) The full address, including a specific number and street name or rural route, of the place of business of the compulsory licensee. A post office box or similar designation will not be sufficient for this purpose, except where it is the only address that can be used in that geographic location;

(iv) The title or titles of the nondramatic musical work or works embodied in phonorecords made under the compulsory license and owned by the copyright owner being served with the Monthly Statement and the name of the author or authors of such work or works, if known;

(v) For each nondramatic musical work that is owned by the same copyright owner being served with the Monthly Statement and that is embodied in phonorecords covered by the compulsory license, a detailed statement of all of the information called for in paragraph (e)(3) of this section;

(vi) The total royalty payable for the month covered by the Monthly Statement, computed in accordance with the requirements of this section and the formula specified in paragraph (e)(4) of this section, together with a statement of account showing in detail how the royalty was computed; and

(vii) In any case where the compulsory licensee falls within the provisions of paragraph (d) of this section, a clear description of the action or proceeding involved, including the date of the final judgment or definitive finding described in that paragraph.

(3) *Specific content of monthly statements: Identification and accounting of phonorecords*. (i) The information called for by paragraph (e)(2)(v) of this section shall, with respect to each nondramatic musical work, include a separate listing of each of the following items of information:

(A) The number of phonorecords, including digital phonorecord deliveries, made during the month covered by the Monthly Statement;

(B) The number of phonorecords that, during the month covered by the Monthly Statement and regardless of when made, were either:

Relinquished from possession for purposes other than sale;

Relinquished from possession for purposes of sale without any privilege of returning unsold phonorecords for credit or exchange;

Relinquished from possession for purposes of sale accompanied by a privilege of returning unsold phonorecords for credit or exchange;

Returned to the compulsory licensee for credit or exchange;

Placed in a phonorecord reserve (except that if a negative reserve balance exists give either the number of phonorecords added to the negative reserve balance, or the number of phonorecords relinquished from possession that have been used to reduce the negative reserve balance);

Never delivered due to a failed transmission; or

Digitally retransmitted in order to complete a digital phonorecord delivery.

(C) The number of phonorecords, regardless of when made, that were relinquished from possession during a month earlier than the month covered by the Monthly Statement but that, during the month covered by the Monthly Statement either have had revenue from their sale "recognized" under paragraph (a)(5)(iii) of this section, or were comprised in a phonorecord reserve that lapsed after nine months under paragraph (B) of §201.19(a)(5)(iii).

(ii) Each of the items of information called for by paragraph (e)(3)(i) of this section shall also include, and if necessary shall be broken down to identify separately, the following:

(A) The catalog number or numbers and label name or names, used on the phonorecords;

(B) The names of the principal recording artist or group engaged in rendering the performances fixed on the phonorecords;

(C) The playing time on the phonorecords of each nondramatic musical work covered by the statement; and

(D) Each phonorecord configuration involved (for example: single disk, long-playing disk, cartridge, cassette, reel-to-reel, digital phonorecord delivery, or a combination of them).

(E) The date of and a reason for each incomplete transmission.

(4) *Royalty payment and accounting.* (i) The total royalty called for by paragraph (e)(2)(vi) of this section shall, as specified in section 115(c)(2) of title 17 of the United States Code, be payable for every phonorecord "voluntarily distributed" during the month covered by the Monthly Statement.

(ii) The amount of the royalty payment shall be calculated in accordance with the following formula:

Step 1: Compute the number of phonorecords shipped for sale with a privilege of return. This is the total of phonorecords that, during the month covered by the Monthly Statement, were relinquished from possession by the compulsory licensee, accompanied by the privilege of returning unsold phonorecords to the compulsory licensee for credit or exchange. This total does *not* include: (1) Any phonorecords relinquished from possession by the compulsory licensee for purposes of sale without the privilege of return; and (2) any phonorecords relinquished from possession for purposes other than sale.

Step 2: Subtract the number of phonorecords reserved. This involves deducting, from the subtotal arrived at in Step 1, the number of phonorecords that have been placed in the phonorecord reserve for the month covered by the Monthly Statement. The number of phonorecords reserved is determined by multiplying the subtotal from Step 1 by the percentage reserve level established under Generally Accepted Accounting Practices. This step should be skipped by a compulsory licensee barred from maintaining reserves under paragraph (d) of this section.

Step 3: Add the total of all phonorecords that were shipped during the month and were not counted in Step 1. This total is the sum of two figures: (1) The number of phonorecords that, during the month covered by the Monthly Statement, were relinquished from possession by the compulsory licensee for purposes of sale, without the privilege of returning unsold phonorecords to the compulsory licensee for credit or exchange; and (2) the number of phonorecords relinquished from possession by the compulsory licensee, during the month covered by the Monthly Statement, for purposes other than sale.

Step 4: Make any necessary adjustments for sales revenue "recognized," lapsed reserves, or reduction of negative reserve balance during the month. If necessary, this step involves adding to or subtracting from the subtotal arrived at in Step 3 on the basis of three possible types of adjustments:

(*a*) *Sales revenue "recognized."* If, in the month covered by the Monthly Statement, the compulsory licensee "recognized" revenue from the sale of phonorecords that had been relinquished from possession in an earlier month, the number of such phonorecords is *added* to the Step 3 subtotal;

(*b*) *Lapsed reserves.* If, in the month covered by the Monthly Statement, there are any phonorecords remaining in the phonorecord reserve for the ninth previous month (that is, any phonorecord reserves from the ninth previous month that have not been offset under FOFI, the first-out-first-in accounting convention, by actual returns during the intervening months), the reserve lapses and the number of phonorecords in it is *added* to the Step 3 subtotal.

(*c*) *Reduction of negative reserve balance.* If, in the month covered by the Monthly Statement, the aggregate reserve balance for all previous months is a negative amount, the number of phonorecords relinquished from possession by the compulsory licensee during that month and used to reduce the negative reserve balance is *subtracted* from the Step 3 subtotal.

(*d*) *Incomplete transmissions.* If, in the month covered by the Monthly Statement, there are any digital transmissions of a sound recording which do not result in specifically identifiable reproductions of the entire sound recording by or for any transmission recipient, as determined by means within the sole control of the distributor, the number of such phonorecords is subtracted from the Step 3 subtotal.

(*e*) *Retransmitted digital phonorecords.* If, in the month covered by the Monthly Statement, there are retransmissions of a digital phonorecord to a recipient who did not receive a complete and usable phonorecord during an initial transmission, and such transmissions are made for the sole purpose of delivering a complete and usable reproduction of the initially requested sound recording to that recipient, the number of such retransmitted digital phonorecords is subtracted from the Step 3 subtotal.

Step 5: Multiply by the statutory royalty rate. The total monthly royalty payment is obtained by multiplying the subtotal from Step 3, as adjusted if necessary by Step 4, by the statutory royalty rate of 5.7 cents or 1.1 cents per minute or fraction of playing time, whichever is larger.

(iii) Each step in computing the monthly payment, including the arithmetical calculations involved in each step, shall be set out in detail in the Monthly Statement.

(5) *Clear statements.* The information required by paragraphs (e) (2) and (3) of this section involves intelligible, legible, and unambiguous statements in the Monthly Statements of Account itself and without incorporation of facts or information contained in other documents or records.

(6) *Oath and signature.* Each Monthly Statement of Account shall include the handwritten signature of the compulsory licensee. If that compulsory licensee is a corporation, the signature shall be that of a duly authorized officer of the corporation; if that compulsory licensee is a partnership, the signature shall be that of a partner. The signature shall be accompanied by:

(i) The printed or typewritten name of the person signing the Monthly Statement of Account;

(ii) The date of signature;

(iii) If the compulsory licensee is a partnership or a corporation, by the title or official position held in the partnership or corporation by the person signing the Monthly Statement of Account;

(iv) A certification of the capacity of the person signing; and

(v) The following statement:

I certify that I have examined this Monthly Statement of Account and that all statements of fact contained herein are true, complete, and correct to the best of my knowledge, information, and belief, and are made in good faith.

(7) *Service.* (i) Each Monthly Statement of Account shall be served on the copyright owner or the agent with authority to receive Monthly Statements of Account on behalf of the copyright owner to whom or which it is directed, together with the total royalty for the month covered by the Monthly Statement, by mail or by reputable courier service on or before the 20th day of the immediately succeeding month. However, in the case where the licensee has served its Notice of Intention upon an agent of the copyright owner pursuant to § 201.18, the licensee is not required to serve Monthly Statements of Account or make any royalty payments until the licensee receives from the agent with authority to receive the Notice of Intention notice of the name and address of the copyright owner or its agent upon whom the licensee shall serve Monthly Statements of Account and the monthly royalty fees. Upon receipt of this information, the licensee shall serve Monthly Statements of Account and all royalty fees covering the intervening period upon the person or entity identified by the agent with authority to receive the Notice of Intention by or before the 20th day of the month following receipt of the notification. It shall not be necessary to file a copy of the Monthly Statement in the Copyright Office.

(ii)(A) In any case where a Monthly Statement of Account is sent by mail or reputable courier service and the Monthly Statement of Account is returned to the sender because the copyright owner or agent is no longer located at that address or has refused to accept delivery, or in any case where an address for the copyright owner is not known, the Monthly Statement of Account, together with any evidence of mailing or attempted delivery by courier service, may be filed in the Licensing Division of the Copyright Office. Any Monthly Statement of Account submitted for filing in the Copyright Office shall be accompanied by a brief statement of the reason why it was not served on the copyright owner. A written acknowledgment of receipt and filing will be provided to the sender.

(B) The Copyright Office will not accept any royalty fees submitted with Monthly Statements of Account under this paragraph (e)(7)(ii).

(C) Neither the filing of a Monthly Statement of Account in the Copyright Office, nor the failure to file such Monthly Statement, shall have effect other than that which may be attributed to it by a court of competent jurisdiction.

(D) No filing fee will be required in the case of Monthly Statements of Account submitted to the Copyright Office under this paragraph (e)(7)(ii). Upon request and payment of the fee specified in § 201.3(e), a Certificate of Filing will be provided to the sender.

(iii) A separate Monthly Statement of Account shall be served for each month during which there is any activity relevant to the payment of royalties under section 115 of Title 17, United States Code, and under this section. The Annual Statement of Account identified in paragraph (f) of this section does not replace any Monthly Statement of Account.

(iv) If a Monthly Statement of Account is sent by certified mail or registered mail, a mailing receipt shall be sufficient to prove that service was timely. If a Monthly Statement of Account is delivered by a reputable courier, documentation from the courier showing the first date of attempted delivery shall also be sufficient to prove that service was timely. In the absence of a receipt from the United States Postal Service showing the date of delivery or documentation showing the first date of attempted delivery by a reputable courier, the compulsory licensee shall bear the burden of proving that the Monthly Statement of Account was served in a timely manner.

(f) *Annual statements of account*—(1) *Forms*. The Copyright Office does not provide printed forms for the use of persons serving Annual Statements of Account.

(2) *Annual period*. Any Annual Statement of Account shall cover the full fiscal year of the compulsory licensee.

(3) *General content*. An Annual Statement of Account shall be clearly and prominently identified as an "Annual Statement of Account Under Compulsory License for Making and Distributing Phonorecords," and shall include a clear statement of the following information:

(i) The fiscal year covered by the Annual Statement;

(ii) The full legal name of the compulsory licensee, together with all fictitious or assumed names used by such person or entity for the purpose of conducting the business of making and distributing phonorecords;

(iii) If the compulsory licensee is a business organization, the name and title of the chief executive officer, managing partner, sole proprietor or other person similarly responsible for the management of such entity.

(iv) The full address, including a specific number and street name or rural route, or the place of business of the compulsory licensee. A post office box or similar designation will not be sufficient for this purpose except where it is the only address that can be used in that geographic location;

(v) The title or titles of the nondramatic musical work or works embodied in phonorecords made under the compulsory license and owned by the copyright owner being served with the Annual Statement and the name of the author or authors of such work or works, if known;

(vi) The playing time of each nondramatic musical work on such phonorecords;

(vii) For each nondramatic musical work that is owned by the same copyright owner being served with the Annual Statement and that is embodied in phonorecords covered by the compulsory license, a detailed statement of all of the information called for in paragraph (f)(4) of this section;

(viii) The total royalty payable for the fiscal year covered by the Annual Statement computed in accordance with the requirements of this section, together with a statement of account showing in detail how the royalty was computed. For these purposes, the applicable royalty as specified in section 115(c)(2) of title 17 of the United States Code, shall be payable for every phonorecord "voluntarily distributed" during the fiscal year covered by the Annual Statement;

(ix) The total sum paid under Monthly Statements of Account by the compulsory licensee to the copyright owner being served with the Annual Statement during the fiscal year covered by the Annual Statement; and

(x) In any case where the compulsory license falls within the provisions of paragraph (d) of this section, a clear description of the action or proceeding involved, including the date of the final judgment or definitive finding described in that paragraph.

(4) *Specific content of annual statements: Identification and accounting of phonorecords*. (i) The information called for by paragraph (f)(3)(vii) of this section shall, with respect to each nondramatic musical work, include a separate listing of each of the following items of information separately stated and

identified for each phonorecord configuration (for example, single disk, long playing disk, cartridge, cassette, or reel-to-reel) made:

(A) The number of phonorecords made through the end of the fiscal year covered by the Annual Statement, including any made during earlier years;

(B) The number of phonorecords which have never been relinquished from possession of the compulsory licensee through the end of the fiscal year covered by the Annual Statement;

(C) The number of phonorecords involuntarily relinquished from possession (as through fire or theft) of the compulsory licensee during the fiscal year covered by the Annual Statement and any earlier years, together with a description of the facts of such involuntary relinquishment;

(D) The number of phonorecords "voluntarily distributed" by the compulsory licensee during all years before the fiscal year covered by the Annual Statement;

(E) The number of phonorecords relinquished from possession of the compulsory licensee for purposes of sale during the fiscal year covered by the Annual Statement accompanied by a privilege of returning unsold records for credit or exchange, but not "voluntarily distributed" by the end of that year;

(F) The number of phonorecords "voluntarily distributed" by the compulsory licensee during the fiscal year covered by the Annual Statement, together with:

(*1*) The catalog number or numbers, and label name or names, used on such phonorecords; and

(*2*) The names of the principal recording artists or groups engaged in rendering the performances fixed on such phonorecords.

(ii) If the information given under paragraphs (f)(4)(i)(A) through (F) of this section does not reconcile, the Annual Statement shall also include a clear and detailed explanation of the difference. For these purposes, the information given under such paragraphs shall be considered not to reconcile if, after the number of phonorecords given under paragraphs (B), (C), (D), and (E) are added together and that sum is deducted from the number of phonorecords given under paragraph (A), the result is different from the amount given under paragraph (F).

(5) *Clear statement.* The information required by paragraph (f)(3) of this section involves intelligible, legible, and unambiguous statements in the Annual Statement of Account itself and without incorporation by reference of facts or information contained in other documents or records.

(6) *Signature and certification.* (i) Each Annual Statement of Account shall include the handwritten signature of the compulsory licensee. If that compulsory licensee is a corporation, the signature shall be that of a duly authorized officer of the corporation; if that compulsory licensee is a partnership, the signature shall be that of a partner. The signature shall be accompanied by: (A) The printed or typewritten name of the person signing the Annual Statement of Account; (B) the date of signature; (C) if the compulsory licensee is a partnership or a corporation, by the title or official position held in the partnership or corporation by the person signing the Annual Statement of Account; and (D) a certification of the capacity of the person signing.

(ii)(A) Each Annual Statement of Account shall also be certified by a licensed Certified Public Accountant. Such certification shall consist of the following statement:

We have examined the attached "Annual Statement of Account Under Compulsory License For Making and Distributing Phonorecords" for the fiscal year ended (date) of (name of the compulsory licensee) applicable to phonorecords embodying (title or titles of nondramatic musical works embodied in phonorecords made under the compulsory license) made under the provisions of section 115 of title 17 of the United States Code, as amended by Pub. L. 94–553, and applicable regulations of the United States Copyright Office. Our examination was made in accordance with generally accepted auditing standards and accordingly, included tests of the accounting records and such other auditing procedures as we considered necessary in the circumstances.

In our opinion the Annual Statement of Account referred to above presents fairly the number of phonorecords embodying each of the above-identified nondramatic musical works made under compulsory license and voluntarily distributed by (name of the compulsory licensee) during the fiscal year ending (date), and the amount of royalties applicable thereto under such compulsory license, on a consistent basis and in accordance with the above cited law and applicable regulations published thereunder.

(City and State of Execution)

(Signature of Certified Public Accountant or CPA Firm)

Certificate Number

Jurisdiction of Certificate

(Date of Opinion)

(B) The certificate shall be signed by an individual, or in the name of a partnership or a professional corporation with two or more shareholders. The certificate number and jurisdiction are not required if the certificate is signed in the name of a partnership or a professional corporation with two or more shareholders.

(7) *Service.* (i) Each Annual Statement of Account shall be served on the copyright owner or the agent with authority to receive Annual Statements of Account on behalf of the copyright owner to whom or which it is directed by mail or by reputable courier service on or before the 20th day of the third month following the end of the fiscal year covered by the Annual Statement. It shall not be necessary to file a copy of the Annual Statement in the Copyright Office. An Annual Statement of Account shall be served for each fiscal year during which at least one Monthly Statement of Account shall be served for each fiscal year during which at least one Monthly Statement of Account was required to have been served under paragraph (e)(7) of this section.

(ii) In any case where the amount required to be stated in the Annual Statement of Account under paragraph (f)(3)(viii) of this section is greater than the amount stated in that Annual Statement under paragraph (f)(3)(ix) of this section, the difference between such amounts shall be delivered to the copyright owner together with the service of the Annual Statement. The delivery of such sum does not require the copyright owner to accept such sum, or to forego any right, relief, or remedy which may be available under law.

(iii)(A) In any case where an Annual Statement of Account is sent by mail or by reputable courier service and is returned to the sender because the copyright owner or agent is not located at that address or has refused to accept delivery, or in any case where an address for the copyright owner is not known, the Annual Statement of Account, together with any evidence of mailing or attempted delivery by courier service, may be filed in the Licensing Division of the Copyright Office. Any Annual Statement of Account submitted for filing shall be accompanied by a brief statement of the reason why it was not served on the copyright owner. A written acknowledgment of receipt and filing will be provided to the sender.

(B) The Copyright Office will not accept any royalty fees submitted with Annual Statements of Account under this paragraph (f)(7)(iii).

(C) Neither the filing of an Annual Statement of Account in the Copyright Office, nor the failure to file such Annual Statement, shall have any effect other than that which may be attributed to it by a court of competent jurisdiction.

(D) No filing fee will be required in the case of Annual Statements of Account submitted to the Copyright Office under this § 201.19(f)(7)(iii). Upon request and payment of the fee specified in § 201.3(e), a Certificate of Filing will be provided to the sender.

(iv) If an Annual Statement of Account is sent by certified mail or registered mail, a mailing receipt shall be sufficient to prove that service was timely. If an Annual Statement of Account is delivered by a reputable courier, documentation from the courier showing the first date of attempted delivery shall also be sufficient to prove that service was timely. In the absence of a receipt from the United States Postal Service showing the date of delivery or documentation showing the first date of attempted delivery by a reputable courier, the compulsory licensee shall bear the burden of proving that the Annual Statement of Account was served in a timely manner.

(g) *Documentation.* All compulsory licensees shall, for a period of at least three years from the date of service of an Annual Statement of Account, keep and retain in their possession all records and documents necessary and appropriate to support fully the information set forth in such Annual Statement and in Monthly Statements served during the fiscal year covered by such Annual Statement.

(17 U.S.C. 115, 702, 708)

[45 FR 79046, Nov. 28, 1980, as amended at 56 FR 7813, Feb. 26, 1991; 56 FR 59885, Nov. 26, 1991; 63 FR 30635, June 5, 1998; 64 FR 29521, June 1, 1999; 64 FR 36574, 36575, July 7, 1999; 64 FR 41289, July 30, 1999; 66 FR 34373, June 28, 2001; 69 FR 34584, June 22, 2004; 73 FR 66181, Nov. 7, 2008]

§ 201.20 Methods of affixation and positions of the copyright notice on various types of works.

(a) *General.* (1) This section specifies examples of methods of affixation and positions of the copyright notice on various types of works that will satisfy the notice requirement of section 401(c) of title 17 of the United States Code, as amended by Pub. L. 94–553. A notice considered "acceptable" under this regulation shall be considered to satisfy the requirement of that section that it be "affixed to the copies in such manner and location as to give reasonable notice of the claim of copyright." As provided by that section, the examples specified in this regulation shall not be considered exhaustive of methods of affixation and positions giving reasonable notice of the claim of copyright.

(2) The provisions of this section are applicable to copies publicly distributed on or after December 1, 1981. This section does not establish any rules concerning the form of the notice or the legal sufficiency of particular notices, except with respect to methods of affixation and positions of notice. The adequacy or legal sufficiency of a copyright notice is determined by the law in effect at the time of first publication of the work.

(b) *Definitions.* For the purposes of this section:

(1) The terms *audiovisual works, collective works, copies, device, fixed, machine, motion picture, pictorial, graphic, and sculptural works,* and their variant forms, have the meanings given to them in section 101 of title 17.

(2) *Title 17* means title 17 of the United States Code, as amended by Pub. L. 94–553.

(3) In the case of a work consisting preponderantly of leaves on which the work is printed or otherwise reproduced on both sides, a "page" is one side of a leaf; where the preponderance of the leaves are printed on one side only, the terms "page" and "leaf" mean the same.

(4) A work is published in *book form* if the copies embodying it consist of multiple leaves bound, fastened, or assembled in a predetermined order, as, for example, a volume, booklet, pamphlet, or multipage folder. For the purpose of this section, a work need not consist of textual matter in order to be considered published in "book form."

(5) A *title page* is a page, or two consecutive pages facing each other, appearing at or near the front of the copies of a work published in book form, on which the complete title of the work is prominently stated and on which the names of the author or authors, the name of the publisher, the place of publication, or some combination of them, are given.

(6) The meaning of the terms *front, back, first, last,* and *following,* when used in connection with works published in book form, will vary in relation to the physical form of the copies, depending upon the particular language in which the work is written.

(7) In the case of a work published in book form with a hard or soft cover, the *front page* and *back page* of the copies are the outsides of the front and back covers; where there is no cover, the "front page," and "back page" are the pages visible at the front and back of the copies before they are opened.

(8) A *masthead* is a body of information appearing in approximately the same location in most issues of a newspaper, magazine, journal, review, or other periodical or serial, typically containing the title of the periodical or

serial, information about the staff, periodicity of issues, operation, and subscription and editorial policies, of the publication.

(9) A *single-leaf work* is a work published in copies consisting of a single leaf, including copies on which the work is printed or otherwise reproduced on either one side or on both sides of the leaf, and also folders which, without cutting or tearing the copies, can be opened out to form a single leaf. For the purpose of this section, a work need not consist of textual matter in order to be considered a "single-leaf work."

(c) *Manner of affixation and position generally.* (1) In all cases dealt with in this section, the acceptability of a notice depends upon its being permanently legible to an ordinary user of the work under normal conditions of use, and affixed to the copies in such manner and position that, when affixed, it is not concealed from view upon reasonable examination.

(2) Where, in a particular case, a notice does not appear in one of the precise locations prescribed in this section but a person looking in one of those locations would be reasonably certain to find a notice in another somewhat different location, that notice will be acceptable under this section.

(d) *Works published in book form.* In the case of works published in book form, a notice reproduced on the copies in any of the following positions is acceptable:

(1) The title page, if any;

(2) The page immediately following the title page, if any;

(3) Either side of the front cover, if any; or, if there is no front cover, either side of the front leaf of the copies;

(4) Either side of the back cover, if any; or, if there is no back cover, either side of the back leaf of the copies;

(5) The first page of the main body of the work;

(6) The last page of the main body of the work;

(7) Any page between the front page and the first page of the main body of the work, if:

(i) There are no more than ten pages between the front page and the first page of the main body of the work; and

(ii) The notice is reproduced prominently and is set apart from other matter on the page where it appears;

(8) Any page between the last page of the main body of the work and back page, if:

(i) There are no more than ten pages between the last page of the main body of the work and the back page; and

(ii) The notice is reproduced prominently and is set apart from the other matter on the page where it appears.

(9) In the case of a work published as an issue of a periodical or serial, in addition to any of the locations listed in paragraphs (d) (1) through (8) of this section, a notice is acceptable if it is located:

(i) As a part of, or adjacent to, the masthead;

(ii) On the page containing the masthead if the notice is reproduced prominently and is set apart from the other matter appearing on the page; or

(iii) Adjacent to a prominent heading, appearing at or near the front of the issue, containing the title of the periodical or serial and any combination of the volume and issue number and date of the issue.

(10) In the case of a musical work, in addition to any of the locations listed in paragraphs (d) (1) through (9) of this section, a notice is acceptable if it is located on the first page of music.

(e) *Single-leaf works.* In the case of single-leaf works, a notice reproduced on the copies anywhere on the front or back of the leaf is acceptable.

(f) *Contributions to collective works.* For a separate contribution to a collective work to be considered to "bear its own notice of copyright," as provided by 17 U.S.C. 404, a notice reproduced on the copies in any of the following positions is acceptable:

(1) Where the separate contribution is reproduced on a single page, a notice is acceptable if it appears:

(i) Under the title of the contribution on that page;

(ii) Adjacent to the contribution; or

(iii) On the same page if, through format, wording, or both, the application of the notice to the particular contribution is made clear;

(2) Where the separate contribution is reproduced on more than one page of

the collective work, a notice is acceptable if it appears:

(i) Under a title appearing at or near the beginning of the contribution;

(ii) On the first page of the main body of the contribution;

(iii) Immediately following the end of the contribution; or

(iv) On any of the pages where the contribution appears, if:

(A) The contribution is reproduced on no more than twenty pages of the collective work;

(B) The notice is reproduced prominently and is set apart from other matter on the page where it appears; and

(C) Through format, wording, or both, the application of the notice to the particular contribution is made clear;

(3) Where the separate contribution is a musical work, in addition to any of the locations listed in paragraphs (f) (1) and (2) of this section, a notice is acceptable if it is located on the first page of music of the contribution;

(4) As an alternative to placing the notice on one of the pages where a separate contribution itself appears, the contribution is considered to "bear its own notice" if the notice appears clearly in juxtaposition with a separate listing of the contribution by title, or if the contribution is untitled, by a description reasonably identifying the contribution:

(i) On the page bearing the copyright notice for the collective work as a whole, if any; or

(ii) In a clearly identified and readily-accessible table of contents or listing of acknowledgements appearing near the front or back of the collective work as a whole.

(g) *Works reproduced in machine-readable copies.* For works reproduced in machine-readable copies (such as magnetic tapes or disks, punched cards, or the like, from which the work cannot ordinarily be visually perceived except with the aid of a machine or device,[1] each of the following constitute examples of acceptable methods of affixation and position of notice:

(1) A notice embodied in the copies in machine-readable form in such a manner that on visually perceptible printouts it appears either with or near the title, or at the end of the work;

(2) A notice that is displayed at the user's terminal at sign on;

(3) A notice that is continuously on terminal display; or

(4) A legible notice reproduced durably, so as to withstand normal use, on a gummed or other label securely affixed to the copies or to a box, reel, cartridge, cassette, or other container used as a permanent receptacle for the copies.

(h) *Motion pictures and other audiovisual works.* (1) The following constitute examples of acceptable methods of affixation and positions of the copyright notice on motion pictures and other audiovisual works: A notice that is embodied in the copies by a photomechanical or electronic process, in such a position that it ordinarily would appear whenever the work is performed in its entirety, and that is located:

(i) With or near the title;

(ii) With the cast, credits, and similar information;

(iii) At or immediately following the beginning of the work; or

(iv) At or immediately preceding the end of the work.

(2) In the case of an untitled motion picture or other audiovisual work whose duration is sixty seconds or less, in addition to any of the locations listed in paragraph (h)(1) of this section, a notice that is embodied in the copies by a photomechanical or electronic process, in such a position that it ordinarily would appear to the projectionist or broadcaster when preparing the work for performance, is acceptable if it is located on the leader of the film or tape immediately preceding the beginning of the work.

(3) In the case of a motion picture or other audiovisual work that is distributed to the public for private use, the notice may be affixed, in addition to the locations specified in paragraph (h)(1) of this section, on the housing or container, if it is a permanent receptacle for the work.

[1] Works published in a form requiring the use of a machine or device for purposes of optical enlargement (such as film, filmstrips, slide films, and works published in any variety of microform) and works published in visually perceptible form but used in connection with optical scanning devices, are not within this category.

(i) *Pictorial, graphic, and sculptural works.* The following constitute examples of acceptable methods of affixation and positions of the copyright notice on various forms of pictorial, graphic, and sculptural works:

(1) Where a work is reproduced in two-dimensional copies, a notice affixed directly or by means of a label cemented, sewn, or otherwise attached durably, so as to withstand normal use, of the front or back of the copies, or to any backing, mounting, matting, framing, or other material to which the copies are durably attached, so as to withstand normal use, or in which they are permanently housed, is acceptable.

(2) Where a work is reproduced in three-dimensional copies, a notice affixed directly or by means of a label cemented, sewn, or otherwise attached durably, so as to withstand normal use, to any visible portion of the work, or to any base, mounting, framing, or other material on which the copies are durably attached, so as to withstand normal use, or in which they are permanently housed, is acceptable.

(3) Where, because of the size or physical characteristics of the material in which the work is reproduced in copies, it is impossible or extremely impracticable to affix a notice to the copies directly or by means of a durable label, a notice is acceptable if it appears on a tag that is of durable material, so as to withstand normal use, and that is attached to the copy with sufficient durability that it will remain with the copy while it is passing through its normal channels of commerce.

(4) Where a work is reproduced in copies consisting of sheet-like or strip material bearing multiple or continuous reproductions of the work, the notice may be applied:

(i) To the reproduction itself;

(ii) To the margin, selvage, or reverse side of the material at frequent and regular intervals; or

(iii) If the material contains neither a selvage nor a reverse side, to tags or labels, attached to the copies and to any spools, reels, or containers housing them in such a way that a notice is visible while the copies are passing through their normal channels of commerce.

(5) If the work is permanently housed in a container, such as a game or puzzle box, a notice reproduced on the permanent container is acceptable.

(17 U.S.C. 401, 702)

[46 FR 58312, Dec. 1, 1981, as amended at 66 FR 34373, June 28, 2001]

§ 201.21 [Reserved]

§ 201.22 Advance notices of potential infringement of works consisting of sounds, images, or both.

(a) *Definitions.* (1) An *Advance Notice of Potential Infringement* is a notice which, if served in accordance with section 411(b) of title 17 of the United States Code, and in accordance with the provisions of this section, enables a copyright owner to institute an action for copyright infringement either before or after the first fixation of a work consisting of sounds, images, or both that is first fixed simultaneously with its transmission, and to enjoy the full remedies of said title 17 for copyright infringement, provided registration for the work is made within three months after its first transmission.

(2) For purposes of this section, the *copyright owner* of a work consisting of sounds, images, or both, the first fixation of which is made simultaneously with its transmission, is the person or entity that will be considered the author of the work upon its fixation (including, in the case of a work made for hire, the employer or other person or entity for whom the work was prepared), or a person or organization that has obtained ownership of an exclusive right, initially owned by the person or entity that will be considered the author of the work upon its fixation.

(3) A *transmission program* is a body of material that, as an aggregate, has been produced for the sole purpose of transmission to the public in sequence and as a unit.

(b) *Form.* The Copyright Office does not provide printed forms for the use of persons serving Advance Notices of Potential Infringement.

(c) *Contents.* (1) An Advance Notice of Potential Infringement shall be clearly and prominently captioned "ADVANCE NOTICE OF POTENTIAL INFRINGEMENT" and must clearly state that the copyright owner objects to the relevant activities of the person responsible for the potential infringement, and must include all of the following:

(i) Reference to title 17 U.S.C. section 411(b) as the statutory authority on which the Advance Notice of Potential Infringement is based;

(ii) The date, specific time, and expected duration of the intended first transmission of the work or works contained in the specific transmission program;

(iii) The source of the intended first transmission of the work or works;

(iv) Clear identification, by title, of the work or works. A single Advance Notice of Potential Infringement may cover all of the works of the copyright owner embodied in a specific transmission program. If any work is untitled, the Advance Notice of Potential Infringement shall include a detailed description of that work;

(v) The name of at least one person or entity that will be considered the author of the work upon its fixation;

(vi) The identity of the copyright owner, as defined in paragraph (a)(2) of this section. If the copyright owner is not the person or entity that will be considered the author of the work upon its fixation, the Advance Notice of Potential Infringement also shall include a brief, general statement summarizing the means by which the copyright owner obtained ownership of the copyright and the particular rights that are owned; and

(vii) A description of the relevant activities of the person responsible for the potential infringement which would, if carried out, result in an infringement of the copyright.

(2) An Advance Notice of Potential Infringement must also include clear and prominent statements:

(i) Explaining that the relevant activities may, if carried out, subject the person responsible to liability for copyright infringement; and

(ii) Declaring that the copyright owner intends to secure copyright in the work upon its fixation.

(d) *Signature and identification.* (1) An Advance Notice of Potential Infringement shall be in writing and signed by the copyright owner, or such owner's duly authorized agent.

(2) The signature of the owner or agent shall be an actual handwritten signature of an individual, accompanied by the date of signature and the full name, address, and telephone number of that person, typewritten or printed legibly by hand.

(3) If an Advance Notice of Potential Infringement is initially served in the form of a telegram or similar communication, as provided by paragraph (e)(2)(iii) of this section, the requirement for an individual's handwritten signature shall be considered waived if the further conditions of said paragraph (e) are met.

(e) *Service.* (1) An Advance Notice of Potential Infringement shall be served on the person responsible for the potential infringement not less than 48 hours before the first fixation and simultaneous transmission of the work as provided by 17 U.S.C. 411(b)(1).

(2) Service of the Advance Notice may be effected by any of the following methods:

(i) Personal service;

(ii) First-class mail; or

(iii) Telegram, cablegram, or similar form of communication, if:

(A) The Advance Notice meets all of the other conditions provided by this section; and

(B) Before the first fixation and simultaneous transmission take place, the person responsible for the potential infringement receives written confirmation of the Advance Notice, bearing the actual handwritten signature of the copyright owner or duly authorized agent.

(3) The date of service is the date the Advance Notice of Potential Infringement is received by the person responsible for the potential infringement or by any agent or employee of that person.

(17 U.S.C. 411, 702)

[46 FR 28849, May 29, 1981, as amended at 63 FR 66042, Dec. 1, 1998; 66 FR 34373, June 28, 2001]

§ 201.23 Transfer of unpublished copyright deposits to the Library of Congress.

(a) *General.* This section prescribes rules governing the transfer of unpublished copyright deposits in the custody of the Copyright Office to the Library of Congress. The copyright deposits may consist of copies, phonorecords, or identifying material deposited in connection with registration of claims to copyright under section 408 of title 17 of the United States Code, as amended by Pub. L. 94–553, 90 Stat. 2541, effective January 1, 1978. These rules establish the conditions under which the Library of Congress is entitled to select deposits of unpublished works for its collections or for permanent transfer to the National Archives of the United States or to a Federal records center in accordance with section 704(b) of title 17 of the United States Code, as amended by Pub. L. 94–553.

(b) *Selection by the Library of Congress.* The Library of Congress may select any deposits of unpublished works for the purposes stated in paragraph (a) of this section at the time of registration or at any time thereafter; *Provided,* That:

(1) A facsimile reproduction of the entire copyrightable content of the deposit shall be made a part of the Copyright Office records before transfer to the Library of Congress as provided by section 704(c) of title 17 of the United States Code, as amended by Pub. L. 94–553, unless, within the discretion of the Register of Copyrights, it is considered impractical or too expensive to make the reproduction;

(2) All unpublished copyright deposits retained by the Library of Congress in its collections shall be maintained under the control of the Library of Congress with appropriate safeguards against unauthorized copying or other unauthorized use of the deposits which would be contrary to the rights of the copyright owner in the work under title 17 of the United States Code, as amended by Pub. L. 94–553; and

(3) At the time selection is made a request for full term retention of the deposit under the control of the Copyright Office has not been granted by the Register of Copyrights, in accordance with section 704(e) of title 17 of the United States Code, as amended by Pub. L. 94–553.

(17 U.S.C. 702, 704)

[45 FR 41414, June 19, 1980]

§ 201.24 Warning of copyright for software lending by nonprofit libraries.

(a) *Definition.* A Warning of Copyright for Software Rental is a notice under paragraph (b)(2)(A) of section 109 of the Copyright Act, title 17 of the United States Code, as amended by the Computer Software Rental Amendments Act of 1990, Public Law 101–650. As required by that paragraph, the "Warning of Copyright for Software Rental" shall be affixed to the packaging that contains the computer program which is lent by a nonprofit library for nonprofit purposes.

(b) *Contents.* A Warning of Copyright for Software Rental shall consist of a verbatim reproduction of the following notice, printed in such size and form and affixed in such manner as to comply with paragraph (c) of this section.

Notice: Warning of Copyright Restrictions

The copyright law of the United States (title 17, United States Code) governs the reproduction, distribution, adaptation, public performance, and public display of copyrighted material.

Under certain conditions specified in law, nonprofit libraries are authorized to lend, lease, or rent copies of computer programs to patrons on a nonprofit basis and for nonprofit purposes. Any person who makes an unauthorized copy or adaptation of the computer program, or redistributes the loan copy, or publicly performs or displays the computer program, except as permitted by title 17 of the United States Code, may be liable for copyright infringement.

This institution reserves the right to refuse to fulfill a loan request if, in its judgement, fulfillment of the request would lead to violation of the copyright law.

(c) *Form and manner of use.* A Warning of Copyright for Software Rental shall be affixed to the packaging that contains the copy of the computer program, which is the subject of a library loan to patrons, by means of a label cemented, gummed, or otherwise durably attached to the copies or to a box, reel, cartridge, cassette, or other container used as a permanent receptacle for the copy of the computer program. The notice shall be printed in such manner as to be clearly legible, comprehensible, and readily apparent to a casual user of the computer program.

[56 FR 7812, Feb. 26, 1991, as amended at 66 FR 34373, June 28, 2001]

§ 201.25 Visual Arts Registry.

(a) *General.* This section prescribes the procedures relating to the submission of Visual Arts Registry Statements by visual artists and owners of buildings, or their duly authorized representatives, for recordation in the Copyright Office under section 113(d)(3) of title 17 of the United States Code, as amended by Public Law 101–650, effective June 1, 1991. Statements recorded in the Copyright Office under this regulation will establish a public record of information relevant to an artist's integrity right to prevent destruction or injury to works of visual art incorporated in or made part of a building.

(b) *Forms.* The Copyright Office does not provide forms for the use of persons recording statements regarding works of visual art that have been incorporated in or made part of a building.

(c) *Recordable statements*—(1) *General.* Any statement designated as a "Visual Arts Regulatory Statement" and which pertains to a work of visual art that has been incorporated in or made part of a building may be recorded in the Copyright Office provided the statement is accompanied by the fee for recordation of documents specified in section 708(a)(4) of title 17 of the United States Code. Upon their submission, the statements and an accompanying documentation or photographs become the property of the United States Government and will not be returned. Photocopies are acceptable if they are clear and legible. Information contained in the Visual Arts Registry Statement should be as complete as possible since the information may affect the enforceability of valuable rights under the copyright law. Visual Arts Registry Statements which are illegible or fall outside of the scope of section 113(d)(3) of title 17 may be refused recordation by the Copyright Office.

(2) *Statements by artists.* Statements by artists regarding a work of visual art incorporated or made part of a building should be filed in a document containing the head: "Registry of Visual Art Incorporated in a Building—Artist's Statement." The statement should contain the following information:

(i) Identification of the artist, including name, current address, age, and telephone number, if publicly listed.

(ii) Identification of the work or works, including the title, dimensions, and physical description of the work and the copyright registration number, if known. Additionally, it is recommended that one or more 8 × 10 photographs of the work on good quality photographic paper be included in the submission; the images should be clear and in focus.

(iii) Identification of the building, including its name and address. This identification may additionally include 8 × 10 photographs of the building and the location of the artist's work in the building.

(iv) Identification of the owner of the building, if known.

(3) *Statements by the owner of the building.* Statements of owners of a building which incorporates a work of visual art should be filed in a document containing the heading: "Registry of Visual Art Incorporated in a Building—Building Owner's Statement." The statement should contain the following information:

(i) Identification of the ownership of the building, the name of a person who represents the owner, and a telephone number, if publicly listed.

(ii) Identification of the building, including the building's name and address. This identification may additionally include 8 × 10 photographs of the building and of the works of visual art which are incorporated in the building.

(iii) Identification of the work or works of visual art incorporated in the building, including the works' title(s), if known, and the dimensions and physical description of the work(s). This identification may include one or more 8 × 10 photographs of the work(s) on high quality photographic paper; the images should be clear and in focus.

(iv) Identification of the artist(s) who have works incorporated in the building, including the current address of each artist, if known.

(v) Photocopy of contracts, if any, between the artist and owners of the building regarding the rights of attribution and integrity.

(vi) Statement as to the measures taken by the owner to notify the artist(s) of the removal or pending removal of the work of visual art, and photocopies of any accompanying documents.

(4) *Updating statements.* Either the artist or owner of the building or both may record statements updating previously recorded information by submitting an updated statement and paying the recording fee specified in paragraph (d) of this section. Such statements should repeat the information disclosed in the previous filing as regarding the name of the artist(s), the name of the work(s) of visual art, the name and address of the building, and the name of the owner(s) of the building. The remaining portion of the statement should correct or supplement the information disclosed in the previously recorded statement.

(d) *Fee.* The fee for recording a Visual Arts Registry Statement, a Building Owner's Statement, or an updating statement is the recordation fee for a document, as prescribed in § 201.3(c).

(e) *Date of recordation.* The date of recordation is the date when all of the elements required for recordation, including the prescribed fee have been received in the Copyright Office. After recordation of the statement, the sender will receive a certificate of record from the Copyright Office. Any documentation or photographs accompanying any submission will be retained and filed by the Copyright Office. They may also be transferred to the Library of Congress, or destroyed after preparing suitable copies, in accordance with usual procedures.

(f) *Effect of recordation.* The Copyright Office will record statements in the Visual Arts Registry without examination or verification of the accuracy or completeness of the statement, if the statement is designated as a "Visual Arts Registry Statement" and pertains to a work of visual art incorporated in or made part of a building. Recordation of the statement and payment of the recording fee shall establish only the fact of recordation in the official record. Acceptance for recordation shall not be considered a determination that the statement is accurate, complete, and otherwise in compliance with section 113(d), title 17, U.S. Code. The accuracy and completeness of the statement is the responsibility of the artist or building owner who submits it for recordation. Artists and building owners are encouraged to submit accurate and complete statements. Omission of any information, however, shall not itself invalidate the recordation, unless a court of competent jurisdiction finds the statement is materially deficient and fails to meet the minimum requirements of section 113(d) of title 17, U.S. Code.

[56 FR 38341, Aug. 13, 1991, as amended at 64 FR 29522, June 1, 1999; 65 FR 39819, June 28, 2000]

§ 201.26 Recordation of documents pertaining to computer shareware and donation of public domain computer software.

(a) *General.* This section prescribes the procedures for submission of legal documents pertaining to computer shareware and the deposit of public domain computer software under section 805 of Public Law 101–650, 104 Stat. 5089 (1990). Documents recorded in the Copyright Office under this regulation will be included in the Computer Shareware Registry. Recordation in this Registry will establish a public record of licenses or other legal documents governing the relationship between copyright owners of computer shareware and persons associated with the dissemination or other use of computer shareware. Documents transferring the ownership of some or all rights under the copyright law of computer shareware and security interests in such software should be recorded under 17 U.S.C. 205, as implemented by § 201.4.

(b) *Definitions*—(1) The term *computer shareware* is accorded its customary meaning within the software industry. In general, shareware is copyrighted software which is distributed for the purposes of testing and review, subject to the condition that payment to the copyright owner is required after a person who has secured a copy decides to use the software.

(2) A *document designated as pertaining to computer shareware* means licenses or other legal documents governing the relationship between copyright owners of computer shareware and persons associated with the dissemination or other use of computer shareware.

(3) *Public domain computer software* means software which has been publicly distributed with an explicit disclaimer of copyright protection by the copyright owner.

(c) *Forms.* The Copyright Office does not provide forms for the use of persons recording documents designated as pertaining to computer shareware or for the deposit of public domain computer software.

(d) *Recordable Documents*—(1) Any document clearly designated as a "Document Pertaining to Computer Shareware" and which governs the legal relationship between owners of computer shareware and persons associated with the dissemination or other use of computer shareware may be recorded in the Computer Shareware Registry.

(2) Submitted documents may be a duplicate original, a legible photocopy, or other legible facsimile reproduction of the document, and must be complete on its face.

(3) Submitted documents will not be returned, and the Copyright Office requests that if the document is considered valuable, that only copies of that document be submitted for recordation.

(4) The Copyright Office encourages the submission of a machine-readable copy of the document in the form of an IBM-PC compatible disk, in addition to a copy of the document itself.

(e) *Fee.* The fee for recording a document pertaining to computer shareware is the recordation fee for a document, as prescribed in §201.3(c).

(f) *Date of recordation.* The date of recordation is the date when all of the elements required for recordation, including the prescribed fee have been received in the Copyright Office. After recordation of the statement, the sender will receive a certificate of record from the Copyright Office. The submission will be retained and filed by the Copyright Office, and may be destroyed at a later date after preparing suitable copies, in accordance with usual procedures.

(g) *Donation of public domain computer software.* (1) Any person may donate a copy of public domain computer software for the benefit of the Machine-Readable Collections Reading Room of the Library of Congress. Decision as to whether any public domain computer software is suitable for accession to the collections rests solely with the Library of Congress. Materials not selected will be disposed of in accordance with usual procedures, including transfer to other libraries, sale, or destruction. Donation of public domain software may be made regardless of whether a document has been recorded pertaining to the software.

(2) In order to donate public domain software, the following conditions must be met:

(i) The copy of the public domain software must contain an explicit disclaimer of copyright protection from the copyright owner.

(ii) The submission should contain documentation regarding the software. If the documentation is in machine-readable form, a print-out of the documentation should be included in the donation.

(iii) If the public domain software is marketed in a box or other packaging, the entire work as distributed, including the packaging, should be deposited.

(iv) If the public domain software is copy protected, two copies of the software must be submitted.

(3) Donations of public domain software with an accompanying letter of explanation must be sent to the following address: Gift Section, Exchange & Gift Division, Library of Congress, Washington, DC 20540–4260.

[58 FR 29107, May 19, 1993, as amended at 60 FR 34168, June 30, 1995; 64 FR 29522, June 1, 1999; 65 FR 39819, June 28, 2000]

§201.27 Initial notice of distribution of digital audio recording devices or media.

(a) *General.* This section prescribes rules pertaining to the filing of an Initial Notice of Distribution in the Copyright Office as required by section

1003(b) of the Audio Home Recording Act of 1992, Public Law 102–563, title 17 of the United States Code, to obtain a statutory license to import and distribute, or manufacture and distribute, any digital audio recording device or digital audio recording medium in the United States.

(b) *Definitions*—(1) *An Initial Notice of Distribution of Digital Audio Recording Devices or Media or Initial Notice* is a notice under section 1003(b) of the Audio Home Recording Act of 1992, Public Law 102–563, title 17 of the United States Code, which is required by that section to be filed in the Copyright Office by an importer or manufacturer of a digital audio recording device or digital audio recording medium who has not previously filed notice of the importation or manufacture for distribution of such device or medium in the United States.

(2) The *product category* of a device or medium is a general class of products made up of functionally equivalent digital audio recording devices or media with substantially the same use in substantially the same environment, including, for example, hand-held portable integrated combination units ("boomboxes"); portable personal recorders; stand-alone home recorders ("tape decks"); home combination systems ("rack systems"); automobile recorders; configurations of tape media (standard cassettes or microcassettes); and configurations of disc media such as 2½," 3" and 5" discs.

(3) The *technology* of a device or medium is a product type distinguished by different technical processes for digitally recording musical sounds, such as digital audio tape recorders (DAT), digital compact cassette, (DCC), or recordable compact discs, including minidiscs (MD).

(4) The terms *digital audio recording device, digital audio recording medium, distribute, manufacture,* and *transfer price,* have the meanings of the same terms as they are used in section 1001 of the Copyright Act, title 17 of the United States Code, as amended by Public Law 102–563.

(c) *Forms.* An Initial Notice form may be obtained from the Copyright Office free of charge, by contacting the Library of Congress, Copyright Office, Licensing Division, 101 Independence Avenue, SE, Washington, DC 20557–6400.

(d) *Filing Deadline.* Initial Notices shall be filed in the Copyright Office no later than 45 days after the commencement of the first distribution of digital audio recording devices or digital audio recording media in the United States, on or after October 28, 1992. A manufacturer or importer shall file an Initial Notice within 45 days of the first distribution for each new product category and each new technology that the manufacturer or importer has not reported in a previous Initial Notice.

(e) *Content of Initial Notices.* An Initial Notice of Distribution of Digital Audio Recording Devices or Media shall be identified as such by prominent caption or heading, and shall include the following:

(1) The designation "Importer" or "Manufacturer," or both, whichever is applicable, followed by the full legal name of the importer or manufacturer of the digital audio recording device or medium, or if the party named is a partnership, the name of the partnership followed by the name of at least one individual partner;

(2) Any trade or business name or names, trademarks, or other indicia of origin that the importer or manufacturer uses or intends to use in connection with the importation, manufacture, or distribution of such digital audio recording device or medium in the United States;

(3) The full United States mailing address of the importer or manufacturer, and the full business address, if different;

(4) The product category and technology of the devices or media imported or manufactured;

(5) The first date (day, month, and year) that distribution commenced, or is to commence;

(6) The signature of an appropriate officer, partner, or agent of the importer or manufacturer, as specified by the Initial Notice form; and

(7) Other information relevant to the importation or manufacture for distribution of digital audio recording devices or media as prescribed on the Initial Notice form provided by the Copyright Office.

(f) *Amendments.* (1) The Copyright Office will record amendments to Initial Notices submitted to correct an error or omission in the information given in an earlier Initial Notice. An amendment is not appropriate to reflect developments or changes in facts occurring after the date of signature of an Initial Notice.

(2) An amendment shall:

(i) Be clearly and prominently identified as an "Amendment to an Initial Notice of Distribution of Digital Audio Recording Devices or Media;"

(ii) Identify the specific Initial Notice intended to be amended so that it may be readily located in the records of the Copyright Office;

(iii) Clearly specify the nature of the amendment to be made; and

(iv) Be signed and dated in accordance with this section.

(3) The recordation of an amendment under this paragraph shall have only such effect as may be attributed to it by a court of competent jurisdiction.

(g) *Recordation.* (1) The Copyright Office will record the Initial Notices and amendments submitted in accordance with this section by placing them in the appropriate public files of the Office. The Copyright Office will advise manufacturers and importers of errors or omissions appearing on the face of documents submitted to it, and will require that any such obvious errors or omissions be corrected before the documents will be recorded. However, recordation by the Copyright Office shall establish only the fact and date thereof; such recordation shall in no case be considered a determination that the document was, in fact, properly prepared or that all of the regulatory requirements to satisfy section 1003 of title 17 have been met.

(2) No fee shall be required for the recording of Initial Notices. The fee for filing an Amendment to an Initial Notice of Distribution of Digital Audio Recording Devices or Media is prescribed in § 201.3(e).

[57 FR 55465, Nov. 25, 1992, as amended at 64 FR 36575, July 7, 1999; 72 FR 33692, June 19, 2007]

§ 201.28 Statements of Account for digital audio recording devices or media.

(a) *General.* This section prescribes rules pertaining to the filing of Statements of Account and royalty fees in the Copyright Office as required by 17 U.S.C. 1003(c) and 1004, in order to import and distribute, or manufacture and distribute, in the United States any digital audio recording device or digital audio recording medium.

(b) *Definitions.* For purposes of this section, the following definitions apply:

(1) *Annual statement of account* is the statement required under 17 U.S.C. 1003, to be filed no later than two months after the close of the accounting period covered by the annual statement.

(2) *Device* and *medium* have the same meaning as *digital audio recording device* and *digital audio recording medium,* respectively, have in 17 U.S.C. 1001.

(3) *Digital audio recording product* means digital audio recording devices and digital audio recording media.

(4) *Generally accepted auditing standards (GAAS),* means the auditing standards promulgated by the American Institute of Certified Public Accountants.

(5) *Manufacturing or importing party* refers to any person or entity that manufactures and distributes, and/or imports and distributes, any digital audio recording device or digital audio recording medium in the United States, and is required under 17 U.S.C. 1003 to file with the Copyright Office quarterly and annual Statements of Account.

(6) *Product category of a device or medium* is a general class of products made up of functionally equivalent digital audio recording products with substantially the same use in substantially the same environment, including, for example, hand-held portable integrated combination units ("boomboxes"); portable personal recorders; stand-alone home recorders ("tape decks"); home combination systems ("rack systems"); automobile recorders; configurations of tape media (standard cassettes or microcassettes); and configurations of disc media, such as 2½ inch, 3 inch, or 5 inch discs.

(7) *Primary auditor* is the certified public accountant retained by the manufacturing or importing party to audit the amounts reported in the annual Statement of Account submitted to the Copyright Office. The primary auditor may be the certified public accountant engaged by the manufacturing or importing party to perform the annual audit of the party's financial statement.

(8) *Quarterly statement of account* is the statement accompanying royalty payments required under 17 U.S.C. 1003, to be filed for each of the first three quarters of the accounting year, and no later than 45 days after the close of the quarterly period covered by the statement.

(9) *Technology of a device or medium* is a digital audio recording product-type distinguished by different technical processes for digitally recording musical sounds, such as digital audio tape recorders (DAT), digital compact cassettes (DCC), or recordable compact discs, including minidiscs (MD).

(10) *Distribute, manufacture, transfer price*, and *serial copying* have the meanings set forth in 17 U.S.C. 1001.

(c) *Accounting periods and filing deadlines*—(1) *Election of filing basis.* Statements of Account may be filed on either a calendar or fiscal year basis at the election of the manufacturing party. The election of a calendar or fiscal year basis must be made when the manufacturing or importing party files its first quarterly Statement of Account by appropriate designation on the Form DART/Q submitted. Thereafter the specific calendar or fiscal-year accounting period must be designated on each quarterly Statement of Account. The filing basis may be changed at any time upon notification in writing to the Register of Copyrights, accompanied by a statement of reasons as to why the change is to be made and a statement that such change will not affect the aggregate royalties due under the earlier basis. The notification of change in filing basis must be made at least two months before the date the next quarterly Statement of Account is due to be filed.

(2) *Quarterly filings.* Quarterly Statements of Account shall be filed on Form DART/Q and shall cover a three-month period corresponding to the calendar or fiscal year of the filing party. A quarterly statement shall be filed no later than 45 days after the close of the period it covers.

(3) *Annual filings.* Annual Statements of Account shall be filed on Form DART/A and shall cover both the fourth quarter of an accounting year and the aggregate of the entire year corresponding to the calendar or fiscal accounting year elected. An annual statement shall be filed no later than two months after the close of the period it covers. As a transitional measure, however, the first annual Statement of Account filed after October 28, 1992, is not due until March 1, 1994, or two months after the end of the calendar or fiscal year in which the manufacturing or importing party first filed a quarterly Statement of Account, whichever is later. The first annual Statement of Account shall cover the entire period from October 28, 1992, to the end of the full accounting year. The appropriate royalty payment, calculated according to the instructions contained in Form DART/A, shall accompany the annual Statement of Account covering royalties due for the filing year: that is, royalties for the fourth quarter and any additional royalties that are due because of adjustments in the aggregate amounts of devices or media distributed.

(4) *Early or late filings.* Statements of Account and royalty fees received before the end of the particular accounting period covered by the statement will not be processed by the Office. The statement must be filed after the close of the relevant accounting period. Statements of Account and royalty fees received after the 45-day deadline for quarterly statements or the two-month deadline for annual statements will be accepted for whatever legal effect they may have and will be assessed the appropriate interest charge for the late filing.

(d) *Forms.* (1) Each quarterly or annual Statement of Account shall be submitted on the appropriate form prescribed by the Copyright Office. Computation of the royalty fee shall be in accordance with the procedures set forth in the forms and this section.

Statement of Account forms are available from the Licensing Division, Library of Congress. Forms and other information may be requested from the Licensing Division by facsimile transmission (FAX), but copies of Statement of Account forms transmitted to the Office by FAX will not be accepted.

(2) Forms prescribed by the Copyright Office are designated Quarterly Statement of Account for Digital Audio Recording Products (Form DART/Q) and Annual Statement of Account for Digital Audio Recording Products (Form DART/A).

(e) *Contents of quarterly Statements of Account*—(1) *Quarterly period and filing.* Any quarterly Statement of Account shall cover the full quarter of the calendar or fiscal accounting year for the particular quarter for which it is filed. A separate quarterly statement shall be filed for each quarter of the first three quarters of the accounting year during which there is any activity relevant to the payment of royalties under 17 U.S.C. 1004. The annual Statement of Account identified in paragraph (f) of this section incorporates the fourth quarter of the accounting year.

(2) *General content.* Each quarterly Statement of Account shall be filed on Form DART/Q, the "Quarterly Statement of Account for Digital Audio Recording Products," and shall include a clear statement of the following information:

(i) A designation of the calendar or fiscal year of the annual reporting period;

(ii) A designation of the period, including the beginning and ending day, month, and year of the period covered by the quarter;

(iii) The full legal name of the manufacturing and/or importing party, together with any "doing-business-as" names used by such person or entity for the purpose of conducting the business of manufacturing, importing, or distributing digital audio recording products;

(iv) The full mailing address of the manufacturing or importing party, including a specific number and street name, or rural route and box number, of the place of business of the person or entity. A post office box or similar designation will not be sufficient for this purpose except where it is the only address that can be used in that geographic location;

(v) A designation of the manufacturing or importing party status, *i.e.*, "Manufacturer," "Importer," or "Manufacturer and Importer;"

(vi) The designation "Product Categories" together with the product categories of the digital audio recording products manufactured or imported and distributed during the quarter covered by the statement;

(vii) The designation "Technologies" together with the technologies of the digital audio recording products manufactured or imported and distributed under the AHRA during the quarter covered by the statement;

(viii) The designation "Series or Model Number" followed by the model or series numbers of the digital audio recording products manufactured or imported and distributed under the AHRA during the quarter covered by the statement;

(ix) The "fee code" associated with the product;

(x) The "source code" for the product category;

(xi) The "transfer price" of the product;

(xii) The "number of units distributed" for each product;

(xiii) The "minimum fee per unit" for each product;

(xiv) The statutory royalty "rate" for digital audio recording devices or media;

(xv) The "rate fee" for each product;

(xvi) The appropriate "maximum fee per unit" for each product;

(xvii) The "maximum fee" for each product; and

(xviii) A computation of the total royalty payable for the quarter covered by the statement. Filing parties may not round off the figures they list in Space C, the computation section of the form, except for the figure representing the total royalty fee due; in that case, numbers ending in 50 to 99 cents may be rounded up to the next dollar, and numbers ending in one to 49 cents may be rounded down to the next dollar;

(3) *Royalty payments and accounting.* (i) The royalty specified in 17 U.S.C.

1004 shall accompany the quarterly and annual Statements of Account. No royalty is payable for redistribution of the same product item unless a credit has been taken for such items. Where royalties are payable for the period covered by the statement, the Statement of Account shall contain the following information for each unique combination of product category, technology, series or model number, fee code, source code, and transfer price:

(A) The total number of digital audio recording media distributed, multiplied by the statutory royalty rate of three percent (3%) of the transfer price;

(B) The total number of digital audio recording devices distributed for which the statutory royalty rate of two percent (2%) of the transfer price is payable, multiplied by such percentage rate of the transfer price;

(C) The total number of digital audio recording devices distributed for which the statutory maximum royalty is limited to eight dollars ($8.00), multiplied by such eight dollar amount;

(D) The total number of digital audio recording devices distributed for which the statutory maximum royalty is limited to twelve dollars ($12.00), multiplied by such twelve dollar amount; and

(E) The total number of digital audio recording devices distributed for which the statutory minimum royalty is limited to one dollar ($1.00), multiplied by such one dollar amount.

(ii) The amount of the royalty payment shall be calculated in accordance with the instructions specified in the quarterly Statement of Account form. Payment shall be made as specified in § 201.28(h).

(4) *Reduction of royalty fee.* (i) Section 1004(a)(2)(A) of title 17 of the United States Code, provides an instance in which royalty payments may be reduced if the digital audio recording device and such other devices are part of a physically integrated unit, the royalty payment shall be based on the transfer price of the unit, but shall be reduced by any royalty payment made on any digital audio recording device included within the unit that was not first distributed in combination with the unit.

(ii) Notice of this provision together with directions for possible application to a product is contained in the DART/Q Form.

(5) *Contact party.* Each Statement of Account shall include the name, address, and telephone and facsimile (FAX) numbers of an individual whom the Copyright Office can write or call about the Statement of Account.

(6) *Credits for returned or exported products.* When digital audio recording products first distributed in the United States for ultimate transfer to United States consumers are returned to the manufacturer or importer as unsold or defective merchandise, or are exported, the manufacturing or importing party may take a credit to be deducted from the royalties payable for the period when the products were returned or exported. The credit may be taken only for returns or exports made within two years following the date royalties were paid for the products. This credit must be reflected in the manufacturing or importing party's quarterly or annual Statement of Account. If the manufacturer or importer later redistributes in the United States any products for which a credit has been taken, these products must be listed on the Statement of Account, and a new computation of the royalty fee must be made based on the transfer price of the products at the time of the new distribution.

(7) *Oath and signature.* Each Statement of Account shall include the handwritten signature of an authorized officer, principal, or agent of the filing party. The signature shall be accompanied by:

(i) The printed or typewritten name of the person signing the quarterly Statement of Account;

(ii) The date the document is signed;

(iii) The following certification:

> I, the undersigned, hereby certify that I am an authorized officer, principal, or agent of the "manufacturing or importing party" identified in Space B.

Penalties for fraud and false statements are provided under 18 U.S.C. 1001 *et. seq.*

(f) *Contents of annual Statements of Account*—(1) *General contents.* Each annual Statement of Account shall be filed on form DART/A, "Annual Statement of Account for Digital Audio Recording Products." It must be filed by any importer or manufacturer that distributed in the United States, during a given calendar or fiscal year, any digital audio recording device or digital audio recording medium. The annual statement shall cover the aggregate of the distribution of devices and media for the entire year corresponding to the calendar or fiscal year elected. The annual Statement of Account shall contain the information, oath, and certification prescribed in paragraphs (e)(2)(i) through (e)(7)(iii) of this section, and shall cover the entire accounting year, including the fourth quarter distribution, and shall also provide for the reconciliation of the aggregated accounting of digital audio recording devices and media for the reported accounting year.

(2) *Reconciliation.* Any royalty payment due under sections 1003 and 1004 of title 17 that was not previously paid with the filing party's first three quarterly Statements of Account, shall be reconciled in the annual statement. Reconciliation in the annual Statement of Account provides for adjustments for reductions, refunds, underpayments, overpayments, credits, and royalty payments paid in Quarters 1, 2, and 3, and shall be computed in accordance with the instructions included in the annual Statement of Account. Errors that require reconciliation shall be corrected immediately upon discovery.

(3) *Accountant's opinion.* Each annual Statement of Account or any amended annual Statement of Account shall be audited by the primary auditor as defined in paragraph (b)(7) of this section. An amendment may be submitted to the Office either as a result of responses to questions raised by a Licensing Division examiner or on the initiative of the manufacturing or importing party to correct an error in the original Statement of Account.

(i) The audit shall be performed in accordance with generally accepted auditing standards (GAAS). The audit may be performed in conjunction with an annual audit of the manufacturing or importing party's financial statements.

(ii) The CPA shall issue a report, the "primary auditor's report," reflecting his or her opinion as to whether the annual statement presents fairly, in all material respects, the number of digital audio recording devices and media that were imported and distributed, or manufactured and distributed, by the manufacturing or importing party during the relevant year, and the amount of royalty payments applicable to them under 17 U.S.C. chapter 10, in accordance with that law and these regulations.

(iii) The primary auditor's report shall be filed with the Copyright Office together with the annual Statement of Account, within two months after the end of the annual period for which the annual Statement of Account is prepared. The report may be qualified to the extent necessary and appropriate.

(iv) The Copyright Office does not provide a specific form, or require a specific format, for the CPA's review; however, in addition to the above, certain items must be named as audited items. These include the variables necessary to complete Space C of the Statement of Account form. The CPA may place his or her opinion, which will serve as the "primary auditor's report," in the space provided on Form DART/A, or may attach a separate sheet or sheets containing the opinion.

(v) The auditor's report shall be signed by an individual, or in the name of a partnership or a corporation, and shall include city and state of execution, certificate number, jurisdiction of certificate, and date of opinion. The certificate number and jurisdiction are not required if the report is signed in the name of a partnership or a corporation.

(g) *Copies of statements of account.* A licensee shall file an original and one copy of the statement of account with the Licensing Division of the Copyright Office.

(h) *Royalty fee payment.* (1) All royalty fees must be paid by a single electronic funds transfer, and must be received in the designated bank by the filing deadline for the relevant accounting period. The following information must be provided as part of the EFT and/or as part of the remittance advice as provided for in circulars issued by the Copyright Office:

(i) Remitter's name and address;

(ii) Name of a contact person, telephone number and extension, and email address;

(iii) The actual or anticipated date that the EFT will be transmitted;

(iv) Type of royalty payment (*i.e.*, DART);

(v) Total amount submitted via the EFT;

(vi) Total amount to be paid by year and period;

(vii) Number of Statements of Account that the EFT covers;

(viii) ID numbers assigned by the Licensing Division;

(ix) Legal name of the owner for each Statement of Account.

(2) The remittance advice shall be attached to the Statement(s) of Account. In addition, a copy of the remittance advice shall be emailed or sent by facsimile to the Licensing Division.

(3) The Office may waive the requirement for payment by electronic funds transfer as set forth in paragraph (1) of this section. To obtain a waiver, the remitter shall submit to the Licensing Division at least 60 days prior to the royalty fee due date a certified statement setting forth the reasons explaining why payment by an electronic funds transfer would be virtually impossible or, alternatively, why it would impose a financial or other hardship on the remitter. The certified statement must be signed by a duly authorized representative of the entity making the payment. A waiver shall cover only a single payment period. Failure to obtain a waiver may result in the remittance being returned to the remitter.

(i) *Documentation.* All filing parties shall keep and retain in their possession, for at least three years from the date of filing, all records and documents necessary and appropriate to support fully the information set forth in quarterly and annual statements that they file.

(j) *Corrections, supplemental payments, and refunds*—(1) *General.* Upon compliance with the procedures and within the time limits set forth in this paragraph (i), corrections to quarterly and annual Statements of Account will be placed on record, and supplemental royalty fee payments will be received for deposit, or refunds without interest will be issued, in the following cases:

(i) Where, with respect to the accounting period covered by the quarterly or annual Statement of Account, any of the information given in the statement filed in the Copyright Office is incorrect or incomplete; or

(ii) Where, for any reason except that mentioned in paragraph (j)(2) of this section, calculation of the royalty fee payable for a particular accounting period was incorrect, and the amount deposited in the Copyright Office for that period was either too high or too low.

(2) Corrections to quarterly or annual Statements of Account will not be placed on file, supplemental royalty fee payments will not be received for deposit, and refunds will not be issued, where the information in the Statements of Account, the royalty fee calculations, or the payments were correct as of the date on which the accounting period ended, but changes (for example, cases where digital audio recording media were exported) took place later.

(3) Requests that corrections to annual or quarterly Statements of Account be accepted, that fee payments be accepted, or that refunds be issued shall be addressed to the Licensing Division of the Copyright Office, and shall meet the following conditions:

(i) The request shall be made in writing and must clearly identify the manufacturing or importing party making the request, the accounting period in question, and the purpose of the request. A request for a refund must be received in the Copyright Office before the expiration of two months from the last day of the applicable Statement of Account filing period. A request made by telephone or by telegraphic or similar unsigned communication will be considered to meet this requirement if it clearly identifies the basis of the request, is received in the Copyright Office within the two-month period, and a written request meeting all the conditions of this paragraph (j)(3) is also received in the Copyright Office within 14 days after the end of such two-month period.

(ii) The request must clearly identify the incorrect or incomplete information formerly filed and must provide the correct or additional information.

(iii) In the case where a royalty fee was miscalculated and the amount deposited with the Copyright Office was too large or too small, the request must be accompanied by an affidavit under the official seal of any officer authorized to administer oaths within the United States, or a statement in accordance with 28 U.S.C. 1746, made and signed in accordance with paragraph (e)(7) of this section. The affidavit or statement shall describe the reasons why the royalty fee was improperly calculated and include a detailed analysis of the proper royalty calculation.

(iv) Following final processing, all requests will be filed with the original Statement of Account in the records of the Copyright Office. Nothing contained in this paragraph shall be considered to relieve manufacturing or importing parties of their full obligations under title 17 of the United States Code, and the filing of a correction or supplemental payment shall have only such effect as may be attributed to it by a court of competent jurisdiction.

(v)(A) The request must be accompanied by a filing fee in the amount prescribed in § 201.3(e) for each Statement of Account involved. Payment of this fee may be in the form of a personal or company check, or a certified check, cashier's check, or money order, payable to the Register of Copyrights. No request will be processed until the appropriate filing fees are received.

(B) Requests that a supplemental royalty fee payment be deposited must be accompanied by a remittance in the full amount of such fee. Payment of the supplemental royalty fee must be in the form of a certified check, cashier's check, money order, or electronic payment payable to the Register of Copyrights. No such request will be processed until an acceptable remittance in the full amount of the supplemental royalty fee has been received.

(vi) All requests submitted under paragraph (j) of this section must be signed by the manufacturing or importing party named in the Statement of Account, or the duly authorized agent of that party in accordance with paragraph (e)(7) of this section.

(vii) A request for a refund is not necessary where the Licensing Division, during its examination of a Statement of Account or related document, discovers an error that has resulted in a royalty overpayment. In this case, the Licensing Division will forward the royalty refund to the manufacturing or importing party named in the Statement of Account. The Copyright Office will not pay interest on any royalty refunds.

(k) *Examination of Statements of Account by the Copyright Office.* (1) Upon receiving a Statement of Account and royalty fee, the Copyright Office will make an official record of the actual date when such statement and fee were physically received in the Copyright Office. Thereafter, the Licensing Division will examine the statement for obvious errors or omissions appearing on the face of the documents and will require that any such obvious errors or omissions be corrected before final processing of the document is completed. If, as the result of communications between the Copyright Office and the manufacturer or importer, an additional fee is deposited or changes or additions are made in the Statement of Account, the date that additional deposit or information was actually received in the Office will be added to the official record.

(2) Completion by the Copyright Office of the final processing of a Statement of Account and royalty fee deposit shall establish only the fact of such completion and the date or dates of receipt shown in the official record. It shall not be considered a determination that the Statement of Account was, in fact, properly prepared and accurate, that the correct amount of the royalty was deposited, that the statutory time limits for filing had been met, or that any other requirements of 17 U.S.C. 1001 *et. seq.* were fulfilled.

(l) *Interest on late payments or underpayments.* (1) Royalty payments submitted as a result of late payments or underpayments shall include interest, which shall begin to accrue on the first day after the close of the period for filing Statements of Account for all late payments or underpayments of royalties for the digital audio recording obligation occurring within that accounting period. The accrual period shall end on the date the electronic payment submitted by the remitter is received. In cases where a waiver of the electronic funds transfer requirement is approved by the Copyright Office, and royalties payments are either late or underpaid, the accrual period shall end on the date the payment is postmarked. If the payment is not received by the Copyright Office within five business days of its date, then the accrual period shall end on the date of the actual receipt by the Copyright Office.

(2) The interest rate applicable to a specific accounting period shall be the Current Value of Funds rate in accordance with the Treasury Financial Manual, at 1 TFM 6–8025.40, in effect on the first business day after the close of the filing deadline for the relevant accounting period. The interest rate for a particular accounting period may be obtained by consulting the FEDERAL REGISTER for the applicable Current Value of Funds Rate, or by contacting the Licensing Division of the Copyright Office.

(3) Interest is not required to be paid on any royalty underpayment or late payment from a particular accounting period if the interest charge is five dollars ($5.00) or less.

(m) *Confidentiality of Statements of Account.* Public access to the Copyright Office files of Statements of Account for digital audio recording products shall not be provided. Access will only be granted to interested copyright parties in accordance with regulations prescribed by the Register of Copyrights pursuant to 17 U.S.C. 1003(c).

[59 FR 4589, Feb. 1, 1994, as amended at 64 FR 36575, July 7, 1999; 65 FR 48914, Aug. 10, 2000; 70 FR 30367, May 26, 2005; 70 FR 38022, July 1, 2005; 71 FR 45740, Aug. 10, 2006; 72 FR 33692, June 19, 2007; 73 FR 29073, May 20, 2008]

§ 201.29 Access to, and confidentiality of, Statements of Account, Verification Auditor's Reports, and other verification information filed in the Copyright Office for digital audio recording devices or media.

(a) *General.* This section prescribes rules covering access to DART Statements of Account, including the Primary Auditor's Reports, filed under 17 U.S.C. 1003(c) and access to a Verifying Auditor's Report or other information that may be filed in the Office in a DART verification procedure as set out in § 201.30. It also prescribes rules to ensure confidential disclosure of these materials to appropriate parties.

(b) *Definitions.* (1) *Access* includes inspection of and supervised making of notes on information contained in Statements of Account including Primary Auditor's Reports, Verification Auditor's Reports, and any other verification information.

(2) *Audit and Verification Information* means the reports of the Primary Auditor and Verifying Auditor filed with the Copyright Office under §§ 201.28 and 201.30, and all information relating to a manufacturing or importing party.

(3) *DART Access Form* means the form provided by the Copyright Office that must be completed and signed by any appropriate party seeking access to DART confidential material.

(4) *DART confidential material* means the Quarterly and Annual Statements of Account, including the Primary Auditor's Report that is part of the Annual Statements of Account, and the Verifying Auditor's Report and any other verification information filed with the Copyright Office. It also includes photocopies of notes made by requestors who have had access to these materials that are retained by the Copyright Office.

(5) *Interested copyright party* means a party as defined in 17 U.S.C. 1001(7).

(6) *A Representative* is someone, such as a lawyer or accountant, who is not an employee or officer of an interested copyright party or a manufacturing or importing party but is authorized to act on that party's behalf.

(7) *Statements of Account* means Quarterly and Annual Statements of Account as required under 17 U.S.C. 1003(c) and defined in § 201.28.

(c) *Confidentiality.* The Copyright Office will keep all DART confidential materials in locked files and disclose them only in accordance with this section. Any person or entity provided with access to DART confidential material by the Copyright Office shall receive such information in confidence and shall use and disclose it only as authorized in 17 U.S.C. 1001 *et. seq.*

(d) *Persons allowed access to DART confidential material.* Access to DART Statements of Account filed under 17 U.S.C. 1003(c) and to Verification Auditor's Reports or other verification information is limited to:

(1) An interested copyright party as defined in §201.29(b)(5) or an authorized representative of an interested copyright party, who has been qualified for access pursuant to paragraph (f)(2) of this section;

(2) The Verifying Auditor authorized to conduct verification procedures under §201.30;

(3) The manufacturing or importing party who filed that Statement of Account or that party's authorized representative(s); and

(4) Staff of the Copyright Office or the Library of Congress who require access in the performance of their duties under title 17 U.S.C. 1001 *et seq.;*

(e) *Requests for access.* An interested copyright party, manufacturing party, importing party, representative, or Verifying Auditor seeking access to any DART confidential material must complete and sign a "DART Access Form." The requestor must submit a copy of the completed DART Access Form to the Licensing Specialist, Licensing Division. The form must be received in the Licensing Division at least 5 working days before the date an appointment is requested. The form may be faxed to the Licensing Division to expedite scheduling, but a copy of the form with the original signature must be filed with the Office.

(1) A representative of an interested copyright party, a manufacturing party or an importing party shall submit an affidavit of his or her authority (e.g., in the form of a letter of authorization from the interested copyright party or the manufacturing or importing party).

(2) An auditor selected to conduct a verification procedure under §201.30 shall submit an affidavit of his or her selection to conduct the verification procedure.

(3) DART Access Forms may be requested from, and upon completion returned to: Library of Congress, Copyright Office, Licensing Division, 101 Independence Avenue, SE, Washington, DC 20557–6400. They may also be requested or submitted in person at the Licensing Division, Room LM–504, James Madison Memorial Building, First and Independence Avenue, SE., Washington, DC, between 8:30 a.m. and 5 p.m.

(f) *Criteria for access to DART confidential material.* (1) A Verifying Auditor will be allowed access to any particular Statement of Account and Primary Auditor's Report required to perform his or her verification function;

(2) Interested copyright parties as defined in paragraph (b)(5) of this section will be allowed access to any DART confidential material as defined in paragraph (b)(4) of this section for verification purposes, except that no interested copyright party owned or controlled by a manufacturing or importing party subject to royalty payment obligations under the Audio Home Recording Act, or who owns or controls such a manufacturing or importing party, may have access to DART confidential material relating to any other manufacturing or importing party. In such cases, a representative of the interested copyright party as defined in paragraph (b)(6) of this section may have access for that party, provided that these representatives do not disclose the confidential information contained in the Statement of Account or Primary Auditor's Report to his or her client.

(3) Access to a Verifying Auditor's Report and any other verification material filed in the Office shall be limited to the interested copyright party(s) requesting the verification procedure and to the manufacturing or importing party whose Statement of Account was the subject of the verification procedure.

(g) *Denial of access.* Any party who does not meet the criteria described in §201.29(f) shall be denied access.

(h) *Content of DART Access Form.* The DART Access Form shall include the following information:

(1) Identification of the Statement of Account and Primary Auditor's Report, the Verification Auditor's Report and other verification materials, or notes prepared by requestors who earlier accessed the same items, to be

accessed, by both the name (of the manufacturing party or importing party) and the quarter(s) and year(s) to be accessed.

(2) The name of the interested copyright party, manufacturing party, importing party, or verification auditor on whose behalf the request is made, plus this party's complete address, including a street address (not a post office box number), a telephone number, and a telefax number, if any.

(3) If the request for access is by or for an interested copyright party, a statement indicating whether the copyright party is owned or controlled by a manufacturing or importing party subject to a royalty payment obligation, or whether the interested copyright party owns or controls a manufacturing or importing party subject to royalty payments.

(4) The name, address, and telephone number of the person making the request for access and his/her relationship to the party on whose behalf the request is made.

(5) The specific purpose for the request for access, for example, access is requested in order to verify a Statement of Account; in order to review the results of a verification audit; for the resolution of a dispute arising from such an audit; or in order for a manufacturing or importing party to review its own Statement of Account, Primary Auditor's Report, Verification Auditor's Report, or related information.

(6) A statement that the information obtained from access to Statements of Account, Primary Auditor's Report, Verification Auditor's Report, and any other verification audit filings will be used only for a purpose permitted under the Audio Home Recording Act (AHRA) and the DART regulations.

(7) The actual signature of the party or the representative of the party requesting access certifying that the information will be held in confidence and used only for the purpose specified by the Audio Home Recording Act and these regulations.

[60 FR 25998, May 16, 1995, as amended at 63 FR 30635, June 5, 1998; 64 FR 36575, July 7, 1999; 73 FR 37839, July 2, 2008]

§ 201.30 Verification of Statements of Account.

(a) *General.* This section prescribes rules pertaining to the verification of information contained in the Statements of Account by interested copyright parties pursuant to section 1003(c) of title 17 of the United States Code.

(b) *Definitions*—(1) *Annual Statement of Account, generally accepted auditing standards (GAAS),* and *primary auditor* have the same meaning as the definition in § 201.28 of this part.

(2) *Filer* is a manufacturer or importer of digital devices or media who is required by 17 U.S.C. 1003 to file with the Copyright Office Quarterly and Annual Statements of Account and a primary auditor's report on the Annual Statement of Account.

(3) *Interested copyright party* has the same meaning as the definition in § 201.29 of this part.

(4) *Verifying auditor* is the person retained by interested copyright parties to perform a verification procedure. He or she is independent and qualified as defined in paragraphs (j)(2) and (j)(3) of this section.

(5) *Verification procedure* is the process followed by the verifying auditor to verify the information reported on an Annual Statement of Account.

(c) *Purpose of verification.* The purpose of verification is to determine whether there was any failure of the primary auditor to conduct the primary audit properly or to obtain a reliable result, or whether there was any error in the Annual Statement of Account.

(d) *Timing of verification procedure*—(1) *Requesting a verification procedure.* No sooner than three months nor later than three years after the filing deadline of the Annual Statement of Account to be verified, any interested copyright party shall notify the Register of Copyrights of its interest in instituting a verification procedure. Such notification of interest shall also be served at the same time on the filer and the primary auditor identified in the Annual Statement of Account. Such notification shall include the year of the Annual Statement of Account to be verified, the name of the filer, information on how other interested copyright parties may contact the party interested in the verification including name, address, telephone number, facsimile number and electronic mail address, if any, and a statement establishing the party filing the notification as an interested copyright party. The notification of interest may apply to more than one Annual Statement of Account and more than one filer.

(2) *Coordination and selection of verifying auditor.* The Copyright Office will publish in the FEDERAL REGISTER notice of having received a notification of interest to institute a verification procedure. Interested copyright parties have one month from the date of publication of the FEDERAL REGISTER notice to notify the party interested in instituting the verification procedure of their intent to join with it and to participate in the selection of the verifying auditor. Any dispute about the selection of the verifying auditor shall be resolved by the parties themselves.

(3) *Notification of the filer and primary auditor.* As soon as the verifying auditor has been selected, and in no case later than two months after the publication in the FEDERAL REGISTER of the notice described in paragraph (d)(2) of this section, the joint interested copyright parties shall notify the Register of Copyrights, the filer, and the primary auditor identified in the Annual Statement of Account to be verified, that they intend or do not intend to initiate a verification procedure.

(4) *Commencement of the verification procedure.* The verification procedure shall begin no sooner than one month after notice of intent to initiate a verification procedure was given to the filer and the primary auditor by the joint interested copyright parties. The joint interested copyright parties shall grant the filer or the primary auditor a postponement of the beginning of the verification procedure of up to one additional month if either one requests it. Verification procedures shall be conducted at reasonable times during normal business hours.

(5) *Anti-duplication rules.* A filer shall be subject to no more than one verification procedure per calendar year. An Annual Statement of Account shall be subject to a verification procedure only once.

(e) *Scope of verification.* The verifying auditor shall limit his or her examination to verifying the information required in the Annual Statement of Account. To the extent possible, the verifying auditor shall inspect the information contained in the primary auditor's report and the primary auditor's working papers. If the verifying auditor believes that access to the records, files, or other materials in the control of the filer is required according to GAAS, he or she may, after consultation with the primary auditor, require the production of these documents as well. The verifying auditor and the primary auditor shall act in good faith using reasonable professional judgment, with the intention of reaching a reasonable accommodation as to the necessity and scope of examination of any additional documents, but the decision to require the production of additional documents is solely that of the verifying auditor.

(f) *Verification report.* Upon concluding the verification procedure, the verifying auditor shall render a report enumerating in reasonable detail the procedures performed by the verifying auditor and his or her findings. Such findings shall state whether there was any failure of the primary auditor to conduct properly the primary audit or obtain a reliable result, and whether there was any error in the Annual Statement of Account, itemized by amount and by the filer's elected fiscal year. If there was such failure or error, the report shall specify all evidence from which the verifying auditor reached such conclusions. Such evidence shall be listed and identified in an appendix to the report in sufficient detail to enable a third party to reasonably understand or interpret the evidence on which the verifying auditor based his or her conclusion. If there was no such failure or error, the report shall so state.

(g) *Distribution of report.* Copies of the verifying auditor's report shall be subject to the confidentiality provisions of § 201.29 and shall be distributed as follows:

(1) One copy, excluding the appendix, if applicable, shall be filed with the Register of Copyrights.

(2) One copy, with the appendix, if applicable, shall be submitted to each of the interested copyright parties who retained the services of the verifying auditor and who are authorized to receive such information according to § 201.29.

(3) One copy, with the appendix, if applicable, shall be submitted to the filer of the Annual Statement of Account.

(4) One copy, with the appendix, if applicable, shall be submitted to the primary auditor.

(h) *Retention of report.* The Register of Copyrights will retain his or her copy of the verifying auditor's report for three years following the date the copy of the verifying auditor's report is filed.

(i) *Costs of verification.* The joint interested copyright parties who requested the verification procedure shall pay the fees of the verifying auditor and the primary auditor for their work performed in connection with the verification procedure, except, if the verification procedure results in a judicial determination or the filer's agreement that royalty payments were understated on the Annual Statement of Account, then,

(1) if the amount is less than five percent (5%) of the amount stated on the Annual Statement of Account, that amount shall first be used to pay the fees of the verifying auditor and the primary auditor, and any remaining amount plus any applicable interest on the total amount shall be deposited, allocated by the filer's elected fiscal year, with the Register of Copyrights, or

(2) if the amount is equal to or greater than five percent (5%) of the amount stated on the Annual Statement of Account, the filer shall pay the fees of the verifying auditor and the primary auditor, and, in addition, shall deposit the amount found to be due plus any applicable interest on the total amount, allocated by the filer's elected fiscal year, with the Register of Copyrights.

(j) *Independence and qualifications of verifying auditor.* (1) The verifying auditor shall be qualified and independent as defined in this section. If the filer has reason to believe that the verifying auditor is not qualified or independent, it shall raise the matter with the joint interested copyright parties before the commencement of the verification procedure, and if the matter is not resolved, it may raise the issue with the American Institute of Certified Public Accountants' Professional Ethics Division and/or the verifying auditor's State Board of Accountancy while the verification procedure is being performed.

(2) A verifying auditor shall be considered qualified if he or she is a certified public accountant or works under the supervision of a certified public accounting firm.

(3) A verifying auditor shall be considered independent if:

(i) He or she is independent as that term is used in the Code of Professional Conduct of the American Institute of Certified Public Accountants, including the Principles, Rules and Interpretations of such Code applicable generally to attest engagements (collectively, the "AICPA Code"); and

(ii) He or she is independent as that term is used in the Statements on Auditing Standards promulgated by the Auditing Standards Board of the AICPA and Interpretations thereof issued by the Auditing Standards Division of the AICPA.

[61 FR 30813, June 18, 1996]

§ 201.31 Procedures for copyright restoration in the United States for certain motion pictures and their contents in accordance with the North American Free Trade Agreement.

(a) *General.* This section prescribes the procedures for submission of Statements of Intent pertaining to the restoration of copyright protection in the United States for certain motion pictures and works embodied therein as required by the North American Free Trade Agreement Implementation Act (NAFTA) of December 8, 1993, Public Law No. 103–182. On or after January 3, 1995, the Copyright Office will publish in the FEDERAL REGISTER a list of works for which potential copyright owners have filed a complete and timely Statement of Intent with the Copyright Office.

(b) *Definitions.* For purposes of this section, the following definitions apply:

(1) *Effective filing.* To be effective a Statement of Intent must be complete and timely.

(2) *Eligible work* means any motion picture that was first fixed or published in Mexico or Canada, and any work included in such motion picture that was first fixed or published with this motion picture, if the work entered the public domain in the United States because it was first published on or after January 1, 1978, and before March 1, 1989, without the notice required by 17 U.S.C. 401, 402, or 403, the absence of which has not been excused by the operation of 17 U.S.C. 405, as such sections were in effect during that period.

(3) *Fixed* means a work 'fixed' in a tangible medium of expression when its embodiment in a copy or phonorecord, by or under the authority of the author, is sufficiently permanent or stable to permit it to be perceived, reproduced, or otherwise communicated for a period of more than transitory duration. A work consisting of sounds, images, or both, that are being transmitted, is 'fixed' for purposes of this title if a fixation of the work is being made simultaneously with its transmission. 17 U.S.C. 101

(4) *Potential copyright owner* means the person who would have owned any of the exclusive rights comprised in a copyright in the United States in a work eligible for copyright restoration under NAFTA, if the work had not fallen into the public domain for failure to comply with the statutory notice requirements in effect at the time of first publication, or any successor in interest to such a person.

(5) *Published* means distribution of copies of a work to the public by sale or other transfer of ownership, or by rental, lease, or lending. The offering to distribute copies to a group of persons for purposes of further distribution, public performance, or public display, constitutes publication. A public performance or display of a work does not of itself constitute publication.

(c) *Forms.* The Copyright Office does not provide Statement of Intent forms for the use of potential copyright owners who want to restore copyright protection in eligible works.

(d) *Requirements for effective Statements of Intent.* (1) The document should be clearly designated as a "Statement of Intent to restore copyright protection in the United States in accordance with the North American Free Trade Agreement".

(2) Statements of Intent must include:

(i) The title(s) of the work(s) for which copyright restoration is sought, including any underlying work(s) that has a title(s) different from the title of the motion picture, provided all works are owned by the same potential copyright owner;

(ii) The nation of first fixation;

(iii) The nation of first publication;

(iv) The date of first publication;

(v) The name and mailing address (and telephone and telefax, if applicable) of the potential copyright owner of the work;

(vi) The following certification (in its entirety); signed and dated by the potential copyright owner or authorized agent:

Certification and Signature: I hereby certify that each of the above titled works was first fixed or first published in

____

(insert Mexico or Canada) and understand that the work(s) have entered the public domain in the United States of America because of first publication on or after January 1, 1978, and before March 1, 1989, without the notice required by U.S. copyright law. I certify that the information given herein is true and correct to the best of my knowledge, and understand that any knowing or willful falsification of material facts may result in criminal liability under 18 U.S.C. 1001.

Signature: ________________

Name (Printed or Typed): ________________

Date: ________________

(3) If copyright restoration is sought for an underlying work only, the Statement of Intent must specify the kind of underlying work covered and give the title if different from the title of the motion picture.

(4) More than one motion picture may be included in a single Statement of Intent provided the potential copyright owner is the same for all the motion pictures. The information required

in § 201.31 (d)(2)(i) through (d)(2)(iv) must be given for each work.

(5) Sports programs that do not have a title can be identified in a Statement of Intent by giving the sporting event, the team names and the date (month, day and year).

(6) Statements of Intent must be received in the Copyright Office on or before December 31, 1994.

(7) Statements of Intent must be in English and either typed or legibly printed by hand, on 8½ inch by 11 inch white paper.

(e) *Fee.* The Copyright Office is not requiring a fee for the processing of Statements of Intent.

(f) *Effective date of restoration of copyright protection.* (1) Potential copyright owners of eligible works who file a complete and timely Statement of Intent with the Copyright Office will have copyright protection restored in these works effective January 1, 1995.

(2) The new section 17 U.S.C. 104A(c) created by the NAFTA Implementation Act gives a one year exemption to U.S. nationals or domiciliaries who made or acquired copies of a motion picture or its contents before December 8, 1993, the date of enactment of the implementing act. These individuals or entities may continue to sell, distribute, or perform publicly such works without liability for a period of one year following the Copyright Office's publication in the FEDERAL REGISTER of the list of the works determined to be properly qualified for protection and for which complete and timely Statements of Intent have been filed.

(g) *Registration of works whose copyright has been restored.* After January 1, 1995, the Copyright Office encourages potential copyright owners to make voluntary copyright registration in accordance with 17 U.S.C. 408 for works that have had copyright restored in accordance with NAFTA.

[59 FR 12164, Mar. 16, 1994, as amended at 59 FR 58789, Nov. 15, 1994; 60 FR 50420, Sept. 29, 1995; 66 FR 34373, June 28, 2001]

§ 201.32 [Reserved]

§ 201.33 Procedures for filing Notices of Intent to Enforce a restored copyright under the Uruguay Round Agreements Act.

(a) *General.* This section prescribes the procedures for submission of Notices of Intent to Enforce a Restored Copyright under the Uruguay Round Agreements Act, as required in 17 U.S.C. 104A(a). On or before May 1, 1996, and every four months thereafter, the Copyright Office will publish in the FEDERAL REGISTER a list of works for which Notices of Intent to Enforce have been filed. It will maintain a list of these works. The Office will also make a more complete version of the information contained in the Notice of Intent to Enforce available on its automated database, which can be accessed over the Internet.

(b) *Definitions*—(1) *NAFTA work* means a work restored to copyright on January 1, 1995, as a result of compliance with procedures contained in the North American Free Trade Agreement Implementation Act of December 8, 1993, Public Law No. 103–182.

(2) *Reliance party* means any person who—

(i) With respect to a particular work, engages in acts, before the source country of that work becomes an eligible country under the URAA, which would have violated 17 U.S.C. 106 if the restored work had been subject to copyright protection and who, after the source country becomes an eligible country, continues to engage in such acts;

(ii) Before the source country of a particular work becomes an eligible country, makes or acquires one or more copies or phonorecords of that work; or

(iii) As the result of the sale or other disposition of a derivative work, covered under the new 17 U.S.C. 104A(d)(3), or of significant assets of a person, described in the new 17 U.S.C. 104 A(d)(3) (A) or (B), is a successor, assignee or licensee of that person.

(3) *Restored work* means an original work of authorship that—

(i) Is protected under 17 U.S.C. 104A(a);

(ii) Is not in the public domain in its source country through expiration of term of protection;

(iii) Is in the public domain in the United States due to—

(A) Noncompliance with formalities imposed at any time by United States copyright law, including failure of renewal, lack of proper notice, or failure to comply with any manufacturing requirements;

(B) Lack of subject matter protection in the case of sound recordings fixed before February 15, 1972; or

(C) Lack of national eligibility; and

(iv) Has at least one author or rightholder who was, at the time the work was created, a national or domiciliary of an eligible country, and if published, was first published in an eligible country and not published in the United States during the 30-day period following publication in such eligible country.

(4) *Source country* of a restored work is—

(i) A nation other than the United States; and

(ii) In the case of an unpublished work—

(A) The eligible country in which the author or rightholder is a national or domiciliary, or, if a restored work has more than one author or rightholder, the majority of foreign authors or rightholders are nationals or domiciliaries of eligible countries; or

(B) If the majority of authors or rightholders are not foreign, the nation other than the United States which has the most significant contacts with the work; and

(iii) In the case of a published work—

(A) The eligible country in which the work is first published; or

(B) If the restored work is published on the same day in two or more eligible countries, the eligible country which has the most significant contacts with the work.

(c) *Forms.* The Copyright Office does not provide forms for Notices of Intent to Enforce filed with the Copyright Office. It requests that filers of such notices follow the format set out in Appendix A of this section and give all of the information listed in paragraph (d) of this section. Notices of Intent to Enforce must be in English, and should be typed or printed by hand legibly in dark, preferably black, ink, on 8½ by 11 inch white paper of good quality, with at least a one inch (or three cm) margin.

(d) *Requirements for Notice of Intent to Enforce a Copyright Restored under the Uruguay Round Agreements Act.* (1) Notices of Intent to Enforce should be sent to the following address: GC/I&R, P.O. Box 70400, Washington, DC 20024, USA.

(2) The document should be clearly designated as "Notice of Intent to Enforce a Copyright Restored under the Uruguay Round Agreements Act".

(3) Notices of Intent to Enforce must include:

(i) Required information:

(A) The title of the work, or if untitled, a brief description of the work;

(B) An English translation of the title if title is in a foreign language;

(C) Alternative titles if any;

(D) Name of the copyright owner of the restored work, or of an owner of an exclusive right therein;

(E) The address and telephone number where the owner of copyright or the exclusive right therein can be reached; and

(F) The following certification signed and dated by the owner of copyright, or the owner of an exclusive right therein, or the owner's authorized agent:

I hereby certify that for each of the work(s) listed above, I am the copyright owner, or the owner of an exclusive right, or the owner's authorized agent, the agency relationship having been constituted in a writing signed by the owner before the filing of this notice, and that the information given herein is true and correct to the best of my knowledge.

Signature __________

Name (printed or typed) __________

As agent for (if applicable) __________

Date: __________

(ii) Optional but essential information:

(A) Type of work (painting, sculpture, music, motion picture, sound recording, book, etc.);

(B) Name of author(s);

(C) Source country;

(D) Approximate year of publication;

(E) Additional identifying information (e.g., for movies: director, leading actors, screenwriter, animator; for photographs or books: subject matter; for books: editor, publisher, contributors);

(F) Rights owned by the party on whose behalf the Notice of Intent to Enforce is filed (e.g., the right to reproduce/distribute/publicly display/publicly perform the work, or to prepare a derivative work based on the work, etc.); and

(G) Telefax number at which owner, exclusive rights holder, or agent thereof can be reached.

(4) Notices of Intent to Enforce may cover multiple works provided that each work is identified by title, all the works are by the same author, all the works are owned by the identified copyright owner or owner of an exclusive right, and the rights owned by the party on whose behalf the Notice of Intent is filed are the same. In the case of Notices of Intent to Enforce covering multiple works, the notice must separately designate for each work covered the title of the work, or if untitled, a brief description of the work; an English translation of the title if the title is in a foreign language; alternative titles, if any; the type of work; the source country; the approximate year of publication; and additional identifying information.

(5) Notices of Intent to Enforce works restored on January 1, 1996, may be submitted to the Copyright Office on or after January 1, 1996, through December 31, 1997.

(e) Fee—(1) *Amount.* The filing fee for recording Notices of Intent to Enforce is prescribed in § 201.3(c).

(2) *Method of Payment*—(i) *Checks, money orders, or bank drafts.* The Copyright Office will accept checks, money orders, or bank drafts made payable to the Register of Copyrights. Remittances must be redeemable without service or exchange fees through a United States institution, must be payable in United States dollars, and must be imprinted with American Banking Association routing numbers. International money orders, and postal money orders that are negotiable only at a post office are not acceptable. CURRENCY WILL NOT BE ACCEPTED.

(ii) *Copyright Office Deposit Account.* The Copyright Office maintains a system of Deposit Accounts for the convenience of those who frequently use its services. The system allows an individual or firm to establish a Deposit Account in the Copyright Office and to make advance deposits into that account. Deposit Account holders can charge copyright fees against the balance in their accounts instead of sending separate remittances with each request for service. For information on Deposit Accounts please write: Copyright Office, Library of Congress, Washington, DC 20559–6000, and request a copy of Circular 5, "How to Open and Maintain a Deposit Account in the Copyright Office."

(iii) *Credit cards.* For URAA filings the Copyright Office will accept VISA, MasterCard and American Express. Debit cards cannot be accepted for payment. With the NIE, a filer using a credit card must submit a separate cover letter stating the name of the credit card, the credit card number, the expiration date of the credit card, the total amount, and a signature authorizing the Office to charge the fees to the account. To protect the security of the credit card number, the filer must not write the credit card number on the Notice of Intent to Enforce.

(f) *Public online access.* (1) Almost all of the information contained in the Notice of Intent to Enforce is available online in the Copyright Office History Documents (COHD) file through the Library of Congress electronic information system LC MARVEL through the Internet. Except on Federal holidays, this information may be obtained on terminals in the Copyright Office at the Library of Congress Monday through Friday 8:30 a.m. - 5:00 p.m. U.S. Eastern Time or over the Internet Monday - Friday 6:30 a.m. - 9:30 p.m. U.S. Eastern Time, Saturday 8:00 a.m. - 5 p.m., and Sunday 1:00 p.m. - 5:00 p.m.

(2) Alternative ways to connect through Internet are: (i) use the Copyright Office Home Page on the World Wide Web at: *http://lcweb.loc.gov/copyright*, (ii) telnet to locis.loc.gov or the numeric address 140.147.254.3, or (iii) telnet to marvel.loc.gov, or the numeric address 140.147.248.7 and log in as marvel, or (iv) use a Gopher Client to connect to marvel.loc.gov.

(3) Information available online includes: the title or brief description if untitled; an English translation of the title; the alternative titles if any; the name of the copyright owner or owner of an exclusive right; the author; the type of work; the date of receipt of the NIE in the Copyright Office; the date of publication in the FEDERAL REGISTER; the rights covered by the notice; and the address, telephone and telefax number (if given) of the copyright owner.

(4) Online records of Notices of Intent to Enforce are searchable by the title, the copyright owner or owner of an exclusive right, and the author.

(g) *NAFTA work.* The copyright owner of a work restored under NAFTA by the filing of a NAFTA Statement of Intent to Restore with the Copyright Office prior to January 1, 1995, is not required to file a Notice of Intent to Enforce under this regulation.

APPENDIX A TO § 201.33—NOTICE OF INTENT TO ENFORCE A COPYRIGHT RESTORED UNDER THE URUGUAY ROUND AGREEMENTS ACT (URAA)

1. Title: ____

(If this work does not have a title, state "No title.") OR

Brief description of work (for untitled works only): ____

2. English translation of title (if applicable):
3. Alternative title(s) (if any): ____
4. Type of work: ____

(e.g. painting, sculpture, music, motion picture, sound recording, book)

5. Name of author(s): ____
6. Source country: ____
7. Approximate year of publication: ____
8. Additional identifying information: ____

(e.g. for movies; director, leading actors, screenwriter, animator, for photographs: subject matter; for books; editor, publisher, contributors, subject matter).

9. Name of copyright owner: ____

(Statements may be filed in the name of the owner of the restored copyright or the owner of an exclusive right therein.)

10. If you are not the owner of all rights, specify the rights you own:

____

(e.g. the right to reproduce/distribute publicly display/publicly perform the work, or to prepare a derivative work based on the work)

11. Address at which copyright owner may be contacted:

____

(Give the complete address, including the country and an "attention" line, or "in care of" name, if necessary.)

12. Telephone number of owner: ____
13. Telefax number of owner: ____
14. Certification and Signature:

I hereby certify that, for each of the work(s) listed above, I am the copyright owner, or the owner of an exclusive right, or the owner's authorized agent, the agency relationship having been constituted in a writing signed by the owner before the filing of this notice, and that the information given herein is true and correct to the best of my knowledge.

Signature: ____
Name (printed or typed): ____
As agent for (if applicable): ____
Date: ____

NOTE: Notices of Intent to Enforce must be in English, except for the original title, and either typed or printed by hand legibly in dark, preferably black, ink. They should be on 8½″ by 11″ white paper of good quality, with at least a 1-inch (or 3 cm) margin.

[60 FR 50420, Sept. 29, 1995, as amended at 63 FR 30635, June 5, 1998; 64 FR 12902, Mar. 16, 1999; 71 FR 31092, June 1, 2006; 73 FR 37839, July 1, 2008]

§ 201.34 Procedures for filing Correction Notices of Intent to Enforce a Copyright Restored under the Uruguay Round Agreements Act.

(a) *General.* This section prescribes the procedures for submission of corrections of Notices of Intent to Enforce a Copyright (NIEs) Restored under the Uruguay Round Agreements Act of December 8, 1994, as required by 17 U.S.C. 104A(e), as amended by Pub. L. 103–465, 108 Stat. 4809, 4976 (1994).

(b) *Definitions.* For purposes of this section, the following definitions apply.

(1) *Major error.* A major error in filing a Notice of Intent to Enforce a Copyright Restored under the Uruguay Round Agreements Act is an error in the name of the copyright owner or rightholder, or in the title of the work (as opposed to its translation, if any) where such error fails to adequately identify the restored work or its owner through a reasonable search of the Copyright Office NIE records. Omission of, or incorrect information regarding, a written agency relationship also constitutes a major error.

(2) *Minor error.* A minor error in filing a Notice of Intent to Enforce a Copyright Restored under the Uruguay Round Agreements Act is any error that is not a major error.

(3) *Restored work.* For the definition of works restored under the URAA, *see* 37 CFR 201.33.

(c) *Forms.* The Copyright Office does not provide forms for Correction Notices of Intent to Enforce filed with the Copyright Office. It requests that filers of such Correction NIEs follow the format set out in Appendix A of this section and give all information listed in paragraph (d) of this section. Correction NIEs must be in English, and should be typed or legibly printed by hand in dark, preferably black ink, on 8½″ by 11″ white paper of good quality with at least a 1″ (or three cm) margin.

(d) *Requirements for Correction Notice of Intent to Enforce a Copyright Restored under the Uruguay Round Agreements Act.* (1) A correction for a Notice of Intent to Enforce should be clearly designated as a "Correction Notice of Intent to Enforce" or "Correction NIE."

(2) Correction Notices of Intent to Enforce should be sent to the following address: URAA/GATT, NIEs and Registrations, PO Box 70400, Washington, DC 20024, USA.

(3) A Correction NIE shall contain the following information:

(i) The volume and document number of the previous NIE which is to be corrected;

(ii) The title of the work as it appears on the previous NIE, including alternative titles, if they appear;

(iii) The English translation of the title, if any, as it appears on the previous NIE;

(iv) A statement of the erroneous information as it appears on the previous NIE;

(v) A statement of the correct information as it should have appeared and an optional explanation of its correction; or

(vi) A statement of the information to be added. This includes optional information such as:

(A) Type of work;

(B) Rights owned by the party on whose behalf the Correction Notice is filed;

(C) Name of author;

(D) Source country;

(E) Year of publication;

(F) Alternative titles;

(G) An optional explanation of the added information.

(vii) The name and address:

(A) To which correspondence concerning the document should be sent; and

(B) To which the acknowledgment of the recordation of the Correction NIE should be mailed; and

(viii) A certification. The certification shall consist of:

(A) A statement that, for each of the works named above, the person signing the Correction NIE is the copyright owner, or the owner of an exclusive right, or the owner's authorized agent, and that the information is correct to the best of that person's knowledge;

(B) The typed or printed name of the person whose signature appears;

(C) The signature and date of signature; and

(D) The telephone and telefax number at which the owner, rightholder, or agent thereof can be reached.

(4) A Correction NIE may cover multiple works in multiple NIE documents for one fee provided that: each work is identified by title; all the works are by the same author; all the works are owned by the same copyright owner or owner of an exclusive right. In the case of Correction NIEs, the notice must separately designate each title to be corrected, noting the incorrect information as it appeared on the previously filed NIE, as well as the corrected information. A single notice covering multiple titles need bear only a single certification.

(5) Copies, phonorecords or supporting documents cannot be made part of the record of a Correction NIE and should not be submitted with the document.

(6) *Time for submitting Correction NIEs.* (i) *Major errors.* The Copyright Office will accept a Correction NIE for a major error concerning a restored work during the 24-month period beginning on the date of restoration of the work, as provided for original NIEs in section 104A(d)(2)(A) of title 17.

(ii) *Minor errors.* The Office will accept a Correction NIE for a minor error or omission concerning a restored work at any time after the original NIE has been filed, as provided in section 104A(e)(1)(A)(iii) of title 17.

(e) Fee—(1) *Amount.* The filing fee for recording Correction NIEs is prescribed in § 201.3(c).

(2) *Method of payment.* See 37 CFR 201.33(e)(1),(2).

(f) *Public online access.* Information contained in the Correction Notice of Intent to Enforce is available online in the Copyright Office History Documents (COHD) file through the Library of Congress electronic information system, available through the Internet. This file is available from computer terminals located in the Copyright Office itself or from terminals located in other parts of the Library of Congress through the Library of Congress Information System (LOCIS). Alternative ways to connect through Internet are the World Wide Web (WWW), using the Copyright Office Home Page at: *http://www.loc.gov/copyright*; directly to LOCIS through the telnet address at locis.loc.gov; or the Library of Congress through gopher LC MARVEL and WWW which are available 24 hours a day. LOCIS is available 24 hours a day, Monday through Friday. For the purpose of researching the full Office record of Correction NIEs on the Internet, the Office has made online searching instructions accessible through the Copyright Office Home Page. Researchers can access them through the Library of Congress Home Page on the World Wide Web by selecting the copyright link. Select the menu item "Copyright Office Records" and/or "URAA, GATT Amends U.S. law." Images of the complete Correction NIEs as filed will be stored on optical disk and will be available from the Copyright Office.

APPENDIX A TO § 201.34—CORRECTION NOTICE OF INTENT TO ENFORCE

CORRECTION OF NOTICE OF INTENT TO ENFORCE

1. Name of Copyright Owner (or owner of exclusive right) If this correction notice is to cover multiple works, the author and the rights owner must be the same for all works covered by the notice.)

______

2. Title(s) (or brief description)
(a) Work No. 1—______
Volume and Document Number: ______
English Translation: ______
(b) Work No. 2 (if applicable)—______
Volume and Document Number: ______
English Translation: ______
(c) Work No. 3 (if applicable)—______
Volume and Document Number: ______
English Translation: ______
(d) Work No. 4 (if applicable)—______
Volume and Document Number: ______
English Translation: ______

3. Statement of incorrect information on earlier NIE:

______

4. Statement of correct (or previously omitted) information:

______

Give the following only if incorrect or omitted on earlier NIE:
(a) Type of work ______
(b) Rights owned ______
(c) Name of author (of entire work) ______
(d) Source Country ______
(e) Year of Publication (Approximate if precise year is unknown) ______
(f) Alternative titles ______

5. Explanation of error:

______

6. Certification and Signature: I hereby certify that for each of the work(s) listed above, I am the copyright owner, or the owner of an exclusive right, or the owner's authorized agent, the agency relationship having been constituted in a writing signed by the owner before the filing of this notice, and that the information given herein is true and correct to the best of my knowledge.

______

Name and Address (typed or printed):

______

Telephone/Fax:

As agent for:

______

Date and Signature:

______

[62 FR 55739, Oct. 28, 1997, as amended at 71 FR 31092, June 1, 2006; 73 FR 37839, July 2, 2008]

§§ 201.35–201.37 [Reserved]

§ 201.38 Designation of agent to receive notification of claimed infringement.

(a) *General.* This section prescribes interim rules under which service providers may provide the Copyright Office with designations of agents to receive notification of claimed infringement under section 512(c)(2) of title 17 of the United States Code, as amended. These interim rules shall remain in effect until more comprehensive rules have been promulgated following a notice of proposed rulemaking and receipt of public comments.

(b) *Forms.* The Copyright Office does not provide printed forms for filing an Interim Designation of Agent to Receive Notification of Claimed Infringement.

(c) *Content.* An "Interim Designation of Agent to Receive Notification of Claimed Infringement" shall be identified as such by prominent caption or heading, and shall include the following information with respect to a single service provider:

(1) The full legal name and address of the service provider;

(2) All names under which the service provider is doing business;

(3) The name of the agent designated to receive notification of claimed infringement;

(4) The full address, including a specific number and street name or rural route, of the agent designated to receive notification of claimed infringement. A post office box or similar designation will not be sufficient except where it is the only address that can be used in that geographic location;

(5) The telephone number, facsimile number, and electronic mail address of the agent designated to receive notification of claimed infringement.

(d) *Signature.* The Interim Designation of Agent to Receive Notification of Claimed Infringement shall include the signature of the appropriate officer or representative of the service provider designating the agent. The signature shall be accompanied by the printed or typewritten name and title of the person signing the Notice, and by the date of signature.

(e) *Filing.* A service provider may file the Interim Designation of Agent to Receive Notification of Claimed Infringement with the Copyright Information Section, Room LM–401, James Madison Memorial Building, Library of Congress, 101 Independence Avenue, SE, Washington, DC, during normal business hours, 9 am to 5 pm. If mailed, the Interim Designation should be addressed to: Copyright GC/I&R, PO Box 70400, Washington, DC 20024. Each designation shall be accompanied by a filing fee for Recordation of an Interim Designation of Agent to Receive Notification of Claimed Infringement under section 512(c)(2) in the amount prescribed in § 201.3(c). Designations and amendments will be posted online on the Copyright Office's website (*http://www.loc.gov/copyright*).

(f) *Amendments.* In the event of a change in the information reported in an Interim Designation of Agent to Receive Notification of Claimed Infringement, a service provider shall file with the Copyright Information Section an amended Interim Designation of Agent to Receive Notification of Claimed Infringement, containing the current information required by § 201.38(c). The amended Interim Designation shall be signed in accordance with the requirements of § 201.38(d) and shall be accompanied by a fee equal to the amount prescribed in § 201.3(c) for Recordation of an Interim Designation of Agent to Receive Notification of Claimed Infringement under section 512(c)(2).

(g) *Termination and dissolution.* If a service provider terminates its operations, the entity shall notify the Copyright Office by certified or registered mail.

[63 FR 59234, Nov. 3, 1998, as amended at 67 FR 38005, May 31, 2002; 72 FR 5932, Feb. 8, 2007; 73 FR 37839, July 2, 2008]

§ 201.39 Notice to Libraries and Archives of Normal Commercial Exploitation or Availability at Reasonable Price.

(a) *General.* This section prescribes rules under which copyright owners or their agents may provide notice to qualified libraries and archives (including a nonprofit educational institution that functions as such) that a published work in its last 20 years of copyright protection is subject to normal commercial exploitation, or that a copy or phonorecord of the work can be obtained at a reasonable price, for purposes of section 108(h)(2) of title 17 of the United States Code.

(b) *Format.* The Copyright Office provides a required format for a Notice to Libraries and Archives of Normal Commercial Exploitation or Availability at Reasonable Price, and for continuation sheets for group notices. The required format is set out in Appendix A to this section, and is available from the Copyright Office website (*http://lcweb.loc.gov/*

copyright). The Copyright Office does not provide printed forms. The Notice shall be in English (except for an original title, which may be in another language), typed or printed legibly in dark ink, and shall be provided on 8½ × 11 inch white paper with a one-inch margin.

(c) *Required content.* A "Notice to Libraries and Archives of Normal Commercial Exploitation or Availability at Reasonable Price" shall be identified as such by prominent caption or heading, and shall include the following:

(1) The acronym NLA in capital, and preferably bold, letters in the top right-hand corner of the page;

(2) A check-box just below the acronym NLA indicating whether continuation sheets for additional works are attached;

(3) The title of the work, or if untitled, a brief description of the work;

(4) The author(s) of the work;

(5) The type of work (e.g., music, motion picture, book, photograph, illustration, map, article in a periodical, painting, sculpture, sound recording, etc.);

(6) The edition, if any (e.g., first edition, second edition, teacher's edition) or version, if any (e.g., orchestral arrangement, translation, French version). If there is no information relating to the edition or version of the work, the notice should so state;

(7) The year of first publication;

(8) The year the work first secured federal copyright through publication with notice or registration as an unpublished work;

(9) The copyright renewal registration number (except this information is not required for foreign works in which copyright is restored pursuant to 17 U.S.C. 104A);

(10) The name of the copyright owner (or the owner of exclusive rights);

(11) If the copyright owner is not the owner of all rights, a specification of the rights owned (e.g., the right to reproduce/distribute/publicly display/publicly perform the work or to prepare a derivative work);

(12) The name, address, telephone number, fax number (if any) and e-mail address (if any) of the person or entity that the Copyright Office should contact concerning the Notice;

(13) The full legal name, address, telephone number, fax number (if any) and e-mail address (if any) of the person or entity that Libraries and Archives may contact concerning the work's normal commercial exploitation or availability at reasonable price; and

(14) A declaration made under penalty of perjury that the work identified is subject to normal commercial exploitation, or that a copy or phonorecord of the work is available at a reasonable price.

(d) *Additional content.* A Notice to Libraries and Archives of Normal Commercial Exploitation or Availability at Reasonable Price may include the following:

(1) The original copyright registration number of the work; and

(2) Additional information concerning the work's normal commercial exploitation or availability at a reasonable price.

(e) *Signature.* The Notice to Libraries and Archives of Normal Commercial Exploitation or Availability at Reasonable Price shall include the signature of the copyright owner or its agent. The signature shall be accompanied by the printed or typewritten name and title of the person signing the Notice, and by the date of signature.

(f) *Multiple works.* A Notice to Libraries and Archives may be filed for more than one work. The first work shall be identified using the format required for all Notices to Libraries and Archives. Each additional work in the group must be identified on a separate continuation sheet. The required format for the continuation sheet is set out in Appendix B to this section, and is available from the Copyright Office website (*http://lcweb.loc.gov/copyright*). A group filing is permitted provided that:

(1) All the works are by the same author;

(2) All the works are owned by the same copyright owner or owner of the exclusive rights therein. If the claimant is not owner of all rights, the claimant must own the same rights with respect to all works in the group;

(3) All the works first secured federal copyright in the same year, through either publication with notice or registration as unpublished works;

(4) All the works were first published in the same year;

(5) The person or entity that the Copyright Office should contact concerning the Notice is the same for all the works; and

(6) The person or entity that Libraries and Archives may contact concerning the work's normal commercial exploitation or availability at reasonable price is the same for all the works.

(g) *Filing*—(1) *Method of filing.* The Notice to Libraries and Archives of Normal Commercial Exploitation or Availability at Reasonable Price should be addressed to: NLA, Library of Congress, Copyright Office, 101 Independence Avenue, SE., Washington, DC 20559–6000. If delivered by hand, it should be delivered during normal business hours, 8:30 a.m. to 5:00 p.m., to the Copyright Information Section, Room LM–401, James Madison Memorial Building, Library of Congress, 101 Independence Avenue, SE., Washington, DC.

(2) *Amount.* The filing fee for recording Notice to Libraries and Archives is prescribed in § 201.3(d).

(3) *Method of payment*—(i) *Checks, money orders, or bank drafts.* The Copyright Office will accept checks, money orders, or bank drafts made payable to the Register of Copyrights. Remittances must be redeemable without service or exchange fees through a United States institution, must be payable in United States dollars, and must be imprinted with American Banking Association routing numbers. Postal money orders that are negotiable only at a post office and international money orders are not acceptable. CURRENCY IS NOT ACCEPTED.

(ii) *Copyright Office Deposit Account.* The Copyright Office maintains a system of Deposit Accounts for the convenience of those who frequently use its services. The system allows an individual or firm to establish a Deposit Account in the Copyright Office and to make advance deposits into that account. Deposit Account holders can charge copyright fees against the balance in their accounts instead of sending separate remittances with each request for service. For information on Deposit Accounts, visit the Copyright Office website or write: Copyright Office, Library of Congress, Washington, DC 20559–6000, and request a copy of Circular 5, "How to Open and Maintain a Deposit Account in the Copyright Office."

APPENDIX A TO § 201.39—REQUIRED FORMAT OF NOTICE TO LIBRARIES AND ARCHIVES OF NORMAL COMMERCIAL EXPLOITATION OR AVAILABILITY AT REASONABLE PRICE

NLA

☐ Check box if continuation sheets for additional works are attached.

Notice to Libraries and Archives of Normal Commercial Exploitation or Availability at Reasonable Price

1. Title of the work (or, if untitled, a brief description of the work): ______.

2. Author(s) of the work: ______.

3. Type of work (e.g. music, motion picture, book, photograph, illustration, map, article in a periodical, painting, sculpture, sound recording, etc.): ______.

4. Edition, if any (e.g., first edition, second edition, teacher's edition) or version, if any (e.g., orchestral arrangement, English translation of French text). If there is no information available relating to the edition or version of the work, the Notice should state, "No information available": ______.

5. Year of first publication: ______.

6. Year the work first secured federal copyright through publication with notice or registration as an unpublished work: ______.

7. Copyright renewal registration number (not required for foreign works restored under 17 U.S.C. 104A): ______.

8. Full legal name of the copyright owner (or the owner of exclusive rights): ______.

9. The person or entity identified in space #8 owns:

☐ all rights.

☐ the following rights (e.g., the right to reproduce/distribute/publicly display/publicly perform the work or to prepare a derivative work): ______.

10. Person or entity that the Copyright Office should contact concerning the Notice:

☐ Name: ______

☐ Address: ______

☐ Telephone: ______

☐ Fax number (if any): ______

☐ E-mail address (if any): ______

11. Person or entity that libraries and archives may contact concerning the work's normal commercial exploitation or availability at a reasonable price:

☐ Name: ______

☐ Address: ______________
☐ Telephone: ______________
☐ Fax number (if any): ______________
☐ E-mail address (if any): ______________

Additional Content (OPTIONAL):

12. Original copyright registration number: ______________

13. Additional information concerning the work's normal commercial exploitation or availability at a reasonable price: ______________

Declaration:

I declare under penalty of perjury under the laws of the United States:

☐ that each work identified in this notice is subject to normal commercial exploitation.
☐ that a copy or phonorecord of each work identified in this notice is available at a reasonable price.

Signature: ______________
Date: ______________
☐ Typed or printed name: ______________
☐ Title: ______________

APPENDIX B TO § 201.39—REQUIRED FORMAT FOR CONTINUATION SHEET

NLA CON
Page ___ of ___ Pages.

Continuation Sheet for NLA Notice to Libraries and Archives of Normal Commercial Exploitation or Availability at Reasonable Price

1. Title of the work (or, if untitled, a brief description of the work): ______________.

2. Type of work (e.g. music, motion picture, book, photograph, illustration, map, article in a periodical, painting, sculpture, sound recording, etc.): ______________.

3. Edition, if any (e.g., first edition, second edition, teacher's edition) or version, if any (e.g., orchestral arrangement, English translation of French text). If there is no information available relating to the edition or version of the work, the Notice should state, "No information available": ______________.

4. Copyright renewal registration number (not required for foreign works restored under 17 U.S.C. 104A): ______________.

Additional Content (OPTIONAL):

5. Original copyright registration number: ______________.

6. Additional information concerning the work's normal commercial exploitation or availability at a reasonable price: ______________.

[63 FR 71787, Dec. 30, 1998, as amended at 66 FR 34373, June 28, 2001; 71 FR 31092, June 1, 2006; 73 FR 37839, July 2, 2008]

§ 201.40 Exemption to prohibition against circumvention.

(a) *General.* This section prescribes the classes of copyrighted works for which the Librarian of Congress has determined, pursuant to 17 U.S.C. 1201(a)(1)(C) and (D), that noninfringing uses by persons who are users of such works are, or are likely to be, adversely affected. The prohibition against circumvention of technological measures that control access to copyrighted works set forth in 17 U.S.C. 1201(a)(1)(A) shall not apply to such users of the prescribed classes of copyrighted works.

(b) *Classes of copyrighted works.* Pursuant to the authority set forth in 17 U.S.C. 1201(a)(1)(C) and (D), and upon the recommendation of the Register of Copyrights, the Librarian has determined that the prohibition against circumvention of technological measures that effectively control access to copyrighted works set forth in 17 U.S.C. 1201(a)(1)(A) shall not apply to persons who engage in noninfringing uses of the following classes of copyrighted works:

(1) Literary works, distributed electronically, that are protected by technological measures which either prevent the enabling of read-aloud functionality or interfere with screen readers or other applications or assistive technologies in the following instances:

(i) When a copy of such a work is lawfully obtained by a blind or other person with a disability, as such a person is defined in 17 U.S.C. 121; provided, however, the rights owner is remunerated, as appropriate, for the price of the mainstream copy of the work as made available to the general public through customary channels; or

(ii) When such work is a nondramatic literary work, lawfully obtained and used by an authorized entity pursuant to 17 U.S.C. 121.

(2) Computer programs that enable wireless telephone handsets to execute lawfully obtained software applications, where circumvention is accomplished for the sole purpose of enabling interoperability of such applications with computer programs on the telephone handset.

(3) Computer programs, in the form of firmware or software, that enable a wireless telephone handset originally acquired from the operator of a wireless telecommunications network or retailer no later than ninety days after the effective date of this exemption to connect to a different wireless telecommunications network, if the operator of the wireless communications network to which the handset is locked has failed to unlock it within a reasonable period of time following a request by the owner of the wireless telephone handset, and when circumvention is initiated by the owner, an individual consumer, who is also the owner of the copy of the computer program in such wireless telephone handset, solely in order to connect to a different wireless telecommunications network, and such access to the network is authorized by the operator of the network.

(4) Motion pictures, as defined in 17 U.S.C. 101, on DVDs that are lawfully made and acquired and that are protected by the Content Scrambling System, where the person engaging in circumvention believes and has reasonable grounds for believing that circumvention is necessary because reasonably available alternatives, such as noncircumventing methods or using screen capture software as provided for in alternative exemptions, are not able to produce the level of high-quality content required to achieve the desired criticism or comment on such motion pictures, and where circumvention is undertaken solely in order to make use of short portions of the motion pictures for the purpose of criticism or comment in the following instances:

(i) In noncommercial videos;

(ii) In documentary films;

(iii) In nonfiction multimedia ebooks offering film analysis; and

(iv) For educational purposes in film studies or other courses requiring close analysis of film and media excerpts, by college and university faculty, college and university students, and kindergarten through twelfth grade educators. For purposes of this exemption, "noncommercial videos" includes videos created pursuant to a paid commission, provided that the commissioning entity's use is noncommercial.

(5) Motion pictures, as defined in 17 U.S.C. 101, that are lawfully made and acquired via online distribution services and that are protected by various technological protection measures, where the person engaging in circumvention believes and has reasonable grounds for believing that circumvention is necessary because reasonably available alternatives, such as noncircumventing methods or using screen capture software as provided for in alternative exemptions, are not able to produce the level of high-quality content required to achieve the desired criticism or comment on such motion pictures, and where circumvention is undertaken solely in order to make use of short portions of the motion pictures for the purpose of criticism or comment in the following instances:

(i) In noncommercial videos;

(ii) In documentary films;

(iii) In nonfiction multimedia ebooks offering film analysis; and

(iv) For educational purposes in film studies or other courses requiring close analysis of film and media excerpts, by college and university faculty, college and university students, and kindergarten through twelfth grade educators. For purposes of this exemption, "noncommercial videos" includes videos created pursuant to a paid commission, provided that the commissioning entity's use is noncommercial.

(6)(i) Motion pictures, as defined in 17 U.S.C. 101, on DVDs that are lawfully made and acquired and that are protected by the Content Scrambling System, where the circumvention, if any, is undertaken using screen capture technology that is reasonably represented and offered to the public as enabling the reproduction of motion picture content after such content has been lawfully decrypted, when such representations have been reasonably relied upon by the user of such technology, when the person engaging in the circumvention believes and has reasonable grounds for believing that the circumvention is necessary to achieve the desired criticism or comment, and where the circumvention is undertaken solely in order to make use of short portions of the motion pictures for the purpose of criticism or comment in the following instances:

(A) In noncommercial videos;

(B) In documentary films;

(C) In nonfiction multimedia ebooks offering film analysis; and

(D) For educational purposes by college and university faculty, college and university students, and kindergarten through twelfth grade educators.

(ii) For purposes of this exemption, "noncommercial videos" includes videos created pursuant to a paid commission, provided that the commissioning entity's use is noncommercial.

(7)(i) Motion pictures, as defined in 17 U.S.C. 101, that are lawfully made and acquired via online distribution services and that are protected by various technological protection measures, where the circumvention, if any, is undertaken using screen capture technology that is reasonably represented and offered to the public as enabling the reproduction of motion picture content after such content has been lawfully decrypted, when such representations have been reasonably relied upon by the user of such technology, when the person engaging in the circumvention believes and has reasonable grounds for believing that the circumvention is necessary to achieve the desired criticism or comment, and where the circumvention is undertaken solely in order to make use of short portions of the motion pictures for the purpose of criticism or comment in the following instances:

(A) In noncommercial videos;

(B) In documentary films;

(C) In nonfiction multimedia ebooks offering film analysis; and

(D) For educational purposes by college and university faculty, college and university students, and kindergarten through twelfth grade educators.

(ii) For purposes of this exemption, "noncommercial videos" includes videos created pursuant to a paid commission, provided that the commissioning entity's use is noncommercial.

(8) Motion pictures and other audiovisual works on DVDs that are protected by the Content Scrambling System, or that are distributed by an online service and protected by technological measures that control access to such works, when circumvention is accomplished solely to access the playhead and/or related time code information embedded in copies of such works and solely for the purpose of conducting research and development for the purpose of creating players capable of rendering visual representations of the audible portions of such works and/or audible representations or descriptions of the visual portions of such works to enable an individual who is blind, visually impaired, deaf, or hard of hearing, and who has lawfully obtained a copy of such a work, to perceive the work; provided however, that the resulting player does not require circumvention of technological measures to operate.

(c) *Definition.* "Specialized format," "digital text" and "authorized entities" shall have the same meaning as in 17 U.S.C. 121.

[65 FR 64574, Oct. 27, 2000, as amended at 68 FR 62018, Oct. 31, 2003; 71 FR 68479, Nov. 27, 2006; 74 FR 55139, Oct. 27, 2009; 75 FR 43839, July 27, 2010; 75 FR 47465, Aug. 6, 2010; 77 FR 65278, Oct. 26, 2012]

PART 202—PREREGISTRATION AND REGISTRATION OF CLAIMS TO COPYRIGHT

Sec.

APPENDIX A TO PART 202—TECHNICAL GUIDELINES REGARDING SOUND PHYSICAL CONDITION

APPENDIX B TO PART 202—"BEST EDITION" OF PUBLISHED COPYRIGHTED WORKS FOR THE COLLECTIONS OF THE LIBRARY OF CONGRESS

AUTHORITY: 17 U.S.C. 408(f), 702

EDITORIAL NOTE: Nomenclature changes to part 202 appear at 76 FR 27898, May 13, 2011.

§ 202.1 Material not subject to copyright.

The following are examples of works not subject to copyright and applications for registration of such works cannot be entertained:

(a) Words and short phrases such as names, titles, and slogans; familiar symbols or designs; mere variations of typographic ornamentation, lettering or coloring; mere listing of ingredients or contents;

(b) Ideas, plans, methods, systems, or devices, as distinguished from the particular manner in which they are expressed or described in a writing;

(c) Blank forms, such as time cards, graph paper, account books, diaries, bank checks, scorecards, address books, report forms, order forms and the like, which are designed for recording information and do not in themselves convey information;

(d) Works consisting entirely of information that is common property containing no original authorship, such as, for example: Standard calendars, height and weight charts, tape measures and rulers, schedules of sporting events, and lists or tables taken from public documents or other common sources.

(e) Typeface as typeface.

[24 FR 4956, June 18, 1959, as amended at 38 FR 3045, Feb. 1, 1973; 57 FR 6202, Feb. 21, 1992]

§ 202.2 Copyright notice.

(a) *General.* (1) With respect to a work published before January 1, 1978, copyright was secured, or the right to secure it was lost, except for works seeking *ad interim* copyright, at the date of publication, *i.e.*, the date on which copies are first placed on sale, sold, or publicly distributed, depending upon the adequacy of the notice of copyright on the work at that time. The adequacy of the copyright notice for such a work is determined by the copyright statute as it existed on the date of first publication.

(2) If before January 1, 1978, publication occurred by distribution of copies or in some other manner, without the statutory notice or with an inadequate notice, as determined by the copyright statute as it existed on the date of first publication, the right to secure copyright was lost. In such cases, copyright cannot be secured by adding the notice to copies distributed at a later date.

(3) Works first published abroad before January 1, 1978, other than works for which *ad interim* copyright has been obtained, must have borne an adequate copyright notice. The adequacy of the copyright notice for such works is determined by the copyright statute as it existed on the date of first publication abroad.

(b) *Defects in notice.* Where the copyright notice on a work published before January 1, 1978, does not meet the requirements of title 17 of the United States Code as it existed on December 31, 1977, the Copyright Office will reject an application for copyright registration. Common defects in the notice include, among others the following:

(1) The notice lacks one or more of the necessary elements (*i.e.*, the word "Copyright," the abbreviation "Copr.", or the symbol ©, or, in the case of a sound recording, the symbol ℗; the name of the copyright proprietor, or, in the case of a sound recording, the name, a recognizable abbreviation of the name, or a generally known alternative designation, of the copyright owner; and, when required, the year date of publication);

(2) The elements of the notice are so dispersed that a necessary element is not identified as a part of the notice; in the case of a sound recording, however, if the producer is named on the label or container, and if no other name appears in conjunction with the notice, his name will be considered a part of the notice;

(3) The notice is not in one of the positions prescribed by law;

(4) The notice is in a foreign language;

(5) The name in the notice is that of someone who had no authority to secure copyright in his name;

(6) The year date in the copyright notice is later than the date of the year in which copyright was actually secured, including the following cases:

(i) Where the year date in the notice is later than the date of actual publication;

(ii) Where copyright was first secured by registration of a work in unpublished form, and copies of the same work as later published without change in substance bear a copyright notice containing a year date later than the year of unpublished registration;

(iii) Where a book or periodical published abroad, for which *ad interim* copyright has been obtained, is later published in the United States without change in substance and contains a year date in the copyright notice later than the year of first publication abroad:

Provided, however, That in each of the three foregoing types of cases, if the copyright was actually secured not more than one year earlier than the year date in the notice, registration may be considered as a doubtful case.

(7) A notice is permanently covered so that it cannot be seen without tearing the work apart;

(8) A notice is illegible or so small that it cannot be read without the aid of a magnifying glass: *Provided, however,* That where the work itself requires magnification for its ordinary use (e.g., a microfilm, microcard or motion picture) a notice which will be readable when so magnified, will not constitute a reason for rejection of the claim;

(9) A notice is on a detachable tag and will eventually be detached and discarded when the work is put in use;

(10) A notice is on the wrapper or container which is not a part of the work and which will eventually be removed and discarded when the work is put to use; the notice may be on a container which is designed and can be expected to remain with the work;

(11) The notice is restricted or limited exclusively to an uncopyrightable element, either by virtue of its position on the work, by the use of asterisks, or by other means.

[24 FR 4956, June 18, 1959; 24 FR 6163, July 31, 1959, as amended at 37 FR 3055, Feb. 11, 1972; 46 FR 33249, June 29, 1981; 46 FR 34329, July 1, 1981; 60 FR 34168, June 30, 1995; 66 FR 34373, June 28, 2001; 66 FR 40322, Aug. 2, 2001; 77 FR 18707, Mar. 28, 20120; 77 FR 20988, Apr. 9, 2012]

§202.3 Registration of copyright.

(a) *General.* (1) This section prescribes conditions for the registration of copyright, and the application to be made for registration under sections 408 and 409 of title 17 of the United States Code, as amended by Pub. L. 94–553.

(2) For the purposes of this section, the terms *audiovisual work, compilation, copy, derivative work, device, fixation, literary work, motion picture, phonorecord, pictorial, graphic and sculptural works, process, sound recording,* and their variant forms, have the meanings set forth in section 101 of title 17. The term *author* includes an employer or other person for whom a work is "made for hire" under section 101 of title 17.

(3) For the purposes of this section, a copyright *claimant* is either:

(i) The author of a work;

(ii) A person or organization that has obtained ownership of all rights under the copyright initially belonging to the author.[1]

(b) *Administrative classification and application forms*—(1) *Classes of works.* For the purpose of registration, the Register of Copyrights has prescribed the classes of works in which copyright may be claimed. These classes, and examples of works which they include, are as follows:

(i) *Class TX: Nondramatic literary works.* This class includes all published and unpublished nondramatic literary works. Examples: Fiction; nonfiction; poetry; textbooks; reference works; directories; catalogs; advertising copy; and compilations of information.

(ii) *Class PA: Works of the performing arts.* This class includes all published and unpublished works prepared for the

[1] This category includes a person or organization that has obtained, from the author or from an entity that has obtained ownership of all rights under the copyright initially belonging to the author, the contractual right to claim legal title to the copyright in an application for copyright registration.

purpose of being performed directly before an audience or indirectly by means of a device or process. Examples: Musical works, including any accompanying words; dramatic works, including any accompanying music; pantomimes and choreographic works; and motion pictures and other audiovisual works.

(iii) *Class VA: Works of the visual arts.* This class includes all published and unpublished pictorial, graphic, and sculptural works. Examples: Two dimensional and three dimensional works of the fine, graphic, and applied arts; photographs; prints and art reproductions; maps, globes, and charts; technical drawings, diagrams, and models; and pictorial or graphic labels and advertisements.

(iv) *Class SR: Sound recordings.* This class includes all published and unpublished sound recordings fixed on and after February 15, 1972. Claims to copyright in literary, dramatic, and musical works embodied in phonorecords may also be registered in this class under paragraph (b)(4) of this section if:

(A) Registration is sought on the same application for both a recorded literary, dramatic, or musical work and a sound recording;

(B) The recorded literary, dramatic, or musical work and the sound recording are embodied in the same phonorecord; and

(C) The same claimant is seeking registration of both the recorded literary, dramatic, or musical work and the sound recording.

(v) Class SE: Serials. A serial is a work issued or intended to be issued in successive parts bearing numerical or chronological designations and intended to be continued indefinitely. This class includes periodicals; newspapers; annuals; and the journals, proceedings, transactions, etc. of societies.

(2) *Submission of application for registration.* For purposes of registration, an applicant may submit an application for registration of individual works and certain groups of works electronically through the Copyright Office's Web site, or by using the printed forms prescribed by the Register of Copyrights.

(i) *Electronic applications.* (A) An applicant may submit an application electronically through the Copyright Office Web site [*www.copyright.gov*] For non-group registrations, an applicant may submit a standard electronic application, or an applicant may submit a "single" application.

(B) A "single" application can be made only for a single work by a single author that is owned by the person who created it, and is not a work made for hire. The claimant and the author must be the same. A third party may remit a "single" application on behalf of the author/claimant, provided that party lists itself as the correspondent. The following categories of work may not be registered using the "single" application: collective works, unpublished collections, units of publication, group registration options, databases, Web sites, works by more than one author, and works with more than one owner. The designation of a work as eligible for a "single" registration does not include work characterized as a "single work" under paragraph (b)(4) of this section.

(C) An online submission requires a payment of the application fee through an electronic fund transfer, credit or debit card, or through a Copyright Office deposit account.

(D) Deposit materials in support of an online application may be submitted electronically in a digital format (if eligible) along with the application and payment, or a remitter may send physical copies or phonorecords as necessary to satisfy the best edition requirements, by mail to the Copyright Office, using the required shipping slip generated during the online registration process.

(ii) (A) Alternatively, an applicant may submit an application on one of the printed forms prescribed by the Register of Copyrights. Each printed form corresponds to a class set forth in paragraph (b)(1) of this section and is so designated ("Form TX"; "Short Form TX", "Form PA"; "Short Form PA", "Form VA"; "Short Form VA", "Form SR"; "Form SE"; "Short Form SE", and "Form SE/Group").

(B) Short form applications may only be used if certain conditions are met. Short Form TX, Short Form PA, and Short Form VA may be used only to register a single work in a case when a living author who is the only author of his or her work is the sole owner of the copyright in the work, the work is not a compilation or derivative work containing a substantial amount of previously published or registered material, and the work is not a work made for hire. Short Form SE may be used only if the claim is in a collective work, the work is essentially an all-new collective work or issue, the author is a citizen or domiciliary of the United States, the work is a work for hire, the author(s) and claimant(s) are the same person(s) or organization(s), and the work was first published in the United States.

(C) Printed form applications should be submitted in the class most appropriate to the nature of the authorship in which copyright is claimed. In the case of contributions to collective works, applications should be submitted in the class representing the copyrightable authorship in the contribution. In the case of derivative works, applications should be submitted in the class most appropriately representing the copyrightable authorship involved in recasting, transforming, adapting, or otherwise modifying the preexisting work. In cases where a work contains elements of authorship in which copyright is claimed which fall into two or more classes, the application should be submitted in the class most appropriate to the type of authorship that predominates in the work as a whole. However, in any case where registration is sought for a work consisting of or including a sound recording in which copyright is claimed, the application shall be submitted on Form SR.

(D) Copies of the printed forms are available on the Copyright Office's Web site [*www.copyright.gov*] and upon request to the Copyright Public Information Office, Library of Congress. Printed form applications may be completed and submitted by completing a printed version or using a PDF version of the applicable Copyright Office application form and mailing it together with the other required elements, *i.e.*, physically tangible deposit copies and/or materials, and the required filing fee, all elements being placed in the same package and sent by mail or hand-delivered to the Copyright Office.

(3) *Continuation sheets.* A continuation sheet (Form CON) is appropriate only in the case when a printed form application is used and where additional space is needed by the applicant to provide all relevant information concerning a claim to copyright. An application may include more than one continuation sheet, subject to the limitations in paragraph (b)(10)(v) of this section.

(4) *Registration as a single work.* (i) For the purpose of registration on a single application and upon payment of a single registration fee, the following shall be considered a single work:

(A) In the case of published works: all copyrightable elements that are otherwise recognizable as self-contained works, that are included in a single unit of publication, and in which the copyright claimant is the same; and

(B) In the case of unpublished works: all copyrightable elements that are otherwise recognizable as self-contained works, and are combined in a single unpublished "collection." For these purposes, a combination of such elements shall be considered a "collection" if:

(*1*) The elements are assembled in an orderly form;

(*2*) The combined elements bear a single title identifying the collection as a whole;

(*3*) The copyright claimant in all of the elements, and in the collection as a whole, is the same; and

(*4*) All of the elements are by the same author, or, if they are by different authors, at least one of the authors has contributed copyrightable authorship to each element.

Registration of an unpublished "collection" extends to each copyrightable element in the collection and to the authorship, if any, involved in selecting and assembling the collection.

(ii) In the case of applications for registration made under paragraphs (b)(4) through (b)(10) of this section, the "year in which creation of this work was completed", as called for by the application, means the latest year in which the creation of any copyrightable element was completed.

(5) *Group registration of related works: Automated databases.* (i) Pursuant to the authority granted by section 408(c)(1) of title 17 of the United States Code, the Register of Copyrights has determined that, on the basis of a single application, deposit, and filing fee, a single registration may be made for automated databases and their updates or other derivative versions that are original works of authorship, if, where a database (or updates or other revisions thereof), if unpublished, is (or are) fixed, or if published is (or are) published only in the form of machine-readable copies, all of the following conditions are met:

(A) All of the updates or other revisions are owned by the same copyright claimant;

(B) All of the updates or other revisions have the same general title;

(C) All of the updates or other revisions are similar in their general content, including their subject;

(D) All of the updates or other revisions are similar in their organization;

(E) Each of the updates or other revisions as a whole, if published before March 1, 1989, bears a statutory copyright notice as first published and the name of the owner of copyright in each work (or an abbreviation by which the name can be recognized, or a generally known alternative designation of the owner) was the same in each notice;

(F) Each of the updates or other revisions if published was first published, or if unpublished was first created, within a three-month period in a single calendar year; and

(G) The deposit accompanying the application complies with § 202.20(c)(2)(vii)(D).

(ii) A single registration may be made on one application for both a database published on a single date, or if unpublished, created on a single date, and also for its copyrightable revisions, including updates covering a three-month period in a single calendar year. An application for group registration of automated databases under section 408(c)(1) of title 17 and this subsection shall consist of:

(A) A form that best reflects the subject matter of the material in the database as set forth in paragraph (b)(2) of this section, completed in accordance with the basic instructions on the form and the Special Instructions for Group Registration of an Automated Database and its Updates or Revisions, except that in the case of an application for group registration of an automated database consisting predominantly of photographs, after consultation and with the permission and under the direction of the Visual Arts Division, the application may be submitted electronically.

(B) The appropriate filing fee, as required in § 201.3(c); and

(C) The deposit required by § 202.20(c)(2)(vii)(D).

(6) *Group registration of related serials.* (i) Pursuant to the authority granted by section 408(c)(1) of title 17 of the United States Code, the Register of Copyrights has determined that, on the basis of a single application, deposit, and filing fee, a single registration may be made for a group of serials published at intervals of a week or longer if all the following conditions are met:

(A) The Library of Congress receives two complimentary copies promptly after publication of each issue of the serial.

(B) The single application covers no more than the issues published in a given three month period.

(C) The claim to copyright for which registration is sought is in the collective work.

(D) The collective work authorship is essentially new material that is being published for the first time.

(E) The collective work is a work made for hire.

(F) The author(s) and claimant(s) of the collective work is the same person(s) or organization(s).

(G) Each issue must have been created no more than one year prior to publication and all issues included in the group registration must have been published in the same calendar year.

(ii) To be eligible for group registration of serials, publishers must submit a letter affirming that two complimentary subscriptions to the particular serial have been entered for the Library of Congress. The letter should be sent to Group Periodicals Registration, Library of Congress, Washington, DC 20540–4161.

(iii) The complimentary subscription copies must be addressed to: Group Periodicals Registration, Library of Congress, Washington, DC 20540–4161.

(iv) The Register of Copyrights may revoke the privilege of group registration of serials for any publisher who fails to submit the required complimentary subscription copies promptly after publication of each issue. Notice of revocation of the group registration of serials privilege shall be given in writing and shall be sent to the individual person or organization applying for group registration of serials, at the last address shown in the records of the Copyright Office. A notice of revocation may be given at any time if the requirements of the regulation are not satisfied, but it shall state a specific date of revocation that is at least 30 days later than the date the notice is mailed.

(v) To apply for registration of a group of serial issues under 408(c)(1) of title 17 and this section, an applicant may file electronically, or submit a completed Form SE/Group.

(A) For applicants filing electronically:

(1) Furnish the requested information for group of serial issues.

(2) Submit the appropriate filing fee, as required in § 201.3(c) of this chapter, for each issue covered by the group registration.

(3) Submit either a digital format which complies with § 202.20(b)(2)(iii) or a deposit consisting of one complete copy of the best edition of each issue included in the group registration.

(B) For applicants filing a completed Form SE/Group, the following must be sent together in the same package:

(1) A completed Form SE/Group, providing the requested information.

(2) The appropriate filing fee, as required in § 201.3(c) of this chapter, for each issue covered by the group registration.

(3) A deposit consisting of one complete copy of the best edition of each issue included in the group registration.

(7) *Group registration of daily newspapers.* (i) Pursuant to the authority granted by 17 U.S.C. 408(c)(1), the Register of Copyrights has determined that, on the basis of a single application, microfilm deposit, and filing fee, a single registration may be made for a group of daily newspapers published in a microfilm format if the following conditions are met:

(A) Registration covers a full month of issues of the same newspaper title published with issue dates in one calendar month.

(B) A completed GDN application form is submitted.

(C) A publication date is specified designating the first and last day that issues in the group were published.

(D) A deposit is made of positive, 35mm silver halide microfilm meeting the Library's best edition criteria that includes all issues published as final editions in the designated calendar month. In addition to the final edition of the daily newspaper, the claim to copyright and the deposit may also include earlier editions published the same day in a given metropolitan area served by the newspaper, but may not include national or regional editions distributed beyond a given metropolitan area.

(E) The appropriate filing fee, as required in § 201.3(c), is included with the submission or charged to an active deposit account.

(F) Registration is sought within three months after the publication date of the last issue included in the group.

(ii) As used in this regulation, newspapers means serials which are classified as newspapers under the policy document "Newspapers Received Currently in the Library of Congress,"which is administered by the Newspaper Section of the Serials & Government Publications Division of the Library of Congress. In general, serials classified as newspapers are serials mainly designed to be a primary source of written information on current events, either local, national, or international in scope. A newspaper contains a broad range of news on all subjects and activities and is not limited to any specific subject matter. Newspapers are intended either for the general public or for a particular ethnic, cultural, or national group.

(8) *Group registration of contributions to periodicals.* (i) As provided by section 408(c)(2) of title 17 of the United States

Code, as amended by Pub. L. 94–553, a single registration, on the basis of a single application, deposit, and registration fee, may be made for a group of works if all of the following conditions are met:

(A) All of the works are by the same author;

(B) The author of each work is an individual, and not an employer or other person for whom the work was made for hire;

(C) Each of the works was first published as a contribution to a periodical (including newspapers) within a twelve-month period;[2]

(D) Each of the works, if first published before March 1, 1989, bore a separate copyright notice, and the name of the owner of copyright in each work (or an abbreviation by which the name can be recognized, or a generally known alternative designation of the owner) was the same in each notice; and

(E) The deposit accompanying the application must consist of one of the following: one copy of the entire issue of the periodical, or, in the case of a newspaper, the entire section containing the contribution; tear sheets or proof copies of the contribution; a photocopy of the contribution itself, or a photocopy of the entire page containing the contribution; the entire page containing the contribution cut or torn from the collective work; the contribution cut or torn from the collective work; or photographs or photographic slides of the contribution or entire page containing the contribution as long as all contents of the contribution to be registered are clear and legible.

(ii) An application for group registration under section 408(c)(2) of title 17 and paragraph (b)(8) of this section shall consist of:

(A) A basic application for registration on Form TX, Form PA, or Form VA,[3] which shall contain the information required by the form and its accompanying instructions;

(B) An adjunct form prescribed by the Copyright Office and designated "Adjunct Application for Copyright Registration for a Group of Contributions to Periodicals (Form GR/CP)", which shall contain the information required by the form and its accompanying instructions; and

(C) The appropriate filing fee, as required in § 201.3(c), and the deposit required by paragraph (b)(8)(i)(E) of this section.

(9) *Group registration of daily newsletters.* Pursuant to the authority granted by 17 U.S.C. 408(c)(1), the Register of Copyrights has determined that, on the basis of a single application, deposit, and filing fee, a single registration may be made for a group of two or more issues of a daily newsletter if the following conditions are met:

(i) As used in this regulation, daily newsletter means a serial published and distributed by mail or electronic media (online or telefacsimile), or in any medium including but not limited to, paper, cassette tape, diskette or CD-ROM. Publication must occur on at least two days each week and the newsletter must contain news or information of interest chiefly to a special group (for example, trade and professional associations, corporate in-house groups, schools, colleges, or churches).

(ii) The works must be essentially all new collective works or all new issues that have not been published before.

(iii) Each issue must be a work made for hire.

(iv) The author(s) and claimant(s) must be the same person(s) or organization(s) for all of the issues.

(v) All the items in the group must bear issue dates within a single calendar month under the same continuing title.

[2] This does not require that each of the works must have been first published during the same calendar year; it does require that, to be grouped in a single application, the earliest and latest contributions must not have been first published more than twelve months apart.

[3] The basic application should be filed in the class appropriate to the nature of authorship in the majority of the contributions. However, if any of the contributions consists preponderantly of nondramatic literary material that is in the English language, the basic application for the entire group should be submitted on Form TX.

(vi) Deposit. (A). The deposit for newsletters registered under this section is one complete copy of each issue included in the group.

(B). In addition, if requested in writing by the Copyright Acquisitions Division before an application for registration is submitted, the claimant must give the Library of Congress whichever of the following the Library prefers: either as many as two complimentary subscriptions of the newsletter in the edition most suitable to the Library's needs, or a single positive, 35 mm silver halide microfilm meeting the Library's best edition criteria that includes all issues published as final editions in the designated calendar month. Subscription copies must be delivered to the separate address specified by the Copyright Acquisitions Division in its request. Subscription copies or a microfilm are not required unless expressly requested by the Copyright Acquisitions Division.

(C) The copyright owner of any newsletter that cannot meet the criteria set out in this section may continue to register on Form SE or Short Form SE.

(vii) Registration is sought within three months after the publication date of the last issue included in the group.

(viii) A Form G/DN shall be submitted for daily newsletters bearing issue dates within a single month, together with one copy of each issue, and a filing fee. The application shall designate the first and last day that issues in the group were published.

(10) *Group registration of published photographs.* Pursuant to the authority granted by 17 U.S.C. 408(c)(1), the Register of Copyrights will accept a single application (on Form VA), deposit and filing fee for registration of a group of photographs if the following conditions are met:

(i) The copyright claimant in all of the photographs must be the same.

(ii) The photographer who photographed each of the photographs submitted for registration as part of the group must be the same person.

(iii) The photographs in the group must have been published within the same calendar year.

(iv) If the photographs in a group were all published on the same date, the date of publication must be identified in space 3b of the application. If the photographs in a group were not all published on the same date, the range of dates of publication (e.g., February 15–September 15, 2004) must be provided in space 3b of the application, and the date of publication of each photograph within the group must be identified either:

(A) On each deposited image;

(B) In a text file on the CD-ROM or DVD that contains the deposited photographic images;

(C) On a list that accompanies the deposit and provides the publication date for each image; or

(D) On a special continuation sheet (Form GR/PPh/CON) provided by the Copyright Office. Dates of publication must be provided in a way that clearly identifies the date of publication for each individual photograph in the group.

(v) If the applicant chooses to identify the date of publication for each photograph in the group on a continuation sheet, the application may include no more than 50 continuation sheets identifying no more than 750 photographs. For these purposes, the applicant must use the special continuation sheet (Form GR/PPh/CON) for registration of a group of photographs made available by the Copyright Office.

(vi) If each photograph within the group was first published within three months before the date on which an acceptable application, an acceptable deposit, and the applicable fee are received in the Copyright Office, the applicant may, in lieu of the procedure set forth in paragraph (b)(10)(iv) of this section, simply state the range of dates of publication (e.g., February 15–May 15, 2001) in space 3b of the application, without specifically identifying the date of publication of each photograph in the group either on the deposited image or on a continuation sheet.

(vii) The deposit(s) and application must be accompanied by the fee set forth in § 201.3(c) of this chapter for a basic registration.

(viii) The applicant must state "Group Registration/Photos" and state the approximate number of photographs included in the group in space 1 of the application Form VA under the heading "Previous or Alternative Titles" (e.g., "Group Registration/ Photos; app. 450 photographs").

(ix) If the photographs in the group are works made for hire, the applicant must note, as part of the applicant's entry in space 2 of the application Form VA for "Name of Author," both the name of the employer for hire and the name of the photographer who photographed the works in the group (e.g., "XYZ Corporation, employer for hire of John Doe").

(x) As an alternative to the best edition of the work, one copy of each photograph shall be submitted in one of the formats set forth in §202.20(c)(2)(xx).

(xi) Instead of using Form VA, an applicant may submit an electronic application for group registration of published photographs after consultation and with the permission and under the direction of the Visual Arts Division.

(11) *One registration per work.* As a general rule only one copyright registration can be made for the same version of a particular work. However:

(i) Where a work has been registered as unpublished, another registration may be made for the first published edition of the work, even if it does not represent a new version;

(ii) Where someone other than the author is identified as copyright claimant in a registration, another registration for the same version may be made by the author in his or her own name as copyright claimant;[4]

(iii) Where an applicant for registration alleges that an earlier registration for the same version is unauthorized and legally invalid, a registration may be made by that applicant; and

(iv) Supplementary registrations may be made, under the conditions of §201.5 of these regulations, to correct or amplify the information in a registration made under this section.

(c) *Application for registration.* (1) An application for copyright registration may be submitted by any author or other copyright claimant of a work, or the owner of any exclusive right in a work, or the duly authorized agent of any such author, other claimant, or owner.

(2) An application for copyright registration shall be submitted by using one of the methods set forth in paragraph (b) of this section. All completed application forms shall be accompanied by the appropriate filing fee, as required in §201.3(c) of this chapter, and the deposit copies and materials required under 17 U.S.C. 408 and §202.20.[6] All applications submitted for registration shall supply the information required by the particular application and shall include a certification. The certification shall consist of:

(i) A designation that the party signing the print application, or submitting the application electronically, falls within an accepted status from among the following: author, claimant, an owner of exclusive rights, or a duly authorized agent of the author, claimant, owner of exclusive rights;

(ii) For print applications, the handwritten signature of the party described in paragraph (c)(2)(i) of this section accompanied by the typed or printed name of that party; or, if an electronically submitted application, a name provided within the certification screen of the electronic application which represents a party described in paragraph (c)(2)(i) of this section;

(iii) A declaration that information provided within the application is correct to the best of that party's knowledge; and,

(iv) For print applications, the date of completion of the application form,

---

[4] An *author* includes an employer or other person for whom a work is "made for hire" under 17 U.S.C. 101. This paragraph does not permit an employee or other person working "for hire" under that section to make a later registration in his or her own name. In the case of authors of a joint work, this paragraph does permit a later registration by one author in his or her own name as copyright claimant, where an earlier registration identifies only another author as claimant.

[5] In the case of applications for group registration of newspapers, contributions to periodicals, and newsletters, under paragraphs (b)(7), (b)(8), and (b)(9) of this section, the deposits shall comply with the deposits specified in the respective paragraphs, and the fees with those specified in §201.3.

with the date (month, day, year) printed, typed, or handwritten; or, if an electronically submitted application, the date of electronic receipt of the application by the Copyright Office, which date shall be provided automatically by the Copyright Office.

An application for registration of a published work will not be accepted if the date of certification is earlier than the date of publication given in the application.

(Pub. L. 94–553; secs. 408, 409, 410, 702)

[43 FR 966, Jan. 5, 1978]

EDITORIAL NOTE: For FEDERAL REGISTER citations affecting § 202.3, see the List of CFR Sections Affected, which appears in the Finding Aids section of the printed volume and at *www.fdsys.gov*.

§ 202.4 Effective date of registration.

The effective date of registration for claims received in the Copyright Office on or after January 3, 1991, and through December 31, 1991, with a short fee of $10 is the date on which the application, deposit, and $10 fee have all been received in the Copyright Office, provided, the claim is later determined to be acceptable for registration by the Register of Copyrights and a supplementary fee of $10 is received in the Copyright Office. If the supplementary fee is not received promptly after notification of the short fee, the Copyright Office will initiate a proceeding to cancel the copyright registration. If the supplementary fee of $10 is not received in the Copyright Office before the cancellation proceeding is completed, the cancellation will become final and will result in the loss of the effective date of registration. After cancellation, registration could be obtained only by submitting a new application, deposit, and filing fee.

[55 FR 50001, Dec. 4, 1990]

§ 202.5 Reconsideration Procedure for Refusals to Register.

(a) *General.* This section prescribes rules pertaining to procedures for administrative review of the Copyright Office's refusal to register a claim to copyright, a mask work, or a vessel hull design upon a finding by the Office that the application for registration does not satisfy the legal requirements of title 17 of the United States Code. If an applicant's initial claim is refused, the applicant is entitled to request that the initial refusal to register be reconsidered.

(b) *First reconsideration.* Upon receiving a written notification from the Registration Program explaining the reasons for a refusal to register, an applicant may request that the Registration Program reconsider its initial decision to refuse registration, subject to the following requirements:

(1) An applicant must request in writing that the Registration Program reconsider its decision. A request for reconsideration must include the reasons the applicant believes registration was improperly refused, including any legal arguments in support of those reasons and any supplementary information. The Registration Program will base its decision on the applicant's written submissions.

(2) The fee set forth in § 201.3(d)(3)(i) of this chapter must accompany the first request for reconsideration.

(3) The first request for reconsideration and the applicable fee must be received by the Copyright Office no later than three months from the date that appears in the Registration Program written notice of its initial decision to refuse registration. When the ending date for the three-month time period falls on a weekend or a Federal holiday, the ending day of the three-month period shall be extended to the next Federal work day.

(4) If the Registration Program decides to register an applicant's work in response to the first request for reconsideration, it will notify the applicant in writing of the decision and the work will be registered. However, if the Registration Program again refuses to register the work, it will send the applicant a written notification stating the reasons for refusal within four months of the date on which the first request for reconsideration is received by the Registration Program. When the ending date for the four-month time period falls on a weekend or a Federal holiday, the ending day of the four-month period shall be extended to the next Federal work day. Failure by the Registration Program to send the written

notification within the four-month period shall not result in registration of the applicant's work.

(c) *Second reconsideration.* Upon receiving written notification of the Registration Program's decision to refuse registration in response to the first request for reconsideration, an applicant may request that the Review Board reconsider the Registration Program's refusal to register, subject to the following requirements:

(1) An applicant must request in writing that the Review Board reconsider the Registration Program's decision to refuse registration. The second request for reconsideration must include the reasons the applicant believes registration was improperly refused, including any legal arguments in support of those reasons and any supplementary information, and must address the reasons stated by the Registration Program for refusing registration upon first reconsideration. The Board will base its decision on the applicant's written submissions.

(2) The fee set forth in § 201.3(d)(3)(ii) of this chapter must accompany the second request for reconsideration.

(3) The second request for reconsideration and the applicable fee must be received in the Copyright Office no later than three months from the date that appears in the Registration Program's written notice of its decision to refuse registration after the first request for reconsideration. When the ending date for the three-month time period falls on a weekend or a Federal holiday, the ending day of the three-month period shall be extended to the next Federal work day.

(4) If the Review Board decides to register an applicant's work in response to a second request for reconsideration, it will notify the applicant in writing of the decision and the work will be registered. If the Review Board upholds the refusal to register the work, it will send the applicant a written notification stating the reasons for refusal.

(d) *Submission of reconsiderations.* (1) All mail, including any that is hand delivered, should be addressed as follows: RECONSIDERATION, Copyright RAC Division, P.O. Box 71380, Washington, DC 20024–1380. If hand delivered by a commercial, non-government courier or messenger, a request for reconsideration must be delivered between 8:30 a.m. and 4 p.m. to: Congressional Courier Acceptance Site, located at Second and D Streets, NE., Washington, DC. If hand delivered by a private party, a request for reconsideration must be delivered between 8:30 a.m. and 5 p.m. to: Room 401 of the James Madison Memorial Building, located at 101 Independence Avenue, SE., Washington, DC.

(2) The first page of the written request must contain the Copyright Office control number and clearly indicate either "FIRST RECONSIDERATION" or "SECOND RECONSIDERATION," as appropriate, on the subject line.

(e) *Suspension or wavier of time requirements.* For any particular request for reconsideration, the provisions relating to the time requirements for submitting a request under this section may be suspended or waived, in whole or in part, by the Register of Copyrights upon a showing of good cause. Such suspension or waiver shall apply only to the request at issue and shall not be relevant with respect to any other request for reconsideration from that applicant or any other applicant.

(f) *Composition of the Review Board.* The Review Board shall consist of three members; the first two members are the Register of Copyrights and the General Counsel or their respective designees. The third member will be designated by the Register.

(g) *Final agency action.* A decision by the Review Board in response to a second request for reconsideration constitutes final agency action.

[69 FR 77636, Dec. 28, 2004, as amended at 70 FR 7177, Feb. 11, 2005; 73 FR 37839, July 2, 2008]

§§ 202.6–202.9 [Reserved]

§ 202.10 Pictorial, graphic, and sculptural works.

(a) In order to be acceptable as a pictorial, graphic, or sculptural work, the work must embody some creative authorship in its delineation or form. The registrability of such a work is not affected by the intention of the author as to the use of the work or the number of copies reproduced. The availability of protection or grant of protection under the law for a utility or design patent will not affect the registrability of a claim in an original work of pictorial, graphic, or sculptural authorship.

(b) A claim to copyright cannot be registered in a print or label consisting solely of trademark subject matter and lacking copyrightable matter. While the Copyright Office will not investigate whether the matter has been or can be registered at the Patent and Trademark Office, it will register a properly filed copyright claim in a print or label that contains the requisite qualifications for copyright even though there is a trademark on it. However, registration of a claim to copyright does not give the claimant rights available by trademark registrations at the Patent and Trademark Office.

[46 FR 33249, June 29, 1981, as amended at 60 FR 15606, Mar. 24, 1995; 61 FR 5445, Feb. 12, 1996]

§202.11 Architectural works.

(a) *General.* This section prescribes rules pertaining to the registration of architectural works, as provided for in the amendment of title 17 of the United States Code by the Architectural Works Copyright Protection Act, title VII of the Judicial Improvements Act of 1990, Public Law 101-650.

(b) *Definitions.* (1) For the purposes of this section, the term *architectural work* has the same meaning as set forth in section 101 of title 17, as amended.

(2) The term *building* means humanly habitable structures that are intended to be both permanent and stationary, such as houses and office buildings, and other permanent and stationary structures designed for human occupancy, including but not limited to churches, museums, gazebos, and garden pavilions.

(c) *Registration*—(1) *Original design.* In general, an original design of a building embodied in any tangible medium of expression, including a building, architectural plans, or drawings, may be registered as an architectural work.

(2) *Registration limited to single architectural work.* For published and unpublished architectural works, a single application may cover only a single architectural work. A group of architectural works may not be registered on a single application form. For works such as tract housing, a single work is one house model, with all accompanying floor plan options, elevations, and styles that are applicable to that particular model.

(3) *Application form.* Registration should be sought on Form VA. Line one of the form should give the title of the building. The date of construction of the building, if any, should also be designated. If the building has not yet been constructed, the notation "not yet constructed" should be given following the title.

(4) *Separate registration for plans.* Where dual copyright claims exist in technical drawings and the architectural work depicted in the drawings, any claims with respect to the technical drawings and architectural work must be registered separately.

(5) *Publication.* Publication of an architectural work occurs when underlying plans or drawings of the building or other copies of the building design are distributed or made available to the general public by sale or other transfer of ownership, or by rental, lease, or lending. Construction of a building does not itself constitute publication for purposes of registration, unless multiple copies are constructed.

(d) *Works excluded.* The following structures, features, or works cannot be registered:

(1) *Structures other than buildings.* Structures other than buildings, such as bridges, cloverleafs, dams, walkways, tents, recreational vehicles, mobile homes, and boats.

(2) *Standard features.* Standard configurations of spaces, and individual standard features, such as windows, doors, and other staple building components.

(3) *Pre-December 1, 1990 building designs*—(i) *Published building designs.* The designs of buildings where the plans or drawings of the building were published before December 1, 1990, or the buildings were constructed or otherwise published before December 1, 1990.

(ii) *Unpublished building designs.* The designs of buildings that were unconstructed and embodied in unpublished plans or drawings on December

1, 1990, and remained unconstructed on December 31, 2002.

[57 FR 45310, Oct. 1, 1992, as amended at 68 FR 38630, June 30, 2003]

§ 202.12 Restored copyrights.

(a) *General.* This section prescribes rules pertaining to the registration of foreign copyright claims which have been restored to copyright protection under section 104A of 17 U.S.C., as amended by the Uruguay Round Agreements Act, Public Law 103–465.

(b) *Definitions.* (1) For the purposes of this section, restored work and source country, have the definition given in the URAA and § 201.33(b) of this chapter.

(2) *Descriptive statement for a work embodied solely in machine-readable format* is a separate written statement giving the title of the work, nature of the work (for example: computer program, database, videogame, etc.), plus a brief description of the contents or subject matter of the work.

(c) *Registration*—(1) *General.* Application, deposit and filing fee for registration of a claim in a restored work under section 104A, as amended, may be submitted to the Copyright Office on or after January 1, 1996. The submission may be a completely electronic submission, with all required elements transmitted to the Office in electronic form; or, the submission may be partially electronic with the application form and fee submitted electronically and the deposit materials sent in physically tangible format(s). If all elements are submitted in physically tangible form, *i.e.*, a completed, printed application form, physically tangible deposit copies/materials, and the appropriate filing fee in check, money order, or deposit account charge, all elements must be placed in the same package and sent to the following address: Library of Congress, Copyright Office, 101 Independence Avenue, SE., Washington, DC 20559–6000.

(2) *GATT form.* Application for registration for single works restored to copyright protection under URAA should be made on Form GATT. Form GATT may be submitted by completing Form GATT electronically, submitting the appropriate filing fee electronically, and sending the deposit copies and materials required by paragraph (c)(4) of this section by postal mail; or by printing Form GATT from the Office's website, sending it with the appropriate filing fee and deposit copies and materials required by paragraph (c)(4) of this section in the same package by mail; or by obtaining a Form GATT, completing it, and sending the appropriate filing fee and the deposit copies and materials required by paragraph (c)(4) of this section in the same package by mail. A printed Form GATT may be obtained by calling or writing the Copyright Office Hotline at 202–707–9100. The GATT deposit materials required by paragraph (c)(4) of this section may be submitted for examination and registration electronically. Where, however, the Library of Congress requests a particular work or its identifying material for its collections, the required print deposit materials must be submitted.

(3) *Fee*—(i) *Amount.* The filing fee for registering a copyright claim in a restored work is prescribed in § 201.3(c).

(ii) *Method of payment*—(A) *Checks, money orders, or bank drafts.* The Copyright Office will accept checks, money orders, or bank drafts made payable to the Register of Copyrights. Remittances must be redeemable without service or exchange fees through a United States institution, must be payable in United States dollars, and must be imprinted with American Banking Association routing numbers. In addition, international money orders, and postal money orders that are negotiable only at a post office are not acceptable. CURRENCY WILL NOT BE ACCEPTED.

(B) *Copyright Office Deposit Account.* The Copyright Office maintains a system of Deposit Accounts for the convenience of those who frequently use its services. The system allows an individual or firm to establish a Deposit Account in the Copyright Office and to make advance deposits into that account. Deposit Account holders can charge copyright fees against the balance in their accounts instead of sending separate remittances with each request for service. For information on Deposit Accounts please write: Register of Copyrights, Copyright Office, Library of Congress, Washington, DC

20559, and request a copy of Circular 5, "How to Open and Maintain a Deposit Account in the Copyright Office."

(C) *Credit cards.* For URAA registrations the Copyright Office will accept VISA, MasterCard, and American Express. Debit cards cannot be accepted for payment. With the registration application, an applicant using a credit card must submit a separate cover letter stating the name of the credit card, the credit card number, the expiration date of the credit card, the total amount authorized and a signature authorizing the Office to charge the fees to the account. To protect the security of the credit card number, the applicant must not write the credit card number on the registration application.

(4) *Deposit*—(i) *General.* The deposit for a work registered as a restored work under the amended section 104A, except for those works listed in paragraphs (c)(4) (ii) through (iv) of this section, should consist of one copy or phonorecord which best represents the copyrightable content of the restored work. In descending order of preference, the deposit should be:

(A) The work as first published;

(B) A reprint or re-release of the work as first published;

(C) A photocopy or identical reproduction of the work as first published; or

(D) A revised version which includes a substantial amount of the copyrightable content of the restored work with an indication in writing of the percentage of the restored work appearing in the revision.

(ii) *Previously registered works.* No deposit is needed for works previously registered in the Copyright Office.

(iii) *Works embodied solely in machine-readable format.* For works embodied only in machine-readable formats, the deposit requirements are as follows:

(A) One machine-readable copy and a descriptive statement of the work; or

(B) Representative excerpts of the work, such as printouts; or, if the claim extends to audiovisual elements in the work, a videotape of what appears on the screen.

(iv) *Pictorial, graphic and sculptural works.* With the exception of 3-dimensional works of art, the general deposit preferences specified under paragraph (c)(4)(i) of this section shall govern. For 3-dimensional works of art, the preferred deposit is one or more photographs of the work, preferably in color.

(v) *Special relief.* An applicant who is unable to submit any of the preferred deposits may seek an alternative deposit under special relief (37 CFR 202.20(d)). In such a case, the applicant should indicate in writing why the deposit preferences cannot be met, and submit alternative identifying materials clearly showing some portion of the copyrightable contents of the restored work which is the subject of registration.

(vi) *Motion pictures.* If the deposit is a film print (16 or 35 mm), the applicant should contact the Performing Arts Division of the Registration Program for delivery instructions. The telephone number is: (202) 707–6040; the telefax number is: (202) 707–1236.

(d) *Works excluded.* Works which are not copyrightable subject matter under title 17 of the U.S. Code, other than sound recordings fixed before February 15, 1972, shall not be registered as restored copyrights.

[60 FR 50422, Sept. 29, 1995, as amended at 64 FR 12902, Mar. 16, 1999; 64 FR 29522, June 1, 1999; 71 FR 31092, June 1, 2006; 72 FR 36888, July 6, 2007; 73 FR 37839, July 2, 2008]

§§ 202.13–202.15 [Reserved]

§ 202.16 Preregistration of copyrights.

(a) *General.* This section prescribes rules pertaining to the preregistration of copyright claims in works eligible for preregistration under Section 408(f) of 17 U.S.C.

(b) *Definitions.* For the purposes of this section—

(1) A work is in a *class of works that the Register of Copyrights has determined has had a history of infringement prior to authorized commercial release* if it falls within one of the following classes of works:

(i) Motion pictures;

(ii) Sound recordings;

(iii) Musical compositions;

(iv) Literary works being prepared for publication in book form;

(v) Computer programs (including videogames); or

(vi) Advertising or marketing photographs.

(2) A work is *being prepared for commercial distribution* if:

(i) The claimant, in a statement certified by the authorized preregistering party, has a reasonable expectation that the work will be commercially distributed to the public; and

(ii) Preparation of the work has commenced and at least some portion of the work has been fixed in a tangible medium of expression, as follows:

(A) For a motion picture, filming of the motion picture must have commenced;

(B) For a sound recording, recording of the sounds must have commenced;

(C) For a musical composition, at least some of the musical composition must have been fixed either in the form of musical notation or in a copy or phonorecord embodying a performance of some or all of the work;

(D) For a literary work being prepared for publication in book form, the actual writing of the text of the work must have commenced;

(E) For a computer program, at least some of the computer code (either source code or object code) must have been fixed; and

(F) For an advertising or marketing photograph, the photograph (or, in the case of a group of photographs intended for simultaneous publication, at least one of the photographs) must have been taken.

(3) A work *eligible for preregistration* is a work that is:

(i) Unpublished;

(ii) Being prepared for commercial distribution; and

(iii) In a class of works that the Register of Copyrights has determined has had a history of infringement prior to authorized commercial release.

(c) *Preregistration*—(1) *General.* A work eligible for preregistration may be preregistered by submitting an application and fee to the Copyright Office pursuant to the requirements set forth in this section.

(2) *Works excluded.* Works that are not copyrightable subject matter under title 17 of the U.S. Code may not be preregistered in the Copyright Office.

(3) *Application form.* An application for preregistration is made using Electronic Form PRE. The application must be submitted electronically on the Copyright Office website at: *http://www.copyright.gov.*

(4) *Preregistration as a single work.* For the purpose of preregistration on a single application and upon payment of a single preregistration fee, all copyrightable elements that are otherwise recognizable as self-contained works, that are to be included and first published in a single unit of publication, and in which the copyright claimant is the same, shall be considered a single work eligible for preregistration.

(5) *Fee*—(i) *Amount.* The filing fee for preregistration is prescribed in § 201.3(c).

(ii) *Method of payment.* (A) Copyright Office deposit account. The Copyright Office maintains a system of Deposit Accounts for the convenience of those who frequently use its services and for those who file applications electronically. The system allows an individual or firm to establish a Deposit Account in the Copyright Office and to make advance deposits in that account. Deposit Account holders can charge preregistration fees against the balance in their accounts instead of using credit cards for each request of service. For information on Deposit Accounts, please download a copy of Circular 5, "How to Open and Maintain a Deposit Account in the Copyright Office," or write the Register of Copyrights, Copyright Office, Library of Congress, Washington, D.C. 20559.

(B) Credit cards, debit cards and electronic funds transfer. The online preregistration filing system will provide options for payment by means of credit or debit cards and by means of electronic funds transfers. Applicants will be redirected to the Department of Treasury's Pay.gov website to make payments with credit or debit cards, or directly from their bank accounts by means of ACH debit transactions.

(C) No refunds. The preregistration filing fee is not refundable.

(6) *Description.* No deposit of the work being preregistered should be submitted with an application for preregistration. The preregistration applicant should submit a detailed description, of not more than 2,000 characters (approximately 330 words), of

the work as part of the application. The description should be based on information available at the time of the application sufficient to reasonably identify the work. Generally, the Copyright Office will not review descriptions for adequacy, but in an action for infringement of a preregistered work, the court may evaluate the adequacy of the description to determine whether the preregistration actually describes the work that is alleged to be infringed, taking into account the information available to the applicant at the time of preregistration and taking into account the legitimate interest of the applicant in protecting confidential information.

(i) For motion pictures, such a description should include the following information to the extent known at the time of filing: the subject matter, a summary or outline, the director, the primary actors, the principal location of filming, and any other information that would assist in identifying the particular work being preregistered.

(ii) For sound recordings, the identifying description should include the following information to the extent known at the time of filing: the subject matter of the work or works recorded, the performer or performing group, the genre of the work recorded (e.g., classical, pop, musical comedy, soft rock, heavy metal, gospel, rap, hip-hop, blues, jazz), the titles of the musical compositions being recorded, the principal recording location, the composer(s) of the recorded musical compositions embodied on the sound recording, and any other information that would assist in identifying the particular work being preregistered.

(iii) For musical compositions, the identifying description should include the following information to the extent known at the time of filing: the subject matter of the lyrics, if any, the genre of the work (for example, classical, pop, musical comedy, soft rock, heavy metal, gospel, rap, hip-hop, blues, jazz), the performer, principal recording location, record label, motion picture, or other information relating to any sound recordings or motion pictures that are being prepared for commercial distribution and will include the musical composition, and any other detail or characteristic that may assist in identifying the particular musical composition.

(iv) For literary works in book form, the identifying description should include to the extent known at the time of filing: the genre of the book, e.g., biography, novel, history, etc., and should include a brief summary of the work including, the subject matter (e.g., a biography of President Bush, a history of the war in Iraq, a fantasy novel); a description (where applicable) of the plot, primary characters, events, or other key elements of the content of the work; and any other salient characteristics of the book, e.g., whether it is a later edition or revision of a previous work, as well as any other detail which may assist in identifying the literary work in book form.

(v) For computer programs (including videogames), the identifying description should include to the extent known at the time of filing, the nature, purpose and function of the computer program, including the programming language in which it is written, any particular organization or structure in which the program has been created; the form in which it is expected to be published, e.g. as an online-only product; whether there have been previous versions (and identification of such previous versions); the identities of persons involved in the creation of the computer program; and, if the work is a videogame, also describe the subject matter of the videogame and the overall object, goal or purpose of the game, its characters, if any, and the general setting and surrounding found in the game.

(vi) For advertising or marketing photographs, the description should include the subject matter depicted in the photograph or photographs, including information such as the particular product, event, public figure, or other item or occurrence which the photograph is intended to advertise or market. To the extent possible and applicable, the description for photographs should give additional details which will assist in identifying the particular photographs, such as the party for whom such advertising photographs are taken; the approximate time periods during which the photographs are taken; the approximate number of photos which may be included in the grouping; any events associated with the photographs; and the location and physical setting or surrounding depicted in the photographs. The description may also explain the general presentation, e.g., the lighting, background scenery, positioning of elements of the subject matter as it is seen in the photographs, and should provide any locations and events, if applicable, associated with the photographs.

(7) *Review of preregistration information.* The Copyright Office will conduct a limited review of applications for preregistration, in order to ascertain whether the application describes a work that is in a class of works that the Register of Copyrights has determined has had a history of infringement prior to authorized commercial release. However, a work will not be preregistered unless an applicant has provided all of the information requested on the application and has certified that all of the information provided on the application is correct to the best of the applicant's knowledge.

(8) *Certification.* The person submitting an application for preregistration must certify on the application that he or she is the author, copyright claimant, or owner of exclusive rights, or the authorized agent of the author, copyright claimant, or owner of exclusive rights, of the work submitted for this preregistration; that the information given in this application is correct to the best of his or her knowledge; that the work is being prepared for commercial distribution; and that he or she has a reasonable expectation that the work will be commercially distributed to the public.

(9) *Effective date of preregistration.* The effective date of a preregistration is the day on which an application and fee for preregistration of a work, which the Copyright Office later notifies the claimant has been preregistered or which a court of competent jurisdiction has concluded was acceptable for preregistration, have been received in the Copyright Office.

(10) *Notification of preregistration.* Upon completion of the preregistration, the Copyright Office will provide the claimant official notification by email of the preregistration.

(11) *Certification of preregistation.* A certified copy of the official notification may be obtained in physical form from the Records Research and Certification Section of the Information and Records Division at the address stated in § 201.1(a)(3) of this chapter.

(12) *Public record of preregistration.* The preregistration record will also be available to the public on the Copyright Office website, *http://www.copyright.gov.*

(13) *Effect of preregistration.* Preregistration of a work offers certain advantages to a copyright owner pursuant to 17 U.S.C. 408(f), 411 and 412. However, preregistration of a work does not constitute prima facie evidence of the validity of the copyright or of the facts stated in the application for preregistration or in the preregistration record. The fact that a work has been preregistered does not create any presumption that the Copyright Office will register the work upon submission of an application for registration.

(14) *Petition for recognition of a new class of works.* At any time an interested party may petition the Register of Copyrights for a determination as to whether a particular class of works has had a history of copyright infringement prior to authorized release that would justify inclusion of that class of works among the classes of works eligible for preregistration.

[70 FR 61906, Oct. 27, 2005, as amended at 71 FR 31092, June 1, 2006; 73 FR 37839, July 2, 2008]

§ 202.17 Renewals

(a) *General.* (1) This section concerns renewal for copyrights originally secured from January 1, 1964, through December 31, 1977, either by publication with the required copyright notice or by registration as an unpublished work. Renewal registration for these works is optional. As provided in Pub. L. No. 102–307, 106 Stat. 264, enacted June 26, 1992, renewal registration made during the last year of the original 28–year term of copyright differs in legal effect from renewal registration made during the 67–year extended renewal term. In the latter instance, the copyright is renewed automatically at the expiration of the original 28–year term. In the former instance, renewal by registration during the last year of the original 28–year term vested the renewal copyright in the statutory claimant living on the date of registration.

(2) Works for which copyright was secured before 1964 are governed by the provisions of 17 U.S.C. 304(a) in effect prior to the 1992 date of enactment of Pub. L. No. 102–307. The copyrights in such works could have been renewed by registration only within the last calendar year of the original 28–year term of copyright protection. If renewal registration was not made during that period of time, copyright protection was lost when the original term of copyright expired and cannot be regained.

(3) Works restored to copyright by the Uruguay Round Agreements Act are governed in their copyright term of protection by Pub. L. No. 103–465, 108 Stat. 4809, 4976 (December 8, 1994). Under 17 U.S.C. 104A(a)(1)(A) and (B), as amended, any work in which copyright is restored subsists for the remainder of the term of copyright that the work would have been otherwise granted in the United States. Such term includes the remainder of any applicable renewal term.

(4) Automatic restoration of copyright in certain foreign works that were in the public domain in the United States may have occurred under the Uruguay Round Agreements Act and may be protected by copyright or neighboring rights in their "source country," as defined at 17 U.S.C. 104A(h)(8).

(b) *Definitions.* (1) For purposes of this section, the terms assignee and successor, as they pertain to 17 U.S.C. 304(a)(3)(A)(ii), refer to a party which has acquired the renewal copyright in a work by assignment or by other means of legal succession from the statutory claimant [as that claimant is defined in 17 U.S.C. 304(a)(1)(B) and (C)] in whom the renewal copyright vested but in whose name no renewal registration was previously made.

(2) For purposes of this section, a work has been copyrighted when it has been published with a proper copyright notice or, in the case of an unpublished work, when it has been registered for copyright.

(3) For purposes of this section, the term posthumous work means a work that was unpublished on the date of the death of the author and with respect to which no copyright assignment or other contract for exploitation of the work occurred during the author's lifetime.

(4) For purposes of this section, the term statutory claimant means:

(i) A party who was entitled to claim copyright for the renewal term at the time renewal registration was made either as a proprietary claimant, 17 U.S.C. 304(a)(2)(A)(i), or as a personal claimant, 17 U.S.C. 304(a)(2)(B)(i), if registration was made during the original term of copyright; or

(ii) If the original copyright term expired, a party who was entitled to claim copyright for the renewal term as of the last day of the original term of copyright as either a proprietary or a personal claimant, 17 U.S.C. 304(a)(2)(A)(ii) and (a)(2)(B)(ii).

(5) For purposes of this section, the term to vest means to give a fixed, non-contingent right of present or future enjoyment of the renewal copyright in a work. If renewal registration was made during the 28th year of the original term of copyright, the renewal copyright vested in the party or parties entitled to claim such copyright at the time of registration as provided by 17 U.S.C. 304(a)(1)(B) and (C). Although the vested right may have been determined by registration during the 28th year of the original term, the exercise of such right did not commence until the beginning of the renewal term, as provided in 17 U.S.C. 304(a)(2). If renewal registration was not made during the 28th year, the renewal copyright automatically vested upon the beginning of the renewal term in the party or parties entitled to claim such copyright on the last day of the original term as provided by 17 U.S.C. 304(a)(2)(A)(ii) and (B)(ii).

(c) *Time limits: original term and renewal term registration.* (1) Under 17 U.S.C. 304(a), prior to its amendment of June 26, 1992, a registration for the original term of copyright must have been made during the 28 years of that original term, and a renewal registration must also have been made during the 28th year of that term. Pub. L. No. 102–307, 106 Stat. 264 (June 26, 1992) amended section 304(a) for works originally copyrighted from January 1, 1964, through December 31, 1977, and provided for optional original-term registration and optional renewal registration. 17 U.S.C. 304(a)(2), (a)(3) and 409(11). For such works, claims to renewal copyright could have been registered during the last year of the original term but such registration was not required in order to enjoy statutory protection during the renewal term. 17 U.S.C. 304(a)(3)(B).

(2) A renewal registration can be made at any time during the renewal term. 17 U.S.C. 304(a)(3)(A)(ii). If no original-term registration was made, renewal registration remains possible; but the Register may request information, under 17 U.S.C. 409(11), regarding the original term of copyright. Such information must demonstrate that the work complies with all requirements of the 1909 Act with respect to the existence, ownership, or duration of the copyright for the original term of the work. The Form RE/Addendum is used to provide this information.

(3) Renewal registration is currently available for works copyrighted from January 1, 1964, through December 31, 1977. Under the provisions of 17 U.S.C. 304(a)(3)(A)(ii), renewal registration may be made any time during the 67–year renewal term for such works according to the procedure indicated in paragraph (h) of this section. Such renewal registration is optional and is not a condition of the subsistence of the copyright for the 67–year renewal term. 17 U.S.C. 304(a)(3)(B). In the case of such works for which no registration was made during the original term of copyright, renewal registration may be made by submission of a Form RE/Addendum. The Addendum, an adjunct to the renewal form, concerns the facts of first publication for a work and assures the Copyright Office that the work as it existed in its original term of copyright was in compliance with the 1909 copyright law, 17 U.S.C. 1, et. seq. (1909 Act, in effect through December 31, 1977), whose provisions govern such works.

(d) *Benefits of 28th-year renewal registration.* Prior to January 1, 2006, renewal registration was available during the 28th year of the original term of copyright for works copyrighted from January 1, 1964, through December 31, 1977. As provided in Pub. L. No. 102–307, 106 Stat. 264, registration made during the 28th year of the original term of copyright provided the following benefits to the registrant:

(1) The certificate of registration constituted prima facie evidence as to the validity of the copyright during its renewal term and of the facts stated in the certificate. 17 U.S.C. 304(a)(4)(B).

(2) A derivative work prepared under the authority of a grant of a transfer or license of copyright in a work made before the expiration of the original term of copyright could not continue to be used under the terms of the grant during the renewal term without the authority of the owner of the renewal copyright. 17 U.S.C. 304(a)(4)(A).

(3) The renewal copyright vested upon the beginning of the renewal term in the party entitled to claim the renewal of copyright at the time the application was made as provided under 17 U.S.C. 304(a)(2)(A)(i) and (B)(i).

(e) *Statutory parties entitled to claim copyright for the renewal term under Section 304(a).* (1) Renewal claims must be registered in the name of the party or parties entitled to claim copyright for the renewal term as provided in paragraphs (e)(2) through (4) of this section and as specified in 17 U.S.C. 304(a). If a work was a new version of a previously published or registered work, renewal registration may be claimed only in the new matter.

(2) If the renewal claim was submitted during the last, *i.e.*, the 28th, year of the original term of copyright, the claim had to be registered in the name[s] of the statutory claimant[s] entitled to claim the renewal copyright on the date on which the claim was submitted to the Copyright Office. If the renewal claim is submitted during the sixty-seven year extended renewal term, the renewal claim can be registered only in the name[s] of the statutory claimant[s] entitled to claim the renewal on the last day (December 31) of the original term of copyright.

These eligible renewal claimants are listed below:

(i) The person who, on the applicable day, was the copyright proprietor is the appropriate renewal claimant in any posthumous work or any periodical, encyclopedia, or other composite work upon which the copyright was originally secured by the proprietor;

(ii) The person who, on the applicable day, was the copyright proprietor is the appropriate claimant in any work copyrighted by a corporate body (otherwise than as assignees or licensees of the individual author), or by an employer for whom such work was made for hire;

(iii) For any other copyrighted work, including a contribution by an individual author to a periodical or to a cyclopedic or other composite work, the appropriate claimants, in descending order of eligibility, are the person who, on the applicable day, was:

(A) The author(s) of the work, if still living;

(B) The widow(er) and/or child(ren) of the author, if the author was deceased on the applicable day;

(C) The author's executor(s), if still acting in that capacity on the applicable day, provided the author had a will and neither the author, nor any widow(er) or child of the author is still living; or

(D) The author's next of kin, in the absence of a will and if neither the author nor any widow, widower or child of the author is living.

(3) The provisions of paragraphs (e)(1) and (2) of this section are subject to the following qualification: Notwithstanding the definition of "posthumous work" in paragraph (b)(4) of this section, a renewal claim may be registered in the name of the proprietor of a work, as well as in the name of the appropriate claimant under paragraph (e)(2)(iii) of this section, in any case in which a contract for exploitation of the work but no copyright assignment in the work has occurred during the author's lifetime. However, registration by the Copyright Office in this case should not be interpreted as evidencing the validity of either claim.

(4) The provisions of paragraphs (e)(2)(iii)(C) and (D) of this section are subject to the following qualifications:

(i) In any case where:

(A) The author has left a will which names no executor;

(B) The author has left a will which names an executor who cannot or will not serve in that capacity; or

(C) The author has left a will which names an executor who has been discharged upon settlement of the estate, removed before the estate has been completely administered, or is deceased at the time of the renewal registration submission, the renewal claim may be registered either in the name of an administrator *cum testamento annexo* (administrator c.t.a.) or an administrator *de bonis non cum testamento annexo* (administrator d.b.n.c.t.a.) so appointed by a court of competent jurisdiction.

(ii) In any case described in paragraph (e) of this section, except in the case where the author has left a will without naming an executor and a court-appointed administrator c.t.a. or administrator d.b.n.c.t.a. is in existence at the time of renewal registration, the renewal claim also may be registered in the name of the author's next of kin. However, registration by the Copyright Office of conflicting renewal claims in such a case should not be interpreted as evidencing the validity of either claim.

(f) *Successors/assignees entitled to file an application for the renewal term under Section 304(a).* The provisions of paragraph (e) of this section are subject to the following qualifications:

(1) Where no renewal registration has been made in the name of a person or entity identified in paragraphs (e)(2)(i), (ii) and (iii) of this section, a renewal application may be filed at any time during the renewal term by any successor or assignee of such person or entity.

(2) In such cases described in paragraph (f)(1)(i) of this section, the renewal application must identify the party in whom the renewal copyright vested; must indicate the basis upon which copyright for the renewal term vested in that party; must identify the party who is the successor or assignee of the statutory claimant under 17

U.S.C. 304(a)(3); and, must give the manner by which such successor/assignee secured the renewal copyright.

(3) When such a claim has been filed by a successor or assignee in the name of the statutory claimant as described in paragraph (e)(2)(i), (ii) and (iii) of this section, generally no subsequent claims may be filed by other successors or assignees whose rights are derived from the same statutory claimant. If a public record of renewal ownership is sought by other successors or assignees of the same statutory claimant, the document of transfer of the renewal copyright, either the renewal in its entirety or in part, may be recorded in the Copyright Office.

(4) Where a successor or assignee claims the renewal right from the same statutory claimant as does another successor or assignee, the Copyright Office may inquire concerning the situation and, if appropriate, may allow adverse renewal claims from the successors/assignees to be placed on the public record. In such cases, correspondence between the parties filing competing renewal claims and the Copyright Office will be, as always, maintained within Office records and subject to public inspection according to regulations found at 37 CFR 201.2.

(g) *Application for renewal registration for a work registered in its original 28-year term.* (1) Each application for renewal registration shall be submitted on Form RE. All forms are available free of charge via the Internet by accessing the Copyright Office homepage at *http://www.copyright.gov*. Copies of Form RE are also available free upon request to the Copyright Information Section, United States Copyright Office, Library of Congress, 101 Independence Avenue, Washington, DC 20559–6000.

(2) (i) An application for renewal registration may be submitted by any eligible statutory renewal claimant as specified in paragraph (e) of this section or by the duly authorized agent of such claimant, or by the successor or assignee of such claimant as provided under paragraph (f) of this section or by the duly authorized agent of such successor or assignee.

(ii) An application for renewal registration shall be accompanied by the required fee as set forth in 37 CFR 201.3. The application shall contain the information required by the form and its accompanying instructions, and shall include a certification. The certification shall consist of:

(A) A designation of whether the applicant is the renewal claimant, or a successor or assignee, or the duly authorized agent of such claimant or of such successor or assignee (whose identity shall also be given);

(B) The handwritten signature of such claimant, successor or assignee, or agent, accompanied by the typewritten or printed name of that person;

(C) A declaration that the statements made in the application are correct to the best of that person's knowledge; and

(D) The date of certification.

(3) Once a renewal registration has been made, the Copyright Office will not accept another application for renewal registration on behalf of the same renewal claimant.

(h) *Renewal with addendum registration for an unregistered work*—(1) *General.* For published works copyrighted from January 1, 1964, through December 31, 1977, where no registration was made during the original term of copyright and where renewal registration is sought during the 67–year renewal term, the Form RE/Addendum must be used to provide information concerning the original term of copyright. The Form RE/Addendum requires a separate fee and the deposit of one copy or phonorecord of the work as first published (or identifying material in lieu of a copy or phonorecord). The effective date of registration for a renewal claim submitted on a Form RE/Addendum is the date the Copyright Office receives an acceptable completed application, the required fees, and an acceptable deposit for the work.

(2) *Time Limits.* A renewal claim accompanied by an Addendum to Form RE may be filed at any time during the 67–year renewal term.

(3) *Content.* The Form RE/Addendum must contain the following information:

(i) The title of the work;

(ii) The name of the author(s);

(iii) The date of first publication of the work;

(iv) The nation of first publication of the work;

(v) The citizenship of the author(s) on the date of first publication of the work;

(vi) The domicile of the author(s) on the date of first publication of the work;

(vii) An averment that, at the time of first publication, and thereafter until March 1, 1989 [effective date of the Berne Implementation Act of 1988], all the copies or phonorecords of the work, including reprints of the work, published, *i.e.*, publicly distributed in the United States or elsewhere, under the authority of the author or other copyright proprietor, bore the copyright notice required by the Copyright Act of 1909 and that United States copyright subsists in the work;

(viii) For works of United States origin which were subject to the manufacturing provisions of section 16 of the Copyright Act of 1909 as it existed at the time the work was published, the Form RE/Addendum must also contain information about the country of manufacture and the manufacturing processes; and

(ix) The handwritten signature of the renewal claimant or successor or assignee, or the duly authorized agent of the claimant or of the successor or assignee. The signature shall be accompanied by the printed or typewritten name of the person signing the Addendum and by the date of the signature; and shall be immediately preceded by a declaration that the statements made in the application are correct to the best of that person's knowledge.

(4) *Fees.* Form RE and Form RE/Addendum must be accompanied by the required fee for each form as required in 37 CFR 201.3.

(5) *Deposit requirement.* One copy or phonorecord or identifying material of the work as first published in accordance with the deposit requirements set out in 37 CFR 202.20 and 202.21 is required.

(6) *Waiver of the deposit requirement.* Where the renewal applicant asserts that it is either impossible or otherwise an undue hardship to satisfy the deposit requirements of 37 CFR 202.20 and 202.21, the Copyright Office, at its discretion, may, upon receipt of an acceptable explanation of the inability to submit such copy or identifying material, permit the deposit of the following in descending order of preference. In every case, however, proof of the copyright notice showing the content and location of the notice as it appeared on copies or phonorecords of the work as first published must be included.

(i) A reproduction of the entire work as first published (e.g., photocopy, videotape, audiotape, CD-ROM, DVD are examples of physical media which may hold reproductions of a work as first published). If the work is a contribution to a periodical, a reproduction of only the contribution (including the relevant copyright notice) will suffice.

(ii) A reprint of the work (e.g., a later edition, a later release of a phonorecord, or the like). The reprint must show the copyright notice as it appeared in the same location within the first published copy of the work as well as the exact content of the copyright notice appearing in the first published edition. If the copyrightable content of the reprint differs from that of the first published edition, an explanation of the differences between the two editions is required.

(iii) Identifying material including a reproduction of the greatest feasible portion of the copyrightable content of a work including a photocopy or photograph of the title page, title screen, record label or the like, as first published, and a photocopy or photograph showing the copyright notice content and location as first published. The Copyright Office may request deposit of additional material if the initial submission is inadequate for examination purposes.

[72 FR 61803, Nov. 1, 2007, as amended at 73 FR 37839, July 2, 2008]

§ 202.18 [Reserved]

§ 202.19 Deposit of published copies or phonorecords for the Library of Congress.

(a) *General.* This section prescribes rules pertaining to the deposit of copies and phonorecords of published works for the Library of Congress under section 407 of title 17 of the United States Code, as amended by

Pub. L. 94–553. The provisions of this section are not applicable to the deposit of copies and phonorecords for purposes of copyright registration under section 408 of title 17, except as expressly adopted in § 202.20 of these regulations.

(b) *Definitions.* For the purposes of this section:

(1)(i) The *best edition* of a work is the edition, published in the United States at any time before the date of deposit, that the Library of Congress determines to be most suitable for its purposes. The "best edition" requirement is described in detail at Appendix B to this part.

(ii) Criteria for selection of the "best edition" from among two or more published editions of the same version of the same work are set forth in the statement entitled "Best Edition of Published Copyrighted Works for the Collections of the Library of Congress" (hereafter referred to as the "Best Edition Statement") in effect at the time of deposit.

(iii) Where no specific criteria for the selection of the "best edition" are established in the Best Edition Statement, that edition which, in the judgment of the Library of Congress, represents the highest quality for its purposes shall be considered the "best edition." In such cases:

(A) When the Copyright Office is aware that two or more editions of a work have been published it will consult with other appropriate officials of the Library of Congress to obtain instructions as to the "best edition" and (except in cases for which special relief is granted) will require deposit of that edition; and

(B) When a potential depositor is uncertain which of two or more published editions comprises the "best edition", inquiry should be made to the Copyright Acquisitions Division.

(iv) Where differences between two or more "editions" of a work represent variations in copyrightable content, each edition is considered a separate version, and hence a different work, for the purpose of this section, and criteria of "best edition" based on such differences do not apply.

(2) A *complete* copy includes all elements comprising the unit of publication of the best edition of the work, including elements that, if considered separately, would not be copyrightable subject matter or would otherwise be exempt from mandatory deposit requirements under paragraph (c) of this section. In the case of sound recordings, a "complete" phonorecord includes the phonorecord, together with any printed or other visually perceptible material published with such phonorecord (such as textual or pictorial matter appearing on record sleeves or album covers, or embodied in leaflets or booklets included in a sleeve, album, or other container). In the case of a musical composition published in copies only, or in both copies and phonorecords:

(i) If the only publication of copies in the United States took place by the rental, lease, or lending of a full score and parts, a full score is a "complete" copy; and

(ii) If the only publication of copies in the United States took place by the rental, lease, or lending of a conductor's score and parts, a conductor's score is a "complete" copy.

In the case of a motion picture, a copy is "complete" if the reproduction of all of the visual and aural elements comprising the copyrightable subject matter in the work is clean, undamaged, undeteriorated, and free of splices, and if the copy itself and its physical housing are free of any defects that would interfere with the performance of the work or that would cause mechanical, visual, or audible defects or distortions. In the case of an electronic work published in the United States and available only online, a copy is "complete" if it includes all elements constituting the work in its published form, *i.e.*, the complete work as published, including metadata and formatting codes otherwise exempt from mandatory deposit.

(3) The terms *architectural works, copies, collective work, device, fixed, literary work, machine, motion picture, phonorecord, publication, sound recording, useful article*, and their variant forms, have the meanings given to them in 17 U.S.C. 101.

(4) For purposes of § 202.19(c)(5) of this regulation, an *electronic serial* is an electronic work published in the

United States and available only online, issued or intended to be issued on an established schedule in successive parts bearing numerical or chronological designations, without subsequent alterations, and intended to be continued indefinitely. This class includes periodicals, newspapers, annuals, and the journals, proceedings, transactions, and other publications of societies.

(c) *Exemptions from deposit requirements.* The following categories of material are exempt from the deposit requirements of section 407(a) of title 17:

(1) Diagrams and models illustrating scientific or technical works or formulating scientific or technical information in linear or three-dimensional form, such as an architectural or engineering blueprint, plan, or design, a mechanical drawing, or an anatomical model.

(2) Greeting cards, picture postcards, and stationery.

(3) Lectures, sermons, speeches, and addresses when published individually and not as a collection of the works of one or more authors.

(4) Literary, dramatic, and musical works published only as embodied in phonorecords. This category does not exempt the owner of copyright, or of the exclusive right of publication, in a sound recording resulting from the fixation of such works in a phonorecord from the applicable deposit requirements for the sound recording.

(5) Electronic works published in the United States and available only online. This exemption includes electronic serials available only online only until such time as a demand is issued by the Copyright Office under the regulations set forth in §202.24 of these regulations. This exemption does not apply to works that are published in both online, electronic formats and in physical formats, which remain subject to the appropriate mandatory deposit requirements.

(6) Three-dimensional sculptural works, and any works published only as reproduced in or on jewelry, dolls, toys, games, plaques, floor coverings, wallpaper and similar commercial wall coverings, textiles and other fabrics, packaging material, or any useful article. Globes, relief models, and similar cartographic representations of area are not within this category and are subject to the applicable deposit requirements.

(7) Prints, labels, and other advertising matter, including catalogs, published in connection with the rental lease, lending, licensing, or sale of articles of merchandise, works of authorship, or services.

(8) Tests, and answer material for tests when published separately from other literary works.

(9) Works first published as individual contributions to collective works. This category does not exempt the owner of copyright, or of the exclusive right of publication, in the collective work as a whole, from the applicable deposit requirements for the collective work.

(10) Works first published outside the United States and later published in the United States without change in copyrightable content, if:

(i) Registration for the work was made under 17 U.S.C. 408 before the work was published in the United States; or

(ii) Registration for the work was made under 17 U.S.C. 408 after the work was published in the United States but before a demand for deposit is made under 17 U.S.C. 407(d).

(11) Works published only as embodied in a soundtrack that is an integral part of a motion picture. This category does not exempt the owner of copyright, or of the exclusive right of publication, in the motion picture, from the applicable deposit requirements for the motion picture.

(12) Motion pictures that consist of television transmission programs and that have been published, if at all, only by reason of a license or other grant to a nonprofit institution of the right to make a fixation of such programs directly from a transmission to the public, with or without the right to make further uses of such fixations.

(d) *Nature of required deposit.* (1) Subject to the provisions of paragraph (d)(2) of this section, the deposit required to satisfy the provisions of section 407(a) of title 17 shall consist of:

(i) In the case of published works other than sound recordings, two complete copies of the best edition; and

(ii) In the case of published sound recordings, two complete phonorecords of the best edition.

(2) In the case of certain published works not exempt from deposit requirements under paragraph (c) of this section, the following special provisions shall apply:

(i) In the case of published three-dimensional cartographic representations of area, such as globes and relief models, the deposit of one complete copy of the best edition of the work will suffice in lieu of the two copies required by paragraph (d)(1) of this section.

(ii) In the case of published motion pictures, the deposit of one complete copy of the best edition of the work will suffice in lieu of the two copies required by paragraph (d)(1) of this section. Any deposit of a published motion picture must be accompanied by a separate description of its contents, such as a continuity, pressbook, or synopsis. The Library of Congress may, at its sole discretion, enter into an agreement permitting the return of copies of published motion pictures to the depositor under certain conditions and establishing certain rights and obligations of the Library with respect to such copies. In the event of termination of such an agreement by the Library it shall not be subject to reinstatement, nor shall the depositor or any successor in interest of the depositor be entitled to any similar or subsequent agreement with the Library, unless at the sole discretion of the Library it would be in the best interests of the Library to reinstate the agreement or enter into a new agreement.

(iii) In the case of any published work deposited in the form of a hologram, the deposit shall be accompanied by:

(A) Two sets of precise instructions for displaying the image fixed in the hologram; and

(B) Two sets of identifying material in compliance with § 202.21 of these regulations and clearly showing the displayed image.

(iv) In any case where an individual author is the owner of copyright in a published pictorial or graphic work and (A) less than five copies of the work have been published, or (B) the work has been published and sold or offered for sale in a limited edition consisting of no more than three hundred numbered copies, the deposit of one complete copy of the best edition of the work or, alternatively, the deposit of photographs or other identifying material in compliance with § 202.21 of these regulations, will suffice in lieu of the two copies required by paragraph (d)(1) of this section.

(v) In the case of a musical composition published in copies only, or in both copies and phonorecords, if the only publication of copies in the United States took place by rental, lease, or lending, the deposit of one complete copy of the best edition will suffice in lieu of the two copies required by paragraph (d)(1) of this section.

(vi) In the case of published multimedia kits, that include literary works, audiovisual works, sound recordings, or any combination of such works, the deposit of one complete copy of the best edition will suffice in lieu of the two copies required by paragraph (d)(1) of this section.

(vii) In the case of published computer programs and published computerized information works, such as statistical compendia, serials, and reference works that are not copy-protected, the deposit of one complete copy of the best edition as specified in the current Library of Congress Best Edition Statement will suffice in lieu of the two copies required by paragraph (d)(1) of this section. If the works are copy-protected, two copies of the best edition are required.

(viii) In the case of published architectural works, the deposit shall consist of the most finished form of presentation drawings in the following descending order of preference:

(A) Original format, or best quality form of reproduction, including offset or silk screen printing;

(B) Xerographic or photographic copies on good quality paper;

(C) Positive photostat or photodirect positive;

(D) Blue line copies (diazo or ozalid process). If photographs are submitted, they should be 8 × 10 inches and should clearly show several exterior and interior views. The deposit should disclose the name(s) of the architect(s) and draftsperson(s) and the building site.

(e) *Special relief.* (1) In the case of any published work not exempt from deposit under paragraph (c) of this section, the Register of Copyrights may, after consultation with other appropriate officials of the Library of Congress and upon such conditions as the Register may determine after such consultation:

(i) Grant an exemption from the deposit requirements of section 407(a) of title 17 on an individual basis for single works or series or groups of works; or

(ii) Permit the deposit of one copy or phonorecord, or alternative identifying material, in lieu of the two copies or phonorecords required by paragraph (d)(1) of this section; or

(iii) Permit the deposit of incomplete copies or phonorecords, or copies or phonorecords other than those normally comprising the best edition; or

(iv) Permit the deposit of identifying material which does not comply with §202.21 of these regulations.

(2) Any decision as to whether to grant such special relief, and the conditions under which special relief is to be granted, shall be made by the Register of Copyrights after consultation with other appropriate officials of the Library of Congress, and shall be based upon the acquisition policies of the Library of Congress then in force.

(3) Requests for special relief under this paragraph shall be made in writing to the Associate Register for Registration Program, shall be signed by or on behalf of the owner of copyright or of the exclusive right of publication in the work, and shall set forth specific reasons why the request should be granted.

(4) The Register of Copyrights may, after consultation with other appropriate officials of the Library of Congress, terminate any ongoing or continuous grant of special relief. Notice of termination shall be given in writing and shall be sent to the individual person or organization to whom the grant of special relief had been given, at the last address shown in the records of the Copyright Office. A notice of termination may be given at any time, but it shall state a specific date of termination that is at least 30 days later than the date the notice is mailed. Termination shall not affect the validity of any deposit made earlier under the grant of special relief.

(f) *Submission and receipt of copies and phonorecords.* (1) All copies and phonorecords deposited in the Copyright Office will be considered to be deposited only in compliance with section 407 of title 17 unless they are accompanied by an application for registration of a claim to copyright in the work represented by the deposit, and either a registration fee or a deposit account number on the application. Copies or phonorecords deposited without such an accompanying application and either a fee or a deposit account notation will not be connected with or held for receipt of separate applications, and will not satisfy the deposit provisions of section 408 of title 17 or §202.20 of these regulations.

(2) All copies and phonorecords deposited in the Copyright Office under section 407 of title 17, unless accompanied by written instructions to the contrary, will be considered to be deposited by the person or persons named in the copyright notice on the work.

(3) Upon request by the depositor made at the time of the deposit, the Copyright Office will issue a certificate of receipt for the deposit of copies or phonorecords of a work under this section. Certificates of receipt will be issued in response to requests made after the date of deposit only if the requesting party is identified in the records of the Copyright Office as having made the deposit. In either case, requests for a certificate of receipt must be in writing and accompanied by the appropriate fee, as required in §201.3(c). A certificate of receipt will include identification of the depositor, the work deposited, and the nature and format of the copy or phonorecord deposited, together with the date of receipt.

[51 FR 6403, Feb. 24, 1986, as amended at 54 FR 42299, Oct. 16, 1989; 56 FR 47403, Sept. 19, 1991; 56 FR 59885, Nov. 26, 1991; 57 FR 45310, Oct. 1, 1992; 60 FR 34168, June 30, 1995; 64 FR 29522, June 1, 1999; 64 FR 62978, Nov. 18, 1999; 66 FR 34373, June 28, 2001; 73 FR 37839, July 2, 2008; 75 FR 3869, Jan. 25, 2010]

§ 202.20 Deposit of copies and phonorecords for copyright registration.

(a) *General.* This section prescribes rules pertaining to the deposit of copies and phonorecords of published and unpublished works for the purpose of copyright registration under section 408 of title 17 of the United States Code, as amended by Pub. L. 94–553. The provisions of this section are not applicable to the deposit of copies and phonorecords for the Library of Congress under section 407 of title 17, except as expressly adopted in § 202.19 of these regulations.

(b) *Definitions.* For the purposes of this section:

(1) *The best edition* of a work has the meaning set forth in § 202.19(b)(1). For purposes of this section, if a work is first published in both hard copy, *i.e.*, in a physically tangible format, and also in an electronic format, the current Library of Congress Best Edition Statement requirements pertaining to the hard copy format apply.

(2) A *complete* copy or phonorecord means the following:

(i) *Unpublished works.* Subject to the requirements of paragraph (b)(2)(vii) of this section, a "complete" copy or phonorecord of an unpublished work is a copy or phonorecord representing the entire copyrightable content of the work for which registration is sought;

(ii) *Published works.* Subject to the requirements of paragraphs (b)(2) (iv) through (vii) of this section, a "complete" copy or phonorecord of a published work includes all elements comprising the applicable unit of publication of the work, including elements that, if considered separately, would not be copyrightable subject matter. However, even where certain physically separable elements included in the applicable unit of publication are missing from the deposit, a copy or phonorecord will be considered "complete" for purposes of registration where:

(A) The copy or phonorecord deposited contains all parts of the work for which copyright registration is sought; and

(B) The removal of the missing elements did not physically damage the copy or phonorecord or garble its contents; and

(C) The work is exempt from the mandatory deposit requirements under section 407 of title 17 of the United States Code and § 202.19(c) of these regulations, or the copy deposited consists entirely of a container, wrapper, or holder, such as an envelope, sleeve, jacket, slipcase, box, bag, folder, binder, or other receptacle acceptable for deposit under paragraph (c)(2) of this section;

(iii) *Works submitted for registration in digital formats.* A 'complete' electronically filed work is one which is embodied in a digital file which contains:

(A) if the work is unpublished, all authorship elements for which registration is sought; and

(B) if the work is published solely in an electronic format, all elements constituting the work in its published form, *i.e.*, the complete work as published, including metadata and authorship for which registration is not sought. Publication in an electronic only format requires submission of the digital file[s] in exact first-publication form and content.

(C) For works submitted electronically, any of the following file formats are acceptable for registration: PDF; TXT; WPD; DOC; TIF; SVG; JPG; XML; HTML; WAV; and MPEG family of formats, including MP3. This list of file formats is non-exhaustive and it may change, or be added to periodically. Changes will be noted in the list of acceptable formats on the Copyright Office website.

(D) Contact with the registration applicant may be necessary if the Copyright Office cannot access, view, or examine the content of any particular digital file that has been submitted for the registration of a work. For purposes of section 410(d) of 17 U.S.C., a deposit has not been received in the Copyright Office until a copy that can be reviewed by the Office is received.

(iv) *Contributions to collective works.* In the case of a published contribution to a collective work, a "complete" copy is one complete copy of the best edition of the entire collective work, the complete section containing the contribution if published in a newspaper, the contribution cut from the paper in which it appeared, or a photocopy of the contribution itself as it was published in the collective work.

(v) *Sound recordings.* In the case of published sound recordings, a "complete" phonorecord has the meaning set forth in § 202.19(b)(2) of these regulations;

(vi) *Musical scores.* In the case of a musical composition published in copies only, or in both copies and phonorecords:

(A) If the only publication of copies took place by the rental, lease, or lending of a full score and parts, a full score is a "complete" copy; and

(B) If the only publication of copies took place by the rental, lease, or lending of a conductor's score and parts, a conductor's score is a "complete" copy;

(vii) *Motion pictures.* In the case of a published or unpublished motion picture, a copy is "complete" if the reproduction of all of the visual and aural elements comprising the copyrightable subject matter in the work is clean, undamaged, undeteriorated, and free of splices, and if the copy itself and its physical housing are free of any defects that would interfere with the performance of the work or that would cause mechanical, visual, or audible defects or distortions.

(3) The terms *architectural works, copy, collective work, device, fixed, literary work, machine, motion picture, phonorecord, publication, sound recording, transmission program,* and *useful article,* and their variant forms, have the meanings given to them in 17 U.S.C. 101.

(4) A *secure test* is a nonmarketed test administered under supervision at specified centers on specific dates, all copies of which are accounted for and either destroyed or returned to restricted locked storage following each administration. For these purposes a test is not marketed if copies are not sold but it is distributed and used in such a manner that ownership and control of copies remain with the test sponsor or publisher.

(5) *Title 17* means title 17 of the United States Code, as amended by Pub. L. 94–553.

(6) For the purposes of determining the applicable deposit requirements under this § 202.20 only, the following shall be considered as unpublished motion pictures: motion pictures that consist of television transmission programs and that have been published, if at all, only by reason of a license or other grant to a nonprofit institution of the right to make a fixation of such programs directly from a transmission to the public, with or without the right to make further uses of such fixations.

(c) *Nature of required deposit.* (1) Subject to the provisions of paragraph (c)(2) of this section, the deposit required to accompany an application for registration of claim to copyright under section 408 of title 17 shall consist of:

(i) In the case of unpublished works, one complete copy or phonorecord.

(ii) In the case of works first published in the United States before January 1, 1978, two complete copies or phonorecords of the work as first published.

(iii) In the case of works first published in the United States on or after January 1, 1978, two complete copies or phonorecords of the best edition.

(iv) In the case of works first published outside of the United States, one complete copy or phonorecord of the work either as first published or of the best edition. For purposes of this section, any works simultaneously first published within and outside of the United States shall be considered to be first published in the United States.

(2) In the case of certain works, the special provisions set forth in this clause shall apply. In any case where this clause specifies that one copy or phonorecord may be submitted, that copy or phonorecord shall represent the best edition, or the work as first published, as set forth in paragraph (c)(1) of this section.

(i) *General.* In the following cases the deposit of one complete copy or phonorecord will suffice in lieu of two copies or phonorecords:

(A) Published three-dimensional cartographic representations of area, such as globes and relief models;

(B) Published diagrams illustrating scientific or technical works or formulating scientific or technical information in linear or other two-dimensional form, such as an architectural or engineering blueprint, or a mechanical drawing;

(C) Published greeting cards, picture postcards, and stationery;

(D) Lectures, sermons, speeches, and addresses published individually and not as a collection of the works of one or more authors;

(E) Musical compositions published in copies only, or in both copies and phonorecords, if the only publication of copies took place by rental, lease, or lending;

(F) Published multimedia kits or any part thereof;

(G) Works exempted from the requirement of depositing identifying material under paragraph (c)(2)(xi)(B)(*5*) of this section;

(H) Literary, dramatic, and musical works published only as embodied in phonorecords, although this category does not exempt the owner of copyright in a sound recording;

(I) Choreographic works, pantomimes, literary, dramatic, and musical works published only as embodied in motion pictures;

(J) Published works in the form of two-dimensional games, decals, fabric patches or emblems, calendars, instructions for needle work, needle work and craft kits; and

(K) Works reproduced on three-dimensional containers such as boxes, cases, and cartons.

(ii) *Motion pictures.* In the case of published or unpublished motion pictures, the deposit of one complete copy will suffice. The deposit of a copy or copies for any published or unpublished motion picture must be accompanied by a separate description of its contents, such as a continuity, pressbook, or synopsis. In any case where the deposit copy or copies required for registration of a motion picture cannot be viewed for examining purposes on equipment in the Registration Program of the Copyright Office, the description accompanying the deposit must comply with § 202.21(h) of these regulations. The Library of Congress may, at its sole discretion, enter into an agreement permitting the return of copies of published motion pictures to the depositor under certain conditions and establishing certain rights and obligations of the Library of Congress with respect to such copies. In the event of termination of such an agreement by the Library, it shall not be subject to reinstatement, nor shall the depositor or any successor in interest of the depositor be entitled to any similar or subsequent agreement with the Library, unless at the sole discretion of the Library it would be in the best interests of the Library to reinstate the agreement or enter into a new agreement. In the case of unpublished motion pictures (including television transmission programs that have been fixed and transmitted to the public, but have not been published), the deposit of identifying material in compliance with § 202.21 of these regulations may be made and will suffice in lieu of an actual copy. In the case of colorized versions of motion pictures made from pre-existing black and white motion pictures, in addition to the deposit of one complete copy of the colorized motion picture and the separate description of its contents as specified above, the deposit shall consist of one complete print of the black and white version of the motion picture from which the colorized version was prepared. If special relief from this requirement is requested and granted, the claimant shall make a good faith effort to deposit the best available, near-archival quality black and white print, as a condition of any grant of special relief.

(iii) *Holograms.* In the case of any work deposited in the form of a three-dimensional hologram, the copy or copies shall be accompanied by:

(A) Precise instructions for displaying the image fixed in the hologram; and

(B) Photographs or other identifying material complying with § 202.21 of these regulations and clearly showing the displayed image.

The number of sets of instructions and identifying material shall be the same as the number of copies required. In the case of a work in the form of a two-dimensional hologram, the image of which is visible without the use of a machine or device, one actual copy of the work shall be deposited.

(iv) *Certain pictorial and graphic works.* In the case of any unpublished pictorial or graphic work, deposit of identifying material in compliance with § 202.21 of these regulations may be made and will suffice in lieu of deposit of an actual copy. In the case of a published pictorial or graphic work, deposit of one complete copy, or of identifying material in compliance with § 202.21 of these regulations, may be made and will suffice in lieu of deposit of two actual copies where an individual author is the owner of copyright, and either:

(A) Less than five copies of the work have been published; or

(B) The work has been published and sold or offered for sale in a limited edition consisting of no more than 300 numbered copies.

(v) *Commercial prints and labels.* In the case of prints, labels, and other advertising matter, including catalogs, published in connection with the rental, lease, lending, licensing, or sale of articles of merchandise, works of authorship, or services, the deposit of one complete copy will suffice in lieu of two copies. Where the print or label is published in a larger work, such as a newspaper or other periodical, one copy of the entire page or pages upon which it appears may be submitted in lieu of the entire larger work. In the case of prints or labels physically inseparable from a three-dimensional object, identifying material complying with § 202.21 of these regulations must be submitted rather than an actual copy or copies except under the conditions of paragraph (c)(2)(xi)(B)(*4*) of this section.

(vi) *Tests.* In the case of tests, and answer material for tests, published separately from other literary works, the deposit of one complete copy will suffice in lieu of two copies. In the case of any secure test the Copyright Office will return the deposit to the applicant promptly after examination: Provided, That sufficient portions, description, or the like are retained so as to constitute a sufficient archival record of the deposit.

(vii) *Computer programs and databases embodied in machine-readable copies other than CD-ROM format.* In cases where a computer program, database, compilation, statistical compendium, or the like, if unpublished is fixed, or if published is published only in the form of machine-readable copies (such as magnetic tape or disks, punched cards, semiconductor chip products, or the like) other than a CD-ROM format, from which the work cannot ordinarily be perceived except with the aid of a machine or device, the deposit shall consist of:

(A) For published or unpublished computer programs, one copy of identifying portions of the program, reproduced in a form visually perceptible without the aid of a machine or device, either on paper or in microform. For these purposes "identifying portions" shall mean one of the following:

(*1*) The first and last 25 pages or equivalent units of the source code if reproduced on paper, or at least the first and last 25 pages or equivalent units of the source code if reproduced in microform, together with the page or equivalent unit containing the copyright notice, if any. If the program is 50 pages or less, the required deposit will be the entire source code. In the case of revised versions of computer programs, if the revisions occur throughout the entire program, the deposit of the page containing the copyright notice and the first and last 25 pages of source code will suffice; if the revisions do not occur in the first and last 25 pages, the deposit should consist of the page containing the copyright notice and any 50 pages of source code representative of the revised material; or

(*2*) Where the program contains trade secret material, the page or equivalent unit containing the copyright notice, if any, plus one of the following: the first and last 25 pages or equivalent units of source code with portions of the source code containing trade secrets blocked-out, provided that the blocked-out portions are proportionately less than the material remaining, and the deposit reveals an appreciable amount of original computer code; or the first and last 10 pages or equivalent units of source code alone with no blocked-out portions; or the first and last 25 pages of object code, together with any 10 or more consecutive pages of source code with no blocked-out portions; or for programs consisting of, or less than, 50 pages or equivalent units, entire source code with the trade secret portions blocked-out, provided that the blocked-out portions are proportionately less than the material remaining, and the remaining portion reveals an appreciable amount of original computer code. If the copyright claim is in a revision not contained in the first and last 25 pages, the deposit shall consist of either 20 pages of source code representative of the revised material with no blocked-out portions, or any 50 pages of source code representative of the revised material with portions of the source code containing trade secrets blocked-out, provided that the blocked-out portions are proportinately less than the material remaining and the deposit reveals an appreciable amount of original computer code. Whatever method is used to block out trade secret material, at least an appreciable amount of original computer code must remain visible.

(B) Where registration of a program containing trade secrets is made on the basis of an object code deposit the Copyright Office will make registration under its rule of doubt and warn that no determination has been made concerning the existence of copyrightable authorship.

(C) Where the application to claim copyright in a computer program includes a specific claim in related computer screen displays, the deposit, in addition to the identifying portions specified in paragraph (c)(2)(vii)(A) of this section, shall consist of:

(*1*) Visual reproductions of the copyrightable expression in the form of printouts, photographs, or drawings no smaller than 3 × 3 inches and no larger than 9 × 12 inches; or

(*2*) If the authorship in the work is predominantly audiovisual, a one-half inch VHS format videotape reproducing the copyrightable expression, except that printouts, photographs, or drawings no smaller than 3 × 3 inches and no larger than 9 × 12 inches must be deposited in lieu of videotape where the computer screen material simply constitutes a demonstration of the functioning of the computer program.

(D) For published and unpublished automated databases, compilations, statistical compendia, and the like, so fixed or published, one copy of identifying portions of the work, reproduced in a form visually perceptible without the aid of a machine or device, either on paper or in microform. For these purposes:

(*1*) *Identifying portions* shall generally mean either the first and last 25 pages or equivalent units of the work if reproduced on paper or in microform.

(*2*) *Datafile* and *file* shall mean a group of data records pertaining to a common subject matter regardless of their size or the number of data items in them.

(*3*) In the case of individual registration of a revised version of the works identified in paragraph (c)(2)(vii)(D) of this section, the identifying portions deposited shall contain 50 representative pages or data records which have been added or modified.

(*4*) If the work is an automated database comprising multiple separate or distinct data files, "identifying portions" shall instead consist of 50 complete data records from each data file or the entire data file, whichever is less, and the descriptive statement required by paragraph (c)(2)(vii)(D)(5) of this section.

(*5*) In the case of group registration for revised or updated versions of a database, the claimant shall deposit identifying portions that contain 50 representative pages or equivalent units, or representative data records which have been marked to disclose (or do in fact disclose solely) the new material added on one representative publication date if published, or on one representative creation date, if unpublished or in the case of applications for automated databases that predominantly consist of photographs, the claimant shall deposit identifying portions that comply with (D)(8) of this section; the claimant shall, also deposit a brief typed or printed descriptive statement containing the notice of copyright information required under paragraphs (c)(2)(vii)(D)(6) or (7) of this section, if the work bears a notice, and;

(*i*) The title of the database;

(*ii*) A subtitle, date of creation or publication, or other information, to distinguish any separate or distinct data files for cataloging purposes;

(*iii*) The name and address of the copyright claimant;

(*iv*) For each separate file, its name and content, including its subject, the origin(s) of the data, and the approximate number of data records it contains; and

(*v*) In the case of revised or updated versions of an automated database, information as to the nature and frequency of changes in the database and some identification of the location within the database or the separate data files of the revisions.

(*6*) For a copyright notice embodied in machine-readable form, the statement shall describe exactly the visually perceptible content of the notice which appears in or with the database, and the manner and frequency with which it is displayed (e.g., at user's terminal only at sign-on, or continuously on terminal display, or on printouts, etc.).

(*7*) If a visually perceptible copyright notice is placed on any copies of the work (or on magnetic tape reels or containers therefor), a sample of such notice must also accompany the statement.

(*8*) In the case of an application for registration of a database that consists predominantly of photographs (including a group registration for revised or updated versions of such a database), "identifying portions" shall instead consist of all individual photographs included in the claim either in one of the formats set forth in paragraph (c)(2)(xx) of this section or in an electronic format submitted along with the electronic application after consultation and with the permission and under the direction of the Visual Arts Division.

(viii) *Machine-readable copies of works other than computer programs, databases, and works fixed in a CD-ROM format.* Where a literary, musical, pictorial, graphic, or audiovisual work, or a sound recording, except for works fixed in a CD-ROM format and literary works which are computer programs, databases, compilations, statistical compendia or the like, if unpublished has been fixed or, if published, has been published only in machine-readable form, the deposit must consist of identifying material. The type of identifying material submitted should generally be appropriate to the type of work embodied in machine-readable form, but in all cases should be that which best represents the copyrightable content of the work. In all cases the identifying material must include the title of the work. A synopsis may also be requested in addition to the other deposit materials as appropriate in the discretion of the Copyright Office. In the case of any published work subject to this section, the identifying material must include a representation of the copyright notice, if one exists. Identifying material requirements for certain types of works are specified below. In the case of the types of works listed below, the requirements specified shall apply except that, in any case where the specific requirements are not appropriate for a given work the form of the identifying material required will be determined by the Copyright Office in consultation with the applicant, but the Copyright Office will make the final determination of the acceptability of the identifying material.

(A) For pictorial or graphic works, the deposit shall consist of identifying material in compliance with § 202.21 of these regulations;

(B) For audiovisual works, the deposit shall consist of either a videotape of the work depicting representative portions of the copyrightable content, or a series of photographs or drawings, depicting representative portions of the work, plus in all cases a separate synopsis of the work;

(C) For musical compositions, the deposit shall consist of a transcription of the entire work such as a score, or a reproduction of the entire work on an audiocassette or other phonorecord;

(D) For sound recordings, the deposit shall consist of a reproduction of the entire work on an audiocassette or other phonorecord;

(E) For literary works, the deposit shall consist of a transcription of representative portions of the work including the first and last 25 pages or equivalent units, and five or more pages indicative of the remainder.

(ix) *Copies containing both visually-perceptible and machine-readable material other than a CD-ROM format.* Where a published literary work is embodied in copies containing both visually-perceptible and machine-readable material, except in the case of a CD-ROM format, the deposit shall consist of the visually-perceptible material and identifying portions of the machine-readable material.

(x) *Works reproduced in or on sheetlike materials.* In the case of any unpublished work that is fixed, or any published work that is published, only in the form of a two-dimensional reproduction on sheetlike materials such as textiles and other fabrics, wallpaper and similar commercial wall coverings, carpeting, floor tile, and similar commercial floor coverings, and wrapping paper and similar packaging material, the deposit shall consist of one copy in the form of an actual swatch or piece of such material sufficient to show all elements of the work in which copyright is claimed and the copyright notice appearing on the work, if any. If the work consists of a repeated pictorial or graphic design, the complete design and at least part of one repetition must be shown. If the sheetlike material in or on which a published work has been reproduced has been embodied in or attached to a three-dimensional object, such as furniture, or any other three-dimensional manufactured article, and the work has been published only in that form, the deposit must consist of identifying material complying with § 202.21 of these regulations instead of a copy. If the sheetlike material in or on which a published work has been reproduced has been embodied in or attached to a two-dimensional object such as wearing apparel, bed linen, or a similar item, and the work has been published only in that form, the deposit must consist of identifying material complying with § 202.21 of these regulations instead of a copy unless the copy can be folded for storage in a form that does not exceed four inches in thickness.

(xi) *Works reproduced in or on three-dimensional objects.* (A) In the following cases the deposit must consist of identifying material complying with § 201.21 of these regulations instead of a copy or copies:

(*1*) Any three-dimensional sculptural work, including any illustration or formulation of artistic expression or information in three-dimensional form. Examples of such works include statues, carvings, ceramics, moldings, constructions, models, and maquettes; and

(*2*) Any two-dimensional or three-dimensional work that, if unpublished, has been fixed, or, if published, has been published only in or on jewelry, dolls, toys, games, except as provided in paragraph (c)(2)(xi)(B)(*3*) of this section, or any three-dimensional useful article.

(B) In the following cases the requirements of paragraph (c)(2)(xi)(A) of this section for the deposit of identifying material shall not apply:

(*1*) Three-dimensional cartographic representations of area, such as globes and relief models;

(*2*) Works that have been fixed or published in or on a useful article that comprises one of the elements of the unit of publication of an educational or instructional kit which also includes a literary or audiovisual work, a sound recording, or any combination of such works;

(*3*) Published games consisting of multiple parts that are packaged and published in a box or similar container with flat sides and with dimensions of no more than 12 × 24 × 6 inches;

(*4*) Works reproduced on three-dimensional containers or holders such as boxes, cases, and cartons, where the container or holder can be readily opened out, unfolded, slit at the corners, or in some other way made adaptable for flat storage, and the copy, when flattened, does not exceed 96 inches in any dimension; or

(*5*) Any three-dimensional sculptural work that, if unpublished, has been fixed, or, if published, has been published only in the form of jewelry cast in base metal which does not exceed four inches in any dimension.

(xii) *Soundtracks.* For separate registration of an unpublished work that is fixed, or a published work that is published, only as embodied in a soundtrack that is an integral part of a motion picture, the deposit of identifying material in compliance with § 202.21 of these regulations will suffice in lieu of an actual copy of the motion picture.

(xiii) *Oversize deposits.* In any case where the deposit otherwise required by this section exceeds 96 inches in any dimension, identifying material complying with § 202.21 of these regulations must be submitted instead of an actual copy or copies.

(xiv) *Pictorial advertising material.* In the case of published pictorial advertising material, except for advertising material published in connection with motion pictures, the deposit of either one copy as published or prepublication material consisting of camera-ready copy is acceptable.

(xv) *Contributions to collective works.* In the case of published contributions to collective works, the deposit of either one complete copy of the best edition of the entire collective work, the complete section containing the contribution if published in a newspaper, the entire page containing the contribution, the contribution cut from the paper in which it appeared, or a photocopy of the contribution itself as it was published in the collective work, will suffice in lieu of two complete copies of the entire collective work.

(xvi) *Phonorecords.* In any case where the deposit phonorecord or phonorecords submitted for registration of a claim to copyright is inaudible on audio playback devices in the Registration Program of the Copyright Office, the Office will seek an appropriate deposit in accordance with paragraph (d) of this section.

(xvii) *Group registration of serials.* For group registration of related serials, as specified in § 202.3(b)(6), for applicants filing electronically, the deposit must consist of one complete copy of the best edition of each issue included in the group registration, or a digital format of a complete copy which complies with § 202.20(b)(2)(iii). For applicants filing a completed Form SE/Group, the deposit must consist of one complete copy of the best edition of each issue included in the group registration. In addition, for all filings for group registration of serial issues, two complimentary subscriptions to any serial for which group registration is sought must be entered and maintained in the name of the Library of Congress, and the copies must be submitted regularly and promptly after publication.

(xviii) *Architectural works.* (A) For designs of unconstructed buildings, the deposit must consist of one complete copy of an architectural drawing or blueprint in visually perceptible form showing the overall form of the building and any interior arrangements of spaces and/or design elements in which copyright is claimed. For archival purposes, the Copyright Office prefers that the drawing submissions consist of the following in descending order of preference:

(*1*) Original format, or best quality form of reproduction, including offset or silk screen printing;

(*2*) Xerographic or photographic copies on good quality paper;

(*3*) Positive photostat or photodirect positive;

(*4*) Blue line copies (diazo or ozalid process).

The Copyright Office prefers that the deposit disclose the name(s) of the architect(s) and draftsperson(s) and the building site, if known.

(B) For designs of constructed buildings, the deposit must consist of one complete copy of an architectural drawing or blueprint in visually perceptible form showing the overall form of the building and any interior arrangement of spaces and/or design elements in which copyright is claimed. In addition, the deposit must also include identifying material in the form of photographs complying with § 202.21 of these regulations, which clearly discloses the architectural works being registered. For archival purposes, the Copyright Office prefers that the drawing submissions constitute the most finished form of presentation drawings and consist of the following in descending order of preference:

(*1*) Original format, or best quality form of reproduction, including offset or silk screen printing;

(*2*) Xerographic or photographic copies on good quality paper;

(*3*) Positive photostat or photodirect positive;

(*4*) Blue line copies (diazo or ozalid process).

With respect to the accompanying photographs, the Copyright Office prefers 8 × 10 inches, good quality photographs, which clearly show several exterior and interior views. The Copyright Office prefers that the deposit disclose the name(s) of the architect(s) and draftsperson(s) and the building site.

(xix) *Works fixed in a CD-ROM format.* (A) Where a work is fixed in a CD-ROM format, the deposit must consist of one complete copy of the entire CD-ROM package, including a complete copy of any accompanying operating software and instructional manual, and a printed version of the work embodied in the CD-ROM, if the work is fixed in print as well as a CD-ROM. A complete copy of a published CD-ROM package includes all of the elements comprising the applicable unit of publication, including elements that if considered separately would not be copyrightable subject matter or could be the subject of a separate registration.

(B) In any case where the work fixed in a CD-ROM package cannot be viewed on equipment available in the Registration Program of the Copyright Office, the Office will seek an appropriate deposit in accordance with paragraph (d) of this section, in addition to the deposit of the CD-ROM package.

(xx) *Photographs: group registration.* For groups of photographs registered with one application under §§ 202.3(b)(4)(i)(B) (unpublished collections) or 202.3(b)(10) (group registration of published photographs) and for automated databases that consist predominantly of photographs under § 202.3(b)(5)(ii)(A), photographs must be deposited in one of the following formats (listed in the Library's order of preference):

(A) Digital form on one or more CD-ROMs (including CD-RW's) or DVD-ROMs, in one of the following formats: JPEG, GIF, TIFF, or PCD;

(B) Unmounted prints measuring at least 3 inches by 3 inches (not to exceed 20 inches by 24 inches);

(C) Contact sheets;

(D) Slides, each with a single image;

(E) A format in which the photograph has been published (e.g., clippings from newspapers or magazines);

(F) A photocopy of each of the photographs included in the group or database, clearly depicting the photograph, provided that if registration is made pursuant to § 202.3(b)(10) for group registration of photographs, the photocopy must be either a photocopy of an unmounted print measuring at least 3 inches by 3 inches (not to exceed 20 inches by 24 inches) or a photocopy of the photograph in a format in which it has been published, and if the photograph was published as a color photograph, the photocopy must be a color photocopy;

(G) Slides, each containing up to 36 images; or

(H) A videotape clearly depicting each photograph.

(d) *Special relief.* (1) In any case the Register of Copyrights may, after consultation with other appropriate officials of the Library of Congress and upon such conditions as the Register may determine after such consultation:

(i) Permit the deposit of one copy or phonorecord, or alternative identifying material, in lieu of the one or two copies or phonorecords otherwise required by paragraph (c)(1) of this section;

(ii) Permit the deposit of incomplete copies or phonorecords, or copies or phonorecords other than those normally comprising the best edition; or

(iii) Permit the deposit of an actual copy or copies, in lieu of the identifying material otherwise required by this section; or

(iv) Permit the deposit of identifying material which does not comply with § 202.21 of these regulations.

(2) Any decision as to whether to grant such special relief, and the conditions under which special relief is to be granted, shall be made by the Register of Copyrights after consultation with other appropriate officials of the Library of Congress, and shall be based upon the acquisition policies of the Library of Congress then in force and the archival and examining requirements of the Copyright Office.

(3) Requests for special relief under this paragraph may be combined with requests for special relief under § 202.19(e) of these regulations. Whether so combined or made solely under this paragraph, such requests shall be made in writing to the Associate Register for Registration Program of the Copyright Office, shall be signed by or on behalf of the person signing the application for registration, and shall set forth specific reasons why the request should be granted.

(4) The Register of Copyrights may, after consultation with other appropriate officials of the Library of Congress, terminate any ongoing or continuous grant of special relief. Notice of termination shall be given in writing

and shall be sent to the individual person or organization to whom the grant of special relief had been given, at the last address shown in the records of the Copyright Office. A notice of termination may be given at any time, but it shall state a specific date of termination that is at least 30 days later than the date the notice is mailed. Termination shall not affect the validity of any deposit or registration made earlier under the grant of special relief.

(e) *Use of copies and phonorecords deposited for the Library of Congress.* Copies and phonorecords deposited for the Library of Congress under section 407 of title 17 and § 202.19 of these regulations may be used to satisfy the deposit provisions of this section if they are accompanied by an application for registration of claim to copyright in the work represented by the deposit, and either a registration fee or a deposit account number on the application.

EDITORIAL NOTE: For FEDERAL REGISTER citations affecting § 202.20, see the List of CFR Sections Affected, which appears in the Finding Aids section of the printed volume and at *www.fdsys.gov*.

§ 202.21 Deposit of identifying material instead of copies.

(a) *General.* Subject to the specific provisions of paragraphs (f) and (g) of this section, and to §§ 202.19(e)(1)(iv) and 202.20(d)(1)(iv), in any case where the deposit of identifying material is permitted or required under § 202.19 or § 202.20 of these regulations for published or unpublished works, the material shall consist of photographic prints, transparencies, photostats, drawings, or similar two-dimensional reproductions or renderings of the work, in a form visually perceivable without the aid of a machine or device. In the case of pictorial or graphic works, such material should reproduce the actual colors employed in the work. In all other cases, such material may be in black and white or may consist of a reproduction of the actual colors.

(b) *Completeness; number of sets.* As many pieces of identifying material as are necessary to show the entire copyrightable content in the ordinary case, but in no case less than an adequate representation of such content, of the work for which deposit is being made, or for which registration is being sought shall be submitted. Except in cases falling under the provisions of § 202.19(d)(2)(iii) or § 202.20(c)(2)(iii) with respect to holograms, only one set of such complete identifying material is required.

(c) *Size.* Photographic transparencies must be at least 35mm in size and, if such transparencies are 3 × 3 inches or less, must be fixed in cardboard, plastic, or similar mounts to facilitate identification, handling, and storage. The Copyright Office prefers that transparencies larger than 3 × 3 inches be mounted in a way that facilitates their handling and preservation, and reserves the right to require such mounting in particular cases. All types of identifying material other than photographic transparencies must be not less than 3 × 3 inches and not more than 9 × 12 inches, but preferably 8 × 10 inches. Except in the case of transparencies, the image of the work must be either lifesize or larger, or if less than lifesize must be large enough to show clearly the entire copyrightable content of the work.

(d) *Title and dimensions.* At least one piece of identifying material must, on its front, back, or mount, indicate the title of the work; and the indication of an exact measurement of one or more dimensions of the work is preferred.

(e) *Copyright notice.* In the case of works published with notice of copyright, the notice and its position on the work must be clearly shown on at least one piece of identifying material. Where necessary because of the size or position of the notice, a separate drawing or similar reproduction shall be submitted. Such reproduction shall be no smaller than 3 × 3 inches and no larger than 9 × 12 inches, and shall show the exact appearance and content of the notice, and its specific position on the work.

(f) For separate registration of an unpublished work that is fixed, or a published work that is published, only as embodied in a soundtrack that is an integral part of a motion picture, identifying material deposited in lieu of an actual copy of the motion picture shall consist of:

(1) A transcription of the entire work, or a reproduction of the entire work on a phonorecord; and

(2) Photographs or other reproductions from the motion picture showing the title of the motion picture, the soundtrack credits, and the copyright notice for the soundtrack, if any.

The provisions of paragraphs (b), (c), (d), and (e) of this section do not apply to identifying material deposited under this paragraph (f).

(g)(1) In the case of unpublished motion pictures (including transmission programs that have been fixed and transmitted to the public, but have not been published), identifying material deposited in lieu of an actual copy shall consist of either:

(i) An audio cassette or other phonorecord reproducing the entire soundtrack or other sound portion of the motion picture, and description of the motion picture; or

(ii) A set consisting of one frame enlargement or similar visual reproduction from each 10-minute segment of the motion picture, and a description of the motion picture.

(2) In either case the "description" may be a continuity, a pressbook, or a synopsis but in all cases it must include:

(i) The title or continuing title of the work, and the episode title, if any;

(ii) The nature and general content of the program;

(iii) The date when the work was first fixed and whether or not fixation was simultaneous with first transmission;

(iv) The date of first transmission, if any;

(v) The running time; and

(vi) The credits appearing on the work, if any.

(3) The provisions of paragraphs (b), (c), (d), and (e) of this section do not apply to identifying material submitted under this paragraph (g).

(h) In the case where the deposit copy or copies of a motion picture cannot be viewed for examining purposes on equipment in the Registration Program of the Copyright Office, the "description" required by § 202.20(c)(2)(ii) of these regulations may be a continuity, a press-book, a synopsis, or a final shooting script but in all cases must be sufficient to indicate the copyrightable material in the work and include

(1) The continuing title of the work and the episode title, if any;

(2) The nature and general content of the program and of its dialogue or narration, if any;

(3) The running time; and

(4) All credits appearing on the work including the copyright notice, if any.

The provisions of paragraphs (b), (c), and (d) of this section do not apply to identifying material submitted under this paragraph (h).

[51 FR 6409, Feb. 24, 1986, as amended at 73 FR 37839, July 2, 2008]

§ 202.22 Acquisition and deposit of unpublished audio and audiovisual transmission programs.

(a) *General.* This section prescribes rules pertaining to the acquisition of phonorecords and copies of unpublished audio and audiovisual transmission programs by the Library of Congress under section 407(e) of title 17 of the United States Code, as amended. It also prescribes rules pertaining to the use of such phonorecords and copies in the registration of claims to copyright, under section 408(b).

(b) *Definitions.* For purposes of this section:

(1) The terms copies, fixed, phonorecords, publication, and transmission program and their variant forms, have the meanings given to them in section 101 of title 17. The term network station has the meaning given it in section 111(f) of title 17. For the purpose of this section, the term transmission includes transmission via the Internet, cable, broadcasting, and satellite systems, and via any other existing or future devices or processes for the communication of a performance or display whereby images or sounds are received beyond the place from which they are sent.

(2) *Title 17* means title 17 of the United States Code, as amended.

(c) *Recording of transmission programs.* (1) Library of Congress employees, including Library of Congress contractors, acting under the general authority of the Librarian of Congress, may make a fixation of an unpublished audio or audiovisual transmission program directly from a transmission to the public in the United States, in accordance with subsections 407(e)(1) and (4) of title 17 of the United States Code. The choice of programs selected for fixation shall be based on the Library of Congress's acquisition policies in effect at the time of fixation. Specific notice of an intent to record a transmission program will ordinarily not be given. In general, the Library of Congress will seek to record a substantial portion of the television programming transmitted by noncommercial educational broadcast stations as defined in section 397 of title 47 of the United States Code, and will record selected programming transmitted by commercial television broadcast stations, both network and independent. The Library will also record a selected portion of the radio programming transmitted by commercial and noncommercial broadcast stations. Additionally, the Library will record a selected portion of unpublished Internet, cable and satellite programming transmitted to the public in the United States.

(2) Upon written request addressed to the Chief, Motion Picture, Broadcasting and Recorded Sound Division by a broadcast station or other owner of the right of transmission, the Library of Congress will inform the requestor whether a particular transmission program has been recorded by the Library.

(3) The Library of Congress will not knowingly record any unfixed or published transmission program under the recording authority of section 407(e) of title 17 of the United States Code.

(4) The Library of Congress is entitled under this paragraph (c) to presume that a radio program transmitted to the public in the United States has been fixed but not published at the time of transmission, and that a television program transmitted to the public in the United States by a noncommercial educational broadcast station as defined in section 397 of title 47 of the United States Code has been fixed but not published.

(5) The presumption established by paragraph (c)(4) of this section may be overcome by written declaration and submission of appropriate documentary evidence to the Chief, Motion Picture, Broadcasting and Recorded Sound Division, either before or after recording of the particular transmission program by the Library of Congress. Such written submission shall contain:

(i) The identification, by title and time of broadcast, of the transmission program in question;

(ii) A brief statement declaring either that the program was not fixed or that it was published at the time of transmission;

(iii) If it is declared that the program was published at the time of transmission, a brief statement of the facts of publication, including the date and place thereof, the method of publication, the name of the owner of the right of first publication, and whether the work was published in the United States; and

(iv) The actual handwritten signature of an officer or other duly authorized agent of the organization which transmitted the program in question.

(6) A declaration that the program was unfixed at the time of transmission shall be accepted by the Library of Congress, unless the Library can cite evidence to the contrary, and the copy or phonorecord will either be

(i) Erased; or

(ii) Retained, if requested by the owner of copyright or of any exclusive right, to satisfy the deposit provision of section 408 of title 17 of the United States Code.

(7) If it is declared that the program was published at the time of transmission, the Library of Congress is entitled under this section to retain the copy or phonorecord to satisfy the deposit requirement of section 407(a) of title 17 of the United States Code.

(8) The Library of Congress shall maintain a list of the radio, cable, Internet and satellite transmission programs that the Library has recorded on the Motion Picture, Broadcasting and Recorded Sound Division Web site at *http://www.loc.gov/rr/record/* for audio transmission programs, or *http://www.loc.gov/rr/mopic/* for audiovisual transmission programs, and, in making fixations of such unpublished transmission programs, shall identify a program that the Library has recorded by including that transmission program on the list no later than fourteen days after such fixation has occurred.

The Library of Congress in making fixations of unpublished television transmission programs transmitted by commercial broadcast stations shall not do so without notifying the transmitting organization or its agent that such activity is taking place. In the case of television network stations, the notification will be sent to the particular network. In the case of any other commercial television broadcasting station, the notification will be sent to the particular broadcast station that has transmitted, or will transmit, the program. Such notice shall, if possible, be given by the Library of Congress prior to the time of broadcast. In every case, the Library of Congress shall transmit such notice no later than fourteen days after such fixation has occurred. Such notice shall contain:

(i) The identification, by title and time of broadcast, of the transmission program in question;

(ii) A brief statement asserting the Library of Congress' belief that the transmission program has been, or will be by the date of transmission, fixed and is unpublished, together with language converting the notice to a demand for deposit under section 407 (a) and (b) of title 17 of the United States Code, if the transmission program has been published in the United States.

(9) The notice required by paragraph (c)(8) of this section shall not cover more than one transmission program except that the notice may cover up to thirteen episodes of one title if such episodes are generally scheduled to be broadcast at the same time period on a regular basis, or may cover all the episodes comprising the title if they are scheduled to be broadcast within a period of not more than two months.

(d) *Demands for deposit of a transmission program.* (1) The Register of Copyrights may make a written demand upon the owner of the right of transmission in the United States to deposit a copy or phonorecord of a specific transmission program for the benefit of the Library of Congress under the authority of section 407(e)(2) of title 17 of the United States Code.

(2) The Register of Copyrights is entitled to presume, unless clear evidence to the contrary is proffered, that the transmitting organization is the owner of the United States transmission right.

(3) Notices of demand shall be in writing and shall contain:

(i) The identification, by title and time of broadcast, of the work in question;

(ii) An explanation of the optional forms of compliance, including transfer of ownership of a copy or phonorecord to the Library, lending a copy or phonorecord to the Library for reproduction, or selling a copy or phonorecord to the Library at a price not to exceed the cost of reproducing and supplying the copy or phonorecord;

(iii) A ninety-day deadline by which time either compliance or a request for an extension of a request to adjust the scope of the demand or the method for fulfilling it shall have been received by the Register of Copyrights;

(iv) A brief description of the controls which are placed on the use of the copies or phonorecords;

(v) A statement concerning the Register's perception of the publication status of the program, together with language converting this demand to a demand for a deposit, under 17 U.S.C. 407, if the recipient takes the position that the work is published; and

(vi) A statement that a *compliance copy*, or in the case of an audio transmission program, a compliance phonorecord, must be made and retained if the notice is received prior to transmission.

(4) With respect to paragraph (d)(3)(ii) of this section, the sale of a copy or phonorecord in compliance with a demand of this nature shall be at a price not to exceed the cost to the Library of reproducing and supplying the copy or phonorecord. The notice of demand should therefore inform the recipient of that cost and set that cost, plus reasonable shipping charges, as the maximum price for such a sale.

(5) Copies and phonorecords transferred, lent, or sold under paragraph (d) of this section shall be of sound physical condition as described in Appendix A to this section.

(6) *Special relief.* In the case of any demand made under paragraph (d) of this section the Register of Copyrights may, after consultation with other appropriate officials of the Library of

Congress and upon such conditions as the Register may determine after such consultation,

(i) Extend the time period provided in subparagraph (d)(3)(iii);

(ii) Make adjustments in the scope of the demand; or

(iii) Make adjustments in the method of fulfilling the demand. Any decision as to whether to allow such extension or adjustments shall be made by the Register of Copyrights after consultation with other appropriate officials of the Library of Congress and shall be made as reasonably warranted by the circumstances. Requests for special relief under paragraph (d) of this section shall be made in writing to the Copyright Acquisitions Division, shall be signed by or on behalf of the owner of the right of transmission in the United States and shall set forth the specific reasons why the request should be granted.

(e) *Disposition and use of copies and phonorecords.* (1) All copies and phonorecords acquired under this section shall be maintained by the Motion Picture, Broadcasting and Recorded Sound Division of the Library of Congress. The Library may make one archival copy or phonorecord of a program which it has fixed under the provisions of section 407(e)(1) of title 17 of the United States Code and paragraph (c) of this section.

(2) All copies and phonorecords acquired or made under this section, except copies and phonorecords of transmission programs consisting of a regularly scheduled newscast or on-the-spot coverage of news events, shall be subject to the following restrictions concerning copying and access: in the case of television or other audiovisual transmission programs, copying and access are governed by Library of Congress Regulation 818–17, Policies Governing the Use and Availability of Motion Pictures and Other Audiovisual Works in the Collections of the Library of Congress, or its successors; in the case of audio transmission programs, copying and access are governed by Library of Congress Regulation 818–18.1, Recorded Sound Listening and Duplication Services, or its successors. Transmission programs consisting of regularly scheduled newscasts or on-the-spot coverage of news events are subject to the provisions of the "American Television and Radio Archives Act," 2 U.S.C. 170, and such regulations as the Librarian of Congress shall prescribe.

(f) *Registration of claims to copyright.* (1) Copies and phonorecords fixed by the Library of Congress under the provisions of paragraph (c) of this section may be used as the deposit for copyright registration provided that:

(i) The application and fee, in a form acceptable for registration, is received by the Copyright Office not later than ninety days after transmission of the program, and

(ii) Correspondence received by the Copyright Office in the envelope containing the application and fee states that a fixation of the instant work was made by the Library of Congress and requests that the copy or phonorecord so fixed be used to satisfy the registration deposit provisions.

(2) Copies and phonorecords transferred, lent, or sold to the Library of Congress under the provisions of paragraph (d) of this section may be used as the deposit for copyright registration purposes only when the application and fee, in a form acceptable for registration, accompany, in the same container, the copy or phonorecord lent, transferred, or sold, and there is an explanation that the copy or phonorecord is intended to satisfy both the demand issued under section 407(e)(2) of title 17 of the United States Code and the registration deposit provisions.

(g) *Agreements modifying the terms of this section.* (1) The Library of Congress may, at its sole discretion, enter into an agreement whereby the provision of copies or phonorecords of unpublished audio or audiovisual transmission programs on terms different from those contained in this section is authorized.

(2) Any such agreement may be terminated without notice by the Library of Congress.

(17 U.S.C. 407, 408, 702)

[48 FR 37208, Aug. 17, 1983, as amended at 56 FR 7815, Feb. 26, 1991; 60 FR 34168, June 30, 1995; 64 FR 36575, July 7, 1999; 66 FR 34373, June 28, 2001; 69 FR 62411, Oct. 26, 2004]

§ 202.23 Full term retention of copyright deposits.

(a) *General.* (1) This section prescribes conditions under which a request for full term retention, under the control of the Copyright Office, of copyright deposits (copies, phonorecords, or identifying material) of published works may be made and granted or denied pursuant to section 704(e) of title 17 of the United States Code. Only copies, phonorecords, or identifying material deposited in connection with registration of a claim to copyright under title 17 of the United States Code are within the provisions of this section. Only the depositor or the copyright owner of record of the work identified by the copyright deposit, or a duly authorized agent of the depositor or copyright owner, may request full term retention. A fee for this service is fixed by this section pursuant to section 708(a)(11) of title 17 of the United States Code.

(2) For purposes of this section, *under the control of the Copyright Office* shall mean within the confines of Copyright Office buildings and under the control of Copyright Office employees, including retention in a Federal records center, but does not include transfer to the Library of Congress collections.

(3) For purposes of this section, *full term retention* means retention for a period of 75 years from the date of publication of the work identified by the particular copyright deposit which is retained.

(4) For purposes of this section, *copyright deposit* or its plural means the copy, phonorecord, or identifying material submitted to the Copyright Office in connection with a published work that is subsequently registered and made part of the records of the Office.

(b) *Form and content of request for full term retention*—(1) *Forms.* The Copyright Office does not provide printed forms for the use of persons requesting full term retention of copyright deposits.

(2) Requests for full term retention must be made in writing addressed to the Chief, Information and Records Division of the Copyright Office, and shall (i) be signed by or on behalf of the depositor or copyright owner of record, and (ii) clearly indicate that full term retention is desired.

(3) The request for full term retention must adequately identify the particular copyright deposit to be retained, preferably by including the title used in the registration application, the name of the depositor or copyright owner of record, the publication date, and, if registration was completed earlier, the registration number.

(c) *Conditions under which requests will be granted or denied*—(1) *General.* A request that meets the requirements of paragraph (b) of this section will generally be granted if the copyright deposit for which full term retention is requested has been continuously in the custody of the Copyright Office and the Library of Congress has not, by the date of the request, selected the copyright deposit for its collections.

(2) *Time of request.* The request for full term retention of a particular copyright deposit may be made at the time of deposit or at any time thereafter; however, the request will be granted only if at least one copy, phonorecord, or set of identifying material is in the custody of the Copyright Office at the time of the request. Where the request is made concurrent with the initial deposit of the work for registration, the requestor must submit one copy or phonorecord more than the number specified in § 202.20 of for the particular work.

(3) *One deposit retained.* The Copyright Office will retain no more than one copy, phonorecord, or set of identifying material for a given registered work.

(4) *Denial of request for full term retention.* The Copyright Office reserves the right to deny the request for full term retention where:

(i) The excessive size, fragility, or weight of the deposit would, in the sole discretion of the Register of Copyrights, constitute an unreasonable storage burden. The request may nevertheless be granted if, within 60 calendar days of the original denial of the request, the requestor pays the reasonable administrative costs, as fixed in the particular case by the Register of Copyrights, of preparing acceptable identifying materials for retention in lieu of the actual copyright deposit;

(ii) The Library of Congress has selected for its collections the single copyright deposit, or both, if two copies or phonorecords were deposited; or

(iii) Retention would result in a health or safety hazard, in the sole judgment of the Register of Copyrights. The request may nevertheless be granted if, within 60 calendar days of the original denial of the request, the requestor pays the reasonable administrative costs, as fixed in the particular case by the Register of Copyrights of preparing acceptable identifying materials for retention in lieu of the actual copyright deposit.

(d) *Form of copyright deposit.* If full term retention is granted, the Copyright Office will retain under its control the particular copyright deposit used to make registration for the work. Any deposit made on or after September 19, 1978, shall satisfy the requirements of §§ 202.20 and 202.21.

(e) *Fee for full term retention.* (1) Pursuant to section 708(a)(11) of title 17 of the United States Code, the Register of Copyrights has fixed the fee for full term retention, as prescribed in § 201.3(d), for each copyright deposit granted full term retention.

(2) A check or money order in the amount prescribed in § 201.3(d) payable to the Register of Copyrights, must be received in the Copyright Office within 60 calendar days from the date of mailing of the Copyright Office's notification to the requestor that full term retention has been granted for a particular copyright deposit.

(3) The Copyright Office will issue a receipt acknowledging payment of the fee and identifying the copyright deposit for which full term retention has been granted.

(f) *Selection by Library of Congress*—(1) *General.* All published copyright deposits are available for selection by the Library of Congress until the Copyright Office has formally granted a request for full term retention. Unless the requestor has deposited the additional copy or phonorecord specified by paragraph (c)(2) of this section, the Copyright Office will not process a request for full term retention submitted concurrent with a copyright registration application and deposit, until the Library of Congress has had a reasonable amount of time to make its selection determination.

(2) A request for full term retention made at the time of deposit of a published work does not affect the right of the Library to select one or both of the copyright deposits.

(3) If one copyright deposit is selected, the second deposit, if any, will be used for full term retention.

(4) If both copyright deposits are selected, or, in the case where the single deposit made is selected, full term retention will be granted only if the additional copy or phonorecord specified by paragraph (c)(2) was deposited.

(g) *Termination of full term storage.* Full term storage will cease 75 years after the date of publication of the work identified by the copyright deposit retained, and the copyright deposit will be disposed of in accordance with section 704, paragraphs (b) through (d), of title 17 of the United States Code.

[52 FR 28822, Aug. 4, 1987, as amended at 60 FR 34168, June 30, 1995; 63 FR 29139, May 28, 1998; 64 FR 29522, June 1, 1999; 64 FR 36575, July 7, 1999; 65 FR 39819, June 28, 2000; 73 FR 37839, July 2, 2008]

§ 202.24 Deposit of published electronic works available only online.

(a) Pursuant to authority under 17 U.S.C. 407(d), the Register of Copyrights may make written demand to deposit one complete copy or a phonorecord of an electronic work published in the United States and available only online upon the owner of copyright or of the exclusive right of publication in the work, under the following conditions:

(1) Demands may be made only for works in those categories identified in § 202.19(c)(5) of these regulations as being subject to demand.

(2) Demands may be made only for works published on or after February 24, 2010.

(3) The owner of copyright or of the exclusive right of publication must deposit the demanded work within three months of the date the demand notice is received.

(4) Copies or phonorecords deposited in response to a demand must be able to be accessed and reviewed by the Copyright Office, Library of Congress,

and the Library's authorized users on an ongoing basis.

(b) *Technical standards*. Technical standards for the transmission of copies of online-only works to the Copyright Office in response to a demand will be available on the Copyright Office website (*www.copyright.gov*).

(c) *Definitions*. (1) "Best edition" has the meaning set forth in § 202.19(b)(1) of these regulations.

(2) "Complete copy" has the meaning set forth in § 202.19(b)(2) of these regulations.

(3) "Electronic works" are works fixed and published solely in an electronic format.

(d) *Special relief*. (1) In the case of any demand made under paragraph (a) of this section, the Register of Copyrights may, after consultation with other appropriate officials of the Library of Congress and upon such conditions as the Register may determine after such consultation,

(i) Extend the time period provided in section 407(d) of Title 17;

(ii) Permit the deposit of incomplete copies or phonorecords; or

(iii) Permit the deposit of copies or phonorecords other than those normally comprising the best edition.

(2) Any decision as to whether to grant such special relief, and the conditions under which special relief is to be granted, shall be made by the Register of Copyrights after consultation with other appropriate officials of the Library of Congress, and shall be based upon the acquisition policies of the Library of Congress then in force.

(3) Requests for special relief under this section shall be made in writing to the Copyright Acquisitions Division, shall be signed by or on behalf of the owner of copyright or of the exclusive right of publication in the work, and shall set forth specific reasons why the request should be granted.

[75 FR 3869, Jan. 25, 2010]

APPENDIX A TO PART 202—TECHNICAL GUIDELINES REGARDING SOUND PHYSICAL CONDITION

To be considered a copy "of sound physical condition" within the meaning of 37 CFR 202.22(d)(5), a copy shall conform to all the technical guidelines set out in this Appendix.

A. *Physical Condition*. All portions of the copy that reproduce the transmission program must be:

1. *Clean:* Free from dirt, marks, spots, fungus, or other smudges, blotches, blemishes, or distortions;

2. *Undamaged:* Free from burns, blisters, tears, cuts, scratches, breaks, erasure, or other physical damage. The copies must also be free from:

(i) Any damage that interferes with performance from the tape or other reproduction, including physical damage resulting from earlier mechanical difficulties such as cassette jamming, breaks, tangles, or tape overflow; and

(ii) Any erasures, damage causing visual or audible defects or distortions or any material remaining from incomplete erasure of previously recorded works.

3. *Unspliced:* Free from splices in any part of the copy reproducing the transmission program, regardless of whether the splice involves the addition or deletion of material or is intended to repair a break or cut.

4. *Undeteriorated:* Free from any visual or aural deterioration resulting from aging or exposure to climatic, atmospheric, or other chemical or physical conditions, including heat, cold, humidity, electromagnetic fields, or radiation. The copy shall also be free from excessive brittleness or stretching, from any visible flaking of oxide from the tape base or other medium, and from other visible signs of physical deterioration or excessive wear.

B. *Physical Appurtenances of Deposit Copy*.

1. *Physical Housing of Video Tape Copy*. (a) In the case of video tape reproduced for reel-to-reel performance, the deposit copy shall consist of reels of uniform size and length. The length of the reels will depend on both the size of the tape and its running time (the last reel may be shorter). (b) In the case of video tape reproduced for cassette, cartridge, or similar performance, the tape drive mechanism shall be fully operable and free from any mechanical defects.

2. *"Leader" or Equivalent*. The copy, whether housed in reels, cassettes, or cartridges, shall have a leader segment both preceding the beginning and following the end of the recording.

C. *Visual and Aural Quality of Copy:*

1. *Visual Quality*. The copy should be equivalent to an evaluated first generation copy from an edited master tape and must reproduce a flawless and consistent electronic signal that meets industry standards for television screening.

2. *Aural Quality*. The sound channels or other portions must reproduce a flawless and consistent electronic signal without any audible defects.

(17 U.S.C. 407, 408, 702)

[48 FR 37209, Aug. 17, 1983, as amended at 60 FR 34168, June 30, 1995]

APPENDIX B TO PART 202—"BEST EDITION" OF PUBLISHED COPYRIGHTED WORKS FOR THE COLLECTIONS OF THE LIBRARY OF CONGRESS

The copyright law (title 17, United States Code) requires that copies or phonorecords deposited in the Copyright Office be of the "best edition" of the work. The law states that "The 'best edition' of a work is the edition, published in the United States at any time before the date of deposit, that the Library of Congress determines to be most suitable for its purposes." (For works first published only in a country other than the United States, the law requires the deposit of the best edition as first published.)

When two or more editions of the same version of a work have been published, the one of the highest quality is generally considered to be the best edition. In judging quality, the Library of Congress will adhere to the criteria set forth below in all but exceptional circumstances.

Where differences between editions represent variations in copyrightable content, each edition is a separate version and "best edition" standards based on such differences do not apply. Each such version is a separate work for the purpose of the copyright law.

The criteria to be applied in determining the best edition of each of several types of material are listed below in descending order of importance. In deciding between two editions, a criterion-by-criterion comparison should be made. The edition which first fails to satisfy a criterion is to be considered of inferior quality and will not be an acceptable deposit. Example: If a comparison is made between two hardbound editions of a book, one a trade edition printed on acid-free paper, and the other a specially bound edition printed on average paper, the former will be the best edition because the type of paper is a more important criterion than the binding.

Under regulations of the Copyright Office, potential depositors may request authorization to deposit copies or phonorecords of other than the best edition of a specific work (e.g., a microform rather than a printed edition of a serial), by requesting "special relief" from the deposit requirements. All requests for special relief should be in writing and should state the reason(s) why the applicant cannot send the required deposit and what the applicant wishes to submit instead of the required deposit.

I. Printed Textual Matter

A. Paper, Binding, and Packaging:

1. Archival-quality rather than less-permanent paper.
2. Hard cover rather than soft cover.
3. Library binding rather than commercial binding.
4. Trade edition rather than book club edition.
5. Sewn rather than glue-only binding.
6. Sewn or glued rather than stapled or spiral-bound.
7. Stapled rather than spiral-bound or plastic-bound.
8. Bound rather than looseleaf, except when future looseleaf insertions are to be issued. In the case of looseleaf materials, this includes the submission of all binders and indexes when they are part of the unit as published and offered for sale or distribution. Additionally, the regular and timely receipt of all appropriate looseleaf updates, supplements, and releases including supplemental binders issued to handle these expanded versions, is part of the requirement to properly maintain these publications.
9. Slip-cased rather than nonslip-cased.
10. With protective folders rather than without (for broadsides).
11. Rolled rather than folded (for broadsides).
12. With protective coatings rather than without (except broadsides, which should not be coated).

B. Rarity:

1. Special limited edition having the greatest number of special features.
2. Other limited edition rather than trade edition.
3. Special binding rather than trade binding.

C. Illustrations:

1. Illustrated rather than unillustrated.
2. Illustrations in color rather than black and white.

D. Special Features:

1. With thumb notches or index tabs rather than without.
2. With aids to use such as overlays and magnifiers rather than without.

E. Size:

1. Larger rather than smaller sizes. (Except that large-type editions for the partially-sighted are not required in place of editions employing type of more conventional size.)

II. Photographs

A. Size and finish, in descending order of preference:

1. The most widely distributed edition.
2. 8 × 10-inch glossy print.
3. Other size or finish.

B. Unmounted rather than mounted.

C. Archival-quality rather than less-permanent paper stock or printing process.

III. Motion Pictures

Film medium is considered a better quality than any other medium. The formats under "film" and "video formats" are listed in descending order of preference:

A. Film

1. Preprint material, by special arrangement

2. 70 mm positive print, if original production negative is greater than 35 mm
3. 35 mm positive prints
4. 16 mm positive prints
B. Video Formats
1. Betacam SP
2. Digital Beta (Digibeta)
3. DVD
4. VHS Cassette

IV. Other Graphic Matter

A. Paper and Printing:
1. Archival quality rather than less-permanent paper.
2. Color rather than black and white.
B. Size and Content:
1. Larger rather than smaller size.
2. In the case of cartographic works, editions with the greatest amount of information rather than those with less detail.
C. Rarity:
1. The most widely distributed edition rather than one of limited distribution.
2. In the case of a work published only in a limited, numbered edition, one copy outside the numbered series but otherwise identical.
3. A photographic reproduction of the original, by special arrangement only.
D. Text and Other Materials:
1. Works with annotations, accompanying tabular or textual matter, or other interpretative aids rather than those without them.
E. Binding and Packaging:
1. Bound rather than unbound.
2. If editions have different binding, apply the criteria in I.A.2–I.A.7, above.
3. Rolled rather than folded.
4. With protective coatings rather than without.

V. Phonorecords

A. Compact digital disc rather than a vinyl disc.
B. Vinyl disc rather than tape.
C. With special enclosures rather than without.
D. Open-reel rather than cartridge.
E. Cartridge rather than cassette.
F. Quadraphonic rather than stereophonic.
G. True stereophonic rather than monaural.
H. Monaural rather than electronically rechanneled stereo.

VI. Musical Compositions

A. Fullness of Score:
1. *Vocal music:*
a. With orchestral accompaniment—
i. Full score and parts, if any, rather than conductor's score and parts, if any. (In cases of compositions published only by rental, lease, or lending, this requirement is reduced to full score only.)
ii. Conductor's score and parts, if any, rather than condensed score and parts, if any. (In cases of compositions published only by rental, lease, or lending, this requirement is reduced to conductor's score only.)
b. Unaccompanied: Open score (each part on separate staff) rather than closed score (all parts condensed to two staves).
2. *Instrumental music:*
a. Full score and parts, if any, rather than conductor's score and parts, if any. (In cases of compositions published only by rental, lease, or lending, this requirement is reduced to full score only.)
b. Conductor's score and parts, if any, rather than condensed score and parts, if any. (In cases of compositions published only by rental, lease, or lending, this requirement is reduced to conductor's score only.)
B. Printing and Paper:
1. Archival-quality rather than less-permanent paper.
C. Binding and Packaging:
1. Special limited editions rather than trade editions.
2. Bound rather than unbound.
3. If editions have different binding, apply the criteria in I.A.2–I.A.12, above.
4. With protective folders rather than without.

VII. Microforms

A. Related Materials:
1. With indexes, study guides, or other printed matter rather than without.
B. Permanence and Appearance:
1. Silver halide rather than any other emulsion.
2. Positive rather than negative.
3. Color rather than black and white.
C. Format (newspapers and newspaper-formatted serials):
1. Reel microfilm rather than any other microform.
D. Format (all other materials):
1. Microfiche rather than reel microfilm.
2. Reel microfilm rather than microform cassetes.
3. Microfilm cassettes rather than micro-opaque prints.
E. Size:
1. 35 mm rather than 16 mm.

VIII. Machine-Readable Copies

A. Computer Programs
1. With documents and other accompanying material rather than without.
2. Not copy-protected rather than copy-protected (if copy-protected then with a backup copy of the disk(s)).
3. *Format:*
a. PC-DOS or MS-DOS (or other IBM compatible formats, such as XENIX):
(i) 5¼″ Diskette(s).
(ii) 3½″ Diskette(s).
(iii) Optical media, such as CD-ROM—best edition should adhere to prevailing NISO standards.

b. Apple Macintosh:

(i) 3½″ Diskette(s).

(ii) Optical media, such as CD-ROM—best edition should adhere to prevailing NISO standards.

B. Computerized Information Works, Including Statistical Compendia, Serials, or Reference Works:

1. With documentation and other accompanying material rather than without.

2. With best edition of accompanying program rather than without.

3. Not copy-protected rather than copy-protected (if copy-protected then with a backup copy of the disk(s)).

4. *Format*

a. PC-DOS or MS-DOS (or other IBM compatible formats, such as XENIX):

(i) Optical media, such as CD-ROM—best edition should adhere to prevailing NISO standards.

(ii) 5¼″ Diskette(s).

(iii) 3½″ Diskette(s).

b. Apple Macintosh:

(i) Optical media, such as CD-ROM—best edition should adhere to prevailing NISO standards.

(ii) 3½″ Diskette(s).

IX. Electronic Works Published in the United States and Available Only Online

For all deposits, UTF–8 encoding is preferred to ASCII encoding and other non UTF–8 encodings for non–Latin character sets in all categories below.

A. Electronic Serials

1. Content Format

a. Level 1: Serials-specific structured/markup format:

(i) Content compliant with the NLM Journal Archiving (XML) Document Type Definition (DTD), with presentation stylesheet(s), rather than without.

(ii) Other widely used serials or journal XML DTDs/schemas, with presentation stylesheet(s), rather than without.

(iii) Proprietary XML format for serials or journals (with documentation), with DTD/schema and presentation stylesheet(s), rather than without.

b. Level 2: Page-oriented rendition:

(i) PDF/A (Portable Document Format/Archival; compliant with ISO 19005).

(ii) PDF (Portable Document Format, with searchable text, rather than without).

c. Level 3: Other formats:

(i) XHTML/HTML, as made available online, with presentation stylesheets(s), rather than without.

(ii) XML (widely used, publicly documented XML–based word-processing formats, e.g., ODF/OpenDocument Format, Office OpenXML), with presentation stylesheets(s), if appropriate, rather than without.

(iii) Plain text.

(iv) Other formats (e.g., proprietary word processing or page layout formats).

2. Metadata Elements:

If it has already been gathered and is available, descriptive data (metadata) as described below should accompany the deposited material.

a. Title level metadata: serial or journal title, ISSN, publisher, frequency, place of publication.

b. Article level metadata, as relevant/applicable: volume(s), number(s), issue dates(s), article title(s), article author(s), article identifier (DOI, etc.).

c. With other descriptive metadata (e.g., subject heading(s), descriptor(s), abstract(s)), rather than without.

3. Technological measures that control access to or use of the work should be removed.

X. Works Existing in More Than One Medium

Editions are listed below in descending order of preference.

A. Newspapers, dissertations and theses, newspaper-formatted serials:

1. Microform.

2. Printed matter.

B. All other materials:

1. Printed matter.

2. Microform.

3. Phonorecord.

[54 FR 42299, Oct. 16, 1989, as amended at 62 FR 51603, Oct. 2, 1997; 69 FR 8822, Feb. 26, 2004; 75 FR 3869, Jan. 25, 2010]

PART 203—FREEDOM OF INFORMATION ACT: POLICIES AND PROCEDURES

ORGANIZATION

PROCEDURES

AVAILABILITY OF INFORMATION

CHARGES FOR SEARCH FOR REPRODUCTION

AUTHORITY: 17 U.S.C 702; 5 U.S.C 552, as amended.

SOURCE: 43 FR 774, Jan. 4, 1978, unless otherwise noted.

ORGANIZATION

§ 203.1 General.

This information is furnished for the guidance of the public and in compliance with the requirements of section 552 of title 5, United States Code, as amended.

[43 FR 774, Jan. 4, 1978, as amended at 66 FR 34373, June 28, 2001]

§ 203.2 Authority and functions.

(a) The administration of the copyright law was entrusted to the Library of Congress by an act of Congress in 1870, and the Copyright Office has been a separate department of the Library since 1897. The statutory functions of the Copyright Office are contained in and carried out in accordance with the Copyright Act. Pub. L. 94–553 (90 Stat. 2541–2602), 17 U.S.C. 101–1101.

[43 FR 774, Jan. 4, 1978, as amended at 62 FR 35421, July 1, 1997]

§ 203.3 Organization.

(a) *In general.* The Office of the Register exercises overall direction of the work of the Copyright Office, including work in conjunction with copyright legislation, litigation and promulgation of copyright regulations. The Office of the Register of Copyrights includes the legal, administrative, and automation staff.

(b) The Copyright Office Chief of Operations has oversight of the operating divisions of the Copyright Office. The operating divisions are:

(1) The Receipt, Analysis and Control Division, which receives incoming materials, dispatches outgoing materials and establishes control over fiscal accounts.

(2) The Registration Program which examines all applications and material presented to the Copyright Office for registration of original and renewal copyright claims, and which determines whether the material deposited constitutes copyrightable subject matter and whether the other legal and formal requirements of title 17 have been met.

(3) The Registration Program, which prepares the bibliographic description of all copyrighted works registered in the Copyright Office, including the recording of legal facts of copyright pertaining to each work, in an on-line database in which copyright records can be searched; and which also examines and catalogs in an on-line database documents submitted for recordation.

(4) The Information and Records Division, which provides a national copyright information service through the Copyright Information Section, educates the public on the copyright law, issues and distributes information materials, responds to reference requests regarding copyright matters, prepares search reports based upon copyright records, certifies copies of legal documents concerned with copyright, and maintains liaison with the United States Customs Service, the Department of the Treasury, and the United States Postal Service on certain matters. The Information and Records Division also develops, services, stores, and preserves the official records and catalogs of the Copyright Office, including applications for registration, historical records, and materials deposited for copyright registration that are not selected by the Library of Congress for addition to its collections.

(5) The Licensing Division, which implements the sections of the Copyright Act dealing with secondary transmissions of radio and television programs, compulsory licenses for making and distributing phonorecords of nondramatic musical, pictorial, graphic, and sculptural works in connection with noncommercial broadcasting. The Licensing Division is in charge of collecting the statutory royalties and distributing these royalties based on either a voluntary agreement among the interested parties or a determination of the Copyright Royalty Board.

(c) The Copyright General Counsel is a principal legal officer of the Office. The General Counsel has overall supervisory responsibility for the legal staff and primary responsibility for providing liaison on legal matters between the Office and the Congress, the Department of Justice and other agencies of Government, the courts, the legal community, and a wide range of interests affected by the copyright law. The

Copyright General Counsel has responsibility for overseeing all functions related to the administration of the compulsory licenses including oversight of the Copyright Royalty Board.

(d) The Associate Register of Copyrights for International Affairs and Policy is a principal legal adviser to the Register with primary responsibility for the international aspects of copyright protection, as well as legislative and policy matters.

(e) The Office has no field organization.

(f) The Office is located in The James Madison Memorial Building of the Library of Congress, 1st and Independence Avenue, SE, Washington, DC. 20559–6000. The Public Information Office is located in Room LM–401. Its hours are 8:30 a.m. to 5 p.m., Monday through Friday except legal holidays. The phone number of the Public Information Office is (202) 707-3000. Informational material regarding the copyright law, the registration process, fees, and related information about the Copyright Office and its functions may be obtained free of charge from the Public Information Office upon request.

(g) All Copyright Office forms may be obtained free of charge from the Public Information Office or by calling the Copyright Office Hotline anytime day or night at (202) 707-9100.

(h) The Copyright Office maintains an "electronic reading room" by making available certain documents and records on its World Wide Web page and by providing access to documents that affect the public in electronic format pursuant to 5 USC 552(a)(2). Copyright Office records in machine-readable form cataloged from January 1, 1978, to the present, including registration information and recorded documents, are available on the Internet. Frequently requested Copyright Office circulars, announcements, and recently proposed as well as final regulations are available on-line. The address for the Copyright Office's home page is: *http://www.loc.gov/copyright;* information may also be accessed by connecting to the Library of Congress' home page on the World Wide Web. The address is: *http://www.loc.gov.* Other Copyright Office documents may be provided on disk when so requested.

[60 FR 34168, June 30, 1995, as amended at 62 FR 55742, Oct. 28, 1997; 64 FR 36575, July 7, 1999; 65 FR 39819, June 28, 2000; 66 FR 34373, June 28, 2001; 73 FR 37839, July 2, 2008; 76 FR 27898, May 13, 2011]

PROCEDURES

§ 203.4 Methods of operation.

(a) In accordance with section 552(a)(2) of the Freedom of Information Act, the Copyright Office makes available for public inspection and copying records of copyright registrations and of final refusals to register claims to copyright; statements of policy and interpretations which have been adopted but are not published in the FEDERAL REGISTER; and administrative staff manuals and instructions to the staff that affect a member of the public.

(b) The Copyright Office also maintains and makes available for public inspection and copying current indexes providing identifying information as to matters issued, adopted, or promulgated after July 4, 1967, that are within the scope of 5 U.S.C. 552(a)(2). The Copyright Office has determined that publication of these indexes is unnecessary and impractical. Copies of the indexes will be provided to any member of the public upon request at the cost of reproduction.

(c) The material and indexes referred to in paragraphs (a) and (b) of this section are available for public inspection and copying at the Public Information Office of the Copyright Office, Room LM–401, The James Madison Memorial Building of the Library of Congress, 1st and Independence Avenue, SE, Washington, DC, between the hours of 8:30 a.m. and 5 p.m., Monday through Friday, except legal holidays.

(d) The Supervisory Copyright Information Specialist is responsible for responding to all initial requests submitted under the Freedom of Information Act. Individuals desiring to obtain access to Copyright Office information under the Act should make a written request to that effect either by mail to the Supervisory Copyright Information

Specialist, Information and Publications Section, Information and Reference Division, Copyright Office, Library of Congress, Washington, DC 20559–6000, or in person between the hours of 8:30 a.m. and 5 p.m. on any working day except legal holidays at Room LM–401, The James Madison Memorial Building, 1st and Independence Avenue, SE, Washington, DC. If a request is made by mail, both the request and the envelope containing it should be plainly marked Freedom of Information Act Request. Failure to so mark a mailed request may delay the Office response.

(e) Records must be reasonably described. A request reasonably describes records if it enables the Office to identify the records requested by any process that is not unreasonably burdensome or disruptive of Office operations. The Supervisory Copyright Information Specialist will, upon request, aid members of the public to formulate their requests in such a manner as to enable the Office to respond effectively and reduce search costs for the requester.

(f) The Office will respond to all properly marked mailed requests and all personally delivered written requests for records within twenty (20) working days of receipt by the Supervisory Copyright Information Specialist. Inquiries should be mailed to: Copyright Office, GC/I&R, P.O. Box 70400, Washington, DC 20024. If hand delivered, materials should go to: Copyright Public Information Office, LM 401, James Madison Memorial Building, Library of Congress, 101 Independence Avenue, SE, Washington, DC. Office hours are from 8:30 a.m. to 5:00 p.m., Monday through Friday, excluding holidays. If it is determined that an extension of time greater than ten (10) working days is necessary to respond to a request due to unusual circumstances, as defined in paragraph (i) of this section, the Supervisory Copyright Information Specialist shall so notify the requester and give the requester the opportunity to:

(1) Limit the scope of the request so that it may be processed within twenty (20) working days, or

(2) Arrange with the Office an alternative time frame for processing the request or a modified request. If a request is denied, the written notification will include the basis for the denial, names of all individuals who participated in the determination, and procedures available to appeal the determination. If a requester wishes to appeal a denial of some or all of his or her request for information, he or she must make an appeal in writing within 30 calendar days of the date of the Office's denial. The request should be directed to the General Counsel of the United States Copyright Office at: Copyright GC/I&R, P.O. Box 70400, Washington, DC 20024. The appeal should be clearly labeled 'Freedom of Information Act Appeal'.

(g) The appeal shall include a statement explaining the basis for the appeal. Determinations of appeals will be set forth in writing and signed by the General Counsel or his or her delegate within 20 working days. If, on appeal, the denial is in whole or in part upheld, the written determination will include the basis for the appeal denial and will also contain a notification of the provisions for judicial review and the names of the persons who participated in the determination.

(h) In unusual circumstances, the General Counsel may extend the time limits prescribed in paragraphs (f) and (g) of this section for not more than 10 working days. The extension period may be split between the initial request and the appeal but the total period of extension shall not exceed 10 working days. Extensions will be by written notice to the person making the request. The Copyright Office will advise the requester of the reasons for the extension and the date the determination is expected. As used in this paragraph "unusual circumstances" means:

(1) The need to search for and collect the requested records from establishments that are physically separate from the office processing the request;

(2) The need to search for, collect, and examine a voluminous amount of separate and distinct records which are demanded in a single request; or

(3) The need for consultation, which shall be conducted with all practical speed, with another agency having a

substantial interest in the determination of the request or among two or more components of the Copyright Office which have a substantial subject matter interest therein.

(i) The Supervisory Copyright Information Specialist will consider requests for expedited processing of requests in cases where the requester demonstrates a compelling need for such processing. The term "compelling need" means:

(1) That a failure to obtain requested records on an expedited basis could reasonably be expected to pose an imminent threat to the life or physical safety of an individual; or

(2) With respect to a request made by a person primarily engaged in disseminating information, urgency to inform the public concerning actual or alleged Federal Government activity. Requesters for expedited processing must include in their requests a statement setting forth the basis for the claim that a "compelling need" exists for the requested information, certified by the requester to be true and correct to the best of his or her knowledge and belief. The Office will determine whether to grant a request for expedited processing and will notify the requester of such determination within ten (10) days of receipt of the request. If a request for expedited processing is approved, documents responsive to the request will be processed as soon as is practicable. Denials of requests for expedited processing may be appealed to the Office of the General Counsel.

[43 FR 774, Jan. 4, 1978, as amended at 47 FR 36820, Aug. 24, 1982; 62 FR 55742, Oct. 28, 1997; 63 FR 1927, Jan 13, 1998; 64 FR 36575, July 7, 1999; 65 FR 39819, June 28, 2000; 66 FR 34373, June 28, 2001; 73 FR 37839, July 2, 2008]

AVAILABILITY OF INFORMATION

§ 203.5 Inspection and copying.

(a) When a request for information has been approved, the person making the request may make an appointment to inspect or copy the materials requested during regular business hours by writing or telephoning the Supervisory Copyright Information Specialist at the address or telephone number listed in § 203.4(d). Such material may be copied manually without charge, and reasonable facilities are available in the Public Information Office for that purpose. Also, copies of individual pages of such materials will be made available at the price per page specified in paragraphs (a) and (b) of § 203.6.

CHARGES FOR SEARCH FOR REPRODUCTION

§ 203.6 Schedule of fees and methods of payment for services rendered.

(a) *General.* The fee schedule of this section does not apply with respect to the charging of fees for those records for which the Copyright Act of 1976, title 17 of the United States Code (Pub. L. 94–553) requires a fee to be charged. The fees required to be charged are contained in § 201.3 of this chapter, or have been established by the Register of Copyrights or Library of Congress pursuant to the requirements of that section. If the Copyright Office receives a request for copies or other services involving the public records or indexes of the Office or for copies of deposited articles for which a fee is required to be charged, the Office will notify the requester of the procedure established to obtain the copies or services and the amount of the chargeable fees. Fees pursuant to title 5 U.S.C., section 552 for all other services not involving the public records of the Copyright Office will be assessed according to the schedule in paragraph (b) of this section. All fees so assessed shall be charged to the requester, except where the charge is limited under paragraph (c) of this section or where a waiver or reduction of fees is granted under paragraph (d) of this section. Requests by record subjects asking for copies of records about themseleves shall be processed under the Privacy Act fee schedule found in 37 CFR 204.6.

(b) *FOIA requests.* In responding to requests under this part the following fees shall be assessed, unless a waiver or reduction in fees has been granted pursuant to paragraph (d) of this section:

(1) For copies of certificates of copyright registration, $25.

(2) For copies of all other Copyright Office records not otherwise provided for in this section a minimum fee of

$15.00 for up to 15 pages and $.50 per page over 15.

(3) For each hour or fraction of an hour spent in searching for a requested record, $65, except that no search fee shall be assessed with respect to requests by educational institutions, non-commercial scientific institutions, and representatives of the news media. Search fees shall be assessed with respect to all other requests, subject to the limitations of paragraph (c) of this section. Fees may be assessed for time spent searching even if the search fails to locate any responsive records or where the records located are subsequently determined to be entirely exempt from disclosure.

(4) For the issuance of any certification, $65 for each hour or fraction of an hour consumed in respect thereto.

(5) Other costs incurred by the Copyright Office in fulfilling a request will be chargeable at the actual cost of the Office.

(6) For computer searches of records, which may be undertaken through the use of existing programing, the actual direct costs of conducting the search including the cost of operating a central processing unit for that portion of operating time that is directly attributable to searching for records responsive to a request, as well as the direct costs of operator/programmer salary apportionable to search (at no less than $65 per hour or fraction thereof).

(7) No review fees will be charged for time spent in resolving legal or policy issues affecting access to Office records. No charge will be made for the time involved in examining records to determine whether some or all such records may be withheld.

(c) *Fee limitations.* The following limitations on fees shall apply:

(1) Except for requesters seeking records for commercial use the following will be provided without charge—

(i) The first 100 pages of duplication (or its cost equivalent), and

(ii) The first two hours of search (or its cost equivalent).

(2) No fees will be charged for ordinary packaging and mailing costs.

(d) *Waiver or reduction of fees.* (1) Records responsive to a request under 5 U.S.C. 552 shall be furnished without charge or at a charge reduced below that established under paragraph (b) of this section where the Office determines, based upon information provided by a requester in support of a fee waiver request or otherwise made known to the Office, that disclosure of the requested information is in the public interest because it is likely to contribute significantly to public understanding of the operations or activities of the government and is not primarily in the commercial interest of the requester. Requests for a waiver or reduction of fees shall be considered on a case-by-case basis.

(2) In order to determine whether the first fee waiver requirement is met—i.e., that disclosure of the requested information is in the public interest because it is likely to contribute significantly to public understanding of the operations or activities of the government—the Office shall consider the following four factors in sequence:

(i) The subject of the request: Whether the subject of the requested records concerns "the operations or activities of the government."

(ii) The informative value of the information to be disclosed: Whether the disclosure is "likely to contribute" to an understanding of government operations or activities.

(iii) The contribution to an understanding of the subject by the public likely to result from disclosures: Whether disclosure of the requested information will contribute to "public understanding."

(iv) The significance of the contribution to public understanding: Whether the disclosure is likely to contribute "significantly" to public understanding of government operations or activities.

(3) In order to determine whether the second fee waiver requirement is met—i.e., that disclosure of the requested information is not primarily in the commercial interest of the requester—the Office shall consider the following two factors in sequence:

(i) The existence and magnitude of a commercial interest: Whether the requester has a commercial interest that would be furthered by the requested disclosure.

(ii) The primary interest in disclosure: Whether the magnitude of the identified commercial interest of the requester is sufficiently large, in comparison with the public interest in disclosure, that disclosure is "primarily in the commercial interest of the requester."

(4) Where only a portion of the requested records satisfies both of the requirements for a waiver or reduction of fees under this paragraph, a waiver or reduction shall be granted only as to that portion.

(e) *Notice of anticipated fees in excess of $25.00.* Where the Office determines or estimates that the fees to be assessed under this section may amoun t to more than $25.00, the Office shall notify the requester as soon as praticable of the actual or estimated amount of the fees, unless the requester has indicated in advance his willingness to pay fees as high as those anticipated. (If only a portion of the fee can be estimated readily, the Office shall advise the requester that the estimated fee may be only a portion of the total fee.) In cases where a requester has been notified that actual or estimated fees may amount to more than $25.00, the requests will be deemed not to have been received until the requester has agreed to pay the anticipated total fee. A notice to a requester pursuant to this paragraph shall offer him the opportunity to confer with Copyright Office personnel in order to reformulate his request to meet his needs at a lower cost.

(f) *Aggregation of requests.* Where the Office reasonably believes that a requester or a group of requesters acting in concert is attempting to divide a request into a series of requests for the purpose of evading the assessment of fees, the Office may aggregate any such requests and charge accordingly.

(g) *Advance payments.* (1) Where the Office estimates that a total fee to be assessed under this section is likely to exceed $250.00, it may require the requester to make an advance payment of an amount up to the entire estimated fee before beginning to process the request, except where it receives a satisfactory assurance of full payment from a requester with a history of prompt payment.

(2) Where a requester has previously failed to pay a records access fee within 30 days of the date of billing, the Office may require the requester to pay the full amount owed, plus any applicable interest (as provided for in paragraph (h) of this section), and to make an advance payment of the full amount of any estimated fee before the Office begins to process a new request or continues to process a pending request from that requester.

(3) For requests other than those described in paragraphs (g)(1) and (g)(2) of this section, the Office shall not require the requester to make an advance payment, *i.e.*, a payment made before work is commenced or continued on a request. Payment owed for work already completed is not an advance payment.

(h) *Charging interest.* The Office may assess interest charges on an unpaid bill starting on the 31st day following the day on which the bill was sent to the requester. Once a fee payment has been received by a component of the Office, even if not processed, the accrual of interest shall be stayed. Interest charges shall be assessed at the rate prescribed in section 3717 of title 31 U.S.C. and shall accrue from the date of billing.

[53 FR 8456, Mar. 15, 1988, as amended at 56 FR 59885, Nov. 26, 1991; 62 FR 55742, Oct. 28, 1997; 63 FR 29139, May 28, 1998; 64 FR 29522, June 1, 1999; 66 FR 34373, June 28, 2001]

PART 204—PRIVACY ACT: POLICIES AND PROCEDURES

Sec.

AUTHORITY: 17 U.S.C. 702; 5 U.S.C. 552(a).

SOURCE: 43 FR 776, Jan. 4, 1978, unless otherwise noted.

§ 204.1 Purposes and scope.

The purposes of these regulations are:

(a) The establishment of procedures by which an individual can determine if the Copyright Office maintains a system of records in which there is a record pertaining to the individual; and

(b) The establishment of procedures by which an individual may gain access to a record or information maintained on that individual and have such record or information disclosed for the purpose of review, copying, correction, or amendment.

§ 204.2 Definitions.

For purposes of this part:

(a) The term *individual* means a citizen of the United States or an alien lawfully admitted for permanent residence;

(b) The term *maintain* includes maintain, collect, use, or disseminate;

(c) The term *record* means any item, collection, or grouping of information about an individual that is maintained by an agency, including, but not limited to, his education, financial transactions, medical history, and criminal or employment history, and that contains his or her name, or the identifying number, symbol, or other identifying particular assigned to the individual, such as a finger or voice print or a photograph;

(d) The term *system of records* means a group of any records under the control of any agency from which information is retrieved by the name of the individual; and

(e) The term *routine use* means, with respect to the disclosure of a record, the use of such record for a purpose which is compatible with the purpose for which it was collected.

§ 204.3 General policy.

The Copyright Office serves primarily as an office of public record. Section 705 of title 17, United States Code, requires the Copyright Office to open for public inspection all records of copyright deposits, registrations, recordations, and other actions taken under title 17. Therefore, a routine use of all Copyright Office systems of records created under section 705 of title 17 is disclosure to the public. All Copyright Office systems of records created under section 705 of title 17 are also available for public copying as required by section 706(a), with the exception of copyright deposits, whose reproduction is governed by section 706(b) and the regulations issued under that section. In addition to the records mandated by section 705 of title 17, the Copyright Office maintains other systems of records which are necessary for the Office effectively to carry out its mission. These systems of records are routinely consulted and otherwise used by Copyright Office employees in the performance of their duties. The Copyright Office will not sell, rent, or otherwise make publicly available any mailing list prepared by the Office.

[47 FR 36821, Aug. 24, 1982]

§ 204.4 Procedure for notification of the existence of records pertaining to individuals.

(a) The Copyright Office will publish in the FEDERAL REGISTER, upon the establishment or revision of the system of records, notices of all Copyright Office systems of records subject to the Privacy Act, as provided by 5 U.S.C., section 552a(e)(4). Individuals desiring to know if a Copyright Office system of records contains a record pertaining to them should submit a written request to that effect either by mail to the Supervisory Copyright Information Specialist, Copyright Information Section, Copyright GC/I&R, P.O. Box 70400,, Washington, DC 20024, or in person between the hours of 8:30 a.m. and 5 p.m. on any working day except legal holidays at Room LM–401, The James Madison Memorial Building, 1st and Independence Avenue, SE, Washington, DC.

(b) The written request should identify clearly the system of records which is the subject of inquiry, by reference, whenever possible, to the system number and title as given in the notices of systems of records in the FEDERAL REGISTER. Both the written request and the envelope carrying it should be plainly marked "Privacy Act Request." Failure to so mark the request may delay the Office response.

(c) The Office will acknowledge all properly marked requests made by individuals wishing to gain access to view or copy their records or any information pertaining to the individual, within a reasonable time. The Office will acknowledge in writing an individual's request to amend a record pertaining to him or her within ten business days.

(d) Since all Copyright Office Records created under section 705 of title 17 are open to public inspection, no identity verification is necessary for individuals who wish to know whether a system of records created under section 705 pertains to them.

[43 FR 776, Jan. 4, 1978, as amended at 47 FR 36821, Aug. 24, 1982; 50 FR 697, Aug. 14, 1985; 60 FR 34169, June 30, 1995; 64 FR 36575, July 7, 1999; 65 FR 39820, June 28, 2000; 73 FR 37839, July 2, 2008]

§204.5 Procedures for requesting access to records.

(a) Individuals desiring to obtain access to Copyright Office information pertaining to them in a system of records other than those created under section 705 of title 17 should make a written request, signed by themselves or their duly authorized agent, to that effect either by mail to the Supervisory Copyright Information Specialist, Copyright Information Section, Copyright GC/I&R, P.O. Box 70400, Washington, DC 20024, or in person between the hours of 8:30 a.m. and 5 p.m. on any working day except legal holidays at Room LM–401, The James Madison Memorial Building, 1st and Independence Avenue, SE, Washington, DC.

(b) The written request should identify clearly the system of records which is the subject of inquiry, by reference, whenever possible, to the system number and title as given in the notices of systems of records in the FEDERAL REGISTER. Both the written request and the envelope carrying it should be plainly marked "Privacy Act Request." Failure to so mark the request may delay the Office response.

(c) The Office will acknowledge all properly marked requests within 20 working days of receipt; and will notify the requester within 30 working days of receipt when and where access to the record will be granted. If the individual requested a copy of the record, the copy will accompany such notification.

[43 FR 776, Jan. 4, 1978, as amended at 47 FR 36821, Aug. 24, 1982; 60 FR 34169, June 30, 1995; 64 FR 36575, July 7, 1999; 65 FR 39820, June 28, 2000; 73 FR 37839, July 2, 2008]

§204.6 Fees.

(a) The Copyright Office will provide, free of charge, one copy to an individual of any record pertaining to that individual contained in a Copyright Office system of records, except where the request is for a copy of a record for which a specific fee is required and identified in §201.3 of this chapter, in which case that fee shall be charged. For additional copies of records not covered by section 708 the fee will be a minimum of $15.00 for up to 15 pages and $.50 per page over 15. The Office will require prepayment of fees estimated to exceed $25.00 and will remit any excess paid or bill an additional amount according to the differences between the final fee charged and the amount prepaid. When prepayment is required, a request is not deemed "received" until prepayment has been made.

(b) The Copyright Office may waive the fee requirement whenever it determines that such waiver would be in the public interest.

[43 FR 776, Jan. 4, 1978, as amended at 47 FR 36821, Aug. 24, 1982; 56 FR 59886, Nov. 26, 1991; 63 FR 29139, May 28, 1998; 64 FR 29522, June 1, 1999]

§204.7 Request for correction or amendment of records.

(a) Any individual may request the correction or amendment of a record pertaining to her or him. With respect to an error in a copyright registration, the procedure for correction and fee chargeable is governed by section 408(d) of title 17 of the United States Code, and the regulations issued as authorized by that section. With respect to an error in any other record, the request shall be in writing and delivered either by mail addressed to the Supervisory Copyright Information Specialist, Copyright Information Section, Copyright GC/I&R, P.O. Box 70400, Washington, DC 20024, or in person between the hours of 8:30 a.m. and 5 p.m. on any working day except legal holidays, at

Room LM–401, The James Madison Memorial Building, 1st and Independence Avenue, SE, Washington, DC. The request shall explain why the individual believes the record to be incomplete, inaccurate, irrelevant, or untimely.

(b) With respect to an error in a copyright registration, the time limit for Office response to requests for correction is governed by section 408(d) of Pub. L. 94–553, and the regulations issued as authorized by that section. With respect to other requests for correction or amendment of records, the Office will respond within ten working days indicating to the requester that the requested correction or amendment has been made or that it has been refused. If the requested correction or amendment is refused, the Office response will indicate the reason for the refusal and the procedure available to the individual to appeal the refusal.

[43 FR 776, Jan. 4, 1978, as amended at 47 FR 36821, Aug. 24, 1982; 60 FR 34169, June 30, 1995; 64 FR 36575, July 7, 1999; 65 FR 39820, June 28, 2000; 73 FR 37839, July 2, 2008]

§ 204.8 Appeal of refusal to correct or amend an individual's record.

(a) An individual who disagrees with a refusal of the Copyright Office to amend his or her record may request a review of the denial. The decision will be made within 30 business days, unless the Office can demonstrate good cause for extending the 30 day period. If the requestor is dissatisfied with the agency's final determination, the individual may bring a civil action against the Office in the appropriate United States district court. appeal the refusal to correct or amend a record pertaining to the individual. The individual should submit a written appeal to the General Counsel, Copyright Office, Copyright GC/I&R, P.O. Box 70400, Washington, DC 20024. Appeals, and the envelopes containing them, should be plainly marked "Privacy Act Appeal." Failure to so mark the appeal may delay the Copyright Office General Counsel's response. An appeal should contain a copy of the request for amendment or correction and a copy of the record alleged to be untimely, inaccurate, incomplete or irrelevant.

(b) The General Counsel will issue a written decision granting or denying the appeal within 30 working days after receipt of the appeal unless, after showing good cause, the General Counsel extends the 30 day period. If the appeal is granted, the requested amendment or correction will be made promptly. If the appeal is denied, in whole or part, the General Counsel's decision will set forth reasons for the denial. Additionally, the decision will advise the requester that he or she has the right to file with the Copyright Office a concise statement of his or her reasons for disagreeing with the refusal to amend the record and that such statement will be attached to the requester's record and included in any future disclosure of such record.

[43 FR 776, Jan. 4, 1978, as amended at 64 FR 36575, July 7, 1999; 65 FR 39820, June 28, 2000; 65 FR 48914, Aug. 10, 2000; 66 FR 34373, June 28, 2001; 73 FR 37840, July 2, 2008]

§ 204.9 Judicial review.

Within two years of the receipt of a final adverse administrative determination, an individual may seek judicial review of that determination as provided in 5 U.S.C. 552a(g)(1).

PART 205—LEGAL PROCESSES

Subpart A—General Provisions

Subpart B—Service of Process

Subpart C—Testimony by Employees and Production of Documents in Legal Proceedings in Which the Office is Not a Party

AUTHORITY: 17 U.S.C. 702.

SOURCE: 69 FR 39334, June 30, 2004, unless otherwise noted.

Subpart A—General Provisions

§205.1 Definitions.

For the purpose of this part:

Demand means an order, subpoena or any other request for documents or testimony for use in a legal proceeding.

Document means any record or paper held by the Copyright Office, including, without limitation, official letters, deposits, recordations, registrations, publications, or other material submitted in connection with a claim for registration of a copyrighted work.

Employee means any current or former officer or employee of the Copyright Office, as well as any individual subject to the jurisdiction, supervision, or control of the Copyright Office.

General Counsel, unless otherwise specified, means the General Counsel of the Copyright Office or his or her designee.

Legal proceeding means any pretrial, trial, and post trial stages of existing or reasonably anticipated judicial or administrative actions, hearings, investigations, or similar proceedings before courts, commissions, boards or other tribunals, foreign or domestic. This phrase includes all phases of discovery as well as responses to formal or informal requests by attorneys or others involved in legal proceedings. This phrase also includes state court proceedings (including grand jury proceedings) and any other state or local legislative and administrative proceedings.

Office means the Copyright Office, including any division, section, or operating unit within the Copyright Office.

Official business means the authorized business of the Copyright Office.

Testimony means a statement in any form, including a personal appearance before a court or other legal tribunal, an interview, a deposition, an affidavit or declaration under penalty of perjury pursuant to 28 U.S.C. 1746, a telephonic, televised, or videotaped statement or any response given during discovery or similar proceeding, which response would involve more than the production of documents, including a declaration under 35 U.S.C. 25 or a declaration under penalty of perjury pursuant to 28 U.S.C. 1746.

United States means the Federal Government, its departments and agencies, individuals acting on behalf of the Federal Government, and parties to the extent they are represented by the United States.

§205.2 Address for mail and service; telephone number.

(a) Mail under this part should be addressed to the General Counsel, Copyright GC/I&R, P.O. Box 70400, Washington, DC 20024–0400.

(b) Service by hand shall be made upon an authorized person from 8:30 a.m. to 5 p.m., Monday through Friday in the Copyright Information Section, U.S. Copyright Office, Library of Congress, James Madison Memorial Building, Room LM–401, 101 Independence Avenue, SE., Washington, DC. Persons authorized to accept service of process are the General Counsel of the Copyright Office and his or her designees.

(c) The Office of the General Counsel may be reached by telephone during normal business hours specified in paragraph (b) of this section at 202–707–8380.

[69 FR 39334, June 30, 2004, as amended at 73 FR 37840, July 2, 2008]

§205.3 Waiver of rules.

In extraordinary situations, when the interest of justice requires, the General Counsel may waive or suspend the rules of this part, *sua sponte* or on petition of an interested party, subject to such requirements as the General Counsel may impose on the parties. However, the inclusion of certain legal processes within the scope of these rules, e.g., state legal proceedings, does not represent a waiver of any claim of immunity, privilege, or other defense by the Office in a legal proceeding, including but not limited to, sovereign immunity, preemption, or lack of relevance. This rule does not create any right or benefit, substantive or procedural, enforceable at law by a party against the Copyright Office, the Library of Congress, or the United States.

§ 205.4 Relationship of this part to the Federal Rules of Civil and Criminal Procedure.

Nothing in this part waives any requirement under the Federal Rules of Civil or Criminal Procedure.

§ 205.5 Scope of this part related to Copyright Office duties under title 17 of the U.S. Code.

This part relates only to legal proceedings, process, requests and demands relating to the Copyright Office's performance of its duties pursuant to title 17 of the United States Code. Legal proceedings, process, requests and demands relating to other matters (e.g., personal injuries, employment matters, etc.) are the responsibility of the General Counsel of the Library of Congress and are governed by 36 CFR part 703.

Subpart B—Service of Process

§ 205.11 Scope and purpose.

(a) This subpart provides the procedures governing service of process on the Copyright Office and its employees in their official capacity. These regulations provide the identity of Copyright Office officials who are authorized to accept service of process. The purpose of this subpart is to provide a centralized location for receipt of service of process to the Office. Such centralization will provide timely notification of legal process and expedite Office response. Litigants also must comply with all requirements pertaining to service of process that are established by statute, court rule and rule of procedure including the applicable provisions of the Federal Rules of Civil Procedure governing service upon the United States.

(b) This subpart does not apply to service of process made on an employee personally for matters not related to official business of the Office. Process served upon a Copyright Office employee in his or her individual capacity must be served in compliance with the applicable requirements for service of process established by statute, court rule, or rule of procedure.

§ 205.12 Process served on the Register of Copyrights or an employee in his or her official capacity.

(a) Summonses, complaints and all other process directed to the Copyright Office, the Register of Copyrights or any other Copyright Office employee in his or her official capacity should be served on the General Counsel of the Copyright Office or his or her designee as indicated in § 205.2 of this part. To effect proper service, the requirements of Rule 4(i) of the Federal Rules of Civil Procedure must also be satisfied by effecting service on both the United States Attorney for the district in which the action is brought and the Attorney General, Attn: Director of Intellectual Property Staff, Commercial Litigation Branch, Civil Division, Department of Justice, Washington, DC 20530.

(b) If, notwithstanding paragraph (a) of this section, any employee of the Office is served with a summons or complaint in connection with the conduct of official business, that employee shall immediately notify and deliver the summons or complaint to the Office of the General Counsel of the Copyright Office.

(c) Any employee receiving a summons or complaint shall note on the summons or complaint the date, hour, and place of service and mode of service.

(d) The Office will accept service of process for an employee only when the legal proceeding is brought in connection with the conduct of official business carried out in the employee's official capacity.

(e) When a legal proceeding is brought to hold an employee personally liable in connection with an action taken in the conduct of official business, rather than liable in an official capacity, the employee is to be served in accordance with any applicable statute, court rule, or rule of procedure. Service of process in this case is inadequate when made only on the General Counsel. An employee sued personally for an action taken in the conduct of official business shall immediately notify and deliver a copy of the summons or complaint to the General Counsel of the Copyright Office.

§ 205.13 Complaints served on the Register of Copyrights pursuant to 17 U.S.C. 411(a).

When an action has been instituted pursuant to 17 U.S.C. 411(a) for infringement of the copyright of a work for which registration has been refused, notice of the institution of the action and a copy of the complaint must be served on the Register of Copyrights by sending such documents by registered or certified mail to the General Counsel of the Copyright Office, GC/I&R, P.O. Box 70400, Washington, DC 20024–0400, or delivery by hand addressed to the General Counsel of the Copyright Office and delivered to the Copyright Information Section, U.S. Copyright Office, Library of Congress, James Madison Memorial Building, Room LM–401, 101 Independence Avenue, SE., Washington, DC. The notice must be in the form of a letter that is clearly identified as a 411(a) notice. Both the letter and the envelope should state: "Section 411(a) Notice to the Register of Copyrights." In compliance with Fed. R. Civ. P. Sec. 4(i), a notice of the institution of the action and a copy of the complaint must also be served on both the United States Attorney for the district in which the action is brought and the United States Department of Justice, directed to the Attorney General, Attn: Director of Intellectual Property Staff, Civil Division, Department of Justice, Washington, DC 20530.

[69 FR 39334, June 30, 2004, as amended at 73 FR 37840, July 2, 2008]

Subpart C—Testimony By Employees and Production of Documents in Legal Proceedings in Which the Office Is Not a Party

§ 205.21 Scope and purpose.

(a) This subpart prescribes policies and procedures of the Copyright Office governing testimony, in legal proceedings in which the Office is not a party, by Office employees in their official capacities and the production of Office documents for use in legal proceedings pursuant to a demand, request, subpoena or order.

(b) The purpose of this subpart is:

(1) To conserve the time of Office employees for conducting official business;

(2) To minimize the possibility of involving the Office in the matters of private parties or other issues which are not related to the mission of the Office;

(3) To prevent the public from confusing personal opinions of Office employees with Office policy;

(4) To avoid spending the time and money of the United States for private purposes;

(5) To preserve the integrity of the administrative process, minimize disruption of the decision-making process, and prevent interference with the Office's administrative functions.

(c) An employee of the Office may not voluntarily appear as a witness or voluntarily testify in a legal proceeding relating to his or her official capacity without proper authorization under this subpart.

(d) This subpart does not apply to any legal proceeding in which:

(1) An employee is to testify regarding facts or events that are unrelated to official business; or

(2) A former employee is asked to testify as an expert on a matter in which that employee did not personally participate while at the Office so long as the former employee testifies concerning his or her personal opinion and does not purport to speak for or on behalf of the Copyright Office.

§ 205.22 Production of documents and testimony.

(a) Generally, all documents and material submitted to the Copyright Office as part of an application to register a claim to copyright are available for public inspection and copying. It is possible, therefore, to obtain those materials without use of a legal process. Anyone seeking such documents must contact the Records Research and Certification Section of the Office. 37 CFR 201.2(b)(1). Certified copies of public documents and public records are self-authenticating. FED. R. EVID. 902 and 1005; *see also*, FED. R. CIV. p. 44(a)(1). In certain specified circumstances, information contained in the in-process files may be obtained by complying with the procedures of 37 CFR 201.2(b)(3). Correspondence between a copyright claimant or his or her agent and the Copyright Office in a completed registration, recordation, or refusal to register is also available for public inspection. Section 201.2(d) of this chapter prescribes the method for requesting copies of copyright registration records. An attorney engaged in actual or prospective litigation who submits a court order or a completed Litigation Statement may obtain a copy of the deposit if his or her request is found to comply with the requirements set out in 37 CFR 201.2(d)(2). The fees associated with various document requests, searches, copies, and expedited handling are listed in 37 CFR 201.3. Other publications containing Copyright Office procedures and practices are available to the public without charge from the Copyright Office or its Web site: *http://www.copyright.gov*. The Office website also allows online searching of copyright registration information and information pertaining to documents recorded with the Copyright Office beginning January 1, 1978. Pre-1978 copyright registration information and document recordation information is available to the public in the Copyright Office during regular business hours. If the information sought to be obtained from the Office is not available through these Office services, demands and subpoenas for testimony or documents may be served as follows:

(1) *Demands for testimony or documents.* All demands, requests, subpoenas or orders for production of documents or testimony in a legal proceeding directed to the Copyright Office, the Register of Copyrights or any other Copyright Office employee in his or her official capacity must be in writing and should be served on the General Counsel of the Copyright Office as indicated in § 205.2 of this part and in accordance with the Federal Rules of Civil or Criminal Procedure.

(2) *Affidavits.* Except when the Copyright Office is a party to the legal proceeding, every demand, request or subpoena shall be accompanied by an affidavit or declaration under penalty of perjury pursuant to 28 U.S.C. 1746. Such affidavit or declaration shall contain a written statement setting forth the title of the legal proceeding; the forum; the requesting party's interest in the legal proceeding; the reasons for the demand, request, or subpoena; a showing that the desired testimony or document is not reasonably available from any published or other written source, (e.g., 37 CFR, Chapter II; Compendium II, Compendium of Copyright Office Practices; other written practices of the Office; circulars; the Copyright Office website) and is not available by other established procedure, e.g., 37 CFR 201.2, 201.3. If testimony is requested in the affidavit or declaration, it shall include the intended use of the testimony, a detailed summary of the testimony desired, and a showing that no document could be provided and used in lieu of the requested testimony. The purpose of these requirements is to permit the Copyright General Counsel to make an informed decision as to whether testimony or production of a document should be authorized. The decision by the General Counsel will be based on consideration of the purposes set forth in § 205.21(b) of this part, on the evaluation of the requesting party's need for the testimony and any other factor warranted by the circumstances. Typically, when the information requested is available through other existing Office procedures or materials, the General Counsel will not authorize production of documents or testimony.

(b) No Copyright Office employee shall give testimony concerning the official business of the Office or produce any document in a legal proceeding other than those made available by the Records Research and Certification Section under existing regulations without the prior authorization of the General Counsel. Without prior approval from the General Counsel, no Office employee shall answer inquiries from a person not employed by the Library of Congress or the Department of Justice regarding testimony or documents in connection with a demand, subpoena or order. All inquiries involving demands, subpoenas, or orders shall be directed to the Copyright General Counsel.

(c) Any Office employee who receives a demand, request, subpoena or order for testimony or the production of documents in a legal proceeding shall immediately notify the Copyright Office General Counsel at the phone number indicated in § 205.2 of this part and shall immediately forward the demand to the Copyright General Counsel.

(d) The General Counsel may consult or negotiate with an attorney for a party or the party, if not represented by an attorney, to refine or limit a demand, request or subpoena to address interests or concerns of the Office. Failure of the attorney or party to cooperate in good faith under this part may serve as the basis for the General Counsel to deny authorization for the testimony or production of documents sought in the demand.

(e) A determination under this part regarding authorization to respond to a demand is not an assertion or waiver of privilege, lack of relevance, technical deficiency or any other ground for noncompliance. The Copyright Office reserves the right to oppose any demand on any appropriate legal ground independent of any determination under this part, including but not limited to, sovereign immunity, preemption, privilege, lack of relevance, or technical deficiency.

(f) *Office procedures when an employee receives a demand or subpoena:*

(1) If the General Counsel has not acted by the return date, the employee must appear at the time and place set forth in the subpoena (unless otherwise advised by the General Counsel) and inform the court (or other legal authority) that the demand has been referred for the prompt consideration of the General Counsel and shall request the court (or other legal authority) to stay the demand pending receipt of the requested instructions.

(2) If the General Counsel makes a determination not to authorize testimony or the production of documents, but the subpoena is not withdrawn or modified and Department of Justice representation cannot be arranged, the employee should appear at the time and place set forth in the subpoena unless advised otherwise by the General Counsel. If legal counsel cannot appear on behalf of the employee, the employee should produce a copy of these rules and state that the General Counsel has advised the employee not to provide the requested testimony or to produce the requested document. If a court (or other legal authority) rules that the demand in the subpoena must be complied with, the employee shall respectfully decline to comply with the demand, citing *United States* ex rel.*Touhy* v. *Ragen*, 340 U.S. 462 (1951).

[69 FR 39334, June 30, 2004, as amended at 73 FR 37840, July 2, 2008]

§ 205.23 Scope of testimony.

(a)(1) If a Copyright Office employee is authorized to give testimony in a legal proceeding, the testimony, if otherwise proper, shall be limited to facts within the personal knowledge of the Office employee. An Office employee is prohibited from giving expert testimony, or opinion, answering hypothetical or speculative questions, or giving testimony with respect to subject matter which is privileged. If an Office employee is authorized to testify in connection with his or her involvement or assistance in a proceeding or matter before the Office, that employee is further prohibited from giving testimony in response to an inquiry about the bases, reasons, mental processes, analyses, or conclusions of that employee in the performance of his or her official functions.

(2) The General Counsel may authorize an employee to appear and give expert testimony or opinion testimony upon the showing, pursuant to § 205.3 of this part, that exceptional circumstances warrant such testimony and that the anticipated testimony will not be adverse to the interest of the Copyright Office or the United States.

(b) If an Office employee is authorized to testify, the employee will generally be prohibited from providing testimony in response to questions which seek, for example:

(1) To elicit information about the employee's:

(i) Qualifications to examine or otherwise consider a particular copyright application.

(ii) Usual practice or whether the employee followed a procedure set out in any Office manual of practice in a particular case.

(iii) Consultation with another Office employee.

(iv) Familiarity with:

(A) Preexisting works that are similar.

(B) Registered works, works sought to be registered, a copyright application, registration, denial of registration, or request for reconsideration.

(C) Copyright law or other law.

(D) The actions of another Office employee.

(v) Reliance on particular facts or arguments.

(2) To inquire into the manner in and extent to which the employee considered or studied material in performing the function.

(3) To inquire into the bases, reasons, mental processes, analyses, or conclusions of that Office employee in performing the function.

(4) In exceptional circumstances, the General Counsel may waive these limitations pursuant to §205.3 of this part.

PART 211—MASK WORK PROTECTION

AUTHORITY: 17 U.S.C. 702 and 908.

SOURCE: 50 FR 26719, June 28, 1985, unless otherwise noted.

§211.1 General provisions.

(a) Mail and other communications with the Copyright Office concerning the Semiconductor Chip Protection Act of 1984, Pub. L. 98–620, chapter 9 of title 17 U.S.C., shall be addressed to: Library of Congress, Department MW, Washington, DC 20540.

(b) Section 201.2 of this chapter relating to the information given by the Copyright Office, and parts 203 and 204 of this chapter pertaining to the Freedom of Information Act and Privacy Act, shall apply, where appropriate, to the administration by the Copyright Office of the Semiconductor Chip Protection Act of 1984, Pub. L. 98–620.

(c) For purposes of this part, the terms *semiconductor chip product, mask work, fixed, commercially exploited,* and *owner,* shall have the meanings set forth in section 901 of title 17 U.S.C.

§211.2 Recordation of documents pertaining to mask works.

The conditions prescribed in §201.4 of this chapter for recordation of transfers of copyright ownership and other documents pertaining to copyright are applicable to the recordation of documents pertaining to mask works under section 903 of title 17 U.S.C.

[50 FR 26719, June 28, 1985, as amended at 66 FR 34373, June 28, 2001]

§211.3 Mask work fees.

(a) Section 201.3 of this chapter prescribes the fees or charges established by the Register of Copyrights for services relating to mask works.

(b) Section 201.6 of this chapter on the payment and refund of Copyright Office fees shall apply to mask work fees.

[50 FR 26719, June 28, 1985, as amended at 56 FR 59886, Nov. 26, 1991; 59 FR 38372, July 28, 1994; 63 FR 29139, May 28, 1998; 64 FR 29522, June 1, 1999]

§211.4 Registration of claims of protection in mask works.

(a) *General.* This section prescribes conditions for the registration of claims of protection in mask works pursuant to section 908 of title 17 U.S.C.

(b) *Application for registration.* (1) For purposes of registration of mask work claims, the Register of Copyrights has designated "Form MW" to be used for all applications submitted on and after January 7, 1985. Copies of the form are available free upon request to the Copyright Information Office, U.S. Copyright Office, Library of Congress, Washington, DC 20559. Applications submitted before January 7, 1985 will be dated January 7, 1985.

(2) An application for registration of a mask work claim may be submitted by the owner of the mask work, or the

duly authorized agent of any such owner.

(i) The owner of a mask work includes a party that has obtained the transfer of all of the exclusive rights in the work, but does not include the transferee of less than all of the exclusive rights, or the licensee of all or less than all of these rights.

(ii) For purposes of eligibility to claim mask work protection pursuant to section 902(a)(1)(A) of 17 U.S.C., the owner of the mask work must be either the initial owner or a person who has obtained by transfer the totality of rights in the mask work under the Act.

(3) An application for registration shall be submitted on Form MW prescribed by the Register under paragraph (b)(1) of this section, and shall be accompanied by the registration fee and deposit required under 17 U.S.C. 908 and §§211.3 and 211.5 of these regulations. The application shall contain the information required by the form and its accompanying instructions, and shall include a certification. The certification shall consist of:

(i) A declaration that the applicant is authorized to submit the application and that the statements made are correct to the best of that person's knowledge; and

(ii) The handwritten signature of the applicant, accompanied by the typed or printed name of that person.

(c) *One registration per mask work.* (1) Subject to the exception specified in paragraph (c)(2) of this section, only one registration can generally be made for the same version of a mask work fixed in an intermediate or final form of any semiconductor chip product. However, where an applicant for registration alleges that an earlier registration for the same version of the work is unauthorized and legally invalid and submits for recordation a signed affidavit, a registration may be made in the applicant's name.

(2) Notwithstanding the general rule permitting only one registration per work, owners of mask works in final forms of semiconductor chip products that are produced by adding metal-connection layers to unpersonalized gate arrays may separately register the entire unpersonalized gate array and the custom metallization layers. Applicants seeking to register separately entire unpersonalized gate arrays or custom metallization layers should make the nature of their claim clear at Space 8 of application Form MW. For these purposes, an "unpersonalized gate array" is an intermediate form chip product that includes a plurality of circuit elements that are adaptable to be personalized into a plurality of different final form chip products, in which some of the circuit elements are, or will be, connected as gates.

(d) *Registration as a single work.* Subject to the exception specified in paragraph (c)(2) of this section, for purposes of registration on a single application and upon payment of a single fee, the following shall be considered a single work.

(1) In the case of a mask work that has not been commercially exploited: All original mask work elements fixed in a particular form of a semiconductor chip product at the time an application for registration is filed and in which the owner or owners of the mask work is or are the same; and

(2) In the case of a mask work that has been commercially exploited. All original mask work elements fixed in a semiconductor chip product at the time that product was first commercially exploited and in which the owner or owners of the mask is or are the same.

(e) *Registration in most complete form.* Owners seeking registration of a mask work contribution must submit the entire original mask work contribution in its most complete form as fixed in a semiconductor chip product. The most complete form means the stage of the manufacturing process which is closest to completion. In cases where the owner is unable to register on the basis of the most complete form because he or she lacks control over the most complete form, an averment of this fact must be made at Space 2 of Form MW. Where such an averment is made, the owner may register on the basis of the most complete form in his or her possession. For applicants seeking to register an unpersonalized gate array or custom metallization layers under paragraph (c)(2) of this section, the most complete form is the entire chip on which the unpersonalized gate array or custom metallization layers reside(s), and registration covers those elements of the chip in which work protection is asserted.

(f) *Corrections and amplifications of prior registration.* Except for errors or omissions made by the Copyright Office, no corrections or amplifications can be made to the information contained in the record of a completed registration after the effective date of the registration. A document purporting to correct or amplify the information in a completed registration may be recorded in the Copyright Office for whatever effect a court of competent jurisdiction may later give to it, if the document is signed by the owner of the mask work, as identified in the registration record, or by a duly authorized agent of the owner.

[50 FR 26719, June 28, 1985, as amended at 56 FR 7818, Feb. 26, 1991; 64 FR 36575, July 7, 1999; 66 FR 34374, June 28, 2001; 73 FR 37840, July 2, 2008]

§ 211.5 Deposit of identifying material.

(a) *General.* This section prescribes rules pertaining to the deposit of identifying material for registration of a claim of protection in a mask work under section 908 of title 17 U.S.C.

(b) *Nature of required deposit.* Subject to the provisions of paragraph (c) of this section, the deposit of identifying material to accompany an application for registration of a mask work claim under § 211.4 of these regulations shall consist of:

(1) In the case of a commercially exploited mask work, four reproductions of the mask work fixed in the form of the semiconductor chip product in which it was first commercially exploited. Defective chips may be deposited under this section provided that the mask work contribution would be revealed in reverse dissection of the chips. The four reproductions shall be accompanied by a visually perceptible representation of each layer of the mask work consisting of:

(i) Sets of plastic color overlay sheets;

(ii) Drawings or plots in composite form on a single sheet or on separate sheets; or

(iii) A photograph of each layer of the work fixed in a semiconductor chip product.

The visually perceptible representation of a mask work deposited under this section shall be reproduced on material which can be readily stored in an 8½ × 11 inch format, and shall be reproduced at a magnification sufficient to reveal the basic circuitry design of the mask work and which shall in all cases be at least 20 times magnification.

(2) In the case of a mask work that has not been commercially exploited, one of the following:

(i) Where the mask work contribution in which registration is sought represents twenty percent or more of the area of the intended final form, a visually perceptible representation of the work in accordance with paragraph (b)(1) (i) or (ii) of this section. In addition to the deposit of visually perceptible representations of the work, an applicant may, at his or her option, deposit four reproductions in the most complete form of the mask work as fixed in a semiconductor product.

(ii) Where the mask work contribution in which registration is sought represents less than twenty percent of the area of the intended final form, a visually perceptible representation of the work which reveals the totality of the mask work contribution to a person trained in the state of the art. The visually perceptible representations may consist of any combination of plastic color overlay sheets, drawing or plots in composite form, or a photograph or photographs of the entire mask set. If the visually perceptible representation fails to identify all of the elements of the mask work contribution, they may be accompanied by additional explanatory material. The visually perceptible representation of a mask work deposited under this section shall be reproduced on material which can be readily stored in an 8½ × 11 inch format and shall be of sufficient magnification and completeness to reveal all elements of the mask work contribution. In addition to the deposit of visually perceptible representations of the work, an applicant may, at his or her option, deposit four reproductions in the most complete form of the mask work as fixed in a semiconductor chip product.

(c) *Trade secret protection.* Where specific layers of a mask work fixed in a semiconductor chip product contain information in which trade secret protection is asserted, certain material may be withheld as follows:

(1) *Mask works commercially exploited.* For commercially exploited mask works no more than two layers of each five or more layers in the work. In lieu of the visually perceptible representations required under paragraph (b)(1) of this section, identifying portions of the withheld material must be submitted. For these purposes, *identifying portions* shall mean (i) a printout of the mask work design data pertaining to each withheld layer, reproduced in microform, or (ii) visually perceptible representations in accordance with paragraph (b)(1) (i), (ii), or (iii) of this section with those portions containing sensitive information maintained under a claim of trade secrecy blocked out, provided that the portions remaining are greater than those which are blocked out.

(2) *Mask work not commercially exploited.* For mask works not commercially exploited falling under paragraph (b)(2)(i) of this section, any layer may be withheld. In lieu of the visually perceptible representations required under paragraph (b)(2) of this section, "identifying portions" shall mean (i) a printout of the mask work design data pertaining to each withheld layer, reproduced in microform, in which sensitive information maintained under a claim of trade secrecy has been blocked out or stripped, or (ii) visually perceptible representations in accordance with paragraph (b)(2)(i) of this section with those portions containing sensitive information maintained under a claim of trade secrecy blocked out, provided that the portions remaining are greater than those which are blocked out. The identifying portions shall be accompanied by a single photograph of the top or other visible layers of the mask work fixed in a semiconductor chip product in which the sensitive information maintained under a claim of trade secrecy has been blocked out, provided that the blocked out portions do not exceed the remaining portions.

(d) *Special relief.* The Register of Copyrights may decide to grant special relief from the deposit requirements of this section, and shall determine the conditions under which special relief is to be granted., Requests for special relief under this paragraph shall be made in writing to the Associate Register for Registration Program, Library of Congress, Copyright Office - RPO, 101 Independence Avenue, SE, Washington, DC 20559–6200, shall be signed by the person signing the application for registration, shall set forth specific reasons why the request should be granted and shall propose an alternative form of deposit.

(e) *Retention and disposition of deposits.* (1) Any identifying material deposited under this section, including material deposited in connection with claims that have been refused registration, are the property of the United States Government.

(2) Where a claim of protection in a mask work is registered in the Copyright Office, the identifying material deposited in connection with the claim shall be retained under the control of the Copyright Office, including retention in Government storage facilities, during the period of protection. After that period, it is within the joint discretion of the Register of Copyrights and the Librarian of Congress to order its destruction or other disposition.

[50 FR 26719, June 28, 1985, as amended at 60 FR 34169, June 30, 1995; 73 FR 37840, July 2, 2008; 76 FR 27898, May 13, 2011]

§211.6 Methods of affixation and placement of mask work notice.

(a) *General.* (1) This section specifies methods of affixation and placement of the mask work notice that will satisfy the notice requirement in section 909 of title 17 U.S.C. A notice deemed "acceptable" under this regulation shall be considered to satisfy the requirement of that section that it be affixed "in such manner and location as to give reasonable notice" of protection. As provided in that section, the examples specified in this regulation shall not be considered exhaustive of the methods of affixation and positions giving reasonable notice of the claim of protection in a mask work.

(2) The acceptability of a mask work notice under these regulations shall depend upon its being legible under normal conditions of use, and affixed in such manner and position that, when affixed, it may be viewed upon reasonable examination.

(b) *Elements of mask work notice.* The elements of a mask work notice shall consist of:

(1) The words *mask work*, the symbol "M" or the symbol "Ⓜ" (the letter M in a circle); and

(2) The name of the owner or owners of the mask work or an abbreviation by which the name is recognized or is generally known.

(c) *Methods of affixation and placement of the notice.* In the case of a mask work fixed in a semiconductor chip product, the following locations are acceptable:

(1) A gummed or other label securely affixed or imprinted upon the package or other container used as a permanent receptacle for the product; or

(2) A notice imprinted or otherwise affixed in or on the top or other visible layer of the product.

[50 FR 26719, June 28, 1985, as amended at 60 FR 34169, June 30, 1995]

§211.7 Reconsideration procedure for refusals to register.

The requirements prescribed in §202.5 of this chapter for reconsideration of refusals to register copyright claims are applicable to requests to reconsider refusals to register mask works under 17 U.S.C. chapter 9, unless otherwise required by this part.

[69 FR 77637, Dec. 28, 2004]

PART 212—PROTECTION OF VESSEL HULL DESIGNS

Sec.

AUTHORITY: 17 U.S.C. chapter 13.

SOURCE: 64 FR 36578, July 7, 1999, unless otherwise noted.

§212.1 Scope.

The provisions of this part apply to the protection and registration of original designs of vessel hulls under chapter 13 of title 17, United States Code. Design protection and registration under this part are separate from copyright protection and registration. Copyright registration is governed by the provisions of part 202 of this subchapter.

§212.2 Fees.

Services related to registration of original designs of vessel hulls are subject to fees prescribed in §§201.3(c) and (d).

[71 FR 31092, June 1, 2006]

§212.3 Registration of claims for protection of eligible designs.

(a) *Limitations.* Protection is not available for, and an application for registration will not be accepted for:

(1) An otherwise eligible design made public prior to October 28, 1998;

(2) An otherwise eligible design made public on a date more than two years prior to the filing of an application for registration under this section;

(3) A design ineligible for any of the reasons set forth in 17 U.S.C. 1302.

(b) *Required elements of application.* An application is considered filed with the Copyright Office on the date on which the following three items have been received by the Copyright Office:

(1) Completed Form D-VH;

(2) Deposit material identifying the design or designs for which registration is sought; and

(3) The appropriate fee.

(c) *Application by owner of design.* An application for registration under this section may be made only by the owner or owners of the design, or by the duly authorized agent or representative of the owner or owners of the design.

(d) *Application form.* Registration must be made on Form D-VH. Forms are available from the Copyright Office and may be reprinted from the Copyright Office's website (*http://www.loc.gov/copyright/forms/formdvh.pdf*).

(e) *Deposit material*—(1) *In General.* Identification of the design to be registered may be made in the form of drawings or photographs. No more than two drawings or photographs of the design may appear on a single sheet. Applicants may submit up to three 8½″ × 11″ sheets containing drawings or photographs as part of the basic application fee. An additional fee shall be assessed for each page beyond the first three pages. No combinations of drawings and photographs may be submitted on a single sheet. The drawings or photographs that accompany the application must reveal those aspects of the design for which protection is claimed. The registration extends only to those aspects of the design which are adequately shown in the drawings or photographs.

(2) *Views.* The drawings or photographs submitted should contain a sufficient number of views to make an adequate disclosure of the appearance of the design, *i.e.*, front, rear, right and left sides, top and bottom. While not required, it is suggested that perspective views be submitted to show clearly the appearance and shape of the three dimensional designs.

(3) *Drawings.* (i) Drawings must be in black ink on white 8½″ × 11″ unruled paper. A drawing of a design should include appropriate surface shading which shows clearly the character and contour of all surfaces of any 3-dimensional aspects of the design. Surface shading is also necessary to distinguish between any open and solid areas of the design. Solid black surface shading is not permitted except when used to represent the black color as well as color contrast.

(ii) The use of broken lines in drawings depicting the design is understood to be for illustrative purposes only and forms no part of the claimed design. Structure that is not part of the design, but that is considered necessary to show the environment in which the design is used, may be represented in the drawing by broken lines. This includes any portion of the vessel hull in which the design is embodied or applied that is not considered part of the design. When the claimed design is only surface ornamentation to the vessel hull, the vessel hull in which it is embodied must be shown in broken lines.

(iii) When broken lines are used, they should not intrude upon or cross the depiction of the design and should not be of heavier weight than the lines used in depicting the design. Where a broken line showing of environmental structure must necessarily cross or intrude upon the representation of the design and obscure a clear understanding of the design, such an illustration should be included as a separate figure, in addition to other figures which fully disclose the subject matter of the design.

(4) *Photographs.* High quality black and white or color photographs will be accepted provided that they are mounted on plain white 8½″ × 11″ unlined paper and do not exceed two photographs per sheet. Photographs must be developed on double weight photographic paper and must be of sufficient quality so that all the details of the design are plainly visible and are capable of reproduction on the registration certificate, if issued.

(f) *Multiple claims*—(1) *In general.* Claims for more than one design may be filed in one of two ways. If multiple designs are contained on a single make and model of a vessel hull (and therefore, the information in Space 1 of Form D-VH—the make and model of the vessel that embodies the design—is the same for each of the designs), a single application form may be used for all designs, provided that the information in spaces 3 through 9 is the same for each of the designs. If multiple designs are contained on more than one make and model of a vessel, or the information in spaces 3 through 9 is not the same for each of the multiple designs, then separate applications must be used for each design.

(2) *Single application.* Where a single application for multiple designs is appropriate, a separate Form D-VH/CON must be used for each design beyond the first appearing on Form D-VH. Each Form D-VH/CON must be accompanied by deposit material identifying the design that is the subject of the

Form D-VH/CON, and the deposit material must be attached to the Form D-VH/CON. The Form D-VH and all the Form D-VH/CONs for the single application must be submitted together.

(3) *Multiple applications.* Where multiple applications for more than one design are required, a Form D-VH must be completed for each design. Deposit material identifying the design must accompany each application. Multiple applications may be filed separately.

(4) *Fees.* The basic application fee prescribed in § 201.3(c) of this chapter applies to each design submitted, regardless of whether a single application or multiple applications are used.

(g) *Written declaration.* In lieu of the oath required by 17 U.S.C. 1312(a), the application shall contain a written declaration, as permitted by 17 U.S.C. 1312(b), signed by the applicant, or the applicant's duly authorized agent or representative. If the design has been made public with the design notice prescribed in 17 U.S.C. 1306, the written declaration shall also describe the exact form and position of the design notice. The written declaration shall read as follows:

The undersigned, as the applicant or the applicant's duly appointed agent or representative, being hereby warned that willful false statements are punishable by fine or imprisonment, or both, under 18 U.S.C. 1001, and that such willful false statements may jeopardize the validity of this application or any resulting registration, hereby declares to the best of his/her knowledge and belief:

(1) That the design has been fixed in a useful article;

(2) That the design is original and was created by the designer(s), or employer if applicable, named in the application;

(3) That those aspects of the design for which registration is sought are not protected by a design patent;

(4) That the design has not previously been registered on behalf of the applicant or the applicant's predecessor in title; and

(5) That the applicant is the person entitled to protection and to registration under chapter 13 of title 17, United States Code.

(h) *Priority claims.* An applicant seeking the benefit of 17 U.S.C. 1311 because the applicant has, within the previous 6 months, filed an application for protection of the same design in a foreign country, must provide:

(1) Identification of the filing date of the foreign application;

(2) Identification of the foreign country in which the application was filed;

(3) The serial number or any other identifying number of the foreign application;

(4) A certified copy of the foreign application;

(5) A translation of the foreign application and a statement, signed by the translator, that the translation is accurate, if the foreign application is in a language other than English; and

(6) If requested by the Copyright Office, proof that the foreign country in which the prior application was filed extends to designs of owners who are citizens of the United States, or to applications filed under chapter 13 of title 17, United States Code, similar protection to that provided under chapter 13 of title 17, United States Code.

(i) *Effective date of registration.* The effective date of registration is the date of publication of the registration by the Copyright Office.

(j) *Publication of registration.* Publication of registrations of vessel hull designs shall be made on the Copyright Office website (*http://www.loc.gov/copyright/vessels*).

[64 FR 36578, July 7, 1999, as amended at 72 FR 33692, June 19, 2007]

§ 212.4 Affixation and placement of design notice.

(a) *General.* (1) This section specifies the methods of affixation and placement of the design notice required by 17 U.S.C. 1306. Sections 1306 and 1307 govern the circumstances under which a design notice must be used and the effect of omission of a design notice. A notice deemed acceptable under this part shall be considered to satisfy the requirements of section 1306 that it be so located and applied as to give reasonable notice of design protection while the useful article embodying the design is passing through its normal channels of commerce. As provided in that section, the examples specified in this part shall not be considered exhaustive of the methods of affixation and locations giving reasonable notice of the claim of protection in the design.

(2) The acceptability of a design notice under these regulations shall depend upon its being legible under normal conditions of use, and affixed in such a manner and position that, when affixed, it may be viewed upon reasonable examination. There is no requirement that a design notice be permanently embossed or engraved into a vessel hull or deck, but it should be affixed in such a manner that, under normal conditions of use, it is not likely to become unattached or illegible.

(b) *Elements of a design notice.* If the design has been registered, the registration number may be included in the design notice in place of the year of the date on which protection for the design commenced and the name of the owner, an abbreviation by which the name can be recognized, or a generally accepted alternative designation of the owner. The elements of a design notice shall consist of:

(1) The words "Protected Design", the abbreviation "Prot'd Des.", or the letter "D" within a circle, or the symbol *D*;

(2) The year of the date on which protection for the design commenced; and

(3) The name of the owner, an abbreviation by which the name can be recognized, or a generally accepted alternative designation of the owner.

(c) *Distinctive identification.* Any distinctive identification of an owner may be used for purposes of paragraph (b)(3) of this section if it has been recorded by the Register of Copyrights pursuant to §212.5 before the design marked with such identification is registered.

(d) *Acceptable locations of notice.* The following are acceptable means of affixing and placement of a design notice:

(1) In close proximity to the hull identification number required by 33 CFR 181.23;

(2) In close proximity to the driver's console such that it is in plain view from the console;

(3) If the vessel is twenty feet in length or less and is governed by 33 CFR 183.21, in close proximity to the capacity marking; and

(4) In close proximity to the make and/or model designation of the vessel.

§212.5 Recordation of distinctive identification of vessel hull designer.

(a) *General.* Any owner of a vessel hull may record a distinctive identification with the Register of Copyrights for purposes of using such distinctive identification in a design protection notice required by 17 U.S.C. 1306. A distinctive identification of an owner may not be used in a design notice before it has first been recorded with the Register.

(b) *Forms.* The Copyright Office does not provide forms for the use of persons recording distinctive identifications of ownership of a vessel hull. However, persons recording distinctive identifications are encouraged to use the suggested format available on the Copyright Office website (*http://www.loc.gov/copyright/vessels*).

(c) *Recording distinctive identifications.* Any distinctive identification of an owner of a vessel hull may be recorded with the Register of Copyrights provided that a document containing the following is submitted:

(1) The name and address of the owner;

(2) A statement of the owner that he/she is entitled to use the distinctive identification;

(3) A statement or depiction of the identification; and

(4) The recordation fee in the amount prescribed in §201.3(c) of this chapter.

(d) The document should be mailed to: Dept. D-VH, Vessel Hull Registration, P.O. Box 71380, Washington, DC 20024–1380.

[64 FR 36578, July 7, 1999, as amended at 67 FR 38005, May 31, 2002; 72 FR 33692, June 19, 2007]

§212.6 Recordation of transfers and other documents.

The conditions prescribed in §201.4 of this chapter for recordation of transfers of copyright ownership and other documents pertaining to copyright are applicable to the recordation of documents pertaining to design protection of vessel hulls under 17 U.S.C. chapter 13.

§212.7 Reconsideration procedure for refusals to register.

The requirements prescribed in §202.5 of this chapter for reconsideration of refusals to register copyright claims are applicable to requests to reconsider refusals to register vessel hull designs under 17 U.S.C. chapter 13, unless otherwise required by this part.

[69 FR 77637, Dec. 28, 2004]

§ 212.8 Correction of errors in certificates of registration.

(a) *General.* (1) This section prescribes conditions relating to the correction of clerical or typographical errors in a certificate of registration of a vessel hull design, under section 1319 of title 17 of the United States Code, as amended by Public Law 105–304.

(2) For the purposes of this section, a *basic registration* means registration of a vessel hull design made under sections 1310 through 1314 of title 17 of the United States Code, as amended by Public Law 105–304.

(3) No correction of the information in a basic registration will be made except pursuant to the provisions of this § 212.8. As an exception, where it is discovered that the record of a vessel hull design registration contains a clerical or typographical error made by the Copyright Office, the Office will take appropriate measures to rectify its error. Correction will be made only of clerical or typographical errors; errors of a different nature cannot be corrected and there is no procedure to amplify the registration record with additional information.

(b) *Application for correction of error in certificate.* At any time after registration of a vessel hull design, the Copyright Office will correct a clerical or typographical error in the registration upon the application of the owner of the registered design or the owner's authorized agent.

(c) *Form and content of application to correct registration.* (1) An application to correct a registration shall be made on a form prescribed by the Copyright Office, shall be accompanied by the appropriate filing fee identified in § 201.3(c) and shall contain the following information:

(i) The make and model of the vessel that embodies the registered design;

(ii) The registration number of the basic registration;

(iii) The year when the basic registration was completed;

(iv) The name or names of the designer or designers of the vessel hull, and the owner or owners of the vessel hull design, as they appear in the basic registration;

(v) The space number and heading or description of the part of the basic registration where the error occurred;

(vi) A transcription of the erroneous information as it appears in the basic registration;

(vii) A statement of the correct information as it should have appeared;

(viii) If desired, an explanation of the error or its correction;

(ix) The name and address:

(A) To which the correspondence concerning the application should be sent; and

(B) To which the certificate of correction should be mailed; and

(x) The certification shall consist of:

(A) The handwritten signature of the owner of the registered design or of the duly authorized agent of such owner (who shall also be identified);

(B) The typed or printed name of the person whose signature appears, and the date of signature; and

(C) A statement that the person signing the application is the owner of the registered design or of the duly authorized agent of such owner, and that the statements made in the application are correct to the best of that person's knowledge.

(2) The form prescribed by he Copyright Office for the foregoing purposes is designated "Application to Correct a Design Registration (Form DC)". Copies of the form are available free upon request to the Public Information Office, Library of Congress, Copyright Office, 101 Independence Avenue, SE., Washington, DC 20559–6000 or on the Copyright Office Web site at *http://www.copyright.gov/forms/formdc.pdf.*

(3) Copies, phonorecords or supporting documents cannot be made part of the record of a corrected certificate of registration and should not be submitted with the application.

(d) *Fee.* The filing fee for an application to correct a certificate of registration of a vessel hull design is prescribed in § 201.3(c).

[71 FR 46402, Aug. 14, 2006]

SUBCHAPTER B—COPYRIGHT ARBITRATION ROYALTY PANEL RULES AND PROCEDURES

EDITORIAL NOTE: Nomenclature changes to subchapter B appear at 58 FR 67691, Dec. 22, 1993, 59 FR 23993, 23994, and 23995, May 9, 1994, as corrected at 59 FR 33201 and 33202, June 28, 1994.

PART 253—USE OF CERTAIN COPYRIGHTED WORKS IN CONNECTION WITH NONCOMMERCIAL EDUCATIONAL BROADCASTING

Sec.

AUTHORITY: 17 U.S.C. 118, 801(b)(1) and 803.

SOURCE: 57 FR 60954, Dec. 22, 1992, unless otherwise noted. Redesignated at 59 FR 23993, May 9, 1994.

§ 253.1 General.

This part 253 establishes terms and rates of royalty payments for certain activities using published nondramatic musical works and published pictorial, graphic and sculptural works during a period beginning on January 1, 2003, and ending on December 31, 2007. Upon compliance with 17 U.S.C. 118, and the terms and rates of this part, a public broadcasting entity may engage in the activities with respect to such works set forth in 17 U.S.C. 118(d).

[57 FR 60954, Dec. 22, 1992. Redesignated at 59 FR 23993, May 9, 1994, as amended at 63 FR 2144, Jan 14, 1998; 67 FR 77171, Dec. 17, 2002]

§ 253.2 Definition of public broadcasting entity.

As used in this part, the term *public broadcasting entity* means a noncommercial educational broadcast station as defined in section 397 of title 47 and any nonprofit institution or organization engaged in the activities described in 17 U.S.C. 118(d)(2).

§ 253.3 [Reserved]

§ 253.4 Performance of musical compositions by PBS, NPR and other public broadcasting entities engaged in the activities set forth in 17 U.S.C. 118(d).

The following schedule of rates and terms shall apply to the performance by PBS, NPR and other public broadcasting entities engaged in activities set forth in 17 U.S.C. 118(d) of copyrighted published nondramatic musical compositions, except for public broadcasting entities covered by §§ 253.5 and 253.6, and except for compositions which are the subject of voluntary license agreements.

(a) Determination of royalty rate. (1) For performance of such work in a feature presentation of PBS:

2003–2007 .... $224.22

(2) For performance of such a work as background or theme music in a PBS program:

2003–2007 .... $56.81

(3) For performance of such a work in a feature presentation of a station of PBS:

2003–2007 .... $19.16

(4) For performance of such a work as background or theme music in a program of a station of PBS:

2003–2007 .... $4.04

(5) For the performance of such a work in a feature presentation of NPR:

2003–2007 .... $22.73

(6) For the performance of such a work as background or theme music in an NPR program:

2003–2007 .... $5.51

(7) For the performance of such a work in a feature presentation of a station of NPR:

2003–2007 .... $1.61

(8) For the performance of such a work as background or theme music in a program of a station of NPR:

2003–2007 .... $.57

(9) For purposes of this schedule the rate for the performance of theme music in an entire series shall be double the single program theme rate.

(10) In the event the work is first performed in a program of a station of PBS or NPR, and such program is subsequently distributed by PBS or NPR, an additional royalty payment shall be made equal to the difference between the rate specified in this section for a program of a station of PBS or NPR, respectively, and the rate specified in this section for a PBS or NPR program, respectively.

(b) *Payment of royalty rate.* The required royalty rate shall be paid to each known copyright owner not later than July 31 of each calendar year for uses during the first six months of that calendar year, and not later than January 31 for uses during the last six months of the preceding calendar year.

(c) *Records of use.* PBS and NPR shall, upon the request of a copyright owner of a published musical work who believes a musical composition of such owner has been performed under the terms of this schedule, permit such copyright owner a reasonable opportunity to examine their standard cue sheets listing the nondramatic performances of musical compositions on PBS and NPR programs. Any local PBS and NPR station that shall be required by the provisions of any voluntary license agreement with ASCAP or BMI covering the license period January 1, 2003, to December 31, 2007, to prepare a music use report shall, upon request of a copyright owner who believes a musical composition of such owner has been performed under the terms of this schedule, permit such copyright owner to examine the report.

(d) *Terms of use.* The fees provided in this schedule for the performance of a musical work in a program shall cover performances of such work in such program for a period of four years following the first performance.

[57 FR 60954, Dec. 22, 1992. Redesignated and amended at 59 FR 23993, May 9, 1994, and amended at 63 FR 2144, Jan 14, 1998; 67 FR 77171, Dec. 17, 2002]

§ 253.5 Performance of musical compositions by public broadcasting entities licensed to colleges and universities.

(a) *Scope.* This section applies to the performance of copyrighted published nondramatic musical compositions by noncommercial radio stations which are licensed to colleges, universities, or other nonprofit educational institutions and which are not affiliated with National Public Radio.

(b) *Voluntary license agreements.* Notwithstanding the schedule of rates and terms established in this section, the rates and terms of any license agreements entered into by copyright owners and colleges, universities, and other nonprofit educational institutions concerning the performance of copyrighted musical compositions, including performances by noncommercial radio stations, shall apply in lieu of the rates and terms of this section.

(c) *Royalty rate.* A public broadcasting entity within the scope of this section may perform published nondramatic musical compositions subject to the following schedule of royalty rates:

(1) For all such compositions in the repertory of ASCAP, $277 annually.

(2) For all such compositions in the repertory of BMI, $277 annually.

(3) For all such compositions in the repertory of SESAC, $90 annually.

(4) For the performance of any other such compositions: $1.

(d) *Payment of royalty rate.* The public broadcasting entity shall pay the required royalty rate to ASCAP, BMI and SESAC not later than January 31 of each year.

(e) *Records of use.* A public broadcasting entity subject to this section shall furnish to ASCAP, BMI and SESAC, upon request, a music-use report during one week of each calendar year. ASCAP, BMI and SESAC shall not in any one calendar year request more than 10 stations to furnish such reports.

[57 FR 60954, Dec. 22, 1992, as amended at 58 FR 63294, Dec. 1, 1993; 60 FR 61655, Dec. 1, 1995; 61 FR 60613, Nov. 29, 1996; 63 FR 2145, Jan. 14, 1998; 63 FR 66042, Dec. 1, 1998; 64 FR 67188, Dec. 1, 1999; 65 FR 75167, Dec. 1, 2000; 66 FR 59699, Nov. 30, 2001; 67 FR 71105, Nov. 29, 2002; 67 FR 77171, Dec. 17, 2002; 68 FR 67045, Dec. 1, 2003; 69 FR 69823, Dec. 1, 2004; 70 FR 72077, Dec. 1, 2005; 71 FR 69486, Dec. 1, 2006]

§ 253.6 Performance of musical compositions by other public broadcasting entities.

(a) *Scope.* This section applies to the performance of copyrighted published nondramatic musical compositions by radio stations not licensed to colleges, universities, or other nonprofit educational institutions and which are not affiliated with National Public Radio.

(b) *Voluntary license agreements.* Notwithstanding the schedule of rates and terms established in this section, the rates and terms of any license agreements entered into by copyright owners and noncommercial radio stations within the scope of this section concerning the performance of copyrighted musical compositions, including performances by noncommercial radio stations, shall apply in lieu of the rates and terms of this section.

(c) Royalty rate. A public broadcasting entity within the scope of this section may perform published nondramatic musical compositions subject to the following schedule of royalty rates:

(1) For all such compositions in the repertory of ASCAP, in 2003, $460; in 2004, $475; in 2005, $495; in 2006, $515; in 2007, $535.

(2) For all such compositions in the repertory of BMI, in 2003, $460; in 2004, $475; in 2005, $495; in 2006, $515; in $2007, $535.

(3) For all such compositions in the repertory of SESAC, in 2003, $98; in 2004, $100; in 2005, $102; in 2006, $104; in 2007, $106.

(4) For the performance of any other such compositions, in 2003 through 2007, $1.

(d) *Payment of royalty rate.* The public broadcasting entity shall pay the required royalty rate to ASCAP, BMI and SESAC not later than January 31 of each year.

(e) *Records of use.* A public broadcasting entity subject to this section shall furnish to ASCAP, BMI and SESAC, upon request, a music-use report during one week of each calendar year. ASCAP, BMI and SESAC each shall not in any one calendar year request more than 5 stations to furnish such reports.

[57 FR 60954, Dec. 22, 1992. Redesignated at 59 FR 23993, May 9, 1994, and amended at 60 FR 8198, Feb. 13, 1995; 63 FR 2145, Jan. 14, 1998; 67 FR 77172, Dec. 17, 2002]

§ 253.7 Recording rights, rates and terms.

(a) *Scope.* This section establishes rates and terms for the recording of nondramatic performances and displays of musical works, other than compositions subject to voluntary license agreements, on and for the radio and television programs of public broadcasting entities, whether or not in synchronization or timed relationship with the visual or aural content, and for the making, reproduction, and distribution of copies and phonorecords of public broadcasting programs containing such nondramatic performances and displays of musical works solely for the purpose of transmission by public broadcasting entities. The rates and terms established in this schedule include the making of the reproductions described in 17 U.S.C. 118(d)(3).

(b) Royalty rate. (1)(i) For uses described in paragraph (a) of this section of a musical work in a PBS-distributed program, the royalty fees shall be calculated by multiplying the following per-composition rates by the number of different compositions in that PBS-distributed program:

	2003–2007
Feature	$112.40
Concert feature (per minute)	33.75
Background	56.81
Theme:	
Single program or first series program	56.81
Other series program	23.06

(ii) For such uses other than in a PBS-distributed television program, the royalty fee shall be calculated by multiplying the following per-composition rates by the number of different compositions in that program:

	2003–2007
Feature	$9.29
Concert feature (per minute)	2.44
Background	4.04
Theme:	
Single program or first series program	4.04
Other series program	1.61

(iii) In the event the work is first recorded other than in a PBS-distributed program, and such program is subsequently distributed by PBS, an additional royalty payment shall be made equal to the difference between the rate specified in this section for other than a PBS-distributed program and the rate specified in this section for a PBS-distributed program.

(2) For uses licensed herein of a musical work in a NPR program, the royalty fees shall be calculated by multiplying the following per-composition rates by the number of different compositions in any NPR program distributed by NPR. For purposes of this schedule "National Public Radio" programs include all programs produced in whole or in part by NPR, or by any NPR station or organization under contract with NPR.

	2003–2007
Feature	$12.17
Concert feature (per minute)	17.86
Background	6.10
Theme:	
Single program or first series program	6.10
Other series program	2.43

(3) For purposes of this schedule, a "Concert Feature" shall be deemed to be the nondramatic presentation in a program of all or part of a symphony, concerto, or other serious work originally written for concert performance or the nondramatic presentation in a program of portions of a serious work originally written for opera performance.

(4) For such uses other than in an NPR-produced radio program:

	2003–2007
Feature	$.78
Feature (concert)(per half hour)	1.63
Background	.39

(5) The schedule of fees covers use for a period of three years following the first use. Succeeding use periods will require the following additional payment: additional one-year period—25 percent of the initial three-year fee; second three-year period—50 percent of the initial three-year fee; each three-year fee thereafter—25 percent of the initial three-year fee; provided that a 100 percent additional payment prior to the expiration of the first three-year period will cover use during all subsequent use periods without limitation. Such succeeding uses which are subsequent to December 31, 2007, shall be subject to the royalty rates established in this schedule.

(c) *Payment of royalty rates.* The required royalty rates shall be paid to each known copyright owner not later than July 31 of each calendar year for uses during the first six months of that calendar year, and not later than January 31 for uses during the last six months of the preceding calendar year.

(d) *Records of use.* (1) Maintenance of cue sheets. PBS and its stations, NPR, or other television public broadcasting entities shall maintain and make available for examination pursuant to subsection (e) copies of their standard cue sheets or summaries of same listing the recording of the musical works of such copyright owners.

(2) Content of cue sheets or summaries. Such cue sheets or summaries shall include:

(i) The title, composer and author to the extent such information is reasonably obtainable.

(ii) The type of use and manner of performance thereof in each case.

(iii) For Concert Feature music, the actual recorded time period on the program, plus all distribution and broadcast information available to the public broadcasting entity.

(e) *Filing of use reports with the Copyright Office. Deposit of cue sheets or summaries.* PBS and its stations, NPR, or other television public broadcasting entity shall deposit with the Copyright

Office copies of their standard music cue sheets or summaries of same (which may be in the form of hard copy of computerized reports) listing the recording pursuant to this schedule of the musical works of copyright owners. Such cue sheets or summaries shall be deposited not later than July 31 of each calendar year for recordings during the first six months of the calendar year and not later than January 31 of each calendar year for recordings during the second six months of the preceding calendar year. PBS and NPR shall maintain at their offices copies of all standard music cue sheets from which such music use reports are prepared. Such music cue sheets shall be furnished to the Copyright Office upon its request and also shall be available during regular business hours at the offices of PBS or NPR for examination by a copyright owner who believes a musical composition of such owner has been recorded pursuant to this schedule.

[57 FR 60954, Dec. 22, 1992; 58 FR 7051, Feb. 4, 1993; 58 FR 8820, Feb. 17, 1993, as amended at 63 FR 2145, Jan. 14, 1998; 63 FR 30635, 30636, June 5, 1998; 67 FR 77172, Dec. 17, 2002]

§253.8 Terms and rates of royalty payments for the use of published pictorial, graphic, and sculptural works.

(a) *Scope.* This section establishes rates and terms for the use of published pictorial, graphic, and sculptural works by public broadcasting entities for the activities described in 17 U.S.C. 118. The rates and terms established in this schedule include the making of the reproductions described in 17 U.S.C. 118(d)(3).

(b) *Royalty rate.* (1) The following schedule of rates shall apply to the use of works within the scope of this section:

(i) For such uses in a PBS-distributed program:

	2003–2007
(A) For featured display of a work	$68.67
(B) For background and montage display	33.49
(C) For use of a work for program identification or for thematic use	135.37
(D) For the display of an art reproduction copyrighted separately from the work of fine art from which the work was reproduced irrespective of whether the reproduced work of fine art is copyrighted so as to be subject also to payment of a display fee under the terms of the schedule	44.47

(ii) For such uses in other than PBS-distributed programs:

	2003–2007
(A) For featured display of a work	$44.47
(B) For background and montage display	22.80
(C) For use of a work for a program identification or for thematic use	90.91
(D) For the display of an art reproduction copyrighted separately from the work of fine art from which the work was reproduced irrespective of whether the reproduced work of fine art is copyrighted so as to be subject also to payment of a display fee under the terms of this schedule	22.80

For the purposes of this schedule the rate for the thematic use of a work in an entire series shall be double the single program theme rate. In the event the work is first used other than in a PBS-distributed program, and such program is subsequently distributed by PBS, an additional royalty payment shall be made equal to the difference between the rate specified in this section for other than a PBS-distributed program and the rate specified in this section for a PBS-distributed program.

(2) "Featured display" for purposes of this schedule means a full-screen or substantially full-screen display appearing on the screen for more than three seconds. Any display less than full-screen or substantially full-screen, or full-screen for three seconds or less,

is deemed to be a "background or montage display".

(3) "Thematic use" is the utilization of the works of one or more artists where the works constitute the central theme of the program or convey a story line.

(4) "Display of an art reproduction copyrighted separately from the work of fine art from which the work was reproduced" means a transparency or other reproduction of an underlying work of fine art.

(c) *Payment of royalty rate.* PBS or other public broadcasting entity shall pay the required royalty fees to each copyright owner not later than July 31 of each calendar year for uses during the first six months of that calendar year, and not later than January 31 for uses during the last six months of the preceding calendar year.

(d) *Records of use.* (1) PBS and its stations or other public broadcasting entity shall maintain and furnish either to copyright owners, or to the offices of generally recognized organizations representing the copyright owners of pictorial, graphic and sculptural works, copies of their standard lists containing the pictorial, graphic, and sculptural works displayed on their programs. Such notice shall include the name of the copyright owner, if known, the specific source from which the work was taken, a description of the work used, the title of the program on which the work was used, and the date of the original broadcast of the program.

(2) Such listings shall be furnished not later than July 31 of each calendar year for displays during the first six months of the calendar year, and not later than January 31 of each calendar year for displays during the second six months of the preceding calendar year.

(e) *Filing of use reports with the Copyright Office.* (1) PBS and its stations or other public broadcasting entity shall deposit with the Copyright Office copies of their standard lists containing the pictorial, graphic, and sculptural works displayed on their programs. Such notice shall include the name of the copyright owner, if known, the specific source from which the work was taken, a description of the work used, the title of the program on which the work was used, and the date of the original broadcast of the program.

(2) Such listings shall be furnished not later than July 31 of each calendar year for displays during the first six months of the calendar year, and not later than January 31 of each calendar year for displays during the second six months of the preceding calendar year.

(f) *Terms of use.* (1) The rates of this schedule are for unlimited use for a period of three years from the date of the first use of the work under this schedule. Succeeding use periods will require the following additional payment: Additional one-year period—25 percent of the initial three-year fee; second three-year period—50 percent of the initial three-year fee; each three-year period thereafter—25 percent of the initial three-year fee; provided that a 100 percent additional payment prior to the expiration of the first three-year period will cover use during all subsequent use periods without limitation. Such succeeding uses which are subsequent to December 31, 2007, shall be subject to the rates established in this schedule.

(2) Pursuant to the provisions of 17 U.S.C. 118 (f), nothing in this schedule shall be construed to permit, beyond the limits of fair use as provided in 17 U.S.C. 107, the production of a transmission program drawn to any substantial extent from a published compilation of pictorial, graphic, or sculptural works.

[58 FR 60954, Dec. 22, 1992; 58 FR 7051, Feb. 4, 1993. Redesignated and amended at 59 FR 23993, May 9, 1994; 63 FR 2145, Jan. 14, 1998; 64 FR 36576, July 7, 1999; 67 FR 77172, Dec. 17, 2002]

§ 253.9 Unknown copyright owners.

If PBS and its stations, NPR and its stations, or other public broadcasting entity is not aware of the identity of, or unable to locate, a copyright owner who is entitled to receive a royalty payment under this part, they shall retain the required fee in a segregated trust account for a period of three years from the date of the required payment. No claim to such royalty fees shall be valid after the expiration of the three year period. Public broadcasting entities may establish a joint trust fund for the purposes of this section. Public broadcasting entities shall make available to the Copyright Office, upon request, information concerning fees deposited in trust funds.

[57 FR 60954, Dec. 22, 1992. Redesignated and amended at 59 FR 23993, May 9, 1994]

§ 253.10 Cost of living adjustment.

(a) (a) On December 1, 2003, the Librarian of Congress shall publish in the FEDERAL REGISTER a notice of the change in the cost of living as determined by the Consumer Price Index (all consumers, all items) during the period from the most recent Index published prior to December 1, 2002, to the most recent Index published prior to December 1, 2003. On each December 1 thereafter the Librarian of Congress shall publish a notice of the change in the cost of living during the period from the most recent index published prior to the previous notice, to the most recent Index published prior to December 1, of that year.

(b) On the same date of the notices published pursuant to paragraph (a) of this section, the Librarian of Congress shall publish in the FEDERAL REGISTER a revised schedule of rates for § 253.5 which shall adjust those royalty amounts established in dollar amounts according to the change in the cost of living determined as provided in paragraph (a) of this section. Such royalty rates shall be fixed at the nearest dollar.

(c) The adjusted schedule of rates for § 253.5 shall become effective thirty days after publication in the FEDERAL REGISTER.

[57 FR 60954, Dec. 22, 1992. Redesignated and amended at 59 FR 23993, May 9, 1994; 59 FR 63042, Dec. 7, 1994; 63 FR 2145, Jan. 14, 1998; 67 FR 77173, Dec. 17, 2002]

§ 253.11 Notice of restrictions on use of reproductions of transmission programs.

Any public broadcasting entity which, pursuant to 17 U.S.C. 118, supplies a reproduction of a transmission program to governmental bodies or nonprofit institutions shall include with each copy of the reproduction a warning notice stating in substance that the reproductions may be used for a period of not more than seven days from the specified date of transmission, that the reproductions must be destroyed by the user before or at the end of such period, and that a failure to fully comply with these terms shall subject the body or institution to the remedies for infringement of copyright.

PART 254—ADJUSTMENT OF ROYALTY RATE FOR COIN-OPERATED PHONORECORD PLAYERS

AUTHORITY: 17 U.S.C. 116, 801(b)(1).

§ 254.1 General.

This part 254 establishes the compulsory license fees for coin-operated phonorecord players beginning on January 1, 1982, in accordance with the provisions of 17 U.S.C. 116.

[45 FR 890, Jan. 5, 1981. Redesignated and amended at 59 FR 23993, May 9, 1994]

§ 254.2 Definition of coin-operated phonorecord player.

As used in this part, the term *coin-operated phonorecord player* is a machine or device that:

(a) Is employed solely for the performance of nondramatic musical works by means of phonorecords upon being activated by insertion of coins, currency, tokens, or other monetary units or their equivalent;

(b) Is located in an establishment making no direct or indirect charge for admission;

(c) Is accompanied by a list of the titles of all the musical works available for performance on it, which list is affixed to the phonorecord player or posted in the establishment in a prominent position where it can be readily examined by the public; and

(d) Affords a choice of works available for performance and permits the choice to be made by the patrons of the establishment in which it is located.

[60 FR 8198, Feb. 13, 1995]

§ 254.3 Compulsory license fees for coin-operated phonorecord players.

(a) Commencing January 1, 1982, the annual compulsory license fee for a coin-operated phonorecord player shall be $25.

(b) Commencing January 1, 1984, the annual compulsory license fee for a coin-operated phonorecord player shall be $50.

(c) Commencing January 1, 1987, the annual compulsory license fee for a coin-operated phonorecord player shall be $63.

(d) If performances are made available on a particular coin-operated phonorecord player for the first time after July 1 of any year, the compulsory license fee for the remainder of that year shall be one half of the annual rate of (a), (b), or (c) of this section, whichever is applicable.

(e) Commencing January 1, 1990, the annual compulsory license fee for a coin-operated phonorecord player is suspended through December 31, 1999, or until such earlier or later time as the March 1990 license agreement between AMOA and ASCAP/BMI/SESAC is terminated.

[51 FR 27537, Aug. 1, 1986, as amended at 55 FR 28197, July 10, 1990. Redesignated at 59 FR 23993, May 9, 1994]

PART 255—ADJUSTMENT OF ROYALTY PAYABLE UNDER COMPULSORY LICENSE FOR MAKING AND DISTRIBUTING PHONORECORDS

AUTHORITY: 17 U.S.C. 801(b)(1) and 803.

§ 255.1 General.

This part 255 adjusts the rates of royalties payable under the compulsory license for making and distributing phonorecords, including digital phonorecord deliveries, embodying nondramatic musical works, under 17 U.S.C. 115.

[60 FR 61657, Dec. 1, 1995]

§ 255.2 Royalty payable under compulsory license.

With respect to each work embodied in the phonorecord, the royalty payable shall be either four cents, or three-quarters of one cent per minute of playing time or fraction thereof, whichever amount is larger, for every phonorecord made and distributed on or after July 1, 1981, subject to adjustment pursuant to § 255.3.

[46 FR 891, Jan. 5, 1981, as amended at 46 FR 62268, Dec. 23, 1981. Redesignated and amended at 59 FR 23993, May 9, 1994]

§ 255.3 Adjustment of royalty rate.

(a) For every phonorecord made and distributed on or after January 1, 1983, the royalty rate payable with respect to each work embodied in the phonorecord shall be either 4.25 cents, or 0.8 cent per minute of playing time or fraction thereof, whichever amount is larger, subject to further adjustment pursuant to paragraphs (b) through (m) of this section.

(b) For every phonorecord made and distributed on or after July 1, 1984, the royalty rate payable with respect to each work embodied in the phonorecord shall be either 4.5 cents, or 0.85 cent per minute of playing time or fraction thereof, whichever amount is larger, subject to further adjustment pursuant to paragraphs (c) through (m) of this section.

(c) For every phonorecord made and distributed on or after January 1, 1986, the royalty rate payable with respect to each work embodied in the phonorecord shall be either 5.0 cents, or 0.95 cent per minute of playing time or fraction thereof, whichever amount is larger, subject to further adjustment pursuant to paragraphs (d) through (m) of this section.

(d) For every phonorecord made and distributed on or after January 1, 1988, the royalty rate payable with respect to each work embodied in the phonorecord shall be either 5.25 cents, or 1.0

cent per minute of playing time or fraction thereof, whichever amount is larger, subject to further adjustment pursuant to paragraphs (e) through (m) of this section.

(e) For every phonorecord made and distributed on or after January 1, 1990, the royalty rate payable with respect to each work embodied in the phonorecord shall be either 5.7 cents, or 1.1 cents per minute of playing time or fraction thereof, whichever amount is larger, subject to further adjustment pursuant to paragraphs (f) through (m) of this section.

(f) For every phonorecord made and distributed on or after January 1, 1992, the royalty rate payable with respect to each work embodied in the phonorecord shall be either 6.25 cents, or 1.2 cents per minute of playing time or fraction thereof, whichever amount is larger, subject to further adjustment pursuant to paragraphs (g) through (m) of this section.

(g) For every phonorecord made and distributed on or after January 1, 1994, the royalty rate payable with respect to each work embodied in the phonorecord shall be either 6.6 cents, or 1.25 cents per minute of playing time or fraction thereof, whichever amount is larger, subject to further adjustment pursuant to paragraphs (h) through (m) of this section.

(h) For every phonorecord made and distributed on or after January 1, 1996, the royalty rate payable with respect to each work embodied in the phonorecord shall be either 6.95 cents, or 1.3 cents per minute of playing time or fraction thereof, whichever amount is larger, subject to further adjustment pursuant to paragraphs (i) through (m) of this section.

(i) For every phonorecord made and distributed on or after January 1, 1998, the royalty rate payable with respect to each work embodied in the phonorecord shall be either 7.1 cents, or 1.35 cents per minute of playing time or fraction thereof, whichever amount is larger, subject to further adjustment pursuant to paragraphs (j) through (m) of this section.

(j) For every phonorecord made and distributed on or after January 1, 2000, the royalty rate payable with respect to each work embodied in the phonorecord shall be either 7.55 cents, or 1.45 cents per minute of playing time or fraction thereof, whichever amount is larger, subject to further adjustment pursuant to paragraphs (k) through (m) of this section.

(k) For every phonorecord made and distributed on or after January 1, 2002, the royalty rate payable with respect to each work embodied in the phonorecord shall be either 8.0 cents, or 1.55 cents per minute of playing time or fraction thereof, whichever amount is larger, subject to further adjustment pursuant to paragraphs (l) through (m) of this section.

(l) For every phonorecord made and distributed on or after January 1, 2004, the royalty rate payable with respect to each work embodied in the phonorecord shall be either 8.5 cents, or 1.65 cents per minute of playing time or fraction thereof, whichever amount is larger, subject to further adjustment pursuant to paragraph (m) of this section.

(m) For every phonorecord made and distributed on or after January 1, 2006, the royalty rate payable with respect to each work embodied in the phonorecord shall be either 9.1 cents, or 1.75 cents per minute of playing time or fraction thereof, whichever amount is larger.

[60 FR 55459, Nov. 1, 1995, as amended at 63 FR 7289, Feb. 13, 1998]

§ 255.4 Definition of digital phonorecord delivery.

A "*digital phonorecord delivery*" is each individual delivery of a phonorecord by digital transmission of a sound recording which results in a specifically identifiable reproduction by or for any transmission recipient of a phonorecord of that sound recording, regardless of whether the digital transmission is also a public performance of the sound recording or any nondramatic musical work embodied therein. The reproduction of the phonorecord must be sufficiently permanent or stable to permit it to be perceived, reproduced, or otherwise communicated for a period of more than transitory duration. Such a phonorecord may be permanent or it may be made available to the transmission recipient for a limited period of time or for a specified number of performances. A digital phonorecord delivery includes all phonorecords that are made for the purpose of making the digital phonorecord delivery.

[73 FR 66182, Nov. 7, 2008]

§ 255.5 Royalty rate for digital phonorecord deliveries in general.

(a) For every digital phonorecord delivery made on or before December 31, 1997, the royalty rate payable with respect to each work embodied in the phonorecord shall be either 6.95 cents, or 1.3 cents per minute of playing time or fraction thereof, whichever amount is larger.

(b) For every digital phonorecord delivery made on or after January 1, 1998, except for digital phonorecord deliveries where the reproduction or distribution of a phonorecord is incidental to the transmission which constitutes the digital phonorecord delivery, as specified in 17 U.S.C. 115(c)(3)(C) and (D), the royalty rate payable with respect to each work embodied in the phonorecord shall be the royalty rate prescribed in § 255.3 for the making and distribution of a phonorecord made and distributed on the date of the digital phonorecord delivery (the "Physical Rate"). In any future proceeding under 17 U.S.C. 115(c)(3)(C) or (D), the royalty rates payable for a compulsory license for digital phonorecord deliveries in general shall be established de novo, and no precedential effect shall be given to the royalty rate payable under this paragraph for any period prior to the period as to which the royalty rates are to be established in such future proceeding.

[64 FR 6223, Feb. 9, 1999]

§ 255.6 Royalty rate for incidental digital phonorecord deliveries.

The royalty rate for digital phonorecord deliveries where the reproduction or distribution of a phonorecord is incidental to the transmission which constitutes a digital phonorecord delivery, as specified in 17 U.S.C. 115(c)(3)(C) and (D), is deferred for consideration until the next digital phonorecord delivery rate adjustment proceeding pursuant to the schedule set forth in § 255.7; provided, however, that any owner or user of a copyrighted work with a significant interest in such royalty rate, as provided in 17 U.S.C. 803(a)(1), may petition the Librarian of Congress to establish a rate prior to the commencement of the next digital phonorecord delivery rate adjustment proceeding. In the event such a petition is filed, the Librarian of Congress shall proceed in accordance with 17 U.S.C. 115(c)(3)(D), and all applicable regulations, as though the petition had been filed in accordance with 17 U.S.C. 803(a)(1).

[64 FR 6223, Feb. 9, 1999]

§ 255.7 Future proceedings.

The procedures specified in 17 U.S.C. 115(c)(3)(C) shall be repeated in 1999, 2001, 2003, and 2006 so as to determine the applicable rates and terms for the making of digital phonorecord deliveries during the periods beginning January 1, 2001, 2003, 2005, and 2008. The procedures specified in 17 U.S.C. 115(c)(3)(D) shall be repeated, in the absence of license agreements negotiated under 17 U.S.C. 115(c)(3)(B) and (C), upon the filing of a petition in accordance with 17 U.S.C. 803(a)(1), in 2000, 2002, 2004, and 2007 so as to determine new rates and terms for the making of digital phonorecord deliveries during the periods beginning January 1, 2001, 2003, 2005, and 2008. Thereafter, the procedures specified in 17 U.S.C. 115(c)(3)(C) and (D) shall be repeated in each fifth calendar year. Notwithstanding the foregoing, different years for the repeating of such proceedings may be determined in accordance with 17 U.S.C. 115(c)(3)(C) and (D).

[64 FR 6223, Feb. 9, 1999]

§ 255.8 Public performances of sound recordings and musical works.

Nothing in this part annuls or limits the exclusive right to publicly perform a sound recording or the musical work embodied therein, including by means of a digital transmission, under 17 U.S.C. 106(4) and 106(6).

[64 FR 6223, Feb. 9, 1999]

PART 256—ADJUSTMENT OF ROYALTY FEE FOR CABLE COMPULSORY LICENSE

AUTHORITY: 17 U.S.C. 702, 802.

§256.1 General.

This part establishes adjusted terms and rates for royalty payments in accordance with the provisions of 17 U.S.C. 111 and 801(b)(2)(A), (B), (C), and (D). Upon compliance with 17 U.S.C 111 and the terms and rates of this part, a cable system entity may engage in the activities set forth in 17 U.S.C. 111.

[47 FR 52159, Nov. 19, 1982. Redesignated at 59 FR 23993, May 9, 1994, and amended at 60 FR 8198, Feb. 13, 1995]

§256.2 Royalty fee for compulsory license for secondary transmission by cable systems.

(a) Commencing with the second semiannual accounting period of 2005 and for each semiannual accounting period thereafter, the royalty rates established by 17 U.S.C. 111(d)(1)(B) shall be as follows:

(1) 1.013 of 1 per centum of such gross receipts for the privilege of further transmitting any nonnetwork programming of a primary transmitter in whole or in part beyond the local service area of such primary transmitter, such amount to be applied against the fees, if any, payable pursuant to paragraphs (a) (2) through (4) and (c);

(2) 1.013 of 1 per centum of such gross receipts for the first distant signal equivalent;

(3) .668 of 1 per centum of such gross receipts for each of the second, third and fourth distant signal equivalents; and

(4) .314 of 1 per centum of such gross receipts for the fifth distant signal equivalent and each additional distant signal equivalent thereafter.

(b) Commencing with the second semiannual accounting period of 2005 and for each semiannual accounting period thereafter, the gross receipts limitations established by 17 U.S.C. 111(d)(1) (C) and (D) shall be adjusted as follows:

(1) If the actual gross receipts paid by subscribers to a cable system for the period covered by the statement for the basic service of providing secondary transmission of primary broadcast transmitters total $263,800 or less, gross receipts of the cable system for the purpose of this paragraph shall be computed by subtracting from such actual gross receipts the amount by which $263,800 exceeds such actual gross receipts, except that in no case shall a cable system's gross receipts be reduced to less than $10,400. The royalty fee payable under this paragraph shall be 0.5 of 1 per centum regardless of the number of distant signal equivalents, if any; and

(2) If the actual gross receipts paid by the subscribers to a cable system for the period covered by the statement, for the basic service of providing secondary transmissions of primary broadcast transmitters, are more than $263,800 but less than $527,600, the royalty fee payable under this paragraph shall be:

(i) 0.5 of 1 per centum of any gross receipts up to $263,800 and

(ii) 1 per centum of any gross receipts in excess of $263,800 but less than $527,600, regardless of the number of distant signal equivalents, if any.

(c) Notwithstanding paragraphs (a) and (d) of this section, commencing with the first accounting period of 1983 and for each semiannual accounting period thereafter, for each distant signal equivalent or fraction thereof not represented by the carriage of:

(1) Any signal which was permitted (or, in the case of cable systems commencing operations after June 24, 1981, which would have been permitted) under the rules and regulations of the Federal Communications Commission in effect on June 24, 1981, or

(2) A signal of the same type (that is, independent, network, or non-commercial educational) substituted for such permitted signal, or

(3) A signal which was carried pursuant to an individual waiver of the rules and regulations of the Federal Communications Commission, as such rules were in effect on June 24, 1981;

the royalty rate shall be, in lieu of the royalty rates specified in paragraphs (a) (2) through (4) and (d) of this section, 3.75 per centum of the gross receipts of the cable systems for each distant signal equivalent; any fraction of a distant signal equivalent shall be computed at its fractional value.

(d) Commencing with the first semiannual accounting period of 1990 and for each semiannual accounting period thereafter, in the case of a cable system located outside the 35-mile specified zone of a commercial VHF station that places a predicted Grade B contour, in whole or in part, over the cable system, and that is not significantly viewed or otherwise exempt from the FCC's syndicated exclusivity rules in effect on June 24, 1981, for each distant signal equivalent or fraction thereof represented by the carriage of such commercial VHF station, the royalty rate shall be, in addition to the amount specified in paragraph (a) of this section,

(1) For cable systems located wholly or in part within a top 50 television market,

(i) .599 per centum of such gross receipts for the first distant signal equivalent;

(ii) .377 per centum of such gross receipts for each of the second, third, and fourth distant signal equivalents; and

(iii) .178 per centum of such gross receipts for the fifth distant signal equivalent and each additional distant signal equivalent thereafter;

(2) For cable systems located wholly or in part within a second 50 television market,

(i) .300 per centum of such gross receipts for the first distant signal equivalent;

(ii) .189 per centum of such gross receipts for each of the second, third, and fourth distant signal equivalents; and

(iii) .089 per centum of such gross receipts for the fifth distant signal equivalent and each additional distant signal equivalent thereafter;

(3) For purposes of this section *top 50 television markets* and "second 50 television markets" shall be defined as the comparable terms are defined or interpreted in accordance with 47 CFR 76.51, as effective June 24, 1981.

[47 FR 52159, Nov. 19, 1982, as amended at 50 FR 18481, May 1, 1985; 54 FR 12619, Mar. 28, 1989; 55 FR 33613, Aug. 16, 1990; 56 FR 12122, Mar. 22, 1991. Redesignated at 59 FR 23993, May 9, 1994, as amended at 63 FR 30636, June 5, 1998; 63 FR 39739, July 24, 1998; 65 FR 39820, June 28, 2000; 65 FR 64623, Oct. 30, 2000; 70 FR 58311, Oct. 6, 2005]

PART 258—ADJUSTMENT OF ROYALTY FEE FOR SECONDARY TRANSMISSIONS BY SATELLITE CARRIERS

Sec.

AUTHORITY: 17 U.S.C. 119, 702, 802.

§ 258.1 General.

This part 258 adjusts the rates of royalties payable under the compulsory license for the secondary transmission of broadcast stations under 17 U.S.C. 119.

[57 FR 19053, May 1, 1992. Redesignated and amended at 59 FR 23994, May 9, 1994; 63 FR 30636, June 5, 1998]

§ 258.2 Definitions.

(a) *Commercial establishment.* The term "commercial establishment" means an establishment used for commercial purposes, such as bars, restaurants, private offices, fitness clubs, oil rigs, retail stores, banks and financial institutions, supermarkets, auto and boat dealerships, and other establishments with common business areas; *provided* that the term "commercial establishment" shall not include a multi-unit permanent or temporary dwelling where private home viewing occurs, such as hotels, dormitories, hospitals, apartments, condominiums and prisons, all of which shall be subject to the rates applicable to private home viewing.

(b) *Syndex-proof signal.* A satellite retransmission of a broadcast signal shall be deemed "syndex proof" for purposes of § 258.3(a) if, during any semi-annual reporting period, the retransmission does not include any program which, if delivered by any cable system in the United States, would be subject to the syndicated exclusivity rules of the Federal Communications Commission.

(c) *Per subscriber per month.* The term "per subscriber per month" means each subscriber subscribing to the station in question, or to a package including such station, on the last day of a given month.

[70 FR 17320, Apr. 6, 2005, as amended at 70 FR 39179, July 7, 2005]

§ 258.3 Royalty fee for secondary transmission of analog signals of broadcast stations by satellite carriers.

(a) Commencing May 1, 1992, the royalty rate for the secondary transmission of analog signals of broadcast stations for private home viewing by satellite carriers shall be as follows:

(1) 17.5 cents per subscriber per month for superstations.

(2) 14 cents per subscriber per month for superstations whose signals are syndex-proof, as defined in § 258.2.

(3) 6 cents per subscriber per month for network stations and noncommercial educational stations.

(b) Commencing January 1, 1998, the royalty fee for secondary transmission of analog signals of broadcast stations for private home viewing by satellite carriers shall be as follows:

(1) 27 cents per subscriber per month for distant superstations.

(2) 27 cents per subscriber per month for distant network stations.

(3) No royalty rate (zero) for a superstation secondarily transmitted within the station's local market, as defined in 17 U.S.C. 119(d)(11).

(4) No royalty rate (zero) for a network station secondarily transmitted within the station's local market, as defined in 17 U.S.C. 119(d)(11), to subscribers residing in unserved households, as defined in 17 U.S.C. 119(d)(10).

(c) Commencing July 1, 1999, the royalty rate for secondary transmission of analog signals of broadcast stations for private home viewing by satellite carriers shall be as follows:

(1) 18.9 cents per subscriber per month for distant superstations.

(2) 14.85 cents per subscriber per month for distant network stations.

(3) 14.85 cents per subscriber per month for the Public Broadcasting Service satellite feed.

(d) Commencing January 1, 2005, the royalty rate for secondary transmission of analog signals of broadcast stations by satellite carriers shall be as follows:

(1) For private home viewing—

(i) 20 cents per subscriber per month for distant superstations.

(ii) 17 cents per subscriber per month for distant network stations.

(2) For viewing in commercial establishments, 40 cents per subscriber per month for distant superstations.

(e) Commencing January 1, 2006, the royalty rate for secondary transmission of analog signals of broadcast stations by satellite carriers shall be as follows:

(1) For private home viewing—

(i) 21.5 cents per subscriber per month for distant superstations.

(ii) 20 cents per subscriber per month for distant network stations.

(2) For viewing in commercial establishments, 43 cents per subscriber per month for distant superstations.

(f) Commencing January 1, 2007, the royalty rate for secondary transmission of analog signals of broadcast stations by satellite carriers shall be as follows:

(1) For private home viewing—

(i) 23 cents per subscriber per month for distant superstations.

(ii) 23 cents per subscriber per month for distant network stations.

(2) For viewing in commercial establishments, 46 cents per subscriber per month for distant superstations.

(g) Commencing January 1, 2008, the royalty rate for secondary transmission of analog signals of broadcast stations by satellite carriers shall be as follows:

(1) For private home viewing—

(i) 24 cents per subscriber per month for distant superstations.

(ii) 24 cents per subscriber per month for distant network stations.

(2) For viewing in commercial establishments, 48 cents per subscriber per month for distant superstations.

(h) Commencing January 1, 2009, the royalty rate for secondary transmission of analog signals of broadcast stations by satellite carriers shall be as follows:

(1) For private home viewing—

(i) 24 cents per subscriber per month for distant superstations.

(ii) 24 cents per subscriber per month for distant network stations.

(2) For viewing in commercial establishments, 48 cents per subscriber per month for distant superstations.

[62 FR 55759, Oct. 28, 1997, as amended at 64 FR 71660, Dec. 22, 1999; 70 FR 17320, Apr. 6, 2005; 70 FR 39179, July 7, 2005; 73 FR 14185, Mar. 17, 2008; 74 FR 12093, Mar. 23, 2009]

§ 258.4 Royalty fee for secondary transmission of digital signals of broadcast stations by satellite carriers.

(a) Commencing January 1, 2005, the royalty rate for secondary transmission of digital signals of broadcast stations by satellite carriers shall be as follows:

(1) For private home viewing—

(i) 20 cents per subscriber per month for distant superstations.

(ii) 17 cents per subscriber per month for distant network stations.

(2) For viewing in commercial establishments, 40 cents per subscriber per month for distant superstations.

(b) Commencing January 1, 2006, the royalty rate for secondary transmission of digital signals of broadcast stations by satellite carriers shall be as follows:

(1) For private home viewing—

(i) 21.5 cents per subscriber per month for distant superstations.

(ii) 20 cents per subscriber per month for distant network stations.

(2) For viewing in commercial establishments, 43 cents per subscriber per month for distant superstations.

(c) Commencing January 1, 2007, the royalty rate for secondary transmission of digital signals of broadcast stations by satellite carriers shall be as follows:

(1) For private home viewing—

(i) 23 cents per subscriber per month for distant superstations.

(ii) 23 cents per subscriber per month for distant network stations.

(2) For viewing in commercial establishments, 46 cents per subscriber per month for distant superstations.

(d) Commencing January 1, 2008, the royalty rate for secondary transmission of digital signals of broadcast stations by satellite carriers shall be as follows:

(1) For private home viewing—

(i) 24 cents per subscriber per month for distant superstations.

(ii) 24 cents per subscriber per month for distant network stations.

(2) For viewing in commercial establishments, 48 cents per subscriber per month for distant superstations.

(e) Commencing January 1, 2009, the royalty rate for secondary transmission of digital signals of broadcast stations by satellite carriers shall be as follows:

(1) For private home viewing—

(i) 24 cents per subscriber per month for distant superstations.

(ii) 24 cents per subscriber per month for distant network stations.

(2) For viewing in commercial establishments, 48 cents per subscriber per month for distant superstations.

(f) For purposes of calculating the royalty rates for secondary transmission of digital signals of broadcast stations by satellite carriers—

(1) In the case of digital multicasting, the rates in paragraphs (a) through (e) of this section apply to each digital stream that a satellite carrier or distributor retransmits pursuant to section 119; *provided*, however that no additional royalty shall be paid for the carriage of any material related to the programming on such stream; and

(2) Satellite carriers and distributors are not required to pay a section 119 royalty for the retransmission of a digital signal to a subscriber who resides in a community where that signal is "significantly viewed," within the meaning of 17 U.S.C. 119(a)(3) and (b)(1), as amended.

[70 FR 39179, July 7, 2005, as amended at 73 FR 14185, Mar. 17, 2008; 74 FR 12093, Mar. 23, 2009]

PART 260—RATES AND TERMS FOR PREEXISTING SUBSCRIPTION SERVICES' DIGITAL TRANSMISSIONS OF SOUND RECORDINGS AND MAKING OF EPHEMERAL PHONORECORDS

AUTHORITY: 17 U.S.C. 114, 801(b)(1).

SOURCE: 63 FR 25413, May 8, 1998, unless otherwise noted.

§ 260.1 General

(a) This part 260 establishes rates and terms of royalty payments for the public performance of sound recordings by nonexempt preexisting subscription services in accordance with the provisions of 17 U.S.C. 114(d)(2), and the making of ephemeral phonorecords in connection with the public performance of sound recordings by nonexempt preexisting subscription services in accordance with the provisions of 17 U.S.C. 112(e).

(b) Upon compliance with 17 U.S.C. 114 and the terms and rates of this part, nonexempt preexisting subscription services may engage in the activities set forth in 17 U.S.C. 114(d)(2).

(c) Upon compliance with 17 U.S.C. 112(e) and the terms and rates of this part, nonexempt preexisting subscription services may engage in the activities set forth in 17 U.S.C. 112(e) without limit to the number of ephemeral phonorecords made.

(d) For purposes of this part, Licensee means any preexisting subscription service as defined in 17 U.S.C. 114(j)(11).

[68 FR 39840, July 3, 2003]

§ 260.2 Royalty fees for the digital performance of sound recordings and the making of ephemeral phonorecords by preexisting subscription services.

(a) Commencing January 1, 2002 and continuing through December 31, 2003, a Licensee's monthly royalty fee for the public performance of sound recordings pursuant to 17 U.S.C. 114(d)(2) and the making of any number of ephemeral phonorecords to facilitate such performances pursuant to 17 U.S.C. 112(e) shall be 7.0% of such Licensee's monthly gross revenues resulting from residential services in the United States.

(b) Commencing January 1, 2004 and continuing through December 31, 2007, a Licensee's monthly royalty fee for the public performance of sound recordings pursuant to 17 U.S.C. 114(d)(2) and the making of any number of ephemeral phonorecords to facilitate such performances pursuant to 17 U.S.C. 112(e) shall be 7.25% of such Licensee's monthly gross revenues resulting from residential services in the United States.

(c) Commencing in the year 2003 and continuing through the year 2007, each Licensee making digital performances of sound recordings pursuant to 17 U.S.C. 114(d)(2) and ephemeral phonorecords pursuant to 17 U.S.C. 112(e) shall make an advance payment of $100,000 per year, payable no later than January 20th of each year; Provided, however, that for 2003, the annual advance payment shall be due on August 20, 2003. The annual advance payment shall be nonrefundable, but the royalties due and payable for a given year or any month therein under paragraphs (a) and (b) of this section shall be recoupable against the annual advance payment for such year; Provided, however, that any unused annual advance payment for a given year shall not carry over into a subsequent year.

(d) A Licensee shall pay a late fee of 1.5% per month, or the highest lawful rate, whichever is lower, for any payment received after the due date. Late fees shall accrue from the due date until payment is received.

(e)(1) For purposes of this section, *gross revenues* shall mean all monies derived from the operation of the programming service of the Licensee and shall be comprised of the following:

(i) Monies received by Licensee from Licensee's carriers and directly from residential U.S. subscribers for Licensee's programming service;

(ii) Licensee's advertising revenues (as billed), or other monies received from sponsors if any, less advertising agency commissions not to exceed 15% of those fees incurred to a recognized advertising agency not owned or controlled by Licensee;

(iii) Monies received for the provision of time on the programming service to any third party;

(iv) Monies received from the sale of time to providers of paid programming such as infomercials;

(v) Where merchandise, service, or anything of value is received by Licensee in lieu of cash consideration for the use of Licensee's programming service, the fair market value thereof or Licensee's prevailing published rate, whichever is less;

(vi) Monies or other consideration received by Licensee from Licensee's carriers, but not including monies received by Licensee's carriers from others and not accounted for by Licensee's carriers to Licensee, for the provision of hardware by anyone and used in connection with the programming service;

(vii) Monies or other consideration received for any references to or inclusion of any product or service on the programming service; and

(viii) Bad debts recovered regarding paragraphs (e)(1) (i) through (vii) of this section.

(2) Gross revenues shall include such payments as set forth in paragraphs (e)(1) (i) through (viii) of this section to which Licensee is entitled but which are paid to a parent, subsidiary, division, or affiliate of Licensee, in lieu of payment to Licensee but not including payments to Licensee's carriers for the programming service. Licensee shall be allowed a deduction from "gross revenues" as defined in paragraph (e)(1) of this section for affiliate revenue returned during the reporting period and for bad debts actually written off during reporting period.

(f) During any given payment period, the value of each performance of each digital sound recording shall be the same.

[63 FR 25413, May 8, 1998, as amended at 64 FR 36576, July 7, 1999; 65 FR 39820, June 28, 2000; 68 FR 36470, June 18, 2003; 68 FR 39840, July 3, 2003]

§ 260.3 Terms for making payment of royalty fees.

(a) All royalty payments shall be made to a designated agent(s), to be determined by the parties through voluntary license agreements or by a duly appointed Copyright Arbitration Royalty Panel pursuant to the procedures set forth in subchapter B of 37 CFR, part 251.

(b) Payment shall be made on the forty-fifth day after the end of each month for that month, commencing with the month succeeding the month in which the royalty fees are set.

(c) The agent designated to receive the royalty payments and the statements of account shall have the responsibility of making further distribution of these fees to those parties entitled to receive such payment according to the provisions set forth at 17 U.S.C. 114(g).

(d) The designated agent may deduct from any of its receipts paid by Licensees under § 260.2, prior to the distribution of such receipts to any person or entity entitled thereto, the reasonable costs permitted to be deducted under 17 U.S.C. 114(g)(3); Provided, however, that the parties entitled to receive royalty payments according to the provisions set forth at 17 U.S.C. 114(g)(1) & (2) who have authorized a designated agent may agree to deduct such other costs agreed to by such other parties and the designated agent.

(e) Until such time as a new designation is made, SoundExchange, which initially is an unincorporated division of the Recording Industry Association of America, Inc., shall be the agent receiving royalty payments and statements of account and shall continue to be designated if it should be separately incorporated.

(f) A Licensee shall make any payments due under § 260.2(a) for digital transmissions or ephemeral phonorecords made between January 1,

2002, and July 31, 2003, to the Designated Agent, less any amounts previously paid by such period to the Recording Industry Association of America, Inc., or SoundExchange by September 15, 2003.

[63 FR 25413, May 8, 1998, as amended at 63 FR 30636, June 5, 1998; 68 FR 36470, June 18, 2003; 68 FR 39841, July 3, 2003]

§260.4 Confidential information and statements of account.

(a) For purposes of this part, confidential information shall include statements of account and any information pertaining to the statements of account designated as confidential by the nonexempt preexisting subscription service filing the statement. Confidential information shall also include any information so designated in a confidentiality agreement which has been duly executed between a nonexempt preexisting subscription service and an interested party, or between one or more interested parties; *Provided* that all such information shall be made available, for the verification proceedings provided for in §§260.5 and 260.6 of this part.

(b) Nonexempt preexisting subscription services shall submit monthly statements of account on a form provided by the agent designated to collect such forms and the monthly royalty payments.

(c) A statement of account shall include only such information as is necessary to verify the accompanying royalty payment. Additional information beyond that which is sufficient to verify the calculation of the royalty fees shall not be included on the statement of account.

(d) Access to the confidential information pertaining to the royalty payments shall be limited to:

(1) Those employees, agents, consultants and independent contractors of the designated agent, subject to an appropriate confidentiality agreement, who are engaged in the collection and distribution of royalty payments hereunder and activities directly related hereto, who are not also employees or officers of a sound recording copyright owner or performing artist, and who, for the purpose of performing such duties during the ordinary course of employment, require access to the records; and

(2) An independent and qualified auditor who is not an employee or officer of a sound recording copyright owner or performing artist, but is authorized to act on behalf of the interested copyright owners with respect to the verification of the royalty payments.

(e) The designated agent or any person identified in paragraph (d) of this section shall implement procedures to safeguard all confidential financial and business information, including, but not limited to royalty payments, submitted as part of the statements of account, using a reasonable standard of care, but no less than the same degree of security used to protect confidential financial and business information or similarly sensitive information belonging to the designated agent or such person.

(f) Books and records relating to the payment of the license fees shall be kept in accordance with generally accepted accounting principles for a period of three years. These records shall include, but are not limited to, the statements of account, records documenting an interested party's share of the royalty fees, and the records pertaining to the administration of the collection process and the further distribution of the royalty fees to those interested parties entitled to receive such fees.

[63 FR 25413, May 8, 1998, as amended at 68 FR 39841, July 3, 2003]

§260.5 Verification of statements of account.

(a) *General.* This section prescribes general rules pertaining to the verification of the statements of account by interested parties according to terms promulgated by a duly appointed copyright arbitration royalty panel, under its authority to set reasonable terms and rates pursuant to 17 U.S.C. 114 and 801(b)(1), and the Librarian of Congress under his authority pursuant to 17 U.S.C. 802(f).

(b) *Frequency of verification.* Interested parties may conduct a single audit of a nonexempt preexisting subscription service during any given calendar year.

(c) *Notice of intent to audit.* Interested parties must submit a notice of intent to audit a particular service with the Copyright Office, which shall publish in the FEDERAL REGISTER a notice announcing the receipt of the notice of intent to audit within 30 days of the filing of the interested parties' notice. Such notification of intent to audit shall also be served at the same time on the party to be audited.

(d) *Retention of records.* The party requesting the verification procedure shall retain the report of the verification for a period of three years.

(e) *Acceptable verification procedure.* An audit, including underlying paperwork, which was performed in the ordinary course of business according to generally accepted auditing standards by an independent auditor, shall serve as an acceptable verification procedure for all parties.

(f) *Costs of the verification procedure.* The interested parties requesting the verification procedure shall pay for the cost of the verification procedure, unless an independent auditor concludes that there was an underpayment of five (5) percent or more; in which case, the service which made the underpayment shall bear the costs of the verification procedure.

(g) *Interested parties.* For purposes of this section, interested parties are those copyright owners who are entitled to receive royalty fees pursuant to 17 U.S.C. 114(g), their designated agents, or the entity designated by the copyright arbitration royalty panel in 37 CFR 260.3 to receive and to distribute the royalty fees.

[63 FR 25413, May 8, 1998, as amended at 68 FR 39841, July 3, 2003]

§ 260.6 Verification of royalty payments.

(a) *General.* This section prescribes general rules pertaining to the verification of the payment of royalty fees to those parties entitled to receive such fees, according to terms promulgated by a duly appointed copyright arbitration royalty panel, under its authority to set reasonable terms and rates pursuant to 17 U.S.C. 114 and 801(b)(1), and the Librarian of Congress under his authority pursuant to 17 U.S.C. 802(f).

(b) *Frequency of verification.* Interested parties may conduct a single audit of the entity making the royalty payment during any given calendar year.

(c) *Notice of intent to audit.* Interested parties must submit a notice of intent to audit the entity making the royalty payment with the Copyright Office, which shall publish in the FEDERAL REGISTER a notice announcing the receipt of the notice of intent to audit within 30 days of the filing of the interested parties' notice. Such notification of interest shall also be served at the same time on the party to be audited.

(d) *Retention of records.* The interested party requesting the verification procedure shall retain the report of the verification for a period of three years.

(e) *Acceptable verification procedure.* An audit, including underlying paperwork, which was performed in the ordinary course of business according to generally accepted auditing standards by an independent auditor, shall serve as an acceptable verification procedure for all interested parties.

(f) *Costs of the verification procedure.* The interested parties requesting the verification procedure shall pay for the cost of the verification procedure, unless an independent auditor concludes that there was an underpayment of five (5) percent or more, in which case, the entity which made the underpayment shall bear the costs of the verification procedure.

(g) *Interested parties.* For purposes of this section, interested parties are those who are entitled to receive royalty payments pursuant to 17 U.S.C. 114(g)(2), or their designated agents.

[68 FR 36470, June 18, 2003, as amended at 68 FR 39841, July 3, 2003]

§ 260.7 Unknown copyright owners.

If the designated collecting agent is unable to identify or locate a copyright owner who is entitled to receive a royalty payment under this part, the collecting agent shall retain the required payment in a segregated trust account for a period of three years from the date of payment. No claim to such payment shall be valid after the expiration of the three-year period. After the expiration of this period, the collecting agent may use the unclaimed funds to offset any costs deductible under 17 U.S.C. 114(g)(3).

[63 FR 25413, May 8, 1998, as amended at 64 FR 36576, July 7, 1999; 68 FR 36470, June 18, 2003; 68 FR 39841, July 3, 2003; 68 FR 57815, Oct. 7, 2003]

PART 261—RATES AND TERMS FOR ELIGIBLE NONSUBSCRIPTION TRANSMISSIONS AND THE MAKING OF EPHEMERAL REPRODUCTIONS

AUTHORITY: 17 U.S.C. 112(e), 114, 801(b)(1).

SOURCE: 67 FR 45272, July 8, 2002, unless otherwise noted.

§ 261.1 General.

(a) This part 261 establishes rates and terms of royalty payments for the public performance of sound recordings in certain digital transmissions by certain Licensees in accordance with the provisions of 17 U.S.C. 114, and the making of ephemeral recordings by certain Licensees in accordance with the provisions of 17 U.S.C. 112(e).

(b) Licensees relying upon the statutory license set forth in 17 U.S.C. 114 shall comply with the requirements of that section and the rates and terms of this part.

(c) Licensees relying upon the statutory license set forth in 17 U.S.C. 112 shall comply with the requirements of that section and the rates and terms of this part.

(d) Notwithstanding the schedule of rates and terms established in this part, the rates and terms of any license agreements entered into by Copyright Owners and services within the scope of 17 U.S.C. 112 and 114 concerning eligible nonsubscription transmissions shall apply in lieu of the rates and terms of this part.

§ 261.2 Definitions.

For purposes of this part, the following definitions shall apply:

Aggregate Tuning Hours mean the total hours of programming that the Licensee has transmitted over the Internet during the relevant period to all end users within the United States from all channels and stations that provide audio programming consisting, in whole or in part, of eligible nonsubscription transmissions. By way of example, if a service transmitted one hour of programming to 10 simultaneous listeners, the service's Aggregate Tuning Hours would equal 10. Likewise, if one listener listened to a service for 10 hours, the service's Aggregate Tuning Hours would equal 10.

Business Establishment Service is a Licensee that is entitled to transmit to the public a performance of a sound recording under the limitation on exclusive rights specified by 17 U.S.C. 114(d)(1)(C)(iv) and that obtains a compulsory license under 17 U.S.C. 112(e) to make ephemeral recordings for the sole purpose of facilitating those exempt transmissions.

Commercial Broadcaster is a Licensee that owns and operates a terrestrial AM or FM radio station that is licensed by the Federal Communications Commission to make over-the-air broadcasts, other than a CPB-Affiliated or Non-CPB-Affiliated, Non-Commercial Broadcaster.

Copyright Owner is a sound recording copyright owner who is entitled to receive royalty payments made under this part pursuant to the statutory licenses under 17 U.S.C. 112(e) or 114.

Designated Agent is the agent designated by the Librarian of Congress for the receipt of royalty payments made pursuant to this part from the Receiving Agent. The Designated Agent shall make further distribution of those royalty payments to Copyright Owners and Performers that have been identified in § 261.4(c).

Ephemeral Recording is a phonorecord created solely for the purpose of facilitating a transmission of a public performance of a sound recording under the limitations on exclusive rights specified by 17 U.S.C. 114(d)(1)(C)(iv) or under a statutory license in accordance with 17 U.S.C. 114(f), and subject to the limitations specified in 17 U.S.C. 112(e).

Gross proceeds mean all fees and payments, as used in § 261.3(d), including those made in kind, received from any source before, during or after the License term which are derived from the use of copyrighted sound recordings pursuant to 17 U.S.C. 112(e) for the sole purpose of facilitating a transmission to the public of a performance of a sound recording under the limitation on the exclusive rights specified in section 114(d)(1)(c)(iv).

Licensee is: (1) A person or entity that has obtained a compulsory license under 17 U.S.C. 112 or 114 and the implementing regulations therefor to make eligible non-subscription transmissions and ephemeral recordings, or

(2) A person or entity entitled to transmit to the public a performance of a sound recording under the limitation on exclusive rights specified by 17 U.S.C. 114(d)(1)(C)(iv) and that has obtained a compulsory license under 17 U.S.C. 112 to make ephemeral recordings.

Listener is a recipient of a transmission of a public performance of a sound recording made by a Licensee or a Business Establishment Service. However, if more than one person is listening to a transmission made to a single machine or device, those persons collectively constitute a single listener.

Non-CPB, Non-Commercial Broadcaster is a Public Broadcasting Entity as defined in 17 U.S.C. 118(g) that is not qualified to receive funding from the Corporation for Public Broadcasting pursuant to the criteria set forth in 47 U.S.C. 396.

Performance is each instance in which any portion of a sound recording is publicly performed to a listener via a Web Site transmission or retransmission (e.g. the delivery of any portion of a single track from a compact disc to one listener) but excluding the following:

(1) A performance of a sound recording that does not require a license (e.g., the sound recording is not copyrighted);

(2) A performance of a sound recording for which the service has previously obtained license from the copyright owner of such sound recording; and

(3) An incidental performance that both: (i) Makes no more than incidental use of sound recordings including, but not limited to, brief musical transitions in and out of commercials or program segments, brief performances during news, talk and sports programming, brief background performances during disk jockey announcements, brief performances during commercials of sixty seconds or less in duration, or brief performances during sporting or other public events; and

(ii) Other than ambient music that is background at a public event, does not contain an entire sound recording and does not feature a particular sound recording of more than thirty seconds (as in the case of a sound recording used as a theme song).

Performer means the respective independent administrators identified in 17 U.S.C. 114(g)(2)(A) and (B) and the parties identified in 17 U.S.C. 114(g)(2)(C).

Receiving Agent is the agent designated by the Librarian of Congress for the collection of royalty payments made pursuant to this part by Licensees and the distribution of those royalty payments to Designated Agents, and that has been identified as such in § 261.4(b). The Receiving Agent may also be a Designated Agent.

Side channel is a channel on the Web Site of a Commercial Broadcaster or a Non-CPB, Non-Commercial Broadcaster, which channel transmits eligible non-subscription transmissions that are not simultaneously transmitted over-the-air by the Licensee.

Webcaster is a Licensee, other than a Commercial Broadcaster, Non-CPB, Non-Commercial Broadcaster or Business Establishment Service, that makes eligible non-subscription transmissions of digital audio programming over the Internet through a Web Site.

Web Site is a site located on the World Wide Web that can be located by an end user through a principal Uniform Resource Locator (a "URL"), e.g., *www.xxxxx.com.*

§ 261.3 Royalty fees for public performances of sound recordings and for ephemeral recordings.

(a) For the period October 28, 1998, through December 31, 2002, royalty rates and fees for eligible digital transmissions of sound recordings made pursuant to 17 U.S.C. 114(d)(2), and the making of ephemeral recordings pursuant to 17 U.S.C. 112(e) shall be as follows:

(1) Webcaster and Commercial Broadcaster Performance Royalty. For all Internet transmissions, including simultaneous Internet retransmissions of over-the-air AM or FM radio broadcasts, a Webcaster and a Commercial Broadcaster shall pay a section 114(f) performance royalty of 0.07¢ per performance.

(2) Non-CPB, Non-Commercial Broadcaster Performance Royalty.

(i) For simultaneous Internet retransmissions of over-the-air AM or FM broadcasts by the same radio station, a non-CPB, Non-Commercial Broadcaster shall pay a section 114(f) performance royalty of 0.02¢ per performance.

(ii) For other Internet transmissions, including up to two side channels of programming consistent with the mission of the station, a Non-CPB, Non-Commercial Broadcaster shall pay a section 114(f) performance royalty of 0.02¢ per performance.

(iii) For Internet transmissions on other side channels of programming, a Non-CPB, Non-Commercial Broadcaster shall pay a section 114(f) performance royalty of 0.07¢ per performance.

(b) Estimate of Performance. Until December 31, 2002, a Webcaster, Commercial Broadcaster, or Non-CPB, Non-Commercial Broadcaster may estimate its total number of performances if the actual number is not available. Such estimation shall be based on multiplying the total number of Aggregate Tuning Hours by 15 performances per hour (1 performance per hour in the case of transmissions or retransmissions of radio station programming reasonably classified as news, business, talk or sports, and 12 performances per hour in the case of transmissions or retransmissions of all other radio station programming).

(c) *Webcaster and Broadcaster Ephemeral Recordings Royalty.* For the making of any number of ephemeral recordings to facilitate the Internet transmission of a sound recording, each Webcaster, Commercial Broadcaster, and Non-CPB, Non-Commercial Broadcaster shall pay a section 112(e) royalty equal to 8.8% of their total performance royalty.

(d) *Business Establishment Ephemeral Recordings Royalty.* For the making of any number of ephemeral recordings in the operation of a service pursuant to the Business Establishment exemption contained in 17 U.S.C. 114(d)(1)(C)(iv), a Business Establishment Service shall pay a section 112(e) ephemeral recording royalty equal to ten percent (10%) of the Licensee's annual gross proceeds derived from the use in such service of the musical programs which are attributable to copyrighted recordings. The attribution of gross proceeds to copyrighted recordings may be made on the basis of:

(1) For classical programs, the proportion that the playing time of copyrighted classical recordings bears to the total playing time of all classical recordings in the program,

(2) For all other programs, the proportion that the number of copyrighted recordings bears to the total number of all recordings in the program.

(e) *Minimum fee.* (1) Each Webcaster, Commercial Broadcaster, and Non-CPB, Non-Commercial Broadcaster licensed to make eligible digital transmissions and/or ephemeral recordings pursuant to licenses under 17 U.S.C. 114(f) and/or 17 U.S.C. 112(e) shall pay a minimum fee of $500 for each calendar year, or part thereof, in which it makes such transmissions or recordings.

(2) Each Business Establishment Service licensed to make ephemeral recordings pursuant to a license under 17 U.S.C. 112(e) shall pay a minimum fee of $10,000 for each calendar year, or part thereof, in which it makes such recordings.

§ 261.4 Terms for making payment of royalty fees and statements of account.

(a) A Licensee shall make the royalty payments due under § 261.3 to the Receiving Agent. If there are more than one Designated Agent representing Copyright Owners or Performers entitled to receive any portion of the royalties paid by the Licensee, the Receiving Agent shall apportion the royalty payments among Designated Agents using the information provided by the Licensee pursuant to the regulations governing records of use of performances for the period for which the royalty payment was made. Such apportionment shall be made on a reasonable basis that uses a methodology that values all performances equally and is agreed upon among the Receiving Agent and the Designated Agents. Within 30 days of adoption of a methodology for apportioning royalties among Designated Agents, the Receiving Agent shall provide the Register of Copyrights with a detailed description of that methodology.

(b) Until such time as a new designation is made, SoundExchange, an unincorporated division of the Recording Industry Association of America, Inc., is designated as the Receiving Agent to receive statements of account and royalty payments from Licensees. Until such time as a new designation is made, Royalty Logic, Inc. and SoundExchange are designated as Designated Agents to distribute royalty payments to Copyright Owners and Performers entitled to receive royalties under 17 U.S.C. 114(g)(2) from the performance of sound recordings owned by such Copyright Owners.

(c) SoundExchange is the Designated Agent to distribute royalty payments to each Copyright Owner and Performer entitled to receive royalties under 17 U.S.C. 114(g)(2) from the performance of sound recordings owned by such Copyright Owners, except when a Copyright Owner or Performer has notified SoundExchange in writing of an election to receive royalties from a particular Designated Agent. With respect to any royalty payment received by the Receiving Agent from a Licensee, a designation by a Copyright Owner or Performer of a particular Designated Agent must be made no later than thirty days prior to the receipt by the Receiving Agent of that royalty payment.

(d) Commencing September 1, 2002, a Licensee shall make any payments due under § 261.3 to the Receiving Agent by the forty-fifth (45th) day after the end of each month for that month. Concurrently with the delivery of payment to the Receiving Agent, a Licensee shall deliver to each Designated Agent a copy of the statement of account for such payment. A Licensee shall pay a late fee of 0.75% per month, or the highest lawful rate, whichever is lower, for any payment received by the Receiving Agent after the due date. Late fees shall accrue from the due date until payment is received by the Receiving Agent.

(e) A Licensee shall make any payments due under § 261.3 for transmissions made between October 28, 1998, and August 31, 2002, to the Receiving Agent by October 20, 2002.

(f) A Licensee shall submit a monthly statement of account for accompanying royalty payments on a form prepared by the Receiving Agent after full consultation with all Designated Agents. The form shall be made available to the Licensee by the Receiving Agent. A statement of account shall include only such information as is necessary to calculate the accompanying royalty payment. Additional information beyond that which is sufficient to calculate the royalty payments to be paid shall not be required to be included on the statement of account.

(g) The Receiving Agent shall make payments of the allocable share of any royalty payment received from any Licensee under this section to the Designated Agent(s) as expeditiously as is reasonably possible following receipt of the Licensee's royalty payment and statement of account as well as the Licensee's Report of Use of Sound Recordings under Statutory License for the period to which the royalty payment and statement of account pertain, with such allocation to be made on the basis determined as set forth in paragraph (a) of this section. The Receiving Agent and the Designated Agent shall agree on a reasonable basis on the sharing on a pro-rata basis of any incremental costs directly associated with the allocation method. A final adjustment, if necessary, shall be agreed and paid or refunded, as the case may be, between the Receiving Agent and a Designated Agent for each calendar year no later than 180 days following the end of each calendar year.

(h) The Designated Agent shall distribute royalty payments on a reasonable basis that values all performances by a Licensee equally based upon the information provided by the Licensee pursuant to the regulations governing records of use of performances; Provided, however, that Copyright Owners and Performers who have designated a particular Designated Agent may agree to allocate their shares of the royalty payments among themselves on an alternative basis.

(i)(1) A Designated Agent shall provide to the Register of Copyrights:

(i) A detailed description of its methodology for distributing royalty payments to Copyright Owners and Performers who have not agreed to an alternative basis for allocating their share of royalty payments (hereinafter, "non-members"), and any amendments thereto, within 30 days of adoption and no later than 60 days prior to the first distribution to Copyright Owners and Performers of any royalties distributed pursuant to that methodology;

(ii) Any written complaint that the Designated Agent receives from a nonmember concerning the distribution of royalty payments, within 30 days of receiving such written complaint; and

(iii) The final disposition by the Designated Agent of any complaint specified by paragraph (i)(1)(ii) of this section, within 60 days of such disposition.

(2) A Designated Agent may request that the Register of Copyrights provide a written opinion stating whether the Agent's methodology for distributing royalty payments to non-members meets the requirements of this section.

(j) A Designated Agent shall distribute such royalty payments directly to the Copyright Owners and Performers, according to the percentages set forth in 17 U.S.C. 114(g)(2), if such Copyright Owners and Performers provide the Designated Agent with adequate information necessary to identify the correct recipient for such payments. However, Performers and Copyright Owners may jointly agree with a Designated Agent upon payment protocols to be used by the Designated Agent that provide for alternative arrangements for the payment of royalties to Performers and Copyright Owners consistent with the percentages in 17 U.S.C. 114(g)(2).

(k) A Designated Agent may deduct from the royalties paid to Copyright Owners and Performers reasonable costs incurred in the collection and distribution of the royalties paid by Licensees under §261.3, and a reasonable charge for administration.

(l) In the event a Designated Agent and a Receiving Agent cannot agree upon a methodology for apportioning royalties pursuant to paragraph (a) of this section, either the Receiving Agent or a Designated Agent may seek the assistance of the Copyright Office in resolving the dispute.

§261.5 Confidential information.

(a) For purposes of this part, "Confidential Information" shall include the statements of account, any information contained therein, including the amount of royalty payments, and any information pertaining to the statements of account reasonably designated as confidential by the Licensee submitting the statement.

(b) Confidential Information shall not include documents or information that at the time of delivery to the Receiving Agent or a Designated Agent are public knowledge. The Receiving Agent or a Designated Agent that claims the benefit of this provision shall have the burden of proving that the disclosed information was public knowledge.

(c) In no event shall the Receiving Agent or Designated Agent(s) use any Confidential Information for any purpose other than royalty collection and distribution and activities directly related thereto; Provided, however, that the Designated Agent may report Confidential Information provided on statements of account under this part in aggregated form, so long as Confidential Information pertaining to any Licensee or group of Licensees cannot directly or indirectly be ascertained or reasonably approximated. All reported aggregated Confidential Information from Licensees within a class of Licensees shall concurrently be made available to all Licensees then in such class. As used in this paragraph, the phrase "class of Licensees" means all Licensees paying fees pursuant to § 261.4(a).

(d) Except as provided in paragraph (c) of this section and as required by law, access to Confidential Information shall be limited to, and in the case of paragraphs (d)(3) and (d)(4) of this section shall be provided upon request, subject to resolution of any relevance or burdensomeness concerns and reimbursement of reasonable costs directly incurred in responding to such request, to:

(1) Those employees, agents, consultants and independent contractors of the Receiving Agent or a Designated Agent, subject to an appropriate confidentiality agreement, who are engaged in the collection and distribution of royalty payments hereunder and activities directly related thereto, who are not also employees or officers of a Copyright Owner or Performer, and who, for the purpose of performing such duties during the ordinary course of employment, require access to the records;

(2) An independent and qualified auditor, subject to an appropriate confidentiality agreement, who is authorized to act on behalf of the Receiving Agent or a Designated Agent with respect to the verification of a Licensee's statement of account pursuant to § 261.6 or on behalf of a Copyright Owner or Performer with respect to the verification of royalty payments pursuant to § 261.7;

(3) In connection with future Copyright Arbitration Royalty Panel proceedings under 17 U.S.C. 114(f)(2) and 112(e), under an appropriate protective order, attorneys, consultants and other authorized agents of the parties to the proceedings, Copyright Arbitration Royalty Panels, the Copyright Office or the courts; and

(4) In connection with *bona fide* royalty disputes or claims by or among Licensees, the Receiving Agent, Copyright Owners, Performers or the Designated Agent(s), under an appropriate confidentiality agreement or protective order, attorneys, consultants and other authorized agents of the parties to the dispute, arbitration panels or the courts.

(e) The Receiving Agent or Designated Agent(s) and any person identified in paragraph (d) of this section shall implement procedures to safeguard all Confidential Information using a reasonable standard of care, but no less than the same degree of security used to protect Confidential Information or similarly sensitive information belonging to such Receiving Agent or Designated Agent(s) or person.

(f) Books and records of a Licensee, the Receiving Agent and of a Designated Agent relating to the payment, collection, and distribution of royalty payments shall be kept for a period of not less than three (3) years.

§ 261.6 Verification of statements of account.

(a) *General.* This section prescribes general rules pertaining to the verification of the statements of account by the Designated Agent.

(b) *Frequency of verification.* A Designated Agent may conduct a single audit of a Licensee, upon reasonable notice and during reasonable business hours, during any given calendar year, for any or all of the prior three (3) calendar years, and no calendar year shall be subject to audit more than once.

(c) *Notice of intent to audit.* A Designated Agent must submit a notice of intent to audit a particular Licensee with the Copyright Office, which shall publish in the FEDERAL REGISTER a notice announcing the receipt of the notice of intent to audit within thirty (30) days of the filing of the Designated Agent's notice. The notification of intent to audit shall be served at the same time on the Licensee to be audited. Any such audit shall be conducted by an independent and qualified auditor identified in the notice, and shall be binding on all Designated Agents, and all Copyright Owners and Performers.

(d) *Acquisition and retention of records.* The Licensee shall use commercially reasonable efforts to obtain or to provide access to any relevant books and records maintained by third parties for the purpose of the audit and retain such records for a period of not less than three (3) years. The Designated

Agent requesting the verification procedure shall retain the report of the verification for a period of not less than three (3) years.

(e) *Acceptable verification procedure.* An audit, including underlying paperwork, which was performed in the ordinary course of business according to generally accepted auditing standards by an independent and qualified auditor, shall serve as an acceptable verification procedure for all Designated Agents with respect to the information that is within the scope of the audit.

(f) *Consultation.* Before rendering a written report to a Designated Agent, except where the auditor has a reasonable basis to suspect fraud and disclosure would, in the reasonable opinion of the auditor, prejudice the investigation of such suspected fraud, the auditor shall review the tentative written findings of the audit with the appropriate agent or employee of the Licensee being audited in order to remedy any factual errors and clarify any issues relating to the audit; Provided that the appropriate agent or employee of the Licensee reasonably cooperates with the auditor to remedy promptly any factual errors or clarify any issues raised by the audit.

(g) *Costs of the verification procedure.* The Designated Agent requesting the verification procedure shall pay the cost of the procedure, unless it is finally determined that there was an underpayment of ten percent (10%) or more, in which case the Licensee shall, in addition to paying the amount of any underpayment, bear the reasonable costs of the verification procedure; Provided, however, that a Licensee shall not have to pay any costs of the verification procedure in excess of the amount of any underpayment unless the underpayment was more than twenty percent (20%) of the amount finally determined to be due from the Licensee and more than $5,000.00.

§ 261.7 Verification of royalty payments.

(a) *General.* This section prescribes general rules pertaining to the verification by any Copyright Owner or Performer of royalty payments made by a Designated Agent; Provided, however, that nothing contained in this section shall apply to situations where a Copyright Owner or a Performer and a Designated Agent have agreed as to proper verification methods.

(b) *Frequency of verification.* A Copyright Owner or a Performer may conduct a single audit of a Designated Agent upon reasonable notice and during reasonable business hours, during any given calendar year, for any or all of the prior three (3) calendar years, and no calendar year shall be subject to audit more than once.

(c) *Notice of intent to audit.* A Copyright Owner or Performer must submit a notice of intent to audit a particular Designated Agent with the Copyright Office, which shall publish in the FEDERAL REGISTER a notice announcing the receipt of the notice of intent to audit within thirty (30) days of the filing of the notice. The notification of intent to audit shall be served at the same time on the Designated Agent to be audited. Any such audit shall be conducted by an independent and qualified auditor identified in the notice, and shall be binding on all Copyright Owners and Performers.

(d) *Acquisition and retention of records.* The Designated Agent making the royalty payment shall use commercially reasonable efforts to obtain or to provide access to any relevant books and records maintained by third parties for the purpose of the audit and retain such records for a period of not less than three (3) years. The Copyright Owner or Performer requesting the verification procedure shall retain the report of the verification for a period of not less than three (3) years.

(e) *Acceptable verification procedure.* An audit, including underlying paperwork, which was performed in the ordinary course of business according to generally accepted auditing standards by an independent and qualified auditor, shall serve as an acceptable verification procedure for all parties with respect to the information that is within the scope of the audit.

(f) *Consultation.* Before rendering a written report to a Copyright Owner or Performer, except where the auditor has a reasonable basis to suspect fraud and disclosure would, in the reasonable opinion of the auditor, prejudice the investigation of such suspected fraud, the auditor shall review the tentative written findings of the audit with the appropriate agent or employee of the Designated Agent being audited in order to remedy any factual errors and clarify any issues relating to the audit; Provided that the appropriate agent or employee of the Designated Agent reasonably cooperates with the auditor to remedy promptly any factual errors or clarify any issues raised by the audit.

(g) *Costs of the verification procedure.* The Copyright Owner or Performer requesting the verification procedure shall pay the cost of the procedure, unless it is finally determined that there was an underpayment of ten percent (10%) or more, in which case the Designated Agent shall, in addition to paying the amount of any underpayment, bear the reasonable costs of the verification procedure; Provided, however, that a Designated Agent shall not have to pay any costs of the verification procedure in excess of the amount of any underpayment unless the underpayment was more than twenty percent (20%) of the amount finally determined to be due from the Designated Agent and more than $5,000.00.

§ 261.8 Unclaimed funds.

If a Designated Agent is unable to identify or locate a Copyright Owner or Performer who is entitled to receive a royalty payment under this part, the Designated Agent shall retain the required payment in a segregated trust account for a period of three (3) years from the date of payment. No claim to such payment shall be valid after the expiration of the three (3) year period. After the expiration of this period, the unclaimed funds of the Designated Agent may first be applied to the costs directly attributable to the administration of the royalty payments due such unidentified Copyright Owners and Performers and shall thereafter be allocated on a pro rata basis among the Designated Agents(s) to be used to offset such Designated Agent(s) other costs of collection and distribution of the royalty fees.

PART 262—RATES AND TERMS FOR CERTAIN ELIGIBLE NON-SUBSCRIPTION TRANSMISSIONS, NEW SUBSCRIPTION SERVICES AND THE MAKING OF EPHEMERAL REPRODUCTIONS

AUTHORITY: 17 U.S.C. 112(e), 114, 801(b)(1).

SOURCE: 69 FR 5695, Feb. 6, 2004, unless otherwise noted.

§ 262.1 General.

(a) *Scope.* This part 262 establishes rates and terms of royalty payments for the public performance of sound recordings in certain digital transmissions by certain Licensees in accordance with the provisions of 17 U.S.C. 114, and the making of Ephemeral Recordings by certain Licensees in accordance with the provisions of 17 U.S.C. 112(e), during the period 2003–2004 and in the case of Subscription Services 1998–2004 (the "License Period").

(b) *Legal compliance.* Licensees relying upon the statutory licenses set forth in 17 U.S.C. 112 and 114 shall comply with the requirements of those sections, the rates and terms of this part and any other applicable regulations.

(c) *Relationship to voluntary agreements.* Notwithstanding the royalty rates and terms established in this part, the rates and terms of any license agreements entered into by Copyright Owners and services shall apply in lieu of the rates and terms of this part to transmissions within the scope of such agreements.

§ 262.2 Definitions.

For purposes of this part, the following definitions shall apply:

(a) *Aggregate Tuning Hours* means the total hours of programming that the Licensee has transmitted during the relevant period to all Listeners within the United States from all channels and stations that provide audio programming consisting, in whole or in part, of eligible nonsubscription transmissions or noninteractive digital audio transmissions as part of a new subscription service, less the actual running time of any sound recordings for which the Licensee has obtained direct licenses apart from 17 U.S.C. 114(d)(2) or which do not require a license under United States copyright law. By way of example, if a service transmitted one hour of programming to 10 simultaneous Listeners, the service's Aggregate Tuning Hours would equal 10. If 3 minutes of that hour consisted of transmission of a directly licensed recording, the service's Aggregate Tuning Hours would equal 9 hours and 30 minutes. As an additional example, if one Listener listened to a service for 10 hours (and none of the recordings transmitted during that time was directly licensed), the service's Aggregate Tuning Hours would equal 10.

(b) *Broadcast Simulcast* means

(1) A simultaneous Internet transmission or retransmission of an over-the-air terrestrial AM or FM radio broadcast, including one with previously broadcast programming substituted for programming for which requisite licenses or clearances to transmit over the Internet have not been obtained and one with substitute advertisements, and

(2) An Internet transmission in accordance with 17 U.S.C. 114(d)(2)(C)(iii) of an archived program, which program was previously broadcast over-the-air by a terrestrial AM or FM broadcast radio station, in either case whether such Internet transmission or retransmission is made by the owner and operator of the AM or FM radio station that makes the broadcast or by a third party.

(c) *Business Establishment Service* means a service making transmissions of sound recordings under the limitation on exclusive rights specified by 17 U.S.C. 114(d)(1)(C)(iv).

(d) *Copyright Owner* is a sound recording copyright owner who is entitled to receive royalty payments made under this part pursuant to the statutory licenses under 17 U.S.C. 112(e) or 114.

(e) *Designated Agent* is the agent designated by the Librarian of Congress as provided in § 262.4(b).

(f) *Ephemeral Recording* is a phonorecord created for the purpose of facilitating a transmission of a public performance of a sound recording under the limitations on exclusive rights specified by 17 U.S.C. 114(d)(1)(C)(iv) or for the purpose of facilitating a transmission of a public performance of a sound recording under a statutory license in accordance with 17 U.S.C. 114(f), and subject to the limitations specified in 17 U.S.C. 112(e).

(g) *Licensee* is a person or entity that

(1) Has obtained a compulsory license under 17 U.S.C. 114 and the implementing regulations therefor to make eligible nonsubscription transmissions, or noninteractive digital audio transmissions as part of a new subscription service (as defined in 17 U.S.C. 114(j)(8)), or that has obtained a compulsory license under 17 U.S.C. 112(e) and the implementing regulations therefor to make Ephemeral Recordings for use in facilitating such transmissions, or

(2) Is a Business Establishment Service that has obtained a compulsory license under 17 U.S.C. 112(e) and the implementing regulations therefor to make Ephemeral Recordings, but not a person or entity that:

(i) Is exempt from taxation under section 501 of the Internal Revenue Code of 1986 (26 U.S.C. 501);

(ii) Has applied in good faith to the Internal Revenue Service for exemption from taxation under section 501 of the Internal Revenue Code and has a commercially reasonable expectation that such exemption shall be granted; or

(iii) Is a State or possession or any governmental entity or subordinate thereof, or the United States or District of Columbia, making transmissions for exclusively public purposes.

(h) *Listener* is a player, receiving device or other point receiving and rendering a transmission of a public performance of a sound recording made by a Licensee, irrespective of the number of individuals present to hear the transmission.

(i) *Nonsubscription Service* means a service making eligible nonsubscription transmissions.

(j) *Performance* is each instance in which any portion of a sound recording is publicly performed to a Listener by means of a digital audio transmission or retransmission (e.g., the delivery of any portion of a single track from a compact disc to one Listener) but excluding the following:

(1) A performance of a sound recording that does not require a license (e.g., the sound recording is not copyrighted);

(2) A performance of a sound recording for which the service has previously obtained a license from the Copyright Owner of such sound recording; and

(3) An incidental performance that both:

(i) Makes no more than incidental use of sound recordings including, but not limited to, brief musical transitions in and out of commercials or program segments, brief performances during news, talk and sports programming, brief background performances during disk jockey announcements, brief performances during commercials of sixty seconds or less in duration, or brief performances during sporting or other public events and

(ii) Other than ambient music that is background at a public event, does not contain an entire sound recording and does not feature a particular sound recording of more than thirty seconds (as in the case of a sound recording used as a theme song).

(k) *Performers* means the independent administrators identified in 17 U.S.C. 114(g)(2)(B) and (C) and the parties identified in 17 U.S.C. 114(g)(2)(D).

(l) *Subscription Service* means a new subscription service (as defined in 17 U.S.C. 114(j)(8)) making noninteractive digital audio transmissions.

(m) *Subscription Service Revenues* shall mean all monies and other consideration paid or payable, including the fair market value of non-cash or in-kind consideration paid or payable by third parties, from the operation of a Subscription Service, as comprised of the following:

(1) Subscription fees and other monies and consideration paid for access to the Subscription Service by or on behalf of subscribers receiving within the United States transmissions made as part of the Subscription Service;

(2) Monies and other consideration (including without limitation customer acquisition fees) from audio or visual advertising, promotions, sponsorships, time or space exclusively or predominantly targeted to subscribers of the Subscription Service, whether

(i) On or through the Subscription Service media player, or on pages accessible only by subscribers or that are predominantly targeted to subscribers, or

(ii) In e-mails addressed exclusively or predominantly to subscribers of the Subscription Service, or

(iii) Delivered exclusively or predominantly to subscribers of the Subscription Service in some other manner, in each case less advertising agency commissions (not to exceed 15% of those monies and other consideration) actually paid to a recognized advertising agency not owned or controlled by Licensee;

(3) Monies and other consideration (including without limitation the proceeds of any revenue-sharing or commission arrangements with any fulfillment company or other third party, and any charge for shipping or handling) from the sale of any product or service directly through the Subscription Service media player or through pages or advertisements accessible only by subscribers or that are predominantly targeted to subscribers (but not pages or advertisements that are not predominantly targeted to subscribers), less

(i) Monies and other consideration from the sale of phonorecords and digital phonorecord deliveries of sound recordings,

(ii) The Licensee's actual, out-of-pocket cost to purchase for resale the products or services (except phonorecords and digital phonorecord deliveries of sound recordings) from third parties, or in the case of products produced or services provided by the Licensee, the Licensee's actual cost to produce the product or provide the service (but not more than the fair market wholesale value of the product or service), and

(iii) Sales and use taxes, shipping, and credit card and fulfillment service fees actually paid to unrelated third parties; provided that:

(A) The fact that a transaction is consummated on a different page than the page/location where a potential customer responds to a "buy button" or other purchase opportunity for a product or service advertised directly through such player, pages or advertisements shall not render such purchase outside the scope of Subscription Service Revenues hereunder, and

(B) Monies and other consideration paid by or on behalf of subscribers for software or any other access device owned by Licensee (or any subsidiary or other affiliate of the Licensee, but excluding, for the avoidance of doubt, any entity that sells a third-party product, whether or not bearing the Licensee's brand) to access the Licensee's Subscription Service shall not be deemed part of Subscription Service Revenues, unless such software or access device is required as a condition to access the Subscription Service and either is purchased by a subscriber contemporaneously with or after subscribing or has no independent function other than to access the Subscription Service;

(4) Monies and other consideration for the use or exploitation of data specifically and separately concerning subscribers or the Subscription Service, but not monies and other consideration for the use or exploitation of data wherein information concerning subscribers or the Subscription Service is commingled with and not separated or distinguished from data that predominantly concern nonsubscribers or other services; and

(5) Bad debts recovered with respect to paragraphs (m)(1) through (4) of this section; provided that the Subscription Service shall be permitted to deduct bad debts actually written off during a reporting period.

[69 FR 5695, Feb. 6, 2004; 69 FR 8822, Feb. 26, 2004]

§ 262.3 Royalty fees for public performances of sound recordings and for ephemeral recordings.

(a) *Basic royalty rate.* Royalty rates and fees for eligible nonsubscription transmissions made by Licensees pursuant to 17 U.S.C. 114(d)(2) during the period January 1, 2003, through December 31, 2004, and the making of Ephemeral Recordings pursuant to 17 U.S.C. 112(e) to facilitate such transmissions; noninteractive digital audio transmissions made by Licensees pursuant to 17 U.S.C. 114(d)(2) as part of a new subscription service during the period October 28, 1998, through December 31, 2004, and the making of Ephemeral Recordings pursuant to 17 U.S.C. 112(e) to facilitate such transmissions; and the making of Ephemeral Recordings by Business Establishment Services pursuant to 17 U.S.C. 112(e) during the period January 1, 2003, through December 31, 2004, shall be as follows:

(1) *Nonsubscription Services.* For their operation of Nonsubscription Services, Licensees other than Business Establishment Services shall, at their election as provided in paragraph (b) of this section, pay at one of the following rates:

(i) *Per Performance Option.* $0.000762 (0.0762¢) per Performance for all digital audio transmissions, except that 4% of Performances shall bear no royalty to approximate the number of partial Performances of nominal duration made by a Licensee due to, for example, technical interruptions, the closing down of a media player or channel switching; Provided that this provision is not intended to imply that permitting users of a service to "skip" a recording is or is not permitted under 17 U.S.C. 114(d)(2). For the avoidance of doubt, this 4% exclusion shall apply to all Licensees electing this payment option irrespective of the Licensee's actual experience in respect of partial Performances.

(ii) *Aggregate Tuning Hour Option*—(A) *Non-Music Programming.* $0.000762 (0.0762¢) per Aggregate Tuning Hour for programming reasonably classified as news, talk, sports or business programming.

(B) *Broadcast Simulcasts.* $0.0088 (0.88¢) per Aggregate Tuning Hour for Broadcast Simulcast programming not reasonably classified as news, talk, sports or business programming.

(C) *Other Programming.* $0.0117 (1.17¢) per Aggregate Tuning Hour for programming other than Broadcast Simulcast programming and programming reasonably classified as news, talk, sports or business programming.

(2) *Subscription Services.* For their operation of Subscription Services, Licensees other than Business Establishment Services shall, at their election as provided in paragraph (b) of this section, pay at one of the following rates:

(i) *Per Performance Option.* $0.000762 (0.0762¢) per Performance for all digital audio transmissions, except that 4% of Performances shall bear no royalty to approximate the number of partial Performances of nominal duration made by a Licensee due to, for example, technical interruptions, the closing down of a media player or channel switching; Provided that this provision is not intended to imply that permitting users of a service to "skip" a recording is or is not permitted under 17 U.S.C. 114(d)(2). For the avoidance of doubt, this 4% exclusion shall apply to all Licensees electing this payment option irrespective of the Licensee's actual experience in respect of partial performances.

(ii) *Aggregate Tuning Hour Option*—(A) *Non-Music Programming.* $0.000762 (0.0762¢) per Aggregate Tuning Hour for programming reasonably classified as news, talk, sports or business programming.

(B) *Broadcast Simulcasts.* $0.0088 (0.88¢) per Aggregate Tuning Hour for Broadcast Simulcast programming not reasonably classified as news, talk, sports or business programming.

(C) *Other Programming.* $0.0117 (1.17¢) per Aggregate Tuning Hour for programming other than Broadcast Simulcast programming and programming reasonably classified as news, talk, sports or business programming.

(iii) *Percentage of Subscription Service Revenues Option.* 10.9% of Subscription Service Revenues, but in no event less than 27¢ per month for each person who subscribes to the Subscription Service for all or any part of the month or to whom the Subscription Service otherwise is delivered by Licensee without a fee (e.g., during a free trial period), subject to the following reduction associated with the transmission of directly licensed sound recordings (if applicable). For any given payment period, the fee due from Licensee shall be the amount calculated under the formula described in the immediately preceding sentence *multiplied by* the following fraction: the total number of Performances (as defined under § 262.2(j), which excludes directly licensed sound recordings) made by the Subscription Service during the period in question, *divided by* the total number of digital audio transmissions of sound recordings made by the Subscription Service during the period in question (inclusive of Performances and equivalent transmissions of directly licensed sound recordings). Any Licensee paying on such basis shall report to the Designated Agent on its statements of account the pertinent music use information upon which such reduction has been calculated. This option shall not be available to a Subscription Service where—

(A) A particular computer software product or other access device must be purchased for a separate fee from the Licensee as a condition of receiving transmissions of sound recordings through the Subscription Service, and the Licensee chooses not to include sales of such software product or other device to subscribers as part of Subscription Service Revenues in accordance with § 262.2(m)(3), or

(B) The consideration paid or given to receive the Subscription Service also entitles the subscriber to receive or have access to material, products or services other than the Subscription Service (for example, as in the case of a "bundled service" consisting of access to the Subscription Service and also access to the Internet in general). In all events, in order to be eligible for this payment option, a Licensee may not engage in pricing practices whereby the Subscription Service is offered to subscribers on a "loss leader" basis or whereby the price of the Subscription Service is materially subsidized by payments made by the subscribers for other products or services.

(3) *Business Establishment Services.* For the making of any number of Ephemeral Recordings in the operation of a service pursuant to the limitation on exclusive rights specified by 17 U.S.C.

114(d)(1)(C)(iv), a Licensee that is a Business Establishment Service shall pay 10% of such Licensee's "Gross Proceeds" derived from the use in such service of musical programs that are attributable to copyrighted recordings. "Gross Proceeds" as used in paragraph (a)(3) of this section means all fees and payments, including those made in kind, received from any source before, during or after the License Period that are derived from the use of copyrighted sound recordings pursuant to 17 U.S.C. 112(e) for the sole purpose of facilitating a transmission to the public of a performance of a sound recording under the limitation on exclusive rights specified in 17 U.S.C. 114(d)(1)(C)(iv). The attribution of Gross Proceeds to copyrighted recordings may be made on the basis of:

(i) For classical programs, the proportion that the playing time of copyrighted classical recordings bears to the total playing time of all classical recordings in the program, and

(ii) For all other programs, the proportion that the number of copyrighted recordings bears to the total number of all recordings in the program.

(b) *Election process.* A Licensee other than a Business Establishment Service shall elect the particular Nonsubscription Service and/or Subscription Service royalty rate categories it chooses (that is, among paragraph (a)(1)(i) or (ii) of this section and/or paragraph (a)(2)(i), (ii) or (iii) of this section) for the License Period by no later than March 8, 2004. Notwithstanding the preceding sentence, where a Licensee has not previously provided a Nonsubscription Service or Subscription Service, as the case may be, the Licensee may make its election by no later than thirty (30) days after the new service first makes a digital audio transmission of a sound recording under the 17 U.S.C. 114 statutory license. Each such election shall be made by notifying the Designated Agent in writing of such election, using an election form provided by the Designated Agent. A Licensee that fails to make a timely election shall pay royalties as provided in paragraphs (a)(1)(i) and (a)(2)(i) of this section, as applicable. Notwithstanding the foregoing, a Licensee eligible to make royalty payments under an agreement entered into pursuant to the Small Webcaster Settlement Act of 2002 may elect to make payments under such agreement as specified in such agreement.

(c) *Ephemeral Recordings.* The royalty payable under 17 U.S.C. 112(e) for any reproduction of a phonorecord made by a Licensee other than a Business Establishment Service during the License Period, and used solely by the Licensee to facilitate transmissions for which it pays royalties as and when provided in this section and § 262.4 shall be deemed to be included within, and to comprise 8.8% of, such royalty payments. The royalty payable under 17 U.S.C. 112(e) for the reproduction of phonorecords by a Business Establishment Service shall be as set forth in paragraph (a)(3) of this section.

(d) *Minimum fee*—(1) *Business Establishment Services.* Each Licensee that is a Business Establishment Service shall pay a minimum fee of $10,000 for each calendar year in which it makes Ephemeral Recordings for use to facilitate transmissions under the limitation on exclusive rights specified by 17 U.S.C. 114(d)(1)(C)(iv), whether or not it does so for all or any part of the year.

(2) *Other Services.* Each Licensee other than a Business Establishment Service shall pay a minimum fee of $2,500, or $500 per channel or station (excluding archived programs, but in no event less than $500 per Licensee), whichever is less, for each calendar year in which it makes eligible nonsubscription transmissions, noninteractive digital audio transmissions as part of a new subscription service or Ephemeral Recordings for use to facilitate such transmissions, whether or not it does the foregoing for all or any part of the year; except that the minimum annual fee for a Licensee electing to pay under paragraph (a)(2)(iii) of this section shall be $5,000.

(3) *In General.* These minimum fees shall be nonrefundable, but shall be fully creditable to royalty payments due under paragraph (a) of this section for the same calendar year (but not any subsequent calendar year).

(e) *Continuing Obligation.* For the limited purpose of the period immediately following the License Period, and on an entirely without prejudice and non-precedential basis relative to other time periods and proceedings, if successor statutory royalty rates for Licensees for the period beginning January 1, 2005, have not been established by January 1, 2005, then Licensees shall pay to the Designated Agent, effective January 1, 2005, and continuing for the period through April 30, 2005, or until successor rates and terms are established, whichever is earlier, an interim royalty pursuant to the same rates and terms as are provided for the License Period. Such interim royalties shall be subject to retroactive adjustment based on the final successor rates. Any overpayment shall be fully creditable to future payments, and any underpayment shall be paid within 30 days after establishment of the successor rates and terms, except as may otherwise be provided in the successor terms. If there is a period of such interim payments, Licensees shall elect the particular royalty rate categories it chooses for the interim period as described in paragraph (b) of this section, except that the election for a service that is in operation shall be made by no later than January 15, 2005.

(f) *Other royalty rates and terms.* This part 262 does not apply to persons or entities other than Licensees, or to Licensees to the extent that they make other types of transmissions beyond those set forth in paragraph (a) of this section. For transmissions other than those governed by paragraph (a) of this section, or the use of Ephemeral Recordings to facilitate such transmissions, persons making such transmissions must pay royalties, to the extent (if at all) applicable, under 17 U.S.C. 112(e) and 114 or as prescribed by other law, regulation or agreement.

§ 262.4 Terms for making payment of royalty fees and statements of account.

(a) *Payment to designated agent.* A Licensee shall make the royalty payments due under § 262.3 to the Designated Agent.

(b) *Designation of agent and potential successor designated agents.* (1) Until such time as a new designation is made, SoundExchange, presently an unincorporated division of the Recording Industry Association of America, Inc. ("RIAA"), is designated as the Designated Agent to receive statements of account and royalty payments from Licensees due under § 262.3 and to distribute such royalty payments to each Copyright Owner and Performer entitled to receive royalties under 17 U.S.C. 112(e) or 114(g). SoundExchange shall continue to be designated after its separate incorporation.

(2) If SoundExchange should fail to incorporate by July 1, 2003, dissolve or cease to be governed by a board consisting of equal numbers of representatives of Copyright Owners and Performers, then it shall be replaced by successor entities upon the fulfillment of the requirements set forth in paragraphs (b)(2)(i) and (ii) of this section.

(i) By a majority vote of the nine copyright owner representatives on the SoundExchange Board as of the last day preceding the condition precedent in paragraph (b)(2) of this section, such representatives shall file a petition with the Copyright Office designating a successor Designated Agent to distribute royalty payments to Copyright Owners and Performers entitled to receive royalties under 17 U.S.C. 112(e) or 114(g) that have themselves authorized such Designated Agent.

(ii) By a majority vote of the nine performer representatives on the SoundExchange Board as of the last day preceding the condition precedent in paragraph (b)(2) of this section, such representatives shall file a petition with the Copyright Office designating a successor Designated Agent to distribute royalty payments to Copyright Owners and Performers entitled to receive royalties under 17 U.S.C. 112(e) or 114(g) that have themselves authorized such Designated Agent.

(iii) The Copyright Office shall publish in the FEDERAL REGISTER within 30 days of receipt of a petition filed under paragraph (b)(2)(i) or (ii) of this section an order designating the Designated Agents named in such petitions. Nothing contained in this section shall prohibit the petitions filed under paragraphs (b)(2)(i) and (ii) of this section from naming the same successor Designated Agent.

(3) If petitions are filed under paragraphs (b)(2)(i) and (ii) of this section, then, following the actions of the Copyright Office in accordance with paragraph (b)(2)(iii) of this section:

(i) Each of the successor entities shall have all the rights and responsibilities of a Designated Agent under this part 262, except as specifically set forth in this paragraph (b)(3).

(ii) Licensees shall make their royalty payments to the successor entity named by the copyright owner representatives under paragraph (b)(2)(i) of this section (the "Receiving Agent") and shall provide statements of account on a form prepared by the Receiving Agent. Licensees shall submit a copy of each statement of account to the collective named by the performer representatives under paragraph (b)(2)(ii) of this section at the same time such statement of account is delivered to the Receiving Agent.

(iii) The Designated Agents shall agree between themselves concerning responsibility for distributing royalty payments to Copyright Owners and Performers that have not themselves authorized either Designated Agent. The Designated Agents also shall agree to a corresponding methodology for allocating royalty payments between them using the information provided by the Licensee pursuant to the regulations governing records of use of performances for the period for which the royalty payment was made. Such methodology shall value all performances equally. Within 30 days after their agreement concerning such responsibility and methodology, the Designated Agents shall inform the Register of Copyrights thereof.

(iv) With respect to any royalty payment received by the Receiving Agent from a Licensee, a designation by a Copyright Owner or Performer of a Designated Agent must be made no later than 30 days prior to the receipt by the Receiving Agent of that royalty payment.

(v) The Receiving Agent shall promptly allocate the royalty payments it receives between the two Designated Agents in accordance with the agreed methodology. A final adjustment, if necessary, shall be agreed and paid or refunded, as the case may be, between the Receiving Agent and the collectives named under paragraph (b)(2) of this section for each calendar year no later than 180 days following the end of each calendar year. The Designated Agents shall agree on a reasonable basis for the sharing on a pro-rata basis of any costs associated with the allocations set forth in paragraph (b)(3)(iii) of this section.

(vi) If a Designated Agent is unable to locate a Copyright Owner or Performer that the Designated Agent otherwise would be required to pay under this paragraph (b) within 3 years from the date of payment by Licensee, such Copyright Owner's or Performer's share of the payments made by Licensees may first be applied to the costs directly attributable to the administration of the royalty payments due such Copyright Owners and Performers by that Designated Agent and shall thereafter be allocated between the Designated Agents on a pro rata basis (based on distributions to entitled parties) to offset any costs permitted to be deducted by a designated agent under 17 U.S.C. 114(g)(3). The foregoing shall apply notwithstanding the common law or statutes of any State.

(c) *Monthly payments.* A Licensee shall make any payments due under § 262.3(a) by the 45th day after the end of each month for that month, except that payments due under § 262.3(a) for the period from the beginning of the License Period through the last day of the month in which these rates and terms are adopted by the Librarian of Congress and published in the FEDERAL REGISTER shall be due 45 days after the end of such period. All monthly payments shall be rounded to the nearest cent.

(d) *Minimum payments.* A Licensee shall make any payment due under § 262.3(d) by January 31 of the applicable calendar year, except that:

(1) Payment due under § 262.3(d) for 2003, and in the case of a Subscription Service any earlier year, shall be due 45 days after the last day of the month in which these rates and terms are adopted by the Librarian of Congress and published in the FEDERAL REGISTER; and

(2) Payment for a Licensee that has not previously made eligible nonsubscription transmissions, noninteractive digital audio transmissions as part of a new subscription service or Ephemeral Recordings pursuant to licenses under 17 U.S.C. 114(f) and/or 17 U.S.C. 112(e) shall be due by the 45th day after the end of the month in which the Licensee commences to do so.

(e) *Late payments.* A Licensee shall pay a late fee of 0.75% per month, or the highest lawful rate, whichever is lower, for any payment received by the Designated Agent after the due date. Late fees shall accrue from the due date until payment is received by the Designated Agent.

(f) *Statements of account.* For any part of the period beginning on the date these rates and terms are adopted by the Librarian of Congress and published in the FEDERAL REGISTER and ending on December 31, 2004, during which a Licensee operates a service, by 45 days after the end of each month during the period, the Licensee shall deliver to the Designated Agent a statement of account containing the information set forth in this paragraph (f) on a form prepared, and made available to Licensees, by the Designated Agent. If a payment is owed for such month, the statement of account shall accompany the payment. A statement of account shall include only the following information:

(1) Such information as is necessary to calculate the accompanying royalty payment, or if no payment is owed for the month, to calculate any portion of the minimum fee recouped during the month, including, as applicable, the Performances, Aggregate Tuning Hours (to the nearest minute) or Subscription Service Revenues for the month;

(2) The name, address, business title, telephone number, facsimile number, electronic mail address and other contact information of the individual or individuals to be contacted for information or questions concerning the content of the statement of account;

(3) The handwritten signature of:

(i) The owner of the Licensee or a duly authorized agent of the owner, if the Licensee is not a partnership or a corporation;

(ii) A partner or delegee, if the Licensee is a partnership; or

(iii) An officer of the corporation, if the Licensee is a corporation;

(4) The printed or typewritten name of the person signing the statement of account;

(5) The date of signature;

(6) If the Licensee is a partnership or a corporation, the title or official position held in the partnership or corporation by the person signing the statement of account;

(7) A certification of the capacity of the person signing; and

(8) A statement to the following effect:

I, the undersigned owner or agent of the Licensee, or officer or partner, if the Licensee is a corporation or partnership, have examined this statement of account and hereby state that it is true, accurate and complete to my knowledge after reasonable due diligence.

(g) *Distribution of payments.* (1) The Designated Agent shall distribute royalty payments directly to Copyright Owners and Performers, according to 17 U.S.C. 114(g)(2); Provided that the Designated Agent shall only be responsible for making distributions to those Copyright Owners and Performers who provide the Designated Agent with such information as is necessary to identify and pay the correct recipient of such payments. The agent shall distribute royalty payments on a basis that values all performances by a Licensee equally based upon the information provided by the Licensee pursuant to the regulations governing records of use of sound recordings by Licensees; Provided, however, Performers and Copyright Owners that authorize the Designated Agent may agree with the Designated Agent to allocate their shares of the royalty payments made by any Licensee among themselves on an alternative basis. Parties entitled to receive payments under 17 U.S.C. 114(g)(2) may agree with the Designated Agent upon payment protocols to be used by the Designated Agent that provide for alternative arrangements for the payment of royalties consistent with the percentages in 17 U.S.C. 114(g)(2).

(2) The Designated Agent shall inform the Register of Copyrights of:

(i) Its methodology for distributing royalty payments to Copyright Owners and Performers who have not themselves authorized the Designated Agent (hereinafter "nonmembers"), and any amendments thereto, within 60 days of adoption and no later than 30 days prior to the first distribution to Copyright Owners and Performers of any royalties distributed pursuant to that methodology;

(ii) Any written complaint that the Designated Agent receives from a nonmember concerning the distribution of royalty payments, within 60 days of receiving such written complaint; and

(iii) The final disposition by the Designated Agent of any complaint specified by paragraph (g)(2)(ii) of this section, within 60 days of such disposition.

(3) A Designated Agent may request that the Register of Copyrights provide a written opinion stating whether the Designated Agent's methodology for distributing royalty payments to nonmembers meets the requirements of this section.

(h) *Permitted deductions.* The Designated Agent may deduct from the payments made by Licensees under §262.3, prior to the distribution of such payments to any person or entity entitled thereto, all incurred costs permitted to be deducted under 17 U.S.C. 114(g)(3); Provided, however, that any party entitled to receive royalty payments under 17 U.S.C. 112(e) or 114(g) may agree to permit the Designated Agent to make any other deductions.

(i) *Retention of records.* Books and records of a Licensee and of the Designated Agent relating to the payment, collection, and distribution of royalty payments shall be kept for a period of not less than 3 years.

§262.5 Confidential information.

(a) *Definition.* For purposes of this part, "Confidential Information" shall include the statements of account, any information contained therein, including the amount of royalty payments, and any information pertaining to the statements of account reasonably designated as confidential by the Licensee submitting the statement.

(b) *Exclusion.* Confidential Information shall not include documents or information that at the time of delivery to the Receiving Agent or a Designated Agent are public knowledge. The Designated Agent that claims the benefit of this provision shall have the burden of proving that the disclosed information was public knowledge.

(c) *Use of Confidential Information.* In no event shall the Designated Agent use any Confidential Information for any purpose other than royalty collection and distribution and activities directly related thereto; Provided, however, that the Designated Agent may disclose to Copyright Owners and Performers Confidential Information provided on statements of account under this part in aggregated form, so long as Confidential Information pertaining to any individual Licensee cannot readily be identified, and the Designated Agent may disclose the identities of services that have obtained licenses under 17 U.S.C. 112(e) or 114 and whether or not such services are current in their obligations to pay minimum fees and submit statements of account (so long as the Designated Agent does not disclose the amounts paid by the Licensee).

(d) *Disclosure of Confidential Information.* Except as provided in paragraph (c) of this section and as required by law, access to Confidential Information shall be limited to:

(1) Those employees, agents, attorneys, consultants and independent contractors of the Designated Agent, subject to an appropriate confidentiality agreement, who are engaged in the collection and distribution of royalty payments hereunder and activities related thereto, who are not also employees or officers of a Copyright Owner or Performer, and who, for the purpose of performing such duties during the ordinary course of their work, require access to the records;

(2) An independent and qualified auditor, subject to an appropriate confidentiality agreement, who is authorized to act on behalf of the Designated Agent with respect to the verification of a Licensee's statement of account pursuant to §262.6 or on behalf of a Copyright Owner or Performer with respect to the verification of royalty payments pursuant to §262.7;

(3) The Copyright Office, in response to inquiries concerning the operation of the Designated Agent;

(4) In connection with future Copyright Arbitration Royalty Panel proceedings under 17 U.S.C. 114(f)(2) and 112(e), and under an appropriate protective order, attorneys, consultants and other authorized agents of the parties to the proceedings, Copyright Arbitration Royalty Panels, the Copyright Office or the courts; and

(5) In connection with bona fide royalty disputes or claims that are the subject of the procedures under § 262.6 or § 262.7, and under an appropriate confidentiality agreement or protective order, the specific parties to such disputes or claims, their attorneys, consultants or other authorized agents, and/or arbitration panels or the courts to which disputes or claims may be submitted.

(e) *Safeguarding of Confidential Information.* The Designated Agent and any person identified in paragraph (d) of this section shall implement procedures to safeguard all Confidential Information using a reasonable standard of care, but no less than the same degree of security used to protect Confidential Information or similarly sensitive information belonging to such Designated Agent or person.

§ 262.6 Verification of statements of account.

(a) *General.* This section prescribes procedures by which the Designated Agent may verify the royalty payments made by a Licensee.

(b) *Frequency of verification.* The Designated Agent may conduct a single audit of a Licensee, upon reasonable notice and during reasonable business hours, during any given calendar year, for any or all of the prior 3 calendar years, but no calendar year shall be subject to audit more than once.

(c) *Notice of intent to audit.* The Designated Agent must file with the Copyright Office a notice of intent to audit a particular Licensee, which shall, within 30 days of the filing of the notice, publish in the FEDERAL REGISTER a notice announcing such filing. The notification of intent to audit shall be served at the same time on the Licensee to be audited. Any such audit shall be conducted by an independent and qualified auditor identified in the notice, and shall be binding on all parties.

(d) *Acquisition and retention of records.* The Licensee shall use commercially reasonable efforts to obtain or to provide access to any relevant books and records maintained by third parties for the purpose of the audit and retain such records for a period of not less than 3 years. The Designated Agent shall retain the report of the verification for a period of not less than 3 years.

(e) *Acceptable verification procedure.* An audit, including underlying paperwork, which was performed in the ordinary course of business according to generally accepted auditing standards by an independent and qualified auditor, shall serve as an acceptable verification procedure for all parties with respect to the information that is within the scope of the audit.

(f) *Consultation.* Before rendering a written report to the Designated Agent, except where the auditor has a reasonable basis to suspect fraud and disclosure would, in the reasonable opinion of the auditor, prejudice the investigation of such suspected fraud, the auditor shall review the tentative written findings of the audit with the appropriate agent or employee of the Licensee being audited in order to remedy any factual errors and clarify any issues relating to the audit; Provided that the appropriate agent or employee of the Licensee reasonably cooperates with the auditor to remedy promptly any factual errors or clarify any issues raised by the audit.

(g) *Costs of the verification procedure.* The Designated Agent shall pay the cost of the verification procedure, unless it is finally determined that there was an underpayment of 10% or more, in which case the Licensee shall, in addition to paying the amount of any underpayment, bear the reasonable costs of the verification procedure.

§ 262.7 Verification of royalty payments.

(a) *General.* This section prescribes procedures by which any Copyright Owner or Performer may verify the royalty payments made by the Designated Agent; Provided, however, that nothing contained in this section shall apply to situations where a Copyright Owner or a Performer and the Designated Agent have agreed as to proper verification methods.

(b) *Frequency of verification.* A Copyright Owner or a Performer may conduct a single audit of the Designated Agent upon reasonable notice and during reasonable business hours, during any given calendar year, for any or all of the prior 3 calendar years, but no calendar year shall be subject to audit more than once.

(c) *Notice of intent to audit.* A Copyright Owner or Performer must file with the Copyright Office a notice of intent to audit the Designated Agent, which shall, within 30 days of the filing of the notice, publish in the FEDERAL REGISTER a notice announcing such filing. The notification of intent to audit shall be served at the same time on the Designated Agent. Any such audit shall be conducted by an independent and qualified auditor identified in the notice, and shall be binding on all Copyright Owners and Performers.

(d) *Acquisition and retention of records.* The Designated Agent shall use commercially reasonable efforts to obtain or to provide access to any relevant books and records maintained by third parties for the purpose of the audit and retain such records for a period of not less than 3 years. The Copyright Owner or Performer requesting the verification procedure shall retain the report of the verification for a period of not less than 3 years.

(e) *Acceptable verification procedure.* An audit, including underlying paperwork, which was performed in the ordinary course of business according to generally accepted auditing standards by an independent and qualified auditor, shall serve as an acceptable verification procedure for all parties with respect to the information that is within the scope of the audit.

(f) *Consultation.* Before rendering a written report to a Copyright Owner or Performer, except where the auditor has a reasonable basis to suspect fraud and disclosure would, in the reasonable opinion of the auditor, prejudice the investigation of such suspected fraud, the auditor shall review the tentative written findings of the audit with the appropriate agent or employee of the Designated Agent in order to remedy any factual errors and clarify any issues relating to the audit; Provided that the appropriate agent or employee of the Designated Agent reasonably cooperates with the auditor to remedy promptly any factual errors or clarify any issues raised by the audit.

(g) *Costs of the verification procedure.* The Copyright Owner or Performer requesting the verification procedure shall pay the cost of the procedure, unless it is finally determined that there was an underpayment of 10% or more, in which case the Designated Agent shall, in addition to paying the amount of any underpayment, bear the reasonable costs of the verification procedure.

§ 262.8 Unclaimed funds.

If a Designated Agent is unable to identify or locate a Copyright Owner or Performer who is entitled to receive a royalty payment under this part, the Designated Agent shall retain the required payment in a segregated trust account for a period of 3 years from the date of payment. No claim to such payment shall be valid after the expiration of the 3-year period. After the expiration of this period, the Designated Agent may apply the unclaimed funds to offset any costs deductible under 17 U.S.C. 114(g)(3). The foregoing shall apply notwithstanding the common law or statutes of any State.

PART 263—RATES AND TERMS FOR CERTAIN TRANSMISSIONS AND THE MAKING OF EPHEMERAL REPRODUCTIONS BY NONCOMMERCIAL LICENSEES

Sec.

AUTHORITY: 17 U.S.C. 112(e), 114, 801(b)(1).

SOURCE: 69 FR 5695, Feb. 6, 2004, unless otherwise noted.

§ 263.1 General.

This part 263 establishes rates and terms of royalty payments for the public performance of sound recordings in certain digital transmissions by certain Noncommercial Licensees in accordance with the provisions of 17 U.S.C. 114, and the making of ephemeral recordings by certain Noncommercial Licensees in accordance with the provisions of 17 U.S.C. 112(e), during the period 2003–2004.

§ 263.2 Definitions.

For purposes of this part, the following definition shall apply:

A *Noncommercial Licensee* is a person or entity that has obtained a compulsory license under 17 U.S.C. 114 and the implementing regulations therefor, or that has obtained a compulsory license under 17 U.S.C. 112(e) and the implementing regulations therefor to make ephemeral recordings for use in facilitating such transmissions, and—

(a) Is exempt from taxation under section 501 of the Internal Revenue Code of 1986 (26 U.S.C. 501);

(b) Has applied in good faith to the Internal Revenue Service for exemption from taxation under section 501 of the Internal Revenue Code and has a commercially reasonable expectation that such exemption shall be granted; or

(c) Is a State or possession or any governmental entity or subordinate thereof, or the United States or District of Columbia, making transmissions for exclusively public purposes.

§ 263.3 Royalty rates and terms.

A Noncommercial Licensee shall in every respect be treated as a "Licensee" under part 262 of this chapter, and all terms applicable to Licensees and their payments under part 262 of this chapter shall apply to Noncommercial Licensees and their payment, except that a Noncommercial Licensee shall pay royalties at the rates applicable to such a "Licensee," as currently provided in § 261.3(a), (c), (d) and (e) of this chapter, rather than at the rates set forth in § 262.3(a) through (d) of this chapter.

PART 270—NOTICE AND RECORDKEEPING REQUIREMENTS FOR STATUTORY LICENSES

AUTHORITY: 17 U.S.C. 702.

SOURCE: 69 FR 11527, Mar. 11, 2004, unless otherwise noted.

§ 270.1 Notice of use of sound recordings under statutory license.

(a) *General.* This section prescribes rules under which copyright owners shall receive notice of use of their sound recordings when used under either section 112(e) or 114(d)(2) of title 17, United States Code, or both.

(b) *Definitions.* (1) A *Notice of Use of Sound Recordings under Statutory License* is a written notice to sound recording copyright owners of the use of their works under section 112(e) or 114(d)(2) of title 17, United States Code, or both, and is required under this section to be filed by a Service in the Copyright Office.

(2) A *Service* is an entity engaged in either the digital transmission of sound recordings pursuant to section 114(d)(2) of title 17 of the United States Code or making ephemeral phonorecords of sound recordings pursuant to section 112(e) of title 17 of the United States Code or both. For purposes of this section, the definition of a Service includes an entity that transmits an AM/FM broadcast signal over a digital communications network such as the Internet, regardless of whether the transmission is made by the broadcaster that originates the AM/FM signal or by a third party, provided that such transmission meets the applicable

requirements of the statutory license set forth in 17 U.S.C. 114(d)(2). A Service may be further characterized as either a preexisting subscription service, preexisting satellite digital audio radio service, nonsubscription transmission service, new subscription service, business establishment service or a combination of those:

(i) A *preexisting subscription service* is a service that performs sound recordings by means of noninteractive audio-only subscription digital audio transmissions, and was in existence and making such transmissions to the public for a fee on or before July 31, 1998, and may include a limited number of sample channels representative of the subscription service that are made available on a nonsubscription basis in order to promote the subscription service.

(ii) A *preexisting satellite digital audio radio service* is a subscription satellite digital audio radio service provided pursuant to a satellite digital audio radio service license issued by the Federal Communications Commission on or before July 31, 1998, and any renewal of such license to the extent of the scope of the original license, and may include a limited number of sample channels representative of the subscription service that are made available on a nonsubscription basis in order to promote the subscription service.

(iii) A *nonsubscription transmission service* is a service that makes noninteractive nonsubscription digital audio transmissions that are not exempt under section 114(d)(1) of title 17 of the United States Code and are made as part of a service that provides audio programming consisting, in whole or in part, of performances of sound recordings, including transmissions of broadcast transmissions, if the primary purpose of the service is to provide to the public such audio or other entertainment programming, and the primary purpose of the service is not to sell, advertise, or promote particular products or services other than sound recordings, live concerts, or other music-related events.

(iv) A *new subscription service* is a service that performs sound recordings by means of noninteractive subscription digital audio transmissions and that is not a preexisting subscription service or a preexisting satellite digital audio radio service.

(v) A *business establishment service* is a service that makes ephemeral phonorecords of sound recordings pursuant to section 112(e) of title 17 of the United States Code and is exempt under section 114(d)(1)(C)(iv) of title 17 of the United States Code.

(c) *Forms and content.* A Notice of Use of Sound Recordings Under Statutory License shall be prepared on a form that may be obtained from the Copyright Office website or from the Licensing Division, and shall include the following information:

(1) The full legal name of the Service that is either commencing digital transmissions of sound recordings or making ephemeral phonorecords of sound recordings under statutory license or doing both.

(2) The full address, including a specific number and street name or rural route, of the place of business of the Service. A post office box or similar designation will not be sufficient except where it is the only address that can be used in that geographic location.

(3) The telephone number and facsimile number of the Service.

(4) Information on how to gain access to the online website or homepage of the Service, or where information may be posted under this section concerning the use of sound recordings under statutory license.

(5) Identification of each license under which the Service intends to operate, including identification of each of the following categories under which the Service will be making digital transmissions of sound recordings: preexisting subscription service, preexisting satellite digital audio radio service, nonsubscription transmission service, new subscription service or business establishment service.

(6) The date or expected date of the initial digital transmission of a sound recording to be made under the section 114 statutory license and/or the date or the expected date of the initial use of the section 112(e) license for the purpose of making ephemeral phonorecords of the sound recordings.

(7) Identification of any amendments required by paragraph (f) of this section.

(d) *Signature.* The Notice shall include the signature of the appropriate officer or representative of the Service that is either transmitting the sound recordings or making ephemeral phonorecords of sound recordings under statutory license or doing both. The signature shall be accompanied by the printed or typewritten name and the title of the person signing the Notice and by the date of the signature.

(e) *Filing notices; fees.* The original and three copies shall be filed with the Licensing Division of the Copyright Office and shall be accompanied by the filing fee set forth in § 201.3(c) of this chapter. Notices shall be placed in the public records of the Licensing Division. The address of the Licensing Division is: Library of Congress, Copyright Office, Licensing Division, 101 Independence Avenue, SE, Washington, DC 20557–6400.

(1) A Service that, prior to April 12, 2004, has already commenced making digital transmissions of sound recordings pursuant to section 114(d)(2) of title 17 of the United States Code or making ephemeral phonorecords of sound recordings pursuant to section 112(e) of title 17 of the United States Code, or both, and that has already filed an Initial Notice of Digital Transmission of Sound Recordings Under Statutory License, and that intends to continue to make digital transmissions or ephemeral phonorecords following July 1, 2004, shall file a Notice of Use of Sound Recordings under Statutory License with the Licensing Division of the Copyright Office no later than July 1, 2004.

(2) A Service that, on or after July 1, 2004, commences making digital transmissions and ephemeral phonorecords of sound recordings under statutory license shall file a Notice of Use of Sound Recordings under Statutory License with the Licensing Division of the Copyright Office prior to the making of the first ephemeral phonorecord of the sound recording and prior to the first digital transmission of the sound recording.

(3) A Service that, on or after July 1, 2004, commences making only ephemeral phonorecords of sound recordings, shall file a Notice of Use of Sound Recordings under Statutory License with the Licensing Division of the Copyright Office prior to the making of the first ephemeral phonorecord of a sound recording under the statutory license.

(f) *Amendment.* A Service shall file a new Notice of Use of Sound Recordings under Statutory License within 45 days after any of the information contained in the Notice on file has changed, and shall indicate in the space provided by the Copyright Office that the Notice is an amended filing. The Licensing Division shall retain copies of all prior Notices filed by the Service.

[69 FR 11527, Mar. 11, 2004, as amended at 69 FR 13127, Mar. 19, 2004]

§ 270.2 Reports of use of sound recordings under statutory license for preexisting subscription services.

(a) *General.* This section prescribes rules under which preexisting subscription services shall serve copyright owners with notice of use of their sound recordings, what the content of that notice should be, and under which records of such use shall be kept and made available.

(b) *Definitions.* (1) A *Collective* is a collection and distribution organization that is designated under the statutory license, either by settlement agreement reached under section 114(f)(1)(A) or section 114(f)(1)(C)(i) of title 17 of the United States Code and adopted pursuant to 37 CFR 251.63(b), or by decision of a Copyright Arbitration Royalty Panel (CARP) under section 114(f)(1)(B) or section 114(f)(1)(C)(ii), or by an order of the Librarian pursuant to 17 U.S.C. 802(f).

(2) A *Report of Use of Sound Recordings Under Statutory License* is the report of use required under this section to be provided by a Service transmitting sound recordings and making ephemeral phonorecords therewith under statutory licenses.

(3) A *Service* is a preexisting subscription service, as defined in 17 U.S.C. 114(j)(11).

(c) *Service.* Reports of Use shall be served upon Collectives that are identified in the records of the Licensing Division of the Copyright Office as having been designated under the statutory license, either by settlement agreement reached under section 114(f)(1)(A) or section 114(f)(1)(C)(i) and adopted pursuant to 37 CFR 251.63(b), or by decision of a Copyright Arbitration Royalty Panel (CARP) under section 114(f)(1)(B) or section 114(f)(1)(C)(ii), or by an order of the Librarian pursuant to 17 U.S.C. 802(f) or pursuant to a settlement agreement reached or statutory license adopted pursuant to section 112(e). Reports of Use shall be served, by certified or registered mail, or by other means if agreed upon by the respective preexisting subscription service and Collective, on or before the forty-fifth day after the close of each month.

(d) *Posting.* In the event that no Collective is designated under the statutory license, or if all designated Collectives have terminated collection and distribution operations, a preexisting subscription service transmitting sound recordings under statutory license shall post and make available online its Reports of Use. Preexisting subscription services shall post their Reports of Use online on or before the forty-fifth day after the close of each month, and make them available to all sound recording copyright owners for a period of 90 days. Preexisting subscription services may require use of passwords for access to posted Reports of Use, but must make passwords available in a timely manner and free of charge or other restrictions. Preexisting subscription services may predicate provision of a password upon:

(1) Information relating to identity, location and status as a sound recording copyright owner; and

(2) A "click-wrap" agreement not to use information in the Report of Use for purposes other than royalty collection, royalty distribution, and determining compliance with statutory license requirements, without the express consent of the preexisting subscription service providing the Report of Use.

(e) *Content.* A "Report of Use of Sound Recordings under Statutory License" shall be identified as such by prominent caption or heading, and shall include a preexisting subscription service's "Intended Playlists" for each channel and each day of the reported month. The "Intended Playlists" shall include a consecutive listing of every recording scheduled to be transmitted, and shall contain the following information in the following order:

(1) The name of the preexisting subscription service or entity;

(2) The channel;

(3) The sound recording title;

(4) The featured recording artist, group, or orchestra;

(5) The retail album title (or, in the case of compilation albums created for commercial purposes, the name of the retail album identified by the preexisting subscription service for purchase of the sound recording);

(6) The marketing label of the commercially available album or other product on which the sound recording is found;

(7) The catalog number;

(8) The International Standard Recording Code (ISRC) embedded in the sound recording, where available and feasible;

(9) Where available, the copyright owner information provided in the copyright notice on the retail album or other product (e.g., following the symbol (P), that is the letter P in a circle) or, in the case of compilation albums created for commercial purposes, in the copyright notice for the individual sound recording;

(10) The date of transmission; and

(11) The time of transmission.

(f) *Signature.* Reports of Use shall include a signed statement by the appropriate officer or representative of the preexisting subscription service attesting, under penalty of perjury, that the information contained in the Report is believed to be accurate and is maintained by the preexisting subscription service in its ordinary course of business. The signature shall be accompanied by the printed or typewritten name and title of the person signing the Report, and by the date of signature.

(g) *Format.* Reports of Use should be provided on a standard machine-readable medium, such as diskette, optical disc, or magneto-optical disc, and should conform as closely as possible to the following specifications:

(1) ASCII delimited format, using pipe characters as delimiter, with no headers or footers;

(2) Carats should surround strings;

(3) No carats should surround dates and numbers;

(4) Dates should be indicated by: MM/DD/YYYY;

(5) Times should be based on a 24-hour clock: HH:MM:SS;

(6) A carriage return should be at the end of each line; and

(7) All data for one record should be on a single line.

(h) *Confidentiality*. Copyright owners, their agents and Collectives shall not disseminate information in the Reports of Use to any persons not entitled to it, nor utilize the information for purposes other than royalty collection and distribution, and determining compliance with statutory license requirements, without express consent of the preexisting subscription service providing the Report of Use.

(i) *Documentation*. All compulsory licensees shall, for a period of at least three years from the date of service or posting of the Report of Use, keep and retain a copy of the Report of Use. For reporting periods from February 1, 1996, through August 31, 1998, the preexisting subscription service shall serve upon all designated Collectives and retain for a period of three years from the date of transmission records of use indicating which sound recordings were performed and the number of times each recording was performed, but is not required to produce full Reports of Use or Intended Playlists for those periods.

[69 FR 11527, Mar. 11, 2004, as amended at 70 FR 24310, May 9, 2005]

§ 270.3 Reports of use of sound recordings under statutory license for nonsubscription transmission services, preexisting satellite digital audio radio services, new subscription services and business establishment services.

(a) *General*. This section prescribes rules under which nonsubscription transmission services, preexisting satellite digital audio radio services, new subscription services, and business establishment services shall maintain reports of use of their sound recordings under section 112(e) or section 114(d)(2) of title 17 of the United States Code, or both.

(b) *Definitions*. (1) *Aggregate Tuning Hours* are the total hours of programming that a nonsubscription transmission service, preexisting satellite digital audio radio service, new subscription service or business establishment service has transmitted during the reporting period identified in paragraph (c)(3) of this section to all listeners within the United States over the relevant channels or stations, and from any archived programs, that provide audio programming consisting, in whole or in part, of eligible nonsubscription service, preexisting satellite digital audio radio service, new subscription service or business establishment service transmissions, less the actual running time of any sound recordings for which the service has obtained direct licenses apart from 17 U.S.C. 114(d)(2) or which do not require a license under United States copyright law. For example, if a nonsubscription transmission service transmitted one hour of programming to 10 simultaneous listeners, the nonsubscription transmission service's Aggregate Tuning Hours would equal 10. If 3 minutes of that hour consisted of transmission of a directly licensed recording, the nonsubscription transmission service's Aggregate Tuning Hours would equal 9 hours and 30 minutes. If one listener listened to the transmission of a nonsubscription transmission service for 10 hours (and none of the recordings transmitted during that time was directly licensed), the nonsubscription transmission service's Aggregate Tuning Hours would equal 10.

(2) An *AM/FM Webcast* is a transmission made by an entity that transmits an AM/FM broadcast signal over a digital communications network such as the Internet, regardless of whether the transmission is made by the broadcaster that originates the AM/FM signal or by a third party, provided that such transmission meets the applicable requirements of the statutory license set forth in 17 U.S.C. 114(d)(2).

(3) A *Collective* is a collection and distribution organization that is designated under one or both of the statutory licenses, either by settlement agreement reached under section 112(e)(3), section 112(e)(6), section 114(f)(1)(A), section 114(f)(1)(C)(i), section 114(f)(2)(A), or section 114(f)(2)(C)(i) and adopted pursuant to § 251.63(b) of this chapter, or by a decision of a Copyright Arbitration Royalty Panel under section 112(e)(4), section 112(e)(6), section 114(f)(1)(B), section (f)(1)(C)(ii), section 114(f)(2)(B), or section 114(f)(2)(C)(ii) or by order of the Librarian of Congress pursuant to 17 U.S.C. 802(f).

(4) A *new subscription service* is defined in § 270.1(b)(2)(iv).

(5) A *nonsubscription transmission service* is defined in § 270.1(b)(2)(iii).

(6) A *preexisting satellite digital audio radio service* is defined in § 270.1(b)(2)(ii).

(7) A *business establishment service* is defined in § 270.1(b)(2)(v).

(8) A *performance* is each instance in which any portion of a sound recording is publicly performed to a Listener by means of a digital audio transmission or retransmission (e.g., the delivery of any portion of a single track from a compact disc to one Listener) but excluding the following:

(i) A performance of a sound recording that does not require a license (e.g., the sound recording is not copyrighted);

(ii) A performance of a sound recording for which the service has previously obtained a license from the Copyright Owner of such sound recording; and

(iii) An incidental performance that both:

(A) Makes no more than incidental use of sound recordings including, but not limited to, brief musical transitions in and out of commercials or program segments, brief performances during news, talk and sports programming, brief background performances during disk jockey announcements, brief performances during commercials of sixty seconds or less in duration, or brief performances during sporting or other public events and

(B) Other than ambient music that is background at a public event, does not contain an entire sound recording and does not feature a particular sound recording of more than thirty seconds (as in the case of a sound recording used as a theme song).

(9) *Play frequency* is the number of times a sound recording is publicly performed by a Service during the relevant period, without respect to the number of listeners receiving the sound recording. If a particular sound recording is transmitted to listeners on a particular channel or program only once during the two-week reporting period, then the play frequency is one. If the sound recording is transmitted 10 times during the two-week reporting period, then the play frequency is 10.

(10) A *Report of Use* is a report required under this section to be provided by a nonsubscription transmission service and new subscription service that is transmitting sound recordings pursuant to the statutory license set forth in section 114(d)(2) of title 17 of the United States Code or making ephemeral phonorecords of sound recordings pursuant to the statutory license set forth in section 112(e) of title 17 of the United States Code, or both.

(c) *Report of Use*—(1) *Separate reports not required.* A nonsubscription transmission service, preexisting satellite digital audio radio service or a new subscription service that transmits sound recordings pursuant to the statutory license set forth in section 114(d)(2) of title 17 of the United States Code and makes ephemeral phonorecords of sound recordings pursuant to the statutory license set forth in section 112(e) of title 17 of the United States Code need not maintain a separate Report of Use for each statutory license during the relevant reporting periods.

(2) *Content.* For a nonsubscription transmission service, preexisting satellite digital audio radio service, new subscription service or business establishment service that transmits sound recordings pursuant to the statutory license set forth in section 114(d)(2) of title 17 of the United States Code, or the statutory license set forth in section 112(e) of title 17 of the United States Code, or both, each Report of Use shall contain the following information, in the following order, for each

sound recording transmitted during the reporting periods identified in paragraph (c)(3) of this section:

(i) The name of the nonsubscription transmission service, preexisting satellite digital audio radio service, new subscription service or business establishment service making the transmissions, including the name of the entity filing the Report of Use, if different;

(ii) The category transmission code for the category of transmission operated by the nonsubscription transmission service, preexisting satellite digital audio radio service, new subscription service or business establishment service:

(A) For eligible nonsubscription transmissions other than broadcast simulcasts and transmissions of non-music programming;

(B) For eligible nonsubscription transmissions of broadcast simulcast programming not reasonably classified as news, talk, sports or business programming;

(C) For eligible nonsubscription transmissions of non-music programming reasonably classified as news, talk, sports or business programming;

(D) For eligible nonsubscription transmissions by a non-Corporation for Public Broadcasting noncommercial broadcaster making transmissions covered by §§ 261.3(a)(2)(i) and (ii) of this chapter;

(E) For eligible nonsubscription transmissions by a non-Corporation for Public Broadcasting noncommercial broadcaster making transmissions covered by § 261.3(a)(2)(iii) of this chapter;

(F) For eligible nonsubscription transmissions by a small webcaster operating under an agreement published in the FEDERAL REGISTER pursuant to the Small Webcaster Settlement Act;

(G) For eligible nonsubscription transmissions by a noncommercial broadcaster operating under an agreement published in the FEDERAL REGISTER pursuant to the Small Webcaster Settlement Act;

(H) For transmissions other than broadcast simulcasts and transmissions of non-music programming made by an eligible new subscription service;

(I) For transmissions of broadcast simulcast programming not reasonably classified as news, talk, sports or business programming made by an eligible new subscription service;

(J) For transmissions of non-music programming reasonably classified as news, talk, sports or business programming made by an eligible new subscription service; and

(K) For eligible transmissions by a business establishment service making ephemeral recordings;

(iii) The featured artist;

(iv) The sound recording title;

(v) The International Standard Recording Code (ISRC) or, alternatively to the ISRC, the

(A) Album title; and

(B) Marketing label;

(vi) The actual total performances of the sound recording during the reporting period or, alternatively, the

(A) Aggregate Tuning Hours;

(B) Channel or program name; and

(C) Play frequency.

(3) *Reporting period.* A Report of Use shall be prepared for a two-week period (two periods of 7 consecutive days) for each calendar quarter of the year. The two weeks need not be consecutive, but both weeks must be completely within the calendar quarter.

(4) *Signature.* Reports of Use shall include a signed statement by the appropriate officer or representative of the service attesting, under penalty of perjury, that the information contained in the Report is believed to be accurate and is maintained by the service in its ordinary course of business. The signature shall be accompanied by the printed or typewritten name and the title of the person signing the Report, and by the date of the signature.

(5) *Confidentiality.* Copyright owners, their agents and Collectives shall not disseminate information in the Reports of Use to any persons not entitled to it, nor utilize the information for purposes other than royalty collection and distribution, without consent of the service providing the Report of Use.

(6) *Documentation.* A Service shall, for a period of at least three years from the date of service or posting of a Report of Use, keep and retain a copy of the Report of Use.

§270.4 Reports of use of sound recordings under statutory license prior to April 1, 2004.

(a) *General.* This section prescribes the rules which govern reports of use of sound recordings by nonsubscription transmission services, preexisting satellite digital audio radio services, new subscription services, and business establishment services under section 112(e) or section 114(d)(2) of title 17 of the United States Code, or both, for the period from October 28, 1998, through March 31, 2004.

(b) *Reports of use.* Reports of use filed by preexisting subscription services for transmissions made under 17 U.S.C. 114(f) pursuant to §270.2 for use of sound recordings under section 112(e) or section 114(d)(2) of title 17 of the United States Code, or both, for the period October 28, 1998, through March 31, 2004, shall serve as the reports of use for nonsubscription transmission services, preexisting satellite digital audio radio services, new subscription services, and business establishment services for their use of sound recordings under section 112(e) or section 114(d)(2) of title 17 of the United States Code, or both, for the period from October 28, 1998, through March 31, 2004.

(c) *Royalty Logic Inc.* If, in accordance with §261.4(c), any Copyright Owners or Performers have provided timely notice to SoundExchange of an election to receive royalties from Royalty Logic, Inc. as a Designated Agent for the period October 28, 1998, through December 31, 2002, or any portion thereof, SoundExchange shall provide to RLI copies of the Reports of Use described in paragraph (b) of this section for that period or the applicable portion thereof.

[69 FR 58262, Sept. 30, 2004]

§270.5 Designated collection and distribution organizations for records of use of sound recordings under statutory license.

(a) *General.* This section prescribes rules under which records of use shall be collected and distributed under section 114(f) of title 17 of the United States Code, and under which records of such use shall be kept and made available.

(b) *Definitions.* (1) A *Collective* is a collection and distribution organization that is designated under the statutory license, either by settlement agreement reached under section 114(f)(1)(A) or section 114(f)(1)(C)(i) and adopted pursuant to 37 CFR 251.63(b), or by decision of a Copyright Arbitration Royalty Panel (CARP) under section 114(f)(1)(B) or section 114(f)(1)(C)(ii), or by an order of the Librarian pursuant to 17 U.S.C. 802(f).

(2) A *Service* is an entity engaged in the digital transmission of sound recordings pursuant to section 114(f) of title 17 of the United States Code.

(c) *Notice of Designation as Collective under Statutory License.* A Collective shall file with the Licensing Division of the Copyright Office and post and make available online a "Notice of Designation as Collective under Statutory License," which shall be identified as such by prominent caption or heading, and shall contain the following information:

(1) The Collective name, address, telephone number and facsimile number;

(2) A statement that the Collective has been designated for collection and distribution of performance royalties under statutory license for digital transmission of sound recordings; and

(3) Information on how to gain access to the online website or home page of the Collective, where information may be posted under this part concerning the use of sound recordings under statutory license. The address of the Licensing Division is: Library of Congress, Copyright Office, Licensing Division, 101 Independence Avenue, SE., Washington, DC 20557–6400.

(d) *Annual Report.* The Collective will post and make available online, for the duration of one year, an Annual Report on how the Collective operates, how royalties are collected and distributed, and what the Collective spent that fiscal year on administrative expenses.

(e) *Inspection of Reports of Use by copyright owners.* The Collective shall make copies of the Reports of Use for the preceding three years available for inspection by any sound recording copyright owner, without charge, during normal office hours upon reasonable notice. The Collective shall predicate inspection of Reports of Use upon information relating to identity, location and status as a sound recording copyright owner, and the copyright owner's written agreement not to utilize the information for purposes other than royalty collection and distribution, and determining compliance with statutory license requirements, without express consent of the Service providing the Report of Use. The Collective shall render its best efforts to locate copyright owners in order to make available records of use, and such efforts shall include searches in Copyright Office public records and published directories of sound recording copyright owners.

(f) *Confidentiality.* Copyright owners, their agents, and Collectives shall not disseminate information in the Reports of Use to any persons not entitled to it, nor utilize the information for purposes other than royalty collection and distribution, and determining compliance with statutory license requirements, without express consent of the Service providing the Report of Use.

(g) *Termination and dissolution.* If a Collective terminates its collection and distribution operations prior to the close of its term of designation, the Collective shall notify the Copyright Office, and all Services transmitting sound recordings under statutory license, by certified or registered mail. The dissolving Collective shall provide each such Service with information identifying the copyright owners it has served.

[69 FR 11527, Mar. 11, 2004, Redesignated at 69 FR 58262, Sept. 30, 2004]

INDEX TO CHAPTER II—COPYRIGHT OFFICE, LIBRARY OF CONGRESS

EDITORIAL NOTE: This listing is provided for informational purposes only. It is compiled and kept current by the Department of Commerce. This index is updated as of July 1, 2013.

[1] *But see* 17 U.S.C. 121 (reproduction for blind or other people with disabilities), added by the Act of September 16, 1996, Pub. L. 104–197, 110 Stat. 2394, 2416.

Index

[2] NAFTA is the acronym for North American Free Trade Agreement.

Index

Index

CHAPTER III—COPYRIGHT ROYALTY BOARD, LIBRARY OF CONGRESS

SUBCHAPTER A—GENERAL PROVISIONS

PART 301—ORGANIZATION

AUTHORITY: 17 U.S.C. 801.

SOURCE: 70 FR 30905, May 31, 2005, unless otherwise noted.

§ 301.1 Copyright Royalty Board.

The Copyright Royalty Board is the institutional entity in the Library of Congress that will house the Copyright Royalty Judges, appointed pursuant to 17 U.S.C. 801(a), and their staff.

§ 301.2 Official addresses.

All claims, pleadings, and general correspondence intended for the Copyright Royalty Board must be addressed as follows:

(a) If sent by mail (including overnight delivery using United States Postal Service Express Mail), the envelope should be addressed to: Copyright Royalty Board, P.O. Box 70977, Southwest Station, Washington, DC 20024–0977.

(b) If hand delivered by a private party, the envelope must be brought to the Copyright Office Public Information Office, Room LM–401 in the James Madison Memorial Building, Monday through Friday, between 8:30 a.m. and 5 p.m., and be addressed as follows: Copyright Royalty Board, Library of Congress, James Madison Memorial Building, 101 Independence Avenue, SE., Washington, DC 20559–6000.

(c) If hand delivered by a commercial courier (excluding Federal Express, United Parcel Service and similar courier services), the envelope must be delivered to the Congressional Courier Acceptance Site (CCAS) located at Second and D Street, NE., Washington, DC, Monday through Friday, between 8:30 a.m. and 4 p.m., and be addressed as follows: Copyright Royalty Board, Library of Congress, James Madison Memorial Building, 101 Independence Avenue, SE., Washington, DC.

(d) Correspondence and filings for the Copyright Royalty Board may not be delivered by means of overnight delivery services such as Federal Express, United Parcel Service, etc., due to delays in processing receipt of such deliveries.

[70 FR 30905, May 31, 2005, as amended at 71 FR 53326, Sept. 11, 2006]

PART 302—PUBLIC ACCESS TO RECORDS

AUTHORITY: 5 U.S.C. 522.

SOURCE: 71 FR 53326, Sept. 11, 2006, unless otherwise noted.

§ 302.1 Public records and access.

(a) *Inspection.* Records of proceedings before the Board will be available for public inspection at the Copyright Royalty Board offices.

(b) *Requests.* Requests for access to records must be directed to the Copyright Royalty Board. No requests for information or access to records shall be directed to or accepted by a Copyright Royalty Judge. Access to records is only available by appointment.

§ 302.2 Fees.

For services rendered in connection with document location, reproduction, *etc.*, fees shall apply in accordance with § 201.3 of this title.

SUBCHAPTER B—COPYRIGHT ROYALTY JUDGES RULES AND PROCEDURES

PART 350—GENERAL ADMINISTRATIVE PROVISIONS

AUTHORITY: 17 U.S.C. 803.

SOURCE: 70 FR 30905, May 31, 2005, unless otherwise noted.

§ 350.1 Scope.

This subchapter governs procedures generally applicable to proceedings before the Copyright Royalty Judges in making determinations and adjustments pursuant to the Copyright Act, 17 U.S.C. 801(b).

[70 FR 30905, May 31, 2005, as amended at 71 FR 53327, Sept. 11, 2006]

§ 350.2 Representation.

Individual parties in proceedings before the Judges may represent themselves or be represented by an attorney. All other parties must be represented by an attorney. Cf. Rule 49(c)(11) of the Rules of the District of Columbia Court of Appeals. The appearance of an attorney on behalf of any party constitutes a representation that the attorney is a member of the bar, in one or more states, in good standing.

[71 FR 53327, Sept. 11, 2006]

§ 350.3 Caption required.

All pleadings and documents filed in a proceeding before the Copyright Royalty Judges must be identified in a caption that identifies the proceeding by caption and docket number.

[70 FR 30905, May 31, 2005, as amended at 71 FR 53327, Sept. 11, 2006]

§ 350.4 Filing and service.

(a) *Filing of pleadings.* For all filings, the submitting party shall deliver an original, five paper copies, and one electronic copy in Portable Document Format (PDF) on compact disk (an optical data storage medium such as a CD-ROM, CD-R or CD-RW) or floppy diskette to the Copyright Royalty Board in accordance with the provisions set forth in § 301.2 of this chapter. In no case shall a party tender any document by facsimile transmission, except with the prior express authorization of the Copyright Royalty Judges.

(b) *Exhibits.* All exhibits must be included with the pleadings they support. In the case of exhibits whose bulk or whose cost of reproduction would unnecessarily encumber the record or burden the party, the Copyright Royalty Judges may reduce the number of required copies.

(c) *English language translations.* Each submission that is in a language other than English shall be accompanied by an English-language translation, duly verified under oath to be a true translation. Any other party to the proceeding may, in response, submit its own English-language translation, similarly verified.

(d) *Affidavits.* The testimony of each witness shall be accompanied by an affidavit or a declaration made pursuant to 28 U.S.C. 1746 supporting the testimony.

(e) *Subscription*—(1) *Parties represented by counsel.* The original of all documents filed by any party represented by counsel shall be signed by at least one attorney of record and shall list the attorney's full name, mailing address, e-mail address (if any), telephone number, facsimile number (if any), and a state bar identification number. Submissions signed by an attorney for a party need not be verified or accompanied by an affidavit. The signature of an attorney constitutes certification that to the best of the person's knowledge, information, and belief, formed after an inquiry reasonable under the circumstances:

(i) It is not being presented for any improper purpose, such as to harass or to cause unnecessary delay or needless increase in the cost of litigation;

(ii) The claims, defenses, and other legal contentions therein are warranted by existing law or by a nonfrivolous argument for the extension, modification, or reversal of existing law or the establishment of new law;

(iii) The allegations and other factual contentions have evidentiary support or, if specifically so identified, are likely to have evidentiary support after a reasonable opportunity for further investigation or discovery; and

(iv) The denials of factual contentions are warranted on the evidence or, if specifically so identified, are reasonably based on a lack of information or belief.

(2) *Parties representing themselves.* The original of all documents filed by a party not represented by counsel shall be signed by that party and list that party's full name, mailing address, email address (if any), telephone number, and facsimile number (if any). The signature will constitute the party's certification that, to the best of his or her knowledge and belief, there is good ground to support the document, and that it has not been interposed for purposes of delay.

(f) *Oppositions and replies.* Oppositions to motions shall be filed within five business days of the filing of the motion, and replies to oppositions shall be filed within four business days of the filing of the opposition.

(g) *Service list.* The Copyright Royalty Judges will compile and distribute, to those parties who have filed a petition to participate that has been accepted by the Copyright Royalty Judges, the official service list of the proceeding. In all filings, a copy shall be served upon counsel of all other parties identified in the service list, or, if the party is unrepresented by counsel, upon the party itself. Proof of service shall accompany the filing. Parties shall notify the Copyright Royalty Judges and all parties of any change in the name or address to which service shall be made.

(h) *Service method.* During the course of a proceeding, each party must serve all motions, objections, oppositions, and replies on the other parties or their counsel by means no slower than overnight express mail on the same day the pleading is filed. If a party is willing to accept service of a document electronically (*i.e.*, by e-mail), followed by a hard copy, first-class mail of the hard copy may be used in lieu of express mail or other expedited delivery.

[70 FR 30905, May 31, 2005, as amended at 71 FR 53327, Sept. 11, 2006; 71 FR 59010, Oct. 6, 2006]

§ 350.5 Time.

(a) *Computation.* To compute the due date for filing and serving any document or performing any other act directed by an order of the Copyright Royalty Judges or the Copyright Royalty Judges' rules:

(1) Exclude the day of the act, event, or default that begins the period.

(2) Exclude intermediate Saturdays, Sundays, and legal holidays when the period is less than 11 days, unless stated in calendar days.

(3) Include the last day of the period unless it is a Saturday, Sunday, legal holiday, or a day on which the weather or other conditions render the Copyright Royalty Board's office inaccessible.

(4) As used in this rule, "legal holiday" means the date designated for the observance of New Year's Day, Martin Luther King, Jr.'s Birthday, Presidents' Day, Memorial Day, Independence Day, Labor Day, Columbus Day, Veterans' Day, Thanksgiving Day, Christmas Day, and any other day declared a holiday by the President or the Congress.

(b) *Extensions.* A party seeking an extension must do so by written motion. Prior to filing such a motion, a party must attempt to obtain consent from the other parties to the proceeding. An extension motion must state:

(1) The date on which the action or submission is due;

(2) The length of the extension sought;

(3) The date on which the action or submission would be due if the extension were allowed;

(4) The reason or reasons why there is good cause for the delay;

(5) The justification for the amount of additional time being sought; and

(6) The attempts that have been made to obtain consent from the other

parties to the proceeding and the position of the other parties on the motion.

[70 FR 30905, May 31, 2005, as amended at 71 FR 53327, Sept. 11, 2006]

§ 350.6 Construction and waiver.

The regulations of the Copyright Royalty Judges are intended to provide efficient and just administrative proceedings and will be construed to advance these purposes. For purposes of an individual proceeding, the provisions of this subchapter may be suspended or waived, in whole or in part, upon a showing of good cause, to the extent allowable by law.

[70 FR 30905, May 31, 2005, as amended at 71 FR 53327, Sept. 11, 2006]

PART 351—PROCEEDINGS

AUTHORITY: 17 U.S.C. 803.

SOURCE: 70 FR 30905, May 31, 2005, unless otherwise noted.

§ 351.1 Initiation of proceedings.

(a) *Notice of commencement; solicitation of petitions to participate.* All proceedings before the Copyright Royalty Judges to make determinations and adjustments of reasonable terms and rates of royalty payments, and to authorize the distribution of royalty fees, shall be initiated by publication in the FEDERAL REGISTER of a notice of the initiation of proceedings calling for the filing of petitions to participate in the proceeding.

(b) *Petitions to participate*—(1) *Royalty rate proceedings*—(i) *Single petition.* Each petition to participate filed in a royalty rate proceeding must include:

(A) The petitioner's full name, address, telephone number, facsimile number (if any), and e-mail address (if any); and

(B) A description of the petitioner's significant interest in the subject matter of the proceeding.

(ii) *Joint petition.* Petitioners with similar interests may, in lieu of filing individual petitions, file a single petition. Each joint petition must include:

(A) The full name, address, telephone number, facsimile number (if any), and e-mail address (if any) of the person filing the petition;

(B) A list identifying all participants to the joint petition;

(C) A description of the participants' significant interest in the subject matter of the proceeding; and

(D) If the joint petition is filed by counsel or a representative of one or more of the participants that are named in the joint petition, a statement from such counsel or representative certifying that, as of the date of submission of the joint petition, such counsel or representative has the authority and consent of the participants to represent them in the royalty rate proceeding.

(2) *Distribution proceedings*—(i) *Single petition.* Each petition to participate filed in a royalty distribution proceeding must include:

(A) The petitioner's full name, address, telephone number, facsimile number (if any), and e-mail address (if any);

(B) In a cable or satellite royalty distribution proceeding, identification of whether the petition covers a Phase I proceeding (the initial part of a distribution proceeding where royalties are divided among the categories or groups of copyright owners), a Phase II proceeding (where the money allotted to each category is subdivided among the various copyright owners within that category), or both; and

(C) A description of the petitioner's significant interest in the subject matter of the proceeding.

(ii) *Joint petition.* Petitioners with similar interests may, in lieu of filing individual petitions, file a single petition. Each joint petition must include:

(A) The full name, address, telephone number, facsimile number (if any), and e-mail address (if any) of the person filing the petition;

(B) A list identifying all participants to the joint petition;

(C) In a cable or satellite royalty distribution proceeding, identification of whether the petition covers a Phase I proceeding (the initial part of a distribution proceeding where royalties are divided among the categories or groups of copyright owners), a Phase II proceeding (where the money allotted to each category is subdivided among the various copyright owners within that category), or both;

(D) A description of the participants' significant interest in the subject matter of the proceeding; and

(E) If the joint petition is filed by counsel or a representative of one or more of the participants that are named in the joint petition, a statement from such counsel or representative certifying that, as of the date of submission of the joint petition, such counsel or representative has the authority and consent of the participants to represent them in the royalty distribution proceeding.

(3) *Filing deadline.* A petition to participate shall be filed by no later than 30 days after the publication of the notice of commencement of a proceeding, subject to the qualified exception set forth in paragraph (d) of this section.

(4) *Filing fee.* A petition to participate must be accompanied with a filing fee of $150 or the petition will be rejected. Payment shall be made to the Copyright Royalty Board. If a check is subsequently dishonored, the petition will be rejected. If the petitioner believes that the contested amount of that petitioner's claim will be $10,000 or less, petitioner shall so state in the petition to participate and should not include payment of the $150 filing fee. If it becomes apparent during the course of the proceedings that the contested amount of the claim is more than $10,000, the Copyright Royalty Judges will require payment of the filing fee at such time.

(c) *Acceptance and rejection of petitions to participate.* A petition to participate will be deemed to have been allowed by the Copyright Royalty Judges unless the Copyright Royalty Judges determine the petitioner lacks a significant interest in the proceeding or the petition is otherwise invalid.

(d) *Late petitions to participate.* The Copyright Royalty Judges may, for substantial good cause shown, and if there is no prejudice to the participants that have already filed petitions, accept late petitions to participate at any time up to the date that is 90 days before the date on which participants in the proceeding are to file their written direct statements. However, petitioners whose petitions are filed more than 30 days after publication of notice of commencement of a proceeding are not eligible to object to a settlement reached during the voluntary negotiation period.

[70 FR 30905, May 31, 2005, as amended at 71 FR 53327, Sept. 11, 2006]

§351.2 Voluntary negotiation period; settlement.

(a) *Commencement; duration.* After the date for filing petitions to participate in a proceeding, the Copyright Royalty Judges will announce the beginning of a voluntary negotiation period and will make a list of the participants available to the participants in the particular proceeding. The voluntary negotiation period shall last three months, after which the parties shall notify the Copyright Royalty Judges in writing as to whether a settlement has been reached.

(b) *Settlement*—(1) *Distribution proceedings.* Pursuant to 17 U.S.C. 801(b)(7)(A), to the extent that a settlement has been reached in a distribution proceeding, that agreement will provide the basis for the distribution.

(2) *Royalty rate proceedings.* If, in a proceeding to determine statutory terms and rates, the participating parties report that a settlement has been reached by some or all of the parties, the Copyright Royalty Judges, pursuant to 17 U.S.C. 801(b)(7)(A), will publish the settlement in the FEDERAL REGISTER for notice and comment from those bound by the terms, rates, or other determination set by the agreement. If an objection to the adoption of an agreement is filed, the Copyright Royalty Judges may decline to adopt the agreement as a basis for statutory terms and rates for participants that are not parties to the agreement if the

Copyright Royalty Judges conclude that the agreement does not provide a reasonable basis for setting statutory terms or rates.

[70 FR 30905, May 31, 2005, as amended at 71 FR 53328, Sept. 11, 2006]

§ 351.3 Controversy and further proceedings.

(a) *Declaration of controversy.* If a settlement has not been reached within the voluntary negotiation period, the Copyright Royalty Judges will issue an order declaring that further proceedings are necessary. The procedures set forth at §§ 351.5, *et seq.*, for formal hearings will apply, unless the abbreviated procedures set forth in paragraphs (b) and (c) of this section are invoked by the Copyright Royalty Judges.

(b) *Small claims in distribution proceedings*—(1) *General.* If, in a distribution proceeding, the contested amount of a claim is $10,000 or less, the Copyright Royalty Judges shall decide the controversy on the basis of the filing of the written direct statement by each participant (or participant group filing a joint petition), the response by any opposing participant, and one optional reply by a participant who has filed a written direct statement.

(2) *Bad faith inflation of claim.* If the Copyright Royalty Judges determine that a participant asserts in bad faith an amount in controversy in excess of $10,000 for the purpose of avoiding a determination under the procedure set forth in paragraph (b)(1) of this section, the Copyright Royalty Judges shall impose a fine on that participant in an amount not to exceed the difference between the actual amount distributed and the amount asserted by the participant.

(c) *Paper proceedings*—(1) *Standard.* The procedure under this paragraph (c) will be applied in cases in which there is no genuine issue of material fact, there is no need for evidentiary hearings, and all participants in the proceeding agree in writing to the procedure. In the absence of an agreement in writing among all participants, this procedure may be applied by the Copyright Royalty Judges either on the motion of a party or by the Copyright Royalty Judges *sua sponte.*

(2) *Procedure.* Paper proceedings will be decided on the basis of the filing of the written direct statement by the participant (or participant group filing a joint petition), the response by any opposing participant, and one optional reply by a participant who has filed a written direct statement.

[70 FR 30905, May 31, 2005, as amended at 71 FR 53328, Sept. 11, 2006]

§ 351.4 Written direct statements.

(a) *Required filing; deadline.* All parties who have filed a petition to participate in the hearing must file a written direct statement. The deadline for the filing of the written direct statement will be specified by the Copyright Royalty Judges, not earlier than 4 months, nor later than 5 months, after the end of the voluntary negotiation period set forth in § 351.2.

(b) *Required content*—(1) *Testimony.* The written direct statement shall include all testimony, including each witness's background and qualifications, along with all the exhibits.

(2) *Designated past records and testimony.* Each participating party may designate a portion of past records, including records of the Copyright Royalty Tribunal or Copyright Arbitration Royalty Panels, that it wants included in its direct statement. If a party intends to rely on any part of the testimony of a witness in a prior proceeding, the complete testimony of that witness (*i.e.*, direct, cross and redirect examination) must be designated. The party submitting such past records and/or testimony shall include a copy with the written direct statement.

(3) *Claim.* In the case of a royalty distribution proceeding, each party must state in the written direct statement its percentage or dollar claim to the fund. In the case of a rate (or rates) proceeding, each party must state its requested rate. No party will be precluded from revising its claim or its requested rate at any time during the proceeding up to, and including, the filing of the proposed findings of fact and conclusions of law.

(c) *Amended written direct statements.* A participant in a proceeding may amend a written direct statement based on new information received during the discovery process, within 15 days after the end of the discovery period. An amended written direct statement must explain how it differs from the written direct statement it will amend and must demonstrate that the amendment is based on new information received during the discovery process. The participant amending its written direct statement may file either the amended portions of the written direct statement or submit complete new copies at its option.

[70 FR 30905, May 31, 2005, as amended at 71 FR 53328, Sept. 11, 2006; 71 FR 59010, Oct. 6, 2006]

§351.5 Discovery in royalty rate proceedings.

(a) *Schedule.* Following the submission to the Copyright Royalty Judges of written direct and rebuttal statements by the participants in a royalty rate proceeding, and after conferring with the participants, the Copyright Royalty Judges will issue a discovery schedule.

(b) *Document production, depositions and interrogatories*—(1) *Document production.* A participant in a royalty rate proceeding may request of an opposing participant nonprivileged documents that are directly related to the written direct statement or written rebuttal statement of that participant. Broad, nonspecific discovery requests are not acceptable. All documents offered in response to a discovery request must be furnished in as organized and useable form as possible. Any objection to a request for production shall be resolved by a motion or request to compel production. The motion must include a statement that the parties had conferred and were unable to resolve the matter.

(2) *Depositions and interrogatories.* In a proceeding to determine royalty rates, the participants entitled to receive royalties shall collectively be permitted to take no more than 10 depositions and secure responses to no more than 25 interrogatories. Similarly, the participants obligated to pay royalties shall collectively be permitted to take no more than 10 depositions and secure responses to no more than 25 interrogatories. Parties may obtain such discovery regarding any matter, not privileged, that is relevant to the claim or defense of any party. Relevant information need not be admissible at hearing if the discovery by means of depositions and interrogatories appears reasonably calculated to lead to the discovery of admissible evidence.

(c) *Motions to request other relevant information and materials.* (1) In any royalty rate proceeding scheduled to commence prior to January 1, 2011, a participant may, by means of written or oral motion on the record, request of an opposing participant or witness other relevant information and materials. The Copyright Royalty Judges will allow such request only if they determine that, absent the discovery sought, their ability to achieve a just resolution of the proceeding would be substantially impaired.

(2) In determining whether such discovery motions will be granted, the Copyright Royalty Judges may consider—

(i) Whether the burden or expense of producing the requested information or materials outweighs the likely benefit, taking into account the needs and resources of the participants, the importance of the issues at stake, and the probative value of the requested information or materials in resolving such issues;

(ii) Whether the requested information or materials would be unreasonably cumulative or duplicative, or are obtainable from another source that is more convenient, less burdensome, or less expensive; and

(iii) Whether the participant seeking the discovery had an ample opportunity by discovery in the proceeding or by other means to obtain the information sought.

[71 FR 53328, Sept. 11, 2006]

§351.6 Discovery in distribution proceedings.

In distribution proceedings, the Copyright Royalty Judges shall designate a 45-day period beginning with the filing of written direct statements within which parties may request of an opposing party nonprivileged underlying documents related to the written exhibits and testimony. However, all parties shall be given a reasonable opportunity to conduct discovery on amended statements.

[71 FR 53328, Sept. 11, 2006]

§ 351.7 Settlement conference.

A post-discovery settlement conference will be held among the participants, within 21 days after the close of discovery, outside of the presence of the Copyright Royalty Judges. Immediately after this conference the participants shall file with the Copyright Royalty Judges a written Joint Settlement Conference Report indicating the extent to which the participants have reached a settlement.

[70 FR 30905, May 31, 2005, as amended at 71 FR 53329, Sept. 11, 2006]

§ 351.8 Pre-hearing conference.

In the absence of a complete settlement in a proceeding not subject to the abbreviated procedures set forth in §§ 351.3(b) and (c), a hearing will be scheduled expeditiously so as to allow the Copyright Royalty Judges to conduct hearings and issue its final determination in the proceeding within the time allowed by the Copyright Act. Prior to the hearing, the Copyright Royalty Judges may conduct a pre-hearing conference to assist in setting the order of presentation of evidence and the appearance of witnesses at the hearing and to provide for the submission of pre-hearing written legal arguments.

[70 FR 30905, May 31, 2005, as amended at 71 FR 53329, Sept. 11, 2006]

§ 351.9 Conduct of hearings.

(a) *By panels.* Subject to paragraph (b) of this section, hearings will be conducted by Copyright Royalty Judges sitting *en banc.*

(b) *Role of Chief Judge.* The Chief Copyright Royalty Judge, or an individual Copyright Royalty Judge designated by the Chief Judge, may preside over such collateral and administrative proceedings, and over such proceedings under section 803(b)(1) through (5) of the Copyright Act, as the Chief Judge considers appropriate. The Chief Judge, or an individual Copyright Royalty Judge designated by the Chief Judge, shall have the responsibility for:

(1) Administering oaths and affirmations to all witnesses;

(2) Announcing the Copyright Royalty Judges' ruling on objections and motions and all rulings with respect to introducing or excluding documentary or other evidence. In all cases, with the exception of a hearing pursuant to 17 U.S.C. 803(a)(2), it takes a majority vote to grant a motion or sustain an objection. A tie vote will result in the denial of a motion or the overruling of the objection;

(c) *Opening statements.* In each distribution or rate proceeding, each party may present its opening statement summarizing its written direct statement.

(d) *Notice of witnesses and prior exchange of exhibits.* Each party must provide all other parties notice of the witnesses who are to be called to testify at least one week in advance of such testimony, unless modified by applicable trial order. Parties must exchange exhibits at least one day in advance of being offered into evidence at a hearing, unless modified by applicable trial order.

(e) *Subpoenas.* The parties may move the Copyright Royalty Judges to issue a subpoena. The object of the subpoena shall be served with the motion and may appear in response to the motion.

(f) *Witnesses sequestered.* Subject to applicable trial order, witnesses, other than party representatives, may not be permitted to listen to any testimony and may not be allowed to review a transcript of any prior testimony.

[70 FR 30905, May 31, 2005, as amended at 71 FR 53329, Sept. 11, 2006]

§ 351.10 Evidence.

(a) *Admissibility.* All evidence that is relevant and not unduly repetitious or privileged, shall be admissible. Hearsay may be admitted to the extent deemed appropriate by the Copyright Royalty Judges. Written testimony and exhibits must be authenticated or identified in order to be admissible as evidence. The requirement of authentication or identification as a condition precedent to admissibility is satisfied by evidence sufficient to support a finding that the matter in question is what its proponent claims. Extrinsic evidence of authenticity as a condition precedent to admissibility is not required with respect to materials that can be self-authenticated under Rule 902 of the Federal Rules of Evidence such as certain public records. No evidence, including exhibits, may be submitted without a sponsoring witness, except for good cause shown.

(b) *Examination of witnesses.* All witnesses shall be required to take an oath or affirmation before testifying. Parties are entitled to conduct direct examination (consisting of the testimony of the witness in the written statements and an oral summary of that testimony); cross-examination (limited to matters raised on direct examination); and redirect examination (limited to matters raised on cross-examination). The Copyright Royalty Judges may limit the number of witnesses or limit questioning to avoid cumulative testimony.

(c) *Exhibits*—(1) *Submission.* Writings, recordings and photographs shall be presented as exhibits and marked by the presenting party. "Writings" and "recordings" consist of letters, words, or numbers, or their equivalent, set down by handwriting, typewriting, printing, photostating, photographing, magnetic impulse, mechanical or electronic recording, or other form of data compilation. "Photographs" include still photographs, video tapes, and motion pictures.

(2) *Separation of irrelevant portions.* Relevant and material matter embraced in an exhibit containing other matter not material or relevant or not intended as evidence must be plainly designated as the matter offered in evidence, and the immaterial or irrelevant parts shall be marked clearly so as to show they are not intended as evidence.

(3) *Summary exhibits.* The contents of voluminous writings, recordings, or photographs which cannot conveniently be examined in the hearing may be presented in the form of a chart, summary, or calculation. The originals, or duplicates, shall be made available for examination or copying, or both, by other parties at a reasonable time and place. The Copyright Royalty Judges may order that they be produced in the hearing.

(d) *Copies.* Anyone presenting exhibits as evidence must present copies to all other participants in the proceedings, or their attorneys, and afford them an opportunity to examine the exhibits in their entirety and offer into evidence any other portion that may be considered material and relevant.

(e) *Introduction of studies and analyses.* If studies or analyses are offered in evidence, they shall state clearly the study plan, the principles and methods underlying the study, all relevant assumptions, all variables considered in the analysis, the techniques of data collection, the techniques of estimation and testing, and the results of the study's actual estimates and tests presented in a format commonly accepted within the relevant field of expertise implicated by the study. The facts and judgments upon which conclusions are based shall be stated clearly, together with any alternative courses of action considered. Summarized descriptions of input data, tabulations of input data and the input data themselves shall be retained.

(f) *Objections.* Parties are entitled to raise objections to evidence on any proper ground during the course of the hearing and to raise an objection that an opposing party has not furnished unprivileged underlying documents.

(g) *New exhibits for use in cross-examination.* Exhibits that have not been identified and exchanged in advance may be shown to a witness on cross-examination. However, copies of such exhibits must be distributed to the Copyright Royalty Judges and to the other participants before being shown to the witness at the time of cross-examination, unless the Copyright Royalty Judges direct otherwise. Such exhibits can be used solely to impeach the witness's direct testimony.

[70 FR 30905, May 31, 2005, as amended at 71 FR 53329, Sept. 11, 2006; 71 FR 59010, Oct. 6, 2006]

§351.11 Rebuttal proceedings.

Written rebuttal statements shall be filed at a time designated by the Copyright Royalty Judges upon conclusion of the hearing of the direct case, in the same form and manner as the written direct statement, except that the claim or the requested rate shall not have to be included if it has not changed from the written direct statement. Further proceedings at the rebuttal stage shall follow the schedule ordered by the Copyright Royalty Judges.

[70 FR 30905, May 31, 2005, as amended at 71 FR 53329, Sept. 11, 2006]

§ 351.12 Closing the record.

To close the record of a proceeding, the presiding Judge shall make an announcement that the taking of evidence has concluded.

[71 FR 53330, Sept. 11, 2006]

§ 351.13 Transcript and record.

(a) An official reporter for the recording and transcribing of hearings shall be designated by the Copyright Royalty Judges. Anyone wishing to inspect the transcript of a hearing may do so at the offices of the Copyright Royalty Board.

(b) The transcript of testimony and written statements, except those portions to which an objection has been sustained, and all exhibits, documents and other items admitted in the course of a proceeding shall constitute the official written record. The written record, along with the Copyright Royalty Judges' final determination, shall be available at the Copyright Royalty Board's offices for public inspection and copying.

[71 FR 53330, Sept. 11, 2006]

§ 351.14 Proposed findings of fact and conclusions of law.

(a) Any party to the proceeding may file proposed findings of fact and conclusions, briefs or memoranda of law, or may be directed by the Copyright Royalty Judges to do so. Such filings, and any replies to them, shall take place after the record has been closed.

(b) Failure to file when directed to do so shall be considered a waiver of the right to participate further in the proceeding unless good cause for the failure is shown. A party waives any objection to a provision in the determination unless the provision conflicts with a proposed finding of fact or conclusion of law filed by the party.

(c) Proposed findings of fact shall be numbered by paragraph and include all basic evidentiary facts developed on the record used to support proposed conclusions, and shall contain appropriate citations to the record for each evidentiary fact. Proposed conclusions shall be stated and numbered by paragraph separately. Failure to comply with this paragraph (c) may result in the offending paragraph being stricken.

[71 FR 53330, Sept. 11, 2006]

§ 351.15 Remand.

In the event of a remand from the United States Court of Appeals for the District of Columbia Circuit of a final determination of the Copyright Royalty Judges, the parties to the proceeding shall within 45 days from the issuance of the mandate from the Court of Appeals file with the Judges written proposals for the conduct and schedule of the resolution of the remand.

[74 FR 38533, Aug. 4, 2009]

PART 352—DETERMINATIONS

Sec.

AUTHORITY: 17 U.S.C. 803.

SOURCE: 70 FR 30905, May 31, 2005, unless otherwise noted.

§ 352.1 How made.

Except for decisions authorized by law to be made by a single Copyright Royalty Judge, determinations in a proceeding will be made by a majority of the Copyright Royalty Judges. The opinion or opinions of the majority and any dissenting opinion will be included in the determination. Each determination will be transmitted to the Register of Copyrights to enable review for consistency with the Copyright Act on the day it is issued.

[70 FR 30905, May 31, 2005, as amended at 71 FR 53330, Sept. 11, 2006]

§ 352.2 Timing.

The Copyright Royalty Judges will issue their determination within 11 months of the date of the post-discovery settlement conference or 15 days before the expiration of the existing rates or terms in a proceeding to determine successors to rates or terms that will expire on a specific date, whichever date first occurs. The date the determination is "issued" refers to the date of the order.

[70 FR 30905, May 31, 2005, as amended at 71 FR 53330, Sept. 11, 2006]

§ 352.3 Final determinations.

Unless a motion for a rehearing is timely filed within 15 days, the determination by the Copyright Royalty Judges pursuant to 17 U.S.C. 803(c) in a proceeding is final when it is issued.

[71 FR 53330, Sept. 11, 2006]

PART 353—REHEARING

AUTHORITY: 17 U.S.C. 803.

SOURCE: 70 FR 30905, May 31, 2005, unless otherwise noted.

§ 353.1 When granted.

A motion for rehearing may be filed by any participant in the relevant proceeding. The Copyright Royalty Judges may grant rehearing upon a showing that any aspect of the determination may be erroneous.

[71 FR 53330, Sept. 11, 2006]

§ 353.2 Form and content of rehearing motions.

A motion for rehearing shall not exceed 10 pages in length and must set forth, in the beginning of its text, a brief summary statement of the aspects of the determination believed by the moving participant to be without evidentiary support in the record or contrary to legal requirements.

§ 353.3 Procedure on rehearing.

Upon receipt of a motion for rehearing, the Copyright Royalty Judges will issue an appropriate order. No participant shall file a response to a rehearing motion, unless such response is allowed by order of the Copyright Royalty Judges.

[70 FR 30905, May 31, 2005, as amended at 71 FR 53330, Sept. 11, 2006]

§ 353.4 Filing deadline.

A motion for rehearing must be filed within 15 days after the date on which the Copyright Royalty Judges issue an initial determination.

[71 FR 53330, Sept. 11, 2006]

§ 353.5 Participation not required.

In any case in which a response to a rehearing motion is allowed, or rehearing is granted, an opposing party shall not be required to participate in the rehearing. The Copyright Royalty Judges will not draw any negative inference from a lack of participation in a rehearing. Nonparticipation in rehearing proceedings may limit the scope of their participation in judicial review proceedings as set forth in 17 U.S.C. 803(d)(1).

[70 FR 30905, May 31, 2005, as amended at 71 FR 53330, Sept. 11, 2006]

PART 354—SUBMISSIONS TO THE REGISTER OF COPYRIGHTS

AUTHORITY: 17 U.S.C. 802.

SOURCE: 70 FR 30905, May 31, 2005, unless otherwise noted.

§ 354.1 Material questions of copyright law.

(a) *Discretionary referrals*. The Copyright Royalty Judges may seek guidance from the Register of Copyrights with respect to a material question of substantive law, concerning an interpretation or construction of those provisions of the Copyright Act, that arises in the course of their proceedings.

(b) *How presented*. A question of substantive law may be referred to the Register of Copyrights at the request of one or more of the Copyright Royalty Judges. A question of substantive law may also be referred to the Register of Copyrights as a request submitted by motion of a participant, provided that one or more of the Copyright Royalty Judges agrees with the participant's request.

(1) *Referral by Judges.* One or more of the Copyright Royalty Judges may refer what he or she believes to be a material question of substantive law to the Register of Copyrights at any time during a proceeding by issuing a written referral that is made part of the record of that proceeding. The referral will state the issue(s) to be referred and the schedule for the filing of briefs by the parties of the issue(s). After the briefs and other relevant materials are received, they will be transmitted to the Register of Copyrights.

(2) *Motion by participant.* Any participant may submit a motion to the Copyright Royalty Judges (but not to the Register of Copyrights) requesting their referral to the Register of Copyrights a question that the participant believes would be suitable for referral under paragraph (a) of this section.

(i) *Content.* The motion should be captioned "Motion of [Participant(s)] Requesting Referral of Material Question of Substantive Law." The motion should set forth, at the outset, the precise legal question for which the moving party is seeking interlocutory referral to the Register of Copyrights. The motion should then proceed to explain, with brevity, why the issue meets the criteria for potential referral under paragraph (a) of this section and why the interests of fair and efficient adjudication would be best served by obtaining interlocutory guidance from the Register of Copyrights. The motion should not include argument on the merits of the issue, but may include a suggested schedule of briefing that would make reasonable provision for comments and legal arguments, in such a way as to avoid delay and duplication.

(ii) *Time of motion.* A motion for referral of a material question of substantive law to the Register of Copyrights should be filed as soon as possible in the relevant proceeding, but no later than any deadline set by the Copyright Royalty Judges.

(iii) *Action on motion*—(A) *Referral granted.* Upon consideration of a Motion Requesting Referral of Material Question of Substantive Law, if one or more of the Copyright Royalty Judges agrees with the request, the Chief Judge shall issue an appropriate referral. The referral will state the issue(s) to be referred and the schedule for the filing of briefs by the parties of the issue(s). After the briefs and other relevant materials are received, they will be transmitted to the Register of Copyrights.

(B) *Referral denied.* If none of the Copyright Royalty Judges agrees with the request, the Board will issue an order denying the request which will provide the basis for the decision. A copy of any order denying a Motion Requesting Referral of Material Question of Substantive Law will be transmitted to the Register of Copyrights.

(c) *No effect on proceedings.* The issuance of a request to the Register of Copyrights for an interpretive ruling under this part does not delay or otherwise affect the schedule of the participants' obligations in the relevant ongoing proceeding, unless that schedule or those obligations are expressly changed by order of the Copyright Royalty Judges.

(d) *Binding effect; time limit.* The Copyright Royalty Judges will not issue a final determination in a proceeding where the discretionary referral of a question to the Register of Copyrights under this part is pending, unless the Register has not delivered the decision to the Copyright Royalty Judges within 14 days after the Register receives all of the briefs of the participants. If the decision of the Register of Copyrights is timely delivered to the Copyright Royalty Judges, the decision will be included in the record of the proceeding. The legal interpretation embodied in the timely delivered response of the Register of Copyrights in resolving material questions of substantive law is binding upon the Copyright Royalty Judges and will be applied by them in their final determination in the relevant proceeding.

[71 FR 53330, Sept. 11, 2006]

§ 354.2 Novel questions.

(a) *Mandatory referrals.* If the material question of substantive law described in § 354.1(a) is a novel question of law, referral to the Register of Copyrights by the Copyright Royalty Judges is mandatory. A "novel question of law" is a question of law that has not been determined in the prior decisions, determinations, or rulings under the Copyright Act of the Copyright Royalty Judges, the Librarian of Congress, the Register of Copyrights, the Copyright Arbitration Royalty Panels (to the extent they are consistent with the current decisions, determinations, or rulings of the Register of Copyrights or the Librarian of Congress), or the former Copyright Royalty Tribunal.

(b) *Procedures.* The procedures set forth for the discretionary referral of material questions of copyright law to the Register of Copyrights by the Copyright Royalty Judges, set forth in § 354.1, shall also govern the mandatory referral of novel questions, except that the Register of Copyrights' decision will be timely if it is delivered to the Copyright Royalty Judges within 30 days after the Register of Copyrights has received all of the briefs or comments of the participants. The Copyright Royalty Judges will not issue a final determination in a proceeding where the referral of a novel question to the Register of Copyrights under this part is pending, unless this 30-day period has expired. The legal interpretation embodied in the timely delivered response of the Register of Copyrights in resolving material questions of substantive law is binding upon the Copyright Royalty Judges and will be applied by them in their final determination in the relevant proceeding.

[70 FR 30905, May 31, 2005, as amended at 71 FR 53331, Sept. 11, 2006]

§ 354.3 Register of Copyrights' authority to redesignate referrals.

If, during the 14-day period of a discretionary referral of a material question of law under § 354.1, the Register of Copyrights determines that the question is a "novel" one within the meaning of § 354.2(a), the Register may notify the Copyright Royalty Judges of that determination. The Copyright Royalty Judges will be bound by such a determination by the Register of Copyrights and will regard the Register's decision as timely delivered if it is received within the 30-day period applicable to novel question referrals.

[70 FR 30905, May 31, 2005, as amended at 71 FR 53331, Sept. 11, 2006]

SUBCHAPTER C—SUBMISSION OF ROYALTY CLAIMS

PART 360—FILING OF CLAIMS TO ROYALTY FEES COLLECTED UNDER COMPULSORY LICENSE

Subpart A—Cable Claims

AUTHORITY: 17 U.S.C. 801, 803, 805.

Subpart A also issued under 17 U.S.C. 111(d)(4).

Subpart B also issued under 17 U.S.C. 119(b)(4).

Subpart C also issued under 17 U.S.C. 1007(a)(1).

SOURCE: 70 FR 30905, May 31, 2005, unless otherwise noted.

Subpart A—Cable Claims

§ 360.1 General.

This subpart prescribes procedures under 17 U.S.C. 111(d)(4)(A) whereby parties claiming to be entitled to cable compulsory license royalty fees shall file claims with the Copyright Royalty Board.

§ 360.2 Time of filing.

During the month of July each year, any party claiming to be entitled to cable compulsory license royalty fees for secondary transmissions of one or more of its works during the preceding calendar year shall file a claim to such fees with the Copyright Royalty Board. No royalty fees shall be distributed to a party for secondary transmissions during the specified period unless such party has timely filed a claim to such fees. Claimants may file claims jointly or as a single claim.

§ 360.3 Form and content of claims.

(a) *Forms.* (1) Each claim to cable compulsory license royalty fees shall be furnished on a form prescribed by the Copyright Royalty Board and shall contain the information required by that form and its accompanying instructions.

(2) Copies of cable claim forms are available:

(i) On the Copyright Royalty Board Web site at *http://www.loc.gov/crb/claims/* for claims filed with the Copyright Royalty Board by mail or by hand delivery in accordance with § 360.4(a)(2)–(4);

(ii) On the Copyright Royalty Board Web site at *http://www.loc.gov/crb/cable/* during the month of July for claims filed online in accordance with § 360.4(a)(1); and

(iii) Upon request to the Copyright Royalty Board, Library of Congress, P.O. Box 70977, Southwest Station, Washington, DC 20024–0977.

(b) *Content*—(1) *Single claim.* A claim filed on behalf of a single copyright owner of a work or works secondarily transmitted by a cable system shall include the following information:

(i) The full legal name and address of the copyright owner entitled to claim the royalty fees.

(ii) A general statement of the nature of the copyright owner's work or works, and identification of at least one secondary transmission by a cable system of such work or works establishing a basis for the claim.

(iii) The name, telephone number, facsimile number, if any, full address, including a specific number and street name or rural route, and e-mail address, if any, of the person or entity filing the single claim. An e-mail address must be provided on claims submitted online through the Copyright Royalty Board Web site.

(iv) The name, telephone number, facsimile number, if any, and e-mail address, if any, of the person whom the Copyright Royalty Board can contact regarding the claim.

(v) An original signature of the copyright owner or of a duly authorized representative of the copyright owner, except for claims filed online through the Copyright Royalty Board Web site. *See* 37 CFR 360.3(b)(1)(vi).

(vi) A declaration of the authority to file the claim and of the veracity of the information contained in the claim and the good faith of the person signing in providing such information. Penalties for fraud and false statements are provided under 18 U.S.C. 1001 *et seq.*

(2) *Joint claim.* A claim filed on behalf of more than one copyright owner whose works have been secondarily transmitted by a cable system shall include the following information:

(i) A list including the full legal name and address of each copyright owner to the joint claim entitled to claim royalty fees.

(ii) A concise statement of the authorization for the person or entity filing the joint claim. For this purpose, a performing rights society shall not be required to obtain from its members or affiliates separate authorizations, apart from their standard membership affiliate agreements, or to list the name of each of its members or affiliates in the joint claim as required by paragraph (b)(2)(i) of this section.

(iii) A general statement of the nature of the copyright owners' works and identification of at least one secondary transmission of one of the copyright owners' works by a cable system establishing a basis for the joint claim and the identification of the copyright owner of each work so identified.

(iv) The name, telephone number, facsimile number, if any, full address, including a specific number and street name or rural route, and e-mail address, if any, of the person or entity filing the joint claim. An e-mail address must be provided on claims submitted online through the Copyright Royalty Board Web site.

(v) The name, telephone number, facsimile number, if any, and e-mail address, if any, of the person whom the Copyright Royalty Board can contact regarding the claim.

(vi) Original signatures of the copyright owners to the joint claim or of a duly authorized representative or representatives of the copyright owners, except for claims filed online through the Copyright Royalty Board Web site. *See* 37 CFR 360.3(b)(2)(vii).

(vii) Notwithstanding paragraph (b)(2)(ii) of this section, a declaration of the authority to file the claim and of the veracity of the information contained in the claim and the good faith of the person signing in providing such information. Penalties for fraud and false statements are provided under 18 U.S.C. 1001 *et seq.*

(c) In the event that the legal name and/or address of the copyright owner entitled to royalties or the person or entity filing the claim changes after the filing of the claim, the Copyright Royalty Board shall be notified of the change. If the good faith efforts of the Copyright Royalty Board to contact the copyright owner or person or entity filing the claim are frustrated because of failure to notify the Copyright Royalty Board of a name and/or address change, the claim may be subject to dismissal.

§ 360.4 Compliance with statutory dates.

(a) Claims filed with the Copyright Royalty Board shall be considered timely filed only if:

(1) They are received online in the Board's server no later than 5 p.m. E.D.T. on July 31. Online claims must be filed through the Copyright Royalty Board Web site at *http://www.loc.gov/crb/cable/* during the month of July.

(2) They are hand delivered by a private party no later than 5 p.m. E.D.T. on July 31. Claims hand delivered by a private party must be delivered to the Copyright Office Public Information Office, in the James Madison Memorial Building, Room LM–401, 101 Independence Avenue, SE., Washington, DC 20559–6000, Monday through Friday, between 8:30 a.m. and 5 p.m., and the envelope must be addressed as follows: Copyright Royalty Board, Library of Congress, James Madison Memorial Building, 101 Independence Avenue, SE., Washington, DC 20559–6000. Claims

hand delivered by a private party must be filed at the Copyright Office Public Information Office during the month of July.

(3) They are hand delivered by a commercial courier (excluding overnight delivery services such as Federal Express, United Parcel Service and similar overnight delivery services) no later than 4 p.m. E.D.T. on July 31. Claims hand delivered by a commercial courier service (excluding overnight delivery services such as Federal Express, United Parcel Service and similar overnight delivery services) must be delivered to the Congressional Courier Acceptance Site (CCAS) located at Second and D Street, N.E., Washington, DC, Monday through Friday, between 8:30 a.m. and 4 p.m., and the envelope must be addressed as follows: Copyright Royalty Board, Library of Congress, James Madison Memorial Building, 101 Independence Avenue, SE., Washington, DC 20559–6000. Claims hand delivered by a commercial courier must be filed at CCAS during the month of July.

(4) They are mailed through the United States Postal Service (USPS) having sufficient postage and bearing a July USPS postmark. Claims mailed through USPS must be addressed as follows: Copyright Royalty Board, P.O. Box 70977, Southwest Station, Washington, DC 20024–0977.

(5) Federal Express, United Parcel Service and similar overnight delivery services may not be used for the filing of claims. A claim sent by means of overnight delivery shall be done via United States Postal Service Express Mail, and the claim shall be addressed in accordance with paragraph (a)(4) of this section.

(b) Claims dated only with a business meter that are received after July 31 will not be accepted as having been timely filed.

(c) Notwithstanding paragraphs (a) and (b) of this section, in any year in which July 31 falls on a Saturday, Sunday, holiday, or other nonbusiness day within the District of Columbia or the Federal Government, claims received by the Copyright Royalty Board by the first business day in August, or properly addressed and deposited with sufficient postage with the United States Postal Service and postmarked by the first business day in August, shall be considered timely filed.

(d) No claim may be filed by facsimile transmission.

(e) In the event that a properly addressed and mailed claim is not timely received by the Copyright Royalty Board, proper filing of the claim may nonetheless be proven if it was sent by certified mail return receipt requested, and a receipt bearing a July date stamp of the United States Postal Service, except where paragraph (c) of this section applies, can be provided. No other offer of proof will be accepted in lieu of the receipt.

(f) The Copyright Royalty Board will accept either the confirmation page generated upon submission of the claim online through the Board's Web site or the electronic mail message from the Board confirming receipt of the claim as proof that a claim submitted online through the Board's Web site was received timely in the Board's server. No other offer of proof will be accepted in lieu thereof.

[70 FR 30905, May 31, 2005, as amended at 71 FR 53331, Sept. 11, 2006]

§ 360.5 Copies of claims.

A claimant shall, for each claim submitted to the Copyright Royalty Board by hand delivery or by mail, file an original and one copy of the claim to cable royalty fees.

Subpart B—Satellite Claims

§ 360.10 General.

This subpart prescribes the procedures under 17 U.S.C. 119(b)(4) whereby parties claiming to be entitled to compulsory license royalty fees for secondary transmissions by satellite carriers of television broadcast signals to the public shall file claims with the Copyright Royalty Board.

§ 360.11 Time of filing.

During the month of July each year, any party claiming to be entitled to compulsory license royalty fees for secondary transmissions by satellite carriers during the previous calendar year of television broadcast signals to the public shall file a claim to such fees with the Copyright Royalty Board. No royalty fees shall be distributed to any party during the specified period unless such party has timely filed a claim to such fees. Claimants may file claims jointly or as a single claim.

§ 360.12 Form and content of claims.

(a) *Forms.* (1) Each claim to compulsory license royalty fees for secondary transmissions by satellite carriers of television broadcast signals to the public shall be furnished on a form prescribed by the Copyright Royalty Board and shall contain the information required by that form and its accompanying instructions.

(2) Copies of satellite claim forms are available:

(i) On the Board's Web site at *http://www.loc.gov/crb/claims/* for claims filed with the Copyright Royalty Board by mail or by hand delivery in accordance with § 360.13(a)(2)–(4);

(ii) On the Board's Web site at *http://www.loc.gov/crb/satellite/* during the month of July for claims filed online in accordance with § 360.13(a)(1); and

(iii) Upon request to the Copyright Royalty Board, Library of Congress, P.O. Box 70977, Southwest Station, Washington, DC 20024–0977.

(b) *Content*—(1) *Single claim.* A claim filed on behalf of a single copyright owner of a work or works secondarily transmitted by a satellite carrier shall include the following information:

(i) The full legal name and address of the copyright owner entitled to claim the royalty fees.

(ii) A general statement of the nature of the copyright owner's work or works, and identification of at least one secondary transmission by a satellite carrier of such work or works establishing a basis for the claim.

(iii) The name, telephone number, facsimile number, if any, full address, including a specific number and street name or rural route, and e-mail address, if any, of the person or entity filing the single claim. An e-mail address must be provided on claims submitted online through the Copyright Royalty Board Web site.

(iv) The name, telephone number, facsimile number, if any, and e-mail address, if any, of the person whom the Copyright Royalty Board can contact regarding the claim.

(v) An original signature of the copyright owner or of a duly authorized representative of the copyright owner, except for claims filed online through the Copyright Royalty Board Web site. *See* 37 CFR 360.12(b)(1)(vi).

(vi) A declaration of the authority to file the claim and of the veracity of the information contained in the claim and the good faith of the person signing in providing such information. Penalties for fraud and false statements are provided under 18 U.S.C. 1001 *et seq.*

(2) *Joint claim.* A claim filed on behalf of more than one copyright owner whose works have been secondarily transmitted by a satellite carrier shall include the following information:

(i) A list including the full legal name and address of each copyright owner to the joint claim entitled to claim royalty fees.

(ii) A concise statement of the authorization for the person or entity filing the joint claim. For this purpose, a performing rights society shall not be required to obtain from its members or affiliates separate authorizations, apart from their standard membership affiliate agreements, or to list the name of each of its members or affiliates in the joint claim as required by paragraph (b)(2)(i) of this section.

(iii) A general statement of the nature of the copyright owners' works, identification of at least one secondary transmission of one of the copyright owners' works by a satellite carrier establishing a basis for the joint claim, and the identification of the copyright owner of each work so identified.

(iv) The name, telephone number, facsimile number, if any, full address, including a specific number and street name or rural route, and e-mail address, if any, of the person or entity filing the joint claim. An e-mail address must be provided on claims submitted online through the Copyright Royalty Board Web site.

(v) The name, telephone number, facsimile number, if any, and e-mail address, if any, of a person whom the Copyright Royalty Board can contact regarding the claim.

(vi) Original signatures of the copyright owners to the joint claim or of a duly authorized representative or representatives of the copyright owners, except for claims filed online through the Copyright Royalty Board Web site. *See* 37 CFR 360.12(b)(2)(vii).

(vii) Notwithstanding paragraph (b)(2)(ii) of this section, a declaration of the authority to file the claim and of the veracity of the information contained in the claim and the good faith of the person signing in providing such information. Penalties for fraud and false statements are provided under 18 U.S.C. 1001 *et seq.*

(c) In the event that the legal name and/or address of the copyright owner entitled to royalties or the person or entity filing the claim changes after the filing of the claim, the Copyright Royalty Board shall be notified of the change. If the good faith efforts of the Copyright Royalty Board to contact the copyright owner or person or entity filing the claim are frustrated because of failure to notify the Copyright Royalty Board of a name and/or address change, the claim may be subject to dismissal.

§ 360.13 Compliance with statutory dates.

(a) Claims filed with the Copyright Royalty Board shall be considered timely filed only if:

(1) They are received online in the Board's server no later than 5 p.m. e.d.t. on July 31. Online claims must be filed through the Copyright Royalty Board Web site at *http://www.loc.gov/crb/satellite/* during the month of July.

(2) They are hand delivered by a private party no later than 5 p.m. e.d.t. on July 31. Claims hand delivered by a private party must be delivered to the Copyright Office Public Information Office, in the James Madison Memorial Building, Room LM–401, 101 Independence Avenue, SE., Washington, DC 20559–6000, Monday through Friday, between 8:30 a.m. and 5 p.m., and the envelope must be addressed as follows: Copyright Royalty Board, Library of Congress, James Madison Memorial Building, 101 Independence Avenue, SE., Washington, DC 20559–6000. Claims hand delivered by a private party must be filed at the Copyright Office Public Information Office during the month of July.

(3) They are hand delivered by a commercial courier (excluding overnight delivery services such as Federal Express, United Parcel Service and similar overnight delivery services) no later than 4 p.m. e.d.t. on July 31. Claims hand delivered by a commercial courier service (excluding overnight delivery services such as Federal Express, United Parcel Service and similar overnight delivery services) must be delivered to the Congressional Courier Acceptance Site (CCAS) located at Second and D Street, NE., Washington, DC, Monday through Friday, between 8:30 a.m. and 4 p.m., and the envelope must be addressed as follows: Copyright Royalty Board, Library of Congress, James Madison Memorial Building, 101 Independence Avenue, SE., Washington, DC 20559–6000. Claims hand delivered by a commercial courier must be filed at CCAS during the month of July.

(4) They are mailed through the United States Postal Service (USPS) having sufficient postage and bearing a July USPS postmark. Claims mailed through USPS must be addressed as follows: Copyright Royalty Board, P.O. Box 70977, Southwest Station, Washington, DC 20024–0977.

(5) Federal Express, United Parcel Service and similar overnight delivery services may not be used for the filing of claims. A claim sent by means of overnight delivery shall be done via United States Postal Service Express Mail, and the claim shall be addressed in accordance with paragraph (a)(4) of this section.

(b) Claims dated only with a business meter that are received after July 31 will not be accepted as having been timely filed.

(c) Notwithstanding paragraphs (a) and (b) of this section, in any year in which July 31 falls on a Saturday, Sunday, holiday, or other nonbusiness day within the District of Columbia or the Federal Government, claims received by the Copyright Royalty Board by the first business day in August, or properly addressed and deposited with sufficient postage with the United States Postal Service and postmarked by the first business day in August, shall be considered timely filed.

(d) No claim may be filed by facsimile transmission.

(e) In the event that a properly addressed and mailed claim is not timely received by the Copyright Royalty Board, proper filing of the claim may nonetheless be proven if it was sent by certified mail return receipt requested, and a receipt bearing a July date stamp of the United States Postal Service, except where paragraph (c) of this section applies, can be provided. No other offer of proof will be accepted in lieu of the receipt.

(f) The Copyright Royalty Board will accept either the confirmation page generated upon submission of the claim online through the Board's Web site or the electronic mail message from the Board confirming receipt of the claim as proof that a claim submitted online through the Board's Web site was received timely in the Board's server. No other offer of proof will be accepted in lieu thereof.

[70 FR 30905, May 31, 2005, as amended at 71 FR 53331, Sept. 11, 2006]

§ 360.14 Copies of claims.

A claimant shall, for each claim submitted to the Copyright Royalty Board by hand delivery or by mail, file an original and one copy of the claim to satellite carrier royalty fees.

§ 360.15 Separate claims required.

If a party intends to file claims for both cable compulsory license and satellite carrier compulsory license royalty fees during the same month of July, that party must file separate claims with the Copyright Royalty Board. Any single claim which purports to file for both cable and satellite carrier royalty fees will be dismissed.

Subpart C—Digital Audio Recording Devices and Media Royalty Claims

§ 360.20 General.

This subpart prescribes procedures pursuant to 17 U.S.C. 1007(a)(1), whereby interested copyright parties, as defined in 17 U.S.C. 1001(7), claiming to be entitled to royalty payments made for the importation and distribution in the United States, or the manufacture and distribution in the United States, of digital audio recording devices and media pursuant to 17 U.S.C. 1006, shall file claims with the Copyright Royalty Board.

§ 360.21 Time of filing.

(a) *General.* During January and February of each succeeding year, every interested copyright party claiming to be entitled to digital audio recording devices and media royalty payments made for quarterly periods ending during the previous calendar year shall file a claim with the Copyright Royalty Board. Claimants may file claims jointly or as a single claim.

(b) *Consequences of an untimely filing.* No royalty payments for the previous calendar year shall be distributed to any interested copyright party who has not filed a claim to such royalty payments during January or February of the following calendar year.

(c) *Authorization.* Any organization or association, acting as a common agent, shall be required to obtain from its members or affiliates separate, specific, and written authorization, signed by members, affiliates, or their representatives, to file claims to the Musical Works Fund or the Sound Recordings Fund, apart from their standard agreements, for purposes of royalties filing and fee distribution. Such written authorization, however, will not be required for claimants to the Musical Works Fund where either:

(1) The agreement between the organization or association and its members or affiliates specifically authorizes such entity to represent its members or affiliates before the Copyright Royalty Board in royalty filing and fee distribution proceedings; or

(2) The agreement between the organization or association and its members or affiliates, as specified in a court order issued by a court with authority to interpret the terms of the contract, authorizes such entity to represent its members or affiliates before the Copyright Royalty Board in royalty filing and fee distribution proceedings.

§ 360.22 Form and content of claims.

(a) *Forms.* (1) Each claim to digital audio recording devices and media royalty payments (DART) shall be furnished on a form prescribed by the Copyright Royalty Board and shall contain the information required by that form and its accompanying instructions.

(2) Copies of DART claim forms are available:

(i) On the Board's Web site at *http://www.loc.gov/crb/claims* for claims filed with the Copyright Royalty Board by mail or by hand delivery in accordance with § 360.24(a)(2)–(4);

(ii) On the Board's Web site at *http://www.loc.gov/crb/dart/* during the months of January and February for claims filed online in accordance with § 360.24(a)(1); and

(iii) Upon request to the Copyright Royalty Board, Library of Congress, P.O. Box 70977, Southwest Station, Washington, DC 20024–0977.

(b) *Content.* Claims filed by interested copyright parties for digital audio recording devices and media royalty payments shall include the following information:

(1) The full legal name and address of the person or entity claiming royalty payments.

(2) The name, telephone number, facsimile number, if any, full address, including a specific number and street name or rural route, and e-mail address, if any, of the person or entity filing the claim. An e-mail address must be provided on claims submitted online through the Copyright Royalty Board Web site.

(3) The name, telephone number, facsimile number, if any, and e-mail address, if any, of a person whom the Copyright Royalty Board can contact regarding the claim.

(4) A statement as to how the claimant fits within the definition of interested copyright party specified in 17 U.S.C. 1001(7).

(5) A statement as to whether the claim is being made against the Sound Recordings Fund or the Musical Works Fund, as set forth in 17 U.S.C. 1006(b), and as to which Subfund of the Sound Recordings Fund (*i.e.*, the copyright owners or featured recording artists Subfund) or the Musical Works Fund (*i.e.*, the music publishers or writers Subfund) the claim is being made against as set forth in 17 U.S.C. 1006(b)(1) through (2).

(6) Identification, establishing a basis for the claim, of at least one musical work or sound recording embodied in a digital musical recording or an analog musical recording lawfully made under title 17 of the United States Code that has been distributed (as that term is defined in 17 U.S.C. 1001(6)), and that, during the period to which the royalty payments claimed pertain, has been (i) Distributed (as that term is defined in 17 U.S.C. 1001(6)) in the form of digital musical recordings or analog musical recordings, or (ii) Disseminated to the public in transmissions.

(7) A declaration of the authority to file the claim and of the veracity of the information contained in the claim and the good faith of the person signing in providing such information. Penalties for fraud and false statements are provided under 18 U.S.C. 1001 *et seq.*

(c) Claims shall bear the original signature of the claimant or of a duly authorized representative of the claimant, except for claims filed online through the Copyright Royalty Board Web site. *See* 37 CFR 360.22(b)(7).

(d) In the event that the legal name and/or address of the claimant changes after the filing of the claim, the claimant shall notify the Copyright Royalty Board of such change. If the good faith efforts of the Copyright Royalty Board to contact the claimant are frustrated because of failure to notify the Copyright Royalty Board of a name and/or address change, the claim may be subject to dismissal.

(e) If the claim is a joint claim, it shall include a concise statement of the authorization for the filing of the joint claim in addition to the declaration required under paragraph (b)(7) of this section and the name of each claimant to the joint claim.

(f) If an interested copyright party intends to file claims against more than one Subfund, each such claim must be filed separately with the Copyright Royalty Board. Any claim that purports to file against more than one Subfund will be rejected.

§ 360.23 Content of notices regarding independent administrators.

(a) The independent administrator jointly appointed by the interested copyright parties, as defined in 17 U.S.C. 1001(7)(A), and the American Federation of Musicians (or any successor entity) for the purpose of managing, and ultimately distributing the royalty payments to nonfeatured musicians as defined in 17 U.S.C. 1006(b)(1), shall file a notice informing the Copyright Royalty Board of his/her name and address.

(b) The independent administrator jointly appointed by the interested copyright parties, as defined in 17 U.S.C. 1001(7)(A), and the American Federation of Television and Radio Artists (or any successor entity) for the purpose of managing, and ultimately distributing the royalty payments to nonfeatured vocalists as defined in 17 U.S.C. 1006(b)(1), shall file a notice informing the Copyright Royalty Board of his/her full name and address.

(c) A notice filed under paragraph (a) or (b) of this section shall include the following information:

(1) The full name of the independent administrator;

(2) The telephone number and facsimile number, if any, full address, including a specific number and street name or rural route, of the place of business of the independent administrator.

(d) Notice shall bear the original signature of the independent administrator or a duly authorized representative of the independent administrator, and shall be filed with the Copyright Royalty Board no later than March 31 of each year, commencing with March 31, 2006.

(e) No notice may be filed by facsimile transmission.

§ 360.24 Compliance with statutory dates.

(a) Claims filed with the Copyright Royalty Board shall be considered timely filed only if:

(1) They are received online in the Board's server no later than 5 p.m. E.S.T. on the last day of February. Online claims must be filed through the Copyright Royalty Board Web site at *http://www.loc.gov/crb/dart/* during the months of January and February.

(2) They are hand delivered by a private party no later than 5 p.m. E.S.T. on the last day of February. Claims hand delivered by a private party must be delivered to the Copyright Office Public Information Office, in the James Madison Memorial Building, Room LM–401, 101 Independence Avenue, SE., Washington, DC 20559–6000, Monday through Friday, between 8:30 a.m. and 5 p.m., and the envelope must be addressed as follows: Copyright Royalty Board, Library of Congress, James Madison Memorial Building, 101 Independence Avenue, SE., Washington, DC 20559–6000. Claims hand delivered by a private party must be filed at the Copyright Office Public Information Office during the months of January and February.

(3) They are hand delivered by a commercial courier (excluding overnight delivery services such as Federal Express, United Parcel Service and similar overnight delivery services) no later than 4 p.m. E.S.T. on the last day of February. Claims hand delivered by a commercial courier service (excluding overnight delivery services such as Federal Express, United Parcel Service and similar overnight delivery services) must be delivered to the Congressional Courier Acceptance Site (CCAS) located at Second and D Street, NE., Washington, DC, Monday through Friday, between 8:30 a.m. and 4 p.m., and the envelope must be addressed as follows: Copyright Royalty Board, Library of Congress, James Madison Memorial Building, 101 Independence Avenue, SE., Washington, DC 20559–6000. Claims hand delivered by a commercial courier must be filed at CCAS during the months of January and February.

(4) They are mailed through the United States Postal Service (USPS) having sufficient postage and bearing a January or February USPS postmark. Claims mailed through USPS must be addressed as follows: Copyright Royalty Board, P.O. Box 70977, Southwest Station, Washington, DC 20024–0977.

(5) Federal Express, United Parcel Service and similar overnight delivery services may not be used for the filing of claims. A claim sent by means of overnight delivery shall be done via

United States Postal Service Express Mail, and the claim shall be addressed in accordance with paragraph (a)(4) of this section.

(b) Claims dated only with a business meter that are received after the last day in February will not be accepted as having been timely filed.

(c) Notwithstanding paragraphs (a) and (b) of this section, in any year in which the last day of February falls on a Saturday, Sunday, a holiday, or other nonbusiness day within the District of Columbia or the Federal Government, claims received by the Copyright Royalty Board by the first business day in March, or properly addressed and deposited with sufficient postage with the United States Postal Service and postmarked by the first business day in March, shall be considered timely filed.

(d) No claim may be filed by facsimile transmission.

(e) In the event that a properly addressed and mailed claim is not timely received by the Copyright Royalty Board, proper filing of the claim may nonetheless be proven if it was sent by certified mail return receipt requested, and a receipt bearing a January or February date stamp of the United States Postal Service, except where paragraph (c) of this section applies, can be provided. No other offer of proof will be accepted in lieu of the receipt.

(f) The Copyright Royalty Board will accept either the confirmation page generated upon submission of the claim online through the Copyright Royalty Board Web site or the electronic mail message from the Copyright Royalty Board confirming receipt of the claim as proof that a claim submitted online through the Copyright Royalty Board Web site was received timely in the Board's server. No other offer of proof will be accepted in lieu thereof.

[70 FR 30905, May 31, 2005, as amended at 71 FR 53331, Sept. 11, 2006]

§ 360.25 Copies of claims.

A claimant shall, for each claim submitted to the Copyright Royalty Board by hand delivery or by mail, file an original and one copy of the claim to digital audio recording devices and media royalty payments.

SUBCHAPTER D—NOTICE AND RECORDKEEPING REQUIREMENTS FOR STATUTORY LICENSES

PART 370—NOTICE AND RECORD-KEEPING REQUIREMENTS FOR STATUTORY LICENSES

AUTHORITY: 17 U.S.C. 112(e)(4), 114(f)(4)(A).

SOURCE: 74 FR 52423, Oct. 13, 2009, unless otherwise noted.

§ 370.1 General definitions.

For purposes of this part, the following definitions apply:

(a) A *Notice of Use of Sound Recordings Under Statutory License* is a written notice to sound recording copyright owners of the use of their works under section 112(e) or 114(d)(2) of title 17, United States Code, or both, and is required under this part to be filed by a Service in the Copyright Office.

(b) A *Service* is an entity engaged in either the digital transmission of sound recordings pursuant to section 114(d)(2) of title 17 of the United States Code or making ephemeral phonorecords of sound recordings pursuant to section 112(e) of title 17 of the United States Code or both. The definition of a Service includes an entity that transmits an AM/FM broadcast signal over a digital communications network such as the Internet, regardless of whether the transmission is made by the broadcaster that originates the AM/FM signal or by a third party, provided that such transmission meets the applicable requirements of the statutory license set forth in 17 U.S.C. 114(d)(2). A Service may be further characterized as either a preexisting subscription service, preexisting satellite digital audio radio service, nonsubscription transmission service, new subscription service, business establishment service or a combination of those.

(c) A *Preexisting Subscription Service* is defined in 17 U.S.C. 114(j)(11).

(d) A *New Subscription Service* is defined in 17 U.S.C. 114(j)(8).

(e) A *Nonsubscription Transmission Service* is a service that makes noninteractive nonsubscription digital audio transmissions that are not exempt under section 114(d)(1) of title 17 of the United States Code and are made as part of a service that provides audio programming consisting, in whole or in part, of performances of sound recordings, including transmissions of broadcast transmissions, if the primary purpose of the service is to provide to the public such audio or other entertainment programming, and the primary purpose of the service is not to sell, advertise, or promote particular products or services other than sound recordings, live concerts, or other music-related events.

(f) A *Preexisting Satellite Digital Audio Radio Service* is defined in 17 U.S.C. 114(j)(10).

(g) A *Business Establishment Service* is a service that makes ephemeral phonorecords of sound recordings pursuant to section 112(e) of title 17 of the United States Code and is exempt under section 114(d)(1)(C)(iv) of title 17 of the United States Code.

(h) A *Collective* is a collection and distribution organization that is designated under one or both of the statutory licenses by determination of the Copyright Royalty Judges.

(i) A *Report of Use* is a report required to be provided by a Service that is transmitting sound recordings pursuant to the statutory license set forth in section 114(d)(2) of title 17 of the United States Code or making ephemeral phonorecords of sound recordings pursuant to the statutory license set forth in section 112(e) of title 17 of the United States Code, or both.

§ 370.2 Notice of use of sound recordings under statutory license.

(a) *General.* This section prescribes rules under which copyright owners shall receive notice of use of their sound recordings when used under either section 112(e) or 114(d)(2) of title 17, United States Code, or both.

(b) *Forms and content.* A Notice of Use of Sound Recordings Under Statutory License shall be prepared on a form that may be obtained from the Copyright Office Web site or from the Licensing Division, and shall include the following information:

(1) The full legal name of the Service that is either commencing digital transmissions of sound recordings or making ephemeral phonorecords of sound recordings under statutory license or doing both.

(2) The full address, including a specific number and street name or rural route, of the place of business of the Service. A post office box or similar designation will not be sufficient except where it is the only address that can be used in that geographic location.

(3) The telephone number and facsimile number of the Service.

(4) Information on how to gain access to the online Web site or homepage of the Service, or where information may be posted under this section concerning the use of sound recordings under statutory license.

(5) Identification of each license under which the Service intends to operate, including identification of each of the following categories under which the Service will be making digital transmissions of sound recordings: Preexisting subscription service, preexisting satellite digital audio radio service, nonsubscription transmission service, new subscription service or business establishment service.

(6) The date or expected date of the initial digital transmission of a sound recording to be made under the section 114 statutory license and/or the date or the expected date of the initial use of the section 112(e) license for the purpose of making ephemeral phonorecords of the sound recordings.

(7) Identification of any amendments required by paragraph (e) of this section.

(c) *Signature.* The Notice shall include the signature of the appropriate officer or representative of the Service that is either transmitting the sound recordings or making ephemeral phonorecords of sound recordings under statutory license or doing both. The signature shall be accompanied by the printed or typewritten name and the title of the person signing the Notice and by the date of the signature.

(d) *Filing notices; fees.* The original and three copies shall be filed with the Licensing Division of the Copyright Office and shall be accompanied by the filing fee set forth in § 201.3(e) of this title. Notices shall be placed in the public records of the Licensing Division. The Notice and filing fee shall be sent to the Licensing Division at either the address listed on the form obtained from the Copyright Office or to: Library of Congress, Copyright Office, Licensing Division, 101 Independence Avenue, SE., Washington, DC 20557–6400. A Service that, on or after July 1, 2004, shall make digital transmissions and/or ephemeral phonorecords of sound recordings under statutory license shall file a Notice of Use of Sound Recordings under Statutory License with the Licensing Division of the Copyright Office prior to the making of the first ephemeral phonorecord of the sound recording and prior to the first digital transmission of the sound recording.

(e) *Amendment.* A Service shall file a new Notice of Use of Sound Recordings under Statutory License within 45 days after any of the information contained in the Notice on file has changed, and shall indicate in the space provided by the Copyright Office that the Notice is an amended filing. The Licensing Division shall retain copies of all prior Notices filed by the Service.

§ 370.3 Reports of use of sound recordings under statutory license for preexisting subscription services.

(a) *General.* This section prescribes the rules for the maintenance and delivery of reports of use for sound recordings under section 112(e) or section 114(d)(2) of title 17 of the United States Code, or both, by preexisting subscription services.

(b) *Delivery.* Reports of Use shall be delivered to Collectives that are identified in the records of the Licensing Division of the Copyright Office as having been designated by determination of the Copyright Royalty Judges. Reports of Use shall be delivered on or before the forty-fifth day after the close of each month.

(c) *Posting.* In the event that no Collective is designated under the statutory license, or if all designated Collectives have terminated collection and distribution operations, a preexisting subscription service transmitting sound recordings under statutory license shall post and make available online its Reports of Use. Preexisting subscription services shall post their Reports of Use online on or before the forty-fifth day after the close of each month, and continue to make them available thereafter to all sound recording copyright owners for a period of 90 days. Preexisting subscription services may require use of passwords for access to posted Reports of Use, but must make passwords available in a timely manner and free of charge or other restrictions. Preexisting subscription services may predicate provision of a password upon:

(1) Information relating to identity, location and status as a sound recording copyright owner; and

(2) A "click-wrap" agreement not to use information in the Report of Use for purposes other than royalty collection, royalty distribution, and determining compliance with statutory license requirements, without the express consent of the preexisting subscription service providing the Report of Use.

(d) *Content.* A "Report of Use of Sound Recordings under Statutory License" shall be identified as such by prominent caption or heading, and shall include a preexisting subscription service's "Intended Playlists" for each channel and each day of the reported month. The "Intended Playlists" shall include a consecutive listing of every recording scheduled to be transmitted, and shall contain the following information in the following order:

(1) The name of the preexisting subscription service or entity;

(2) The channel;

(3) The sound recording title;

(4) The featured recording artist, group, or orchestra;

(5) The retail album title (or, in the case of compilation albums created for commercial purposes, the name of the retail album identified by the preexisting subscription service for purchase of the sound recording);

(6) The marketing label of the commercially available album or other product on which the sound recording is found;

(7) The catalog number;

(8) The International Standard Recording Code (ISRC) embedded in the sound recording, where available and feasible;

(9) Where available, the copyright owner information provided in the copyright notice on the retail album or other product (e.g., following the symbol (P), that is the letter P in a circle) or, in the case of compilation albums created for commercial purposes, in the copyright notice for the individual sound recording;

(10) The date of transmission; and

(11) The time of transmission.

(e) *Signature.* Reports of Use shall include a signed statement by the appropriate officer or representative of the preexisting subscription service attesting, under penalty of perjury, that the information contained in the Report is believed to be accurate and is maintained by the preexisting subscription service in its ordinary course of business. The signature shall be accompanied by the printed or typewritten name and title of the person signing the Report, and by the date of signature.

(f) *Format.* Reports of Use should be provided on a standard machine-readable medium, such as diskette, optical disc, or magneto-optical disc, and should conform as closely as possible to the following specifications:

(1) ASCII delimited format, using pipe characters as delimiter, with no headers or footers;

(2) Carats should surround strings;

(3) No carats should surround dates and numbers;

(4) Dates should be indicated by: YYYY/MM/DD;

(5) Times should be based on a 24-hour clock: HH:MM:SS;

(6) A carriage return should be at the end of each line; and

(7) All data for one record should be on a single line.

(g) *Confidentiality.* Copyright owners, their agents and Collectives shall not disseminate information in the Reports of Use to any persons not entitled to it, nor utilize the information for purposes other than royalty collection and distribution, and determining compliance with statutory license requirements, without express consent of the preexisting subscription service providing the Report of Use.

(h) *Documentation.* All compulsory licensees shall, for a period of at least three years from the date of service or posting of the Report of Use, keep and retain a copy of the Report of Use.

(i) In any case in which a preexisting subscription service has not provided a report of use required under this section for use of sound recordings under section 112(e) or section 114 of title 17 of the United States Code, or both, prior to January 1, 2010, reports of use for the corresponding calendar year filed by other preexisting subscription services shall serve as the reports of use for the non-reporting service, solely for purposes of distribution of any corresponding royalties by the Collective.

[74 FR 52423, Oct. 13, 2009, as amended at 76 FR 45696, Aug. 1, 2011]

§370.4 Reports of use of sound recordings under statutory license for nonsubscription transmission services, preexisting satellite digital audio radio services, new subscription services and business establishment services.

(a) *General.* This section prescribes rules for the maintenance and delivery of reports of use of sound recordings under section 112(e) or section 114(d)(2) of title 17 of the United States Code, or both, by nonsubscription transmission services, preexisting satellite digital audio radio services, new subscription services, and business establishment services.

(b) *Definitions.* (1) *Aggregate Tuning Hours* are the total hours of programming that a nonsubscription transmission service, preexisting satellite digital audio radio service, new subscription service or business establishment service has transmitted during the reporting period identified in paragraph (d)(3) of this section to all listeners within the United States over the relevant channels or stations, and from any archived programs, that provide audio programming consisting, in whole or in part, of eligible nonsubscription service, preexisting satellite digital audio radio service, new subscription service or business establishment service transmissions, less the actual running time of any sound recordings for which the service has obtained direct licenses apart from 17 U.S.C. 114(d)(2) or which do not require a license under United States copyright law. For example, if a nonsubscription transmission service transmitted one hour of programming to 10 simultaneous listeners, the nonsubscription transmission service's Aggregate Tuning Hours would equal 10. If 3 minutes of that hour consisted of transmission of a directly licensed recording, the nonsubscription transmission service's Aggregate Tuning Hours would equal 9 hours and 30 minutes. If one listener listened to the transmission of a nonsubscription transmission service for 10 hours (and none of the recordings transmitted during that time was directly licensed), the nonsubscription transmission service's Aggregate Tuning Hours would equal 10.

(2) An *AM/FM Webcast* is a transmission made by an entity that transmits an AM/FM broadcast signal over a digital communications network such as the Internet, regardless of whether the transmission is made by the broadcaster that originates the AM/FM signal or by a third party, provided that such transmission meets the applicable requirements of the statutory license set forth in 17 U.S.C. 114(d)(2).

(3) A *minimum fee broadcaster* is a nonsubscription service that meets the definition of a broadcaster pursuant to §380.2(b) of this chapter and the service's payments for eligible transmissions do not exceed the annual minimum fee established for licensees relying upon the statutory licenses set forth in 17 U.S.C. 112 and 114.

(4) A *performance* is each instance in which any portion of a sound recording

is publicly performed to a Listener by means of a digital audio transmission or retransmission (e.g., the delivery of any portion of a single track from a compact disc to one Listener) but excluding the following:

(i) A performance of a sound recording that does not require a license (e.g., the sound recording is not copyrighted);

(ii) A performance of a sound recording for which the service has previously obtained a license from the Copyright Owner of such sound recording; and

(iii) An incidental performance that both:

(A) Makes no more than incidental use of sound recordings including, but not limited to, brief musical transitions in and out of commercials or program segments, brief performances during news, talk and sports programming, brief background performances during disk jockey announcements, brief performances during commercials of sixty seconds or less in duration, or brief performances during sporting or other public events; and

(B) Other than ambient music that is background at a public event, does not contain an entire sound recording and does not feature a particular sound recording of more than thirty seconds (as in the case of a sound recording used as a theme song).

(5) *Play frequency* is the number of times a sound recording is publicly performed by a Service during the relevant period, without respect to the number of listeners receiving the sound recording. If a particular sound recording is transmitted to listeners on a particular channel or program only once during the reporting period, then the play frequency is one. If the sound recording is transmitted 10 times during the reporting period, then the play frequency is 10.

(c) *Delivery*. Reports of Use shall be delivered to Collectives that are identified in the records of the Licensing Division of the Copyright Office as having been designated by determination of the Copyright Royalty Judges. Reports of Use shall be delivered on or before the forty-fifth day after the close of each reporting period identified in paragraph (d)(3) of this section.

(d) *Report of Use*. (1) *Separate reports not required*. A nonsubscription transmission service, preexisting satellite digital audio radio service or a new subscription service that transmits sound recordings pursuant to the statutory license set forth in section 114(d)(2) of title 17 of the United States Code and makes ephemeral phonorecords of sound recordings pursuant to the statutory license set forth in section 112(e) of title 17 of the United States Code need not maintain a separate Report of Use for each statutory license during the relevant reporting periods.

(2) *Content*. For a nonsubscription transmission service, preexisting satellite digital audio radio service, new subscription service or business establishment service that transmits sound recordings pursuant to the statutory license set forth in section 114(d)(2) of title 17 of the United States Code, or the statutory license set forth in section 112(e) of title 17 of the United States Code, or both, each Report of Use shall contain the following information, in the following order, for each sound recording transmitted during the reporting periods identified in paragraph (d)(3) of this section:

(i) The name of the nonsubscription transmission service, preexisting satellite digital audio radio service, new subscription service or business establishment service making the transmissions, including the name of the entity filing the Report of Use, if different;

(ii) The category transmission code for the category of transmission operated by the nonsubscription transmission service, preexisting satellite digital audio radio service, new subscription service or business establishment service:

(A) For eligible nonsubscription transmissions other than broadcast simulcasts and transmissions of non-music programming;

(B) For eligible nonsubscription transmissions of broadcast simulcast programming not reasonably classified as news, talk, sports or business programming;

(C) For eligible nonsubscription transmissions of non-music programming reasonably classified as news, talk, sports or business programming;

(D)–(G) [Reserved]

(H) For transmissions other than broadcast simulcasts and transmissions of non-music programming made by an eligible new subscription service;

(I) For transmissions of broadcast simulcast programming not reasonably classified as news, talk, sports or business programming made by an eligible new subscription service;

(J) For transmissions of non-music programming reasonably classified as news, talk, sports or business programming made by an eligible new subscription service; and

(K) For eligible transmissions by a business establishment service making ephemeral recordings;

(iii) The featured artist;

(iv) The sound recording title;

(v) The International Standard Recording Code (ISRC) or, alternatively to the ISRC, the:

(A) Album title; and

(B) Marketing label;

(vi) For a nonsubscription transmission service except those qualifying as minimum fee broadcasters: The actual total performances of the sound recording during the reporting period.

(vii) For a preexisting satellite digital audio radio service, a new subscription service, a business establishment service or a nonsubscription service qualifying as a minimum fee broadcaster: The actual total performances of the sound recording during the reporting period or, alternatively, the

(A) Aggregate Tuning Hours;

(B) Channel or program name; and

(C) Play frequency.

(3) *Reporting period.* A Report of Use shall be prepared:

(i) For each calendar month of the year by all services other than a nonsubscription service qualifying as a minimum fee broadcaster; or

(ii) For a two-week period (two periods of 7 consecutive days) for each calendar quarter of the year by a nonsubscription service qualifying as a minimum fee broadcaster and the two-week period need not consist of consecutive weeks, but both weeks must be completely within the calendar quarter.

(4) *Signature.* Reports of Use shall include a signed statement by the appropriate officer or representative of the service attesting, under penalty of perjury, that the information contained in the Report is believed to be accurate and is maintained by the service in its ordinary course of business. The signature shall be accompanied by the printed or typewritten name and the title of the person signing the Report, and by the date of the signature.

(5) *Confidentiality.* Copyright owners, their agents and Collectives shall not disseminate information in the Reports of Use to any persons not entitled to it, nor utilize the information for purposes other than royalty collection and distribution, without consent of the service providing the Report of Use.

(6) *Documentation.* A Service shall, for a period of at least three years from the date of service or posting of a Report of Use, keep and retain a copy of the Report of Use.

(e) *Format and delivery.* (1) *Electronic format only.* Reports of use must be maintained and delivered in electronic format only, as prescribed in paragraphs (e)(2) through (8) of this section. A hard copy report of use is not permissible.

(2) *ASCII text file delivery; facilitation by provision of spreadsheet templates.* All report of use data files must be delivered in ASCII format. However, to facilitate such delivery, SoundExchange shall post and maintain on its Internet Web site a template for creating a report of use using Microsoft's Excel spreadsheet and Corel's Quattro Pro spreadsheet and instruction on how to convert such spreadsheets to ASCII text files that conform to the format specifications set forth below. Further, technical support and cost associated with the use of spreadsheets is the responsibility of the service submitting the report of use.

(3) *Delivery mechanism.* The data contained in a report of use may be delivered by File Transfer Protocol (FTP), e-mail, or CD–ROM according to the following specifications:

(i) A service delivering a report of use via FTP must obtain a username, password and delivery instructions from SoundExchange. SoundExchange shall maintain on a publicly available portion of its Web site instructions for applying for a username, password and delivery instructions. SoundExchange shall have 15 days from date of request to respond with a username, password and delivery instructions.

(ii) A service delivering a report of use via e-mail shall append the report as an attachment to the e-mail. The main body of the e-mail shall identify:

(A) The full name and address of the service;

(B) The contact person's name, telephone number and e-mail address;

(C) The start and end date of the reporting period;

(D) The number of rows in the data file. If the report of use is a file using headers, counting of the rows should begin with row 15. If the report of use is a file without headers, counting of the rows should begin with row 1; and

(E) The name of the file attached.

(iii) A service delivering a report of use via CD–ROM must compress the reporting data to fit onto a single CD–ROM per reporting period. Each CD–ROM shall be submitted with a cover letter identifying:

(A) The full name and address of the service;

(B) The contact person's name, telephone number and e-mail address;

(C) The start and end date of the reporting period;

(D) The number of rows in the data file. If the report of use is a file using headers, counting of the rows should begin with row 15. If the report of use is a file without headers, counting of the rows should begin with row 1; and

(E) The name of the file attached.

(4) *Delivery address.* Reports of use shall be delivered to SoundExchange at the following address: SoundExchange, Inc., 1121 14th Street, NW., Suite 700, Washington, DC 20005; (Phone) (202) 640–5858; (Facsimile) (202) 640–5859; (E-mail) *reports@soundexchange.com.* SoundExchange shall forward electronic copies of these reports of use to all other collectives defined in this section.

(5) *File naming.* Each data file contained in a report of use must be given a name by the service followed by the start and end date of the reporting period. The start and end date must be separated by a dash and in the format of year, month, and day (YYYYMMDD). Each file name must end with the file type extension of ".txt". (*Example:* AcmeMusicCo20050101–20050331.txt).

(6) *File type and compression.* (i) All data files must be in ASCII format.

(ii) A report of use must be compressed in one of the following zipped formats:

(A) .zip—generated using utilities such as WinZip and/or UNIX zip command;

(B) .Z—generated using UNIX compress command; or

(C) .gz—generated using UNIX gzip command.

(iii) Zipped files shall be named in the same fashion as described in paragraph (e)(5) of this section, except that such zipped files shall use the applicable file extension compression name described in this paragraph (e)(6).

(7) *Files with headers.* (i) If a service elects to submit files with headers, the following elements, in order, must occupy the first 14 rows of a report of use:

(A) Name of service;

(B) Name of contact person;

(C) Street address of the service;

(D) City, state and zip code of the service;

(E) Telephone number of the contact person;

(F) E-mail address of the contact person;

(G) Start of the reporting period (YYYYMMDD);

(H) End of the reporting period (YYYYMMDD);

(I) Report generation date (YYYYMMDD);

(J) Number of rows in data file, beginning with 15th row;

(K) Text indicator character;

(L) Field delimiter character;

(M) Blank line; and

(N) Report headers (Featured Artist, Sound Recording Title, etc.).

(ii) Each of the rows described in paragraphs (e)(7)(i)(A) through (F) of this section must not exceed 255 alphanumeric characters. Each of the rows described in paragraphs (e)(7)(i)(G) through (I) of this section should not exceed eight alphanumeric characters.

(iii) Data text fields, as required by paragraph (d) of this section, begin on row 15 of a report of use with headers. A carriage return must be at the end of each row thereafter. Abbreviations within data fields are not permitted.

(iv) The text indicator character must be unique and must never be found in the report's data content.

(v) The field delimiter character must be unique and must never be found in the report's data content. Delimiters must be used even when certain elements are not being reported; in such case, the service must denote the blank data field with a delimiter in the order in which it would have appeared.

(8) *Files without headers.* If a service elects to submit files without headers, the following format requirements must be met:

(i) ASCII delimited format, using pipe (|) characters as delimiters, with no headers or footers;

(ii) Carats (^) should surround strings;

(iii) No carats (^) should surround dates and numbers;

(iv) A carriage return must be at the end of each line;

(v) All data for one record must be on a single line; and

(vi) Abbreviations within data fields are not permitted.

(f) In any case in which a nonsubscription transmission service, preexisting satellite digital audio radio service, new subscription service, or business establishment service has not provided a report of use required under this section for use of sound recordings under section 112(e) or section 114 of title 17 of the United States Code, or both, prior to January 1, 2010, reports of use for the corresponding calendar year filed by other services of the same type shall serve as the reports of use for the non-reporting service, solely for purposes of distribution of any corresponding royalties by the Collective.

[74 FR 52423, Oct. 13, 2009, as amended at 76 FR 45696, Aug. 1, 2011]

§ 370.5 Designated collection and distribution organizations for reports of use of sound recordings under statutory license.

(a) *General.* This section prescribes rules under which reports of use shall be collected and distributed under section 114(f) of title 17 of the United States Code, and under which reports of such use shall be kept and made available.

(b) *Notice of Designation as Collective under Statutory License.* A Collective shall file with the Licensing Division of the Copyright Office and post and make available online a "Notice of Designation as Collective under Statutory License," which shall be identified as such by prominent caption or heading, and shall contain the following information:

(1) The Collective name, address, telephone number and facsimile number;

(2) A statement that the Collective has been designated for collection and distribution of performance royalties under statutory license for digital transmission of sound recordings; and

(3) Information on how to gain access to the online Web site or home page of the Collective, where information may be posted under this part concerning the use of sound recordings under statutory license. The address of the Licensing Division is: Library of Congress, Copyright Office, Licensing Division, 101 Independence Avenue, SE., Washington, DC 20557–6400.

(c) *Annual Report.* The Collective will post and make available online, for the duration of one year, an Annual Report on how the Collective operates, how royalties are collected and distributed, and what the Collective spent that fiscal year on administrative expenses.

(d) *Inspection of Reports of Use by copyright owners.* The Collective shall make copies of the Reports of Use for the preceding three years available for inspection by any sound recording copyright owner, without charge, during normal office hours upon reasonable notice. The Collective shall predicate inspection of Reports of Use upon information relating to identity, location and status as a sound recording copyright owner, and the copyright owner's written agreement not to utilize the information for purposes other than royalty collection and distribution, and determining compliance with statutory license requirements, without express consent of the Service providing the Report of Use. The Collective shall render its best efforts to locate copyright owners in order to make available reports of use, and such efforts shall include searches in Copyright Office public records and published directories of sound recording copyright owners.

(e) *Confidentiality.* Copyright owners, their agents, and Collectives shall not disseminate information in the Reports of Use to any persons not entitled to it, nor utilize the information for purposes other than royalty collection and distribution, and determining compliance with statutory license requirements, without express consent of the Service providing the Report of Use.

(f) *Termination and dissolution.* If a Collective terminates its collection and distribution operations prior to the close of its term of designation, the Collective shall notify the Licensing Division of the Copyright Office, the Copyright Royalty Board and all Services transmitting sound recordings under statutory license, by certified or registered mail. The dissolving Collective shall provide each such Service with information identifying the copyright owners it has served.

SUBCHAPTER E—RATES AND TERMS FOR STATUTORY LICENSES

PART 380—RATES AND TERMS FOR CERTAIN ELIGIBLE NON-SUBSCRIPTION TRANSMISSIONS, NEW SUBSCRIPTION SERVICES AND THE MAKING OF EPHEMERAL REPRODUCTIONS

AUTHORITY: 17 U.S.C. 112(e), 114(f), 804(b)(3).

SOURCE: 76 FR 13046, Mar. 9, 2011, unless otherwise noted.

Subpart A—Commercial Webcasters and Noncommercial Webcasters

§ 380.1 General.

(a) *Scope.* This subpart establishes rates and terms of royalty payments for the public performance of sound recordings in certain digital transmissions by Licensees as set forth in this subpart in accordance with the provisions of 17 U.S.C. 114, and the making of Ephemeral Recordings by Licensees in accordance with the provisions of 17 U.S.C. 112(e), during the period January 1, 2011, through December 31, 2015.

(b) *Legal compliance.* Licensees relying upon the statutory licenses set forth in 17 U.S.C. 112(e) and 114 shall comply with the requirements of those sections, the rates and terms of this subpart, and any other applicable regulations.

(c) *Relationship to voluntary agreements.* Notwithstanding the royalty rates and terms established in this subpart, the rates and terms of any license agreements entered into by Copyright Owners and Licensees shall apply in lieu of the rates and terms of this subpart to transmission within the scope of such agreements.

§ 380.2 Definitions.

For purposes of this subpart, the following definitions shall apply:

Aggregate Tuning Hours (ATH) means the total hours of programming that the Licensee has transmitted during the relevant period to all listeners within the United States from all channels and stations that provide audio programming consisting, in whole or in part, of eligible nonsubscription transmissions or noninteractive digital audio transmissions as part of a new subscription service, less the actual running time of any sound recordings for which the Licensee has obtained direct licenses apart from 17 U.S.C. 114(d)(2) or which do not require a license under United States copyright law. By way of example, if a service transmitted one hour of programming to 10 simultaneous listeners, the service's Aggregate Tuning Hours would equal 10. If 3 minutes of that hour consisted of transmission of a directly licensed recording, the service's Aggregate Tuning Hours would equal 9 hours and 30 minutes. As an additional example, if one listener listened to a service for 10 hours (and none of the recordings transmitted during that time was directly licensed), the service's Aggregate Tuning Hours would equal 10.

Broadcaster is a type of Licensee that owns and operates a terrestrial AM or FM radio station that is licensed by the Federal Communications Commission.

Collective is the collection and distribution organization that is designated by the Copyright Royalty Judges. For the 2011–2015 license period, the Collective is SoundExchange, Inc.

Commercial Webcaster is a Licensee, other than a Noncommercial Webcaster, that makes eligible digital audio transmissions.

Copyright Owners are sound recording copyright owners who are entitled to royalty payments made under this subpart pursuant to the statutory licenses under 17 U.S.C. 112(e) and 114.

Ephemeral Recording is a phonorecord created for the purpose of facilitating a transmission of a public performance of a sound recording under a statutory license in accordance with 17 U.S.C. 114, and subject to the limitations specified in 17 U.S.C. 112(e).

Licensee is a person that has obtained a statutory license under 17 U.S.C. 114, and the implementing regulations, to make eligible nonsubscription transmissions, or noninteractive digital audio transmissions as part of a new subscription service (as defined in 17 U.S.C. 114(j)(8)) other than a Service as defined in §383.2(h) of this chapter, or that has obtained a statutory license under 17 U.S.C. 112(e), and the implementing regulations, to make Ephemeral Recordings for use in facilitating such transmissions, but that is not—

(1) A Broadcaster as defined in §380.11; or

(2) A Noncommercial Educational Webcaster as defined in §380.21.

Noncommercial Webcaster is a Licensee that makes eligible digital audio transmissions and

(1) Is exempt from taxation under section 501 of the Internal Revenue Code of 1986 (26 U.S.C. 501),

(2) Has applied in good faith to the Internal Revenue Service for exemption from taxation under section 501 of the Internal Revenue Code and has a commercially reasonable expectation that such exemption shall be granted, or

(3) Is operated by a State or possession or any governmental entity or subordinate thereof, or by the United States or District of Columbia, for exclusively public purposes.

Performance is each instance in which any portion of a sound recording is publicly performed to a listener by means of a digital audio transmission (*e.g.*, the delivery of any portion of a single track from a compact disc to one listener) but excluding the following:

(1) A performance of a sound recording that does not require a license (*e.g.*, a sound recording that is not copyrighted);

(2) A performance of a sound recording for which the service has previously obtained a license from the Copyright Owner of such sound recording; and

(3) An incidental performance that both:

(i) Makes no more than incidental use of sound recordings including, but not limited to, brief musical transitions in and out of commercials or program segments, brief performances during news, talk and sports programming, brief background performances during disk jockey announcements, brief performances during commercials of sixty seconds or less in duration, or brief performances during sporting or other public events and

(ii) Other than ambient music that is background at a public event, does not contain an entire sound recording and does not feature a particular sound recording of more than thirty seconds (as in the case of a sound recording used as a theme song).

Performers means the independent administrators identified in 17 U.S.C. 114(g)(2)(B) and (C) and the parties identified in 17 U.S.C. 114(g)(2)(D).

Qualified Auditor is a Certified Public Accountant.

Side Channel is a channel on the Web site of a Broadcaster which channel transmits eligible transmissions that are not simultaneously transmitted over the air by the Broadcaster.

§ 380.3 Royalty fees for the public performance of sound recordings and for ephemeral recordings.

(a) *Royalty rates.* Royalty rates and fees for eligible digital transmissions of sound recordings made pursuant to 17 U.S.C. 114, and the making of ephemeral recordings pursuant to 17 U.S.C. 112(e) are as follows:

(1) *Commercial Webcasters:* For all digital audio transmissions, including simultaneous digital audio retransmissions of over-the-air AM or FM radio broadcasts, and related Ephemeral Recordings, a Commercial Webcaster will pay a royalty of: $0.0019 per performance for 2011; $0.0021 per performance for 2012; $0.0021 per performance for 2013; $0.0023 per performance for 2014; and $0.0023 per performance for 2015.

(2) *Noncommercial Webcasters:* (i) For all digital audio transmissions totaling not more than 159,140 Aggregate Tuning Hours (ATH) in a month, including simultaneous digital audio retransmissions of over-the-air AM or FM radio broadcasts, and related Ephemeral Recordings, a Noncommercial Webcaster will pay an annual per channel or per station performance royalty of $500 in 2011, 2012, 2013, 2014, and 2015.

(ii) For all digital audio transmissions totaling in excess of 159,140 Aggregate Tuning Hours (ATH) in a month, including simultaneous digital audio retransmissions of over-the-air AM or FM radio broadcasts, and related Ephemeral Recordings, a Noncommercial Webcaster will pay a royalty of: $0.0019 per performance for 2011; $0.0021 per performance for 2012; $0.0021 per performance for 2013; $0.0023 per performance for 2014; and $0.0023 per performance for 2015.

(b) *Minimum fee*—(1) *Commercial Webcasters.* Each Commercial Webcaster will pay an annual, nonrefundable minimum fee of $500 for each calendar year or part of a calendar year of the period 2011–2015 during which it is a Licensee pursuant to 17 U.S.C. 112(e) or 114. This annual minimum fee is payable for each individual channel and each individual station maintained by Commercial Webcasters, and is also payable for each individual Side Channel maintained by Broadcasters who are Commercial Webcasters, provided that a Commercial Webcaster shall not be required to pay more than $50,000 per calendar year in minimum fees in the aggregate (for 100 or more channels or stations). For each such Commercial Webcaster, the annual minimum fee described in this paragraph (b)(1) shall constitute the minimum fees due under both 17 U.S.C. 112(e)(4) and 114(f)(2)(B). Upon payment of the minimum fee, the Commercial Webcaster will receive a credit in the amount of the minimum fee against any additional royalty fees payable in the same calendar year.

(2) *Noncommercial Webcasters.* Each Noncommercial Webcaster will pay an annual, nonrefundable minimum fee of $500 for each calendar year or part of a calendar year of the period 2011–2015 during which it is a Licensee pursuant to 17 U.S.C. 112(e) or 114. This annual minimum fee is payable for each individual channel and each individual station maintained by Noncommercial Webcasters, and is also payable for each individual Side Channel maintained by Broadcasters who are Noncommercial Webcasters. For each such Noncommercial Webcaster, the annual minimum fee described in this paragraph (b)(2) shall constitute the minimum fees due under both 17 U.S.C. 112(e)(4) and 114(f)(2)(B). Upon payment of the minimum fee, the Noncommercial Webcaster will receive a credit in the amount of the minimum fee against any additional royalty fees payable in the same calendar year.

(c) *Ephemeral recordings.* The royalty payable under 17 U.S.C. 112(e) for the making of all Ephemeral Recordings used by the Licensee solely to facilitate transmissions for which it pays royalties shall be included within, and constitute 5% of, the total royalties payable under 17 U.S.C. 112(e) and 114.

§ 380.4 Terms for making payment of royalty fees and statements of account.

(a) *Payment to the Collective.* A Licensee shall make the royalty payments due under § 380.3 to the Collective.

(b) *Designation of the Collective.* (1) Until such time as a new designation is made, SoundExchange, Inc., is designated as the Collective to receive statements of account and royalty payments from Licensees due under § 380.3 and to distribute such royalty payments to each Copyright Owner and Performer, or their designated agents, entitled to receive royalties under 17 U.S.C. 112(e) or 114(g).

(2) If SoundExchange, Inc. should dissolve or cease to be governed by a board consisting of equal numbers of representatives of Copyright Owners and Performers, then it shall be replaced by a successor Collective upon the fulfillment of the requirements set forth in paragraph (b)(2)(i) of this section.

(i) By a majority vote of the nine Copyright Owner representatives and the nine Performer representatives on the SoundExchange board as of the last day preceding the condition precedent in this paragraph (b)(2), such representatives shall file a petition with the Copyright Royalty Judges designating a successor to collect and distribute royalty payments to Copyright Owners and Performers entitled to receive royalties under 17 U.S.C. 112(e) or 114(g) that have themselves authorized the Collective.

(ii) The Copyright Royalty Judges shall publish in the FEDERAL REGISTER within 30 days of receipt of a petition filed under paragraph (b)(2)(i) of this section an order designating the Collective named in such petition.

(c) *Monthly payments.* A Licensee shall make any payments due under § 380.3 on a monthly basis on or before the 45th day after the end of each month for that month. All monthly payments shall be rounded to the nearest cent.

(d) *Minimum payments.* A Licensee shall make any minimum payment due under § 380.3(b) by January 31 of the applicable calendar year, except that payment for a Licensee that has not previously made eligible nonsubscription transmissions, noninteractive digital audio transmissions as part of a new subscription service or Ephemeral Recordings pursuant to the licenses in 17 U.S.C. 114 and/or 17 U.S.C. 112(e) shall be due by the 45th day after the end of the month in which the Licensee commences to do so.

(e) *Late payments and statements of account.* A Licensee shall pay a late fee of 1.5% per month, or the highest lawful rate, whichever is lower, for any payment and/or statement of account received by the Collective after the due date. Late fees shall accrue from the due date until payment and the related statement of account are received by the Collective.

(f) *Statements of account.* Any payment due under § 380.3 shall be accompanied by a corresponding statement of account. A statement of account shall contain the following information:

(1) Such information as is necessary to calculate the accompanying royalty payment;

(2) The name, address, business title, telephone number, facsimile number (if any), electronic mail address and other contact information of the person to be contacted for information or questions concerning the content of the statement of account;

(3) The handwritten signature of:

(i) The owner of the Licensee or a duly authorized agent of the owner, if the Licensee is not a partnership or corporation;

(ii) A partner or delegee, if the Licensee is a partnership; or

(iii) An officer of the corporation, if the Licensee is a corporation.

(4) The printed or typewritten name of the person signing the statement of account;

(5) The date of signature;

(6) If the Licensee is a partnership or corporation, the title or official position held in the partnership or corporation by the person signing the statement of account;

(7) A certification of the capacity of the person signing; and

(8) A statement to the following effect:

I, the undersigned owner or agent of the Licensee, or officer or partner, have examined this statement of account and hereby state that it is true, accurate, and complete to my knowledge after reasonable due diligence.

(g) *Distribution of royalties.* (1) The Collective shall promptly distribute royalties received from Licensees to Copyright Owners and Performers, or their designated agents, that are entitled to such royalties. The Collective shall only be responsible for making distributions to those Copyright Owners, Performers, or their designated agents who provide the Collective with such information as is necessary to identify the correct recipient. The Collective shall distribute royalties on a basis that values all performances by a Licensee equally based upon the information provided under the reports of use requirements for Licensees contained in § 370.4 of this chapter.

(2) If the Collective is unable to locate a Copyright Owner or Performer entitled to a distribution of royalties under paragraph (g)(1) of the section within 3 years from the date of payment by a Licensee, such royalties shall be handled in accordance with § 380.8.

(h) *Retention of records.* Books and records of a Licensee and of the Collective relating to payments of and distributions of royalties shall be kept for a period of not less than the prior 3 calendar years.

§ 380.5 Confidential Information.

(a) *Definition.* For purposes of this subpart, "Confidential Information" shall include the statements of account and any information contained therein, including the amount of royalty payments, and any information pertaining to the statements of account reasonably designated as confidential by the Licensee submitting the statement.

(b) *Exclusion.* Confidential Information shall not include documents or information that at the time of delivery to the Collective are public knowledge. The party claiming the benefit of this provision shall have the burden of proving that the disclosed information was public knowledge.

(c) *Use of Confidential Information.* In no event shall the Collective use any Confidential Information for any purpose other than royalty collection and distribution and activities related directly thereto.

(d) *Disclosure of Confidential Information.* Access to Confidential Information shall be limited to:

(1) Those employees, agents, attorneys, consultants and independent contractors of the Collective, subject to an appropriate confidentiality agreement, who are engaged in the collection and distribution of royalty payments hereunder and activities related thereto, for the purpose of performing such duties during the ordinary course of their work and who require access to the Confidential Information;

(2) An independent and Qualified Auditor, subject to an appropriate confidentiality agreement, who is authorized to act on behalf of the Collective with respect to verification of a Licensee's statement of account pursuant to § 380.6 or on behalf of a Copyright Owner or Performer with respect to the verification of royalty distributions pursuant to § 380.7;

(3) Copyright Owners and Performers, including their designated agents, whose works have been used under the statutory licenses set forth in 17 U.S.C. 112(e) and 114 by the Licensee whose Confidential Information is being supplied, subject to an appropriate confidentiality agreement, and including those employees, agents, attorneys, consultants and independent contractors of such Copyright Owners and Performers and their designated agents, subject to an appropriate confidentiality agreement, for the purpose of performing their duties during the ordinary course of their work and who require access to the Confidential Information; and

(4) In connection with future proceedings under 17 U.S.C. 112(e) and 114 before the Copyright Royalty Judges, and under an appropriate protective order, attorneys, consultants and other authorized agents of the parties to the proceedings or the courts.

(e) *Safeguarding of Confidential Information.* The Collective and any person identified in paragraph (d) of this section shall implement procedures to safeguard against unauthorized access to or dissemination of any Confidential Information using a reasonable standard of care, but no less than the same degree of security used to protect Confidential Information or similarly sensitive information belonging to the Collective or person.

§ 380.6 Verification of royalty payments.

(a) *General.* This section prescribes procedures by which the Collective may verify the royalty payments made by a Licensee.

(b) *Frequency of verification.* The Collective may conduct a single audit of a Licensee, upon reasonable notice and during reasonable business hours, during any given calendar year, for any or all of the prior 3 calendar years, but no calendar year shall be subject to audit more than once.

(c) *Notice of intent to audit.* The Collective must file with the Copyright Royalty Judges a notice of intent to audit a particular Licensee, which shall, within 30 days of the filing of the notice, publish in the FEDERAL REGISTER a notice announcing such filing. The notification of intent to audit shall be served at the same time on the Licensee to be audited. Any such audit shall be conducted by an independent and Qualified Auditor identified in the notice, and shall be binding on all parties.

(d) *Acquisition and retention of report.* The Licensee shall use commercially reasonable efforts to obtain or to provide access to any relevant books and records maintained by third parties for the purpose of the audit. The Collective shall retain the report of the verification for a period of not less than 3 years.

(e) *Acceptable verification procedure.* An audit, including underlying paperwork, which was performed in the ordinary course of business according to generally accepted auditing standards by an independent and Qualified Auditor, shall serve as an acceptable verification procedure for all parties with respect to the information that is within the scope of the audit.

(f) *Consultation.* Before rendering a written report to the Collective, except where the auditor has a reasonable basis to suspect fraud and disclosure would, in the reasonable opinion of the auditor, prejudice the investigation of such suspected fraud, the auditor shall review the tentative written findings of the audit with the appropriate agent or employee of the Licensee being audited in order to remedy any factual errors and clarify any issues relating to the audit; Provided that an appropriate agent or employee of the Licensee reasonably cooperates with the auditor to remedy promptly any factual errors or clarify any issues raised by the audit.

(g) *Costs of the verification procedure.* The Collective shall pay the cost of the verification procedure, unless it is finally determined that there was an underpayment of 10% or more, in which case the Licensee shall, in addition to paying the amount of any underpayment, bear the reasonable costs of the verification procedure.

§ 380.7 Verification of royalty distributions.

(a) *General.* This section prescribes procedures by which any Copyright Owner or Performer may verify the royalty distributions made by the Collective; provided, however, that nothing contained in this section shall apply to situations where a Copyright Owner or Performer and the Collective have agreed as to proper verification methods.

(b) *Frequency of verification.* A Copyright Owner or Performer may conduct a single audit of the Collective upon reasonable notice and during reasonable business hours, during any given calendar year, for any or all of the prior 3 calendar years, but no calendar year shall be subject to audit more than once.

(c) *Notice of intent to audit.* A Copyright Owner or Performer must file with the Copyright Royalty Judges a notice of intent to audit the Collective, which shall, within 30 days of the filing of the notice, publish in the FEDERAL REGISTER a notice announcing such filing. The notification of intent to audit shall be served at the same time on the Collective. Any audit shall be conducted by an independent and Qualified Auditor identified in the notice, and shall be binding on all Copyright Owners and Performers.

(d) *Acquisition and retention of report.* The Collective shall use commercially reasonable efforts to obtain or to provide access to any relevant books and records maintained by third parties for the purpose of the audit. The Copyright Owner or Performer requesting the verification procedure shall retain the report of the verification for a period of not less than 3 years.

(e) *Acceptable verification procedure.* An audit, including underlying paperwork, which was performed in the ordinary course of business according to generally accepted auditing standards by an independent and Qualified Auditor, shall serve as an acceptable verification procedure for all parties with respect to the information that is within the scope of the audit.

(f) *Consultation.* Before rendering a written report to a Copyright Owner or Performer, except where the auditor has a reasonable basis to suspect fraud and disclosure would, in the reasonable opinion of the auditor, prejudice the investigation of such suspected fraud, the auditor shall review the tentative written findings of the audit with the appropriate agent or employee of the Collective in order to remedy any factual errors and clarify any issues relating to the audit; Provided that the appropriate agent or employee of the Collective reasonably cooperates with the auditor to remedy promptly any factual errors or clarify any issues raised by the audit.

(g) *Costs of the verification procedure.* The Copyright Owner or Performer requesting the verification procedure shall pay the cost of the procedure, unless it is finally determined that there was an underpayment of 10% or more, in which case the Collective shall, in addition to paying the amount of any underpayment, bear the reasonable costs of the verification procedure.

§ 380.8 Unclaimed funds.

If the Collective is unable to identify or locate a Copyright Owner or Performer who is entitled to receive a royalty distribution under this subpart, the Collective shall retain the required payment in a segregated trust account for a period of 3 years from the date of distribution. No claim to such distribution shall be valid after the expiration of the 3-year period. After expiration of this period, the Collective may apply the unclaimed funds to offset any costs deductible under 17 U.S.C. 114(g)(3). The foregoing shall apply notwithstanding the common law or statutes of any State.

Subpart B—Broadcasters

§ 380.10 General.

(a) *Scope.* This subpart establishes rates and terms of royalty payments for the public performance of sound recordings in certain digital transmissions made by Broadcasters as set forth herein in accordance with the provisions of 17 U.S.C. 114, and the making of Ephemeral Recordings by Broadcasters as set forth herein in accordance with the provisions of 17 U.S.C. 112(e), during the period January 1, 2011, through December 31, 2015.

(b) *Legal compliance.* Broadcasters relying upon the statutory licenses set forth in 17 U.S.C. 112(e) and 114 shall comply with the requirements of those sections, the rates and terms of this subpart, and any other applicable regulations not inconsistent with the rates and terms set forth herein.

(c) *Relationship to voluntary agreements.* Notwithstanding the royalty rates and terms established in this subpart, the rates and terms of any license agreements entered into by Copyright Owners and digital audio services shall apply in lieu of the rates and terms of this subpart to transmission within the scope of such agreements.

§ 380.11 Definitions.

For purposes of this subpart, the following definitions shall apply:

Aggregate Tuning Hours means the total hours of programming that the Broadcaster has transmitted during the relevant period to all listeners within the United States from any channels and stations that provide audio programming consisting, in whole or in part, of Eligible Transmissions.

Broadcaster means an entity that:

(1) Has a substantial business owning and operating one or more terrestrial AM or FM radio stations that are licensed as such by the Federal Communications Commission;

(2) Has obtained a compulsory license under 17 U.S.C. 112(e) and 114 and the implementing regulations therefor to

make Eligible Transmissions and related ephemeral recordings;

(3) Complies with all applicable provisions of Sections 112(e) and 114 and applicable regulations; and

(4) Is not a noncommercial webcaster as defined in 17 U.S.C. 114(f)(5)(E)(i).

Broadcaster Webcasts mean eligible nonsubscription transmissions made by a Broadcaster over the Internet that are not Broadcast Retransmissions.

Broadcast Retransmissions mean eligible nonsubscription transmissions made by a Broadcaster over the Internet that are retransmissions of terrestrial over-the-air broadcast programming transmitted by the Broadcaster through its AM or FM radio station, including ones with substitute advertisements or other programming occasionally substituted for programming for which requisite licenses or clearances to transmit over the Internet have not been obtained. For the avoidance of doubt, a Broadcast Retransmission does not include programming that does not require a license under United States copyright law or that is transmitted on an Internet-only side channel.

Collective is the collection and distribution organization that is designated by the Copyright Royalty Judges. For the 2011–2015 license period, the Collective is SoundExchange, Inc.

Copyright Owners are sound recording copyright owners who are entitled to royalty payments made under this subpart pursuant to the statutory licenses under 17 U.S.C. 112(e) and 114(f).

Eligible Transmission shall mean either a Broadcaster Webcast or a Broadcast Retransmission.

Ephemeral Recording is a phonorecord created for the purpose of facilitating an Eligible Transmission of a public performance of a sound recording under a statutory license in accordance with 17 U.S.C. 114(f), and subject to the limitations specified in 17 U.S.C. 112(e).

Performance is each instance in which any portion of a sound recording is publicly performed to a listener by means of a digital audio transmission (*e.g.*, the delivery of any portion of a single track from a compact disc to one listener) but excluding the following:

(1) A performance of a sound recording that does not require a license (*e.g.*, a sound recording that is not copyrighted);

(2) A performance of a sound recording for which the Broadcaster has previously obtained a license from the Copyright Owner of such sound recording; and

(3) An incidental performance that both:

(i) Makes no more than incidental use of sound recordings including, but not limited to, brief musical transitions in and out of commercials or program segments, brief performances during news, talk and sports programming, brief background performances during disk jockey announcements, brief performances during commercials of sixty seconds or less in duration, or brief performances during sporting or other public events and

(ii) Other than ambient music that is background at a public event, does not contain an entire sound recording and does not feature a particular sound recording of more than thirty seconds (as in the case of a sound recording used as a theme song).

Performers means the independent administrators identified in 17 U.S.C. 114(g)(2)(B) and (C) and the parties identified in 17 U.S.C. 114(g)(2)(D).

Qualified Auditor is a Certified Public Accountant.

Small Broadcaster is a Broadcaster that, for any of its channels and stations (determined as provided in §380.12(c)) over which it transmits Broadcast Retransmissions, and for all of its channels and stations over which it transmits Broadcaster Webcasts in the aggregate, in any calendar year in which it is to be considered a Small Broadcaster, meets the following additional eligibility criteria:

(1) During the prior year it made Eligible Transmissions totaling less than 27,777 Aggregate Tuning Hours; and

(2) During the applicable year it reasonably expects to make Eligible Transmissions totaling less than 27,777 Aggregate Tuning Hours; provided that, one time during the period 2011–2015, a Broadcaster that qualified as a Small Broadcaster under the foregoing definition as of January 31 of one year, elected Small Broadcaster status for

that year, and unexpectedly made Eligible Transmissions on one or more channels or stations in excess of 27,777 aggregate tuning hours during that year, may choose to be treated as a Small Broadcaster during the following year notwithstanding paragraph (1) of the definition of "Small Broadcaster" if it implements measures reasonably calculated to ensure that it will not make Eligible Transmissions exceeding 27,777 aggregate tuning hours during that following year. As to channels or stations over which a Broadcaster transmits Broadcast Retransmissions, the Broadcaster may elect Small Broadcaster status only with respect to any of its channels or stations that meet all of the foregoing criteria.

§ 380.12 Royalty fees for the public performance of sound recordings and for ephemeral recordings.

(a) *Royalty rates.* Royalties for Eligible Transmissions made pursuant to 17 U.S.C. 114, and the making of related ephemeral recordings pursuant to 17 U.S.C. 112(e), shall, except as provided in § 380.13(g)(3), be payable on a per-performance basis, as follows:

(1) 2011: $0.0017;

(2) 2012: $0.0020;

(3) 2013: $0.0022;

(4) 2014: $0.0023;

(5) 2015: $0.0025.

(b) *Ephemeral royalty.* The royalty payable under 17 U.S.C. 112(e) for any reproduction of a phonorecord made by a Broadcaster during this license period and used solely by the Broadcaster to facilitate transmissions for which it pays royalties as and when provided in this section is deemed to be included within such royalty payments and to equal the percentage of such royalty payments determined by the Copyright Royalty Judges for other webcasting as set forth in § 380.3.

(c) *Minimum fee.* Each Broadcaster will pay an annual, nonrefundable minimum fee of $500 for each of its individual channels, including each of its individual side channels, and each of its individual stations, through which (in each case) it makes Eligible Transmissions, for each calendar year or part of a calendar year during 2011–2015 during which the Broadcaster is a licensee pursuant to licenses under 17 U.S.C. 112(e) and 114, provided that a Broadcaster shall not be required to pay more than $50,000 in minimum fees in the aggregate (for 100 or more channels or stations). For the purpose of this subpart, each individual stream (*e.g.*, HD radio side channels, different stations owned by a single licensee) will be treated separately and be subject to a separate minimum, except that identical streams for simulcast stations will be treated as a single stream if the streams are available at a single Uniform Resource Locator (URL) and performances from all such stations are aggregated for purposes of determining the number of payable performances hereunder. Upon payment of the minimum fee, the Broadcaster will receive a credit in the amount of the minimum fee against any additional royalties payable for the same calendar year for the same channel or station. In addition, an electing Small Broadcaster also shall pay a $100 annual fee (the "Proxy Fee") to the Collective for the reporting waiver discussed in § 380.13(g)(2).

§ 380.13 Terms for making payment of royalty fees and statements of account.

(a) *Payment to the Collective.* A Broadcaster shall make the royalty payments due under § 380.12 to the Collective.

(b) *Designation of the Collective.* (1) Until such time as a new designation is made, SoundExchange, Inc., is designated as the Collective to receive statements of account and royalty payments from Broadcasters due under § 380.12 and to distribute such royalty payments to each Copyright Owner and Performer, or their designated agents, entitled to receive royalties under 17 U.S.C. 112(e) and 114(g).

(2) If SoundExchange, Inc. should dissolve or cease to be governed by a board consisting of equal numbers of representatives of Copyright Owners and Performers, then it shall be replaced by a successor Collective upon the fulfillment of the requirements set forth in paragraph (b)(2)(i) of this section.

(i) By a majority vote of the nine Copyright Owner representatives and the nine Performer representatives on the SoundExchange board as of the last day preceding the condition precedent in this paragraph (b)(2), such representatives shall file a petition with the Copyright Royalty Board designating a successor to collect and distribute royalty payments to Copyright Owners and Performers entitled to receive royalties under 17 U.S.C. 112(e) or 114(g) that have themselves authorized such Collective.

(ii) The Copyright Royalty Judges shall publish in the FEDERAL REGISTER within 30 days of receipt of a petition filed under paragraph (b)(2)(i) of this section an order designating the Collective named in such petition.

(c) *Monthly payments and reporting.* Broadcasters must make monthly payments where required by § 380.12, and provide statements of account and reports of use, for each month on the 45th day following the month in which the Eligible Transmissions subject to the payments, statements of account, and reports of use were made. All monthly payments shall be rounded to the nearest cent.

(d) *Minimum payments.* A Broadcaster shall make any minimum payment due under § 380.12(b) by January 31 of the applicable calendar year, except that payment by a Broadcaster that was not making Eligible Transmissions or Ephemeral Recordings pursuant to the licenses in 17 U.S.C. 114 and/or 17 U.S.C. 112(e) as of said date but begins doing so thereafter shall be due by the 45th day after the end of the month in which the Broadcaster commences to do so.

(e) *Late fees.* A Broadcaster shall pay a late fee for each instance in which any payment, any statement of account or any report of use is not received by the Collective in compliance with applicable regulations by the due date. The amount of the late fee shall be 1.5% of a late payment, or 1.5% of the payment associated with a late statement of account or report of use, per month, or the highest lawful rate, whichever is lower. The late fee shall accrue from the due date of the payment, statement of account or report of use until a fully compliant payment, statement of account or report of use is received by the Collective, provided that, in the case of a timely provided but noncompliant statement of account or report of use, the Collective has notified the Broadcaster within 90 days regarding any noncompliance that is reasonably evident to the Collective.

(f) *Statements of account.* Any payment due under § 380.12 shall be accompanied by a corresponding statement of account. A statement of account shall contain the following information:

(1) Such information as is necessary to calculate the accompanying royalty payment;

(2) The name, address, business title, telephone number, facsimile number (if any), electronic mail address (if any) and other contact information of the person to be contacted for information or questions concerning the content of the statement of account;

(3) The handwritten signature of:

(i) The owner of the Broadcaster or a duly authorized agent of the owner, if the Broadcaster is not a partnership or corporation;

(ii) A partner or delegee, if the Broadcaster is a partnership; or

(iii) An officer of the corporation, if the Broadcaster is a corporation.

(4) The printed or typewritten name of the person signing the statement of account;

(5) The date of signature;

(6) If the Broadcaster is a partnership or corporation, the title or official position held in the partnership or corporation by the person signing the statement of account;

(7) A certification of the capacity of the person signing; and

(8) A statement to the following effect:

I, the undersigned owner or agent of the Broadcaster, or officer or partner, have examined this statement of account and hereby state that it is true, accurate, and complete to my knowledge after reasonable due diligence.

(g) *Reporting by Broadcasters in General.* (1) Broadcasters other than electing Small Broadcasters covered by paragraph (g)(2) of this section shall submit reports of use on a per-performance basis in compliance with the regulations set forth in part 370 of this chapter, except that the following provisions shall apply notwithstanding the provisions of such part 370 of this chapter from time to time in effect:

(i) Broadcasters may pay for, and report usage in, a percentage of their programming hours on an Aggregate Tuning Hour basis as provided in paragraph (g)(3) of this section.

(ii) Broadcasters shall submit reports of use to the Collective on a monthly basis.

(iii) As provided in paragraph (d) of this section, Broadcasters shall submit reports of use by no later than the 45th day following the last day of the month to which they pertain.

(iv) Except as provided in paragraph (g)(3) of this section, Broadcasters shall submit reports of use to the Collective on a census reporting basis (*i.e.*, reports of use shall include every sound recording performed in the relevant month and the number of performances thereof).

(v) Broadcasters shall either submit a separate report of use for each of their stations, or a collective report of use covering all of their stations but identifying usage on a station-by-station basis;

(vi) Broadcasters shall transmit each report of use in a file the name of which includes:

(A) The name of the Broadcaster, exactly as it appears on its notice of use, and

(B) If the report covers a single station only, the call letters of the station.

(vii) Broadcasters shall submit reports of use with headers, as presently described in § 370.4(e)(7) of this chapter.

(viii) Broadcasters shall submit a separate statement of account corresponding to each of their reports of use, transmitted in a file the name of which includes:

(A) The name of the Broadcaster, exactly as it appears on its notice of use, and

(B) If the statement covers a single station only, the call letters of the station.

(2) On a transitional basis for a limited time in light of the unique business and operational circumstances currently existing with respect to Small Broadcasters and with the expectation that Small Broadcasters will be required, effective January 1, 2016, to report their actual usage in compliance with then-applicable regulations. Small Broadcasters that have made an election pursuant to paragraph (h) of this section for the relevant year shall not be required to provide reports of their use of sound recordings for Eligible Transmissions and related Ephemeral Recordings. The immediately preceding sentence applies even if the Small Broadcaster actually makes Eligible Transmissions for the year exceeding 27,777 Aggregate Tuning Hours, so long as it qualified as a Small Broadcaster at the time of its election for that year. In addition to minimum royalties hereunder, electing Small Broadcasters will pay to the Collective a $100 Proxy Fee to defray costs associated with this reporting waiver, including development of proxy usage data.

(3) Broadcasters generally reporting pursuant to paragraph (g)(1) of this section may pay for, and report usage in, a percentage of their programming hours on an Aggregate Tuning Hours basis, if

(i) Census reporting is not reasonably practical for the programming during those hours, and

(ii) If the total number of hours on a single report of use, provided pursuant to paragraph (g)(1) of this section, for which this type of reporting is used is below the maximum percentage set forth below for the relevant year:

(A) 2011: 16%;

(B) 2012: 14%;

(C) 2013: 12%;

(D) 2014: 10%;

(E) 2015: 8%.

(iii) To the extent that a Broadcaster chooses to report and pay for usage on an Aggregate Tuning Hours basis pursuant to this paragraph (g)(3), the Broadcaster shall

(A) Report and pay based on the assumption that the number of sound recordings performed during the relevant programming hours is 12 per hour;

(B) Pay royalties (or recoup minimum fees) at the per-performance rates provided in § 380.12 on the basis of paragraph (g)(3)(iii)(A) of this section;

(C) Include Aggregate Tuning Hours in reports of use; and

(D) Include in reports of use complete playlist information for usage reported on the basis of Aggregate Tuning Hours.

(h) *Election of Small Broadcaster Status.* To be eligible for the reporting waiver for Small Broadcasters with respect to any particular channel in a given year, a Broadcaster must satisfy the definition set forth in § 380.11 and must submit to the Collective a completed and signed election form (available on the SoundExchange Web site at *http://www.soundexchange.com*) by no later than January 31 of the applicable year. Even if a Broadcaster has once elected to be treated as a Small Broadcaster, it must make a separate, timely election in each subsequent year in which it wishes to be treated as a Small Broadcaster.

(i) *Distribution of royalties.* (1) The Collective shall promptly distribute royalties received from Broadcasters to Copyright Owners and Performers, or their designated agents, that are entitled to such royalties. The Collective shall only be responsible for making distributions to those Copyright Owners, Performers, or their designated agents who provide the Collective with such information as is necessary to identify and pay the correct recipient. The Collective shall distribute royalties on a basis that values all performances by a Broadcaster equally based upon information provided under the report of use requirements for Broadcasters contained in § 370.4 of this chapter and this subpart, except that in the case of electing Small Broadcasters, the Collective shall distribute royalties based on proxy usage data in accordance with a methodology adopted by the Collective's Board of Directors.

(2) If the Collective is unable to locate a Copyright Owner or Performer entitled to a distribution of royalties under paragraph (g)(1) of this section within 3 years from the date of payment by a Broadcaster, such distribution may be first applied to the costs directly attributable to the administration of that distribution. The foregoing shall apply notwithstanding the common law or statutes of any State.

(j) *Retention of records.* Books and records of a Broadcaster and of the Collective relating to payments of and distributions of royalties shall be kept for a period of not less than the prior 3 calendar years.

§ 380.14 Confidential Information.

(a) *Definition.* For purposes of this subpart, "Confidential Information" shall include the statements of account and any information contained therein, including the amount of royalty payments, and any information pertaining to the statements of account reasonably designated as confidential by the Broadcaster submitting the statement.

(b) *Exclusion.* Confidential Information shall not include documents or information that at the time of delivery to the Collective are public knowledge. The party claiming the benefit of this provision shall have the burden of proving that the disclosed information was public knowledge.

(c) *Use of Confidential Information.* In no event shall the Collective use any Confidential Information for any purpose other than royalty collection and distribution and activities related directly thereto.

(d) *Disclosure of Confidential Information.* Access to Confidential Information shall be limited to:

(1) Those employees, agents, attorneys, consultants and independent contractors of the Collective, subject to an appropriate confidentiality agreement, who are engaged in the collection and distribution of royalty payments hereunder and activities related thereto, for the purpose of performing such duties during the ordinary course of their work and who require access to the Confidential Information;

(2) An independent and Qualified Auditor, subject to an appropriate confidentiality agreement, who is authorized to act on behalf of the Collective with respect to verification of a Broadcaster's statement of account pursuant to § 380.15 or on behalf of a Copyright Owner or Performer with respect to the verification of royalty distributions pursuant to § 380.16;

(3) Copyright Owners and Performers, including their designated agents, whose works have been used under the statutory licenses set forth in 17 U.S.C. 112(e) and 114(f) by the Broadcaster whose Confidential Information is being supplied, subject to an appropriate confidentiality agreement, and including those employees, agents, attorneys, consultants and independent contractors of such Copyright Owners

and Performers and their designated agents, subject to an appropriate confidentiality agreement, for the purpose of performing their duties during the ordinary course of their work and who require access to the Confidential Information; and

(4) In connection with future proceedings under 17 U.S.C. 112(e) and 114(f) before the Copyright Royalty Judges, and under an appropriate protective order, attorneys, consultants and other authorized agents of the parties to the proceedings or the courts.

(e) *Safeguarding of Confidential Information.* The Collective and any person identified in paragraph (d) of this section shall implement procedures to safeguard against unauthorized access to or dissemination of any Confidential Information using a reasonable standard of care, but not less than the same degree of security used to protect Confidential Information or similarly sensitive information belonging to the Collective or person.

§ 380.15 Verification of royalty payments.

(a) *General.* This section prescribes procedures by which the Collective may verify the royalty payments made by a Broadcaster.

(b) *Frequency of verification.* The Collective may conduct a single audit of a Broadcaster, upon reasonable notice and during reasonable business hours, during any given calendar year, for any or all of the prior 3 calendar years, but no calendar year shall be subject to audit more than once.

(c) *Notice of intent to audit.* The Collective must file with the Copyright Royalty Board a notice of intent to audit a particular Broadcaster, which shall, within 30 days of the filing of the notice, publish in the FEDERAL REGISTER a notice announcing such filing. The notification of intent to audit shall be served at the same time on the Broadcaster to be audited. Any such audit shall be conducted by an independent and Qualified Auditor identified in the notice, and shall be binding on all parties.

(d) *Acquisition and retention of report.* The Broadcaster shall use commercially reasonable efforts to obtain or to provide access to any relevant books and records maintained by third parties for the purpose of the audit. The Collective shall retain the report of the verification for a period of not less than 3 years.

(e) *Acceptable verification procedure.* An audit, including underlying paperwork, which was performed in the ordinary course of business according to generally accepted auditing standards by an independent and Qualified Auditor, shall serve as an acceptable verification procedure for all parties with respect to the information that is within the scope of the audit.

(f) *Consultation.* Before rendering a written report to the Collective, except where the auditor has a reasonable basis to suspect fraud and disclosure would, in the reasonable opinion of the auditor, prejudice the investigation of such suspected fraud, the auditor shall review the tentative written findings of the audit with the appropriate agent or employee of the Broadcaster being audited in order to remedy any factual errors and clarify any issues relating to the audit; Provided that an appropriate agent or employee of the Broadcaster reasonably cooperates with the auditor to remedy promptly any factual error or clarify any issues raised by the audit.

(g) *Costs of the verification procedure.* The Collective shall pay the cost of the verification procedure, unless it is finally determined that there was an underpayment of 10% or more, in which case the Broadcaster shall, in addition to paying the amount of any underpayment, bear the reasonable costs of the verification procedure.

§ 380.16 Verification of royalty distributions.

(a) *General.* This section prescribes procedures by which any Copyright Owner or Performer may verify the royalty distributions made by the Collective; Provided, however, that nothing contained in this section shall apply to situations where a Copyright Owner or Performer and the Collective have agreed as to proper verification methods.

(b) *Frequency of verification.* A Copyright Owner or Performer may conduct a single audit of the Collective upon reasonable notice and during reasonable business hours, during any given calendar year, for any or all of the prior 3 calendar years, but no calendar year shall be subject to audit more than once.

(c) *Notice of intent to audit.* A Copyright Owner or Performer must file with the Copyright Royalty Board a notice of intent to audit the Collective, which shall, within 30 days of the filing of the notice, publish in the FEDERAL REGISTER a notice announcing such filing. The notification of intent to audit shall be served at the same time on the Collective. Any audit shall be conducted by an independent and Qualified Auditor identified in the notice, and shall be binding on all Copyright Owners and Performers.

(d) *Acquisition and retention of report.* The Collective shall use commercially reasonable efforts to obtain or to provide access to any relevant books and records maintained by third parties for the purpose of the audit. The Copyright Owner or Performer requesting the verification procedure shall retain the report of the verification for a period of not less than 3 years.

(e) *Acceptable verification procedure.* An audit, including underlying paperwork, which was performed in the ordinary course of business according to generally accepted auditing standards by an independent and Qualified Auditor, shall serve as an acceptable verification procedure for all parties with respect to the information that is within the scope of the audit.

(f) *Consultation.* Before rendering a written report to a Copyright Owner or Performer, except where the auditor has a reasonable basis to suspect fraud and disclosure would, in the reasonable opinion of the auditor, prejudice the investigation of such suspected fraud, the auditor shall review the tentative written findings of the audit with the appropriate agent or employee of the Collective in order to remedy any factual errors and clarify any issues relating to the audit; Provided that the appropriate agent or employee of the Collective reasonably cooperates with the auditor to remedy promptly any factual errors or clarify any issues raised by the audit.

(g) *Costs of the verification procedure.* The Copyright Owner or Performer requesting the verification procedure shall pay the cost of the procedure, unless it is finally determined that there was an underpayment of 10% or more, in which case the Collective shall, in addition to paying the amount of any underpayment, bear the reasonable costs of the verification procedure.

§ 380.17 Unclaimed funds.

If the Collective is unable to identify or locate a Copyright Owner or Performer who is entitled to receive a royalty distribution under this subpart, the Collective shall retain the required payment in a segregated trust account for a period of 3 years from the date of distribution. No claim to such distribution shall be valid after the expiration of the 3-year period. After expiration of this period, the Collective may apply the unclaimed funds to offset any costs deductible under 17 U.S.C. 114(g)(3). The foregoing shall apply notwithstanding the common law or statutes of any State.

Subpart C—Noncommercial Educational Webcasters

§ 380.20 General.

(a) *Scope.* This subpart establishes rates and terms, including requirements for royalty payments, recordkeeping and reports of use, for the public performance of sound recordings in certain digital transmissions made by Noncommercial Educational Webcasters as set forth herein in accordance with the provisions of 17 U.S.C. 114, and the making of Ephemeral Recordings by Noncommercial Educational Webcasters as set forth herein in accordance with the provisions of 17 U.S.C. 112(e), during the period January 1, 2011, through December 31, 2015.

(b) *Legal compliance.* Noncommercial Educational Webcasters relying upon the statutory licenses set forth in 17 U.S.C. 112(e) and 114 shall comply with the requirements of those sections, the rates and terms of this subpart, and any other applicable regulations not inconsistent with the rates and terms set forth herein.

(c) *Relationship to voluntary agreements.* Notwithstanding the royalty rates and terms established in this subpart, the rates and terms of any license agreements entered into by Copyright Owners and digital audio services shall apply in lieu of the rates and terms of this subpart to transmissions within the scope of such agreements.

§ 380.21 Definitions.

For purposes of this subpart, the following definitions shall apply:

ATH or Aggregate Tuning Hours means the total hours of programming that a Noncommercial Educational Webcaster has transmitted during the relevant period to all listeners within the United States over all channels and stations that provide audio programming consisting, in whole or in part, of Eligible Transmissions, including from any archived programs, less the actual running time of any sound recordings for which the Noncommercial Educational Webcaster has obtained direct licenses apart from 17 U.S.C. 114(d)(2) or which do not require a license under United States copyright law. By way of example, if a Noncommercial Educational Webcaster transmitted one hour of programming to 10 simultaneous listeners, the Noncommercial Educational Webcaster's Aggregate Tuning Hours would equal 10. If three minutes of that hour consisted of transmission of a directly licensed recording, the Noncommercial Educational Webcaster's Aggregate Tuning Hours would equal 9 hours and 30 minutes. As an additional example, if one listener listened to a Noncommercial Educational Webcaster for 10 hours (and none of the recordings transmitted during that time was directly licensed), the Noncommercial Educational Webcaster's Aggregate Tuning Hours would equal 10.

Collective is the collection and distribution organization that is designated by the Copyright Royalty Judges. For the 2011–2015 license period, the Collective is SoundExchange, Inc.

Copyright Owners are sound recording copyright owners who are entitled to royalty payments made under this subpart pursuant to the statutory licenses under 17 U.S.C. 112(e) and 114(f).

Eligible Transmission means an eligible nonsubscription transmission made by a Noncommercial Educational Webcaster over the Internet.

Ephemeral Recording is a phonorecord created for the purpose of facilitating an Eligible Transmission of a public performance of a sound recording under a statutory license in accordance with 17 U.S.C. 114(f), and subject to the limitations specified in 17 U.S.C. 112(e).

Noncommercial Educational Webcaster means Noncommercial Webcaster (as defined in 17 U.S.C. 114(f)(5)(E)(i)) that

(1) Has obtained a compulsory license under 17 U.S.C. 112(e) and 114 and the implementing regulations therefor to make Eligible Transmissions and related ephemeral recordings;

(2) Complies with all applicable provisions of Sections 112(e) and 114 and applicable regulations;

(3) Is directly operated by, or is affiliated with and officially sanctioned by, and the digital audio transmission operations of which are staffed substantially by students enrolled at, a domestically accredited primary or secondary school, college, university or other post-secondary degree-granting educational institution; and

(4) Is not a "public broadcasting entity" (as defined in 17 U.S.C. 118(g)) qualified to receive funding from the Corporation for Public Broadcasting pursuant to the criteria set forth in 47 U.S.C. 396.

Performance is each instance in which any portion of a sound recording is publicly performed to a listener by means of a digital audio transmission (*e.g.*, the delivery of any portion of a single track from a compact disc to one listener) but excluding the following:

(1) A performance of a sound recording that does not require a license (*e.g.*, a sound recording that is not copyrighted);

(2) A performance of a sound recording for which the Noncommercial Educational Webcaster has previously obtained a license from the Copyright Owner of such sound recording; and

(3) An incidental performance that both:

(i) Makes no more than incidental use of sound recordings, including, but not limited to, brief musical transitions in and out of commercials or program segments, brief performances during news, talk and sports programming, brief background performances during disk jockey announcements, brief performances during commercials of sixty seconds or less in duration, or brief performances during sporting or other public events; and

(ii) Other than ambient music that is background at a public event, does not contain an entire sound recording and does not feature a particular sound recording of more than thirty seconds (as in the case of a sound recording used as a theme song).

Performers means the independent administrators identified in 17 U.S.C. 114(g)(2)(B) and (C) and the parties identified in 17 U.S.C. 114(g)(2)(D).

Qualified Auditor is a Certified Public Accountant.

§ 380.22 Royalty fees for the public performance of sound recordings and for ephemeral recordings.

(a) *Minimum fee.* Each Noncommercial Educational Webcaster shall pay an annual, nonrefundable minimum fee of $500 (the "Minimum Fee") for each of its individual channels, including each of its individual side channels, and each of its individual stations, through which (in each case) it makes Eligible Transmissions, for each calendar year it makes Eligible Transmissions subject to this subpart. For clarity, each individual stream (*e.g.*, HD radio side channels, different stations owned by a single licensee) will be treated separately and be subject to a separate minimum. In addition, a Noncommercial Educational Webcaster electing the reporting waiver described in § 380.23(g)(1), shall pay a $100 annual fee (the "Proxy Fee") to the Collective.

(b) *Additional usage fees.* If, in any month, a Noncommercial Educational Webcaster makes total transmissions in excess of 159,140 Aggregate Tuning Hours on any individual channel or station, the Noncommercial Educational Webcaster shall pay additional usage fees ("Usage Fees") for the Eligible Transmissions it makes on that channel or station after exceeding 159,140 total ATH at the following per-performance rates:

(1) 2011: $0.0017;

(2) 2012: $0.0020;

(3) 2013: $0.0022;

(4) 2014: $0.0023;

(5) 2015: $0.0025.

(6) For a Noncommercial Educational Webcaster unable to calculate actual total performances and not required to report ATH or actual total performances under § 380.23(g)(3), the Noncommercial Educational Webcaster may pay its Usage Fees on an ATH basis, provided that the Noncommercial Educational Webcaster shall pay its Usage Fees at the per-performance rates provided in paragraphs (b)(1) through (5) of this section based on the assumption that the number of sound recordings performed is 12 per hour. The Collective may distribute royalties paid on the basis of ATH hereunder in accordance with its generally applicable methodology for distributing royalties paid on such basis. In addition, and for the avoidance of doubt, a Noncommercial Educational Webcaster offering more than one channel or station shall pay Usage Fees on a per-channel or -station basis.

(c) *Ephemeral royalty.* The royalty payable under 17 U.S.C. 112(e) for any ephemeral reproductions made by a Noncommercial Educational Webcaster and covered by this subpart is deemed to be included within the royalty payments set forth in paragraphs (a) and (b)(1) through (5) of this section and to equal the percentage of such royalty payments determined by the Copyright Royalty Judges for other webcasting in § 380.3.

§ 380.23 Terms for making payment of royalty fees and statements of account.

(a) *Payment to the Collective.* A Noncommercial Educational Webcaster shall make the royalty payments due under § 380.22 to the Collective.

(b) *Designation of the Collective.* (1) Until such time as a new designation is made, SoundExchange, Inc., is designated as the Collective to receive statements of account and royalty payments from Noncommercial Educational Webcasters due under § 380.22 and to distribute such royalty payments to each Copyright Owner and Performer, or their designated agents, entitled to receive royalties under 17 U.S.C. 112(e) or 114(g).

(2) If SoundExchange, Inc., should dissolve or cease to be governed by a board consisting of equal numbers of representatives of Copyright Owners and Performers, then it shall be replaced by a successor Collective upon the fulfillment of the requirements set forth in paragraph (b)(2)(i) of this section.

(i) By a majority vote of the nine Copyright Owner representatives and the nine Performer representatives on the SoundExchange board as of the last day preceding the condition precedent in this paragraph (b)(2), such representatives shall file a petition with the Copyright Royalty Board designating a successor to collect and distribute royalty payments to Copyright Owners and Performers entitled to receive royalties under 17 U.S.C. 112(e) or 114(g) that have themselves authorized such Collective.

(ii) The Copyright Royalty Judges shall publish in the FEDERAL REGISTER within 30 days of receipt of a petition filed under paragraph (b)(2)(i) of this section an order designating the Collective named in such petition.

(c) *Minimum fee.* Noncommercial Educational Webcasters shall submit the Minimum Fee, and Proxy Fee if applicable, accompanied by a statement of account, by January 31st of each calendar year, except that payment of the Minimum Fee, and Proxy Fee if applicable, by a Noncommercial Educational Webcaster that was not making Eligible Transmissions or Ephemeral Recordings pursuant to the licenses in 17 U.S.C. 114 and/or 17 U.S.C. 112(e) as of said date but begins doing so thereafter shall be due by the 45th day after the end of the month in which the Noncommercial Educational Webcaster commences doing so. Payments of minimum fees must be accompanied by a certification, signed by an officer or another duly authorized faculty member or administrator of the institution with which the Noncommercial Educational Webcaster is affiliated, on a form provided by the Collective, that the Noncommercial Educational Webcaster.

(1) Qualifies as a Noncommercial Educational Webcaster for the relevant year; and

(2) Did not exceed 159,140 total ATH in any month of the prior year for which the Noncommercial Educational Webcaster did not submit a statement of account and pay any required Usage Fees. At the same time the Noncommercial Educational Webcaster must identify all its stations making Eligible Transmissions and identify which of the reporting options set forth in paragraph (g) of this section it elects for the relevant year (provided that it must be eligible for the option it elects).

(d) *Usage fees.* In addition to its obligations pursuant to paragraph (c) of this section, a Noncommercial Educational Webcaster must make monthly payments of Usage Fees where required by § 380.22(b), and provide statements of account to accompany these payments, for each month on the 45th day following the month in which the Eligible Transmissions subject to the Usage Fees and statements of account were made. All monthly payments shall be rounded to the nearest cent.

(e) *Late fees.* A Noncommercial Educational Webcaster shall pay a late fee for each instance in which any payment, any statement of account or any report of use is not received by the Collective in compliance with the applicable regulations by the due date. The amount of the late fee shall be 1.5% of the late payment, or 1.5% of the payment associated with a late statement of account or report of use, per month, compounded monthly for the balance due, or the highest lawful rate, whichever is lower. The late fee shall accrue from the due date of the payment, statement of account or report of use until a fully compliant payment, statement of account or report of use (as applicable) is received by the Collective, provided that, in the case of a timely provided but noncompliant statement of account or report of use, the Collective has notified the Noncommercial Educational Webcaster within 90 days regarding any noncompliance that is reasonably evident to the Collective.

(f) *Statements of account.* Any payment due under § 380.22 shall be accompanied by a corresponding statement of account. A statement of account shall contain the following information:

(1) The name of the Noncommercial Educational Webcaster, exactly as it appears on the notice of use, and if the statement of account covers a single station only, the call letters or name of the station;

(2) Such information as is necessary to calculate the accompanying royalty payment as prescribed in this subpart;

(3) The name, address, business title, telephone number, facsimile number (if any), electronic mail address (if any) and other contact information of the person to be contacted for information or questions concerning the content of the statement of account;

(4) The handwritten signature of an officer or another duly authorized faculty member or administrator of the applicable educational institution;

(5) The printed or typewritten name of the person signing the statement of account;

(6) The date of signature;

(7) The title or official position held by the person signing the statement of account;

(8) A certification of the capacity of the person signing; and

(9) A statement to the following effect:

I, the undersigned officer or other duly authorized faculty member or administrator of the applicable educational institution, have examined this statement of account and hereby state that it is true, accurate, and complete to my knowledge after reasonable due diligence.

(g) *Reporting by Noncommercial Educational Webcasters in general*—(1) *Reporting waiver.* In light of the unique business and operational circumstances currently existing with respect to Noncommercial Educational Webcasters, and for the purposes of this subpart only, a Noncommercial Educational Webcaster that did not exceed 55,000 total ATH for any individual channel or station for more than one calendar month in the immediately preceding calendar year and that does not expect to exceed 55,000 total ATH for any individual channel or station for any calendar month during the applicable calendar year may elect to pay to the Collective a nonrefundable, annual Proxy Fee of $100 in lieu of providing reports of use for the calendar year pursuant to the regulations at §370.4 of this chapter. In addition, a Noncommercial Educational Webcaster that unexpectedly exceeded 55,000 total ATH on one or more channels or stations for more than one month during the immediately preceding calendar year may elect to pay the Proxy Fee and receive the reporting waiver described in this paragraph (g)(1) during a calendar year, if it implements measures reasonably calculated to ensure that it will not make Eligible Transmissions exceeding 55,000 total ATH during any month of that calendar year. The Proxy Fee is intended to defray the Collective's costs associated with this reporting waiver, including development of proxy usage data. The Proxy Fee shall be paid by the date specified in paragraph (c) of this section for paying the Minimum Fee for the applicable calendar year and shall be accompanied by a certification on a form provided by the Collective, signed by an officer or another duly authorized faculty member or administrator of the applicable educational institution, stating that the Noncommercial Educational Webcaster is eligible for the Proxy Fee option because of its past and expected future usage and, if applicable, has implemented measures to ensure that it will not make excess Eligible Transmissions in the future.

(2) *Sample-basis reports.* A Noncommercial Educational Webcaster that did not exceed 159,140 total ATH for any individual channel or station for more than one calendar month in the immediately preceding calendar year and that does not expect to exceed 159,140 total ATH for any individual channel or station for any calendar month during the applicable calendar year may elect to provide reports of use on a sample basis (two weeks per calendar quarter) in accordance with the regulations at §370.4 of this chapter, except that, notwithstanding §370.4(d)(2)(vi), such an electing Noncommercial Educational Webcaster shall not be required to include ATH or actual total performances and may in lieu thereof provide channel or station

name and play frequency. Notwithstanding the foregoing, a Noncommercial Educational Webcaster that is able to report ATH or actual total performances is encouraged to do so. These reports of use shall be submitted to the Collective no later than January 31st of the year immediately following the year to which they pertain.

(3) *Census-basis reports.* If any of the following three conditions is satisfied, a Noncommercial Educational Webcaster must report pursuant to this paragraph (g)(3):

(i) The Noncommercial Educational Webcaster exceeded 159,140 total ATH for any individual channel or station for more than one calendar month in the immediately preceding calendar year;

(ii) The Noncommercial Educational Webcaster expects to exceed 159,140 total ATH for any individual channel or station for any calendar month in the applicable calendar year; or

(iii) The Noncommercial Educational Webcaster otherwise does not elect to be subject to paragraphs (g)(1) or (2) of this section. A Noncommercial Educational Webcaster required to report pursuant to this paragraph (g)(3) shall provide reports of use to the Collective quarterly on a census reporting basis (*i.e.*, reports of use shall include every sound recording performed in the relevant quarter), containing information otherwise complying with applicable regulations (but no less information than required by § 370.4 of this chapter), except that, notwithstanding § 370.4(d)(2)(vi), such a Noncommercial Educational Webcaster shall not be required to include ATH or actual total performances, and may in lieu thereof provide channel or station name and play frequency, during the first calendar year it reports in accordance with this paragraph (g)(3). For the avoidance of doubt, after a Noncommercial Educational Webcaster has been required to report in accordance with this paragraph (g)(3) for a full calendar year, it must thereafter include ATH or actual total performances in its reports of use. All reports of use under this paragraph (g)(3) shall be submitted to the Collective no later than the 45th day after the end of each calendar quarter.

(h) *Distribution of royalties.* (1) The Collective shall promptly distribute royalties received from Noncommercial Educational Webcasters to Copyright Owners and Performers, or their designated agents, that are entitled to such royalties. The Collective shall only be responsible for making distributions to those Copyright Owners, Performers, or their designated agents who provide the Collective with such information as is necessary to identify and pay the correct recipient. The Collective shall distribute royalties on a basis that values all performances by a Noncommercial Educational Webcaster equally based upon the information provided under the report of use requirements for Noncommercial Educational Webcasters contained in § 370.4 of this chapter and this subpart, except that in the case of Noncommercial Educational Webcasters that elect to pay a Proxy Fee in lieu of providing reports of use pursuant to paragraph (g)(1) of this section, the Collective shall distribute the aggregate royalties paid by electing Noncommercial Educational Webcasters based on proxy usage data in accordance with a methodology adopted by the Collective's Board of Directors.

(2) If the Collective is unable to locate a Copyright Owner or Performer entitled to a distribution of royalties under paragraph (h)(1) of this section within 3 years from the date of payment by a Noncommercial Educational Webcaster, such distribution may first be applied to the costs directly attributable to the administration of that distribution. The foregoing shall apply notwithstanding the common law or statutes of any State.

(i) *Server logs.* Noncommercial Educational Webcasters shall retain for a period of no less than three full calendar years server logs sufficient to substantiate all information relevant to eligibility, rate calculation and reporting under this subpart. To the extent that a third-party Web hosting or service provider maintains equipment or software for a Noncommercial Educational Webcaster and/or such third party creates, maintains, or can reasonably create such server logs, the Noncommercial Educational Webcaster shall direct that such server logs be created and maintained by said third party for a period of no less than three full calendar years and/or that such server logs be provided to, and maintained by, the Noncommercial Educational Webcaster.

§380.24 Confidential Information.

(a) *Definition.* For purposes of this subpart, "Confidential Information" shall include the statements of account and any information contained therein, including the amount of Usage Fees paid, and any information pertaining to the statements of account reasonably designated as confidential by the Noncommercial Educational Webcaster submitting the statement.

(b) *Exclusion.* Confidential Information shall not include documents or information that at the time of delivery to the Collective are public knowledge. The party claiming the benefit of this provision shall have the burden of proving that the disclosed information was public knowledge.

(c) *Use of Confidential Information.* In no event shall the Collective use any Confidential Information for any purpose other than royalty collection and distribution and activities related directly thereto.

(d) *Disclosure of Confidential Information.* Access to Confidential Information shall be limited to:

(1) Those employees, agents, attorneys, consultants and independent contractors of the Collective, subject to an appropriate confidentiality agreement, who are engaged in the collection and distribution of royalty payments hereunder and activities related thereto, for the purpose of performing such duties during the ordinary course of their work and who require access to Confidential Information;

(2) An independent Qualified Auditor, subject to an appropriate confidentiality agreement, who is authorized to act on behalf of the Collective with respect to verification of a Noncommercial Educational Webcaster's statement of account pursuant to §380.25 or on behalf of a Copyright Owner or Performer with respect to the verification of royalty distributions pursuant to §380.26;

(3) Copyright Owners and Performers, including their designated agents, whose works have been used under the statutory licenses set forth in 17 U.S.C. 112(e) and 114(f) by the Noncommercial Educational Webcaster whose Confidential Information is being supplied, subject to an appropriate confidentiality agreement, and including those employees, agents, attorneys, consultants and independent contractors of such Copyright Owners and Performers and their designated agents, subject to an appropriate confidentiality agreement, for the purpose of performing their duties during the ordinary course of their work and who require access to the Confidential Information; and

(4) In connection with future proceedings under 17 U.S.C. 112(e) and 114(f) before the Copyright Royalty Judges, and under an appropriate protective order, attorneys, consultants and other authorized agents of the parties to the proceedings or the courts.

(e) *Safeguarding of Confidential Information.* The Collective and any person identified in paragraph (d) of this section shall implement procedures to safeguard against unauthorized access to or dissemination of any Confidential Information using a reasonable standard of care, but no less than the same degree of security used to protect Confidential Information or similarly sensitive information belonging to the Collective or person.

§380.25 Verification of royalty payments.

(a) *General.* This section prescribes procedures by which the Collective may verify the royalty payments made by a Noncommercial Educational Webcaster.

(b) *Frequency of verification.* The Collective may conduct a single audit of a Noncommercial Educational Webcaster, upon reasonable notice and during reasonable business hours, during any given calendar year, for any or all of the prior 3 calendar years, but no calendar year shall be subject to audit more than once.

(c) *Notice of intent to audit.* The Collective must file with the Copyright Royalty Board a notice of intent to audit a particular Noncommercial Educational Webcaster, which shall, within 30 days of the filing of the notice, publish in the FEDERAL REGISTER a notice announcing such filing. The notification of intent to audit shall be served at the same time on the Noncommercial Educational Webcaster to be audited. Any such audit shall be conducted by an independent Qualified Auditor identified in the notice and shall be binding on all parties.

(d) *Acquisition and retention of report.* The Noncommercial Educational Webcaster shall use commercially reasonable efforts to obtain or to provide access to any relevant books and records maintained by third parties for the purpose of the audit. The Collective shall retain the report of the verification for a period of not less than 3 years.

(e) *Acceptable verification procedure.* An audit, including underlying paperwork, which was performed in the ordinary course of business according to generally accepted auditing standards by an independent Qualified Auditor, shall serve as an acceptable verification procedure for all parties with respect to the information that is within the scope of the audit.

(f) *Consultation.* Before rendering a written report to the Collective, except where the auditor has a reasonable basis to suspect fraud and disclosure would, in the reasonable opinion of the auditor, prejudice the investigation of such suspected fraud, the auditor shall review the tentative written findings of the audit with the appropriate agent or employee of the Noncommercial Educational Webcaster being audited in order to remedy any factual errors and clarify any issues relating to the audit; Provided that an appropriate agent or employee of the Noncommercial Educational Webcaster reasonably cooperates with the auditor to remedy promptly any factual errors or clarify any issues raised by the audit.

(g) *Costs of the verification procedure.* The Collective shall pay the cost of the verification procedure, unless it is finally determined that there was an underpayment of 10% or more, in which case the Noncommercial Educational Webcaster shall, in addition to paying the amount of any underpayment, bear the reasonable costs of the verification procedure.

§ 380.26 Verification of royalty distributions.

(a) *General.* This section prescribes procedures by which any Copyright Owner or Performer may verify the royalty distributions made by the Collective; Provided, however, that nothing contained in this section shall apply to situations where a Copyright Owner or Performer and the Collective have agreed as to proper verification methods.

(b) *Frequency of verification.* A Copyright Owner or Performer may conduct a single audit of the Collective upon reasonable notice and during reasonable business hours, during any given calendar year, for any or all of the prior 3 calendar years, but no calendar year shall be subject to audit more than once.

(c) *Notice of intent to audit.* A Copyright Owner or Performer must file with the Copyright Royalty Board a notice of intent to audit the Collective, which shall, within 30 days of the filing of the notice, publish in the FEDERAL REGISTER a notice announcing such filing. The notification of intent to audit shall be served at the same time on the Collective. Any audit shall be conducted by an independent Qualified Auditor identified in the notice, and shall be binding on all Copyright Owners and Performers.

(d) *Acquisition and retention of report.* The Collective shall use commercially reasonable efforts to obtain or to provide access to any relevant books and records maintained by third parties for the purpose of the audit. The Copyright Owner or Performer requesting the verification procedure shall retain the report of the verification for a period of not less than 3 years.

(e) *Acceptable verification procedure.* An audit, including underlying paperwork, which was performed in the ordinary course of business according to generally accepted auditing standards by an independent Qualified Auditor, shall serve as an acceptable verification procedure for all parties with respect to the information that is within the scope of the audit.

(f) *Consultation.* Before rendering a written report to a Copyright Owner or Performer, except where the auditor has a reasonable basis to suspect fraud and disclosure would, in the reasonable opinion of the auditor, prejudice the investigation of such suspected fraud, the auditor shall review the tentative written findings of the audit with the appropriate agent or employee of the Collective in order to remedy any factual errors and clarify any issues relating to the audit; Provided that the appropriate agent or employee of the Collective reasonably cooperates with the auditor to remedy promptly any factual errors or clarify any issues raised by the audit.

(g) *Costs of the verification procedure.* The Copyright Owner or Performer requesting the verification procedure shall pay the cost of the procedure, unless it is finally determined that there was an underpayment of 10% or more, in which case the Collective shall, in addition to paying the amount of any underpayment, bear the reasonable costs of the verification procedure.

§ 380.27 Unclaimed funds.

If the Collective is unable to identify or locate a Copyright Owner or Performer who is entitled to receive a royalty distribution under this subpart, the Collective shall retain the required payment in a segregated trust account for a period of 3 years from the date of distribution. No claim to such distribution shall be valid after the expiration of the 3-year period. After expiration of this period, the Collective may apply the unclaimed funds to offset any costs deductible under 17 U.S.C. 114(g)(3). The foregoing shall apply notwithstanding the common law or statutes of any State.

PART 381—USE OF CERTAIN COPYRIGHTED WORKS IN CONNECTION WITH NONCOMMERCIAL EDUCATIONAL BROADCASTING

Sec.

AUTHORITY: 17 U.S.C. 118, 801(b)(1) and 803.

SOURCE: 72 FR 67647, Nov. 30, 2007, unless otherwise noted.

§ 381.1 General.

This part establishes terms and rates of royalty payments for certain activities using published nondramatic musical works and published pictorial, graphic and sculptural works during a period beginning on January 1, 2013, and ending on December 31, 2017. Upon compliance with 17 U.S.C. 118, and the terms and rates of this part, a public broadcasting entity may engage in the activities with respect to such works set forth in 17 U.S.C. 118(c).

[72 FR 67647, Nov. 30, 2007, as amended at 77 FR 71105, Nov. 29, 2012]

§ 381.2 Definition of public broadcasting entity.

As used in this part, the term *public broadcasting entity* means a noncommercial educational broadcast station as defined in section 397 of title 47 and any nonprofit institution or organization engaged in the activities described in 17 U.S.C. 118(c).

§ 381.3 [Reserved]

§ 381.4 Performance of musical compositions by PBS, NPR and other public broadcasting entities engaged in the activities set forth in 17 U.S.C. 118(c).

The following schedule of rates and terms shall apply to the performance by PBS, NPR and other public broadcasting entities engaged in activities set forth in 17 U.S.C. 118(c) of copyrighted published nondramatic musical compositions, except for public broadcasting entities covered by §§ 381.5 and 381.6, and except for compositions which are the subject of voluntary license agreements.

(a) *Determination of royalty rate.*

(1) For performance of such work in a feature presentation of PBS:	
2013–2017	$232.18
(2) For performance of such a work as background or theme music in a PBS program:	
2013–2017	$58.51
(3) For performance of such a work in a feature presentation of a station of PBS:	
2013–2017	$19.84
(4) For performance of such a work as background or theme music in a program of a station of PBS:	
2013–2017	$4.18
(5) For the performance of such a work in a feature presentation of NPR:	
2013–2017	$23.53
(6) For the performance of such a work as background or theme music in an NPR program:	
2013–2017	$5.70
(7) For the performance of such a work in a feature presentation of a station of NPR:	
2013–2017	$1.66
(8) For the performance of such a work as background or theme music in a program of a station of NPR:	
2013–2017	$.59

(9) For purposes of this schedule the rate for the performance of theme music in an entire series shall be double the single program theme rate.

(10) In the event the work is first performed in a program of a station of PBS or NPR, and such program is subsequently distributed by PBS or NPR, an additional royalty payment shall be made equal to the difference between the rate specified in this section for a program of a station of PBS or NPR, respectively, and the rate specified in this section for a PBS or NPR program, respectively.

(b) *Payment of royalty rate.* The required royalty rate shall be paid to each known copyright owner not later than July 31 of each calendar year for uses during the first six months of that calendar year, and not later than January 31 for uses during the last six months of the preceding calendar year.

(c) *Records of use.* PBS and NPR shall, upon the request of a copyright owner of a published musical work who believes a musical composition of such owner has been performed under the terms of this schedule, permit such copyright owner a reasonable opportunity to examine their standard cue sheets listing the nondramatic performances of musical compositions on PBS and NPR programs. Any local PBS and NPR station that shall be required by the provisions of any voluntary license agreement with ASCAP, BMI or SESAC covering the license period January 1, 2013, to December 31, 2017, to provide a music use report shall, upon request of a copyright owner who believes a musical composition of such owner has been performed under the terms of this schedule, permit such copyright owner to examine the report.

(d) *Terms of use.* The fees provided in this schedule for the performance of a musical work in a program shall cover performances of such work in such program for a period of four years following the first performance.

[72 FR 67647, Nov. 30, 2007, as amended at 77 FR 71105, Nov. 29, 2012]

§ 381.5 Performance of musical compositions by public broadcasting entities licensed to colleges and universities.

(a) *Scope.* This section applies to the performance of copyrighted published nondramatic musical compositions by noncommercial radio stations which are licensed to accredited colleges, accredited universities, or other accredited nonprofit educational institutions and which are not affiliated with National Public Radio. For purposes of this section, accreditation of institutions providing post-secondary education shall be determined by a regional or national accrediting agency recognized by the Council for Higher Education Accreditation or the United States Department of Education; and accreditation of institutions providing elementary or secondary education shall be as recognized by the applicable state licensing authority.

(b) *Voluntary license agreements.* Notwithstanding the schedule of rates and terms established in this section, the rates and terms of any license agreements entered into by copyright owners and colleges, universities, and other nonprofit educational institutions concerning the performance of copyrighted musical compositions, including performances by noncommercial radio stations, shall apply in lieu of the rates and terms of this section.

(c) *Royalty rate.* A public broadcasting entity within the scope of this section may perform published nondramatic musical compositions subject to the following schedule of royalty rates:

(1) For all such compositions in the repertory of ASCAP, the royalty rates shall be as follows:

(i)

	Number of full-time students	2013	2014	2015	2016	2017
Level 1	<1,000	$319	$325	$332	$339	$345
Level 2	1,000–4,999	369	376	384	392	399
Level 3	5,000–9,999	505	515	525	535	546
Level 4	10,000–19,999	655	668	681	695	708
Level 5	20,000 +	822	838	855	872	890

(ii) Level 1 rates as set forth in paragraph (c)(1)(i) of this section, shall also apply to College Radio Stations with an authorized effective radiated power (ERP), as that term is defined in 47 CFR 73.310(a), of 100 Watts or less, as specified on its current FCC license, regardless of the size of the student population.

(2) For all such compositions in the repertory of BMI, the royalty rates shall be as follows:

(i)

	Number of full-time students	2013	2014	2015	2016	2017
Level 1	<1,000	$319	$325	$332	$339	$345
Level 2	1,000–4,999	369	376	384	392	399
Level 3	5,000–9,999	505	515	525	535	546
Level 4	10,000–19,999	655	668	681	695	708
Level 5	20,000 +	822	838	855	872	890

(ii) Level 1 rates, as set forth in paragraph (c)(2)(i) of this section, shall also apply to College Radio Stations with an authorized effective radiated power (ERP), as that term is defined in 47 CFR 73.310(a), of 100 Watts or less, as specified on its current FCC license, regardless of the size of the student population.

(3) For all such compositions in the repertory of SESAC, the royalty rates shall be as follows:

(i) 2013: $140.00 per station;

(ii) 2014: $140 per station, subject to an annual cost of living adjustment in accordance with paragraph (c)(3)(vi) of this section;

(iii) 2015: The 2014 rate, subject to an annual cost of living adjustment in accordance with paragraph (c)(3)(vi) of this section;

(iv) 2016: The 2015 rate, subject to an annual cost of living adjustment in accordance with paragraph (c)(3)(vi) of this section;

(v) 2017: The 2016 rate, subject to an annual cost of living adjustment in accordance with paragraph (c)(3)(vi) of this section.

(vi) Such cost of living adjustment to be made in accordance with the greater of

(A) The change, if any, in the Consumer Price Index (all consumers, all items) published by the U.S. Department of Labor, Bureau of Labor Statistics during the twelve (12) month period from the most recent Index, published before December 1 of the year immediately prior to the applicable year, or

(B) Two percent (2%).

(4) For the performance of any other such compositions: $1.

(d) *Payment of royalty rate.* The public broadcasting entity shall pay the required royalty rate to ASCAP, BMI and SESAC not later than January 31 of each year. Each annual payment to ASCAP, BMI and SESAC shall be accompanied by a signed declaration stating the number of full-time students enrolled in the educational entity operating the station and/or the effective radiated power (ERP) as specified in its current FCC license. An exact copy of such declaration shall be furnished to each of ASCAP, BMI and SESAC.

(e) *Records of use.* A public broadcasting entity subject to this section shall furnish to ASCAP, BMI and SESAC, upon request, a music-use report during one week of each calendar year. ASCAP, BMI and SESAC shall not in any one calendar year request more than 10 stations to furnish such reports.

[72 FR 67647, Nov. 30, 2007, as amended at 73 FR 72726, Dec. 1, 2008; 74 FR 62705, Dec. 1, 2009; 75 FR 74623, Dec. 1, 2010; 76 FR 74703, Dec. 1, 2011; 77 FR 71105, Nov. 29, 2012]

§ 381.6 Performance of musical compositions by other public broadcasting entities.

(a) *Scope.* This section applies to the performance of copyrighted published nondramatic musical compositions by radio stations not licensed to colleges, universities, or other nonprofit educational institutions and which are not affiliated with NPR. In the event that a station owned by a public broadcasting entity broadcasts programming by means of an in-band, on-channel ("IBOC") digital radio signal and such programming is different than the station's analog broadcast programming, then any such programming shall be deemed to be provided by a separate station requiring a separate royalty payment.

(b) *Definitions.* As used in paragraphs (d) and (e) of this section, the following terms and their variant forms mean the following:

(1) *Feature Music* shall mean any performance of a musical work, whether live or recorded, that is the principal focus of audience attention. Feature Music does not include bridge, background, or underscore music, themes or signatures, interstitial music between programs such as in public service announcements or program sponsorship identifications, brief musical transitions in and out of program segments (not to exceed 60 seconds in duration), incidental performances of music during broadcasts of public, religious, or sports events, or brief performances during news, talk, religious, and sports programming of no more than 30 seconds in duration.

(2) *Population Count.* The combination of:

(i) The number of persons estimated to reside within a station's Predicted 60 dBu Contour, based on the most recent available census data; and

(ii) The nonduplicative number of persons estimated to reside in the Predicted 60 dBu Contour of any Translator or Booster Station that extends a public broadcasting entity's signal beyond the contours of a station's Predicted 60 dBu Contour.

(iii) In determining Population Count, a station or a Translator or Booster Station may use and report the total population data, from a research company generally recognized in the broadcasting industry, for the radio market within which the station's community license is located.

(3) *Predicted 60 dBu Contour* shall be calculated as set forth in 47 CFR 73.313.

(4) *Talk Format Station* shall mean a noncommercial radio station:

(i) Whose program content primarily consists of talk shows, news programs, sports, community affairs or religious sermons (or other non-music-oriented programming);

(ii) That performs Feature Music in less than 20% of its programming annually; and

(iii) That performs music-oriented programming for no more than four (4) programming hours during the hours from 6 a.m. to 10 p.m. each weekday, with no two (2) hours of such programming occurring consecutively, with the exception of up to five (5) weekdays during the year.

(5) *Weekday* shall mean the 24-hour period starting at 12 a.m. through 11:59 p.m. on Mondays, Tuesdays, Wednesdays, Thursdays and Fridays occurring

between January 1 of a given year up to and including Thanksgiving day of that year.

(6) *Translator Station* and *Booster Station* shall have the same meanings as set forth in 47 CFR 74.1201.

(c) *Voluntary license agreements.* Notwithstanding the schedule of rates and terms established in this section, the rates and terms of any license agreements entered into by copyright owners and noncommercial radio stations within the scope of this section concerning the performance of copyrighted musical compositions, including performances by noncommercial radio stations, shall apply in lieu of the rates and terms of this section.

(d) *Royalty rate.* A public broadcasting entity within the scope of this section may perform published nondramatic musical compositions subject to the following schedule of royalty rates:

(1) For all such compositions in the repertory of ASCAP, the royalty rates shall be as follows:

(i) Music Fees (Stations with 20% or more programming containing Feature Music):

	Population count	2013	2014	2015	2016	2017
Level 1	0–249,999	$631	$644	$657	$670	$683
Level 2	250,000–499,999	1,126	1,149	1,171	1,195	1,219
Level 3	500,000–999,999	1,688	1,722	1,756	1,791	1,827
Level 4	1,000,000–1,499,999.	2,251	2,296	2,342	2,389	2,437
Level 5	1,500,000–1,999,999.	2,814	2,870	2,928	2,986	3,046
Level 6	2,000,000–2,499,999.	3,377	3,445	3,513	3,584	3,655
Level 7	2,500,000–2,999,999.	3,939	4,018	4,098	4,180	4,264
Level 8	3,000,000 and above.	5,628	5,741	5,855	5,972	6,092

(ii) Talk Format Station Fees (Stations with <20% Feature Music programming):

	Population count	2013	2014	2015	2016	2017
Level 1	0–249,999	$631	$644	$657	$670	$683
Level 2	250,000–499,999	631	644	657	670	683
Level 3	500,000–999,999	631	644	657	670	683
Level 4	1,000,000–1,499,999.	788	804	820	836	853
Level 5	1,500,000–1,999,999.	985	1,005	1,025	1,045	1,066
Level 6	2,000,000–2,499,999.	1,182	1,206	1,230	1,254	1,279
Level 7	2,500,000–2,999,999.	1,379	1,406	1,434	1,463	1,492
Level 8	3,000,000 and above.	1,970	2,009	2,049	2,090	2,132

(2) For all such compositions in the repertory of BMI, the royalty rates shall be as follows:

(i) Music Fees (Stations with 20% or more programming containing Feature Music):

	Population count	2013	2014	2015	2016	2017
Level 1	0–249,999	$631	$644	$657	$670	$683
Level 2	250,000–499,999	1,126	1,149	1,171	1,195	1,219
Level 3	500,000–999,999	1,688	1,722	1,756	1,791	1,827
Level 4	1,000,000–1,499,999.	2,251	2,296	2,342	2,389	2,437
Level 5	1,500,000–1,999,999.	2,814	2,870	2,928	2,986	3,046

	Population count	2013	2014	2015	2016	2017
Level 6	2,000,000–2,499,999.	3,377	3,445	3,513	3,584	3,655
Level 7	2,500,000–2,999,999.	3,939	4,018	4,098	4,180	4,264
Level 8	3,000,000 and above.	5,628	5,741	5,855	5,972	6,092

(ii) Talk Format Station Fees (Stations with <20% Feature Music programming):

	Population count	2013	2014	2015	2016	2017
Level 1	0–249,999	$631	$644	$657	$670	$683
Level 2	250,000–499,999	631	644	657	670	683
Level 3	500,000–999,999	631	644	657	670	683
Level 4	1,000,000–1,499,999.	788	804	820	836	853
Level 5	1,500,000–1,999,999.	985	1,005	1,025	1,045	1,066
Level 6	2,000,000–2,499,999.	1,182	1,206	1,230	1,254	1,279
Level 7	2,500,000–2,999,999.	1,379	1,406	1,434	1,463	1,492
Level 8	3,000,000 and above.	1,970	2,009	2,049	2,090	2,132

(3) For all such compositions in the repertory of SESAC, the royalty rates shall be as follows:

(i) Music fees for stations with >=20% Feature Music programming:

	Population count	2013	2014	2015	2016	2017
Level 1	0–249,999	$138	$140	$143	$146	$149
Level 2	250,000–499,999	230	234	239	244	248
Level 3	500,000–999,999	345	352	359	366	373
Level 4	1,000,000–1,499,999.	459	468	478	487	497
Level 5	1,500,000–1,999,999.	574	586	597	609	622
Level 6	2,000,000–2,499,999.	689	702	716	731	745
Level 7	2,500,000–2,999,999.	804	820	836	853	870
Level 8	3,000,000 and above.	1,149	1,171	1,195	1,219	1,243

(ii) Talk fees for stations with <20% Feature Music programming:

	Population count	2013	2014	2015	2016	2017
Level 1	0–249,999	$138	$140	$143	$146	$149
Level 2	250,000–499,999	138	140	143	146	149
Level 3	500,000–999,999	138	140	143	146	149
Level 4	1,000,000–1,499,999.	161	164	167	170	174
Level 5	1,500,000–1,999,999.	201	205	209	213	218
Level 6	2,000,000–2,499,999.	241	246	251	256	261
Level 7	2,500,000–2,999,999.	281	287	293	299	305

	Population count	2013	2014	2015	2016	2017
Level 8	3,000,000 and above.	402	410	418	427	435

(4) For the performance of any other such compositions, in 2013 through 2017, $1.

(e) *Payment of royalty rate.* The public broadcasting entity shall pay the required royalty rate to ASCAP, BMI and SESAC not later than January 31 of each year. Each annual payment shall be accompanied by a signed declaration stating the Population Count of the public broadcasting entity and the source for such Population Count. An exact copy of such declaration shall be furnished to each of ASCAP, BMI and SESAC. Upon prior written notice thereof from ASCAP, BMI and SESAC, a public broadcasting entity shall make its books and records relating to its Population Count available for inspection. In the event that a public broadcasting entity wishes to be deemed a Talk Format Station, then such entity shall provide a signed declaration stating that Feature Music is performed in less than 20% of its annual programming and that it complies with the caps set forth in paragraph (b)(4) of this section. An exact copy of such declaration shall be furnished to each of ASCAP, BMI and SESAC. Upon prior written notice thereof from ASCAP, BMI or SESAC, a public broadcasting entity shall make its program schedule or other documentation supporting its eligibility as a Talk Format Station available for inspection.

(f) *Records of use.* A public broadcasting entity subject to this section shall furnish to ASCAP, BMI and SESAC, upon request, a music-use report during one week of each calendar year. ASCAP, BMI and SESAC each shall not in any one calendar year request more than 10 stations to furnish such reports.

[72 FR 67647, Nov. 30, 2007, as amended at 77 FR 71106, Nov. 29, 2012]

§381.7 Recording rights, rates and terms.

(a) *Scope.* This section establishes rates and terms for the recording of nondramatic performances and displays of musical works, other than compositions subject to voluntary license agreements, on and for the radio and television programs of public broadcasting entities, whether or not in synchronization or timed relationship with the visual or aural content, and for the making, reproduction, and distribution of copies and phonorecords of public broadcasting programs containing such nondramatic performances and displays of musical works solely for the purpose of transmission by public broadcasting entities. The rates and terms established in this schedule include the making of the reproductions described in 17 U.S.C. 118(c)(3).

(b) *Royalty rate.* (1)(i) For uses described in paragraph (a) of this section of a musical work in a PBS-distributed program, the royalty fees shall be calculated by multiplying the following per-composition rates by the number of different compositions in that PBS-distributed program:

	2013–2017
(A) Feature	$116.37
(B) Concert feature (per minute)	34.95
(C) Background	58.81
(D) Theme:	
(*1*) Single program or first series program	58.81
(*2*) Other series program	23.88

(ii) For such uses other than in a PBS-distributed television program, the royalty fee shall be calculated by multiplying the following per-composition rates by the number of different compositions in that program:

	2013–2017
(A) Feature	$ 9.62
(B) Concert feature (per minute)	2.53
(C) Background	4.18
(D) Theme:	
(*1*) Single program or first series of program	4.18
(*2*) Other series program	1.66

(iii) In the event the work is first recorded other than in a PBS-distributed program, and such program is subsequently distributed by PBS, an additional royalty payment shall be made equal to the difference between the rate specified in this section for other than a PBS-distributed program and the rate specified in this section for a PBS-distributed program.

(2) For uses licensed herein of a musical work in a NPR program, the royalty fees shall be calculated by multiplying the following per-composition rates by the number of different compositions in any NPR program distributed by NPR. For purposes of this schedule "National Public Radio" programs include all programs produced in whole or in part by NPR, or by any NPR station or organization under contract with NPR.

	2013–2017
(i) Feature	$ 12.60
(ii) Concert feature (per minute)	18.49
(iii) Background	6.31
(iv) Theme:	
(A) Single program or first series program	6.31
(B) Other series program	2.52

(3) For purposes of this schedule, a "Concert Feature" shall be deemed to be the nondramatic presentation in a program of all or part of a symphony, concerto, or other serious work originally written for concert performance, or the nondramatic presentation in a program of portions of a serious work originally written for opera performance.

(4) For such uses other than in an NPR-produced radio program:

	2013–2017
(i) Feature	$.79
(ii) Feature (concert) (per half hour)	1.65
(iii) Background	.40

(5) The schedule of fees covers use for a period of three years following the first use. Succeeding use periods will require the following additional payment: Additional one-year period—25 percent of the initial three-year fee; second three-year period—50 percent of the initial three-year fee; each three-year fee thereafter—25 percent of the initial three-year fee; provided that a 100 percent additional payment prior to the expiration of the first three-year period will cover use during all subsequent use periods without limitation. Such succeeding uses which are subsequent to December 31, 2017, shall be subject to the royalty rates established in this schedule.

(c) *Payment of royalty rates.* The required royalty rates shall be paid to each known copyright owner not later than July 31 of each calendar year for uses during the first six months of that calendar year, and not later than January 31 for uses during the last six months of the preceding calendar year.

(d) *Records of use*—(1) *Maintenance of cue sheets.* PBS and its stations, NPR, or other public broadcasting entities shall maintain and make available for examination pursuant to paragraph (e) of this section copies of their standard cue sheets or summaries of same listing the recording of the musical works of such copyright owners.

(2) *Content of cue sheets or summaries.* Such cue sheets or summaries shall include:

(i) The title, composer and author to the extent such information is reasonably obtainable.

(ii) The type of use and manner of performance thereof in each case.

(iii) For Concert Feature music, the actual recorded time period on the program, plus all distribution and broadcast information available to the public broadcasting entity.

(e) *Filing of use reports with the Copyright Royalty Judges. Deposit of cue sheets or summaries.* PBS and its stations, NPR, or other television public broadcasting entity shall deposit with the Copyright Royalty Judges one electronic copy in Portable Document Format (PDF) on compact disk (an optical data storage medium such as a CD-ROM, CD-R or CD-RW) or floppy diskette of their standard music cue sheets or summaries of same listing the recording pursuant to this schedule of the musical works of copyright owners. Such cue sheets or summaries shall be deposited not later than July 31 of each calendar year for recordings during the first six months of the calendar year and not later than January 31 of each calendar year for recordings during the second six months of the preceding calendar year. PBS and NPR shall maintain at their offices copies of all standard music cue sheets from which such music use reports are prepared. Such music cue sheets shall be furnished to the Copyright Royalty Judges upon their request and also shall be available during regular business hours at the offices of PBS or NPR for examination by a copyright owner who believes a musical composition of such owner has been recorded pursuant to this schedule.

[72 FR 67647, Nov. 30, 2007, as amended at 77 FR 71108, Nov. 29, 2012]

§ 381.8 Terms and rates of royalty payments for the use of published pictorial, graphic, and sculptural works.

(a) *Scope.* This section establishes rates and terms for the use of published pictorial, graphic, and sculptural works by public broadcasting entities for the activities described in 17 U.S.C. 118. The rates and terms established in this schedule include the making of the reproductions described in 17 U.S.C. 118(c).

(b) *Royalty rate.* (1) The following schedule of rates shall apply to the use of works within the scope of this section: (i) For such uses in a PBS-distributed program:

	2013–2017
(A) For featured display of a work	$70.75
(B) For background and montage display	34.50
(C) For use of a work for program identification or for thematic use	139.46
(D) For the display of an art reproduction copyrighted separately from the work of fine art from which the work was reproduced irrespective of whether the reproduced work of fine art is copyrighted so as to be subject also to payment of a display fee under the terms of the schedule	45.82

(ii) For such uses in other than PBS-distributed programs:

	2013–2017
(A) For featured display of a work	$45.82
(B) For background and montage display	23.48
(C) For use of a work for program identification or for thematic use	93.65
(D) For the display of an art reproduction copyrighted separately from the work of fine art from which the work was reproduced irrespective of whether the reproduced work of fine art is copyrighted so as to be subject also to payment of a display fee under the terms of the schedule	23.49

(2) For the purposes of the schedule in paragraph (b)(1) of this section the rate for the thematic use of a work in an entire series shall be double the single program theme rate. In the event the work is first used other than in a PBS-distributed program, and such program is subsequently distributed by PBS, an additional royalty payment shall be made equal to the difference between the rate specified in this section for other than a PBS-distributed program and the rate specified in this section for a PBS-distributed program.

(3) "Featured display" for purposes of this schedule means a full-screen or substantially full-screen display appearing on the screen for more than three seconds. Any display less than full-screen or substantially full-screen, or full-screen for three seconds or less, is deemed to be a "background or montage display".

(4) "Thematic use" is the utilization of the works of one or more artists where the works constitute the central theme of the program or convey a story line.

(5) "Display of an art reproduction copyrighted separately from the work of fine art from which the work was reproduced" means a transparency or other reproduction of an underlying work of fine art.

(c) *Payment of royalty rate.* PBS or other public broadcasting entity shall pay the required royalty fees to each copyright owner not later than July 31 of each calendar year for uses during the first six months of that calendar year, and not later than January 31 for uses during the last six months of the preceding calendar year.

(d) *Records of use.* (1) PBS and its stations or other public broadcasting entity shall maintain and furnish either to copyright owners, or to the offices of generally recognized organizations representing the copyright owners of pictorial, graphic and sculptural works, copies of their standard lists containing the pictorial, graphic, and sculptural works displayed on their programs. Such notice shall include the name of the copyright owner, if known, the specific source from which the work was taken, a description of the work used, the title of the program on which the work was used, and the date of the original broadcast of the program.

(2) Such listings shall be furnished not later than July 31 of each calendar year for displays during the first six months of the calendar year, and not later than January 31 of each calendar year for displays during the second six months of the preceding calendar year.

(e) *Filing of use reports with the Copyright Royalty Judges.* (1) PBS and its stations or other public broadcasting entity shall deposit with the Copyright Royalty Judges one electronic copy in Portable Document Format (PDF) on compact disk (an optical data storage medium such as a CD-ROM, CD-R or CD-RW) or floppy diskette of their standard lists containing the pictorial, graphic, and sculptural works displayed on their programs. Such notice shall include the name of the copyright owner, if known, the specific source from which the work was taken, a description of the work used, the title of the program on which the work was used, and the date of the original broadcast of the program.

(2) Such listings shall be furnished not later than July 31 of each calendar year for displays during the first six months of the calendar year, and not later than January 31 of each calendar year for displays during the second six months of the preceding calendar year.

(f) *Terms of use.* (1) The rates of this schedule are for unlimited use for a period of three years from the date of the first use of the work under this schedule. Succeeding use periods will require the following additional payment: Additional one-year period—25 percent of the initial three-year fee; second three-year period—50 percent of the initial three-year fee; each three-year period thereafter—25 percent of the initial three-year fee; provided that a 100 percent additional payment prior to the expiration of the first three-year period will cover use during all subsequent use periods without limitation. Such succeeding uses which are subsequent to December 31, 2017, shall be subject to the rates established in this schedule.

(2) Pursuant to the provisions of 17 U.S.C. 118(e), nothing in this schedule shall be construed to permit, beyond the limits of fair use as provided in 17 U.S.C. 107, the production of a transmission program drawn to any substantial extent from a published compilation of pictorial, graphic, or sculptural works.

[72 FR 67647, Nov. 30, 2007, as amended at 77 FR 71108, Nov. 29, 2012]

§ 381.9 Unknown copyright owners.

If PBS and its stations, NPR and its stations, or other public broadcasting entity is not aware of the identity of, or unable to locate, a copyright owner who is entitled to receive a royalty payment under this part, they shall retain the required fee in a segregated trust account for a period of three years from the date of the required payment. No claim to such royalty fees shall be valid after the expiration of the three-year period. Public broadcasting entities may establish a joint trust fund for the purposes of this section. Public broadcasting entities shall make available to the Copyright Royalty Judges, upon request, information concerning fees deposited in trust funds.

§ 381.10 Cost of living adjustment.

(a) On or before December 1, 2013, the Copyright Royalty Judges shall publish in the FEDERAL REGISTER a notice of the change in the cost of living as determined by the Consumer Price Index (all consumers, all items) during the period from the most recent Index published prior to December 1, 2012, to the most recent Index published prior to December 1, 2013. On or before each December 1 thereafter the Copyright Royalty Judges shall publish a notice of the change in the cost of living during the period from the most recent index published prior to the previous notice, to the most recent Index published prior to December 1, of that year.

(b) On the same date of the notices published pursuant to paragraph (a) of this section, the Copyright Royalty Judges shall publish in the FEDERAL

REGISTER a revised schedule of the rates for § 381.5(c)(3), the rate to be charged for compositions in the repertory of SESAC, which shall adjust the royalty amounts established in a dollar amount according to the greater of

(1) The change in the cost of living determined as provided in paragraph (a) of this section, or

(2) Two percent (2%).

(3) Such royalty rates shall be fixed at the nearest dollar.

(c) The adjusted schedule for the rates for § 381.5(c)(3) shall become effective thirty (30) days after publication in the FEDERAL REGISTER.

[72 FR 67647, Nov. 30, 2007, as amended at 77 FR 71109, Nov. 29, 2012]

§ 381.11 Notice of restrictions on use of reproductions of transmission programs.

Any public broadcasting entity which, pursuant to 17 U.S.C. 118, supplies a reproduction of a transmission program to governmental bodies or nonprofit institutions shall include with each copy of the reproduction a warning notice stating in substance that the reproductions may be used for a period of not more than seven days from the specified date of transmission, that the reproductions must be destroyed by the user before or at the end of such period, and that a failure to fully comply with these terms shall subject the body or institution to the remedies for infringement of copyright.

PART 382—RATES AND TERMS FOR DIGITAL TRANSMISSIONS OF SOUND RECORDINGS AND THE REPRODUCTION OF EPHEMERAL RECORDINGS BY PREEXISTING SUBSCRIPTION SERVICES AND PREEXISTING SATELLITE DIGITAL AUDIO RADIO SERVICES

Subpart A—Preexisting Subscription Services

Sec.

Subpart B—Preexisting Satellite Digital Audio Radio Services

AUTHORITY: 17 U.S.C. 112(e), 114 and 801(b)(1).

SOURCE: 72 FR 71796, Dec. 19, 2007, unless otherwise noted.

Subpart A—Preexisting Subscription Services

§ 382.1 General.

(a) This subpart establishes rates and terms of royalty payments for the public performance of sound recordings by nonexempt preexisting subscription services in accordance with the provisions of 17 U.S.C. 114, and the making of Ephemeral Recordings in connection with the public performance of sound recordings by nonexempt preexisting subscription services in accordance with the provisions of 17 U.S.C. 112(e).

(b) Upon compliance with 17 U.S.C. 114 and the terms and rates of this subpart, nonexempt preexisting subscription services may engage in the activities set forth in 17 U.S.C. 114(d)(2).

(c) Upon compliance with 17 U.S.C. 112(e) and the terms and rates of this subpart, nonexempt preexisting subscription services may engage in the activities set forth in 17 U.S.C. 112(e) without limit to the number of Ephemeral Recordings made.

[72 FR 71796, Dec. 19, 2007, as amended at 78 FR 23096, Apr. 17, 2013]

§ 382.2 Definitions.

For purposes of this subpart, the following definitions shall apply:

Collective is the collection and distribution organization that is designated by the Copyright Royalty Judges. For the 2013–2017 license term, the Collective is SoundExchange, Inc.

Copyright Owners are sound recording copyright owners who are entitled to royalty payments made under this subpart pursuant to the statutory licenses under 17 U.S.C. 112(e) and 114.

Ephemeral Recording is a phonorecord created for the purpose of facilitating a transmission of a public performance of a sound recording under a statutory license in accordance with 17 U.S.C. 114 and subject to the limitations specified in 17 U.S.C. 112(e).

GAAP shall mean generally accepted accounting principles in effect from time to time in the United States.

Gross Revenues. (1) Gross Revenues shall mean all monies derived from the operation of the programming service of the Licensee and shall be comprised of the following:

(i) Monies received by Licensee from Licensee's carriers and directly from residential U.S. subscribers for Licensee's programming service;

(ii) Licensee's advertising revenues (as billed), or other monies received from sponsors, if any, less advertising agency commissions not to exceed 15% of those fees incurred to a recognized advertising agency not owned or controlled by Licensee;

(iii) Monies received for the provision of time on the programming service to any third party;

(iv) Monies received from the sale of time to providers of paid programming such as infomercials;

(v) Where merchandise, service, or anything of value is received by Licensee in lieu of cash consideration for the use of Licensee's programming service, the fair market value thereof or Licensee's prevailing published rate, whichever is less;

(vi) Monies or other consideration received by Licensee from Licensee's carriers, but not including monies received by Licensee's carriers from others and not accounted for by Licensee's carriers to Licensee, for the provision of hardware by anyone and used in connection with the programming service;

(vii) Monies or other consideration received for any references to or inclusion of any product or service on the programming service; and

(viii) Bad debts recovered regarding paragraphs (1)(i) through (vii) of this definition.

(2) Gross Revenues shall include such payments as set forth in paragraphs (1)(i) through (viii) of this definition to which Licensee is entitled but which are paid to a parent, subsidiary, division, or affiliate of Licensee, in lieu of payment to Licensee but not including payments to Licensee's carriers for the programming service. Licensee shall be allowed a deduction from "Gross Revenues" as defined in paragraph (1) of this definition for affiliate revenue returned during the reporting period and for bad debts actually written off during reporting period.

Licensee means any preexisting subscription service as defined in 17 U.S.C. 114(j)(11).

Performers means the independent administrators identified in 17 U.S.C. 114(g)(2)(B) and (C), and the parties identified in 17 U.S.C. 114(g)(2)(D).

Qualified Auditor is a Certified Public Accountant.

[78 FR 23096, Apr. 17, 2013]

§ 382.3 Royalty fees for the digital performance of sound recordings and the making of ephemeral recordings by preexisting subscription services.

(a) Commencing January 1, 2013, and continuing through December 31, 2017, the monthly royalty fee to be paid by a Licensee for the public performance of sound recordings pursuant to 17 U.S.C. 114 and the making of any number of Ephemeral Recordings to facilitate such performances pursuant to 17 U.S.C. 112(e) shall be a percentage of monthly Gross Revenues resulting from residential services in the United States as follows: for 2013, 8%; and for 2014 through 2017, 8.5%.

(b) Each Licensee making digital performances of sound recordings pursuant to 17 U.S.C. 114 and Ephemeral Recordings pursuant to 17 U.S.C. 112(e) shall make an advance payment to the Collective of $100,000 per year, payable no later than January 20th of each year. The annual advance payment shall be nonrefundable, but it may be counted as an advance of the section

112 royalties due and payable for a given year or any month therein under paragraph (a) of this section; Provided, however, that any unused portion of an annual advance payment for a given year shall not carry over into a subsequent year.

(c) The royalty payable under 17 U.S.C. 112(e) for the making of phonorecords used by the Licensee solely to facilitate transmissions for which it pays royalties as and when provided in this subpart shall be included within, and constitute 5% of, the total royalties payable under 17 U.S.C. 112(e) and 114.

(d) A Licensee shall pay a late fee of 1.5% per month, or the highest lawful rate, whichever is lower, for each payment or statement of account, or either of them, received by the Collective after the due date. Late fees shall accrue from the due date until payment and the statement of account are received.

[78 FR 23096, Apr. 17, 2013]

§ 382.4 Terms for making payment of royalty fees and statements of account.

(a) *Payment to the Collective.* A Licensee shall make the royalty payments due under § 382.3 to the Collective.

(b) *Timing of payment.* A Licensee shall make any payments due under § 382.3 on a monthly basis on or before the 45th day after the end of each month for that month.

(c) *Statements of Account.* Licensees shall submit monthly statements of account on a form provided by the Collective. A statement of account shall contain the following information:

(1) Such information as is necessary to calculate the accompanying royalty payments;

(2) The name, address, business title, telephone number, facsimile (if any), electronic mail address and other contact information of the person to be contacted for information or questions concerning the content of the statement of account;

(3) The signature of a duly authorized officer or representative of the Licensee;

(4) The printed or typewritten name of the person signing the statement of account;

(5) The date of signature;

(6) The title or official position held in relation to the Licensee by the person signing the statement of account;

(7) A certification of the capacity of the person signing; and

(8) A statement to the following effect:

I, the undersigned officer or representative of the Licensee, have examined this statement of account and hereby state that it is true, accurate, and complete to my knowledge after reasonable due diligence.

(d) *Distribution of royalties.* (1) The Collective shall promptly distribute royalties received from Licensees to Copyright Owners and Performers, or their designated agents, that are entitled to such royalties. The Collective shall be responsible only for making distributions to those Copyright Owners, Performers, or their designated agents who provide the Collective with such information as is necessary to identify the correct recipient. The Collective shall distribute royalties on a basis that values all performances by a Licensee equally based upon the information provided under the reports of use requirements for Licensees contained in § 370.3 of this chapter.

(2) If the Collective is unable to locate a Copyright Owner or Performer entitled to a distribution of royalties under paragraph (d)(1) of this section within 3 years from the date of payment by a Licensee, such royalties shall be handled in accordance with § 382.8.

(e) *Retention of records.* Both Licensees and the Collective shall maintain books and records relating to the payment of the license fees in accordance with generally accepted accounting principles for a period of three years after the end of the period for which the payment is made. These records shall include, but are not limited to, the statements of account, records documenting an interested party's share of the royalty fees, and the records pertaining to the administration of the collection process and the further distribution of the royalty fees to those interested parties entitled to receive such fees.

[78 FR 23097, Apr. 17, 2013]

§ 382.5 Confidential information.

(a) For purposes of this subpart, confidential information shall include statements of account and any information pertaining to the statements of account designated as confidential by the nonexempt preexisting subscription service filing the statement. Confidential information shall also include any information so designated in a confidentiality agreement duly executed between a nonexempt preexisting subscription service and an interested party, or between one or more interested parties; Provided that all such information shall be made available, for the verification proceedings provided for in §§ 382.6 and 382.7.

(b) Access to the confidential information pertaining to the royalty payments shall be subject to an appropriate confidentiality agreement and limited to:

(1) Those employees, agents, consultants and independent contractors of the Collective who are engaged in the collection and distribution of royalty payments hereunder and activities directly related hereto, who are not also employees or officers of a sound recording Copyright Owner or Performer, and who, for the purpose of performing such duties during the ordinary course of employment, require access to the records; and

(2) An independent and Qualified Auditor who is not an employee or officer of a sound recording Copyright Owner or Performer, but is authorized to act on behalf of the interested Copyright Owners with respect to the verification of the royalty payments; and

(3) Copyright Owners and Performers whose works have been used under the statutory licenses set forth in 17 U.S.C. 112(e) and 114 by the Licensee whose Confidential Information is being supplied, or agents thereof provided that the only confidential information that may be shared pursuant to this paragraph (b)(3) are the monthly statements of account that accompany royalty payments.

(c) The Collective or any person identified in paragraph (b) of this section shall implement procedures to safeguard all confidential financial and business information, including, but not limited to royalty payments, submitted as part of the statements of account, using a reasonable standard of care, but no less than the same degree of security used to protect confidential financial and business information or similarly sensitive information belonging to the Collective or such person.

[72 FR 71796, Dec. 19, 2007. Redesignated at 78 FR 23096, Apr. 17, 2013 and amended at 78 FR 23097, Apr. 17, 2013]

§ 382.6 Verification of statements of account.

(a) *General.* This section prescribes general rules pertaining to the verification of the statements of account by interested parties according to terms promulgated by the Copyright Royalty Board.

(b) *Frequency of verification.* Interested parties may conduct a single audit of a nonexempt preexisting subscription service during any given calendar year.

(c) *Notice of intent to audit.* Interested parties must submit a notice of intent to audit a particular service to the Copyright Royalty Board, which shall publish in the FEDERAL REGISTER a notice announcing the receipt of the notice of intent to audit within 30 days of the filing of the interested party's notice. Such notification of intent to audit shall also be delivered at the same time to the party to be audited.

(d) *Retention of records.* The party requesting the verification procedure shall retain the report of the verification for a period of three years from the date of completion of the verification process.

(e) *Acceptable verification procedure.* An audit, including underlying paperwork, which was performed in the ordinary course of business according to generally accepted auditing standards by an independent and Qualified Auditor, shall serve as an acceptable verification procedure for all parties.

(f) *Costs of the verification procedure.* The interested party or parties requesting the verification procedure shall pay all costs of the verification procedure, unless an independent and Qualified Auditor concludes that during the period audited, the Licensee underpaid royalties by an amount of five (5) percent or more; in which case, the service that made the underpayment shall bear the costs of the verification procedure.

(g) *Interested parties.* For purposes of this section, interested parties are those Copyright Owners who are entitled to receive royalty fees pursuant to 17 U.S.C. 114(g), their designated agents, or the Collective.

[72 FR 71796, Dec. 19, 2007. Redesignated at 78 FR 23096, Apr. 17, 2013 and amended at 78 FR 23097, Apr. 17, 2013]

§ 382.7 Verification of royalty payments.

(a) *General.* This section prescribes general rules pertaining to the verification of the payment of royalty fees to those parties entitled to receive such fees, according to terms promulgated by the Copyright Royalty Board.

(b) *Frequency of verification.* Interested parties may conduct a single audit of the Collective during any given calendar year.

(c) *Notice of intent to audit.* Interested parties must submit a notice of intent to audit the entity making the royalty payment to the Copyright Royalty Board, which shall publish in the FEDERAL REGISTER a notice announcing the receipt of the notice of intent to audit within 30 days of the filing of the interested party's notice. Such notification of intent shall also be delivered at the same time to the party to be audited.

(d) *Retention of records.* The interested party requesting the verification procedure shall retain the report of the verification for a period of three years after completion of the verification process.

(e) *Acceptable verification procedure.* An audit, including underlying paperwork, which was performed in the ordinary course of business according to generally accepted auditing standards by an independent and Qualified Auditor, shall serve as an acceptable verification procedure for all interested parties.

(f) *Costs of the verification procedure.* The interested party or parties requesting the verification procedure shall pay for all costs associated with the verification procedure, unless an independent and Qualified Auditor concludes that, during the period audited, the Licensee underpaid royalties in the amount of five (5) percent or more, in which case, the entity that made the underpayment shall bear the costs of the verification procedure.

(g) *Interested parties.* For purposes of this section, interested parties are those who are entitled to receive royalty payments pursuant to 17 U.S.C. 114(g)(2), or their designated agents.

[72 FR 71796, Dec. 19, 2007. Redesignated at 78 FR 23096, Apr. 17, 2013 and amended at 78 FR 23098, Apr. 17, 2013]

§ 382.8 Unclaimed funds.

If the Collective is unable to identify or locate a Copyright Owner or Performer who is entitled to receive a royalty distribution under this subpart, the Collective shall retain the required payment in a segregated trust account for a period of 3 years from the date of the last distribution from the royalty fund at issue. No claim to such distribution shall be valid after the expiration of the 3-year period. After expiration of the three-year claim period, the Collective may apply the unclaimed funds to offset any costs deductible under 17 U.S.C. 114(g)(3). The foregoing shall apply notwithstanding the common law or statutes of any State.

[72 FR 71796, Dec. 19, 2007. Redesignated at 78 FR 23096, Apr. 17, 2013 and amended at 78 FR 23098, Apr. 17, 2013]

Subpart B—Preexisting Satellite Digital Audio Radio Services

AUTHORITY: 17 U.S.C. 112(e), 114(f), 804(b)(3).

SOURCE: 73 FR 4102, Jan. 24, 2008, unless otherwise noted.

§ 382.10 General.

(a) *Scope.* This subpart establishes rates and terms of royalty payments for the public performance of sound recordings in certain digital transmissions by Licensees in accordance with the provisions of 17 U.S.C. 114, and the making of Ephemeral Recordings by Licensees in accordance with the provisions of 17 U.S.C. 112(e), during the period from January 1, 2013, through December 31, 2017.

(b) *Legal compliance.* Licensees relying upon the statutory licenses set forth in 17 U.S.C. 112(e) and 114 shall comply with the requirements of those sections, the rates and terms of this subpart, and any other applicable regulations.

(c) *Relationship to voluntary agreements.* Notwithstanding the royalty rates and terms established in this subpart, the rates and terms of any voluntary license agreements entered into by Copyright Owners and Licensees shall apply in lieu of the rates and terms of this subpart to transmission within the scope of such agreements.

[73 FR 4102, Jan. 24, 2008, as amended at 78 FR 23098, Apr. 17, 2013]

§ 382.11 Definitions.

For purposes of this subpart, the following definitions shall apply:

Collective is the collection and distribution organization that is designated by the Copyright Royalty Judges. For the 2013–2017 license term, the Collective is SoundExchange, Inc.

Copyright Owners are sound recording copyright owners who are entitled to royalty payments made under this subpart pursuant to the statutory licenses under 17 U.S.C. 112(e) and 114.

Directly-Licensed Recording is a sound recording for which the Licensee has previously obtained a license of all relevant rights from the Copyright Owner of such sound recording.

Ephemeral Recording is a phonorecord created for the purpose of facilitating a transmission of a public performance of a sound recording under a statutory license in accordance with 17 U.S.C. 114 and subject to the limitations specified in 17 U.S.C. 112(e).

GAAP shall mean generally accepted accounting principles in effect from time to time in the United States.

Gross Revenues. (1) Gross Revenues shall mean revenue recognized by the Licensee in accordance with GAAP from the operation of an SDARS, and shall be comprised of the following:

(i) Subscription revenue recognized by Licensee directly from U.S. subscribers for Licensee's SDARS; and

(ii) Licensee's advertising revenues, or other monies received from sponsors, if any, attributable to advertising on channels other than those that use only incidental performances of sound recordings, less advertising agency and sales commissions.

(2) Gross Revenues shall include such payments as set forth in paragraphs (1)(i) and (ii) of the definition of "Gross Revenues" to which Licensee is entitled but which are paid to a parent, wholly-owned subsidiary or division of Licensee.

(3) Gross Revenues shall exclude:

(i) Monies or other consideration attributable to the sale and/or license of equipment and/or other technology, including but not limited to bandwidth, sales of devices that receive the Licensee's SDARS and any taxes, shipping and handling fees therefor;

(ii) Royalties paid to Licensee for intellectual property rights;

(iii) Monies or other consideration received by Licensee from the sale of phonorecords and digital phonorecord deliveries;

(iv) Sales and use taxes, shipping and handling, credit card, invoice, and fulfillment service fees;

(v) Bad debt expense, and

(vi) Revenues recognized by Licensee for the provision of

(A) Current and future data services offered for a separate charge (e.g., weather, traffic, destination information, messaging, sports scores, stock ticker information, extended program associated data, video and photographic images, and such other telematics and/or data services as may exist from time to time);

(B) Channels, programming, products and/or other services offered for a separate charge where such channels use only incidental performances of sound recordings;

(C) Channels, programming, products and/or other services provided outside of the United States; and

(D) Channels, programming, products and/or other services for which the performance of sound recordings and/or the making of Ephemeral Recordings is exempt from any license requirement or is separately licensed, including by a statutory license and, for the avoidance of doubt, webcasting, audio services bundled with television programming, interactive services, and transmissions to business establishments.

Licensee is a person that has obtained a statutory license under 17 U.S.C. 114, and the implementing regulations, to make transmissions over a preexisting satellite digital audio radio service, and has obtained a statutory license under 17 U.S.C. 112(e), and the implementing regulations, to make Ephemeral Recordings for use in facilitating such transmissions.

Performers means the independent administrators identified in 17 U.S.C. 114(g)(2)(B) and (C), and the parties identified in 17 U.S.C. 114(g)(2)(D).

Pre-1972 Recording is a sound recording fixed before February 15, 1972.

Qualified Auditor is a Certified Public Accountant.

SDARS means the preexisting satellite digital audio radio services as defined in 17 U.S.C. 114(j)(10).

Term means the period commencing January 1, 2013, and continuing through December 31, 2017.

[73 FR 4102, Jan. 24, 2008, as amended at 78 FR 23098, Apr. 17, 2013]

§382.12 Royalty fees for the public performance of sound recordings and the making of ephemeral recordings.

(a) *In general.* The monthly royalty fee to be paid by a Licensee for the public performance of sound recordings pursuant to 17 U.S.C. 114(d)(2) and the making of any number of Ephemeral Recordings to facilitate such performances pursuant to 17 U.S.C. 112(e) shall be a percentage of monthly Gross Revenues as follows: for 2013, 9.0%; for 2014, 9.5%; for 2015, 10.0%; for 2016, 10.5%; and for 2017, 11.0%, except that the royalty fee so determined may be reduced by the Direct License Share or the Pre-1972 Recording Share as described in paragraphs (d) and (e), respectively, of this section.

(b) *Ephemeral recordings.* The royalty payable under 17 U.S.C. 112(e) for the making of phonorecords used by the Licensee solely to facilitate transmissions for which it pays royalties as and when provided in this subpart shall be included within, and constitute 5% of, the total royalties payable under 17 U.S.C. 112(e) and 114.

(c) *Ephemeral recordings minimum fee.* Each Licensee making Ephemeral Recordings pursuant to 17 U.S.C. 112(e) shall make an advance payment to the Collective of $100,000 per year, payable no later than January 20th of each year. The annual advance payment shall be nonrefundable, but it shall be considered as an advance of the Ephemeral Recordings royalties due and payable for a given year or any month therein under paragraphs (a) and (b) of this section; Provided, however, that any unused annual advance payment for a given year shall not carry over into a subsequent year.

(d) *Direct license share.* The percentage of monthly Gross Revenues royalty fee specified in paragraph (a) of this section may be reduced by a percentage as set forth in this paragraph (referred to herein as the "Direct License Share").

(1) Subject to paragraph (d)(3) of this section, for each month, the Direct License Share is the result of dividing the Internet Performances of Directly-Licensed Recordings on the Reference Channels by the total number of Internet Performances of all sound recordings on the Reference Channels.

(2) For purposes of paragraph (d)(1) of this section:

(i) A "Performance" is each instance in which any portion of a sound recording is publicly performed to a listener within the United States by means of a digital audio transmission or retransmission (e.g., the delivery of any portion of a single track from a compact disc to one listener) but excluding an incidental performance that both:

(A) Makes no more than incidental use of sound recordings including, but not limited to, brief musical transitions in and out of commercials or program segments, brief performances during news, talk and sports programming, brief background performances during disk jockey announcements, brief performances during commercials of sixty seconds or less in duration, or brief performances during sporting or other public events; and

(B) Other than ambient music that is background at a public event, does not contain an entire sound recording and does not feature a particular sound recording of more than thirty seconds (as in the case of a sound recording used as a theme song).

(ii) The "Reference Channels" are Internet webcast channels offered by the Licensee that directly correspond to channels offered on the Licensee's SDARS that are capable of being received on all models of Sirius radio, all models of XM radio, or either or both, and on which the programming consists primarily of music.

(3) A Direct License Share adjustment as described in paragraph (d) of this section is available to a Licensee only if—

(i) The Reference Channels constitute a large majority of the music channels offered on the Licensee's SDARS and are generally representative of the music channels offered on the Licensee's SDARS; and

(ii) The Licensee timely provides the relevant information required by § 382.13(h).

(4) No performance shall be credited as an Internet Performance of a Directly-Licensed Sound Recording under this section if that performance is separately credited as an Internet Performance of a Pre-1972 sound recording under paragraph (e)(1) of this section.

(e) *Pre-1972 Recording Share.* The percentage of monthly Gross Revenues royalty fee specified in paragraph (a) of this section may be reduced by a percentage as set forth in this paragraph (referred to herein as the "Pre-1972 Recording Share").

(1) Subject to paragraph (e)(3) of this section, for each month, the Pre-1972 Recording Share is the result of dividing the Internet Performances of Pre-1972 Sound Recordings on the Reference Channels by the total number of Internet Performances of all sound recordings on the Reference Channels.

(2) For purposes of paragraph (e)(1) of this section:

(i) A "Performance" is each instance in which any portion of a sound recording is publicly performed to a listener within the United States by means of a digital audio transmission or retransmission (e.g., the delivery of any portion of a single track from a compact disc to one listener) but excluding an incidental performance that both:

(A) Makes no more than incidental use of sound recordings including, but not limited to, brief musical transitions in and out of commercials or program segments, brief performances during news, talk and sports programming, brief background performances during disk jockey announcements, brief performances during commercials of sixty seconds or less in duration, or brief performances during sporting or other public events; and

(B) Other than ambient music that is background at a public event, does not contain an entire sound recording and does not feature a particular sound recording of more than thirty seconds (as in the case of a sound recording used as a theme song).

(ii) The "Reference Channels" are Internet webcast channels offered by the Licensee that directly correspond to channels offered on the Licensee's SDARS that are capable of being received on all models of Sirius radio, all models of XM radio or both, and on which the programming consists primarily of music.

(3) A Pre-1972 Recording Share adjustment as described in paragraph (e) of this section is available to a Licensee only if—

(i) The Reference Channels constitute a large majority of the music channels offered on the Licensee's SDARS and are generally representative of the music channels offered on the Licensee's SDARS; and

(ii) The Licensee timely provides the relevant information required by § 382.13(h).

[78 FR 23098, Apr. 17, 2013]

§ 382.13 Terms for making payment of royalty fees and statements of account.

(a) *Payment to the Collective.* A Licensee shall make the royalty payments due under § 382.12 to the Collective.

(b) *Designation of the Collective.* (1) Until such time as a new designation is made, SoundExchange, Inc., is designated as the Collective to receive statements of account and royalty payments from Licensees due under § 382.12 and to distribute such royalty payments to each Copyright Owner and Performer, or their designated agents, entitled to receive royalties under 17 U.S.C. 112(e) or 114.

(2) If SoundExchange, Inc. should dissolve or cease to be governed by a board consisting of equal numbers of representatives of Copyright Owners and Performers, then it shall be replaced by a successor Collective upon the fulfillment of the requirements set forth in paragraph (b)(2)(i) of this section.

(i) By a majority vote of the nine Copyright Owner representatives and the nine Performer representatives on the SoundExchange board as of the last day preceding the condition precedent in paragraph (b)(2) of this section, such representatives shall file a petition with the Copyright Royalty Judges designating a successor to collect and distribute royalty payments to Copyright Owners and Performers entitled to receive royalties under 17 U.S.C. 112(e) or 114 that have themselves authorized the Collective.

(ii) The Copyright Royalty Judges shall publish in the FEDERAL REGISTER within 30 days of receipt of a petition filed under paragraph (b)(2)(i) of this section an order designating the Collective named in such petition.

(c) *Monthly payments.* A Licensee shall make any payments due under § 382.12 on a monthly basis on or before the 45th day after the end of each month for that month. All payments shall be rounded to the nearest cent.

(d) *Late payments and statements of account.* A Licensee shall pay a late fee of 1.5% per month, or the highest lawful rate, whichever is lower, each for any payment or statement of account, or either of them received by the Collective after the due date. Late fees shall accrue from the due date until payment and the statement of account are received by the Collective.

(e) *Statements of account.* Any payment due under § 382.12 shall be accompanied by a corresponding statement of account. A statement of account shall contain the following information:

(1) Such information as is necessary to calculate the accompanying royalty payments;

(2) The name, address, business title, telephone number, facsimile number (if any), electronic mail address and other contact information of the person to be contacted for information or questions concerning the content of the statement of account;

(3) The signature of a duly authorized officer or representative of the Licensee;

(4) The printed or typewritten name of the person signing the statement of account;

(5) The date of signature;

(6) The title or official position held in relation to the Licensee by the person signing the statement of account;

(7) A certification of the capacity of the person signing; and

(8) A statement to the following effect:

I, the undersigned officer or representative of the Licensee, have examined this statement of account and hereby state that it is true, accurate, and complete to my knowledge after reasonable due diligence.

(f) *Distribution of royalties.* (1) The Collective shall promptly distribute royalties received from Licensees to Copyright Owners and Performers, or their designated agents, that are entitled to such royalties. The Collective shall only be responsible for making distributions to those Copyright Owners, Performers, or their designated agents who provide the Collective with such information as is necessary to identify the correct recipient. The Collective shall distribute royalties on a basis that values all performances by a Licensee equally based upon the information provided under the reports of use requirements for Licensees contained in § 370.4 of this chapter.

(2) If the Collective is unable to locate a Copyright Owner or Performer entitled to a distribution of royalties under paragraph (f)(1) of this section within 3 years from the date of payment by a Licensee, such royalties shall be handled in accordance with § 382.17.

(g) *Retention of records.* Books and records of a Licensee and of the Collective relating to payments of and distributions of royalties shall be kept for a period of not less than the prior 3 calendar years.

(h) *Notification of exclusions.* (1) As a condition to a Licensee's taking a Direct License Share adjustment as described in § 382.12(d), by no later than the due date for the relevant payment under paragraph (c) of this section, the Licensee must provide the Collective a list of each Copyright Owner from which the Licensee claims to have a direct license of rights to Directly-Licensed Recordings that is in effect for the month for which the payment is made, and of each sound recording as to which the Licensee takes such an adjustment (identified by featured artist name, sound recording title, and International Standard Recording Code (ISRC) number or, alternatively to the ISRC, album title and copyright owner name). Notwithstanding § 382.14, the Collective may disclose such information as reasonably necessary for it to confirm whether a claimed direct license exists and claimed sound recordings are properly excludable.

(2) As a condition to a Licensee's taking a Pre-1972 Recording Share adjustment as described in § 382.12(e), by no later than the due date for the relevant payment under paragraph (c) of this section, the Licensee must provide the Collective a list of each Pre-1972 Recording as to which the Licensee takes such an adjustment (identified by featured artist name, sound recording title, and International Standard Recording Code (ISRC) number or, alternatively to the ISRC, album title and copyright owner name).

[73 FR 4102, Jan. 24, 2008, as amended at 76 FR 45696, Aug. 1, 2011; 78 FR 23099, Apr. 17, 2013]

§ 382.14 Confidential information.

(a) *Definition.* For purposes of this subpart, "Confidential Information" shall include the statements of account and any information contained therein, including the amount of royalty payments, and any information pertaining to the statements of account reasonably designated as confidential by the Licensee submitting the statement.

(b) *Exclusion.* Confidential Information shall not include documents or information that at the time of delivery to the Collective are public knowledge. The party claiming the benefit of this provision shall have the burden of proving that the disclosed information was public knowledge.

(c) *Use of Confidential Information.* In no event shall the Collective use any Confidential Information for any purpose other than royalty collection and distribution and activities related directly thereto.

(d) *Disclosure of Confidential Information.* Access to Confidential Information shall be limited, subject to an appropriate confidentiality agreement, to:

(1) Those employees, agents, attorneys, consultants and independent contractors of the Collective, who are engaged in the collection and distribution of royalty payments hereunder and activities related thereto, for the purpose of performing such duties during the ordinary course of their work and who require access to the Confidential Information;

(2) An independent and Qualified Auditor, who is authorized to act on behalf of the Collective with respect to verification of a Licensee's statement of account pursuant to § 382.15 or on behalf of a Copyright Owner or Performer with respect to the verification of royalty distributions pursuant to § 382.16;

(3) Copyright Owners and Performers, including their designated agents, whose works have been used under the statutory licenses set forth in 17 U.S.C. 112(e) and 114 by the Licensee whose Confidential Information is being supplied, and including those employees, agents, attorneys, consultants and independent contractors of such Copyright Owners and Performers and their designated agents, for the purpose of performing their duties during the ordinary course of their work and who require access to the Confidential Information; and

(4) In connection with future proceedings under 17 U.S.C. 112(e) and 114 before the Copyright Royalty Judges, and under an appropriate protective order, attorneys, consultants and other authorized agents of the parties to the proceedings or the courts.

(e) *Safeguarding of Confidential Information.* The Collective and any person identified in paragraph (d) of this section shall implement procedures to safeguard against unauthorized access to or dissemination of any Confidential Information using a reasonable standard of care, but no less than the same degree of security used to protect Confidential Information or similarly sensitive information belonging to the Collective or person.

[73 FR 4102, Jan. 24, 2008, as amended at 78 FR 23099, Apr. 17, 2013]

§ 382.15 Verification of royalty payments.

(a) *General.* This section prescribes procedures by which the Collective may verify the royalty payments made by a Licensee.

(b) *Frequency of verification.* The Collective may conduct a single audit of a Licensee, upon reasonable notice and during reasonable business hours, during any given calendar year, for any or all of the prior 3 calendar years, but no calendar year shall be subject to audit more than once.

(c) *Notice of intent to audit.* The Collective must file with the Copyright Royalty Judges a notice of intent to audit a particular Licensee, which shall, within 30 days of the filing of the notice, publish in the FEDERAL REGISTER a notice announcing such filing. The notification of intent to audit shall be served at the same time on the Licensee to be audited. Any such audit shall be conducted by an independent and Qualified Auditor identified in the notice, and shall be binding on all parties.

(d) *Acquisition and retention of report.* The Licensee shall use commercially reasonable efforts to obtain or to provide access to any relevant books and records maintained by third parties for the purpose of the audit. The Collective shall retain the report of the verification for a period of not less than 3 years.

(e) *Acceptable verification procedure.* An audit, including underlying paperwork, which was performed in the ordinary course of business according to generally accepted auditing standards by an independent and Qualified Auditor, shall serve as an acceptable verification procedure for all parties with respect to the information that is within the scope of the audit.

(f) *Consultation.* Before rendering a written report to the Collective, except where the auditor has a reasonable basis to suspect fraud and disclosure would, in the reasonable opinion of the auditor, prejudice the investigation of such suspected fraud, the auditor shall review the tentative written findings of the audit with the appropriate agent or employee of the Licensee being audited in order to remedy any factual errors and clarify any issues relating to the audit; Provided that an appropriate agent or employee of the Licensee reasonably cooperates with the auditor to remedy promptly any factual errors or clarify any issues raised by the audit.

(g) *Costs of the verification procedure.* The Collective shall pay all costs associated with the verification procedure, unless it determines that the Licensee underpaid royalties in an amount of 10% or more, in which case the Licensee shall, in addition to paying the amount of any underpayment, bear the reasonable costs of the verification procedure.

[73 FR 4102, Jan. 24, 2008, as amended at 78 FR 23099, Apr. 17, 2013]

§ 382.16 Verification of royalty distributions.

(a) *General.* This section prescribes procedures by which any Copyright Owner or Performer may verify the royalty distributions made by the Collective; Provided, however, that nothing contained in this section shall apply to situations where a Copyright Owner or Performer and the Collective have agreed as to proper verification methods.

(b) *Frequency of verification.* A Copyright Owner or Performer may conduct a single audit of the Collective upon reasonable notice and during reasonable business hours, during any given calendar year, for any or all of the prior 3 calendar years, but no calendar year shall be subject to audit more than once.

(c) *Notice of intent to audit.* A Copyright Owner and Performer must file with the Copyright Royalty Judges a notice of intent to audit the Collective, which shall, within 30 days of the filing of the notice, publish in the FEDERAL REGISTER a notice announcing such filing. The notification of intent to audit shall be served at the same time on the Collective. Any audit shall be conducted by an independent and Qualified Auditor identified in the notice, and shall be binding on all Copyright Owners and Performers.

(d) *Acquisition and retention of report.* The Collective shall use commercially reasonable efforts to obtain or to provide access to any relevant books and records maintained by third parties for the purpose of the audit. The Copyright Owner or Performer requesting the verification procedure shall retain the report of the verification for a period of not less than 3 years.

(e) *Acceptable verification procedure.* An audit, including underlying paperwork, which was performed in the ordinary course of business according to generally accepted auditing standards by an independent and Qualified Auditor, shall serve as an acceptable verification procedure for all parties with respect to the information that is within the scope of the audit.

(f) *Consultation.* Before rendering a written report to a Copyright Owner or Performer, except where the auditor has a reasonable basis to suspect fraud and disclosure would, in the reasonable opinion of the auditor, prejudice the investigation of such suspected fraud, the auditor shall review the tentative written findings of the audit with the appropriate agent or employee of the Collective in order to remedy any factual errors and clarify any issues relating to the audit; Provided that the appropriate agent or employee of the Collective reasonably cooperates with the auditor to remedy promptly any factual errors or clarify any issues raised by the audit.

(g) *Costs of the verification procedure.* The Copyright Owner or Performer requesting the verification procedure shall pay all costs associated with the procedure, unless it is finally determined that the Licensee underpaid royalties in an amount of 10% or more, in which case the Collective shall, in addition to paying the amount of any underpayment, bear the reasonable costs of the verification procedure.

[73 FR 4102, Jan. 24, 2008, as amended at 78 FR 23100, Apr. 17, 2013]

§ 382.17 Unclaimed funds.

If the Collective is unable to identify or locate a Copyright Owner or Performer who is entitled to receive a royalty distribution under this subpart, the Collective shall retain the required payment in a segregated trust account for a period of 3 years from the date of distribution. No claim to such distribution shall be valid after the expiration of the 3-year period. After expiration of this period, the Collective may apply the unclaimed funds to offset any costs deductible under 17 U.S.C. 114(g)(3). The foregoing shall apply notwithstanding the common law or statutes of any State.

PART 383—RATES AND TERMS FOR SUBSCRIPTION TRANSMISSIONS AND THE REPRODUCTION OF EPHEMERAL RECORDINGS BY NEW SUBSCRIPTION SERVICES

AUTHORITY: 17 U.S.C. 112(e), 114, and 801(b)(1).

SOURCE: 72 FR 72254, Dec. 20, 2007, unless otherwise noted.

§ 383.1 General.

(a) *Scope.* This part 383 establishes rates and terms of royalty payments for the public performance of sound recordings in certain digital transmissions by Licensees in accordance with the provisions of 17 U.S.C. 114, and the making of certain ephemeral recordings by Licensees in accordance with the provisions of 17 U.S.C. 112(e), during the period commencing from the inception of the Licensees' Services and continuing through December 31, 2015.

(b) *Legal compliance.* Licensees relying upon the statutory licenses set forth in 17 U.S.C. 112(e) and 114 shall comply with the requirements of those sections and the rates and terms of this part.

(c) *Relationship to voluntary agreements.* Notwithstanding the royalty rates and terms established in this part, the rates and terms of any license agreements entered into by Copyright Owners and Licensees shall apply in lieu of the rates and terms of this part to transmissions with the scope of such agreements.

[72 FR 72254, Dec. 20, 2007, as amended at 75 FR 14075, Mar. 24, 2010]

§ 383.2 Definitions.

For purposes of this part, the following definitions shall apply:

(a) *Applicable Period* is the period for which a particular payment to the designated collection and distribution organization is due.

(b) *Bundled Contracts* means contracts between the Licensee and a Provider in which the Service is not the only content licensed by the Licensee to the Provider.

(c) *Copyright Owner* is a sound recording copyright owner who is entitled to receive royalty payments under 17 U.S.C. 112(e) or 114(g).

(d) *License Period* means the period commencing from the inception of the Licensees' Services and continuing through December 31, 2015.

(e) *Licensee* is a person that has obtained statutory licenses under 17 U.S.C. 112(e) and 114, and the implementing regulations, to make digital audio transmissions as part of a Service (as defined in paragraph (h) of this section), and ephemeral recordings for use in facilitating such transmissions.

(f) *Provider* means a "multichannel video programming distributor" as that term is defined in 47 CFR 76.1000(e); notwithstanding such definition, for purposes of this part, a Provider shall include only a distributor of programming to televisions, such as a cable or satellite television provider.

(g) *Revenue*. (1) "Revenue" means all monies and other considerations, paid or payable, recognizable during the Applicable Period as revenue by the Licensee consistent with Generally Accepted Accounting Principles ("GAAP") and the Licensee's past practices, which is derived by the Licensee from the operation of the Service and shall be comprised of the following:

(i) Revenues recognizable by Licensee from Licensee's Providers and directly from residential U.S. subscribers for Licensee's Service;

(ii) Licensee's advertising revenues recognizable from the Service (as billed), or other monies received from sponsors of the Service if any, less advertising agency commissions not to exceed 15% of those fees incurred to a recognized advertising agency not owned or controlled by Licensee;

(iii) Revenues recognizable for the provision of time on the Service to any third party;

(iv) Revenues recognizable from the sale of time to Providers of paid programming, such as infomercials, on the Service;

(v) Where merchandise, service, or anything of value is receivable by Licensee in lieu of cash consideration for the use of Licensee's Service, the fair market value thereof or Licensee's prevailing published rate, whichever is less;

(vi) Monies or other consideration recognizable as revenue by Licensee from Licensee's Providers, but not including revenues recognizable by Licensee's Providers from others and not accounted for by Licensee's Providers to Licensee, for the provision of hardware for the Service by anyone and used in connection with the Service;

(vii) Monies or other consideration recognizable as revenue for any references to or inclusion of any product or service on the Service; and

(viii) Bad debts recovered regarding paragraphs (g)(1)(i) through (vii) of this section.

(2) "Revenue" shall include such payments as set forth in paragraphs (g)(1)(i) through (viii) of this section to which Licensee is entitled but which are paid or payable to a parent, subsidiary, division, or affiliate of Licensee, in lieu of payment to Licensee but not including payments to Licensee's Providers for the Service. Licensee shall be allowed a deduction from "Revenue" as defined in paragraph (g)(1) of this section for bad debts actually written off during the reporting period.

(h) A *Service* is a non-interactive (consistent with the definition of "interactive service" in 17 U.S.C. 114(j)(7)) audio-only subscription service (including accompanying information and graphics related to the audio) that is transmitted to residential subscribers of a television service through a Provider which is marketed as and is in fact primarily a video service where

(1) Subscribers do not pay a separate fee for audio channels.

(2) The audio channels are delivered by digital audio transmissions through a technology that is incapable of tracking the individual sound recordings received by any particular consumer.

(3) However, paragraph (h)(2) of this section shall not apply to the Licensee's current contracts with Providers that are in effect as of the effective date of this part if such Providers become capable in the future of tracking the individual sound recordings received by any particular consumer, provided that the audio channels continued to be delivered to Subscribers by digital audio transmissions and the Licensee remains incapable of tracking the individual sound recordings received by any particular consumer.

(i) *Subscriber* means every residential subscriber to the underlying service of the Provider who receives Licensee's Service in the United States for all or any part of a month; provided, however, that for any Licensee that is not able to track the number of subscribers on a per-day basis, "Subscribers" shall be calculated based on the average of the number of subscribers on the last day of the preceding month and the last day of the applicable month, unless the Service is paid by the Provider based on end-of-month numbers, in which event "Subscribers" shall be counted based on end-of-month data.

(j) *Stand-Alone Contracts* means contracts between the Licensee and a Provider in which the only content licensed to the Provider is the Service.

[72 FR 72254, Dec. 20, 2007, as amended at 75 FR 14075, Mar. 24, 2010]

§ 383.3 Royalty fees for public performances of sound recordings and the making of ephemeral recordings.

(a) *Royalty rates.* Royalty rates for the public performance of sound recordings by eligible digital transmissions made over a Service pursuant to 17 U.S.C. 114, and for ephemeral recordings of sound recordings made pursuant to 17 U.S.C. 112(e) to facilitate such transmissions during the License Period, are as follows. Each Licensee will pay, with respect to content covered by the License that is provided via the Service of each such Licensee:

(1) For Stand-Alone Contracts, the greater of:

(i) 15% of Revenue, or

(ii) The following monthly minimum payment per Subscriber to the Service of such Licensee—

(A) From inception through 2006: $0.0075

(B) 2007: $0.0075

(C) 2008: $0.0075

(D) 2009: $0.0125

(E) 2010: $0.0150

(F) 2011: $0.0155

(G) 2012: $0.0159

(H) 2013: $0.0164

(I) 2014: $0.0169

(J) 2015: $0.0174 and

(2) For Bundled Contracts, the greater of:

(i) 15% of Revenue allocated to reflect the objective value of the Licensee's Service, or

(ii) The following monthly minimum payment per Subscriber to the Service of such Licensee:

(A) From inception through 2006: $0.0220

(B) 2007: $0.0220

(C) 2008: $0.0220

(D) 2009: $0.0220

(E) 2010: $0.0250

(F) 2011: $0.0258

(G) 2012: $0.0265

(H) 2013: $0.0273

(I) 2014: $0.0281

(J) 2015: $0.0290

(b) *Minimum fee.* Each Licensee will pay an annual, non-refundable minimum fee of one hundred thousand dollars ($100,000), payable on January 31 of each calendar year in which the Service is provided pursuant to the section 112(e) and 114 statutory licenses, but payable pursuant to the applicable regulations for all years 2007 and earlier. Such fee shall be recoupable and credited against royalties due in the calendar year in which it is paid.

(c) *Ephemeral recordings.* The royalty payable under 17 U.S.C. 112(e) for the making of phonorecords used by the Licensee solely to facilitate transmissions during the License Period for which it pays royalties as and when provided in this part shall be included within, and constitute 5% of, such royalty payments.

[72 FR 72254, Dec. 20, 2007, as amended at 75 FR 14075, Mar. 24, 2010]

§383.4 Terms for making payment of royalty fees.

(a) *Terms in general.* Subject to the provisions of this section, terms governing timing and due dates of royalty payments to the Collective, late fees, statements of account, audit and verification of royalty payments and distributions, cost of audit and verification, record retention requirements, treatment of Licensees' confidential information, distribution of royalties by the Collective, unclaimed funds, designation of the Collective, and any definitions for applicable terms not defined herein and not otherwise inapplicable shall be those adopted by the Copyright Royalty Judges for subscription transmissions and the reproduction of ephemeral recordings by preexisting satellite digital audio radio services in 37 CFR part 382, subpart B of this chapter, for the license period 2007–2012. For purposes of this section, the term "Collective" refers to the collection and distribution organization that is designated by the Copyright Royalty Judges. For the License Period through 2015, the sole Collective is SoundExchange, Inc.

(b) *Reporting of performances.* Without prejudice to any applicable notice and recordkeeping provisions, statements of account shall not require reports of performances.

(c) *Applicable regulations.* To the extent not inconsistent with this part, all applicable regulations, including part 370 of this chapter, shall apply to activities subject to this part.

[75 FR 14075, Mar. 24, 2010]

PART 384—RATES AND TERMS FOR THE MAKING OF EPHEMERAL RECORDINGS BY BUSINESS ESTABLISHMENT SERVICES

Sec.

AUTHORITY: 17 U.S.C. 112(e), 801(b)(1).

SOURCE: 73 FR 16199, Mar. 27, 2008, unless otherwise noted.

§384.1 General.

(a) *Scope.* This part 384 establishes rates and terms of royalty payments for the making of Ephemeral Recordings by a Business Establishment Service, as defined in §384.2(a), in accordance with the provisions of 17 U.S.C. 112(e), during the period 2009–2013 (the "License Period").

(b) *Legal compliance.* Licensees relying upon the statutory licenses set forth in 17 U.S.C. 112 shall comply with the requirements of that section, the rates and terms of this part and any other applicable regulations.

(c) *Relationship to voluntary agreements.* Notwithstanding the royalty rates and terms established in this part, the rates and terms of any license agreements entered into by Copyright Owners and services shall apply in lieu of the rates and terms of this part to the making of Ephemeral Recordings within the scope of such agreements.

§384.2 Definitions.

For purposes of this part, the following definitions shall apply:

Business Establishment Service means a service making transmissions of sound recordings under the limitation on exclusive rights specified by 17 U.S.C. 114(d)(1)(C)(iv).

Collective is the collection and distribution organization that is designated by the Copyright Royalty Judges. For the License Period, the Collective is SoundExchange, Inc.

Copyright Owner is a sound recording copyright owner who is entitled to receive royalty payments made under this part pursuant to the statutory license under 17 U.S.C. 112(e).

Ephemeral Recording is a phonorecord created for the purpose of facilitating a transmission of a public performance of a sound recording under the limitations on exclusive rights specified by 17 U.S.C. 114(d)(1)(C)(iv), and subject to the limitations specified in 17 U.S.C. 112(e).

Licensee is a Business Establishment Service that has obtained a compulsory license under 17 U.S.C. 112(e) and the implementing regulations therefor to make Ephemeral Recordings.

Performers means the independent administrators identified in 17 U.S.C. 114(g)(2)(B) and (C) and the parties identified in 17 U.S.C. 114(g)(2)(D).

Qualified Auditor is a certified public accountant.

§ 384.3 Royalty fees for ephemeral recordings.

(a) *Basic royalty rate.* For the making of any number of Ephemeral Recordings in the operation of a service pursuant to the limitation on exclusive rights specified by 17 U.S.C. 114(d)(1)(C)(iv), a Licensee shall pay 10% of such Licensee's "Gross Proceeds" derived from the use in such service of musical programs that are attributable to copyrighted recordings. "Gross Proceeds" as used in this section means all fees and payments, including those made in kind, received from any source before, during or after the License Period that are derived from the use of copyrighted sound recordings during the License Period pursuant to 17 U.S.C. 112(e) for the sole purpose of facilitating a transmission to the public of a performance of a sound recording under the limitation on exclusive rights specified in 17 U.S.C. 114(d)(1)(C)(iv). The attribution of Gross Proceeds to copyrighted recordings may be made on the basis of:

(1) For classical programs, the proportion that the playing time of copyrighted classical recordings bears to the total playing time of all classical recordings in the program, and

(2) For all other programs, the proportion that the number of copyrighted recordings bears to the total number of all recordings in the program.

(b) *Minimum fee.* Each Licensee shall pay a minimum fee of $10,000 for each calendar year in which it makes Ephemeral Recordings for use to facilitate transmissions under the limitation on exclusive rights specified by 17 U.S.C. 114(d)(1)(C)(iv), whether or not it does so for all or any part of the year. These minimum fees shall be nonrefundable, but shall be fully creditable to royalty payments due under paragraph (a) of this section for the same calendar year (but not any subsequent calendar year).

(c) *Other royalty rates and terms.* This part 384 does not apply to persons or entities other than Licensees, or to Licensees to the extent that they make other types of ephemeral recordings beyond those set forth in paragraph (a) of this section. For ephemeral recordings other than those governed by paragraph (a) of this section, persons making such ephemeral recordings must pay royalties, to the extent (if at all) applicable, under 17 U.S.C. 112(e) or as prescribed by other law, regulation or agreement.

§ 384.4 Terms for making payment of royalty fees and statements of account.

(a) *Payment to Collective.* A Licensee shall make the royalty payments due under § 384.3 to the Collective.

(b) *Designation of the Collective.* (1) Until such time as a new designation is made, SoundExchange, Inc., is designated as the Collective to receive statements of account and royalty payments from Licensees due under § 384.3 and to distribute such royalty payments to each Copyright Owner, or their designated agents, entitled to receive royalties under 17 U.S.C. 112(e).

(2) If SoundExchange, Inc. should dissolve or cease to be governed by a board consisting of equal numbers of representatives of Copyright Owners and Performers, then it shall be replaced by a successor Collective upon the fulfillment of the requirements set forth in paragraph (b)(2)(i) of this section.

(i) By a majority vote of the nine Copyright Owner representatives and the nine Performer representatives on the SoundExchange board as of the last day preceding the condition precedent in paragraph (b)(2) of this section, such representatives shall file a petition with the Copyright Royalty Judges designating a successor to collect and distribute royalty payments to Copyright Owners entitled to receive royalties under 17 U.S.C. 112(e) that have themselves authorized such Collective.

(ii) The Copyright Royalty Judges shall publish in the FEDERAL REGISTER within 30 days of receipt of a petition filed under paragraph (b)(2)(i) of this section an order designating the Collective named in such petition.

(c) *Monthly payments.* A Licensee shall make any payments due under § 384.3(a) by the 45th day after the end of each month for that month, except that if the Copyright Royalty Judges issue their final determination adopting these rates and terms after the commencement of the License Period, then payments due under § 384.3(a) for the period from the beginning of the License Period through the last day of the month in which the Copyright Royalty Judges issue their final determination adopting these rates and terms shall be due 45 days after the end of such period. All monthly payments shall be rounded to the nearest cent.

(d) *Minimum payments.* A Licensee shall make any payment due under § 384.3(b) by January 31 of the applicable calendar year, except that:

(1) If the Copyright Royalty Judges issue their final determination adopting these rates and terms after the commencement of the License Period, then payment due under § 384.3(b) for 2009 shall be due 45 days after the last day of the month in which these rates and terms are adopted by the Copyright Royalty Judges and published in the FEDERAL REGISTER; and

(2) Payment for a Licensee that has not previously made Ephemeral Recordings pursuant to the license under 17 U.S.C. 112(e) shall be due by the 45th day after the end of the month in which the Licensee commences to do so.

(e) *Late payments.* A Licensee shall pay a late fee of 0.75% per month, or the highest lawful rate, whichever is lower, for any payment received by the Collective after the due date. Late fees shall accrue from the due date until payment is received by the Collective.

(f) *Statements of account.* For any part of the period beginning on the date the Copyright Royalty Judges issue their final determination adopting these rates and terms and ending on December 31, 2013, during which a Licensee operates a Business Establishment Service, by 45 days after the end of each month during the period, the Licensee shall deliver to the Collective a statement of account containing the information set forth in this paragraph (f) on a form prepared, and made available to Licensees, by the Collective. If a payment is owed for such month, the statement of account shall accompany the payment. A statement of account shall contain only the following information:

(1) Such information as is necessary to calculate the accompanying royalty payment, or if no payment is owed for the month, to calculate any portion of the minimum fee recouped during the month;

(2) The name, address, business title, telephone number, facsimile number, electronic mail address and other contact information of the individual or individuals to be contacted for information or questions concerning the content of the statement of account;

(3) The handwritten signature of:

(i) The owner of the Licensee or a duly authorized agent of the owner, if the Licensee is not a partnership or a corporation;

(ii) A partner or delegee, if the Licensee is a partnership; or

(iii) An officer of the corporation, if the Licensee is a corporation;

(4) The printed or typewritten name of the person signing the statement of account;

(5) The date of signature;

(6) If the Licensee is a partnership or a corporation, the title or official position held in the partnership or corporation by the person signing the statement of account;

(7) A certification of the capacity of the person signing; and

(8) A statement to the following effect:

I, the undersigned owner or agent of the Licensee, or officer or partner, if the Licensee is a corporation or partnership, have examined this statement of account and hereby state that it is true, accurate and complete to my knowledge after reasonable due diligence.

(g) *Distribution of payments.* The Collective shall distribute royalty payments directly to Copyright Owners; Provided that the Collective shall only be responsible for making distributions to those Copyright Owners who provide the Collective with such information as is necessary to identify and pay the correct recipient of such payments.

The Collective shall distribute royalty payments on a basis that values all Ephemeral Recordings by a Licensee equally based upon the information provided by the Licensee pursuant to the regulations governing reports of use of sound recordings by Licensees; Provided, however, that Copyright Owners that authorize the Collective may agree with the Collective to allocate their shares of the royalty payments made by any Licensee among themselves on an alternative basis. Copyright Owners entitled to receive payments may agree with the Collective upon payment protocols to be used by the Collective that provide for alternative arrangements for the payment of royalties.

(h) *Permitted deductions.* The Collective may deduct from the payments made by Licensees under § 384.3, prior to the distribution of such payments to any person or entity entitled thereto, all incurred costs permitted to be deducted under 17 U.S.C. 114(g)(3); Provided, however, that any party entitled to receive royalty payments under 17 U.S.C. 112(e) may agree to permit the Collective to make any other deductions.

(i) *Retention of records.* Books and records of a Licensee and of the Collective relating to the payment, collection, and distribution of royalty payments shall be kept for a period of not less than 3 years.

§ 384.5 Confidential information.

(a) *Definition.* For purposes of this part, "Confidential Information" shall include the statements of account, any information contained therein, including the amount of royalty payments, and any information pertaining to the statements of account reasonably designated as confidential by the Licensee submitting the statement.

(b) *Exclusion.* Confidential Information shall not include documents or information that at the time of delivery to the Collective are public knowledge. The Collective shall have the burden of proving that the disclosed information was public knowledge.

(c) *Use of Confidential Information.* In no event shall the Collective or any other person or entity authorized to have access to Confidential Information pursuant to paragraph (d) of this section use any Confidential Information for any purpose other than royalty collection and distribution and activities directly related thereto.

(d) *Disclosure of Confidential Information.* Access to Confidential Information shall be limited to:

(1) Those employees, agents, attorneys, consultants and independent contractors of the Collective, subject to an appropriate confidentiality agreement, who are engaged in the collection and distribution of royalty payments hereunder and activities related thereto, who are not also employees or officers of a Copyright Owner or Performer, and who, for the purpose of performing such duties during the ordinary course of their work, require access to the records;

(2) Board members of the Collective, and members of Collective committees whose primary functions are directly related to royalty collection and distribution, subject to an appropriate confidentiality agreement and for the sole purpose of performing their duties as board or committee members of the Collective, as applicable, provided that the sole confidential information that may be shared pursuant to this paragraph (d)(2) is confidential information contained in monthly statements of accounts provided pursuant to § 384.4(f) that accompany royalty payments;

(3) An independent and Qualified Auditor, subject to an appropriate confidentiality agreement, who is authorized to act on behalf of the Collective with respect to the verification of a Licensee's royalty payments pursuant to § 384.6 or on behalf of a Copyright Owner with respect to the verification of royalty distributions pursuant to § 384.7;

(4) Copyright owners whose works have been used under the statutory license set forth in 17 U.S.C. 112(e) by the Licensee whose Confidential Information is being supplied, or agents thereof, subject to an appropriate confidentiality agreement, provided that the sole confidential information that may be shared pursuant to paragraph (d)(4) of this section are monthly statements of account provided pursuant to § 384.4(f) that accompany royalty payments;

(5) In connection with future proceedings under 17 U.S.C. 112(e) before the Copyright Royalty Judges, and under an appropriate protective order, attorneys, consultants and other authorized agents of the parties to the proceedings or the courts; and

(6) In connection with bona fide royalty disputes or claims that are the subject of the procedures under § 384.6 or § 384.7, and under an appropriate confidentiality agreement or protective order, the specific parties to such disputes or claims, their attorneys, consultants or other authorized agents, and/or arbitration panels or the courts to which disputes or claims may be submitted.

(e) *Safeguarding of Confidential Information.* The Collective and any person or entity identified in paragraph (d) of this section shall implement procedures to safeguard all Confidential Information using a reasonable standard of care, but no less than the same degree of security used to protect Confidential Information or similarly sensitive information belonging to such Collective, person, or entity.

§ 384.6 Verification of royalty payments.

(a) *General.* This section prescribes procedures by which the Collective may verify the royalty payments made by a Licensee.

(b) *Frequency of verification.* The Collective may conduct a single audit of a Licensee, upon reasonable notice and during reasonable business hours, during any given calendar year, for any or all of the prior 3 calendar years, but no calendar year shall be subject to audit more than once.

(c) *Notice of intent to audit.* The Collective must file with the Copyright Royalty Judges a notice of intent to audit a particular Licensee, which shall, within 30 days of the filing of the notice, publish in the FEDERAL REGISTER a notice announcing such filing. The notification of intent to audit shall be served at the same time on the Licensee to be audited. Any such audit shall be conducted by an independent and Qualified Auditor identified in the notice, and shall be binding on all parties.

(d) *Acquisition and retention of records.* The Licensee shall use commercially reasonable efforts to obtain or to provide access to any relevant books and records maintained by third parties for the purpose of the audit and retain such records for a period of not less than 3 years. The Collective shall retain the report of the verification for a period of not less than 3 years.

(e) *Acceptable verification procedure.* An audit, including underlying paperwork, which was performed in the ordinary course of business according to generally accepted auditing standards by an independent and Qualified Auditor, shall serve as an acceptable verification procedure for all parties with respect to the information that is within the scope of the audit.

(f) *Consultation.* Before rendering a written report to the Collective, except where the auditor has a reasonable basis to suspect fraud and disclosure would, in the reasonable opinion of the auditor, prejudice the investigation of such suspected fraud, the auditor shall review the tentative written findings of the audit with the appropriate agent or employee of the Licensee being audited in order to remedy any factual errors and clarify any issues relating to the audit; Provided that the appropriate agent or employee of the Licensee reasonably cooperates with the auditor to remedy promptly any factual errors or clarify any issues raised by the audit.

(g) *Costs of the verification procedure.* The Collective shall pay the cost of the verification procedure, unless it is finally determined that there was an underpayment of 10% or more, in which case the Licensee shall, in addition to paying the amount of any underpayment, bear the reasonable costs of the verification procedure.

§ 384.7 Verification of royalty distributions.

(a) *General.* This section prescribes procedures by which any Copyright Owner may verify the royalty distributions made by the Collective; Provided, however, that nothing contained in this section shall apply to situations where a Copyright Owner and the Collective have agreed as to proper verification methods.

(b) *Frequency of verification.* A Copyright Owner may conduct a single audit of the Collective upon reasonable notice and during reasonable business hours, during any given calendar year, for any or all of the prior 3 calendar years, but no calendar year shall be subject to audit more than once.

(c) *Notice of intent to audit.* A Copyright Owner must file with the Copyright Royalty Judges a notice of intent to audit the Collective, which shall, within 30 days of the filing of the notice, publish in the FEDERAL REGISTER a notice announcing such filing. The notification of intent to audit shall be served at the same time on the Collective. Any such audit shall be conducted by an independent and Qualified Auditor identified in the notice, and shall be binding on all Copyright Owners.

(d) *Acquisition and retention of records.* The Collective shall use commercially reasonable efforts to obtain or to provide access to any relevant books and records maintained by third parties for the purpose of the audit and retain such records for a period of not less than 3 years. The Copyright Owner requesting the verification procedure shall retain the report of the verification for a period of not less than 3 years.

(e) *Acceptable verification procedure.* An audit, including underlying paperwork, which was performed in the ordinary course of business according to generally accepted auditing standards by an independent and Qualified Auditor, shall serve as an acceptable verification procedure for all parties with respect to the information that is within the scope of the audit.

(f) *Consultation.* Before rendering a written report to a Copyright Owner, except where the auditor has a reasonable basis to suspect fraud and disclosure would, in the reasonable opinion of the auditor, prejudice the investigation of such suspected fraud, the auditor shall review the tentative written findings of the audit with the appropriate agent or employee of the Collective in order to remedy any factual errors and clarify any issues relating to the audit; Provided that the appropriate agent or employee of the Collective reasonably cooperates with the auditor to remedy promptly any factual errors or clarify any issues raised by the audit.

(g) *Costs of the verification procedure.* The Copyright Owner requesting the verification procedure shall pay the cost of the procedure, unless it is finally determined that there was an underpayment of 10% or more, in which case the Collective shall, in addition to paying the amount of any underpayment, bear the reasonable costs of the verification procedure.

§ 384.8 Unclaimed funds.

If a Collective is unable to identify or locate a Copyright Owner who is entitled to receive a royalty payment under this part, the Collective shall retain the required payment in a segregated trust account for a period of 3 years from the date of payment. No claim to such payment shall be valid after the expiration of the 3-year period. After the expiration of this period, the Collective may apply the unclaimed funds to offset any costs deductible under 17 U.S.C. 114(g)(3). The foregoing shall apply notwithstanding the common law or statutes of any State.

PART 385—RATES AND TERMS FOR USE OF MUSICAL WORKS UNDER COMPULSORY LICENSE FOR MAKING AND DISTRIBUTING OF PHYSICAL AND DIGITAL PHONORECORDS

Subpart A—Physical Phonorecord Deliveries, Permanent Digital Downloads and Ringtones

Subpart B—Interactive Streaming, Other Incidental Digital Phonorecord Deliveries and Limited Downloads

AUTHORITY: 17 U.S.C. 115, 801(b)(1), 804(b)(4).

SOURCE: 74 FR 4529, Jan. 26, 2009, unless otherwise noted.

Subpart A—Physical Phonorecord Deliveries, Permanent Digital Downloads and Ringtones

§385.1 General.

(a) *Scope.* This subpart establishes rates and terms of royalty payments for making and distributing phonorecords, including by means of digital phonorecord deliveries, in accordance with the provisions of 17 U.S.C. 115.

(b) *Legal compliance.* Licensees relying upon the compulsory license set forth in 17 U.S.C. 115 shall comply with the requirements of that section, the rates and terms of this subpart, and any other applicable regulations.

(c) *Relationship to voluntary agreements.* Notwithstanding the royalty rates and terms established in this subpart, the rates and terms of any license agreements entered into by Copyright Owners and Licensees shall apply in lieu of the rates and terms of this subpart to use of musical works within the scope of such agreements.

§385.2 Definitions.

For purposes of this subpart, the following definitions apply:

Copyright owners are nondramatic musical work copyright owners who are entitled to royalty payments made under this subpart pursuant to the compulsory license under 17 U.S.C. 115.

Digital phonorecord delivery means a digital phonorecord delivery as defined in 17 U.S.C. 115(d).

Licensee is a person or entity that has obtained a compulsory license under 17 U.S.C. 115, and the implementing regulations, to make and distribute phonorecords of a nondramatic musical work, including by means of a digital phonorecord delivery.

Permanent digital download means a digital phonorecord delivery that is distributed in the form of a download that may be retained and played on a permanent basis.

Ringtone means a phonorecord of a partial musical work distributed as a digital phonorecord delivery in a format to be made resident on a telecommunications device for use to announce the reception of an incoming telephone call or other communication or message or to alert the receiver to the fact that there is a communication or message.

§385.3 Royalty rates for making and distributing phonorecords.

(a) *Physical phonorecord deliveries and permanent digital downloads.* For every physical phonorecord and permanent digital download made and distributed, the royalty rate payable for each work embodied in such phonorecord shall be either 9.1 cents or 1.75 cents per minute of playing time or fraction thereof, whichever amount is larger.

(b) *Ringtones.* For every ringtone made and distributed, the royalty rate payable for each work embodied therein shall be 24 cents.

§385.4 Late payments.

A Licensee shall pay a late fee of 1.5% per month, or the highest lawful rate, whichever is lower, for any payment received by the Copyright Owner after the due date set forth in (201.19(e)(7)(i) of this title. Late fees shall accrue from the due date until payment is received by the Copyright Owner.

Subpart B—Interactive Streaming, Other Incidental Digital Phonorecord Deliveries and Limited Downloads

§385.10 General.

(a) *Scope.* This subpart establishes rates and terms of royalty payments for interactive streams and limited downloads of musical works by subscription and nonsubscription digital music services in accordance with the provisions of 17 U.S.C. 115.

(b) *Legal compliance.* A licensee that makes or authorizes interactive streams or limited downloads of musical works through subscription or nonsubscription digital music services pursuant to 17 U.S.C. 115 shall comply with the requirements of that section, the rates and terms of this subpart, and any other applicable regulations.

§ 385.11 Definitions.

For purposes of this subpart, the following definitions shall apply:

Interactive stream means a stream of a sound recording of a musical work, where the performance of the sound recording by means of the stream is not exempt under 17 U.S.C. 114(d)(1) and does not in itself or as a result of a program in which it is included qualify for statutory licensing under 17 U.S.C. 114(d)(2).

Licensee means a person that has obtained a compulsory license under 17 U.S.C. 115 and its implementing regulations.

Licensed activity means interactive streams or limited downloads of musical works, as applicable.

Limited download means a digital transmission of a sound recording of a musical work to an end user, other than a stream, that results in a specifically identifiable reproduction of that sound recording that is only accessible for listening for—

(1) An amount of time not to exceed 1 month from the time of the transmission (unless the service, in lieu of retransmitting the same sound recording as another limited download, separately and upon specific request of the end user made through a live network connection, reauthorizes use for another time period not to exceed 1 month), or in the case of a subscription transmission, a period of time following the end of the applicable subscription no longer than a subscription renewal period or 3 months, whichever is shorter; or

(2) A specified number of times not to exceed 12 (unless the service, in lieu of retransmitting the same sound recording as another limited download, separately and upon specific request of the end user made through a live network connection, reauthorizes use of another series of 12 or fewer plays), or in the case of a subscription transmission, 12 times after the end of the applicable subscription.

(3) A limited download is a general digital phonorecord delivery under 17 U.S.C. 115(c)(3)(C) and (D).

Offering means a service's offering of licensed activity that is subject to a particular rate set forth in § 385.13(a) (e.g., a particular subscription plan available through the service).

Promotional royalty rate means the statutory royalty rate of zero in the case of certain promotional interactive streams and certain promotional limited downloads, as provided in § 385.14.

Publication date means January 26, 2009.

Record company means a person or entity that

(1) Is a copyright owner of a sound recording of a musical work;

(2) In the case of a sound recording of a musical work fixed before February 15, 1972, has rights to the sound recording, under the common law or statutes of any State, that are equivalent to the rights of a copyright owner of a sound recording of a musical work under title 17, United States Code;

(3) Is an exclusive licensee of the rights to reproduce and distribute a sound recording of a musical work; or

(4) Performs the functions of marketing and authorizing the distribution of a sound recording of a musical work under its own label, under the authority of the copyright owner of the sound recording.

Relevant page means a page (including a Web page, screen or display) from which licensed activity offered by a service is directly available to end users, but only where the offering of licensed activity and content that directly relates to the offering of licensed activity (e.g., an image of the artist or artwork closely associated with such offering, artist or album information, reviews of such offering, credits and music player controls) comprises 75% or more of the space on that page, excluding any space occupied by advertising. A licensed activity is directly available to end users from a page if sound recordings of musical works can be accessed by end users for limited downloads or interactive streams from such page (in most cases this will be the page where the limited download or interactive stream takes place).

Service means that entity (which may or may not be the licensee) that, with respect to the licensed activity,

(1) Contracts with or has a direct relationship with end users in a case where a contract or relationship exists, or otherwise controls the content made available to end users;

(2) Is able to report fully on service revenue from the provision of the licensed activity to the public, and to the extent applicable, verify service revenue through an audit; and

(3) Is able to report fully on usage of musical works by the service, or procure such reporting, and to the extent applicable, verify usage through an audit.

Service revenue. (1) Subject to paragraphs (2) through (5) of the definition of "Service revenue," and subject to U.S. Generally Accepted Accounting Principles, *service revenue* shall mean the following:

(i) All revenue recognized by the service from end users from the provision of licensed activity;

(ii) All revenue recognized by the service by way of sponsorship and commissions as a result of the inclusion of third-party "in-stream" or "in-download" advertising as part of licensed activity (*i.e.*, advertising placed immediately at the start, end or during the actual delivery, by way of interactive streaming or limited downloads, as applicable, of a musical work); and

(iii) All revenue recognized by the service, including by way of sponsorship and commissions, as a result of the placement of third-party advertising on a relevant page of the service or on any page that directly follows such relevant page leading up to and including the limited download or interactive streaming, as applicable, of a musical work; provided that, in the case where more than one service is actually available to end users from a relevant page, any advertising revenue shall be allocated between such services on the basis of the relative amounts of the page they occupy.

(2) In each of the cases identified in paragraph (1) of the definition of "Service revenue," such revenue shall, for the avoidance of doubt,

(i) Include any such revenue recognized by the service, or if not recognized by the service, by any associate, affiliate, agent or representative of such service in lieu of its being recognized by the service;

(ii) Include the value of any barter or other nonmonetary consideration;

(iii) Not be reduced by credit card commissions or similar payment process charges; and

(iv) Except as expressly set forth in this subpart, not be subject to any other deduction or set-off other than refunds to end users for licensed activity that they were unable to use due to technical faults in the licensed activity or other bona fide refunds or credits issued to end users in the ordinary course of business.

(3) In each of the cases identified in paragraph (1) of the definition of "Service revenue," such revenue shall, for the avoidance of doubt, exclude revenue derived solely in connection with services and activities other than licensed activity, provided that advertising or sponsorship revenue shall be treated as provided in paragraphs (2) and (4) of the definition of "Service revenue." By way of example, the following kinds of revenue shall be excluded:

(i) Revenue derived from non-music voice, content and text services;

(ii) Revenue derived from other non-music products and services (including search services, sponsored searches and click-through commissions); and

(iii) Revenue derived from music or music-related products and services that are not or do not include licensed activity.

(4) For purposes of paragraph (1) of the definition of "Service revenue," advertising or sponsorship revenue shall be reduced by the actual cost of obtaining such revenue, not to exceed 15%.

(5) Where the licensed activity is provided to end users as part of the same transaction with one or more other products or services that are not a music service engaged in licensed activity, then the revenue deemed to be recognized from end users for the service for the purpose of the definition in paragraph (1) of the definition of "Service revenue" shall be the revenue recognized from end users for the bundle less the standalone published price for end users for each of the other component(s) of the bundle; provided that, if there is no such standalone published

price for a component of the bundle, then the average standalone published price for end users for the most closely comparable product or service in the U.S. shall be used or, if more than one such comparable exists, the average of such standalone prices for such comparables shall be used. In connection with such a bundle, if a record company providing sound recording rights to the service

(i) Recognizes revenue (in accordance with U.S. Generally Accepted Accounting Principles, and including for the avoidance of doubt barter or nonmonetary consideration) from a person or entity other than the service providing the licensed activity and;

(ii) Such revenue is received, in the context of the transactions involved, as consideration for the ability to make interactive streams or limited downloads of sound recordings, then such revenue shall be added to the amounts expensed by the service for purposes of § 385.13(b). Where the service is the licensee, if the service provides the record company all information necessary for the record company to determine whether additional royalties are payable by the service hereunder as a result of revenue recognized from a person or entity other than the service as described in the immediately preceding sentence, then the record company shall provide such further information as necessary for the service to calculate the additional royalties and indemnify the service for such additional royalties. The sole obligation of the record company shall be to pay the licensee such additional royalties if actually payable as royalties hereunder; provided, however, that this shall not affect any otherwise existing right or remedy of the copyright owner nor diminish the licensee's obligations to the copyright owner.

Stream means the digital transmission of a sound recording of a musical work to an end user—

(1) To allow the end user to listen to the sound recording, while maintaining a live network connection to the transmitting service, substantially at the time of transmission, except to the extent that the sound recording remains accessible for future listening from a streaming cache reproduction;

(2) Using technology that is designed such that the sound recording does not remain accessible for future listening, except to the extent that the sound recording remains accessible for future listening from a streaming cache reproduction; and

(3) That is also subject to licensing as a public performance of the musical work.

Streaming cache reproduction means a reproduction of a sound recording of a musical work made on a computer or other receiving device by a service solely for the purpose of permitting an end user who has previously received a stream of such sound recording to play such sound recording again from local storage on such computer or other device rather than by means of a transmission; provided that the user is only able to do so while maintaining a live network connection to the service, and such reproduction is encrypted or otherwise protected consistent with prevailing industry standards to prevent it from being played in any other manner or on any device other than the computer or other device on which it was originally made.

Subscription service means a digital music service for which end users are required to pay a fee to access the service for defined subscription periods of 3 years or less (in contrast to, for example, a service where the basic charge to users is a payment per download or per play), whether such payment is made for access to the service on a standalone basis or as part of a bundle with one or more other products or services, and including any use of such a service on a trial basis without charge as described in § 385.14(b).

[74 FR 4529, Jan. 26, 2009, as amended at 74 FR 6834, Feb. 11, 2009]

§ 385.12 Calculation of royalty payments in general.

(a) *Applicable royalty.* Licensees that make or authorize licensed activity pursuant to 17 U.S.C. 115 shall pay royalties therefor that are calculated as provided in this section, subject to the minimum royalties and subscriber-based royalty floors for specific types of services provided in § 385.13, except as provided for certain promotional uses in § 385.14.

(b) *Rate calculation methodology.* Royalty payments for licensed activity shall be calculated as provided in paragraph (b) of this section. If a service includes different offerings, royalties must be separately calculated with respect to each such offering. Uses subject to the promotional royalty rate shall be excluded from the calculation of royalties due, as further described in this section and the following § 385.13.

(1) *Step 1:* Calculate the All-In Royalty for the Service. For each accounting period, the all-in royalty for each offering of the service is the greater of

(i) The applicable percentage of service revenue as set forth in paragraph (c) of this section (excluding any service revenue derived solely from licensed activity uses subject to the promotional royalty rate), and

(ii) The minimum specified in § 385.13 of the offering involved.

(2) *Step 2:* Subtract Applicable Performance Royalties. From the amount determined in step 1 in paragraph (b)(1) of this section, for each offering of the service, subtract the total amount of royalties for public performance of musical works that has been or will be expensed by the service pursuant to public performance licenses in connection with uses of musical works through such offering during the accounting period that constitute licensed activity (other than licensed activity subject to the promotional royalty rate). While this amount may be the total of the service's payments for that offering for the accounting period under its agreements with performing rights societies as defined in 17 U.S.C. 101, it will be less than the total of such public performance payments if the service is also engaging in public performance of musical works that does not constitute licensed activity. In the latter case, the amount to be subtracted for public performance payments shall be the amount of such payments allocable to licensed activity uses (other than promotional royalty rate uses) through the relevant offering, as determined in relation to all uses of musical works for which the public performance payments are made for the accounting period. Such allocation shall be made on the basis of plays of musical works or, where per-play information is unavailable due to bona fide technical limitations as described in step 4 in paragraph (b)(4) of this section, using the same alternative methodology as provided in step 4.

(3) *Step 3:* Determine the Payable Royalty Pool. This is the amount payable for the reproduction and distribution of all musical works used by the service by virtue of its licensed activity for a particular offering during the accounting period. This amount is the greater of

(i) The result determined in step 2 in paragraph (b)(2) of this section, and

(ii) The subscriber-based royalty floor resulting from the calculations described in § 385.13.

(4) *Step 4:* Calculate the Per-Work Royalty Allocation for Each Relevant Work. This is the amount payable for the reproduction and distribution of each musical work used by the service by virtue of its licensed activity through a particular offering during the accounting period. To determine this amount, the result determined in step 3 in paragraph (b)(3) of this section must be allocated to each musical work used through the offering. The allocation shall be accomplished by dividing the payable royalty pool determined in step 3 for such offering by the total number of plays of all musical works through such offering during the accounting period (other than promotional royalty rate plays) to yield a per-play allocation, and multiplying that result by the number of plays of each musical work (other than promotional royalty rate plays) through the offering during the accounting period. For purposes of determining the per-work royalty allocation in all calculations under this step 4 only (*i.e.*, after the payable royalty pool has been determined), for sound recordings of musical works with a playing time of over 5 minutes, each play on or after October 1, 2010 shall be counted as provided in paragraph (d) of this section. Notwithstanding the foregoing, if the service is not capable of tracking play information due to bona fide limitations of the available technology for services of that nature or of devices useable with the service, the per-work royalty allocation may instead be accomplished in a manner consistent

with the methodology used by the service for making royalty payment allocations for the use of individual sound recordings.

(c) *Percentage of service revenue.* The percentage of service revenue applicable under paragraph (b) of this section is 10.5%, except that such percentage shall be discounted by 2% (*i.e.*, to 8.5%) in the case of licensed activity occurring on or before December 31, 2007.

(d) *Overtime adjustment.* For licensed activity on or after October 1, 2010, for purposes of the calculations in step 4 in paragraph (b)(4) of this section only, for sound recordings of musical works with a playing time of over 5 minutes, adjust the number of plays as follows:

(1) 5:01 to 6:00 minutes—Each play = 1.2 plays

(2) 6:01 to 7:00 minutes—Each play = 1.4 plays

(3) 7:01 to 8:00 minutes—Each play = 1.6 plays

(4) 8:01 to 9:00 minutes—Each play = 1.8 plays

(5) 9:01 to 10:00 minutes—Each play = 2.0 plays

(6) For playing times of greater than 10 minutes, continue to add .2 for each additional minute or fraction thereof.

(e) *Accounting.* The calculations required by paragraph (b) of this section shall be made in good faith and on the basis of the best knowledge, information and belief of the licensee at the time payment is due, and subject to the additional accounting and certification requirements of 17 U.S.C. 115(c)(5) and § 201.19 of this title. Without limitation, a licensee's statements of account shall set forth each step of its calculations with sufficient information to allow the copyright owner to assess the accuracy and manner in which the licensee determined the payable royalty pool and per-play allocations (including information sufficient to demonstrate whether and how a minimum royalty or subscriber-based royalty floor pursuant to § 385.13 does or does not apply) and, for each offering reported, also indicate the type of licensed activity involved and the number of plays of each musical work (including an indication of any overtime adjustment applied) that is the basis of the per-work royalty allocation being paid.

§ 385.13 Minimum royalty rates and subscriber-based royalty floors for specific types of services.

(a) *In general.* The following minimum royalty rates and subscriber-based royalty floors shall apply to the following types of licensed activity:

(1) *Standalone non-portable subscription—streaming only.* Except as provided in paragraph (a)(4) of this section, in the case of a subscription service through which an end user can listen to sound recordings only in the form of interactive streams and only from a non-portable device to which such streams are originally transmitted while the device has a live network connection, the minimum for use in step 1 of § 385.12(b)(1) is the lesser of subminimum II as described in paragraph (c) of this section for the accounting period and the aggregate amount of 50 cents per subscriber per month. The subscriber-based royalty floor for use in step 3 of § 385.12(b)(3) is the aggregate amount of 15 cents per subscriber per month.

(2) *Standalone non-portable subscription—mixed.* Except as provided in paragraph (a)(4) of this section, in the case of a subscription service through which an end user can listen to sound recordings either in the form of interactive streams or limited downloads but only from a non-portable device to which such streams or downloads are originally transmitted, the minimum for use in step 1 of § 385.12(b)(1) is the lesser of the subminimum I as described in paragraph (b) of this section for the accounting period and the aggregate amount of 50 cents per subscriber per month. The subscriber-based royalty floor for use in step 3 of § 385.12(b)(3) is the aggregate amount of 30 cents per subscriber per month.

(3) *Standalone portable subscription service.* Except as provided in paragraph (a)(4) of this section, in the case of a subscription service through which an end user can listen to sound recordings in the form of interactive streams or limited downloads from a portable device, the minimum for use in step 1 of § 385.12(b)(1) is the lesser of subminimum I as described in paragraph (b) of this section for the accounting period and the aggregate amount of 80 cents

per subscriber per month. The subscriber-based royalty floor for use in step 3 of §385.12(b)(3) is the aggregate amount of 50 cents per subscriber per month.

(4) *Bundled subscription services.* In the case of a subscription service made available to end users with one or more other products or services as part of a single transaction without pricing for the subscription service separate from the product(s) or service(s) with which it is made available (e.g., a case in which a user can buy a portable device and one-year access to a subscription service for a single price), the minimum for use in step 1 of §385.12(b)(1) is subminimum I as described in paragraph (b) of this section for the accounting period. The subscriber-based royalty floor for use in step 3 of §385.12(b)(3) is the aggregate amount of 25 cents per month for each end user who has made at least one play of a licensed work during such month (each such end user to be considered an "active subscriber").

(5) *Free nonsubscription/ad-supported services.* In the case of a service offering licensed activity free of any charge to the end user, the minimum for use in step 1 of §385.12(b)(1) is subminimum II described in paragraph (c) of this section for the accounting period. There is no subscriber-based royalty floor for use in step 3 of §385.12(b)(3).

(b) *Computation of subminimum I.* For purposes of paragraphs (a)(2), (3) and (4) of this section, and with reference to paragraph (5) of the definition of "service revenue" in §385.11 if applicable, subminimum I for an accounting period means the aggregate of the following with respect to all sound recordings of musical works used in the relevant offering of the service during the accounting period—

(1) In cases in which a record company is the licensee under 17 U.S.C. 115 and a third-party service has obtained from the record company the rights to make interactive streams or limited downloads of a sound recording together with the right to reproduce and distribute the musical work embodied therein, 17.36% of the total amount expensed by the service in accordance with U.S. Generally Accepted Accounting Principles, which for the avoidance of doubt shall include the value of any barter or other nonmonetary consideration provided by the service, for such rights for the accounting period, except that for licensed activity occurring on or before December 31, 2007, subminimum I for an accounting period shall be 14.53% of the amount expensed by the service for such rights for the accounting period.

(2) In cases in which the relevant service is the licensee under 17 U.S.C. 115 and the relevant service has obtained from a third-party record company the rights to make interactive streams or limited downloads of a sound recording without the right to reproduce and distribute the musical work embodied therein, 21% of the total amount expensed by the service in accordance with U.S. Generally Accepted Accounting Principles, which for the avoidance of doubt shall include the value of any barter or other nonmonetary consideration provided by the service, for such sound recording rights for the accounting period, except that for licensed activity occurring on or before December 31, 2007, subminimum I for an accounting period shall be 17% of the amount expensed by the service for such sound recording rights for the accounting period.

(c) *Computation of subminimum II.* For purposes of paragraphs(a)(1) and (5) of this section, subminimum II for an accounting period means the aggregate of the following with respect to all sound recordings of musical works used by the relevant service during the accounting period—

(1) In cases in which a record company is the licensee under 17 U.S.C. 115 and a third-party service has obtained from the record company the rights to make interactive streams and limited downloads of a sound recording together with the right to reproduce and distribute the musical work embodied therein, 18% of the total amount expensed by the service in accordance with U.S. Generally Accepted Accounting Principles, which for the avoidance of doubt shall include the value of any barter or other nonmonetary consideration provided by the service, for such rights for the accounting period, except that for licensed activity occurring on

or before December 31, 2007, subminimum II for an accounting period shall be 14.53% of the amount expensed by the service for such rights for the accounting period.

(2) In cases in which the relevant service is the licensee under 17 U.S.C. 115 and the relevant service has obtained from a third-party record company the rights to make interactive streams or limited downloads of a sound recording without the right to reproduce and distribute the musical work embodied therein, 22% of the total amount expensed by the service in accordance with U.S. Generally Accepted Accounting Principles, which for the avoidance of doubt shall include the value of any barter or other nonmonetary consideration provided by the service, for such sound recording rights for the accounting period, except that for licensed activity occurring on or before December 31, 2007, subminimum II for an accounting period shall be 17% of the amount expensed by the service for such sound recording rights for the accounting period.

(d) *Computation of subscriber-based royalty rates.* For purposes of paragraph (a) of this section, to determine the minimum or subscriber-based royalty floor, as applicable to any particular offering, the service shall for the relevant offering calculate its total number of subscriber-months for the accounting period, taking into account all end users who were subscribers for complete calendar months, prorating in the case of end users who were subscribers for only part of a calendar month, and deducting on a prorated basis for end users covered by a free trial period subject to the promotional royalty rate as described in § 385.14(b)(2), except that in the case of a bundled subscription service, subscriber-months shall instead be determined with respect to active subscribers as defined in paragraph (a)(4) of this section. The product of the total number of subscriber-months for the accounting period and the specified number of cents per subscriber (or active subscriber, as the case may be) shall be used as the subscriber-based component of the minimum or subscriber-based royalty floor, as applicable, for the accounting period.

§ 385.14 Promotional royalty rate.

(a) *General provisions.* (1) This section establishes a royalty rate of zero in the case of certain promotional interactive streaming activities, and of certain promotional limited downloads offered in the context of a free trial period for a digital music subscription service under a license pursuant to 17 U.S.C. 115. Subject to the requirements of 17 U.S.C. 115 and the additional provisions of paragraphs (b) through (e) of this section, the promotional royalty rate shall apply to a musical work when a record company transmits or authorizes the transmission of interactive streams or limited downloads of a sound recording that embodies such musical work, only if—

(i) The primary purpose of the record company in making or authorizing the interactive streams or limited downloads is to promote the sale or other paid use of sound recordings by the relevant artists, including such sound recording, through established retail channels or the paid use of one or more established retail music services through which the sound recording is available, and not to promote any other good or service;

(ii) Either—

(A) The sound recording (or a different version of the sound recording embodying the same musical work) is being lawfully distributed and offered to consumers through the established retail channels or services described in paragraph (a)(1)(i) of this section; or

(B) In the case of a sound recording of a musical work being prepared for commercial release but not yet released, the record company has a good faith intention of lawfully distributing and offering to consumers the sound recording (or a different version of the sound recording embodying the same musical work) through the established retail channels or services described in paragraph (a)(1)(i) of this section within 90 days after the commencement of the first promotional use authorized under this section (and in fact does so, unless it can demonstrate that notwithstanding its bona fide intention, it unexpectedly did not meet the scheduled release date);

(iii) In connection with authorizing the promotional interactive streams or limited downloads, the record company has obtained from the service it authorizes a written representation that—

(A) In the case of a promotional use commencing on or after October 1, 2010, except interactive streaming subject to paragraph (d) of this section, the service agrees to maintain for a period of no less than 5 years from the conclusion of the promotional activity complete and accurate records of the relevant authorization and dates on which the promotion was conducted, and identifying each sound recording of a musical work made available through the promotion, the licensed activity involved, and the number of plays of such recording;

(B) The service is in all material respects operating with appropriate license authority with respect to the musical works it is using for promotional and other purposes; and

(C) The representation is signed by a person authorized to make the representation on behalf of the service;

(iv) Upon receipt by the record company of written notice from the copyright owner of a musical work or agent of the copyright owner stating in good faith that a particular service is in a material manner operating without appropriate license authority from such copyright owner, the record company shall within 5 business days withdraw by written notice its authorization of such uses of such copyright owner's musical works under the promotional royalty rate by that service;

(v) The interactive streams or limited downloads are offered free of any charge to the end user and, except in the case of interactive streaming subject to paragraph (d) of this section in the case of a free trial period for a digital music subscription service, no more than 5 sound recordings at a time are streamed in response to any individual request of an end user;

(vi) The interactive streams and limited downloads are offered in a manner such that the user is at the same time (e.g., on the same Web page) presented with a purchase opportunity for the relevant sound recording or an opportunity to subscribe to a paid service offering the sound recording, or a link to such a purchase or subscription opportunity, except—

(A) In the case of interactive streaming of a sound recording being prepared for commercial release but not yet released, certain mobile applications or other circumstances in which the foregoing is impracticable in view of the current state of the relevant technology; and

(B) In the case of a free trial period for a digital music subscription service, if end users are periodically offered an opportunity to subscribe to the service during such free trial period; and

(vii) The interactive streams and limited downloads are not provided in a manner that is likely to cause mistake, to confuse or to deceive, reasonable end users as to the endorsement or association of the author of the musical work with any product, service or activity other than the sale or paid use of sound recordings or paid use of a music service through which sound recordings are available. Without limiting the foregoing, upon receipt of written notice from the copyright owner of a musical work or agent of the copyright owner stating in good faith that a particular use of such work under this section violates the limitation set forth in this paragraph (a)(1)(vii), the record company shall promptly cease such use of that work, and within 5 business days withdraw by written notice its authorization of such use by all relevant third parties it has authorized under this section.

(2) To rely upon the promotional royalty rate, a record company making or authorizing interactive streams or limited downloads shall keep complete and accurate contemporaneous written records of such uses, including the sound recordings and musical works involved, the artists, the release dates of the sound recordings, a brief statement of the promotional activities authorized, the identity of the service or services where each promotion is authorized (including the Internet address if applicable), the beginning and end date of each period of promotional activity authorized, and the representation required by paragraph (a)(1)(iii) of this section; provided that, in the case of trial subscription uses, such records

shall instead consist of the contractual terms that bear upon promotional uses by the particular digital music subscription services it authorizes; and further provided that, if the record company itself is conducting the promotion, it shall also maintain any additional records described in paragraph (a)(1)(iii)(A) of this section. The records required by this paragraph (a)(2) shall be maintained for no less time than the record company maintains records of usage of royalty-bearing uses involving the same type of licensed activity in the ordinary course of business, but in no event for less than 5 years from the conclusion of the promotional activity to which they pertain. If the copyright owner of a musical work or its agent requests a copy of the information to be maintained under this paragraph (a)(2) with respect to a specific promotion or relating to a particular sound recording of a musical work, the record company shall provide complete and accurate documentation within 10 business days, except for any information required under paragraph (a)(1)(iii)(A) of this section, which shall be provided within 20 business days, and provided that if the copyright owner or agent requests information concerning a large volume of promotions or sound recordings, the record company shall have a reasonable time, in view of the amount of information requested, to respond to any request of such copyright owner or agent. If the record company does not provide required information within the required time, and upon receipt of written notice citing such failure does not provide such information within a further 10 business days, the uses will be considered not to be subject to the promotional royalty rate and the record company (but not any third-party service it has authorized) shall be liable for any payment due for such uses; provided, however, that all rights and remedies of the copyright owner with respect to unauthorized uses shall be preserved.

(3) If the copyright owner of a musical work or its agent requests a copy of the information to be maintained under paragraph (a)(1)(iii)(A) of this section by a service authorized by a record company with respect to a specific promotion, the service shall provide complete and accurate documentation within 20 business days, provided that if the copyright owner or agent requests information concerning a large volume of promotions or sound recordings, the service shall have a reasonable time, in view of the amount of information requested, to respond to any request of such copyright owner or agent. If the service does not provide required information within the required time, and upon receipt of written notice citing such failure does not provide such information within a further 10 business days, the uses will be considered not to be subject to the promotional royalty rate and the service (but not the record company) will be liable for any payment due for such uses; provided, however, that all rights and remedies of the copyright owner with respect to unauthorized uses shall be preserved.

(4) The promotional royalty rate is exclusively for audio-only interactive streaming and limited downloads of musical works subject to licensing under 17 U.S.C. 115. The promotional royalty rate does not apply to any other use under 17 U.S.C. 115; nor does it apply to public performances, audiovisual works, lyrics or other uses outside the scope of 17 U.S.C. 115. Without limitation, uses subject to licensing under 17 U.S.C. 115 that do not qualify for the promotional royalty rate (including without limitation interactive streaming or limited downloads of a musical work beyond the time limitations applicable to the promotional royalty rate) require payment of applicable royalties. This section is based on an understanding of industry practices and market conditions at the time of its development, among other things. The terms of this section shall be subject to de novo review and consideration (or elimination altogether) in future proceedings before the Copyright Royalty Judges. Nothing in this section shall be interpreted or construed in such a manner as to nullify or diminish any limitation, requirement or obligation of 17 U.S.C. 115 or other protection for musical works afforded by the Copyright Act, 17 U.S.C. 101 *et seq.*

(b) *Interactive streaming and limited downloads of full-length musical works through third-party services.* In addition to those of paragraph (a) of this section, the provisions of this paragraph (b) apply to interactive streaming, and limited downloads (in the context of a free trial period for a digital music subscription service), authorized by record companies under the promotional royalty rate through third-party services (including Web sites) that is not subject to paragraphs (c) or (d) of this section. Such interactive streams and limited downloads may be made or authorized by a record company under the promotional royalty rate only if—

(1) No cash, other monetary payment, barter or other consideration for making or authorizing the relevant interactive streams or limited downloads is received by the record company, its parent company, any entity owned in whole or in part by or under common ownership with the record company, or any other person or entity acting on behalf of or in lieu of the record company, except for in-kind promotional consideration used to promote the sale or paid use of sound recordings or the paid use of music services through which sound recordings are available;

(2) In the case of interactive streaming and limited downloads offered in the context of a free trial period for a digital music subscription service, the free trial period does not exceed 30 consecutive days per subscriber per two-year period; and

(3) In contexts other than a free trial period for a digital music subscription service, interactive streaming subject to paragraph (b) of this section of a particular sound recording is authorized by the record company on no more than 60 days total for all services (*i.e.*, interactive streaming under paragraph (b) of this section of a particular sound recording may be authorized on no more than a total of 60 days, which need not be consecutive, and on any one such day, interactive streams may be offered on one or more services); provided, however, that an additional 60 days shall be available each time the sound recording is re-released by the record company in a remastered form or as a part of a compilation with a different set of sound recordings than the original release or any prior compilation including such sound recording.

(4) In the event that a record company authorizes promotional uses in excess of the time limitations of paragraph (b) of this section, the record company, and not the third-party service it has authorized, shall be liable for any payment due for such uses; provided, however, that all rights and remedies of the copyright owner with respect to unauthorized uses shall be preserved. In the event that a third-party service exceeds the scope of any authorization by a record company, the service, and not the record company, shall be liable for any payment due for such uses; provided, however, that all rights and remedies of the copyright owner with respect to unauthorized uses shall be preserved.

(c) *Interactive streaming of full-length musical works through record company and artist services.* In addition to those of paragraph (a) of this section, the provisions of this paragraph (c) apply to interactive streaming conducted or authorized by record companies under the promotional royalty rate through a service (e.g., a Web site) directly owned or operated by the record company, or directly owned or operated by a recording artist under the authorization of the record company, and that is not subject to paragraph (d) of this section. For the avoidance of doubt and without limitation, an artist page or site on a third-party service (e.g., a social networking service) shall not be considered a service operated by the record company or artist. Such interactive streams may be made or authorized by a record company under the promotional royalty rate only if—

(1) The interactive streaming subject to this paragraph (c) of a particular sound recording is offered or authorized by the record company on no more than 90 days total for all services (*i.e.*, interactive streaming under this paragraph (c) of a particular sound recording may be authorized on no more than a total of 90 days, which need not be consecutive, and on any such day, interactive streams may be offered on one or more services operated by the record company or artist, subject to

the provisions of paragraph (b)(2) of this section); provided, however, that an additional 90 days shall be available each time the sound recording is re-released by the record company in a remastered form or as part of a compilation with a different set of sound recordings than prior compilations that include that sound recording;

(2) In the case of interactive streaming through a service devoted to one featured artist, the interactive streams subject to this paragraph (c) of this section of a particular sound recording are made or authorized by the record company on no more than one official artist site per artist and are recordings of that artist; and

(3) In the case of interactive streaming through a service that is not limited to a single featured artist, all interactive streaming on such service (whether eligible for the promotional royalty rate or not) is limited to sound recordings of a single record company and its affiliates and the service would not reasonably be considered to be a meaningful substitute for a paid music service.

(d) *Interactive streaming of clips.* In addition to those in paragraph (a) of this section, the provisions of this paragraph (d) apply to interactive streaming conducted or authorized by record companies under the promotional royalty rate of segments of sound recordings of musical works with a playing time that does not exceed the greater of:

(1) 30 seconds, or

(2) 10% of the playing time of the complete sound recording, but in no event in excess of 60 seconds. Such interactive streams may be made or authorized by a record company under the promotional royalty rate without any of the temporal limitations set forth in paragraphs (b) and (c) of this section (but subject to the other conditions of paragraphs (b) and (c) of this section, as applicable). For clarity, this paragraph (d) is strictly limited to the uses described herein and shall not be construed as permitting the creation or use of an excerpt of a musical work in violation of 17 U.S.C. 106(2) or 115(a)(2) or any other right of a musical work owner.

[74 FR 4529, Jan. 26, 2009, as amended at 74 FR 6834, Feb. 11, 2009]

§ 385.15 [Reserved]

§ 385.16 Reproduction and distribution rights covered.

A compulsory license under 17 U.S.C. 115 extends to all reproduction and distribution rights that may be necessary for the provision of the licensed activity, solely for the purpose of providing such licensed activity (and no other purpose).

§ 385.17 Effect of rates.

In any future proceedings under 17 U.S.C. 115(c)(3)(C) and (D), the royalty rates payable for a compulsory license shall be established de novo.

PART 386—ADJUSTMENT OF ROYALTY FEES FOR SECONDARY TRANSMISSIONS BY SATELLITE CARRIERS

Sec.

AUTHORITY: 17 U.S.C. 119(c), 801(b)(1).

SOURCE: 75 FR 53198, Aug. 31, 2010, unless otherwise noted.

§ 386.1 General.

This part 386 adjusts the rates of royalties payable under the statutory license for the secondary transmission of broadcast stations under 17 U.S.C. 119.

§ 386.2 Royalty fee for secondary transmission by satellite carriers.

(a) *General.* (1) For purposes of this section, *Per subscriber per month* shall mean for each subscriber subscribing to the station in question (or to a package including such station) on the last day of a given month.

(2) In the case of a station engaged in digital multicasting, the rates set forth in paragraph (b) of this section shall apply to each digital stream that a satellite carrier or distributor retransmits pursuant to 17 U.S.C. 119, provided however that no additional royalty shall be paid for the carriage of any material

related to the programming on such stream.

(b) *Rates*—(1) *Private home viewing.* The rates applicable to Satellite Carriers' carriage of each broadcast signal for private home viewing shall be as follows:

(i) 2010: 25 cents per subscriber per month (for each month of 2010);

(ii) 2011: 25 cents per subscriber per month;

(iii) 2012: 26 cents per subscriber per month;

(iv) 2013: 27 cents per subscriber per month;

(v) 2014: The 2013 rate, adjusted for the amount of inflation as measured by the change in the Consumer Price Index for all Urban Consumers All Items from October 2012 to October 2013.

(2) *Viewing in commercial establishments.* The rates applicable to Satellite Carriers' carriage of each broadcast signal for viewing in commercial establishments shall be as follows:

(i) 2010: 50 cents per subscriber per month (for each month of 2010);

(ii) 2011: 51 cents per subscriber per month;

(iii) 2012: 53 cents per subscriber per month;

(iv) 2013: 54 cents per subscriber per month;

(v) 2014: The 2013 rate, adjusted for the amount of inflation as measured by the change in the Consumer Price Index for all Urban Consumers All Items from October 2012 to October 2013.

[75 FR 53198, Aug. 31, 2010, as amended at 75 FR 75624, Dec. 6, 2010; 76 FR 74704, Dec. 1, 2011; 77 FR 70374, Nov. 26, 2012]

CHAPTER IV—NATIONAL INSTITUTE OF STANDARDS AND TECHNOLOGY, DEPARTMENT OF COMMERCE

PART 401—RIGHTS TO INVENTIONS MADE BY NONPROFIT ORGANIZATIONS AND SMALL BUSINESS FIRMS UNDER GOVERNMENT GRANTS, CONTRACTS, AND COOPERATIVE AGREEMENTS

AUTHORITY: 35 U.S.C. 206; DOO 30–2A.

SOURCE: 52 FR 8554, Mar. 18, 1987, unless otherwise noted.

§401.1 Scope.

(a) Traditionally there have been no conditions imposed by the government on research performers while using private facilities which would preclude them from accepting research funding from other sources to expand, to aid in completing or to conduct separate investigations closely related to research activities sponsored by the government. Notwithstanding the right of research organizations to accept supplemental funding from other sources for the purpose of expediting or more comprehensively accomplishing the research objectives of the government sponsored project, it is clear that the ownership provisions of these regulations would remain applicable in any invention "conceived or first actually reduced to practice in performance" of the project. Separate accounting for the two funds used to support the project in this case is not a determining factor.

(1) To the extent that a non-government sponsor established a project which, although closely related, falls outside the planned and committed activities of a government-funded project and does not diminish or distract from the performance of such activities, inventions made in performance of the non-government sponsored project would not be subject to the conditions of these regulations. An example of such related but separate projects would be a government sponsored project having research objectives to expand scientific understanding in a field and a closely related industry sponsored project having as its objectives the application of such new knowledge to develop usable new technology. The time relationship in conducting the two projects and the use of new fundamental knowledge from one in the performance of the other are not important determinants since most inventions rest on a knowledge base built up by numerous independent research efforts extending over many years. Should such an invention be claimed by the performing organization to be the product of non-government sponsored research and be challenged by the sponsoring agency as being reportable to the government as a "subject invention", the challenge is appealable as described in §401.11(d).

(2) An invention which is made outside of the research activities of a government-funded project is not viewed as a "subject invention" since it cannot be shown to have been "conceived or first actually reduced to practice" in performance of the project. An obvious example of this is a situation where an instrument purchased with government funds is later used, without interference with or cost to the government-funded project, in making an invention all expenses of which involve only non-government funds.

(b) This part inplements 35 U.S.C. 202 through 204 and is applicable to all Federal agencies. It applies to all funding agreements with small business firms and nonprofit organizations executed after the effective date of this part, except for a funding agreement made primarily for educational purposes. Certain sections also provide guidance for the administration of funding agreements which predate the effective date of this part. In accordance with 35 U.S.C. 212, no scholarship, fellowship, training grant, or other funding agreement made by a Federal agency primarily to an awardee for educational purposes will contain any provision giving the Federal agency any rights to inventions made by the awardee.

(c) The *march-in* and appeals procedures in §§ 401.6 and 401.11 shall apply to any march-in or appeal proceeding under a funding agreement subject to Chapter 18 of Title 35, U.S.C., initiated after the effective date of this part even if the funding agreement was executed prior to that date.

(d) At the request of the contractor, a funding agreement for the operation of a government-owned facility which is in effect on the effective date of this part shall be promptly amended to include the provisions required by §§ 401.3(a) unless the agency determines that one of the exceptions at 35 U.S.C. 202(a)(i) through (iv) § 401.3(a)(8) through (iv) of this part) is applicable and will be applied. If the exception at § 401.3(a)(iv) is determined to be applicable, the funding agreement will be promptly amended to include the provisions required by § 401.3(c).

(e) This regulation supersedes OMB Circular A–124 and shall take precedence over any regulations dealing with ownership of inventions made by small businesses and nonprofit organizations which are inconsistent with it. This regulation will be followed by all agencies pending amendment of agency regulations to conform to this part and amended Chapter 18 of Title 35. Only deviations requested by a contractor and not inconsistent with Chapter 18 of Title 35, United States Code, may be made without approval of the Secretary. Modifications or tailoring of clauses as authorized by §§ 401.5 or 401.3, when alternative provisions are used under § 401.3(a)(1) through (4), are not considered deviations requiring the Secretary's approval. Three copies of proposed and final agency regulations supplementing this part shall be submitted to the Secretary at the office set out in § 401.16 for approval for consistency with this part before they are submitted to the Office of Management and Budget (OMB) for review under Executive Order 12291 or, if no submission is required to be made to OMB, before their submission to the FEDERAL REGISTER for publication.

(f) In the event an agency has outstanding prime funding agreements that do not contain patent flow-down provisions consistent with this part or earlier Office of Federal Procurement Policy regulations (OMB Circular A–124 or OMB Bulletin 81–22), the agency shall take appropriate action to ensure that small business firms or nonprofit organizations that are subcontractors under any such agreements and that received their subcontracts after July 1, 1981, receive rights in their subject inventions that are consistent with Chapter 18 and this part.

(g) This part is not intended to apply to arrangements under which nonprofit organizations, small business firms, or others are allowed to use government-owned research facilities and normal technical assistance provided to users of those facilities, whether on a reimbursable or nonreimbursable basis. This part is also not intended to apply to arrangements under which sponsors reimburse the government or facility contractor for the contractor employee's time in performing work for the sponsor. Such arrangements are not considered "funding agreements" as defined at 35 U.S.C. 201(b) and § 401.2(a) of this part.

§ 401.2 Definitions.

As used in this part—

(a) The term *funding agreement* means any contract, grant, or cooperative agreement entered into between any Federal agency, other than the Tennessee Valley Authority, and any contractor for the performance of experimental, developmental, or research work funded in whole or in part by the Federal government. This term also includes any assignment, substitution of parties, or subcontract of any type entered into for the performance of experimental, developmental, or research work under a funding agreement as defined in the first sentence of this paragraph.

(b) The term *contractor* means any person, small business firm or nonprofit organization which is a party to a funding agreement.

(c) The term *invention* means any invention or discovery which is or may be patentable or otherwise protectable under Title 35 of the United States Code, or any novel variety of plant which is or may be protectable under the Plant Variety Protection Act (7 U.S.C. 2321 *et seq.*).

(d) The term *subject invention* means any invention of a contractor conceived or first actually reduced to practice in the performance of work under a funding agreement; provided that in the case of a variety of plant, the date of determination (as defined in section 41(d) of the Plant Variety Protection Act, 7 U.S.C. 2401(d)) must also occur during the period of contract performance.

(e) The term *practical application* means to manufacture in the case of a composition of product, to practice in the case of a process or method, or to operate in the case of a machine or system; and, in each case, under such conditions as to establish that the invention is being utilized and that its benefits are, to the extent permitted by law or government regulations, available to the public on reasonable terms.

(f) The term *made* when used in relation to any invention means the conception or first actual reduction to practice of such invention.

(g) The term *small business firm* means a small business concern as defined at section 2 of Pub. L. 85–536 (15 U.S.C. 632) and implementing regulations of the Administrator of the Small Business Administration. For the purpose of this part, the size standards for small business concerns involved in government procurement and subcontracting at 13 CFR 121.5 will be used.

(h) The term *nonprofit organization* means universities and other institutions of higher education or an organization of the type described in section 501(c)(3) of the Internal Revenue Code of 1954 (26 U.S.C. 501(c) and exempt from taxation under section 501(a) of the Internal Revenue Code (26 U.S.C. 501(a)) or any nonprofit scientific or educational organization qualified under a state nonprofit organization statute.

(i) The term *Chapter 18* means Chapter 18 of Title 35 of the United States Code.

(j) The term *Secretary* means the Director of the National Institute of Standards and Technology.

(k) The term *electronically filed* means any submission of information transmitted by an electronic or optical-electronic system.

(l) The term *electronic or optical-electronic system* means a software-based system approved by the agency for the transmission of information.

(m) The term *patent application* or "application for patent" includes a provisional or nonprovisional U.S. national application for patent as defined in 37 CFR 1.9 (a)(2) and (a)(3), respectively, or an application for patent in a foreign country or in an international patent office.

(n) The term *initial patent application* means a nonprovisional U.S. national application for patent as defined in 37 CFR 1.9(a)(3).

[52 FR 8554, Mar. 18, 1987, as amended at 60 FR 41812, Aug. 14, 1995; 78 FR 4766, Jan. 23, 2013]

§401.3 Use of the standard clauses at §401.14.

(a) Each funding agreement awarded to a small business firm or nonprofit organization (except those subject to 35 U.S.C. 212) shall contain the clause found in §401.14(a) with such modifications and tailoring as authorized or required elsewhere in this part. However, a funding agreement may contain alternative provisions—

(1) When the contractor is not located in the United States or does not have a place of business located in the United States or is subject to the control of a foreign government; or

(2) In exceptional circumstances when it is determined by the agency that restriction or elimination of the right to retain title to any subject invention will better promote the policy and objectives of Chapter 18 of Title 35 of the United States Code; or

(3) When it is determined by a government authority which is authorized

by statute or executive order to conduct foreign intelligence or counter-intelligence activities that the restriction or elimination of the right to retain title to any subject invention is necessary to protect the security to such activities; or

(4) When the funding agreement includes the operation of the government-owned, contractor-operated facility of the Department of Energy primarily dedicated to that Department's naval nuclear propulsion or weapons related programs and all funding agreement limitations under this subparagraph on the contractor's right to elect title to a subject invention are limited to inventions occurring under the above two programs.

(5) If any part of the contract may require the contractor to perform work on behalf of the Government at a Government laboratory under a Cooperative Research and Development Agreement (CRADA) pursuant to the statutory authority of 15 U.S.C. 3710a, the contracting officer may include alternate paragraph (b) in the basic patent rights clause in § 401.14. Because the use of the alternate is based on a determination of exceptional circumstances under § 401.3(a)(2), the contracting officer shall ensure that the appeal procedures of § 401.4 are satisfied whenever the alternate is used.

(b) When an agency exercises the exceptions at § 401.3(a)(2) or (3), it shall use the standard clause at § 401.14(a) with only such modifications as are necessary to address the exceptional circumstances or concerns which led to the use of the exception. For example, if the justification relates to a particular field of use or market, the clause might be modified along lines similar to those described in § 401.14(b). In any event, the clause should provide the contractor with an opportunity to receive greater rights in accordance with the procedures at § 401.15. When an agency justifies and exercises the exception at § 401.3(a)(2) and uses an alternative provision in the funding agreement on the basis of national security, the provision shall provide the contractor with the right to elect ownership to any invention made under such funding agreement as provided by the Standard Patent Rights Clause found at § 401.14(a) if the invention is not classified by the agency within six months of the date it is reported to the agency, or within the same time period the Department of Energy does not, as authorized by regulation, law or Executive order or implementing regulations thereto, prohibit unauthorized dissemination of the invention. Contracts in support of DOE's naval nuclear propulsion program are exempted from this paragraph.

(c) When the Department of Energy exercises the exception at § 401.3(a)(4), it shall use the clause prescribed at § 401.14(b) or substitute thereto with such modification and tailoring as authorized or required elsewhere in this part.

(d) When a funding agreement involves a series of separate task orders, an agency may apply the exceptions at § 401.3(a)(2) or (3) to individual task orders, and it may structure the contract so that modified patent rights provisions will apply to the task order even though the clauses at either § 401.14(a) or (b) are applicable to the remainder of the work. Agencies are authorized to negotiate such modified provisions with respect to task orders added to a funding agreement after its initial award.

(e) Before utilizing any of the exceptions in § 401.3(a) of this section, the agency shall prepare a written determination, including a statement of facts supporting the determination, that the conditions identified in the exception exist. A separate statement of facts shall be prepared for each exceptional circumstances determination, except that in appropriate cases a single determination may apply to both a funding agreement and any subcontracts issued under it or to any funding agreement to which such an exception is applicable. In cases when § 401.3(a)(2) is used, the determination shall also include an analysis justifying the determination. This analysis should address with specificity how the alternate provisions will better achieve the objectives set forth in 35 U.S.C. 200. A copy of each determination, statement of facts, and, if applicable, analysis shall be promptly provided to the contractor or prospective contractor along with a notification to the contractor or prospective contractor of its rights to appeal the determination of the exception under 35 U.S.C. 202(b)(4) and §401.4 of this part.

(f) Except for determinations under §401.3(a)(3), the agency shall also provide copies of each determination, statement of fact, and analysis to the Secretary. These shall be sent within 30 days after the award of the funding agreement to which they pertain. Copies shall also be sent to the Chief Counsel for Advocacy of the Small Business Administration if the funding agreement is with a small business firm. If the Secretary of Commerce believes that any individual determination or pattern of determinations is contrary to the policies and objectives of this chapter or otherwise not in conformance with this chapter, the Secretary shall so advise the head of the agency concerned and the Administrator of the Office of Federal Procurement Policy and recommend corrective actions.

(g) To assist the Comptroller General of the United States to accomplish his or her responsibilities under 35 U.S.C. 202, each Federal agency that enters into any funding agreements with nonprofit organizations or small business firms shall accumulate and, at the request of the Comptroller General, provide the Comptroller General or his or her duly authorized representative the total number of prime agreements entered into with small business firms or nonprofit organizations that contain the patent rights clause in this part or under OMB Circular A-124 for each fiscal year beginning with October 1, 1982.

(h) To qualify for the standard clause, a prospective contractor may be required by an agency to certify that it is either a small business firm or a nonprofit organization. If the agency has reason to question the status of the prospective contractor as a small business firm, it may file a protest in accordance with 13 CFR 121.9. If it questions nonprofit status, it may require the prospective contractor to furnish evidence to establish its status as a nonprofit organization.

[52 FR 8554, Mar. 18, 1987, as amended at 69 FR 17301, Apr. 2, 2004]

§401.4 Contractor appeals of exceptions.

(a) In accordance with 35 U.S.C. 202(b)(4) a contractor has the right to an administrative review of a determination to use one of the exceptions at §401.3(a) (1) through (4) if the contractor believes that a determination is either contrary to the policies and objectives of this chapter or constitutes an abuse of discretion by the agency. Paragraph (b) of this section specifies the procedures to be followed by contractors and agencies in such cases. The assertion of such a claim by the contractor shall not be used as a basis for withholding or delaying the award of a funding agreement or for suspending performance under an award. Pending final resolution of the claim the contract may be issued with the patent rights provision proposed by the agency; however, should the final decision be in favor of the contractor, the funding agreement will be amended accordingly and the amendment made retroactive to the effective date of the funding agreement.

(b)(1) A contractor may appeal a determination by providing written notice to the agency within 30 working days from the time it receives a copy of the agency's determination, or within such longer time as an agency may specify in its regulations. The contractor's notice should specifically identify the basis for the appeal.

(2) The appeal shall be decided by the head of the agency or by his/her designee who is at a level above the person who made the determination. If the notice raises a genuine dispute over the material facts, the head of the agency or the designee shall undertake, or refer the matter for, fact-finding.

(3) Fact-finding shall be conducted in accordance with procedures established by the agency. Such procedures shall be as informal as practicable and be consistent with principles of fundamental fairness. The procedures should afford the contractor the opportunity to appear with counsel, submit documentary evidence, present witnesses and confront such persons as the agency may rely upon. A transcribed record shall be made and shall be available at cost to the contractor upon request. The requirement for a transcribed

record may be waived by mutual agreement of the contractor and the agency.

(4) The official conducting the fact-finding shall prepare or adopt written findings of fact and transmit them to the head of the agency or designee promptly after the conclusion of the fact-finding proceeding along with a recommended decision. A copy of the findings of fact and recommended decision shall be sent to the contractor by registered or certified mail.

(5) Fact-finding should be completed within 45 working days from the date the agency receives the contractor's written notice.

(6) When fact-finding has been conducted, the head of the agency or designee shall base his or her decision on the facts found, together with any argument submitted by the contractor, agency officials or any other information in the administrative record. In cases referred for fact-finding, the agency head or the designee may reject only those facts that have been found to be clearly erroneous, but must explicitly state the rejection and indicate the basis for the contrary finding. The agency head or the designee may hear oral arguments after fact-finding provided that the contractor or contractor's attorney or representative is present and given an opportunity to make arguments and rebuttal. The decision of the agency head or the designee shall be in writing and, if it is unfavorable to the contractor shall include an explanation of the basis of the decision. The decision of the agency or designee shall be made within 30 working days after fact-finding or, if there was no fact-finding, within 45 working days from the date the agency received the contractor's written notice. A contractor adversely affected by a determination under this section may, at any time within sixty days after the determination is issued, file a petition in the United States Claims Court, which shall have jurisdiction to determine the appeal on the record and to affirm, reverse, remand, or modify as appropriate, the determination of the Federal agency.

§ 401.5 Modification and tailoring of clauses.

(a) Agencies should complete the blank in paragraph (g)(2) of the clauses at § 401.14 in accordance with their own or applicable government-wide regulations such as the Federal Acquisition Regulation. In grants and cooperative agreements (and in contracts, if not inconsistent with the Federal Acquisition Regulation) agencies wishing to apply the same clause to all subcontractors as is applied to the contractor may delete paragraph (g)(2) of the clause and delete the words "to be performed by a small business firm or domestic nonprofit organization" from paragraph (g)(1). Also, if the funding agreement is a grant or cooperative agreement, paragraph (g)(3) may be deleted. When either paragraph (g)(2) or paragraphs (g) (2) and (3) are deleted, the remaining paragraph or paragraphs should be renumbered appropriately.

(b) Agencies should complete paragraph (l), "Communications", at the end of the clauses at § 401.14 by designating a central point of contact for communications on matters relating to the clause. Additional instructions on communications may also be included in paragraph (l).

(c) Agencies may replace the italicized words and phrases in the clauses at § 401.14 with those appropriate to the particular funding agreement. For example, "contracts" could be replaced by "grant," "contractor" by "grantee," and "contracting officer" by "grants officer." Depending on its use, "Federal agency" can be replaced either by the identification of the agency or by the specification of the particular office or official within the agency.

(d) When the agency head or duly authorized designee determines at the time of contracting with a small business firm or nonprofit organization that it would be in the national interest to acquire the right to sublicense foreign governments or international organizations pursuant to any existing treaty or international agreement, a sentence may be added at the end of paragraph (b) of the clause at § 401.14 as follows:

This license will include the right of the government to sublicense foreign governments, their nationals, and international organizations, pursuant to the following treaties or international agreements:

________________.

The blank above should be completed with the names of applicable existing treaties or international agreements, agreements of cooperation, memoranda of understanding, or similar arrangements, including military agreements relating to weapons development and production. The above language is not intended to apply to treaties or other agreements that are in effect on the date of the award but which are not listed. Alternatively, agencies may use substantially similar language relating the government's rights to specific treaties or other agreements identified elsewhere in the funding agreement. The language may also be modified to make clear that the rights granted to the foreign government, and its nationals or an international organization may be for additional rights beyond a license or sublicense if so required by the applicable treaty or international agreement. For example, in some exclusive licenses or even the assignment of title in the foreign country involved might be required. Agencies may also modify the language above to provide for the direct licensing by the contractor of the foreign government or international organization.

(e) If the funding agreement involves performance over an extended period of time, such as the typical funding agreement for the operation of a government-owned facility, the following language may also be added:

The *agency* reserves the right to unilaterally amend this *funding agreement* to identify specific treaties or international agreements entered into or to be entered into by the government after the effective date of this *funding agreement* and effectuate those license or other rights which are necessary for the government to meet its obligations to foreign governments, their nationals and international organizations under such treaties or international agreements with respect to subject inventions made after the date of the amendment.

(f) Agencies may add additional subparagraphs to paragraph (f) of the clauses at § 401.14 to require the contractor to do one or more of the following:

(1) Provide a report prior to the close-out of a funding agreement listing all subject inventions or stating that there were none.

(2) Provide, upon request, the filing date, patent application number and title; a copy of the patent application; and patent number and issue date for any subject invention in any country in which the contractor has applied for a patent.

(3) Provide periodic (but no more frequently than annual) listings of all subject inventions which were disclosed to the agency during the period covered by the report.

(g) If the contract is with a nonprofit organization and is for the operation of a government-owned, contractor-operated facility, the following will be substituted for paragraph (k)(3) of the clause at § 401.14(a):

(3) After payment of patenting costs, licensing costs, payments to inventors, and other expenses incidental to the administration of subject inventions, the balance of any royalties or income earned and retained by the *contractor* during any fiscal year on subject inventions under this or any successor *contract* containing the same requirement, up to any amount equal to five percent of the budget of the facility for that fiscal year, shall be used by the contractor for scientific research, development, and education consistent with the research and development mission and objectives of the facility, including activities that increase the licensing potential of other inventions of the facility. If the balance exceeds five percent, 75 percent of the excess above five percent shall be paid by the contractor to the Treasury of the United States and the remaining 25 percent shall be used by the *contractor* only for the same purposes as described above. To the extent it provides the most effective technology transfer, the licensing of subject inventions shall be administered by *contractor* employees on location at the facility.

(h) If the contract is for the operation of a government-owned facility, agencies may add the following at the end of paragraph (f) of the clause at § 401.14(a):

(5) The contractor shall establish and maintain active and effective procedures to ensure that subject inventions are promptly identified and timely disclosed and shall submit a description of the procedures to the

contracting officer so that the *contracting officer* may evaluate and determine their effectiveness.

[52 FR 8554, Mar. 18, 1987, as amended at 60 FR 41812, Aug. 14, 1995]

§ 401.6 Exercise of march-in rights.

(a) The following procedures shall govern the exercise of the march-in rights of the agencies set forth in 35 U.S.C. 203 and paragraph (j) of the clause at § 401.14.

(b) Whenever an agency receives information that it believes might warrant the exercise of march-in rights, before initiating any march-in proceeding, it shall notify the contractor in writing of the information and request informal written or oral comments from the contractor as well as information relevant to the matter. In the absence of any comments from the contractor within 30 days, the agency may, at its discretion, proceed with the procedures below. If a comment is received within 30 days, or later if the agency has not initiated the procedures below, then the agency shall, within 60 days after it receives the comment, either initiate the procedures below or notify the contractor, in writing, that it will not pursue march-in rights on the basis of the available information.

(c) A march-in proceeding shall be initiated by the issuance of a written notice by the agency to the contractor and its assignee or exclusive licensee, as applicable and if known to the agency, stating that the agency is considering the exercise of march-in rights. The notice shall state the reasons for the proposed march-in in terms sufficient to put the contractor on notice of the facts upon which the action would be based and shall specify the field or fields of use in which the agency is considering requiring licensing. The notice shall advise the contractor (assignee or exclusive licensee) of its rights, as set forth in this section and in any supplemental agency regulations. The determination to exercise march-in rights shall be made by the head of the agency or his or her designee.

(d) Within 30 days after the receipt of the written notice of march-in, the contractor (assignee or exclusive licensee) may submit in person, in writing, or through a representative, information or argument in opposition to the proposed march-in, including any additional specific information which raises a genuine dispute over the material facts upon which the march-in is based. If the information presented raises a genuine dispute over the material facts, the head of the agency or designee shall undertake or refer the matter to another official for fact-finding.

(e) Fact-finding shall be conducted in accordance with the procedures established by the agency. Such procedures shall be as informal as practicable and be consistent with principles of fundamental fairness. The procedures should afford the contractor the opportunity to appear with counsel, submit documentary evidence, present witnesses and confront such persons as the agency may present. A transcribed record shall be made and shall be available at cost to the contractor upon request. The requirement for a transcribed record may be waived by mutual agreement of the contractor and the agency. Any portion of the march-in proceeding, including a fact-finding hearing that involves testimony or evidence relating to the utilization or efforts at obtaining utilization that are being made by the contractor, its assignee, or licensees shall be closed to the public, including potential licensees. In accordance with 35 U.S.C. 202(c)(5), agencies shall not disclose any such information obtained during a march-in proceeding to persons outside the government except when such release is authorized by the contractor (assignee or licensee).

(f) The official conducting the fact-finding shall prepare or adopt written findings of fact and transmit them to the head of the agency or designee promptly after the conclusion of the fact-finding proceeding along with a recommended determination. A copy of the findings of fact shall be sent to the contractor (assignee or exclusive licensee) by registered or certified mail. The contractor (assignee or exclusive licensee) and agency representatives will be given 30 days to submit written arguments to the head of the agency or designee; and, upon request by the contractor oral arguments will be held before the agency head or designee that will make the final determination.

(g) In cases in which fact-finding has been conducted, the head of the agency or designee shall base his or her determination on the facts found, together with any other information and written or oral arguments submitted by the contractor (assignee or exclusive licensee) and agency representatives, and any other information in the administrative record. The consistency of the exercise of march-in rights with the policy and objectives of 35 U.S.C. 200 shall also be considered. In cases referred for fact-finding, the head of the agency or designee may reject only those facts that have been found to be clearly erroneous, but must explicitly state the rejection and indicate the basis for the contrary finding. Written notice of the determination whether march-in rights will be exercised shall be made by the head of the agency or designee and sent to the contractor (assignee of exclusive licensee) by certified or registered mail within 90 days after the completion of fact-finding or 90 days after oral arguments, whichever is later, or the proceedings will be deemed to have been terminated and thereafter no march-in based on the facts and reasons upon which the proceeding was initiated may be exercised.

(h) An agency may, at any time, terminate a march-in proceeding if it is satisfied that it does not wish to exercise march-in rights.

(i) The procedures of this part shall also apply to the exercise of march-in rights against inventors receiving title to subject inventions under 35 U.S.C. 202(d) and, for that purpose, the term "contractor" as used in this section shall be deemed to include the inventor.

(j) An agency determination unfavorable to the contractor (assignee or exclusive licensee) shall be held in abeyance pending the exhaustion of appeals or petitions filed under 35 U.S.C. 203(2).

(k) For purposes of this section the term *exclusive licensee* includes a partially exclusive licensee.

(l) Agencies are authorized to issue supplemental procedures not inconsistent with this part for the conduct of march-in proceedings.

§ 401.7 Small business preference.

(a) Paragraph (k)(4) of the clauses at § 401.14 Implements the small business preference requirement of 35 U.S.C. 202(c)(7)(D). Contractors are expected to use efforts that are reasonable under the circumstances to attract small business licensees. They are also expected to give small business firms that meet the standard outlined in the clause a preference over other applicants for licenses. What constitutes reasonable efforts to attract small business licensees will vary with the circumstances and the nature, duration, and expense of efforts needed to bring the invention to the market. Paragraph (k)(4) is not intended, for example, to prevent nonprofit organizations from providing larger firms with a right of first refusal or other options in inventions that relate to research being supported under long-term or other arrangements with larger companies. Under such circumstances it would not be resonable to seek and to give a preference to small business licensees.

(b) Small business firms that believe a nonprofit organization is not meeting its obligations under the clause may report their concerns to the Secretary. To the extent deemed appropriate, the Secretary will undertake informal investigation of the concern, and, if appropriate, enter into discussions or negotiations with the nonprofit organization to the end of improving its efforts in meeting its obligations under the clause. However, in no event will the Secretary intervene in ongoing negotiations or contractor decisions concerning the licensing of a specific subject invention. All the above investigations, discussions, and negotiations of the Secretary will be in coordination with other interested agencies, including the Small Business Administration; and in the case of a contract for the operation of a government-owned, contractor operated research or production facility, the Secretary will coordinate with the agency responsible for the facility prior to any discussions or negotiations with the contractor.

§ 401.8 Reporting on utilization of subject inventions.

(a) Paragraph (h) of the clauses at § 401.14 and its counterpart in the clause at Attachment A to OMB Circular A–124 provides that agencies have the right to receive periodic reports from the contractor on utilization of inventions. Agencies exercising this right should accept such information, to the extent feasible, in the format that the contractor normally prepares it for its own internal purposes. The prescription of forms should be avoided. However, any forms or standard questionnaires that are adopted by an agency for this purpose must comply with the requirements of the Paperwork Reduction Act. Copies shall be sent to the Secretary.

(b) In accordance with 35 U.S.C. 202(c)(5) and the terms of the clauses at § 401.14, agencies shall not disclose such information to persons outside the government. Contractors will continue to provide confidential markings to help prevent inadvertent release outside the agency.

§ 401.9 Retention of rights by contractor employee inventor.

Agencies which allow an employee/inventor of the contractor to retain rights to a subject invention made under a funding agreement with a small business firm or nonprofit organization contractor, as authorized by 35 U.S.C. 202(d), will impose upon the inventor at least those conditions that would apply to a small business firm contractor under paragraphs (d)(1) and (3); (f)(4); (h); (i); and (j) of the clause at § 401.14(a).

§ 401.10 Government assignment to contractor of rights in invention of government employee.

In any case when a Federal employee is a co-inventor of any invention made under a funding agreement with a small business firm or nonprofit organization and the Federal agency employing such co-inventor transfers or reassigns the right it has acquired in the subject invention from its employee to the contractor as authorized by 35 U.S.C. 202(e), the assignment will be made subject to the same conditions as apply to the contractor under the patent rights clause of its funding agreement. Agencies may add additional conditions as long as they are consistent with 35 U.S.C. 201–206.

§ 401.11 Appeals.

(a) As used in this section, the term *standard clause* means the clause at § 401.14 of this part and the clauses previously prescribed by either OMB Circular A–124 or OMB Bulletin 81–22.

(b) The agency official initially authorized to take any of the following actions shall provide the contractor with a written statement of the basis for his or her action at the time the action is taken, including any relevant facts that were relied upon in taking the action.

(1) A refusal to grant an extension under paragraph (c)(4) of the standard clauses.

(2) A request for a conveyance of title under paragraph (d) of the standard clauses.

(3) A refusal to grant a waiver under paragraph (i) of the standard clauses.

(4) A refusal to approve an assignment under paragraph (k)(1) of the standard clauses.

(5) A refusal to grant an extension of the exclusive license period under paragraph (k)(2) of the clauses prescribed by either OMB Circular A–124 or OMB Bulletin 81–22.

(c) Each agency shall establish and publish procedures under which any of the agency actions listed in paragraph (b) of this section may be appealed to the head of the agency or designee. Review at this level shall consider both the factual and legal basis for the actions and its consistency with the policy and objectives of 35 U.S.C. 200–206.

(d) Appeals procedures established under paragraph (c) of this section shall include administrative due process procedures and standards for fact-finding at least comparable to those set forth in § 401.6 (e) through (g) whenever there is a dispute as to the factual basis for an agency request for a conveyance of title under paragraph (d) of the standard clause, including any dispute as to whether or not an invention is a subject invention.

(e) To the extent that any of the actions described in paragraph (b) of this section are subject to appeal under the

Contract Dispute Act, the procedures under the Act will satisfy the requirements of paragraphs (c) and (d) of this section.

§401.12 Licensing of background patent rights to third parties.

(a) A funding agreement with a small business firm or a domestic nonprofit organization will not contain a provision allowing a Federal agency to require the licensing to third parties of inventions owned by the contractor that are not subject inventions unless such provision has been approved by the agency head and a written justification has been signed by the agency head. Any such provision will clearly state whether the licensing may be required in connection with the practice of a subject invention, a specifically identified work object, or both. The agency head may not delegate the authority to approve such provisions or to sign the justification required for such provisions.

(b) A Federal agency will not require the licensing of third parties under any such provision unless the agency head determines that the use of the invention by others is necessary for the practice of a subject invention or for the use of a work object of the funding agreement and that such action is necessary to achieve practical application of the subject invention or work object. Any such determination will be on the record after an opportunity for an agency hearing. The contractor shall be given prompt notification of the determination by certified or registered mail. Any action commenced for judicial review of such determination shall be brought within sixty days after notification of such determination.

§401.13 Administration of patent rights clauses.

(a) In the event a subject invention is made under funding agreements of more than one agency, at the request of the contractor or on their own initiative the agencies shall designate one agency as responsible for administration of the rights of the government in the invention.

(b) Agencies shall promptly grant, unless there is a significant reason not to, a request by a nonprofit organization under paragraph (k)(2) of the clauses prescribed by either OMB Circular A–124 or OMB Bulletin 81–22 inasmuch as 35 U.S.C. 202(c)(7) has since been amended to eliminate the limitation on the duration of exclusive licenses. Similarly, unless there is a significant reason not to, agencies shall promptly approve an assignment by a nonprofit organization to an organization which has as one of its primary functions the management of inventions when a request for approval has been necessitated under paragraph (k)(1) of the clauses prescribed by either OMB Circular A–124 or OMB Bulletin 81–22 because the patent management organization is engaged in or holds a substantial interest in other organizations engaged in the manfacture or sale of products or the use of processes that might utilize the invention or be in competition with embodiments of the invention. As amended, 35 U.S.C. 202(c)(7) no longer contains this limitation. The policy of this subsection should also be followed in connection with similar approvals that may be required under Institutional Patent Agreements, other patent rights clauses, or waivers that predate Chapter 18 of Title 35, United States Code.

(c) The President's Patent Policy Memorandum of February 18, 1983, states that agencies should protect the confidentiality of invention disclosure, patent applications, and utilization reports required in performance or in consequence of awards to the extent permitted by 35 U.S.C. 205 or other applicable laws. The following requirements should be followed for funding agreements covered by and predating this part 401.

(1) To the extent authorized by 35 U.S.C. 205, agencies shall not disclose to third parties pursuant to requests under the Freedom of Information Act (FOIA) any information disclosing a subject invention for a reasonable time in order for a patent application to be filed. With respect to subject inventions of contractors that are small business firms or nonprofit organizations, a reasonable time shall be the time during which an initial patent application may be filed under paragraph (c) of the standard clause found at §401.14(a) or such other clause may be

used in the funding agreement. However, an agency may disclose such subject inventions under the FOIA, at its discretion, after a contractor has elected not to retain title or after the time in which the contractor is required to make an election if the contractor has not made an election within that time. Similarly, an agency may honor a FOIA request at its discretion if it finds that the same information has previously been published by the inventor, contractor, or otherwise. If the agency plans to file itself when the contractor has not elected title, it may, of course, continue to avail itself of the authority of 35 U.S.C. 205.

(2) In accordance with 35 U.S.C. 205, agencies shall not disclose or release for a period of 18 months from the filing date of the patent application to third parties pursuant to requests under the Freedom of Information Act, or otherwise, copies of any document which the agency obtained under this clause which is part of an application for patent with the U.S. Patent and Trademark Office or any foreign patent office filed by the contractor (or its assignees, licensees, or employees) on a subject invention to which the contractor has elected to retain title. This prohibition does not extend to disclosure to other government agencies or contractors of government agencies under an obligation to maintain such information in confidence.

(3) A number of agencies have policies to encourage public dissemination of the results of work supported by the agency through publication in government or other publications of technical reports of contractors or others. In recognition of the fact that such publication, if it included descriptions of a subject invention could create bars to obtaining patent protection, it is the policy of the executive branch that agencies will not include in such publication programs copies of disclosures of inventions submitted by small business firms or nonprofit organizations, pursuant to paragraph (c) of the standard clause found at §401.14(a), except that under the same circumstances under which agencies are authorized to release such information pursuant to FOIA requests under paragraph (c)(1) of this section, agencies may publish such disclosures.

(4) Nothing in this paragraph is intended to preclude agencies from including in the publication activities described in the first sentence of paragraph (c)(3), the publication of materials describing a subject invention to the extent such materials were provided as part of a technical report or other submission of the contractor which were submitted independently of the requirements of the patent rights provisions of the contract. However, if a small business firm or nonprofit organization notifies the agency that a particular report or other submission contains a disclosure of a subject invention to which it has elected title or may elect title, the agency shall use reasonable efforts to restrict its publication of the material for six months from date of its receipt of the report or submission or, if earlier, until the contractor has filed an initial patent application. Agencies, of course, retain the discretion to delay publication for additional periods of time.

(5) Nothing in this paragraph is intended to limit the authority of agencies provided in 35 U.S.C. 205 in circumstances not specifically described in this paragraph.

[52 FR 8554, Mar. 18, 1987, as amended at 60 FR 41812, Aug. 14, 1995]

§401.14 Standard patent rights clauses.

(a) The following is the standard patent rights clause to be used as specified in §401.3(a).

Patent Rights (Small Business Firms and Nonprofit Organizations)

(a) Definitions

(1) *Invention* means any invention or discovery which is or may be patentable or otherwise protectable under Title 35 of the United States Code, or any novel variety of plant which is or may be protected under the Plant Variety Protection Act (7 U.S.C. 2321 *et seq.*).

(2) *Subject invention* means any invention of the *contractor* conceived or first actually reduced to practice in the performance of work under this *contract*, provided that in the case of a variety of plant, the date of determination (as defined in section 41(d) of the Plant Variety Protection Act, 7 U.S.C. 2401(d))

must also occur during the period of *contract* performance.

(3) *Practical Application* means to manufacture in the case of a composition or product, to practice in the case of a process or method, or to operate in the case of a machine or system; and, in each case, under such conditions as to establish that the invention is being utilized and that its benefits are, to the extent permitted by law or government regulations, available to the public on reasonable terms.

(4) *Made* when used in relation to any invention means the conception or first actual reduction to practice of such invention.

(5) *Small Business Firm* means a small business concern as defined at section 2 of Pub. L. 85–536 (15 U.S.C. 632) and implementing regulations of the Administrator of the Small Business Administration. For the purpose of this clause, the size standards for small business concerns involved in government procurement and subcontracting at 13 CFR 121.3–8 and 13 CFR 121.3–12, respectively, will be used.

(6) *Nonprofit Organization* means a university or other institution of higher education or an organization of the type described in section 501(c)(3) of the Internal Revenue Code of 1954 (26 U.S.C. 501(c) and exempt from taxation under section 501(a) of the Internal Revenue Code (25 U.S.C. 501(a)) or any nonprofit scientific or educational organization qualified under a state nonprofit organization statute.

(b) Allocation of Principal Rights

The *Contractor* may retain the entire right, title, and interest throughout the world to each subject invention subject to the provisions of this clause and 35 U.S.C. 203. With respect to any subject invention in which the *Contractor* retains title, the Federal government shall have a nonexclusive, nontransferable, irrevocable, paid-up license to practice or have practiced for or on behalf of the United States the subject invention throughout the world.

(c) Invention Disclosure, Election of Title and Filing of Patent Application by *Contractor*

(1) The *contractor* will disclose each subject invention to the *Federal Agency* within two months after the inventor discloses it in writing to *contractor* personnel responsible for patent matters. The disclosure to the agency shall be in the form of a written report and shall identify the *contract* under which the invention was made and the inventor(s). It shall be sufficiently complete in technical detail to convey a clear understanding to the extent known at the time of the disclosure, of the nature, purpose, operation, and the physical, chemical, biological or electrical characteristics of the invention. The disclosure shall also identify any publication, on sale or public use of the invention and whether a manuscript describing the invention has been submitted for publication and, if so, whether it has been accepted for publication at the time of disclosure. In addition, after disclosure to the *agency*, the *Contractor* will promptly notify the *agency* of the acceptance of any manuscript describing the invention for publication or of any on sale or public use planned by the *contractor*.

(2) The *Contractor* will elect in writing whether or not to retain title to any such invention by notifying the *Federal agency* within two years of disclosure to the *Federal agency*. However, in any case where publication, on sale or public use has initiated the one year statutory period wherein valid patent protection can still be obtained in the United States, the period for election of title may be shortened by the *agency* to a date that is no more than 60 days prior to the end of the statutory period.

(3) The *contractor* will file its initial patent application on a subject invention to which it elects to retain title within one year after election of title or, if earlier, prior to the end of any statutory period wherein valid patent protection can be obtained in the United States after a publication, on sale, or public use. The *contractor* will file patent applications in additional countries or international patent offices within either ten months of the corresponding initial patent application or six months from the date permission is granted by the Commissioner of Patents and Trademarks to file foreign patent applications where such filing has been prohibited by a Secrecy Order.

(4) Requests for extension of the time for disclosure, election, and filing under subparagraphs (1), (2), and (3) may, at the discretion of the *agency*, be granted.

(d) Conditions When the Government May Obtain Title

The *contractor* will convey to the *Federal agency*, upon written request, title to any subject invention—

(1) If the *contractor* fails to disclose or elect title to the subject invention within the times specified in (c), above, or elects not to retain title; provided that the *agency* may only request title within 60 days after learning of the failure of the *contractor* to disclose or elect within the specified times.

(2) In those countries in which the *contractor* fails to file patent applications within the times specified in (c) above; provided, however, that if the *contractor* has filed a patent application in a country after the times specified in (c) above, but prior to its receipt of the written request of the *Federal agency*, the *contractor* shall continue to retain title in that country.

(3) In any country in which the *contractor* decides not to continue the prosecution of

any application for, to pay the maintenance fees on, or defend in reexamination or opposition proceeding on, a patent on a subject invention.

(e) Minimum Rights to *Contractor* and Protection of the *Contractor* Right to File

(1) The *contractor* will retain a nonexclusive royalty-free license throughout the world in each subject invention to which the Government obtains title, except if the *contractor* fails to disclose the invention within the times specified in (c), above. The *contractor's* license extends to its domestic subsidiary and affiliates, if any, within the corporate structure of which the *contractor* is a party and includes the right to grant sublicenses of the same scope to the extent the *contractor* was legally obligated to do so at the time the *contract* was awarded. The license is transferable only with the approval of the *Federal agency* except when transferred to the sucessor of that party of the *contractor's* business to which the invention pertains.

(2) The *contractor's* domestic license may be revoked or modified by the *funding Federal agency* to the extent necessary to achieve expeditious practical application of the subject invention pursuant to an application for an exclusive license submitted in accordance with applicable provisions at 37 CFR part 404 and *agency* licensing regulations (if any). This license will not be revoked in that field of use or the geographical areas in which the *contractor* has achieved practical application and continues to make the benefits of the invention reasonably accessible to the public. The license in any foreign country may be revoked or modified at the discretion of the *funding Federal agency* to the extent the *contractor*, its licensees, or the domestic subsidiaries or affiliates have failed to achieve practical application in that foreign country.

(3) Before revocation or modification of the license, the *funding Federal agency* will furnish the *contractor* a written notice of its intention to revoke or modify the license, and the *contractor* will be allowed thirty days (or such other time as may be authorized by the *funding Federal agency* for good cause shown by the *contractor*) after the notice to show cause why the license should not be revoked or modified. The *contractor* has the right to appeal, in accordance with applicable regulations in 37 CFR part 404 and *agency* regulations (if any) concerning the licensing of Government-owned inventions, any decision concerning the revocation or modification of the license.

(f) *Contractor* Action to Protect the Government's Interest

(1) The *contractor* agrees to execute or to have executed and promptly deliver to the *Federal agency* all instruments necessary to (i) establish or confirm the rights the Government has throughout the world in those subject inventions to which the *contractor* elects to retain title, and (ii) convey title to the *Federal agency* when requested under paragraph (d) above and to enable the government to obtain patent protection throughout the world in that subject invention.

(2) The *contractor* agrees to require, by written agreement, its employees, other than clerical and nontechnical employees, to disclose promptly in writing to personnel identified as responsible for the administration of patent matters and in a format suggested by the *contractor* each subject invention made under *contract* in order that the *contractor* can comply with the disclosure provisions of paragraph (c), above, and to execute all papers necessary to file patent applications on subject inventions and to establish the government's rights in the subject inventions. This disclosure format should require, as a minimum, the information required by (c)(1), above. The *contractor* shall instruct such employees through employee agreements or other suitable educational programs on the importance of reporting inventions in sufficient time to permit the filing of patent applications prior to U.S. or foreign statutory bars.

(3) The *contractor* will notify the *Federal agency* of any decisions not to continue the prosecution of a patent application, pay maintenance fees, or defend in a reexamination or opposition proceeding on a patent, in any country, not less than thirty days before the expiration of the response period required by the relevant patent office.

(4) The *contractor* agrees to include, within the specification of any United States patent applications and any patent issuing thereon covering a subject invention, the following statement, "This invention was made with government support under (identify the *contract*) awarded by (identify the Federal agency). The government has certain rights in the invention."

(g) Subcontracts

(1) The *contractor* will include this clause, suitably modified to identify the parties, in all subcontracts, regardless of tier, for experimental, developmental or research work to be performed by a small business firm or domestic nonprofit organization. The subcontractor will retain all rights provided for the *contractor* in this clause, and the *contractor* will not, as part of the consideration for awarding the subcontract, obtain rights in the subcontractor's subject inventions.

(2) The *contractor* will include in all other subcontracts, regardless of tier, for experimental developmental or research work the patent rights clause required by (*cite section of agency implementing regulations or FAR*).

(3) In the case of subcontracts, at any tier, when the prime award with the Federal agency was a contract (but not a grant or cooperative agreement), the *agency*, subcontractor, and the contractor agree that the mutual obligations of the parties created by this clause constitute a contract between the subcontractor and the Federal agency with respect to the matters covered by the clause; provided, however, that nothing in this paragraph is intended to confer any jurisdiction under the Contract Disputes Act in connection with proceedings under paragraph (j) of this clause.

(h) Reporting on Utilization of Subject Inventions

The *Contractor* agrees to submit on request periodic reports no more frequently than annually on the utilization of a subject invention or on efforts at obtaining such utilization that are being made by the *contractor* or its licensees or assignees. Such reports shall include information regarding the status of development, date of first commerical sale or use, gross royalties received by the contractor, and such other data and information as the *agency* may reasonably specify. The *contractor* also agrees to provide additional reports as may be requested by the *agency* in connection with any march-in proceeding undertaken by the *agency* in accordance with paragraph (j) of this clause. As required by 35 U.S.C. 202(c)(5), the *agency* agrees it will not disclose such information to persons outside the government without permission of the *contractor*.

(i) Preference for United States Industry

Notwithstanding any other provision of this clause, the *contractor* agrees that neither it nor any assignee will grant to any person the exclusive right to use or sell any subject inventions in the United States unless such person agrees that any products embodying the subject invention or produced through the use of the subject invention will be manufactured substantially in the United States. However, in individual cases, the requirement for such an agreement may be waived by the *Federal agency* upon a showing by the *contractor* or its assignee that reasonable but unsuccessful efforts have been made to grant licenses on similar terms to potential licensees that would be likely to manufacture substantially in the United States or that under the circumstances domestic manufacture is not commerically feasible.

(j) March-in Rights

The *contractor* agrees that with respect to any subject invention in which it has acquired title, the *Federal agency* has the right in accordance with the procedures in 37 CFR 401.6 and any supplemental regulations of the *agency* to require the *contractor*, an assignee or exclusive licensee of a subject invention to grant a nonexclusive, partially exclusive, or exclusive license in any field of use to a responsible applicant or applicants, upon terms that are reasonable under the circumstances, and if the *contractor*, assignee, or exclusive licensee refuses such a request the *Federal agency* has the right to grant such a license itself if the *Federal agency* determines that:

(1) Such action is necessary because the *contractor* or assignee has not taken, or is not expected to take within a reasonable time, effective steps to achieve practical application of the subject invention in such field of use.

(2) Such action is necessary to alleviate health or safety needs which are not reasonably satisfied by the *contractor*, assignee or their licensees;

(3) Such action is necessary to meet requirements for public use specified by Federal regulations and such requirements are not reasonably satisfied by the *contractor*, assignee or licensees; or

(4) Such action is necessary because the agreement required by paragraph (i) of this clause has not been obtained or waived or because a licensee of the exclusive right to use or sell any subject invention in the United States is in breach of such agreement.

(k) Special Provisions for *Contracts* with Nonprofit Organizations

If the *contractor* is a nonprofit organization, it agrees that:

(1) Rights to a subject invention in the United States may not be assigned without the approval of the *Federal agency*, except where such assignment is made to an organization which has as one of its primary functions the management of inventions, provided that such assignee will be subject to the same provisions as the *contractor;*

(2) The *contractor* will share royalties collected on a subject invention with the inventor, including Federal employee co-inventors (when the agency deems it appropriate) when the subject invention is assigned in accordance with 35 U.S.C. 202(e) and 37 CFR 401.10;

(3) The balance of any royalties or income earned by the *contractor* with respect to subject inventions, after payment of expenses (including payments to inventors) incidential to the administration of subject inventions, will be utilized for the support of scientific research or education; and

(4) It will make efforts that are reasonable under the circumstances to attract licensees of subject invention that are small business firms and that it will give a preference to a small business firm when licensing a subject invention if the *contractor* determines that the small business firm has a plan or proposal for marketing the invention which, if executed, is equally as likely to bring the invention to practical application as any plans

or proposals from applicants that are not small business firms; provided, that the *contractor* is also satisfied that the small business firm has the capability and resources to carry out its plan or proposal. The decision whether to give a preference in any specific case will be at the discretion of the *contractor*. However, the *contractor* agrees that the Secretary may review the *contractor's* licensing program and decisions regarding small business applicants, and the *contractor* will negotiate changes to its licensing policies, procedures, or practices with the Secretary when the Secretary's review discloses that the *contractor* could take reasonable steps to implement more effectively the requirements of this paragraph (k)(4).

(l) Communication

(Complete According to Instructions at 401.5(b))

(b) When the Department of Energy (DOE) determines to use alternative provisions under §401.3(a)(4), the standard clause at §401.14(a), of this section, shall be used with the following modifications unless a substitute clause is drafted by DOE:

(1) The title of the clause shall be changed to read as follows: *Patent Rights to Nonprofit DOE Facility Operators*

(2) Add an "(A)" after "(1)" in paragraph (c)(1) and add subparagraphs (B) and (C) to paragraph (c)(1) as follows:

(B) If the subject invention occurred under activities funded by the naval nuclear propulsion or weapons related programs of *DOE*, then the provisions of this subparagraph (c)(1)(B) will apply in lieu of paragraphs (c)(2) and (3). In such cases the contractor agrees to assign the government the entire right, title, and interest thereto throughout the world in and to the subject invention except to the extent that rights are retained by the contractor through a greater rights determination or under paragraph (e), below. The contractor, or an employee-inventor, with authorization of the contractor, may submit a request for greater rights at the time the invention is disclosed or within a reasonable time thereafter. *DOE* will process such a request in accordance with procedures at 37 CFR 401.15. Each determination of greater rights will be subject to paragraphs (h)–(k) of this clause and such additional conditions, if any, deemed to be appropriate by the *Department of Energy*.

(C) At the time an invention is disclosed in accordance with (c)(1)(A) above, or within 90 days thereafter, the contractor will submit a written statement as to whether or not the invention occurred under a naval nuclear propulsion or weapons-related program of the *Department of Energy*. If this statement is not filed within this time, subparagraph (c)(1)(B) will apply in lieu of paragraphs (c)(2) and (3). The contractor statement will be deemed conclusive unless, within 60 days thereafter, the Contracting Officer disagrees in writing, in which case the determination of the Contracting Officer will be deemed conclusive unless the contractor files a claim under the Contract Disputes Act within 60 days after the Contracting Officer's determination. Pending resolution of the matter, the invention will be subject to subparagraph (c)(1)(B).

(3) Paragraph (k)(3) of the clause will be modified as prescribed at §401.5(g).

(c) As prescribed in §401.3, replace (b) of the basic clause with the following paragraphs (1) and (2):

(b) Allocation of principal rights. (1) The Contractor may retain the entire right, title, and interest throughout the world to each subject invention subject to the provisions of this clause, including (2) below, and 35 U.S.C. 203. With respect to any subject invention in which the Contractor retains title, the Federal Government shall have a nonexclusive, nontransferable, irrevocable, paid-up license to practice or have practiced for or on behalf of the United States the subject invention throughout the world.

(2) If the Contractor performs services at a Government owned and operated laboratory or at a Government owned and contractor operated laboratory directed by the Government to fulfill the Government's obligations under a Cooperative Research and Development Agreement (CRADA) authorized by 15 U.S.C. 3710a, the Government may require the Contractor to negotiate an agreement with the CRADA collaborating party or parties regarding the allocation of rights to any subject invention the Contractor makes, solely or jointly, under the CRADA. The agreement shall be negotiated prior to the Contractor undertaking the CRADA work or, with the permission of the Government, upon the identification of a subject invention. In the absence of such an agreement, the Contractor agrees to grant the collaborating party or parties an option for a license in its inventions of the same scope and terms set forth in the CRADA for inventions made by the Government.

[52 FR 8554, Mar. 18, 1987, as amended at 69 FR 17301, Apr. 2, 2004]

§401.15 Deferred determinations.

(a) This section applies to requests for greater rights in subject inventions made by contractors when deferred determination provisions were included in the funding agreement because one of the exceptions at §401.3(a) was applied, except that the Department of Energy is authorized to process deferred determinations either in accordance with its waiver regulations or this section. A contractor requesting greater rights should include with its request information on its plans and intentions to bring the invention to practical application. Within 90 days after receiving a request and supporting information, or sooner if a statutory bar to patenting is imminent, the agency should seek to make a determination. In any event, if a bar to patenting is imminent, unless the agency plans to file on its own, it shall authorize the contractor to file a patent application pending a determination by the agency. Such a filing shall normally be at the contractor's own risk and expense. However, if the agency subsequently refuses to allow the contractor to retain title and elects to proceed with the patent application under government ownership, it shall reimburse the contractor for the cost of preparing and filing the patent application.

(b) If the circumstances of concerns which originally led the agency to invoke an exception under §401.3(a) are not applicable to the actual subject invention or are no longer valid because of subsequent events, the agency should allow the contractor to retain title to the invention on the same conditions as would have applied if the standard clause at §401.14(a) had been used originally, unless it has been licensed.

(c) If paragraph (b) is not applicable the agency shall make its determination based on an assessment whether its own plans regarding the invention will better promote the policies and objectives of 35 U.S.C. 200 than will contractor ownership of the invention. Moreover, if the agency is concerned only about specific uses or applications of the invention, it shall consider leaving title in the contractor with additional conditions imposed upon the contractor's use of the invention for such applications or with expanded government license rights in such applications.

(d) A determination not to allow the contractor to retain title to a subject invention or to restrict or condition its title with conditions differing from those in the clause at §401.14(a), unless made by the head of the agency, shall be appealable by the contractor to an agency official at a level above the person who made the determination. This appeal shall be subject to the procedures applicable to appeals under §401.11 of this part.

§401.16 Electronic filing.

Unless otherwise requested or directed by the agency,

(a) The written report required in (c)(1) of the standard clause in §401.14(a) may be electronically filed;

(b) The written election required in (c)(2) of the standard clause in §401.14(a) may be electronically filed; and

(c) The close-out report in (f)(1) and the information identified in (f)(2) and (f)(3) of §401.5 may be electronically filed.

[60 FR 41812, Aug. 14, 1995]

§401.17 Submissions and inquiries.

All submissions or inquiries should be directed to the Chief Counsel for NIST, National Institute of Standards and Technology, 100 Bureau Drive, Mail Stop 1052, Gaithersburg, Maryland 20899–1052; telephone: (301) 975–2803; email: *nistcounsel@nist.gov*.

[78 FR 4766, Jan. 23, 2013]

PART 404—LICENSING OF GOVERNMENT-OWNED INVENTIONS

Sec.

AUTHORITY: 35 U.S.C. 207–209, DOO 30–2A.

SOURCE: 50 FR 9802, Mar. 12, 1985, unless otherwise noted.

§404.1 Scope of part.

This part prescribes the terms, conditions, and procedures upon which a federally owned invention, other than an invention in the custody of the Tennessee Valley Authority, may be licensed. This part does not affect licenses which:

(a) Were in effect prior to April 7, 2006;

(b) May exist at the time of the Government's acquisition of title to the invention, including those resulting from the allocation of rights to inventions made under Government research and development contracts;

(c) Are the result of an authorized exchange of rights in the settlement of patent disputes, including interferences; or

(d) Are otherwise authorized by law or treaty, including 35 U.S.C. 202(e), 35 U.S.C. 207(a)(3) and 15 U.S.C. 3710a, which also may authorize the assignment of inventions. Although licenses on inventions made under a cooperative research and development agreement (CRADA) are not subject to this regulation, agencies are encouraged to apply the same policies and use similar terms when appropriate. Similarly, this should be done for licenses granted under inventions where the agency has acquired rights pursuant to 35 U.S.C. 207(a)(3).

[71 FR 11512, Mar. 8, 2006]

§404.2 Policy and objective.

It is the policy and objective of this subpart to use the patent system to promote the utilization of inventions arising from federally supported research or development.

§404.3 Definitions.

(a) *Government owned invention* means an invention, whether or not covered by a patent or patent application, or discovery which is or may be patentable or otherwise protectable under Title 35, the Plant Variety Protection Act (7 U.S.C. 2321 *et seq.*) or foreign patent law, owned in whole or in part by the United States Government.

(b) *Federal agency* means an executive department, military department, Government corporation, or independent establishment, except the Tennessee Valley Authority, which has custody of a federally owned invention.

(c) *Small business firm* means a small business concern as defined in section 2 of Pub. L. 85–536 (15 U.S.C. 632) and implementing regulations of the Administrator of the Small Business Administration.

(d) *Practical application* means to manufacture in the case of a composition or product, to practice in the case of a process or method, or to operate in the case of a machine or system; and, in each case, under such conditions as to establish that the invention is being utilized and that its benefits are to the extent permitted by law or Government regulations available to the public on reasonable terms.

(e) *United States* means the United States of America, its territories and possessions, the District of Columbia, and the Commonwealth of Puerto Rico.

[50 FR 9802, Mar. 12, 1985, as amended at 71 FR 11512, Mar. 8, 2006]

§404.4 Authority to grant licenses.

Federally owned inventions shall be made available for licensing as deemed appropriate in the public interest and each agency shall notify the public of these available inventions. The agencies having custody of these inventions may grant nonexclusive, co-exclusive, partially exclusive, or exclusive licenses thereto under this part. Licenses may be royalty-free or for royalties or other consideration. They may be for all or less than all fields of use or in specified geographic areas and may include a release for past infringement. Any license shall not confer on any person immunity from the antitrust laws or from a charge of patent misuse, and the exercise of such rights pursuant to this part shall not be immunized from the operation of state or federal law by reason of the source of the grant.

[71 FR 11512, Mar. 8, 2006]

§404.5 Restrictions and conditions on all licenses granted under this part.

(a)(1) A license may be granted only if the applicant has supplied the Federal agency with a satisfactory plan for development or marketing of the invention, or both, and with information about the applicant's capability to fulfill the plan. The plan for a non-exclusive research license may be limited to describing the research phase of development.

(2) A license granting rights to use or sell under a Government owned invention in the United States shall normally be granted only to a licensee who agrees that any products embodying the invention or produced through the use of the invention will be manufactured substantially in the United States. However, this condition may be waived or modified if reasonable but unsuccessful efforts have been made to grant licenses to potential licensees that would be likely to manufacture substantially in the United States or if domestic manufacture is not commercially feasible.

(b) Licenses shall contain such terms and conditions as the Federal agency determines are appropriate for the protection of the interests of the Federal Government and the public and are not in conflict with law or this part. The following terms and conditions apply to any license:

(1) The duration of the license shall be for a period specified in the license agreement, unless sooner terminated in accordance with this part.

(2) Any patent license may grant the licensee the right of enforcement of the licensed patent without joining the Federal agency as a party as determined appropriate in the public interest.

(3) The license may extend to subsidiaries of the licensee or other parties if provided for in the license but shall be nonassignable without approval of the Federal agency, except to the successor of that part of the licensee's business to which the invention pertains.

(4) The license may provide the licensee the right to grant sublicenses under the license, subject to the approval of the Federal agency. Each sublicense shall make reference to the license, including the rights retained by the Government, and a copy of such sublicense with any modifications thereto, shall be promptly furnished to the Federal agency.

(5) The license shall require the licensee to carry out the plan for development or marketing of the invention, or both, to bring the invention to practical application within a reasonable time as specified in the license, and continue to make the benefits of the invention reasonably accessible to the public.

(6) The license shall require the licensee to report periodically on the utilization or efforts at obtaining utilization that are being made by the licensee, with particular reference to the plan submitted but only to the extent necessary to enable the agency to determine compliance with the terms of the license.

(7) Where an agreement is obtained pursuant to §404.5(a)(2) that any products embodying the invention or produced through the use of the invention will be manufactured substantially in the United States, the license shall recite such an agreement.

(8) The license shall provide for the right of the Federal agency to terminate the license, in whole or in part, if the agency determines that:

(i) The licensee is not executing its commitment to achieve practical application of the invention, including commitments contained in any plan submitted in support of its request for a license and the licensee cannot otherwise demonstrate to the satisfaction of the Federal agency that it has taken, or can be expected to take within a reasonable time, effective steps to achieve practical application of the invention;

(ii) Termination is necessary to meet requirements for public use specified by Federal regulations issued after the date of the license and such requirements are not reasonably satisfied by the licensee;

(iii) The licensee has willfully made a false statement of or willfully omitted a material fact in the license application or in any report required by the license agreement;

(iv) The licensee commits a substantial breach of a covenant or provision contained in the license agreement, including the requirement in §404.5(a)(2); or

(v) The licensee has been found by a court of competent jurisdiction to have violated the Federal antitrust laws in connection with its performance under the license agreement.

(9) The license may be modified or terminated, consistent with this part, upon mutual agreement of the Federal agency and the licensee.

(10) The license may be modified or terminated, consistent with this part, upon mutual agreement of the Federal agency and the licensee.

(11) Nothing relating to the grant of a license, nor the grant itself, shall be construed to confer upon any person any immunity from or defenses under the antitrust laws or from a charge of patent misuse, and the acquisition and use of rights pursuant to this part shall not be immunized from the operation of state or Federal law by reason of the source of the grant.

[50 FR 9802, Mar. 12, 1985, as amended at 71 FR 11512, Mar. 8, 2006]

§ 404.6 Nonexclusive licenses.

Nonexclusive licenses may be granted under Government owned inventions without a public notice of a prospective license.

[71 FR 11513, Mar. 8, 2006]

§ 404.7 Exclusive, co-exclusive and partially exclusive licenses.

(a)(1) Exclusive, co-exclusive or partially exclusive domestic licenses may be granted on Government owned inventions, only if;

(i) Notice of a prospective license, identifying the invention and the prospective licensee, has been published in the FEDERAL REGISTER, providing opportunity for filing written objections within at least a 15-day period;

(ii) After expiration of the period in § 404.7(a)(1)(i) and consideration of any written objections received during the period, the Federal agency has determined that;

(A) The public will be served by the granting of the license, in view of the applicant's intentions, plans and ability to bring the invention to the point of practical application or otherwise promote the invention's utilization by the public.

(B) Exclusive, co-exclusive or partially exclusive licensing is a reasonable and necessary incentive to call forth the investment capital and expenditures needed to bring the invention to practical application or otherwise promote the invention's utilization by the public; and

(C) The proposed scope of exclusivity is not greater than reasonably necessary to provide the incentive for bringing the invention to practical application, as proposed by the applicant, or otherwise to promote the invention's utilization by the public;

(iii) The Federal agency has not determined that the grant of such a license will tend substantially to lessen competition or create or maintain a violation of the Federal antitrust laws; and

(iv) The Federal agency has given first preference to any small business firms submitting plans that are determined by the agency to be within the capability of the firms and as having equal or greater likelihood as those from other applicants to bring the invention to practical application within a reasonable time.

(2) In addition to the provisions of § 404.5, the following terms and conditions apply to domestic exclusive, co-exclusive and partially exclusive licenses:

(i) The license shall be subject to the irrevocable, royalty-free right of the Government of the United States to practice or have practiced the invention on behalf of the United States and on behalf of any foreign government or international organization pursuant to any existing or future treaty or agreement with the United States.

(ii) The license shall reserve to the Federal agency the right to require the licensee to grant sublicenses to responsible applicants, on reasonable terms, when necessary to fulfill health or safety needs.

(iii) The license shall be subject to any licenses in force at the time of the grant of the exclusive, co-exclusive or partially exclusive license.

(b)(1) Exclusive, co-exclusive or partially exclusive foreign licenses may be granted on a Government owned invention provided that;

(i) Notice of the prospective license, identifying the invention and prospective licensee, has been published in the

FEDERAL REGISTER, providing opportunity for filing written objections within at least a 15-day period and following consideration of such objections received during the period;

(ii) The agency has considered whether the interests of the Federal Government or United States industry in foreign commerce will be enhanced; and

(iii) The Federal agency has not determined that the grant of such a license will tend substantially to lessen competition or create or maintain a violation of the Federal antitrust laws.

(2) In addition to the provisions of §404.5, the following terms and conditions apply to foreign exclusive, co-exclusive and partially exclusive licenses:

(i) The license shall be subject to the irrevocable, royalty-free right of the Government of the United States to practice and have practiced the invention on behalf of the United States and on behalf of any foreign government or international organization pursuant to any existing or future treaty or agreement with the United States.

(ii) The license shall be subject to any licenses in force at the time of the grant of the exclusive, co-exclusive or partially exclusive license.

(iii) The license may grant the licensee the right to take any suitable and necessary actions to protect the licensed property, on behalf of the Federal Government.

(c) Federal agencies shall maintain a record of determinations to grant exclusive, co-exclusive or partially exclusive licenses.

[71 FR 11513, Mar. 8, 2006]

§404.8 Application for a license.

An application for a license should be addressed to the Federal agency having custody of the invention and shall normally include:

(a) Identification of the invention for which the license is desired including the patent application serial number or patent number, title, and date, if known;

(b) Identification of the type of license for which the application is submitted;

(c) Name and address of the person, company, or organization applying for the license and the citizenship or place of incorporation of the applicant;

(d) Name, address, and telephone number of the representative of the applicant to whom correspondence should be sent;

(e) Nature and type of applicant's business, identifying products or services which the applicant has successfully commercialized, and approximate number of applicant's employees;

(f) Source of information concerning the availability of a license on the invention;

(g) A statement indicating whether the applicant is a small business firm as defined in §404.3(c)

(h) A detailed description of applicant's plan for development or marketing of the invention, or both, which should include:

(1) A statement of the time, nature and amount of anticipated investment of capital and other resources which applicant believes will be required to bring the invention to practical application;

(2) A statement as to applicant's capability and intention to fulfill the plan, including information regarding manufacuturing, marketing, financial, and technical resources;

(3) A statement of the fields of use for which applicant intends to practice the invention; and

(4) A statement of the geographic areas in which applicant intends to manufacture any products embodying the invention and geographic areas where applicant intends to use or sell the invention, or both;

(i) Identification of licenses previously granted to applicant under federally owned inventions;

(j) A statement containing applicant's best knowledge of the extent to which the invention is being practiced by private industry or Government, or both, or is otherwise available commercially; and

(k) Any other information which applicant believes will support a determination to grant the license to applicant.

§404.9 [Reserved]

§404.10 Modification and termination of licenses.

Before modifying or terminating a license, other than by mutual agreement, the Federal agency shall furnish the licensee and any sublicensee of record a written notice of intention to modify or terminate the license, and the licensee shall be allowed 30 days after such notice to remedy any breach of the license or show cause why the license shall not be modified or terminated.

[71 FR 11514, Mar. 8, 2006]

§ 404.11 Appeals.

(a) In accordance with procedures prescribed by the Federal agency, the following parties may appeal to the agency head or designee any decision or determination concerning the grant, denial, modification, or termination of a license:

(1) A person whose application for a license has been denied;

(2) A licensee whose license has been modified or terminated, in whole or in part; or

(3) A person who timely filed a written objection in response to the notice required by § 404.7(a)(1)(i) or § 404.7(b)(1)(i) and who can demonstrate to the satisfaction of the Federal agency that such person may be damaged by the agency action.

(b) An appeal by a licensee under paragraph (a)(2) of this section may include a hearing, upon the request of the licensee, to address a dispute over any relevant fact. The parties may agree to Alternate Dispute Resolution in lieu of an appeal.

[71 FR 11514, Mar. 8, 2006]

§ 404.12 Protection and administration of inventions.

A Federal agency may take any suitable and necessary steps to protect and administer rights to Government owned inventions, either directly or through contract.

[71 FR 11514, Mar. 8, 2006]

§ 404.13 Transfer of custody.

A Federal agency having custody of a federally owned invention may transfer custody and administration, in whole or in part, to another Federal agency, of the right, title, or interest in such invention.

§ 404.14 Confidentiality of information.

Title 35, United States Code, section 209, requires that any plan submitted pursuant to § 404.8(h) and any report required by § 404.5(b)(6) shall be treated as commercial or financial information obtained from a person and privileged and confidential and not subject to disclosure under section 552 of Title 5 of the United States Code.

[71 FR 11514, Mar. 8, 2006]

PART 501—UNIFORM PATENT POLICY FOR RIGHTS IN INVENTIONS MADE BY GOVERNMENT EMPLOYEES

Sec.

AUTHORITY: Sec. 4, E.O. 10096, 3 CFR, 1949–1953 Comp., p. 292, as amended by E.O. 10930, 3 CFR, 1959–1963 Comp., p. 456 and by E.O. 10695, 3 CFR, 1954–1958 Comp., p. 355, DOO 30–2A.

SOURCE: 53 FR 39735, Oct. 11, 1988, unless otherwise noted.

EDITORIAL NOTE: At 78 FR 4766, Jan. 23, 2013, parts 500–599 were transferred from Title 37, Chapter V, to Title 37, Chapter IV. Chapter V was removed and reserved.

§ 501.1 Purpose.

The purpose of this part is to provide for the administration of a uniform patent policy for the Government with respect to the rights in inventions made by Government employees and to prescribe rules and regulations for implementing and effectuating such policy.

[61 FR 40999, Aug. 7, 1996]

§ 501.2 Scope.

This part applies to any invention made by a Government employee and to any action taken with respect thereto.

§501.3 Definitions.

(a) The term *Secretary*, as used in this part, means the Director of the National Institute of Standards and Technology.

(b) The term *Government agency*, as used in this part, means any Executive department or independent establishment of the Executive branch of the Government (including any independent regulatory commission or board, any corporation wholly owned by the United States, and the Smithsonian Institution), but does not include the Department of Energy for inventions made under the provisions of 42 U.S.C. 2182, the Tennessee Valley Authority, or the Postal Service.

(c) The term *Government employee*, as used in this part, means any officer or employee, civilian or military, of any Government agency, including any special Government employee as defined in 18 U.S.C. 202 or an individual working for a Federal agency pursuant to the Intergovernmental Personnel Act (IPA), 5 U.S.C. 1304 and 3371–3376, or a part-time consultant or part-time employee as defined in 29 U.S.C. 2101(a)(8) except as may otherwise be provided by agency regulation approved by the Secretary.

(d) The term *invention*, as used in this part, means any art or process, machine, manufacture, design, or composition of matter, or any new and useful improvement thereof, or any variety of plant, which is or may be patentable under the patent laws of the United States.

(e) The term *made* as used in this part in relation to any invention, means the conception or first actual reduction to practice of such invention as stated in *In re King*, 3 USPQ2d (BNA) 1747 (Comm'r Pat. 1987).

[61 FR 40999, Aug. 7, 1996, as amended at 78 FR 4766, Jan. 23, 2013]

§501.4 Determination of inventions and rights.

Each Government agency has the approval of the Secretary to determine whether the results of research, development, or other activity in the agency constitute an invention within the purview of Executive Order 10096, as amended by Executive Order 10930 and Executive Order 10695, and to determine the rights in and to the invention in accordance with the provisions of §§501.6 and 501.7.

[61 FR 40999, Aug. 7, 1996]

§501.5 Agency liaison officer.

Each Government agency shall designate a liaison officer to represent the agency before the Secretary; Provided, however, that the Departments of the Army, the Navy, and the Air Force may each designate a liaison officer.

§501.6 Criteria for the determination of rights in and to inventions.

(a) The following rules shall be applied in determining the respective rights of the Government and of the inventor in and to any invention that is subject to the provisions of this part:

(1) The Government shall obtain, except as herein otherwise provided, the entire right, title and interest in and to any invention made by any Government employee:

(i) During working hours, or

(ii) With a contribution by the Government of facilities, equipment, materials, funds or information, or of time or services of other Government employees on official duty, or

(iii) Which bears a direct relation to or is made in consequence of the official duties of the inventor.

(2) In any case where the contribution of the Government, as measured by any one or more of the criteria set forth in paragraph (a)(1) of this section, to the invention is insufficient equitably to justify a requirement of assignment to the Government of the entire right, title and interest in and to such invention, or in any case where the Government has insufficient interest in an invention to obtain the entire right, title and interest therein (although the Government could obtain same under paragraph (a)(1) of this section), the Government agency concerned shall leave title to such invention in the employee, subject however, to the reservation to the Government of a nonexclusive, irrevocable, royalty-free license in the invention with power to grant licenses for all governmental purposes. The terms of such

reservation will appear, where practicable, in any patent, domestic or foreign, which may issue on such invention. Reference is made to section 15 of the Federal Technology Transfer Act of 1986 (15 U.S.C. 3710d) which requires a Government agency to allow the inventor to retain title to any covered invention when the agency does not intend to file a patent application or otherwise promote commercialization.

(3) In applying the provisions of paragraphs (a)(1) and (2) of this section to the facts and circumstances relating to the making of a particular invention, it shall be presumed that an invention made by an employee who is employed or assigned:

(i) To invent or improve or perfect any art or process, machine, design, manufacture, or composition of matter;

(ii) To conduct or perform research, development work, or both,

(iii) To supervise, direct, coordinate, or review Government financed or conducted research, development work, or both, or

(iv) To act in a liaison capacity among governmental or non-governmental agencies or individuals engaged in such research or development work,

falls within the provisions of paragraph (a)(1) of this section, and it shall be presumed that any invention made by any other employee falls within the provisions of paragraph (a)(2) of this section. Either presumption may be rebutted by a showing of the facts and circumstances in the case and shall not preclude a determination that these facts and circumstances justify leaving the entire right, title and interest in and to the invention in the Government employee, subject to law.

(4) In any case wherein the Government neither:

(i) Obtains the entire right, title and interest in and to an invention pursuant to the provisions of paragraph (a)(1) of this section nor

(ii) Reserves a nonexclusive, irrevocable, royalty-free license in the invention, with power to grant licenses for all governmental purposes, pursuant to the provisions of paragraph (a)(2) of this section,

the Government shall leave the entire right, title and interest in and to the invention in the Government employee, subject to law.

[53 FR 39735, Oct. 11, 1988, as amended at 61 FR 40999, Aug. 7, 1996]

§ 501.7 Agency determination.

(a) If the agency determines that the Government is entitled to obtain title pursuant to § 501.6(a)(1) and the employee does not appeal, no further review is required.

(b) In the event that a Government agency determines, pursuant to paragraph (a)(2) or (a)(4) of § 501.6, that title to an invention will be left with the employee, the agency shall notify the employee of this determination. In cases pursuant to § 501.6(a)(2) where the Government's insufficient interest in the invention is evidenced by its decision not to file a patent application, the agency may impose on the employee any one or all of the following conditions or any other conditions that may be necessary in a particular case:

(1) That a patent application be filed in the United States and/or abroad, if the Government has determined that it has or may need to practice the invention;

(2) That the invention not be assigned to any foreign-owned or controlled corporation without the written permission of the agency; and

(3) That any assignment or license of rights to use or sell the invention in the United States shall contain a requirement that any products embodying the invention or produced through the use of the invention be substantially manufactured in the United States. The agency shall notify the employee of any conditions imposed.

(c) In the case of a determination under either paragraph (a) or (b) of this section, the agency shall promptly provide the employee with:

(1) A signed and dated statement of its determination and reasons therefor; and

(2) A copy of 37 CFR part 501.

[53 FR 39735, Oct. 11, 1988, as amended at 61 FR 40999, Aug. 7, 1996]

§ 501.8 Appeals by employees.

(a) Any Government employee who is aggrieved by a Government agency determination pursuant to §§ 501.6(a)(1) or (a)(2), may obtain a review of any agency determination by filing, within 30 days (or such longer period as the Secretary may, for good cause shown in writing, fix in any case) after receiving notice of such determination, two copies of an appeal with the Secretary. The Secretary then shall forward one copy of the appeal to the liaison officer of the Government agency.

(b) On receipt of a copy of an appeal filed pursuant to paragraph (a) of this section, the agency liaison officer shall, subject to considerations of national security, or public health, safety or welfare, promptly furnish both the Secretary and the inventor with a copy of a report containing the following information about the invention involved in the appeal:

(1) A copy of the agency's statement specified in §501.7(c);

(2) A description of the invention in sufficient detail to identify the invention and show its relationship to the employee's duties and work assignments;

(3) The name of the employee and employment status, including a detailed statement of official duties and responsibilities at the time the invention was made; and

(4) A detailed statement of the points of dispute or controversy, together with copies of any statements or written arguments filed with the agency, and of any other relevant evidence that the agency considered in making its determination of Government interest.

(c) Within 25 days (or such longer period as the Secretary may, for good cause shown, fix in any case) after the transmission of a copy of the agency report to the employee, the employee may file a reply with the Secretary and file one copy with the agency liaison officer.

(d) After the time for the inventor's reply to the Government agency's report has expired and if the inventor has so requested in his or her appeal, a date will be set for hearing of oral arguments before the Secretary, by the employee (or by an attorney whom he or she designates by written power of attorney filed before, or at the hearing) and a representative of the Government agency involved. Unless it shall be otherwise ordered before the hearing begins, oral arguments will be limited to thirty minutes for each side. The employee need not retain an attorney or request an oral hearing to secure full consideration of the facts and his or her arguments. The employee may expedite such consideration by notifying the Secretary when he or she does not intend to file a reply to the agency report.

(e) After a hearing on the appeal, if a hearing was requested, or after expiration of the period for the inventor's reply to the agency report if no hearing is set, the Secretary shall issue a decision on the matter within 120 days, which decision shall be final after a thirty day period for requesting reconsideration expires or on the date that a decision on a petition for reconsideration is finally disposed of. Any request for reconsideration or modification of the decision must be filed within 30 days from the date of the original decision (or within such an extension thereof as may be set by the Secretary before the original period expires). The decision of the Secretary shall be made after consideration of the statements of fact in the employee's appeal, the agency's report, and the employee's reply, but the Secretary at his or her discretion and with due respect to the rights and convenience of the inventor and the Government agency, may call for further statements on specific questions of fact or may request additional evidence in the form of affidavits or depositions on specific facts in dispute.

[53 FR 39735, Oct. 11, 1988, as amended at 61 FR 41000, Aug. 7, 1996]

§501.9 Patent protection.

(a) A Government agency, upon determining that an invention coming within the scope of §§501.6(a)(1) or (a)(2) has been made, shall promptly determine whether patent protection will be sought in the United States by or on behalf of the agency for such invention. A controversy over the respective rights of the Government and of the employee shall not unnecessarily delay the filing of a patent application by the agency to avoid the loss of patent rights. In cases coming within the scope of §501.6(a)(2), the filing of a patent application shall be contingent upon the consent of the employee.

(b) Where there is an appealed dispute as to whether §§ 501.6 (a)(1) or (a)(2) applies in determining the respective rights of the Government and of an employee in and to any invention, the agency may determine whether patent protection will be sought in the United States pending the Secretary's decision on the dispute. If the agency decides that an application for patent should be filed, the agency will take such rights as are specified in § 501.6(a)(2), but this shall be without prejudice to acquiring the rights specified in paragraph (a)(1) of that section should the Secretary so decide.

(c) Where an agency has determined to leave title to an invention with an employee under § 501.6(a)(2), the agency will, upon the filing of an application for patent, take the rights specified in that paragraph without prejudice to the subsequent acquisition by the Government of the rights specified in paragraph (a)(1) of that section should the Secretary so decide.

(d) Where an agency has filed a patent application in the United States, the agency will, within 8 months from the filing date of the U.S. application, determine if any foreign patent applications should also be filed. If the agency chooses not to file an application in any foreign country, the employee may request rights in that country subject to the conditions stated in § 501.7(b) that may be imposed by the agency. Alternatively, the agency may permit the employee to retain foreign rights by including in any assignment to the Government of an unclassified U.S. patent application on the invention an option for the Government to acquire title in any foreign country within 8 months from the filing date of the U.S. application.

[61 FR 41000, Aug. 7, 1996]

§ 501.10 Dissemination of this part and of implementing regulations.

Each Government agency shall disseminate to its employees the provisions of this part, and any appropriate implementing agency regulations and delegations. Copies of any such regulations shall be sent to the Secretary. If the Secretary identifies an inconsistency between this part and the agency regulations or delegations, the agency, upon being informed by the Secretary of the inconsistency, shall take prompt action to correct it.

§ 501.11 Submissions and inquiries.

All submissions or inquiries should be directed to the Chief Counsel for NIST, National Institute of Standards and Technology, 100 Bureau Drive, Mail Stop 1052, Gaithersburg, MD 20899–1052; telephone: (301) 975–2803; email: *nistcounsel@nist.gov*.

[78 FR 4766, Jan. 23, 2013]

CHAPTER V [RESERVED]

FINDING AIDS

A list of current CFR titles, subtitles, chapters, subchapters and parts and an alphabetical list of agencies publishing in the CFR are included in the CFR Index and Finding Aids volume to the Code of Federal Regulations, which is published separately and revised annually.

Table of CFR Titles and Chapters

(Revised as of July 1, 2013)

Title 1—General Provisions

I Administrative Committee of the Federal Register (Parts 1—49)
II Office of the Federal Register (Parts 50—299)
III Administrative Conference of the United States (Parts 300—399)
IV Miscellaneous Agencies (Parts 400—500)

Title 2—Grants and Agreements

SUBTITLE A—OFFICE OF MANAGEMENT AND BUDGET GUIDANCE FOR GRANTS AND AGREEMENTS

I Office of Management and Budget Governmentwide Guidance for Grants and Agreements (Parts 2—199)
II Office of Management and Budget Circulars and Guidance (200—299)

SUBTITLE B—FEDERAL AGENCY REGULATIONS FOR GRANTS AND AGREEMENTS

III Department of Health and Human Services (Parts 300— 399)
IV Department of Agriculture (Parts 400—499)
VI Department of State (Parts 600—699)
VII Agency for International Development (Parts 700—799)
VIII Department of Veterans Affairs (Parts 800—899)
IX Department of Energy (Parts 900—999)
XI Department of Defense (Parts 1100—1199)
XII Department of Transportation (Parts 1200—1299)
XIII Department of Commerce (Parts 1300—1399)
XIV Department of the Interior (Parts 1400—1499)
XV Environmental Protection Agency (Parts 1500—1599)
XVIII National Aeronautics and Space Administration (Parts 1800—1899)
XX United States Nuclear Regulatory Commission (Parts 2000—2099)
XXII Corporation for National and Community Service (Parts 2200—2299)
XXIII Social Security Administration (Parts 2300—2399)
XXIV Housing and Urban Development (Parts 2400—2499)
XXV National Science Foundation (Parts 2500—2599)
XXVI National Archives and Records Administration (Parts 2600—2699)
XXVII Small Business Administration (Parts 2700—2799)
XXVIII Department of Justice (Parts 2800—2899)

Title 2—Grants and Agreements—Continued

Chap.	
XXX	Department of Homeland Security (Parts 3000—3099)
XXXI	Institute of Museum and Library Services (Parts 3100—3199)
XXXII	National Endowment for the Arts (Parts 3200—3299)
XXXIII	National Endowment for the Humanities (Parts 3300—3399)
XXXIV	Department of Education (Parts 3400—3499)
XXXV	Export-Import Bank of the United States (Parts 3500—3599)
XXXVII	Peace Corps (Parts 3700—3799)
LVIII	Election Assistance Commission (Parts 5800—5899)

Title 3—The President

I	Executive Office of the President (Parts 100—199)

Title 4—Accounts

I	Government Accountability Office (Parts 1—199)
II	Recovery Accountability and Transparency Board (Parts 200—299)

Title 5—Administrative Personnel

I	Office of Personnel Management (Parts 1—1199)
II	Merit Systems Protection Board (Parts 1200—1299)
III	Office of Management and Budget (Parts 1300—1399)
V	The International Organizations Employees Loyalty Board (Parts 1500—1599)
VI	Federal Retirement Thrift Investment Board (Parts 1600—1699)
VIII	Office of Special Counsel (Parts 1800—1899)
IX	Appalachian Regional Commission (Parts 1900—1999)
XI	Armed Forces Retirement Home (Parts 2100—2199)
XIV	Federal Labor Relations Authority, General Counsel of the Federal Labor Relations Authority and Federal Service Impasses Panel (Parts 2400—2499)
XV	Office of Administration, Executive Office of the President (Parts 2500—2599)
XVI	Office of Government Ethics (Parts 2600—2699)
XXI	Department of the Treasury (Parts 3100—3199)
XXII	Federal Deposit Insurance Corporation (Parts 3200—3299)
XXIII	Department of Energy (Parts 3300—3399)
XXIV	Federal Energy Regulatory Commission (Parts 3400—3499)
XXV	Department of the Interior (Parts 3500—3599)
XXVI	Department of Defense (Parts 3600— 3699)
XXVIII	Department of Justice (Parts 3800—3899)
XXIX	Federal Communications Commission (Parts 3900—3999)
XXX	Farm Credit System Insurance Corporation (Parts 4000—4099)
XXXI	Farm Credit Administration (Parts 4100—4199)

Chap.	
LXXXIII	Special Inspector General for Afghanistan Reconstruction (Parts 9300—9399)
LXXXIV	Bureau of Consumer Financial Protection (Parts 9400—9499)
LXXXVI	National Credit Union Administration (9600—9699)
XCVII	Department of Homeland Security Human Resources Management System (Department of Homeland Security—Office of Personnel Management) (Parts 9700—9799)
XCVII	Council of the Inspectors General on Integrity and Efficiency (Parts 9800—9899)

Title 6—Domestic Security

I	Department of Homeland Security, Office of the Secretary (Parts 1—99)
X	Privacy and Civil Liberties Oversight Board (Parts 1000—1099)

Title 7—Agriculture

	Subtitle A—Office of the Secretary of Agriculture (Parts 0—26)
	Subtitle B—Regulations of the Department of Agriculture
I	Agricultural Marketing Service (Standards, Inspections, Marketing Practices), Department of Agriculture (Parts 27—209)
II	Food and Nutrition Service, Department of Agriculture (Parts 210—299)
III	Animal and Plant Health Inspection Service, Department of Agriculture (Parts 300—399)
IV	Federal Crop Insurance Corporation, Department of Agriculture (Parts 400—499)
V	Agricultural Research Service, Department of Agriculture (Parts 500—599)
VI	Natural Resources Conservation Service, Department of Agriculture (Parts 600—699)
VII	Farm Service Agency, Department of Agriculture (Parts 700—799)
VIII	Grain Inspection, Packers and Stockyards Administration (Federal Grain Inspection Service), Department of Agriculture (Parts 800—899)
IX	Agricultural Marketing Service (Marketing Agreements and Orders; Fruits, Vegetables, Nuts), Department of Agriculture (Parts 900—999)
X	Agricultural Marketing Service (Marketing Agreements and Orders; Milk), Department of Agriculture (Parts 1000—1199)
XI	Agricultural Marketing Service (Marketing Agreements and Orders; Miscellaneous Commodities), Department of Agriculture (Parts 1200—1299)
XIV	Commodity Credit Corporation, Department of Agriculture (Parts 1400—1499)
XV	Foreign Agricultural Service, Department of Agriculture (Parts 1500—1599)

Title 7—Agriculture—Continued

Chap.	
XVI	Rural Telephone Bank, Department of Agriculture (Parts 1600—1699)
XVII	Rural Utilities Service, Department of Agriculture (Parts 1700—1799)
XVIII	Rural Housing Service, Rural Business-Cooperative Service, Rural Utilities Service, and Farm Service Agency, Department of Agriculture (Parts 1800—2099)
XX	Local Television Loan Guarantee Board (Parts 2200—2299)
XXV	Office of Advocacy and Outreach, Department of Agriculture (Parts 2500—2599)
XXVI	Office of Inspector General, Department of Agriculture (Parts 2600—2699)
XXVII	Office of Information Resources Management, Department of Agriculture (Parts 2700—2799)
XXVIII	Office of Operations, Department of Agriculture (Parts 2800—2899)
XXIX	Office of Energy Policy and New Uses, Department of Agriculture (Parts 2900—2999)
XXX	Office of the Chief Financial Officer, Department of Agriculture (Parts 3000—3099)
XXXI	Office of Environmental Quality, Department of Agriculture (Parts 3100—3199)
XXXII	Office of Procurement and Property Management, Department of Agriculture (Parts 3200—3299)
XXXIII	Office of Transportation, Department of Agriculture (Parts 3300—3399)
XXXIV	National Institute of Food and Agriculture (Parts 3400—3499)
XXXV	Rural Housing Service, Department of Agriculture (Parts 3500—3599)
XXXVI	National Agricultural Statistics Service, Department of Agriculture (Parts 3600—3699)
XXXVII	Economic Research Service, Department of Agriculture (Parts 3700—3799)
XXXVIII	World Agricultural Outlook Board, Department of Agriculture (Parts 3800—3899)
XLI	[Reserved]
XLII	Rural Business-Cooperative Service and Rural Utilities Service, Department of Agriculture (Parts 4200—4299)

Title 8—Aliens and Nationality

I	Department of Homeland Security (Immigration and Naturalization) (Parts 1—499)
V	Executive Office for Immigration Review, Department of Justice (Parts 1000—1399)

Title 9—Animals and Animal Products

I	Animal and Plant Health Inspection Service, Department of Agriculture (Parts 1—199)

Title 9—Animals and Animal Products—Continued

Chap.

Chap.	
II	Grain Inspection, Packers and Stockyards Administration (Packers and Stockyards Programs), Department of Agriculture (Parts 200—299)
III	Food Safety and Inspection Service, Department of Agriculture (Parts 300—599)

Title 10—Energy

Chap.	
I	Nuclear Regulatory Commission (Parts 0—199)
II	Department of Energy (Parts 200—699)
III	Department of Energy (Parts 700—999)
X	Department of Energy (General Provisions) (Parts 1000—1099)
XIII	Nuclear Waste Technical Review Board (Parts 1300—1399)
XVII	Defense Nuclear Facilities Safety Board (Parts 1700—1799)
XVIII	Northeast Interstate Low-Level Radioactive Waste Commission (Parts 1800—1899)

Title 11—Federal Elections

Chap.	
I	Federal Election Commission (Parts 1—9099)
II	Election Assistance Commission (Parts 9400—9499)

Title 12—Banks and Banking

Chap.	
I	Comptroller of the Currency, Department of the Treasury (Parts 1—199)
II	Federal Reserve System (Parts 200—299)
III	Federal Deposit Insurance Corporation (Parts 300—399)
IV	Export-Import Bank of the United States (Parts 400—499)
V	Office of Thrift Supervision, Department of the Treasury (Parts 500—599)
VI	Farm Credit Administration (Parts 600—699)
VII	National Credit Union Administration (Parts 700—799)
VIII	Federal Financing Bank (Parts 800—899)
IX	Federal Housing Finance Board (Parts 900—999)
X	Bureau of Consumer Financial Protection (Parts 1000—1099)
XI	Federal Financial Institutions Examination Council (Parts 1100—1199)
XII	Federal Housing Finance Agency (Parts 1200—1299)
XIII	Financial Stability Oversight Council (Parts 1300—1399)
XIV	Farm Credit System Insurance Corporation (Parts 1400—1499)
XV	Department of the Treasury (Parts 1500—1599)
XVI	Office of Financial Research (Parts 1600—1699)
XVII	Office of Federal Housing Enterprise Oversight, Department of Housing and Urban Development (Parts 1700—1799)
XVIII	Community Development Financial Institutions Fund, Department of the Treasury (Parts 1800—1899)

Title 13—Business Credit and Assistance

Chap.

I Small Business Administration (Parts 1—199)

III Economic Development Administration, Department of Commerce (Parts 300—399)

IV Emergency Steel Guarantee Loan Board (Parts 400—499)

V Emergency Oil and Gas Guaranteed Loan Board (Parts 500—599)

Title 14—Aeronautics and Space

I Federal Aviation Administration, Department of Transportation (Parts 1—199)

II Office of the Secretary, Department of Transportation (Aviation Proceedings) (Parts 200—399)

III Commercial Space Transportation, Federal Aviation Administration, Department of Transportation (Parts 400—1199)

V National Aeronautics and Space Administration (Parts 1200—1299)

VI Air Transportation System Stabilization (Parts 1300—1399)

Title 15—Commerce and Foreign Trade

SUBTITLE A—OFFICE OF THE SECRETARY OF COMMERCE (PARTS 0—29)

SUBTITLE B—REGULATIONS RELATING TO COMMERCE AND FOREIGN TRADE

I Bureau of the Census, Department of Commerce (Parts 30—199)

II National Institute of Standards and Technology, Department of Commerce (Parts 200—299)

III International Trade Administration, Department of Commerce (Parts 300—399)

IV Foreign-Trade Zones Board, Department of Commerce (Parts 400—499)

VII Bureau of Industry and Security, Department of Commerce (Parts 700—799)

VIII Bureau of Economic Analysis, Department of Commerce (Parts 800—899)

IX National Oceanic and Atmospheric Administration, Department of Commerce (Parts 900—999)

XI Technology Administration, Department of Commerce (Parts 1100—1199)

XIII East-West Foreign Trade Board (Parts 1300—1399)

XIV Minority Business Development Agency (Parts 1400—1499)

SUBTITLE C—REGULATIONS RELATING TO FOREIGN TRADE AGREEMENTS

XX Office of the United States Trade Representative (Parts 2000—2099)

SUBTITLE D—REGULATIONS RELATING TO TELECOMMUNICATIONS AND INFORMATION

XXIII National Telecommunications and Information Administration, Department of Commerce (Parts 2300—2399)

Title 16—Commercial Practices

Chap.

I Federal Trade Commission (Parts 0—999)

II Consumer Product Safety Commission (Parts 1000—1799)

Title 17—Commodity and Securities Exchanges

I Commodity Futures Trading Commission (Parts 1—199)

II Securities and Exchange Commission (Parts 200—399)

IV Department of the Treasury (Parts 400—499)

Title 18—Conservation of Power and Water Resources

I Federal Energy Regulatory Commission, Department of Energy (Parts 1—399)

III Delaware River Basin Commission (Parts 400—499)

VI Water Resources Council (Parts 700—799)

VIII Susquehanna River Basin Commission (Parts 800—899)

XIII Tennessee Valley Authority (Parts 1300—1399)

Title 19—Customs Duties

I U.S. Customs and Border Protection, Department of Homeland Security; Department of the Treasury (Parts 0—199)

II United States International Trade Commission (Parts 200—299)

III International Trade Administration, Department of Commerce (Parts 300—399)

IV U.S. Immigration and Customs Enforcement, Department of Homeland Security (Parts 400—599)

Title 20—Employees' Benefits

I Office of Workers' Compensation Programs, Department of Labor (Parts 1—199)

II Railroad Retirement Board (Parts 200—399)

III Social Security Administration (Parts 400—499)

IV Employees' Compensation Appeals Board, Department of Labor (Parts 500—599)

V Employment and Training Administration, Department of Labor (Parts 600—699)

VI Office of Workers' Compensation Programs, Department of Labor (Parts 700—799)

VII Benefits Review Board, Department of Labor (Parts 800—899)

VIII Joint Board for the Enrollment of Actuaries (Parts 900—999)

IX Office of the Assistant Secretary for Veterans' Employment and Training Service, Department of Labor (Parts 1000—1099)

Title 21—Food and Drugs

Chap.

I Food and Drug Administration, Department of Health and Human Services (Parts 1—1299)

II Drug Enforcement Administration, Department of Justice (Parts 1300—1399)

III Office of National Drug Control Policy (Parts 1400—1499)

Title 22—Foreign Relations

I Department of State (Parts 1—199)

II Agency for International Development (Parts 200—299)

III Peace Corps (Parts 300—399)

IV International Joint Commission, United States and Canada (Parts 400—499)

V Broadcasting Board of Governors (Parts 500—599)

VII Overseas Private Investment Corporation (Parts 700—799)

IX Foreign Service Grievance Board (Parts 900—999)

X Inter-American Foundation (Parts 1000—1099)

XI International Boundary and Water Commission, United States and Mexico, United States Section (Parts 1100—1199)

XII United States International Development Cooperation Agency (Parts 1200—1299)

XIII Millennium Challenge Corporation (Parts 1300—1399)

XIV Foreign Service Labor Relations Board; Federal Labor Relations Authority; General Counsel of the Federal Labor Relations Authority; and the Foreign Service Impasse Disputes Panel (Parts 1400—1499)

XV African Development Foundation (Parts 1500—1599)

XVI Japan-United States Friendship Commission (Parts 1600—1699)

XVII United States Institute of Peace (Parts 1700—1799)

Title 23—Highways

I Federal Highway Administration, Department of Transportation (Parts 1—999)

II National Highway Traffic Safety Administration and Federal Highway Administration, Department of Transportation (Parts 1200—1299)

III National Highway Traffic Safety Administration, Department of Transportation (Parts 1300—1399)

Title 24—Housing and Urban Development

SUBTITLE A—OFFICE OF THE SECRETARY, DEPARTMENT OF HOUSING AND URBAN DEVELOPMENT (PARTS 0—99)

SUBTITLE B—REGULATIONS RELATING TO HOUSING AND URBAN DEVELOPMENT

I Office of Assistant Secretary for Equal Opportunity, Department of Housing and Urban Development (Parts 100—199)

Title 24—Housing and Urban Development—Continued

Chap.

Chap.	
II	Office of Assistant Secretary for Housing-Federal Housing Commissioner, Department of Housing and Urban Development (Parts 200—299)
III	Government National Mortgage Association, Department of Housing and Urban Development (Parts 300—399)
IV	Office of Housing and Office of Multifamily Housing Assistance Restructuring, Department of Housing and Urban Development (Parts 400—499)
V	Office of Assistant Secretary for Community Planning and Development, Department of Housing and Urban Development (Parts 500—599)
VI	Office of Assistant Secretary for Community Planning and Development, Department of Housing and Urban Development (Parts 600—699) [Reserved]
VII	Office of the Secretary, Department of Housing and Urban Development (Housing Assistance Programs and Public and Indian Housing Programs) (Parts 700—799)
VIII	Office of the Assistant Secretary for Housing—Federal Housing Commissioner, Department of Housing and Urban Development (Section 8 Housing Assistance Programs, Section 202 Direct Loan Program, Section 202 Supportive Housing for the Elderly Program and Section 811 Supportive Housing for Persons With Disabilities Program) (Parts 800—899)
IX	Office of Assistant Secretary for Public and Indian Housing, Department of Housing and Urban Development (Parts 900—1699)
X	Office of Assistant Secretary for Housing—Federal Housing Commissioner, Department of Housing and Urban Development (Interstate Land Sales Registration Program) (Parts 1700—1799)
XII	Office of Inspector General, Department of Housing and Urban Development (Parts 2000—2099)
XV	Emergency Mortgage Insurance and Loan Programs, Department of Housing and Urban Development (Parts 2700—2799)
XX	Office of Assistant Secretary for Housing—Federal Housing Commissioner, Department of Housing and Urban Development (Parts 3200—3899)
XXIV	Board of Directors of the HOPE for Homeowners Program (Parts 4000—4099)
XXV	Neighborhood Reinvestment Corporation (Parts 4100—4199)

Title 25—Indians

Chap.	
I	Bureau of Indian Affairs, Department of the Interior (Parts 1—299)
II	Indian Arts and Crafts Board, Department of the Interior (Parts 300—399)
III	National Indian Gaming Commission, Department of the Interior (Parts 500—599)
IV	Office of Navajo and Hopi Indian Relocation (Parts 700—799)
V	Bureau of Indian Affairs, Department of the Interior, and Indian Health Service, Department of Health and Human Services (Part 900)

Title 25—Indians—Continued

Chap.

VI Office of the Assistant Secretary-Indian Affairs, Department of the Interior (Parts 1000—1199)

VII Office of the Special Trustee for American Indians, Department of the Interior (Parts 1200—1299)

Title 26—Internal Revenue

I Internal Revenue Service, Department of the Treasury (Parts 1—End)

Title 27—Alcohol, Tobacco Products and Firearms

I Alcohol and Tobacco Tax and Trade Bureau, Department of the Treasury (Parts 1—399)

II Bureau of Alcohol, Tobacco, Firearms, and Explosives, Department of Justice (Parts 400—699)

Title 28—Judicial Administration

I Department of Justice (Parts 0—299)

III Federal Prison Industries, Inc., Department of Justice (Parts 300—399)

V Bureau of Prisons, Department of Justice (Parts 500—599)

VI Offices of Independent Counsel, Department of Justice (Parts 600—699)

VII Office of Independent Counsel (Parts 700—799)

VIII Court Services and Offender Supervision Agency for the District of Columbia (Parts 800—899)

IX National Crime Prevention and Privacy Compact Council (Parts 900—999)

XI Department of Justice and Department of State (Parts 1100—1199)

Title 29—Labor

SUBTITLE A—OFFICE OF THE SECRETARY OF LABOR (PARTS 0—99)

SUBTITLE B—REGULATIONS RELATING TO LABOR

I National Labor Relations Board (Parts 100—199)

II Office of Labor-Management Standards, Department of Labor (Parts 200—299)

III National Railroad Adjustment Board (Parts 300—399)

IV Office of Labor-Management Standards, Department of Labor (Parts 400—499)

V Wage and Hour Division, Department of Labor (Parts 500—899)

IX Construction Industry Collective Bargaining Commission (Parts 900—999)

X National Mediation Board (Parts 1200—1299)

XII Federal Mediation and Conciliation Service (Parts 1400—1499)

XIV Equal Employment Opportunity Commission (Parts 1600—1699)

Title 29—Labor—Continued

Title 30—Mineral Resources

Title 31—Money and Finance: Treasury

Title 32—National Defense

Title 32—National Defense—Continued

Chap.	
V	Department of the Army (Parts 400—699)
VI	Department of the Navy (Parts 700—799)
VII	Department of the Air Force (Parts 800—1099)
	SUBTITLE B—OTHER REGULATIONS RELATING TO NATIONAL DEFENSE
XII	Defense Logistics Agency (Parts 1200—1299)
XVI	Selective Service System (Parts 1600—1699)
XVII	Office of the Director of National Intelligence (Parts 1700—1799)
XVIII	National Counterintelligence Center (Parts 1800—1899)
XIX	Central Intelligence Agency (Parts 1900—1999)
XX	Information Security Oversight Office, National Archives and Records Administration (Parts 2000—2099)
XXI	National Security Council (Parts 2100—2199)
XXIV	Office of Science and Technology Policy (Parts 2400—2499)
XXVII	Office for Micronesian Status Negotiations (Parts 2700—2799)
XXVIII	Office of the Vice President of the United States (Parts 2800—2899)

Title 33—Navigation and Navigable Waters

I	Coast Guard, Department of Homeland Security (Parts 1—199)
II	Corps of Engineers, Department of the Army (Parts 200—399)
IV	Saint Lawrence Seaway Development Corporation, Department of Transportation (Parts 400—499)

Title 34—Education

	SUBTITLE A—OFFICE OF THE SECRETARY, DEPARTMENT OF EDUCATION (PARTS 1—99)
	SUBTITLE B—REGULATIONS OF THE OFFICES OF THE DEPARTMENT OF EDUCATION
I	Office for Civil Rights, Department of Education (Parts 100—199)
II	Office of Elementary and Secondary Education, Department of Education (Parts 200—299)
III	Office of Special Education and Rehabilitative Services, Department of Education (Parts 300—399)
IV	Office of Vocational and Adult Education, Department of Education (Parts 400—499)
V	Office of Bilingual Education and Minority Languages Affairs, Department of Education (Parts 500—599)
VI	Office of Postsecondary Education, Department of Education (Parts 600—699)
VII	Office of Educational Research and Improvement, Department of Education (Parts 700—799) [Reserved]
	SUBTITLE C—REGULATIONS RELATING TO EDUCATION
XI	National Institute for Literacy (Parts 1100—1199)
XII	National Council on Disability (Parts 1200—1299)

Title 35 [Reserved]

Chap.

Title 36—Parks, Forests, and Public Property

I National Park Service, Department of the Interior (Parts 1—199)

II Forest Service, Department of Agriculture (Parts 200—299)

III Corps of Engineers, Department of the Army (Parts 300—399)

IV American Battle Monuments Commission (Parts 400—499)

V Smithsonian Institution (Parts 500—599)

VI [Reserved]

VII Library of Congress (Parts 700—799)

VIII Advisory Council on Historic Preservation (Parts 800—899)

IX Pennsylvania Avenue Development Corporation (Parts 900—999)

X Presidio Trust (Parts 1000—1099)

XI Architectural and Transportation Barriers Compliance Board (Parts 1100—1199)

XII National Archives and Records Administration (Parts 1200—1299)

XV Oklahoma City National Memorial Trust (Parts 1500—1599)

XVI Morris K. Udall Scholarship and Excellence in National Environmental Policy Foundation (Parts 1600—1699)

Title 37—Patents, Trademarks, and Copyrights

I United States Patent and Trademark Office, Department of Commerce (Parts 1—199)

II Copyright Office, Library of Congress (Parts 200—299)

III Copyright Royalty Board, Library of Congress (Parts 300—399)

IV Assistant Secretary for Technology Policy, Department of Commerce (Parts 400—599)

Title 38—Pensions, Bonuses, and Veterans' Relief

I Department of Veterans Affairs (Parts 0—199)

II Armed Forces Retirement Home (Parts 200—299)

Title 39—Postal Service

I United States Postal Service (Parts 1—999)

III Postal Regulatory Commission (Parts 3000—3099)

Title 40—Protection of Environment

I Environmental Protection Agency (Parts 1—1099)

IV Environmental Protection Agency and Department of Justice (Parts 1400—1499)

V Council on Environmental Quality (Parts 1500—1599)

VI Chemical Safety and Hazard Investigation Board (Parts 1600—1699)

Title 40—Protection of Environment—Continued

Chap.

VII Environmental Protection Agency and Department of Defense; Uniform National Discharge Standards for Vessels of the Armed Forces (Parts 1700—1799)

Title 41—Public Contracts and Property Management

SUBTITLE A—FEDERAL PROCUREMENT REGULATIONS SYSTEM [NOTE]

SUBTITLE B—OTHER PROVISIONS RELATING TO PUBLIC CONTRACTS

50 Public Contracts, Department of Labor (Parts 50–1—50–999)

51 Committee for Purchase From People Who Are Blind or Severely Disabled (Parts 51–1—51–99)

60 Office of Federal Contract Compliance Programs, Equal Employment Opportunity, Department of Labor (Parts 60–1—60–999)

61 Office of the Assistant Secretary for Veterans' Employment and Training Service, Department of Labor (Parts 61–1—61–999)

62—100 [Reserved]

SUBTITLE C—FEDERAL PROPERTY MANAGEMENT REGULATIONS SYSTEM

101 Federal Property Management Regulations (Parts 101–1—101–99)

102 Federal Management Regulation (Parts 102–1—102–299)

103—104 [Reserved]

105 General Services Administration (Parts 105–1—105–999)

109 Department of Energy Property Management Regulations (Parts 109–1—109–99)

114 Department of the Interior (Parts 114–1—114–99)

115 Environmental Protection Agency (Parts 115–1—115–99)

128 Department of Justice (Parts 128–1—128–99)

129—200 [Reserved]

SUBTITLE D—OTHER PROVISIONS RELATING TO PROPERTY MANAGEMENT [RESERVED]

SUBTITLE E—FEDERAL INFORMATION RESOURCES MANAGEMENT REGULATIONS SYSTEM [RESERVED]

SUBTITLE F—FEDERAL TRAVEL REGULATION SYSTEM

300 General (Parts 300–1—300–99)

301 Temporary Duty (TDY) Travel Allowances (Parts 301–1—301–99)

302 Relocation Allowances (Parts 302–1—302–99)

303 Payment of Expenses Connected with the Death of Certain Employees (Part 303–1—303–99)

304 Payment of Travel Expenses from a Non-Federal Source (Parts 304–1—304–99)

Title 42—Public Health

I Public Health Service, Department of Health and Human Services (Parts 1—199)

IV Centers for Medicare & Medicaid Services, Department of Health and Human Services (Parts 400—599)

Title 42—Public Health—Continued

Title 43—Public Lands: Interior

Title 44—Emergency Management and Assistance

Title 45—Public Welfare

Title 45—Public Welfare—Continued

Chap.

XVI Legal Services Corporation (Parts 1600—1699)

XVII National Commission on Libraries and Information Science (Parts 1700—1799)

XVIII Harry S. Truman Scholarship Foundation (Parts 1800—1899)

XXI Commission on Fine Arts (Parts 2100—2199)

XXIII Arctic Research Commission (Part 2301)

XXIV James Madison Memorial Fellowship Foundation (Parts 2400—2499)

XXV Corporation for National and Community Service (Parts 2500—2599)

Title 46—Shipping

I Coast Guard, Department of Homeland Security (Parts 1—199)

II Maritime Administration, Department of Transportation (Parts 200—399)

III Coast Guard (Great Lakes Pilotage), Department of Homeland Security (Parts 400—499)

IV Federal Maritime Commission (Parts 500—599)

Title 47—Telecommunication

I Federal Communications Commission (Parts 0—199)

II Office of Science and Technology Policy and National Security Council (Parts 200—299)

III National Telecommunications and Information Administration, Department of Commerce (Parts 300—399)

IV National Telecommunications and Information Administration, Department of Commerce, and National Highway Traffic Safety Administration, Department of Transportation (Parts 400—499)

Title 48—Federal Acquisition Regulations System

1 Federal Acquisition Regulation (Parts 1—99)

2 Defense Acquisition Regulations System, Department of Defense (Parts 200—299)

3 Health and Human Services (Parts 300—399)

4 Department of Agriculture (Parts 400—499)

5 General Services Administration (Parts 500—599)

6 Department of State (Parts 600—699)

7 Agency for International Development (Parts 700—799)

8 Department of Veterans Affairs (Parts 800—899)

9 Department of Energy (Parts 900—999)

10 Department of the Treasury (Parts 1000—1099)

12 Department of Transportation (Parts 1200—1299)

13 Department of Commerce (Parts 1300—1399)

14 Department of the Interior (Parts 1400—1499)

Chap.

15 Environmental Protection Agency (Parts 1500—1599)

16 Office of Personnel Management, Federal Employees Health Benefits Acquisition Regulation (Parts 1600—1699)

17 Office of Personnel Management (Parts 1700—1799)

18 National Aeronautics and Space Administration (Parts 1800—1899)

19 Broadcasting Board of Governors (Parts 1900—1999)

20 Nuclear Regulatory Commission (Parts 2000—2099)

21 Office of Personnel Management, Federal Employees Group Life Insurance Federal Acquisition Regulation (Parts 2100—2199)

23 Social Security Administration (Parts 2300—2399)

24 Department of Housing and Urban Development (Parts 2400—2499)

25 National Science Foundation (Parts 2500—2599)

28 Department of Justice (Parts 2800—2899)

29 Department of Labor (Parts 2900—2999)

30 Department of Homeland Security, Homeland Security Acquisition Regulation (HSAR) (Parts 3000—3099)

34 Department of Education Acquisition Regulation (Parts 3400—3499)

51 Department of the Army Acquisition Regulations (Parts 5100—5199)

52 Department of the Navy Acquisition Regulations (Parts 5200—5299)

53 Department of the Air Force Federal Acquisition Regulation Supplement (Parts 5300—5399) [Reserved]

54 Defense Logistics Agency, Department of Defense (Parts 5400—5499)

57 African Development Foundation (Parts 5700—5799)

61 Civilian Board of Contract Appeals, General Services Administration (Parts 6100—6199)

63 Department of Transportation Board of Contract Appeals (Parts 6300—6399)

99 Cost Accounting Standards Board, Office of Federal Procurement Policy, Office of Management and Budget (Parts 9900—9999)

Title 49—Transportation

SUBTITLE A—OFFICE OF THE SECRETARY OF TRANSPORTATION (PARTS 1—99)

SUBTITLE B—OTHER REGULATIONS RELATING TO TRANSPORTATION

I Pipeline and Hazardous Materials Safety Administration, Department of Transportation (Parts 100—199)

II Federal Railroad Administration, Department of Transportation (Parts 200—299)

III Federal Motor Carrier Safety Administration, Department of Transportation (Parts 300—399)

IV Coast Guard, Department of Homeland Security (Parts 400—499)

Title 49—Transportation—Continued

Title 50—Wildlife and Fisheries

CFR Index and Finding Aids

Alphabetical List of Agencies Appearing in the CFR

(Revised as of July 1, 2013)

Agency	CFR Title, Subtitle or Chapter
Administrative Committee of the Federal Register	1, I
Administrative Conference of the United States	1, III
Advisory Council on Historic Preservation	36, VIII
Advocacy and Outreach, Office of	7, XXV
Afghanistan Reconstruction, Special Inspector General for	22, LXXXIII
African Development Foundation	22, XV
Federal Acquisition Regulation	48, 57
Agency for International Development	2, VII; 22, II
Federal Acquisition Regulation	48, 7
Agricultural Marketing Service	7, I, IX, X, XI
Agricultural Research Service	7, V
Agriculture Department	2, IV; 5, LXXIII
Advocacy and Outreach, Office of	7, XXV
Agricultural Marketing Service	7, I, IX, X, XI
Agricultural Research Service	7, V
Animal and Plant Health Inspection Service	7, III; 9, I
Chief Financial Officer, Office of	7, XXX
Commodity Credit Corporation	7, XIV
Economic Research Service	7, XXXVII
Energy Policy and New Uses, Office of	2, IX; 7, XXIX
Environmental Quality, Office of	7, XXXI
Farm Service Agency	7, VII, XVIII
Federal Acquisition Regulation	48, 4
Federal Crop Insurance Corporation	7, IV
Food and Nutrition Service	7, II
Food Safety and Inspection Service	9, III
Foreign Agricultural Service	7, XV
Forest Service	36, II
Grain Inspection, Packers and Stockyards Administration	7, VIII; 9, II
Information Resources Management, Office of	7, XXVII
Inspector General, Office of	7, XXVI
National Agricultural Library	7, XLI
National Agricultural Statistics Service	7, XXXVI
National Institute of Food and Agriculture	7, XXXIV
Natural Resources Conservation Service	7, VI
Operations, Office of	7, XXVIII
Procurement and Property Management, Office of	7, XXXII
Rural Business-Cooperative Service	7, XVIII, XLII, L
Rural Development Administration	7, XLII
Rural Housing Service	7, XVIII, XXXV, L
Rural Telephone Bank	7, XVI
Rural Utilities Service	7, XVII, XVIII, XLII, L
Secretary of Agriculture, Office of	7, Subtitle A
Transportation, Office of	7, XXXIII
World Agricultural Outlook Board	7, XXXVIII
Air Force Department	32, VII
Federal Acquisition Regulation Supplement	48, 53
Air Transportation Stabilization Board	14, VI
Alcohol and Tobacco Tax and Trade Bureau	27, I
Alcohol, Tobacco, Firearms, and Explosives, Bureau of	27, II
AMTRAK	49, VII
American Battle Monuments Commission	36, IV
American Indians, Office of the Special Trustee	25, VII

Agency	CFR Title, Subtitle or Chapter
Animal and Plant Health Inspection Service	7, III; 9, I
Appalachian Regional Commission	5, IX
Architectural and Transportation Barriers Compliance Board	36, XI
Arctic Research Commission	45, XXIII
Armed Forces Retirement Home	5, XI
Army Department	32, V
Engineers, Corps of	33, II; 36, III
Federal Acquisition Regulation	48, 51
Bilingual Education and Minority Languages Affairs, Office of	34, V
Blind or Severely Disabled, Committee for Purchase from People Who Are	41, 51
Broadcasting Board of Governors	22, V
Federal Acquisition Regulation	48, 19
Bureau of Ocean Energy Management, Regulation, and Enforcement	30, II
Census Bureau	15, I
Centers for Medicare & Medicaid Services	42, IV
Central Intelligence Agency	32, XIX
Chemical Safety and Hazardous Investigation Board	40, VI
Chief Financial Officer, Office of	7, XXX
Child Support Enforcement, Office of	45, III
Children and Families, Administration for	45, II, III, IV, X
Civil Rights, Commission on	5, LXVIII; 45, VII
Civil Rights, Office for	34, I
Council of the Inspectors General on Integrity and Efficiency	5, XCVIII
Court Services and Offender Supervision Agency for the District of Columbia	5, LXX
Coast Guard	33, I; 46, I; 49, IV
Coast Guard (Great Lakes Pilotage)	46, III
Commerce Department	2, XIII; 44, IV; 50, VI
Census Bureau	15, I
Economic Analysis, Bureau of	15, VIII
Economic Development Administration	13, III
Emergency Management and Assistance	44, IV
Federal Acquisition Regulation	48, 13
Foreign-Trade Zones Board	15, IV
Industry and Security, Bureau of	15, VII
International Trade Administration	15, III; 19, III
National Institute of Standards and Technology	15, II
National Marine Fisheries Service	50, II, IV
National Oceanic and Atmospheric Administration	15, IX; 50, II, III, IV, VI
National Telecommunications and Information Administration	15, XXIII; 47, III, IV
National Weather Service	15, IX
Patent and Trademark Office, United States	37, I
Productivity, Technology and Innovation, Assistant Secretary for	37, IV
Secretary of Commerce, Office of	15, Subtitle A
Technology Administration	15, XI
Technology Policy, Assistant Secretary for	37, IV
Commercial Space Transportation	14, III
Commodity Credit Corporation	7, XIV
Commodity Futures Trading Commission	5, XLI; 17, I
Community Planning and Development, Office of Assistant Secretary for	24, V, VI
Community Services, Office of	45, X
Comptroller of the Currency	12, I
Construction Industry Collective Bargaining Commission	29, IX
Consumer Financial Protection Bureau	5, LXXXIV; 12, X
Consumer Product Safety Commission	5, LXXI; 16, II
Copyright Office	37, II
Copyright Royalty Board	37, III
Corporation for National and Community Service	2, XXII; 45, XII, XXV
Cost Accounting Standards Board	48, 99
Council on Environmental Quality	40, V
Court Services and Offender Supervision Agency for the District of Columbia	5, LXX; 28, VIII

Agency	CFR Title, Subtitle or Chapter
Foreign Service Labor Relations Board	22, XIV
Foreign-Trade Zones Board	15, IV
Forest Service	36, II
General Services Administration	5, LVII; 41, 105
Contract Appeals, Board of	48, 61
Federal Acquisition Regulation	48, 5
Federal Management Regulation	41, 102
Federal Property Management Regulations	41, 101
Federal Travel Regulation System	41, Subtitle F
General	41, 300
Payment From a Non-Federal Source for Travel Expenses	41, 304
Payment of Expenses Connected With the Death of Certain Employees	41, 303
Relocation Allowances	41, 302
Temporary Duty (TDY) Travel Allowances	41, 301
Geological Survey	30, IV
Government Accountability Office	4, I
Government Ethics, Office of	5, XVI
Government National Mortgage Association	24, III
Grain Inspection, Packers and Stockyards Administration	7, VIII; 9, II
Harry S. Truman Scholarship Foundation	45, XVIII
Health and Human Services, Department of	2, III; 5, XLV; 45, Subtitle A,
Centers for Medicare & Medicaid Services	42, IV
Child Support Enforcement, Office of	45, III
Children and Families, Administration for	45, II, III, IV, X
Community Services, Office of	45, X
Family Assistance, Office of	45, II
Federal Acquisition Regulation	48, 3
Food and Drug Administration	21, I
Human Development Services, Office of	45, XIII
Indian Health Service	25, V
Inspector General (Health Care), Office of	42, V
Public Health Service	42, I
Refugee Resettlement, Office of	45, IV
Homeland Security, Department of	2, XXX; 6, I; 8, I
Coast Guard	33, I; 46, I; 49, IV
Coast Guard (Great Lakes Pilotage)	46, III
Customs and Border Protection	19, I
Federal Emergency Management Agency	44, I
Human Resources Management and Labor Relations Systems	5, XCVII
Immigration and Customs Enforcement Bureau	19, IV
Transportation Security Administration	49, XII
HOPE for Homeowners Program, Board of Directors of	24, XXIV
Housing and Urban Development, Department of	2, XXIV; 5, LXV; 24, Subtitle B
Community Planning and Development, Office of Assistant Secretary for	24, V, VI
Equal Opportunity, Office of Assistant Secretary for	24, I
Federal Acquisition Regulation	48, 24
Federal Housing Enterprise Oversight, Office of	12, XVII
Government National Mortgage Association	24, III
Housing—Federal Housing Commissioner, Office of Assistant Secretary for	24, II, VIII, X, XX
Housing, Office of, and Multifamily Housing Assistance Restructuring, Office of	24, IV
Inspector General, Office of	24, XII
Public and Indian Housing, Office of Assistant Secretary for	24, IX
Secretary, Office of	24, Subtitle A, VII
Housing—Federal Housing Commissioner, Office of Assistant Secretary for	24, II, VIII, X, XX
Housing, Office of, and Multifamily Housing Assistance Restructuring, Office of	24, IV
Human Development Services, Office of	45, XIII
Immigration and Customs Enforcement Bureau	19, IV
Immigration Review, Executive Office for	8, V

Agency	CFR Title, Subtitle or Chapter
Rural Telephone Bank	7, XVI
Rural Utilities Service	7, XVII, XVIII, XLII, L
Saint Lawrence Seaway Development Corporation	33, IV
Science and Technology Policy, Office of	32, XXIV
Science and Technology Policy, Office of, and National Security Council	47, II
Secret Service	31, IV
Securities and Exchange Commission	5, XXXIV; 17, II
Selective Service System	32, XVI
Small Business Administration	2, XXVII; 13, I
Smithsonian Institution	36, V
Social Security Administration	2, XXIII; 20, III; 48, 23
Soldiers' and Airmen's Home, United States	5, XI
Special Counsel, Office of	5, VIII
Special Education and Rehabilitative Services, Office of	34, III
State Department	2, VI; 22, I; 28, XI
Federal Acquisition Regulation	48, 6
Surface Mining Reclamation and Enforcement, Office of	30, VII
Surface Transportation Board	49, X
Susquehanna River Basin Commission	18, VIII
Technology Administration	15, XI
Technology Policy, Assistant Secretary for	37, IV
Tennessee Valley Authority	5, LXIX; 18, XIII
Thrift Supervision Office, Department of the Treasury	12, V
Trade Representative, United States, Office of	15, XX
Transportation, Department of	2, XII; 5, L
Commercial Space Transportation	14, III
Contract Appeals, Board of	48, 63
Emergency Management and Assistance	44, IV
Federal Acquisition Regulation	48, 12
Federal Aviation Administration	14, I
Federal Highway Administration	23, I, II
Federal Motor Carrier Safety Administration	49, III
Federal Railroad Administration	49, II
Federal Transit Administration	49, VI
Maritime Administration	46, II
National Highway Traffic Safety Administration	23, II, III; 47, IV; 49, V
Pipeline and Hazardous Materials Safety Administration	49, I
Saint Lawrence Seaway Development Corporation	33, IV
Secretary of Transportation, Office of	14, II; 49, Subtitle A
Surface Transportation Board	49, X
Transportation Statistics Bureau	49, XI
Transportation, Office of	7, XXXIII
Transportation Security Administration	49, XII
Transportation Statistics Bureau	49, XI
Travel Allowances, Temporary Duty (TDY)	41, 301
Treasury Department	5, XXI; 12, XV; 17, IV; 31, IX
Alcohol and Tobacco Tax and Trade Bureau	27, I
Community Development Financial Institutions Fund	12, XVIII
Comptroller of the Currency	12, I
Customs and Border Protection	19, I
Engraving and Printing, Bureau of	31, VI
Federal Acquisition Regulation	48, 10
Federal Claims Collection Standards	31, IX
Federal Law Enforcement Training Center	31, VII
Financial Crimes Enforcement Network	31, X
Fiscal Service	31, II
Foreign Assets Control, Office of	31, V
Internal Revenue Service	26, I
Investment Security, Office of	31, VIII
Monetary Offices	31, I
Secret Service	31, IV
Secretary of the Treasury, Office of	31, Subtitle A
Thrift Supervision, Office of	12, V
Truman, Harry S. Scholarship Foundation	45, XVIII
United States and Canada, International Joint Commission	22, IV

List of CFR Sections Affected

All changes in this volume of the Code of Federal Regulations (CFR) that were made by documents published in the FEDERAL REGISTER since January 1, 2008 are enumerated in the following list. Entries indicate the nature of the changes effected. Page numbers refer to FEDERAL REGISTER pages. The user should consult the entries for chapters, parts and subparts as well as sections for revisions.

For changes to this volume of the CFR prior to this listing, consult the annual edition of the monthly List of CFR Sections Affected (LSA). The LSA is available at *www.fdsys.gov*. For changes to this volume of the CFR prior to 2001, see the "List of CFR Sections Affected, 1949–1963, 1964–1972, 1973–1985, and 1986–2000" published in 11 separate volumes. The "List of CFR Sections Affected 1986–2000" is available at *www.fdsys.gov*.

2008

37 CFR

73 FR Page

Chapter I

1.1 (d) revised 47540
1.4 (d)(3) and (4)(i) revised; (d)(4)(ii)(C) added 47684
1.8 (a)(2)(iii)(A) revised 47684
1.9 (j) revised 47685
1.16 Authority citation added after undesignated center heading; (a) through (e), (h) through (k) and (m) through (s) revised 47540
1.17 (a), (l) and (m) revised 47540
1.18 (a), (b) and (c) revised 47541
1.20 (c)(3), (4) and (d) through (g) revised 47541
1.21 (a)(3) removed; (a)(7), (8) and (9) added 67756
1.25 (c)(3) revised; (c)(4) removed 47541
1.401—1.499 (Subpart C) Authority citation revised 66759
1.445 (a)(1), (2) and (3) revised 66759
1.492 (a), (b)(3), (4), (c)(2), (d), (e), (f) and (j) revised 47541
2.2 (c) revised 47685
2.6 (a)(8), (13), (19), (b)(3) and (6) revised 67767
2.11 Revised 47685
2.17 (a), (b) and (c) revised 47685
2.18 (a) revised 47685
2.19 (b) revised 47685
2.21 (a) introductory text and (b) revised; (c) removed 67767

37 CFR—Continued

73 FR Page

Chapter I—Continued

2.23 (a)(2) revised 67768
2.24 Revised 47685
2.25 Revised 67768
2.26 Removed 67768
2.27 (d) revised 67768
2.32 (a)(8) added 13784
2.32 (a)(3)(iii), (6) and (8) revised; (a)(3)(iv), (9) and (10) added 67768
2.33 (a)(3) revised 47685
(b)(1) revised 67768
2.34 (a)(1)(i), (2), (3)(i) and (4)(ii) revised; (a)(1)(v) added 67768
2.37 Revised 13784
2.41 (a) revised 67768
2.44 (b) revised 67769
2.45 (b) revised 67769
2.47 (a) revised 67769
2.48 Added 67769
2.52 (b)(5) revised 13784
2.52 (b) introductory text and (1) revised 67769
2.53 (a) revised 67769
2.56 (b)(1), (d)(2) and (4) revised 67769
2.62 Revised 67769
2.64 (c)(1) revised 67769
2.65 (a) revised 67769
2.66 (a)(1), (d) and (f)(1) revised 67769
2.73 Revised 67770
2.74 Revised 67770
2.76 (d) revised 67770
2.77 Revised 67770
2.81 (b) revised 67770
2.84 (b) revised 67770
2.85 Revised 67770

37 CFR—Continued

37 CFR—Continued

37 CFR—Continued

73 FR Page

37 CFR—Continued

73 FR Page

37 CFR—Continued

73 FR Page

Chapter II—Continued

201.2 (b)(1), (2), (3) introductory text, (i) introductory text, (4), (5), (7) and (d)(1)(iv) correctly amended....37838
201.5 (c)(2) correctly amended....37838
201.8 (g) correctly amended....37838
201.11 (i)(1) revised....29072
201.17 (i)(4) added....29073
201.18 (a)(2) through (6) redesignated as (a)(4) through (8); new (a)(2) and (3) added; interim....66181
201.19 (a)(1) amended; (a)(3) through (12) redesignated as (a)(4) through (13); new (a)(3) added; interim....66181
201.28 (l)(1) revised....29073
201.29 (e)(3) correctly amended....37839
201.33 (d)(1) correctly amended....37839
201.34 (d)(2) correctly amended....37839
201.38 (e) and (f) correctly amended....37839
201.39 (g)(1) correctly amended....37839
202.3 (b)(2)(i), (ii) introductory text and (6)(ii) correctly amended....37839
202.5 (b) introductory text, (1), (3), (4), (c) introductory text, (1), (3) and (d)(1) correctly amended....37839
202.12 (c)(4)(vi) correctly amended....37839
202.16 (c)(11) correctly amended....37839
202.17 (g)(1) correctly amended....37839
202.19 (e)(3) correctly amended....37839
202.20 (c)(2)(ii), (xvi), (xix)(B) and (d)(3) correctly amended....37839
202.21 (h) correctly amended....37839
202.23 (b)(2) correctly amended....37839
203.3 (b) introductory text, (1) through (5) and (c) correctly amended; (e) correctly removed; (f) through (i) correctly redesignated as new (e) through (h)....37839
203.4 (f) correctly amended....37839
204.4 (a) correctly amended....37839
204.5 (a) correctly amended....37839
204.7 (a) correctly amended....37839
204.8 (a) correctly amended....37840
205.2 (a) and (b) correctly amended....37840
205.13 Correctly amended....37840
205.22 (a) and (b) correctly amended....37840
211.4 (b)(1) correctly amended....37840
211.5 (d) correctly amended....37840

37 CFR—Continued

73 FR Page

Chapter II—Continued

255.4 Revised; interim....66182
258.3 (g) revised....14185
258.4 (d) revised....14185

Chapter III

381.5 (c)(1), (2) and (3) revised....72726
382.10—382.17 (Subpart B) Added....4102
384 Added; eff. 1–1–09....16199

2009

37 CFR

74 FR Page

Chapter I

1.17 (f) revised....52688
1.26 (a) and (b) revised....52688
1.52 (d)(2) revised....52688
1.53 (b) and (c)(4) revised....52688
1.75 (b) and (c) revised....52688
1.76 (b)(5) revised....52689
1.78 Revised....52689
1.104 (a)(1) and (b) revised....52690
1.105 (a)(1)(ix) removed....52690
1.110 Revised....52690
1.114 (a) and (d) revised; (f), (g) and (h) removed....52691
1.117 Removed....52691
1.136 (a)(1) revised....52691
1.142 (a) revised; (c) removed....52691
1.145 Revised....52691
1.265 Removed....52691
1.485 Revised....31373
1.495 (g) revised....52691
1.704 (c)(11) removed; (c)(12) redesignated as new (c)(11)....52691
2.17 Revised....54906
2.18 Revised....54906
2.19 Revised....54907
2.22 (a)(11) revised....54907
2.24 Revised....54907
2.33 (a) revised; (d) removed....54908
2.62 (b) revised....54908
2.64 (b) revised....54908
2.68 Revised....54908
2.74 (b) revised....54908
2.76 (b)(1) introductory text revised....54908
2.87 (f) revised....54908
2.88 (b)(1) introductory text revised....54908
2.89 (a)(3) and (b)(3) revised....54908
2.101 (b) introductory text revised....54909
2.102 (a) introductory text revised....54909
2.111 (b) revised....54909

37 CFR—Continued

74 FR Page

Chapter I—Continued

2.119 (d) revised....54909
2.146 (c) revised....54909
2.153 Revised....54909
2.161 (b) revised....54910
2.163 (b) revised....54910
2.167 (a) revised....54910
2.171 (b)(1) revised....54910
2.172 Revised....54910
2.184 (b)(2) revised....54910
2.193 Revised....54910
11.18 (a) revised....54912

Chapter II

201.1 (b)(2) revised....12556
201.3 (c)(16) amended....12556
(c), (d) and (e) revised....32807
201.4 (c)(3) revised....12556
201.6 (c) revised....32809
201.10 (f)(4) redesignated as (f)(5); (f)(1)(iii), new (f)(4) and (6) added; new (f)(5) revised....12556
201.15 Added; eff. through 7-1-11....39902
201.40 (b) introductory text amended; interim....55139
258.3 (h) revised....12093
258.4 (e) revised....12093

Chapter III

351 Authority citation revised....38533
351.15 Added; interim....38533
370 Revised....52423
381.5 (c)(1) and (2) revised....62705
385 Added....4529
385.11 Amended....6834
385.14 (a)(4) amended; (e) removed....6834
385.15 Removed....6834

2010

37 CFR

75 FR Page

Chapter I

1.1 (a)(3)(ii) and (iii) revised....36295
2.160 (a)(3) revised; interim....35976
2.161 (d)(2) revised; interim....35976
2.163 Revised; interim....35976
2.164 Revised; interim....35976
2.168 Heading and (a) revised; interim....35976
7.6 (a)(8) added; interim....35977
7.25 (a) revised; interim....35977
7.36 (b)(2) revised; (b)(3) and (c) added; interim....35977
7.37 (d)(2) revised; interim....35977
7.39 Revised; interim....35977
41.200 (b) removed....19559

37 CFR—Continued

75 FR Page

Chapter I—Continued

102.2 (a) revised....36295
104.2 (a) revised....36295

Chapter II

201 Policy statement....52267
201.11 Amended; (a) and (b) amended; (b)(1) revised; interim....56872
201.17 (b)(5) revised; (e)(9)(vii), (viii) and (g) through (l) redesignated as (e)(9)(ix), (x) and (h) through (m); new (j) through (m) redesignated as new (k) through (n); (e)(5)(iii), new (9)(vii), (viii), new (g), new (i)(10) and new (j) added; (e)(5)(i), new (9)(ix), new (m) and (3)(v) amended; interim....56872
(i)(4) amended....20526
201.40 (b) revised....43839
(b) introductory text correctly amended....47465
202.19 Undesignated text following (b)(2)(ii) amended; (b)(4) added; (c)(5) revised; interim....3869
202.24 Added; interim....3869
202 Appendix B amended; interim....3869
256.2 (b)(2)(i) and (ii) corrected; CFR correction....32857

Chapter III

380 Order....56873
380.3 (b) revised....6098
381.5 (c)(1), (2) and (3) revised....74623
382.12 Revised....5513
383.1 (a) and (b) amended; eff. 1-1-11....14075
383.2 (d) and (e) amended; eff. 1-1-11....14075
383.3 (a) introductory text, (1)(ii)(E) and (b) amended; (a)(1)(ii)(F) through (J), (2)(ii)(F) through (J) and (c) added; eff. 1-1-11....14075
383.4 Revised; eff. 1-1-11....14075
386 Added....53198
386.2 (b)(1)(ii) and (2)(ii) revised....75624

2011

37 CFR

76 FR Page

Chapter I

1.16 (t) added....70653
1.17 (c) added; (i) revised....18407

37 CFR—Continued

76 FR Page

37 CFR—Continued

76 FR Page

37 CFR—Continued

76 FR Page

2012

37 CFR

77 FR Page

37 CFR—Continued

77 FR Page

37 CFR—Continued

77 FR Page

Chapter I—Continued

1.303 Removed 48669
1.304 Removed 48669
1.313 (b)(4) revised 46626
1.321 (b) revised 48822
1.322 (a)(3) revised 46626
1.323 Revised 46626
1.324 Revised 48822
1.414 (c)(2) revised 48823
1.421 Revised 48823
1.422 Revised 48823
1.423 Removed 48823
1.424 Added 48823
1.431 (b)(3)(iii) revised 48823
1.491 Heading and (b) revised; (c) added 48823
1.492 (h) revised 48823
(a), (b)(3), (4), (c)(2), (d), (e), (f) and (j) revised 54366
1.495 (a), (c), (g) and (h) revised 48824
1.496 Revised 48824
1.497 Revised 48824
1.501 Undesignated center heading and section revised 46626
1.510 (a) and (b)(2) revised; (b)(6) added 46626
1.515 (a) revised 46626
1.530 (l)(1) revised 48825
1.550 (i) added 48851
1.552 (d) added 46627
1.601—1.625 (Subpart E) added 48851
1.701 (a)(1), (3), (c)(1)(i), (ii), (2)(iii) and (3) revised 46627
1.702 (a)(3), (b)(2), (4), (c) and (e) revised 46627
1.703 (a)(5), (b)(2), (3)(iii), (c)(1), (2) and (d)(3) revised 46628
(b)(4) and (e) revised 49360
1.704 (c)(9) introductory text revised 46628
(c)(10)(ii) and (11) revised; (c)(12) added 49360
1.730 (b)(1) revised 48825
1.937 (a) revised 46628
(d) added 48853
1.959 Undesignated center heading and section revised 46628
1.979 Revised 46628
1.981 Revised 46628
1.983 (a), (c), (d) and (f) revised 46628
1.985 Revised 46629
1.993 Revised 46629
2.34 (a)(1)(iv) revised 30207
2.56 (a) revised 30207
2.61 (b) revised 30207
2.76 (b)(2) revised 30207

37 CFR—Continued

77 FR Page

Chapter I—Continued

2.86 (a)(3) and (b) revised 30207
2.88 (b)(2) revised 30207
2.161 (g) introductory text revised; (h) added 30207
2.173 (b)(3) revised; (b)(4) added 30207
3.31 (h) added 48825
3.71 (a), (b) and (c) revised 48825
3.73 Revised 48825
5.25 (a)(3)(iii) and (b) revised 48826
5.3 (b) revised 46629
6.1 Revised 47529
7.37 (g) revised; (h) added 30208
10.1 (s) revised 46629
10.23 (c)(11) removed 48826
11.1 Amended 45251
11.5 (b)(1) introductory text revised 46629
11.6 (d) revised 46629
11.10 (b)(3)(iii) revised 46630
11.22 (c) removed 45251
11.34 (d) and (e) added 45251
11.58 (b)(1)(i) revised 46630
41 Heading revised 46630
41.1 (a) revised 46630
41.2 Amended 46630
41.9 (a) revised 48826
41.10 Revised 46630
41.20 (b) revised 54366
41.30 Amended 46630
41.37 (c)(1)(ii) and (iii) revised 46630
41.67 (c)(1)(ii) and (v) revised 46630
41.68 (b)(1)(ii) revised 46631
41.77 (a) revised 46631
41.110 (b)(2) revised 46631
41.201 Amended 46631
41.202 (b) revised 42174
42 Added 48669
Policy statement 48756
Authority citation revised 56090
42.100—42.123 (Subpart B) Added 48727
42.200—42.224 (Subpart C) Added 48729
42.300—42.304 (Subpart D) Added 48731
42.400—42.412 (Subpart E) Added 56090
42.301 Added 48753
90 Added 48677

Chapter II

201 Policy statement 37605
201.3 (b)(2) amended; (f) added 18705
(c) amended 18707
201.4 (a)(1)(iii) amended 71103

37 CFR—Continued

77 FR Page

Chapter II—Continued

201.18 (a)(4) revised; (g) redesignated as (h); (e)(5), new (g) and (i) added....71103
201.40 (b) revised....65278
202.2 (b)(1) amended....18707
(b)(1) corrected....20988
202.3 (b)(2) and (3) revised; (b)(10)(iv)(D), (v) and (c)(2) introductory text amended; footnotes 3 through 6 redesignated as footnotes 2 through 5....18707
(b)(6)(v) revised....66921
202.20 (c)(2)(vii)(D)(*5*) introductory text, (*8*) and (xx) introductory text amended....40270
(c)(2)(xvii) revised....66921

Chapter III

381.1 Amended....71105
381.4 (a)(1) through (8) revised; (c) amended....71105
381.5 (c) and (d) revised....71105
381.6 (f) removed; (b) through (e) redesignated as (c) through (f); new (b) added; new (d) and (e) revised....71106
381.7 (b)(1)(i)(A) through (D), (ii)(A) through (D) and (2)(i) through (iv) revised; (b)(4) and (5) amended....71108
381.8 (b)(1)(i) and (ii) revised; (f) amended....71108
381.10 (a) and (c) amended; (b) revised....71109
386.2 (b)(1)(iv) and (2)(iv) revised....70374

2013

(Regulations published from January 1, 2013, through July 1, 2013)

37 CFR

78 FR Page

Chapter I

1 Policy statement....11059
1 Authority citation amended....4284
1.4 (d)(4)(i) revised....20196
1.9 (d), (e) and (f) added....11052
1.14 (f) revised....11052
1.16—1.28 Authority citation revised....4284
1.16 (a) through (s) revised....4284
1.17 (a) through (i), (k), (l), (m) and (p) through (t) revised....4285
(g) and (i) revised; (n) and (o) removed....11052
Revised; interim....17105

37 CFR—Continued

78 FR Page

Chapter I—Continued

1.18 Revised; eff. in part 1-1-14....4286
1.19 Revised....4287
1.20 Revised....4287
Revised; interim....17108
1.21 (a), (e), (g) through (k) and (n) revised; (d) removed; eff. in part 1-1-14....4288
(a)(7) and (8) removed....20196
1.27 (c)(3) introductory text revised....4289
1.48 (c) added....4289
1.53 (b) introductory text, (c)(2)(ii), (iii) and (4) revised; (c)(2)(iv) and (j) removed....11053
1.55 Revised....11053
Correctly revised....16182
1.71 (g)(1) revised....11055
1.76 (b)(5) and (6) revised....11055
1.77 (b)(2) revised; (b)(6) through (12) redesignated as (b)(7) through (13); new (b)(6) added....11055
1.78 Revised....11055
1.84 (a)(2) introductory text revised....11057
1.103 (g) removed....11057
1.104 (c)(4) and (5) revised; (c)(6) added....11057
1.109 Added....11057
1.110 Revised....11058
1.130 Revised....11058
1.131 Revised....11058
1.293 Removed....11059
1.294 Removed....11059
1.295 Removed....11059
1.296 Removed....11059
1.297 Removed....11059
1.321 (d) introductory text revised....11059
1.445 (a) introductory text, (1)(i), (2), (3), (4) and (b) revised; eff. in part 1-1-14....4289
Revised; interim....17109
1.482 Revised; eff. in part 1-1-14....4289
Revised; interim....17110
1.492 Revised....4290
1.702 (a)(1) and (b) heading revised; interim....19420
1.703 (a)(1) revised; interim....19420
1.704 (e) revised; interim....19420
1.705 (d) and (e) removed; (f) redesignated as new (d); (a), (b) introductory text and (c) introductory text revised; interim....19420
2.2 (c) revised....20197

37 CFR—Continued

78 FR Page

37 CFR—Continued

78 FR Page

○

www.ingramcontent.com/pod-product-compliance
Lightning Source LLC
LaVergne TN
LVHW052011200926
848481LV00005B/1463
* 9 7 8 1 6 2 7 7 3 1 3 6 2 *